Handbook of
The Psychology of Aging

The Handbooks of Aging

Consisting of Three Volumes

Critical comprehensive reviews of
research knowledge, theories, concepts, and issues

Editor-in-chief
James E. Birren

Handbook of the Biology of Aging
Edited by Edward J. Masoro and Steven N. Austad

Handbook of the Psychology of Aging
Edited by James E. Birren and K. Warner Schaie

Handbook of Aging and the Social Sciences
Edited by Robert H. Binstock and Linda K. George

Handbook of
The Psychology of Aging
Fifth Edition

Editors
James E. Birren and K. Warner Schaie

Associate Editors
Ronald P. Abeles, Margaret Gatz,
and Timothy A. Salthouse

ACADEMIC PRESS

A Harcourt Science and Technology Company

San Diego   San Francisco   New York   Boston   London   Sydney   Tokyo

Academic Press
A Harcourt Science and Technology Company
525 B Street, Suite 1900, San Diego, California 92101–4495, USA
http://www.academicpress.com

Academic Press
Harcourt Place, 32 Jamestown Road, London NW1 7BY, UK
http://www.academicpress.com

Library of Congress Catalog Card Number: 2001088189

International Standard Book Number: 0–12–101262–X (casebound)
                                       0–12–101263–8 (paperback)

PRINTED IN THE UNITED STATES OF AMERICA
01 02 03 04 05 06 QW 9 8 7 6 5 4 3 2

Contents

Part One
Concepts, Theory, and Methods in the Psychology of Aging

Part Two
Biological and Social Influences on Behavior

Part Three
Behavioral Processes and Psychological Functions

Part Four
Behavior in Social Contexts

23. Elder Abuse and Victimization
Kathleen H. Wilber and Dennis P. McNeilly

24. Quality of Life and the End of Life
M. Powell Lawton

Contributors and Editors

Numbers in parentheses indicate the page number on which the author's contribution begins.

Ronald P. Abeles, Office of Behavioral and Social Sciences Research, National Institutes of Health Bethesda, Maryland 20892–9205

Marilyn S. Albert (161), Department of Psychiatry, Massachusetts Hospital, Boston, Massachusetts 02114

Toni C. Antonucci (427), Institute for Social Research, University of Michigan, Ann Arbor, Michigan 48109

Lars Bäckman (349), Department of Psychology, Uppsala University, SE-751 42 Uppsala, Sweden

James E. Birren (3), UCLA Center on Aging, Los Angeles, California 90095–6980

Edith Burns (186), Zabolocki Veterans Administration Medical Center, Milwaukee, Wisconsin 53295

Sarah J. Czaja (547), Miami Center for Human Factors, Department of Industrial Engineering, University of Miami, Miami, Florida 33133

Arthur D. Fisk (267), School of Psychology, Georgia Institute of Technology, Atlanta, Georgia 30332–0170

James L. Fozard (241), [1]Morton Plant Mease Health Care, Clearwater, Florida 35756

Margaret Gatz (522), Department of Psychology, University of Southern California, Los Angeles, California 90089–1061

Sandra Gordon-Salant (241), Department of Hearing and Speech Sciences, University of Maryland College Park, Maryland 20742

Scott M. Hofer (53), The Pennsylvania State University, Department of Human Development and Family Studies, University Park, Pennsylvania 16802

[1]Present Address: Florida Gerontological Research and Training Services, Palm Harbor, Florida 34684–4039

Susan Kemper (378), Department of Psychology, University of Kansas, Lawrence, Kansas 66045

Caroline J. Ketcham (313), Exercise and Sports Science Institute, Arizona State University, Tempe, Arizona 85287

Ronald J. Killiany (161), Department of Psychiatry, Massachusetts Hospital, Boston, Massuchsetts 02114

Christine M. L. Kwan (477), Department of Psychology, University of Wisconsin, Madison, Wisconsin 53706

M. Powell Lawton (592), [2]Philadelphia Geriatric Center, Philadelphia, Pennsylvania 19141

Howard Leventhal (186), Center for Research on Health and Behavior, Rutgers University, New Brunswick, New Jersey 08903

Elaine A. Leventhal (186), Gerontological Institute and Department of Medicine, Robert Wood Johnson School of Medicine, University of Medicine and Dentistry of New Jersey, New Brunswick, New Jersey 08901

Todd I. Lubart (499), Universite Rene Descartes, Laboratoire Cognition et Developpement 75006 Paris, France

David J. Madden (288), Medical Center, Duke University, Durham, North Carolina 27710–0001

Carol Magai (399), Psychology Department, Long Island University, Brooklyn, New York 11201

Gerald McClearn (109), Pennsylvania State University, University Park, Pennsylvania 16802

Dennis P. McNeilly (569), Andrus Gerontology Center, University of Southern California, Los Angeles, California 90089–0191

Tracy L. Mitzner (378), Department of Psychology, University of Kansas, Lawrence, Kansas 66045

Carolyn Rabin (186), Center for Research on Health and Behavior, Rutgers University, New Brunswick, New Jersey 08903

Christian Rietz (29), Psychologisches Institut, Universität Bonn, 53117 Bonn, Germany

Wendy A. Rogers (267), School of Psychology, Georgia Institute of Technology, Atlanta, Georgia 30332–0170

Georg Rudinger (29), Psychologisches Institut, Universität Bonn, 53117 Bonn, Germany

Carol D. Ryff (477), Department of Psychology, University of Wisconsin, Madison, Wisconsin 53706

Timothy A. Salthouse, Georgia Institute of Technology, School of Psychology, Atlanta, Georgia 30332

K. Warner Schaie (53), The Pennsylvania State University, Department of Human Development and Family Studies, University Park, Pennsylvania 16802

Johannes J. F. Schroots (3), [3]UCLA Center on Aging, Los Angeles, California 90095–6980

Kim Shifren (454), Psychology Department, Towson University, Baltimore, Maryland 21204

Burton H. Singer (477), Population Research, Princeton University, Princeton, New Jersey 08544

[2] Deceased
[3]Present address: University of Amsterdam, Department of Psychology, 1018 WB Amsterdam, The Netherlands

Jan D. Sinnot (454), Psychology Department, Towson University, Baltimore, Maryland 21204

Brent J. Small (349), Department of Gerontology, University of South Florida, Tampa, Florida 33620

Michael A. Smyer (522), Graduate School of Arts & Sciences, Boston College, Boston, Massachusetts 02167

George E. Stelmach (313), Exercise and Sports Science Institute, Arizona State University, Tempe, Arizona 85287

Robert J. Sternberg (499), Department of Psychology, Yale University, New Haven, Connecticut 06520–8205

Harry V. Vinters (135), Department of Neuropathology, UCLA Medical Center, Los Angeles, California 90095

George P. Vogler (109), Pennsylvania State University, University Park, Pennsylvania 16802

Hans-Werner Wahl (215), Deutsches Institut für Alternsforschung, Universität Heidelberg, 69115 Heidelberg, Germany

Åke Wahlin (349), Stockholm Gerontology Research Center and Department of Clinical Neuroscience, Occupational Therapy, and Elderly Care Research (NEUROTEC), Division of Geriatric Medicine, Karolinska Institute, Stockholm, Sweden

Kathleen H. Wilber (569), Andrus Gerontology Center, University of Southern California, Los Angeles, California 90089–0191

Sherry L. Willis (78), Department of Human Development and Family Studies, Pennsylvania State University, University Park, PA 16802

Foreword

This volume is one of a series of three handbooks on aging, *Handbook of the Biology of Aging*, *Handbook of the Psychology of Aging*, and *Handbook of Aging and the Social Sciences*. The series is in its fifth edition, which reflects the growth of research and publication on aging.

The handbook series is used by research personnel, graduate students, and professional personnel for access not only to the rapidly growing volume of literature, but also to the perspectives provided by the integration and interpretations of the findings by experienced and well-informed scholars. The subject matter of aging has matured and expanded in recent years, with much research and education being conducted. It has become a mainstream topic in the sciences, ranging from the biological to the social, and also in the many professions that serve older persons.

A by-product of this exponential growth of research literature on aging and the speed of access in the information age is that an overwhelming amount of information is quickly available to individuals. One result of such information overload can be an adaptive narrowing of interests and scope. This is particularly relevant to understanding a complex field such as aging, in which many factors interact. More than ever, students of aging need integration and interpretations from experts in subtopics adjacent to their special interests. The handbook series provides the opportunity to read to not only a topic of special interest but also adjacent subject matter that may have important implications. This opportunity particularly significant in aging, which is not a lock-and-key issue solved by one discipline, one study, or one insight.

Rapid changes in the 20th century provided that environmental factors can contribute much to both the length and the quality of life. Aging is a dynamic process, with shifts in the magnitude of what contributes to the aging process. There is little doubt that our genetic background as a species and our individual heredity contribute to our prospects for length of life and life-limiting and disabling diseases. We can expect much more understanding of the genetic factors in aging as contemporary research continues to expand. However, environmental factors, both physical and social, and our behavior modulate the expression of our genetic predispositions. In a broad perspective, aging is a product of ecological forces. For this reason researchers and students of aging must be aware of diverse factors contributing to the phenomena of aging. The handbook series makes available interpretations of a vast literature and contributes to the integration of a highly complex but vital subject matter.

Public interest in aging has grown along with the impressive increases in life expectancy and in the numbers and proportion of older persons. This interest presumably has led to the increased support of research and scholarship by governments and foundations. Aging has become a topic of daily life discussions. Further improvements in our life expectancy and reductions in limitations on the quality of life with advancing age may be expected to emerge from the efforts of those who have written chapters for the series of handbooks on aging.

Without the intense efforts and cooperation of the editors and associate editors of the individual volumes, the series would not be possible. I thank Edward J. Masoro and Steven N. Austad, the editors of the *Handbook of the Biology of Aging*, and their associate editors, Judith Campisi, George M. Martin, and Charles V. Mobbs; Robert H. Binstock and Linda K. George, editors of the *Handbook of Aging and the Social Sciences*, and their associate editors, Victor W. Marshall, Angela M. O'Rand, and James H. Schulz; K. Warner Schaie, my co-editor of the *Handbook of the Psychology of Aging*, and the associate editors, Ronald P. Abeles, Margaret Gatz, and Timothy A. Salthouse.

I also express my appreciation to Nikki Levy, Publisher at Academic Press, whose long-standing interest and cooperation have facilitated the publication of the series of handbooks on aging.

James E. Birren

Preface

This fifth edition of the *Handbook of the Psychology of Aging* provides reviews and evaluations of the growing volume of literature on adult development and aging. It is a definitive reference source in the behavioral sciences for researchers, graduate students, and professionals. The emphasis is on the basic behavioral processes and how they change over the adult years.

Research on the psychology of aging is expanding rapidly. In the 1977 edition of the handbook, K. Riegel gave a quantitative analysis of the growth of literature and noted an exponential increase beginning a 1950. The breadth and depth of the subject matter have continued to expand. From its early 20th- century beginning, it grew from a marginal interest in psychology to become a mainline subject, with many universities currently having specialized teaching and research programs in both basic and applied aspects of aging. Funding of training programs and research on the psychology of aging by public and private institutions has been given high priority.

Data from the growing number of longitudinal studies of long periods of the life span are providing clues about causal variables of changes in the adult organism. Unlike limited experimental studies, they not only provide a broad time perspective but also offer evidence of behavioral changes in the contexts of possible biological, health, and social influences and their interactions. Advances in methodology make it possible to explore the interactions of the variables in greater detail, leading to the anticipation that patterns and subpatterns of aging of behavior will be identified.

There are few topics, if any, in psychology that have the inherent complexity of aging. At the same time psychology is trying to answer the question of how behavior is organized, it is trying to answer the question of how change is organized.

The chapters of this volume give promise to the idea of replacing chronological age with causal variables of change. It is tempting to forget that chronological age is but a convenient index to vast areas of behavioral data and does not in itself point to the antecedent conditions or causes of change. As part of the scientific quest for understanding, new theoretical metaphors are suggested. Often they express the motives of the investigators more clearly than they explicate the patterns of aging (e.g., successful aging, productive aging, adaptation with compensation, gerotranscendence, counterpart, branching, and chaos). A fundamental issue to be faced is the diversity among the contributing variables and their consequences. The present chapters indicate that the field has moved away from the simplistic views common in the early part of the 20th century that a single process of senscence characterized the later adult years (e.g., you are as old as your arteries).

Public interest in aging has risen, undoubtedly reflecting the dramatic increase in life expectancy in the 20th century and the rise in the proportion of older adults in the population. There has been a notable accompanying increase in the applications of psychology for individuals and society. Issues of the psychology of aging touch upon many facets of daily life, from the workplace and family life to important policy matters of retirement, health care and medical insurance, to social security and pensions.

The increase in the volume of published literature and the emergence of new topics require the editors to make decisions about which topics need to be updated and also which new topics warrant inclusion. Growth is by no means uniform, with notable increases in findings from longitudinal research, neuropsychology, behavioral genetics, and cognitive psychology. Past editions include chapters on topics not included in the present volume, and readers are advised to consult those volumes. Also, past chapters on the same topics often have different perspectives and may be read for contrasts with those in the present volume. The editors deliberately try to seek new authors to encourage new approaches to established topics. In this edition, 18 of the chapters are written by new authors and 6 by authors who had contributed chapters to previous editions. Of the 6 repeat authors, 3 are writing on new topics. Thus an important feature of the successive editions of the *Handbook on the Psychology of Aging* is that the subject matter is developed by new authors.

New topics include behavioral interventions and clinical trials, gender and aging, mental health and aging, technological change and the older worker, abuse and victimization, and end-of-life changes and prospects. Some of the new topics of earlier editions that do not reappear in this volume are brain and life span in primates; religion, spirituality, and aging; posture, gait, and falls; activity, exercise, and behavior; aging, behavior, and terminal decline; and everyday problem solving. For this reason the previous editions should be consulted for a perspective on the continuing development of the subject matter.

The chapters are organized into four divisions: Part One: Concepts, Theory, and Methods; Part Two: Biological and Social Influences on Behavior; Part Three: Behavioral Processes and Psychological Functions; and Part Four: Behavior in Social Contexts. Choosing the topics and the authors of the chapters was not a simple process but a product of the senior editors consulting with the associate editors. The draft of each chapter was revised after being reviewed by two readers, one of the senior editors, and one of the associate editors.

The senior editors thank the associate editors, Ronald P. Abeles, Margaret Gatz, and Timothy A. Salthouse, for their advice and for reading the manuscripts. The assistance of Anna Shuey in the editorial process is gratefully acknowledged.

James E. Birren
K. Warner Schaie

About the Editors

James E. Birren

is associate director of the Center on Aging at the University of California, Los Angeles, and serves as an adjunct professor in medicine, psychiatry, and biobehavioral sciences. Dr. Birren's previous positions include serving as chief of the section on aging of the National Institute of Mental Health, founding executive director and dean of the Ethel Percy Andrus Gerontology Center of the University of Southern California, founding director of the Anna and Harry Borun Center for Gerontological Research at UCLA, and president of the Gerontological Society of America, The Western Gerontological Society, and the Division on Adult Development and Aging of the American Psychological Association. His awards include the Brookdale Award for Gerontological Research, the Sandoz Prize for Gerontological Research, and the award for outstanding contribution to gerontology by the Canadian Association of Gerontology. Author of over 250 scholarly publications, Dr. Birren's research interests include the causes and consequences of slowed information processing in the older nervous system and the relation of age to decision-making processes. He has developed a program of guided autobiography for research purposes and for application to groups of older adults.

K. Warner Schaie

is the Evan Pugh Professor of Human Development and Psychology and director of the Gerontology Center at the Pennsylvania State University. He also holds an appointment as Affiliate Professor of Psychiatry and Behavioral Science at the University of Washington. He received the Kleemeier Award for Distinguished Research Contributions from the Gerontological Society of America and the Distinguished Scientific Contributions award from the American Psychological Association. He was awarded an honorary doctorate by the Friedrich Schiller University of Jena, Germany. He is a fellow of the Gerontological Society and the American Psychological Association and has served as president of the APA Division of Adult Development and Aging and as editor of the *Journal of Gerontology: Psychological Sciences*. He chaired National Institutes of Health review groups on human development and aging. He is author or editor of 35 books, including the textbook *Adult Development and Aging* (with S. L. Willis), now in its fifth edition. He has directed the Seattle Longitudinal Study of cognitive aging since 1956 and is the author of more than 250 journal articles and chapters on the psychology of aging. His special area of interest is the life course of adult intelligence, its antecedents and modifiability, as well as methodological issues in the developmental sciences.

Ronald P. Abeles

is the special assistant to the director of the Office of Behavioral and Social Sciences Research in the Office of the Director, National Institutes of Health (NIH). Previously, he was the associate director for behavioral and Social Research at the National Institute on Aging, NIH. He is also the chair of the NIH Coordinating committee for Behavioral and Social Sciences Research. He is the president-elect of the Division on Adult Development and Aging of the American Psychological Association (APA) and past-chair of the Section on Aging and the Life Course of the American Sociological Association. Dr. Abeles is a fellow of the APA, the American Psychological Society, and the Society of Behavioral Medicine. He is the recipient of the NIH Director's Award and the NIH Award of Merit for "leadership and contributions to the advancement of behavioral and social research on aging." He has edited books or published articles and chapters on aging and social psychology, health behaviors, quality of life, sense of control and the interface between social structure and behavior.

Margaret Gatz

is professor of psychology [and gerontology] at the University of Southern California and foreign adjunct professor in medical epidemiology at the Karolinska Institute in Stockholm, Sweden. She is a fellow of the American Psychological Association, American Psychological Society, and Gerontological Society of America. She has served as chair of the Behavioral and Social Sciences Section of the Gerontological Society of America and associate editor of *Psychology and Aging*. Author of over 120 scholarly publications. Dr. Gatz's research interests encompass risk and protective factors for Alzheimer's disease, age-related change in depressive symptoms, and evaluation of the effects of psychological interventions. She has been recognized by the Master Mentor Award of the Retirement Research Foundation and Division 20 of the American Psychological Association, the Distinguished Mentorship Award from the Gerontological Society BSS section, and by the Apple of Knowledge for important contributions to development of research through the University College of Health Sciences, Jönköping, Sweden.

Timothy A. Salthouse

is the Brown-Forman Professor of Psychology at the University of Virginia. He is a fellow of the Gerontological Society of America, the American Association for the Advancement of Science, the American Psychological Society, and Divisions 3 and 20 of the American Psychological Association. He is a former president of Division 20 (Adult Development and Aging) of the American Psychological Association, and a past editor of the journal *Psychology and Aging*. He has received the Distinguished Research Contribution

Award from Division 20 and the William James Fellow Award from the American Psychological Society. His primary research areas are age-related effects on cognitive functioning and the role of experience and knowledge in minimizing the consequences of those effects.

Part One

Concepts, Theory, and Methods in the Psychology of Aging

One

The History of Geropsychology

James E. Birren and Johannes J. F. Schroots

I. Introduction

Aging is one of the most complex subjects for humans to face and for science to analyze, and its subjective aspects have long been reflected upon and written about. The history of geropsychology is long or short depending upon whether one includes the long cultural history of ideas about aging or whether the subject is restricted to the emergence of research on the changes and transformations that may occur in behavior. Research in geropsychology is a relatively new subject matter. One might use the arbitrary date of 1950 to mark the beginnings of organized university research and education and the granting of doctoral degrees to graduate students doing research in the psychology of aging. Preceding that time, humans speculated for thousands of years about destiny and how we grow old. Such thoughts have undoubtedly influenced contemporary concepts of growing old.

Writers and philosophers throughout history have reflected on aging and noted changes in themselves and others as they grew older. Lacking empirical methods to sort implausible from plausible ideas, myths were generated and passed on for generations. In many myths, supernatural forces ordained the transition to old age and beyond, and in nature were vaguely understood to influence how long one lived and whether one could obtain immortality.

Geropsychology focuses on the manifest changes or transformations that occur in human and animal behavior related to the length of life. Use of the word *behavior* restricts the scope of the study to processes mediated by the central nervous system. Modification of our behavior is often required by a change in bones and muscle or an illness. Also, behavior is modified as we adapt to the institutions in which we grow up and grow old. For example, there is the process of retirement and adapting to its economic effects. In its fullest view, human aging is the result of ecological relationships; a particular genetic background is expressed in particular social and physical environments and modified by the strategic capacities of the individual. Aging has always reminded people of the likelihood of disease, dying, and the transition of death. Simplifying the complexity of such changes to mythical forces has served as an escape from the threat of the unknown. In contemporary life, aging is viewed as though it is explainable by deterministic forces through the efforts of science, but death and life beyond are separate subjects.

The present history of geropsychology does not include a review of non-Western literature because it was not accessible. It remains for future scholars to present an account of non-Western cultural and philosophical concepts about aging and their influence on the emergence of psychology as an academic discipline.

II. Mythical Origins
(c. 3000–800 B.C.)

The historian Gruman (1966) reviewed the mythical origins of aging and death in literature and identified three dominant themes: the antediluvian theme (literally, "before the deluge"), the hyperborean theme (literally "beyond the north wind"), and the "fountain of youth" or rejuvenation quest. The antediluvian theme emerges from myths that are based on the belief that people lived much longer in the past. This theme is exemplified in the book of Genesis, where the life spans of 10 Hebrew patriarchs are recorded: for instance, Adam, is said to have lived for 930 years, Noah for 950 years, and Methuselah, whose name has become a byword for longevity, lived for 969 years.

Confronted by the fact that old people tended to change in appearance and die, it was characteristic in many cultures to assume that the course of life was under the control of cosmic forces and life continued beyond death in some form. Many cultures assumed that humankind once had immortality, but lost it through its own actions. Thus myths evolved, providing roots for myths that continue to the present day in modified form. Western conceptions of life and death, for example, can be traced back to the Sumerian

epic of Gilgamesh, which is about 5000 years old and was written in cuneiform script in the 14th century B.C. (Sandars, 1983). In brief, the story is as follows:

Gilgamesh is the vigorous but tyrannical king of the Mesopotamian city of Uruk. He ruins his subjects' happiness and the gods decide to teach him a lesson. This idea is not entirely successful, because muscular Enkidu, whom they send for the purpose, becomes his best friend after a vigorous battle. Gilgamesh and Enkidu now set out to do great things that should bring them immortal fame. After several heroic adventures, they finally cut off the horrible monster Huwawa's head, like St. George. Highly pleased with themselves, the heroes go home and then make a fatal mistake: They call the elderly but very powerful goddess of Uruk "old harlot" (after she has tried to seduce Gilgamesh, who is very masculine) and thus violate the divine law. From then on the epic develops like a Greek tragedy. The gods decree that Enkidu should become ill and die. Gilgamesh is confronted with death for the first time in his life.

Gilgamesh for Enkidu, his friend,
Weeps bitterly and roams over the desert.
O' When I die, shall I not be like unto Enkidu!
Sorrow has entered my heart.
I am afraid of death and roam over the desert..."
(Ninth song, verse 1–5; cf. Sandars, 1983)

After a Odyssey of untiring wandering Gilgamesh finally finds himself in the distant country of his ancestor Utnapishtim, the only man who has escaped the mortal destiny and who may show him the way to immortality. Unfortunately, Utnapishtim's message does not augur well: Man is a mortal creature and he can only acquiesce in this fate. Nevertheless Gilgamesh is given the opportunity to obtain immortality (by staying awake for six days and seven nights) but, as befits a mortal, he fails to seize it by falling asleep immediately. He is also allowed to bathe in the source of life for a rejuvenation cure, but he is not allowed to take the water home with him. Utnapishtim then takes pity on Gilgamesh, who is desperate, and finally shows him the herb of life, which is growing in the deepest part of the well of life:

Gilgamesh brings the herb to the surface... It is a herb that brings life. Man's most ardent wish is fulfilled, he is given the full vigour of youth... I shall bring it to my well-fortified city of Uruk ... and I shall make everybody eat of it. The name of the plant is "When a grey-beard, man becomes young again"... For twice twenty hours he travelled on. After thirty hours he pitched his camp. Gilgamesh saw a pool and bathed.... A snake inhaled the odor of the herb, slunk closer and stole the herb. It shed its skin and was rejuvenated.... That day Gilgamesh sat down and wept. (cf. Sandars, 1983)

His chance of immortality was stolen.

Gilgamesh should be compulsory reading for all students of life and death, as well as the related biblical story of Adam and Eve who lost immortality and the earthly paradise. Both stories show some remarkable parallels. For example, the Tree of Life, placed in the center of the Garden of Eden, provided immortality to the first human couple through its fruit, and might be compared with the herb of life, which makes older people as young again. It should be noted that the Tree of Life is hidden behind the obtrusive Tree of the Knowledge of Good and Evil, which in an earlier version of the paradise story is the Tree of Death (Frazer, in Gruman, 1966, p. 13). The serpent, who loses its skin, also appears in both stories as the symbol of rejuvenation or life and death: in Gilgamesh he steals the herb of life, and in the paradise story he seduces Adam and Eve to eat from the Tree of Knowledge, which leads to death. Compared with the herb of life, the Tree of Life is far more apt for the description of a person's life through the annual cycle of budding, blooming, growing, dying, and falling leaves. However, there can be no Tree of Life without a source of life, the well from which the tree derives its sap. The similarity between the well from which Gilgamesh obtains the herb of life

and the paradisian source of life need not surprise us. The sap of life has always been regarded as the giver of life, the elixir of life which promises immortality. This is what the alchemists were looking for, and fluid gold was an important ingredient, as the 15th- and 16th-century adventurers had hoped to find in their search for El Dorado (literally "the gilded") and the Fountain of Youth.

The hyperborean theme, originating with the Greeks, arises from the belief that in some distant place, beyond the north wind, there is a culture or society whose fortunate people enjoy a remarkably long life, free from all natural ills. One of the most popular hyperborean legends is the medieval "Voyage of St. Brandan," the Christianized version of the old Celtic story that recounts the adventures of mortals seeking an island in the West where the golden age still exists. This type of legend long served as a stimulus to geographical exploration. Columbus, for example, on his third voyage in 1498, concluded that he had located the earthly paradise along the coast of Venezuela near the island of Trinidad.

A third theme found in many legends and myths is the rejuvenation quest, which is often expressed through a fountain whose waters are purported to rejuvenate (cf. the epic of Gilgamesh). Americans are familiar with the legend of Juan Ponce de Leon, whose search for the fountain of youth led accidentally to the discovery of Florida in 1513. In the ancient Near East the story of Alexander the Great's search for the fountain of youth has inspired many imaginative writers. In one version, Alexander has a cook who, while cleaning a dried fish in a spring, is astounded to see it leap into life. Realizing that this must be the fountain of life, the cook bathes in the waters and becomes immortal. Alexander, unable to discover the fountain himself, decides to kill the cook but, finding him invulnerable to death, has him thrown into the sea where he lives on as a demon. The fountain in this story is located near paradise (cf. the paradisian well of life).

Recently, the American classicist De-Luce (1996) has reviewed Greco-Roman mythology and identified one general image and four specific images of old age that have become part of Western tradition. The general image originates from Hesiod's *Works and Days* (ca. 700 B.C.), in which the poet describes the history of humankind in terms of five ages, varying from the Golden Age (the first and the best of the five, in which humans lived comfortably and did not actually grow old and die) to the Iron Age, the fifth and last age of increasing labor and misery. Hesiod laments that he was born in this age and predicts that people will grow old more and more quickly to the point that children will be born already gray-haired. The poem includes also the Prometheus myth with the story of the first woman, Pandora, who opened the box given her by the gods as a punishment for humans, releasing all the ills of human experience including old age into the world (cf. the story of Adam and Eve).

The four more specific images of old age are concerned with physical frailty, moral strength, elders as advisers, and elders in action (DeLuce, 1996, pp. 191–193). Physical frailty is illustrated by the story of the Trojan youth Tithonus who was loved by Eos, the amorous goddess of the Dawn. Eos asked Zeus that her mortal lover be made immortal but failed to request eternal youth for him as well. As he aged and grew increasingly feeble, the goddess lost interest in him and shut him away, although she continued to feed him ambrosia. Finally, all that remained of him was his voice emanating from the chamber.

Moral strength is exemplified by Ovid's story of a poor elderly couple, Baucis and Philemon, who—unlike their neighbours—welcomed strangers and entertained them from their meager supply of food, unaware that they have received gods into their home. The gods drown the rest of the neighborhood, but grant the couple a wish: because they have lived together for so long and because it would be too painful for one to survive the other, Baucis and Philemon request that they die at precisely the same moment. They not only die simultaneously, but they are transformed into an oak tree and a linden tree that continue to grow side by side (cf. tree of death).

DeLuce presents the third image of elders as advisors in the mythic figure of Teiresias, the great Theban seer from the Oedipus myth, and in the figure of Nestor, who had lived seven generations and acted as an adviser to the Greeks in Homer's *Iliad* and *Odyssey*.

Although elders may not be as physically vigorous as they had once been, they may provide more than advice when action is required, the fourth image of old age. The *Odyssey*, for example, tells the story of the old goat herd Eumaeus, who is a central figure in effecting Odysseus's vengeance on the suitors who are harassing his wife, have threatened the life of his son, and are eating up his wealth. In concluding this section on the mythical origins of ideas about aging, the riddle of the Sphinx should be told, as this story has implications for a concept of the life span. According to tradition, the Sphinx sat outside of Thebes and asked passersby a riddle. If they could not answer the riddle, she killed and ate them. In its simplest form, the Sphinx asked: What has one voice and is four-footed, two-footed, and three-footed? What goes slowest when it has the most feet? Oedipus answered that the riddle fit human experience, because infancy goes on all fours, maturity on two feet, and old age with the help of a cane (the third "foot"). At hearing the correct answer, the Sphinx killed herself. The answer may imply that to some degree the human life span is circular; that is, it begins in dependency in childhood and returns to dependency in old age.

III. Greco-Roman Philosophers (c. 800 B.C.–100 A.D.)

Originally, there was no sharp distinction between mythology and philosophy, between *mythos* (speech or narrative) and *logos* (argument or reason). However, the distinction between the two developed between the eight and fourth centuries B.C., when there was a change from oral to written literature. Generally speaking, the Greek philosophical tradition has a somewhat critical but realistic view of aging and death. The pre-Socratic philosopher Democritus, for example, criticized people for their senseless longing for life, fearing death rather than old age, and in the fourth century B.C. Epicurus thought that if people developed the right attitude about the end of life and death, they lost their fear of them and lived a more peaceful life. A short life could be just as happy as a long one so that prolongation of life was not important. A similar view is expressed by the Roman poet and Epicurean philosopher Lucretius (96?–55? B.C.), who emphasized that life, however prolonged, will always remain insignificant compared to how long we shall be dead:

What is this deplorable lust of life that holds us trembling in bondage to such uncertainties and dangers? . . . By prolonging life, we cannot subtract or whittle away one jot from the duration of our death . . . However many generations you may add to your store by living, there waits for you none the less the same eternal death." The claim by Lucretius that aging and death are necessary to prevent overpopulation makes him a forerunner of the early 19th-century political economist Malthus. (Lucretius, *On the Nature of the Universe*, from Gruman, 1966, p. 14, 19).

Successful aging is in the eye of the beholder. Falkner and DeLuce (1992) point out that neither Democritus nor Plato (427–327 B.C.) regarded wisdom as a necessary by-product of age or experience:

In the *Republic*, where belief and behavior will be carefully regimented, the "philosopher-kings" are a select group of men and women aged 50 and older, but they rule not by virtue of their age but of their grueling education. In fact, Plato begins the dialogue with a portrait of the complacent old Cephalus, who excuses himself from the deliberations precisely when they become difficult. (p. 10)

Like Epicurus, Plato emphasizes the personal experience of aging. The feeling of "being old" is very much dependent on the person's view of young and old people. To age "wisely" and peacefully, it is necessary to live a righteous life. For this reason, the youth should be educated to live with a sense of duty in order to enjoy old age. According to Lehr (1977), the Platonist view of healthy aging is reflected in the modern conception of *geroprophylaxis*, which emphasizes educating people in healthy lifestyles, management of stress, the need for adequate exercise and nutrition, and the prevention of loss of autonomy as well as prevention of disease. This process must begin in young adulthood in order to be fully effective.

Aristotle (384–322 B.C.), pupil of Plato and teacher of Alexander the Great, gives not even the benefit of the doubt to growing old smoothly, let alone to healthy or successful aging. In characterizing the three stages of life (i.e., youth, the prime of life, and old age), he presents a very unsympathetic picture of elderly men:

They have lived many years; they have often been taken in, and often made mistakes; and life on the whole is a bad business. The result is that they are sure about nothing and *underdo* everything. They "think", but they never "know"; and because of their hesitation they always add a "possibly" or a "perhaps", putting everything this way and nothing positively. They are cynical; that is, they tend to put the worst construction on everything. Further, their experience makes them distrustful and therefore suspicious of evil. . . . They are small-minded, because they have been humbled by life. . . . They are not generous, because money is one of the things they must have. . . . They are cowardly, and are always anticipating danger.... They are too fond of themselves.... They are not shy, but shameless rather.... They lack confidence in the future.... They live by memory rather than by hope (*Rhetoric*, 2, 12–14; quoted in Cole & Winkler, 1994, pp. 25–26).

Aristotle's negative characterization of old age must be inspired by the humoral theories of the Hippocratic physicians of the fifth century B.C. They based their conceptions of physiological functioning across the life span on a scheme of four humors (blood, yellow bile, black bile, phlegm) and four qualities (hot, cold, moist, dry). According to this scheme, Aristotle thought that the old body was cold and dry, leading to death. Metaphorically, he likened the diminished innate heat of old age to a feeble flame that could be extinguished readily. The preservation of heat was necessary for vitality, which was diminished in old age. An echo of this theory is reflected in the suggestion of the famous 17th-century physician Herman Boerhaave, that the old burgomaster of Amsterdam might regain both his strength and his spirits if he would only sleep between two young girls. According to Gruman (1966, p. 65) the inspiration for this idea came directly from the Old Testament (I Kings 1: 1–4), in which it is related how the aged King David (c. 1000–762 B.C.) was warmed by lying abed with a beautiful maiden, with whom, it is stated, he did not have sexual intercourse.

Cicero (106–42 B.C.), the renowned Roman statesman and man of letters, might be conceived as the Epicurian counterpart of Aristotle. In his essay on senescence, *Cato maior de senectute*, the 62-year old Cicero argues that it is not old age that is at fault but rather our attitude towards it. Cicero listed the four principal complaints against old age and rebutted each of them:

And, indeed, when I reflect on this subject I find four reasons why old age appears to be unhappy: first, that it withdraws us from active pursuits; second, that it makes the body weaker; third, that it deprives us of almost all physical pleasures; and, fourth, that it is not far removed from death.

To the complaint that "old age withdraws us from active pursuits" Cicero replies that courageous old men can find a way to make themselves useful in various advisory, intellectual, and administrative functions. But, "it is alleged, the memory is impaired. Of course, if you do not exercise it (....) Such was the case with Solon, whom we see boasting in his verses that he grows old learning something every day."

To the charge that senescence "makes the body weaker" Cicero answers that bodily development counts for little as compared with the cultivations of mind and character. Yet,

it may be urged, many old men are so feeble that they can perform no function that duty or indeed any position in life demands. True, but that is not particular to old age; generally it is a characteristic of ill-health.... But it is our duty, my young friends, to resist old age; to compensate for its defects by a watchful care; to fight against it as we would fight against disease; to adopt a regimen of health; to practise moderate exercise; and to take just enough of food and drink to restore our strength and not to overburden it. Nor, indeed, are we to give our attention solely to the body; much greater care is due to the mind and soul; for they, too, like lamps, grow dim with time, unless we keep them supplied with oil. Moreover, exercise causes the body to become heavy with fatigue, but intellectual activity gives buoyancy to the mind.

To the complaint that aging "deprives us of almost all physical pleasures" Cicero replies that such a loss is good riddance, because it allows the aged to concentrate on the promotion of reason and virtue:

No more deadly curse ... has been given by nature to man than carnal pleasure, through eagerness for which the passions are driven recklessly and uncontrollably to its gratification. From it come treason and the overthrow of states; and from it spring secret and corrupt conferences with public foes. In short, there is no criminal purpose and no evil deed which the lust for pleasure will not drive men to undertake.... But if some concession must be made to pleasure, since her allurements are difficult to resist, and she is, as Plato happily says, "the bait of sin,"—evidently because men are caught therewith like fish—then I admit that old age, though it lacks immoderate banquets, may find delight in temperate repasts.

Finally, to the charge that old age "is not far removed from death" Cicero answers along Epicurean lines that death should be considered a blessing, because it frees the immortal soul from its bodily prison on this imperfect earth:

When old men die it is as if a fire had gone out without the use of force and of its own accord, after the fuel had been consumed.... For as Nature has marked the bounds of everything else, so she has marked the bounds of life. Moreover, old age is the final scene, as it were, in life's drama, from which we ought to escape when it grows wearisome and, certainly, when we have had our fill. (quotations re. Cicero are from Gruman, 1966; and Cole & Winkler, 1994, pp. 48–53)

In concluding this section, we quote Cole's (1988) summary view of the Greco-Roman philosophy of aging and the life cycle:

Beginning at conception, the physiological process of drying out and growing cold continued inexorably until death. The stages of life were nature's milestones, marking the diminution of natural heat and increased desiccation. Each change dictated its own behavior pattern. This approach to aging and the life cycle took shape in an intellectual world without boundaries between science and philosophy; hence it combined the physical and the moral, interpreting behavioral signs in the light of physiology as well as individual character. (p. 49)

IV. Philosophy to Protoscience (c. 100–1600 A.D.)

In the time of Aristotle there was no sharp distinction between (natural) philosophy and science. Hippocratic medicine was a mixture of both, in the sense that physicians made use freely of biological and philosophical principles in explanation of the course of life and the afflictions of the aging body. The works of

Galen (129–216 A.D.), the Greek physician of the second century who followed Aristotle's lead and ultimately practiced in Rome, represent the culmination of Greco-Roman medicine. Galen who was born in Pergamum (Asia Minor), was pre-eminent in the medical world of his time, and became a model for physicians and for medicine far into the Middle Ages. The most complete presentation of Galen's gerontology appears in his book on hygiene, *De sanitate tuenda*. Galen believed, like others of his time, that aging is a lifelong process and begins at the very conception of the organism. Arguing that blood and semen, as sources of generation, required a drying element to produce tissues and organs, he posited that vital heat dried the substances to create an embryo. Because of this drying, the tissues and organs are formed as the body grows and develops. However, there comes a time in early adulthood when the balance shifts, and the drying ceases to be beneficial and becomes malignant. That is when the fuel of the body, the "innate moisture," begins to dry up, and, as a result, the body becomes more and more cold.

Galen did not attempt to interfere with what was regarded as the inevitable changes in the body's balance of heat and cold and the drying out of tissues. He limited himself to cautious hygienic measures designed to moderate, but not basically to alter, the inexorable development of the constitutional imbalance of old age. Galen's writings reflect the syllogistic assumption that nature does everything for the best, that old age is not contrary to nature, and thus old age is not a disease. This thought is diametrically opposed to the Aristotelian view, as expressed by the Roman philosopher and statesman Seneca (4? B.C.–65 A.D.), that senescence is an incurable illness, *senectus insanabilis morbus* (Freeman, 1979).

In the early Middle Ages, Galen's interpretation of the biology of life was shared by an Arabic philosopher and physician Avicenna (980–1037), who was said to have known all of Aristotle's writings from memory. His *Canon of Medicine* followed the anatomy of Galen and the clinical observations of Hippocrates. He believed that the drying-out process began in the embryo and continued as a beneficial influence until growth and development ceased at about the age of 30. The lamp metaphor explains the decline of the body that begins at that time. The "innate moisture" is the fuel of the body, and, like the oil of a lamp, it feeds the flame, the "innate" heat. As the innate moisture dries up, the innate heat decreases and thus, the aging body becomes cold and dry. This led to a pessimistic outlook about the capacity of medicine to interfere in the decline of function of an aging body. Avicenna believed that senescence is an inevitable concomitant of life and that extending the life was not a legitimate medical goal, because each individual had a predetermined fixed term of life (Birren, 1996b, p. 658).

The real object of conserving the energies of the body lies in the attainment of spiritual development. The actual bodily occupation is itself, if we will it so, the practical means of that attainment. The energy of will to associate this means of worship with the subjugation of the vices inherent in our frailty must be employed during the early years if we are not to find ourselves in old age powerless to advance along the critical stages of the journey to the only true Goal. This principle underlies the idea of "right Regimen." (Quoted in Cole & Winkler, 1994, p. 340)

Avicenna's thought blended with that of St. Augustine (354–430), the Christian philosopher and theologian, and many of the medieval Scholastics. Christianity added a new dimension, a fundamental cause for illness and death that went far beyond the natural explanation of Hippocratic medicine. In medieval Christian theology, sickness, aging, and death were not the original fate of humankind; rather, they resulted from the rebellion of Adam and Eve against God's commandment. In paradise, Adam and Eve had lived in perfect health, their humors in balance—immune to the aging process. St. Augustine, who is well known for his *Confessions*, perhaps the first autobiography, explained Adam's and Eve's youthful health:

[Their] bodies were not indeed growing old and senile, so as to be brought in the end to an inevitable death. This condition was granted them by the wonderful grace of God, and was derived from the tree of life which was in Paradise.

Once expelled from Paradise, however, they were no longer protected by the tree, and became subject to the processes of aging and illness which have been the lot of humankind ever since. (quotations re. St. Augustine in Cole, 1998, p. 50)

In the medieval synthesis, medicine and theology interact: although it is natural to age and die, the reason for doing so is attributed to the Fall of Man. The religious and theological underpinnings of medieval life encouraged the view that one should not tamper with God's will. Because of such religious beliefs, the study of aging became the study of proper preparation for death and eternity. This view not only discouraged attempts to modify the course of life but also discouraged science generally, because its attempts to understand nature were intrusions into the organization of the cosmos as designed and desired by God. As recently as the 18th and 19th centuries, there was evidence that the dominant Christian theology discouraged an empirical approach to demography and epidemiology that could ascribe the length of life to natural phenomena (Birren, 1996b, p. 659).

In addition to the dominant thoughts of medieval Scholastics, there was some room for alchemy, the precursor of the modern science of chemistry. Alchemy may be defined as the art which sought to transmute ordinary metals into silver and gold, and which attempted to prepare a chemical medicine that would cure all diseases and greatly prolong life. Originally an Arabic science and philosophy, alchemy was widely practiced in the 13th and 14th centuries. Roger Bacon (c. 1220–c. 1292), a Franciscan friar and Oxford scholar, was one of the great figures in the popularization of alchemy. In his *Opus majus*, he presented four reasons why the brevity of life must be considered accidental, and therefore, subject to improvement. The first reason is based on the Judeo-Christian traditions about Eden and the ten partriarchs:

The possibility of the prolongation of life is confirmed by the consideration that the soul naturally is immortal and capable of not dying. So, after the fall, a man might live for a thousand years [i.e., Methuselah]; and since that time the length of life has been gradually shortened. Therefore it follows that this shortening is accidental and may be remedied wholly or in part. (Gruman, 1966, p. 63)

As second and third reasons, Bacon argued that longevity was decreased by widespread immorality and by the neglect of hygiene. The detrimental influence of these factors is compounded with each succeeding generation: "Thus a weakened constitution passes from father to sons, until a final shortening of life has been reached, as is the case in these days" (p. 63).

As the fourth reason for regarding the life span to be flexible, Bacon asserted there were numerous instances in which individuals, by "secret arts," had added remarkably to their years. Bacon's favorite story was one about a Sicilian farmer: "While ploughing he found a golden vessel in the fields hidden in the earth, which contained an excellent liquor. Thinking this liquor was dew from the sky he drank it and washed his face, and was renewed in mind and body beyond measure" (cited in Gruman, 1966, p. 63). The implication of this story is that the farmer had benefited from a solution of gold, and this was in accord with the

alchemical quest for potable gold, i.e., the elixer of life.

The above reasons moved Bacon to assert that human longevity could be extended significantly. As such, Bacon is diametrically opposed to the medical tradition of Galen and Avicenna, who did not have any aspirations for retarding age, let alone reversing the aging process. Historically, Bacon stands in the Aristotelian tradition, given his grim portrayal of senescence: "excess of mucus, foul phlegm, inflammation of the eyes, general injury to the organs of sense, forgetfulness," etc. etc. p. 64). The significance of Roger Bacon's work is that he offered something radically new in the Western world in terms of a methodical rationale for prolonging life (quotations re. Bacon in Gruman, 1966, pp. 63–64).

The 14th and 15th centuries mark the Renaissance of literature, learning, and art in Western Europe. Stimulated by the prosperity of the Italian economy and its culture, many new expressions were spawned in the humanities and science. In the 16th century, the Renaissance was joined by a Reformation movement in which Protestant churches separated from the Roman Catholic church. The Reformation brought with it a new freedom of thought but also new tensions about social controls, religious beliefs, and desirable life activities, though it still carried with it an emphasis on doing good works during one's lifetime. In brief, the Renaissance and Reformation permitted a shift in attitudes that supported the growth of natural science and the gathering of systematic data.

In Italy, mid-16th century, the Renaissance hygienist Cornaro (1467–1565) published his Discourses (*Discorsi della vita sobria*), which were very influential in Western Europe well into the 19th century. The ideas of Cornaro were derived of Cicero and Galen, but he interpreted them differently by arguing the desirability and possibility of a long and healthy life. The first argument is a simple affirmation of the worth of long life: "I ceaselessly keep repeating, Live, live, that you may become better servants of God." The second reason for the desirability of longevity is that old age is a happy phase of life is that he has "an ardent desire that every man should strive to attain my age, in order that he may enjoy...the most beautiful period of life." Cornaro's third argument is simply that longevity pays:

Men endowed with fine talents ought to prize a long life very highly....if he is a public official, how much greater is the possibility of his being called to the highest dignity in the state; if a man of letters, he will be looked upon as a god on earth; and the same is true of all others, according to their various occupations

As a fourth reason Cornaro remarks that if one lives long enough, he will attain the blessing of a "natural death": "For, in them, the end is caused merely by the failure of the radical ['innate'] moisture; which, consumed by degrees, finally becomes completely exhausted, after the manner of a lamp which gradually fails. Hence they pass away peacefully, and without any kind of sickness" (cited in Gruman, 1966, pp. 69–70).

The keystone of Cornaro's regimen was sobriety, especially in regard to diet. As one matured, it was absolutely essential to reduce the amount of food taken in: every individual is born with a certain amount of innate moisture that gradually is used up by the body's activities. As this principle of life is consumed, it cannot be regained, but, by leading a temperate life, one may determine that the supply will last for the time allotted to man by God and Nature, 100 to 120 years. The major obstacle on the road to long life is disease, for when one is ill, the innate moisture is expended at an abnormally rapid rate. Cornaro claimed that the great usefulness of his regimen, which essentially consists of some very simple hygienic practices, is that it keeps the four humors of the body nicely balanced and, therefore, prevents

all disease (quotations re. Cornaro in Gruman, 1966, pp. 68–71). This view has its counterparts today, that personal dietary habits, exercise and activity patterns, exposure to noxious environmental influences, and stress influence how long and how well we live.

V. Protoscience
(c. 1600–1800 A.D.)

In Great Britain, the view of the philosopher Francis Bacon (1561–1626) encouraged the growth of natural sciences and serious inquiry into the processes of aging. Bacon's (1638) implications for gerontology was that by undertaking a systematic study of the processes of aging one might discover the causes of aging. In the introduction to *The Historie of Life and Death, with Observations Naturall and Experimentall for the Prolonging of Life*, Bacon formulated his program. In four admonitions he criticized physicians for neglecting the prolongation of life, the "principal part of their art":

First, that, to date, all works on the subject have been unsound; Aristotle's contribution was only of slight value, while more modern writers (apparently, the alchemists and iatrochemists) were vain and superstitious. Second, that naive efforts to preserve natural warmth and moisture do more harm than good. Third, and perhaps the most apt, that prolongevity is a long and complex undertaking.... And fourth, that it is necessary to distinguish between the regimen for health and that for longevity, for that which exhilarates the body and spirit is not necessarily conducive to long life. (Gruman, 1966, p. 81)

In spite of his criticism, Francis Bacon was more impressive as a philosopher and prophet of science than in doing the scientific work itself. Both his theory of aging and the hygienic regimen were largely derivative of Aristotle and Galen. To postpone the decline of the body forces, Bacon had the following suggestions:

First, the spirits must be conserved and their actions modified: they may be "condensed" by certain drugs (e.g., opium and nitre), their escape may be blocked by coating with oil the pores of the skin, and their harmful effects on the blood may be decreased by baths (which cool the blood). Secondly, one may attempt to aid those processes, which restore and regenerate the body: for example, certain herbs strengthen the vital organs, while a proper

regimen (diet, exercise, etc.) helps to improve the digestion and assimilation of food. Finally, there are efforts directed at rejuvenation: thus, overly dry parts may be softened and moistened by massage and special baths, while periodically one may take herbs and purgatives for the purging away of old juice and supplying of new juice. (Gruman, 1966, p. 82)

The significance of Bacon's work is that it brought great prestige to the experimental study of aging and that it stimulated the formation of the Royal Society (UK), which became the model for all scientific societies.

The 18th century of Enlightenment is characterized by a firm belief in reason and the progress of science. The American statesman, philosopher and scientist Benjamin Franklin (1706–1790) looked to the future optimistically and wrote to the English chemist Joseph Priestly (who discovered oxygen) that the time would come when "all diseases may by sure means be prevented or cured, not excepting even that of old age, and our lives lenghtened at pleasure even beyond the antediluvian standard" (Gruman, 1966, p. 74). Franklin was a versatile thinker with serious interests in many subjects including the prolongation of life. Because of his involvement with the discovery of the lightning rod and thereby controlling the flow of electrical discharge, he thought that the loss of electricity or the loss of vitality might be the cause of aging and death. As he wrote in a letter to a close friend,

Your observations on the causes of death and the experiments which you propose for recalling to life those who appear to be killed by lightning,

demonstrate equally your sagacity and your humanity. It appears that the doctrines of life and death in general are yet but little understood. (Gruman, 1966, p. 84)

Franklin's speculations about the cause of aging underscores many uncertainties in the field of gerontology. That is, it is uncertain whether a particular characteristic of the organism associated with advancing age is the cause of general aging or is a result of it. This dilemma is seen, for example, in the earlier emphasis on vital heat and the body, which led to the assumption that the drying process or the loss of innate moisture was the cause of aging, and if moisture was added to the body, aging would be stopped or reversed. In a similar way, because sexual intercourse seems to decline with age, it was thought that stimulating increased sexual activity might fend off the more general effects of aging (Birren, 1996b, p. 661).

In the last quarter of the Enlightment, the German philosophers Johann Nikolas Tetens (1736–1807) and Friedrich August Carus (1770–1808) published their thoughts about human development. In the following we are quoting liberally from Reinert (1979) and Baltes (1983). Tetens's work on natural philosophy, for example, dealing with the *Perfectability and Development of Man* (1777), emphasized observation as the method of psychological analysis. Tetens said that "the strength of this method was dependent upon how well the generalizations of the experiential principles obtained from individual cases would succeed. Such generalizations would be derived on the basis of hypotheses and arguments by analogy, especially between physical and psychical development" (Reinert, 1979, p. 212). According to Baltes (1983), Tetens posits three fundamental issues about the nature and explanation of geropsychology:

(1) the question of whether performance decrement as observed in older persons necessarily indexes decline or whether certain aspects of apparent performance decrement can be seen instead as evidence for

further development; (2) the question of to what degree performance decrement in older persons is a function of "nonuse" (disuse) of functions; and (3) whether decline in old age should be conceptualized as regression, that is, as a process that occurs in reverse order from that observed in the first half of life.... Tetens uses concrete examples such as memory functioning to illustrate these issues. In the case of memory, for example, he emphasizes that memory decrement in elderly persons could be seen as adaptive and that a major problem in memory performance of older persons is not one of memory trace but one of retrieval, of reaching the 'enveloped' memory material. (pp. 84–85)

F. A. Carus, not to be confused with his relative, the well-known romanticist Carl Gustav Carus, died at a young age and his work of historical significance was published posthumously under the title *Special Psychology* (1808). Carus, who—just like Tetens—was a sensitive observer but not a scientist, identified four periods of the life-span: childhood, youth, adulthood, and senescence. According to Reinert (1979), he understood that "in and of itself chronological age ... was not a psychological determinant. (hence), the freedom of human development should not be bound to years" Instead of speaking of age, he preferred to speak more psychologically of periods of life, or chronological stages that are not clearly separable. Such periods, therefore, are more aptly described as inwardly psychological stages that all individuals must go through or at least run through, (pp. 219–220). To depict Carus's theoretical stance, Baltes (1983) uses his view of psychological aging as an illustration. Carus is

not only concerned with aging as decline but also as a stage of progression. For example, Carus emphasized that if one were to take a teleological view of the developmental periods, one should expect to find in old age the most perfect human being.... He goes on to state that age as senescence denotes the last and highest stage of development, maturity (p. 86)

Tetens's and Carus's notions of geropsychology make a surprisingly modern impression. However, it must not be forgotten that these notions are based on reflections rather than on experiments and empirical science. As such, Tetens and Carus are among the last representatives in the history of geropsychology who were engaged somewhere on the borderline between philosophy and science.

VI. The Rise of Science (c. 1800–1900 A.D.)

The roots of geropsychology as a science lie in European scientific developments of the 19th century. The European Zeitgeist fostered a strong conviction that the scientific method could be applied to all phenomena and that rational and logical explanations of their causes could be ascertained. Science and its methodology became the doorway to knowledge. The optimism of the 19th century belief in the lawfulness of nature, even the lawfulness of death, is illustrated in a paper published by an English actuary, Benjamin Gompertz (1779–1865), *On the nature of the Function Expressive of the Law of Human Mortality* (1825).

Gompertz studied human vital statistics from four locations, Northampton, Deparcieux, Sweden, and Carlisle. He noted that the mortality rate increases in geometric progression (i.e., by a constant ratio in successive equal age intervals). Hence, a straight line, known as the Gompertz function, results when death rates are plotted on a logarithmic (ratio) scale. The prevalence of many diseases and disabilities rises in the same geometrical manner as does the mortality rate. The regularity of Gompertz's observations has led to much speculation and research into the genetic and biological basis of aging and the causes of death. An explanation, however, for the relationship between rate of death and age is still a subject for research. Nevertheless, Gompertz's law can now be seen to be slightly less than a natural law, but it serves a reasonably accurate description of human mortality (Strehler, 1977).

While scientific effort was devoted to identifying specific relationships like Gompertz's law, the Belgian scientist, mathematician, statistician, and astronomer Adolphe Quetelet (1796–1874) attempted to demonstrate that all facets of the changes in human behavior across the life span were lawful. The data he reported covered such topics as birth rate, mortality trends by age, stature, weight, and strength, as well as the development of "moral and intellectual qualities of man." The first sentence in Quetelet (1835/1842) reflects his scientific orientation: "Man is born, grows up, and dies, according to certain laws which have never been properly investigated, either as a whole or in the mode of their mutual reactions" (p. 1). This is followed by statements about his program for probing the regularity or lawfulness of human development and aging. In commenting about previous work Quetelet said,

They have not determined the age at which his faculties reach their maximum or highest energy, nor the time when they commence to decline. Neither have they determined the relative value of his faculties at different epochs or periods of his life, nor the mode according to which they mutually influence each other, nor the modifying causes. In like manner, the progressive development of moral and intellectual man has scarcely occupied their attention; nor have they noted how the faculties of his mind are at every age influenced by those of the body, nor how his faculties mutually react. (p. 1)

Quetelet was a distinguished scientist of his day, and he visited and corresponded widely with other leaders in science in Western Europe. It is of interest to note that it is difficult to classify him in terms of contemporary science. He wrote and studied at a time before there were few formal university departments in many of the disciplines. Trained as a mathematician, he became interested in probabilities and developed the concept of *l'homme moyen*, the "average man," around whom values or measurements

were distributed according to the law of accidental causes. In this he anticipated the work of Gauss on the binomial distribution, which is commonly known as the normal or bell-shaped curve. Quetelet's work opened the way for the study of the regularities in social and behavioral phenomena in relation to age, sex, profession, season of year, and economic and religious institutions. He even anticipated the later interest in creativity and age and examined the dramatic works of French and English dramatists in relation to age and included an analysis of the number of works that would have been produced had the sample not been reduced by death:

Quetelet's writing reveals that he recognized clearly the influences of both social and biological influences on how humans develop and how long and how well they live. In this regard he was the forerunner of the view that geropsychology lies between the biological and social sciences. (Birren, 1961, pp. 69–70)

After Quetelet, the British naturalist Charles Darwin (1809–1882) gave a further rationale for studying human development and aging, as a part of the natural world. Darwin placed the human species in a chain of evolution in which a common biological history was shared with other species. His book, *On the Origin of Species by Means of Natural Selection or the Preservation of Favoured Races in the Struggle for Life*, was published in 1859, and sparked a flurry of scientific activity, which continues to this day. Through his observations of various species, Darwin concluded that there had been an evolution of species from simple early forms to later more complex species, including human.

Essentially, Darwin's theory of evolution contains two explanatory concepts. The first is *natural selection*, or the idea that those characteristics of plants and animals that aid survival within a particular environment will persist. Poorly adapted forms disappear. As environmental conditions change and mutations occur, new species develop. Thus humanity is seen as an evolving member of the animal kingdom that shares a common origin with other species. The second concept is the mechanism for transmitting advantageous characteristics, which we now accept as being *heredity*. In this context, the central question, as far as geropsychology concerns, is whether adaptation continues in the postreproductive phase of life. Darwin didn't have a clear answer, but he assumed that the force of natural selection declines with age and there may be indirect, selective pressures for senescence.

Although evolutionary theory did give humans a superior position in the sense that it was a late evolved species, it clearly broke with the creationist tradition, which regarded humankind as a unique and immediate purposive product of a Divine Being. Darwin's notions that selective pressures shape the development of specific biological characteristics had tremendous impact on how scientists viewed human biology and behavior. Darwin influenced the development of psychology; a casual inspection of the articles referenced in the *Psychological Index*, from the founding of the American Psychological Association in 1894 to 1920, showed a major focus of research on genetic influences on behavior (Birren, 1996b).

Darwin's ideas influenced his cousin, Francis Galton (1822–1911), who was perhaps the most prominent 19th-century investigator in the field of human development and aging. Galton had been in contact with Quetelet, and both men were interested in quantifying the relationship of functional aspects of organisms with the age of the organism. Galton, like Quetelet, had broad interests. He was originally trained in medicine and mathematics and later studied geography, anthropology, and psychology.

He became increasingly interested in anthropometric measurements and, like Quetelet, included measurements of physical and mental functions in his research. By 1879, he had already gathered relevant data on the upper limits of hearing, using variable-pitch whistles, and made what is probably the first report of the late-life decline in audibility of high-frequency tones. In 1883, Galton published a book, *Inquiries into Human Faculty and Its Development*, as his biographer Pearson points out, after 7 years of work. Some of his notes were labelled "Psychometric Inquiries 1876." A clear statement of Galton's recognition of developmental psychology and geropsychology is shown in a request he made in 1884 to gather together an exhibit of

means of defining and measuring personal peculiarities of Form and Faculty, more especially to test whether any given person, regarded as a human machine, was at the time of trial more or less effective than others of the same age and sex. Again, to show by means of testings repeated at intervals during life, whether the rate of his development and decay was normal. (Pearson, 1914, vol. II, p. 213)

Here we find an early call for longitudinal studies of development and aging, a later 20th-century emphasis.

Galton used the term *human machine*, which undoubtedly reflects his earlier background in physiology. He was interested in fitting the facts of both development and aging of human beings into a broader framework of human evolution and science. One of his major contributions to the study of aging was his gathering of data at the International Health Exhibition of London of 1884. Over 9,337 males and females aged 5–80 years were measured on 17 different functions. Because of his exposure to large masses of data, Galton developed an index of correlation to measure the degree of association of two variables (e.g., age and strength). This was a large step forward because it enabled scholars to separate factors according to the degree to which they were related to age or to some purported causal factors of aging. Galton's interests later turned away from the study of development and aging to the application of Darwin's ideas of evolution. He began studies of twins, because observations suggest that twins are more similar in appearance and behavior than other children within the same family. Twin studies are used today for a variety of purposes, including attempts to establish the roles of heredity and environment in determining differences in intelligence, personality, and other characteristics. Galton also attempted to develop principles of eugenics for application in the population at large. He wanted to encourage selective breeding of the population so that persons with high intelligence levels would have more offspring.

In concluding this section on the rise of science, Galton should be quoted when he mentions in an insightful manner the loss of criticism from his peers:

Among the many things of which age deprives us, I regret few more than the loss of contemporaries. When I was young I felt diffident in the presence of my seniors, partly owing to a sense that the ideas of the young cannot be in complete sympathy with those of the old. Now that I myself am old it seems to me that my much younger friends keenly perceive the same difference, and I lose much of that outspoken criticism which is an invaluable help to all who investigate. (Pearson, 1914, vol. III, p. 318)

Here we find the notion that aging is not only a matter of measurement but also an inner process.

VII. The Emergence of Geropsychology (c. 1900–1950)

Geropsychology is primarily a product of the 20th century, and particularly it is a product of post-World War II research and scholarship. Its early years are marked by few publications, and it trailed the expansion of the study of child development by about 50 years. This gives rise to questions about why geropsychology was such a late emerging field of specialization, as presumably it had the stimulation of Francis Galton's 1884 health exhibit in London that measured over 9,337 subjects aged 5 to 80 years on 17 different measures. In 1923, Koga and Morandt (1923) reanalyzed some of Galton's data using a partial correlation technique, which made it possible to remove the effect of intervening variables. In this case they established the fact that a large component of the slowness of reaction time with age was associated with the central nervous system rather than with peripheral sensory changes. This work is rarely cited and it apparently did not influence further research.

Galton was a gentleman scholar who did not need an academic appointment to maintain himself. However, having no students, his career did not have much lasting direct impact. This is in dramatic contrast to Wundt, who founded the experimental psychology department at the University of Leipzig in 1879 and whose students influenced the course of psychology in many universities, although it had no content of developmental psychology or geropsychology. Apparently the institutionalization or departmentalization of a subject matter appears to be a factor in its growth and intellectual influence.

Child development had the encouragement of the practical necessity of providing textbooks and instructions for teachers in training as well as providing advice to parents who wanted their children to grow up and utilize their talents. Early in the 20th century, the development of mental tests to measure child intelligence became a major activity of psychologists. Later the same measurements were applied to older adults, and the results, interpreted as reflecting decrements and increments in capacities with advancing age, precipitated discussions about their interpretation. Soon discussion focused on the matter of whether the same validating criteria of measures of intelligence could be used for children and adults. In the case of children, the criterion widely accepted was school achievement or grades. No such obvious consensual criterion was at hand for older adults, and age norms were often created that left avoided the issue of what the tests measured. Later scores were interpreted more in terms of poor scores or deficits related to physical conditions.

Contributing to the slow rise of geropsychology as a subject matter was a strong orientation of behaviorism, particularly in America, which attributed the shaping of behavior to external reinforcement. This left little room for emerging internal psychophysiological and emotional variables to influence measurements and their interpretation. An early developmental psychologist, Lewis Terman, took a rather extreme view of behaviorism:

That the Watsonian brand of behaviorism is a cult, and that its presumption in claiming the whole of psychology and in basing a theory of child training and a denial of heredity on a few minor experiments in the emotional conditioning of infants is ridiculous. (Terman, 1932, p. 330)

Despite his early studies, which only involved animal behavior in a psychobiological context, John Watson turned to the study of infants to formulate his views on radical behaviorism. Late in his career his autobiography reveals his deep commitment to the interpretations of behaviorism. "I still believe as firmly as ever in the general behavioristic position I took over in 1912" (Watson, 1936, p. 281). Excluded from consideration were the effects of genetics and other organismic variables. Obviously a tension has existed on the interpretation of development between the behaviorist position and that of broader organismic views.

By extension, the behaviorist position about older persons could be viewed narrowly as a product of their early rewards and punishments. This logic has an ele-

ment in common with the psychodynamic interpretation of the development of behavior by Freud, who viewed the experiences of the first few years of life as structuring the predispositions or personality throughout adult life. In both streams of thought, the interpretations of changes in the adult organisms related to their early experience and did not encourage the detailed study of adults themselves. For Freud, the early emotional experiences were important and for the behaviorists in the Watson tradition, early cognitive conditioning was of dominant importance. Both behaviorism and psychoanalysis contributed to the slow emergence of the study of older adults and a broader view of developmental and geropsychology.

Another negative influence on the encouragement given to geropsychology was the great influence that the Swiss psychologist Piaget had in developing his concepts of stages of cognitive development during childhood (Piaget, 1928). In his autobiography he expressed the view that a next step for him would be to link the stages of mental development with "stages of nervous development" (Piaget, 1952, p. 256). Presumably by nervous development he meant the nervous system not emotional behaviors. However, this still left little reason to study older adults. Piaget's interests in the early life succession of mental stages was highly productive, but he left little need to explore the dynamics of the cognitive abilities of older adults. An exception to the lack of encouragement the Piagetian influence provided geropspsychology was the work of Kohlberg. His studies of stages of moral development opened the door to the life span study of higher levels of moral behavior (Kohlberg, 1982).

Erik Erikson, trained as a psychoanalyst, used concepts of stages to develop a psychosocial theory of personality development across the life span. He posed eight stages of life, each with its own crises arising from conflicts between opposite behavioral tendencies, and viewed development as a function of both individual and cultural factors. His book, *Childhood and Society* (Erikson, 1950), encouraged research in geropsychology.

The traditions of experimental psychology retarded the growth of geropsychology, with its bias toward isolating an aspect of behavior and subjecting it to manipulation and interpretation within a microtheoretical context. When experimental psychologists interpreted the performance of their subjects in relation to age, it was done within the context of what had been discovered in work on age-constant subjects.

One of the early exceptions was G. S. Hall, who after he retired as president of Clark University wrote a book on senescence (Hall, 1922). Apparently he was concerned about growing older and made a comprehensive review of the literature in biology and medicine as well as in psychology. He reported the findings of some interviews he had done with older adults that included attitudes toward death. His sample of subjects would hardly meet contemporary standards, but he did believe there was a shift with age in attitudes toward death that is still relevant to today's discussions about the circumstances of dying in later life and assisted death or euthanasia. A student of G. S. Hall had already published in 1896 an article on the psychology of aging and death (Scott, 1896); however, he is not cited in a biography of Hall (Ross, 1972).

Although G. S. Hall was prepotent as an American psychologist and as a creator of the field of adolescent development, he left little impact on the evolution of geropsychology. He was the organizer and first president of the American Psychological Association. One may infer that his late life turn to the study of aging transmitted little encouragement to young students who were influenced by the growth

of behaviorism and the narrow views of much of experimental psychology.

John B. Watson, the founder of behaviorism, did little to encourage geropsychology, although he was the mentor to one of the earliest women to earn a Ph.D. in America, Helen Hubbert. She did her dissertation at Johns Hopkins University on learning in rats of different ages and followed them longitudinally (Hubbert, 1915). She was both a gender pioneer and a subject matter pioneer, although there is little evidence that she or her dissertation was cited and had an impact on subsequent thinking or research.

Perhaps the first organized attempt to stimulate research on the psychology of aging was at Stanford University from about 1927–1932, under the direction of Walter Miles and encouraged by Louis Terman, a developmental psychologist who created the Stanford Binet test of intelligence. There were five doctoral dissertations supervised by Miles and one postdoctoral study. The department of psychology had received a grant of $10,000 in 1928, and also a second grant in 1932 from the Carnegie Corporation in support of the Stanford Later Maturity Study (Miles, 1967, p. 240). This was rather impressive fiscal support for research in that period and may have been the first organized program of research in geropsychology. Applying for the Carnegie funds was an outstanding group of professors: Terman, Strong, Stone, and Miles. Despite the fiscal and intellectual prosperity at Stanford, the graduate students left no obvious trail of influence in the evolution of geropsychology. This may be due to the fact that they emerged from their studies at the time of the Great Depression, when there were few job opportunities, and it was important to secure any position rather than set a precondition that it must provide opportunities for research on aging. Also, Walter Miles left Stanford University in 1933 to take a position at Yale, which broke the continuity of the research on aging at Stanford. There were subsequent reports of longitudinal studies of Terman's gifted children into adult life that represented a continuity of faculty interest but little graduate student activity. An early splinter activity from the Stanford faculty was the guidance center for older adults established in San Francisco in 1929 by Lillian Martin after she retired from the psychology faculty at Stanford.

The doctoral study of Elsa Frenkel-Brunswick (1939) on the psychology of aging was encouraged by Charlotte Bühler at the University of Vienna. However any potential programmatic interest died with the onset of World War II and the scattering of faculty.

In 1945 at Cambridge University, Frederick Bartlett created a productive center for research on aging headed by Alan Welford. About the same time Hans Thomae began his studies in the psychology of aging at the University of Bonn, Germany. It is probably not wise to neglect the role of economics and other social influences on developing academic programs. Certainly the Great Depression and World War II had wide influences on careers and the topics that faculty members chose to study. In 1941 the U.S. Public Health Service founded its research program on aging in Baltimore under the direction of Nathan Shock, but because of the war its efforts were diverted until 1945, when physiological investigations were started joined by psychological research in 1947. This program has been maintained to date, and numerous research fellows have gained experience there, and the longitudinal studies have gained significance.

In America a group headed by Sydney Pressey organized a division of the American Psychological Association devoted to the psychology of aging. He became its first president and its first meeting was held in 1947 attended by such persons as

Walter Miles and Charlotte Bühler among others. Pressey had started innovative studies by interviewing competent older persons. Although Pressey had strong interests in the measurement of mental deterioration he came to realize that "deterioration might not be a major feature of age" (Pressey, 1967, p. 334). Perhaps Pressey had the broadest perspective about the gains and losses of growing up and growing old and was clearly one of the pioneers in psychology who gave support in ideas, research, and professional activities that encouraged the emergence of geropsychology.

VIII. Recent Developments (c. 1950–Present)

Following World War II, active research on aging was encouraged in many countries perhaps stimulated by the growing awareness of the dramatically increasing life expectancy and the growth of the older populations. There was a rising need for information about the conditions of life that influenced disabilities and for practical information about treatment, care, housing, and the functional capacities of older adults.

Other developments favored the growth of geropsychology and the knowledge it might provide. Medicine was beginning to recognize that the nervous system is an active agent in the changes in the organism with advancing age. Early opinions left the nervous system as a passive bystander in the processes of aging. It began to be recognized that the brain was the primary regulator of both physiological functions and behavior.

The Gerontological Society of America was founded in 1946 with participation by biologists, physicians, psychologists, and social scientists. The International Association of Gerontology was founded shortly after, which led to sharing of data across countries as well as across disciplines. One may infer from these developments that much stimulation for geropsychology came from outside organized psychology. This is supported by the fact that the *Journal of Gerontology* published articles of the psychology of aging beginning in 1946, whereas the journal *Psychology and Aging*, published by the American Psychological Association, did not appear until 1985.

The post-World War II period was undoubtedly the launching period of geropsychology, as shown by Riegel's (1977) analysis. Riegel (1977) did a quantitative analysis of publications in what he called psychological gerontology. In the 31-year period 1919–1950, he identified 33 persons who were senior authors on eight or more publications. By coincidence, in the 10-year period 1951 to 1961, there were the same number of leaders in publications, 33, illustrating the growing interest in the subject matter. Similar results were seen in Riegel's list of major human studies in the psychology of aging. He identified 24 major research studies from 1884 to 1950, and 25 major studies from 1951–61. Thus in a 10-year interval nearly the same number of studies were undertaken as in the previous 60 years. In Riegel's analysis of the year of publication of 3,449 articles or books from 1873–1968, there appeared to be an exponential increase in the publication rate after 1950, reaching a peak in the last year of his survey of 247 articles or books. Thus in 1 year, 1969, almost as many articles and books were published as in the entire pre-World War II period. This staggering rate of growth of the field is clearly encouraging for a field that might be judged to be lagging behind other areas of psychology. It does, however, portend a problem for the future of geropsychology, the difficulty of integrating what is known. The large and growing volume of publications makes it difficult for researchers and scholars to get a comprehensive and integrated picture of available knowledge,

perhaps a situation facing the whole subject matter of psychology as we move into the 21st century.

A. Theory

Birren was the first to study systematically the age-related slowing of behavior as a fundamental characteristic of the process of aging (for an overview, see Birren & Fisher, 1995). Till today the scientific debate focuses on the question of whether there is a pervasive general slowing of behavior by the central nervous system or whether there are specific localized mechanisms. Sufficient research, however, has been conducted to indicate that there are specific factors as well as a general process associated with the slowing of behavior with advancing age (Birren's strong hypothesis of speed of behavior). Whether such slowing is a primary (strong hypothesis) or secondary (weak hypothesis) cause of age differences in cognitive processes is a significant scientific issue, of which its origins remain to be understood in greater detail, as well as its relationship to the health and well-being of the individual.

Since the beginning of the 1980s, Baltes and colleagues have conducted a series of studies on psychological processes of development and aging from a life-span perspective (for an overview, see Baltes, 1997). Their work resulted in a psychological model, called "selective optimization with compensation." The central focus of this life span model is the management of the dynamics between gains and losses (i.e., a general process of adaptation), consisting of three interacting elements: selection, optimization, and compensation. Selection refers to an increasing restriction of one's life to fewer domains of functioning because of an age-related loss in the range of adaptive potential. Optimization reflects the view that people engage in behaviors to enrich and augment their general reserves and to maximize their chosen life courses (and associated forms of behavior) with regard to quantity and quality. Finally, compensation results also (like selection) from restrictions in the range of adaptive potential. It becomes operative when specific behavioral capacities are lost or are reduced below a standard required for adequate functioning. The lifelong process of selective optimization with compensation allows people to age successfully (i.e., to engage in life tasks that are important to them despite a reduction in energy).

Recent developments in the psychology of aging concern the emerging field of gerodynamics, which studies the organization of behavior over the course of life from a gerontological perspective (for an overview, see Schroots & Yates, 1999). Gerodynamics is based on general and dynamic systems theory, and conceptualizes the aging of living systems (individuals) as a nonlinear series of transformations into higher and/or lower order structures or processes of entropic origin, showing a progressive trend toward more disorder than order over the life span, and resulting in the system's death. The concept of intraindividual variability of functions, as a measure for entropic processes, plays an important role in describing and explaining behavioral transformations over the life span.

B. Methods

The decades since 1950 have seen the growth of longitudinal studies on aging (Schroots, 1993). A strong addition to the growing sources of important information about the psychology of aging have been the twin studies. Such studies have included the longitudinal following of identical twins raised together and apart providing information that differentiates the magnitude of environmental and genetic influences on behavior in the later adult years (Pedersen, 1996).

The analysis of data proposed by Schaie (1986) into three components has had a pervasive effect on the design and interpretation of data. He proposed the separation of measurements into those reflecting cohort differences, differences associated with time changes within the individual, and the time of measurement. This has come to be known as the effects of APC—age, period, and cohort—and has greatly increased the sophistication of analyses of data in relation to time and the attribution of causality (Schaie, 1986).

Measurements of individuals characterized as growth curves are often summarized as a mean curve. Collins (1996) cautions that group curves can be misleading and that there is a need to shed light on the correlations between initial status and subsequent change. Obviously there has been a great increase in methodological and design sophistication in studies of the psychology of aging. In the area of cognition, Herzog (1996) made the summary statement that "experimental research in the area of aging and cognition is currently characterized by an unprecedented increase in the technological and methodological quality of those aspects of the research that are associated with experimental methods for assessing cognition" (p. 35).

The increased sophistication in the design of research and methods of analysis of data would seem to insure greater objectivity in the interpretation of causal influences in aging and minimizing unjustified and premature applications to improve the well-being of older persons.

C. New Subject Matter

The exponential increase in the literature after 1950 was accompanied by the study and publication of articles on many new issues. A large growth of interest can be seen in the broad domain of health behavior and aging with questions whether observed behavioral changes are the antecedent of illness or result from illness (Schroots, Birren, & Svanborg, 1988). This has in turn led to growing questioning about the diversity and patterns of late life terminal decline (Berg, 1996). Increased research has taken place to answer questions about the origin of later life changes in behavior as being inevitable or a results of disuse and lack of stimulation (Willis, 1996).

The neurosciences have added a new chapter in the exploration of aging, and the neuropsychology of aging has become an interest area of large scope (Woodruff-Pak, 1997). Partly this is a product of the need for differential diagnoses and treatment of older persons with behavioral changes suspect of having pathological origins, such as Alzheimer's Disease.

Recognition of different patterns of late-life diseases and disabilities between men and women has led to research on gender differences. However, gender research about social influences on the behavior and life careers of men and women has also emerged as an area of study. Some research topics that have emerged appear to have little counterpart with studies of child developmental or experimental psychology. Topics linked closely with later life that are active areas of research are creativity and wisdom (Simonton, 1996; Sternberg, 1990). To this should be added the study of the role of spiritual outlook and religion in the adult life. Overlooked in the past, spirituality and religion has come to be an active subject of research on aging (McFadden, 1996). Closely related is the growth of interest in the inner experience of aging or of being old. What is referred to as narrative content, the oral reports of persons of their inner experiences, interpretations of life and its events, and emotions has greatly expanded in recent years (Birren, Kenyon, Ruth, Schroots, & Svensson, 1996). Subjective oral reports have also become an adjunct to research on aging

and health including self-appraisal of health status.

It is conceivable that careers will develop that are devoted to integration of the volume of information generated in geropsychology. Such careers would supplement the more typical pattern of individuals who develop careers through research on the particulars of behavior (Birren & Schroots, 2000). We may also scc more publication of metanalyses, handbooks, annual reviews, and mini-encyclopedias to encourage integration and supplement the information provided by individual studies. The pressure for integration may arise outside of universities that cultivate individual research and come from agencies and foundations responsible for funding research. The latter may be more concerned with the evaluation of a field or cultivating an area of research and the pursuit of of generalizations.

Both the complexity of phenomena of aging and the growth of knowledge may in the future require more multidisciplinary teams of investigators not only within psychology (e.g., those pursuing research in cognition, memory, personality, and neuropsychology), but also geneticists, epidemiologists, and physiologists. One may also see a broadening of the scope of the methodologies, with borrowings from clinical, experimental, and epidemiological methods, as we seek the efficient pursuit of answers to important but complex questions. As the growth of knowledge about the psychology of aging continues, there will also be opportunities for applications. Contemporary science has supported research, but it is also interested in applications of research knowledge to raise the quality of life.

IX. Epilogue

Although the emergence of geropsychology is primarily a phenomenon of the second half of the 20th century, it has deep roots in early beliefs and cultural traditions. Many elements of contemporary ideas about aging have similarity if not continuity with ancient beliefs that bred extreme optimism or extreme pessimism about death, dying, and the course of life. Death and dying were the province of early religious beliefs, which dictated the interpretation of aging and its processes.

During the period when Greco-Roman philosophers dominated intellectual life, there was an increased emphasis on logic. Though more rigorous in reasoning, they lacked evidence for their views. However, they did begin free thinking about underlying natural processes, such as drying of the body and becoming colder. The Renaissance prepared the way for further steps in the discarding of mythical views of the control of aging and the growth of empirical research. Finally, the rise of science in the 19th century opened the door to research on aging including psychology.

Geropsychology trailed the growth of experimental psychology and child development by many decades. One may speculate on the factors that contributed to this slower emergence of the study of geropsychology and then about the factors that released its dramatic growth after 1950. Perhaps the answer lies in the high birth rates and the short life expectancy in the early 20th century and the need for psychology to meet practical needs of providing principles of development for the training of school teachers and helping parents raise children.

Because of the pressures for knowledge about the development of children, it seems likely that psychology departments added faculty members who were specialized in early life development. One might detect today a negative view of the emergence of geropsychology because of its implications of competition with child development for faculty positions and financial support.

It is of more than passing interest that a large 1994 history of a century of developmental psychology did not index aging, adult development, or gerontology and devoted only about a paragraph to life span developmental psychology (Parke, Ornstein, Rieser, & Zahn-Waxler, 1994). Although the book was published by the American Psychological Association, it made no reference to a 1956 book (published by the same organization) on the psychological aspects of aging that was attended by a broad spectrum of psychologists (Anderson, 1956). Apparently, developmental psychology is commonly interpreted as referring to child development, and there has been a wide gap and lack of integration of the subject matters of the child and adult phases of the life span. Perhaps the expanding skills of childhood are an optimistic context for research in contrast to the more threatening rising probability of death associated with aging. However, some discouragement of a liasion between the study of childhood and adulthood results from early psychodynamic concepts that early life events were basically formative, and adult life was a scenario derived from early childhood experiences (e.g., Freud). Similarly, Piaget's stage theory of cognitive development didn't encourage study of the later years of life. It was as though adults lived out their later years from the patterns established primarily during early development.

Another negative influence was perhaps the emphasis on experimental psychology in the post-Wundt days, when researchers studied particulars of behavior such as perception and memory using college-aged students as their subjects. Evidence that early psychology had little or no contact with subjects in the second half of life is seen in reviews of research in psychology in Europe and North America that characterized the contents of psychology up to 1930. No reference is made to aging (Murchison,

1930). The model for experimental research was then the success of physics in developing laws of natural phenomena such as gravity. Investigating particular aspects of behavior by experimental means was thought to have the potential for giving rise to important scientific generalizations, such as those related to atoms, ions, and electrons. One may contrast the microperspective of experimental psychology with the macrovision of the complexity of the organization of adult behavior adopted by many geropsychologists.

If geropsychology did not receive much encouragement from its psychology neighbors, other influences nourished it. In the mid-1930s, there was a realization in medicine that the infectious diseases were coming under control and that the chronic diseases were becoming the major sources of mortality. This led to a multidisciplinary perspective that aging is a product of biological, behavioral, and social interactions. This is shown in the E. V. Cowdry (1938) edited volume and later in the 1943 U.S. Public Health Service report on mental health in later maturity based upon a multidisciplinary conference (U.S. Public Health Service, 1943).

World War II delayed the expression of interest in aging, though it rapidly expanded after the war with the establishment of research grants by the National Institutes of Health as well as an intramural program of research on aging that included psychology. The founding of the Gerontological Society in 1946 and the creation of a division of the American Psychological Association on Maturity and Old Age, whose name was changed later to Adult Development and Aging, led to the creation of a specialized journal and annual meetings participated in by psychologists dealing with aspects of adult life.

With the growth of research some new issues have emerged for geropsychology.

One issue concerns questions about the behavioral contributions to the differences in mortality and morbidity of men and women. Another issue is the large diversity among older individuals, which is often obscured by focusing solely on trends in mean values. Still another emerging topic is the study of the inner experience of aging, the ways individuals experience and interpret their lives. Thus supplementing an experimental orientation is the growth of interest in the personal or autobiographical interpretation of life.

Geropsychology clearly stands between the biological sciences on the one hand and the social sciences on the other. In its searches for explanations of changes in human and animal behavior, geropsychology observes influences from these adjacent areas of science as well as from the domains of thought, emotions, and actions that may spring from the organization of the nervous system and its capacities for knowing, feeling, planning and strategic action, and the emergence of individual identity and self.

What is now becoming clear in the history of the subject matter is that *age* itself doesn't cause anything. Age is a convenient index to group phenomena, but it does not reflect the dynamic processes that bring about the changes associated with age. As the science of geropsychology becomes increasingly knowledge based, chronological age will become replaced with the variables that bring about change. More research may be expected to be devoted to the antecedents of change, although chronological age may never disappear as a useful index in the initial organization of data.

Geropsychology seeks to identify the antecedents of change in relation to length of life, whether they be beneficial or detrimental to the organism. Some of the antecedents may go back to the unique genetic inheritance of an individual or group, to the circumstance of fertilization and fetal development, and to the process of learning in a particular society and the unique experiences that accompany the growing up and growing old of a particular person. Given the complexity of human aging, it is perhaps not surprising that geropsychology was relatively recent to emerge as an area of study. It required the development of methodological sophistication and controlled sampling of study populations.

A view of the history of geropsychology is that the subject matter is complex; many avenues of research are necessary because so many systems interact. Increasing sophistication of our longitudinal studies and statistical methodology will undoubtedly make possible new insights and also quantify the relative importance of different contributing factors to how well we grow up, grow old, and the quality of lives we lead at different phases of life.

References

Anderson, J. E. (Ed.) (1956). *Psychological aspects of aging.* Washington, DC: American Psychological Association.

Bacon, F. (1638). *The historie of life and death.* London: I. Okes H. Mosley.

Baltes, P. B. (1983). Life-span developmental psychology: Observations on history and theory revisited. In R. M. Lerner (Ed.), *Developmental psychology: Historical and philosophical perspectives* (pp. 79–111). Hillsdale, NJ: Lawrence Erlbaum.

Baltes, P. B. (1997). On the incomplete architecture of human ontogeny: Selection, optimization, and compensation as foundation of developmental theory. *American Psychologist, 52,* 366–380.

Berg, S. (1996). Aging, behavior, and terminal decline. In J. E. Birren & K. W. Schaie (Eds.), *Handbook of the psychology of aging,* (4th ed.) (pp. 323–337). San Diego, CA: Academic Press.

Birren, J. E. (1961). A brief history of the psychology of aging. *The Gerontologist, 1,* 69–77; 127–134.

Birren, J. E. (1996a). James Emmett Birren. In D. Thompson & J. D. Hogan (Eds.), *A history of developmental psychology in autobiography* (pp. 24–45). Boulder, CO: Westview Press.

Birren, J. E. (1996b). History of gerontology. In J. E. Birren (Ed.), *Encyclopedia of gerontology* (Vol. 1, pp. 655–665). San Diego: Academic Press.

Birren, J. E. (Ed.). (1996c). *Encyclopedia of gerontology.* San Diego: Academic Press.

Birren, J. E., & Fisher, L. (1995). Aging and speed of behavior: Possible consequences for psychological functioning. *Annual Review of Psychology, 46,* 329–353.

Birren, J. E., Kenyon, G., Ruth, J. E., Schroots, J. J. F., & Svensson, T. (Eds.) (1996). *Aging and biography: Explorations in adult development.* New York: Springer.

Birren, J. E., & Schroots, J. J. F. (Eds.) (2000). *A history of geropsychology in autobiography.* Washington, DC: American Psychological Association.

Cole, T. R. (1988). Aging, history, and health: Progress and paradox. In J. J. F. Schroots, J. E. Birren, & A. Svanborg (Eds.), *Health and aging: Perspectives and prospects* (pp. 45–63). New York: Springer.

Cole, T. R. & Winkler, M. G. (Eds.) (1994). *The Oxford book of aging: Reflections on the journey of life.* New York: Oxford University Press.

Collins, L. M. (1996). Measurement of change in research on aging: old and new issues from an individual growth perspective. In J. E. Birren & K. W. Schaie (Eds.), *Handbook of the psychology of aging* (pp. 38–56). San Diego, CA: Academic Press.

Cowdry, E. V. (Ed.) (1938). *Problems of ageing.* Baltimore: Williams and Wilkins.

Darwin, C. (1859). *On the origin of the species by natural selection.* London: John Murray.

DeLuce, J. (1996). Mythology. In J. E. Birren (Ed.), *Encyclopedia of gerontology* (Vol. 2, pp. 187–195). San Diego: Academic Press.

Erikson, E. H. (1950) *Childhood and society.* New York: W. W. Norton.

Falkner, T. M., & DeLuce, J. (1992). A view from antiquity: Greece, Rome, and elders. In T. R. Cole, D. D. Van Tassel, & R. Kastenbaum (Eds.), *Handbook of the humanities and aging* (pp. 3–39). New York: Springer.

Freeman, J. T. (1979). *Aging: Its history and literature.* New York: Human Sciences Press.

Galton, F. (1883). *Inquiries into human faculty and its development*. London: Macmillan & Co.

Gompertz, B. (1825). On the nature of the function expressive of the law of human mortality, and on a new mode of determining the value of life contingencies. *Philosophical Transactions of the Royal Society, 115*, 513–585.

Gruman, G. J. (1966). *A history of ideas about the prolongation of life* (Transactions of the American Philosophical Society; New Series, Volume 56, Part 9). Philadelphia: The American Philosophical Society.

Hall, G. S. (1922). *Senescence: The last half of life*. New York: D. Appleton.

Herzog, C. (1996). Research design in studies of aging and cognition. In J. E. Birren & K. W. Schaie (Eds.), *Handbook of the psychology of aging* (4th ed.) (pp. 24–37). San Diego: Academic Press.

Hubbert, H. B. (1915). The effect of age on habit formation in the albino rat. *Behavior Monographs, 2* (6), 55.

Koga, Y., & Morandt, G. M. (1923). On the degree of association between reaction times in the case of different senses. *Biometrika, 15*, 346–372.

Kohlberg, L. (1982) Moral development. In J. M. Broughton & D. J. Freeman-Moir (Eds.), *The cognitive developmental psychology of James Mark Baldwin: Current theory and research in genetic epistemology* (pp. 277–325). Norwood, NJ: Ablex.

Lehr, U. (1977). *Psychologie des Alterns [Psychology of aging]*. Heidelberg: Quelle & Meyer.

McFadden, S. (1996). Religion, spirituality, and aging. In J. E. Birren & K. W. Schaie (Eds.), *Handbook of the psychology of aging* (4th ed.) (pp. 162–177). San Diego: Academic Press.

Miles, W. R. (1967). Walter R. Miles. In E. G. Boring & G. Lindzey (Eds.), *A history of psychology in autobiography* (Vol V, pp. 223–252). New York: Appleton Century Crofts.

Murchison, C. (Ed.), (1930). *Psychologies of 1930*. Worcester, MA: Clark University Press.

Parke, D. P., Ornstein, P. A., Rieser, J. J., & Zahn-Waxler, C. (Eds.) (1994). *A century of developmental psychology*. Washington, DC: American Psychological Association.

Pearson, K. (1914). *The life, letters and labours of Francis Galton*. (4 vols.). Cambridge: University of Cambridge Press.

Pedersen, N. (1996). Gerontological behavior genetics. In, J. E. Birren & K. W. Schaie (Eds.), *Handbook of the psychology of aging*, 4th edition, pp. 59–77. San Diego, CA: Academic Press.

Piaget, J. (1928) *Judgment and reasoning in the child*. London: Kegan Paul, Dtrench & Trubner.

Piaget, J. (1952). Jean Piaget. In E. G. Boring, H. S. Langfeld, H. Werner, & R. M. Yerkes (Eds.), *A history of psychology in autobiography* (Vol. IV, pp. 237–256). Worcester, MA: Clark University Press.

Pressey, S. L. (1967). Sidney Leavitt Pressey. In E. G. Boring & G. Lindzey (Eds.), *A history of psychology in autobiography* (pp. 313–339). New York: Appleton Century Crofts.

Quetelet, A. (1835/1842) *A treatise on man and the development of his faculties*. Edinburgh: William and Robert Chambers.

Reinert, G. (1979). Prolegomena to a history of life-span developmental psychology. In P. B. Baltes & O. G. Brim, Jr. (Eds.), *Life-span development and behavior* (Vol. 2, pp. 205–253). New York: Academic Press.

Riegel, K. (1977). History of psychological gerontology. In J. E. Birren & K. W. Schaie (Eds.), *Handbook of the psychology of aging* (pp. 70–102). New York: Van Nostrand Reinhold.

Ross, D. (1972). *G. Stanley Hall: The psychologist as prophet*. Chicago: University of Chicago Press.

Sandars, N. K. (1983). *The epic of Gilgamesh*. New York: Penguin Books.

Schaie, K. W. (1986). Beyond calendar definitions of age, time, and cohort: The general developmental model revisited. *Developmental Review, 6*, 252–277.

Schroots, J. J. F. (Ed.) (1993). *Aging, health, and competence: The next generation of longitudinal research*. Amsterdam: Elsevier.

Schroots, J. J. F., Birren, J. E., & Svanborg, A. (Eds.) (1988). *Health and aging*. New York: Springer.

Schroots, J. J. F., & Yates, F. E. (1999). On the dynamics of development and aging. In V. L. Bengtson & K. W. Schaie (Eds.), *Handbook of theories of aging* (pp. 317–433). New York: Springer.

Scott, C. (1896). Old age and death. *American Journal of Psychology, 8,* 67–122.

Simonton, D. K. (1996). Creativity and wisdom in aging. In J. E. Birren & K. W. Schaie (Eds.), *Handbook of the psychology of aging* (4th ed.) (pp. 320–329). San Diego: Academic Press.

Sternberg, R. J. (Ed.) (1990). *Wisdom: its nature, origins, and development.* New York: Cambridge University Press.

Strehler, B. L. (1977). *Time, cells, and aging.* New York: Academic Press.

Terman, L. M. (1932). Trails to psychology. In C. Murchison, (Ed.), *A history of psychology in autobiography* (Vol. II, pp. 297–331). Worcester, MA: Clark University Press.

U.S. Public Health Service (1943). Mental health in later maturity. *Public Health Reports,* suppl. No. 168. Washington, DC: Government Printing Office.

Watson, J., B. (1936). John Broadus Watson. In C. Murchison (Ed.), *A history of psychology in autobiography* (Vol. III, pp. 271–281). Worcester, MA: Clark University Press.

Willis, S. L. (1996). Everyday problem solving. In J. E. Birren & K. W. Schaie (Eds.), *Handbook of the psychology of aging* (4th ed.) (pp. 287–308). San Diego: Academic Press.

Woodruff-Pak, D. (1997). *The neuropsychology of aging.* Oxford, UK: Blackwell.

Two

Structural Equation Modeling in Longitudinal Research on Aging

Georg Rudinger and Christian Rietz

I. Longitudinal Research on Aging

Research on aging is a very broad and exponentially growing field. It is characterized by a large diversity of substantive research areas (Binstock & George, 1996; Birren & Schaie, 1996; Schneider & Rowe, 1996) and, corresponding to this growth, by a large variety of methodological approaches (Cavanaugh & Whitbourne, 1999; Cohen & Reese, 1994; Magnusson, Bergman, Rudinger, & Törestad, 1994; Rudinger & Rietz, 1999; von Eye & Clogg, 1994). Important questions in developmental research and especially in aging research undoubtedly could and should be answered using longitudinal methodology (Baltes & Mayer, 1999; Nesselroade & Baltes, 1979; Schaie, 1996; Schroots, Fernandez-Ballesteros, & Rudinger, 1999).

In longitudinal studies the entity of interest usually is observed repeatedly as it evolves over time (McCall, 1977). In every longitudinal data set, invariance and change, as basic characteristics of time-bound processes, can be viewed from different conceptual perspectives (e.g., Buss, 1979; Nesselroade, 1991) that are also found in more complex systems, such as chaos and catastrophe theory, transitions, and nonlinear system theory (Newell & Molenaar, 1998).

The longitudinal approach offers unique opportunities to investigate determinants and characteristics of transitional processes (e.g., Anderson et al., 1998; Hartelsman, van der Maas, & Molenaar, 1998), interindividual differences and intraindividual changes (Nesselroade, 1991; Nesselroade & Boker, 1994; Nesselroade & Featherman, 1997), as well as changes in structure or structures of change (McArdle & Nesselroade, 1994; Schaie, Maitland, Willis, & Intrieri, 1998). Longitudinal designs offer not only many advantages, but also suffer from drawbacks such as selection effects, systematic attrition, and different types of selectivity (Bosworth & Schaie, 1999; Lindenberger et al., 1999; Pedersen, Steffensson, Berg, Johansson, & McClearn, 1999; Rudinger & Rietz, 1998a), and from incomplete data sets related to the processes (McArdle & Hamagami, 1991, 1992; Rubin, 1987).

From a statistician's point of view, this situation creates severe problems, because mathematical assumptions (concerning distributions and concepts of

Handbook of the Psychology of Aging

independency) for the application of "classical" test statistics are often violated. Some ways to finesse these assumptions have been described by Edgington (1995), Efron and Tibshirani (1993), and by Wilcox (1997). Regardless of these problems, linear structural equation models (SEMs) have become well established for analyzing developmental and aging research data (Hertzog, 1987, 1990; McArdle & Nesselroade, 1994; Raykov, Tomer, & Nesselroade, 1991). The merits of linear SEM in the context of longitudinal research will be explicated by means of some very elementary concepts at the beginning of this chapter (also see Collins, 1996).[1]

A. Facets of Change in Observed Variables

The fundamental concepts of invariance and change will be illustrated by means of a miniaturized two occasion situation and one observed variable (measuring change). Figures 2.1a–1c (adapted from Rogosa, Brandt, & Zimowski, 1982) provide selected examples of invariance and change under at least three perspectives.

Tisak and Meredith (1990) differentiate several types of stability. Strict stability (no change at all, neither in means nor in variances), parallel stability (individuals develop linearily, but individual differences do not vary across time, Figure 2.1a), and monotonic stability (individuals maintain their same rank order over the measured time periods, Figure 2.1c).

Figure 2.1a illustrates low interindividual differences in intraindividual changes, as almost all individual paths follow the same increasing slope. Examples of this type of individual and

[1] The input streams of the models are available as a file: Appendix.doc (Word document) on the FTP-server at the following addresses: ftp.seniorweb.uni-bonn.de/zem/handbook

group trajectories can be found as overall effects in cognitive intervention programs (see Dunlosky & Hertzog, 1998; Hagen, Oswald, & Rupprecht, 1998).

Change in everyday competence in old age might provide an example for Figure 2.1c (Baltes, Maas, Willms, Borchelt, & Little, 1999; Diehl, Willis, & Schaie, 1995; Schaie & Willis, 1999). The figure shows decreasing level, increasing (fan-spread) variances, and stable positions of individuals across time (high correlation of everyday competences over time). Nevertheless, the interindividual differences in intraindividual changes are considerable, because the slopes of the individual trajectories across time differ (dependent on the initial level): The lower the competence, the more rapid the decrease.

The counterpart of stability (i.e., inconsistency or instability) has two faces: random changes of relative positions from first to second occasion (Figure 2.1b) or systematic changes of relative positions, (e.g., an entire exchange of relative positions from first to second occasion).

Figure 2.1b shows stable level, growing interindividual differences (i.e., increasing variances) and unstable positions of persons across time (numerous crossing time paths, i.e., low correlation across time, usually considered as low "stability"); additionally, it shows large interindividual differences in intraindividual changes (= different slopes). This figure could be characteristic of individual trajectories of life satisfaction at two different far distant points in time. Numerous events could have occurred that differentiate life satisfaction in different persons, such as loss of a spouse or gaining a new partner, retirement (positive for some persons, negative for others), changes in housing conditions, change in financial situation, and changing health conditions (Holahan, Holahan, & Wonacott, 1999; McCamish-Svensson, Samuelsson, Hagverg, Svensson, & Dehlin,

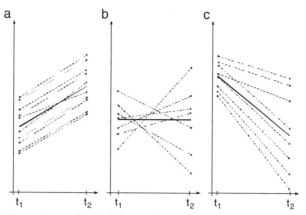

Figure 2.1 Individual time paths (a–c) for two points of measurement. Bold lines: means, broken lines: individual trajectories.

1999; Penninx et al., 1999; Perrig-Chiello, Perrig, & Staehlin, 1999).

Rogosa, Brandt, and Zimowski (1982) used similar illustrations to operationalize interindividual differences in intraindividual changes. The core of their approach consists of correlating the initial scores with the slopes of the individual trajectories. This individualized approach has to be carefully differentiated from an aggregated approach, such as SEM; modeling changes by structural equations is usually not modeling of the individual trajectories, but of aggregated data. The (individual) slopes contain the combined information of amount and direction of intraindividual change. As Rogosa and his co-workers (Rogosa, Brandt, & Zimowski, 1982; Rogosa & Willett, 1983, 1985a) argue, this approach circumvents almost all classical problems in measuring change (Harris, 1963): reliability of difference scores, regression towards the mean, correlation of differences with third variables, law of initial value, and so on (Collins & Horn, 1991; Raykov, 1994, 1999). The correlation between the individual initial scores and the individual slopes provides information on the existence of interindividual differences in intraindividual changes that depend on the initial level. The correlation is equal or close to

zero in Figures 2.1a und 2.1b, and high positive in Figure 2.1c.

The different features are separate facets of change:—first, level of functioning or performance correspond to their statistical counterpart the means, second, interindividual differences in variables under study or variability among individuals corresponding to, variances, and third, relative positions of subjects within their reference group across time (stability), corresponding to the "test–retest correlation."

B. Facets of Change in Latent Variables

In addition to means, variances, and individual slopes, as a fourth aspect it has to be taken into account whether the change is located on the observed or on the latent level. Increasing variances of the observed variables across time could indicate a "real" fan-spread change on the latent level (i.e., growing variances of the latent variables across time) or could indicate decreasing reliability across time, (i.e., increasing error variances across time). It is possible that behind every facet of change in the observed world (see Figure 2.1a–c) a convergent or divergent process of change is hidden in the latent world. This is illustrated in Figure 2.2.

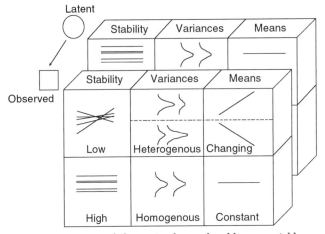

Figure 2.2   Facets of change in observed and latent variables.

The above considerations provide the reasons why SEM—explicitly differentiating between observed and latent variables—is extremely useful for the analysis of longitudinal data. However, complex multivariate statistical techniques require strong a priori distributional assumptions that are rarely met in the longitudinal context. Nevertheless we take a pragmatic and optimistic view and hope that future developments will solve those problems, which are mathematical rather than conceptual. We pay this pragmatic price for the good value obtained with SEM: SEM separates the observed variables from the latent universe. It allows the test of otherwise separated hypotheses, and most importantly, SEM is able to explicitly model the directionality of time.

C. Time

The longitudinal orientation corresponds to a conceptualization of time as an ordered dimension (Riegel, 1972). Time sequence and directionality of time *a priori* explicitly enter modeling and statistical analyses. An example, which we will use later again, is as follows: instead of describing time-ordered empirical covariances or correlations by (confirmatory) factor analysis (CFA) type models, it is preferred to explain the covariances or correlations by autoregressive models, which take directionality into account. It seems undesirable to reintroduce the time order *post hoc* in interpreting results of statistical analyses, as is typical in classical analyses for repeated measures, such as *t*-tests for dependent samples, multivariate analysis of variance (MANOVA) for repeated measures, and so on (for a detailed discussion of (MANOVA for longitudinal research see Hertzog, 1994). Time series analysis, which is more sensitive to the order of measurement occasions, and their derivates (Molenaar & Nesselroade, 1998) are not focused in this chapter because in conventional longitudinal studies the number of measurement points is too small for an appropriate application of this technique. In addition, the basic assumption of stationarity is not compatible with most of the research questions in longitudinal aging research.

II. Stability and Reliability

The conceptual distinction between reliability and stability has a central role and long history in longitudinal research (see Heise, 1969; McArdle & Woodcock, 1997; Rudinger; 1998; Wiley & Wiley, 1970). Initially separation of reliability and stability here is limited to covariances and correlations, ignoring mean levels. In SEM terms, the definition of reliability refers to the assumptions about relations of theoretical concepts to a set of measured variables. Reliability describes the quality of measurement of the phenomena under study (Alwin, 1999). The definition of stability refers to the structural model, specifying the relations hypothesized within a set of theoretical concepts. Stability is operationalized as the correlation of latent variables adjacent in time. Stability in this sense mirrors the consistency of interindividual differences at the level of latent constructs and refers to theoretical assumptions about the time-bound process. Stability does not exclude interindividual differences in intraindividual changes at the observed (see Figure 2.1) or latent level.

Every empirical correlation (connecting one variable observed at two points in time: r_{12}) contains reliability information at each time point (rel_i) as well as stability information (ρ_{12} correlation of the true scores across time). Every empirically observed correlation is a nonlinear function of at least five unknowns, because rel_i is a function of true score variances and error variances, which are unknown, too:

$$r_{12} = \rho_{12} \cdot \sqrt{rel_1 \cdot rel_2}.$$

For alternative decompositions of r_{12} see McArdle and Woodcock (1997).

In the case of two measurement points and one variable, the equation is not solvable (not identified) unless reliability and/or stability coefficients are known. If they are unknown, the solution is only possible if the model is extended to more than one observed variable per construct and/or to more than two measurement points. We will demonstrate the separation of stability and reliability by means of SEM by extending the measurement points to four. This separation can be accomplished most appropriately by means of structural regression models that involve the estimation or regression coefficients representing a sequence of time-ordered direct relationships between antecedent and consequent variables.

Another class of longitudinal SEMs just contains covariances among latent variables across time. They represent CFA-type models, sometimes with correlated factors. Figure 2.3 illustrates two different families of models, CFA-type models (represented by a one factor model) versus "real" longitudinal models (represented by a quasi-Markov-simplex model), which explicitly takes the time sequence into account.

The question of the adequacy of CFA-type models versus autoregressive models is also part of the trait–state debate (see Hertzog & Nesselroade, 1987; Kim, Nesselroade, & Featherman, 1996; Nesselroade, & Bartsch, 1977; Usala & Hertzog, 1991). However, a state-theoretical assumption about the relational system under study can be modeled by autoregressive coefficients estimated close to zero. Because the classical definition of trait and state contains a time-bound component (Cattell, 1950), CFA-type models do not seem optimal to disentangle trait and state variance.

It is a drawback of CFA-type models that sequentiality of time, the essential feature of a longitudinal data set, is lost (Rudinger, Andres, & Rietz, 1994) (see Figure 2.3). In CFA-type models, the order of measurement points is part of the external information possessed by the researcher. The researcher refers to the knowledge *post hoc* in interpreting the results, but no time-related assumptions are specified *a priori* and explicitly at the stage of modeling.

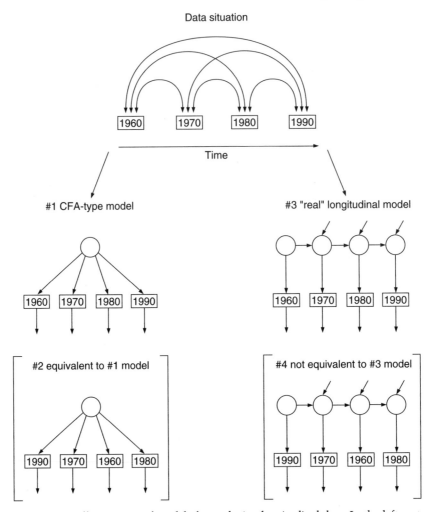

Figure 2.3 Different types of models for analyzing longitudinal data. In the left part, the time order of measurements can be changed—as in the model in brackets below— and the CFA-type models remain statistically equivalent; in the right part every change of the time order (e.g., 1990, 1970, 1980 instead of 1960, 1970, 1980, 1990) of measurements connected autoregressively yields different results.

A. The Quasi-Markov Simplex (Single Indicator)

We next consider estimation of reliability and stability in the framework of autoregressive models. The classic model for analyzing reliability and stability of longitudinal data is the quasi-Markov simplex (Jöreskog, 1970). However, this model is still appropriate for longitudinal questions (Boomsma & Molenaar, 1987; Man-dys, Dolan, & Molenaar, 1994; Raykov, 1998). Figure 2.4 illustrates this type of model.

Separation of reliability and stability will be illustrated with intelligence data (Wechsler Adult Intelligence Scale—(WAIS) from the Bonn Longitudinal Study of Aging (BOLSA; Lehr & Thomae, 1987). The BOLSA was started in 1965 with a sample of 221 women and men, born in 1890–1895 (cohort 1) and 1900–1905 (co-

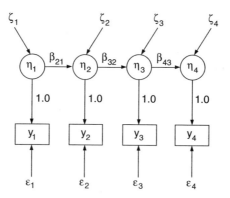

measurement equations

$$y_1 = \eta_1 + \varepsilon_1$$
$$y_2 = \eta_2 + \varepsilon_2$$
$$y_3 = \eta_3 + \varepsilon_3$$
$$y_4 = \eta_4 + \varepsilon_4$$

structural equations

$$\eta_1 = \zeta_1$$
$$\eta_2 = \beta_{21}\eta_1 + \zeta_2$$
$$\eta_3 = \beta_{32}\eta_2 + \zeta_3$$
$$\eta_4 = \beta_{43}\eta_3 + \zeta_4$$

variances

$$\mathrm{Var}(y_1) = \psi_{11} + \mathrm{Var}(\varepsilon_1)$$
$$\mathrm{Var}(y_2) = \mathrm{Var}(\eta_2) + \mathrm{Var}(\varepsilon_2)$$
$$\mathrm{Var}(y_3) = \mathrm{Var}(\eta_3) + \mathrm{Var}(\varepsilon_3)$$
$$\mathrm{Var}(y_4) = \mathrm{Var}(\eta_4) + \mathrm{Var}(\varepsilon_4)$$

$$\mathrm{Var}(\eta_1) = \psi_{11}$$
$$\mathrm{Var}(\eta_2) = \beta^2_{21}\psi_{11} + \psi_{22}$$
$$\mathrm{Var}(\eta_3) = \beta^2_{32}(\beta^2_{21}\psi_{11} + \psi_{22}) + \psi_{33}$$
$$\mathrm{Var}(\eta_4) = \beta^2_{43}(\beta^2_{32}(\beta^2_{21}\psi_{11} + \psi_{22}) + \psi_{33} + \psi_{44}$$

covariances

$$\mathrm{Cov}(\eta_1, \eta_2) = \beta_{21}\psi_{11}$$
$$\mathrm{Cov}(\eta_2, \eta_3) = \beta_{32}\beta^2_{21}\psi_{11} + \beta_{32}\psi_{22}$$
$$\mathrm{Cov}(\eta_3, \eta_4) = \beta_{43}\beta^2_{32}\beta^2_{21}\psi_{11} + \beta_{43}\beta^2_{32}\psi_{22} + \beta_{43}\psi_{33}$$

Figure 2.4   A quasi-Markov simplex.

hort 2). In some of the following analyses, we refer to four of the eight measurement points $(t_1 = 1965, t_2 = 1967, t_3 = 1969, t_4 = 1972)$ with a sample of 105 subjects. The intention is to test hypotheses concerning equal reliabilities of assessments across time, equal stabilities from time t to time $t + 1$, and equal variances of the latent variables across time simultaneously. As pointed out earlier, the variances of the latent variables indicate change or invariance of interindividual differences across time. When correlations are analyzed, these possible differences are removed by definition, and tests of hypotheses concerning variances are no

longer possible. Consequently, the covariance matrix must be analyzed. Table 2.1 shows the covariance matrix of four successive intelligence measures (Comprehension subtest of WAIS) across 7 years with a sample of 105 subjects from the BOLSA.

Because of the unequal latent variances and covariances, the reliabilities and the stabilities are generally also unequal. To test hypotheses about reliability and stability, such as equality, it is necessary to specify *a priori* assumptions about variances and covariances of the dependent and independent latent variables, which is impossible within the model in Figure 2.4,

Table 2.1
Covariance Matrix of Four Successive Intelligence
Measures across Seven Years[a]

		1965 (y_1)	1967 (y_2)	1969 (y_3)	1972 (y_4)
1965	(y_1)	4.861			
1967	(y_2)	3.093	4.537		
1969	(y_3)	3.607	3.564	6.765	
1972	(y_4)	3.195	3.154	4.285	6.592

[a]WAIS: Comprehension $N = 105$.

because the assumptions lead to the non-linear equations (i.e., a nonstandard application of SEM).

Figure 2.5 shows the principle of an autoregressive model, which is suitable for superimposing nonlinear constraints in such a way that the nonlinear equations displayed above can be solved (more technical details are available in Rudinger & Rietz, 1993; Rudinger, et al., 1994).

To get "control" over the variances of the latent variables, a trick is used: the variance of the latent variable at time t (Ψ_t) is subtracted from the variance of the latent variable at time $t+1$ using phantom variables (Green & Palmquist,

1991; Rindskopf, 1983, 1984); the latent variable at time $t + 1$ gets a "new" controllable variance (Ψ_{t+1}). This procedure is schematically illustrated in Figure 2.5. Using this basic idea, every hypothesis about variances and connected to this about stability and reliability is testable.

In the following section, some prototypical results are presented, as yielded by appling this model to the intelligence data in old age (Table 2.1). This model was designed to test simultaneously the hypothesis of equal reliabilities, equal stabilities, and equal variances of the latent construct across time. This restrictive hypothesis implies the estimation of three parameters: (a) the four residual variances of the observed variables, (b) the four variances of the latent variables, and (c) the three structural regression coefficients between the latent variables. The structural regression coefficient (stability) is 0.93 between the measurement occasions, the residual variance of the observed variables is 1.74, and the variance of the latent variables is 3.96. The resulting estimated reliability of the measurements is 0.69 at each point in time. The model fit is acceptable ($\chi^2 = 11.49$, $df = 7, p = 0.12$). Satisfying an autoregressive structure with covariances by just three parameters is not trivial at all. Thus, the slogan-like critics of Rogosa and Willett (1985b) and Raykov (1998) have to be rejected resolutely for this type of (quasi-Markov simplex) model.

A closer look shows that the spacing of the four measurements in BOLSA is unbalanced, 2 years between the first and the second and between the second and the third, and 3 years between the third and the fourth. To overcome this incommensurability problem, phantom variables—illustrated in Figure 2.6—are used: 1 year between 1965 and 1967, another year between 1967 and 1969, and 2 years between 1969 and 1972. They slice the stream of time into equal (virtual) units of 1 year.

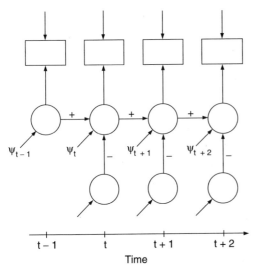

Figure 2.5　A simplex model with nonlinear constraints.

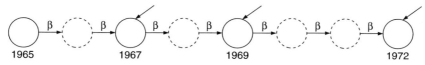

Figure 2.6 Using phantom variables between measurement points.

Using the phantom variables, the structural regression coefficients (β) can be constrained to equality for identical time units. The purpose of this equality constraint is the specification of the hypothesis that the 1-year stabilities are equal. This reflects the assumption of stationarity (i.e., invariant change process over time). The stability across n years is equal to 1-year stability *power n*. The corresponding analysis (model fit: $\chi^2 = 10.80, df = 7, p = 0.15$) yields a 7-year stability of $0.963^7 = 0.768$.

B. More Specific Hypotheses in the Frame of the Quasi-Markov Simplex

A possible hypothesis in psychometric intelligence research in midlife (see Willis & Schaie, 1999) might be the following one: the true score variances no longer change (i.e. the interindividual variability in middle age remains constant over time); the reliabilities of the measurement, however, change over time. Additionally, as an independent process, stability decreases with increasing age. Another substantive hypothesis in intellectual development in old age might propose an increment in interindividual variability over time (fan-spread). The measurement instrument, however, should not change its reliability; stability is expected to be invariant (i.e., in spite of increasing latent variances the correlation between adjacent latent variables is hypothesized to be unchanged; examples of this type of hypotheses are given in Berg & Johansson, 1998; Hultsch, Hertzog, Dixon, & Small, 1998).

Within the model presented in Figure 2.5, the researcher is also in the position

to specify in a general way different types of inequalities between parameters, and particularly inequalities between the variances (true score and/or error variances). Proportional changes of both variances that do not affect the ratio of these variances and that lead to constant reliabilities in the context of changing variances can also be modeled. Specifying the hypothesis of equal reliabilities $rel_1 = rel_2 = rel_3 = rel_4$ in the context of changing variances across time leads to the following generic equations:

$$\frac{1 \cdot Var(\eta_1)}{1 \cdot Var(\eta_1) + 1 \cdot \Theta_{\varepsilon_{11}}} = \frac{a \cdot Var(\eta_1)}{a \cdot Var(\eta_1) + a \cdot \Theta_{\varepsilon_{11}}} =$$

$$\frac{b \cdot Var(\eta_1)}{b \cdot Var(\eta_1) + b \cdot \Theta_{\varepsilon_{11}}} = \frac{c \cdot Var(\eta_1)}{c \cdot Var(\eta_1) + c \cdot \Theta_{\varepsilon_{11}}}$$

The relations between the parameters a, b, and c can be constrained with respect to several substantive hypotheses: $1 < a < b < c$, for example, implies increasing variances (combined with equal reliabilities). To illustrate the basic mechanism of modeling proportionality, the covariance matrix in Table 2.2 was analyzed under the assumption of equal reliabilities over time.

Table 2.2
Covariance Matrix of Four Successive Intelligence Measures[a]

		1965 (y_1)	1967 (y_2)	1969 (y_3)	1972 (y_4)
1965	(y_1)	6.796			
1967	(y_2)	4.005	5.890		
1969	(y_3)	3.672	3.623	4.875	
1972	(y_4)	3.326	3.126	3.061	4.194

[a]WAIS: Similarities; $N = 105$.

The main results of this analysis are the following: the variances of the latent variables are estimated as $Var(\eta_1) = 4.48$, $Var(\eta_2) = 3.96$, $Var(\eta_3) = 3.30$, and $Var(\eta_4) = 2.77$. The estimated residual variances of the corresponding observed variables are $Var(\varepsilon_1) = 2.19$, $Var(\varepsilon_2) = 1.94$, $Var(\varepsilon_3) = 1.61$ and $Var(\varepsilon_4) = 1.36$. As a consequence, the reliabilities (i.e., the ratio of latent variances to observed variances) are estimated equal over time ($rel_1 = rel_2 = rel_3 = rel_4 = 0.67$). This very specific model fits the data well ($\chi^2 = 0.707$, $df = 4$, $p = 0.950$). In analogy, the same principle of proportionality can be used to model stabilities in the context of changing variances.

Every example presented so far focuses on a subset of plausible hypotheses. The examples can be considered as tools for building more complex models (and testing more complex hypotheses). Combining the features of the reported models enables one to test all these types of longitudinal hypotheses.

C. Autoregressive Model with Multiple Indicators

As mentioned above, a solution to the reliability–stability dilemma is also possible if the model is extended to more than one observed variable per construct. In the following, an example of this situation is presented briefly with life satisfaction data from the Interdisciplinary Longitudinal Study of Adulthood and Aging (ILSE). Details for this study are provided by Rudinger and Minnemann (1997). The covariance matrix of the two measures of life satisfaction (ls1 = life satisfaction in general, ls2 = life satisfaction under financial aspects) across three years (1996 and 1999) is given in Table 2.3. The covariance matrix is computed for a sample of 201 subjects from the birth cohort 1930–1932.

The model displayed in the following Figure 2.7 fits the data well ($\chi^2 = 0.76$,

Table 2.3
Covariance Matrix between Two Measures of Life Satisfaction at Two Points of Measurement from the ILSE-Study

		1996		1999	
		ls1	ls2	ls1	ls2
1996	ls1	0.63			
	ls2	0.19	0.94		
1999	ls1	0.18	0.17	0.43	
	ls2	0.22	0.26	0.22	0.54

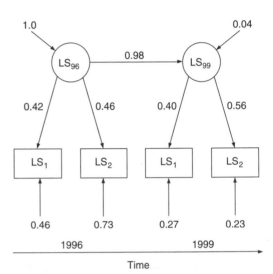

Figure 2.7 Autoregressive model: two measurement points with two indicators.

$df = 1$, $p = 0.38$), and yields as a result low reliabilities (0.27 and 0.23 for the measures in the year 1996, 0.37 and 0.57 in 1999) and a very high stability between the constructs (0.98).

The model in Figure 2.7 can be extended in the same way presented above to test explicitly hypotheses about equal or proportional reliabilities across time in the context of changing covariances.

The variances of the constructs, the stabilities (indicating the relative positions of the subjects), and the reliabilities are conceptually independent features of the "system" (i.e., of the sample respectively of the population) under study. It becomes clear that different assumptions concerning developmental processes lead to different partitions of the total variance due to different sources, including measurement errors (i.e., to different models) (for example from another field, see Finkel, Pedersen, Plomin, & McClearn, 1998). Although these are well-known theoretical facts, they are nevertheless neglected very often in empirical longitudinal research.

III. Mean Structures

In empirical research, investigations initially attend to the means. Analyses of differences or changes in means by *t*-tests, (M)ANOVA, or nonparametric counterparts seem very simple and easily interpretable. In SEM by contrast, the basic analysis starts with variances and covariances. The analysis of mean structures in SEM is a nonstandard procedure.

A. Latent Growth Curve Models

An early model that considers mean structures and covariances simultaneously in a longitudinal context was introduced by Roskam (1976). Other fundamental work has also been done by Jöreskog, van Thiello, and Gruveaus (1970). One of the first explicit latent growth curve (LGC) models for analyzing covariances and mean structures as well in a longitudinal context was published by McArdle (1986) and McArdle and Epstein (1987) (for more recent developments see McArdle, 1998).

The latter authors used SEM to combine traditional ideas from repeated measures ANOVA with some ideas from (longitudinal) factor analysis. The most prominent feature of the McArdle and Epstein (1987) LGC model is the inclusion of at least one common factor (see Figure 2.8). The latent growth factors are

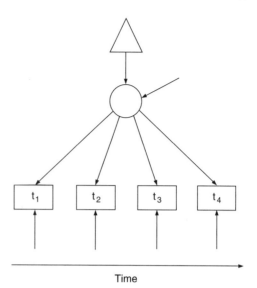

Figure 2.8 A latent growth curve model developed by McArdle and Epstein (1987). A triangle symbolizes the integration of means in the models.

estimated from the repeated observation of a single variable and are used to characterize longitudinal correlations and variances as well as the means. McArdle and Epstein (1987) consider it an advantage of their model that it is possible to study these longitudinal dynamic patterns without any need to reference time-to-time stability or autoregression coefficients. They prefer the (M)ANOVA-type LGC, because they are—as they point out—interested in "studying individual change as a function of time" (p. 111).

The McArdle and Epstein model assumes the same growth process for means and variances; for example, if the means increase linearly, the variances also have to increase by the same linear rule. If the means remain constant, the variances also have to remain stable across time. Therefore we name this type of model an identical process model. This is a very restrictive hypothesis. Referring again to Figures 2.1a–c just a minor subset of all possible hypotheses concerning longitudinal growth processes of means and variances can be tested by the identical process model.

A more liberal and for some research questions also a more appropriate model allows the specification of different growth processes for means and variances (Rudinger & Rietz, 1998b). Schematically this type of model is illustrated in Figure 2.9.

The original McArdle and Epstein model (1987) as well as the unfolded version do not take into account the sequentiality and direction of time, because the models do not contain any time-bound components. Every permutation of the sequence of times of measurement yields exactly the same model fit (i.e., these models are equivalent, irrespective of time order) (see Figure 2.3). However, in the domain of autoregressive models, the order of measurement points plays an important and crucial role. Most permutations of the sequence of time of measurement yield different parameters and different model fits (i.e., these models are not equivalent). The LGC models have this limitation in common with (M)ANOVA of repeated measures, as well as with almost all longitudinal factor analysis models.

B. Latent Growth Curve Models Including Level and Slope Factors

McArdle and Hamagami (1991, 1992) presented an LGC model for the analysis of incomplete longitudinal data sets. We will focus on the model itself and not on the problem of incomplete data sets. Distinctive to the models described in the last section, this extension considers the means by introducing two chronometric correlated factors, level (L) and slope (S) (see Figure 2.10).

The meaning of L and S in this model is as follows. The L-factor represents individual differences in *level of performance* as a base level or as an average level. In either case the L-score is constant for

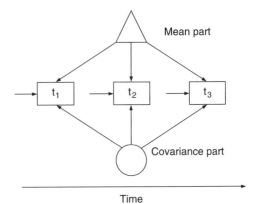

Figure 2.9 An unfolded latent growth curve model.

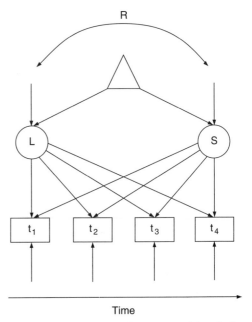

Figure 2.10 Latent growth curve model including level and slope factors.

each individual across the entire time series. The S-factor represents individual differences in the rate of *change in performance* over time. The sign of this score gives the direction of change over time. Like the L-score, this score remains the same for any individual across the entire time series. The distinction between L and S makes it easier to specify and interpret more clearly different growth functions (e.g., linear growth, exponential growth, polynomial growth, or no growth). For example, if L is defined as base level, S represents the increments or decrements according to the specified growth function.

It has to be re-emphasized that differentiation between L and S in the enlarged model also involves the identical process modeled for the behavior of variances and means across time. A distinction between the covariances and means is only possible if these two sets of parameters are unfolded in the manner described above (compare Figure 2.9). The analyzed model still implies insensitivity to time order and directionality.

The correlation between L and S is the innovation of this model. This correlation resembles the correlation between L and S conceptualized by Rogosa and Willett (1985a) and by Rogosa et al. (1982). Some researchers (e.g., Raykov, 1996, 1997) claim that there is a strong parallelism between these two L–S concepts. However, within the structural equations approach, the core information (individual slopes) as used by Rogosa et al. (1982) is simply not available, because the model is based on the supraindividual augmented moment matrix, which does not contain information on covariance or correlation between base status and individual slopes. It is difficult to find a substantive interpretation of R (see also Rovine & Molenaar, 1998; Rudinger & Rietz, 1998b).

C. Latent Growth Curve Models Including a Simplex Structure

Dolan, Molenaar, and Boomsma (1989, 1991, 1992) developed another LGC model for applications in the field of behavior genetics. In the field of behavior genetics, more complex models are needed that incorporate at least two influential factors across time (i.e., genetic and environmental factors) (Molenaar, Boosma, &

Dolan, 1999). The purpose of these models is to test explicitly the hypothesis that the structure of phenotypic means and covariances can be modeled by the same environmental and genetic factors. These more complex models are not presented here, since their basic format is identical to the model depicted in Figure 2.11.

The model is based on the assumption that structuring both means and covariances is equally interesting and represents complementary information for understanding the ontogenesis of a behavioral trait. Longitudinal data have to be examined from the perspectives of stability of individual differences and the continuity in the average growth curves. Consequently, the authors in the preceding paragraph present a longitudinal model based on the simplex model to test the hypothesis that means and covariances can be attributed to a common developmental process (i.e., that the average growth curve and the stability of individual differences are functionally

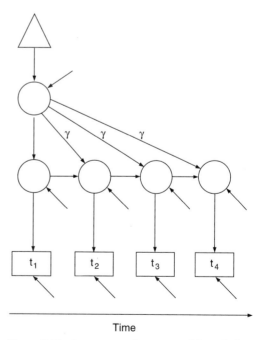

Figure 2.11 Latent growth curve models including a simplex structure.

related). There are some striking differences between this type of model and most of the McArdle and associates studies. Incorporating the simplex property, this model takes into account the time relatedness of the ontogenetic processes under study. Additionally, the authors term their model as a *real latent mean model*, because the means are expressed through the latent variables to the observed variables. Basically, this model is also conceptualized as an *identical process model*. This characteristic also holds for later work (e.g., Mandys et al. 1994). Implementing γ as (different) innovation increments neutralizes the same process model. Only if the γ parameters are zero, the model remains a same process model; otherwise, the developmental processes for means and variances are different, but unfortunately still partly confounded.

IV. Integration: Growth, Interindividual Differences, Stability, and Reliability

We have now presented the ingredients for a family of models that allow tests of longitudinal hypotheses regarding growth, interindividual differences, and relative position of subjects (stability). By integrating the components of modeling stability and reliability and modeling means, it is possible to test all of the combined hypotheses that can be derived from Figure 2.2. The essential characteristic of a real longitudinal LGC model consists of a mean part separated from the covariance part modeled in an autoregressive manner (see Figure 2.12).

The defining characteristic of the separate process model is that all features of the part modeling means (parameters, latent constructs, model equations) are distinct from the part modeling covariances. The identical process model can be expressed as a special case of the different process model. By applying the different process model, it is possible to test a large variety of longitudinal hypotheses concerning means, variances, covariances, and correlations of latent variables. Because of its generality, this model allows testing of a hierarchy of partially nested hypotheses. We will demonstrate the power of this approach in the following example, analyzing

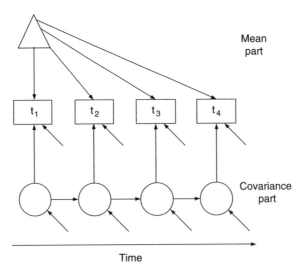

Figure 2.12 Latent growth curve separate process model with autoregressive covariance part.

intelligence across 7 years and including means (also see de Ribaupierre & Bailleux, 1995).

Intellectual development in old age, at least in the domain of fluid intelligence, is characterized by a loss of intellectual abilities (decreasing means) and in some studies by increasing interindividual variability (increasing variances). The available LGC models described in the preceeding paragraphs are not suitable for testing simultaneously a hypothesis of different developmental processes for means and variances.

The analysis of different and divergent developmental processes is once again demonstrated with intelligence data (WAIS: Digit Span) from the BOLSA. The analysis is based on the augmented moment matrix displayed in Table 2.4.

The model in the example specifies weak assumptions about the developmental processes (monotonicity). However, the processes are specified as different or separate ones. The model fits the data well ($\chi^2 = 5.00, df = 5, p = 0.42$). Other types of hypotheses (linearity, exponential growth, etc.) could be specified by equality constraints and/or fixing parameters.

The assumption of a common cause of mean change and variance change is not compatible with the longitudinal intelligence data in the old aged BOLSA sample. Neither the McArdle and Epstein model nor the Dolan, Molenaar, and Boomsma model are suitable to parameterize these separate or "no common cause" processes that characterize the BOLSA data. The model fit using the basic McArdle LGC model is $\chi^2 = 36.36$, $df = 5, p = 0.00$; the model fit using the Dolan, Molenaar and Boomsma model is $\chi^2 = 25.79, df = 3, p = 0.00$. Both models do not fit.

Of course, the same process models are the more parsimonious ones, and should be preferred, if they are confirmed by the data, because they explain the time-varying means and (co-) variances in terms of a single underlying dynamic process model. However, we believe that a *falsified* same process model delivers very little information about the underlying developmental processes, as analyses with the McArdle and Dolan model demonstrate. In this case, the different process model is able to substantiate the (different) types of dynamic processes, as in the example.

V. Structuring Change and Changing Structures

One topic frequently addressed by developmental psychologists, particularly in the field of aging, involves assessment of invariance of constructs over time (Horn & McArdle, 1992; Labouvie, 1980; McArdle, 1996; Nesselroade & Thompson, 1995; Rietz, 1996; Schaie et al., 1998). From the traditional perspective, the invariance definition of constructs over time is synonymous with definitions of factorial invariance. This involves the same relative magnitude of factor loadings of variables on factors (measurement equivalence) as well as the same degree of relations between the factors (structural equivalence). The degree of relation between (oblique) factors can range from

Table 2.4
Augmented Moment Matrix of Four Successive Intelligence Measures[a]

		1965 (y_1)	1967 (y_2)	1969 (y_3)	1972 (y_4)	(y_5)
1965	(y_1)	164.36				
		(6.86)				
1967	(y_2)	151.38	145.01			
		(5.05)	(9.05)			
1969	(y_3)	130.37	122.75	111.65		
		(5.37)	(6.62)	(12.45)		
1972	(y_4)	84.48	79.86	70.75	55.62	
		(6.28)	(6.87)	(8.40)	(16.43)	
(means)	(y_5)	12.55	11.66	9.96	6.26	1.00

[a]WAIS: Digit Span; $N = 105$. [Variances and Covariances]

zero to one in correlational terms. The emergence of qualitatively new structures can be mirrored by relations between factors changing from measurement point to measurement point. Differentiation can be indicated by weaker and weaker relations across time, and dedifferentiation by increasing relations across time. If the relations get perfect, the factors collapse to one factor.

An example from the BOLSA serves as an illustration for the analysis of (factorial) invariance. Table 2.5 gives the covariance matrix of four intelligence subtests of the WAIS measured at two occasions.

The main theoretical assumptions with respect to the "development" of intelligence in old age are the following: invariance of the measurement model over time and structural stability of the fluid and crystallized components (i.e., the correlation between the two constructs at the two points of measurement is hypothesized to be numerically equal). The measurement model is operationalized for the crystallized component by the

subtests Information (y_1 resp. y_5) and Similarities (y_2 resp. y_6); the fluid component is defined by the subtests Digit Symbol (y_3 resp. y_7) and Block Design (y_4 resp. y_8). The invariance of the measurement model over time implies certain assumptions, constraints, and restrictions on the factor loadings and residual variances, comparable to the procedure illustrated in the simplex paragraph of this contribution. Additionally, it is of interest whether the correlation between fluid and crystallized components is stable across time or growing (dedifferentiation) or whether it is fading away (differentiation).

For the sake of simplicity we remain in the context of two wave models. Figure 2.13 displays the autoregressive model for fluid and crystallized intelligence.

Computing the SEM specified in Figure 2.13 without any restriction leads to a very acceptable model fit ($\chi^2 = 7.69$, $df = 12$, $p = 0.81$). This model does not allow a comprehensive answer to the research questions mentioned above. Neverthe-

Table 2.5

Covariance Matrix of Four Intelligence Subtests of WAIS Measured at Two Occasions[a]

		t_1 (1965)				t_2 (1976)			
		Information (y_1)	Similarities (y_2)	Digit symbol (y_3)	Block design (y_4)	Information (y_5)	Similarities (y_6)	Digit symbol (y_7)	Block design (y_8)
t_1 (1965)	Information (y_1)	5.371							
	Similarities (y_2)	3.547	5.040						
	Digit symbol (y_3)	2.598	2.069	5.162					
	Block design (y_4)	2.127	1.663	3.141	6.347				
t_2 (1976)	Information (y_5)	4.606	3.484	2.732	1.868	6.493			
	Similarities (y_6)	3.838	3.470	2.161	1.716	4.074	6.037		
	Digit symbol (y_7)	2.462	2.021	3.313	3.023	2.912	2.449	4.585	
	Block design (y_8)	2.937	1.808	3.506	4.802	3.393	2.920	3.892	6.694

[a]$N = 78$.

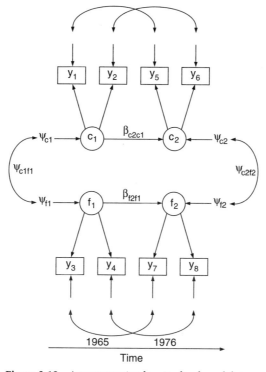

Figure 2.13 Autoregressive longitudinal model: two measurement points, four observed variables per occasion, and fluid (f) and crystallized (c) intelligence as the two latent variables per occasion.

less, the results of the 11-year longitudinal study give some evidence for the appropriateness of the specified measurement model. The model shows high structure regression coefficients (.96 and .94) and the structural correlation (i.e., the correlation between fluid and crystallized intelligence) is .66 at the first measurement point and .74 at the second measurement point. The correlations are numerically different, but we cannot be certain whether these correlations are also statistically different. However, it is precisely invariance or change of these correlations that is subject of the differentiation or integration hypothesis. How can we actually test hypotheses about structural features such as strong (numerical) measurement invariance and strong (numerical) structural invariance?

Invariance of the measurement model is usually specified by pairwise equality constraints among the factor loadings and by pairwise equality constraints of the corresponding residual variances of the observed variables (e.g., constraining the loading from $c1$ on Information at the first measurement point and $c2$ on Information at the second point of measurement to equality, and constraining the residual variances of the observed variables Information at both points of measurement to equality, too). These equality constraints are considered to be a presupposition of measurement equivalence. However, this procedure fails in the context of longitudinal autoregressive models, as already mentioned in section II, Stability and Reliability. Testing the equality of the structural correlations between $c1$ and $f1$, and $c2$ and $f2$ fails for the same reason. The hypothesis of the equality of the structural correlations $(\rho_{c1f1} = \rho_{c2f2})$ leads to this equation:

$$\rho_{c2f2} = \frac{\beta_{c2c1} \cdot \beta_{f2f1} \cdot \Psi_{c1f1} + \Psi_{c2f2}}{\sqrt{(\beta_{c2c1}^2 \cdot \Psi_{c1} + \Psi_{c2}) \cdot (\beta_{f2f1}^2 \cdot \Psi_{f1} + \Psi_{f2})}}$$

$$= \frac{\Psi_{c1f1}}{\sqrt{\Psi_{c1} \cdot \Psi_{f1}}} = \rho_{c1f1}.$$

The variances (Ψ_{c2}, Ψ_{f2}), the covariance, and the correlation of the latent variables following the first assessment are nonlinear functions of the variances of the latent variables of the first measurement (Ψ_{c1}, Ψ_{f1}) and of the structural regression coefficients $(\beta_{c2c1}, \beta_{f2f1})$ connecting the first assessment with subsequent assessments (see Figure 2.13). In the autoregressive type of models there is no direct way to test any assumptions about correlations or covariances between the latent variables. This holds for structural correlations $(\rho_{c1f1}, \rho_{c2f2})$ as well as for the structural regression coefficients resp. the stability coefficients $(\beta_{c2c1}, \beta_{f2f1})$.

Nonautoregressive CFA-type models avoid the nonlinearity problem, since they contain just covariances among latent variables across time and imply no independent–dependent variable distinction. The nonautoregressive models allow one to test measurement equivalence and structural invariance in a rather uncomplicated manner (Hertzog & Schaie, 1986, 1988).

However, CFA-type models (even including hierarchically nested testing) neglect the sequential time order of assessments: the time order is no longer part of the model. On the other hand, autoregressive models yield information about temporal stability, conceptualized as predictability in an autoregressive way. Both families of models are qualitatively different.

Both sets of hypotheses, measurement equivalence (same reliability included) and invariance of structural correlations on the one hand, and invariance of structural regression coefficients on the other hand, can only be tested simultaneously by a model that is a conjunction of an autoregressive and a nonautoregressive CFA-type model. This hybrid model reparameterizes both models (see Rudinger et al., 1994). To integrate the features of both models the hybrid model employs numerous phantom variables to deal with the nonlinearity problem effectively. The hybrid model enables the researcher to test a hierarchy from strong models implying invariant variances and covariances of latent variables across time to weak ones, implying changing variances and covariances of latent variables across time to weak ones, implying changing variances and covariances of latent variables across time. It is possible to test hypotheses about differentiation or dedifferentiation.

Applying the hybrid model to the data from Table 2.5 and testing the mentioned hypotheses of (a) strong (numerical) measurement equivalence combined with equal variances and (b) invariant structural correlations yields the following results: the model fits the data $(\chi^2 = 19.10,\ df = 21, p = 0.58)$, the structural correlations are 0.69 at both times of measurement, and the measurement models across time are numerically equal.

Multiconstruct and multiwave longitudinal models of the type presented here can also be enriched by including LGC components for modeling the mean part in the way described.

VI. Conclusion

The principal purpose of this chapter was to illustrate the mapping of longitudinal hypotheses into SEMs. Time order and directionality of time must explicitly be taken into account in modeling and statistical analyses of longitudinal data. To test longitudinal hypotheses about reliability, stability, interindividual differences, and growth curves appropriately, as well as about structural invariance and measurement equivalence across time, we presented autoregressive separate process models. These models go beyond the classic models of the autoregressive type, the classic LGC models, as well as the classic models of CFA-type. Each of the five models presented focuses on specific questions of longitudinal data analysis. The concepts developed for answering these research questions can be used as tools and can be adapted to various problems. In this sense, the models presented can lead to new answers to long-standing longitudinal research questions.

The most conceptual problems associated with longitudinal aging research are solvable with SEM. Future research has to focus on the statistical-mathematical problems of the application of SEM, for example, on the problem of robust estimators based on small samples, on the influence of selectivity concerning the distribution of variables and statistics, and on so-called correct statistical test of models.

Acknowledgments

The authors thank Ute Hormes, Jane Janser, Johannes Andres, and Dirk Zander for their comments on earlier drafts of this chapter and for their editorial help.

References

Alwin, D. F. (1999). Aging and errors of measurement: Implications for the study of lifespan development. In N. Schwarz & D. C. Park (Eds.), *Cognition, aging, and self-reports* (pp. 365–385). Hove: Psychology Press.

Anderson, R. T., James, M. K., Miller, M. E., Worley, A. S., & Longino, C. F. Jr. (1998). The timing of change: Patterns in transitions in functional status among elderly persons. *Journals of Gerontology, 53B*(1), S17–S27.

Baltes, M. M., Maas, I., Willms, H. U., Borchelt, M., & Little, T. D. (1999). Everyday competence in old and very old: Theoretical considerations and empirical findings. In P. B. Baltes & K. U. Mayer (Eds.), *The Berlin Aging Study. Aging from 70 to 100* (pp. 384–402). Cambridge: Cambridge University Press.

Baltes, P. B., & Mayer, K. U. (1999). *The Berlin Aging Study, Aging from 70 to 100.* Cambridge: Cambridge University Press.

Berg, S., & Johansson, B. (1998). *Intelligens och aldrande: Resultat gran en svensk longitudinell studie* [Intelligence and aging: Results from a Swedish longitudinal study]. *Tidsskrift for Norsk Psykologrorening, 35*(8), 768–774.

Binstock, R. H., & George, L. K. (Eds.) (1996). *Handbook of aging and the social sciences* (4th ed.). San Diego, CA: Academic Press.

Birren, J. E., & Schaie, K. W. (Eds.) (1996). *Handbook of the psychology of aging* (4th ed.). San Diego, CA: Academic Press.

Boomsma, D. I., & Molenaar, P. C. M. (1987). The genetic analysis of repeated measures: I. Simplex models. *Behavior Genetics, 17*(2), 111–123.

Bosworth, H. B., & Schaie, K. W. (1999). Survival effects in cognitive function, cognitive style and sociodemographic variables in the Seattle Longitudinal Study. *Experimental Aging Research, 25*(2), 121–139.

Buss, A. R. (1979). Toward a unified framework for psychometric concepts in the multivariate development situation: Intraindividual change and inter- and intraindividual differences. In J. R. Nesselroade & P. B. Baltes (Eds.), *Longitudinal research and the study of behavior and development* (pp. 41–59). New York: Academic Press.

Cattell, R. B. (1950). *Personality: A systematically, theoretical and factual study.* New York: McGraw Hill.

Cavanaugh, J. C., & Whitbourne, S. K. (1999). Research methods. In J. C. Cavanaugh & S. K. Whitbourne (Eds.), *Gerontology: An interdisciplinary perspective* (pp. 33–64). New York: Oxford University Press.

Cohen, S. H., & Reese, H. W. (Eds.) (1994). *Life-span developmental psychology: Methodological contributions. The West Virginia University conferences on life-span developmental psychology.* Hillsdale, NJ: Lawrence Erlbaum.

Collins, L. M. (1996). Measurement of change in research of aging: Old and new issues from an individual growth perspective. In J. E. Birren & K. W. Schaie (Eds.), *Handbook of the psychology of aging* (4th ed.) (pp. 38–56). San Diego, CA: Academic Press.

Collins, L. M., & Horn, J. L. (Eds.) (1991). *Best methods for the analysis of change.* New York: American Psychological Association.

Diehl, M., Willis, S. L., & Schaie, K. W. (1995). Everyday problem solving in older adults: Observational assessment and cognitive correlates. *Psychology and Aging, 10*(3), 478–491.

Dolan, C. V., Molenaar, P. C. M., & Boomsma, D. I. (1989). LISREL analysis of twin data with structured means. *Behavior Genetics, 19*, 51–62.

Dolan, C. V., Molenaar, P. C. M., & Boomsma, D. I. (1991). Simultaneously genetic analysis of longitudinal means and covariance structure in the simplex model using twin data. *Behavior Genetics, 21*, 49–65.

Dolan, C. V., Molenaar, P. C. M., & Boomsma, D. I. (1992). Decomposition of group-related differences in multivariate phenotypic means in genetic covariance structure analysis. *Behavior Genetics, 22*, 319–335.

Dunlosky, J., & Hertzog, C. (1998). Training programs to improve learning in later adulthood: Helping older adults educate themselves. In D. J. Hacker & J. Dunlosky (Eds.), *Metacognition in educational theory and practice. The educational psychology series* (pp. 249–275). Mahwah, NJ: Lawrence Erlbaum.

Edgington, E. S. (1995). *Randomization tests* (3rd ed.). New York: Dekker.

Efron, B., & Tibshirani, R. J. (1993). *An introduction to the Bootstrap.* New York: Chapman & Hall.

Finkel, D., Pedersen, N. L., Plomin, R., & McClearn, G. E. (1998). Longitudinal and cross-sectional twin data on cognitive abilities in adulthood: The Swedish Adoption/Twin Study of Aging. *Developmental Psychology, 34*(6), 1400–1413.

Green, D. P., & Palmquist, B. L. (1991). More "tricks of the trade": Reparameterizing LISREL models using negative variances. *Psychometrika, 56*, 137–145.

Hagen, B., Oswald, W. D., & Rupprecht, R. (1998). *Bedingungen der Erhaltung und Förderung von Selbständigkeit im höheren Lebensalter (SIMA)—Teil XII: Verlaufsanalyse der Selbständigkeit und der Alltagsbewältigung* [Maintaining and supporting independent living in old age (SIMA)—Part XII: Longitudinal analysis of long-term training effects on independent living and coping with everyday problems]. *Zeitschrift für Gerontopsychologie und-Psychiatrie, 11*(4), 240–254.

Harris, C. W. (Ed.) (1963). *Problems in measuring change.* Madison: University of Wisconsin Press.

Hartelsman, P. A., van der Maas, H. L. J., & Molenaar, P. C. M. (1998). Detecting and modelling developmental transitions. *British Journal of Developmental Psychology, 16*, 97–122.

Heise, D. R. (1969). Separating reliability and stability in test–retest correlations. *American Sociological Review, 34*, 93–101.

Hertzog, C. (1987). Applications of structural equation models in gerontological research. In K. W. Schaie (Ed.), *Annual review of gerontology and geriatrics, Vol. 7. Annual review of gerontology and geriatrics* (pp. 265–293). New York: Springer.

Hertzog, C. (1990). On the utility of structural equation models for developmental research. In P. B. Baltes & D. L. Featherman (Eds.), *Life-span development and behavior,* (Vol. 10, pp. 257–290). Hillsdale, NJ: Lawrence Erlbaum.

Hertzog, C. (1994). Repeated measures analysis in developmental research: What our ANOVA text didn't tell us. In S. H. Cohen & H. W. Reese (Eds.), *Life-span developmental psychology: Methodological contributions* (pp. 187–222). Hillsdale, NJ: Lawrence Erlbaum.

Hertzog, C., & Nesselroade, J. R. (1987). Beyond autoregressive models: Some implications of the trait-state-distinction for the structural modelling of developmental change. *Child Development, 58*, 93–109.

Hertzog, C., & Schaie, K. W. (1986). Stability and change in adult intelligence: I. Analysis of longitudinal covariance structures. *Psychology and Aging, 1* (2), 159–171.

Hertzog, C., & Schaie, K. W. (1988). Stability and change in adult intelligence: II. simultaneous analysis of longitudinal means and covariance structures. *Psychology and Aging, 3*(2), 122–130.

Holahan, C. K., Holahan, C. J., & Wonacutt, N. L. (1999). Self-appraisal, life satisfaction, and retrospective life choices across one and three decades. *Psychology and Aging, 14*(2), 238–244.

Horn, J. L., & McArdle, J. J. (1992). A practical and theoretical guide to measurement invariance in aging research. *Experimental Aging Research, 18*(3–4), 117–144.

Hultsch, D. F., Hertzog, C., Dixon, R. A., & Small, B. J. (Eds.) (1998). *Memory change in the aged.* New York: Cambridge University Press.

Jöreskog, K. G. (1970). Estimation and testing of simplex models. *British Journal of Mathematical and Statistical Psychology, 23,* 121–145.

Jöreskog, K. G., van Thiello, M., & Gruveaus, G. T. (1970). *ACOVSM–A general computer program for analysis of covariance structure including generalized MANOVA (Research Bulletin, 70–01).* Princeton, NJ: Educational Testing Service.

Kim, J. E., Nesselroade, J. R., & Featherman, D. L. (1996). The state component in self-reported worldview and religious beliefs of older adults: The MacArthur Successful Aging studies. *Psychology and Aging, 11*(3), 396–407.

Labouvie, E. W. (1980). Identity versus equivalence of psychological measures and constructs. In L. W. Poon (Ed.), *Aging in the 1980's: Selected contemporary issues in the psychology of aging* (pp. 493–502). Washington, DC: American Psychological Association.

Lehr, U., & Thomae, H. (Eds.) (1987). *Formen seelischen Alterns. Ergebnisse der Bonner gerontologischen Längsschnittstudie* [Pattern of aging. Results from the Bonn Longitudinal Study of Aging]. Stuttgart: Enke.

Lindenberger, U., Gilberg, R., Little, T. D., Nuthmann, R., Pötter, U., & Baltes, P. B. (1999). Sample selectivity and generalizability of the results of the Berlin Aging Study. In P. B. Baltes & K. U. Mayer (Eds.), *The Berlin Aging Study: Aging from 70 to 100* (pp. 56–82). Cambridge: Cambridge University Press.

Magnusson, D., Bergman, L. R., Rudinger, G., & Törestad. B. (Eds.) (1994). *Problems and methods in longitudinal research: Stability and change.* Cambridge: Cambridge University Press.

Mandys, F., Dolan, C. V., & Molenaar, P. C. M. (1994). Two aspects of the simplex model: Goodness of fit to linear growth curve structures and the analysis of mean trends. *Journal of Educational and Behavioral Statistics, 19*(3), 201–215.

McArdle, J. J. (1986). Latent variable growth within behavior genetic models. *Behavior Genetics, 16,* 163–200.

McArdle, J. J. (1996). Current directions in structural factor analysis. *Current Directions in Psychological Science, 5*(1), 11–18.

McArdle, J. J. (1998). Modeling longitudinal data by Latent Growth Curve methods. In G. A. Marcoulides (Ed.), *Modern methods for business research. Methodology for business and management* (pp. 359–406). Mahwah, NJ: Lawrence Erlbaum.

McArdle, J. J., & Epstein, D. (1987). Latent growth curves within developmental structural equation models. *Child Development, 58,* 110–133.

McArdle, J. J., & Hamagami, F. (1991). Modeling incomplete longitudinal and cross sectional data using latent growth structural models. In L. M. Collins & J. L. Horn (Eds.), *Best methods for the analysis of change. Recent advances, unanswered questions, future directions* (pp. 276–304). Washington, DC: American Psychological Association.

McArdle, J. J., & Hamagami, F. (1992). Modeling incomplete and cross-sectional data using latent growth structural models. *Experimental Aging Research, 18*(3–4), 145–166.

McArdle, J. J., & Nesselroade, J. R. (1994). Using multivariate data to structure developmental change. In S. H. Cohen & H. W. Reese (Eds.), *Life-span developmental psychology: Methodological contributions. The West Virginia University conferences on life-span developmental psychology* (pp. 223–267). Hillsdale, NJ: Lawrence Erlbaum.

McArdle, J. J., & Woodcock, R. W. (1997). Expanding test–retest designs to include developmental time-lag components. *Psychological Methods, 2*(4), 403–435.

McCall, R. B. (1977). Challenges to a science of developmental psychology. *Child Development, 48*, 333–344.

McCamish-Svensson, C., Samuelsson, G., Hagverg, B., Svensson, T., & Dehlin, O. (1999). Social relationships and health as predictor of life satisfaction in advanced old age: Results from a Swedish longitudinal study. *International Journal of Aging and Human Development, 48*(4), 301–324.

Molenaar, P. C. M., & Nesselroade, J. R. (1998). A comparison of pseudo-maximum likelihood and asymptotically distribution-free dynamic factor analysis parameter estimation in fitting covariance-structure models to Block-Toeplitz matrices representing single-subject multivariate time-series. *Multivariate Behavioral Research, 33* (3), 313–342.

Molenaar, P. C. M., Boomsma, D. I., & Dolan, C. V. (1999). The detection of genotype–environment interaction in longitudinal genetic models. In M. C. LaBuda & E. L. Grigorenko (Eds.), *On the way to individuality: Current methodological issues in behavioral genetics* (pp. 53–70). Commack, NY: Nova Science.

Nesselroade, J. R. (1991). Interindividual differences in intraindividual changes. In L. M. Collins & J. L. Horn (Eds.), *Best methods for the analysis of change: Recent advances, unanswered questions, future directions* (pp. 92–105). Washington, DC: American Psychological Association.

Nesselroade, J. R., & Baltes, P. B. (Eds.) (1979). *Longitudinal research in the study of behavior and development.* New York: Academic Press.

Nesselroade, J. R., & Bartsch, T. W. (1977). Multivariate perspectives on the construct validity of the trait-state distinction. In R. B. Cattell & R. M. Dreger (Eds.), *Handbook of modern personality theory* (pp. 374–401). New York: Wiley.

Nesselroade, J. R., & Boker, S. M. (1994). Assessing constancy and change. In T. F. Heatherton & J. L. Weinberger (Eds.), *Can personality change?* (pp. 121–147). Washington, DC: American Psychological Association.

Nesselroade, J. R., & Featherman, D. L. (1997). Establishing a reference frame against which to chart age-related changes. In M. A. Hardy (Ed.), *Studying aging and social change: Conceptual and methodological issues* (pp. 191–205). Thousand Oaks, CA: Sage.

Nesselroade, J. R., & Thompson, W. W. (1995). Selection and related threats to group comparisons: An example comparing factorial structures of higher and lower ability groups of adult twins. *Psychological Bulletin, 117*(2), 271–284.

Newell, K. M., & Molenaar, P. C. M. (Eds.) (1998). *Applications of nonlinear dynamics to developmental process modeling.* Mahwah, NJ: Lawrence Erlbaum.

Pedersen, N. L., Steffensson, B., Berg, S., Johansson, B. & McClearn, G. E. (1999). The importance of genetic and environmental effects for self-reported health symptoms: A 30-year follow-up considering survival and selection effects. *Journal of Aging and Health, 11* (4), 475–493.

Penninx, B. W. J. H., van Tilburg, T., Kriegsman, D. M. W., Boeke, A. J. P., Deeg, D. J. H., & van Eijk, J. Th. M. (1999). Social network, social support, and loneliness in older persons with different chronic diseases. *Journal of Aging and Health, 11*(2), 151–168.

Perrig-Chiello, P., Perrig, W. G., & Staehlin, H. B. (1999). Health control beliefs in old age—relationship with subjective and objective health, and health behavior. *Psychology, Health and Medicine, 4* (1), 83–94.

Raykov, T. (1994). On two-wave measurement of individual change and initial value dependence. *Zeitschrift für Psychologie, 202*(3), 275–290.

Raykov, T. (1996) Plasticity in fluid intelligence of older adults: An individual latent growth curve modeling application. *Structural Equation Modeling, 3* (3), 248–265.

Raykov, T. (1997). Simultaneous study of individual and group patterns of latent longitudinal change using structural equation modeling. *Structural Equation Modeling, 4* (3), 212–236.

Raykov, T. (1998). Satisfying a simplex structure is simpler than it should be: A latent curve analysis revisit. *Multivariate Behavioral Research, 33* (3), 343–363.

Raykov, T. (1999). Are simple change scores obsolet? An approach to studying correlates and predicators of change. *Applied Psychological Measurement, 23* (2), 120–126.

Raykov, T., Tomer, A., & Nesselroade, J. R. (1991). Reporting structural equation modeling results in Psychology and Aging: Some proposed guidelines. *Psychology and Aging, 6* (4), 499–503.

Ribaupierre, A., de; & Bailleux, C. (1995). Development of attentional capacity in childhood: A longitudinal study. In F. E. Weinert & W. Schneider (Eds.), *Memory performance and competencies: Issues in growth and development* (pp. 45–70). Mahwah, NJ: Lawrence Erlbaum.

Riegel, K. F. (1972). Time and change in the development of the individual and society. In H. W. Reese (Ed.), *Advances in child development and behavior* (Vol. 7) (pp. 81–113). New York: Academic Press.

Rietz, C. (1996). *Faktorielle Invarianz—Die inferenzstatistische Absicherung von Faktorstrukturvergleichen* [Factorial invariance—inference statistics for factor comparisons]. Bonn: PACE.

Rindskopf, D. M. (1983). Parameterizing inequality constraints on unique variances in linear structural equation models. *Psychometrika, 48,* 73–83.

Rindskopf, D. M. (1984). Using phantom and imaginary latent variables to parameterize constraints in linear structural models. *Psychometrika, 49,* 37–49.

Rogosa, D., & Willett, J. B. (1983). Demonstrating the reliability of the difference score in the measurement of change. *Journal of Educational Measurement, 20,* 335–343.

Rogosa, D., & Willett, J. B. (1985a). Understanding correlates of change by modeling indidual differences in growth. *Psychometrika, 50,* 203–228.

Rogosa, D., & Willett, J. B. (1985b). Satisfying a simplex structure is simpler as ist should be. *Journal of Educational Statistics, 10,* 99–107.

Rogosa, D., Brandt, D., & Zimowski, M. (1982). A growth curve approach to the measurement of change. *Psychological Bulletin, 92,* 726–748.

Roskam, E. E. (1976). Multivariate analysis of change and growth: A critical review. In D. N. M. de Gruijter & L. J. Th. van der

Kamp (Eds.), *Advances in psychological and educational measurement* (pp. 111–134). London: Wiley.

Rovine, M. J., & Molenaar, P. C. M. (1998). A nonstandard method for estimating a linear growth model in LISREL. *International Journal of Behavioral Development, 22* (3), 453–473.

Rubin, D. B. (1987). *Multiple imputation for nonresponse in surveys.* New York: Wiley.

Rudinger, G. (1998). *Strukturgleichungsmodelle in der Entwicklungspsychologie* [Structural equation modelling in developmental psychology]. In R. Oerter & L. Montada (Eds.), *Entwicklungspsychologie* (4th ed) (pp. 1177–1190). Weinheim: Psychologie Verlags Union.

Rudinger, G., & Minnemann, E. (1997). *Die Lebenssituation von älteren Frauen und Männern in Ost—und Westdeutschland: Ergebnisse der Interdisziplinären Langzeitstudie des Erwachsenenalters* (ILSE) [The life situation of older women and men in East and West Germany: Results of the Interdisciplinary Longitudinal Study of Middle and Old Age]. *Zeitschrift für Gerontopsychologie und—psychiatrie, 10,* 205–212.

Rudinger, G., & Rietz, C. (1993). *Und mal wieder: Reliabilität und Stabilität in Panelmodellen* [And once again: Reliability and stability in panel models]. *ZUMA-Nachrichten, 17* (32), 60–75.

Rudinger, G., & Rietz, C. (1998a). *Intelligenz und Selektivität im höheren Alter: Neuere Ergebnisse aus der Bonner Längsschnittstudie des Alterns* [Intelligence and selectivity in old age: New findings from the Bonn Longitudinal Study of Aging]. In A. Kruse (Ed.), *Jahrbuch der Medizinischen Psychologie, 15, Psychosoziale Gerontologie, Band 1: Grundlagen* (pp. 147–174). Göttingen: Hogrefe.

Rudinger, G., & Rietz, C. (1998b). The neglected time dimension? Introducing a longitudinal model testing latent growth curves, stability, and reliability as time bound processes. *Methods of Psychological Research Online, 3*(2), 109–130.

Rudinger, G., & Rietz, C. (1999). Methodological issues in a cross-European study. In J. J. F. Schroots, R. Fernandez-Ballesteros & G. Rudinger (Eds.), *Aging in Europe* (pp. 157–167). Amsterdam: IOS.

Rudinger, G., Andres, J., & Rietz, C. (1994). Structural equation models for studying intellectual development. In D. Magnusson, L. R. Bergman, G. Rudinger & B. Törestad (Eds.), *Problems and methods in longitudinal research* (paperback ed., pp. 274–307). Cambridge: Cambridge University Press.

Schaie, K. W. (1996). *Intellectual development in adulthood: The Seattle Longitudinal Study.* Cambridge: Cambridge University Press.

Schaie, K. W., Maitland, S. B., Willis, S. L., & Intrieri, R. C. (1998). Longitudinal invariance of adult psychometric ability factor structures across 7 years. *Psychology and Aging,* 13(1), 8–20.

Schaie, K. W., & Willis, S. L. (1999). Theories of everyday competence and aging. In V. L. Bengtson & K. W. Schaie (Eds.), *Handbook of theories of aging* (pp. 174–195). New York, NY: Springer.

Schneider, E. L., & Rowe, J. W. (1996). *Handbook of the biology of aging* (4th ed.). San Diego, CA: Academic Press.

Schroots, J. J. F., Fernandez-Ballesteros, R., & Rudinger, G. (Eds.) (1999). *Aging in Europe.* Amsterdam: IOS.

Tisak, J., & Meredith, W. (1990). Descriptive and associative developmental models. In A. von Eye (Ed.), *Statistical methods in longitudinal research* (Vol. II, pp. 387–406). San Diego, CA: Academic Press.

Usala, P. D., & Hertzog, C. (1991). Evidence of differential stability of state and trait anxiety in adults. *Journal of Personality and Social Psychology,* 60 (3), 471–479.

von Eye, A., & Clogg, C. C. (Eds.) (1994). *Latent variable analysis: Applications for developmental research.* Thousand Oaks, CA: Sage.

Wilcox, R. R. (1997). *Introducing to robust estimation and hypothesis testing.* San Diego, CA: Academic Press.

Wiley, D. E., & Wiley, J. A. (1970). The estimation of measurement error in panel data. *American Sociological Review,* 35, 112–117.

Willis, S. L., & Schaie, K. W. (1999). Intellectual functioning in midlife. In S. L. Willis & J. D. Reid (Eds.), *Life in the middle: Psychological and social development in the middle age* (pp. 233–247). San Diego, CA: Academic Press.

Three

Longitudinal Studies in Aging Research

K. Warner Schaie and Scott M. Hofer

I. Introduction

The purpose of this chapter is to review the current status and role of longitudinal studies in the psychology of aging. There seems to be wide recognition now of the importance of longitudinal studies if we are to go beyond the description of age-related differences in behavior to the discovery of mechanisms that explain the human progression from young adulthood to old age. We will begin our discussion by reminding the reader why longitudinal studies are such important contributors to the aging literature. We then turn to the problems of longitudinal studies as quasi-experiments. There follows a brief discussion of other issues that plague longitudinal inquiries, such as the matter of invariance of the relation between latent constructs and observed variables over time and cohorts, issues of unequal intervals and missing data, and retesting effects. The contributions of relevant recent methodological advances that can address these problems will then be discussed. Finally, we provide a review of current long-term as well as recently initiated longitudinal studies that should be brought to the attention of serious aging researchers.

Only in the past decade or so has there been an increased recognition that it is possible to apply longitudinal methodologies over relatively short intervals and that data sets already in existence can readily be converted into longitudinal studies by another wave of data collection. Funding agencies have been more willing to support such efforts, and archived long-term data sets are becoming available for secondary analyses by the broader scientific community. It seems timely, therefore, to review some of the principal methodological concerns that become important in the analysis of longitudinal data in aging research and to provide a review of the major longitudinal studies that have impacted the aging literature during the past decade.

For several decades the aging literature has been replete with exhortations that longitudinal studies are the methods of choice for data collections designed to contribute towards issues of behavioral change and decline of functions from young adulthood to old age. Nevertheless, the aging literature has continued to be largely dominated by cross-sectional age-comparative studies. Many reasons have been cited for this disconnect in theoretical understanding and research practice.

Handbook of the Psychology of Aging
Copyright © 2001 by Academic Press.
All rights of reproduction in any form reserved.

They include practical issues, such as the need to complete theses and dissertations (and publishable projects by tenure-seeking junior scientists) in a timely fashion, the reluctance of funding agencies to enter into long-term commitments, as well as difficulties in managing archives over long time periods. Experimentally trained scientists also tend to prefer short-term experiments rather than the long-term quasi-experiments represented by the longitudinal approach. It is our hope that this chapter will encourage better understanding of the longitudinal approach in aging research and reassure those who contemplate designing new longitudinal studies.

II. Why Should One Conduct Longitudinal Studies?

Early empirical inquiries in the study of adult development were conducted primarily in the areas of intelligence and personality traits. Investigators interested in the age-related aspects of learning and memory largely adopted the paradigms popular in early experimental child psychology and thus limited themselves to age-comparative studies of young and old adults. Only recently have we seen studies that investigate developmental mechanisms by use of longitudinal paradigms (see Salthouse, 1999). Even in the study of intellectual development, cross-sectional studies predominated until the late 1930s and clouded our understanding of adult development due to the confusion of age-related development with secular changes expressed as cohort effects (also see Schaie, 2000).

Although the explicit differences in information from cross-sectional and longitudinal inquiries were not fully explicated until the 1960s (cf. Mason, Mason, Winsborough, & Poole, 1973; Ryder, 1965; Schaie, 1965), it has always

been clear that longitudinal data are needed in order to study intraindividual development, to elucidate antecedent-consequent relationships in time-bound developmental mechanisms, and to distinguish typologies of alternative courses of development (Baltes & Nesselroade, 1979). Longitudinal data are also essential to decompose different influences that impact age-related change. By contrast, cross-sectional studies provide data and allow inferences only about interindividual differences. Even successive independent samples drawn over time from the same population cohort would allow inferences only about changes in level for the population examined. Of course, longitudinal studies also provide information on interindividual differences.

Five rationales have been identified for the utility of longitudinal study of behavioral development. Three of these involve descriptions of the course of development whereas two are concerned with explanatory issues (cf. Baltes & Nesselroade, 1979; Schaie, 1983):

1. *Direct identification of intraindividual change.* Changes within individuals may be continuous or may involve transformation of one behavior into another. They may also involve changes in the relation of observed variables to the underlying theoretical constructs. Single-occasion observations would be inappropriate for the identification of such changes.

2. *Identification of interindividual variability in intraindividual change.* Different individuals vary in their behavioral course over time. The identification of typologies of growth curves requires the examination of similarities and differences in developmental change within individuals. Without such data, it would be impossible to determine whether group parameters were characteristic of the development of any particular individual.

3. *Relationships among intraindividual changes.* Longitudinal studies allow the discovery of structural relationships among behavior changes occurring over more than a single variable. Longitudinal data are therefore essential to the discovery of constancies and change for the entire organism. They are also required for tests of differentiation and de-differentiation of functional capabilities (see below).

4. *Determinants of intraindividual change.* Longitudinal studies are also required to identify time-ordered antecedents to provide the necessary conditions for causal interpretations. Only longitudinal studies can provide data that show whether a causal process involves discontinuities, whether causal chains are multidirectional, or whether multivariate patterns of influence are implicated.

5. *Interindividual variability in determinants of intraindividual change.* Longitudinal data also permit inferences regarding whether individuals who have similar patterns of intraindividual change are determined by different change processes. Variations in interindividual patterns of change may be attributable to alternative combinations of causal sequences, or differential patterns related to different levels of social, psychological, or biological attributes.

Longitudinal studies that have informed our understanding of adult development are of three different types. First, certain studies were begun to examine development and child-rearing practices in early childhood, but panel members were given continued follow-up when adulthood was reached. A classic example of this genre of studies is the follow-up of the Berkeley Growth and Guidance studies (Bayley & Oden, 1955; Eichorn, Clausen, Haan, Honzik, & Mussen, 1981). A second group of studies traced participants who had been assessed as young adults during their college experience and were reassessed in midlife or later.

An example of such studies is Owens's (1953, 1966) follow-up of persons in their 50s who had first been assessed as ROTC members during World War I. Finally, beginning with work such as the Bonn Longitudinal Study (Rott, 1993; Schmitz-Scherzer & Thomae, 1983), the Duke Longitudinal Study (Palmore, Busse, Maddox, Nowlin, & Siegler, 1985), and the Seattle Longitudinal Study (Schaie, 1958, 1996), a concerted effort was made to obtain reasonably representative samples selected from adult populations.

III. Longitudinal Studies as Quasi-Experiments

Campbell and Stanley (1963) have described a number of threats to the internal validity of quasi-experiments such as longitudinal studies. These include maturation, effects of history, reactivity, instrumentation, statistical regression, experimental mortality, selection, and the selection–maturation interaction. The first two, history and maturation, have special meaning for scientists studying individual development. *Maturation*, quite obviously, is not a threat to the validity of developmentally oriented longitudinal studies, but rather is the topic of primary interest to the investigator. Maturation here is simply the normal developmental course of individuals over their life span, given their genetic predispositions and the characteristic demands of the culture and environment within which such maturation occurs.

On the other hand, *historical* effects can be seen as the primary internal validity problem of longitudinal studies. History is directly involved in both cohort and time-of-measurement (period) effects. Cohort effects represent the impact of historical influences upon a group of individuals that share similar environmental circumstances at equivalent temporal points in their life course. By contrast, time-of-measurement effects represent common historical exposures that influence all members of a population regardless of cohort membership. Historical effects may threaten the internal validity of longitudinal designs that seek to measure effects of maturation (aging effects). In other words, effects thought to be age-dependent must be carefully disaggregated from those due to historically limited environmental impacts. This disaggregation is only possible if a minimum of two cohorts are followed over similar age ranges (Schaie, 1977, 1988).

Longitudinal studies are also affected by the other six threats to internal validity described by Campbell and Stanley. *Reactivity* may simply involve practice effects on performance measures to the extent that study participants spend less time figuring out problems previously solved and therefore improve their performance because of previous exposure to the experimental protocol. On the other hand, longitudinal study participants might also respond on subsequent test occasions very differently than they would if they had not been previously tested, a behavior change that could be confused with the effects of maturation. Methods for assessing practice effects are available when at least two subsamples are available at different levels of measurement exposure (cf. Schaie, 1988). Alternative designs with differing individual measurement intervals can also provide useful avenues for estimating practice effects and provide less biased estimates of maturation (McArdle & Woodcock, 1997).

The threat of *instrumentation* refers to differences in experimental protocols that covary with measurement occasions. Such differences are likely to occur in long-term longitudinal studies when study personnel changes, or when records regarding study protocol on previous occasions are lost and slight variations in protocol are inadvertently introduced. As a consequence, erroneous inferences might be made regarding maturational trends or the impact of societal interventions.

Statistical regression is the tendency of variables containing measurement error to regress towards the population mean from one occasion to the next. This problem is particularly serious when only two data points are available (see Baltes, Nesselroade, Schaie, & Labouvie, 1972, and Schaie & Willis, 1986, for examples of applications of the time-reversal method, which can be used to test for the effect of regression in such studies). It has been shown, however, that regression effects do not necessarily cumulate over extended longitudinal series (Nesselroade, Stigler, & Baltes, 1980). If evidence for statistical regression is found, one can either adjust for reliability of the base line scores, or model change at the latent construct level, thus permitting better control of error variance.

Members of longitudinal panels obviously cannot be coerced to continue their participation. Hence, another serious internal validity threat is that of *experimental mortality*. This term refers to the loss of participants between measurement occasions, whether due to biological mortality, morbidity, or simply experimenter ineptness in maintaining his or her sample. Empirical studies of experimental mortality suggest that attrition is nonrandom at least between the first and second measurement occasion (Cooney, Schaie, & Willis, 1989; Schaie, 1988, 1996). Distinctions should always be made between "natural" mortality (i.e., attrition caused by death or disability) and attrition caused by refusal to continue participation or by experimenters' failure to locate or access participants for logistical reasons.

Selection refers to the process of obtaining a sample from the population such that the observed effect is a function of the specific sample characteristics rather than of the maturational effect we wish to estimate (cf. Nesselroade, 1986). The *selection–maturation interaction* refers to the case where maturational effects may be found in some samples but not in others.

It is not possible to control for or measure the effects of any of the internal validity threats in single-cohort longitudinal studies. When multiple samples are available and certain assumptions are made, however, the magnitude and significance of these effects can be estimated and appropriate corrections applied in the substantive studies. Specific designs for appropriate analyses have previously been presented by Schaie (1977, 1988, 1996).

IV. Invariance of Latent Constructs across Time

When we wish to compare observations across periods of time (age) within individuals, which is the basic rationale for a longitudinal study, we make the implicit assumption that observations have the same relation to the underlying hypothetical construct at all points of measurement. This relationship is expressed technically as the equivalence across time of the factor loadings of the observed variables on the latent constructs. Only when the invariance of these relationships can be shown to hold can meaningful longitudinal inferences be drawn.

Horn, McArdle, and Mason (1983) drew attention to an important distinction between two levels of invariance in factor loadings (a distinction first introduced by Thurstone [1947, pp. 360–369]) that may have different implications for age change and age difference research: *configural invariance* and *metric invariance*. Meredith (1993) has explicated in greater detail the necessary conditions required to satisfy factorial invariance at different levels of

stringency, known as weak, strong, and strict factorial invariance (see Hofer, Horn, & Eber, 1997).

For meaningful longitudinal comparisons it is necessary to show at a minimum that the factor pattern across groups or time display configural invariance. In this case, all measures marking the factors (latent constructs) have their primary nonzero loading on the *same* factor construct across test occasions. They must also have zero or low loadings on the same nonsalient measures for all other factor dimensions. Note, however, that it is possible that the factor loadings can differ in magnitude across groups or time, making the comparative basis for interpretation less than ideal.

A second (more satisfactory) level of factorial invariance (metric invariance, termed *weak factorial invariance* by Meredith, 1993) requires that the unstandardized factor pattern weights (factor loadings) can be constrained equal across time without loss of overall measurement model fit. The technical and substantive considerations for this level of factorial invariance have found extensive discussion in the literature (cf. Hofer, et al., 1997; Horn, 1991; Horn & McArdle, 1992; Jöreskog, 1971, 1979; Meredith, 1993; Schaie & Hertzog, 1985; Thurstone, 1947). Additional equality constraints on the intercepts, known as *strong factorial invariance*, permit the evaluation of mean differences at the factor level. If the measurements are comparable (when factorial invariance constraints do not significantly result in a model misfit), it becomes possible to test substantive hypotheses about the latent factor means, variances, and covariances over time and across groups.

However, we should stress that it is perhaps questionable whether even the assumptions of weak factorial invariance can be met in complex empirical data sets such as are found in many aging studies. In fact, Horn, et al. (1983) argued that configural invariance is likely to be the best solution obtainable with empirical data. Nevertheless, it ought to be possible to demonstrate more stringent levels of invariance for subsystems of variables across at least some ages. Byrne, Shavelson, and Muthén (1989) have proposed therefore that one should also test for partial measurement invariance. This proposition is controversial in the factor-analytic literature because it results in factors that are not completely comparable. However, testing for partial invariance is reasonable from the point of view of the substantively oriented scientist. Inspection of the particular measures that produce the misfit in the factor model can lead to better understanding of the factor construct and measurement properties of the instruments and to further development of "age invariant" measurement instruments. Nevertheless, it should be stressed that tests of factorial invariance should precede the interpretation of longitudinal age changes whenever possible (also see Chapter 2, Rudinger & Rietz, this volume, for relevant structural equation models). In certain circumstances, departures from factorial invariance might be predicted on theoretical grounds or when measurement properties of particular instruments are out of range. Arguments might then be made that a specific analysis ought to be restricted over that age range where the specific construct of interest remains invariant.

V. The Issue of Dedifferentiation in Advanced Old Age

A related issue here is the possibility of changes in the factor space of the domains covered in a given longitudinal study. Considerable attention has recently been devoted to observations that performance on many behavioral attributes and measures of sensory capabilities converge in advanced old age (cf. Baltes & Lindenberger, 1997). One interpretation of this phenomenon might be to suggest that the study of physiological processes should be given priority as outcome events in old age, even though behavioral dimensions might have greater salience as indicators of life quality.

The hypothesized convergence of factor space in old age has a long history. Its conceptual basis comes from the theorizing of Kurt Lewin (1935; also see Schaie, 1962) and particularly Heinz Werner (1948), who argued that the cognitive structures of young children were amorphous and undifferentiated, but that the process of development would lead to a greater differentiation of distinct mental processes. The reason for the original lack of differentiation was attributed to the fact that all psychological processes are heavily dependent on their physiological infrastructures during early development and hence would need to develop in an undifferentiated tandem with the physiological development. As adulthood is reached, however, environmental and experiential phenomena come to dominate the psychological processes, with much less dependence on their physiological bases. However, once late midlife is reached, the decline of sensorimotor and central nervous system functions are presumed to lead to a renewed dependence of individual differences on physiological infrastructures. Hence, a reversal of the earlier differentiation is to be expected, as psychological processes increasingly depend on the physiological infrastructure (cf. Baltes & Lindenberger, 1997). This dedifferentiation can be expressed in statistical terms as the progressive increase of individual differences covariances and the corresponding decrease in variances. Other substantive domains such as personality, self-concepts, or values might, of course, experience alternate forms of structural reorganizations with age, but data are relatively sparse as yet with respect to the latter domains.

Evidence for the dedifferentiation phenomenon has been reported for individual variables since the 1940s (e.g., Balinsky, 1941; Cornelius, Willis, Nesselroade, & Baltes, 1983; Garrett, 1946; Reinert, 1970). More recent work has also demonstrated increases in correlations between cognitive and sensory functions (e.g., Lindenberger & Baltes, 1997; Salthouse, Hancock, Meinz & Hambrick, 1996). Much of this work, however, has either been at the level of individual marker variables or has relied heavily on cross-sectional data (e.g., Schaie, Willis, Jay, & Chipuer, 1989). However, there is now work, particularly in the Seattle Longitudinal Study (Maitland, Intrieri, Schaie, & Willis, 2000; Schaie, Maitland, Willis, & Intrieri, 1998) as well as the Victoria Longitudinal Study (Hultsch, Herzog, Dixon, & Small, 1998), suggesting that dedifferentiation can also be demonstrated at the latent construct level. The literature is not yet clear, however, whether the dedifferentiation phenomenon can be demonstrated to hold across all domains of behavior. Latent factor analysis allows a formal test of this hypothesis.

Once factorial invariance across time has been demonstrated at least at the configural invariance level, it is then possible to proceed with a formal test of the dedifferentiation hypothesis. This test requires that the variance–covariance matrices for successive ages be constrained equal across time. If there is no loss in model fit over a competing model that allows independent estimates of the different variance–covariance matrices, then the hypothesis would be disconfirmed. It is most likely that a subset of variables can be constrained to be equal across age groups. Evaluation of models such as these have important substantive implications because it would specify the latent dimensions for which convergence of factor space can or cannot be demonstrated.

VI. Missing Data and Unequal Intervals

Longitudinal studies extending over long time intervals typically experience participants attrition (or dropping out and returning at a later date) as well as failure to respond to certain variables (i.e., sparse missing data). Fortunately, substantial advances have been made in conducting missing data analyses, and the application of statistical methods for treating missing data using maximum likelihood (e.g., structural equation modeling) or multiple imputation (Schafer, 1997) methods is becoming routine. These new methods provide more consistent and efficient estimates of population parameters than otherwise might be obtained with traditional methods relying on complete cases, available pairwise, mean imputation, or single-imputation regression methods (e.g., Graham, Hofer, & MacKinnon, 1996; Graham, Hofer, & Piccinin, 1993; Little & Rubin, 1986; Schafer, 1997).

Following the work of Little and Rubin (1987; Rubin, 1976), a distinction can be made between dropouts missing completely at random (MCAR), missing at random (MAR), and not missing at random (NMAR). The key distinction is whether the cause of the missingness is related directly to levels of the outcome variable (NMAR) or whether the missingness is due to other variables that are either irrelevant (MCAR) or measured and included in the model (MAR). Whether valid inferences can be drawn from analysis of longitudinal data with participant loss depends on the relationship between the outcome variables and the dropout mechanism (i.e., the reason for dropout), whether the dropout mechanism has been measured and included in the analysis (MAR), and the method of analysis (e.g., maximum likelihood). For most studies, the measurement of the dropout mechanism is critical and may include covariates that predict dropout, such as health-related variables, time to death, age, and numerous demographic variables. Assuming the data are MCAR or MAR, inferences derived from likelihood-based methods will be unbiased (Little & Rubin, 1987). The interpretation of these results based on missing data is as if all individuals continued participation in the study—the differences between participants and nonparticipants carried by the covariates and previous outcome measurements. The utility of these methods has been demonstrated in a number of studies (e.g., Graham, et al., 1993; 1996; McArdle, 1994; McArdle & Hamagami, 1991). In addition to nonparticipation, many surveys also have sparse missing values that do not allow for complete case analysis of the data without further (often substantial) loss of information. Sparse missingness can be handled using the same likelihood-based methods. Although these methods are certainly useful and represent substantial progress in dealing with selection issues, other methods of analyses (e.g., mixture models) may be more appropriate when the underlying population of individuals is considered to be different across distinct patterns of age-based nonparticipation.

Estimation of rates of change in longitudinal studies is often complicated by unequal schedules of data collection at either the group or individual level. Most random coefficients models, including implementations of the latent growth model, permit estimation of change curves with unequal intervals as long as all participants have the same approximate interval between test occasions (cf. Bryk & Raudenbush, 1987; Mehta & West, 2000; Rogosa, Brandt, & Zimowsky, 1982; Rogosa & Willett, 1985; Willett & Sayer, 1994). Other approaches permit unequal testing schedules at the level of the individual. McArdle and Woodcock (1997) propose a model for analyzing longitudinal data based on multiple groups with different test–retest intervals and show how such methods can permit the statistical separation of testing–practice effects, factor stability, change, and state fluctuation.

Important issues in longitudinal research include the description of normative aging trends and the estimation of correlations between rates of aging, concomitants, and predictors of change and consequents of changes (e.g., mortality). There are numerous challenges to obtaining proper inferences given any research design. Assuming that some process is declining over time, nonrandom dropout and retest–practice effects will have an effect of decreasing observed longitudinal changes, particularly changes measured over short intervals. Cohort effects will have the opposite effect; if assumed to be uniformly in favor of more recent generations, older individuals in the study will exhibit greater change and poorer outcomes. Both cross-sectional and longitudinal research are troubled by initial recruitment selection, typically favoring more highly functioning individuals. It is also the case that systematic intraindividual variability in performance may lead to less than optimal estimates of change over time. Nevertheless, longitudinal aging studies are the standard by which to evaluate changes in rates of aging within people. Advances in statistical methods and research designs are better equipping us for dealing with these challenges. Missing data methods for treating nonrandom attrition and sparse missing data, structural equation modeling methods that permit the analysis of reliable variance, designs using "measurement bursts" to model intraindividual fluctuation (Nesselroade & Schmidt-McCollam, 2000), and multivariate models to estimate reliable change and covariates of change offer promising ways to overcome many of these difficulties.

VII. Archiving and Data Sharing

Most long-term longitudinal studies eventually become important resources that should be shared with the broader scientific community. It is a rare that a single group of investigators will be able to exhaustively mine the rich resources that have been accumulated at great expense, time, and effort. Although the transition to a younger investigator may keep some studies alive, others will be become dormant for periods of time, to be picked up by others who discover that important questions can be addressed by follow-up of previously assessed populations. It becomes important therefore to plan the development of archives of raw data as well as derived scores on media that have the promise of preserving data over time. In long-term studies, however, one must also deal with changes of technology and make certain that records are promptly transferred to newer media when technology changes.

At some point investigators must seriously consider whether their archives should be transferred to public depositories such as the Murray Center or the National Archive of Computerized Data on Aging (NACDA). Such deposition, however, may require complex negotiation regarding the confidentiality of the individuals whose data are being deposited. Although it is relatively simple to de-identify past data for reanalysis, it is also necessary to maintain appropriate rosters of the identity of individual data if there is a likelihood that a further longitudinal follow-up may be warranted.

An alternative approach to placing entire studies into archives is to make data available to other investigators on particular variables or variable domains. This approach is particularly promising where individual investigators can acquire only relatively small data sets that provide low analytic power. An important example of this kind of data sharing is the acquisition of cross-sectional and longitudinal Wechsler Adult Intelligence Scale (WAIS) data by McArdle and associates (e.g., McArdle, 1994), demonstrating the possibility of covering larger portions of the adult life span by combining data from multiple studies.

VIII. Longitudinal Studies of Psychological Aging

The contributions of longitudinal studies to the psychology of aging have been significant but are, in many ways, only a beginning. Longitudinal studies, by definition, are necessary to address issues relating to intraindividual change and correlates of such changes. Questions regarding individual differences in aging, whether different processes "age" at different rates and in different individuals, and, indeed, whether "aging" is a universal or multidimensional process must be answered using longitudinal designs. This is not to say that cross-sectional findings are always misleading, but rather to say that they are not conclusive. Indeed, comparison of longitudinal to cross-sectional findings provides evidence of both concordance and disagreements (either full or in part). For example, the fluid–crystallized distinction (Horn & Cattell, 1967)—the observation and explanation that certain abilities are relatively maintained with age while others exhibit declines—was initially observed across people of different ages but has since been demonstrated in both cross-sectional and longitudinal studies (Horn & Hofer, 1992; Schaie, 1996). Disagreements between cross-sectional and longitudinal findings in the fluid–crystallized distinction involve primarily the ages at which declines are first observed as well as the magnitudes of decline.

Other direct comparisons between cross-sectional and longitudinal results include some of the variables found to account for age differences in cognitive functioning. A recent review of 34 longitudinal studies by Anstey and Christensen (2000) concluded that longitudinal findings regarding the effect of education, health, cardiovascular disease, hypertension, and apolipoprotein E genotype on cognitive change were consistent with cross-sectional findings, although results regarding the effect of physical activity were mixed and considered inconclusive. Although this comparative study provides support that between-individual differences are indicating important within-individual aging-related changes, this may not be the case for all processes of change.

Certain questions can only be asked of longitudinal data, particularly where the individual's "history" is required. Most longitudinal studies emphasize the interface between health status, change in health, and the association with psychological variables, and a major component of these studies includes the collection of extensive medical and clinical data. This is important for separating poor primary aging outcomes from insidious onset disease processes (secondary aging). A recent example of this is the study of "preclinical" dementia, which requires that preclinical cases of dementia be ascertained retrospectively. A finding from the Einstein Aging Study demonstrates decline in cognitive functioning initiating several years prior to meeting a threshold leading to diagnosis of clinical dementia (Sliwinski, Lipton, Buschke, & Stewart, 1996). An implication of this finding is that a significant proportion of "normal" cognitive change in both cross-sectional and longitudinal studies with shorter follow-up periods may be due to the preclinical phase of a dementing illness. A related research issue that requires long-term follow-up of individuals has to do with

the effect of apolipoprotein E(apoE) genotype, which has been shown to have a link with the incidence of dementia and also to influence "normal" cognitive decline. The influence of apoE has been evaluated in several longitudinal studies and found to be related to declines in both memory and speed in nondemented samples (Anstey & Christensen, 2000). A major contribution of longitudinal designs is the ability to separate change in functional capabilities from disease-related processes retrospectively, thereby permitting the evaluation of patterns and rates of aging for particular subgroups and individuals.

The study of stability and change in personality has benefited from long-term longitudinal studies. A recent longitudinal study of participants in the Berkeley Growth Study (1928–present), Berkeley Guidance Study (1928–present), and the Oakland Growth Study (1931–present) included data from participants at 14, 18, 30, 40, 50, and 62 years of age on an index of psychological health (Jones & Meredith, 2000). Latent growth curve models indicated that psychological health is relatively stable during adolescence and increases after age 30. Individuals having greater psychological health in adolescence and early adulthood tend to show the greatest increase in middle adulthood.

Hypotheses and theories regarding psychological aging phenomenon must account for within-person changes and, if derived from between-person observations, be validated on longitudinal data. Aging is a dynamic phenomenon, and the appropriate unit of analysis is the person followed over time. However, it is the case that most evidence for theories of aging are derived from cross-sectional analysis of samples varying broadly in age with the implicit assumption that the single occasion study of individuals varying in age provides a good estimate of how individuals change over time. The focus of these studies is typically on the amount of shared age-related individual differences and on the variables that account for most of the age-related variance (e.g., speed, sensorimotor, working memory; e.g., Salthouse, 1994). Two hypotheses of age-related mediation of cognitive functioning—the general slowing hypothesis (e.g., Birren & Fisher, 1995; Salthouse, 1999) and the "common cause" hypothesis (e.g., Lindenberger & Baltes, 1997)—have emphasized measures of processing speed and sensorimotor functioning, respectively. There have been few longitudinal evaluations of these hypotheses. In one longitudinal evaluation of the speed hypothesis, processing speed accounted for far less of the total longitudinal age effect compared to the total cross-sectional age effect (Sliwinski & Buschke, 1999).

There are, of course, numerous potential reasons for discrepancies between cross-sectional and longitudinal findings, including the relative age range available for study. Cross-sectional studies, however, must be regarded to provide a very poor basis for inference regarding whether change (aging) in one variable is associated with change (aging) in another variable. Indeed, a review of the cross-sectional literature on shared age-related effects finds that a highly diverse set of variables, all exhibiting mean differences across people of different ages, are moderately to highly associated in terms of shared age-related variance. An often overlooked reason for this is that in cross-sectional analysis of age-related variables, associations between time-dependent processes may arise simply due to average changes in the population and therefore tell us nothing about associations between rates of aging within individuals (Hofer, Berg, & Era, 1998; Hofer & Flaherty, 2000; Wohlwill, 1973). The potential for spurious associations among age-related variables is one of the major problems of cross-sectional designs for the study of associations between de-

velopmental and aging-related phenomenon. The foundation for scientific hypotheses and theories of aging involving the estimation of patterns and rates of decline, associations between rates of aging, the proper account of early or initial individual differences, and predictors of such changes in patterns and rates of aging must be based on appropriate longitudinal designs. Cross-sectional designs are important, particularly for the development of measurement instruments (e.g., evaluating factorial invariance across age groups), but do not provide a strong basis for understanding within-individual aging.

In the following section we describe briefly longitudinal studies of aging that have addressed psychological constructs, whether as a central objective or as a substantial emphasis. We cannot, of course, provide an exhaustive listing or more than a cursory overview of each study. Table 3.1 shows basic design and sample characteristics for each of the longitudinal studies that include major components focusing on psychological aging. Each longitudinal study necessarily began as a cross-sectional study, and numerous publications describe this first wave of data. In several cases, longitudinal data collection is quite recent; hence, publications on the longitudinal aspects of these studies are often still in progress.

We have limited this review to studies currently in progress and provide brief descriptions and references to some of the research associated with each major study as entry points to their characteristics and findings. The date given is the year when the study commenced. Several earlier completed studies are referenced in the introductory sections of this chapter. Other completed longitudinal studies not described here in detail include the Bonn Longitudinal Study (1965–1984, Rott, 1993; Thomae, 1993), The First Duke Longitudinal Study (1955–1976;

Table 3.1
Longitudinal Studies of Psychological Aging

Study Title	Start yr	N (T1)	Age (T1)	Follow-up (yrs)[a]	Occ Interval	Curr # Occ	Type sample	New cohort?
Australian Longitudinal Study of Aging	1992	1947	70–85+	4.0	1	2	Stratified sample of community-dwelling and institutional care facilities	
Asset and Health Dynamics Among the Oldest Old	1994	7447	70+	4.0	2	3	HRS Screening sample, Medicare enrollment, minority oversample	y
Baltimore Longitudinal Study of Aging	1958	260	20–96	42	2		Volunteer sample	y
Berkeley Older Generation Study	1968	94	59–79	14	14	2	Participants of Berkeley Growth and Guidance Studies	
Berlin Aging Study	1990	516	70–100+	6.0	2	4	Volunteer sample, former West-Berlin	
The Betula Project	1988	3000+	35–80	10.0	5	3	Stratified	y
Canberra Longitudinal Study	1991	897	70–93	10.5	3.5	4	Community sample (electoral role), institutional care, oversampling of very old	
Einstein Aging Studies	1980	488	70–90	20.0	1	20	Volunteer sample	y
Gender Study of Unlike-Sex DZ Twins	1995	498	69–81	4.0	2	2	Opposite sex twins in Sweden born between 1906 and 1925	
Groningen Longitudinal Aging Study	1993	753	57–99	2.0	1	3	Patient population with physical limitations	
The Gerontological and Geriatric Population Studies in Göteborg, Sweden	1971	1000	70	29.0	varies	12	Representative sample: Gothenberg	y
Health and Retirement Study	1992	12600	50–60	6.0	2	4	National sample, minorities oversampled	y
Interdisciplinary Longitudinal Study of Adult Development	1996	1384	45, 65	4	4	2	Former East and West Germany	
The Kungsholmen Project	1987	327	75+	12.0	4	4	Population from Kungsholmen district, Stockholm	y
Long Beach Longitudinal Study	1978	509	55–87	21.0	varies	4	Recruited from Health Maintenance Organization	y
Longitudinal Aging Study Amsterdam	1991	3107	55–85	6.0	3	3	Urban and rural municipal registries	y
Lund 80+ Study	1988	80+		10.0	5	3	Population of Lund 80+ years old	y
Maastricht Aging Study	1992	2000	24–81	6.0	3	3	Recruitment from Registration Network Family Practices	y
Manchester and Newcastle Longitudinal Studies of Aging	1982	~6400	49–96	14.0	varies	4	Community volunteer sample	y
McArthur Studies of Successful Aging	1988	1192	70–79	2.5	2.5	2	Selected from three cohorts of the Established Populations for Epidemiologic Studies of the Elderly	
Normative Aging Study	1963	2032	25–75		5	3	Community residents	
Nordic Research on Aging	1989	1204	75	5.0	5	2	Representative city samples	
The Nun Study	1991	678	75–103	9	~1.5	6	American members of the School Sisters of Notre Dame	
Octogenarian Twin Study	1990	702	80+	6	2	4	Swedish Twin Registry	
Seattle Longitudinal Study	1956	5000+ Cumul.	22–95	42	7	7	Health Maintenance Organization	y
The Swedish Adoption/Twin Study of Aging	1984	1500	40–84	6	3	3	Swedish Twin Registry	
The Victoria Longitudinal Study	1986	484	55–86	12	3	5	Community volunteers	y

[a]Total follow-up is as of year 2000.

Botwinick & Siegler, 1980), Second Duke Longitudinal Study (1968–1976; Palmore et al. 1985), Intergenerational Growth Study (1932–1982), Iowa State Study (1919–1976), New York State Psychiatric Institute Study of Aging Twins (1946–1973), New York Longitudinal Study (1956–1988), National Institute of Mental Health Study (1955), The OCTO Study (Johansson, Allen-Burge, & Zarit, 1997), and the Terman-Stanford Study (Bayley & Oden, 1955).

IX. Ongoing Longitudinal Studies

A. Australian Longitudinal Study of Aging (1992)

This study aims to determine features of successful aging in regards to physical, mental, and social variables. The participants include both community-dwelling and institutionalized individuals obtained using stratified sampling of 5-year age and sex groups over 70 years of age. Cross-sectional analysis of individual differences in memory performance found that processing speed was the major mediator of age-related variance in memory, with measures of depression, activity, gender, and health having mimimal influence (Luszcz, Bryan, & Kent, 1997). In longitudinal analyses of the Australian Longitudinal Study of Aging (ALSA) data, Luszcz (1998) reported decline in speed, picture memory, depression, morale, and self-esteem over the 2-year period.

B. Baltimore Longitudinal Study of Aging (1958)

Participants include healthy, community-dwelling, middle-to upper-middle-class volunteers aged 40–89 at the first occasion. The study began with men in 1958, with the additional inclusion of women in 1978. The findings include age-related changes for tests of paired associate learning and serial recall (Arenberg, 1983) and on the Benton Visual Retention test (Giambra, Arenberg, Zonderman, Kawas, & Costa, 1995).

C. Berkeley Older Generation Study (1958)

Members of this study began as participants in the earlier Berkeley Guidance and Berkeley Growth Studies. Evidence for continuity in friendships was found from young-old to old-old age, particularly among women, where the number of new friends and the desire for close and intimate friendships exhibited was stable, with some decline in these found for men (Field, 1999). Family involvement was found to increase with age, while beyond-family contacts declined for men but not for women (Field & Minkler, 1988). Health and socioeconomic status were found to account for the largest proportion of variance in family contact, with participants in better health having greater amounts of contact (Field, Minkler, Falk, & Leino, 1993).

D. Berlin Aging Study (1990)

The sample for this multidisciplinary study of persons over age 70 (Baltes & Mayer, 1999) includes 516 individuals drawn from former West Berlin (1990–1993) who participated in the intensive assessments (14 sessions). Of the cross-sectional findings, sensory and sensorimotor functioning have been shown to account for most of the age-related declines in cognitive functioning cross-sectionally (Lindenberger & Baltes, 1994). These findings were further replicated in a larger sample of older adults over 70 years of age and extended to younger adults between 25 and 69 years old (Baltes & Lindenberger, 1997).

E. The Betula Project (1988)

This prospective study of aging and dementia focuses on memory changes with age, with particular emphasis on risk factors and signs of preclinical dementia (Nilsson, et al., 1997). This study includes extensive memory measures, health indicators (e.g., clinical interviews, blood samples) and measures of social factors. Over 3000 participants from Umea, Sweden, born between the years 1908 and 1960 make up the sample. Stability for verbal fluency and vocabulary was found from age 35 to 50, followed by gradual decline, and education was a key factor associated with level of semantic memory (Bäckman & Nilsson, 1996).

F. Canberra Longitudinal Study (1991)

This prospective study of cognitive functioning and dementia is composed of a random sample of people aged 70 years and older drawn from the electoral roll for Canberra and the neighboring town of Queanbeyan, Australia (Korten, et al., 1997). Longitudinal results include the finding that education is associated with long-term individual differences in cognitive functioning but has little influence on timing or amount of cognitive change in late life (Christensen, et al., 2001). Changes in memory and speed functioning over 3.5 years were associated with decline in grip strength, more illnesses, and higher depression (Christensen, et al., 1999).

G. Einstein Aging Studies (1980)

The Einstein Aging Study has emerged from several longitudinal aging studies that began more than 20 years ago. These studies include the Bronx Aging Study, a longitudinal study of community-residing elderly individuals focused on assessing risk factors for dementia and the incidence of dementia; the Teach-

ing Nursing Program Project examined age-associated memory impairment and the cognitive deficits in Alzheimer's disease; and the Mechanisms of Age-Associated Memory Impairment Study focused on the study of cognitive mediators and mechanisms underlying memory differences between young and elderly adults. Longitudinal studies in this program have demonstrated that cognitive changes associated with normal aging are significantly influenced by contamination of normative samples by individuals with unidentified preclinical dementia (Sliwinski, Lipton, Buschke, & Stewart, 1996). Others findings demonstrate that although processing speed mediates longitudinal changes in memory and cognition to some degree (6% to 29%), longitudinal mediation accounts for much less variance compared to cross-sectional age mediation models (70–100%; Sliwinski & Buschke, 1999).

H. The Gender Study of Unlike-Sex Dizygotic Twin Pairs (1995)

A major aim of this study is to understand the sex differences in health and health-related variables. The sampling frame is based on all living pairs of opposite-sex twins in Sweden born between 1906 and 1925 and includes 249 complete pairs of unlike-sex dizygotic (DZ) twins.

I. Groningen Longitudinal Aging Study (1993)

This study focuses on functional status and the need for supportive and institutional care. Assessment includes a variety of person characteristics, and environmental factors are combined with multiple measures of outcomes (i.e., disease-related impairments, symptoms, functional limitations, disability, and quality of life) to achieve greater insight into the complex adaptation process resulting from impairment in late life. Findings from this study include changes in cognitive functioning (Jelicic & Kempen, 1997), personality and health-related quality of life (Kempen, Jelicic, & Ormel, 1997), and depressive symptoms and chronic health problems (Ormel, et al., 1998).

J. The Gerontological and Geriatric Population Studies in Gothenburg, Sweden (1971)

The aims of this study include description of "normal" aging, prevalence and incidence of disease, and the evaluation of the potential for preventing functional decline in late life (Rinder, Roupe, Steen, & Svanborg, 1975). The initial representative sample of 70-year-olds was obtained in the city of Gothenburg in 1971–1972. The study is multidisciplinary and includes extensive physiological exams as well as demographic, social, and cognitive variables. The examination of aging-related changes in cognitive functioning related to education, disease, and survival (terminal drop) has been a central focus of psychologically oriented analyses (Berg, 1987; Maxson, Berg, & McClearn, 1996).

K. Interdisciplinary Longitudinal Study of Adult Development (1996)

This study focuses on predictors and determinants of successful physiological and mental aging (Rudinger & Minnemann, 1997). The sample includes 1390 participants from two age cohorts (1930–1932 and 1950–1952 born before and after WWII) and 4 years between measurement occasions. Reports include adjustment to retirement (Lehr, et al., in press), changes in cognitive ability across participants from former East and West Germany (Oswald, Rupprecht, & Hagen, 1997), and age differences in stress, social resources, and well-being (Martin, Grunendahl, & Martin, in press).

L. The Kungsholmen Project (1987)

This longitudinal population-based study of individuals aged 75 and over focuses on aging and the incidence of dementia (Fratiglioni, et al., 1991). The initial sample includes residents of the Kungsholmen district of Stockholm, with later expansion to include individuals from two other areas in Sweden. Recent findings include differential change in memory performance over 3 years across groups defined by apoE-epsilon 4 allele (Small, Basun, & Bäckman, 1998), predictors of cognitive changes in memory, visuospatial, and verbal performance (Small & Bäckman, 1998), and negative and positive affect associations with health and life satisfaction in late life (Hillerås, Jorm, Herlitz, & Winblad, 1998).

M. Long Beach Longitudinal Study (1978)

This study, which focuses on mechanisms and models of change in cognitive functioning, was initiated in 1978. Recent results include comparison of both cross-sectional and longitudinal age trends on memory performance (Zelinski, Gilewski, & Schaie, 1993). Zelinski and Burnight (1997) report age declines in list and text recall with no evidence for differential decline across cohorts over a 16-year longitudinal period. However, no reliable decline was observed for recognition memory (Zelinski & Stewart, 1998).

N. Longitudinal Aging Study Amsterdam (1992)

This study is guided by questions concerning changes in physical, cognitive, emotional, and social components of aging, predictors of changes with age, association between aging-related changes, and consequences of such changes in terms of quality of life, adjustment, and need for care (Deeg, Beekman, Kriegsman, & Westendorp-de Serière,

1998). Findings from this study demonstrate a link between depression and incidence of physical disability, providing evidence that risk for physical disability may be related to less physical activity and having fewer social contacts among depressed individuals (Penninx, Leveille, Ferruci, van Eijk, & Guralnik, 1999). Smits, Deeg, Kriegsman, and Schmand (1999) found that measures of cognitive functioning (i.e., processing speed, fluid intelligence) independently predicted mortality after controlling for health, age, depressive symptoms, and other covariates.

O. The (Lund) 80+ Studies (1988)

The initial 80+ study was based in Lund, Sweden, (Svensson, Dehlin, Hagberg, & Samuelsson, 1993) and has since expanded to include other 80+ studies in Reykjavik, Iceland (1993) and Fredericton, New Brunswick, Canada (1998), which permit cross-cultural cohort comparisons. Each study is based on a cohort-sequential design and includes yearly assessments of medical, social, and psychological variables (similar forms across studies). Recent research has focused on predictors of life satisfaction (McCamish-Svensson, Samuelsson, Hagberg, Svensson, & Dehlin, 1999b) and formal and informal support (McCamish-Svensson, Samuelsson, Hagberg, Svensson, & Dehlin, 1999a).

P. Manchester and Newcastle Longitudinal Studies of Aging (1982)

The Manchester and Newcastle Longitudinal Studies of Cognitive Performance include data on approximately 6400 self-selected volunteers aged between 49 and 96 years and approximately 75% female (Rabbitt, 1990, 1993; Rabbitt, Donlan, Bent, McInnes, & Abson, 1993). Age, distance and cause of death, self-reports of health status and recent medical care, and

activities of daily living were found to be predictive of cognitive ability (Rabbitt, Bent, & McInnes, 1997). An analysis of four trials of a letter-letter coding test, similar to the WAIS Digit-Symbol Substitution Subtest, given in succession within a single test occasion suggests that memory plays an important role in substitution coding tests (Piccinin & Rabbitt, 1999).

Q. MacArthur Studies of Successful Aging (1988)

This study emphasizes the prediction of cognitive function in a healthy sample of individuals. Education was found to be the strongest predictor of cognitive change assessed over a 2.0–2.5-year period in participants aged 70–79 years (Albert, et al., 1995). A previous cross-sectional study reported that level of cognitive performance was predicted by educational attainment, with income and race having smaller influences (Inouye, Albert, Mohs, Sun, & Berkman, 1993).

R. Normative Aging Study (1963)

This study was established as an intramural research program within the Department of Veterans Affairs and focused on describing the biomedical, psychosocial, and disease-related changes associated with aging. The initial sample was composed of 2,280 men with an average age of 72 years, most of whom were veterans from WWII and the Korean War. Clinical health data were collected at 3-year intervals and supplemented with mailed surveys.

S. Nordic Research on Ageing (1989)

This study (Heikkinen, Berg, Schroll, Steen, & Viidik, 1997) is a comparative study of functional capacity and health in 75-year-old men and women. This international collaborative study is composed of systematic random samples of 75-year-old residents of Glostrup in Denmark ($n = 481$), Gothenburg in Sweden ($n = 368$), and residents of Jyvaskyla in Finland ($n = 355$). Results focus on functional ability status (Heikkinen et al., 1997) and memory and cognitive functioning (Steen, Fromholt, Äystö, & Berg, 1997).

T. The Nun Study (1986)

Participants in the Nun Study include 678 members of the School Sisters of Notre Dame who were 75–103 years of age in 1986. The focus is on aging and Alzheimer's disease, with annual medical and psychological assessments and full access to archival and medical records. Results from this study indicate that those without the apoE epsilon 4 allele had half the risk of decline in cognitive functioning compared to those with the allele (Riley, et al., 2000). Low linguistic ability early in life was found to be predictive of lower cognitive functioning and Alzheimer's disease in old age (Snowden, et al., 1996) and of mortality (Snowdon, Greiner, Kemper, Nanayakkara, & Mortimer, 1999).

U. Origins of Variance in the Old-Old (1991)

Participants in this study included 351 twin pairs, 149 monozygotic (MZ) and 202 same-sex DZ twin pairs, aged 80 and older. The gender ratio, education, socioeconomic status, marital status, and housing for this unique sample corresponds to population statistics for this age segment of the Swedish population (Simmons, et al., 1997). A broad spectrum of biobehavioral measures of health and functional capacity, personality, well-being, interpersonal functioning, as well as memory and cognition were obtained. Findings from this study include evidence for substantial genetic influence on cog-

nitive capabilities late in life (McClearn, et al., 1997) and somewhat less genetic influence on measures of memory (Johansson et al., 1999).

V. Seattle Longitudinal Study (1956)

The Seattle Longitudinal Study (SLS) has been a major resource for monitoring age and cohort trends in adult cognitive development, providing normative data for assessment instruments used with older adults, exploring the causes of individual differences in aging, and assessing the effects of targeted cognitive interventions within the context of a longitudinal study (Schaie, 1996). The SLS began in 1956 and has operated continuously with new participant recruitment at each wave of measurement at 7-year intervals. Extensions of the study include longitudinal data on second-generation family members and assessment of grandchildren of the original participants. Recent findings include evidence for longitudinal factorial invariance of the cognitive structure (Schaie, et al., 1998) and evidence for cognitive and other risk factors for mortality (Bosworth, Schaie, & Willis, 1999)

W. The Swedish Adoption/Twin Study of Aging (1984)

Central to the aims of the Swedish Adoption/Twin Study of Aging (SATSA) study is understanding the relative importance of genetic and environmental influences that account for individual differences in aging-related outcomes. SATSA includes longitudinal data from both comprehensive questionnaires (measured every 3 years) and in-person interviews on a subset of the total Swedish Twin Registry sample, which included twins who were reared apart. Findings from the SATSA suggest individual differences in cognition are under substantial genetic involvement in middle to late adulthood and that stability in cognitive functioning in late life is largely genetic (Plomin, Pederson, Lichtenstein, & McClearn, 1994). Finkel, Pederson, Plomin, and McClearn (1998) examined cross-sectional and longitudinal age changes in cognition and found that genetic variance decreased for a cognitive factor when studied longitudinally. Emery, Pedersen, Svartengren, and McClearn (1998) found that forced expiratory volume shared genetic effects with fluid abilities, but not crystallized knowledge, in late life.

X. The Victoria Longitudinal Study (1986)

The objective of the Victoria Longitudinal Study (VLS) is to examine profiles and predictors of cognitive changes in healthy, community-dwelling older adults ranging in age from 55 to 85 years (Hultsch, Hertzog, Dixon, & Small, 1998). Findings from the VLS include the association between intellectually demanding lifestyle activities and maintenance of cognitive functioning (Hultsch, Hertzog, Small, & Dixon, 1999). Declines in quantitative word and text recall were observed, whereas overall qualitative (number of categories and intrusions) levels were relatively maintained over a 6-year period (Small, Dixon, Hultsch, & Hertzog, 1999).

X. Summary and Conclusions

This chapter began by reminding the reader why longitudinal studies are such important contributors to the aging literature, examined problems of longitudinal studies as quasi-experiments, and discussed some of the methodological issues in cross-sectional and longitudinal inquiries. Recent methodological advances that can address some of these issues were indicated. We then provided a brief review of major long-term as well as recently begun longitudinal studies that

should be of interest to serious aging researchers.

Several themes have served as motivations for longitudinal studies of psychological aging. What are the normative (nonpathological) changes in cognitive functioning with increasing age? What are the predictors or concomitants of change in cognitive functioning? Does speed account for most of the age-related variability in intellectual functioning? What are the consequences of changes in cognitive functioning in terms of older persons' contributions to society, their adjustment, and their need for care? As we have indicated above, the study of aging is the study of change, and the appropriate unit of analysis is the individual followed over time. These longitudinal studies are producing valuable answers to many of these questions.

We do not feel a need to lobby for more emphasis on longitudinal studies; that message has apparently been well heard and accepted by the aging community. However, we must now call attention to the need of attending to issues of comparability of data that will make possible adequate comparison of data collected with widely differing instruments, in different samples of people, and over differing temporal intervals. It is unlikely that any single investigator can cover the broad field of the psychology of aging, nor is it likely that many investigators will have the resources to both collect data from representative populations and oversample subgroups of special interest. Hence, the role of collaborative longitudinal research, meta-analysis, and pooling of data archives will become increasingly important. In this context, efforts are needed to identify a small number of standard reference measures that should be included in all studies to facilitate cross-battery analysis. Many of the major ongoing studies represent important scientific resources that merit careful documentation and archiving for eventual release to the broader scientific community. For this purpose, it would be important to develop standard protocols for the archiving of longitudinal data.

Previous reviews of the status of the psychology of aging have often bemoaned the lack of adequate longitudinal studies covering the period from young adulthood to advanced old age. As this chapter shows, that call has been heeded in many substantive areas. It is our hope that this chapter will provide greater accessibility to the longitudinal literature, particularly for other reviewers and textbook authors. We look particularly to the latter to now provide appropriate corrections for popular misconceptions based largely on cross-sectional data. However, we would also urge them to call attention to the continuing importance of cross-sectional studies for the identification of age-related phenomena and development of age-appropriate measurement instruments as well as to provide data that can form a basis for time-specific policy formulation with regard to problems and needs of the present aging population.

References

Albert, M. S., Jones, K., Savage, C. R., Berkman, L., Seeman, T., Blazer, D., & Rowe, J. W. (1995). Predictors of cognitive change in older persons: MacArthur Studies of Successful Aging, *Psychology and Aging, 10,* 578–589.

Anstey, K., & Christensen, H. (2000). Education, activity, health, blood pressure, and apolipoprotein E as predictors of cognitive change in old age: A review. *Gerontology, 46,* 163–177.

Arenberg, D. (1983). Memory and learning do decline late in life. In J. E. Birren, J. M. A. Munnichs, H. Thomae, & M. Marios (Eds.), *Aging: A challenge to science and society, Vol. 3, Behavioural sciences and conclusions.* Oxford, UK: Oxford University Press.

Bäckman, L., & Nilsson, L.-G. (1996). Semantic memory functioning across the adult life span. *European Psychologist, 1,* 27–33.

Balinsky, B. (1941). An analysis of the mental factors of various age groups from nine to sixty. *Genetic Psychology Monographs, 23,* 191–234.

Baltes, P. B., & Lindenberger, U. (1997). Emergence of a powerful connection between sensory and cognitive functions across the adult life span: A new window to the study of cognitive aging. *Psychology and Aging, 12,* 12–21.

Baltes, P. B., & Mayer, K. U. (1999). *The Berlin Aging Study: Aging from 70 to 100.* New York: Cambridge University Press.

Baltes, P. B., & Nesselroade, J. R. (1979). History and rationale of longitudinal research. In J. R. Nesselroade & P. B. Baltes (Eds.), *Longitudinal research in the study of behavior and development.* New York: Academic Press.

Baltes, P. B., Nesselroade, J. R., Schaie, K. W., & Labouvie, E. W. (1972). On the dilemma of regression effects in examining ability-level-related differentials in ontogenetic patterns of intelligence. *Developmental Psychology, 6,* 78–84.

Bayley, N., & Oden, M. H. (1955). The maintenance of intellectual ability in gifted adults. *Journal of Gerontology, 10,* 91–107.

Bell, R. Q. (1953). Convergence: An accelerated longitudinal approach. *Child Development, 24,* 145–152.

Berg S. (1987). Intelligence and terminal decline. In G. L. Maddox & E. W. Busse (Eds.), *Aging, the universal human experience* (pp. 411–416). New York: Springer Publishing Company.

Birren, J. E., & Fisher, L. M. (1995). Aging and speed of behavior: Possible consequences for psychological functioning. *Annual Review of Psychology, 46,* 329–353.

Bosworth, H. B., Schaie, K. W., & Willis, S. L. (1999). Cognitive and sociodemographic risk factors for mortality in the Seattle Longitudinal Study. *Journal of Gerontology: Psychological Sciences, 54B,* P273–P282.

Botwinick, J., & Siegler, I. C. (1980). Intellectual ability among the elderly: Simultaneous cross-sectional and longitudinal comparisons, *Developmental Psychology, 16,* 49–53.

Bryk, A. S., & Raudenbush, S. W. (1987). Application of hierarchical linear models to assessing change. *Psychological Bulletin, 101,* 147–158.

Byrne, B. M., Shavelson, R. J., & Muthén, B. (1989). Testing for the equivalence of factor covariance and mean structures: The issue of partial measurement invariance. *Psychological Bulletin, 105*, 456–466.

Campbell, W. T., & Stanley, J. C. (1963). *Experimental and quasi-experimental designs for research.* Chicago: Rand McNally.

Christensen, H., Hofer, S. M., MacKinnon, A. J., Korten, A. E., Jorm, A. F., Henderson, A. S., & Jacomb, P. (2001). Age is no kinder to the better educated: Absence of an association established using latent growth techniques in a community sample. *Psychological Medicine, 31*, 15–27.

Christensen, H., MacKinnon, A. J., Korten, A. E., Jorm, A. F., Henderson, A. S., Jacomb, P., & Rodgers, B. (1999). An analysis of diversity in the cognitive performance of elderly community dwellers: Individual differences in change scores as a function of age. *Psychology and Aging, 14*, 365–379.

Cooney, T. M., Schaie, K. W., & Willis, S. L. (1988). The relationship between prior functioning of cognitive and personality dimensions and subject attrition in longitudinal research. *Journal of Gerontology: Psychological Sciences, 43*, P12–17.

Cornelius, S. W., Willis, S. L., Nesselroade, J. R., & Baltes, P. B. (1983). Convergence between attention variables and factors of psychometric intelligence in older adults. *Intelligence, 7*, 253–269.

Deeg, D. J. H., Beekman, A. T. F., Kriegsman, D. M. W., & Westendorp-de Serière, M. (1998). *Autonomy and well-being in the aging population II: Report from the Longitudinal Aging Study Amsterdam 1995–1996.* Amsterdam, The Netherlands: VU University Press.

Eichorn, D. H., Clausen, J. A., Haan, N., Honzik, M. P., & Mussen, P. H. (1981). *Present and past in middle life.* New York: Academic Press.

Emery, C. F., Pedersen, N. L., Svartengren, M., & McClearn, G. E. (1998). Longitudinal and genetic effects in the relationship between pulmonary function and cognitive performance. *Journal of Gerontology: Psychological Sciences, 53B*, P311–P317.

Field, D. (1999). Continuity and change in friendships in advanced old age: Findings from the Berkeley Older Generation Study, *International Journal of Aging & Human Development, 48*, 325–346.

Field, D., & Minkler, M. (1988). Continuity and change in social support between young-old and old-old or very-old age. *Journal of Gerontology: Psychological Sciences, 43*, P100–P106.

Field, D., Minkler, M., Falk, R., & Leino, E. V. (1993). The influence of health on family contacts and family feelings in advanced old age: A longitudinal study. *Journal of Gerontology: Psychological Sciences, 48*, P18–P28.

Finkel, D., Pedersen, N. L., Plomin, G. E., & McClearn, G. E. (1998). Longitudinal and cross-sectional twin data on cognitive abilities in adulthood: The Swedish Adoption/Twin Study of Aging, *Developmental Psychology, 34*, 1400–1413.

Fratiglioni, L., Grut, M., Forsell, Y., Viitanen, M., Grafström, M., Holmen, K., Ericsson, K., Bäckman, L., Ahlbom, A. & Winblad, B. (1991). Prevalence of Alzheimer's disease in an elderly urban population: Relationship with sex and education. *Neurology, 41*, 1886–1891.

Garrett, H. E. (1946). A developmental theory of intelligence. *American Psychologist, 1*, 372–378.

Giambra, L. M., Arenberg, D., Zonderman, A. B., Kawas, C. & Costa, P. T. (1995). Adult life span changes in immediate visual memory and verbal intelligence. *Psychology and Aging, 10*, 123–139.

Graham, J. W., Hofer, S. M., & MacKinnon, D. P. (1996). Maximizing the usefulness of data obtained with planned missing value patterns: An application of maximum likelihood procedures. *Multivariate Behavioral Research, 31*, 197–218.

Graham, J. W., Hofer, S. M., & Piccinin, A. M. (1994). Analysis with missing data in drug prevention research. In L. Collins and L. Seitz (Eds.), *National Institute on Drug Abuse Research Monograph Series, 142*, (pp. 13–62). Washington, DC: National Institute on Drug Abuse.

Heikkinen, E., Berg, S., Schroll, M., Steen, B., & Viidik, A. (Eds.) (1997). *Functional status, health and aging: The NORA study.* Paris, France: Serdi Publishers.

Hilleräs, P., Jorm, A., Herlitz, A., & Winblad B. (1998). Negative and positive affect among the very old: A survey on a sample aged 90 years or above. *Research on Ageing, 20,* 593–610.

Hofer, S. M., Berg, S., & Era, P. (1998, November). *Evidence for independent aging effects on perceptual acuity, balance, and cognitive capabilities: The NORA study.* Paper presented at the annual meeting of the Gerontological Society of America, Philadelphia, PA.

Hofer, S. M., & Flaherty, B. P. (2000, November). *Narrow age-cohort analysis of cross-sectional data.* Paper presented at the annual meeting of the Gerontological Society of Americae, Washington, DC.

Hofer, S. M., Horn, J. L., & Eber, H. W. (1997). A robust five-factor structure of the 16PF: Evidence from independent rotation and confirmatory factorial invariance procedures. *Personality and Individual Differences, 23,* 247–269.

Horn, J. L. (1991). Comments on issues in factorial invariance. In L. M. Collins & J. L. Horn (Eds.), *Best methods for the analysis of change* (pp. 114–125). Washington, DC: American Psychological Association.

Horn, J. L., & Cattell, R. B. (1967). Age differences in fluid and crystallized intelligence. *Acta Psychologica, 26,* 107–129.

Horn, J. L., & Hofer, S. M. (1992). Major abilities and development in the adult period. In R. J. Sternberg & C. A. Berg (Eds.), *Intellectual development* (pp. 44–99). New York: Cambridge University Press.

Horn, J. L., & McArdle, J. J. (1992). A practical and theoretical guide to measurement invariance in aging research. *Experimental Aging Research, 18,* 117–144.

Horn, J. L., McArdle, J. J., & Mason, R. (1983). When is invariance not invariant: A practical scientist's look a the ethereal concept of factor invariance. *Southern Psychologist, 1,* 179–188.

Hultsch, D. F., Hertzog, C., Dixon, R. A., & Small, B. J. (1998). *Memory changes in the aged.* New York: Cambridge University Press.

Hultsch, D. F., Hertzog, C., Small, B. J., & Dixon, R. A. (1999). Use it or lose it: Engaged lifestyle as a buffer of cognitive decline in aging? *Psychology and Aging, 14,* 245–263.

Inouye, S. K., Albert, M. S., Mohs, R., Sun, K., & Berkman, L. F. (1993). Cognitive performance in a high-functioning community-dwelling elderly population. *Journal of Gerontology: Medical Sciences, 48,* M146–M151.

Jelicic, M., & Kempen G. I. J. M. (1997). Cognitive function in community-dwelling elderly with chronic medical conditions. *International Journal of Geriatric Psychiatry, 12,* 1039–1041.

Johansson, B., Allen-Burge, R., & Zarit, S. H. (1997). Self-reports on memory functioning in a longitudinal study of the oldest-old: Relation to current, prospective, and retrospective performance. *Journal of Gerontology: Psychological Sciences, 52B,* P139–P146.

Johansson, B., Whitfield, K., Pedersen, N. L., Hofer, S. M., Ahern, F., & McClearn, G. E. (1999). Origins of individual differences in episodic memory in the oldest-old: A population-based study of identical and same-sex fraternal twins aged 80 and above. *Journal of Gerontology: Psychological Sciences, 54B,* P173–P179.

Jones, C. J., & Meredith, W. (2000). Developmental paths of psychological health from early adolescence to later adulthood. *Psychology and Aging, 15,* 351–360.

Jöreskog, K. G. (1971). Simultaneous factor analysis in several populations. *Psychometrika, 36,* 409–426.

Jöreskog, K. G. (1979). Statistical estimation of structural models in longitudinal developmental investigations. In J. R. Nesselroade & P. B. Baltes (Eds.), *Longitudinal research in the study of behavior and development* (pp. 303–351). New York: Academic Press.

Kempen, G. I. J. M., Jelicic, M., & Ormel, J. (1997). Personality, chronic medical morbidity and health-related quality of life among older persons. *Health Psychology, 16,* 539–546.

Korten, A. E., Henderson, A. S., Christensen, H., Jorm A. F., Rodgers, B., Jacomb, P., & Mackinnon, A. J. (1997). A prospective study of cognitive functioning in the elderly. *Psychological Medicine, 27,* 919–930.

Lehr, U., Jüchtern, J.-C., Schmitt, M., Sperling, U., Fischer, A., Grünendahl, M., & Minnemann, E. (in press). Anticipation of and adjustment to retirement. *Aging: Clinical and Experimental Research.*

Lewin, K. (1935). *Dynamic theory of personality*. New York: McGraw-Hill.

Lindenberger, U., & Baltes, P. B. (1994). Sensory functioning and intelligence in old age: A strong connection. *Psychology and Aging, 9*, 339–355.

Lindenberger, U., & Baltes, P. B. (1997). Intellectual functioning in old and very old age: Cross-sectional results from the Berlin Aging Study. *Psychology and Aging, 12*, 410–432.

Little, R. J. A., & Rubin, D. B. (1987). *Statistical analysis with missing data*. New York: Wiley.

Luszcz, M. A. (1998). A longitudinal study of psychological changes in cognition and self in late life. *The Australian Educational and Developmental Psychologist, 15*, 39–61.

Luszcz, M. A., Bryan, J., & Kent, P. (1997). Predicting episodic memory performance of very old men and women: Contributions from age, depression activity, cognitive ability, and speed. *Psychology and Aging, 12*, 340–351.

Maitland, S. B., Intrieri, R. C., Schaie, K. W., & Willis, S. L. (2000). Gender differences in cognitive abilities: Invariance of covariance and latent mean structures. *Aging, Neuropsychology and Cognition, 7*, 32–53.

Martin, M., Grunendahl, M., & Martin, P. (in press). Age differences in stress, social resources, and well-being in middle and older age. *Journal of Gerontology: Psychological Sciences*.

Mason, K. G., Mason, W. H., Winsborough, H. H., & Poole, W. K. (1973). Some methodological problems in cohort analyses of archival data. *American Sociological Review, 38*, 242–258.

Maxson, P. J., Berg, S., & McClearn, G. (1996). Multidimensional patterns of aging in 70-year-olds. Survival differences. *Journal of Aging and Health, 8*, 320–333.

McCamish-Svensson, C., Samuelsson, G., Hagberg, B., Svensson, T. & Dehlin, O. (1999a). Informal and formal support from a multi-disciplinary perspective: a Swedish follow-up between 80 and 82 years of age. *Health and Social Care in the Community, 7*, 163–176.

McCamish-Svensson, C., Samuelsson, G., Hagberg, B., Svensson, T. & Dehlin, O. (1999b). Social relationships and health as predictors of life satisfaction in advanced age: Results from a Swedish longitudinal study. *International Journal of Aging and Human Development, 48*, 301–324.

McArdle, J. J. (1994). Structural factor analysis experiments with incomplete data. *Multivariate Behavioral Research, 29*, 63–113.

McArdle, J. J., & Hamagami, F. (1991). Modeling incomplete longitudinal and cross-sectional data using latent growth structural models. In L. M. Collins & J. L. Horn (Eds.), *Best methods for the analysis of change* (pp. 276–304). Washington, DC: American Psychological Association.

McArdle, J. J., & Woodcock, R. W. (1997). Expanding test-retest designs to include developmental time-lag components. *Psychological Methods, 4*, 403–435.

McClearn, G. E., Johansson, B., Berg, S., Pedersen, N. L., Ahern, F., Petrill, S. A., & Plomin, R. (1997). Substantial genetic influence on cognitive abilities in twins 80+ years old. *Science, 276*, 1560–1563.

Mehta, P. D., & West, S. G. (2000). Putting the individual back into individual growth curves. *Psychological Methods, 5*, 23–43.

Meredith, W. (1993). Measurement invariance, factor analysis and factorial invariance. *Psychometrika, 58*, 525–543.

Nesselroade, J. R. (1986). Selection and generalization in investigations of interrelationships in among variables: Some commentary on aging research. *Educational Gerontology, 12*, 395–402.

Nesselroade, J. R., & Schmidt-McCollam, K. M. (2000). Putting the process in developmental process. *International Journal of Behavioral Development, 24*, 295–300.

Nesselroade, J. R., Stigler, J. R., & Baltes, P. B. (1980). Regression toward the mean and the study of change. *Psychological Bulletin, 88*, 622–637.

Nilsson, L.-G., Bäckman, L., Erngrund, K., Nyberg, L., Adolfsson, R., Bucht, G., Karlsson, S., Widing, M., & Winblad, B. (1997). The Betula prospective cohort study: Memory, health, and aging. *Aging, Neuropsychology, and Cognition, 4*, 1–32.

Ormel, J., Kempen, G. I. J. M., Deeg, D. J. H., Brilman, E. I., van Sonderen, E., & Relyveld, J (1998). Functioning, well-being and health perception in late middle aged and older people. Comparing the effects of depressive symptoms and chronic medical conditions. *Journal of the American Geriatrics Society, 46*, 39–48.

Owens, W. A., Jr. (1953). Age and mental abilities: A longitudinal study. *Genetic Psychology Monographs, 48*, 3–54.

Owens, W. A., Jr. (1966). Age and mental abilities: A second adult follow-up. *Journal of Educational Psychology, 57*, 311–325.

Oswald, W. D., Rupprecht, R., & Hagen, B. (1997). *Aspekte der kognitiven Leistungsfähigkeit bei 60–62jährigen aus Ost- und Westdeutschland* [Aspects of cognitive ability among participants from East and West Germany]. *Zeitschrift für Gerontopsychologie und Psychiatrie, 10*, 213–230.

Palmore, E., Busse, E. W., Maddox, G. L., Nowlin, J. B., & Siegler, I. C. (1985). *Normal aging III*. Durham, NC: Duke University Press.

Pedersen, N. L., & Reynolds, C. A. (1998). Stability and change in adult personality: Genetic and environmental components. *European Journal of Personality, 12*, 365–386.

Penninx, B. W. J. H., Leveille, S., Ferruci, L., van Eijk, J. Th. M., & Guralnik, J. M. (1999). Exploring the effect of depression on physical disability: longitudinal evidence from the established populations for epidemiologic studies of the elderly. *American Journal of Public Health, 9*, 1346–1352.

Piccinin, A. M., & Rabbitt, P. M. A. (1999). Contribution of cognitive abilities to performance and improvement on a substitution coding task. *Psychology and Aging, 14*, 539–551.

Plomin, R., Pederson, N. L., Lichtenstein, P., & McClearn, G. E. (1994). Variability and stability in cognitive abilities are largely genetic later in life. *Behavior Genetics, 24*, 207–215.

Rabbitt, P. (1990). Applied cognitive gerontology: Some problems, methodologies and data. *Applied Cognitive Psychology, 4*, 225–246.

Rabbitt, P. (1993). Does it all go together when it goes? *Quarterly Journal of Experimental Psychology: Human Experimental Psychology, 46A*, 385–434.

Rabbitt, P., Bent, N., & McInnes, L. (1997). Health, age and mental ability. *Irish Journal of Psychology, 18*, 104–131.

Rabbitt, P., Donlan, C., Bent, N., McInnes, L., & Abson, V. (1993). The University of Manchester Age and Cognitive Performance Research Centre and the North East Age Research Longitudinal Programmes, 1982 to 1997. *Zeitschrift für Gerontologie, 26*, 176–183.

Reinert, G. (1970). Comparative factor analytic studies of intelligence through the human life-span. In L. R. Goulet & P. B. Baltes (Eds.), *Life-span developmental psychology: Research and theory* (pp. 468–485). New York: Academic Press.

Riley, K. P., Snowdon, D. A., Saunders, A. M., Roses, A. D., Mortimer, J. A., Nanayakkara. N. (2000). Cognitive function and apolipoprotein-E in the very old: findings from the Nun Study. *Journal of Gerontology: Social Sciences, 55*, S69–S75.

Rinder L., Roupe, S., Steen, B., & Svanborg A. (1975). Seventy-year-old people in Gothenburg. A population study in an industrialized Swedish city. I. General presentation of the study. *Acta Medica Scandinavica, 198*, 397–407.

Rogosa, D., Brandt, D., & Zimowsky, M. (1982). A growth curve approach to the measurement of change. *Psychological Bulletin, 92*, 726–748.

Rogosa, D., & Willett, J. B. (1985). Understanding correlates of change by modeling individual differences in growth. *Psychometrika, 50*, 203–228.

Rott, C. (1993). Three components of intellectual development in old age: Results from the Bonn Longitudinal Study on Aging. *Zeitschrift für Gerontologie, 26*, 184–190.

Rubin, D. B. (1976). Inference with missing data. *Biometrika, 63*, 581–592.

Rudinger, G., & Minnemann, E. (1997). Die Lebenssituation von älteren Frauen und Männern in Ost-und Westdeutschland: Ergebnisse der Interdisziplinären Langzeitstudie des Erwachsenenalters (ILSE) [The lives of older women and men in East and West Germany: Results from the Interdisciplinary Longitudinal Study of Adulthood (ILSE)]. *Zeitschrift für Gerontopsychologie und Psychiatrie, 10*, 205–212.

Ryder, N. B. (1965). The cohort as a concept in the study of social changes. *American Sociological Review, 30*, 843–861.

Salthouse, T. (1994). How many causes are there of aging-related decrements in cognitive functioning, *Developmental Review*, *14*, 413–437.

Salthouse, T. (1999). Theories of cognition. In V. L. Bengtson & K. W. Schaie (Eds.), *Handbook of theories of aging* (pp. 196–208). New York: Springer Publishing Co.

Salthouse, T. A., Hancock, H. E., Meinz, E. J., & Hambrick, D. Z. (1996). Interrelations of age, visual acuity, and cognitive functioning. *Journal of Gerontology: Psychological Sciences, 51B*, P317–P330.

Schafer, J. L. (1997). *Analysis of incomplete multivariate data*. London, UK: Chapman & Hall.

Schaie, K. W. (1958). Rigidity-flexibility and intelligence: A cross-sectional study of the adult life span from 20 to 70 years. *Psychological Monographs, 72* (No. 462, Whole No. 9).

Schaie, K. W. (1962). A field-theory approach to age changes in cognitive behavior. *Vita Humana, 5*, 129–141.

Schaie, K. W. (1965). A general model for the study of developmental problems. *Psychological Bulletin, 64*, 92–107.

Schaie, K. W. (1977). Quasi-experimental designs in the psychology of aging. In J. E. Birren & K. W. Schaie (Eds.), *Handbook of the psychology of aging* (pp. 39–58). New York: Van Nostrand Reinhold.

Schaie, K. W. (1983). What can we learn from the longitudinal study of adult psychological development. In K. W. Schaie (Ed.), *Longitudinal studies of adult psychological development* (pp. 1–19). New York: Guilford Press.

Schaie, K. W. (1988). Internal validity threats in studies of adult cognitive development. In M. L. Howe & C. J. Brainard (Eds.), *Cognitive development in adulthood: Progress in cognitive development research* (pp. 241–272). New York: Springer-Verlag.

Schaie, K. W. (1996). *Intellectual development in adulthood: The Seattle Longitudinal Study*. New York: Cambridge University Press.

Schaie, K. W. (2000). The impact of longitudinal studies on understanding development from young adulthood to old age. *International Journal of Behavioral Development, 24*, 267–275.

Schaie, K. W., & Hertzog, C. (1985). Measurement in the psychology of adulthood and aging. In J. E. Birren & K. W. Schaie (Eds.), *Handbook of the psychology of aging*, (2nd ed., pp. 61–92). New York: Van Nostrand Reinhold.

Schaie, K. W., Maitland, S. B., Willis, S. L., & Intrieri, R. L. (1998). Longitudinal invariance of adult psychometric ability factor structures across seven years. *Psychology and Aging, 13*, 8–20.

Schaie, K. W., & Willis, S. L. (1986). Can decline in adult intellectual functioning be reversed? *Development Psychology, 22*, 223–232.

Schaie, K. W., Willis, S. L., Jay, G., & Chipuer, H. (1989). Structural invariance of cognitive abilities across the adult life span: A cross-sectional study. *Developmental Psychology, 25*, 652–662.

Schmitz-Scherzer, R., & Thomae, H. (1983). Constancy and change of behavior in old age: Findings from the Bonn Longitudinal Study. In K. W. Schaie (Ed.), *Longitudinal studies of adult psychological development* (pp. 191–221). New York: Guilford Press.

Simmons, S. F., Johansson, B., Zarit, S. H., Ljungquist, B., Plomin, R., & McClearn, G. E. (1997). Selection bias in samples of older twins? A comparison between octogenarian twins and singeltons in Sweden. *Journal of Aging and Health, 9*, 553–567.

Sliwinski, M., & Buschke, H. (1999). Cross-sectional and longitudinal relationships among age, memory and processing speed. *Psychology and Aging, 14*, 18–33.

Sliwinski, M., Lipton, R. B., Buschke, H., & Stewart, W. F. (1996). The effect of preclinical dementia on estimates of normal cognitive function in aging. *Journal of Gerontology: Psychological Sciences, 51B*, P217–P225.

Small, B. J., & Bäckman, L. (1998). Predictors of longitudinal changes in memory, visuospatial and verbal performance in very old demented adults. *Dementia, 9*, 258–266.

Small, B. J., Basun, H., & Bäckman, L. (1998). Three-year changes in cognitive performance as a function of apolipoprotein E genotype: Evidence from very old adults without dementia. *Psychology and Aging, 13*, 80–87.

Small, B. J., Dixon, R. A., Hultsch, D. F., & Hertzog, C. (1999). Longitudinal changes in quantitative and qualitative indicators of word and story recall in young-old and old-old adults. *Journal of Gerontology: Psychological Sciences, 54B*, P107–P115.

Smits, C. H. M., Deeg, D. J. H., Kriegsman, D. M. W., & Schmand, B. (1999). Cognitive functioning and health as determinants of mortality in an older population. *American Journal of Epidemiology, 150*, 978–986.

Snowdon, D. A., Greiner, L. H., Kemper, S. J., Nanayakkara, N., Mortimer, J. A. (1999). Linguistic ability in early life and longevity: Findings from the Nun Study In J. M. Robine, B. Forette, B, C. Franceschi, & M. Allard (Eds.). *The paradoxes of longevity*, (pp. 103–113) Berlin, Germany: Springer-Verlag.

Snowdon, D. A., Kemper, S., Mortimer, J. A., Greine, L. H., Wekstei, D. R., & Markesbery, W. R. (1996). Linguistic ability in early life and cognitive function and Alzheimer's disease in late life: Findings from the Nun Study. *Journal of the American Medical Association, 275*, 528–532.

Steen, G., Fromholt, P., Äystö, S., Berg, S. (1997). Cognitive functioning in 75-year-olds: A study in three Nordic localities. In E. Heikkinen, S. Berg, M. Schroll, B. Steen, & A. Viidik (Eds.), *Functional status, health and aging: The NORA Study* (pp. 66–77). Paris, France: Serdi Publishers.

Svensson, T., Dehlin, O., Hagberg, B., & Samuelsson, G. (1993). The Lund 80+ study: Some general findings. In J. J. F. Schroots (Ed.), *Aging, health and competence: The next generation of longitudinal research.* Amsterdam, The Netherlands: Elsevier.

Thomae, H. (1993). Die Bonner Gerontologische Längsschnittstudie (BOLSA) [The Bonn Longitudinal Study on Ageing]. *Zeitschrift für Gerontologie, 26*, 142–150.

Thurstone, L. L. (1947). *Multiple factor analysis.* Chicago: University of Chicago Press.

Werner, H. (1948). *Comparative psychology of mental development.* New York: International Universities Press.

Wohlwill, J. B. (1973). *The study of behavioral development.* New York: Academic Press.

Willett, J. B., & Sayer, A. G. (1994). Using covariance structure analysis to detect correlates and predictors of individual change over time. *Psychological Bulletin, 116*, 363–381.

Zelinski, E. M., & Burnright, K. P. (1997) Sixteen-year longitudinal and time-lag changes in memory and cognition in older adults. *Psychology and Aging, 12*, 503–523.

Zelinski, E. M., Gilewski, M. J., & Schaie, K. W. (1993). Individual differences in cross-sectional and three-year longitudinal memory performance across the adult lifespan. *Psychology and Aging, 8*, 176–186.

Zelinski, E. M., & Stewart, S. (1998). Individual differences in 16-year memory changes. *Psychology and Aging, 13*, 622–630.

Four

Methodological Issues in Behavioral Intervention Research with the Elderly

Sherry L. Willis

I. Introduction

There has been the assumption that the primary goal of behavioral intervention research should be to assess the efficacy of a given intervention—to examine whether there is positive gain in functioning as a result of training. In large-scale intervention research, such as clinical trials research, the primary focus is on the efficacy of an intervention to produce a specific outcome. There is relatively less concern with such issues as the role of individual differences or the specific processes and mechanisms underlying the desired outcome.

Although determining the efficacy of a given intervention is an important objective, programmatic intervention research should be aimed at the broader goal of answering a series of theoretically important empirical questions (Baltes & Willis, 1977; Hazlett-Stevens & Borkovec, 1999; Schulz & Martire, 1999). When couched within a particular theory or conceptual framework, programmatic intervention research seeks to address questions such as: What is the nature of the problem or deficit? What specific mechanisms, processes, or components of the inter-

vention are responsible for the desired change? What individual-difference variables are associated with responsivity to change? How can the change be maintained?

Kastenbaum (1968) has suggested that until the 1960s, gerontological researchers were largely satisfied with "counting and classifying the wrinkles of aged behavior" (p. 282). Since the 1960s there has been increasing focus on the "why" or explanations of aging. The step from explanation to experimentation and intervention was a relatively small and expected one (Baltes & Danish, 1979). In the 1970s a new movement of behavioral intervention research in aging began to appear. Cognitive training research was one manifestation of this trend. These intervention studies were typically small scale, conducted by a single investigator in a single laboratory (Camp, 1999; Kliegl, Smith, & Baltes, 1989; Neely & Backman, 1995; Willis, 1990; Yesavage et al., 1990). In the 1980s and particularly in the 1990s, there has been a shift toward larger scale intervention studies, involving multiple sites and investigators (Appel et al., 1995; Jobe et al., in press; LaRosa et al., 1994; Ory et al., 1993). These large-scale

Handbook of the Psychology of Aging

interventions were often an outgrowth of the findings of the earlier smaller scale intervention work. Although there have been recent reviews of substantive findings from these training studies (Schulz, Maddox, & Lawton, 1999), the evolution of intervention research with the elderly has also resulted in methodological issues specific to behavioral interventions, particularly when conducted from a psychosocial or life span developmental perspective (Baltes & Danish, 1979; Smyer & Gatz, 1986).

This chapter serves as a vehicle for a discussion of what we consider to be some of the most salient current methodological issues in behavioral intervention research with the elderly. Many of the methodological issues discussed are relevant to different types of behavioral interventions with the elderly, such as those involving exercise and nutrition. Given the author's research interests and experiences, however, many of the exemplars are drawn from cognitive training research. The chapter begins by considering several definitions of intervention and by enumerating characteristics that are common to most behavioral interventions. The second section consists of a review of the primary experimental designs employed in behavioral training studies, with discussion of the strengths and limitations of each design. In the third section of the chapter, there is a discussion of the mechanisms or processes that are assumed to underlie the intervention and how these mechanisms mediate intervention outcomes. A final section focuses on several factors related to treatment outcomes. Levels of treatment outcomes are considered, and the critical but difficult phenomenon of training transfer is discussed.

There are numerous other important methodological issues that are not considered in this chapter, such as sampling, attrition, training of the interventionist, quality control, follow-up assessment, and measurement characteristics of the outcome measures (see Schulz et al., 1999). The topics focused on in this chapter, such as mechanisms accounting for treatment outcomes and transfer effects, reflect methodological issues that have recently been identified in the literature as relatively understudied but of particular salience (Salomon & Perkins, 1989; Schulz & Martire, 1999).

II. Defining Behavioral Intervention Research

The concept of behavioral intervention does not have a singular meaning. Schulz and Martire (1999) state that "an intervention study involves actions that alter, or are intended to alter, relationships between observable phenomena" (p. 2). The goal of intervention is that some agent under human control can be manipulated to bring about desired change; thus, the design of choice in most cases is a randomized trial. The action of interest typically has a definable onset and in many cases a clear termination. In a chapter on interventions in life span development and aging, Baltes and Danish (1979) consider a gerontological intervention as programmatic attempts aimed at modification of the course of psychological aging. In a prior edition of the *Handbook of the Psychology of Aging*, a psychological intervention was defined as planned processes of behavioral change that employ a deliberate application of psychological principles and theory (Smyer, Zarit, & Qualls, 1990).

In this chapter, behavioral interventions will be considered to have in general the following characteristics. The intervention is a planned effort with the goal of manipulating or altering behavior. The key independent variable is behavioral in nature. In many instances, the dependent variable(s) are also behaviors (outcomes). The target of the intervention is an individual, typically an older adult. Given that it is a planned effort, the intervention typically has a defined onset and often a defined duration and termination. The design should involve a comparison group, and individuals are randomly assigned to groups. Ideally, the intervention is grounded in one or more theoretical or conceptual framework(s) and is based on prior descriptive research. The hypothesized causal links between the intervention and the outcome should be stated, and the mechanisms or processes that mediate the intervention should be explicated. Many of the above characteristics are representative of the broader domain of experimental research of which behavioral intervention research is a class. In contrast to many experiments, intervention studies are often of a longer duration involving multiple training sessions, and the temporal durability of outcome(s) is expected to be longer. Moreover, intervention studies often involve multiple levels of outcomes and a broader assessment battery.

III. Design Issues in Behavioral Interventions

The particular experimental design chosen for an intervention study serves to address some of the above issues. That is, the specific control or comparison groups chosen in between-group experimental designs contribute knowledge regarding the nature of the problem or deficit and the processes or mechanisms hypothesized to be responsible for the change. In this section of the chapter, some of the more common between-group designs used in behavioral intervention research are reviewed (Borkovec, 1994; Campbell & Stanley, 1963; Kazdin, 1992). Exemplar cognitive training studies representing a particular design are cited.

A. No-Treatment Control Group

The most common comparison employed in intervention research is the no-treatment group. In clinical research, this group is often referred to as "treatment as usual." This design examines the magnitude of change associated with the intervention compared with the amount of change that would have occurred without the intervention. The no-treatment group receives the same pre- and postintervention assessment battery but otherwise no intervention or contact. The no-treatment control permits assessment of the amount of change that could have occurred simply due to the passage of time, including the pre–post assessment. Change in the no-treatment control group may occur due to factors such as maturation, sociocultural and history-related events, spontaneous remission, effects of repeated testing, changes in measurement procedures, statistical regression, attrition, or the interaction of these factors with each other or participant variables (Campbell & Stanley, 1963). The effect of maturation has traditionally been cited as of particular concern with younger age groups in which ongoing developmental process may result in acquisition of the target cognitive skill, without any specific intervention. In older groups, maturation may represent the normative age-related decline in cognitive functioning that occurs with no intervention; or in pathological conditions, the normative progression of the disease, such as Alzheimer's disease without a treatment.

A no-treatment control group is considered to be essential in early phases of studying a new intervention procedure to provide initial evidence of treatment efficacy. It is also less expensive than other comparison groups, because it involves no time or expenditures for alternative interventions or contact hours. In addition, the largest effect is often obtained in comparisons of the intervention with the no-treatment group, hence allowing a reduction in the number of subjects needed for adequate statistical power.

There are some particular limitations of a no-treatment control that are related to the recruitment and maintenance of a sample, ethical considerations, and the information gained from the comparison (Hazlett-Stevens & Borkovec, 1999). First, if the problem being addressed is of particular concern to a certain segment of participants or the intervention is believed to be of considerable merit, then participants with these concerns may be reluctant to enroll in the trial, given the possibility of being randomized to the no-treatment group. Hence, the parent population from which the sample is recruited may be biased. For example, persons who believe themselves to have memory problems or who have recently been diagnosed with Alzheimer's disease may be less willing to risk being assigned to a no-treatment group and to make the commitment not to seek other treatment during the intervention trial. Assessment of the long-term maintenance of the intervention, furthermore, may be compromised due to no-treatment controls dropping out of the study as newer, promising treatments become available. Moreover, there is the ethical issue of not providing any treatment to participants with a known problem or deficit.

It is often stated that the no-treatment control group provides the least information regarding the processes or mechanisms associated with the intervention in relation to any other comparison group. There is, however, particularly in cognitive training research, a critical type of information that is best provided by a no-treatment control group. Specifically, the pre–post change in performance of the no-treatment control on cognitive outcome measures provides the best estimate of the magnitude of change that can

accrue from repeated testing or being exposed to the assessment battery (see also Schaie, 1988, 1996, for discussion of practice effects in repeated testing in a longitudinal design). The magnitude of pre–post change shown by any comparison group other than the no-treatment control represents a confound of practice effects and the possible enhancement associated with the activity in which the comparison group was involved.

The magnitude of pre–post practice effects is not inconsequential when participants are low-educated elderly and have had little experience with the types of tests or assessment involved in psychological research. Simply becoming familiar with the assessment routine and practicing the tests can lead to significant improvement. In some of our studies of training on fluid abilities, the magnitude of retest effects has approached one-quarter of a standard deviation (Willis, Blieszner, & Baltes, 1981). The magnitude of practice effects or reactivity may vary for different mental abilities or assessment procedures. The largest practice effects are often shown for measures of abstract reasoning or speeded performance representing the fluid abilities that decline earlier and thus have been the target of many cognitive training studies. For example, verbal memory tests or inductive reasoning measures may exhibit larger retest effects than a vocabulary test, representing crystallized intelligence. Differences in reactivity among measures have also been reported in other behavioral interventions (Hazlett-Stevens & Borkovec, 1999).

Given the relative brevity of many cognitive training interventions, the time involved in the pre–post assessment battery may equal or exceed the time spent in the intervention itself. The likelihood of this occurring increases if multiple measures of an outcome are included in order to assess the target outcome at the construct level, as is currently supported from a methodological perspective (Bentler, 1980; Schaie, 1996). Hence, participating in the pre–post battery becomes an intervention in itself! The challenge for the target training program, then, is to produce an effect that exceeds the performance improvement associated with practice and with increasing familiarity with the assessment routine. The impact of practice effects becomes of further concern with follow-up assessments conducted in order to examine the maintenance of the intervention. The follow-up assessment may serve as a mini-booster intervention, making it difficult to distinguish retest effects versus maintenance effects ascribed solely to the intervention. Additional control groups varying in number of assessment occasions would need to be added at each follow-up occasion to disentangle completely the retest effects versus maintenance.

Although practice effects are more obvious and can be directly measured for objective cognitive ability measures, reactivity effects also occur for other forms of assessment included in pre–post batteries (Hazlett-Stevens & Borkovec, 1999). For example, responding to questionnaires or interviews regarding their self-efficacy beliefs or metacognitive knowledge may increase older adults' awareness of such issues and lead to their further consideration or monitoring of these factors. Many researchers have had the experience, for example, of having an older participant return to a follow-up session and make statements, such as "I've been thinking about those questions you asked me regarding how often I cannot remember someone's name..."

B. Nonspecific Comparison Group

Since at least the 1950s (Rosenthal & Frank, 1956), placebo or nonspecific comparison groups have been given special attention in psychopharmacological and clinical trial interventions. Some have argued that placebo groups provide the only adequate control group and are the sine qua non of adequate experimental design (Klein, 1996; Rosenthal & Frank, 1956). Recently, there has been considerable discussion of the limitations of the traditional placebo control in psychologically oriented interventions (Brown, 1994; Kazdin, 1992; O'Leary & Borkovec, 1978; Strayhorn, 1987)

A brief discussion of the evolution of a placebo control is useful to understand the current debate (O'Leary & Borkovec, 1978; Rosenthal & Frank, 1956). From a historical perspective, there is evidence that many traditional medicines and cures were inert and probably were effective due to psychological placebo-type effects (Shapiro, 1971). Hence the necessity of a placebo control—known as the "sugar pill"—became an important design feature in current pharmacological research. The classical criteria for a placebo condition was that it involved a theoretically *inert* procedure that did not include factors considered critical to the intervention (O'Leary & Borkovec, 1978). A critical aspect of the criteria is that the placebo procedure is assumed to be *inert*. There was no theoretical rationale for why the placebo should result in the hypothesized positive outcome predicted for the treatment condition. A second critical aspect of the placebo effect was the assumption that the same type and level of *expectancies* regarding outcomes would be generated by participants in the treatment and in the placebo groups. The placebo and treatment conditions were presented to participants in such a manner that both groups should form the same expectancies regarding outcomes.

With the increase in psychological-based interventions and in interventions with both pharmaceutical and behavioral intervention arms, a placebo-type control was argued to be critical to the design of these types of interventions also (Parloff,

1986). The placebo-type control is sometimes known as the *nonspecific control* condition. The assumption was that a placebo-type control would account or control for nonspecific factors that were not considered critical to the treatment in behavioral or psychological interventions. The nonspecific-type factors assumed to be represented in a placebo-type control has grown to include variables such as social contact, personal contact with the trainer, expectancy effects, and opportunities for the participant to verbalize their concerns and to receive attention (Brown, 1994; Hazlett-Stevens & Borkovec, 1999; O'Leary & Borkovec, 1978).

There is a growing debate regarding the appropriateness of nonspecific, placebo-type controls for psychological and behavioral interventions (Hazlett-Stevens & Borkovec, 1999; Strayhorn, 1987; Wilkins, 1983). Conceptual, methodological, and ethical questions have been raised. First, it has been questioned whether a truly theoretically *inert* placebo procedure can be developed in psychologically oriented interventions. Nonspecific elements such as social contact, personal contact with the interventionist, and participation in multiple sessions are not psychologically inert. These nonspecific elements can have psychological effects that are not directly analogous to a pharmaceutical inert placebo, which can be assumed to have no beneficial physiological effect.

These nonspecific factors, moreover, are often considered to be necessary for the delivery of the critical theory-specific elements of the intervention (Parloff, 1986). For example, both in cognitive training and in therapeutic interventions, formation of some form of therapeutic alliance between interventionist and participant may enhance or be necessary in the delivery of the critical elements of the intervention (Hazlett-Stevens & Borkovec, 1999). Nonspecific factors such as personal contact with the trainer, positive feedback and support, development of trust and respect are often seen as salient aspects in the development of the therapeutic alliance. It might be argued that although factors such as a therapeutic alliance are considered salient in the traditional manner of treatment delivery, successful interventions have been administered via computers or the internet with less emphasis on a therapeutic alliance (Ball & Owsley, 2000; Finkel & Yesavage, 1989). However, research has also shown that treatment is often more effective when administered by an in-person trainer when recipients are cognitively low functioning individuals or have more severe pathologies (Rebok, Rasmusson, & Brandt, 1997).

A second concern regarding placebo-type controls in behavioral interventions is whether participants can be truly blinded to the assigned conditions and whether equivalent levels of expectancies can be created and maintained across conditions (Kazdin, 1992; Morin, Colecchi, Brink, & Astruc, 1995). The "sugar pill" in pharmaceutical interventions had much more face validity than can be created in many psychological interventions; moreover, recent advances in pharmaceuticals have resulted in reduced side effects such that the patient is even less able to judge the condition to which he or she was assigned (Brown, 1994). In contrast, in psychological interventions it is much more difficult to create a placebo condition that is equally credible compared to the treatment condition. Such credibility is based not only on the type of activities involved in the placebo condition, but also the ability of the intervener to generate and manifest enthusiasm and expectations that are equivalent in treatment and placebo. Many recent studies have involved placebo conditions that bore little similarity to the treatment of interest and thus further limited the likelihood of equivalent expectancies across groups (Clark et al., 1997; Tinetti et al., 1993).

Given these difficulties in developing comparable treatment and placebo–control conditions, some studies have reported a higher drop-out rate for participants assigned to placebo–control versus treatment (Nicholas, Wilson, & Goyen, 1991).

Maintaining the credibility of a placebo condition and of equivalent expectancies across groups becomes more difficult when the treatment is lengthy, which is more common when the intervention is dealing with serious, real-life problems. Expectancies are likely to dissipate across time in the placebo group if there are no effects or there are less effects over time (Brown, 1994). Likewise, maintaining equivalent motivation and enthusiasm in the intervener across groups becomes more challenging with lengthy interventions.

Relatively few cognitive training studies have included a social contact or placebo-type control; studies have more typically included a no-treatment or an alternative treatment condition. The few studies including such a control have generally found the mean performance of the treatment group to exceed that of the social contact control group (Clark et al., 1997). In our lab we compared cognitive training on attention and flexibility to a social contact group that met for an equivalent number of hours focusing on social support and friendship (Willis, Cornelius, Blow, & Baltes, 1983). The social contact group's performance on the target ability measures was significantly below the treatment group and did not differ from the no-treatment control.

The impact of placebo conditions has been more thoroughly examined in behavioral interventions focusing on psychological conditions such as depression, anxiety, and phobias. In these studies, placebo controls have shown greater effects when the intervention involved fewer sessions, when the participant was suffering from a less severe level of the condition, such as depression, and the episode of the condition was brief (Brown, 1994). Findings appear to be mixed from the few studies comparing the long-term maintenance of placebo effects versus treatment effects (Jacobson & Hollon, 1996; Rush, 1994).

C. Component Control Condition

A control condition that is considered by some researchers to avoid not only many of the limitations of the placebo control but also to provide additional valuable theoretical information regarding the nature of the treatment effect has been referred to as a *component comparison* approach (Hazlett-Stevens & Borkovec, 1999). An essential aspect of this approach is the ability to identify and to implement independently the various components of the total intervention package. The component approach is a between-group design in which various components of the intervention are implemented separately and in combination. This approach examines which specific elements of the intervention are responsible for particular observed changes by providing some participants with the entire intervention and some with only selected components.

This approach offers considerable flexibility to examine the optimal packaging of the treatment. Components can be combined in different sequences to examine whether ordering of components enhances magnitude of outcome effects. Moreover, the component control design can be achieved in two different ways. The researcher can approach the issue by systematically adding components until the whole intervention package is examined. Alternatively, the researcher can begin by first examining the entire intervention package and then selectively dismantling or deleting components. Again, this approach is only possible if the components of the intervention package are well specified and can be easily componentialized (Basham, 1986).

The component approach avoids some of the limitations of the placebo or nonspecific control condition. Each treatment group includes one or more components that is considered to be efficacious and thus should lead to more equivalent expectancies across groups and enhance the credibility of each treatment group. Nonspecific factors are represented in all treatment components. This approach allows for increased specificity in studying cause and effect relationships, addressing specifically what aspects of the intervention are causing a certain outcome (Neely & Bäckman, 1995). In addition, there are less ethical concerns because all components are potentially efficacious.

This approach is represented in cognitive training studies in which imagery instruction and/or training in relaxation techniques were administered in combination with memory training on the method of loci (Gratzinger, Sheikh, Friedman, & Yesavage, 1990; Hill, Sheikh, & Yesavage, 1989; Kotler-Cope & Camp, 1990; Yesavage, 1990; Yesavage, Rose, & Bower, 1983; Zarit, Cole & Guider, 1981). In successive studies, imagery instruction, relaxation techniques, and both were paired with traditional method-of-loci training. Another componential approach has compared memory efficacy training alone or in combination with training on self-generated memory strategies (Lachman, Weaver, Bandura, Elliot, & Lewkowicz, 1992).

D. Parametric Design

This approach addresses the question of whether quantitative changes in one specific aspect of the intervention can increase the effectiveness of the intervention (Kazdin, 1992). An example of the parametric approach is systematically varying the dosage or number of training sessions to examine changes in the magnitude of training effects. The investigator can hold all experimental factors constant except for the one that is being manipulated (e.g., dosage, number of sessions). A unique strength of the parametric approach is that multiple levels of the variable can be examined. Quantitative increments in one specific aspect of the intervention may not be associated with linear changes or increases in the magnitude of treatment effects. For example, as the number of training sessions increases, there may be a diminishing return in terms of increases in treatment outcome.

There have been relatively few studies involving a parametric design approach in cognitive training research, and further utilization of this approach is needed. On the negative side, execution of this design is expensive in terms of factors such as the number of subjects needed and the number of treatment groups required to thoroughly examine incremental approaches in a treatment variable, such as number of training sessions. Hence, the cost and labor of conducting research using this design can be high. On the other hand, such a design has the potential to address some of the most salient cost–benefit and pragmatic issues in intervention research. This approach can address practical questions such as, What is the minimal number of training sessions required to produce an effect of a given magnitude? Can the treatment be administered as effectively in varying sized groups versus one-on-one? Over how long an interval is there maintenance of the outcomes? In the long term, such a systematic, incremental approach can provide important information on the relative cost and labor involved in an intervention when issues related to dissemination or generalization of the intervention arise.

Prior training studies have taken an incremental or parametric approach primarily to various issues dealing with time and with size. A parametric approach has been used to address factors, such as number of training or practice sessions (Hofland, Willis, & Baltes, 1981); increased efficacy from delayed booster sessions (McDougall, 1999; Willis & Nesselroade, 1990; Willis & Schaie, 1994); varying the number of participants in training sessions, small group versus one-on-one (Rebok et al., 1997); variations in latency or response time (Baltes & Kliegl, 1992; Kliegl, Smith, & Baltes, 1989, 1990); long-term durability of treatment effects (Neely Bäckman, 1993; Scogin & Bienias, 1988; Willis & Nesselroade, 1990; Willis & Schaie, 1994); breadth of training transfer and number of measures used to assess effects (Willis & Schaie, 1986); and variations in level of competence and training of the intervener (Quayhagen & Quayhagen, 1989).

E. Comparative Design

A final type of design for intervention research involves contrasting two or more distinctly different intervention approaches to the same problem (Borkovec & Castonguay, 1998; Kazdin, 1986). The two or more interventions are assumed to represent different conceptual or theoretical views of the nature of the problem and of the optimal mechanisms for intervention. The key question is which of the existing approaches is more effective?

This approach is based on the implicit assumptions that there are two or more intervention approaches to the same problem and that initial research has shown both interventions to have some promise of efficacy. In clinical trial research on psychological disorders, the comparative design has been used to compare the efficacy of pharmacological versus behavioral interventions. This is sometimes described as an intervention with two arms—pharmacological and behavioral. Examples of this approach include clin-ical trials involving comparisons of the efficacy of pharmacological versus behavioral interventions for conditions such as depression (Jacobson & Hollon, 1996; Klein, 1996), panic disorder (National Institutes of Health, 1991), and insomnia (Morin, Culbert, & Schwartz, 1994).

At first glance, this might be thought to be one of the most common and useful types of intervention designs, but a number of problems and limitations in utilizing this design have been noted (Borkovec & Castonguay, 1998; Hazlett-Stevens & Borkovec, 1999; O'Leary & Borkovec, 1978). First, when comparing two established intervention programs, they often vary in so many ways that there are few variables that can be held constant across interventions. The interventions may vary in factors such as dosing (number of sessions), method of delivery of the program (e.g., delivered by person, computer, pill), and degree of social contact and/or therapeutic alliance. Although the two intervention programs may be modified to equate factors such as number of sessions, the question then arises of whether the modified program is truly comparable to the original version of the intervention that was shown to be effective. Eysenck (1994) has argued that the differences among intervention approaches in terms of treatment parameters and dependent measures stem from very important and often irreconcilable differences in scientific paradigms and methods of acquiring and interpreting knowledge. Such differences are reflected in important qualitative differences in treatment delivery and in the particular outcome measures considered to be most salient.

A second challenge to the comparative design focuses on internal validity issues arising from the need for comparable expertise and therapeutic allegiance of the trainers for each intervention approach (Borkovec, 1994; Jacobson & Hollon, 1996). Are the individuals who administer the interventions comparable in their understanding and expertise across all interventions and does their allegiance vary across interventions? Administering each intervention at only one site may limit interpretation of results due to staff or sampling differences or problems. If each intervention is only administered at one site by the originators or adherents of the intervention, differences between interventions may be due to factors other than the efficacy of the intervention. Likewise, if each intervention is administered at only one site, sampling variations in the study population may make interpretation of results difficult. Ideally, each of the interventions to be compared should be administered at multiple sites by staff equated in level of expertise or allegiance across intervention approaches. Quality checks need to be made for variations in program implementation across the intervention trial (Hazlett-Stevens. & Borkovec, 1999).

A third challenge to the comparative approach is the development of a common assessment battery across interventions. Different approaches to the same problem often vary in the specific outcome measures deemed to be of particular salience. One approach may be more concerned with affective or self-report measures of the phenomenon, whereas another approach may focus on behavioral outcomes. *Reach* is a clinical trial currently in progress that involves the same core assessment battery (as well as site-specific measures) to compare different intervention approaches for caregivers of demented patients (Coon et al., 1999)

The comparative design approach has been less common in cognitive aging intervention research, particularly, with nondemented elderly, than might be expected. This may be due, in part, to the strong focus on strategies as the primary mechanism studied in cognitive intervention research. Because strategies are considered quite specific to a given cognitive ability or skill (Salthouse, 1991), compari-

son of distinctly different cognitive strategies for the same cognitive ability or process is less likely. It might be suggested that alternative interventions could be developed focusing on different mechanisms for cognitive deficits, such as limitations in perceived self-efficacy versus strategy use. However, these different approaches have more typically been viewed as separate components in a total intervention package (Lachman et al., 1992) and thus examined within a componential rather than comparative design approach.

As the range of pharmaceutical options for cognitive deficits increases, there may be an increase in outcome or evidence-based trials, with cognitive factors as outcomes that involve pharmaceutical and behavioral intervention arms. However, again, it can be argued that a componential approach involving a combination of pharmaceutical and behavioral interventions may be more efficacious rather than a comparative either–or approach. That is, it might be hypothesized that the optimal approach is to examine the efficacy of a pharmaceutical agent to stabilize cognitive functioning or to retard decline followed by a behavioral intervention to maximize the patient's potential to utilize the existing cognitive resources.

IV. Understanding the Mechanisms for Intervention Effectiveness

A primary goal of intervention studies is to produce a desired outcome—a change in behavior. An equally important objective, but one that is often not addressed adequately, is understanding how and *why* a certain outcome is achieved. A strong theoretical or conceptual framework for the intervention is critical in examining the processes or mechanisms underlying a change in behavior. The conceptual framework specifies in detail the processes or mechanisms through which a given outcome is to occur. In a recent chapter on intervention research with the elderly, Schulz and Martire (1999) identified one of the most common shortcomings of existing intervention studies to be the failure to articulate a theoretical model that specified the mechanisms for achieving intervention outcomes. An associated deficit in intervention studies has been the lack of appropriate measurement of hypothesized mechanisms.

A. Cognitive Strategies

In cognitive training research, instruction on some form of cognitive strategy is hypothesized to be one of the primary mechanisms or processes by which change in cognitive behavior occurs (Charness, 1985; Kliegl, Smith & Baltes, 1989; Salthouse, 1991). A strategy can be defined as one of several alternative methods for performing a particular cognitive task (Salthouse, 1991). Verbal memory training studies have focused on strategies including the method of loci (Kliegl et al., 1989, 1990; Rebok & Balcerak, 1989; Yesavage, 1990), organization, visualization or imagery (Hill, Sheikh, & Yesavage, 1989; Yesavage, 1990; Zarit, Cole, & Guider, 1981), and formation of associations (Dunlosky & Hertzog, 1998a, in press). Camp's intervention work with demented elderly has utilized a technique or strategy known as spaced retrieval (Camp, 1999). Charness and colleagues have taught adults strategies for squaring two-digit numbers mentally (Charness & Campbell, 1988). Training on spatial orientation ability has focused on strategies facilitating mental rotation of objects, including identifying two salient features of the object and naming of abstract objects (Schaie & Willis, 1986). Our training research on inductive reasoning has involved strategies for identifying a serial pattern, including saying the pattern aloud, underlining repetitions in the pattern, and marking skips in a pattern (Willis & Schaie, 1986).

Study of the mechanisms underlying an outcome involves not only a conceptual framework that specifies the particular processes or mechanisms of interest but also developing procedures for independent assessment of the mechanisms (e.g., strategies; Dunlosky & Hertzog, in press; Saczynski, Willis, & Schaie, in press). Theory-guided intervention research requires assessing both whether use of the processes or strategies becomes more proficient or frequent as the intervention progresses, and whether increased usage of the strategies is associated with enhanced performance on training outcome (Saczynski et al., in press). For example, if utilization of the method of loci is the strategy hypothesized to enhance list learning, then (a) increased usage and/or improvement in the ease with which the loci strategy is implemented must be demonstrated, and (b) increased frequency or improvement in strategy use should be shown to be associated with recall of a greater number of words on the list.

A number of different questions regarding strategy usage may be important to address, depending on the nature of the strategy and outcome variables. Probably the most common strategy variable is frequency of usage of the strategy. Other aspects of strategy usage include the proficiency or speed with which the strategy is employed. Speed or proficiency of usage is important if the task is timed or speeded or if processing of significant information is involved.

B. Criteria for the Study of Strategies

Salthouse (1991) has specified a number of criteria for the study of strategies in cognitive aging. These criteria may be stated in the following manner when applied to intervention research. First, strategies are assumed to be specific to the outcome that is the target of training. Second, all participants involved in the intervention are assumed to be capable of learning and executing the strategy. Third, the evidence provided to demonstrate use of strategies must be distinct from the measure of the outcome variable. Fourth, it is assumed that differences in performance on the outcome will be associated with strategy use. In training research, it is important first to show an increase in appropriate strategy usage from baseline to posttraining for the treatment group when compared with control groups. In addition, the increased strategy usage must be shown to account for significant variance in enhanced performance on the related outcome measure.

These assumptions regarding the strategies or mechanisms underlying the effectiveness of the intervention have important implications for intervention study design and methodology. The assumption that a strategy or mechanism is specific to a particular cognitive outcome has implications for specification of the hypothesized pattern of training transfer and for the measures selected to assess training outcomes. The issue of training transfer will be discussed in a later section of this chapter. It is important to note here, however, that the assumption that a particular strategy is specific to a given task implies an ability-specific model of training transfer. Training a particular strategy should result in improvement only on the cognitive ability or process with which the strategy is assumed to be associated.

There is increasing pressure to include outcome measures in cognitive training research that involve "real-world" problems that are often cognitively complex or that involve physical as well as cognitive processes. For example, medication compliance may be proposed as an outcome for a memory training program focusing on cognitive strategies and mnemonics. Park and colleagues (Park &

Jones, 1997), however, have shown that medication compliance is a cognitively complex task that involves a variety of distinct memory processes, including working memory, verbal memory, and prospective memory. Moreover, for some individuals, medication compliance involves sensory and manual processes required to read the label or open the medicine bottle.

The research literature indicates that distinct memory strategies are associated with each type of memory process. The memory training program may be effective only for those aspects of medication compliance that involve the memory processes associated with the strategies trained. Thus, when specific strategies or mechanisms are the focus of training and hypothesized to account for intervention outcomes, it is critical that the outcome measures map carefully on the strategies and cognitive processes trained. Weaker training effects are to be expected for complex outcome measures involving cognitive processes that are not directly trained in the intervention.

The second and third criteria that all participants being compared are capable of learning and using the strategy and that level of performance on the outcome is associated with strategies also have implications for training programs. A strong interpretation of the second and third assumptions is the "strategy-as-cause" position, assuming that all participants are capable of learning and using the strategy regardless of their ability level (Salthouse, 1991). Performance on the outcome variable is moderated by strategy usage. Some researchers, however, have suggested that certain strategies place heavy demands on memory or other cognitive resources and hence may be beyond the capabilities of some participants (Charness, 1981, 1985; Finkel & Yesavage, 1989). In a related vein, investigators have suggested that strategy utilization may be associated with factors such as motivation, efficacy beliefs, and social constraints (Cavanaugh, Krammer, Sinnott, Camp & Markley, 1985; Dunlosky & Hertzog, 1998a, in press). Yesavage and colleagues have found personality characteristics such as openness to experience related to learning of strategies associated with face–name recall (Gratzinger et al., 1990). An individual-differences approach to training would in this case be called for, with screening of participants for the required level of ability or other person characteristics deemed necessary to learn and use the strategy.

C. Factors Facilitating Learning of a Strategy and Strategy Usage

Cognitive aging research has found that many older adults do not spontaneously use appropriate strategies (Kausler, 1994). This finding may suggest that older adults find certain strategies difficult to learn and to use and thus need additional assistance in mastering a particular strategy. Alternatively, older adults may question the utility of the strategy or doubt their ability (i.e., efficacy) to use the strategy successfully. Finally, older adults may have difficulty determining the problems or contexts in which a particular strategy would be useful.

Some training studies have employed pretraining components to facilitate learning of strategies shown to be particularly difficult for older adults. The method of loci and forming associations through imagery are two strategies that have been shown to be highly effective in learning unrelated words, yet are difficult for older adults to master (Gratzinger et al., 1990; Hill et al., 1989). Two forms of pretraining have been used to facilitate the learning of these strategies; each form of pretraining focuses on a different hypothesis regarding the difficulty in learning the strategy. The first form of pretraining focuses on enhancing imagery skills. There is some support for a decline

in imagery processes with age; moreover, some older adults question the utility of forming images, particularly fanciful images, or find it stressful (Verhaegen & Marcoen, 1994, 1996). Practice in imagery has been administered prior to memory training in work by Yesavage and colleagues (Hill et al., 1989; Yesavage, 1990). Similarly, pretraining in relaxation techniques has been employed prior to training (Hayslip, 1989; Yesavage, 1990). Relaxation techniques are employed to reduce the stress of using the imagery procedure or of learning a difficult strategy, such as method of loci. In a related vein, Bandura (1989) has suggested that affect is important in developing and maintaining self-efficacy. Induced positive mood has been shown to enhance perceived self-efficacy, whereas despondent mood diminishes perceived self-efficacy (Hertzog, McGuire & Lineweaver, 1998; Kavanagh & Bower, 1985; Berry, West, & Dennehey, 1989).

If the treatment outcome variable is cognitively complex or involves multiple components, the participant may be required to determine for which outcome measures the strategy trained is appropriate and useful (Dunlosky & Hertzog, 1998b). For example, if the list of words is unrelated, then the method of loci may be a more productive strategy. In contrast, with a list of related words, formation of meaningful categories may be more effective. The intervention procedure in this case may need to train not only on the specific strategies but also give guidance in determining in what instances a given strategy is likely to be most useful. The intervention would then involve not only training on a specific strategy but enhancing executive or metacognitive processes (see also Salomon & Perkins, 1989), which are hypothesized to affect the selection and monitoring of strategies over a wider range of cognitive tasks. The intervention would require training of metacognitive strategies or skills, on which there is much less empirical research, and also provide practice not only on problems for which the strategy is relevant but also problems for which the strategy is not relevant (McKeough, Lupart, & Marini, 1995).

These higher order skills and metacognition have been discussed as a part of self-regulated learning and memory monitoring (Dunlosky & Hertzog, 1998a). Bandura (1989) has suggested that development of self-regulatory capabilities requires instilling a resilient sense of efficacy as well as imparting skill in using a given strategy. If the elderly are not fully convinced of their personal efficacy, they rapidly abandon the strategy they have been taught when they fail to get quick results or it requires bothersome effort.

The mnemonic training research of Rebok and Balcerak (1989) on the method of loci found use of the strategy improved the memory performance of older adults but did not raise their beliefs in their memory efficacy. The lack of an association between the strategy and self-efficacy may explain why only 39% of participants used method of loci during generalization tests of memory for digits. In contrast, younger adults whose self-efficacy increased as a result of mnemonic training spontaneously used the loci aid in generalization memory tasks.

Bandura argues that training in cognitive strategies can produce more generalized and lasting effects if self-efficacy beliefs are increased and participants see an association between strategy use and increased control of their memory. Bandura (1989) sees direct mastery experiences as a particularly effective way of building efficacy beliefs. Participants perform memory tasks with and without mnemonic aids and compare the results. Evidence of better memory performance with mnemonic aids provides participants with persuasive demonstrations that they can exercise some control over their memory by enlisting cognitive strategies. Such efficacy-validating trials not only serve as efficacy builders, but also put on trial the value of the techniques being taught.

D. Measurement of Strategy Usage

As noted by Schulz (Schulz & Martire, 1999), prior behavior intervention research has often lacked not only specification of the process or mechanisms underlying the intervention, but also distinct measurement of the targeted strategies. There have been several common procedures for determining strategy usage, each having limitations (Dunlosky & Hertzog, 1998a). The most common and simplest procedure for determining strategy usage has been to ask participants to report on the strategy used after they have completed the task (Cohen & Faulkner, 1986; Rice & Meyer, 1986). The validity of these reports is unknown, as there is often no means of verifying the accuracy of the self-reports. In a recent study, Dunlosky and Hertzog (in press) found that retrospective reports were not completely consistent with concurrent reports, suggesting that the validity of retrospective reports is somewhat diminished by forgetting, particularly in older adults. Other procedures for assessing strategy usage include thinking aloud and then analyzing recordings for indications of strategy use. Analyzing time allocated to each portion of a sequential task (Salthouse & Prill, 1987) can also provide evidence of strategy use. The distribution of these times forms a profile of processing durations, which can be considered a reflection of the strategy used.

In our training research on inductive reasoning ability, the strategies trained provide an objective record of strategy use. Participants are taught to mark the patterns in reasoning problems with specific types of markings to indicate pattern repetitions, pattern skips, and pattern replications (Willis & Schaie, 1986).

Reliable instances of pattern usage at pre- and posttest were coded. Significant pre–posttest increases in pattern usage were shown for the reasoning training group compared to participants trained on spatial orientation. Moreover, increases in strategy usage accounted for significant variance in factor scores of reasoning ability performance (Saczynski, et al. in press).

V. Levels of Outcome and Mediators

As stated at the beginning of this chapter, a primary goal of evidence-based interventions or of clinical trials in the behavioral sciences is to examine whether treatment results in a greater improvement for the intervention group on the outcome measures than for the comparison groups. Although treatment effects are often stated in terms of improvement, the goal of treatment may alternatively involve a reduction in negative outcomes (e.g., memory complaints, incidents of forgetting) or even an outcome of stability, maintenance, or consistency (e.g., maintaining a certain level of accuracy and speed in a driving task; no increase in visits to emergency rooms or need for home health services).

Most behavioral interventions, particularly those with some commitment to real-world problems, will consider multiple domains of participants' functioning in assessing outcomes. First, real-world problems rarely involve only a single domain of an individual's functioning. Second, psychosocial phenomena (e.g., cognition, personality, efficacy, affect) that are of interest to social scientists and that are likely to be the target of psychological behavioral interventions are most adequately assessed in multiple domains (at the neural or physiological level, through behavior, and through per-

ceptions). Third, an intervention may affect not only the cognitive ability or skill that is the target of the intervention but may result in transfer to other domains of the individual's life or other aspects of behavior and perception. Thus, measurement of intervention outcomes often involves multiple levels of outcome and involves outcomes that vary in how close they map on the process, skill, or ability that was the specific target of the intervention.

The importance of a strong theoretical or conceptual framework to guide all major aspects of a behavioral intervention program is a crucial principle stressed throughout this chapter and in the work and writings of other researchers in the field (Baltes, 1987; Borkovec, 1994; Camp, 1999; Lerner, 1986; Schulz & Martare, 1999). An adequate conceptual framework often begins with a basic theory of some aspect of life span development and then is extended and enriched by decades of descriptive and intervention research. The conceptual framework needs to be viewed as dynamic, a work in progress, rather than a theory established by a former giant in the field (or at an earlier stage in the researcher's own professional career) and set in stone. Ideally, a developmental theory or framework *describes* the life span developmental trajectory of a phenomenon, articulates possible *explanatory mechanisms* for development and change in the phenomenon, and based on these components of description and explanation, offers insight regarding the plasticity or *modifiability* of the phenomenon, either across the life span or at specific developmental periods (Baltes & Willis, 1977; Bandura, 1989; Lerner, 1986; Schaie, 2000).

At least three major levels of outcomes are generally recognized in behavioral intervention research: proximal, primary, and distal outcomes. The remaining part of this section will deal with a discussion of these three levels of outcomes.

A. Proximal Intervention Outcome

The proximal outcome in cognitive training research is the key cognitive process, skill, or ability that is the target of training. The proximal outcome represents the nearest level of training transfer. In our intervention research on fluid intelligence, the abilities of figural relations, inductive reasoning, or spatial orientation have been the proximal outcomes (Willis et al., 1981; Willis & Schaie, 1986). In memory intervention research, the proximal outcomes have been variables, such as recall of long word lists, recall of face–name pairs, or recall of text material (Kliegl et al., 1990; Yesavage, 1990). Most cognitive training research has focused almost exclusively on training effects and training transfer at the level of proximal outcome measures. There has been relatively little attention given to the remaining two levels of intervention outcomes, primary and distal outcomes, as discussed below.

An issue that has been examined with regard to proximal outcomes in cognitive training research has been breadth of transfer within the proximal outcome domain. Cognitive training studies have been subject to criticism of "teaching the test" when a single measure of proximal outcome was employed. Training studies have increasingly employed multiple measures of the proximal outcome (Willis & Schaie, 1986). If training effects are shown for multiple measures of the proximal outcome or if the proximal outcome is represented in terms of factor scores, then it can be argued that training effects have been demonstrated at the latent construct level. That is, the shared variance among multiple measures of the proximal outcome has been impacted by the intervention (Schaie, Willis, Hertzog & Schulenberg, 1987).

The proximal outcome must be specified in a consistent, congruent manner in at least three places in the reporting of a study (a) the statement of the objectives of the intervention, (b) the tests or measures used to assess the target of training, and (c) the intervention protocol.

An unfortunate common mistake in interventions is a lack of congruence and specificity in description of the proximal outcome in the aims, measures, and treatment protocol. The aims or goals of the intervention are often stated in much more general or broad terms than what is actually measured by the tests or questionnaire employed. Likewise, a careful examination of the treatment protocol or training manual often indicates that relatively little time is spent focusing directly on the target ability or cognitive skill—or that the treatment protocol is not specified in the detail required to determine whether the majority of the time is spent in practice or training on the target skill or ability.

1. Mechanisms and Cognitive Strategies: The Mediators of Proximal Outcomes

As discussed in the previous section on cognitive strategies, it is critical that the conceptual framework for the intervention specify the types of mechanisms that are hypothesized to change performance on the proximal outcome or training target. In much cognitive training research, the key mechanisms are cognitive strategies. In training a skill, a series of skill components may be specified. An important point is that, at least in cognitive interventions, the mechanisms, strategies, or skill components are likely to be highly specific to the ability or skill (proximal outcome) being trained. Unique strategies or skill components have usually been identified for a given ability or skill. Thus, mechanisms (e.g., strategies) and proximal outcomes go hand-in-glove.

Another common mistake in cognitive training research is that the particular mechanisms to enhance the proximal outcome are not clearly specified and are not the primary focus of the training protocol. To a large extent, the strategies, skill components, or mechanisms taught during training define the proximal outcome. If the proximal outcome is complex, then multiple strategies or skill components may need to be taught and proportional time devoted to each strategy in accord with its hypothesized salience to the proximal outcome as a totality.

The mechanisms or strategies specified to underlie the proximal outcomes then become a critical mediator of change in the proximal outcome. Enhancement in performance on the proximal outcome should occur as a function of an increase in frequency of strategy usage and/or increased expertise in applying or executing the strategy. Thus, competence with and use of the key mechanism or strategy should account for significant variance in individual differences in improvement on the proximal outcome (Dunlosky & Hertzog, 1998, 1998b; Saczynski, Willis, & Schaie, in press).

B. Primary Intervention Outcomes

The second level of intervention outcomes is often known as primary outcomes. Primary outcomes should be a product of the proximal outcome, share significant common variance with the proximal outcome, or both. At least two very significant criteria must be met in order for there to be the possibility of significant training transfer at the primary outcome level: (a) there must be evidence of considerable shared variance between the proximal and primary outcomes, and (b) a significant training effect should be demonstrated at the level of the proximal outcome. That is, in order for a training effect at the level of the primary outcome to be ascribed to the treatment, a training effect must first be demonstrated for the proximal outcome that was the target of

the intervention (Salomon & Perkins, 1989).

For example, in our cognitive training research on fluid abilities, one possible primary outcome would be enhanced performance on cognitively demanding tasks of daily living (comprehending medication labels, interpreting phone bills, etc). Prior research has shown a significant association between fluid abilities such as inductive reasoning and cognitively demanding tasks of daily living (Willis, 1996). Moreover, in lagged analyses, fluid and crystallized abilities measured at the first occasion have been shown to predict performance on cognitively demanding tasks of daily living 7 years later (Willis, Jay, Diehl, & Marsiske, 1992). In addition, it would need to be shown that participants who showed significant training on fluid ability were more likely to show reliable improvement on measures of cognitively demanding tasks of daily living.

C. Distal Intervention Outcomes

The third level of intervention outcomes are distal or secondary outcomes. In terms of training transfer, these would be referred to as far transfer. These are the least studied of the three levels of intervention outcomes. It is generally argued that if distal intervention outcomes occur, they are the result of "spill over" from treatment-related change in primary and proximal outcomes. For example, enhanced performance on cognitively demanding tasks of daily living might lead to distal outcomes, such as improved medication adherence or maintenance of the current level of medication adherence as the individual ages. Theoretical rationales for how distal intervention outcomes would occur are not well developed and need considerable further study. Bandura's (1986) theory of the role of self-efficacy at multiple phases in an intervention is one exemplar of the type of theory and research that needs to be done in this area. Also, the discussion of far transfer by Salomon and Perkins (1989) reviewed in the next section of this chapter may provide important insights.

VI. Issues in Training Transfer

Transfer is a central concept in learning theory and in training research that has been studied and debated over much of the past century (Detterman & Sternberg, 1993). Discussion regarding the construct is usually traced back as far as the writings of Thorndike and Woodworth (1901). Although issues related to transfer have been occasionally addressed in cognitive training studies with the elderly (Donaldson, 1981; Fisk, Rogers, Cooper, & Gilbert, 1997; Willis & Baltes, 1981; Willis, 1987, 1990), discussion of the history and assumptions regarding transfer have received relatively limited attention in cognitive aging. However, transfer is becoming a critical issue, as large-scale behavioral clinical trials targeting psychological and social constructs become more frequent in gerontology. These trials often examine whether intervention into the cognitive and social constructs studied by gerontologists have implications for maintaining (i.e., transferring to) competence in activities associated with the health and independence of the elderly (Coon et al., 1999; Jobe et al., in press).

This section begins with a brief review of the broader transfer literature (Cormier & Hagman, 1987; Detterman & Sternberg, 1993; McKeough et al., 1995; Voss, 1990), followed by a more in-depth discussion of the literature on mechanisms to foster transfer and the specification of a continuum of transfer. It is important to note that although transfer has been extensively studied and debated for over a decade, there is still often limited consensus on critical aspects of the construct (Detterman & Sternberg, 1993).

A. Defining Transfer and a Brief History

The first task is to define transfer as a construct. Transfer is said to occur when learning in one context enhances performance in a somewhat different context (Salomon & Perkins, 1989), or transfer occurs when prior learned knowledge and skill affect the way in which new knowledge and skills are learned and performed (Cormier & Hagman, 1987). Detterman (1993) has defined transfer as the degree to which a behavior will be repeated in a new situation. Transfer refers to a recognition that various terms and entities of one set can be mapped onto those of another set (Ceci & Ruiz, 1993). In job training, transfer has been defined as the application in the workplace of the knowledge, skills, and attitudes learned in training (Yelon, 1992). Although definitions of transfer differ, there is a common often unstated but critical assumption: A prerequisite for transfer is that some form of initial learning has occurred—there must be at least a minimal mastery of information or skills for the opportunity for transfer to exist (Salomon & Perkins, 1989)

The concept of transfer is closely tied to that of learning, and hence as various theories of learning have come and gone over the past century, definitions of transfer have evolved and changed (Voss, 1990). Ferguson (1956) argued that if improvements occur from learning trial to learning trial, then transfer had occurred between trials; this would be a very near form of transfer. At the time of Thorndike's and Woodworth's (1901) early research on transfer, the dominant theory of human learning was associationism. Early explanations of transfer were, thus, typically based on the theory of identical elements and couched in stimulus–response (S–R) language (Cormier &

Hagman, 1987). Thorndike concluded that when transfer occurs it occurs because of common elements in the two situations. The amount of transfer that occurs can be predicted from the proportion of common elements shared by two situations. Given this orientation, Thorndike concluded that only near transfer is likely to occur.

On the other hand, throughout the history of the study of intelligence, a hallmark of intelligence and of an intelligent person has been the ability to think abstractly and to derive general principles from concrete exemplars. The core of intelligence, g, from Cattell's notion of fluid intelligence (Cattell, 1963) to Sternberg's triarchic theory (Sternberg, 1985) has been described in terms of linear reasoning, thinking abstractly, and making inductions. Intelligence involves the ability to adapt to new situations. A major adaptive mechanism of the human species is the ability to profit from experience. Humans learn to abstract relevant knowledge and skills from prior experiences to their advantage in new or novel situations. They *transfer* the essence of knowledge, skills, and principles acquired in prior contexts to how they think and-behave in sometimes dramatically new situations.

These two different views regarding transfer are reflected in two classic theories of education (Ceci & Ruiz, 1993; Detterman, 1993) that continue to have followers into the present day. Early in the 20th century the doctrine of formal disciplines was a dominant educational approach. This approach held that training in one discipline enabled one to think more effectively and hopefully abstractly in many other disciplines. For example, specific training in Latin or chess was regarded as an exercise that fostered the development of logical reasoning in general. Learning how to reason in one context was thought to transfer to reasoning in other contexts. Recent expressions of

this approach can be found in research that touts the benefits of learning computer programming languages to develop rigorous thinking, to learn the use of heuristics, and to teach the process of problem solving (Salomon & Perkins, 1989). The research of Thorndike arguing for only near transfer was in response to the widespread acceptance of the formal disciplines approach in the early 20th century.

The second educational approach has focused on domain-specific learning—explicitly teaching information, principles, and strategies within each domain. The individual can learn to transfer knowledge and principles to multiple situations *within* a given substantive domain. However, training in a specific domain such as Latin is not likely to result in enhanced reasoning and understanding in another domain such as physics (Detterman, 1993).

B. Four Aspects or Dimensions of Transfer

Major issues studied and debated throughout the 20th century regarding transfer can be summarized in terms of four aspects or dimensions: (a) The *how* or *mechanisms* of transfer; (b) *what* is transferred; (c) the *amount* of transfer; and (d) the *distance* or *breadth* of transfer.

1. The How or Mechanisms of Transfer

A major question regarding transfer, even near transfer, has focused on the mechanisms by which transfer occurs. Salomon and Perkins (1989) have proposed that transfer can occur by different routes or mechanisms or combinations of mechanisms. They hypothesize two major internal mechanisms by which transfer can occur: low-road transfer and high-road transfer. Because of the unintentional "negative transfer" associated with the term *low-road transfer*, in this discussion, the two mechanisms are referred to as *transfer due to automaticity and transfer due to mindful abstraction.*

Transfer due to automaticity involves the processes of (a) extensive practice in varied contexts, (b) stimulus control, and (c) automaticity. A skill or other cognitive element is learned and practiced in a variety of contexts until it becomes automated. If practiced in a variety of somewhat related and expanding contexts, execution of the skill or cognitive element can become increasingly flexible. Automatization occurs as a result of extensive practice (Shiffrin & Schneider, 1977). The processing and behavior becomes fast, effortless, and relatively unlimited by processing capacity. The behaviors and cognitions are stimulus controlled. One's cognitive system automatically applies the learned behavior whenever it identifies situational cues it takes to be prototypical of a particular category of situations.

A plus of this form of transfer is that it usually increases the efficiency of the behavior; the behavior is performed fast, effortlessly, and with reduced processing demands. The limitation of this mechanism for transfer is that automaticity inhibits analytic reflection. Conscious control and analytic awareness is reduced by automaticity.

In an extensive, ongoing, well-designed program of research, Fisk, Rogers, and colleagues are conducting training studies with older adults that address many issues related to automaticity as a mechanism for transfer (Fisk, Lee, & Rogers, 1991; Fisk, Rogers, & Giambra, 1991; Fisk et al. 1997).

Transfer due to mindful abstraction is the second mechanism of training transfer proposed by Salomon and Perkins (1989). The processes involved in this mechanism of transfer are (a) mindful, deliberate, deep processing of information

(Langer, 1989) and (b) the abstraction or decontextualization of cognitions. Abstractions generally take the form of a rule, principle, schema, or prototype. Abstraction is the principle by which transfer occurs; abstraction provides a bridge from one context to another. Formation of the abstraction is a mindful, deliberate process that typically occurs during the learning process (although see the backward-reaching process next).

Salomon and Perkins (1989) suggest two alternative ways in which mindful abstraction may lead to transfer. The first type is called *forward reaching*. In this case, the participant mindfully abstracts basic elements during the initial learning situation in anticipation of making a later application. The information is learned or encoded as a general principle in the initial learning, and new applications of the general principle occur almost spontaneously in later situations (transfer). In the second type called *backward reaching*, the abstraction actually occurs in the transfer situation rather than in the initial learning situation. One is faced with a new situation and deliberately searches for relevant information from prior situations that might be applicable in the new transfer context. The principle is learned originally for a context-specific purpose, but the individual at a later occasion is able to reformulate the information or principle to a higher level of abstraction.

Transfer due to mindful abstraction probably better characterizes the training process conducted in training on fluid abilities (Schaie & Willis, 1986) and perhaps in application of some memory strategies (Dunlosky & Hertzog, in press; Hill et al., 1989; Rasmussion Rebok, & Brandt, 1999). The elder is trained on general rules or strategies (e.g., looking for certain types of patterns in inductive reasoning problems, applying method of loci to list of words) and is given practice in applying (transferring) these rules or strategies to new instances of the problem. As discussed in the section on cognitive strategies, the participant must not only learn to apply the rule or strategy to the next instance of the problem, but also must determine whether or not a given strategy applies or which strategy applies when faced with problems varying in the specific cognitive strategy needed to solve a problem.

2. What Is Transferred

As noted above, the concepts of learning and transfer are closely intertwined. *What* is hypothesized to be transferred will depend on the researcher's or interventionist's theories of learning and of intelligence or cognition. In an associative approach to learning, transfer is viewed as being narrow or near to the initial learning and context. *What* is transferred is defined in S-R terms, in terms of identical or similar elements between the learning and the transfer situation. In contrast, theories of intelligence and learning approaches that focus on concepts such as learning-to-learn, procedural knowledge, and expertise are concerned with the ability of the individual to form abstractions, develop hierarchies of knowledge, and identify general principles. This approach should lead to broader transfer across contexts. *What* is transferred is more likely to be described in terms of a subroutine, learning strategy, overarching principle, or generalized skill.

Moreover, Salomon and Perkins (1989) have argued that *what* is transferred interacts with the *mechanisms* of transfer. What is transferred through the mechanism of automaticity and practice is hypothesized to involve behavior that is unintentional, implicit, based on modeling, and driven by reinforcement. These activities are involved in processes such as socialization, acculturation, and experience-based cognitive development.

In contrast, transfer via mindful abstraction is more likely to occur during explicit instruction that is aimed at teaching or provoking the learner to identify a generalization. Transfer results from the *mindful* generation of an abstraction developed during the learning process (Langer, 1989). Teaching strategies and mnemonics to mildly retarded children was effective only when skills of mindful attention and metacognition were taught along with the strategies and mnemonics (Brown & Kane, 1988; Campione, Shapiro, & Brown, 1995).

3. Amount of Transfer

Amount of transfer refers to how much improvement results in the transfer context from attaining some level of performance in the learning context. Salomon and Perkins (1989) hypothesized that the extensive practice involved in transfer due to automaticity affects mainly the *amount* of transfer — practice leads to the automatic activation of whole "bundles" of interrelated responses. Because of bundling, amount of transfer is likely to involve the entire set of skill components or the entire knowledge set, rather than selected components of a skill or fragments of the knowledge set. For example, in transferring driving skill from one car to another, the entire repertoire of driving skills is transferred, even though certain skill components (e.g., reaching for the clutch on a car with automatic transmission) might not be needed or appropriate.

What about amount of transfer from a mindful abstraction approach to transfer? The goal of this type of transfer is to form an abstraction or generalization that can be applied in new situations. However, the amount of transfer may depend in part on the fit or match between the level of abstraction at which a principle is learned and the level of abstraction required in a particular transfer situation. If abstraction occurs at too high a level in the initial learning, then it may interfere with applying the principle to a transfer situation. The principle is not encoded at the level of concreteness that would most easily facilitate transfer to a particular context. For example, a traveler learns a precise algebraic formula for converting Euros to dollars and vice versa. However, during a particular interval when one Euro is almost equivalent to one dollar, applying the precise algebraic formula to determine the price of an inexpensive item may be overkill.

Addressing the issue of the amount of transfer involves two questions: at which of the levels of intervention outcomes, discussed previously, is amount of transfer most directly studied and upon what factors might the amount of transfer depend? Amount of transfer refers to *how much improvement* results in the transfer context as a result of the level of mastery attained in the learning context. In terms of the previous section on levels of outcome, the *primary outcomes* are of particular concern with respect to transfer. The central question is whether pre–posttest gain in the primary outcomes for the treatment group exceeds the pre–posttest gain in the primary outcomes for the comparison groups.

The second question that focuses on what factors might be associated with variability in the amount of transfer attained is complex. It depends in part on factors such as the investigator's theory of learning, the mechanisms of transfer, and perhaps participant characteristics. Such factors can only be briefly considered here. Based on the discussion above, Salomon and Perkins (1989) suggest that automaticity as the mechanisms of transfer may lead to a high incidence of transfer, but that the breadth of transfer will be more specific or narrow. That is, once a skill is automated, there should be a high likelihood that the skill will be performed in a transfer situation if the stimulus cues are present, and that it will be performed nearly flawlessly.

With regard to amount of transfer and characteristics of the trainee, there is ongoing debate on the relationship between transfer and intelligence (Ceci & Ruiz, 1993; Detterman, 1993; Singley & Anderson, 1989; Sternberg & Frensch, 1993). The debate appears to focus primarily on far (general) transfer, rather than on near transfer. There seems to be more agreement that lower cognitively functioning individuals are less likely to show near transfer. This finding has demonstrated primarily with young mildly retarded individuals (Brown & Kane, 1988), although some evidence with older adults (compared with younger adults) is also reported by Fisk and associates (1997). The more debatable issue across the life span appears to be the extent to which far transfer can be trained and the extent to which successful training in far transfer would reduce broad cognitive deficits. Several educational programs based on this premise are ongoing with young or retarded children (Campione, Shapiro & Brown, 1995) and with young adults (McKeough et al., 1995).

4. Distance or Breadth of Transfer

Distance of transfer concerns how far learning transfers and to which tasks: very similar tasks, somewhat related ones, or even quite remote tasks. Transfer can be conceptualized as a continuum of situations progressively more different from the original learning experience. The major debate in training centers on how broad or far across the continuum transfer should be expected. Two general types of transfer are often distinguished; these two types of transfer have been described in terms of near/far, specific/nonspecific, and deep/surface structure (Cormier & Hagman, 1987; Detterman, 1993; Mayer & Greeno, 1972).

Near transfer occurs when the skills or abilities acquired in training are demonstrated in situations that are similar to the original learning situation except for a few important differences. The more different the original versus new situations, the more likely transfer is to be called *far* transfer.

Salomon and Perkins (1989) have made some hypotheses regarding near versus far transfer when transfer involves mechanisms of automaticity versus mindful abstraction. In transfer associated with automaticity, the individual does not consciously analyze a new situation in terms of similarities or differences compared with the initial learning situation. Similarities of prototypical cues across contexts are detected automatically. Thus, transfer to new situations occurs primarily if these situations activate these response clusters because of automatically detected similarity of prototypical cues (Schneider & Fisk, 1984). Transfer to situations more remote from the learning context are less likely because identification of similarities would require intentional (conscious) examination of the similarities. As discussed under the section on amount of transfer, partial components of a skill or fragments of knowledge that might be relevant in a new situation are not likely to be transferred, because the complete skill or knowledge set is bundled and activated as a totality.

What of near versus far transfer is associated with mindful abstraction? While far or distant transfer appears less likely via the mechanism of automaticity, transfer to more distant contexts is hypothesized to be more likely to occur via the mechanism of mindful abstraction. The higher the level of generality at which a principle is abstracted, the broader or more distal the range of situations to which it might be possible to apply the principle.

Although the near–far distinction is most common in discussions of the breadth or distance of transfer, several other types of contrasts have been noted. In *specific* transfer the learner transfers the contents of learning to a new situations. In *nonspecific* transfer, general skills or principles transfer to the new situations. More recently a distinction has been made between the *deep structure* and *surface structure* in a situation. An example is that all car dashboards give similar information but their dial configurations are different. Deep structure is the same but surface structure is different. On the other hand, airplane dashboards contain dials similar to a car's, but the information presented by the dials is different. For the car and plane dashboards, there is similar surface structure but different deep structure.

In terms of the three levels of training outcomes discussed in the previous section, proximal outcomes would be considered to represent very near or specific transfer. *Primary* outcomes would be considered to include moderately far transfer further along the continuum involving the transfer of either general skills or principles or transfer to markedly different situations. Distal outcomes would represent the furthest form of transfer. In training, the greatest interest has been in whether moderately far (i.e., primary outcomes), nonspecific, or deep structure transfer could be achieved and what factors enhance or impeded such transfer. Whether transfer of general principles can occur between different situations, as examined in primary outcomes, is particularly important in training research.

VII. Summary and Future Directions

The background for this chapter lies in the significant increase in behavioral intervention research with the elderly that has occurred over the last three decades.

Behavioral interventions with the elderly have evolved from experimental research conducted by a single investigator in his or her laboratory to large-scale multisite studies (Schulz, Maddox, & Lawton, 1999). Behavioral intervention research with the elderly is increasingly represented in the clinical trial arena (Coon et al., 1999; Jobe et al., in press). Journal articles and book chapters reporting the substantive findings from these studies are beginning to appear in the literature. An aim of this chapter was to review and discuss selected methodological issues with respect to behavioral intervention research with the elderly. The cognitive training research literature provides many of the exemplars cited throughout the chapter.

A plea is made throughout the chapter that strong conceptual and theoretical frameworks should continue to guide the future evolution of behavioral intervention research. In the first generation of behavioral intervention research, the single investigator typically had considerable knowledge of the existing descriptive and explanatory models of the psychology of aging and grounded the intervention protocol and measurement system within these models. Thus, not only was the issue of invention outcomes addressed, but the training research made significant contributions to the broader psychological aging literature. A reciprocal relationship existed; gerontological behavioral interventions were deeply rooted in developmental and experimental theories of aging, and intervention findings contributed to further theory development.

Although the recent and ongoing large-scale, multisite behavioral intervention studies will make significant contributions to issues regarding the generalizability and representativeness of the earlier training literature, there is also the concern that the reciprocal contributing relationship between gerontological descriptive and experimental research and behavioral interventions may diminish.

It is essential that the strong, almost singular emphasis on outcomes and treatment effectiveness that is characteristic of outcome intervention research and in clinical trials be complemented and even tempered by an equally strong commitment to the grounding of the intervention in a conceptual framework—with theory-based assumptions and hypotheses required and made explicit. Moreover, the role of the conceptual framework must be reviewed at each stage in the development and implementation of the intervention. Furthermore, it is important that the methodological procedures and assumptions upon which outcome interventions and clinical trials are based, which are often rooted in pharmacological intervention research, be reexamined and their applicability reevaluated as they are extended to behavioral interventions with the elderly. Behavioral intervention research must not lose its roots and heritage in the psychology of aging, both substantively and methodologically. Each branch of research must continue to maintain a dialogue and contribute to their mutual development.

In the first section of this chapter, the major between-group designs employed in behavioral intervention research were reviewed and their relative utility examined. The between-group perspective is based on examining the treatment efficacy of various types of control or comparison groups, compared to the intervention group. These control groups have included no-treatment control, a nonspecific effects group, component approach, alternative treatment groups, and a parametric approach. Although each alternative has important strengths and limitations, the component approach appears at this time to be the most flexible approach and to be most likely to provide further theory-based knowledge regarding the intervention. Many behavioral interventions began, in honesty, with the "kitchen sink" approach, including a wide array of factors that might contribute to a positive training effect. Having shown significant effects with the total-package intervention, it is now important to systematically examine the relative contribution of each component. In addition, the parametric approach, although labor intensive and costly in subjects, has the potential to provide critical information in the form of a cost–benefit analysis of the relative gain achieved by increasing or decreasing the amount or intensity of various components of the intervention.

The second section of the chapter considered the essential role of mechanisms, processes, and strategies in behavioral interventions with the elderly. The field of cognitive aging is noteworthy for the theoretical and research efforts made to identify and understand the mechanisms underlying cognitive functioning (Baltes, 1987; Craik & Salthouse, 1992; Kausler, 1994). The early cognitive training research is to be commended for grounding the intervention protocols in conceptual frameworks derived from the cognitive aging literature. Prior training research has been successful in teaching older adults that a particular strategy is useful for a particular cognitive task and how to use the strategy. It is becoming evident that knowing how to use a skill in a highly structured training session does not equate with older adults accepting the efficacy of the skill or being able to determine in what contexts in the real world such a strategy is appropriate and useful. The next generation of training studies will need to take into account to a greater extent the role of context and factors such as motivation and efficacy. Perhaps even more challenging is the likelihood that facilitating the older adult's use of a particular cognitive strategy in appropriate real-world contexts may require some form of executive or metacognitive training in addition to strategy-specific instruction.

Concern with the possible need for training at the executive or metacognitive level led to the final section on training transfer. It bears repeating that transfer is one of the most challenging phenomena in the field of learning and training and one for which there is relatively little consensus. Cognitive aging research can make a unique and very valuable contribution to research on transfer. Many of the major concepts discussed in the transfer literature, including automaticity, prior knowledge, and abstraction, are areas of important current research in cognitive aging. Moreover, there appear to be quantitative and/or qualitative changes in these phenomena with age that may well provide insight into the role of transfer in learning and training.

In summary, the field of behavior intervention research with the elderly is relatively young, but it has experienced a period of near exponential growth in the last two decades, from single-investigator studies involving less than 100 participants to large-scale studies involving several thousand older adults. Given the movement toward larger-scale behavioral intervention studies in aging, it appears that rapid growth of this literature will continue. Perhaps behavioral intervention research in aging is now in its adolescence. It is hoped that as it experiences the growth spurts, mood swings, and unlimited horizons characteristic of adolescence that it will continue to seek guidance from and affiliation with its parent disciplines in the psychology of cognition and aging, particularly with regard to theory and methods.

References

Appel, L. J., Espeland, M., Whelton, P. K., Dolecek, T., Kumanyika, S., Applegate, W. B., Ettinger, W. H., Jr., Dostis, J. B., Wilson, A. C. & Lacy, C. (1995). Trial of nonpharmacologic intervention in the elderly (TONE): Design and rationale of a blood pressure control trial. *Annals of Epidemiology, 5,* 119–129.

Ball, K., & Owsley C. (2000). Increasing mobility and reducing accidents in older drivers. In K. W. Schaie & M. Pietrucha (Eds.), *Mobility and transportation in the elderly.* New York: Springer.

Baltes, P. B. (1987). Theoretical propositions of life-span developmental psychology. On the dynamics between growth and decline. *Developmental Psychology, 23,* 611–626.

Baltes, P. B., & Danish, S. J. (1979). Gerontological interventions based on a life-span developmental psychology: Problems and concepts. *Zeitschrift Fuer entwicklungspsychologie und Paedagogische Psychologie, 11,* 112–140.

Baltes, P. B., & Kliegl R. (1992). Further testing of limits of cognitive plasticity: Negative age differences in a mnemonic skill are robust. *Developmental Psychology, 28,* 121–125.

Baltes, P. B., & Willis, S. L. (1977). Toward psychological theories of aging and development. In J. Birren & K. W. Schaie (Eds.), *The handbook of the psychology of aging* (pp. 128–154). New York: Van Nostrand-Reinhold.

Bandura, A. (1986). *Social foundations of thought and action: A social cognitive theory.* Englewood Cliffs, NJ: Prentice-Hall.

Bandura, A. (1989). Regulation of cognitive processes through perceived self-efficacy. *Developmental Psychology, 25,* 729–735.

Basham, R. B. (1986). Scientific and practical advantages of comparative design in psychotherapy outcome research. *Journal of Consulting and Clinical Psychology, 54,* 88–94.

Bentler, P. M. (1980). Multivariate analysis with latent variables: Causal modeling. *Annual Review of Psychology, 31,* 332–456.

Berry, J. M., West, R. L., & Dennehey, D. M. (1989). Reliability and validity of the Memory Self-Efficacy Questionnaire. *Developmental Psychology, 25,* 701–713.

Borkovec, T. D. (1994). Between-group therapy outcome research: Design and methodology. In L S. Onken & J. D. Blaine (Eds.), *Behavioral treatments for drug abuse and dependence. NIDA Research Monograph #137* (pp. 249–289). Rockville, MD: National Institute of Drug Abuse.

Borkovec, T. D., & Castonguay, L. G. (1998). What is the scientific meaning of empirically supported therapy? *Journal of Consulting and Clinical Psychology, 66,* 136–142.

Brown, W. A. (1994). Placebo as a treatment for depression. *Neuropsychopharmacology, 10,* 265–269.

Brown, A. L. & Kane, L. R. (1988). Preschool children can learn to transfer: Learning to learn and learning from example. *Cognitive Psychology, 20,* 493–523.

Camp, C. (1999). Memory interventions for normal and pathological older adults. In R. Schulz, G. Maddox, & M. P. Lawton (Eds.), *Annual review of gerontology and geriatrics: Focus on interventions research with older adults,* (pp. 1–16). New York: Springer.

Campbell, D. T., & Stanley, J. C. (1963). Experimental and quasi-experimental designs for research in teaching. In N. L. Gage (Ed.), *Handbook of research on teaching* (pp. 171–246). Skokie, IL: Rand McNally.

Campione, J. C., Shapiro, A. M., & Brown, A. L. (1995). Forms of transfer in a community of learners: Flexible learning and understanding. In A. McKeough, J. Lupart, & A. Marini (Eds.), *Teaching for transfer: Fostering generalization in learning.* (pp. 35–68) Mahwah, NJ: Erlbaum.

Cattell, R. B. (1963). Theory of fluid and crystallized intelligence: A critical experiment. *Journal of Educational Psychology, 54,* 1–22.

Cavanaugh, J. C., Krammer, D. A., Sinnott, J. D., Camp, C. J., & Markley, R. P (1985). On missing links and such: interfaces between cognitive research and everyday problem solving. *Human Development, 28,* 146–168.

Ceci, S., & Ruiz, A. (1993). Transfer, abstractness and intelligence. In D. K. Detterman & R. J. Sternberg (Eds.), *Transfer on trial: Intelligence, cognition, and instruction* (pp 168–191). Norwood, NJ: Ablex.

Charness, N. (1981). Search in chess: Age and skill differences. *Journal of Experimental Psychology: Human Perception and Performance, 7,* 467–476.

Charness, N. (1985). Aging and problem solving performance. In N. Charness (Ed.), *Aging and human performance* (pp. 225–259). Chichester: Wiley.

Charness, N. & Campbell, J. I. (1988). Acquiring skill at mental calculation in adulthood: A task decomposition. *Journal of Experimental Psychology: General, 117*, 115–129.

Clark, F., Azen, S., Zemke, R., Jackson, J., Carlson, M., Mandel, D., Hay, J., Hosephson, K., Cherry, B., Hessel, C., Palmer, J., & Lipson, L. (1997). Occupational therapy for independent living older adults. *JAMA, 278*, 1321–1326.

Cohen, G., & Faulkner, D. (1986). Memory for proper names: Age differences in retrieval. *British Journal of Developmental Psychology, 4*, 187–190.

Coon D. W., Schulz, R., Ory, M. G., & The REACH study group (1999). Innovative intervention approaches for Alzheimer's disease caregivers. In D. E. Biegel & A. Blum (Eds.), *Innovations in practice and service delivery across the lifespan* (pp. 295–325). New York: Oxford University Press.

Cormier, S. M., & Hagman, J. D. (Eds.). (1987). *Transfer of learning: Contemporary research and applications*. San Diego, CA: Academic Press.

Craik, F. I. M., & Salthouse, T. A. (1992). *Handbook of aging and cognition*. Hillsdale, NJ: Erlbaum.

Detterman, D. K. (1993). The case for the prosecution: Transfer as an epiphenomenon. In D. K. Detterman & R. J. Sternberg (Eds.), *Transfer on trial: Intelligence, cognition, and instruction* (pp 1–24). Norwood, NJ: Ablex.

Detterman, D. K., & Sternberg, R. J. (Eds.) 1993 *Transfer on trial: Intelligence, cognition, and instruction*. Norwood, NJ: Ablex.

Donaldson, G. (1981). Letter to the editor. *Journal of Gerontology, 36*, 634–636.

Dunlosky, J., & Hertzog, C. (1998a). Aging and deficits in associative memory: What is the role of strategy production? *Psychology and Aging, 13*, 597–607.

Dunlosky, J., & Hertzog, C. (1998b). Training programs to improve learning in later adulthood: Helping older adults educate themselves. In D. J. Hacker & J. D. Dunlosky (Eds.), Metacognition in educational theory and practice. The educational psychology series (pp. 249–275). Mahwah, NJ: Lawrence Erlbaum.

Dunlosky, J., & Hertzog, C. (in press). Measuring strategy production during associative learning: The relative utility of concurrent versus retrospective reports. *Memory and Cognition*.

Eysenck, H. J. (1994). The outcome problem in psychotherapy: What have we learned? *Behavior Research and Therapy, 32*, 477–495.

Ferguson, G. A. (1956). On transfer and the abilities of man. *Canadian Journal of Psychology, 10*, 121–131.

Finkel, S. I., & Yesavage, J. A. (1989). Learning mnemonics: A preliminary evaluation of a computer-aided instruction package for the elderly. *Experimental Aging Research, 15*, 199–201.

Fisk, A. D., Lee, M. D., & Rogers, W. A. (1991). Recombination of automatic processing components: The effects of transfer, reversal, and conflict situations. *Human Factors, 33*, 267–280.

Fisk, A. D., Rogers, W. A., Cooper, B. P., & Gilbert, D. K. (1997). Automatic category search and its transfer: Aging, type of search and level of learning. *Journal of Gerontology: Psychological Sciences, 52B*, P91–P102.

Fisk, A. D., Rogers, W. A., & Giambra, L. M. (1990). Consistent and varied memory/visual search: Is there an interaction between age and response-set effects? *Journal of Gerontology: Psychological Sciences, 45*, P81–87.

Gratzinger, P., Sheikh, J. I., Friedman, L., & Yesavage, J. A. (1990). Cognitive interventions to improve face-name recall: The role of personality trait differences. *Developmental Psychology, 26*, 889–893.

Hayslip, B. (1989). Alternative mechanisms for improvements in fluid ability performance among older adults. *Psychology and Aging, 4*, 122–124.

Hazlett-Stevens, H., & Borkovec, T. D. (1999). Experimental design and methodology in between-group intervention outcome research. In R. Schulz, G. Maddox, & M. P. Lawton (Eds.). *Annual review of gerontology and geriatrics: Focus on interventions research with older adults.* (pp. 17–47). New York: Springer.

Hertzog, C., McGuire, C. L., & Lineweaver, T. T. (1998). Aging, attributions, perceived control, and strategy use in a free recall task. *Aging, Neuropsychology, and Cognition, 5*, 85–106.

Hill, R. D., Sheikh, J. I., & Yesavage, J. A. (1989). Pretraining enhances mnemonic training in elderly adults. *Experimental Aging Research, 14*, 207–211.

Hofland, B. F., Willis, S. L., & Baltes, P. B. (1981). Fluid intelligence performance in the elderly: Intraindividual variability and conditions of assessment. *Journal of Educational Psychology, 73*, 573–586.

Jacobson, N. S., & Hollon, S. D. (1996). Cognitive-behavior therapy versus pharmacotherapy: Now that the jury's returned its verdict, it's time to present the rest of the evidence. *Journal of Consulting and Clinical Psychology, 64*, 74–80.

Jobe, J. B., Smith, D. M., Ball, K., Tennstedt, S. Marsiske, M., Rebok, G., Morris, J. N., Willis, S. L., Helmers, K., Leveck, M. D., & Kleinman, K. (2000). *ACTIVE: A cognitive intervention trial to promote independence in older adults.* Washington, DC: National Institutes of Health.

Kastenbaum, R. (1968). Perspectives on the development and modification of behavior in the aged: A developmental-field perspective. *Gerontologist, 8*, 280–283.

Kausler, D. (1994). *Learning and memory in normal aging.* San Diego, CA: Academic Press.

Kavanagh, D. J., & Bower, G. H. (1985). Mood and self-efficacy: Impact of joy and sadness on perceived capabilities. *Cognitive Therapy and Research, 9*, 507–525.

Kazdin, A. E. (1986). Comparative outcome studies of psychotherapy: Methodological issues and strategies. *Journal of Consulting and Clinical Psychology, 54*, 95–105.

Kazdin, A. E. (1992). *Research design in clinical psychology* (2nd ed.). Needham Heights, MA: Allyn & Bacon.

Kliegl, R., Smith, J., & Baltes, P. B. (1989). Testing-the-limits and the study of adult age differences in cognitive plasticity of a mnemonic skill. *Developmental Psychology, 25*, 247–256.

Kliegl, R., Smith, J., & Baltes, P. B. (1990). On the locus and process of magnification of age differences during mnemonic training. *Developmental Psychology, 26*, 894–904.

Klein, D. F. (1996). Preventing hung juries about therapy studies. *Journal of Consulting and Clinical Psychology, 64*, 81–87.

Kotler, S., & Camp, C. J. (1990). Memory interventions and aging. In E. Lovelace (Ed.), *Aging and cognition: Mental processes, self awareness, and interventions.* Amsterdam: North Holland.

Lachman, M. E., Weaver, S. L., Bandura, M., Elliot, E., & Lewkowicz, C. (1992). Improving memory and control beliefs through cognitive restructuring and self-generated strategies. *Journal of Gerontology: Psychological Sciences, 47*, P293–P298.

Langer, E. J. (1989). *Mindfulness.* Reading, MA: Addison-Wesley.

LaRosa, J. C, Applegate, W., Crouse, J. R., Hunninghake, D. B., Grimm, R., Knopp, R., Eckfeldt, J. H., Davis, C. E., & Gordon, D. J. (1994). Cholesterol-lowering in the elderly: Results of the cholesterol reduction in seniors program (CRISP) pilot study. *Archives of Internal Medicine, 154*, 529–539.

Lerner, R. M. (1986). *Concepts and theories of human development.* New York: Random.

Mayer, R. E., & Greeno, J. G. (1972). Structural differences between learning outcomes produced by different instructional methods. *Journal of Educational Psychology, 63*, 165–173.

McDougall, G. J. Jr. (1999). Cognitve interventiosn among older adults. In J. J. Fitzpatrick (Ed.), *Annual review of nursing research, vol. 17* (pp. 219–240). New York: Springer.

McKeough, A., Lupart, J., & Marini, A. (Eds). (1995). *Teaching for transfer: Fostering generalization in learning.* Mahwah, NJ: Erlbaum.

Mohs, R. C., Ashman, T. A., Jatzen, K., Albert, M., Brandt, J., Gordon, B., Rasmusson, X., Grossman, M., Jacobs, D., & Stern, Y. (1998). A study of the efficacy of a comprehensive memory enhancement program in healthy elderly persons. *Psychiatry Research, 77*, 183–195.

Morin, C., Colecchi, C., Brink, D., & Abstruc, M. (1995). How "blind" are double-blind placebo-controlled trials of benzodiazepine hynotics? *Sleep, 18*, 240–245.

Morin, C. M., Culbert, J. P., & Schwartz, S. M. (1994). Nonpharmacological interventions for insomnia: A meta-analysis of treatment efficacy. *American Journal of Psychiatry, 151*, 1172–1180.

National Institutes of Health (1991, September 25–27). *Treatment of panic disorder.* Bethesda, MD: National Institutes of Health Consensus Development Conference Consensus Statement.

Neely, A. S., & Bäckman, L. (1993). Long-term maintenance of gains from memory training in older adults: Two 3 -year follow-up studies. *Journal of Gerontology, 48,* P233–P237.

Neely, A. S., & Bäckman, L. (1995). Effect of multifactorial training in old age:

Nicholas, M. K., Wilson, P. H., & Goyen, J. (1991). Operant-behavioural and cognitive-behavioural treatment for chronic low back pain. *Behavioral Research Therapy, 29,* 225–238.

O'Leary, K. D., & Borkovec, T. D. (1978). Conceptual, methodological, and ethical problems of placebo groups in psychotherapy research. *American Psychologist, 33,* 821–830.

Ory, M. G., Schechtman, K. B., Miller, J. P., Hadley, E. C., Fiatarone, M. A., Province, M. A., Arfken, C. L., Morgan, D., Weiss, S., & Kaplan, M. (1993). Frailty and injuries in later life: The FICSIT trials. *Journal of the American Geriatrics Society, 41,* 283–296.

Parloff, M. B. (1986). Placebo controls in psychotherapy research: A sine qua non or a placebo for research problems? *Journal of Consulting and Clinical Psychology, 54,* 79–87.

Park, D. C., & Jones, T. R. (1997). Medication adherence and aging. In A. D. Fisk & W. A. Rogers (Eds.), *Handbook of human factors and the older adult* (pp. 257–287). New York: Academic Press.

Quayhagen, M. P., & Quayhagen, M. (1989). Differential effects of family-based strategies on Alzheimer's disease. *The Gerontologist, 29,* 150–155.

Rasmusson, D. X., Rebok, G. W., Bylsma, F. W., & Brandt, J. (1999). Effects of three types of memory training in normal elderly. *Aging, Neuropsychology, and Cognition, 6,* 56–66.

Rebok, G. W., & Balcerak, L. J. (1989). Memory self-efficacy and performance differences in young and old adults: The effect of mnemonic training. *Developmental Psychology, 25,* 714–721.

Rebok, G. W., Rasmusson, D. X., & Brandt, J. (1997). Improving memory in community

elderly though group-based and individualized memory training. In D. G. Payne & F. G. Conrad (Eds.), *Intersections in basic and applied memory* (pp. 327–343) Hillsdale, NJ: Lawrence Erlbaum Associates.

Rice, G. E., & Meyer, B. J. (1986). Prose recall: Effects of aging, verbal ability, and reading behavior. *Journal of Gerontology, 41,* 469–480.

Rosenthal, D., & Frank, J. D. (1956). Psychotherapy and the placebo effect. *Psychological Bulletin, 53,* 294–302.

Rush, A. J. (1994). Placebo responsiveness does not imply that placebo is a sufficient treatment. *Neuropsychopharmacology, 10,* 281–283.

Saczynski, J., Willis, S. L., Schaie, K. W. (in press). *Strategy use in reasoning training in older adults. Aging, Neuropsychology, and Cognition.*

Salomon, G., & Perkins, D. N. (1989). Rocky roads to transfer: Rethinking mechanisms of a neglected phenomenon. *Educational Psychologist, 24,* 113–142.

Salthouse, T. A. (1991). *Theoretical perspective on cognitive aging.* Hillsdale, NJ: Erlbaum.

Salthouse, T. A., & Prill, K. A., (1987). Inferences about age impairments in inferential reasoning. *Psychology and Aging, 2,* 43–51.

Schaie, K. W. (1988). Internal validity threats in studies of adult cognitive development. In M. L. Howe & C. J. Brainard (Eds), *Cognitive development in adulthood: Progress in cognitive development research* (pp. 241–272). New York: Springer Verlag.

Schaie, K. W. (1996). *Intellectual development in adulthood: The Seattle Longitudinal Study.* Cambridge: Cambridge University Press.

Schaie, K. W. (2000). Impact of longitudinal studies on understanding development from young adulthood to old age. *International Journal of Behavioral Development, 24,* 257–266.

Schaie, K. W., & Willis, S. L. (1986). Can decline in adult intellectual functioning be reversed? *Developmental Psychology, 22,* 223–232.

Schaie, K. W., Willis, S. L., Hertzog, C., Schulenberg, J. E. (1987). Effects of cognitive training on primary mental ability structure. *Psychology and Aging, 2,* 233–242.

Schneider, W., & Fisk, D. (1984). Automatic category search and its transfer. *Journal of Experimental Psychology: Learning Memory and Cognition, 10,* 1–15.

Schulz, R., Maddox, G., & Lawton, M. P. (Eds). (1999). *Annual review of gerontology and geriatrics: Focus on interventions research with older adults.* New York: Springer.

Schulz, R., & Martire, L. M. (1999). Intervention research with older adults: Introduction, overview, and future directions. In R. Schulz, G. Maddox, & M. P. Lawton (Eds.), *Annual review of gerontology and geriatrics: Focus on interventions research with older adults* (pp. 1–16). New York: Springer.

Scogin, F., & Bienias, J. L. (1988). A three-year follow-up of older adult participants in a memory skills training program. *Psychology and Aging, 3,* 334–37.

Shapiro, A. K. (1971). Placebo effects in medicine, psychotherapy, and psychoanalysis. In A. E. Bergin & S. L. Garfield (Eds.), *Handbook of psychotherapy and behavior change.* New York: Wiley.

Shiffrin, R. M., & Schneider, W. (1977). Controlled and automatic human information processing: II. Perceptual learning, automatic attending, and a general theory. *Psychological Review, 84,* 127–190.

Singley, M. K., & Anderson, J. R. (1989). *The transfer of cognitive skill.* Cambridge, MA: Harvard University Press.

Smyer, M. A., & Gatz, M. (1986). Intervention research approaches. *Research on Aging, 8,* 536–558.

Smyer, M. A, Zarit, S. H., & Qualls, S. H. (1990). Psychological intervention with the aging individual. Chapter in J. E. Birren & K. W. Schaie (Eds.), Handbook of the psychology of aging, 3rd ed., (pp. 375–403). San Diego, CA: Academic Press.

Sternberg, R. L. (1985). *Beyond IQ: A triarchic theory of human intelligence.* New York: Cambridge University of Press.

Sternberg, R. J., & Frensch, P. A. (1993). Mechanisms of transfer. In D. K. Detterman & R. J. Sternberg (Eds.), *Transfer on trial: Intelligence, cognition, and instruction* (pp. 25–38). Norwood, NJ: Ablex.

Strayhorn, J. (1987). Control groups for psychosocial intervention outcome studies. *American Journal of Psychiatry, 144,* 275–282.

Thorndike, E. L., & Woodworth, R. S. (1901) The influence of improvement in one mental function upon the efficiency of other functions. *Psychological Review, 8,* 247–261.

Tinetti, M. E., Baker, D. I., Garrett, P. A., Gottschalk, M., Koch, M. L., & Horwitz, R. I. (1993). Yale Ficsit: Risk factor abatement strategy for fall prevention. *Journal of the American Geriatric Society, 41,* 315–320.

Verhaeghen, P., & Marcoen, A. (1994). The production deficiency hypothesis revisited: Adult age differences in strategy use as a function of processing resources. *Aging and Cognition, 1,* 32–338.

Verhaeghen, P., & Marcoen, A. (1996). On the mechanisms of plasticity in young and older adults after instruction in the Method of Loci: Evidence for and amplification model. *Psychology and Aging, 11,* 164–178.

Voss, J. F. (1990). Learning and transfer in subject matter learning: A problem-solving model. In P. J. D., Drenth & J. A. Sergeant (Eds.), *European perspectives in psychology, Vol. 1: Theoretical, psychometrics, personality, developmental, educational, cognitive, gerontological* (pp 607–621). Chichester, UK: John Wiley.

Wilkins, W. (1983). Failure of placebo groups to control for nonspecific events in therapy outcome research. *Psychotherapy: Theory, Research and Practice, 20,* 31–37.

Willis S. L. (1987). Cognitive training and everyday competence. In K. W. Schaie (Ed.), *Annual review of gerontology and geriatrics (Vol. 7),* New York: Springer.

Willis S. L. (1990). Current issues in cognitive training research. In E. A., Lovelace (Ed.), *Aging and cognition: Mental processes, self awareness, and interventions* (pp. 263–280). Amsterdam: Elsevier.

Willis, S. L. (1996). Everyday cognitive competence in elderly persons: conceptual issues and empirical findings. *Gerontologist, 36,* 595–601.

Willis, S. L., & Baltes, P. B. (1981). Derivation of gerontological training research from the Gf-Gc theory of intelligence: A reply to Donaldson and some critical observations. *Journal of Gerontology, 36,* 634–638.

Willis, S. L., Blieszner, R., & Baltes, P. B. (1981). Intellectual training research in aging: Modification of performance on the fluid ability of figural relations. *Journal of Educational Psychology, 73,* 41–50.

Willis S. L., Cornelius S. W., Blow F. C., & Baltes P. B. (1983). Training in research in aging: Attentional processes. *Journal of Educational Psychology, 75,* 257–270.

Willis S. L., Jay G. M., Diehl, M., & Marsiske M. (1992). Longitudinal change and prediction of everyday task performance in the elderly. *Research on Aging, 14,* 68–91.

Willis, S. L., & Nesselroade, C. S. (1990). Long term effects of fluid ability training in old age. *Developmental Psychology, 26,* 905–910.

Willis S. L., & Schaie, K. W. (1986). Training the elderly on the ability factors of spatial orientation and inductive reasoning. *Psychology and Aging, 1,* 129–247.

Willis, S. L., & Schaie, K. W. (1994). Cognitive training in the normal elderly. In F. Forette, Y. Christen, & F. Boller (Eds.), *Plasticité*

cérébrale et stimulation cognitive (pp. 91–113). Paris: Foundation National de Gérontologie.

Yelon, S. (1992) M.A.S.S.: A model for producing transfer. *Performance Improvement Quarterly, 5,* 13–23.

Yesavage, J. A. (1990). Age-associated memory impairment: Conceptual background and treatment approaches. In *Challenges in aging: The 1990 Sandoz Lectures in gerontology.* (pp. 53–72). London: Academic Press.

Yesavage, J. A., Rose, T. L., & Bower, G. H. (1983). Interactive imagery and affective judgements improve face-name learning in the elderly. *Journal of Gerontology, 38,* 197–203.

Zarit, S., H., Cole, K. D., & Guider, R. L. (1981). Memory training strategies and subjective complaints of memory in the aged. *The Gerontologist, 21,* 158–164.

Five

The Genetics of Behavioral Aging

Gerald E. McClearn and George P. Vogler

The general topic of the genetics of behavioral aging has been addressed previously in several forums. Kallman and Jarvik summarized the field in 1959, as did Goodrick in 1978. Each of the previous editions of this handbook has included a discussion of the genetics of behavioral aging (McClearn & Foch, 1985; Omenn, 1977; Pedersen, 1996; Plomin & McClearn, 1990). Collectively, these papers, spanning nearly four decades, have presented the theoretical and logical bases for behavioral genetics research in general, and have provided a wide variety of illustrative applications specific to behavioral aging. During these years, there have been many changes in each of the parent disciplines of gerontology, psychology, and genetics. Of particular relevance to this presentation have been the recent developments in genetic science, about which adjectives such as revolutionary, explosive, or breathtaking seem to be necessary. This chapter will therefore not provide a detailed reiteration of the material that has previously been presented. We shall present an abbreviated review of basic genetic principles, together with selected examples, particularly of recent contributions, that illustrate the theoretical underpinnings of

the research venture, the methodologies employed, and the nature of the evidence concerning the genetics of behavioral aging. However, we shall concentrate on some recent developments, both empirical and theoretical, from genetics and from several other areas that provide new or enriched perspectives that should provide a foundation for interpretation of the current and rapidly forthcoming literature on the genetic and environmental origins of variability in behavioral aging. Together with some older examples that take on new significance in light of these recent developments, a picture emerges of the likely agenda, strategies, and tactics for future research in the area of gerontological genetics.

I. Genetic Perspectives on Aging: Basic Logic

As briefly sketched below, the various subdisciplines of genetics address different facets of the phenomena of aging.

A. Mendelian Genetics

Mendel's paradigm-establishing discoveries were based on studies of the distribution

Handbook of the Psychology of Aging

of categorically distinct traits or phenotypes in parents and offspring. The brilli-
ant hypothesis at the core of Mendelian
theory was that the hereditary material
was composed of paired elements, with
one member of each pair provided by the
mother and one by the father. These
elements may exist in different forms,
and the trait of an individual depended
upon what combination of these elements
it possessed. The "Mendelian rules"
pertained to the way in which these elements (at a considerably later date termed
genes) were singly parceled out into eggs
and sperm, to be paired anew in the offspring, and the rules that related the
phenotypic category of the offspring to
whether it had zero, one, or two of a
particular form (later to be termed *allele*)
of the particular gene.

Strictly speaking, no information concerning the physical nature of the genetic
material is necessary for the conduct of a
basic Mendelian analysis. Mendelian elements were hypothetical elements. However, when it became evident that genes
had a physical existence on the recently
discovered chromosomes within the nuclei of cells, new conceptual and methodological tools became available.

Mendelian genetics has been particularly successful in uncovering the etiology of medical disorders that result
from the action of a major gene (a single
gene that has a very strong influence on
the expression of a disease). There are over
11,000 entries catalogued in Online Mendelian Inheritance in Man (OMIM, 2000).
Major genes often exhibit a characteristic
pattern of expression. For example, a
major gene is recessive if two copies of a
particular allelic form are required for the
trait to be observed. A major gene is dominant if a single copy of the relevant allele
is sufficient for a trait to be expressed.
Other regular patterns of expression of
major genes can also be observed. The
mode of inheritance for a trait of major
gene etiology can be characterized using

the statistical tools of segregation analysis, which uses patterns of transmission
in large, multigenerational extended pedigrees (Elston & Stewart, 1971), nuclear
families (Morton & MacLean, 1974), a
combined approach (Lalouel, Rao, Morton, & Elston, 1983), or regressive models
developed by Bonney (1984, 1986). Together, these approaches provide a comprehensive set of tools for using patterns
of transmission to distinguish among
competing Mendelian models. Some also
provide a way to determine if familial
resemblance is consistent with a single-
gene Mendelian model in contrast to
multifactorial transmission due to many
genetic and environmental influences of
smaller effect.

Although segregation analysis permits
assessment of mode of transmission, it
does not provide information about the
identity of specific genes or their location
on specific chromosomes. A methodological breakthrough that permits the localization of genes on specific chromosomal
addresses is a tool called linkage analysis.
Linkage analysis (Ott, 1991) is a sophisticated statistical methodology that makes
it possible to locate a gene at a particular
site (or locus) on a particular chromosome
by relating variability in a trait to measurable variability in a fragment of DNA (the
fragment is called a *marker* and variability occurs as *polymorphisms* or multiple
forms of the alleles at the fragment). Because the marker is at a known chromosomal location, it is possible to infer the
presence of a functional gene for the trait
at or near the DNA marker. Libraries of
these markers have been developed so
that there are measurable markers distributed throughout the entire genome.
There are several classes of markers, including restriction fragment length polymorphisms (RFLPs, Lander & Botstein,
1989) in which the variability (polymorphism) consists of either presence or
absence of a particular precise DNA sequence that is cut by a restriction en-

zyme. Other classes of markers result from variability in the size of a DNA fragment that results from differences in the number of times that a short sequence of base pairs is repeated. A newer class of markers consists of DNA fragments that show differences in the sequence at a single nucleotide (single nucleotide polymorphisms). These markers have made it routinely possible to map specific loci to chromosomal regions using linkage analysis. Although many of the genetic influences related to behavior in aging are not Mendelian, this approach has been successfully applied to map a gene that has a major influence on Huntington's disease (Gusella et al., 1983) and is promising as a tool for specifying major gene influences on traits such as Alzheimer's disease.

B. Population Genetics

The field of population genetics pertains to the frequencies of different alleles in a population, to differences in allelic frequencies in different populations, and to the dynamics of the processes, such as mutation, selection, migration, and random "drift" that influence the rate and direction of changes in these frequencies (see, for example, Crow, 1986; Hartl & Clark, 1997; Roff, 1997; Roughgarden, 1996; Wallace, 1981). For present purposes, a major consideration from population genetics is the fact that the gene pools of different populations may differ in allelic frequencies sufficiently to impair the generalizability of results, concerning either genetic influence or environmental influence, from one population to another.

C. Quantitative Genetics

Genes that conform to Mendelian expectations are sometimes called "major" genes, in contrast to the genes of individually small influence that constitute the collective hereditary influence on continuously distributed phenotypes, as discussed below.

Extensive theoretical development has occurred in quantitative genetics over nearly a century. Summaries of this work are very accessible (e.g., Falconer & Mackay, 1996, and earlier editions; Lynch & Walsh, 1998). The basis of the quantitative genetic model is that variability in traits arises from the cumulative action of an indefinitely large number of influences of vanishingly small effect. Although geneticists have traditionally focused on genetic influences, environmental influences of individually small effect also contribute to variability in phenotypic expression. These influences result in a continuous phenotypic distribution on a quantitative scale that has theoretically well-described characteristics—most commonly a normal distribution describing the population variability and a multivariate normal distribution describing covariation among relatives. In reality, it takes a relatively small number of jointly acting influences, perhaps even fewer than 10, to produce a quantitative distribution that can be reasonably robustly characterized by such a theoretical distribution.

These types of distributions provide a theoretical underpinning to predictions regarding patterns of variation and covariation under a multifactorial model in both experimental and naturalistic studies. A wide assortment of sophisticated models has been developed to decompose the population phenotypic variance into its components. These models permit the distinction between genetic components and environmental components. Classical approaches in animal studies use patterns of means and variances in inbred strains and derived generations primarily to investigate polygenic influences (additive, dominant, and interaction effects). Classical approaches in human studies use models of covariance among relatives (twins, families, extended pedigrees, and adoptees) to investigate both genetic effects and, in some designs, cultural transmission effects (Cloninger, Rice, & Reich, 1979a, 1979b; Rice, Cloninger, & Reich, 1978). It is important to note that these models consider latent, unobserved components of variance that are not directly measurable, although a recent trend is to merge these approaches with gene-mapping studies to incorporate the effect of individual quantitative trait loci (QTLs; see below). There is no theoretical reason why such approaches cannot also be extended to incorporate the effect of individual environmental factors as well. The incorporation of measurable genetic and environmental influences into the quantitative model has the potential to ease some of the limitations of this approach regarding its ability to explore non-additive, interaction effects such as genotype-environment interaction and gene-gene interaction (epistasis).

The traditional description of this model as a quantitative genetic model is perhaps unfortunate. A more appropriate descriptor might be a "differential" model, given that genetic and environmental influences are explored simultaneously. It does not imply a competition of "nature versus nurture," but rather nature and nurture considered together in two-part harmony. This kind of influence is frequently observed in traits of significance in aging, such as cognitive function, memory, and chronic disease.

D. Molecular Genetics

As has been noted, both Mendelian genes and polygenes are hypothetical entities. Neither their physical nature nor the mechanisms through which their influence is exerted was known initially, nor was such information necessary to the development of the pertinent theories and methodologies. But gradually it became evident that genetic effects were expressed via the anatomy and physiology —the basic biology—of the organism. No special or mystical routes of genetic influence bypassing this basic biology needed to be invoked. Attempts to characterize the chemical nature of the gene metamorphosed into a truly paradigm-shifting domain, molecular genetics, which has come to dominate, and to permeate, modern life sciences.

In this new genetics, a locus was now definable in terms of DNA, allelic differences in terms of differences in the base sequences in the DNA, the allelic influence mediated through transcription from DNA to RNA, and translation from RNA into a protein, and thus into the biochemical, endocrinological, neurological, immunological, anatomical, (etc.) processes of the basic biology. (However, see Rosenberg [1985] for a discussion of the extent to which Mendelian genetics is reducible, in the philosophy-of-science meaning of the term, to molecular genetics.)

The term "causal field" (Mackie, 1974) (perhaps "influence field" for those with particular philosophical convictions about the meaning of causality) is convenient to represent the complex of physiological processes that constitute the pathways of influence from gene product to phenotype. A representation of the situation can be rendered as in Figure 5.1.

This schema identifies two broad classes of influence—genetic and environmental—on two phenotypes. The mediating causal routes from genes and environments to phenotypes are represented by a network of elements that display converging and diverging influences providing alternative pathways of influence with feedback relationships that render dubious unidirectional interpretations of causation. Collectively, these constitute the causal field. In addition to illustrating pleiotropy (the fanning out of influence from a given gene), polygeny (multiple factors; the influence of many genes on one phenotype), the route that

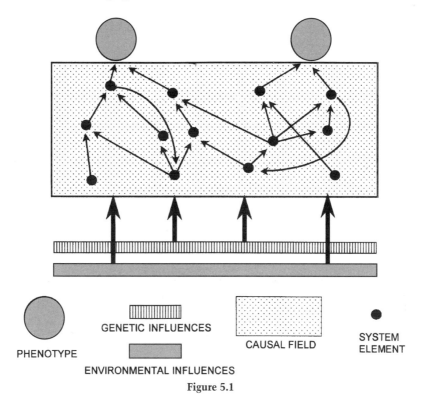

GENETIC INFLUENCES

CAUSAL FIELD

SYSTEM ELEMENT

PHENOTYPE

ENVIRONMENTAL INFLUENCES

Figure 5.1

can be traced from one phenotype through the causal network to the other phenotype rationalizes the source of genetic correlation. Of particular importance is the representation that genetic and environmental influences operate through the same causal field.

"Explanations" of individual differences in the phenotype in terms of the predecessor variables is essentially a reductionist strategy. If the explanatory variables are part of the causal field, as here defined, this effort is within the purview of the established physiological and anatomical sciences. Another tactic can overleap the causal field and relate the phenotype directly "back" to one or all of the elements of the central, molecular dogma: DNA, RNA, protein. A comprehensive explanatory trail will lead all the way from the DNA to the phenotype, and many different disciplines will be required for the enterprise. Beginning with

phenotypic differences and attempting to relate these to DNA (or to Mendelian genes) is sometimes rather awkwardly described as "forward genetics." The ability to characterize differences in the DNA per se has led to "backward genetics," which begins with the molecular differences and seeks to discover the phenotypic consequences. In this endeavor, proceeding from the molecular to the level of complex phenotypes, integrative issues arise, as will be discussed later.

The same causal field is the mediator of influence both of genetic and of environmental factors. It constitutes the arena in which genetic and environmental factors co-act and interact in the generation of the phenotype. Understanding that the genes operate through basic biological processes provides a counter to the early objections of critics of behavioral genetics that nothing as flexible, pliant, and adaptable as behavior could possibly be influenced by the fixed genotypes of individuals: the organ systems—nervous system, endocrine system, musculature, etc.—upon which behavioral flexibility is based are the very systems through which the genes' influence is exerted.

E. Developmental Genetics

The fledgling science of genetics in the early part of the century concentrated on understanding the rules of transmission of the genes from one generation to the next. An equally intriguing issue concerned the way in which the genetic information, however it was transmitted, engaged in developmental processes that eventuated in another adult organism. This latter became the subject matter of embryology, and a considerable rivalry emerged between these sibling disciplines (Keller, 1994). About mid-century, vigorous and ingenious efforts began to effect a merging both of Mendelian and of quantitative genetics with developmental science.

A memorable heuristic model of the time was that of Waddington's (1957) developmental landscape that incorporated a chronological dimension into a scheme that identified both genetic and environmental influences in developmental phenomena. The phenotype was represented as a ball rolling down an inclined terrain. Genetic factors were portrayed as agents determining features of the terrain (the depth of the valleys, the steepness of their walls, the location of points of divergence, and so on), and environmental factors were regarded as acting laterally on the phenotypic ball. The displaced phenotype would return to the developmental trajectory (valley floor) more or less rapidly depending upon the width of the valley floor, steepness of sides, etc., unless the displacement happened to occur just at a branching of the valley. In that case, one or the other trajectory would be followed thereafter. Individual

differences in alleles at pertinent loci affect the terrain differences that eventuate in differential developmental labilities and susceptibilities.

This conception provided a new perspective on phenomena typically modeled by notions of thresholds and critical periods; it captured the dynamic coaction and interaction of genetic and environmental factors, and is now recognized as a major early contribution to the sciences of complexity (Stein & Varela, 1993). With the Waddingtonian landscape in mind, the thoughtless conceptualization of genetics and environment as contraposed agencies is hard to maintain.

As molecular geneticists began to clarify the mechanisms of regulation of gene expression, the application to developmental processes were obvious, and the field of molecular developmental genetics burgeoned into its current status at the cutting-edge of molecular biology. The essential fact was that some genes can be turned on or off, in the sense that RNA may or may not be transcribed from the DNA, or that the amount of gene product can be up- or down-regulated. This fact, in principle, made comprehensible the role of genes in development. Just as environmental factors experienced by an organism change throughout the life course, different subsets of his or her genotype may be called into play at different stages.

Whereas developmental genetics has often focused on growth and development of the organism to adulthood, change over time that is related to the aging process is also a developmental process. Whether one views aging as an accumulation of random errors (Curtis, 1966) resulting in a change in random environmental influences over time, a progressive deterioration of homeostatic control and repair (Kirkwood, 1977), or the result of some other mechanism, the patterns of not only means but also the expected degree of similarity among classes of relatives (for example, parents and offspring, siblings, monozygotic twins, dizygotic twins, and other relative pairings) will show predictable patterns of change over time. One approach to quantitative modeling of aging as a dynamic process is through the application of time series methods. Eaves et al. (Eaves, Long, & Heath, 1986; Eaves, Hewitt, & Heath, 1988) developed a biometrical model of familial resemblance using time series theory to determine whether genetic and environmental influences are the same or different at different ages and whether there are differences in the relative accumulation of genetic and environmental influences at different ages. Change in homeostatic control mechanisms can result in changes in epistasis (in the case of gene control of homeostasis) or changes in sensitivity to the environment (genotype–environment interaction). Such changes will alter means, variances, and family correlations (Eaves, 1984; Eaves, Hewitt, Meyer, & Neale, 1990; Mather & Jinks, 1982). In theory, developmental patterns of means, variances, and correlations would provide insight into changes in underlying homeostatic mechanisms, although practical application of this approach in genetic epidemiology is limited by issues of power to detect epistasis and genotype–environment interactions in realistic samples.

F. Evolutionary Genetics

One of the fundamental issues concerning aging processes is their evolutionary origin. Indeed, it seems fair to say that all other perspectives on aging must ultimately be interpreted in the evolutionary context. Basic data of this approach to aging are differences among species in longevity or in other variables hypothesized to be consequences, covariates, or mechanisms of aging. Gerontology has been well served by the evolutionary perspective, which has been a rich source of theories and hypotheses of relevance to

the whole broad spectrum of the sciences of aging. This central area falls, however, outside the scope of this chapter, which concentrates on intraspecific genetics. There are many excellent accounts of evolutionary gerontology (see, for example, Arking, 1991; Finch, 1990; Rose, 1991) that can be consulted for details.

II. The Tools of Gerontological Genetics

Any of the theoretical perspectives or methodological tools of any of the genetic sciences can be brought to bear on one or another aspect of aging processes. Because so much of the information concerning aging behavioral phenotypes has been derived from twin studies in humans and from studies of inbred strains or selected lines of rodents, and because many of our examples concern these groups, the basic logic of these methods warrants brief review.

A. Inbred Strains

Inbred strains are the common currency of much biomedical research (Festing, 1979). Successive generations of mating of relatives (~ 20 generations in the case of matings of siblings, which is the usual case in rodents) from a genetically heterogeneous population will eventuate in a strain of animals of (very nearly) homogeneous genotype. The qualification refers to the facts that the approach to genetic uniformity is asymptotic, that selection can maintain heterozygosity at some few loci, and that mutational events can occur. But, as a useful approximation, all animals within an inbred strain have essentially the same genotype, except, of course, for the difference in sex chromosomes between males and females. Furthermore, at each genetic locus, the animals are homozygous (i.e., have two copies of the same allele). Because the inbreeding process involves a largely sto-chastic element in respect to which allele of those available in the heterogeneous parent population is "fixed" at each locus, another inbred strain will have a different characteristic overall genotype. Each strain thus provides a standard, re-peatable element comparable to a fixed environmental variable in an experiment. This stability of genotype is a powerful advantage, making possible the replica-tion of a fundamental property of the experimental animals in different labora-tories and at different times. Because of the inevitable genetic differences be-tween different inbred strains, a phenoty-pic difference between strains maintained under the same environmental circum-stances constitutes ipso facto evidence of genetic influence on the phenotype. Ob-servations made on generations derived by matings between the strains and among the strains and the derived genera-tions, such as F1s and F2s, can provide evidence concerning the proportions of variance due to the genetic differences (heritability) and to the environmental differences among individuals. The logic of these analyses is applicable even if the genes that differ between the strains re-main totally anonymous, as is usually the case.

A substantial body of literature on aging has been generated from studies of inbred strains of rats and mice. Festing (1979), for example, reviewed several stu-dies that, in the aggregate, assessed life span in over 24 inbred strains of mice. A huge range of life spans was identified. In 1981, the Committee on Animal Models for Research on Aging of the National Research Council surveyed the available data, which provided substantial concur-rence that a particular inbred strain of mice called C57BL/6J are relatively longer lived than many other strains. In part as a consequence of these results, the C57BL/6 has become a strain of choice in much gerontological research.

In respect to behavioral aging, there have been several studies that have as-sessed inbred strains of mice on batteries of various behavioral measures. Ingram (1990), for example, described compari-sons of another inbred strain, A/J, to C57BL/6J mice and to the F1 generation derived by mating the two strains over age ranges from about 5 months to 23–29 months on psychomotor measures of activity, balance beam, and tightrope per-formance, grip strength, exploratory beha-vior, and on maze learning. Animals of another mouse strain, CBA/HT6J, were also compared to C57BL/6 mice on the psychomotor measures. Dramatic strain differences were evident in many of these phenotypes. In this report, Ingram made an important distinction between the observations of strain differences in level of a phenotype, but with parallel trajectories across age, and cases of diver-gent or convergent trajectories. Genetic influence on rate of behavioral aging is clearly more evident in the latter case, as observed in rotorod performance and run-ning speed in the CBA/HT6J–C57BL/6J comparisons, and errors in a 14-unit T-maze and exploratory activity in the C57BL/6J–A/J (and F1) comparisons.

The results from these and other stu-dies are straightforward. The logic is sim-ple and the results are compelling: animals of different (though unspecified) genotypes differ in the rate and pattern of change with chronological age of a wide array of behavioral phenotypes. Such strain comparisons are powerful for de-tecting the presence of genetic influence, but not powerful for further characteriza-tion of the nature of that genetic influ-ence. It should be emphasized, however, that negative evidence—the lack of a sig-nificant phenotypic difference between compared strains—does not constitute evidence that there are no genes that can affect the phenotype. It simply means either that the particular strains com-pared did not differ at any relevant loci, or, more likely, that different combinations of alleles happened to produce similar phenotypic values.

The use of inbred strains and derived generations is not without its limitations. The same genetic uniformity of animals within strains that constitutes their principal merit is also their principal limitation. Any observation on the effect of a particular environmental manipulation, for example, may be idiosyncratic. However many animals of a strain are included in the design, only one genotype is represented from the indefinitely large number of uniform genotypes that could be generated by the inbreeding process. Generalizability of results from one strain is an empirical question, and cannot be assumed a priori. Furthermore, the lack of genetic variation limits any study that seeks to evaluate covariation between two phenotypes within a single strain.

Thus, for many purposes, other methods offer advantages. In particular, systematically derived and maintained genetically heterogeneous stocks have merit for correlational studies, as normative reference groups, for circumvention of generalization limitations, and as foundation stocks for selective breeding (Austad, 1993; McClearn, 1999; McClearn & Hofer, 1999; Miller et al., 1999). Because of the demonstrated power of this latter procedure in behavioral and biological research, it will be briefly outlined.

B. Selectively Bred Lines

Whether inbred strains will be useful for a research project depends upon the identification of one or more strains with phenotypic characteristics of interest. Selective breeding procedures, by contrast, permit the investigator to construct animal models to her or his phenotypic specification. The essential ingredient is a genetically heterogeneous stock displaying diversity in the phenotype of interest.

If animals of like extreme values for the phenotype are mated, and, if the variability is influenced to some extent by genes (i.e., has a nonzero heritability), then the offspring will display a mean phenotypic value that deviates from the mean of their parents' generation in the direction of the mean of their select parents. Depending upon the heritability and such matters as the number of polygenic loci that influence the phenotype and their dominance relationships, successive generations of such selection will result in the accumulation of increasing percentages of alleles influencing the trait in the desired direction and a phenotypic mean that changes to a plateau level. For research purposes, the selection is usually bidirectional, providing for an upward- and a downward-selected line. Certain genetic conclusions can be reached by the rate and symmetry of divergence of the "high" line and a "low" line; furthermore, the two lines provide powerful model systems for testing hypotheses concerning the causal field.

There have been several programs of selective breeding for postponed age in *Drosophila* (see review by Rose, 1991, for a review of this literature, including his own contributions). An example with some behavioral aspects was that of Arking (1987), who selected for increased longevity by propagating the selected strain by mating of "elite" survivors. Parents were those surviving and fertile after 75% of their generation had died. Substantial extension of median life span occurred by the ninth generation of selection, and it was nearly doubled after 25 generations. These lines have proven valuable for the study of biomarkers of aging, in addition to longevity per se (Arking & Wells, 1990). The chronological age was determined at which 50% of the animals could not meet specified criteria for fecundity, in vivo amino acid incorporation, metabolic rate, and two behavioral tests—positive phototaxis and negative geotaxis. Both the extended longevity strain and a control strain were examined. There was a characteristic order in which these functions were lost in both strains, with the behavioral performance loss presaging the rapid drop in the survival curve. The results were interpreted to indicate that, whatever the genes involved, their effect was to delay the onset of senescence.

C. Twin Studies

Twin studies have long been a tool in behavioral genetics. The basic logic of using twins is straightforward—since members of identical (monozygotic) twin pairs share 100% of their genes and fraternal (dizygotic) twin pairs share 50% of their genes, greater resemblance for monozygotic than dizygotic twins is consistent with genetic influences. If members of twin pairs are correlated but the magnitude of the correlation is not a function of zygosity, it implies that there are environmental influences on the trait that are shared by twins but no genetic influences. This approach can be applied to qualitative traits by looking at how often members of twin pairs have the same expressed form of the trait (concordance) in contrast to how often they have a different form of the trait (discordance). The approach is applied to quantitative traits by looking at the magnitude of twin-pair similarity using correlations or covariances. Highly sophisticated refinements of this method include the incorporation of models of development (Eaves et al., 1986, 1988) and latent variable growth (McArdle, 1986) and frailty models of survival data (e.g., Iachine et al., 1998). Twin studies are useful for studying a wide array of phenomena related to aging, including health-related traits. A key application of twin studies in behavioral genetics of aging is the study of change in cognitive performance because of its impact on issues of quality of life

and functionality. In a chapter on gerontological behaviora genetics in the last edition of the *Handbook of the Psychology of Aging*, Pedersen (1996) summarized heritability estimates and longitudinal quantitative genetic analyses from the key twin studies of aging. These include a subsample of 303 twin pairs aged 50 years or older in the longitudinal Swedish Adoption/Twin Study of Aging (SATSA; Pedersen, Friberg, Floderus-Myrhed, McClearn, & Plomin, 1984); 287 adult twin pairs aged 27 to 88 from the Minnesota Study of Adult Development and Aging (Finkel & McGue, 1993), and OCTO-Twin (Berg et al., 1992), which is a study of 351 pairs of Swedish twins aged 80 or older. Smaller studies and other twin registries that have followed twins that are now entering ages of gerontological interest are also described.

Results of analysis of heritability of cognitive abilities in older samples provide convincing evidence of fairly stable and substantial genetic influences on cognitive abilities. Overall, genetic influences on cognitive abilities appear to increase in adulthood, accounting for approximately half of the variance in childhood and adolescence and increasing to 80% in early and middle adulthood (McCartney, Harris, & Bernieri, 1990; McGue, Hirsch, & Lykken, 1993). Analysis of cross-sectional subsamples of young (27–49 years), middle-aged (50–64 years), and older (65–88 years) adults in the Minnesota and SATSA twins (Finkel, Pedersen, McGue, & McClearn, 1995) indicate that heritability remains quite high (81%) in younger and middle-aged adults and begins to drop (54%) for older adults. Heritability estimates from the OCTO-Twin sample of octogenarians confirms that heritability is reduced from the maximum to 62% for general cognitive ability (McClearn et al., 1997). Using cross-sequential methods of analysis of longitudinal and cross-sectional data of three measurement occasions separated by 3-

year intervals in the SATSA data, Finkel, Pedersen, Plomin, and McClearn (1998) confirm that heritability declines over the 6-year interval from about 80% to nearly 60%.

In general, the results of these longitudinal and cross-sectional analyses indicate that the relative importance of genetic influences is reduced from its maximum in older adults but still remains substantial. Thus even in the presence of generally declining heritability there remains general stability in the significance of genetic influences. As these cohorts are followed over the long-term, and information on mortality becomes available, it will be possible to test more sophisticated hypotheses regarding whether this stability and change is related to terminal decline (Berg, 1996).

III. Changing Perspectives

Here we wish to identify some of the fast-breaking news on the genetics scene that seems most likely to affect the way we view the role of genes in behavioral development and aging, and in the way in which future research will be conducted.

A. Individuation of Polygenes

The success in mapping the genomes of human beings and of various model species, including yeast, nematodes, fruit flies, and mice, has provided the opportunity to begin the localization and identification of some of the loci in polygenic systems. Although it is sometimes algebraically convenient to assume that the genes in a polygenic collective are of equal, small effect, it has long been appreciated that some of them might have a greater effect than others. Prior to the availability of the dense chromosome maps now in hand, the effort to locate these loci was almost prohibitive.

The search for these QTLs is now increasingly feasible and popular in various agricultural and biomedical genetic domains, including that of behavioral genetics.

Several methods are available for the search. One that has been applied to aging phenomena is the study of recombinant inbred strains (RIs). The first step in generating RIs is the mating of two different progenitor inbred strains to provide an F1 generation. These F1 individuals are mated to provide an F2 generation. Although the F1s, like their parents, are uniform genotypically, the alleles get shuffled during the generation of gametes by the F1s, and the F2s are thus genetically variable. If inbreeding is undertaken from this F2 population, the resulting (recombinant) inbred strains represent different combinations of the genetic differences originally existing between the progenitor strains. Several series of RIs have been generated, with the initial purpose of detecting major genes. As more and more chromosomal markers have been identified in the RIs, the power has grown rapidly to locate QTLs—with effect size too small to be found by Mendelian procedures, but of sufficient size to be associated with a chromosomal marker. Basically, each known marker is examined for a relationship to the phenotype. On average, for all loci for which the progenitor strains had different alleles, half of the RIs will have one allele, and the other half will have the other allele in homozygous state. A mean difference between these two groups suggests that there is, somewhere in the neighborhood of the marker, a locus that has an influence on the phenotype.

The RI–QTL method is being utilized in an increasing number of phenotypic areas. In respect to aging phenomena, it has yielded valuable results in three different model species: *C. elegans*, *D. melanogaster*, and the laboratory mouse.

A pioneering application of the RI–QTL approach to longevity was undertaken by

Gelman, Watson, Bronson, and Yunis (1988), who studied the life spans of female mice of 20 RI strains of the BXD series (derived from C57BL/6 and DBA/2 progenitor strains). Strain identity accounted for 29% of the variance in longevity, reflecting large intrastrain variability. Six QTLs, distributed over four chromosomes, were identified that influenced longevity. This same laboratory (de Haan, Gelmen, Watson, Yunis, & van Zant, 1998) later provided evidence for the existence of a QTL that, perhaps through affecting sensitivity to environmental factors, is related to within-strain variance. This phenomenon explored as "laxity of control" genes by Murphy and Trojak (1986) and as "variability" genes by Berg (1987), may be of considerable relevance to explorations of the frequent (but not invariable) increase in phenotypic variability in older individuals.

In *Drosophila*, Nuzhdin, Pasyukova, Dilda, Zeng, and Mackay (1997) identified five QTLs affecting life span. These QTLs account for 37 to 47% of the genetic variance between the progenitor strains. The effects were strongly sex-specific, with one marker accounting for about one-third of the genetic variance in females, whereas four different markers collectively account for nearly half of the genetic variance in males. Four of the QTLs were also age-specific. The female marker significantly affected mortality from days 4–12 and again at days 36 and 46; the effect of one of the male markers was detectable from days 26–36, another from days 28–34, and another from days 28–38. As the authors note, the genotype X sex interaction demonstrates that a genotype does not have the same effect in males and females, and the late age-specific QTLs support the mutation-accumulation theory of aging.

Ebert et al. (1993) compared elite agers of *Caenorhabditis elegans* (the last surviving 5% of the population of RIs) to young controls, and identified five chromosomal regions containing loci differing significantly in frequency between the groups. Longevity was evaluated under two environmental conditions, and four of the five loci were common to the two situations, suggesting some generalizability of genetic influence with respect to the environmental milieu.

The results of these studies give clear demonstration of the fruitfulness of exploring the polygenic architecture of longevity and offer a hint as to the type of phenomena to be described by several current programs of aging–QTL research that include behavioral measures.

There has been an explosion of methodological advances in recent years for individuation of polygenes in human studies. Sib pair QTL gene-mapping techniques are based on the approach developed by Haseman and Elston (1972). This capitalizes on the fact that siblings vary in the degree to which they share alleles at a locus identical-by-descent (IBD), which means the alleles in two siblings are identical because they have both been inherited from the same common ancestor. Sibs can share neither, one, or both alleles, and linkage between a quantitative trait and a marker is inferred if there is a relationship between the degree of similarity at the marker locus and the degree of similarity at a trait locus for members of sib pairs. Methodological refinements of this approach in recent years include maximum likelihood and variance component approaches, integration into more complex models of familial resemblance, multipoint mapping using more than one genetic marker, and integration of linkage and association methods (Almasy & Blangero, 1998; Amos, 1994; Fulker & Cherny, 1996; Fulker, Cherny, Sham, & Hewitt, 1999; Xu & Atchley, 1995). This approach has yet to be applied systematically to behavioral aging phenotypes, primarily because the sample sizes required to detect loci of modest impact are quite large.

A second class of QTL analysis that is increasingly employed involves association studies using candidate genes or tightly linked markers that are assumed to be in linkage disequilibrium with another nearby gene. Association can be detected using a simple case-control design for qualitative traits or a test of mean differences as a function of genotype for a quantitative trait (Risch & Merikangas, 1996). Because statistical association can arise for reasons unrelated to physical linkage between a marker and trait locus (Ewens & Spielman, 1995; Lander & Schork, 1994), within-family tests of association have been developed under the general name of transmission/disequilibrium tests (TDT). For aging-related traits, sibling-based tests are more appropriate than parent–offspring tests, because it is frequently difficult or impractical to obtain multigenerational data on aging-related phenotypes. Substantial developments of sibling-based TDT tests for quantitative traits have recently occurred (Abecasis, Cardon, & Cookson, 2000; Allison, Heo, Kaplan, & Martin, 1999; Fulker et al., 1999). These methods show great promise for individuation of polygenes for age-related traits.

A trait that has received substantial attention in the context of detecting specific genetic risk factors is Alzheimer's disease. Several findings in genetic studies are of note. In a population-based study in Rouen, France, *presenilin 1* and the *amyloid precursor protein* genes account for 71% of the early-onset autosomal dominant Alzheimer's disease cases (Campion et al., 1999). This study confirms findings that have been fairly consistent since key work identifying the roles of the amyloid precursor protein (Goate et al., 1991), *presenilin 1*, and *presenilin 2* (Levy-Lahad et al., 1995). However, the prevalence rates reported for early-onset Alzheimer's disease (defined as prior to age 60 or 65, depending on the investigator) and the autosomal dominant form indicate that these cases account for only a small percentage of the total. The picture for late-onset Alzheimer's is quite different. Linkage studies to the regions where *presenilin 1* and the *amyloid precursor protein* genes are located have been largely negative for late-onset cases. Instead, there is convincing evidence that the *apolipoprotein* E (APOE) gene influences late-onset cases (Saunders et al., 1993). There are three common allele forms for APOE (Utermann et al., 1980): $\varepsilon 3$ is the most common (77%), followed by $\varepsilon 4$ (15%), and $\varepsilon 2$ (8%), although the frequencies vary among human subpopulations. The $\varepsilon 4$ allele appears to result in increased risk for late-onset Alzheimer's disease and earlier age at onset (Corder et al., 1993). The $\varepsilon 2$ allele, in contrast, appears to confer a protective effect (Corder et al., 1994). The presence of $\varepsilon 4$ alleles can account for as many as 65% of late-onset cases with an additional 23% of cases resulting from absence of an $\varepsilon 2$ allele. These results appear to result both from APOE-related increases in plaque deposition and earlier onset of the histopathological process (Corder, Lannfelt, Bogdanovic, Fratiglioni, & Mori, 1998). Alzheimer's disease is an example of a trait that is most likely heterogeneous in etiology, with different causes among ethnic groups, presenting particular challenges for the detection of specific genetic (and nongenetic) influences.

B. Systems Perspectives

The "sciences of complexity" have undergone striking developments in recent decades. Many of these developments remain at a theoretical level, but applications are gradually permeating all variety of scientific disciplines. Here follow a few nontechnical considerations that concern the role of the contexts in which any given variable exerts an influence in a complex system.

1. The Genetics of Complex Developing Systems

Causal fields like those we propose to be mediating the influence of a gene or of a set of polygenes on a complex phenotype exhibit a number of features that have major implications for design and interpretation of studies in gerontological genetics. Such causal fields characteristically possess feedback processes and redundant pathways with cross-communication. The influence of any input variable, genetic or environmental, to such a system is, as a result, context-dependent. In brief, the effect size of allelic substitutions at a given locus can well depend upon the allelic constitution of other loci involved in the same metabolic pathway.

Self-construction is another attribute of many complex systems. Although the technical concept of a self-constructing system is far richer than that which will be discussed here, we note that the concept will likely provide a useful frame of interpretation for the new developmental genetics. An amazing view of the complexities of development has been provided by research on the development of *Drosophila*. Details being far beyond the scope of this presentation, this domain can here be represented only by the briefest glimpse.

The differentiation of the body form of *Drosophila* begins with a gradient within the egg of RNA from a gene named *bicoid*. This RNA is not derived from the corresponding DNA within the egg; it is instead provided by the mother during oogenesis. The RNA is concentrated in the anterior end of the egg, and the protein translated from it extends backward from the anterior end. Another maternally derived RNA, nanos, is concentrated at the posterior end of the egg. These and other maternal gene effects are at the top of a developmental hierarchy of genes of the zygote itself that affect

properties of the segments of the developing organism in subtle and complex interactions. For example, the bicoid protein stimulates the transcription of one of the egg's own genes, *hunchback* (named for the phenotypic effect of its mutation). The nanos protein has the function of repressing translation of the hunchback RNA into protein. As a consequence, the abdominal-structure permitting genes can be expressed. More than 25 maternal genes have been identified, 5 so-called "gap" genes (of which *hunchback* is one), 7 "pair-rule" genes, 11 "segment polarity" genes, and 7 "homoeotic" genes.

Although these examples do not bear directly upon aging processes, as usually defined, they present a strong heuristic picture of change in living systems. These are the sorts of complex interactions, serial and simultaneous, that we can expect to encounter throughout the life trajectory.

An example pertaining to the full life span is provided by the same organism. Rogina and Helfand (1995) measured the expression of a gene in *Drosophila* antennae. From no detectable activity at the time of hatching, the expression of this gene increases to a peak in early midlife, and then shows a subsequent decline. When the rearing temperature was raised above standard, the life span was reduced and the pattern of gene expression was scaled to the new life trajectory rather than to simple chronology. Similarly, in two studies involving flies possessing a life-shortening gene, the pattern was proportional to the shortened life span. The authors discuss the relevance of these results to the rate-of-living theory. For present purposes, the message is that we can expect the expression of some genes to be changing throughout the life course in a systematic manner. A veridical model of the genotype in aging thus cannot be static. The operational part of an individual's genotype will be changing from infancy through to senescence and death. Some genes presumably will be operating throughout the life; some may be turning on in mid- or late-life; others may be turning off. Still others may be cycling according to seasons, or to some biorhythm. And, of course, the particular pattern of change and stability of gene expression will differ in different cells, tissues, and organs.

An illustration from early development is provided by Cheverud et al. (1996), who observed two different sets of QTLs associated with mouse growth. One set exhibited diminishing influence by about 6 weeks of age; the influence of the other set became apparent during the interval from 3 to 6 weeks. In a behavioral example, McClearn, Tarantino, Hofer, Jones, and Plomin (1998) found that a mouse QTL on chromosome 15 that was associated with voluntary alcohol consumption in early adulthood (about 100 days of age) was not relevant to that phenotype in early midlife (at 300 days).

One often-cited attribute of complex developing systems is the tendency for change to occur by saltation. Such changes are the focus of catastrophe and chaos theory but, in some cases, may also be addressed by more familiar threshold or step-function models. As yet there are few data that merge genetic perspectives with those of nonlinear dynamic theories, but these processes may be of central importance in understanding the etiological and pathophysiological dynamics of late-onset disorders such as Parkinson's disease, Alzheimer's disease, Type II diabetes, and other diseases associated with advanced age.

Consideration of abrupt, step-function changes in aging processes also suggests the possibility of limitations to predictability from age to age. For example, in an aging process subject to chaotic bifurcation, because of the unpredictable (even though determined) nature of that event, it may well be that our capability of pre- diction of later-life phenomena from earlier phenomena is practicable only between bifurcation events.

2. Interactions

a. Gene/gene Interactions The basic observation of interactions among genes (epistasis) is that the effect of differences in genotype at one locus depends upon the allelic state at some other locus or loci. The prototype example is that of albinism, in which a particular genotype at the albino locus renders irrelevant any other pigment genes the individual may have. Such interactions can be understood to occur either as gene regulation, in which one locus influences the expression of another locus, or in terms of the interactions of the downstream metabolic products of the interacting genes in their shared causal field.

A plethora of examples exists of epistatic relationships at the molecular level of analysis of major genes and their immediate products. More pertinent to present purposes are data that show the importance of polygenic contexts. A classic example to illustrate the point is the demonstration by Coleman and Hummel (1975) that the pathophysiology, symptomatology, and prognosis of the condition resulting from homozygosity for the allele, *db*, at the *diabetes* locus in mouse differ strikingly depending upon the inbred strain in which the genotype occurs.

The capability of "knocking-out" genes is leading to many pertinent new examples of the importance of genetic context. Bowers et al. (1999) incapacitated a gene involved in production of a protein kinase enzyme that had been shown to have an influence on ethanol-related processes. On the genetic background on which the null mutant mice were generated (a mixture of C57BL/6J and 129/SvJ), the effect was decreased ethanol sensitivity and failure to develop chronic tolerance both in terms of sedative-hypnotic sensitivity and hypothermia. When transferred to the C57BL/6J background alone, both types of tolerance were restored, but when animals were outcrossed to another mixed (C57BL/6J X 129/SvEvTac) background, hypothermia tolerance was still present, but sedative effect tolerance was not.

This work clearly illustrates the methodological problem that gene-context sensitivity poses for characterizing the effect of single loci, but it also provides a powerful object lesson in respect to both animal model and human research: the impact of a gene may differ substantially in different populations that have differing allelic frequencies for loci that interact with the gene in question. A case in point may be the observation that the *ApoE ε4* allele has no or reduced risk implications for Alzheimer's disease in African (Osuntokun et al., 1995) and African-American populations (Sahota et al., 1997). Alternatively, these observations may reflect gene/environment interactions, as discussed next.

b. Gene–Environment Interactions A clear-cut example of gene–environment interaction in behavioral aging is provided by Ingram (1990), who found an age-related decline in activity under white light testing conditions in C57BL/6J but not in the A/J strains. Under dark conditions, both strains displayed the age-related decline.

In gerontological behavioral genetics, as in other gerontological areas, there has been a particular concern with animal models of cognitive functioning. An early demonstration of the dependence of the effect of polygenic differences on the environmental milieu was provided by Cooper and Zubek (1958), who examined the maze performance of rat lines selectively bred for maze-learning ability. Performance of animals from the "maze-bright" and "maze-dull" lines that had been reared in environmentally enriched or environmentally impoverished cage conditions was compared to that of animals reared "normally." The impact of environment is dramatic—the number of errors declined from the restricted to normal to enriched conditions. Under the normal condition (under which the strains were maintained during the program of selective breeding), the impact of genes is equally dramatic. But under either the impoverished or the enriched conditions, whatever genes that influenced the phenotypic difference shown in the normal condition were not now expressed phenotypically. As a capsule summary, the consequences of restriction did not appreciably impair the "maze-dull" rats, and enrichment did not much improve the "maze-bright" rats.

McGaugh and Cole (1965) investigated the influence of the specific environmental circumstances of the learning situation on performance of other strains in a Lashley III maze at two ages: 29–33 days and 142–164 days of age under conditions of hunger motivation and food reward. Half of the animals were tested under massed practice (30-sec intertrial interval) and half under distributed practice (30-min intertrial interval). Significant main effects were obtained for strain and interval, and age interacted significantly with sex, strain, and interval. At the younger age, the maze-bright animals were superior to the maze-dulls under distributed practice conditions, but there were no differences when practice was massed. Older bright males made fewer errors than did older dull males under massed practice, but not under distributed practice, and older females of the two strains did not differ under either condition. All older animals benefited from distribution of practice, however.

Sprott (1972) provided further evidence of gene–environment interaction in a different learning situation—passive-avoidance conditioning—in C57BL/6J and

DBA/2J strains and their F1. Animals were tested at about 5 weeks or at about 5 months of age. The intensity of the foot shock was varied systematically. An interesting interaction was observed: DBA/2J mice performed best at 5 months of age with foot shock of at least 0.1 ma., but at this age and under this condition, C57BL/6J mice performed poorly. At 5 weeks, and under the 0.1 ma. condition, C57BL/6J mice performed significantly better than the DBA/2J.

These results clearly implicate interactions between the anonymous polygenic differences between the selected lines and environment—a long-term developmental influence—in the first example and immediate environmental circumstances in the latter examples. Succinctly put, genetic differences are manifest in some environments but not others; equally, environmental influences are effective on some genotypes, but not others. This generalization has important implications for the search for, and implementation of, prevention and remediation (McClearn & Vogler, 1996).

A somewhat different and subtle relationship between genes and environment arises from the facts that an active organism can select from the array of environmental niches that are accessible to it, and that the selection of environment can be influenced by genetic factors. There are abundant illustrations of the latter from the active ecological genetic research area of microhabitat selection (see Powell, 1997, for review). Sokolowski et al. (1986), for example, described a relationship between genetically influenced activity levels and selection of pupation site in *Drosophila* larvae. In a similar vein, Cavener (1979) showed that *D. melanogaster* larvae with different genotypes affecting alcohol dehydrogenase activity display selective preference for environments with or without the presence of alcohol. A mammalian example with an aging dimension is provided by Wax and Goodrick

(1974), who found mouse strain differences in voluntary exposure to light via lever press, along with a variety of interactions of strain-by-illumination level, age-by-illumination level, and age-by-strain.

By suggestive extrapolation, one might consider a human being whose genotype promotes avidity for alcohol (this example is not intended to imply that environment has no role in this proclivity). The consumed alcohol is clearly a potent environmental factor, not only with an immediate effect on neuropsychological processes, but also resulting in metabolic and tissue tolerance, which processes undoubtedly involve enzymatic processes, and their predecessor gene expression processes. And these adjustments may in turn promote or facilitate further alcohol consumption.

This summary—organisms may choose particular subsets of the environmental features offered within any macrohabitat, and that choice may be influenced by the genotype—illustrates well the complexity and subtlety of the gene–environment relationship. In effect, genetic factors may influence the operative array of environmental circumstances; in turn, these environmental circumstances may have an influence on gene expression. This nonrecursivity constitutes a challenge to the linear analytical procedures that are the workaday tools of contemporary analysis of the genetic and environmental influences operating in complex developing systems.

A fitting conclusion to an exposition of gene–gene and gene–environment interaction possibilities is the work of Vieira and colleagues (2000). The longevity of *Drosophila* flies was measured in five different environments—a standard culture, one with elevated temperature, one with reduced temperature, one involving heat-shock, and one involving starvation stress. Seventeen QTLs were identified, and each of them displayed environment specificity, sex specificity, or both. Furthermore, in a quantitative genetic analysis, all of the genetic variation was found to be in the interactions of genotype with sex and environment.

IV. The Agenda

The perspective of the genotype that is emerging is a dynamic one, with some elements in continuous operation, but with others changing, some in response to programmed (or system) properties, some in response to environmental features and events. Some of the onsets and offsets of gene expression may be permanent, others transient; some changes may be slow, occurring once a lifetime, the timetable of others may be expressed in minutes. Characterizing the effects of this kaleidoscopic genome on behavioral aging will require some new research designs and new methods, and, most of all, new perspectives.

Prominent among the new perspectives will be the genetics of dynamics of nonlinear systems, such as the parameters of negative feedback homeostatic and homeorhetic systems, the contours of catastrophe surfaces (reminiscent of the Waddingtonian [1957] landscape) or the frequency and spacing of bifurcation events. It is clear that we need to squeeze as much as possible from our relatively tractable present linear models, but we must be prepared for the possibility that a significant fraction of the variability in any given phenomenon of interest will be due to nonlinear processes, and we must be likewise prepared with conceptualizations such as those cited, and we must be ready to appropriate or invent suitable research designs and analytical procedures.

Among the new tools that are available for the new agenda are those provided by the individuation of polygenes—either the loci themselves or QTLs. The mole-cular characterization of these loci is an obvious and enticing research direction. But the identification of these hereditary units also permits integrative research. The effects of genes can be studied in the specifiable context of other genes, and, in the case of animal model research, the relevant genes (either identified and characterized genes or QTLs) can be assembled to specification, offering unprecedented opportunities not only to describe the interactions of genes with genes and of genes with environments, but to explore the routes in the causal field that mediate these interactions.

A powerful tool for dealing with temporal changes in gene complexes has opened vistas unimaginable only a few years ago. Microarrays permit the assessment of the expression state of thousands of genes simultaneously. When this method, so recently astonishing but now becoming standard, is joined to the other methods, procedures, and perspectives that have been here but briefly sketched, our understanding of the complexities of the co-actions and interactions of genes and environment in affecting individuality in behavioral aging should grow exponentially.

Effective use of the dramatic advances in molecular genetics can be made only if they can be successfully incorporated into comprehensive analytical tools that accurately model complex behavioral processes in aging. "The genes" can only be sensibly interpreted when viewed within the context of the many other causal factors that operate and interact in complex systems.

The prospect of having measurable genetic influences for complex multifactorial traits is particularly exciting because it provides new opportunities to explore influences at a level that are vastly more complex than the overly simple models that are the limit of latent variable approaches. These new models are much more likely to be able to describe the true mechanism of action of multiple influences on a complex system than has previously been possible.

Equally exciting is the prospect of detecting and incorporating measurable effects of specific environmental influences into a comprehensive model. Geneticists, by and large, have focused on the exciting advances in genetics in recent years for gene mapping and identification. However, it is not reasonable to ignore nongenetic effects on complex traits. Genetic influences are likely to be complex and dynamic, with genes turning on and off in response to conditions of the system that are influenced by other genes and by environmental influences. As a result, true understanding of the influences that lead to a phenotype is likely to occur only in the context of a comprehensive model of interacting genetic and environmental influences. Gene expression technology is likely to provide further dramatic opportunities for model refinement by providing a means to quantify effects such as tissue specificity, developmental effects, genetic response to environmental agents, and so on.

The success of this integrated approach will lie in effective cross-communication between researchers who are expert in exploiting genetic information and those who are expert in environmental assessment. Clearly it will not be adequate simply to take a moderate sample, measure everything, and conduct a huge multiple regression analysis. Collaborative, large-scale data collection efforts will be essential to provide adequate power to detect small effects and especially to characterize interactions among small effects. Certain steps towards comprehensive integrated models can be taken rather rapidly with extensions to available technology. Some issues, however, will require innovative new ideas from a multidisciplinary perspective.

Acknowledgements

The cited examples from the authors' own work were supported variously by the Mac-Arthur Foundation Research Network on Successful Aging; NIA grants AG04948, AG09333, AG08861, AG04563, AG10175, and AG14731; NIAAA grant AA08125; NHLBI grant HL55976, and by funds from the Center for Developmental and Health Genetics.

References

Abecasis, G. R., Cardon, L. R., & Cookson, W. O. C. (2000). A general test of association for quantitative traits in nuclear families. *American Journal of Human Genetics, 66,* 279–292.

Allison, D. B., Heo, M., Kaplan, N., & Martin, E. R. (1999). Sibling-based tests of linkage and association for quantitative traits. *American Journal of Human Genetics, 64,* 1754–1764.

Almasy, L., & Blangero, J. (1998). Multipoint quantitative-trait linkage analysis in general pedigrees. *American Journal of Human Genetics, 62,* 1198–1211.

Amos, C. I. (1994). Robust variance-components approach for assessing genetic linkage in pedigrees. *American Journal of Human Genetics, 54,* 535–543.

Arking, R. (1987). Successful selection for increased longevity in Drosophila: analysis of the survival data and presentation of a hypothesis on the genetic regulation of longevity. *Experimental Gerontology, 22,* 199–220.

Arking, R. (1991). *Biology of aging.* Englewood Cliffs, NJ: Prentice Hall.

Arking, R., & Wells, R. A. (1990). Genetic alteration of normal aging processes is responsible for extended longevity in Drosophila. *Developmental Genetics, 11,* 141–148.

Austad, S. N. (1993). The comparative perspective and choice of animal models in aging research. *Aging* (Milano), 5, 259–267.

Berg, K. (1987). Genetics of coronary heart disease and its risk factors. In G. Bock & G. M. Collins (Eds.), *Molecular approaches to human polygenic disease* (pp. 14–33). Chichester, UK: John Wiley & Sons, Ltd.

Berg, S. (1996). Aging, behavior, and terminal decline. In J. E. Birren & K. W. Schaie (Eds.),

Handbook of the psychology of aging (4th ed.), (pp. 323–337). New York: Academic Press.

Berg, S., Johansson, B., Plomin, R., Ahern, F. M., Pedersen, N. L., & McClearn, G. E. (1992). Origins of variance in the old-old: The first presentation of the OCTO-Twin Study in Sweden. *Behavior Genetics, 22,* 708–709.

Bonney, G. E. (1984). On the statistical determination of major gene mechanisms in continuous human traits: Regressive models. *American Journal of Medical Genetics, 18,* 731–749.

Bonney, G. E. (1986). Regressive logistic models for familial and other binary traits. *Biometrics, 42,* 611–625.

Bowers, B. J., Owen, E. H., Collins, A. C., Abeliovich, A., Tonegawa, S., & Wehner, J. M. (1999). Decreased ethanol sensitivity and tolerance development in gamma-protein kinase C null mutant mice is dependent on genetic background. *Alcoholism: Clinical and Experimental Research, 23,* 387–397.

Campion, D., Dumanchin, C., Hannequin, D., Dubois, B., Belliard, S., Puel, M., Thomas-Anterion, C., Michon, A., Martin, C., Charbonnier, F., Raux, G., Camuzat, A., Penet, C., Mesnage, V., Martinez, M., Clerget-Darpoux, F., Brice, A., & Frebourg, T. (1999). Early-onset autosomal dominant Alzheimer Disease: Prevalence, genetic heterogeneity, and mutation spectrum. *American Journal of Human Genetics, 65,* 664–670.

Cavener, D. (1979). Preference for ethanol in *Drosophila melanogaster* associated with the alcohol dehydrogenase polymorphism. *Behavior Genetics, 9,* 359–365.

Cheverud, J. M., Routman, E. J., Duarte, F. A. M., van Swinderen, B., Cothran, K., & Perel, C. (1996). Quantitative trait loci for murine growth. *Genetics, 142,* 1305–1319.

Cloninger, C. R., Rice, J., & Reich, T. (1979a). Multifactorial inheritance with cultural transmission and assortative mating. II. A general model of combined polygenic and cultural inheritance. *American Journal of Human Genetics, 31,* 176–198.

Cloninger, C. R., Rice, J., & Reich, T. (1979b). Multifactorial inheritance with cultural transmission and assortative mating. III. Family structure and the analysis of separation

experiments. *American Journal of Human Genetics, 31,* 366–388.

Coleman, D. L., & Hummel, K. P. (1975). Influence of genetic background on the expression of mutations at the diabetes locus in the mouse. II. Studies on background modifiers. *Israeli Journal of Medical Science, 11,* 708–713.

Committee on Animal Models for Research on Aging (1981). *Mammalian models for research on aging.* Washington, DC: National Academy Press.

Cooper, R. M., & Zubek, J. P. (1958). Effects of enriched and restricted early environments on the learning ability of bright and dull rats. *Canadian Journal of Psychology, 12,* 159–164.

Corder, E. H., Saunders, A. M., Strittmatter, W. J., Wchmechel, D. E., Gaskell, P. C., Small, G. W., Roses, A. D., Haines, J. L., & Pericak-Vance, M. A. (1993). Gene dose of apolipoprotein E type 4 allele and the risk of Alzheimer's disease in late onset families. *Science, 261,* 921–923.

Corder, E. H., Saunders, A. M., Risch, N. J., Strittmatter, W. J., Schmechel, D. E., Gaskell, P. C. Jr., Rimmler, J. B., Locke, P. A., Conneally, P. M., Schmader, K. E., Small, G. W., Roses, A. D., Haines, J. L., & Pericak-Vance, M. A. (1994). Protective effect of apolipoprotein E type 2 allele for late onset Alzheimer disease. *Nature Genetics, 7,* 180–184.

Corder, E. H., Lannfelt, L., Bogdanovic, N., Fratiglioni, L., & Mori, H. (1998). The role of APOE polymorphisms in late-onset dementias. *Cell and Molecular Life Sciences, 54,* 928–934.

Crow, J. F. (1986). *Basic concepts in population, quantitative, and evolutionary genetics.* New York: W. H. Freeman and Co.

Curtis, H. J. (1966). *Biological mechanisms of aging.* Springfield, IL: C. C. Thomas.

de Haan, G., Gelman, R., Watson, A., Yunis, E., & van Zant, G. (1998). A putative gene causes variability in lifespan among genotypically identical mice. *Nature Genetics, 19,* 114–116.

Eaves, L. J. (1984). The resolution of genotype x environment interaction in segregation analysis of nuclear families. *Genetic Epidemiology, 1,* 215–228.

Eaves, L. J., Hewitt, J. K., & Heath, A. C. (1988). The quantitative study of developmental change: A model and its limitations. In B. S. Weir, E. J. Eisen, M. M. Goodman, & G. Nomkoong (Eds.), *The Second International Conference on Quantitative Genetics*. Sunderland, MA: Sinauer Associates.

Eaves, L. J., Hewitt, J. K., Meyer, J., & Neale, M. (1990). Approaches to quantitative genetic modeling of development and age-related changes. In M. E. Hahn, J. K. Hewitt, N. D. Henderson & R. Benno (Eds.), Developmental Behavior Genetics: Nueral, Biometrical, and Evolutionary Approaches (pp. 266–280). New York: Oxford University Press.

Eaves, L. J., Long, J., & Heath, A. C. (1986). A theory of developmental change in quantitative phenotypes applied to cognitive development. *Behavior Genetics, 16,* 143–162.

Ebert, R. H. 2nd, Cherkasova, V. A., Dennis, R. A., Wu, J. H., Ruggles, S., Perrin, T. E., & Shmookler Reis, R. J. (1993). Longevity-determining genes in Caenorhabditis elegans: chromosomal mapping of multiple noninteractive loci. Genetics, 135, 1003–1010.

Elston, R. C., & Stewart, J. (1971). A general model for the genetic analysis of pedigree data. *Human Heredity, 21,* 523–542.

Ewens, W. J., & Spielman, R. S. (1995). The transmission/disequilibrium test: History, subdivision, and admixture. *American Journal of Human Genetics, 57,* 455–464.

Falconer, D. C., & Mackay, T. F. C. (1996). *Introduction to quantitative genetics* (4th ed.). Harlow, UK: Longman.

Festing, M. F. W. (1979). *Inbred strains in biomedical research.* London: The Macmillan Press, Ltd.

Finch, C. E. (1990). *Longevity, senescence, and the genome.* Chicago: The University of Chicago Press.

Finkel, D., & McGue, M. (1993). The origins of individual differences in memory among the elderly: A behavior genetic analysis. *Psychology and Aging, 8,* 527–537.

Finkel, D., Pedersen, N. L., McGue, M., & McClearn, G. E. (1995). Heritability of cognitive abilities in adult twins: Comparison of Minnesota and Swedish data. *Behavior Genetics, 25,* 421–431.

Finkel, D., Pedersen, N. L., Plomin, R., & McClearn, G. E. (1998). Longitudinal and cross-sectional twin data on cognitive abilities in adulthood: The Swedish Adoption/Twin Study of Aging. *Developmental Psychology, 34,* 1400–1413.

Fulker, D. W., & Cherny, S. S. (1996). An improved multipoint sib-pair analysis of quantitative traits. *Behavior Genetics, 26,* 527–532.

Fulker, D. W., Cherny, S. S., Sham, P. C., & Hewitt, J. K. (1999). Combined linkage and association sib-pair analysis for quantitative traits. *American Journal of Human Genetics, 64,* 259–267.

Gelman, R., Watson, A., Bronson, R., & Yunis, E. (1988). Murine chromosomal regions correlated with longevity. *Genetics, 118,* 693–704.

Goate, A., Chartier-Harlin, M. C., Mullan, M., Brown, J., Crawford, F., Fidani, L., Giuffra, L., Haynes, A., Irving, N., James, L., et al. (1991). Segregation of a missense mutatin in the amyloid precursor protein gene with familial Alzheimer's disease. *Nature, 349,* 704–706.

Goodrick, C. L. (1978). *Behavior genetics and aging.* In E. L. Schneider (Ed.), *The genetics of aging* (pp. 403–415). New York: Plenum Press

Gusella, J. F., Wexler, N. S., Conneally, P. M., Naylor, S. L., Anderson, M. A., Tanzi, R. E., Watkins, P. C., Ottina, K., Wallace, M. R., & Sakaguchi, A. Y. (1983). A polymorphic DNA marker genetically linked to Huntington's disease. *Nature, 3–6,* 234–238.

Hartl, D. L., & Clark, A. G. (1997). *Principles of population genetics* (3rd ed.). Sunderland, MA: Sinauer Associates, Inc.

Haseman, J. K., & Elston, R. C. (1972). The investigation of linkage between a quantitative trait and a marker locus. *Behavior Genetics, 15,* 15–30.

Iachine, I. A., Holm, N. V., Harris, J. R., Begun, A. Z., Iachina, M. K., Laitinen, M., Kaprio, J., & Yashin, A. I. (1998). How heritable is individual susceptibility to death? The results of an analysis of survival data on Danish, Swedish and Finnish twins. *Twin Research, 1,* 196–205.

Ingram, D. K. (1990). Perspectives on genetic variability in behavioral aging of mice. In D. E. Harrison (Ed.), *Genetic effects on aging* II (pp. 205–231). Caldwell, NJ: The Telford press.

Kallmann, F. J., & Jarvik, L. (1959). Individual differences in constitution in genetic background. In J. E. Birren (Ed.), *Handbook of aging in the individual* (pp. 216–275). Chicago: University of Chicago Press.

Keller, E. F. (1994). Rethinking the meaning of genetic determinism. In G. B. Peterson (Ed.), *The Tanner Lectures on human values* (pp. 115–139). Salt Lake City: University of Utah Press.

Kirkwood, T. B. L. (1977). The evolution of ageing. *Nature, 270,* 301–304.

Lalouel, J. M., Rao, D. C., Morton, N. E., & Elston, R. C. (1983). A unified model for complex segregation analysis. *American Journal of Human Genetics, 35,* 816–826.

Lander, E. S., & Botstein, D. (1989). Mapping Mendelian factors underlying quantitative traits using RFLP linkage maps. *Genetics, 121,* 185–199.

Lander, E. S., & Schork, N. J. (1994). Genetic dissection of complex traits. *Science, 265,* 2037–2048.

Levy-Lahad, E., Wasco, W., Poorkaj, P., Romano, D. M., Oshima, J., Pettingell, W. H., Yu, C. E., Jondro, P. D., Schmidt, S. D., Wang, K., et al (1995). Candidate gene for the chromosome 1 familial Alzheimer's disease locus. *Science, 269,* 973–977.

Lynch, M., & Walsh, B. (1998). *Genetics and analysis of quantitative traits.* Sunderland, MA: Sinauer Associates.

Mackie, J. L. (1974). *The cement of the universe.* Oxford: Clarendon Press.

Mather, K., & Jinks, J. L. (1982). Biometrical Genetics: The Study of Continuous Variation (3rd ed.). London: Chapman and Hall.

McArdle, J. J. (1986). Latent variable growth within behavior genetic models. *Behavior Genetics, 16,* 163–200.

McCartney, K., Harris, M. J., & Bernieri, F. (1990). Growing up and growing apart: A developmental meta-analysis of twin studies. *Psychological Bulletin, 107,* 226–237.

McClearn, G. E. (1999). Commentary. Exotic mice as models for aging research: polemic and prospectus by R. Miller et al. *Neurobiology of Aging, 20,* 233–236.

McClearn, G. E., & Foch, T. T. (1985). Behavioral genetics. In J. Birren & K. W. Schaie (Eds.), Handbook of the Psychology of Aging (2nd ed.). New York: Van Nostrand Reinhold Co. (pp. 113–143).

McClearn, G. E., & Hofer, S. M. (1999). Genes as gerontological variables: Uses of geneti-

cally heterogeneous stocks. Neurobiology of Aging, 20, 147–156.

McClearn, G. E., Johansson, B., Berg, S., Pedersen, N. L., Ahern, F., Petrill, S. A., & Plomin, R. (1997). Substantial genetic influence on cognitive abilities in twins 80 or more years old. *Science, 276,* 1560–1563.

McClearn, G. E., Tarantino, L. M., Hofer, S. M., Jones, B., & Plomin, R. (1998). Developmental loss of effect of a chromosome 15 QTL on alcohol acceptance. Mammalian Genome, 9, 991–994.

McClearn, G. E., & Vogler, G. P. (1996). Genetics and behavioral medicine. Behavioral Medicine, 22, 93–102.

McGaugh, J. L., & Cole, J. M. (1965). Age and strain differences in the effect of distribution of practice on maze learning. Psychonomic Science, 2, 253–254.

McGue, M., Hirsch, B., & Lykken, D. T. (1993). Age and the self-perception of ability: A twin study analysis. *Psychology and Aging, 8,* 72–80.

Miller, R. A., Austad, S., Burke, D., Chrisp, C., Dysko, R., Galecki, Jackson, & Monnier, V. (1999). Exotic mice as models for aging research: polemic and prospectus. *Neurobiology of Aging, 20,* 217–231.

Morton, N. E., & MacLean, C. J. (1974). Analysis of family resemblance. III. Complex segregation analysis of quantitative traits. *American Journal of Human Genetics, 26,* 489–503.

Murphy, E. A., & Trojak, J. L. (1986). The genetics of quantifiable homeostasis: I. The general issues. *American Journal of Medical Genetics, 24,* 159–169.

Nuzhdin, S. V., Pasyukova, E. G., Dilda, C. L., Zeng, Z-B., & Mackay, T. F. C. (1997). Sex-specific quantitative trait loci affecting longevity in Drosophila melanogaster. *Proceedings of the National Academy of Sciences, 94,* 9734–9739.

Omenn, G. S. (1977). Behavior genetics. In J. E. Birren & K. W. Schaie (Eds.), *Handbook of the psychology of aging* (pp. 190–218). New York: Van Nostrand Reinhold.

Online Mendelian Inheritance in Man OMIM™, (2000). McKusick-Nathans Institute for Genetic Medicine, Johns Hopkins University (Baltimore, MD) and National Center for Biotechnology Information, National Library of Medicine (Bethesda, MD).

Available: http://www.ncbi.nlm.nih.gov/omim/

Osuntokun, B. O., Sahota, A., Ogunniyi, A. O., Gureje, O., Baiyewu, O., Adeyinka, A., Oluwole, S. O., Komolafe, O., Hall, K. S., Unverzagt, F. W., Jui, S. L., Yang, M., & Hendrie, H. C. (1995). Lack of an association between apolipoprotein E epsilon 4 and Alzheimer's disease in elderly Nigerians. *Annals of Neurology, 38*, 463–465.

Ott, J. (1991). *Analysis of human genetic linkage* (Rev. ed.). Baltimore, MD: Johns Hopkins University Press.

Pedersen, N. (1996). Gerontological behavior genetics. In J. E. Birren & K. W. Schaie (Eds.), *Handbook of the psychology of aging* (4th ed.). (pp. 59–77). San Diego: Academic Press.

Pedersen, N. L., Friberg, L., Floderus-Myrhed, B., McClearn, G. E., & Plomin, R. (1984). Swedish early separated twins: Identification and characterization. *Acta Geneticae Medicae et Gemellologiae, 33*, 243–250.

Plomin, R., & McClearn, G. E. (1990). Human behavioral genetics of aging. In J. E. Birren & K. W. Schaie (Eds.), *Handbook of the psychology of aging* (3rd ed.) (pp. 66–77). New York: Academic Press.

Powell, J. R. (1997). *Progress and prospects in evolutionary biology: The Drosophila model*. New York: Oxford University Press.

Rice, J., Cloninger, C. R., & Reich, T. (1978). Multifactorial inheritance with cultural transmission and assortative mating. I. Description and basic properties of the unitary model. *American Journal of Human Genetics, 30*, 618–643.

Risch, N. J., & Merikangas, K. (1996). The future of genetic studies of complex human diseases. *Science, 273*, 1516–1517.

Roff, D. A. (1997). *Evolutionary quantitative genetics*. New York: Chapman and Hall.

Rogina, B., & Helfand, S. L. (1995). Regulation of gene expression is linked to life span in adult Drosophila. *Genetics, 14*, 1043–1048.

Rose, M. R. (1991). *Evolutionary biology of aging*. New York: Oxford University Press.

Rosenberg, A. (1985). *The structure of biological science*. Cambridge: Cambridge University Press.

Roughgarden, J. (1996). *Theory of population genetics and evolutionary ecology*. Upper Saddle River: Prentice-Hall, Inc.

Sahota, A., Yang, M., Gao, S., Hui, S. L., Baiyewu, O., Gureje, O., Oluwole, S., Ogunniyi, A., Hall, K. S., & Hendrie, H. C. (1997). Apolipoprotein E-associated risk for Alzheimer's disease in the African-American population is genotype dependent. *Annals of Neurology, 42*, 659–661.

Saunders, A. M., Strittmatter, W. J., Schmechel, D., George-Hyslop, P. H., Pericak-Vance, M. A., Joo, S. H., Rosi, B. L., Gusella, J. F., Crapper-MacLachlan, D. R., Alberts, M. J. et al. (1993). Association of apolipoprotein E allele 4 with late-onset familial and sporadic Alzheimer's disease. *Neurology, 43*, 1467–1472.

Sokolowski, M. B., Bauer, S. J., Wai-Ping, V., Rodriguez, L., Wong, J. L., & Kent, C. (1986). Ecological genetics and behaviour of *Drosophila melanogaster* larvae in nature. *Animal Behavior, 34*, 403–408.

Sprott, R. L. (1972). Passive-avoidance conditioning in inbred mice: effects of shock intensity, age, and genotype. *Journal of Comparative and Physiological Psychology, 80*, 327–334.

Stein, W. E., & Varela, F. J. (1993). Thinking about biology: An introductory essay. In W. D. Stein & F. J. Varela (Eds.), *Thinking about biology* (pp. 1–13). Reading, MA: Addison-Wesley Publishing Company.

Utermann, G., Langenbeck, U., Beisiegel, U., & Weber, W. (1980). Genetics of the apolipoprotein E system in man. *American Journal of Human Genetics, 32*, 339–347.

Vieira, C., Pasyukova, E. G., Zeng, Z-B., Hackett, J. B., Lyman, R. F., & Mackay, T. F. C. (2000). Genotype-environment interaction for quantitative trait loci affecting life span in *Drosophila melanogaster*. *Genetics, 154*, 213–227.

Waddington, C. H. (1957). *The strategy of the genes*. New York: The Macmillan Company.

Wallace, B. (1981). *Basic population genetics*. New York: Columbia University Press.

Wax, T. M., & Goodrick, C. L. (1974). Voluntary exposure to light by young and aged albino and pigmented inbred mice as a function of light intensity. *Developmental Psychobiology, 8*, 297–303.

Xu, S., & Atchley, W. R. (1995). A random model approach to interval mapping of quantitative trait loci. *Genetics, 141*, 1189–1197.

Part Two

Biological and Social Influences on Behavior

Six

Aging and the Human Nervous System

Harry V. Vinters

I. Introduction

It is a question that has intrigued human beings since recorded time: Why do some people age well and others badly? Asked with specific reference to the brain and other components of the central nervous system (CNS), the query becomes, Why do some individuals retain normal or near normal mental, neurobehavioral, and motor capacities into advanced old age, whereas others slow down and develop senility, which we now recognize (most commonly) as senile dementia of the Alzheimer type (simply, Alzheimer's disease or AD)? The brain is unquestionably the primary regulatory organ of the body. The endocrine system is tightly regulated in large part by hypothalamic-releasing hormones, through their influence on the anterior pituitary gland. The regulation of respiration is influenced by brain functions determined at numerous anatomical levels, including the forebrain and all regions of the brain stem—so much so that specific breathing abnormalities can be empirically linked to structural lesions at these different sites (Plum & Posner, 1972). The gastrointestinal system is linked to the CNS by way of auto-

nomic ganglia within the gut, which in turn receive input from the spinal cord. Thus the effects of aging in the CNS can be disseminated into many other organ systems; *abnormal* aging probably affects visceral function indirectly in ways we do not yet even recognize. The CNS may play a greater role in somatic aging and survival than is currently appreciated. Slowing the aging process in the brain and spinal cord may therefore have beneficial consequences for end organs that receive CNS input (i.e., virtually every organ and and tissue in the body). As well, age-related abnormalities of the sensory system—especially blindness and deafness—that interfere with a clinician's ability to accurately evaluate cognitive and neurobehavioral function may create the *erroneous* impression of dementia in the very old (Hauw et al., 1986).

Since it came to be recognized as the major neuropathologic substrate of dementia in the mid-to late 1960s, AD has been studied as a model of CNS aging gone astray, especially because (as we shall discuss) virtually all of the microscopic lesions that accumulate dramatically in AD brain accumulate much less prominently in the normal aging CNS

Handbook of the Psychology of Aging

(i.e., the brains of individuals who are judged to be cognitively intact, even normal, until the time of death). Therefore the huge advances that have revolutionized our understanding of AD through the methodologies of cellular and experimental neuropathology, biochemistry, and molecular genetics have also taught us much about normal aging of the CNS. The most important lesson from this mountain of work may simply be this: although AD is extremely common in the ninth and tenth decades of life, it is not an *inevitable* consequence of growing old. A key theme of research on CNS aging therefore continues to be a search for the determinant(s) of healthy brain aging.

Human life expectancy has increased dramatically, even in this century, as a result of improvements in housing, public health, nutrition, and the successful treatment of many common infectious diseases. As a result, life span is now limited in large part by intrinsic senescence and its associated illnesses, two of the most common of which are vascular disease and AD (Kirkwood, 1996). This chapter will focus on basic mechanisms of cell aging as they may or may not apply to the CNS, briefly consider normal versus abnormal CNS aging, and finally discuss structural changes in the brain that appear to correlate with AD. The approach to examining morphologic correlates of brain senescence will be a cell biologic and morphologic one (i.e., alterations in neurons, synapses and neuropil, and blood vessels will be considered separately). Other forms of dementia will also be discussed, though only briefly, because AD is more common than these other entities combined, and is even more prevalent as a cause of dementia in advanced age. The author's goal is to build upon the excellent foundation laid in a comparable chapter in an earlier edition of this text (Scheibel, 1996), though

with a slightly different emphasis. Indeed, a direct quotation from another of Dr. Scheibel's articles seems highly appropriate at the introduction to this review: "The phenomenon of aging should be considered a part of a continuous developmental sequence commencing with embryogenesis and proceeding through a number of maturational phases during the life span of the organism" (Scheibel, 1992, p. 147).

II. Basic Principles of Cellular Aging

Much of the basic biological, genetic, and biochemical research on the cell biology of aging has been carried out on cultured human cells that originate outside the CNS (e.g., skin fibroblasts) or comparatively simple life forms such as yeast, *C. elegans* and *Drosophila* (Dimri & Campisi, 1994; Jazwinski, 1996). The field of biogerontology has now clearly come of age. Results of basic studies on aging suggest that there are multiple mechanisms, some genetically determined, by which this complex process takes place. In *C. elegans* a group of genes designated as *daf* plays an important role in the determination of longevity. Epigenetic effects during animal development and aging are also important determinants of how an organism grows old. Caloric restriction in animals is the only widely accepted method by which life span can be extended and senescence postponed (Jazwinski, 1996; Sohal & Weindruch, 1996), probably through its effect on lowering steady-state levels of oxidative stress and damage. Stress-associated oxidative damage may contribute to accelerated aging phenomena and age-related neurodegenerative diseases (for a review, see Liu & Mori, 1999). Moderate caloric restriction has been shown, in experimental animals, to attenuate age-related decreases in cerebral arteriolar density, interarteriolar anastomoses, and venular density—all of which appear to mediate cerebral blood flow (CBF) (Lynch et al., 1999).

Because senescent cells are blocked in the G1 phase of the cell cycle and are unable to reinitiate DNA synthesis, particular emphasis has been placed upon studying genes involved in regulation of this cycle (Smith & Pereira-Smith, 1996). Telomeres, regions of DNA that cap the tips of linear chromosomes, progressively shorten in somatic cells, to the point where the chromosomes become unstable and the cell incapable of further replication (Mera, 1998; Pardue & DeBaryshe, 1999). This telomere shortening appears to represent a determinant of *replicative senescence*, simply defined as any given somatic cell's finite capacity for division. The enzyme telomerase is capable of restoring telomere ends that are lost during cell division. Whereas most somatic cells have negligible telomerase activity, germ cells retain the enzyme and neoplastic cells acquire the ability to activate it, ensuring their immortality, though often to the detriment of the patient who harbors the neoplasm.

It remains to be determined how much of what has been learned about the phenomenology of aging from these simple systems applies to the human CNS. If a senescent cell is defined as one that is incapable of further DNA synthesis or self-replication, most neurons—even those within the brain of an infant—are postmitotic, therefore senescent, even though they must serve the organism for many decades in a terminally differentiated state. Why and how such cell bodies survive for years, then start to die in advanced age—more rapidly in some humans than others—is at present unknown, but probably is a key to understanding the pathogenesis of many neurodegenerative and dementing disorders. Although neurons are considered terminally differentiated postmitotic cells, however, there has been recent interest in the possibility that an aberrant attempt on the part of such cells to reenter the cell cycle may be a pivotal event in the pathogenesis of AD (Raina et al. 2000). The phenomenon of programmed cell death (apoptosis), by which cells implode or "commit suicide" through an orderly process of disassembly, avoiding an inflammatory reaction, is one that probably takes place in at least a subpopulation of aged neurons. Distinct from necrosis, apoptosis (which may take place through several distinctive pathways) is a complex process involving caspases, the tumor suppressor gene *p53*, *bcl*-2, and a variety of inhibitors (Barnes & MacKenzie, 1999; Sastry & Rao, 2000). Damage to DNA within the human brain can be demonstrated, even in the absence of typical apoptotic cytologic morphology, in aging and AD (Lucassen, Chung, Kamphorst, & Swaab, 1997). Antibodies to caspase-cleaved actin can detect apoptosis-related events in human autopsy brain specimens (Yang et al., 1998).

Mitochondrial abnormalities may play a yet to be defined role in brain aging. Since the existence of a mitochondrial genome (composed of mitochondrial DNA, mtDNA) was proven in the early 1990s, many severe metabolic disorders—some affecting the CNS but most involving skeletal muscle—have been shown to result from mutations in, or deletions of mtDNA (Kiechle, Kaul, & Farkas, 1996). How the progression of decades may impact on mitochondrial function in the context of CNS aging is not yet fully appreciated. Note below, however, a brief discussion of possible mitochondrial abnormalities that may figure in the development of (neuronal) neurofibrillary tangles.

III. Normal versus Abnormal Aging in the Human Central Nervous System

Studies on normal human brain aging have included clinical, neuropsychologic, morpho-anatomic or neuropathologic, and neurochemical investigations. More recently, neuroimaging (including metabolic) studies of the aging brain have been possible, given the rapid advances in our ability to gain a precise look into a person's CNS while he or she is still alive. The methodology of functional magnetic resonance imaging (fMRI) has taken on a key role in studying how the normal and diseased CNS works, and it is likely to become an invaluable tool in studies of brain aging (Prichard & Cummings, 1997). An important caveat, however, is that fMRI *infers* focal brain activity from parameters related to adjacent blood flow. Some experiments using this technique show that, depending on the specific task being performed, elderly adults may display *greater or lesser activity* in task-relevant brain regions when compared with younger adults (Grady & Craik, 2000). Recent studies suggest that fMRI used to measure patterns of brain activation during tasks requiring memory may predict a subsequent decline in this function for patients at genetic risk for developing AD (Bookheimer et al., 2000).

Excellent reviews of brain aging from both neuropathologic and functional perspectives have appeared (Creasey & Rapoport, 1985; Mrak, Griffin, & Graham, 1997). For practical purposes, abnormal brain aging can be defined as any disorder that leads to brain atrophy and nonphysiologic neuron loss; the most common of these is AD. Even in the absence of organic disease, brain weight (average normal is 1400 g for adult men, 1250 g for women) decreases gradually beyond the age of 60 yr, at a rate estimated to be 2–3 g/yr, largely due to tissue losses in the white matter, which are accentuated in the frontal lobes. Another measure of brain size, the ratio of brain: skull volume, is approximately 95% up to age 60 yr, then declines to 80% in people in their 90s. With advancing age, ventricular enlargement and widening of the sulci takes place. Mean ventricular volume (lateral and third ventricles) is 15 ml in teens, increasing to 55 ml in those over 60 yr of age. Cerebral hemispheric volume decreases progressively after the start of the third decade of life, at a more rapid rate in men than women (i.e., 3.5% per decade vs. 2% per decade). The initial volume decrease primarily involves cortical structures (Mrak et al., 1997). Many authors emphasize the variability of these age-related phenomena among individuals; many elderly subjects do not show either cortical atrophy or lateral ventricular enlargement (as measured using magnetic resonance imaging), suggesting that neither phenomenon is an inevitable consequence of aging (Coffey et al. 1992).

Assessments of age-associated changes (declines) in neuronal number and density that have been made historically, though certainly of archival value, may need to be reevaluated in view of modern cell-counting techniques. Currently, *unbiased stereology* is the most widely used technique employed to obtain estimates of numbers of neurons or nonneuronal cells in defined brain regions (Hyman, Gomez-Isla, & Irizarry, 1998; Coggeshall & Lekan, 1996; Long et al., 1998). Earlier studies have suggested that the widely accepted view of pronounced (cortical) neuron loss with normal aging was erroneous, in part because large neurons may simply shrink to become smaller ones, with overall negligible change in their total number (Terry, 1986). Aging appears to affect frontal and temporal lobes more than parietal, and glia appear to increase with age (Terry, DeTeresa, & Hansen, 1987). In select specialized regions of the brain (e.g., Ammon's horn or hippocampus), the granule cell layer may retain its normal neuronal number over decades, and may actually show some proliferative potential even in advanced age. Changes in neocortical synaptic density with advancing age have also been documented, initially by ultrastructural study (Huttenlocher, 1979; Gibson, 1983) and more recently by quantitative immunohistochemistry employing sensitive primary antibodies to synapse-specific proteins such as synaptophysin, a calcium-binding glycoprotein situated in the membranes of small presynaptic vesicles (Masliah, Terry, DeTeresa, & Hansen, 1989). Several studies using a variety of techniques have shown that there is a profound and widespread loss of neocortical synapses in AD (up to 50% decrease vs. age-matched controls) and other neurodegenerative disorders such as Pick disease (Masliah et al, 1989; Scheff, DeKosky, & Price, 1990). Furthermore, loss of synapses in AD appears to be out of proportion to loss of neuronal cell bodies, and has been implicated as the physical basis of cognitive impairment in AD (Davies, Mann, Sumpter & Yates, 1987; Terry et al., 1991).

Of potentially greater interest than age-associated loss of synapses is the possible selective loss of one or more neurotransmitters and/or their receptors. Increasing age brings with it loss of choline acetyltransferase (ChAT) and muscarinic binding sites. The dopamine system is affected, with documented declines in levels of striatal dopamine uptake sites, transporters, and levels of the transmitter itself (Mrak et al., 1997); extreme dopamine loss (together with accumulation of Lewy bodies within pigmented brain stem neurons of the substantia nigra and locus ceruleus) is associated with Parkinson disease (Figure 6.1). (Ellison et al., 1998; Vinters, Farrell, Mischel, & Anders,

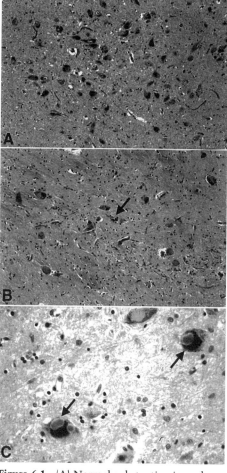

Figure 6.1 (A) Normal substantia nigra, showing pigmented neurons containing abundant cytoplasmic neuromelanin. (B) Substantia nigra from a patient with severe Parkinson's disease. Note striking loss of pigmented neurons; many of the small cells in the neuropil represent reactive astrocytes. Note also foci of pigment incontinence (arrow, panel B), visualized as neuromelanin in the neuropil remaining after cell bodies have disappeared. (C) Cytoplasmic Lewy bodies (arrows) in residual pigmented neurons. In this and subsequent micrographs, sections have been stained with hematoxylin and eosin *unless* otherwise indicated.

1998). Binding sites and/or receptors for serotonin, adrenergic transmitters, and gamma aminobutyric acid (GABA) all decline with normal aging.

AD, to be considered in detail below, is characterized by accumulation within the CNS of characteristic microscopic lesions, including senile plaques, neurofibrillary tangles, and amyloid (congophilic) angiopathy, these will be discussed and described in detail. There is ongoing debate as to which of these lesions—if any!—when present in excess in the aging cortex, correlates best with the cognitive decline of AD. This debate began with the landmark comparison, in the late 1960s and early 1970s, of structural features of brains from patients with carefully documented dementia versus those without dementia (Tomlinson, Blessed, & Roth, 1968, 1970), but it continues robustly to the present day. Centers that have expertise in the study of patients with AD have turned their attention, in many cases, to examination of the oldest old who age well, with negligible or minimal neuropsychological impairment into the ninth and tenth decades of life. One such study has demonstrated an increasing burden of senile plaques and neurofibrillary tangles in those who manifest cognitive decline but appear not to be functionally impaired, and do not meet criteria for dementia (Green, Kaye, & Ball, 2000), suggesting that AD lesions, even when not especially numerous, may represent something other than benign senescent changes. Others who have examined neuropathological and neuropsychological changes in normal aging also find evidence for preclinical AD in cognitively normal patients as old as 105 yr (Hulette et al., 1998). On the other hand, senile plaques, especially of the diffuse type, are often found within surgical resection specimens of middle-aged patients undergoing temporal lobectomy for intractable seizure disorder. When such patients are followed over several years, they have shown negligible evidence of cognitive deterioration (Mackenzie, McLachlan, Kubu & Miller, 1996).

IV. Microscopic Central Nervous System Lesions Associated with Aging

A. Changes in Nerve Cell Bodies and Their Processes, Neuropil

Simple inspection of a histologic section of human cerebral neocortex in any individual (free of neurologic disease) over the age of 12–13 yr does not provide specific clues as to the age of the person from which the specimen originated. Subtle accumulation of aging pigments and a variety of nuclear or cytoplasmic inclusions occurs with the passage of years, but appears not to be associated with clinically apparent neurologic disease. Lipofuscin, a poorly soluble intracellular pigment that accumulates within secondary lysosomes of neurons and other postmitotic cells, becomes especially prominent within the cytoplasm of nerve cell bodies of the cranial nerve motor nuclei and spinal cord anterior horn cells, thalamus, globus pallidus, inferior olivary nuclei of the medulla oblongata, and dentate nuclei of the cerebellum. Corpora amylacea, round prominently basophilic structures 5–20 μm in diameter, become more conspicuous with advancing age, especially at subpial and subependymal locations (Figure 6.2) throughout the brain. Marinesco bodies are small oval or round glassy eosinophilic intranuclear structures that appear in the late 20s and 30s and are more commonly found in elderly patients, but have no known disease association (Mrak et al., 1997).

1. Neurofibrillary Tangles

These intraneuronal lesions are visible on routine (H & E-stained) sections of brain—especially hippocampus or neocortex—but are much more easily visualized using silver stains, especially the modified Bielschowsky or Gallyas techniques (Figure 6.3) or immunohistochemical

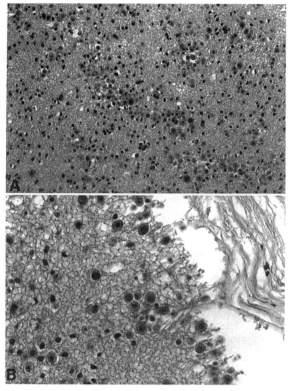

Figure 6.2 Corporal amylacea are round or oval basophilic structures (sometimes referred to as *brain sand*) most commonly found at pial and ependymal interfaces. (A) intermediate magnification, (B) higher magnification in a subpial location. They are of unknown, but probably minimal, neuropathologic significance, but are often found in the brains of elderly patients. (Magnifications A ×220, B ×435).

methods using appropriate primary antibodies. Because they are composed, like other amyloids, of beta-pleated protein sheets, neurobrillary tangles (NFT) can also be highlighted with a Congo red-gallocyanin method, using polarized light (Ball, 1978). Small to moderate numbers of these lesions may be seen within the hippocampi of brains from neurologically normal elderly, and it has been suggested that a few NFTs may even be present in the neocortex (especially the temporal lobes) of elderly (75 yr and older) nondemented persons, and sometimes even younger individuals (Mann, Tucker, & Yates, 1987). Beyond the mid-70s, NFT appear to increase in concentration or density exponentially (Price & Morris, 1999). Ultrastructurally, NFT are composed of bifilar helices or paired helical filaments (PHFs), twisted ribbon-like structures that represent two protofilaments wrapped around each other with a periodic crossover every 80 nm, and a variable width of 8–20 nm (Vinters, 1998; Vinters et al., 1994). Immunohistochemically, NFT can be labeled with antibodies to the microtubule-associated protein tau, ubiquitin, and amyloid P component (Duong, Doucette, Zidenberg, Jacobs, & Scheibel, 1993; Duong & Gallagher, 1994). Indeed, tau has long been known to be a major component of the PHFs within NFT (Grundke-Iqbal et al.,

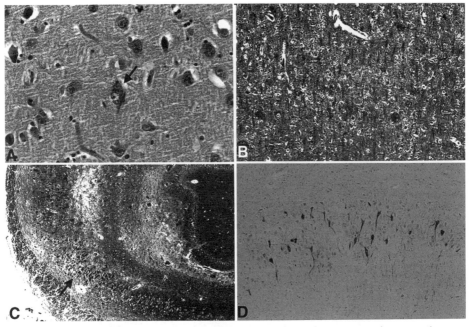

Figure 6.3 Neurofibrillary tangles (NFTs). (A) Hematoxylin and eosin-stained section showing faintly fibrillar cytoplasmic material (NFT, arrow) in some neurons. (B) Bielschowsky-stained histologic section from cortex of a patient with NFT-predominant Alzheimer's disease (AD), (i.e., there were relatively few senile plaques within the cortex by comparison to high density of NFTs). (C) Hippocampus from the same patient as illustrated in (B), also stained with the Bielschowsky technique. Note that virtually all neurons in the CA1 sector of hippocampus (arrow) contain NFTs. (D) Tau-immunostained section from hippocampus of a patient with AD, showing prominent immunoreactivity of many NFTs. (magnifications A ×435, B ×110, C ×45.)

1986), and excessive or abnormal (hyper-) phosphorylation of tau may be a pivotal event in the transformation of normal adult tau into PHF-tau in the course of evolution of AD brain changes (Matsuo et al., 1994).

Various investigations have sought structural or functional correlates of NFT development within neuronal cell bodies. Early stages of NFT formation may occur in a subpopulation of comparatively healthy neurons, but NFT progression appears to be accompanied by increasing neuronal morbidity, as measured using the TUNEL assay for (neuronal) DNA damage (Sheng, Mrak, & Griffin, 1998). Loss of alpha-amino-3-hydroxy-5-methyl-4-isoxazole propionate (AMPA) glutamate receptor subunits, GluR2(3) (evaluated immunohistochemically) appears to

precede the formation of NFTs within neuronal cell bodies (Ikonomovic, Mizukami, Davies, Hamilton, Sheffield, & Armstrong, 1997). Declines in neuronal activity, as inferred by examining intraneuronal markers of mitochondrial energy metabolism, are noted in early stages of NFT formation (Hatanpää, Brady, Stoll, Rapoport, & Chandrasekaran, 1996).

2. Granulovacuolar Degeneration

Granulovacular degeneration (GVD) might appropriately be regarded as the forgotten lesion of AD and brain aging; since the discovery in 1984 of Abeta protein and increasing recognition of its contribution to the evolution and structural integrity of senile plaques and amyloid angiopathy (see below), molecular studies have focused on trying to define the role of Abeta (as well as that of neuronal tau) in brain aging and AD. GVD neurons show evidence of neither cytoplasmic Abeta nor NFT-like cytoskeletal abnormalities, and are anatomically more circumscribed than the other microscopic lesions that define AD. A cellular lesion that is almost always confined to the hippocampus and (less often, especially in the Pick type of frontotemporal dementia) deep central grey matter nuclei, GVD imparts a characteristic appearance to involved neurons. As the descriptor suggests, the cytoplasm of affected cells becomes distended by vacuoles that contain small basophilic granules, which can be immunolabeled with antibodies to ubiquitin and may represent breakdown products of tau protein (Figure 6.4) (Ellison et al., 1998). In AD, both NFT and GVD have been shown to increase in number in hippocampal subfields in a stereotypical fashion, the subiculum and CA1/H1 segments having an apparent predilection for development of neurons manifesting GVD (Ball, 1978).

3. Senile Plaques

The pathogenesis of these enigmatic lesions is inextricably linked to an understanding of how Abeta protein comes to be deposited within the brain (Hardy & Higgins, 1992; Hendriks & van Broeckhoven, 1996; Maury, 1995; Selkoe, 1994; Vinters, Wang, & Secor, 1996). Excellent reviews on the subject of senile plagues (SPs) have recently appeared (Dickson, 1997; Verbeek, Eikelenboom & de Waal, 1997). SPs are recognized in human brain using the modified Bielschowsky, Campbell-Switzer, or other silver stains. Because their protein components are now fairly well understood, they can be decorated immunohistochemically using various primary antibodies, especially those directed against Abeta (Delaère, Duyckaerts, He, Piette, & Hauw, 1991; Dickson, 1997; Mak, Yang, Vinters, Frautschy, & Cole, 1994; Mann, Jones, Prinja, & Purkiss, 1990; Yamaguchi, Hirai, Morimatsu, Shoji, & Ihara, 1988) (Figure 6.5). SPs may be subdivided into the diffuse type (dSP), probably an early manifestation of Abeta deposition in the neuropil and arguably the earliest event in the cellular pathogenesis of AD. Mature or neuritic SPs (ntSP) appear as tufts of argyrophilic material within the neuropil, often centered on a core of amyloid (Figure 6.5). It has been hypothesized (Dickson, 1997) that SPs originate in neuropil as diffuse neurocentric amyloid deposits possibly composed of P3, comprising amino acids

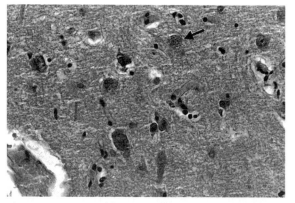

Figure 6.4 Scattered hippocampal neurons from a patient with Alzheimer's disease show granulovacuolar degeneration (e.g., arrow) (magnification ×435).

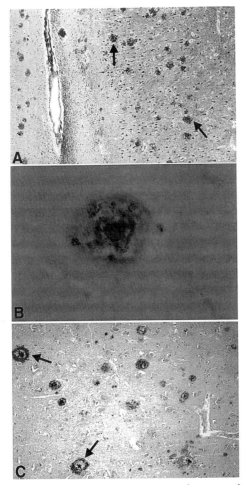

Figure 6.5 (A) Bielschowsky-stained section of cortex from an Alzheimer's disease (AD) patient shows numerous tuft-like globules of argentophilic material (e.g., arrows) (i.e., neuritic senile plaques). (B) Magnified view of an SP showing dense amyloid core, surrounded by neurites. Silver stain. (C) Histologic section of AD brain immunostained with antibodies to Abeta protein. Note numerous plaque-like Abeta-immunoreactive deposits (e.g., arrows).

results in preamyloid localization within cerebral cortex.

The *presence* of SPs within (temporal) neocortex correlates strongly with patient age, though surprisingly neither the mean nor maximum SP *density* shows any increase with advancing age in large autopsy studies of neurologically intact adults (Mackenzie, 1994). The density of ntSP also does *not* show a significant increase with age in this same patient population, though the *proportion* of ntSP does.

For as yet unclear reasons that may include disease-specific metabolic imbalance(s) within neuroglial elements, in AD there occurs also a subsequent deposition within the neuropil of a 42-amino acid cleavage product of APP (Abeta 1–42) through the endosomal-lysosomal, amyloidogenic pathway. These focal deposits may represent sites on which additional amyloid is deposited, by a process with precisely defined and regulated physicochemical parameters (Esler et al., 1996, 1999; Maggio et al., 1992). The larger Abeta proteins, though apparently not P3, contain motifs or domains that permit binding and activation of complement and facilitate the process of glycation; the latter leads to nonenzymatic modification of long-lived proteins. The ensuing pathogenetic cascade is thought to involve local recruitment of microglia, which may secrete compounds that are neurotoxic, including excitatory amino acids, proteases, interleukins, and tumor necrosis factor-alpha. Microglia may also have important phagocytic functions that include *removal* and processing of brain amyloid, as well as the transformation of insoluble Abeta into amyloid fibrils (Kalaria, 1999; Mackenzie, Hao, & Munoz, 1995). Astrocytic hypertrophy and proliferation (gliosis) may follow, and these astrocytes are capable of releasing cytokines and nitric oxide (NO) as well as factors that can lead to additional microglial activation and proliferation, perpetuating a vicious cycle of brain injury that affects

17–42 of Abeta. P3 originates from the amyloid precursor protein (APP), a large membrane-spanning protein encoded by a gene on chromosome 21, by way of the secretory or *non* amyloidogenic pathway. Many neuropathologists consider deposition of this peptide in diffuse plaque-like structures as a largely benign process that

both axons and dendrites. This damage to neuronal processes results in their degeneration, visualized within silver-stained brain sections as the prominently argyrophilic neurites of ntSP. SP neurites may also be immunoreactive for ubiquitin (a proteolysis-related peptide) and, on ultrastuctural examination, show degenerating synaptic elements including lysosomal dense bodies and membranous lamellar components, and PHFs—the latter described above as major components of NFTs. Not surprisingly, excessive accumulation of neocortical ntSP (rather than simply dSP) has been thought to correlate with the clinical manifestations of AD (Blessed, Tomlinson, & Roth, 1968; Dickson, 1997). However, large numbers of dSPs (and even ntSPs) may be seen at autopsy in the brains of elderly patients judged to be cognitively normal as recently as a few days or weeks prior to death (Price & Morris, 1999).

4. Dendritic Abnormalities

Quantitative evaluation of dendritic spine abnormalities within neuropil is possible using Golgi impregnation techniques, which have—despite their limitations—been exploited in numerous investigations aimed at understanding dendritic loss and plasticity as a function of aging (Jacobs & Scheibel, 1993). The dendritic arbors of nerve cell bodies are said to constitute 80–95% of the total synaptic receptive surface area of each neuron, not surprising given the role of dendritic connections in maintenance of the structural and functional integrity of the CNS (Scheibel, 1992). It appears that the number of synaptic terminals present in a given neuronal soma-dendrite unit varies markedly with location, age of the organism, and possibly the intensity or frequency with which a neural system is utilized during life. Dendritic growth starts just after neurons have positioned themselves appropriately in the CNS dur-

ing intrauterine life, continues through puberty, and slows during maturity. Dendritic regression occurs in the eigth decade of life, though experimental evidence suggests some retention of dendritic plasticity (in response to environmental stimuli) into old age.

It is unclear how much dendritic loss must occur before it manifests as an individual's showing psychosocial, neurobehavioral, or cognitive impairment. Dendritic alterations and loss imply functional changes in a nerve cell body, not necessarily its imminent death (Scheibel, 1992, 1996). Quantitative investigations of dendritic neuropil within cytoarchitecturally defined cortical regions (e.g., Wernicke's) as a function of normal aging in humans have shown that there is clearly dendritic degeneration that takes place as a function of aging (Jacobs & Scheibel, 1993). This important study, carried out on selected neurons from patients in the age range of 18–79 years, showed decreases in both total and mean dendritic length. As well, interhemispheric dendritic asymmetries appeared to decrease with age, patients under the age of 50 years having significantly greater total dendritic lengths within the left cerebral hemisphere.

B. Changes in Blood Vessels

Cerebrovascular disease resulting in stroke is, together with AD, the most common brain affliction of the elderly (Vinters, 2000). Whereas the former results in devastation diffusely throughout much of the neocortex and hippocampal formation, the latter can produce well-defined regions of brain injury or necrosis (encephalomalacia) or brain hemorrhage. Stroke represents the third leading cause of death in industrialized nations, with an incidence that increases from approximately 100 per 100,000 for individuals of age 45–54 years, to 1800 per 100,000 for those over 85 years of age (Ellison et al.,

1998). In North America, ischemic brain infarcts are about ten times more frequent than hemorrhages as a presentation of stroke, whereas in the Orient spontaneous intracranial bleeding occurs almost as often as cerebral infarcts. A detailed discussion of the pathogenesis of stroke in the elderly is well beyond the scope of this chapter. However, certain vasculopathies that are common—and often clinically important—in the elderly merit brief consideration.

Atherosclerosis of the cervical arteries that supply blood to the brain is arguably the most common cause of ischemic brain infarcts in the geriatric population (Barnett, Mohr, Stein, & Yatsu, 1998). It is a systemic disease of epidemic proportions in developed nations that may affect the CNS or any other organ, especially the heart (to produce myocardial infarct). Advances in cell and molecular biological techniques over the past 25–30 years have led to a detailed understanding of its pathogenesis; though medication and lifestyle alterations (e.g., exercise, cessation of smoking cigarettes, lowering of serum lipids) can alter the progression of atheroma (the physical manifestation of atherosclerosis within arteries), the disease remains a huge clinical problem (Ross, 1993, 1999).

Small vessels (primarily arterioles and capillaries) in the basal ganglia, especially the globus pallidus, often develop deposits of calcium and iron in their walls, together with punctate calcifications in adjacent brain parenchyma (Slager & Wagner, 1956). This phenomenon, also known as ferruginization or siderocalcinosis (Figure 6.6) is more common in the brains of elderly individuals and can also be seen in microvessels adjacent to the hippocampal endplate region. Though microscopically rather dramatic, this microvascular siderocalcinosis is thought to be a benign age-related process *not* associated with significant brain parenchymal injury or encephalomalacia. Glomeruloid

microvascular loops or reduplication of capillaries, small veins, or arteries (Figure 6.7) is also occasionally encountered as an incidental finding in the neocortex of elderly patients (Hassler, 1967).

Two forms of cerebral microangiopathy—arteriosclerosis/lipohyalinosis (AS/LH) and cerebral amyloid (congophilic) angiopathy (CAA)—are extremely common in the brains of geriatric patients (Ellison et al., 1998; Vinters et al., 1998). The evolution of AS/LH has historically been linked to long-standing hypertension. However, a recent investigation of 70 patients in whom significant AS/LH was discovered at autopsy disclosed that almost a third of affected individuals had neither a significant history of high blood pressure, nor other pathologic sequelae (cardiomegaly, left ventricular hypertrophy) to suggest a history of hypertension (Lammie, Brannan, Slattery, & Warlow, 1997). This form of cerebral microangiopathy was hypothesized to result from abnormal microvascular permeability during life. Microscopic features of AS/LH include the following: hyaline thickening of arteriolar walls with variable degeneration of the internal elastic membrane, intimal fibromuscular hyperplasia, and concentric "onion-skin" type smooth muscle cell proliferation that results in variable narrowing of the vascular lumen (Ellison et al., 1998) (Figure 6.8).

CAA describes a microvascular abnormality that affects both cerebral cortical parenchymal and overlying leptomeningeal arteries and arterioles (Vinters, 1987; Vinters et al., 1996). In the evolution of CAA, arterial medial and/or adventitial components are replaced by an eosinophilic hyaline material with distinctive biochemical and molecular properties (Verbeek, de Waal, & Vinters, 2000). CAA is associated clinically with both stroke (especially cerebral hemorrhage) and dementia. It is a microvascular abnormality that is included among the key microscopic lesions that, when seen

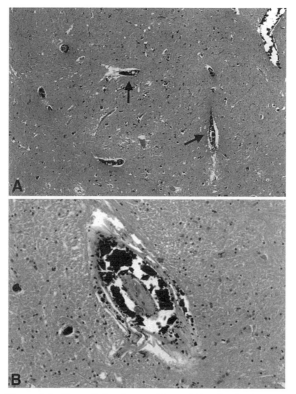

Figure 6.6 Ferruginization or siderocalcinosis of microvessels in globus pallidus from an elderly patient. (A) Note both microvessel-associated (arrows) and granular deposits of densely basophilic material. (B) Magnified view of a severely involved arteriole (magnifications A ×45, B ×220).

in abundance in the CNS, provide morphologic evidence in support of the clinical diagnosis of AD. Indeed, the Abeta protein discussed above in the context of SPs was initially isolated in 1984 from brain meningeal arteries affected by severe CAA (Glenner & Wong, 1984). CAA is thus associated with deposition, within arterial and capillary walls, of this Abeta protein, a 4.2-kiloDalton peptide cleaved from the APP (Vinters, Pardridge, & Yang, 1988; Vinters, Secor, Pardridge, & Gray, 1990) (Figure 6.9). Over 80% of brains taken at autopsy from patients with AD show some degree of Abeta CAA, often affecting cerebral vessels in one or more cortical regions (Ellis et al., 1996; Vinters & Gilbert, 1983). Brains with a moderate to severe degree of CAA show a significantly higher frequency of hemorrhagic or ischemic lesions than do those with minimal or insignificant CAA; furthermore, in cross-sectional studies, CAA increases in extent and severity with advancing age (Verbeek et al., 2000). Moderate to severe CAA is found in as many as 12–15% of brains examined from unselected patients over age 85 yr. Among consecutive necropsies on AD patients, however, moderate to severe degrees of CAA were noted in over 25% (Greenberg, 1998; Greenberg & Vonsattel, 1997).

All regions of the neocortex and overlying meninges may be affected by CAA, with relatively minor topographic variation among lobes in the distribution of

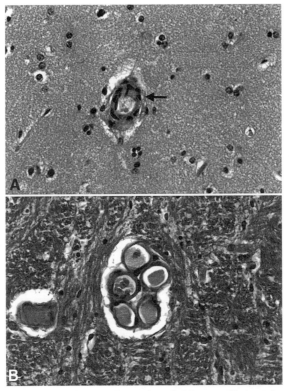

Figure 6.7 (A) Normal vessel, probably a small arteriole, in brain (arrow). (B) By comparison, a glomerular loop collection of small vessels is seen in brain from an elderly patient (magnification both panels ×435).

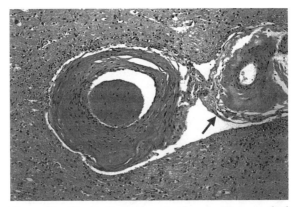

Figure 6.8 Lipohaylinosis/arteriosclerosis. Note marked thickening of two arterioles in brain of a patient with a history of vascular dementia (for details, see Vinters et al., 2000). Vessel on the left shows more prominent smooth muscle cell hyperplasia, whereas artery on the right (arrow) shows more hyaline thickening (mag. ×110).

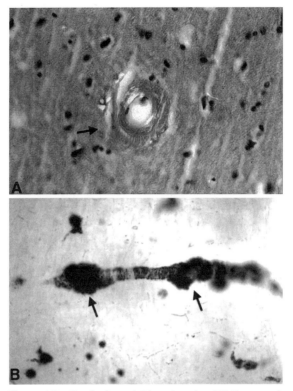

Figure 6.9 Cerebral amyloid angiopathy. (A) Congo red-stained section of brain viewed under polarized light. A thickened artery (arrow) cut in transverse section shows birefringence, which was apple-green. (B) Thick section of brain stained with the Campbell-Switzer technique. Vessel at center of the micrograph, cut in longintudinal section, shows marked thickening as a result of amyloid deposition, which is focally accentuated (arrows).

affected arteries (Vinters & Gilbert, 1983). By contrast, this microvascular lesion is almost never found within deep central gray matter or brain stem, and only rarely within subcortical white matter. The descriptor CAA defines amyloid protein deposition within the walls of both arterioles and capillaries; the latter is sometimes referred to, in part for historical reasons, as *dyshoric* angiopathy—especially when (on histologic sections) amyloid suggests an appearance of leaking from the capillary lumen into adjacent brain.

The severity of CAA within a brain region—or even an arteriolar segment—can be graded. The grade of CAA depends upon the extent of smooth muscle cell (SMC) replacement by amyloid within the media. Grade 1 CAA correlates with deposition of amyloid among SMCs in an otherwise intact arteriolar segment, whereas grade 3 CAA describes an arterial segment, media of which has been entirely replaced by amyloid, with extensive disruption of the vessel wall (Vonsattel et al., 1991). Risk of cerebral hemorrhage correlates with the extent of amyloid deposition within vessel walls. The pathogenesis of this intriguing brain microangiopathy is, as yet, poorly understood. SMCs appear capable of synthesizing

APP messenger RNA and Abeta protein, whether this is assessed by *in situ* hybridization or immunohistochemistry in human brain specimens (Natté et al., 1999; Kawai et al., 1993; Shoji, Hirai, Harigaya, Kawarabayashi, & Yamaguchi, 1990). Transgenic mouse models of Abeta overproduction in which CAA is found, are certain to clarify key pathogenetic questions, such as why it develops in only selected brain regions.

The cerebral microvasculature, especially its capillaries—site of the blood–brain barrier (BBB), an important metabolic interface between the blood and brain parenchyma—undergoes alterations with normal aging and appears to become increasingly leaky in AD. Ultrastructural morphometric investigations of human brain biopsies reveal that in *non*demented individuals examined from the second to the eighth decades of life, capillary walls in the white matter—normally thicker than those in cortex—undergo progressive thinning. However, mitochondrial content of brain capillary endothelium remains stable over the decades, as do presumed nonspecific permeability routes through the BBB (Stewart et al., 1987). By contrast, in AD there is a diminution in endothelial mitochondrial density, together with the development of features among interendothelial junctions that suggest increasing permeability, higher numbers of pinocytotic vesicles, and increased numbers of pericytes, the latter an indirect measure of a second line of defense when capillary endothelial function becomes impaired (Claudio, 1996; Stewart, Hayakawa, Akers, & Vinters, 1992).

V. Alzheimer's Disease and Other Dementias

Neurodegenerative diseases are among the most common afflictions of old age, clinically immensely challenging, yet biologically intriguing. For example, AD, the most common member of this group, has become an epidemic as people more commonly live to an age at which its prevalence is extremely high. As human life span increases, and in the absence of preventive measures that might be taken as prophylaxis against AD and its kindred ailments, they are certain to become an even greater challenge in the coming decades for those who provide health care to the elderly, attempting to guide them into mentally sound and relatively healthy old age. Degenerative diseases of the (central) nervous system are a heterogeneous group that share certain unifying clinicopathologic features (Vinters et al., 1998):

1. Until recently, the etiology of most was unknown. However, many CNS degenerations are now understood to have a specific genetic or metabolic basis. Some diseases—AD is the best example —though usually sporadic, have hereditary forms which are, from a neuropathologic standpoint, identical to the familial forms; understanding the molecular genetics of those variants has been immensely instructive.

2. They show highly selective involvement of specific families or groups of neurons and/or fiber tracts. Affected neurons and tracts may be widespread within the CNS (as with AD) or fairly localized (Parkinson's disease). A key event in the onset and progression of most of these disorders is progressive loss of neurons and tracts (their axons, insulating myelin, or both), with resultant scarring—this manifests in the CNS as proliferation of astrocytes, also described as astrocytic gliosis or simply gliosis. In many neurodegenerative disorders, characteristic nuclear and/or cytoplasmic inclusions and abnormalities of the cytoskeleton or neuropil may develop. These commonly serve as markers for a disease, though they are not necessarily informative as to its pathogenesis or etiology.

3. Most are relentlessly progressive, leading to decline over months or years, though the tempo of their progression may be extremely variable. As an example, AD may become increasingly symptomatic over more than a decade, or may lead to death within 3–4 years of onset. Death from a neurodegenerative disease often results from intercurrent problems, especially infections, to which a bedridden and incapacitated individual is prone.

4. Clinically, neurodegenerative disorders present with dementia (a global decline in higher intellectual functions including abnormalities of memory storage and retrieval, and personality changes), or abnormalities of the sensory and motor systems, or both. A recent meta-analysis (Jorm & Jolley, 1998) has shown that the incidence of dementia rises exponentially in virtually all populations up to the age of 90 years, though with some variation among demographic groups in terms of the relative frequencies of different *causes* of dementia. The presentation of a given disorder usually leads the neurologist to a (probable) etiologic diagnosis. This diagnosis may be supported by neuroimaging and electrodiagnostic (EEG) studies, though occasionally a brain biopsy is performed to confirm a specific disease entity, especially when the clinical presentation appears somewhat anomalous. I shall consider only the most common neurodegenerative diseases in this section.

A. Alzheimer's Disease

AD was first described in 1907 and, for the first half of this century, regarded as a most unusual cause of dementia. It is now recognized as the most common cause of both presenile and senile dementia (Tomlinson et al., 1970; Joachim, Morris, & Selkoe, 1988), having a prevalence of 5–10% among individuals over 65 yr and 20–40% in people over the age of 80 yr. AD most often presents with the insidious onset of memory disturbance, especially affecting short-term memory, and sometimes psychiatric illness, including severe paranoia. In elderly patients, true dementia must be distinguished from delirium or a subacute confusional state (Patterson, Hogan, Bergman, & Gold, 2000; Fleming, Adams, & Peterson, 1995). Other features include personality change and speech abnormalities. In early stages, motor, sensory, and visual systems are spared. At autopsy, the brain of a patient with AD may appear grossly normal or it may show diffuse atrophy that ranges from mild to severe (Figure 6.10), the latter associated with pronounced widening of the sulci and shrinkage or atrophy of the gyri. Cut sections of the atrophic brain usually show marked enlargement of the lateral ventricles, described as hydrocephalus *ex vacuo*.

There has been substantial debate as to how the diagnosis of AD is most appropriately confirmed by examining histologic sections of brain. All of the brain parenchymal and microvascular lesions seen in the brains of AD patients have already been described and discussed above; they include SPs (especially ntSP), NFTs, CAA, and GVD (usually confined to the hippocampus). Many of these are best visualized using silver stains and immunohistochemistry, incorporating primary antibodies to amyloid and cytoskeletal components. Though virtually all are present in small numbers in the CNS of neurologically intact elderly (Price & Morris, 1999), all of them occur in excess (in numbers and densities greater than would be seen in a *non*demented individual of comparable age) in AD (i.e., it is a quantitative or semiquantitative diagnosis). The gradual accumulation of parenchymal AD-associated lesions over time has been documented in the brains of patients who have undergone both biopsy and, years later, autopsy examination of the CNS (DiPatre et al., 1999).

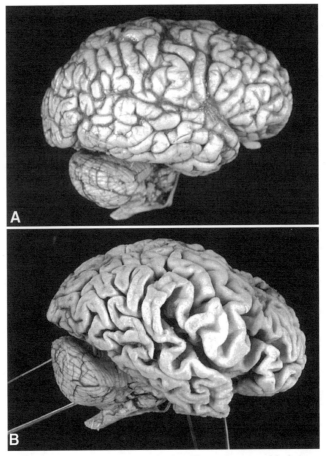

Figure 6.10 (A) Lateral view of a fixed brain from an elderly, non demented individual. (B) Similar view of the brain from a patient with Alzheimer's disease (AD). Note striking atrophy of gyri and widening of sulci. Cerebellum and brain stem, however, are largely unremarkable and preserved in the AD brain.

Specific, semiquantitative neuropathologic criteria for the diagnosis of AD have been discussed and promulgated since the 1980s (Khachaturian, 1985). Braak and Braak (1991) have characterized the key neuropathologic event in AD as a gradual accumulation within the CNS of NFTs. They have proposed that AD can thus be subdivided into stages, depending upon loci at which NFT are found: in its early stages, NFT are confined to the entorhinal or transentorhinal cortex, later they appear in the hippocampal formation, and finally in neocortical or isocortical regions, associated with destruction of these areas. A consortium of AD researchers has, in a series of papers over the past 10 years, wrestled with ways to standardize the clinical, neuroimaging and neuropathologic evaluation of patients with dementia, including that caused by AD (Davis et al. 1992; Gearing et al., 1995; Mirra et al., 1991). The consortium to Establish a Registry for Alzheimer's Disease (CERAD) criteria for the neuropathologic diagnosis of AD place slightly more emphasis upon SP counts or scores, particularly densities of ntSPs within several regions of the neocortex, in arriving at a firm statement as to AD being the cause of a given patient's dementia. Finally, consensus criteria or recommendations for the autopsy diagnosis of AD have recently been enunciated and editorialized (Duyckaerts & Hauw, 1997; Wisniewski & Silverman, 1997; Hyman, 1998; NIA-Reagan Institute Working Group, 1997). The National Institute on Aging–Reagan criteria attempt to fuse Braak and Braak, and CERAD approaches to the morphologic diagnosis and staging of AD. They furthermore emphasize that AD is a heterogeneous clinicopathologic entity, that *any* AD changes in the post mortem brain should be considered abnormal (even though we have discussed above how they may be present in the CNS of neuropsychologically intact nonagenarians), and that dementia in the elderly may arise from more than one disorder—hence the presence of comorbid neuropathologic change should be carefully evaluated in any brain showing typical AD features.

The molecular pathogenesis of AD has, over the past two decades, become well (though still incompletely) understood (for review, see Cummings et al., 1998). The amyloid cascade hypothesis (Hardy & Higgins, 1992) as an explanation for much of the morbid anatomy of AD has been described above, while inflammation has become recognized as a potentially important—and treatable—contributor to AD-associated neuropathologic changes (Mrak & Griffin, 2000). Mutations in genes other than APP (presenilin-1 on chromosome 14, presenilin-2 on chromosome 1) are associated with familial AD (FAD) (Hardy, 1997). The apolipoprotein E (APOE) e4 isoform is a major risk factor for the development of late onset AD (Roses, 1996; Strittmatter & Roses, 1995). Other disease-causing mutations and risk factors for the development of AD are aggressively being sought.

B. Non-Alzheimer's Dementias

Non-Alzheimer's dementias are numerous but, by comparison to AD, relatively infrequent. Dementia with Lewy bodies (DLB) is a disorder in which these intraneuronal inclusions occur not only in the substantia nigra, but also within neocortex, where they are best demonstrated immunohistochemically utilizing antibodies to ubiquitin and/or alpha-synuclein. Patients with DLB often have significant SP plaque load within the neocortex, thus DLB may represent a variant of AD in which SPs predominate over NFTs (Hansen & Galasko, 1992; Harding & Halliday, 1998; McKeith et al., 1996; Mega et al., 1996). Abnormalities of the synuclein protein, a component of Lewy bodies, are increasingly recognized in many neurodegenerative disorders, including DLB, to the extent that many are now referred to as synucleinopathies (Duda, Lee, & Trojanowski, 2000). Fronto-temporal dementias (FTDs) are currently recognized as a group of disorders showing preferential atrophy of the frontal and temporal lobes. Pick disease (circumscribed lobar atrophy) is one subtype of FTD, in which Pick bodies are found within residual swollen neurons of involved neocortex (Vinters et al., 1998). Many examples of familial FTD appear to be linked to mutations of the tau gene on chromosome 17, hence are now often described as chromosome 17-linked dementias or even *tauopathies* (Mann, 1998; Spillantini, Bird, & Ghetti, 1998). The cumulative effect of multiple large and small cerebral infarcts can result in multiinfarct or ischemic vascular dementia (Vinters et al., 2000).

VI. Concluding Remarks

Although this chapter has attempted to discuss mechanisms of normal brain aging in the context of *abnormal* CNS aging, especially resulting in AD, the two variations on how senescence occurs are inextricably linked. A key question for psychogeriatricians over the coming decades will be, Does the prevention or slowing of the rate of formation of lesions associated with AD within brain result in the preservation of normal cognitive function? The increasing numbers of individuals living to 100 yr of age or older—it is estimated that by midcentury there will be 100s of thousands of centenarians in the United States—will provide a marvelous "experiment of nature" in which to test this important question. Molecular genetics and structural biochemistry are at a point where the neuronal and extracellular lesions of AD will become manipulatable in the brain, possibly even preventable. Will this result in preserved cognitive function into advanced old age, or (as some students of brain amyloid fear) not prevent dementia? The hypothesis will soon be testable.

Another important issue that has not been adequately studied is that of CNS reserve. Does one 75-yr-old person remain psychologically alert, animated, and active because of a reserve capacity of "recruitable" brain tissue, while his 70-yr-old neighbor, lacking this resource, slips into senile dementia? And if so, what are the determinants of such a reserve, this plasticity of the brain that allows for adaptation and learning after 70, 80, or 90 years of activity? Might growth factors be developed and administered that will prevent loss of this reserve or, if it is lost, allow for its reconstitution? Does remaining intellectually active into old age enhance the reserve? Answers to a modification of the question posed at the outset, Why do some peoples' brains age well, others badly?, may soon be at hand.

Acknowledgments

Work in the author's laboratory supported in part by NIH/PHS Grants # P01 AG12435 and P50 AG 16570. Figures prepared by Ms. Carol Appleton.

References

Ball, M. J. (1978). Topographic distribution of neurofibrillary tangles and granulovacuolar degeneration in hippocampal cortex of aging and demented patients. A quantitative study. *Acta Neuropathologica (Berlin), 42,* 73–80.

Barnes, D. G., & MacKenzie, A. (1999). Recent recognition and molecular delineation of apoptosis: Beginnings of a therapeutic revolution? *Annals of the Royal College of Physicians & Surgeons of Canada, 32,* 376–382.

Barnett, H. J. M., Mohr, J. P., Stein, B. M., & Yatsu, F. M. (Eds.). (1998). *Stroke Pathophysiology, diagnosis, and management.* (3rd ed.). New York: Churchill Livingstone.

Blessed, G., Tomlinson, B. E., & Roth, M. (1968). The association between quantitative measures of dementia and of senile change in the cerebral grey matter of elderly subjects. *British Journal of Psychiatry, 114,* 797–811.

Bookheimer, S. Y., Strojwas, M. H., Cohen, M. S., Saunders, A. M., Pericak-Vance, M. A., Mazziotta, J. C., & Small, G. W. (2000). Patterns of brain activation in people at risk for Alzheimer's disease. *The New England Journal of Medicine, 343,* 450–456.

Braak, H., & Braak, E. (1991). Neuropathological staging of Alzheimer-related changes. *Acta Neuropathologica, 82,* 239–259.

Claudio, L. (1996). Ultrastructural features of the blood-brain barrier in biopsy tissue from Alzheimer's disease patients. *Acta Neuropathologica, 91,* 6–14.

Coffey, C. E., Wilkinson, W. E., Parashos, I. A., Soady, S. A. R., Sullivan, R. J., Patterson, L. J., Figiel, S. J., Webb, M. C., Spritzer, C. E., & Djang, W. T. (1992). Quantitative cerebral anatomy of the aging human brain: A cross-sectional study using magnetic resonance imaging. *Neurology, 42,* 527–536.

Coggeshall, R. E., & Lekan, H. A. (1996). Methods for determining numbers of cells and synapses: A case for more uniform standards of review. *The Journal of Comparative Neurology, 364,* 6–15.

Creasey, H., & Rapoport, S. I. (1985). The aging human brain. *Annals of Neurology, 17,* 2–10.

Cummings, J. L., Vinters, H. V., Cole G. M., & Khachaturian, Z. S. (1998). Alzheimer's disease. Etiologies, pathophysiology, cognitive reserve, and treatment opportunities. *Neurology, 51* (Suppl. 1), S2–S17.

Davies, C. A., Mann, D. M. A., Sumpter, P. Q., & Yates, P. O. (1987). A quantitative morphometric analysis of the neuronal and synaptic content of the frontal and temporal cortex in patients with Alzheimer's disease. *Journal of the Neurological Sciences, 78,* 151–164.

Davis, P. C., Gray, L., Albert, M., Wilkinson, W., Hughes, J., Heyman, A., Gado, M., Kumar, A. J., Destian, S., Lee, C., Duvall, E., Kido, D., Nelson, M. J., Bello, J., Weathers, S., Jolesz, F., Kikinis, R., & Brooks, M. (1992). The Consortium to Establish a Registry for Alzheimer's Disease (CERAD). Part III. Reliability of a standardized MRI evaluation of Alzheimer's disease. *Neurology, 42,* 1676–1680.

Delaère, P., Duyckaerts, C., He, Y., Piette, F., & Hauw, J. J. (1991). Subtypes and differential laminar distributions of betaA4 deposits in Alzheimer's disease: Relationship with the intellectual status of 26 cases. *Acta Neuropathologica, 81,* 328–335.

Dickson, D. W. (1997). The pathogenesis of senile plaques. *Journal of Neuropathology and Experimental Neurology, 56,* 321–339.

Dimri, G. P., & Campisi, J. (1994). Molecular and cell biology of replicative senescence. *Cold Spring Harbor Symposia on Quantitative Biology, 54,* 67–73.

Di Patre, P. L., Read, S. L., Cummings, J. L., Tomiyasu, U., Vartavarian, L. M., Secor, D. L., & Vinters, H. V. (1999). Progression of clinical deterioration and pathological changes in patients with Alzheimer disease evaluated at biopsy and autopsy. *Archives of Neurology, 56,* 1254–1261.

Duda, J. E., Lee, V. M.-Y., & Trojanowski, J. Q. (2000). Neuropathology of synuclein aggregates: New insights into mechanisms of neurodegenerative diseases. *Journal of Neuroscience Research, 61,* 121–127.

Duong, T., Doucette, T., Zidenberg, N. A., Jacobs, R. W., & Scheibel, A. B. (1993). Microtubule-associated proteins tau and amyloid P component in Alzheimer's disease. *Brain Research, 603,* 74–86.

Duong, T., & Gallagher, K. A. (1994). Immunoreactivity patterns in neurofibrillary tangles of the inferior temporal cortex in Alzheimer disease. *Molecular and Chemical Neuropathology, 22,* 105–122.

Duyckaerts, C., & Hauw, J.-J. (1997). Diagnosis and staging of Alzheimer disease. *Neurobiology of Aging, 18* (S4), S33–S42.

Ellis, R. J., Olichney, J. M., Thal, L. J., Mirra, S. S., Morris, J. C., Beekly, D., & Heyman, A. (1996). Cerebral amyloid angiopathy in the brains of patients with Alzheimer's disease: The CERAD experience, part XV. *Neurology, 46,* 1592–1596.

Ellison, D., Love, S., Chimelli, L., Harding, B., Lowe, J., Roberts, G. W., & Vinters, H. V. (1998). *Neuropathology. A reference text of CNS pathology.* London: Mosby.

Esler, W. P., Stimson, E. R., Fishman, J. B., Ghilardi, J. R., & Vinters, H. V., Mantyh, P. W., & Maggio, J. E. (1999). Stereochemical specificity of Alzheimer's disease beta-peptide assembly. *Biopolymers, 49,* 505–514.

Esler, W. P., Stimson, E. R., Ghilardi, J. R., Lu, Y-A., Felix, A. M., Vinters, H. V., Mantyh, P. W., Lee, J. P., & Maggio, J. E. (1996). Point substitution in the central hydrophobic cluster of a human beta-amyloid congener disrupts peptide folding and abolishes plaque competence. *Biochemistry, 35,* 13914–13921.

Fleming, K. C., Adams, A. C., & Peterson, R. C. (1995). Dementia: Diagnosis and evaluation. *Mayo Clinic Proceedings, 70,* 1093–1107.

Gearing, M., Mirra, S. S., Hedreen, J. C., Sumi, S. M., Hansen, L. A., & Heyman, A. (1995). The Consortium to Establish a Registry for Alzheimer's disease (CERAD). Part X. Neuropathology confirmation of the clinical diagnosis of Alzheimer's disease. *Neurology, 45,* 461–466.

Gibson, P. H. (1983). EM study of the numbers of cortical synapses in the brains of ageing people and people with Alzheimer-type dementia. *Acta Neuropathologica (Berlin), 62,* 127–133.

Glenner, G. G., & Wong, C. W. (1984). Alzheimer's disease: Initial report of the purification and characterization of a novel cerebrovascular amyloid protein. *Biochemical Biophysical Research Communications, 120,* 885–890.

Grady, C. L., & Craik, F. I. (2000). Changes in memory processing with age. *Current Opinion in Neurobiology, 10,* 224–231.

Green, M. S., Kaye, J. E. A., & Ball, M. J. (2000). The Oregon Brain Aging Study—Neuropathology accompanying healthy aging in the oldest old. *Neurology, 54,* 105–113.

Greenberg, S. M. (1998). Cerebral amyloid angiopathy. Prospects for clinical diagnosis and treatment. *Neurology, 51,* 690–694.

Greenberg, S. M., & Vonsattel, J-P. G. (1997). Diagnosis of cerebral amyloid angiopathy. Sensitivity and specificity of cortical biopsy. *Stroke, 28,* 1418–1422.

Grundke-Iqbal, I., Iqbal, K., Quinlan, M., Tung, Y-C., Zaidi, M. S., & Wisniewski, H. M. (1986). Microtubule-associated protein tau. A component of Alzheimer paired helical filaments. *The Journal of Biological Chemistry, 261,* 6084–6089.

Hansen, L. A., & Galasko, D. (1992). Lewy body disease. *Current Opinion in Neurology and Neurosurgery, 5,* 889–894.

Harding, A. J., & Halliday, G. M. (1998). Simplified neuropathological diagnosis of dementia with Lewy bodies. *Neuropathology and Applied Neurobiology, 24,* 195–201.

Hardy, J. (1997). Amyloid, the presenilins and Alzheimer's disease. *Trends in Neuroscience, 20,* 154–159.

Hardy, J. A., & Higgins, G. A. (1992). Alzheimer's disease: The amyloid cascade hypothesis. *Science, 256,* 184–185.

Hassler, O. (1967). Arterial deformities in senile brains. *Acta Neuropathologica, 8,* 219–229.

Hatanpää, K., Brady, D. R., Stoll, J., Rapoport, S. I., & Chandrasekaran, K. (1996). Neuronal activity and early neurofibrillary tangles in Alzheimer's disease. *Annals of Neurology, 40,* 411–420.

Hauw, J.-J., Vignolo, P., Duyckaerts, C., Beck, H., Forette, F., Henry, J.-F., Laurent, M., Piette, F., Sachet, A., & Berthaux, P. (1986). Étude neuropathologique de 12 centenaires. *Revue Neurologique (Paris), 142,* 107–115.

Hendriks, L., & van Broeckhoven, C. (1996). The betaA4 amyloid precursor protein gene and Alzheimer's disease. *European Journal of Biochemistry, 237,* 6–15.

Hulette, C. M., Welsh-Bohmer, K. A., Murray, M. G., Saunders, A. M., Mash, D. C., & McIntyre, L. M. (1998). Neuropathological

and neuropsychological changes in "normal" aging: Evidence for preclinical Alzheimer disease in cognitively normal individuals. *Journal of Neuropathology and Experimental Neurology, 57,* 1168–1174.

Huttenlocher, P. R. (1979). Synaptic density in human frontal cortex—developmental changes and effects of aging. *Brain Research, 163,* 195–205.

Hyman, B. T. (1998). New neuropathological criteria for Alzheimer disease. *Archives of Neurology, 55,* 1174–1176.

Hyman, B. T., Gomez-Isla, T., & Irizarry, M. C. (1998). Stereology: A practical primer for neuropathology. *Journal of Neuropathology and Experimental Neurology, 57,* 305–310.

Ikonomovic, M. D., Mizukami, K., Davies, P., Hamilton, R., Sheffield, R., & Armstrong, D. M. (1997). The loss of GluR2(3) immunoreactivity precedes neurofibrillary tangle formation in the entorhinal cortex and hippocampus of Alzheimer brains. *Journal of Neuropathology and Experimental Neurology, 56,* 1018–1027.

Jacobs, B., & Scheibel, A. B. (1993). A quantitative dendritic analysis of Wernicke's area in humans. I. Lifespan changes. *The Journal of Comparative Neurology, 327,* 83–96.

Jazwinski, S. M. (1996). Longevity, genes, and aging. *Science, 273,* 54–59.

Joachim, C. L., Morris, J. H., & Selkoe, D. J. (1988). Clinically diagnosed Alzheimer's disease: Autopsy results in 150 cases. *Annals of Neurology, 24,* 50–56.

Jorm, A. F., & Jolley, D. (1998). The incidence of dementia. A meta-analysis. *Neurology, 51,* 728–733.

Kalaria, R. N. (1999). Microglia and Alzheimer's disease. *Current Opinion in Hematology, 6,* 15–24.

Kawai, M., Kalaria, R. N., Cras, P., Siedlak, S. L., Velasco, M. E., Shelton, E. R., Chan, H. W., Greenberg, B. D., & Perry, G. (1993). Degeneration of vascular muscle cells in cerebral amyloid angiopathy of Alzheimer disease. *Brain Research, 623,* 142–146.

Khachaturian, Z. S. (1985). Diagnosis of Alzheimer's disease. *Archives of Neurology, 42,* 1097–1105.

Kiechle, F. L., Kaul, K. L., & Farkas, D. H. (1996). Mitochondrial disorders. Methods and specimen selection for diagnostic molecular pathology. *Archives of Pathology and Laboratory Medicine, 120,* 597–603.

Kirkwood, T. B. L. (1996). Human senescence. *BioEssays, 18,* 1009–1016.

Lammie, A. G., Brannan, F., Slattery, J., & Warlow, C. (1997). Nonhypertensive cerebral small vessel disease. *Stroke, 28,* 2222–2229.

Liu, J. K., & Mori, A. (1999). Stress, aging, and brain oxidative damage. *Neurochemical Research, 24,* 1479–1497.

Long, J. M., Kalehua, A. N., Muth, N. J., Hengemihle, J. M., Jucker, M., Calhoun, M. E., Ingram, D. K., & Mouton, P. R. (1998). Stereological estimation of total microglia number in mouse hippocampus. *Journal of Neuroscience Methods, 84,* 101–108.

Lucassen, P., Chung, W. C. J., Kamphorst, W., & Swaab, D. F. (1997). DNA damage distribution in the human brain as shown by in situ end labelling; Area-specific differences in aging and Alzheimer disease in the absence of apoptotic morphology. *Journal of Neuropathology and Experimental Neurology, 56,* 887–900.

Lynch, C. D., Cooney, P. T., Bennett, S. A., Thornton, P. L., Khan, A. S., Ingram, R. L., & Sonntag, W. E. (1999). Effects of moderate caloric restriction on cortical microvascular density and local cerebral blood flow in aged rats. *Neurobiology of Aging, 20,* 191–200.

Mackenzie, I. R. A. (1994). Senile plaques do not progressively accumulate with normal aging. *Acta Neuropathologica, 87,* 520–525.

Mackenzie, I. R. A., Hao, C., & Munoz, D. G. (1995). Role of microglia in senile plaque formation. *Neurobiology of Aging, 16,* 797–804.

Mackenzie, I. R. A., McLachlan, R. S., Kubu, C. S., & Miller, L. A. (1996). Prospective neuropsychological assessment of nondemented patients with biopsy proven senile plaques. *Neurology, 46,* 425–429.

Maggio, J. E., Stimson, E. R., Ghilardi, J. R., Allen, C. J., Dahl, C. E., Whitcomb, D. C., Vigna, S. R., Vinters, H. V., Labenski, M. E., & Mantyh, P. W. (1992). Reversible *in vitro* growth of Alzheimer disease beta-amyloid plaques by deposition of labeled amyloid peptide. *Proceedings of the National Academy of Sciences of the U.S.A., 89,* 5462–5466.

Mak, K., Yang, F., Vinters, H. V., Frautschy, S. A., & Cole, G. M. (1994). Polyclonals to beta-amyloid (1–42) identify most plaque

and vascular deposits in Alzheimer cortex, but not striatum. *Brain Research, 667,* 138–142.

Mann, D. M. A. (1998). Dementia of frontal type and dementias with subcortical gliosis. *Brain Pathology, 8,* 325–338.

Mann, D. M. A., Jones, D., Prinja, D., & Purkiss, M. S. (1990). The prevalence of amyloid (A4) protein deposits within the cerebral and cerebellar cortex in Down's syndrome and Alzheimer's disease. *Acta Neuropathologica, 80,* 318–327.

Mann, D. M. A., Tucker, C. M., & Yates, P. O. (1987). The topographic distribution of senile plaques and neurofibrillary tangles in the brains of non-demented persons of different ages. *Neuropathology and Applied Neurobiology, 13,* 123–139.

Masliah, E., Terry, R. D., DeTeresa, R. M., & Hansen, L. A. (1989). Immunohistochemical quantification of the synapse-related protein synaptophysin in Alzheimer disease. *Neuroscience Letters, 103,* 234–239.

Matsuo, E. S., Shin, R-W., Billingsley, M. L., de Voorde, A. V., O'Connor, M., Trojanowski, J. Q., & Lee, V. M.-Y. (1994). Biopsy-derived adult human brain tau is phosphorylated at many of the same sites as Alzheimer's disease paired helical filament tau. *Neuron, 13,* 1–20.

Maury, C. P. J. (1995). Molecular pathogenesis of beta-amyloidosis in Alzheimer's disease and other cerebral amyloidoses. *Laboratory Investigation, 72,* 4–16.

McKeith, I. G., Galasko, D., Kosaka, K., Perry, E. K., Dickson, D. W., Hansen, L. A., Salmon, D. P., Lowe, J., Mirra, S. S., Byrne, E. J., Lennox, G., Quinn, N. P., Edwardson, J. A., Ince, P. G., Bergeron, C., Burns, A., Miller, B. L., Lovestone, S., Collerton, D., Jansen, E. N. H., Ballard, C., de Vos, R. A. I., Wilcock, G. K., Jellinger, K. A., Perry, R. H., for the Consortium on Dementia with Lewy Bodies. (1996). Consensus guidelines for the clinical and pathologic diagnosis of dementia with Lewy bodies (DLB): Report of the consortium on DLB international workshop. *Neurology, 47,* 1113–1124.

Mega, M. S., Masterman, D. L., Benson, D. F., Vinters, H. V., Tomiyasu, U., Craig, A. H., Foti, D. J., Kaufer, D., Scharre, D. W., Fairbanks, L., & Cummings, J. L. (1996). Dementia with Lewy bodies: Reliability and validity of clinical and pathologic criteria. *Neurology, 47,* 1403–1409.

Mera, S. L. (1998). The role of telomeres in ageing and cancer. *British Journal of Biomedical Sciences, 55,* 221–225.

Mirra, S. S., Heyman, A., McKeel, D., Sumi, S. M., Crain, B. J., Brownlee, L. M., Vogel, F. S., Hughes, J. P., van Belle, G., Berg, L., and participating CERAD neuropathologists. (1991). The Consortium to Establish a Registry for Alzheimer's disease (CERAD). Part II. Standardization of the neuropathologic assessment of Alzheimer's disease. *Neurology, 41,* 479–486.

Mrak, R. E., & Griffin, W. S. T. (2000). Interleukin-1 and the immunogenetics of Alzheimer disease. *Journal of Neuropathology and Experimental Neurology, 59,* 471–476.

Mrak, R. E., Griffin, W. S. T., & Graham, D. I. (1997). Aging-associated changes in human brain. *Journal of Neuropathology and Experimental Neurology, 56,* 1269–1275.

National Institute on Aging, and Reagan Institute Working Group on Diagnostic Criteria for the Neuropathological Assessment of Alzheimer's Disease. (1997). Consensus recommendations for the postmortem diagnosis of Alzheimer's disease. *Neurobiology of Aging, 18* (S4), S1–S2.

Natté, R., de Boer, W. I., Maat-Schieman, M. L. C., Baelde, H. J., Vinters, H. V., Roos, R. A. C., & van Duinen, S. G. (1999). Amyloid beta precursor protein-mRNA is expressed throughout cerebral vessel walls. *Brain Research, 828,* 179–183.

Pardue, M-L., & DeBaryshe, P. G. (1999). Telomeres and telomerase: more than the end of the line. *Chromosoma, 108,* 73–82.

Patterson, C., Hogan, D. B., Bergman, H., & Gold, S. (2000). Update in geriatrics. *Annals of the Royal College of Pysicians & Surgeons of Canada, 33,* 212–218.

Plum, F., & Posner, J. B. (1972). *Diagnosis of stupor and coma.* (2nd ed.) (pp. 25–32). Philadelphia: F. A. Davis Company.

Price, J. L., & Morris, J. C. (1999). Tangles and plaques in nondemented aging and 'preclinical' Alzheimer's disease. *Annals of Neurology, 45,* 358–368.

Prichard, J. W., & Cummings, J. L. (1997). The insistent call from functional MRI. *Neurology, 48,* 797–800.

Raina, A. K., Zhu, X., Rottkamp, C. A., Monteiro, M., Takeda, A., & Smith, M. A. (2000). Cyclin' toward dementia: Cell cycle abnormalities and abortive oncogenesis in Alzheimer disease. *Journal of Neuroscience Research, 61,* 128–133.

Roses, A. D. (1996). The Alzheimer diseases. *Current Opinion in Neurobiology, 6,* 644–650.

Ross, R. (1993). The pathogenesis of atherosclerosis: a perspective for the 1990s. *Nature, 362,* 801–809.

Ross, R. (1999). Atherosclerosis—an inflammatory disease. *New England Journal of Medicine, 340,* 115–126.

Sastry, P. S., & Rao, K. S. (2000). Apoptosis and the nervous system. *Journal of Neurochemistry, 74,* 1–20.

Scheff, S. W., DeKosky, S. T., & Price, D. A. (1990). Quantitative assessment of cortical synaptic density in Alzheimer's disease. *Neurobiology of Aging, 11,* 29–37.

Scheibel, A. B. (1992). Structural changes in the aging brain. In J. E. Birren, R. B. Sloane, & G. D. Cohen (Eds.), *Handbook of mental health and aging.* (2 ed.) (pp. 147–173). San Diego, CA: Academic Press.

Scheibel, A. B. (1996). Structural and functional changes in the aging brain. In J. E. Birren & K. W. Schaie (Eds.), *Handbook of the psychology of aging* (4 edn.) (pp. 105–128). San Diego, CA: Academic Press.

Selkoe, D. J. (1994). Alzheimer's disease: A central role for amyloid. *Journal of Neuropathology and Experimental Neurology, 53,* 438–447.

Sheng, J. G., Mrak, R. E., & Griffin, W. S. T. (1998). Progressive neuronal DNA damage associated with neurofibrillary tangle formation in Alzheimer disease. *Journal of Neuropathology and Experimental Neurology, 57,* 323–328.

Shoji, M., Hirai, S., Harigaya, Y., Kawarabayashi, T., & Yamaguchi, H. (1990). The amyloid beta-protein precursor is localized in smooth muscle cells of leptomeningeal vessels. *Brain Research, 530,* 113–116.

Slager, U. T., & Wagner, J. A. (1956). The incidence, composition, and pathological significance of intracerebral vascular deposits in the basal ganglia. *Journal of Neuropathology and Experimental Neurology, 15,* 417–431.

Smith, J. R., & Pereira-Smith, O. M. (1996). Replicative senescence: Implications for in vivo aging and tumor suppression. *Science*, *273*, 63–67.

Sohal, R. S., & Weindruch, R. (1996). Oxidative stress, caloric restriction, and aging. *Science*, *273*, 59–62.

Spillantini, M. G., Bird, T. D., & Ghetti, B. (1998). Frontotemporal dementia and Parkinsonism linked to chromosome 17: A new group of tauopathies. *Brain Pathology*, *8*, 387–402.

Stewart, P. A., Hayakawa, K., Akers, M-A., & Vinters, H. V. (1992). A morphometric study of the blood-brain barrier in Alzheimer's disease. *Laboratory Investigation*, *67*, 734–742.

Stewart, P. A., Magliocco, M., Hayakawa, K., Farrell, C. L., Del Maestro, R. F., Girvin, J., Kaufmann, J. C. E., Vinters, H. V. & Gilbert, J. (1987). A quantitative analysis of blood-brain barrier ultrastructure in the aging human. *Microvascular Research*, *33*, 270–282.

Strittmatter, W. J., & Roses, A. D. (1995). Apolipoprotein E and Alzheimer disease. *Proceedings of the National Academy of Sciences of the U.S.A.*, *92*, 4725–4727.

Terry, R. D. (1986). Interrelations among the lesions of normal and abnormal aging of the brain. *Progress in Brain Research*, *70*, 41–48.

Terry, R. D., DeTeresa, R., & Hansen, L. A. (1987). Neocortical cell counts in normal human adult aging. *Annals of Neurology*, *21*, 530–539.

Terry, R. D., Masliah, E., Salmon, D. P., Butters, N., DeTeresa, R., Hill, R., Hansen, L. A., & Katzman, R. (1991). Physical basis of cognitive alterations in Alzheimer's disease: Synapse loss is the major correlate of cognitive impairment. *Annals of Neurology*, *30*, 572–580.

Tomlinson, B. E., Blessed, G., & Roth, M. (1968). Observations on the brains of nondemented old people. *Journal of the Neurological Sciences*, *7*, 331–356.

Tomlinson, B. E., Blessed, G., & Roth, M. (1970). Observations on the brains of demented old people. *Journal of the Neurological Sciences*, *11*, 205–242.

Verbeek, M. M., Eikelenboom, P., & de Waal, R. M. W. (1997). Differences between the pathogenesis of senile plaques and congophilic angiopathy in Alzheimer disease. *Journal of Neuropathology and Experimental Neurology*, *56*, 751–761.

Verbeek, M. M., de Waal, R. M. W., & Vinters, H. V. (Eds.) (2000). *Cerebral amyloid angiopathy in Alzheimer's disease and related disorders*. Dordrecht, The Netherlands: Kluwer Academic Publishers.

Vinters, H. V. (1987). Cerebral amyloid angiopathy—a critical review. *Stroke*, *18*, 311–324.

Vinters, H. V. (1998). Alzheimer's disease: a neuropathologic perspective. *Current Diagnostic Pathology*, *5*, 109–117.

Vinters, H. V. (2000). Cerebrovascular disease in the elderly. In S. Duckett, J. de la Torre (Eds.), *Pathology of the aging nervous system* (2nd ed.) New York: Oxford University Press.

Vinters, H. V., Ellis, W. G., Zarow, C., Zaias, B. W., Jagust, W. J., Mack, W. J., & Chui, H. C. (2000). Neuropathologic substrates of ischemic vascular dementia. *Journal of Neuropathology and Experimental Neurology*, *59*, 931–945.

Vinters, H. V., Farrell, M. A., Mischel, P. S., & Anders, K. H. (1998). *Diagnostic neuropathology*. New York: Marcel Dekker.

Vinters, H. V., & Gilbert, J. J. (1983). Cerebral amyloid angiopathy: incidence and complications in the aging brain. II. The distribution of amyloid vascular changes. *Stroke*, *14*, 924–928.

Vinters, H. V., Pardridge, W. M., & Yang, J. (1988). Immunohistochemical study of cerebral amyloid angiopathy: use of an antiserum to a synthetic 28-amino-acid peptide fragment of the Alzheimer's disease amyloid precursor. *Human Pathology*, *19*, 214–222.

Vinters, H. V., Secor, D. L., Pardridge, W. M., & Gray, F. (1990). Immunohistochemical study of cerebral amyloid angiopathy. III. Widespread Alzheimer A4 peptide in cerebral microvessel walls colocalizes with gamma trace in patients with leukoencephalopathy. *Annals of Neurology*, *28*, 34–42.

Vinters, H. V., Secor, D. L., Read, S. L., Frazee, J. G., Tomiyasu, U., Stanley, T. M., Ferreiro, J. A., & Akers, M-A. (1994). The microvasculature in brain biopsy specimens from patients with Alzheimer's disease: An immunohistochemical and ultrastructural study. *Ultrastructural Pathology*, *18*, 333–348.

Vinters, H. V., Wang, Z. Z., & Secor, D. L.
(1996). Brain parenchymal and microvascular amyloid in Alzheimer's disease. *Brain
Pathology, 6,* 179–195.

Vonsattel, J. P., Myers, R. H., Hedley-Whyte,
E. T., Ropper, A. H., Bird, E. D., & Richard-
son, E. P. Jr. (1991). Cerebral amyloid angiopathy without and with cerebral
hemorrhages: a comparative histological
study. *Annals of Neurology, 30,* 637–649.

Wisniewski, H. M., & Silverman, W. (1997).
Diagnostic criteria for the neuropathological
assessment of Alzheimer's disease: Current
status and major issues. *Neurobiology of
Aging, 18* (S4), S43–S50.

Yamaguchi, H., Hirai, S., Morimatsu, M.,
Shoji, M., & Ihara, Y. (1988). A variety of
cerebral amyloid deposits in the brains of
the Alzheimer-type dementia demonstrated
by beta protein immunostaining. *Acta Neuropathologica, 76,* 541–549.

Yang, F., Sun, X., Beech, W., Teter, B., Wu, S.,
Sigel, J., Vinters, H. V., Frautschy, S. A., &
Cole, G. M. (1998). Antibody to caspase-
cleaved actin detects apoptosis in differentiated neuroblastoma and plaque-associated
neurons and microglia in Alzheimer's disease. *American Journal of Pathology, 152,*
379–389.

Seven

Age-Related Cognitive Change and Brain–Behavior Relationships

Marilyn S. Albert and Ronald J. Killiany

I. Introduction

There is considerable evidence for age-related declines in cognition. They are described in detail in other chapters and include declines in explicit memory (Chapter 14, Bäckman et al.), executive functions (such as divided attention) (Chapter 11, Rogers & Fisk), and language (Chapter 15, Kemper & Mitzner). Moreover, such changes are observed among carefully screened individuals, with no evidence of clinical disease (e.g., Albert, Duffy, & Naeser, 1987), suggesting that the increased prevalence of disease with advancing age is not the only mechanism causing age-related changes in cognition. It has been hypothesized that alterations in brain structure and function are, at least in part, responsible for age-related cognitive change. Within the last two decades, technological advances in noninvasive imaging and neuropathological evaluation have significantly expanded the capacity to evaluate the contribution of brain alterations to cognitive change with age. Likewise, the cognitive evaluation of nonhuman primates across the age range has served as an important model for studies of brain–behavior relation-

ships, as they apply to cognitive change with age.

In this chapter we will summarize the information these advances have provided regarding alterations in brain structure and function with age, and their relationship to cognitive aging. The chapter begins with a brief historical overview of brain–behavior relations and some of the methodologic and technologic issues related to their investigation. We then review the imaging methods and findings pertaining to structural changes seen in the brain with advancing age and their relationship to cognition. This is followed by a presentation of the methods and findings concerned with changes in brain function with age, and what is known about their associations with cognitive performance. Studies of nonhuman primates, both behavioral and pathological, will be included, where they shed additional light on these issues. In general, the goal of this chapter is to provide an overview of what is known about the brain–behavior relationships associated with cognitive aging.

The emphasis in this chapter will be on the age-related changes that one sees in cognition in the absence of clinical

Handbook of the Psychology of Aging
Copyright © 2001 by Academic Press.

disease. To put these findings in perspective, we also include a brief discussion of the brain–behavior alterations observed in Alzheimer's disease (AD), the disorder that most commonly causes cognitive decline among older individuals.

II. Historical Perspective on Brain– Behavior Relationships

Studies that relate various structures in the brain to specific functions originated with the classic works of investigators such as Broca (1865), Dax (1865a, 1865b), Jackson (1876), and Luria (1962). Each of these investigators believed that discrete behavioral and cognitive functions were subserved by unique, separate regions of the brain. Over time, the notion of identifying specific brain–behavior relationships became known as regionalization.

For a period of time, in the early part of the 20th century, this position was criticized by Karl Lashley (1929) and his colleagues. They argued that no specific brain–behavior relationships could be identified because considerable cortical damage could occur, particularly in the young (Hebb, 1942), and many cognitive and behavioral functions could be adequately performed. This point of view, known as the "theory of equipotentiality," has been proven untenable with respect to the adult brain by the accumulation of carefully controlled studies in mature humans, nonhuman primates, and rodents (Kandel, Schwartz, & Jessell, 2000).

These studies have employed several well-known strategies for making scientific inferences about brain–behavior relationships. The first is the classical method based on postmortem examination of brain structures among individuals with carefully documented health and cognitive assessments. The second classical method is the collection of behavioral data following brain stimula-

tion or insults, either surgical or accidental (e.g., brain lesions, infections). A third more recent and less invasive methodology is based on the collection of data on brain structures and activity, using imaging techniques. The first and third methods have successfully been applied to the study of brain–behavior relationships as they relate to aging. They will be the focus of this chapter.

III. Methodologic and Technologic Advances

A. Focus on Optimally Healthy Older Individuals

One of the major changes to occur in the study of brain–behavior relationships in aging is the focus on optimally healthy participants. This permits one to differentiate changes related to disease from those related to age. Among human subjects, this requires careful exclusion of subjects in the early stages of AD. However, many medical diseases are common in older individuals (e.g., hypertension, respiratory or cardiac disease, vitamin deficiency), all of which may impair intellectual function. Ideally, if one wants to study healthy individuals, these disorders should be excluded as well. Subjects selected without evidence of clinical disease will differ greatly from a group of older persons that is chosen at random from a population, because individuals chosen in order to be representative of the average will include many individuals with serious medical illness. Some of these illnesses will include those with considerable impact on cognitive function, such as AD (Odenheimer et al. 1994). Thus, optimally healthy individuals, although nonrepresentative, can be of heuristic value, and may ultimately make it easier to identify interventions that can minimize age-related cognitive change.

B. Postmortem Examination of Carefully Screened Subjects

Postmortem examination of well-studied individuals represent the most long-standing method for establishing brain–behavior relationships, as described above. Nevertheless, recent technological and methodological advances in the evaluation of postmortem tissue have produced a dramatic revision of our concepts of brain aging. The major technological advance pertains to the development of nonbiased stereological techniques, which permit investigators to accurately count neurons within a prescribed volume of tissue. It is this technological advance, combined with careful screening to assure that subjects with evidence of any relevant disease are excluded from examination, that has changed our concepts of the amount and nature of neuronal loss with advancing age.

C. Noninvasive Imaging Techniques

The advent of modern imaging techniques, beginning in about the mid-1970s, provided another major advance in the ability to study structure–function relationships. For the first time it was possible to study the living brain. This was particularly advantageous for the study of aging, because it became possible to examine optimally healthy individuals and determine whether changes in the brain occurred in the absence of clinical disease and, if so, how this related to changes in cognition. These imaging techniques can loosely be divided into two basic types: structural scans and functional scans (see Table7.1). The structural scans produce highly detailed images of the anatomical features of the brain. In fact, the images produced by the most advanced of these techniques look very similar in detail to that seen on postmortem examination of brain tissue. Examples of this type of structural scan include computerized tomography (CT) and magnetic resonance imaging (MRI). Functional scans, on the other hand, provide an indication of the activity of the brain, but do not tend to produce high anatomical detail. Examples of functional imaging scans include positron emission tomography (PET) and functional MRI (fMRI). When these functional methods are combined with structural scans, as is now commonly done, considerable localization of function is possible. Studies of aging, using each of these imaging modalities, will be presented here. Wherever possible, cognitive measurements obtained in conjunction with these scanning procedures will be discussed.

As will be seen by this review, noninvasive imaging procedures have demonstrated that changes in the brain are, at least in part, responsible for age-related declines in cognition. However, a comprehensive explication of the reasons for these declines has not yet been provided by either the structural imaging procedures currently available, or by the initial functional methods that have been applied to this question. There is increasing evidence, however, that fMRI, the newest noninvasive imaging technique that has been applied to the study of cognitive aging, is capable of providing the answers to these long sought questions. Moreover, as this review highlights, structural imaging procedures have been highly informative with respect to diseases of the brain that are caused by structural change,

Table 7.1
Types of Imaging

Structural	Functional
• X-rays	• Single photon emission computerized tomography
• Computerized tomography	
• Magnetic resonance imaging	• Positron emission tomography
	• Functional magnetic resonance imaging

such as AD. Structural imaging and, more recently functional imaging, have been able to take advantage of what has been learned about the location of the underlying pathology and the nature of the cognitive changes that accompany them. Progress in this area has advanced to the point that they are being considered as endpoints in clinical trials of new medications.

IV. Structural Imaging Studies of Normal Aging

A. Computerized Tomography

CT scanning provided the first major break through for investigators interested in viewing the living human brain. It is based on X-ray technology and can provide images of relatively high resolution for differentiating between structures of different density in the brain, such as bone, soft tissue, and fluid. CT's greatest drawback has been an inability to adequately differentiate between different types of soft tissues, such as the gray matter and white matter of the brain. For this reason, most CT studies of aging have focused on measures of general brain volume. With CT, brain volume can be quantified directly, or can be inferred by quantifying the size of the large cavities in the brain, known as *ventricles*, which are filled with cerebral spinal fluid (CSF). These measurements can be made by computer programs that are almost entirely automated, requiring little input from an operator. Thus the tissue and CSF volume estimates are highly reproducible.

The first striking finding to emerge from studies of healthy adults across the age range was that there is clear evidence of decreases in the amount of brain tissue in older individuals compared with younger ones. This is commonly referred to as brain atrophy. In general, CT studies

have concluded that the average individual above 55 to 65 years of age demonstrates brain atrophy and increasing amounts of atrophy are seen as people get older. Thus, as people get older, the volume of CSF within the ventricles increases and the volume of brain tissue decreases (Barrow, Jacobs, & Kinkel, 1976; Brinkman, Sarwar, Levin, & Morris, 1981; de Leon et al., 1989; Gado, Hughes, Danziger & Chi, 1983; Gado et al. 1982; Huckman, Fox, & Topel, 1975; Hughes & Gado, 1981; Kasezniak, Garron, Fox, Bergen, & Huckman, 1979; Roberts & Caird, 1976; Stafford, Albert, Naeser, Sandor & Garvey, 1988; Zatz, Jernigan, & Ahumada, 1982).

CT studies conducted in the same individuals over time have demonstrated this phenomenon as well. Longitudinal evaluation over a 1-yr period (Gado et al., 1983) and a 3-yr period (e.g., de Leon et al., 1989) have demonstrated an approximate rate of atrophy of 2% per year among healthy older individuals over the age of 64. This rate of change is relatively low compared to the 9% rate of atrophy seen in the brains of patients with AD (de Leon et al., 1989).

Several studies have demonstrated a relationship between increased atrophy in the brain, as measured by CT, and decreases in cognition (Jacoby, Levy, & Dawson, 1980; Soininen, Puranen, & Riekkinen, 1982; Stafford et al., 1988). In general, the greater the amount of atrophy, the lower the cognitive test score is likely to be. For example, after adjusting for age, positive correlations have been demonstrated between the volume of the left temporal lobe and a composite measure of cognitive performance largely reflecting memory ability (Soininen et al., 1982). Likewise, a measure of ventricular volume showed an inverse correlation with a composite measure of attention and abstraction (Stafford et al., 1988). Moreover, where this has been examined, these relationships appear to be nonlinear, in that greater atrophy and corresponding declines in cognition are generally seen after age 60 (e.g., Albert et al., 1987; Sullivan, Marsh, Mathalon, Lim, & Pfefferbaum, 1995).

There is, in addition, increasing evidence that changes in cognition are functionally related to changes in brain structure. This has been demonstrated by a number of studies in which structural equation modeling (SEM) has been employed. The SEM method of analysis was designed for situations in which there are a number of independent variables within a set of variables that potentially have effects on one another. A computer program known as LISREL is one commonly available method for applying SEM methods.

In the first study in which SEM was employed, CT variables were used in conjunction with other measures of physiological and behavioral status, to predict cognitive performance (Jones et al., 1991). The data were all from one point in time, thus the question addressed by the analysis was whether age-related alterations in cognition could be attributed, at least in part, to changes in the brain. The conclusion from the study was that the status of the brain was mediating, to a substantial degree, the observed effect of age on cognitive function. A similar finding was reported in a study that examined the relationship between MRI measures of the frontal lobe and mental imagery tasks (Raz, Briggs, Marks, & Acker, 1999).

This technique has also been applied to longitudinal data in which CT and explicit memory measurements have been examined, using a novel growth model based on SEM (McArdle et al., 2001). The individuals in the study were examined over a 7-yr interval, and health status was carefully evaluated, thus it was possible to assess the role of health in the model, as well as factors such as the gender of the participant. The analysis revealed that the size of the largest fluid-containing structures in the brain (the lateral ventricles) and memory performance were coupled over time in such a way that ventricular size was a leading indicator (i.e., predictor) of subsequent memory performance. Although these findings cannot conclusively prove causality, they demonstrate a strong association between age-related changes in brain structure and subsequent changes in memory.

The measures of gross brain atrophy provided by CT imaging have not, however, been capable of examining specific structure–function relationships. Imaging techniques, such as structural MRI, provide higher spatial resolution (and thus greater anatomical detail) and can therefore address some of the limitations of CT.

B. Magnetic Resonance Imaging

Structural MRI provides much greater anatomical detail than is possible with CT, because it can differentiate the two major classes of brain tissue (white matter and gray matter) and can reveal CSF spaces with greater accuracy. Two different imaging sequences are used to highlight these differing aspects of brain structure. The first image sequence, which is primarily used to examine details of brain tissue, is known as a T1 weighted image. When images of the brain are produced with this imaging procedure, the white matter (W) appears white, the gray matter (G) appears gray and the CSF and blood appear black (see Figure 7.1a). It should be noted that the gray appearance of the gray matter is because it contains the neuronal cell bodies, whereas the extension of the neurons (the axons and dendrites) are primarily within the white matter. The type of image sequence primarily used to examine CSF volumes in the brain is known as a T2 weighted image. When images of the brain are produced with this imaging

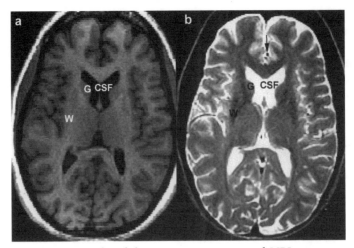

Figure 7.1 Examples of the two common structural MRI sequences. The image sequence on the left (a) is known as a T1 weighted image, and is primarily used to examine details of brain tissue. In such images, the white matter (W) appears white, the gray matter (G) appears gray, and the cerebrospinal fluid (CSF) and blood appear black. The image on the right (b) is known as a T2 weighted image and is primarily used to examine CSF volumes in the brain. When images of the brain are produced with this imaging procedure, the white matter (W) and blood have a dark, black appearance, the gray matter (G) appears gray and the cerebrospinal fluid (CSF) appears lighter, or white.

procedure, the white matter and blood have a dark, black appearance, the gray matter appears gray, and the CSF appears lighter, or white (see Figure 7.1b). Numerous specialty image sequences, such as diffusion-weighted imaging and fluid-attenuated inversion recovery, also exist. However, these image types are beyond the scope of this chapter. As with CT, the global measures of CSF and tissue volume (both gray matter and white matter) can be obtained by computer programs that are highly automated.

1. Global Change in Tissue Volume Assessed by MRI

MRI studies of healthy adults across the age range have confirmed the findings described above for CT. That is, regardless of the sequence type, overall brain volume shows a decrease with age, while the amount of CSF increases, even if in-

dividuals are healthy (Christiansen, Larsson, Thomsen, Wieslander, & Henriksen, 1994; Coffey et al., 1992; Harris et al., 1994; Jernigan, Press & Hesselink, 1990; Jernigan et al., 1991; Lim, Zipursky, Watts, & Pfefferbaum, 1992; Murphy, DeCarli, Schapiro, Rapoport & Horwitz, 1992; Matsumae et al., 1996; Pfefferbaum et al., 1994; Tanna et al., 1991).

2. Selective Change in Tissue Volume

MRI studies have extended the findings based on CT by examining specific changes in the volume of the gray and white matter. However, unlike the global measures on MRI described above, there is less agreement among studies about age-related changes in the volumes of these brain tissue types. Some studies have reported changes in gray matter, but have found no significant changes in the white matter (Coffey et al., 1992; Lim et al., 1992; Murphy et al., 1992; Pfefferbaum et al., 1994; Sullivan, Marsh, Mathalon, Lim, & Pfefferbaum, 1995). Conversely, a number of studies have reported significant decreases in white matter with age (Christiansen et al., 1994; Double et al., 1996; Guttmann et al., 1998; Harris et al., 1994; Jernigan et al., 1990, 1991; Resnick et al., 2000; Yue et al., 1997).

Moreover, a number of studies have reported that changes in the white matter appear to predominate over those of the gray matter (Double et al., 1996; Guttmann et al., 1998; Resnick et al., 2000). For example, among a group of healthy adults aged approximately 20–80, a highly significant age-related decrease in the percentage of white matter was seen, with a concomitant increase in the percentage of CSF (Guttmann et al., 1998). The percentage of gray matter showed only a relatively small decline with age; the only significant difference in gray matter was found between subjects 20 through 40 versus those in their 50s. A recent study by Resnick and colleagues (Resnick et al., 2000) provides further support for the notion that changes in white matter are more prevalent with aging than those of the gray matter. In this study of participants in the Baltimore Longitudinal Study of Aging, subjects between the ages of 59 and 85 were reevaluated over a 1-year period. The results showed a significant ventricular enlargement over time, along with an interaction between age and tissue type. This was interpreted by the authors as suggesting that aging has a greater effect on white matter than it does on gray matter.

These latter findings are consistent with morphological data in humans (Haug, 1984; Leuba & Garey, 1989; Terry, De Teresa, & Hansen, 1987), which indicate that, with advancing age, neuronal loss in the cortex is either not significant or not as extensive as reports prior to 1984 had suggested (Anderson,

Hubbard, Coghill, & Slidders, 1983; Brody, 1955, 1970; Colon, 1972; Henderson, Tomlinson, & Gibson, 1980; Shefer, 1973). Although large neurons appear to shrink, few are lost (Terry et al., 1987).

There are, in addition, comparable data in monkeys. Minimal neuronal cortical loss with age in monkeys has now been demonstrated in the striate cortex (Vincent, Peters, & Tigger, 1989), motor cortex (Tigges, Herndon, & Peters, 1992), frontal cortex (Peters, Leahu, Moss, & McNally, 1994), and the entorhinal cortex (Amaral, 1993). These general conclusions have been reached not only on the basis of a comparison of counts of neurons in young (5 to 6 years) and old (over 25 years of age) monkeys, but also on the basis of an examination of the cortical tissue by electron microscopy (Peters et al., 1994). Beyond an accumulation of lipofuscin granules in the cell body of some neurons and some cellular debris in neuroglial cells, there is very little evidence of changes with age in the neurons of these cortical regions (Peters, Josephson, & Vincent, 1991).

In addition, age-related alterations in the white matter have been described in some detail (Nielson & Peters, 2000; Peters, 1996; Peters, Leahu, Moss, & McNally, 1994). At first glance, the data suggesting loss of white matter in the brain without a loss of gray matter can be difficult to understand. Conventional knowledge suggests that white matter consists of the axons of neurons, and that if there is a loss of axons, there should be cell death and a loss of gray matter. However, the white matter of the brain is also composed of a number of glial elements such as oligodendrocytes. Evidence from the nonhuman primate suggests that the oligodendrocytes, which are responsible for forming the myelin sheath surrounding the axons, may be less efficient with age. For example, when the oligodendrocytes of old and young monkeys were compared

(Peters, 1996) it was found that the myelin sheaths in the old monkeys were abnormal and appeared to be degenerating. However, when the number of axons in old and young monkeys was compared by the same investigators (Nielsen & Peters, 2000), relatively few degenerating axons were found in the old monkeys. Taken together, these findings suggest changes in myelin, rather than axonal loss, are at least in part responsible for age-related changes in white matter observed with advancing age.

Visual examination of an MRI image from a healthy young and older individual exemplifies some of the changes described above. Figure 7.2 shows an MRI image, taken at approximately the same anatomical level, in a healthy, young adult (see Figure 7.2a) and a healthy, older adult (see Figure 7.2b). As can be seen, the general shape and size of the bone around the brain is nearly equal in both subjects. However, the image on the right appears to have less tissue than the image on the left. The cavities within the brain that contain CSF are also larger in the older individual than in the young. The largest CSF spaces in the brain, the lateral and third ventricles, clearly appear larger in the older person, but it is more difficult to determine visually whether the lower portion of the lateral ventricle (known as the *inferior horn of the lateral ventricle*) is enlarged. In addition, the folds of tissue on the cortical surface (known as the *sulci*) appear to be more spread apart in the older than in the younger subject. The space between the temporal lobes (known as the *supracellar cistern* [SC]) also appears to be wider in the older person than the young.

However, the gray matter of the brain does not appear to be as changed as the CSF spaces. The ribbon of gray matter forming the outer surface of the cortex appears as thick in the older subject as it does in the young. The hippocampal (H) formation is of nearly equal size in the two subjects. The deep gray matter structures, such as the thalamus (TH), also appear to be of approximately equivalent size in the two individuals. Close inspection of the images suggests that the white matter of the brain may be changed in the older person. Overall, there appears to be less white matter in the older individual than in the young; however, this is difficult to assess convincingly with visual inspection.

3. *Global MRI Measures and Cognitive Performance*

As with the CT studies described above, there is evidence that global MRI meas-

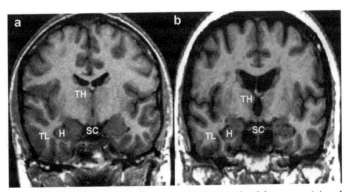

Figure 7.2 An example of a structural MRI in a healthy young (a) and healthy older individual (b). H = hippocampus, TH = thalamus, SC = suprasellar cistern.

ures of tissue volume or percentage of CSF correlate with global measures of cognitive performance. For example, both the gray–white ratio in the medial temporal lobe and an overall measure of total tissue volume were positively correlated with performance on nonverbal reasoning tasks (Raz, Millman, & Sarpel, 1990; Raz et al., 1993). However, a number of studies have either found weak correlations or no correlation between global MRI measures of tissue volume or CSF and measures of cognitive functioning (e.g., Tisserand, Visser, van Boxtel, & Jolles, 2000; Wahlund, Almkvist, Basun, & Julin, 1996). There are, to our knowledge, no reports that white matter volume correlates with measures of speed, thus it is unclear whether changes in white matter may contribute to the well-known slowing associated with age and to the observed association between slowing and cognitive change among older individuals (Salthouse, 1996), as has been suggested by some investigators (Meyerson, Hale, Wagstaff, Poon, & Smith, 1990).

4. The Hippocampus and Memory Performance

The visual detail provided by structural MRI also makes it possible to examine the volume of specific brain regions. However, this has been automated for only a small number of brain structures. For most regions, reliable assessment currently requires an individual skilled in neuroanatomy to outline the region, using objectively defined, easily reproducible boundaries. The brain region that has been the most widely studied with respect to age-related change is the hippocampus. This is not surprising, as changes in explicit memory are among the most well-studied change in cognition with age (see Bäckman et al., Chapter 14), and the hippocampus and adjacent structures are part of a memory-related neural system in the brain (Squire, Zola-Morgan, & Chen, 1988).

Although the MRI studies of the hippocampus vary methodologically in many ways, fourteen of them are consistent in finding mild to moderate age-related reductions in volume with increasing age (see Raz, 2000, for a review). In contrast, three studies (Jack et al., 1989; Sullivan, March, Mathalon, Lim, & Pferrerbaum, 1995; Zipursky et al., 1994) have reported a lack of correlation between hippocampal volume and age.

Although it is tempting to dismiss the results of these latter three studies on the basis of methodological differences, the weight of the evidence from postmortem studies supports their conclusion that the hippocampus shows minimal structural change with advancing age. The postmortem data in humans and monkeys indicate that neuronal loss is surprisingly low in most subfields of the hippocampus. For example, the subiculum shows a significant age-related loss in humans, with a similar trend in monkeys, however, the CA1, CA2 and CA3 subfields of the hippocampus show no evidence of age-related neuronal loss (Amaral, 1993; Gomez-Isla et al., 1996; Rosene, 1993; West, Coleman, Flood, & Troncoso, 1994). Equivalent data have recently been reported in rodents, where it was shown that even in the subset of animals with declines on a memory task, there was no decrease in the number of neurons in the various hippocampal subfields (Rapp & Gallagher, 1996). (See Morrison & Hof, 1997, for a more detailed discussion of these issues.)

Thus, it is important to consider the potential reasons why many structural MRI studies of the hippocampus show age-related decreases in volume when neuronal loss is minimal. The first reason pertains to the definition of the hippocampus itself. Most of the studies that included the anterior portion of the hippocampus demonstrate an age-related decrease in volume, while many of those that do not, fail to demonstrate this relationship. It has been argued that there is a true anterior–posterior gradient of age-related vulnerability in the hippocampus, with the more anterior regions showing the most age-related declines in volume. An alternative explanation is that the apparent decrease in volume comes from inclusion of part of the amygdala, which is found at the most anterior boundary of the hippocampus. The amygdala is reported to show age-related decreases in neuronal number (Navarro & Ganzalo, 1991), thus inclusion of part of this region may be responsible for the volumetric decrease seen in the hippocampus. In addition, the hippocampus has some white matter within it, and more importantly, white matter pathways leading from the hippocampus (the fimbria and the fornix) are generally included in any hippocampal MRI measure (see Figure 7.3). If there are selective decreases in white matter volume with age,

as suggested above, then inclusion of white matter may artificially show decrease in volume of the hippocampus. Certainly more morphological and imaging studies need to be conducted to determine the basis for this discrepancy.

The results of studies comparing the volume of the hippocampus to memory performance are also varied. Some have found a significant positive correlation (Golomb et al., 1994; O'Brien et al., 1997). However, a number of studies have either found weak correlations or no correlation between measures of this region and measures of cognitive functioning (Petersen et al., 2000; Raz et al., 1998; Sullivan et al., 1995; Tisserand, Visser, van Boxtel, Jolles, 2000; Ylikoski et al., 2000). These differences may be due to a number of factors, such as the definitions of the anatomical structures, the nature of the cognitive assessments, or the timing

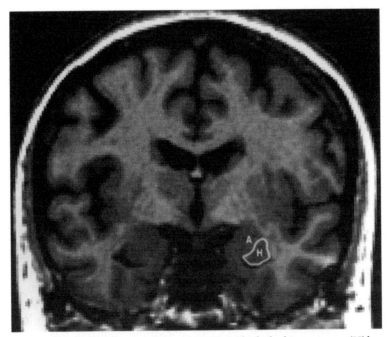

Figure 7.3 An example of a structural MRI on which the hippocampus (H) has been outlined. The general position of the amygdala (A), at the anterior end of the hippocampus is indicated.

of the changes in either structure or function.

The variations in correlational studies involving the hippocampus and memory performance may also be due to the fact that neurochemical changes outside the hippocampus may play a role in age-related declines in memory. There is substantial neuronal loss in selected subcortical regions responsible for the production of neurotransmitters important for memory ability, such as the basal forebrain and the locus coeruleus (e.g., Chan-Palay & Asan, 1989; Rosene, 1993). For example, in humans and monkeys there is approximately a 50% neuronal loss with age in the basal forebrain and 35–40% loss in the locus coeruleus and dorsal raphe (Kemper, 1993). This compares with an approximate loss of 5% in the CA1 subfield of the hippocampus.

The neuronal loss in these subcortical nuclei may be very important for memory function, as these brain regions influence the production of several neurotransmitters important for memory (such as acetylcholine and serotonin). Though subcortical, these nuclei have extensive connections with the cortex, and thus are responsible for the level of many neurotransmitters within the cortex. Perhaps as a result, a number of cortical regions have recently been shown to be important for memory, as described below, thus a structural evaluation of the hippocampus alone would underestimate the total contribution of age-related changes in the brain to memory performance.

It should also be noted that there are alterations in at least one receptor type (i.e., N-methyl-D-aspartate [NMDA] receptors) within the hippocampus that play an important role in memory function (Gazzaley, Siegel, Kordower, Muffson, & Morrison, 1996; Barnes, Suster, Shen, & McNaughton, 1997), suggesting another reason why structural measures per se may not consistently correlate with memory performance.

5. The Frontal Lobes and Executive Function Performance

MRI volumetric measurements have also looked for evidence of differential cortical atrophy, particularly with respect to the frontal lobes. Several studies have reported greater decreases in frontal lobe volume than in the other cortical regions (Coffey et al., 1992; Cowell et al., 1994; Murphy et al., 1996; Raz et al., 1997).

This is consistent with reports, based on postmortem examination, that the prefrontal cortex shows greater age-related declines than other cortical areas. Although the data suggest that there is minimal neuronal loss in frontal cortex with age, there is clear evidence for white matter losses below this cortical tissue (Peters, 1996; Peters et al., 1994), including declines in synaptic density and dendritic arborization (e.g., Liu, Erikson, & Brun, 1996). Studies of the frontal lobe on MRI likely include the white matter as well as gray matter of the frontal lobe, which may account for the observed decreases in frontal lobe volume that have been reported.

In addition, there is a selective age-related alteration in dopamine levels in the frontal lobe that appear to result from a decrease in neuronal number in the substantia nigra, another subcortical nucleus. For example, the substantia nigra loses neurons at a rate of about 6% per year (McGeer, McGeer, & Suzuki, 1977). Dopaminergic binding sites in the caudate nucleus and substantia nigra are also decreased (Severson, Marcusson, Winblad, & Finch, 1982). There is increasing evidence that this important neurotransmitter influences performance on tasks that require working memory and cognitive flexibility. Declines in working memory have, for example, been demonstrated in monkeys, who have an age-related loss of dopamine, and treatment with medication that increases dopamine levels improves performance (Arnsten,

Cai, Steere, & Goldman-Rakic, 1995). More severe declines in dopamine are also thought to be associated with the changes in cognitive flexibility seen in patients with Parkinson's disease (a disorder associated with a loss of cells in the substantia nigra and a severe decline in dopamine levels). These cognitive deficits have variably been described as mental inflexibility (Lees & Smith, 1983), a disorder of the shifting attitude (Cools, Van Den Bercken, Horstink, Van Spaendonck, & Berger, 1984), an instability of cognitive set (Flowers & Robertson, 1985), and difficulty with set formation, maintenance, and shifting (Taylor, Saint-Cyr, & Lang, 1987). Thus, age-related declines in dopamine may, at least in part, explain the changes seen in executive function with advancing age. It is interesting to note that this loss of dopamine may also be responsible for many of the common neurological signs that increase in frequency with age, including decreased arm swing and increased rigidity (Odenheimer et al., 1994).

Thus, correlations might be anticipated between volumetric measures of the frontal cortex and tasks that pertain to executive function, particularly if the measures include some of the adjacent white matter. Such data are limited but are consistent with this hypothesis. For example, it has been reported that the volume of prefrontal cortex is inversely correlated with performance on the Wisconsin Card Sorting Test (Raz et al., 1998).

There are, in addition, numerous studies of the relationship between cognition and white matter hyperintensities. Hyperintensities represent areas of increased signal on MRI and are generally associated with increased prevalence of diseases such as hypertension, diabetes, and heart disease. Few studies have examined hyperintensities in relation to specific brain regions; however, it has been found that when they are present in large numbers among healthy individuals, they are associated with lower frontal lobe perfusion and lower cognitive scores (DeCarli et al., 1995).

C. Functional Imaging Studies of Normal Aging

One of the most important innovations for the study of brain–behavior relationships has been the development of functional imaging. The most commonly employed functional imaging tools are PET and fMRI. In PET scanning, a radioactive isotope is either injected or inhaled by the subject, and the scanning machine evaluates the differential decay of radioactivity in order to assess regional changes in blood flow in the brain. The blood flow is considered a surrogate for neuronal activity. Likewise, fMRI uses the magnetic qualities of water molecules to evaluate the differential distribution of oxygenated blood in the brain, and the ratio of oxygenated to deoxygenated blood is thought to be an indirect measure of neuronal activity.

To obtain information about how the brain performs cognitive tasks, these imaging techniques are combined with cognitive paradigms, which produce a range of brain activations. Through careful design of such paradigms, it becomes possible to obtain information about the brain regions that are involved in a specific cognitive activity. Perceptual and emotional experience can also be interrogated in a similar manner. When such functional imaging procedures are combined with structural imaging, one can obtain data with highly accurate anatomical detail. The newest of these approaches, fMRI, provides such information in close to real time (i.e., the latency between stimulus onset and fMRI response is typically 2 sec).

1. Positron Emission Tomography

Most PET studies that have included older individuals have focused on the examination of memory changes with age. Due to the technological limitations of PET, these studies have generally focused on either the encoding or the retrieval phase of memory.

The most important general concept to emerge from such studies is that multiple brain regions are essential for encoding or retrieving new information. Moreover, some of the brain regions that appear to be integral to so-called memory networks have not been easy to evaluate by other imaging modalities. The most important in this regard is the frontal lobes, which are activated during both encoding and retrieval in normal young individuals (Buckner, Kelley, & Petersen, 1999; Demb, Desmond, Wagner, Waidya, Glover, & Gabrieli, 1995; Fletcher et al., 1995; Wagner et al., 1998; Madden et al., 1999; Kapur et al., 1994, 1996).

The hippocampus, known to be essential for normal memory based primarily on lesion studies (Squire et al., 1988), is more difficult to activate than many other brain regions, for reasons that are not entirely clear. Nevertheless, many recent PET studies have shown that significant activations of the hippocampus may be demonstrated when an individual is attempting to learn or retreive new information. The parahippocampal gyrus, a cortical region adjacent to the hippocampus, is also frequently activated in cognitive paradigms focused on explicit memory (Brewer, Zhao, Desmond, Glover, & Gabrieli, 1998; Gabrielli, Brewer, Desmond, & Glover, 1997; Martin, Wiggs, & Weisberg, 1997; Schacter & Wagner, 1999; Stern et al., 1996; Wagner et al., 1998), as is the prefrontal cortex (e.g., Haxby et al., 1995; Wagner et al., 1998), as peviously mentioned.

The most consistent finding to emerge from PET studies of aging is that there are alterations in the activation of the frontal lobes during encoding and/or retrieval of new information, (e.g., Cabeza, Anderson, Houle, Mangels, & Nyberg, 2000; Cabeza

et al., 1997; Grady, McIntosh, Rajah, Beig, & Crak, 1999; Hazlett et al., 1998), although the specific nature of these age-related differences remains to be clarified. Some researchers have found increased activity; others have found decreases. However, the nature of the activation paradigms have differed considerably among these studies, no doubt contributing to the differential findings.

There has been even less agreement about age-related changes in the hippocampus. For example, a PET study in which young subjects demonstrated significant hippocampal and prefrontal activation during an encoding task failed to produce similar activations in the elderly (Grady et al., 1995). Conversely, a PET study that examined subjects during a recall task reported similar activations in the hippocampus and/or parahippocampal gyrus in both young and elderly subjects, but substantial differences between the age groups in other brain regions, particularly the frontal lobes (Schacter, Savage, Alpert, Rauch, & Albert, 1996). Differences between the cognitive paradigms in the two studies, particularly in the degree to which the subjects learned the to-be-remembered material, are the most likely cause of these discrepancies.

2. Functional Magnetic Resonance Imaging

Since fMRI does not involve exposure to radioactivity, and measurements are closer to real time, many investigators who previously employed PET are turning to fMRI. Though few such studies have been published, a number have been reported at meetings. They concur with the PET studies in finding altered prefrontal activity during encoding (as mentioned previously). Most of these fMRI studies have demonstrated decreased activation of the prefrontal lobe when older individuals are trying to learn new information (e.g., Bates et al.,

2000; Sperling et al., 1999). It has been hypothesized that the differences in prefrontal activation between the young and the elderly subjects may reflect the fact that the two age groups use differing strategies to perform the task (e.g., Cabeza et al., 1997; Grady et al., 1999). This is consistent with numerous reports showing that elderly individuals are less likely to spontaneously use mnemonic strategies than the young when trying to learn new information (for reviews see Arenberg & Robertson-Tchabo, 1977; Craik, 1977). An alternate possibility is that the same strategy is being applied in different ways by the two age groups.

Interestingly, increased activation in the elderly compared with the young has also been demonstrated. For example, in tasks where the stimuli to-be-remembered are visual in nature, older individuals have shown greater activity than the young in the parietal cortex (one of the brain regions involved with spatial organization) (Bates et al., 2000; Sperling et al., 1999). This may also be a reflection of the differential deployment of cognitive strategies during the task, as mentioned above.

In this context, one should mention the hypothesis of *dedifferentiation* with age. This term is often applied to the finding that intercorrelations among tests of different cognitive domains increase with advancing age. At the neural level, this has been interpreted by some to mean that brain functions that are mediated by different brain regions in the young are mediated by larger combinations of brain regions as individuals get older. This latter hypothesis is not, however, supported by the large body of neuropsychological studies of adult humans and animals with brain lesions (e.g., Squire & Butters, 1992; Heilman & Satz, 1983; Lesak, 1983; Nadeau, Gonzalezrothi, Crosson, & Gonzalez-Rothi, 2000). However, the differential application of cognitive strategies among older individuals might explain

studies in which healthy older individuals demonstrate more widespread activation of brain regions than younger persons.

It should also be noted that some investigators have reported differences between the young and the elderly in hemodynamic response (D'Esposito, Zarahn, Aguirre, & Rypma, 1999; Ross et al., 1997; Taoka et al., 1998). Although the nature of these changes is still controversial, ranging from the possibility of decreased hemodynamic response (and therefore signal change) in the elderly, to increased noise with no absolute reduction in the magnitude of signal change, it is clearly possible that these differences are, at least in part, responsible for some of the fMRI differences between healthy young and older individuals. It is, however, reasonable to hypothesize that if such underlying hemodynamic changes exist, they might effect the ability to remember new information.

V. Brain–Behavior Relationships in Alzheimer's Disease

The cognitive changes that occur in normal aging are considerably different from that seen in AD, the most common cause of dementia among older persons. It should therefore not be surprising that the brain–behavior relationships that are observed differ both in nature and degree from what is seen in normal aging.

There is broad consensus that the earliest symptom of AD is a memory deficit that is characterized by impaired retention over delay intervals (e.g., Cummings & Benson, 1983). This is not the pattern of memory loss seen in aging. As healthy people get older, it takes longer to learn new information, thus given a limited period of time, older individuals learn less than younger ones (see Bäckman et al., Chapter 14). However, information that is well learned tends to be retained over delays in both healthy young and older individuals (e.g., Petersen, Smith, Kokmen, Ivnit, & Tangalos, 1992). Even in the early stage of AD, this pattern of retention is lost. Over brief delays, recall of newly learned information is severely impaired (Moss, Albert, Butters, & Payne, 1986; Welsh, Butters, Hughes, Mohs, & Heyman, 1992).

In addition, there is broad agreement, based on postmortem studies, that the hippocampal formation and adjacent regions within the medial temporal lobe are severely and selectively damaged in the early stage of AD (Braak & Braak, 1991; Hyman, Van Hoesen, Kromer, & Damasio, 1984). Neuronal loss and the pathological hallmarks of the disease (known as neuritic plaques and neurofibrillary tangles) are evident in large numbers throughout this region.

Thus, many MRI studies have focused on measurements of the hippocampus and the temporal horn (a part of the ventricle immediately adjacent to the hippocampus). These studies demonstrate that such measures differentiate patients with mild AD from controls with high levels of accuracy (e.g., Convit et al., 1993; Jack, Petersen, O'Brien, & Tangalos, 1992; Killiany, Moss, Albert, Sandor, Tieman, & Jolesz, 1993). MRI measures of these areas vary according to the severity of disease (Murphy et al., 1993). They also differentiate AD patients from patients with other neurologic and psychiatric disorders (O'Brien et al., 1997).

Recently, it has become apparent that MRI measures focused on an even smaller structure in this area are a sensitive marker of the early stage of AD. This structure is known as the entorhinal cortex (see Figure 7.4). It is a portion of the anterior parahippocampal gyrus that receives projections from widespread areas of the cortex and gives rise to the perforant pathway, the major cortical excitatory input to the hippocampus itself (Gomez-Isla et al., 1996; Hyman et al., 1984). Postmortem studies indicate that layers of the entorhinal cortex undergo 40–60% neuronal loss, even in the earliest phase of AD, when memory impairments and patient complaints are subtle and the symptoms do not reach threshold for a diagnosis of AD (Gomez-Isla et al., 1996). Recent MRI studies have demonstrated a highly significant difference between mild AD patients and controls, based on a measure of the entorhinal cortex alone (Bobinski et al., 1999; Killiany et al., 2000) (see Figure 7.4a and b). In addition, the volume of the entorhinal cortex is significantly correlated with

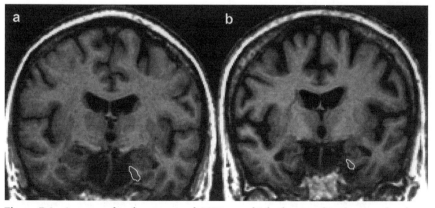

Figure 7.4 An example of a structural MRI on which the entorhinal cortex has been outlined. The image on the left is taken from a healthy older individual (a) and the image on the right is from an individual with mild Alzheimer's disease (b).

memory test performance. Moreover, the difference in the volume of the entorhinal cortex between AD patients and controls is similar to the degree of neuronal loss between these groups when measured in neuropathological tissue from this same region (Gomez-Isla et al., 1996; Killiany et al., 2000).

These findings suggest that measures of the entorhinal cortex and related structures may be useful as either an early marker of disease or as an outcome measure in a treatment trial of medication for AD. They also exemplify the potential of neuroimaging measures that are based on an understanding of the underlying neuropathology of a disorder and the cognitive deficits associated with it.

VI. Methodologic Issues Pertaining to Studies of Brain–Behavior Relations

There are several methodological issues pertaining to the studies that have just been discussed. These include the interindividual differences associated with age, secular trends or cohort effects, and changes in technology.

A. Interindividual Differences and Aging

It is important to emphasize the increased interindividual differences that occur with advancing age, even among optimally healthy individuals. Thus, the general statements made throughout this chapter apply to the changes for the average individual in the group, but cannot be said to apply to all individuals. Within a group of healthy older individuals there are invariably individuals whose brain structure and function appears similar to that of persons many decades younger than themselves. This phenomenon is exemplified in Figure 7.5, where the mean volume in white matter clearly decreases with age, but many older individuals have white matter volumes that are equivalent to that of younger persons. The cause of this increase in inter individual difference is an area of intense interest, as it suggests that there may be ways of reducing change among a larger number of older persons.

B. Secular Trends or Cohort Effects

Most, though not all, of the data presented here are cross-sectional in nature. It is therefore important to point out that secular trends or cohort effects can potentially effect these findings (see Haug, 1985, for a review) in the population. In essence, the problem is that humans born and raised at different time points have experienced different life events that can have long-term consequences on them. For example, individuals born in the early 1900s typically constitute the aging subjects in any curent cross-sectional study of aging, and those born and raised in the 1970s to 1980s would constitute the sample of young adult subjects. During the 70+-year period from the 1900s, countless improvements in health care have taken place that have resulted in a dramatic change in the average human. For example, the improvements in prenatal care, postnatal care, nutrition, and antibiotics have resulted in a population of young adults that not only are taller and heavier in body weight than their grandparents or great-grandparents but who also have bigger brains. This can be verified by comparing brain weights of young adults who died in the 1990s with young adults who died in the 1920s. Although all brain measures described in the present chapter are quantified as percentages in relation to brain size, the effect of these differences are not entirely understood.

In addition, major worldwide events that have taken place at particular time points in history have had profound impacts on particular segments of a cohort.

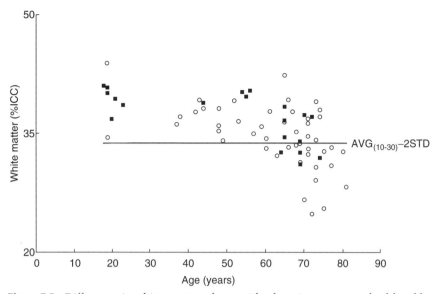

Figure 7.5 Differences in white matter volume with advancing age among healthy older individuals are shown as an example of the variability that can be seen in measures of brain structure among healthy individuals. The white matter measure is presented as a percent of intracranial cavity volume (%ICC) for each subject (circles = females; squares = males). A horizontal line is drawn 2 SD below the mean for the 20-year-old subjects. Note that only subjects 60 and older fall below this horizontal line, but there remain many older individuals who fall above the line.

For example, large numbers of males were killed at relatively young ages by various wars. At the time of these wars, the screening process for determining who was potentially placed at greatest risk was not always socioeconomically or socioeducationally unbiased, suggesting that the remaining population of males, in particular, may have been biased by this selection process.

Longitudinal studies are designed to reduce these secular trends, and thus are important to note, where available. Although such studies must overcome the difficulties associated with the loss of subjects due to drop out, they nonetheless provide us with greater insights into the direct affects of age.

C. Gender Differences

Since the days of the earliest studies of the brain, in the second half of the 19th century, the notion has existed that men have, on average, larger brains than women. Indeed, studies of brain size have been politically charged in the past (see Gould, 1981, for a review).

A variety of morphologic and imaging studies have, however, confirmed the suggestion that brain size differs between the sexes. Here again, it is hoped that the use of percent volume rather than absolute size, will reduce this bias. However, even matching by gender does not insure that the results have not been skewed by greater changes with age in one gender. Indeed, the literature suggests that males show greater age-specific changes than females (see Coffey et al., 1998, for a review) at least in terms of some CSF spaces. Future studies will provide greater detail about the extent to which gender may interact with age or other variables of interest. It should be noted that some investigations have reported a differential prevalence of AD between the genders, but this is not a consistent finding (see Katzman & Kawas, 1994, for a review).

D. Changes in Technology

All of the forms of imaging we have discussed in this chapter rely at least in part upon computer systems. At this point in time, as we enter a new century, we find ourselves in an amazing period of technological advances and change. These advances are rapidly being utilized by the scanning industry to produce ever more advanced scanners. More and more investigators have begun to use longitudinal studies to examine aging and disorders associated with it, as such studies are quite powerful in addressing issues, such as progression of change over time. However, more and more frequently, investigators are finding themselves having to change or upgrade technologically midstudy, potentially producing confounds in their data. A major challenge is to design a state-of-the-art scanning protocol that will at least be adequate to address the issues over time.

VII. Conclusion

There has been a major revision in our understanding of the type of changes that occur in the brain with advancing age. There is increasing evidence that widespread neuronal loss does not take place and produce ever increasing amounts of cognitive decline over time. Instead, it appears that a variety of neurobiological changes in the brain occur as people get older, including functional changes at the molecular level, alterations in dendritic branching, and neuronal loss in selective subcortical regions. If the changes in the brain with healthy aging are, in fact, more subtle than previously thought, it is not surprising that imaging modalities that look solely at brain structure appear not to adequately assess brain–behavior relationship. The advent of new ways of simultaneously examining both brain structure and function, as is done in fMRI, thus offers researchers interested in these issues a powerful tool for answering questions concerning how the brain changes with age, and how this impacts on cognition. It is hoped that these new approaches will ultimately lead to ways of reducing cognitive alterations among older individuals.

References

Albert, M. S., Duffy, F. H., & Naeser, M. (1987) Non-linear changes in cognition with age and their neurophysiological correlated. *Canadian Journal of Psychology*, *41*, 141–157.

Amaral, D. (1993). Morphological analyses of the brains of behaviorally characterized aged nonhuman primates. *Neurobiology and Aging*, *14*, 671–672.

Anderson, J. M., Hubbard, B. M., Coghill, G. R. & Slidders, W. (1983). The effect of advanced old age on the neurone content of the cerebral cortex. Observations with an automatic image analyser point counting method. *Journal of Neurological Sciences*, *58*, 233–244.

Arenberg, D., & Robertson-Tchabo, E. (1977). Learning and aging. In J. Birren & K. Schaie (eds.), *Handbook of the psychology of aging* (pp. 421–449). New York: Van Nostrand Reinhold.

Arnsten, A., Cai, J., Steere, J., & Goldman-Rakic, P. (1995). Dopamine D2 receptor mechanisms contribute to age-related cognitive decline: the effects of quinpirole on memory and motor performance in monkeys. *Journal of Neuroscience*, *15*, 3429–3439.

Barnes, C. A., Suster, M. S., Shen, J., & McNaughton, B. L. (1997). Multistability of cognitive maps in the hippocampus of old rats. *Nature*, *388*, 272–275.

Barrow, S. A., Jacobs, L., & Kinkel, W. R. (1976). Changes in size of normal lateral ventricles during aging determined by computerized tomography. *Neurology*, *26*, 1011–1013.

Bates, J., Savage, C., Schacter, D., Buckner, R., McInerney, S., Hyman, B., Rosen, B., Stern, C., Weisskoff, R., & Albert, M. (2001). Differential patterns of cortical but not hippocampal activity between young and elderly subjects during a visual encoding task. Manuscript submitted for publication.

Bobinski, M., deLeon, M., Convit, A., DeSanti, S., Weigiel, J., Tarshish, C., Saint Louis, L., Wisniewski, H. (1999). MRI of entorhinal cortex in mild Alzheimer's disease. *Lancet*, *353*, 38–40.

Boone, K. B., Miller, B. L., Leser, I. M., Mehringer, M., Hill-Gutierrez, E., Goldberg, M. A., & Berman, N. G. (1992). Neuropsychological correlates of white-matter lesions in healthy elderly subjects: A threshold effect. *Archives of Neurology*, *49*, 549–554.

Braak, H., & Braak, E. (1991). Neuropathological staging of Alzheimer-related changes. *Acta Neuropathologica*, *82*, 239–259.

Brewer, J., Zhao Z., Desmond, J., Glover, G., & Gabrieli, J. (1998). Making memories: Brain activity that predicts how well visual experience will be remembered. *Science*, *281*, 1185–87.

Brinkman, A. D., Sarwar, M., Levin, H. S., & Morris, H. H. (1981). Quantitative indexes of computed tomography in dementia and normal aging. *Radiology*, *138*, 89–92.

Broca, P. (1865). Du siege de la faculté du langage articule. *Bulletin of the Society of Anthropologists*, *6*, 377–393.

Brody, H. (1955). Organization of cerebral cortex. III. A study of aging in the human cerebral cortex. *Journal of Comparative Neurology*, *102*, 511–556.

Brody, H. (1970). Structural changes in the aging nervous system. *Interdisciplinary Topics in Gerontology*, *7*, 9–21.

Buckner, R., Kelley, W., & Petersen, W. (1999). Frontal cortex contributes to human memory formation. *Nature Neuroscience*, *2*, 1–4.

Cabeza, R., Anderson, N., Houle, S., Mangels, J., & Nyberg, L. (2000). Age-related differences in neural activity during item and temporal-order memory retrieval: A positron emission tomography study. *Journal of Cognitive Neuroscience*, *12*, 197–206.

Cabeza, R., Grady, C., Nyberg L., McIntosh A., Tulving, E., Kapur, S., Jennings, J., Houle, S., & Craik, F. (1997). Age-related differences in neural activity during memory encoding and retrieval: A positron emission tomography study. *Journal of Neuroscience*, *17*, 391–400.

Chan-Palay, V., & Asan, E. (1989). Quantitation of catecholamine neurons in the locus ceruleus in human brains of normal young and older adults in depression. *Journal of Comparative Neurology*, *287*, 357–372.

Christiansen, P., Larsson, H. B., Thomsen, C., Wieslander, S. B., & Henriksen, O. (1994). Age dependent white matter lesions and brain volume changes in healthy volunteers. *Acta Radiologica*, *35*, 117–122.

Coffey, C. E., Lucke, J. E., Saxton, J. A., Ratcliff, G., Unitas, L. J., Billig, B., & Bryan, R. N. (1998). Sex differences in brain aging: A quantitative magnetic resonance imaging study. *Archives of Neurology*, *55*, 169–179.

Coffey, C. E., Wilkinson, W. E., Parashos, I. A., Soady, S. A., Sullivan, R. J., Patterson, L. J., Figiel, G. S., Webb, M. C., Spritzer, C. E., & Djang, W. T. (1992). Quantitative cerebral anatomy of the aging human brain: A cross-sectional study using magnetic resonance imaging. *Neurology*, *42*, 527–536.

Colon, E. J. (1972). The elderly brain. A quantitative analysis of the cerebral cortex in two cases. *Psychiatria Neurologia, Neurochirugia*, *75*, 261–270.

Convit, A., deLeon, M., Golomb, J., George, A., Tarshish, S., Bobinski, M., Tsui, W., DeSanti, S., Wegiel, J., & Wisniewski, H. (1993). Hippocampal atrophy in early Alzheimer's disease: Anatomic specificity and validation. *Psychiatric Quarterly*, *64*, 371–87.

Cools, A., Van Den Bercken, J., Horstink, M., Van Spaendonck, L., & Berger H. (1984). Cognitive and motor shifting aptitude disorder in Parkinson's disease. *Journal of Neurology, Neurosurgery and Psychiatry*, *4*, 443–453.

Cowell, P. E., Turetsky, B. I., Gur, R. C., Grossman, R. I., Shtasel, D. L. & Gur, R. E. (1994). Sex differences in aging of the human frontal and temporal lobes. *Journal of Neuroscience*, *14*, 4748–4755.

Craik, F. (1977). Age differences in human memory. In J. Birren, & K. Schaie, (Eds.), *Handbook of the psychology of aging* (pp. 384–420). New York: Van Nostrand Reinhold.

Cummings, J., & Benson, D. (1983). *Dementia: A clinical approach*. Woburn, MA: Butterworth.

Dax, M. (1865a). *Lesions de la moitié gauche de líencephale coincidant avec líouble des signes de al pensée. Gazzeta Internazionale Di Medicina Chirurgia, 2*, 259–260.

Dax, M. (1865b). *Sur le même sujet. Gazzeta Internazionale di Medicine e Chirurgia, 2*, 260–262.

DeCarli, C., Murphy, D. G., Trahn, M., Grady, C. L., Haxby, J. V., Gillette, J. A., Salerno, J. A., Gonzales-Aviles, A., Horwitz, B., Rapoport, S., & Shapiro, M. B. (1995). The effect of white matter hyperintensity volume on brain structure, cognitive performance, and cerebral metabolism of glucose in 51 healthy adults. *Neurology, 45*, 2077–2084.

de Leon, M. J., George, A. E., Reisberg, B., Ferris, S. H., Kluger, A., Stylopoulos, L. A., Miller, J. D., La Regina, M. E., Chen, C. & Cohen, J. (1989). Alzheimer's disease: Longitudinal CT studies of ventricular change. *American Journal of Neuroradiology, 10*, 371–376.

Demb, J., Desmond, J., Wagner, A., Waidya, C., Glover, G., & Gabrieli, J. (1995). Semantic encoding and retrieval in the left inferior prefrontal cortex: A functional MRI study of task difficulty and process specificity. *Journal of Neuroscience, 15*, 5870–5878.

D'Esposito, M., Zarahn, E., Aguirre, G., & Rypma, B. (1999). The effect of normal aging on the coupling of neural activity to the BOLD hemodynamic response. *Neuroimage, 10*, 6–14.

Double, K., Halliday, G., Kril, J., Harasty, J., Cullen, K, Brooks, W., Creasey, H., & Broe, G. (1996). Topography of brain atrophy during normal aging and Alzheimer's disease. *Neurobiology of Ageing, 17*, 513–521.

Fletcher, P., Frith, C., Grasby, P., Shallice, T., Frackowiack, R., & Dolan, R. (1995). Brain systems for encoding and retrieval of auditory-verbal memory: An in vivo study in humans. *Brain, 118*, 401–416.

Flowers, K., & Robertson, C. (1985). The effect of Parkinson's disease on the ability to maintain mental set. *Journal of Neurology, Neurosurgery, and Psychiatary, 48*, 517–529.

Gabrielli, J., Brewer, J., Desmond, J., & Glover, G. (1997). Separate neural bases of two fundamental memory processes in the human medial temporal lobe. *Science, 276*, 264–266.

Gado, M., Hughes, C. P. Danziger, W., & Chi, D. (1983). Aging, dementia, and brain atrophy: A longitudinal computed tomographic study. *American Journal of Neuroradiology, 4*, 699–702.

Gado, M., Hughes, C. P., Danziger, W., Chi, D., Jost, G., & Berg, L. (1982). Volumetric measurements of cerebrospinal fluid spaces in demented subjects and controls. *Radiology, 144*, 535–538.

Gazzaley, A., Siegel, R., Kordowe, J., Mufson, E., & Morrison J. (1996). Circuit-specific alterations of N-methyl-D-aspartate receptor subunit 1 in the dentate gyrus of aged monkeys. *Procedures of the National Academy of Science, 93*, 3121–3125.

Golomb, J., Kluger, A., de Leon, M. J., Ferris, S. H., Convit, A., Mittelman, M., Cohen, J., Rusinek, H., De Santi, S., & George, A. E. (1994). Hippocampal formation size in normal human aging: A correlate of delayed secondary memory performance. *Learning and Memory, 1*, 45–54.

Gomez-Isla, T., Price, J. L., McKeel, D. W. Jr. Morris, J. C., Growdon, J. H., & Hyman, B. T. (1996). Profound loss of layer II entorhinal cortex neurons occurs in very mild Alzheimer's disease. *Journal of Neuroscience, 16*, 4491–4500.

Grady, C., Masoig, J., Horwitz, B., Ungerleider, L., Mentis, M., Salerno, J., Pietrini, P., Wagner, E., & Haxby, J. (1995). Age-related reductions in human recognition memory due to impaired encoding. *Science, 269*, 218–221.

Grady, C., McIntosh, A., Rajah, N., Beig, S., & Craik, F. (1999). The effects of age on the neural correlates of episodic encoding. *Cerebral Cortex, 9*, 805–814.

Gould, S. J. (1981). *The mismeasure of man.* New York: W. W. Norton and Company.

Guttmann, C. R. G., Jolesz, F. A., Kikinis, R., Killiany, R. J., Moss, M. B., Sandor, T., & Albert, M. S. (1998). White matter changes with normal aging. *Neurology, 50*, 972–978.

Harris, G. J., Schlaepfer, T. E., Peng, L. W., Lee, S., Federman, E. B. & Pearlson, G. (1994). Magnetic resonance imaging evaluation of the effects of ageing on grey-white ratio in the human brain. *Neuropathology, and Applied Neurobiology, 20*, 290–293.

Haug, H. (1984). Macroscopic and microscopic morphometry of the human brain and cortex. A survey in the light of new results. *Brain Pathology, 1,* 123–149.

Haug, H. (1985). Are neurons of the human cerebral cortex really lost during aging? A morphometric examination. In J. Traber & W. Gispen (Eds.), *Senile dementia of the Alzheimer's type* (pp. 150–63). Berlin: Springer-Verlag.

Haxby J, Ungerleider L, Horwitz B, Maisog J, Rapaport S., & Grady C. (1996). Face encoding and recognition in human brain. *Proceedings of the National Academy of Science, 93,* 922–927.

Hazlett, E., Buchsbaumm M., Mohs, R., Spiegel-Cohen, J., Wei, T., Azueta, R., Haznedar, M., Singer, M., Shihabuddin, L., Luu-Hsia, C., & Harvey, P. (1998). Age-related shift in brain region activity during successful memory performance. *Neurobiology of Aging, 19,* 437–445.

Hebb, D. O. (1942). The effect of early and late brain injury upon test scores and the nature of normal adult intelligence. *Proceedings of the American Philosophical Society, 85,* 275–292.

Heilman, K., & Satz, P. (1983). *Neuropsychology of human emotion.* New York: Guilford Press.

Henderson, G., Tomlinson, B., & Gibson, P. (1980). Cell counts in human cerebral cortex in normal adults throughout life, using an image analysing computer. *Journal of Neurological Science, 46,* 113–136.

Huckman, M. S., Fox, J., & Topel, J. (1975). The validity of criteria for the evaluation of cerebral atrophy by computed tomography. *Radiology, 116,* 85–92.

Hughes, C. P., & Gado, M. H. (1981). Computed tomography and aging of the brain. *Radiology, 139,* 391–396.

Hyman, B. T., Van Hoesen, G. W., Kromer, C., & Damasio, A. R. (1984). Alzheimer's disease: Cell specific pathology isolates the hippocampal formation. *Science, 225,* 1168–1170.

Jack, C., Petersen, R., O'Brien, P., & Tangalos, E. (1992). MR-based hippocampal volumetry in the diagnosis of Alzheimer's disease. *Neurology, 42,* 183–188.

Jack, C. R., Twomey, C. K., March, W. R., Zinsmeister, A. R., Sharbrough, F. W., Petersen, R. C., & Cascino, G. D. (1989). Anterior temporal lobes and hippocampal forma-

tions: Normative volumetric measurements from MR images in young adults. *Radiology, 172,* 549–554.

Jackson, J. H. (1876). Case of large cerebral tumor with optic neuritis and with left hemiplegia and imperception. *Royal London Ophthalmic Hospital Reports, 8,* 434–444.

Jacoby, R., Levy, R., & Dawson, J. (1980). Computed tomography in the elderly: 1. The normal population. *British Journal of Psychiatry, 136,* 249–255.

Jernigan, T. L., Archibald, S., Berhow, M., Sowell, E., Foster, D., & Hesselink, J. (1991). Cerebral structure on MRI. I. Localization of age-related changes. *Biological Psychiatry, 29,* 55–67.

Jernigan, T. L., Press, G. A., & Hesselink, J. R. (1990). Methods for measuring brain morphologic features on magnetic resonance images. *Archives of Neurology, 47,* 27–32.

Jones, K. J., Albert, M. S., Duffy, F. H., Hyde, M. R., Naeser, M., & Aldwin, C. (1991). Modeling age using cognitive psychosocial and physiological variables: The Boston normative aging study. *Experimental Aging Research, 17,* 227–242.

Kandel, E., Schwartz, J., & Jessell, T. (2000). *Principles of neural science.* New York: McGraw-Hill.

Kapur, S., Craik, F., Tulving, E., Wilson, A., Houle, S., & Brown, G. (1994). Neuroanatomical correlates of encoding in episodic memory: Levels of processing effects. *Proceedings of the National Academy of Science, 91,* 2008–2011.

Kapur, S., Tulving, E., Cabeza, R., McIntosh, A., Houle, S., & Craik, F. (1996). The neural correlates of intentional learning of verbal materials: A PET study in humans. *Cognitive Brain Research, 4,* 243–249.

Kaszniak, A. W., Garron, D. C., Fox, J. H., Bergen, D., & Huckman, M. S. (1979). Cerebral atrophy, EEG slowing age, education and cognitive functioning in suspected dementia. *Neurology, 29,* 1273–1279.

Katzman, R., & Kawas, C. (1994). The epidemiology of dementia and Alzheimer disease. In R. D. Terry, R. Katzman, & K. Bick (Eds), Alzheimer's Disease (pp. 105–122). New York: Raven Press.

Kemper, T. (1993). The relationship of cerebral cortical changes to nuclei in the brainstem. *Neurobiology of Ageing, 14,* 659–660.

Killiany, R., Gomez-Isla, T., Moss, M., Kikinis, R., Sandor, T., Jolesz, F., Tanzi, R., Jones, K., Hyman, B., & Albert, M. (2000). Use of structural MRI to predict who will get Alzheimer's Disease. *Neurology, 47,* 430–439.

Killiany, R. J., Moss, M. B., Albert, M. S., Sandor, T., Tieman, J., & Jolesz, F. (1993). Temporal lobe regions on magnetic resonance imaging identify patients with early Alzheimer's disease. *Archives of Neurology, 50,* 949–954.

Lashley, K. S. (1929). *Brain mechanism and intelligence.* Chicago: University of Chicago Press.

Lees, A., & Smith, E. (1983). Cognitive deficits in the early stages of Parkinson's disease. *Brain, 106,* 257–270.

Lesak, M. (1983). *Neuropsychological assessment.* New York: Oxford University Press.

Leuba, B., & Garey, L. (1989). Comparison of neuronal and glial numerical density in primary and secondary visual cortex. *Experimental Brain Research, 77,* 31–38.

Lim, K. O., Zipursky, R. B., Watts, M. C., & Pfefferbaum, A. (1992). Decreased gray matter in normal aging: An in vivo magnetic resonance study. *Journal of Gerontology, 47,* B26–30.

Liu, X., Erikson, C., & Brun, A. (1996). Cortical synaptic changes and gliosis in normal aging, Alzheimer's disease and frontal lobe degeneration. *Dementia, 3,* 128–134.

Luria, A. R. (1962). *Higher cortical functions in man.* Moscow: Moscow University Press.

Madden, D. J., Turkington, T. G., Provenzale, J. M., Denny, L. L., Hawk, T. C., Gottlob, L. R., Coleman, R. E. (1999). Adult age differences in the functional neuroanatomy of verbal recognition memory. *Human Brain Mapping, 7,* 115–135.

Martin, A., Wiggs, C., & Weisberg, J. (1997). Modulation of human medial temporal lobe activity by form, meaning and experience. *Hippocampus, 7,* 587–573.

Matsumae, M., Kikinis, R., Morocz, I. A., Lorenzo, A., Sandor, T., Albert, M., Black, P., & Jolesz, F. (1996). Age-related changes in intracranial compartment volumes in normal adults assessed by magnetic resonance imaging. *Journal of Neurosurgery, 84,* 982–991.

McArdle, J. J., Hamgami, F., Jones, K. J., Jolesz, F., Sandor, T., Kikinis, R., Spiro, R. & Albert, M. S. (2001). Structural modeling of dynamic changes in memory and brain structure: Longitudinal data from the normative aging study. *Journal of Gerontology, in press.*

McGeer, P., McGeer, E., & Suzuki, J. (1977). Aging and extrapyramidal function. *Archives of Neurology, 34,* 33–35.

Meyerson, J., Hale, S., Wagstaff, D., Poon, L. W., & Smith, G. A. (1990). The information-loss model: A mathematical theory of age-related cognitive slowing. *Psychological Review, 97,* 475–487.

Morrison, J. H., & Hof, R. P. (1997). Life and death of neurons in the aging brain. *Science, 278,* 412–419.

Moss, M. B., Albert, M. S., Butters, N., & Payne. M. (1986). Differential patterns of memory loss among patients with Alzheimer's disease, Huntington's disease and Alcoholic Korsakoff's Syndrome. *Archives of Neurology, 43,* 239–246.

Murphy, D., DeCarli, C., Daly, E., Gillette, J., McIntosh, A. R., Haxby, J., Teichberg, D., Shapiro, M., Rapoport, S., & Horwitz, B. (1993). Volumetric magnetic resonance imaging in men with dementia of the Alzheimer type: Correlations with disease severity. *Biological Psychiatry, 34,* 612–621.

Murphy, D. G., DeCarli, C., McIntosh, A. R., Daly, E., Mentis, M. J., Pietrini, P., Szczepanik, J., Schapiro, M. B., Grady, C. L., Horwitz, B., & Rapoport, S. (1996). Sex differences in human brain morphometry and metabolism: An in vivo quantitative magnetic resonance imaging and positron emission tomography study on the effect of aging. *Archives of General Psychiatry, 53,* 585–94.

Murphy, D. G., DeCarli, C., Schapiro, M. B., Rapoport, S. I., & Horwitz, B. (1992). Age-related differences in volume of subcortical nuclei, brain matter, and cerebrospinal fluid in healthy men as measured with magnetic resonance imaging. *Archives of Neurology, 49,* 839–845.

Nadeau, S., Gonzalezrothi, L., Crosson, B., & Gonzalez-Rothi, L. (2000). *Aphasia and language: Theory and practice.* New York: Guilford.

Navarro, C., & Gonzalo, L. M. (1991). Changes in the human amygdaloid complex due to age. *Revista Medica de Universidad de Navarra, 35,* 7–12.

Neilsen, K., & Peters, A. (2000). The effects on the frequency of nerve fibers in rhesus monkey striate cortex. *Neurobiology of Ageing, 21,* 621–628.

O'Brien, J. T., Desmond, P., Ames, D., Schweitzer, I., Chiu, E., & Tress, B. (1997). Magnetic resonance imaging correlates of memory impairment in the healthy elderly: Association with medial temporal lobe atrophy but not white matter lesions. *International Journal of Geriatric Psychiatry, 12,* 369–374.

Odenheimer, G., Funkenstein, H., Beckett, L., Chown, M., Pilgrim, D., Evans, D., & Albert, M. (1994). Comparison of neurologic changes in successfully aging persons vs the total aging population. *Archives of Neurology, 51,* 573–580.

Peters, A. (1996). Age-related changes in oligodendrocytes in monkey cerebral cortex. *Journal of Comparactive Neurology, 371,* 153–163.

Peters, A., Josephson, K., & Vincent, S. (1991). Effects of aging on the neuroglial cells and pericytes within area 17 of the rhesus monkey (Macaca mulatta). *Anatomical Record, 229,* 384–398.

Peters, A., Leahu, D., Moss, M. B., & McNally, K. (1994). The effects of aging on area 46 of the frontal cortex of the aging monkey. *Cerebral Cortex, 6,* 621–635.

Petersen, R. C., Jack, C. R., Xu, Y. C., Waring, S. C., O'Brien, P. C., Smith, G. E., Ivnik, R. J., Tangalos, E. G., Boeve, B. F., & Kokmen, E. (2000). Memory and MRI-based hippocampal volumes in aging and AD. *Neurology, 54,* 581–587.

Petersen, R. C., Smith, G., Kokmen, E., Ivnik, R., & Tangalos, E. (1992). Memory function in normal aging. *Neurology, 42,* 396–401.

Pfefferbaum, A., Mathalon, D. H., Sullivan, E. V., Rawles, J. M., Zipursky, R. B. & Lim, K. O. (1994). A quantitative magnetic resonance imaging study of changes in brain morphology from infancy to late adulthood. *Archives of Neurology, 51,* 874–887.

Rapp, P. R., & Gallagher, M. (1996). Preserved neuron number in the hippocampus of aged rats with spatial learning deficits. *Proceedings of the National Academy of Science, 93,* 9926–9930.

Raz, N. (2000). Aging of the brain and its impact on cognitive performance: Integration of structural and functional findings. In F. I. M. Craik & T. A. Salthouse (Eds.), *Handbook of aging and cognition.* Mahwah, NJ; Erlbaum.

Raz, N., Briggs, S., Marks, W., & Acker, J. (1999). Age-related deficits in generation and manipulation of mental images. II. The role of the dorsolateral prefrontal cortex. *Psychology and Aging, 14,* 436–444.

Raz, N., Gunning-Dixon, F., Head, D., Dupuis, J., & Acker, J. (1998). Neuroanatomical correlates of cognitive aging: evidence from structural magnetic resonance imaging. *Journal of Neuropsychology, 121,* 95–114.

Raz, N., Gunning, F. M., Head, D., Dupuis, J. H., McQuain, J., Briggs, S. D., Loken, W. J., Thornton, A. E., & Acker, J. D. (1997). Selective aging of the human cerebral cortex observed in vivo: differential vulnerability of the prefrontal gray matter. *Cerebral Cortex, 7,* 268–82.

Raz, N., Millman, D., & Sarpel, G. (1990). Cerebral correlates of cognitive aging: Grey–white matter differentiation in the medial temporal lobes, and fluid vs. crystallized abilities. *Psychobiology, 18,* 475–481.

Raz, N., Torres, I. J., Spencer, W. D., Baertschie, J. C., Millman, D., & Sarpel, G. (1993). Neuroanatomical correlates of age-sensitive and age-invariant cognitive abilities: An in vivo MRI investigation. *Intelligence, 17,* 407–422.

Resnick, S. M., Goldszal, A. F., Davatzikos, C., Golski, S., Kraut, M. A., Metter, E. J., Bryan, R. N., & Zonderman, A. B. (2000). One-year age changes in MRI brain volumes in older adults. *Cerebral Cortex, 10,* 464–472.

Roberts, M. A., & Caird, F. I. (1976). Computerized tomography and intellectual impairment in the elderly. *Journal of Neurology, Neurosurgery, and Psychiatry, 39,* 986–989.

Rosene, D. (1993). Comparing age-related changes in the basal forebrain and hippocampus of the rhesus monkey. *Neurobiology of Ageing, 14,* 669–670.

Ross, P., Yurgelon-Todd, D., Renshaw, P., Maas, L., Mendelson, J., Mello, N., Cohen, B., & Levin, J. (1997). Age-related reduction in functional MRI response to photic stimulation. *Neurology, 48,* 173–176.

Salthouse, T. A. (1996). The processing-speed theory of adult age differences in cognition. *Psychological Review, 103,* 403–428.

Schacter, D. L., Savage, C. R., Alpert, N. M., Rauch, S. L., & Albert, M. S. (1996). The role of the hippocampus and frontal cortex in age-related memory changes: A PET study. NeuroReport, 7, 1165–1169.

Schacter, D., & Wagner, A. (1999). Medial temporal lobe activations in fMRI and PET studies of episodic encoding and retrieval. Hippocampus, 9, 7–24.

Severson, J., Marcusson, J., Winblad, B., & Finch, C. (1982). Age-correlated loss of dopaminergic binding sites in human basal ganglia. Journal of Neurochemistry, 39, 1623–1631.

Shefer, V. (1973). Absolute number of neurons and thickness of cerebral cortex during aging, senile and vascular dementia and Pick's and Alzheimer's disease. Neuroscience and Behavioral Physiology, 6, 319–324.

Soininen, H., Puranen, M., & Riekkinen, P. (1982). Computed tomography findings in senile dementia and normal aging. Journal of Neurology, Neursurgery and Psychiatry, 45, 50–54.

Sperling, R., Bates, J., Cocchiarella, A., Zaheer, A., Campbell, T., Rentz, D., Schacter, D., Rosen, B., & Albert, M. (1999). fMRI of face-name association in healthy young and older subjects. Society for Neuroscience, 25, 646.

Squire, L., & Butters, N. (1992). Neuropsychology of memory. New York: Guilford Press.

Squire, L., Zola-Morgan, S., & Chen, K. (1988). Human amnesia and animal models of amnesia: performance of amnesic patients on tests designed for the monkey. Behavioral Neuroscience, 11, 210–221.

Stafford, J., Albert, M. s., Naeser, M., Sandor, T., & Garvey, A. (1988). Age related differences in CT scan measurements. Archives of Neurology, 45, 409–419.

Stern, C., Corkin, S., Gonzalez, R., Guimaraes, A., Baker, J., Jennings, P., Carr, C., Sugiura, R., Vedantham, V., & Rosen, B. (1996). The hippocampus participates in novel picture encoding: Evidence from functional magnetic resonance imaging. Proceedings of the National Academy of Science, 93, 8660–8665.

Sullivan, E. V., Marsh, L., Mathalon, D. H., Lim, K. O., & Pfefferbaum, A. (1995). Age-related decline in MRI volumes of temporal lobe gray matter but not hippocampus. Neurobiology of Ageing, 16, 591–606.

Tanna, N. K., Kohn, M. I., Horwich, D. N., Jolles, P. R., Zimmerman, R. A., Alves, W. M., & Alavi, A. (1991). Analysis of brain and cerebrospinal fluid volumes with MR imaging: Impact on PET data correction for atrophy. Part II. Aging and Alzheimeris dementia. Radiology, 178, 123–130.

Taoka, T., Iwasaki, S., Uchida, H., Fukusumi, A, Nakagawa, H., Kichikawa, K., Yoshioka, T., Takewa, M., & Ohishi, H. (1998). Age correlation of the time lag in signal change on EPI-fMRI. Journal of Computer Assisted Tomography, 22, 514–517.

Taylor, A., Saint-Cyr, J., & Lang, A. (1987). Parkinson's disease: Cognitive changes in relation to treatment response. Brain, 110, 35–51.

Terry, R. D., DeTeresa, R., & Hansen, L. A. (1987). Neocortical cell counts in normal human adult aging. Annals of Neurology, 21, 530–539.

Tigges, J., Herndon, J., & Peters, A. (1992). Neuronal population of area 4 during life span of rhesus monkeys. Neurobiology of Ageing, 11, 201–208.

Tisserand, D., Visser, P., van Boxtel, M., & Jolles, J. (2000). The relation between global and limbic brain volumes in MRI and cognitive performance in healthy individuals across the age range. Neurobiology of Ageing, 21, 569–576.

Vincent, S., Peters, A., & Tigges J. (1989). Effects of aging on neurons within area 17 of rhesus monkey cerebral cortex. Anatomical Record, 223, 329–341.

Wagner, A., Poldrack, R., Eldridge, L., Desmond, J., Glover, G., & Gabrieli, J. (1998). Material-specific lateralization of prefrontal activation during episodic encoding and retrieval. NeuroReport, 9, 3711–3717.

Wagner, A., Schacter, D., Rotte M., Koutstaal, W., Maril, A., Dale, A., Rosen, B., & Buckner, R. (1998). Building memories: Remembering and forgetting verbal experiences as predicted by brain activity. Science, 281, 1188–1191.

Wahlund, L., Almkvist, O., Basun, H., & Julin, P. (1996). MRI in successful aging, a 5-year follow-up study from the eighth to ninth decade of life. Magnetic Resonance Imaging, 14, 601–608.

Welsh, K., Butters, N., Hughes, J., Mohs, R., & Heyman, A. (1992). Detection and staging in Alzheimer's disease: Use of the neuropsychological measures developed for the Consortium to Establish a Registry for Alzheimer's Disease. *Archives of Neurology, 49,* 448–452.

West, M., Coleman, P., Flood, D., & Troncoso, J. (1994). Differences in the pattern of hippocampal neuronal loss in normal aging and Alzheimer's disease. *Lancet, 344,* 769–772.

Ylikoski, R., Salonen, O., Mantyla, R., Ylikoski, A., Keskivaara, P., Leskela, M., & Erkinjuntti, T. (2000). Hippocampal and temporal lobe atrophy and age-related decline in memory. *Acta Neurologica Scandanavica, 101,* 273–280.

Yue, N., Arnold, A., Longstreth, W., Elster, Al., Jungreis, C., O'Leary, D., Poirier, V., & Bryan, R. N. (1997). Sulcal, ventricular, and white matter changes at MR imaging in the aging brain: Data from the Cardiovascular Health Study. *Radiology, 202,* 33–39.

Zatz, L., Jernigan, T. L., & Ahumada, A. J. (1982). Changes on computed cranial tomography with aging: Intracranial fluid volume. *American Journal of Neuroradiology, 3,* 1–11.

Zipursky, R. B., Marsh, L., Lim, K. E., DeMent, S., Shear, P. K., Sullivan, E. V., Murphy, G. M., Csernansky, R. G., & Pfefferbaum, A. (1994). Volumetric MRI assessment of temporal lobe structures in schizophrenia. *Biological Psychiatry, 35,* 501–516.

Eight

Health Risk Behaviors and Aging

Howard Leventhal, Carolyn Rabin, Elaine A. Leventhal and Edith Burns

I. Introduction

Four questions come immediately to mind when we address the issue of health behavior and aging: (a) What are health and risk behaviors? (b) Are there clear benefits to so-called health promoting behaviors, and are these benefits visible for older persons or are they restricted to young and middle aged persons? (c) What motivates older persons to adopt and sustain healthy behaviors and stop risky behaviors that have significant health effects? (d) Can older persons change their behaviors (i.e., adopt new health behaviors of known efficacy and desist from behaviors that carry known risk), and what can be done to assist them in making these changes?

Our focus on the elderly moderates the answers to each of these questions. The later years of life bring physical changes that may or may not be alterable. Some are normal changes of aging or senescence, and others are wrought by illness, or cognitive decline. Although aging begins in the womb, changes attributed to senescence usually begin in the postpubertal years. Evolutionary pressures for sustaining health and function are less intense beyond puberty (i.e., the age at which the next generation can be conceived) (Hafez, 1973). From age 20 onward, cognitive functions such as fluid or working memory, speed of processing, and so on, show steady decline with each decade (Park & Hedden, in press); crystalized knowledge does not. In fact, domain-specific knowledge among the intact elderly may exceed that for younger persons (Charness, 2000). The rate of decline is swifter, however, in some physiological systems than others. For example, pulmonary function declines more rapidly than physical strength (Timiras & Atherton, 1988).

Aging is also associated with multiple changes wrought by illness or cognitive decline. Some of these changes are gradual (e.g., the onset of osteoarthritis), and others are abrupt (e.g., diagnoses of life-threatening illness) and introduce unexpected changes to the self. Illness, whether of gradual or sudden onset, brings dysfunction, and efforts to overcome these changes can lead to complex and sometimes debilitating treatments. Illness-induced functional decline and actual and perceived stigmatization can lead to withdrawal from social roles and reductions in economic resources. In addition, illness often requires participation in complex and unfamiliar institutional and social structures while dealing with personal, physical dysfunction (H. Leventhal, Idler, & Leventhal, 1999).

The reductions in physical function and participation in daily activities caused by senescence and cognitive decline are associated with increases in negative affect and declines in positive affect (Benyamini, Idler, Leventhal, & Leventhal, 2000; Stewart et al., 1989; Williamson, 1998; Zeiss, Lewinsohn, Rohde, & Seeley, 1996). They also result in reduced assessments of health (Benyamini, Leventhal, & Leventhal, 1999), and these reductions, in association with lowered expectations of functional ability and life expectancy, can affect the use of medical care (Idler & Benyamini, 1997; Tissue, 1972). The added burden of managing unfamiliar disease can contribute to the sense of hopelessness that is an integral component of depression. Thus, failure to recover or slow recovery from disease-induced disability can sustain emotional distress and lower quality of life and self-esteem (Reich, Zautra, & Guarnaccia, 1989; Stewart et al., 1989). In summary, the evidence indicates that functional decline associated with both senescence and cognitive decline carries psychological hazards, and these psychological changes feed-forward and reinforce the very functional deficits that initiated them.

Can health behaviors minimize the physical and psychological burdens of aging and illness? In the section immediately following, we discuss behaviors that are presumed to benefit and behaviors that are presumed to pose risks to health. Our review will focus on evidence for the benefit for elderly persons of activities such as exercise and diet. The section following that turns to issues of motivation, and discusses some of the barriers to the adoption of health practices that are known to be effective for improving physical and psychological well-being. We

focus on two sets of such factors. The first set involves common-sense beliefs that self-management of both aging and illness requires special strategies both for survival and for maintaining physical and psychological function. The belief that illness and age weaken the body can encourage elderly persons to conserve energy in order to ensure a longer and healthier life, (i.e., it will encourage a *self-regulation strategy* of conservation of resources) (E. A. Leventhal & Crouch, 1997). This strategy can be a barrier to engaging in health-promoting activities such as physical exercise. Belief in the value of conservation will likely be stronger among older persons who experience painful and/or threatening symptoms when active. For example, elderly men whose cardiac conditions generate angina in response to physical activity are likely to believe that conservation is essential for survival, and become the quintessential couch potatoes (Aikens, Michael, Levin, & Lowry, 1998; Wenger, 1981). Thus, beliefs about the self, one's psychological and physical resources given one's age and morbidities, and those about strategies and specific procedures for promoting health and preventing disease will interact to generate motivation for health promotive and risk-reducing actions. As the belief is likely shared by family members and friends, social influences will reinforce the individual's approach to self-management (Botwinick, 1984). The consequence of this motivational mix is that the elderly may be more willing and able to adopt and maintain some specific health-promotive behaviors but unwilling and/or unable to adopt others.

The second set of factors that we discuss can be grouped under the heading of *social influence*. We prefer to use the phrase social influence rather than the more widely used phrase, *social support*, as the latter implies that social influences are beneficial for health behaviors. But not all social influences are beneficial;

some are burdensome demands that may or may not be beneficial for health. Social support typically refers to providing assistance with instrumental activities (e.g., driving the patient to the doctor) and/or to listening to the individual's expression of feelings and providing emotional and self-esteem support (Cohen & Hoberman, 1983). *Social demand*, on the other hand, refers to obligations to others, many of which are distressing, and *social control* refers to the variety of ways in which someone may attempt to regulate another person's behavior (Rook & Pietromonaco, 1987). Moreover, different procedures can be used to provide supports, create demands, and implement social controls. Thus, each of these three ways of relating to others can affect health and risk behaviors and can do so in different ways depending upon the procedures accompanying them (Lewis & Rook, 1999; Tucker & Mueller, 2000).

II. Healthy and Risky Behaviors: What Are They?

Health behaviors can enhance physical and psychological function and well-being, and in some cases, reduce vulnerability to disease and/or slow disease progression. The list of health behaviors believed to reduce vulnerability to disease (i.e., to be effective for primary prevention) includes items such as never smoking, maintaining average weight and sleeping 7 to 8 hours per night (Belloc & Breslow, 1972; Wingard, Berkman, & Brand, 1982), consuming a diet rich in fruits and vegetables (Chandalia et al., 2000; De Lorgeri et al., 1998; Steinmaus, Nunez, & Smith, 2000), using dietary supplements including B vitamins (Gey, 1993), micronutrients such as calcium (deJong, et al., 2000), low-dose aspirin reducing myocardial infarction (Hansson et al., 1998), green tea (Imai, Suga, & Nakachi, 1997), and exercising (Blumenthal et

al., 1989; Fiatarone, et al., 1994; Moore & Blumenthal, 1998). Some are related to decreased mortality (Wingard, Berkman, & Brand, 1982), others to increased lean body mass, physical function, and bone density (deJong et al., 2000; Fiatarone et al., 1994). Although many other procedures are presumed to offer benefits, many fail to deliver as promised (Apple, 1996). A recent report from the Institute of Medicine points to the absence of data to support the claims for prevention of disease made for a host of nutritional supplements including vitamin C, beta carotine, and so on. (Institute of Medicine, 2000). Evidence is lacking for a host of other, "alternative" and complementary procedures, such as massage therapy and herbal remedies, that are widely used (Cassileth, 1998; Collacott, Zimmerman, White, & Rindone, 2000; Eisenberg et al., 1993, 1998).

Risk behaviors, on the other hand, can undermine general health and cause disease even though they are enhancing an individual's sense of well-being. Cigarette smoking is a prime example: it generates feelings of calmness and well-being while being responsible for an estimated 85% of all lung cancer deaths, 80% of all chronic obstructive pulmonary disease deaths, and 30% of all heart disease deaths (McGinnis & Foege, 1993; U.S. Department of Health and Human Services, 1990), in addition to precipitating early menopause and increasing risk of osteoporosis for elderly women (Ensrud et al., 1994). By contrast, stopping smoking can both slow and even reverse harmful somatic changes (Shopland & Burns 1993) and increase negative affect (Hatsukami, Dahlgren, Zimmerman, & Hughes, 1988). Thus, cigarette smoking is likely the outstanding performer for risky behaviors, with actions such as excessive use of alcohol, overeating, improper use of medications, and failure to heed warnings following close by (Rodin & Salovey, 1989).

The healthy and risky behaviors mentioned were selected because of their relationship to mortality. Behaviors that avoid or slow mortality make the healthy behavior list; those that create and or speed mortality are designated as risky. Mortality is not, however, the only endpoint for generating a list of health-relevant behaviors. Behaviors can be classified with respect to their association with specific diseases (e.g., any one of the 200 or more cancers, cardiac, endocrine, and musculoskeletal disorders), and for disrupting particular functions (e.g., difficulties with walking; coordination; sleep; memory; etc.). As the endpoints vary so too will the behaviors on the list, and so too will their rank order. For example, consumption of 3 to 4 ounces of alcohol per day may be bad for the liver, a risk for cancer and memory loss, but reduce the risk of coronary artery disease (Keil, Chambless, Doring, Filipiak, & Stieber, 1997). Although case control studies suggested that high-fiber diets were effective in reducing colon cancer risk (Howe et al., 1992), randomized trials do not show protective effects (Alberts et al., 2000; Schatzkin et al., 2000), though a well-controlled, small-scale trial shows that a high-fiber diet lowered blood glucose in diabetics (Chandalia et al., 2000).

The list of health and risky behaviors and the position of the items on it will change with the age of the population under consideration. Thus, some behaviors may convey more benefit or risk at early rather than later ages, and others more harm and less benefit at later ages. For example, elevation of cholesterol (240 mg/ml) and mild overweight (10 to 15 pounds over age-recommended figures) appear more serious at age 29 than at age 85 (Andres, Elahi, Tobin, Muller, & Brant, 1985; Cornoni-Huntley et al., 1991), though overweight is hazardous at any age (Calle, Thun, Petrelli, Rodriguez, & Heath, 1999). Slight overweight at age 70 and above may be associated with increased life expectancy, though it may be harmful to musculoskeletal function in physically active persons.

A. Which Health Behaviors Benefit the Elderly?

The maintenance of good health is typically described as a life span issue. The ideal view is that maximal benefit is expected when healthy behaviors begin and risky behaviors are avoided from birth onward. The ideal is not, however, incompatible with a late start, as there are clear benefits for health and physical function when healthy behaviors are initiated later in life, and risky behaviors, such as smoking, are eliminated. Relatively few behaviors with claims to preventive and health-promoting value have been subjected to randomized clinical trails, the presumed "gold standard" for the evaluation of efficacy: exercise and dietary practices are the exceptions among health-promotive behaviors. A wide variety of procedures designed to screen for early detection of disease and the prevention of disease spread and disability have been studied in considerable detail, though not always with randomized trails. We will discuss each in turn.

1. Exercise

The benefits of exercise are well established in the elderly. For example, moderate exercise by older persons has been shown to maintain strength and physical function (Fiatarone et al., 1994), to prevent adverse sequelae of myocardial infarction (death and subsequent heart attacks; Blumenthal et al., 1989), to increase life expectancy (Hakim et al., 1998), and enhance function and reduce morbidity in the final years of life (Fries, 1983). Exercise also appears to be as effective as pharmacotherapy and psychotherapy for the treatment of clinically depressed older adults (Moore &

Blumenthal, 1998). Exercise, however, is not risk free. The possibility of injury, particularly among the elderly, is always present, and the risk is greater if the activity is unsupervised and/or conducted with insufficient attention to safety (Lox, Burns, Treasure, & Wasley, 1999; Pollock et al., 1991). And though exercise in the later years is clearly beneficial (e.g., merely walking 2 miles or more a day is associated with an increased life expectancy of 5 years in healthy older men (Hakim et al., 1998), it will be of greater benefit for those who have previously been sedentary (Blair et al., 1995). The benefit of exercise may be slight for those maintaining a life-long pattern of vigorous activity.

2. Diet

Among dietary practices, epidemiological data suggest that consumption of fruits and vegetables and green tea can reduce the rates of colon and bladder cancers (Steinmaus, Nunez, & Smith, 2000; Kohlmeier, Weterings, Steck, & Kok, 1997), and data from case control studies (e.g., comparisons of persons with specific diseases with otherwise similar, age-matched individuals), cross-national studies, and clinical trials concur in showing that low-fat diets reduce rates of coronary disease and in some instances appear to lower all-cause mortality among those in their fifties and sixties (Ornish et al., 1998). Although most participants in dietary studies are in their middle, late middle, and early late years, the data suggest that the efficacy of these dietary changes are equivalent across age groups (Ornish et al., 1998). However, adherence to extremely low-fat diets may be expensive both in the cost of low-fat products and the effort involved in adherence, and runs the danger of malnutrition, particularly in older individuals. Although many older adults express concern about elevated cholesterol and ask for medication for

cholesterol reduction, preliminary results—on samples including middle-aged and late middle-aged participants—suggest that medications prescribed to lower elevated cholesterol may have small, adverse effects on attention and psychomotor speed as assessed by neuropsychological tests (Muldoon et al., 2000; Wardle et al., 2000). Evidence for the efficacy of specific diets and food supplements also is often contradictory. Most of the data in this domain are from retrospective, epidemiological surveys using case control methodology, and failure to replicate is frequent. The evidence from longitudinal studies is limited and not overly encouraging. As mentioned earlier, high-fiber diets have proven ineffective in preventing recurrence of colon polyps in samples of adults aged 40 to 80 (Alberts et al., 2000) and 35 years of age or older (Schatzkin et al., 2000), though they do appear effective in the control of diabetes (Chandalia et al., 2000).

3. Supplements: Calcium and Hormonal Agents

Studies of the control of osteoporosis, confined largely to investigations of women's health, have focused on calcium supplements and exercise (Lau, Woo, Leung, Swaminathan, & Leung, 1992; Ulrich, Georgiou, Snow-Harter, & Gillis, 1996), estrogen replacement (Nachtigall, Nachtigall, Nachtigall, & Beckman, 1979), and more recently, estrogen antagonists such as tamoxifen and raloxifene, which show substantial benefits for the preservation of bone density (Tamoxifen; Love et al., 1992; Raloxifene: Delmas et al., 1997) and the reduction of breast cancer in women over 35 years of age (Tamoxifen: Fisher et al., 1998). Calcium deficiency is also serious for the elderly male population with regard to both the preservation of bone density and possible prevention of colon cancer (Baron et al., 1999). Exercise has been demonstrated to increase bone density and improve aerobic fitness in elderly men as well (Blumenthal et al., 1991). Once again, however, one must weigh costs (both financial and risk of cardiovascular problems) against potential benefits for behavioral interventions using more potent pharmacological agents such as tamoxifen or raloxifene.

4. Screening

Screening for the detection and early treatment of disease (i.e., secondary prevention) is presumed to minimize the progression and threat to life of cancers and cardiovascular diseases. Debate about the age at which to initiate screening has been stimulated by recent biomedical advances that have created noninvasive procedures for the early detection of these diseases. Screening to detect cancers (e.g., breast, colon, and prostate) is generally recommended to begin when people are in their forties and fifties and to continue into the sixties and early seventies; screening for cardiac disease is generally recommended to begin earlier, particularly for individuals from families with a history of coronary disease. These issues are extremely relevant to the elderly, as the incidence of cardiovascular diseases and many cancers increase with age (American Heart Association, 1999). The incidence of coronary heart disease (CHD) is greatest for men in their fifties and sixties, and greatest for women in the seventies. And CHD in older women is underrecognized by both patients, families, and professionals (Martin, Gordon, & Lounsbury, 1998). Although the evidence favors most screening procedures, not all meet expectations. Data from both case-control studies and clinical trials indicate benefit for early detection for breast cancer, however (Demissie, Mills, & Rhoads, 1998; Kerlikowske, Grady, Rubin, Sandrock, & Ernster, 1995; UK Trial, 1988).

Unfortunately, despite evidence to support the use of some screening procedures, compliance is less than optimal. The diagnosis and control of hypertension by use of medication, weight reduction, and exercise can have a major impact on the occurrence of stroke and myocardial infarction. Though these actions are known to be effective, only 1/3 to 1/2 of those with hypertension have been screened and diagnosed, 1/3 to 1/2 who have been diagnosed are in active treatment, and only 1/3 to 1/2 of those in treatment have blood pressure that is controlled (Leventhal, Zimmerman, & Gutmann, 1984), figures that differ little from those 25 years earlier.

Similarly, though regular mammography appears to be effective in reducing mortality from breast cancer, 25% of women with a family history of breast cancer have never had a mammogram (Costanza, 1992; Kerlikowske et al., 1995; Lerman, Kash, & Stefanek, 1994 Thompson et al., 1994: the typical effect size of screening on mortality is small to moderate in size). The deficit in screening may reflect the debate over the appropriate age of onset, frequency, and duration of mammography, as there are contradictory suggestions from the National Cancer Institute, the American Cancer Society, U.S. Preventive Services Task Force, American College of Obstetrics and Gynecology, and American Geriatrics Society. Data suggest deficits in screening for other forms of cancer. For example, Myers et al. (1994) study found that two successive yearly mailings urging the use of a fecal occult blood test (FOBT) to detect colon cancer generated a 50% response rate in the first year, but that rates of screening declined in the second year to approximately 25% for those under 65 years of age. In this instance, rates of screening remained approximately the same (50%) for those over 65. Thus, the elderly seemed more attuned to screening for colon cancer. Screening for prostate cancer, digital examination by the physician, and the prostate specific antigen test (PSA) makes the important point that not all screening behaviors involve patient choice, as the former should be part of the physical examination. The extent of patient choice for PSA testing, however, will likely be related to the practitioners' beliefs in the efficacy of testing and benefits of treatment; the latter is not entirely clear at this time (Canadian Task Force, 1991; Goldberg & Chavin, 1997).

Given the late onset of many diseases, it would appear that the elderly are prime candidates for screening for early detection, and many public health authorities encourage mass screening for breast and prostate cancer and coronary disease. The heavy use of screening, at least by elderly women, suggests that public perception is congruent with such public health policies. Recent, epidemiological data on the efficacy of screening casts doubt, however, on such broadly drawn policies. First, the value of screening is doubted for detection of diseases for which there is no clear evidence for effective treatment. Prostate cancer is a prime example; it is a disease of elderly men, and its incidence increases with age (it is estimated that >40% of men over 70 years of age have a prostate tumor). Most prostate cancers, however, are slow growing and do not threaten life. In addition, there is currently insufficient evidence that treatment is effective, and treatment, and even diagnosis, can cause morbidities that sacrifice quality of life for questionable gains. Some believe that screening may do more harm than good, but others suggest that repeated screening (with PSA) may help to distinguish slow-growing, nonlife-threatening tumors best treated with watchful waiting, from rapidly growing malignancies that merit invasive treatments with surgery and radiation (Balducci, Pow-Sang, Friedland, & Diaz, 1997). Second, questions have been raised about the benefit of screening for the el-

derly (i.e., whether screening for individuals over 70 to 75 years of age will gain more than a few extra days of life) (Robinson & Beghe, 1997; Balducci & Lyman, 1997). These debates and biomedical advances in genetics will undoubtedly influence the elderly public's perception of the value of both behavioral change for prevention and screening for early detection.

III. Motivation for Healthy Behaviors and Reduction of Risky Behaviors among the Elderly

The biomedical focus of health professionals and researchers will lead them to rank the importance of health and risk behaviors on the basis of data from epidemiological studies and clinical trials. These data identify links between behaviors and health outcomes. Focusing only on these data risks ignoring the public perception of these behaviors. That which has been validated as healthy in an "objective" clinical trial may not be seen as such by laypersons. In the lay view, healthy actions may be seen as risky (e.g., mammography screening) and risky actions as healthy (e.g., sun exposure), and specific healthy and risky behaviors may simply be absent from the laypersons' screen (Manderbacka, Lundberg, & Martikainen, 1999). Moreover, a wide range of factors may be involved in generating motivation for engaging in healthy behaviors and stopping risky ones, and many of these factors may have little or no relationship to health concerns or health values. Sun exposure is an example. A tan skin has long been seen as sexually attractive and a sign of vigor and health; the relationship of sun exposure and tanning to skin cancer has only recently entered the public domain. Although cigarette smoking is now recognized as a health risk, its adoption has relatively little to do with health concerns. Indeed, for over 400 years smoking has been perceived, at times simultaneously, as a boon to health and as a plague (Borgatta, 1968; H. Leventhal & Clearly, 1980). People adopt alternative procedures for prevention and treatment as they fit themes that underlie commonsense thinking about health (e.g., that the "natural" is superior to the artificial), that our innate, vital potential is critical for health, etc. (Kaptchuk & Eisenberg, 1998). Most of these alternative procedures have neither proven efficacy nor are they likely to prove effective when tested. Although the elderly may be somewhat less prone to use alternatives therapies, they will likely find many of these themes appealing. Identifying the conditions for generating motivation for engaging in healthy actions and reducing risky ones among the elderly is an important focus for research. So too is determining whether the conditions involved in the maintenance of healthy behaviors are the same or different from those involved in their initiation.

Unfortunately, the domains in which deficits in motivation for healthy behavior, are clearly visible are also those in which the epidemiological evidence favoring action are most clear (i.e., exercise and diet). The very same studies that report the success of exercise in strengthening muscle and balance illustrate the enormous motivational barriers to participation in health-promoting activity. For example, Fiatarone et al. (1994) induced only 29% of their population of elderly nursing home residents to participate in their exercise program. Despite the offer from a recognized group of investigators from a prestigious medical school, 71% of the residents declined to participate. Although low participation rates in institutional settings are complicated by a significant number of individuals with dementia, problems with recruitment are clearly present in noninstitutional studies. For example, Ettinger and colleagues (1997) identified 1164 individuals as eligible for participation in the FAST trial (a comparison of aerobic exercise, resistance exercise, and health education for adults over 60 years of age with knee osteoarthritis). Of the 841 adults remaining after exclusion for medical reasons, only 52% agreed to participate and only 43% completed the program. Another example is the study by Rubenstein and associates in which only 10% of 7054 men aged 70 or older at risk for falls and eligible for participation in a carefully designed, medically supervised exercise study responded to the informational flyer used as the initial contact for recruitment (Rubenstein et al., 2000). Recruitment is not, however, the only barrier to improving health through exercise: missing sessions and dropping out are clear barriers to improvement in health, though they occur with sufficient frequency to serve as a good outcome measure for studies of adherence (e.g., Duncan, McAuley, Stoolmiller, & Duncan, 1993).

Adoption and maintenance of simple dietary practices fare little better. Although drinking green tea and consuming low-fat diets appear to be effective in lowering rates of cardiovascular disease and colon cancer (Bushman, 1998), and green tea has been shown to have a direct effect on the destruction of cancer cells in the colon (Ahmad et al., 1997), it may be difficult to persuade many to implement these behaviors; a 1992 review of participation in health-promotion programs indicates that rates of participation are often disappointing (Carter, Elward, Malmgren, Martin, & Larson, 1992). Though reluctant to perform such simple dietary alterations, elderly individuals spend billions of dollars each year on dietary supplements for which there is no proven efficacy (Comsumer Reports, 2000). Public willingness to make use of supplements, cleansing agents (e.g., antibacterial soaps and cleansers), and avoidance of specific foods (e.g., red meats), and the growth of the organic food industry suggests substantial public belief in ideas such as, "You are what you eat!", "Poisons in foods need to be avoided", "The system needs to be cleansed of poisons", and "Proper intake can strengthen (the immune system and) resistance to disease."

A. A Model for the Motivation and Performance of Health Behaviors

A variety of theoretical models have been used to structure studies to analyze the determinants of participation and adherence to health behaviors among both young and older persons. The models have also served as the basis for intervention studies, though such studies are greatly outnumbered by studies describing correlates of participation and adherence. Utility models are among the most common. They include the health belief model (Rosenstock, 1974; Rosenstock, Strecher, & Becker, 1988), protection motivation theory (Rogers, 1984), the theory of reasoned action (Ajzen & Fishbein, 1977), and the modification of the latter model, the theory of planned behavior (Ajzen, 1985). Models in this class propose that motivation to act is a function of beliefs in personal vulnerability to a health threat and beliefs respecting its seriousness. Preference for one or another specific, protective action depends upon beliefs about the benefits (including efficacy) and costs of each available act. A second set of models—cognitive behavioral theory (Bandura, 1997) and self-regulation theory (Carver & Scheier, 1982, 1998; Lazarus, 1966; Lazarus & Folkman, 1984; Leventhal, 1970; H. Leventhal, Meyer, & Nerenz, 1980)—place greater emphasis on how specific life events are interpreted as health threats and the development of skills for performing protective actions.

Though their terms differ, all theories of health action agree that the mechanism underlying the performance of healthy behaviors involves both motivation and behavioral plans and skills, though significant and subtle differences exist in the way motivation and behavioral factors are conceptualized by each. As our focus is not on a review of these similarities and differences, we have selected self-regulation models to guide our analysis as we believe they offer the most comprehensive view of the factors that are important for motivation by elderly persons. They should prove useful, therefore, both to the researcher and clinician (Petrie & Weinman, 1997; Skelton & Croyle, 1991).

1. Hierarchical Structures Involved Self-regulation

a. Contextual Structure Self-regulation theories posit two hierarchies for the analysis of the initiation and maintenance of health and risk behaviors (see Figure 8.1). The first nests the psychological factors controlling the ongoing regulation of behavior, the *problem level*, in the context of four, consecutive levels formed by the self and the social environment. The second involves a hierarchy of mental operations, some automatic, perceptual or experiential, and others volitional or controlled.

The *problem level* forms the base of the first hierarchy of mental process. It consists of the overt and covert–mental activity involved in the interpretation of somatic experience, symptoms, and function as indicators of health risks, and the performance of procedures for managing these risks. The *self system* forms the most proximal contextual level (Bronfenbrenner, 1992; Brownlee, Leventhal, & Leventhal, 2000). It consists of a set of self identities, problem-solving strategies, beliefs about the self's competency in various domains, and personality traits that moderate the individual's behaviors at the *problem level*. Next is the *neighbor-*

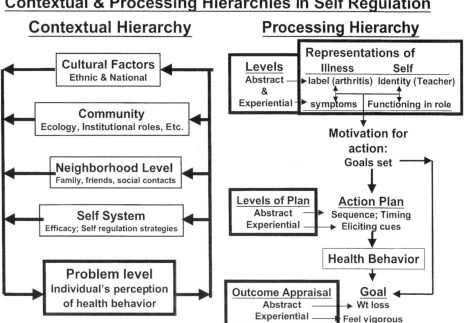

Figure 8.1 The contextual hierarchy (left side) shows the problem level (representation of health threats and health behaviors for prevention and control of these threats) nested under and influenced by the self, neighborhood, community and cultural factors. Experience with behavioral outcomes at the problem level feedback and influence the self, neighborhood, community, and culture, though we can expect weaker feedback effects as we move from the self and neighborhood to the community and cultural levels. To avoid a too busy diagram, we do not show arrows for interactions among the cultural, community, neighborhood and self. The processing hierarchy (right side) shows how the abstract and experiential levels of representations of illness threats and the self interact to form motivation for the performance of healthy behaviors and the elimination of risky behaviors. Motivation involves setting goals, which can be abstract (cure arthritis) or experiential (reduce arthritis pain and stiffness), generating action plans, and the performance of specific health behaviors for goal attainment. Goal attainment can be appraised at the abstract (arthritis cured) and experiential levels (exercise-reduced pain and stiffness). A health behavior (e.g., exercise) may meet expectations for both or for one or the other of the abstract (disease cure) or experiential goals motivating action.

hood level, what Chrisman and Kleinman (1983) called the "popular level" (i.e., the social contacts and influences from family and peers). A variety of social processes influence healthy and risky behaviors at this level: examples include social support, direct efforts at social control, perceived demands, social conflict, and social isolation. Emotional distress due to social conflict can encourage and sustain risky behaviors and interfere with the possibility for movement toward healthy behaviors. Another contextual level is formed by structural factors including *roles* defined by formal and informal organizations and ecological factors reflecting the orderliness or disruptiveness of the physical environment (Park et al., 1999). The final contextual level involves ethnic, national, and regional *cultural norms* that encourage healthy and/or risky actions.

Contextual factors influence and are influenced by the individual's ongoing experience with specific health and risk behaviors. The reciprocal nature of these influences creates direct and indirect paths among levels (e.g., ethnic, national culture and the local ecology influencing one another and the individual's sense of self). The individual's perceptions of relationships among the levels (e.g., an elderly person's perception that his community is looked down upon by powerful others), or the perception that her ethnic and cultural values are discrepant with national values, can affect her relationship with other individuals at the neighborhood level. These reflected perceptions further complicate the analysis of the interacting effects of these levels on physical and psychological health.

b. Psychological Structure The second hierarchy is that identified with the mental mechanisms regulating ongoing behavior. The perceptual or experiential level of the *problem-based processes* includes factors such as the somatic sensations, functional changes, and affective reactions generated by the performance of specific behaviors (e.g., leg muscle or chest pain during exercise and feelings of energy and/or fatigue postexercise). The conceptual level of problem-based processes involves the interpretation and emergent meaning of these experiential factors. Meanings are a product of the integration of experiential factors with the propositionally structured system of categories comprising declarative knowledge. For example, muscular pain during exercise and postexercise fatigue may be interpreted as fatigue due to emotional distress or as indicators of cardiac risk; the latter interpretation would lead to seeking health care (Cameron, Leventhal, & Leventhal, 1995). It is critical to recognize that somatic experience is more likely to be interpreted as relevant to age and/or health by elderly than by younger persons (H. Leventhal, Patrick-Miller, Leventhal, & Burns, 1997; Prohaska, Keller, Leventhal, & Leventhal, 1987; Prohaska, Leventhal, Leventhal, & Keller, 1985), as

with advancing age people accumulate a substantial number of illness experiences. Indeed, when questioned about their medical histories, the 851 older persons participating in a just completed longitudinal study reported an average of 10 illnesses, the vast majority of which were chronic conditions. Thus, the distinction between health and illness behaviors is clearly less relevant for older than for younger persons, as virtually any health-promoting activity by older persons is undertaken in the context of a complex history of experience with multiple medical conditions.

2. Motivation, Procedures, and Appraisals in the Self-Regulation Process

a. The System at Work Unfortunately, educational programs promoting healthy behaviors rarely make use of these hierarchical conceptualizations. Most national, regional, and statewide efforts, and even the majority of local efforts, develop health messages that present abstract information on the relationships of healthy or risky actions to specific diseases and fail to address how the members of their audience experience risk (i.e., whether they base personal feelings of risk on family history, observations of others, their physical symptoms, or emotional reactions, (H. Leventhal, Kelley, & Leventhal, 1999). Pictorial material is often used to personalize information (e.g., testimonials expressing a person's beliefs about a recommended action are designed to encourage identification with the source and enhance the personal relevance of the message). This may be effective if the source matches the recipient on critical factors, such as sharing vulnerabilities and potential gains from the action or sharing a similar life situation (Mazen & Leventhal, 1972). Connecting with the recipient's experiences may require, however, sharing of information that is neither understood as relevant nor typically used in media messages.

We can picture how these hierarchical systems work by imagining two examples of elderly individuals engaging in vigorous, potentially health-promotive activities, Mr. X, a 59-year-old, working male, and Mrs. Y, a 73-year-old, retired female. Assume for the moment that both Mr. X and Mrs. Y experience identical symptoms after moderately vigorous physical activity. After walking up a hill on a hot afternoon as part of their daily "fitness routine," each of them experiences mild chest discomfort and difficulty breathing. Both have been under considerable stress, Mr. X concerned that he may be replaced by a younger, less expensive employee, Mrs. Y concerned about a serious marital conflict between her son and daughter-in-law. Given the symptoms, his age, 59, and work stress, Mr. X is likely to interpret the cues as cardiac-related (Rushton et al., 1998). That is Mr. X will elaborate upon his experience in three of the domains of the commonsense representations of illness (See Figure 8.2): the identity (symptoms fit the cardiac label), cause (work stress), and timeline (age of 59) as his experience fits the schema for cardiovascular disease (Lau & Hartman, 1983; Leventhal, Myer, & Nerenz, 1980). This schema will likely be shared with others, (i.e., friends and family), and they also are likely to share images and beliefs for the two remaining domains of illness representations—consequences (X's report activating images of George Y who unexpectedly died of a heart attack), and control (modern medicine can manage coronary disease). This shared schema will lead X's associates to encourage him to see a doctor as soon as possible (Leventhal, Diefenbach, & Leventhal, 1992; Suls, Martin, & Leventhal, 1997). In summary, both Mr. X and the members of his neighborhood will elaborate a *representation* of the experience that fits that of a cardiac-related event. A fearful image of sudden death (consequences for self), at an age (timeline for self) when one is still functional and fulfilling family and work roles (self-identity), and this representation will motivate a *plan for action*, a doctor visit. As Martin, Gordon, and Lounsbury (1998) have shown, both laypeople and practitioners will hold a gender bias that, under these circumstances, will make them likely to request a series of tests for myocardial infarction. Thus, the interaction of the individual's schema for heart attack with his self-schema, and the support of it by neighborhood factors (friends schema of CHD and the vulnerable male) converge for a common interpretation of symptoms and a common, behavioral outcome. Efforts to change lifestyle factors (e.g., smoking cessation if Mr. X is a smoker, low fat diets, etc.) are likely to follow, encouraged by his own beliefs and those of the members of his immediate social environment.

The older, Mrs. Y is likely to fare quite differently with the same experience. The schema for heart attack is gender biased (women are not perceived as likely targets and, thus, the identity of self does not match identity of disease; Martin et al., 1998; van Tiel, van Vliet, & Moerman, 1998). Second, heart attacks are perceived to be more common for people in their fifties and sixties and not their seventies (a mismatch on perceived timeline), the decade for which the incidence of heart attack is highest among women (Wilcox & Stefanick, 1999). Third, work stress not family stress is perceived as the cause of cardiac incidents. In addition, women are known to report more vague psychophysiological symptoms when under stress (Macintyre, Hunt, & Sweeting, 1996). Thus, neither Mrs. Y nor her friends are likely to interpret her symptoms as signs of cardiac problem. Not surprisingly, older women are more likely to minimize cardiac symptoms, delay in seeking care, and when they arrive in the

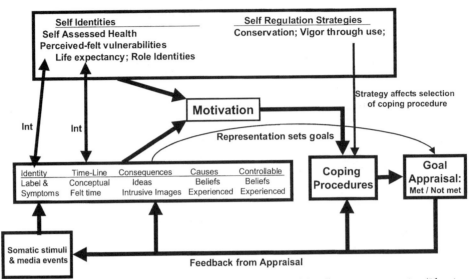

Figure 8.2 Interactions (Int) among the five content domains of the illness representation (Identity: heart attack and symptoms) with similar domains in the self system (pain and heart attack expected for male at this age) generates motivation for action. The representations define goals for action (reduce pain) and in combination with self-regulation strategies (vigor maintained through use) identifies relevant coping procedures (exercise to strengthen heart and eliminate pain). The efficacy of the procedure (exercise did/did not eliminate pain) is appraised against the goal. If the goal is not met a new procedure will be sought.

medical system, are less likely to be diagnosed with CHD, receive emergency procedures when hospitalized, and are more likely to die after admission due to failure to treat (Dracup et al., 1997; Marrugat et al., 1998). A recent study confirms that age and gender is related to treatment and mortality for individual's experiencing asymptomatic (i.e., silent) heart attacks (Canto et al., 2000).

b. Summary The key points emerging from our examples are as follows: First, both the individual experiencing a somatic event and the persons in their surround, lay and professional, elaborate representations that give the event its meaning. The elaboration at the problem level (i.e., the understanding and experience of the disease) is based on the schema of the disease and its relationship to self-schema. The interaction among these two belief structures establishes the relevance of a diagnosis of heart at-

tack to the self and does so by comparing the self and the disease schemata in five domains: identity (self-identities and diagnosed illnesses and symptoms), timelines (expectations regarding own age, life span, and age of onset and duration of disease, etc.), control (resources for control and is the disease treatable), consequences (death, disability, economic loss), and cause (own health, family health history, and cause of disease).

Second, procedures are selected to manage the threat, and the selection and its expected efficacy (e.g., symptom removal over a time frame) is shaped by the representation of the threat. The procedures are appraised for efficacy against the criteria or goals set by the representation. Third, the individual's affective reactions will impact performance: fear of the consequences of not controlling the illness threat will enhance performance, whereas fear of the procedures for prevention and/or control will interfere. For example, fear of medications, that they are dangerous and or addictive, can be a barrier to use of medication to control hypertension and depression (Horne & Weinmann, 1999). Fourth, performance of the procedure will be affected by the individual's beliefs in his or her ability to complete the required actions and manage any fears about the procedure itself. Fifth, the process unfolds over time in an ecological and social context, and the context can support and enhance performance or create barriers and inhibit performance. Finally, the potential exists for misunderstanding about the disease and the effects of treatment among the individual and the social environment (i.e., family, friends, and practitioners), as many of the factors driving performance are experiential and private, whereas communication from the individual to family, friends, physicians, and nurses is conceptual (i.e., expressed in words).

B. Initiating and Maintaining Health Behaviors for the Elderly

Some would object to our using the examples of Mr. X and Mrs. Y seeking health care in a chapter on health behavior as they would regard their actions as *illness behaviors*, (i.e., behavioral processes brought into play by somatic indicators of illness). These investigators might restrict the term *health behavior* to behavioral processes initiated by factors such as social influence, functional changes (need to get in shape for athletics), and alterations in morphology, (e.g., summer clothes that are too tight or the appearance of facial wrinkles) (Kasl & Cobb, 1966). Behaviors motivated by symptoms and disease interpretations would be labeled illness behaviors. In our judgment the distinction is both arbitrary and misleading as the same, self-regulatory mechanism underlies both types of behavior. Thus, both health and illness behavior are regulated by motivational variables involving

the perception of a need for improved health or the avoidance of a health threat (e.g., cancer or heart disease) action plans for performing one or more procedures that are available and perceived to be effective for preventing disease and promoting health, and an appraisal of the degree to which the behavior has moved toward one's goals. Indeed, as people age and have more experience with illness, they are more likely to focus on the health implications of functional and somatic sensations, increasing the likelihood that these experiences will motivate health-promotive behavior. This age-related increase in health focus on somatic changes further blurs any differentiation between health and illness behaviors (H. Leventhal et al., 1997).

1. Content of Interventions: Motivation and Barriers

Self-regulation models suggest that an effective intervention must contain information to meet at least four different goals: increasing motivation for change and reducing barriers to change; a plan for executing change within the context of the individual's life situation; evidence that the individual or individuals like him or her has the capacity to make such changes; and suggestions for ways of creating environmental supports and reducing environmental barriers to change. Interventions to achieve these goals will need to be sensitive to age, gender, ethnic, and cultural differences, and more importantly perhaps, to differences in disease, disease history, and the individual's ecological context. Timing is a major issue for all interventions. Specifically what are the optimal points in the individual's life situation for generating motivation needed to initiate and sustain behavioral change? Motivation must be sufficiently strong to develop the skills and sense of self-competence for sustaining change once it has occurred.

2. Timing Interventions

Both the initiation and cessation of smoking behavior provides a good example of timing. Smoking typically begins during the adolescent years motivated by the need to belong and create an identity for the self (Mosbach & Leventhal, 1988). Cessation usually occurs decades later, and although it can be motivated by non-health factors, severe illness has proven to be the strongest motivator for quitting; heavy smokers are most likely to quit following episodes of lifethreatening cardiovascular disease (Taylor, Houstone-Miller, Killen, DeBusk, 1990). Indeed, in one study severity of illness was the only predictor of quitting smoking, and psychological factors such as self-efficacy failed to predict behavior (Ockene et al., 1992). (Evidence for lifestyle changes following cancer is less clear; Pinto, Eakin, & Maruyama, 2000.) Thus, it is reasonable to assume that interventions to increase healthy actions (i.e., smoking cessation and dietary change) will be more effective if they are connected in some way with the occurrence of illness and/or with medical contacts. As cardiac disease and cancer tend to strike during the late-middle and young-old years of life, these findings are clearly relevant for older people.

Despite the encouraging reductions in risk behavior following major episodes of cardiovascular disease, clinical trials conducted in medical settings show relatively small benefits for health behaviors such as smoking cessation, dietary changes (low-fat diet), and exercise (Pinto et al., 2000). One reason for the modest size of these interventions is that healthy behaviors often increase in the nonintervention control groups. Another is likely the timing of the antismoking or dietary intervention (e.g., is it presented during a wellness visit or during a visit to for a specific illness?). If delivered during an illness visit, is the intervention given at the same time as diagnostic information? If so, the patient is likely to be more concerned with the implications of the diagnosis for his life situation and inattentive to the recommendations for lifestyle change. Interventions to encourage healthy behavior delivered at the time of diagnosis also may have to cope with feelings of helplessness (i.e., beliefs that it is too late for prevention as disease has already evaded the body's defenses). Waiting till treatment has terminated may also be inappropriate, as by that point in time the patient is likely to have formulated his own plan for prevention based upon beliefs as to what is optimal for survival. Unfortunately, these beliefs may focus on procedures that are of little biological benefit, such as stress control or the use of complementary medicine. If the illness episode involved cardiovascular disease, the patient's a priori beliefs may encourage reduced activity and conservation of energy as a way of reducing stress and enhancing survival (Aikens et al., 1998; Eifert, Hodson, Tracey, Seville, & Gunawardane, 1996), resulting in avoidance of active rehabilitation.

We suspect that the optimal time for intervention for older persons afflicted with serious, life-threatening disease is at some point prior to the termination of invasive treatment when the individual and members of his or her immediate social network begin to address issues related to returning to a normal, daily life. This is likely to be a day or two prior to discharge from hospital after cardiac surgery, or one or two cycles prior to the termination of extended chemotherapy for treatment of cancer. These points appear optimal as they are times when the patient must begin to address plans for reintegrating him- or herself and prescribed behavioral changes into everyday activities (Rose, Suls, Green, Lounsbury, & Gordon, 1996). Thus, the individual is looking forward to restructuring his or her existence and an intervention would mesh with that goal. More research is needed, however, to establish whether age-related differences in orientation toward the future have implications for the efficacy of such interventions.

3. Intervening during the Clinical Exam: Framing Motives for Change

Communications from physicians during annual medical check-ups and examinations for nonlife-threatening diseases can be effective for achieving behavioral changes if the information is properly framed. This is likely to be true for interventions to encourage screening for serious illness as well as interventions for lifestyle changes such as smoking cessation (Brown & Kutner, 1993). If information on the risk of smoking and benefits of exercise is delivered during the physical examination, the practitioner can stress the nature of risk to specific organs while these parts of the body are being listened to and palpated. While listening to the heart and looking in the mouth, the physician can indicate that she is looking for possible signs of smoking-induced, precancerous changes; that fortunately, no signs of disease are currently visible; and if he, the patient, stops smoking, he can maintain his disease-free status and resume his daily activities with less need to worry about heart disease and cancer. Thus, by presenting the message during the physical examination, the clinician can emphasize her special access to somatic information and place the behavioral change message in a positive frame (Rothman & Salovey, 1997) (i.e., acknowledging the absence of current disease and stating that behavioral changes can help to maintain a disease-free state and a renewed sense of safety). Combining such interventions with counseling programs for behavioral change could prove especially effective for reducing risk and enhancing healthy behaviors. Communications delivered at these times and in these ways are likely similar to the delivery of health-promoting messages to individuals returning to daily living after treatment for serious medical conditions: they are strong messages that combine both threat and hope in appealing for behavioral change (Diefenbach, Miller, & Daly, 1999; Keller & Block, 1999).

4. Removing Barriers by Correcting Misunderstandings

Eliminating barriers to change is especially valuable as removing a single barrier creates a more favorable motivational balance than adding a reason for change. When a person's baseline is four motives for and four motives against adopting a healthy behavior, subtracting a motive against change creates a 4:3 ratio for action, while adding a motive for change creates a less favorable, 5:4 ratio (H. Leventhal, 1993). Age, gender, disease history, and cohort and cultural factors are of special importance for the removal of barriers, as doing so requires identification of beliefs and experiences that inhibit lifestyle change. As mentioned earlier in this chapter, representations of the aging body as fragile, and representations that a disease requires reduced activity (e.g., physical action producing somatic distress for patients with cardiac conditions) may inhibit engaging in the physical activities needed to strengthen and sustain an ailing organ system. Petrie, Cameron, Ellis, Buick, and Weinman (2000) have shown that a brief intervention distinguishing the physical sensations of exercise from the sensations of a heart attack, the former associated with a beneficial activity the latter with risk, and clarifying the meaning of cardiac injury (i.e., that symptoms are due to insufficient oxygen and not an indication that the heart is about to burst) can change the interpretation of somatic sensations and remove a barrier to entering rehabilitation. Empirical data indicate that such distinctions are possible with other diseases. For example, the "breath-lessness" experienced by elderly persons with chronic obstructive lung disease differs from that of patients with congestive heart failure and interstitial lung disease. As symptoms encourage inactivity in pulmonary patients, the result is the added risk of cardiovascular deconditioning. Helping elderly persons to understand the source of these symptoms, those which do and those which do not imply danger, can play a role in returning them to activity and the recovery of cardiac function (Mahler, Harver, Lentine, Scott, & Schwartzstein, 1996).

The effect of symptoms on nonadherence is not restricted to coronary disease. Studies focusing on a variety of medical conditions have demonstrated that the presence of symptoms diminishes treatment compliance among middle-aged and older adults if the symptoms are interpreted as threatening. Symptoms played a key role in nonadherence to chemoprevention in the P1 trial examining the efficacy of tamoxifen for cancer prevention (Fisher et al., 1998), and symptoms are repeatedly identified as causes of nonadherence to treatment for controlling risk factors such as hypertension. Symptoms were also among the most important factor for nonadherence in the Carotene and Retinol Efficacy Trial, the majority of whose participants were over 60 years of age, although they were a less potent deterrent to adherence than they had been in exercise trials for persons with cardiovascular disease (Bowen, Cartmel, Barnett, Goodman, & Omen, 1999). Interestingly, efforts to cope with chronic conditions, such as arthritis, are associated with positive affect for individuals focused on coping with their symptoms; patients who are trying to alter the underlying disease, which is essentially unalterable, report more distress the more intense their coping efforts (Affleck, Ten-nen, Pfeiffer, & Fifield, 1987). Coping with symptoms may also be facilitated, as data have shown that providing patients with information about what they are about to experience reduces distress during unpleasant medical procedures (Johnson & Leventhal, 1974); a logical extension of this finding is that providing older persons with clear descriptions of the various somatic experiences that will accompany health behaviors (e.g., changes in diet and exercise) and the meaning of these somatic events (i.e., that they are normal and not indications of disease), will facilitate adherence to healthy actions.

5. Action Plans and Outcome Appraisals

An early contribution of self-regulation theory was the clear evidence that interventions focused upon motivation are not sufficient for behavioral change (H. Leventhal, 1970; H. Leventhal, Singer & Jones, 1965). To produce action, a motive-generating message needs to be combined with a plan for action. As elaborated in self-regulation theory, action plans have several critical components. First, as with representations, they are both conceptual and experiential. The conceptual level is most easily understood: it consists of an overall image or schema of the sequence of times and places for executing specific behaviors to reach a specific goal. Schemas exist even for quite simple behaviors, such as keeping medical appointments. Memory for appointments can be enhanced and appointment keeping improved by designing communications for appointments in accord with the schema underlying such apparently simple behaviors (Morrow, Leirer, Carver, & Tanke, 1998). Mail reminders are effective for increasing rates of mammography, and reminders that specify a specific appointment time are more effective than those leaving the time open (Wagner, 1998). The more complex schema to initiate an exercise program can be set out in a series of simple, achievable actions, each of which requires a simple plan. For example, one must first decide what type of exercise to do, jogging versus walking, muscle building, or aerobic, and so on. Next, one defines the specific tasks needed to start the program, including obtaining a medical check-up, setting out a program with an appropriate sequence for levels of performance, purchasing clothing, footgear, and a membership in an exercise club or a treadmill for the home, and so on. Information is collected on these tasks from friends and media, and the individual moves forward in his or her program step by step.

Three additional factors, the hierarchical nature of plans, their relationship to ongoing activity, and their automatic characteristic, are important features at the experiential level and are less well understood and less often discussed. They involve defining specific cues and associated actions at each of the many steps needed to put a new health behavior in place. Completing these steps requires the examination of the individual's ecology; his or her physical environment and daily schedules can provide opportunities and pose barriers for identifying times, places, and means for action (e.g., initiating an exercise program). For example, complex daily environments pose barriers to adherence to treatment for arthritis (Park et al., 1999), and a far greater number of barriers can delay and even prevent the purchase of appropriate equipment, signing up at a gym, or purchasing a treadmill and finding time to exercise. Identifying a specific time for visiting a gym or equipment store, posting a reminder to do so, and integrating the visit with existent and familiar activity ensures its performance. The individual may discover that a minor alteration in the route chosen for biweekly trips to the supermarket can facilitate and indeed, ensure a visit to the sporting goods shop or gym. Finding a companion eager to make the side trip provides additional insurance for completing the visit. The critical aspect of these "subroutines" is their nesting in ongoing activities that are evoked by dependable cues. Thus, the subplan is likely to be executed even if one has forgotten about the larger plan or forgotten about the subplan (e.g., taking the altered route to the supermarket); an act that can be automatic rather than decisional will activate and ensure completion of the subroutine. One can retain and use information without remembering that one is doing so (Roediger, 1990). Successful initiation of the behavioral change requires multiple, experientially directed subplans of this type; they are nested within subroutines that are in turn nested within the overall plan to adopt a health action (i.e., exercise).

6. Outcome Appraisals, Self-Competence and Social Validation

Perhaps the most important contribution of self-regulation theory to the appraisal of the efficacy of health actions is the assumption that appraisals of success and/or failure can be made at both an abstract, propositional level or a concrete, experiential level. Indeed, outcome appraisals and feelings of benefit from diet or exercise, or feelings of risk and/or failure, are often influenced to a greater degree by experiential feedback from performance than from abstract knowledge. Thus, if chest pain was a critical factor initiating muscle-strengthening exercise, reductions in frequency of tripping and avoiding falls may have little impact in evaluating exercise efficacy, though they are important benefits. The nature of the feedback and how it is understood will vary as a function of the biology of the individual, the intensity of the exercise, and how the individual interprets or assigns meaning to chest pain or to tripping and falling. The evaluation can encourage or discourage further exercise depending upon the meaning of these experiences, and meaning can be affected by context (i.e., preparatory communication from practitioners and the social context).

One would hope that successful performance of each step of a plan will not only validate achievement of each specific goal, but will increase commitment to the overall objective and enhance the individual's sense of competence to perform and reach the desired outcome. This may not, however, occur for all persons or for any single person on all occasions. Data strongly suggest that framing activities (i.e., providing ways of interpreting success and setbacks and placing activities in a supportive social context) can help ensure validation of self-efficacy for initiating and sustaining change. For example, exercising in a supportive social context appears to enhance beliefs that one can and will continue exercising in the absence of social support (Duncan & McAuley, 1993; Duncan, McAuley, Stoolmiller, & Duncan, 1993; McAuley, Blissmer, Katula, & Duncan, 2000). It is important to recognize, however, the privacy of experience! The experience of the elderly person when exercising, dieting, or engaging in any health-promotive action is private, and not readily shared with others. Indeed, discrepancies will exist between the social environment (e.g., an elderly person's spouse) and the individual actor's experience and interpretations of that experience. These differences can have negative impact on the elderly individual's adjustment (e.g., Heijmans, deRidder, & Bensing, 2000). Health-promotion programs that communicate to the social "neighborhood" and increase public understanding of the experiences and hurdles facing the active participant, and emphasizing how they can support change, are very likely to be more effective than those that focus on the individual alone.

IV. Conclusions

Existent data make abundantly clear that a number of health behaviors can enhance physical and psychological well-being and do so in the later years. It is also clear that these behaviors are smaller in number than one might expect. Exercise, a low-fat diet, and adherence to treatment for high blood pressure and hypercholesterolemia appear of clear benefit, though the evidence also suggests that greater benefits are likely to accrue from the cessation of risky behaviors such as smoking and excessive use of alcohol. Indeed, Christensen and Jensen (1994) speculate that, "an inadequate response to psychosocial stress and the choice of dysfunctional coping strategies may be more harmful and cause more 'ill health,' than hypersecretion of stress hormones like epinephrine and cortisol" (p. 81). Evidence for the efficacy of a multitude of other actions is minimal to nonexistent. But even beneficial activities have risk. Estrogen replacement therapy substantially lowers the risk of osteoporosis, but raises the risk of endometrial and breast cancer, and treatment for hypercholesterolemia can have small, but adverse effects on attention and psychomotor speed assessed by neuropsychological tests (Muldoon et al., 2000; Wardle et al., 2000); whether these deficits are important either clinically or for daily function is unknown. Although there are few if any panaceas for a disease-free life, and little evidence that healthy actions or medical treatment will produce enormous gains in life span, evidence suggests that healthy behaviors will make a major contribution to the maintenance of function even in the final year of life (Liao, McGee, Cao, & Cooper, 2000; Vita, Terry, Hubert, & Fries, 1998). It is also important to remember that the gain in life expectancy and function are greater when interventions and treatments target those at highest risk (Wright & Weinstein, 1998).

Second, it is clear that beliefs (i.e., representations of illness threats and beliefs about the aging self) are important sources of motivation for healthy action and the elimination of risky actions. Effective action depends, however, on the combination of motivation with action plans, multilevel representations of sequences of actions necessary for the adoption and maintenance of healthy actions. The self and social contexts will moderate the motivation generated by representations of health threats and the formation and execution of plans. Thus, individuals confronting a conflicted and unsupportive social environment and lacking a plan for managing that environment are less likely to initiate and sustain difficult health actions. The perception of which action is healthy and belief that one is capable of its execution will also be moderated by the strategies the individual and his peers, family, and friends believe to be effective for sustaining physical well-being. Beliefs that inactivity and conservation of energy is the best way to avoid death from coronary disease, and the belief that physical and/or mental activity are effective for enhancing well-being and protecting against cancer and dementia will influence decisions to participate in regular exercise and sustain active involvement in social and cognitively stimulating activities. There is also evidence suggesting that people are skeptical about the value of medical care and that this skepticism may deter adoption of effective medical procedures and increase the likelihood of mortality (Fiscella, Franks, Clancy, Doescher, & Banthin, 1999). Intervention programs need to recognize the presence of these beliefs at all levels (i.e., the individual, the neighborhood—family and peers—, the institutional, and cultural) and to search for ways of building upon them, and if need be, to confront and point to their limitations. For example, it is known that individuals in non-Western cultures will adopt Western medical practices in preference to traditional practices when they see when and for whom Western practices prove to be effective (Lock, 1980).

On the assumption that healthy behaviors are interrelated, interventions to promote health-enhancing behaviors should target multiple actions. This suggestion may be fruitful for cessation of risky behaviors and for promotion of healthy actions that reduce risk for a common threat or are linked to a common, underlying mechanism (e.g., the complementary role of exercise to diet for weight loss). Data suggest, however, that although risky behaviors are modestly interrelated for most individuals, health-promotive behaviors show weak or no interrelatedness (H. Leventhal, Prohaska, & Hirschmann, 1985). Thus, interventions at best may focus on two or three activities, and in the worst-case scenario, one at a time. Focusing on several health behaviors may prove costly, however; though it is often said that "an ounce of prevention is worth a pound of cure," the total cost will be high and effectiveness low if a moderately effective preventive intervention is used for the entire population where the incidence of the disease is very low.

It is also clear that an individual's behavior can create an environment that is health damaging, hostile persons creating competitive situations that add to cardiovascular risk (Suls & Martin, in press). In addition, the physical structure of a neighborhood and its social history can create a context that encourages groups and individual residents to feel that they have or that they lack control over their lives (Putnam, 1993), and these beliefs may affect the adoption of behaviors that lead to healthy and/or risky outcomes as assessed by indicators of mortality and morbidity (Yen & Syme, 1999). Interventions targeting these individual and contextual factors to improve health behavior and health outcomes make demands that go beyond the usual health-promoting intervention that is focused on changing a specific health behavior.

Studies assessing the effects of different programs on initiating and sustaining behavioral change for exercise and diet have appeared in increasing numbers during the past two decades and have been reviewed in recent publications (e.g., Wing, Voorhees, & Hill, 2000). In our judgment, most interventions for enhancing healthy action are based on low-level empirical hypotheses and fail to reflect a comprehensive view of the social and psychological processes affecting adult action. Self-regulation theory is a useful guide for generating questions and specific hypotheses respecting the behavior of elderly persons with respect to initiating and maintaining behaviors for disease prevention and health promotion. As the theory is more fully differentiated, and better methods are developed for testing the effects of multiple factors on the adoption and maintenance of action, it will provide a richer source of hypotheses for intervention and better tools for their evaluation. The questions and hypotheses will reflect the hierarchical structure and content of the regulatory system underlying behavior and the contextual hierarchy formed by the self, neighborhood, institutional, and cultural context within which the regulatory system resides. Large-scale national and regional programs that set specific set of interlocking goals for each level in this hierarchy (i.e., from behavioral change for the self through supportive action for family and friends), to linking a health action to a communities cultural values, are likely to be more effective than those targeting only one level in the system (e.g., the individual), or those using the same message and goal (e.g., walk for a half an hour every day) for every level of the system.

Acknowledgment

Preparation of this manuscript was supported by grant AG03501.

References

Ahmad, N., Feyes, D. K., Nieminen, A. L., Agarwal, R., & Mukhtar, H. (1997). Green tea constituent epigallocatechin-3-gallate and induction of apoptosis and cell cycle arrest in human carcinoma cells. *Journal of the National Cancer Institute, 89,* 1881–1886.

Affleck, G., Tennen, H., Pfeiffer, C., & Fifield, J. (1987). Appraisals of control and predictability in adapting to a chronic disease. *Journal of Personality and Social Psychology, 53,* 273–279.

Aikens, J. E., Michael, E., Levin, T., & Lowry, E. (1998). Symptom awareness, fear, and cardiophobic cognition in noncardiac chest pain patients. *Annals of Behavioral Medicine, 20* (Suppl.) S-172.

Ajzen, I. (1985). From intentions to actions: A theory or planned behavior. In J. Kuhn & J. Beckman (Eds.), *Action control: From cognition to behavior* (pp. 11–39). Heidelberg: Springer.

Ajzen, I., & Fishbein, M. (1977). Attitude-behavior relations: A theoretical analysis and review of empirical research, *Psychological Bulletin, 84,* 888–918.

Alberts, D. S., Martinex, M. E., Roe, D. J., Guillen-Rodriguex, J. M., Marshall, J. R., van Leeuwen, J. B., Reid, M. E., Ritenbaugh, C., Vargas, P. A., Bhattacharyya, A. B., Earnest, D. L., Sampliner, R. E., & The Phoenix Colon Cancer Prevention Physicians' Network (2000). Lack of effect of a high-fiber cereal supplement on the recurrence of colorectal adenomas. *New England Journal of Medicine, 342,* 1156–1162

American Heart Association (1999). *Biostatistical fact sheets.* [On-line]. Available: http://www.americanheart.org/statistics/biostats

Andres, R., Elahi, D., Tobin, J. D., Muller, D. C., & Brant, L. (1985). Impact of age on weight goals. *Annals of Internal Medicine, 103,* 1030–1033.

Apple, R. D. (1996). Vitamania: Vitamins. In *American culture.* New Brunswick, NJ: Rutgers University Press.

Balducci, L., Pow-Sang, J., Friedland, J., & Diaz, J. I. (1997). Prostate cancer. *Clinics in Geriatric Medicine, 13,* 283–306.

Balducci, L., & Lyman, G. H. (1997). Cancer in the elderly. Epidemiologic and clinical implications. *Clinics in Geriatric Medicine, 13:* 1–14.

Bandura, A. (1997). *Self-efficacy: The exercise of control.* New York: W. H. Freeman & Co., Publishers.

Baron, J. A., Beach, M., Mandel, J. S., van Stolk, R. U., Haile, R. W., Sandler, R. S., Rothstein, R., Summers, R. W., Snover, D. C., Beck, G. J., Bond, J. H., & Greendberg, E. R. (1999). Calcium supplements for the prevention of colorectal adenomas. *New England Journal of Medicine, 340,* 101–107.

Belloc, N. B., & Breslow, L. (1972). Relationship of physical health status and family practices. *Preventative Medicine, 1,* 409–421.

Benyamini, Y. B., Leventhal, H., & Leventhal, E. A. (1999). Self assessments of health: What do people know that predicts their mortality. *Research on Aging, 21,* 477–500.

Benyamini, Y., Idler, E. L., Leventhal, H., & Leventhal, E. A. (2000). Positive affect and function as influences on self-assessments of health: Expanding our view beyond illness and disability. *Journal of Gerontology, 55B,* P107–P116.

Blair, S. N., Kohl, H. W., III, Barlow, C. E., Paffenbarger, R. S., Jr., Gibbons, L. W., & Macera, C. A. (1995). Changes in physical fitness and all-cause mortality. *Journal of the American Medical Association, 273,* 1093–1098.

Blumenthal, J. A., Emery, C. F., Madden, D. J., George, L. K., Coleman, R. E., Riddle, M. W., McKee, D. C., Reasoner, J., & Williams, R. S. (1989). Cardiovascular and behavioral effects of aerobic exercise training in healthy older men and women. *Journal of Gerontology: Medical Sciences, 44,* M147–M157.

Blumenthal, J. A., Emery, C. F., Madden, D. J., Schniebolk, S., Walsh-Riddle, M., George, L. K., McKee, D. C., Higginbotham, M. B., Cobb, G. R., & Colman, R. E. (1991). Long-term effects of exercise on psychological functioning in older men and women. *Journal of Gerontology, 46,* 352–361.

Borgatta, E. F. (1968). Some notes on the history of tobacco use. In E. F. Borgatta & R. R. Evans (Eds.) *Smoking, health, and behavior* (pp. 3–11). Chicago, II: Aldine.

Botwinick, J. (1984). *Aging and behavior,* (3rd ed.). New York: Springer.

Bowen, D. J., Cartmel, B., Barnett, M., Goodman, G., & Omenn, G. S. (1999). Predicators of participant retention in two chemoprevention feasibility trials. *Annals of Behavioral Medicine, 21,* 210–215.

Bronfenbrenner, U. (1992). Ecological systems theory. In R. Vasta et al. (Ed.) *Six theories of child development: Revised formulations and current issues* (pp. 187–249). London, UK: Jessica Kingsley Publishers.

Brown, H., & Kutner, G. (1993). *Older women and the Medicare mammography benefit: 1992 awareness and usage levels.* Washington, DC: American Association of Retired Persons.

Brownlee, S., Leventhal, E. A., & Leventhal, H. (2000). Regulation, self regulation and regulation of the self in maintaining physical health. In M. Boekartz, P. R. Pintrich, & M. Ziedner (Eds.), *Handbook of self regulation* (pp. 369–416). San Diego, CA: Academic Press.

Bushman, J. L. (1998). Green tea and cancer in humans: A review of the literature. *Nutrition and Cancer, 31,* 151–159.

Calle, E. E., Thun, M. J., Petrelli, J. M., Rodriguez, C., & Heath, C. W. (1999). Body-mass index and mortality in a prospective cohort of U.S. adults. *The New England Journal of Medicine, 341,* 1097–1105.

Cameron, L. C., Leventhal, E. A., & Leventhal, H. (1995). Seeking medical care in response to symptoms and life stress. *Psychosomatic Medicine, 57,* 37–47.

Canadian Task Force on the Periodic Health Examination (1991). Periodic health examination, update: 3: Secondary prevention of prostate cancer. *Canadian Medical Association Journal, 145,* 413–428.

Canto, J. G., Shlipak, M. G., Rogers, W. J., Malmgren, J. A., Frederick, P. D., Costas, T. L., Ornato, J. P., Barron, H. V., & Kiefe, C. I. (2000). Prevalence, clinical characteristics, and mortality among patients with myocardial infarction presenting without chest pain. *Journal of the American Medical Association, 283,* 3223–3229.

Carter, W. B., Elward, K., Malmgren, J., Martin, M. L., & Larson, E. (1992). Participation of older adults in health programs and research: A critical review of the literature. *Gerontologist, 31,* 584–592.

Carver, C. S., & Scheier, M. F. (1982). Control theory: A useful conceptual framework for personality, social, clinical, and health psychology. *Psychological Bulletin, 92,* 111–135.

Carver, C. S., & Scheier, M. F. (1998). *On the self-regulation of behavior.* New York: Cambridge University Press.

Cassileth, B. R. (1998). *The alternative medicine handbook: The complete reference guide to alternative and complementary therapies.* New York: W. W. Norton.

Chandalia, M., Garg, A., Lutjohann, D., von Bergmann, K., Grundy, S. M., & Brinkley, L. J. (2000). Beneficial effects of high dietary fiber intake in patients with type 2 diabetes mellitus. *The New England Journal of Medicine, 342,* 1392–1398.

Charness, N. (2000). Can acquired knowledge compensate for age-related declines in cognitive efficiency? In S. H. Qualls & N. Abeles (Eds.), *Psychology and the aging revolution: How we adapt to longer life* (pp. 99–117). Washington, DC: American Psychological Association.

Chrisman, N. J., & Kleinman, A. (1983). Popular Health Care, Social Networks, and Cultural Meanings: The Orientation of Medical Anthropology. In D. Mechanic (Ed.), *Handbook of health, health care, and the health professions* (pp. 569–590). New York: Free Press.

Christensen, N. J., & Jensen, E. W. (1994). Effect of psychosocial stress and age on plasma norepinephrine levels: A review. *Psychosomatic Medicine, 56,* 77–83.

Consumer Reports (2000, May). *The mainstreaming of alternative medicine,* 17–25.

Cohen, S., & Hoberman, H. M. (1983). Positive events and social supports as buffers of life change stress. *Journal of Applied Social Psychology, 13*(2), 99–125.

Collacott, E. A., Zimmerman, J. T., White, D. W., & Rindone, J. P. (2000). Bipolar permanent magnets for the treatment of chronic low back pain: A pilot study. *Journal of the American Medical Association, 283,* 1322–1325.

Cornoni-Huntley, J. C., Harris, R. B., Eferett, D. F., et al. (1991). An overview of body weight of older persons, including the im-

pact of mortality. The National Health and Nutrition Examination Survey I—Epidemiologic follow-up study. *Journal of Clinical Epidemiology, 44,* 743–753.

Costanza, M. E., (1992). Breast cancer screening in older women: Synopsis of a forum. *Cancer, 69,* 1925–1931.

de Jong, N., Chin, A., Paw, M. J. M., de Groot, L. C. P. G. M., Hiddink, G. J., & van Staveren, W. A. (2000). Dietary supplements and physical exercise affecting bone and body composition in frail elderly persons. *American Journal of Public Health, 90,* 947–954.

De Lorgeril, M., Salen, P., & Martin, J. L., et al. (1998). Mediterranean dietary pattern in a randomized trial: prolonged survival and possible reduced cancer rate. *Archives of International Medicine, 8,* 1181–1187.

Delmas, P. D., Bjarnason, N. H., Mitlak, B. H., Ravoux, A. C., Shah, A. S., Huster, W. J., Draper, M., & Christiansen, C. (1997). Effects of raloxifene on bone mineral density, serum cholesterol concentrations, and uterine endometrium in postmenopausal women. *New England Journal of Medicine, 337,* 1641–1647.

Demissie, K., Mills, O. F., & Rhoads, G. G. (1998). Empirical comparison of the results of randomized controlled trials and case-control studies in evaluating the effectiveness of screening mammography. *Journal of Clinical Epidemiology, 51,* 81–91.

Diefenbach, M. A., Miller, S. M., & Daly, M. B. (1999). Specific worry about breast cancer predicts mammography use in women at risk for breast and ovarian cancer. *Health Psychology, 18,* 532–536.

Dracup, K., Alonzo, A. A., Atkins, J. M., Bennett, N. M., Braslow, A., Clark, L. T., Eisenberg, M., Ferdinand, K., Frye, R., Green, L., Hill, M. M. Kennedy, J. W., Kline-Rogers, E., Moser, D. K., Ornato, J. PI, Pitt, B., Scott, J. D., Selker, H. P., Silva, S. J., Thies, W., Weaver, W. D., Wenger, N. K., & White, S. K. (1997). The physician's role in minimizing prehospital delay in patients at high risk of acute myocardial infarction: Recommendations from the National Heart Attack Alert Program. *Annals of Internal Medicine, 126,* 645–651.

Duncan, T. E., & McAuley E. (1993). Social support and efficacy cognitions in exercise adherence: A latent growth curve analysis. *Journal of Behavioral Medicine, 16,* 199–218.

Duncan, T. E., McAuley, E., Stoolmiller, M., & Duncan, S. C. (1993). Serial fluctuations in exercise behavior as a function of social support and efficacy cognitions. *Journal of Applied Social Psychology, 23,* 1498–1522.

Eifert, G. H., Hodson, S. T., Tracey, D. R., Seville, J. L., & Gunawardane, K. (1996). Heart-focused anxiety, illness beliefs, and behavioral impairment: Comparing healthy heart-anxious patients with cardiac and surgical inpatients. *Journal of Behavioral Medicine, 19,* 385–398.

Eisenberg, D. M., Kessler, R. C., Foster, C., Norlock, F. E., Calkins, D. R., & Delbanco, T. L. (1993). Unconventional medicine in the United States: prevalence, costs, and patterns of use. *New England Journal of Medicine, 328,* 246–252.

Eisenberg, D. M., Davis, R. B., Ettner, S. L., Appel, S., Wilkey, S., Van Rompay, M., & Kessler, R. C. (1998). Trends in alternative medicine use in the United States, 1990–1997: Results of a follow-up national survey. *Journal of the American Medical Association, 280,* 1569–75.

Ensrud, K. E., Nevitt, M. C., Yunis, C., Cauley, J. A., Seeley, D. G., Fox, K. M., & Cummings, S. R. (1994). Correlates of impaired function in older women. *Journal of the American Geriatric Society, 42*(5), 481–489.

Ettinger, W. H., Burns, R., Messier, S. P., Applegate, W., Rejeski, W. J., Morgan, T., Shumaker, S., Berry, M. J., O'Toole, M., Monu, J., & Craven, T. (1997). A randomized trial comparing aerobic exercise and resistance exercise with a health education program in older adults with knee osteoarthritis: the fitness and seniors trial (FAST). *Journal of the American Medical Association, 277,* 25–31.

Fiatarone, M. A., O'Neill, E. F., Ryan, N. D., Clements, K. M., Solares, G. R., Nelson, M. E., Roberts, S. B., Kehayias, J. J., Lipsitz, L. A., & Evans, W. J. (1994). Exercise training and nutritional supplementation for physical frailty in very elderly people. *New England Journal of Medicine, 330,* 1769–1775.

Fiscella, K., Franks, P., Clancy, C. M., Doescher, M. P., & Banthin, J. S. (1999). Does skepticism towards medical care predict mortality? *Medical Care, 37,* 409–414.

Fisher, B., Costantino, J. P., Wickerham, D. L., Redmond, C. K., Kavanah, M., Cronin, W. M., Vogel, V., Robidoux, A., Dimitrov, N., Atkins, J., Daly, M., Wieand, S., Tan-Chiu, E., Ford, L. & Wolmark, N. (1998). Tamoxifen for prevention of breast cancer: report of the National Surgical Adjuvant Breast and Bowel Project P-1 Study. *Journal of the National Cancer Institute, 90,* 1371–1388.

Fries, J. F. (1983). The compression of morbidity. *Milbank Memorial Fund Quarterly Health and Society, 61,* 397–419.

Gey K. F. (1993). Prospects for the prevention of free radical disease, regarding cancer and cardiovascular disease. *British Medical Bulletin, 49,* 679–99.

Goldberg, T. H., & Chavin, S. I. (1997). Preventive medicine and screening in older adults. *Journal of the American Geriatric Society, 45,* 344–354.

Hafez, E. S. E. (1973). Reproductive Life Cycle. In E. S. E. Hafez (Ed.), *Human reproduction: Conception and contradiction* (pp. 157–200). Hagerstown, MD: Harper and Row.

Hakim, A. A., Petrovitch, H., Burchfiel, C. M., Ross, W. G., Rodriguez, B. L., White, L. R., Katsuhiko, Y., Curb, D., & Abbott, R. D. (1998). Effects of walking on mortality among nonsmoking retired men. *New England Journal of Medicine, 338,* 94–99.

Hansson, L., Zanchetti, A., Carruthers, S. G., Dahlog, B., Elmfeldt, D., Julius, S., Menard, J., Rahn, K. H., Wedel, H., Westerling, S. for the HOT study group (1998). Effects of intensive blood-pressure lowering and low-dose aspirin in patients with hypertension: Principal results of the hypertension optimal treatment (HOT) randomized trial. *Lancet, 351,* 1755–1762.

Hatsukami, D. K., Dahlgren, L., Zimmerman, R., & Hughes, J. R. (1988). Symptoms of tobacco withdrawal from total cigarette cessation versus partial cigarette reduction. *Psychopharmacology, 94,* 242–247.

Heijmans, M., deRidder, D., & Bensing, J. (1999). Dissimilarity in patients' and spouses' representations of chronic disease: Explorations of relations to patient adaptation. *Psychology and Health 14*(3), 451–466.

Horne, R., & Weinmann, J. (1999). Patients' beliefs about prescribed medicines and their role in adherence to treatment in chronic physical illness. *Journal of Psychosomatic Research, 47*(6), 555–67.

Howe, G. R., Benito, E., Castelleto, R., Cornee, J., Esteve, J., Gallagher, R. P., Iscovich, J. M., Dengao, J., & Kaaks–Kune, G. A. (1992). Dietary intake of fiber and decreased risk of cancers of the colon and rectum: Evidence form the combined analysis of 13 case-control studies. *Journal of the National Cancer Institute, 84*, 1887–1896.

Idler, E. L., & Benyamini, Y. (1997). Self-rated health and mortality: a review of twenty-seven community studies. *Journal of Health and Social Behavior, 39*, 21–37.

Imai, K., Suga, K., & Nakachi, K. (1997). Cancer-preventive effects of drinking green tea among a Japanese population. *Preventive Medicine, 26*, 769–775.

Institute of Medicine (2000). *Overview: Nutritional health in the older person.* [On-line]. Available: http://books.NAP.edu/books/0309068460/html/46.html

Johnson, J. E., & Leventhal, H. (1974). Effects of accurate expectations and behavioral instructions on reactions during a noxiuos medical examination. *Journal of Personality and Social Psychology, 29* (5), 710–718.

Kaptchuk, T. J., & Eisenberg, D. M. (1998). The persuasive appeal of alternative medicine. *Annals of Internal Medicine, 129*, 1061–1065.

Kasl, S., & Cobb, S. (1966). Health behavior, illness behavior, and sick role behavior—part 1 sick role behavior. *Archives of Environmental Health, 12*, 530–541.

Keil, U., Chambless, L. E., Doring, A., Filipiak, B., & Stieber, J. (1997). The relationship of alcohol intake to coronary heart disease and all-cause mortality in a beer-drinking population. *Epidemiology, 8* (6), 687–688.

Keller, P. A., & Block, L. G. (1999). The effect of affect-based dissonance versus cognition-based dissonance on motivated reasoning and health-related persuasion. *Journal of Experimental Psychology: Applied, 5*, 302–313.

Kerlikowske, K., Grady, D., Rubin, S. M., Sandrock, C., & Ernster, V. L. (1995). Efficacy of screening mammography. A meta-analysis. *Journal of the American Medical Association, 273*, 149–154.

Kohlmeier, L., Weterings, K. G. C., Steck, S., & Kok, F. J. (1997). Tea and cancer prevention: An evaluation of the epidemiologic literature. *Nutrition and Cancer, 27*, 1–13.

Lau, E. M., Woo, J., Leung, P. C., Swaminathan, R., & Leung, D. (1992). The effects of calcium supplementation and exercise on bone density in elderly Chinese women. *Osteoporosis International, 2*, 168–173.

Lazarus, R. S. (1966). *Psychological stress and the coping process.* New York: McGraw-Hill

Lazarus, R. S., & Folkman, S. (1984). *Stress, appraisal and coping.* New York: Springer Publishing Co.

Lerman, C., Kash, K., & Stefanek, M. (1994) Younger women at increased risk for breast cancer: Perceived risk, psychological well-being, and surveillance behavior. *Journal of the NCI Monographs, 16*, 171–176.

Leventhal, E. A., & Crouch, M. (1997). Are there differences in perceptions of illness across the lifespan? In K. J. Petrie & J. A. Weinman (Eds.), *Perceptions of health and illness: Current research and applications* (pp. 77–102). Singapore: Harwood Academic Publishers.

Leventhal, H. (1970). Findings and theory in the study of fear communications. *Advances in Experimental Social Psychology, 5*, 119–186.

Leventhal, H. (1993). Theories of compliance, and turning necessitites into preferences: Application to adolescent health action. In N. A. Krasnegor, L. Epstein, S. Bennett-Johnson, & S. J. Yaffe (Eds.), *Developmental aspects of health compliance behavior* (pp. 91–124). Hillsdale, NJ: Lawrence Erlbaum.

Leventhal, H., & Cleary, P. D. (1980). The smoking problem: A review of the research and theory in behavioral risk modification. *Psychological Bulletin, 88*, 370–405.

Leventhal, H., Diefenbach, M., & Leventhal, E. A. (1992). Illness cognition: Using common sense to understand treatment adherence and affect cognition interactions. *Cognitive Therapy and Research, 16*, 143–163.

Leventhal, H., Idler, E., & Leventhal, E. A. (1999). The impact of chronic illness on the self system. In R. J. Contrada & R. D. Ashmore (Eds.), *Self, Social Identity, and Physical Health: Interdisciplinary Explorations.* Second Rutgers Symposium on Self and Social Identity (pp. 185–208). New York: Oxford Univ. Press.

Leventhal, H., & Kelley, K., & Leventhal, E. A. (1999). Population risk, actual risk, perceived risk, and cancer control. *Journal of the National Cancer Institute Monographs, 25*

Leventhal, H., Meyer, D., & Nerenz, D. (1980). The common sense representation of illness danger. In S. Rachman (Ed.), *Contributions to medical psychology* (Vol. II, pp. 7–30). New York: Pergamon Press.

Leventhal, H., Patrick-Miller, L., Leventhal, E. A., & Burns, E. A. (1997). Does stress-emotion cause illness in elderly people? In K. W. Schaie & M. P. Lawton (Eds.), *Annual Review of Gerontology and Geriatrics: Focus on, emotion and adult development* (Vol 17, pp. 138–184). New York: Springer Publishing Co.

Leventhal, H., Prohaska, T. R., & Hirschman, R. S. (1985). Preventive health behavior across the life span. In J. C. Rosen & L. J. Solomon (Eds.), *Prevention in health psychology* (Vol. 8, pp. 191–235). Hanover, NH: University Press of New England.

Leventhal, H., Singer, R., & Jones, S. (1965). Effects of fear and specificity of recommendations upon attitudes and behavior, *Journal of Personality and Social Psychology, 2,* 20–29.

Leventhal, H., Zimmerman, R., & Gutmann, M. (1984). Compliance: A self-regulation perspective. In W. D. Gentry (Ed.), *Handbook of Behavioral Medicine* (pp. 369–436). New York: The Guilford Press.

Lewis, M. A., & Rook, K. S. (1999). Social control in personal relationships: Impact on health behaviors and psychological distress. *Health Psychology, 18,* 63–71.

Liao, Y., McGee, D. L., Cao, G., & Cooper, R. S. (2000). Quality of the last year of life of older adults: 1986 vs. 1993. *Journal of the American Medical Association, 283,* 512–518.

Lock, M. (1980). *East Asian medicine in urban Japan.* Berkeley, CA: University of California Press.

Lox, C. L., Burns, S. P., Treasure, D. C., & Wasley, D. A. (1999). Physical and psychological predictors of exercise dosage in healthy adults. *Medicine & Science in Sports & Exercise, 31,* 1060–1064.

Love, R. R., Mazess, R. B., Barden, H. S., Epstein, S., Newcomb, P. A., Jordan, V. C., Carbone, P. P., & DeMets, D. L. (1992). Effects of tamoxifen on bone mineral density in postmenopausal women with breast cancer. *New England Journal of Medicine, 326,* 852–856.

Macintyre, S., Hunt, K., & Sweeting, H. (1996). Gender differences in health: Are things really as simple as they seem? *Social Science and Medicine, 42,* 617–624.

Mahler, D. A., Harver, A., Lentine, T., Scott, B., & Schwartzstein, R. M. (1996) Descriptors of breathlessness in cardiorespiratory diseases. *American Journal Respiratory Critical Care Medicine, 154,* 1357–1363.

Manderbacka, K., Lundberg, O., & Martikainen, P. (1999) Do risk factors and health behaviours contribute to self-ratings of health. *Social Science & Medicine, 48,* 1713–1720.

Marrugat, J., Sala, J., Masia, R., Pavesi, M., Sanz, G., Valle, V., Molina, L., Seres, L. & Elosua, R. (1998). Mortality differences between men and women following first myocardial infarction. *JAMA, 280,* 1405–1409.

Martin, R., Gordon, E. E. I., & Lounsbury, P. (1998). Gender disparities in the interpretation of cardiac-related symptoms: The contribution of common sense models of illness. *Health Psychology, 17,* 346–357.

Mazen, R., & Leventhal, H. (1972). The influence of communicator-recipient similarity upon the beliefs and behavior of pregnant women. *Journal of Experimental Social Psychology, 8,* 289–302.

McGinnis, J. M., & Foege, W. H. (1993). Actual cause of death in the United States. *Journal of the American Medical Association, 270,* 2207–2212.

McAuley, E., Blissmer, B., Katula, J., & Duncan, T. E. (2000). Exercise environment, self-efficacy, and affective responses to acute exercise in older adults. *Psychology and Health, 2000, (1,* 341–355).

Moore, K. A., & Blumenthal, J. A. (1998). Exercise training as an alternative treatment for depression among older adults. *Alternative Therapies in Health & Medicine, 4(1),* 48–56.

Morrow, D. G., Leirer, V. O., Carver, L. M., & Tanke, E. D. (1998). Older and younger adult memory for health appointment information: Implications for automated telephone messaging design. *Journal of Experimental Psychology: Applied, 4(4),* 352–374.

Mosbach, P., & Leventhal, H. (1988). Peer group identification and smoking: Implications for intervention. *Journal of Abnormal Psychology, 97*, 238–245.

Muldoon, M. F., Barger, S. D., Ryan, C. M., Flory, J. D., Lehoczky, J. P., Matthews, K. A., & Manuck, S. B. (2000). Effects of lovastatin on cognitive function and psychological well-being. *American Journal of Medicine, 108*, 538–46.

Myers, R. E., Ross, E., Jepson, C., Wolf, T., Balshem, A., Millner, L., & Leventhal, H. (1994). Modelingadherence to colorectal cancer screening. *Preventative Medicine, 23*, 142–151.

Nachtigall, L. E., Nachtigall, R. H., Nachtigall, R. D., & Beckman, E. M. (1979). Estrogen replacement therapy I: A 10-year prospective study in the relationship to osteoporosis. *Obstetrics & Gynecology, 53*, 277–281.

Ockene, J., Kristeller, J. L., Goldberg, R., Ockene, I., Merriam, P., & Barrett, S. (1992). Smoking cessation and severity of disease: The Coronary Artery Smoking Intervention Study. *Health Psychology, 11*, 119–126.

Ornish, D., Scherwitz, L. W., Billings, J. H., Brown, S. E., Gould, K. L., Merritt, T. A., Sparler, S., Armstrong, W. T., Ports, T. A., Kirkeeide, R. L., Hogeboom C., & Brand, R. J. (1998). Intensive lifestyle changes for reversal of coronary heart disease. *Journal of the American Medical Association, 280*, 2001–7.

Park, D. C., & Hedden, T. (in press). Working memory and aging. In M. Naveh-Benjamin, M. Moscovitch & H. L. Roediger (Eds.), *Perspectives on human memory and cognitive aging: Essays in honour of Fergus Craik*. East Sussex, UK: Psychology Press.

Park, D. C., Hertzog, C., Leventhal, H., Morrell, R., Leventhal, E., Birchmore, D., Martin, M., & Bennett, J. (1999). Medication adherence in rheumatoid arthritis patients: Older is wiser. *Journal of the American Geriatrics Society, 47*, 172–183.

Petrie, K. J., Cameron, L. D., Ellis, C. J., Buick, D., & Weinman, J. (2000). *Changing illness perceptions following myocardial infarction: An early intervention randomized controlled trial*. Manuscript submitted for publication.

Petrie, K. J., & Weinman, J. A. (1997.). Perceptions of health and illness: Current research

and applications. Amsterdam, The Netherlands: Harwood Academic Publishers.

Pinto, B. M., Eaken, E., & Maruyama, N. C. (2000). Health behavior changes after a cancer diagnosis: What do we know and where do we go from here. *Annals of Behavioral Medicine, 22*, 38–52.

Pollock, M. L., Carroll, J. F., & Graves, J. E., Leggett, S. H., Braith, R. W., Limacher, M. & Hagberg, J. M. (1991). Injuries and adherence to walk/jog and resistance training programs in the elderly. *Medical Science Sports and Exercise, 23*, 1194–1200.

Prohaska, T. R., Keller, M. L., Leventhal, E. A., & Leventhal, H. (1987). Impact of symptoms and aging attribution on emotions and coping. *Health Psychology, 6*, 495–514.

Prohaska, T. R., Leventhal, E. A., Leventhal, H., & Keller, M. L. (1985). Health practices and illness cognition in young, middle-aged, and elderly adults. *Journal of Gerontology, 40*, 569–578.

Putnam, R. D. (1993). *Making demoracy work: Civic traditions in modern Italy*. Princeton, NJ: Princeton University Press.

Reich, J. W., Zautra, A. J., & Guarnaccia, C. A. (1989). Effects of disability and bereavement on the mental health and recovery of older adults. *Psychology and Aging, 4*, 57–65.

Robinson, B., & Beghe, C. (1997). Cancer screening in the older patient. *Clinics in Geriatric Medicine, 13*, 97–118.

Rodin, J., & Salovey, P. (1989). Health psychology. *Annual Review of Psychology, 40*, 533–579.

Roediger III, H. L. (1990). Implicit memory—retention without remembering. *American Psychologist, 45*, 1043–1056.

Rogers, R. (1984). Changing health-related attitudes and behavior: The role of preventive health psychology. In J. H., Harvey, J. E., Maddux, R. P. McGlynn, & C. D., Stoltenberg (Eds.), *Social perception in clinical and counseling psychology* (pp. 291–312). Lubbock, TX: Texas Tech University Press.

Rook, K. S., & Pietromonaco, P. (1987). Close relationships: Ties that heal or ties that bind? In W. H. Jones & D. Perlman (Eds.), *Advances in personal relationship* (Vol. 1 pp. 1–35). Greenwich, CT: JAI Press.

Rose, G., Suls, J., Green, P., Lounsbury, P., & Gordon, E. (1996). Comparison of adjustment, activity and tangible support in men and women patients and their spouses during the six months post myocardial infarction. *Annals of Behavioral Medicine, 18,* 264–272.

Rosenstock, I. M. (1974). The health belief model and preventive health behavior. *Health Education Monographs, 2,* 354–386.

Rosenstock, I. M., Strecher, V. J. & Becker, M. (1988). Social learning theory and the health belief model. *Health Education Quarterly, 15,* 175–183.

Rothman, A. J., & Salovey, P. (1997). Shaping perceptions to motivate healthy behavior: The role of message framing. *Psychological Bulletin, 121,* 3–19.

Rubenstein, L. Z., Josephson, K. R., Trueblood, P. R., Loy, S., Harker, J. O., Pietruszka F. M., & Robbins, A. S. (2000). Effects of a group exercise program on strength, mobility and falls among fall-prone elderly men. *Journal of Gerontology: Medical Sciences, 55A,* M317–M321.

Rushton, A., Clayton, J., & Calnan, M. (1998). Patients' action during their cardiac event: Qualitative study exploring differences and modifiable factors. *British Medical Journal, 316,* 1060–1064.

Schatzkin, A., Lanza, E., Corle, D., Lance, P., Iber, F., Caan, B., Shike, M., Weissfeld, J., Burt, R., Cooper, M. R., Kikendall, J. W., Cahill, J., & The Polyp Prevention Trial Study Group (2000). Lack of effect of a low-fat, high fiber diet on the recurrence of colorectal adenomas. *New England Journal of Medicine, 342,* 1149–1155.

Shopland, D. R., & Burns, D. M. (1993). Medical and public health implications of tobacco addiction. In C. T. Orleans & J. D. Slade (Eds.), *Nicotine addiction: Principles and management* (pp 105–128). New York: Oxford University Press.

Skelton, J. A., & Croyle, R. T. (1991). *Mental representation in health and illness.* New York: Springer-Verlag.

Steinmaus, C. M., Nunez, S., & Smith, A. H. (2000). Diet and bladder cancer: A meta-analysis of six dietary variables. *American Journal of Epidemiology, 151,* 693–702.

Stewart, A. L., Greenfield, S., Hays, R. D., Wells, K., Rogers, W. H., Berry, S. D., McGlynn, E. A., & Ware, J. E. (1989). Functional status and well-being of patients with chronic conditions. *Journal of the American Medical Association, 262,* 907–913.

Suls, J., & Martin, R. (in press). Linear and dynamical thinking about psychosocial factors and cardiovascular risk. In K. W. Schaie, H. Leventhal, & S. L. Willis (Eds.), *Social structures and health behavior in the elderly.* New York: Springer Publishing Co.

Suls, J., Martin, R., & Leventhal, H., (1997). Social comparison, lay referral, and the decision to seek medical care. In B. Buunk & F. X. Gibbons (Eds.), *Health, coping and well being: Perspectives from social comparison theory* (pp. 195–226). Hillsdale, NJ: Lawrence Erlbaum.

Taylor, C. B., Houston-Miller, N., Killen, J. D., & DeBusk, R. K. (1990). Smoking cessation after acute myocardial infarction: Effects of a nurse-managed intervention. *Annals of Internal Medicine, 113,* 118–23.

Thompson, R. S., Barlow, W. E., Taplin, S. H., Grothaus, L., Immanuel, V., Salazar, A., & Wagner, E. H. (1994). A population-based case-cohort evaluation of the efficacy of mammographic screening for breast cancer. *American Journal of Epidemiology, 140*(10), 889–901.

Timiras, P. S., & Atherton, R. W. (1988). Aging of respiration, erythrocytes, and the hematopoitic system. In *Physiological Basis of Aging and Geriatrics* (pp. 225–228). Boca Raton, FL: CRC Press.

Tissue, T. (1972). Another look at self-rated health among the elderly. *Journal of Gerontology, 27*(1), 91–94.

Tucker, J. S., & Mueller, J. S. (2000). Spouses' social control of health behaviors: Use and effectiveness of specific strategies. *Personality and Social Psychology Bulletin, 26,* 1120–1130.

Ulrich, C. M., Georgiou, C. C., Snow-Harter, C. M., & Gillis, D. E. (1996). Bone mineral density in mother-daughter pairs: Relations to lifetime exercise, lifetime milk consumption, and calcium supplements. *American Journal of Clinical Nutrition, 63,* 72–79.

UK Trial of Early Detection of Breast Cancer Group (1988). First results on mortality reduction in the UK trial of early detection of breast cancer. *Lancet, 2,* 411–416.

U.S. Department of Health and Human Services. (1996). *Physical activity and health: A report of the Surgeon General.* Atlanta,

GA: Centers for Disease Control and Prevention, National Center for Chronic Disease Prevention and Health Promotion.

van Tiel, D., van Vliet, K. P., & Moerman, C. J. (1998). Sex differences in illness beliefs and illness and behaviour in patients with suspected coronary artery disease. *Patient Education and Counseling, 33*, 143–147.

Vita, A. J., Terry, R. B., Hubert, H. B., & Fries, J. F. (1998). Aging, health risks, and cumulative disability. *New England Journal of Medicine, 338*, 1035–41.

Wagner, T. H. (1998). The effectiveness of mailed patient reminders on mammography screening: A meta-analysis. *American Journal of Preventive Medicine, 14*, 64–70.

Wardle, J., Rogers, P., Judd, P., Taylor, M. A., Rapoport, L., Green, M., & Perry, K. N. (2000). Randomized trial of the effects of cholesterol-lowering dietary treatment on psychological function. *The American Journal of Medicine, 108*, 547–553.

Wenger, N. K. (1981). Rehabilitation of the elderly cardiac patient. *Cardiovascular Clinic, 12*, 221–230.

Wilcox, S., & Stefanick, M. L. (1999). Knowledge and perceived risk of major diseases in middle-aged and older women. *Health Psychology, 18*, 346–353.

Williamson, G. (1998). The central role of restricted normal activities in adjustment to illness and disability: A model of depressed affect. *Rehabilitation Psychology, 43*, 327–347.

Wing, R. R., Voorhees, C. C., & Hill, D. R. (2000). Maintenance of behavior change in cardiorespiratory risk reduction. *Health Psychology, 19*, 3–4.

Wingard, D. L., Berkman, L. F., & Brand, R. J. (1982). A multivariate analyses of health-related practices: A nine-year mortality follow-up of the Alameda County study. *American Journal of Epidemiology, 116*, 765–775.

Wright, J. C., & Weinstein, M. C. (1998). Gains in life expectancy from medical interventions–standardizing data on outcomes. *The New England Journal of Medicine, 339*, 380–386.

Yen, I. H., & Syme, S. L. (1999). The social environment and health: A discussion of the epidemiologic literature. *Annual Review of Public Health, 20*, 287–308.

Zeiss, A. M., Lewinsohn, P. M., Rohde, P., & Seeley, J. R. (1996). Relationship of physical disease and functional impairment to depression in older people. *Psychology and Aging, 11*, 572–581.

Nine

Environmental Influences on Aging and Behavior

Hans-Werner Wahl

I. Introduction and Overview

Understanding the role of the environment on the course and outcome of aging is a classic field of gerontological research that has been included in this handbook since its first edition (Lawton, 1977). However, purposefully omitting a chapter on the ecology of aging in the fourth edition of the handbook, because "there had not been sufficient progress since the previous handbook edition to warrant a new presentation" (Birren & Schaie, 1996, p. XVI), raises questions with respect to the recent progress, current status, and future of this area of gerontology. This chapter offers a critical, but (I hope) constructive view on the influences of environment on aging and behavior by summarizing, integrating, and evaluating empirical research and theoretical contributions published since Parmelee and Lawton's (1990) thoughtful chapter in the third edition of the handbook.

Reviewing the outlook, discussion, and recommendation sections of chapters on environmental issues in earlier editions of this handbook, as well as key work written

by well-known scholars in the field (Carp, 1987, 1994; Lawton, 1977; Moos & Lemke, 1985; Parmelee & Lawton, 1990; Scheidt & Windley, 1985), was a major starting point for preparing this chapter. This chapter will examine whether the questions they raised have been successfully addressed in research during the last decade. Based on their writing, four interrelated key challenges of environmental gerontology can be identified: (a) empirical research—the challenge to further a consistent and heuristically fruitful empirical research perspective and to ensure progression and a high research standard in the field; (b) theory—the challenge to develop theoretical accounts of the person–environment relation in the later years, an account that must begin with the "old" theories in the field (see Lawton, Windley, & Byerts, 1982), but should also consider recent theoretical progress (Scheidt & Windley, 1998b), including new ideas from social and psychological gerontology; (c) comprehensiveness—the challenge to address the whole scope of older adults and their respective living settings; a comprehensive account would thus include the entire gamut of elderly

This chapter is dedicated to Dr. M. Powell Lawton, who passed away in January 2001.

individuals, from different groups of frail elderly to "normal" or "successfully" aging older individuals, as well as various kinds of living contexts, from urban to rural settings[1] and from ordinary housing to highly specific purpose-built living environments, such as assisted living facilities and institutions; (d) basic research and application—the challenge to use existing findings in order to directly or indirectly enhance the life quality of elders by optimizing their living arrangements (Sanford & Connell, 1998; Schwarz & Brent, 1999).[2]

This chapter is organized as follows. First, I review the empirical research on environmental gerontology by roughly distinguishing between private home environments, institutional settings, and residential decisions. To do so, I shall rely on Lawton's (1989) description of the sociophysical environment's three basic functions, namely, maintenance, stimulation, and support. The environmental function of *maintenance* highlights the important role of constancy and predictability of the environment. The meaning of home and processes of place attachment, satisfaction with one's retirement setting, the role of the sociophysical environment on the course and outcome of dementia—all of these are examples of the maintenance function. The environmental function of *stimulation* typically means the departure from the usual in the

environment, the appearance of a novel array of stimuli and their effects on behavior. Findings that show how aspects of the sociophysical environment can facilitate or hinder leisure time activities and social behaviors, including so-called problem behaviors, such as agitation and disruptive vocalization, are examples of the stimulating function. The environmental function of *support* can typically be seen in the environment's potential to compensate for reduced or lost competencies. Specific environmental designs in institutions that improve safety and facilitate orientation, or the modification of private home environments to enhance independence in activities of daily living (ADL) and instrumental ADL (IADL) functioning are examples of the supporting function. The three environmental functions described above are also used to interpret research findings on residential decisions. Although these environmental functions are closely related to each other in real person–environment interchanges, it seems helpful to highlight each of these environmental functions separately in a research analysis.

In the second half of this chapter, I discuss theoretical developments in the field. First, I evaluate new theoretical suggestions in light of the "old" theories of environmental gerontology, then go on to discuss which theoretical approaches from psychological gerontology may be fruitful for environmental gerontology. Finally, I provide suggestions for integrating existing concepts in a more cohesive manner.

---

[1]Although undoubtedly very important, rural aging issue are not explicitly addressed in this chapter due to space limitations (e.g., Coward & Krout, 1998).

[2]To these four challenges, one might add methodological challenges, typically expressed in the need for good measurement instruments in order to assess the sociophysical environment or in what Parmelee and Lawton (1990) have described as interactional versus transactional research. Methodological issues, however, are not addressed in this chapter due to excellent reviews and contributions that have appeared during the 1990s (Car, 1994; Gitlin, 1998; Lawton, 1999; Lawton, Weisman, Sleane & Calkins, 1997).

II. Review of Empirical Research in the Field

A. Staying Put: Person–Environment Processes in the Private Home Environment

The psychoecological varieties of this major theme of environmental gerontology have been addressed in many excellent books and articles in the last 10 to 15 years (among them Gitlin, 1998; Golant, 1992; Regnier, 1994; Schwarz & Brent, 1999). The goal of this section is to review new empirical material that focuses on the link between behavior and the private home environment and extends research conducted in the 1960s, 1970s, and 1980s. The term *private home environment* includes all housing options that are not strictly institutional—even though institutions certainly can serve as one's *home*.

1. Maintaining Functions of the Home Environment

Several major research questions address the maintenance function of the home environment: What kind of place-related feelings and cognitive representations are evoked by the long-term environment as the individual ages? What functions do these cognitive–affective associations have? What role does personal aging, as well as the aging of homes, neighborhoods, and communities themselves, play in the person–environment interchange process? Classic empirical research from the 1980s (e.g., Rowles, 1983), has been extended into the 1990s in order to search for answers to these questions.

Rubinstein's (Rubinstein, Kilbride, & Nagy, 1992) work on the *meaning of home* draws upon case examples and lengthy ethnographic interviews. The cornerstone of his work is the view that the active management of the environment in itself represents a major source of well-being and the "good life" for older people, especially those who are frail or living alone. Rubinstein identifies three classes of psychosocial processes that give meaning to the home environment, namely social-centered (ordering of the home environment based on a person's version of sociocultural rules for domestic order), person-centered (expression of one's life course in features of the home),

and body-centered processes (the ongoing relationship of the body to the environmental features that surround it). Sixsmith and Sixsmith's (1991) findings also clearly underline the important role of the home as the major physical-spatial location in old age, where critical life transitions, such as physical impairment or widowhood, are (re)integrated within one's life structure by relying upon the resources and enduring nature of the physical home environment. Oswald's (1996) analysis sheds further light on these processes by identifying how chronic conditions (in this case, ongoing mobility impairment) affects representations of the home environment. When subjects were asked what "being at home" means, mobility-impaired elders reported significantly more aspects of familiarity and accustomization compared to unimpaired elders. Furthermore, several studies support the notion that staying in the home environment is highly desirable for elders at risk, such as those who lose their capacity to function autonomously (Krothe, 1997), recently experience widowhood (Swenson, 1998), or live in suboptimal environments (e.g., single-room elderly occupants in New York City; Crystal & Beck, 1992). This fits well with other results showing that elders, when forced to make housing choices, generally prefer to remain in their own home (e.g., Groves & Wilson, 1992).

Another perspective on the meaning of home is provided by the environmental construct of *place attachment*, which in recent years has increasingly been tied to the so-called aging-in-place construct. Place attachment has been defined as "a set of feelings about a geographic location that emotionally binds a person to that place as a function of its role as a setting for experience" (Rubinstein & Parmelee, 1992, p. 139). From a life span view of development, it is worth noting that place attachment was higher among older compared to younger persons in a study of over 500 adults aged 14 to 93 years in Bern, Switzerland (Fuhrer & Kaiser, 1991). Zingmark, Norberg, and Sandman (1995), in a study of persons aged 2 to 102 years, found additional support for a steady progression in the experience of being at home throughout the life span.

Still another perspective on cognitive-emotional bonding to the home is reflected in the *housing satisfaction* construct, typically acknowledged to be an important component of well-being, autonomy, and continuity in the later years. Research in the 1990s replicated and extended the classic finding of earlier studies that elders (both frail and healthy) tend to score highly on this construct, regardless of their objective home and neighborhood conditions; instead, subjective housing evaluations seem to be the best predictors of housing satisfaction (Christensen, Carp, Cranz, & Whiley, 1992).

To summarize, research on the meaning of home, place attachment, and housing satisfaction supports the view that beyond social bonding, the strongest tie between elders and the sociophysical environment is the one to their own home or apartment. They strongly prefer to cope on their own with the environmental challenges associated with the aging process, and relocation is (for most) neither a pleasant nor a promising adjustment option for their personal future.

2. Stimulating Functions of the Home Environment

Most of the research on stimulating functions of the home environment examines neighborhoods and communities. The guiding hypothesis behind this work is that neighborhood and community characteristics are powerful forces that shape the elderly person's life quality; they can trigger or hinder social and nonsocial activities, obligatory or discretionary, and thus exert a strong influence on satisfaction with daily life and the course of aging.

For example, Krause and colleagues' work (e.g., Krause, 1993; Thompson & Krause, 1998) showed that outcomes such as received social support and self-rated health (a variable critical for the use of outdoor areas) were negatively influenced by neighborhood deterioration and fear of crime. Fear of crime has also, in accordance with earlier studies (see for review, Lawton, 1977; Scheidt & Windley, 1985), shown negative correlations with the use of neighborhood opportunities (Bazargan, 1994) and with outdoor mobility in general (Mollenkopf, Marcellini, & Ruoppila, 1998). However, as can be expected, this variable varies significantly within as well as between countries, as has been shown in a comparison study of urban areas in Germany, Italy, and Finland (Finland had the lowest fear of crime; Mollenkopf et al., 1998).

Results on activity and interaction patterns in other public areas of the community further add to our understanding of the stimulating function of the environment for old age. Smith's (1991) data on the grocery shopping patterns of elders revealed their dependence on urban, inner suburban, or outer suburban location, with those in the inner city being disadvantaged in their access to discount supermarkets. The dominance of small shops in the inner city, as well as the lower availability of cars among elderly downtown residents, both contributed to lower supermarket access. The variables that influence the elderly individual's use of community resources are quite diverse. At the personal level, health-related variables and cognitive performance (e.g., spatial cognitive abilities) are prerequisites for exploring and maneuvering through the many different kinds of outdoor environments (Simon, Walsh, Regnier, & Krauss, 1992). In terms of the physical or built environment, long distances to environmental resources, such as supermarkets or pharmacies, are often difficult to bridge; consequently, the availability of a private car is crucial for ensuring the action range of elders (Mollenkopf et al., 1998). Of course, cultural, regional, as well as cohort differences have to be taken into consideration. The differences in car use between elders in the U.S. and most European countries are obvious to most, but there are also interesting differences within any single country. For example, elders from the eastern regions of Germany (former German Democratic Republic) less frequently have a car at their disposal than their western counterparts (Mollenkopf et al., 1998). In addition, the growing number of older women who can drive a car will significantly alter the outdoor mobility of future cohorts.

To sum up, there appear to be relatively close associations between the older person's behavior and the outside home environment. The search for explanations of variation in outdoor mobility and outdoor social and leisure activities patterns should include a whole scope of variables, ranging from sociodemographic and personality variables to physical and social environmental features at the micro- meso-, and macrolevel.

3. Supportive Functions of the Home Environment

Using the supportive potential of the home environment as a complementary strategy to person-centered intervention (such as rehabilitation) and as a means to prevent relocation became a very prominent issue during the 1990s. The literature on the possibilities and varieties of home modification for older people is extensive (e.g., Pynoos & Regnier, 1991) but controlled outcome studies are still the exception. This is particularly true with respect to demented elders cared for at home by family members and professionals (Gitlin, 1998).

Gill, Robinson, Williams, and Tinetti (1999) examined the home environment of 1088 adults aged 72 years or older and found no differences between physically impaired and unimpaired elders in the prevalence of environmental hazards (except for the presence of grab bars). In many cases, the frequency of environmental hazards was higher in impaired elders; for example, the frequencies of obstructed pathways was 47% (impaired) versus 37% (unimpaired) and loose throw rugs were observed at a frequency of 72% in both groups. These rather high percentages, however, do not necessarily show the elderly individual to be a pawn of physical environmental conditions. In line with the proactivity argument put forth by Lawton (1985), Reschovsky and Newman (1990) found the majority of elders or households in which elders live undertake at least some home modifications or repair themselves (only 9% reported no such activities during the 12 months previous to the interview). Similarly, visually impaired older people have been found to employ a wide variety of person and environment-related compensations in order to reduce existing gaps between their competence and environmental demands (Wahl, Oswald, & Zimprich, 1999).

Further insights into natural existing links between behavior and characteristics of the home environment, as well as into day-to-day adjustment processes in the home, come from German and Dutch studies. Based on a large study with elderly Germans from East and West Germany with data collection dating back to 1992, substandard housing conditions were significantly associated with ADL and IADL performance deficits, and higher care needs among elders in East Germany could be partly explained by the stronger prevalence of substandard housing (Olbrich & Diegritz, 1995). Wahl et al. (1999) examined person–physical environment fit in visually impaired and sighted elders; in line with Lawton and Brody's (1969) assumption, the visually impaired were more vulnerable to environmental press in IADL but not in ADL. The findings support the environmental docility hypothesis as originally suggested by Lawton and Simon (1968), yet also underscore the need for differentiation. Slangen-de Kort's (1999) work on how the elderly solve problems in their home environment demonstrates once more that good solutions take a number of factors into account (such as being alone or with a partner, ease of use, costs, ease of realization). Active person–environment adaptations in the home setting (that is, direct modifications) appeared to be more effective than passive ones, although they did not correlate with subjective well-being scores. Dispositional variables that might predict different ways of coping with housing problems, such as the distinction between tenacious goal pursuit and flexible goal adjustment (Brandtstädter & Renner, 1990), were used to explain why some elders tend to modify the environment while others employ personal modes of adaptation. As expected, tenacious goal pursuit predicted direct home modification effort, whereas flexible goal adjustment predicted person-centered adjustment to the physical environment.

To conclude, research on the home environment must be buttressed by more psychological research in order to understand the complex interchange processes that can lead to dramatic adjustments in the physical surroundings of some elderly, to practically none in others. Again, a mixture of person variables (including personality characteristics) and physical–social environment variables must be considered in order to account for the pronounced interindividual variability between elderly people.

B. Institutional Environments

Institutional settings serving the elderly have long been the subject of inquiry for environmental psychologists and gerontologists. However, although more competent residents were a major focus of basic and intervention-oriented research in the 1970s and even into the 1970s, the theme of dementia has sparked the most interest in institutional research in the last decade.

1. Maintaining Functions of the Institutional Environment

Empirical research has addressed maintenance within the institutional environment context in a twofold manner, first, by addressing the meaning of the (new) institutional home (Can an institution be a home?) as well as indicators of general well-being in the institution setting, and second, by approaching the very specific but highly important issue of whether institutional environments can be "therapeutic" in the sense of truly impacting on the course and progression of dementia in a positive manner.

With respect to the first issue, most of the gerontology literature automatically associates the meaning of home with private home settings. Is it possible to live in an institution and truly feel at home? Questions such as these were posed as early as the 1970s; a particularly poignant example is Gubriums's (1975) classic book "Living and Dying at Murray Manor." Among the rare empirical work contributing to this issue in the 1990s is a qualitative study by Groger (1995) based on 20 cognitively unimpaired African-American elders, of whom 10 were nursing home residents and another 10 homecare clients. According to her results, the nursing home can become a home, but the development of this affective-cognitive-behavioral conglomerate depends on at least three factors, including the circumstances of placement (e.g., enough time for anticipation of the new living situation contributes to the "home" feeling), the subjective criteria that define "home" (e.g., those who had associated home more with social relations and less with competence and independence were better able to feel "at home"), and the degree of continuity achieved after relocation to the nursing home (e.g., being able to transfer selected activities from one's previous life into the institution helps to maintain feeling "at home").

Feeling at "home" is a powerful, albeit circumscribed indicator of environmental well-being. What about more general, long-term cognitive-emotional adaptation to institutions? Nursing home satisfaction has been found to be more strongly influenced by personal than organizational factors (Kruzich, Clinton, & Kelber, 1992), but interaction effects between person and environmental factors play a role as well. For example, O'Connor and Vallerand (1994) provide empirical evidence that the person–environment congruence model predicts subjective well-being (see also Kahana, Liang, & Felton, 1980). In particular, residents with self-determined motivational styles were better adjusted when they lived in homes that provided opportunities for freedom and choice, whereas residents with less self-determined motivational styles were better adjusted when they lived in highly constrained environments. Interactions between residents and the institutional environment were also illustrated by Timko and Moos's (1990) findings from a large, U.S. nationwide sample of facilities, showing that the institution's organizational and physical environment can significantly foster (or hinder) interpersonal support and self-direction among residents.

Overall, research on the meaning of home and well-being among nursing home residents has been sparse. There seem to be good reasons to assert that living in an institution and being "at home" is not a contradiction in terms.

Rather, it seems to depend on a variety of factors, including the circumstances of relocation and personal preferences, as well as the social and organizational features of the institution itself. The general subjective well-being of residents may be expected to be influenced by environmental features of the institution, but the person–environment fit must also be taken into account.

Regarding the second issue, the term *therapeutic environment* which is often used in conjunction with institutional environments specifically designed for demented elders, implies that environments have a curative effect on their residents, and this basic assumption underlies a whole series of outstanding books and articles on the issue that have appeared since the end of the 1980s (e.g., Calkins, 1988; Cohen & Weisman, 1991; Lawton et al., 1997; Regnier & Pynoos, 1992; Weisman, Lawton, Sloane, Calkins, & Norris-Baker, 1996). Although the literature is full of suggestions for designing "good" environments for the demented, the very notion of a therapeutic environment is in dire need of empirical testing.

A host of studies from different countries show diverse results. No study supports the view of a broad, strong, and long-lasting impact of skilled care units (SCUs) on the course and outcome of dementia. Among the "some beneficial effect" studies is an Italian one by Bianchetti et al. (1997), who found a reduction in behavioral problems—but no change in functional capacity and cognitive performance—after 6 months of stay in a SCU. Kihlgren et al.'s (1992) study in the U.S. covered a relatively long observation period of 22 months and included behavioral as well as physiological measures (electroencephologram). They found slight positive effects on the overall collective living group setting compared to traditional nursing home settings. The Swedish researchers Annerstedt,

Gustafson, and Nilsson (1993) found that residents in group living units showed improvement (e.g., less depression, less dyspraxia and dysphasia, reduction in neuroleptic treatment) 6 and 12 months after introducing the new treatment environment.

With respect to the studies that report no effect (but make certain reservations), the Swedish researchers Elmstahl, Annerstedt, and Ahlund (1997) evaluated two group living units with different architectural features at 6-month and 1-year follow-ups. Both groups of demented residents deteriorated continually after one year, but decline was more pronounced in the corridor-like environment, which illustrates the differential effects of physical design.

Finally, the clear "no effect" studies include a French one (Ritchie, Colvez, Ankri, & Ledesert, 1992) of 241 demented elders in traditional nursing homes and 110 residents of so-called "cantous" (a place providing nonmedical care more akin to an ordinary living situation than to an institution); 50 matched pairs showed no effect on the progression of dementia 1 year after the intake assessment.

To sum up, the evidence of the impact of SCUs on the course and outcome of dementia is still very mixed (see also Sloane, Lindemann, Phillips, Moritz, & Koch, 1995). Nevertheless, the notion of specially designed environments for demented elders (at least until effective pharmacological treatment has been found) still seems to be a worthy goal. Probably, Zeisel's (1999) statement is the best evaluation of the current state of knowledge: "The future will tell if the approaches being developed at the end of the twentieth century in environmental design and caregiving for people with Alzheimer's disease and other dementias take hold in the twenty-first century or are discarded as short-lived fads" (p. 129).

2. Stimulating Functions of the Institutional Environment

The institutional environment can provide a broad range of potential stimulating functions. Empirical research on this topic can be divided into the following three domains: social interaction as dependent on physical conditions, activity and autonomy, and the use of environmental stimuli to regulate problem behaviors, such as agitation and disruptive behavior.

Regarding the first of these domains, the "old" issue of multiple versus single occupancy rooms has been raised with respect to demented elders. Morgan and Stewart (1998a) were able to follow demented elders relocating from a high to a low social density unit with private bedrooms. Residents in the low social density unit spent more time in their rooms during the day, required less interventions (including medication) to promote sleep at night, and had fewer conflicts with fellow residents. However, staff's perception of the single occupancy rooms revealed certain disadvantages, such as reduced efficiency because they could not supervise more than one resident at a time. One may add here the results of a study conducted by Kovach and Robinson (1996) addressing the role of the roommate relationship. The study showed that nearly half of the residents never talked to their roommates and a positive correlation between roommate relationship and well-being held true only for those residents who talked to their roommates.

Teresi, Holmes, and Monaco (1993) conducted one of the very few studies that examined how social and physical proximity to cognitively impaired residents affects cognitively unimpaired residents. Generally, the latter report negative feelings and behaviors when thrust into this person–environment constellation. However, factors influencing the willingness of alert residents to cohabit with cognitively impaired peers have been found to be multifaceted, covering, among other variables, the alert resident's emotional reaction to living with the cognitively impaired as well as the alert resident's perception of the benefits of cohabitation for the cognitively impaired.

Turning now to research on activity and autonomy, one should note that keeping residents active is among the highest priorities of most institutions today. Voelkl, Fries, and Galecki (1995) analyzed data on activity involvement and on predictors of activity from more than 2500 nursing home residents and found only one quarter of their subjects were not involved in some sort of structured activity over the course of 1 week. However, the staff spent an average of only 12 minutes per resident per week. Among the major influencing factors were depression (higher depression predicted lower activity involvement) and gender (women were more involved than men), but space-related variables (preferring to stay in one's own room had a dampening effect on activity involvement) were influential also. Bowie and Mountain (1997) found a link between the sociophysical environment and resident's behavior, that is, options provided by the physical environment stimulated different activities, but space availability per se was not related to any of these behaviors. Morgan and Stewart's (1997) study even underscores the possibility that a transition from cramped to roomier quarters may well lead from overstimulation to understimulation and induce boredom in some residents.

With respect to autonomy or the independent functioning of nursing home residents (with little or no cognitive impairment), Margret Baltes and associates initiated a whole empirical research program during the 1980s and 1990s (Baltes, 1996). The major and very robust finding was that social interactions between older adults and social partners are prone to a *dependence-support script*, that is, dependent behavior among elders is reinforced by their social partners (typically by direct helping behavior), whereas autonomous behaviors are typically ignored. As was also found, the dependence-support script is more pronounced in institutional settings compared to home health care and family care settings (Baltes & Wahl, 1992). It is also subject to change when proper interventions with professional caregivers are employed (Baltes, Neumann, & Zank, 1994).

And finally, research has addressed the so-called problem behaviors exhibited by demented elders in institutions by using a learning theory approach combined with other theoretical and methodological facets such as behavior mapping or manipulating the acoustic environment. This combination has proved to be a powerful tool for describing, explaining, and modifying behaviors such as agitation. Cohen-Mansfield, Werner, and Marx (1990) found the agitation of demented residents to be associated with a variety of physical locations within institutional settings, such as the toilet, corridor, nurses' station, and other resident's rooms. However, it was not observed in the target person's room, despite the fact that the demented person generally spends a great deal of time there. Among the interventions tested, medication and behavioral strategies have been found to be particularly successful (Burgio, Scilley, Hardin, Hsu, & Yancey, 1996).

Verbally disruptive behaviors are another class of problem behaviors typically exhibited by demented residents. Morgan and Stewart (1998b) found low social density to ameliorate verbal disruptions. Cohen-Mansfield and Werner (1997) tested different environmental conditions experimentally for their effectiveness in reducing verbally disruptive behaviors

(VDB) in cognitively impaired nursing home residents. One-to-one social interactions provided by trained research assistants outperformed two other conditions (exposure to videotape, exposure to music), leading to a 56% reduction in VDBs.

To sum up, research in the 1990s has gathered a variety of evidence for the stimulating role of the institutional environment. As has been shown, different characteristics of the sociophysical environment are linked with social behavior, activity and autonomy, and problem behaviors. Of course, personal determinants for these behaviors must be considered as well. Intervention-oriented research in these fields has clear practical implications but also supports, from a basic science point of view, some degree of plasticity in nursing home resident's behaviors, even among those who suffer from dementia.

3. Supportive Functions of the Institutional Environment

Institutional environments are generally designed to compensate for age-related loss in competence. However, institutions vary greatly with respect to their physical-architectural features and program characteristics (e.g., Moos & Lemke, 1985), and thus in their ability to support the elderly resident in a comprehensive manner.

Dementia patients typically experience orientation and way-finding difficulties that may at least in part be due to the physical environment. In a carefully conducted experimental study, Passini, Rainville, Marchand, and Joanette (1998) compared the way-finding capability of demented elders with matched normals. All subjects were asked to reach a prescribed destination in a large hospital, and all verbalizations were recorded and the content analyzed. Results showed most dementia patients to be capable of

developing an overall plan to solve the way-finding task, but incapable of making decisions involving memory or inferences. Conversely, they were better able to make decisions based on information of an explicitly architectural nature, such as different colors in different corridors. Furthermore, patients performed poorly when forced to extract relevant information from graphic displays and tended to be confused by irrelevant information displays. Netten (1989), in a study of 104 demented elders in 13 institutions, found clear relations between wayfinding and architectural features; for example, finding one's room was easier when the residents' rooms were located around a central area compared to rooms situated along long corridors.

Among the most controversially discussed program features of institutions to compensate for lost behavioral competencies is the use of physical restraints—mostly for those with severe cognitive and ADL impairment (Burton et al., 1992; Karlsson, Bucht, Erksson, & Sandman, 1996). The benefits of this method, or the advantages and disadvantages that emerge due to the reduction of restraints, are not altogether clear. An increased risk of falls, particularly nonserious falls, has been shown to accompany the reduction of restraints (Ejaz, Jones, & Rose, 1994), but in another study, the finding was only replicated among confused ambulatory subjects (Capezuti, Evans, Strumpf, & Maiskn, 1996). By and large, Capezuti et al.'s (1996) call for individualized assessment instead of routine use of physical restraints seems to be the best advice for the practical field, given the current state of knowledge.

In conclusion, physical and program features of the institutional environment can well serve to support residents in compensating for their loss in cognitive and behavioral functioning. Nevertheless there is probably a pronounced gap between what is suggested and implemented in the practical field and what has been evaluated in a rigorous manner.

C. Residential Decisions

The question Hamlet might have posed regarding one's residency in old age—to move or not to move—is among the most important decisions to make in later life. Although relocation can be a stressful life event at any age, old people have traditionally been seen as particularly vulnerable. Today, two qualifications are important for reconsidering this issue: on the one hand, relocation to the nursing home is now predominantly a move of the oldest old, and among these persons, many suffer from different degrees of dementia or very severe chronic illness. On the other hand, relocation in the later years, particularly home-to-home relocation, is increasingly being motivated by the desire for new stimulation and achieving a better person–environment fit with respect to "higher order" needs (Carp & Carp, 1984).

1. Moving from Home-to-Home

Much research in the 1990s tried to better understand why older people move from one private household to another. Obviously, the strong attachment to one's home environment that is typically found in old age must be considered as a basic factor in any relocation decision. As proxy variables for place attachment, living in one's residence for a long period of time and owning one's home are both associated with an inclination to stay put (e.g., Speare, Avery, & Lawton, 1991). In contrast, personal variables, such as degree of disability, do not seem to play a major role in home-to-home relocation decisions (Speare et al., 1991).

Litwak and Longino (1987) have suggested a distinction between first, second, and third moves, which also have overlap with the functions of the environment suggested above. First moves are expected to predominantly appear in the early years after retirement and are driven by the desire for new stimulation (e.g., "Sun Belt Moves"). Second moves are expected to appear later in the course of old age and are motivated by the supportive function of the environment, but more in terms of reducing risk or ensuring against potential need. Relocating to be closer to one's children is typical of this category. Third moves directly target the supportive function of the sociophysical environment and may best be exemplified by a relocation to a nursing home among those of very advanced age. Although the distinction between first, second, and third moves and the hypothesized time periods are probably not mutually exclusive, this conception has found at least partial empirical support (Hazelrigg & Hardy, 1995) and can help to understand why elders move.

Haas and Serow (1993) propose another useful distinction: push-versus-pull factors in the relocation process. Whereas push factors are more on the reactive side of the reason-to-move motivation continuum, representing factors such as impaired health or negative neighborhood changes, pull factors are attractions of the new environment that are actively sought by the would-be mover. Pull factors have been found to be more important than push factors and particularly triggered by amenity motives and "higher order" needs (Haas & Serow, 1993; Oswald, Wahl, & Gäng, 1999). Serow, Friedrich, and Haas (1996) have also found a prevalence of amenity motives in a United States–German comparison study; moving closer to other family members appeared to be equally strong in both cultures, whereas, as expected, climate was only a strong pull motive among American elders.

Ryff and Essex (1992; Kling, Seltzer, & Ryff, 1997) provided a more in-depth psychological analysis of the dynamics between push and pull motives among older women followed in the Wisconsin Study of Community Relocation. These authors were able to highlight the important role of discrepancies between push-and-pull factors for psychological relocation outcomes such as psychological well-being. Overall, greater discrepancies were associated with lower psychological well-being, especially personal growth, purpose in life, and self-acceptance.

2. Moving from Home to Institutional Environments and Intrainstitutional Relocation

Research in the 1990s supports the consensus in the empirical literature regarding the three sets of variables that impact on relocation to a nursing home: (a) sociodemographic characteristics, such as age, gender, and marital status, (b) health characteristics, such as ADL dependency and cognitive impairment, and (c) social support characteristics, such as living alone or having no children (e.g., Salive, Collins, Foley, & George, 1993; Speare et al., 1991). Approaching the issue from a more subjective perspective, McCullough, Wilson, Teasdale, Kolpakchi, and Skelly (1993) conducted a qualitative study of elders living in different residency situations (including nursing homes) and their significant others (including professionals) and found that elders predominantly emphasized personal values such as independence, whereas professionals stressed health-related issues.

In general, intrainstitutional relocation has not been found to produce negative consequences for either physically or mentally frail elders (Grant, Skinkle, & Lipps, 1992). Nevertheless, well-planned relocation preparation programs are essential (Tesch, Nehrke, & Whitbourne, 1989) and may have differential effects on the older mover. For example, in a controlled study of intrainstitutional moves, Gallagher and Walker (1990)

found the move to have a negative impact on those who had moved temporarily (due to renovations) but a positive one on those moving permanently.

Overall, recent research on residential decisions in later life has contributed a lot to the understanding of the relocation process. In particular, relocation research has followed the current trend in today's aging societies by emphasizing home-to-home relocation motivation and processes. By and large, there is reason to assume that the environmental function of stimulation has become a major pull factor in today's cohorts of healthy elders. (Sun Belt movers represent the most typical subgroup of this trend.) In contrast to 40 or 50 years ago, those attracted by the support (and stimulation) provided by long-term institutions are predominantly the oldest old and mentally or physically frail. However, when reviewing the field of relocation research, one must never forget that the maintenance function of the environment can be powerful, and probably only a minority of tomorrow's elders will decide to move.

III. Theoretical Status of the Field

From its inception, environmental gerontology has been strongly theoretical (e.g., Lawton, Windley, & Byerts, 1982; Saup, 1993; Wahl, in press). However, the pervasive feeling nowadays is that little theorizing has occurred in environmental gerontology over the last 15 years or so (Scheidt & Windley, 1998a). This section provides the reader with an update of the concepts used in the field over the last 10 years, differentiating between classic approaches to environmental gerontology and theoretical work from psychological gerontology with direct relevance for environmental gerontology. Finally, avenues toward better integration of theoretical conceptions and, hence, more frutiful empirical research, are proposed.

A. Major Theoretical Approaches within Environmental Gerontology: Old and New

The classic theoretical accounts in environmental gerontology in the 1970s and 1980s (reviewed by Lawton et al., 1982, and, more recently, by Scheidt & Windley, 1998b) stimulated considerable empirical research. Six major models have been developed (see also Table 9.1): (a) Competence Press Model (Lawton & Nahemow, 1973), (b) Person–Environment Congruence Model (Kahana, 1975), (c) Social Ecological Model (Moos, 1976), (d) Transactional View of Person–Environment Relations (Rowles, 1983), (e) Person–Environment Stress Model (Schooler, 1982), and (6) Complementary/Congruence Model (Carp & Carp, 1984). Lawton and Nahemow's Press-Competence Model has remained among the most frequently cited theoretical approaches within psychological gerontology in general and

their famous Figure 1 (p. 661) is among the most frequently reproduced figures in the field.

More recent theoretical approaches have followed and extended these classic research traditions and deepened our understanding of all three major realms of person–environment interchange in the later years: Aging in the private home environment, aging in institutions, and residential decisions. Rubinstein (1998) has argued that a phenomenological and anthropological approach to the home environment has great potential. Using extensive data from case histories, Rubinstein has demonstrated the fruitfulness of a perspective that integrates societal and cultural influences on the macrolevel with the development of the home environment as a symbolic extension of the self on the microlevel. Other classic constructs from environmental psychology, such as Roger Barker's concept of behavior setting (Norris-Baker, 1998) or Kurt

Table 9.1
Classic Theoretical Accounts of Environmental Gerontology in Chronological Order

Theoretical account	Main proposition	Key reference
Competence Press Model	Behavior as a function of personal competence and environmental press	Lawton & Nahemow, 1973
Person–Environment Congruence Model	Behavior as a function of the congruence between personal characteristics and what the environment has to offer	Kahana, 1975
Social Ecology Model	Influence of physical and social environments on individual behavior and vice versa	Moos, 1976
Transactional view of older persons in their environments	Physical, social, and autobiographical insideness as consequences of long-term living and aging in one place	Rowles, 1983
Stress–Theoretical Model	Dynamic process of appraisal, coping, and reappraisal constitutes person–environment transactions	Schooler, 1982
Complementary/Congruence Model	Well-being as influenced by the match between environmental resources and personal needs	Carp & Carp, 1984

Lewin's concept of life space (Parmelee, 1998), have been recently rediscovered and act as theoretical catalysts to further empirical research on the home environment and beyond.

Aging in the institutional and institution-like context has also been of ongoing theoretical interest in environmental gerontology. First, the conceptualization of institutions as social ecologies (Moos & Lemke, 1985) has stimulated a very productive research program based on a theory-guided operationalization, the Multiphasic Environmental Assessment Procedure (MEAP) (Moos & Lemke, 1994, 1996). Second, institutions have proved to be an ideal arena for applying the learning theory perspective to aging. Two of the productive research programs alluded to earlier, namely, the description, explanation, and modification of dependency in old age (M. Baltes, 1996) and selected problem behaviors of demented elders (Burgio et al., 1996), have been conducted in institutional settings. In the 1990s, Margret Baltes expanded her theoretical view of institutional aging by applying the model of selective optimization with compensation to these settings as well (Baltes, 1994). Third, the issue of providing good environments for demented elders has challenged scholars in the field to develop concepts that help to understand and optimize person–environment interchange processes characteristic of this very specific human condition. In this regard, Weisman's (1997; Weisman, Chaudhury, & Diaz Moore, 2000) *model of place* has received due recognition. Weisman highlights the concept of *place experience*, which is framed within the physical setting, but also in the social and organizational context. According to Weisman, environmental attributes addressing the microlevel of institutional life "bring to the surface the integrated nature of place experiences in a way that is meaningful for environmental design"

(Weisman et al., 2000, p. 12). Numerous such environmental attributes have been suggested by different scholars (Calkins, 1988; Cohen & Weisman, 1991; Regnier & Pynoos, 1992), ranging from basic safety to privacy and personal control.

The explanation of residential decisions and their outcomes in old age has always attracted environmental gerontologists. Golant (1998), for example, has recently proposed a conceptual model to better understand how older persons experience changes in their personal and environmental outcomes as a result of relocation. Although not directly related to the Golant model the relocation-oriented research of Ryff and her colleagues (Ryff & Essex, 1992; Kling et al., 1997) has particularly contributed to a differential view of the relocation process. Based on the theoretical assumption that elders have quite different psychological resources interacting with push-and-pull motives, these scholars have significantly enhanced our understanding of why relocation leads to different levels of subjective well-being.

B. Psychological Gerontology Theories Important for Environmental Gerontology

Two observations can be made: First, although the so-called ecological equation always incorporated the person, the sociophysical environment, and the interaction between the two (Lawton, 1982), there has been a tendency to neglect the person in the equation. Recently, Lawton (1998) stressed the one-sidedness of current theorizing in environment gerontology. Second, although there are theoretical accounts within psychological gerontology with direct implications for analyzing person–environment relations in old age, most of these fail to explicitly address the sociophysical environment. At best, research tends to speak about environmental resources or constraints without further detailed clarification.

A consensus among environmental gerontologists is emerging that one of the most relevant psychological conceptions in this regard is control theory (e.g., Gitlin, 1998; Parmelee & Lawton, 1990). New developments in control theory, such as the life-span theory of control suggested by Heckhausen and Schulz (1995), are based on the distinction between primary and secondary control and on the expectation of different trajectories of both of these control modes across the adult life span. Primary control is seen as the universal human effort to maintain influence over the external environment, whereas secondary control encompasses a variety of personal adjustments to failure, indirectly supporting primary control processes. Furthermore, whereas the tendency toward primary control is expected to remain stable across the adult life span, secondary control is assumed to increase in old age due to the culmination of loss experiences. A life span theory of control, emphasizing development across middle adulthood and into advanced age, can help us to interpret how older people use the sociophysical home environment as a resource and adapt to existing physical constraints.

Another growing consensus among environmental gerontologists is that differential aspects of person–environment processes in the later years deserve more attention (Gitlin, 1998; Golant, 1998; Lawton, 1998). To address this need, psychological gerontology can draw upon concepts old and new. Among the classics are personality traits such as extraversion and openness to experience (McCrae & Costa, 1990; see also Lawton, 1998). Among the newer concepts worth considering is Brandstädter and Renner's (1990) theoretical distinction between tenacious goal pursuit and flexible goal adjustment. The dynamic interplay between both of these processes—as well as the elderly individual's facility to adjust personal preferences to existing standards—may help to explain why some persons successfully adjust to their living environment and others decide to relocate (Slangen-de Kort, 1999).

C. Pathways toward Better Integration of Environmental Gerontology: Theoretical Accounts

Despite theoretical developments in both environmental gerontology and psychological gerontology, the general lack of conceptual integration is still a major shortcoming in the field. The need for integration can be elaborated in a threefold manner.

1. Better Integration of the Physical and the Social Environment

The need to consider the physical and the social environment with equal strengths in ecological theorizing has always been emphasized by the "big names" in social ecology, environmental psychology, and gerontology (such as Barker, Bronfenbrenner, Lawton, Lewin, or Moos). However, much empirical work gives precedence to the physical environment over the social environment (Parmelee, 1998; Parmelee & Lawton, 1990). Interestingly, one of the most classic studies in the field (Lawton & Simon, 1968), which gave rise to the so-called Environmental Docility Hypothesis, linked patterns of social interaction with physical distances. Future theorizing—if it hopes to further empirical research in environmental gerontology—should consider both the physical and the social environment. Pragmatically, this will require stronger collaboration between those interested in social support networks and those interested in physical ecology.

2. Better Integration of Environmental and Psychological Gerontology

When considering how to advance this field of research, one interesting question concerns where to find the best ideas: Is it more heuristically fruitful to dig back to the theoretical roots of environmental gerontology (as others have done, such as Parmelee, 1998, by referring to Kurt Lewin, or Norris-Baker, 1998, by referring to Roger Barker), or to move ahead with new ideas by drawing from ongoing theory development in gerontology, particularly in psychological gerontology? Although these alternatives are not mutually exclusive, I would argue strongly for the latter path: psychological gerontology has a great deal to offer, especially in terms of differential analysis. Future theoretical accounts should use ecological approaches (which explicitly consider the sociophysical environment) in combination with psychological gerontology conceptions (which typically do not). The combination works to the advantage of both fields of research, but in practice, requires stronger collaboration between ecologists and developmental and personality psychologists.

3. Better Integration of the Micro- and Macrolevels of Analysis

Theoretical accounts addressing the microlevel of person–environment relations in old age (e.g., the Press-Competence Model) and those addressing this relation from a molar or macroperspective (in social gerontology, Krause, 1993; in housing policy, Sheehan, 1995) are still mostly separate worlds. Moreover, environmental characteristics such as housing standard can also be seen as a proxy for social class, despite the fact that high-quality housing and neighborhoods are not necessarily "good" environments for aging. However, this fact is seldom considered in environmental research that focuses mostly on the objective, physical features of the home environment per se. A "collective social psychology" (M. Baltes & Carstensen, 1999) could be informative and stimulating to environmental gerontologists and sociologists as well. Future theoretical accounts should more strongly combine the microlevel of analysis with the macrolevel. Research should investigate the influence of culture and society on adapting to one's home environment, living and aging in an institution, or deciding to move. Again, in terms of practice, stronger collaboration between ecologists, sociologists, and social policy researchers becomes necessary.

IV. Conclusions and Outlook

Noted scholars in environmental gerontology have often provided recommendations and advice that might advance their field of research (Carp, 1987, 1994; Lawton, 1977; Moos & Lemke, 1985; Parmelee & Lawton, 1990; Scheidt & Windley, 1985); unfortunately, most of these suggestions cannot be easily incorporated into research paradigms in a satisfactory manner or in a reasonable amount of time. Parmelee and Lawton (1990) nevertheless ended their handbook chapter with the hope that something can be done "to move the field beyond its current languishing state" (p. 483). Has something, in fact, been done since then?

I would answer this question with a qualified yes. Let us consider again the four main challenges for environmental gerontology described in the introduction: Empirical research, theory, comprehensiveness, and basic research and application. This review has clearly shown that the first of these challenges has been adequately addressed; there have been many empirical contributions to environmental gerontology during the 1990s, adding significantly to our understanding of environmental–behavior links in private home settings, institutional life, and residential decision making. Furthermore, this research, particularly work focusing on the home environment and institutions, can be well organized according to the environment's three major functions in later life, namely maintenance, stimulation, and support (Lawton, 1989). This conceptual scheme is also helpful in interpreting findings on residential satisfaction. Thus, a considerable amount of consistency in empirical research in the field has been achieved and furthered in the 1990s.

Recent theoretical progress in the field presents a less rosy picture. Although some new conceptual proposals have been introduced, most of these lack the vision and grand scale found among the classic theoretical approaches in the field (see again Table 9.1). On the other hand, classic theories are too entrenched in the well-worn concepts from yesterday's gerontology and psychology and tend to neglect individual differences in behavior–environment links (Lawton, 1999). This unsatisfactory conceptual balance sheet of today's environmental gerontology is critical due to the important role that theory plays in interpreting empirical results (see again Birren's statement that gerontology is "data-rich and theory-poor," Birren, 1999, p. 459). As was argued in this chapter, the situation in environmental gerontology can best be solved by better integration of already existing theoretical accounts on three levels: Better integration of theories addressing the physical and the social environment, better integration of theories of environmental gerontology and psychological gerontology, and better integration of the micro- and macrolevel of analysis by use of theories incorporating a psychological perspective on person–environment relations in old age as well as a sociological and social policy points of view.

With respect to the comprehensiveness of environmental gerontology, concern has been expressed that too much research deals with elders suffering from chronic conditions (Carp, 1987). The empirical research reviewed in this chapter shows that elders, ranging from the healthy and active Sun Belt movers to very frail Alzheimer's patients, have been the research focus in the 1990s. Research on aging has also investigated a broad variety of ecologies. Environmental gerontology, as well as other areas of psychological gerontology, must nevertheless be characterized as predominately "urban" in nature (Coward & Krout, 1998; see again footnote 1). In addition, future research would do well to examine the new person–environment settings that arise from forthcoming cohorts of older adults (the baby boomers, in particular) and new technologies and new media (Stokols, 1999). For example, one important question in this regard is how the meaning of home and thus the maintaining function of the home environment will change due to Internet use and intelligent home facilities (Graafmans, Taipale, & Charness, 1998).

Finally, the tension between basic science and application in environmental gerontology creates some natural pitfalls (as well as opportunities) in the field. On the one hand, environmental gerontology is a shining example of an area of psychological gerontology that produces valuable findings from basic research and controlled intervention studies. Results can be directly applied to the practical field, such as to planned housing, designing institutions, or promoting the age-friendliness of neighborhoods or whole communities. The applied potential of environmental gerontology has contributed much to the societal recognition of gerontology in recent years. On the other hand, scholars in the field would be wise to resist the temptation of producing ever more field guides to practical problems, which runs the risk of remaking the wheel. Instead, the future focus of environmental gerontology should be on producing and replicating basic findings.

Acknowledgments

This chapter has substantially profited from the comments of and talks with the following colleagues: David Burmedi, Laura Gitlin, M. Powell Lawton, Frank Oswald, and Gerald Weisman. Helpful comments from the editors of this handbook were very much appreciated as well. Also, I would like to thank numerous colleagues all over the world who have sent me their latest work in the field.

References

Annerstedt, L., Gustafson, L., & Nilsson, K. (1993). Medical outcome of psychosocial intervention in demented patients: One-year clinical follow-up after relocation into group living units. *International Journal of Geriatric Psychiatry, 8*, 833–841.

Baltes, M. M. (1994). Aging well and institutional living: A paradox? In R. P. Abeles, H. C. Gift, & M. G. Ory (Eds.), *Aging and quality of life* (pp. 185–201). New York: Springer.

Baltes, M. M. (1996). *The many faces of dependency in old age.* Cambridge: Cambridge University Press.

Baltes, M. M., & Carstensen, L. L. (1999). Social-psychological theories and their applications to aging: From individual to collective. In V. L. Bengtson & K. W. Schaie (Eds.), *Handbook of the theories of aging* (pp. 209–226). New York: Springer.

Baltes, M. M., Neumann, E.-M., & Zank, S. (1994). Maintenance and rehabilitation of independence in old age: An Intervention program for staff. *Psychology and Aging, 9*, 179–188.

Baltes, M. M., & Wahl, H.-W. (1992). The dependency-support script in institutions: Generalization to community settings. *Psychology and Aging, 7*, 409–418.

Bazargan, M. (1994). The effects of health, environmental, and socio-psychological variables on fear of crime and its consequences among urban black elderly individuals. *International Journal of Aging and Human Development, 38*, 99–115.

Bianchetti, A., Benvenuti, P., Ghisla, K. M., Frisoni, G. et al. (1997). An Italian model of dementia special care unit: Results of a pilot study. *Alzheimer Disease and Associated Disorders, 11*, 53–56.

Birren, J. E. (1999). Theories of aging: A personal perspective. In V. L. Bengtson & K. W. Schaie (Eds.), *Handbook of the theories of aging* (pp. 459–472). New York: Springer.

Birren, J. E., & Schaie, K. W. (Eds.). (1996). *Handbook of the psychology of aging* (4th ed.). New York: Academic Press.

Bowie, P., & Mountain, G. (1997). The relationship between patient behaviour and environmental quality for the dementing. *International Journal of Geriatric Psychiatry, 12*, 718–723.

Brandstädter, J., & Renner, G. (1990). Tenacious goal pursuit and flexible goal adjustment: Explication and age-related analysis of assimilation and accommodation strategies of coping. *Psychology and Aging, 5*, 58–67.

Burgio, L., Scilley, K., Hardin, J. M., Hsu, C., & Yancey, J. (1996). Environmental "White Noise": An intervention for verbally agitated nursing home residents. *Journal of Gerontology: Psychological Sciences, 51B*, P364–P373.

Burton, L., German, P. S., Rovner, B. W., Brant, L., & Clark, R. D. (1992). Mental illness and the use of restraints in nursing homes. *The Gerontologist, 32*, 164–170.

Calkins, M. (1988). *Design for dementia.* Owings Mills, MD: National Health Publishing.

Capezuti, E., Evans, L., Strumpf, N., & Maislin, G. (1996). Physical restraint use and falls in nursing home residents. *Journal of the American Geriatrics Society, 44*, 627–633.

Carp, F. M. (1987). Environment and aging. In D. Stokols & I. Altman (Eds.), *Handbook of environmental psychology* (pp. 329–360). New York: Wiley.

Carp, F. M. (1994). Assessing the environment. In M. P. Lawton & J. A. Teresi (Eds.), *Focus on assessment techniques. Annual Review of gerontology and geriatrics* (Vol. 14, pp. 302–323). New York: Springer.

Carp, F. M., & Carp, A. (1984). A complementary/congruence model of well-being or mental health for the community elderly.

In I. Altman, P. M. Lawton, & J. F. Wohlwill (Eds.), *Human behavior and environment, Vol 7: Elderly people and the environment* (pp. 279–336). New York: Plenum Press.

Christensen, D. L., Carp, F. M., Cranz, G. L., & Whiley, J. A. (1992). Objective housing indicators as predictors of the subjective evaluations of elderly residents. *Journal of Environmental Psychology, 12,* 225–236.

Cohen, U., & Weisman, G. (1991). *Holding on to home: Designing environments for people with dementia.* Baltimore, MD: Johns Hopkins University Press.

Cohen-Mansfield, J., & Werner, P. (1997). Management of verbally disruptive behaviors in nursing home residents. *Journal of Gerontology: Medical Sciences, 52A,* M369–M377.

Cohen-Mansfield, J., Werner, P., & Marx, M. S. (1990). The spatial distribution of agitation in agitated nursing home residents. *Environment and Behavior, 22,* 408–419.

Coward, R. T., & Krout, J. A. (Eds.). (1998). *Aging in rural settings.* New York: Springer Publ.

Crystal, S., & Beck, P. (1992). A room of one's own: The SRO and the single elderly. *The Gerontologist, 32,* 684–692.

Ejaz, F. K., Jones, J. A., & Rose, M. S. (1994). Falls among nursing home residents: An examination of incident reports before and after restraint reduction programs. *Journal of the American Geriatrics Society, 42,* 960–964.

Elmstahl, S., Annerstedt, L., & Ahlund, O. (1997). How should a group living unit for demented elderly be designed to decrease psychiatric symptoms? *Alzheimer Disease and Associated Disorders, 11,* 47–52.

Fuhrer, U., & Kaiser, F. G. (1991). *Ortsbindung und Verkehrsdichte. Ortsbindung im Lichte räumlich-sozialer und individueller Merkmale* [Place attachment and traffic density. Place attachment in the light of socio-physical and individual characteristics]. *Zeitschrift für experimentelle und angewandte Psychologie. 38,* 365–378.

Gallagher, E. M., & Walter, G. (1990). Vulnerability of nursing home residents during relocations and renovations. *Journal of Aging Studies, 4,* 31–46.

Gill, T. M., Robinson, J. T., Williams, C. S., & Tinetti, M. E. (1999). Mismatches between the home environment and physical capabilities among community-living older persons. *Journal of the American Geriatric Society, 47,* 88–92.

Gitlin, L. N. (1998). Testing home modification interventions: Issues of theory, measurement, design, and implementation. In R. Schulz, G. Maddox, & M. P. Lawton (Eds.), *Focus on interventions research with older adults.* Annual Review of Gerontology and Geriatrics, (Vol. 18, pp. 190–246). New York: Springer.

Golant S. M. (1992). *Housing America's elderly: Many possibilities/few choices.* Newbury Park, CA: Sage.

Golant, S. M. (1998). Changing an older person's shelter and care setting: A model to explain personal and environmental outcomes. In R. J. Scheidt & P. G. Windley (Eds.), *Environment and aging theory. A focus on housing* (pp. 33–60). Westport, CT: Greenwood Press.

Graafmans, J., Taipale, V., & Charness, N. (Eds.). (1998). *Gerontechnology. A sustainable investment in the future.* Amsterdam: IOS Press.

Grant, P. R., Skinkle, R. R., & Lipps, G. (1992). The impact of an interinstitutional relocation on nursing home residents requiring a high level of care. *The Gerontologist, 32,* 834–842.

Groger, L. (1995). A nursing home can be a home. *Journal of Aging Studies, 9,* 137–153.

Groves, M. A., & Wilson, V.-F. (1992). To move or not to move? Factors influencing the housing choice of elderly persons. *Journal of Housing for the Elderly, 10,* 33–47.

Gubrium, J. (1975). *Living and dying at Murray Mannor.* Charlottesville: University Press of Virginia. (published again 1997).

Haas, W. H., & Serow, W. J. (1993). Amenity retirement migration process: A model and preliminary evidence. *The Gerontologist, 33,* 212–220.

Hazelrigg, L. E., & Hardy, M. A. (1995). Older adult migration to the sunbelt. *Research on Aging, 17,* 209–234.

Heckhausen, J., & Schulz, R. (1995). A lifespan theory of control. *Psychological Review, 102,* 284–304.

Kahana, E. (1975). A congruence model of person-environment interaction. In P. G. Windley & G. Ernst (Eds.), *Theory development in environment and aging*. Washington, DC: Gerontological Society.

Kahana, E., Liang, J., & Felton, B. J. (1980). Alternative models of person-environment fit: Predicting morale in three homes for the aged. *Journal of Gerontology, 35*, 584–595.

Karlsson, S., Bucht, G., Eriksson, S., & Sandman, P. O. (1996). Physical restraints in geriatric care in Sweden: Prevalence and patient characteristics. *Journal of the American Geriatrics Society, 44*, 1348–1354.

Kihlgren, M., Brane, G., Karlsson, I., Kuremyr, D., et al. (1992). Long-term influence on demented patients in different caring milieus, a collective living unit and a nursing home: A descriptive study. *Dementia, 3*, 342–349.

Kling, K. C., Seltzer, M. M., & Ryff, C. D. (1997). Distinctive late-life challenges: Implications for coping and well-being. *Psychology and Aging, 12*, 288–295.

Kovach, S. S., & Robinson, J. D. (1996). The roommate relationship for elderly nursing home resident. *Journal of Social and Personal Relationships, 13*, 627–634.

Krause, N. (1993). Neighborhood deterioration and social isolation in later life. *International Journal of Aging and Human Development, 36*, 9–38.

Krothe, J. S. (1997). Giving voice to elderly people: Community-based long-term care. *Public Health Nursing, 14*, 217–226.

Kruzich, J. M., Clinton, J. F., & Kelber, S. T. (1992). Personal and environmental influences on nursing home satisfaction. *The Gerontologist, 32*, 342–350.

Lawton, M. P. (1977). The impact of the environment on aging and behavior. In J. E. Birren & K. W. Schaie (Eds.), *Handbook of the psychology of aging* (pp. 276–301). New York: Van Nostrand Reinhold.

Lawton, M. P. (1982). Competence, environmental press, and the adaptation of older people. In M. P. Lawton, P. G. Windley, & T. O. Byerts (Eds.), *Aging and the environment. Theoretical approaches* (pp. 33–59). New York: Springer.

Lawton, M. P. (1985). The elderly in context. Perspectives from environmental psychology and gerontology. *Environment and Behavior, 17*, 501–519.

Lawton, M. P. (1989). Three functions of the residential environment. *Journal of Housing for the Elderly, 5*, 35–50.

Lawton, M. P. (1998). Environment and aging: Theory revisited. In R. J. Scheidt & P. G. Windley (Eds.), *Environment and aging theory. A focus on housing* (pp. 1–31). Westport, CT: Greenwood Press.

Lawton, M. P. (1999). Environmental taxonomy: Generalizations from research with older adults. In S. L. Friedman & T. D. Wachs (Eds.), *Measuring environment across the life span* (pp. 91–124). Washington, DC: American Psychological Association.

Lawton, M. P., & Brody, E. M. (1969). Assessment of older people: Self-maintaining and instrumental activities of daily living. *The Gerontologist, 9*, 179–186.

Lawton, M. P., & Nahemow, L. (1973). Ecology and the aging process. In C. Eisdorfer & M. P. Lawton (Eds.), *The psychology of adult development and aging* (pp. 132–160). Washington, DC: American Psychology Association.

Lawton, M. P., & Simon, B. B. (1968). The ecology of social relationships in housing for the elderly. *The Gerontologist, 8*, 108–115.

Lawton, M. P., Weisman, G. D., Sloane, P., & Calkins, M. (1997). Assessing environments for older people with chronic illness. In J. Teresi, M. P. Lawton, D. Holmes (Eds.), *Measurement in elderly chronic care populations* (pp. 193–209). New York: Springer.

Lawton, M. P., Windley, P. G., & Byerts, T. O. (Eds). (1982). *Aging and the environment. Theoretical approaches*. New York: Springer.

Litwak, E., & Longino, C. F., Jr. (1987). Migration patterns among the elderly: A developmental perspective. *The Gerontologist, 27*, 266–272.

McCrae, R. R., & Costa, P. T. (1990). *Personality in adulthood*. New York: Guilford.

McCullough, L. G., Wilson, N. L., Teasdale, T. A., Kolpakchi, A. L., & Skelly, J. R. (1993). Mapping personal, familial, and professional values in long-term care decisions. *The Gerontologist, 33*, 324–332.

Mollenkopf, H., Marcellini, F., & Ruoppila, I., (1998). The outdoor mobility of elderly people—a comparative study in three European countries. In J. Graafmans, V. Taipale, & N. Charness (Eds.), *Gerontechnology. A sustainable investment in the* future (pp. 204–211). Amsterdam: IOS Press.

Moos, R. H. (1976). Conceptualizations of human environments. In R. Moos (Ed.), *The human context: Environmental determinants of behavior* (pp. 3–35). New York: Wiley.

Moos, R. H., & Lemke, S. (1985). Specialized living environments for older people. In J. E. Birren & K. W. Schaie (Eds.), *Handbook of the psychology of aging* (pp. 864–889). New York: Van Nostrand Reinhold.

Moos, R. H., & Lemke, S. (1994). *Group residences for older adults: Physical features, policies, and social climate.* New York: Oxford University Press.

Moos, R. H., & Lemke, S. (1996). *Evaluating residential facilities: The multiphasic environmental assessment procedure.* Thousand Oaks, CA: Sage.

Morgan, D. G., & Stewart, N. J. (1997). The importance of the social environment in dementia care. *Western Journal of Nursing Research, 19,* 740–761.

Morgan, D. G., & Stewart, N. J. (1998a). High versus low density special care units: Impact on the behaviour of elderly residents with dementia. *Canadian Journal on Aging, 17,* 143–165.

Morgan, D., & Stewart, N. J. (1998b). Multiple occupancy versus private rooms on dementia care units. *Environmental and Behavior, 30,* 487–503.

Netten, A. (1989). The effect of design of residential homes in creating dependency among confused elderly residents. A study of elderly demented residents and their ability to find their way around homes for the elderly. *International Journal of Geriatric Psychiatry, 4,* 14.

Norris-Baker, C. (1998). The evolving concept of behavior settings: Implications for housing older adults. In R. J. Scheidt & P. G. Windley (Eds.), *Environment and aging theory. A focus on housing* (pp. 141–160). Westport, CT: Greenwood Press.

O'Connor, B. P., & Vallerand, R. J. (1994). Motivation, self-determination, and person-environment fit as predictors of psychological adjustment among nursing home residents. *Psychology and Aging, 9,* 189–194.

Olbrich, E., & Diegritz, U. (1995). *Das Zusammenwirken von Person-und Umweltfakto-*

ren im Alltag: Eine kritische Diskussion von Aktivitäten des täglichen Lebens und instrumentalen Aktivitäten des täglichen Lebens [The transaction between person and situation in everyday behavior: A critical discussion of Activities of Daily Living and Instrumental Activities of Daily Living]. *Zeitschrift für Gerontopsychologie und -psychiatrie, 8,* 199–212.

Oswald, F. (1996). *Hier bin ich zu Hause. Zur Bedeutung des Wohnens: Eine empirische Studie mit gesunden und gehbeeinträchtigten Älteren* [On the meaning of home: An empirical study with healthy and mobility impaired elders]. Regensburg: Roderer.

Oswald, F., Wahl, H.-W., & Gäng, K. (1999). *Umzug im Alter: Eine ökogerontologische Studie zum Wohnungswechsel privatwohnender Älterer in Heidelberg Älteren* [Relocation in old age: An environmental gerontology study on home-to-home moves of elders in Heidelberg]. *Zeitschrift für Gerontopsychologie und—psychiatrie, 12,* 1–19.

Parmelee, P. A. (1998). Theory of research on housing for the elderly: The legacy of Kurt Lewin. In R. J. Scheidt & P. G. Windley (Eds.), *Environment and aging theory* (pp. 161–185). Westport, CT: Greenwood Press.

Parmelee, P. A., & Lawton, M. P. (1990). The design of special environments for the aged. In J. E. Birren & K. W. Schaie (Eds.), *Handbook of the psychology of aging* (3rd ed.) (pp. 464–488). New York: Academic Press.

Passini, R., Rainville, C., Marchand, N., & Joanette, Y. (1998). Wayfinding and dementia: Some research findings and a new look at design. *Journal of Architectural and Planning Research, 15,* 133–151.

Pynoos, J., & Regnier, V. (1991). Improving residential environments for the frail elderly: Bridging the gap between theory and application. In J. Birren, J. Lubben, J. Rowe, & D. Deutchman (Eds.), *The concept and measurement of quality of life in the frail elderly.* New York: Academic press.

Regnier, V. (1994). *Assisted living housing for the elderly. Design innovations from the United States and Europe.* New York: Van Nostrand Reinhold.

Regnier, V., & Pynoos, J. (1992). Environmental intervention for cognitively impaired older persons. In J. E. Birren, R. B. Sloane, & G. D. Cohen (Eds.), *Handbook of mental health and aging* (2nd ed.) (pp. 763–792). San Diego, CA: Academic Press.

Reschovsky, J. D., & Newman, S. J. (1990). Adaptations for independent living by older frail housholds. *The Gerontologist, 30,* 543–552.

Ritchie, K., Colvez, A., Ankri, J., & Ledesert, B. (1992). The evaluation of long-term care for the dementing elderly: A comparative study of hospital and collective non-medical care in France. *International Journal of Geriatric Psychiatry, 7,* 549–557.

Rowles, G. D. (1983). Geographical dimensions of social support in rural Appalachia. In G. D. Rowles & R. J. Ohta (Eds.), *Aging an milieu. Environmental perspectives on growing old* (pp. 111–130). New York: Academic Press.

Rubinstein, R. L. (1998). The phenomenology of housing for older people. In R. J. Scheidt & P. G. Windley (Eds.), *Environment and aging theory* (pp. 89–110). Westport, CT: Greenwood Press.

Rubinstein, R. L., Kilbride, J., & Nagy, S. (1992). *Elders living alone: Frailty and the perception of choice.* Hawthorne, NY: Aldine de Gruyter.

Rubinstein, R. L., & Parmelee, P. A. (1992). Attachment to place and representation of life course by the elderly. In I. Altman & S. M. Low (Eds.), *Human behavior and environment, Vol. 12: Place attachment* (pp. 139–163). New York: Plenum Press.

Ryff, C. D., & Essex, M. J. (1992). The interpretation of life experience and well-being: The sample case of relocation. *Psychology and Aging, 7,* 507–517.

Salive, M. E., Collins, K. S., Foley, D. J., & George, L. K. (1993). Predictors of nursing home admission in a biracial population. *American Journal of Public Health, 83,* 1765–1767.

Sanford, J., & Connell, B. R. (Eds.). (1998). *People, places and public policy.* Edmond, OK: Environmental Design Research Association.

Saup, W. (1993). *Alter und Umwelt. Eine Einführung in die Ökologische Gerontologie* [Old age and the environment. An introduction into environmental gerontology]. Stuttgart: Kohlhammer.

Scheidt, R. J., & Windley, P. G. (1985). The ecology of aging. In J. E. Birren & K. W. Schaie (Eds.), *Handbook of the psychology of aging* (2nd ed.) (pp. 245–258). New York: Van Nostrand Reinhold.

Scheidt, R. J., & Windley, P. G. (1998a). Preface. In R. J. Scheidt & P. G. Windley (Eds.), *Environment and aging theory* (pp. ix–xii). Westport, CT: Greenwood Press.

Scheidt R. J., & Windley P. G. (Eds.). (1998b). *Environment and aging theory.* Westport, CT: Greenwood Press.

Schooler, K. K. (1982). Response of the elderly to environment: A stress-theoretical perspective. In M. P. Lawton, P. G. Windley & T. O. Byerts (Eds.), *Aging and the environment: Theoretical approaches* (pp. 80–96). New York: Springer.

Schwarz, B., & Brent, R. (Eds.). (1999). *Aging, autonomy, and architecture. Advances in assisted living.* Baltimore: Johns Hopkins University Press.

Serow, W. J., Friedrich, F., & Haas, W. H. (1996). Residential relocation and regional redistribution of the elderly in the USA and Germany. *Journal of Cross-Cultural Gerontolgy, 11,* 293–306.

Sheehan, N. W. (1995). Bringing together housing and aging services: The experiences of Area Agencies on Ageing. *Journal of Aging & Social Policy, 7,* 41–58.

Simon, S. L., Walsh, D. A., Regnier, V. A., & Krauss, I. K. (1992). Spatial cognition and neighborhood use. The relationship in older adults. *Psychology and aging, 7,* 389–394.

Sixsmith, A., & Sixsmith, J. A. (1991). Transitions in home experience in later life. *Journal of Architectural and Planning Research, 8,* 181–191.

Slangen-de Kort, Y. (1999). *A tale of two adaptations. Coping processes of older persons in the domain of independent living.* Dissertation, Eindhoven University of Technology, The Netherlands.

Sloane, P. D., Lindemann, D. A., Phillips, C., Moritz, D. J., & Koch, G. (1995). Evaluating Alzheimer's spesial care units: Reviewing the evidence and identifying potential sources of study bias. *The Gerontologist, 35,* 103–111.

Smith, G. C. (1991). Grocery shopping patterns of the ambulatory urban elderly. *Environment and Behavior, 23,* 86–114.

Speare, A., Avery, R., & Lawton, L. (1991). Disability, residential mobility, and changes in living arrangements. *Journal of Gerontology: Social Sciences, 46,* S133–142.

Stokols, D. (1999). Human development in the age of the internet: Conceptual and methodological horizons. In S. L. Friedman & T. D. Wachs (Eds.), *Measuring environment across the life span* (pp. 327–356). Washington, DC: American Psychological Association.

Swenson, M. M. (1998). The meaning of home to five elderly women. *Health Care for Women International, 19,* 381–393.

Teresi, J. A., Holmes, D., & Monaco, C. (1993). An evaluation of the effects of commingling cognitively and noncognitively impaired individuals in long-term care facilities. *The Gerontologist, 33,* 350–358.

Tesch, S., Nehrke, M. F., &, Whitbourne, S. K. (1989). Social relationships, psychosocial adaptation, and intrainstitutional relocation of elderly men. *The Gerontologist, 29,* 517–523.

Thompson, E. E., & Krause, N. (1998). Living alone and neighborhood characteristics as predictors of social support in late life. *Journal of Gerontology: Social Sciences, 53B,* S354–S364.

Timko, C., & Moos, R. H. (1990). Determinants of interpersonal support and self-direction in group residentail facilities. *Journals of Gerontology, 45,* S184–S192.

Voelkl, J. E., Fries, B. E., & Galecki, A. T. (1995). Predictors of nursing home residents' participation in activity programs. *The Gerontologist, 35,* 44–51.

Wahl, H.-W. (in press). Ecology of aging. In N. J. melser & P. B. Baltes (Eds.), *International Encyclopedia of the Social and Behavioral Sciences.* Pergamon/Elsevier Sciences.

Wahl, H.-W., Oswald, F., & Zimprich, D. (1999). Everyday competence in visually impaired older adults: A case for person-environment perspectives. *The Gerontologist, 39,* 140–149.

Weisman, G. D. (1997). Environments for older persons with cognitive impairments. In G. Moore & R. Marans (Eds.), *Environment, behavior and design* (Vol. 4, pp. 315–346). New York: Plenum Press.

Weisman, G. D., Chaudhury, H., & Diaz Moore, K. (2000). Theory and practice of place: Toward a integrative model. In R. Rubenstein, M. Moss, & M. Kleban (Eds.), *The many dimensions of aging. Essays in honor of M. Powell Lawton* (pp. 3–21). New York: Springer.

Weisman, J., Lawton, M. P., Sloane, P. S., Calkins, M., & Norris-Baker, L. (1996). *The professional environmental assessment protocol.* Milwaukee, WI: School of Architecture, University of Wisconsin.

Zeisel, J. (1999). Life-quality Alzheimer care in assisted living. In B. Schwarz & R. Brent (Eds.), *Aging, autonomy, and architecture* (pp. 110–129). Baltimore: Johns Hopkins University Press.

Zinkmark, K., Norberg, A., & Sandman, P.-O. (1995). The experience of being at home throughout the life span. Investigation of persons aged from 2 to 102. *International Journal of Aging and Human Development, 41,* 47–62.

Part Three

Behavioral Processes and Psychological Functions

Ten

Changes in Vision and Hearing with Aging

James L. Fozard and Sandra Gordon-Salant

I. Introduction

Similar in outline to its two predecessors (Fozard, 1990; Kline & Scialfa, 1996), the present chapter is based on a search of over 600 articles published in 1994–1999. The number of relevant published articles is significantly greater than available for earlier *handbook* reviews—only about 29% could be cited in the present chapter—and the diversity of specialty journals in which they are published is much greater. The current review emphasizes research differentiating functions that change or stay constant over age. Research conducted in the last 5 years is characterized by careful control of visual and auditory sensitivity between younger and older subjects and precision in stimulus presentation paradigms. Convergence of laboratory findings with findings from population-based studies and longitudinal studies indicate that senescent changes in certain auditory and visual functions are only observed in the oldest age decades (over 75 or 80 years). However, when challenged by complex stimuli and tasks, age-related deficits emerge among younger individuals. Efficacy of intervention strategies, such as control of glare

and noise and use of focused illumination and amplification is discussed briefly, reflecting the recent interest in accommodation technologies applied specifically for older people. The list of modifiable risk factors for age-associated losses in vision and hearing has been extended beyond bright sunlight and loud noise to include tobacco use (Cruickshanks et al., 1998) and blood pressure (e.g., McLeod, West, Quigley, & Fozard, 1990; Brant et al., 1996).

II. Vision

The efforts made to control factors that complicate the interpretation of the age differences in visual function have increased significantly. The use of trial lenses to assure equal acuity for different observers, various techniques to ensure equal luminance of visual displays, and techniques such as interferometry to control for age differences in lens density are now the rule. The descriptions of observers, including the direct evaluation of visual pathology, obtaining relevant medical histories, and so on, has improved significantly. The term, *screened*

Handbook of the Psychology of Aging

observers, serves as a summary description of these efforts later in the text.

A. What People Say about Their Vision

The significance of sensory functioning is best understood in terms of the context of specific tasks and disorders of the visual system (Mangione et al., 1998). The Salisbury Eye Evaluation project (West et al., 1997) provides a population-based assessment of visual function including acuity, contrast sensitivity with and without glare, stereoacuity and visual fields, self-reported limitations in activities of daily living (ADLs), instrumental ADLs (IADLs), and mobility. Poor acuity was associated with difficulties requiring good resolution and adaptation to changing light conditions, whereas contrast sensitivity was associated with difficulty in tasks requiring distance judgments, night driving, and mobility (Rubin, Roche, Prasado-Rao, & Fried, 1994).

Wahl, Oswald, and Zimprich (1999) measured personal and environmental compensations made by blind, visually impaired, and nonvisually impaired adults. Trained observers rated the participant's living environments in terms of supportiveness and safety—person–environment fit. Visual impairment was an important predictor of the other variables only in situations in which the environmental challenges were high. In the IADLs, the correlation between good person–environment fit and functioning was strong in the blind and visually impaired.

B. Ocular Media and Visual Pathways

Over a dozen studies documented age differences in ocular media and visual pathways. Guirao and colleagues (1999) measured age differences in the width of the retinal image by computing the modular transfer function (MTF), a measure of the level and rate of change of retinal luminance from the source. Differences in refraction, pupil dilation, and retinal luminance were controlled and pupil centering was monitored to minimize artifacts during the tests. MTF declined with age and increasing artificial pupil diameter.

Muir, Barlow, and Morrison (1996) measured the pattern electroretinograms of screened observers ranging from 20 to 99 years while their contrast sensitivity thresholds were determined. Display luminance threshold was equated individually, and suprathreshold test gratings were presented while latencies of the electroretinogram were determined. The patterns for the psychophysically equivalent stimuli did not vary across age, leading the authors to conclude that age declines in contrast sensitivity were before or at the level of the retinal ganglion cells.

Age differences in visual evoked responses (VEP) were reviewed by Tobimatsu (1995), who concluded that age differences in VEPs were larger for small, foveally projected targets than for ones that included parafoveal stimulation. The P 100 latency increases little with age at lowered luminance levels but does with poorer contrast. However, in one study in which the contrast was adjusted psychophysically to the same level in young and elderly observers (Morrison & Reilly, 1989), the age difference in VEPs disappeared. Positron emission tomography (PET) activation studies show lower response by older persons in many visual functions (Grady et al., 1994).

C. Binocular Vision

Is the gain from binocular versus monocular vision the same across age; and is there an age difference in stereoptic vision? The answers are a qualified "no" to the first question and "yes" to the second.

Wood and Bullimore (1996) found no systematic age differences in the variability of interocular function for visual acuity and contrast, functions that are known to differ by age. Pardhan (1996) measured binocular and monocular contrast sensitivity and found that binocular summation, the ratio of binocular sensitivity to monocular sensitivity for the better eye, was lower for the older observers.

Age differences in binocular cues for depth perception are of special interest in gerontological research because stereoptic vision depends on integration of visual information at neurological levels beyond the optic chiasma (See Fozard, 1990, Figure 1 and related discussion). Rubin and colleagues (1997) provided population-based data on this topic. They found that after age 75, the stereothreshold increased as did the prevalence of stereoblindness.

D. Eye Movements and Vestibular-Ocular Interactions

Two studies related eye movements to movements of the observer. Paige (1994) studied age differences in vestibular-ocular and visual-vestibular interactions in screened adults ranging in age from 18 to 89 years. Pursuit movements were studied with a point light spot and optokinetic movement with a moving pattern of vertical light and dark bars, which effectively filled the visual field. To measure the vestibular-ocular interactions, observers sat with head position fixed in a chair that oscillated horizontally. The vestibular-ocular reflex measured in the dark was stable across age with respect to gain, the peak velocity of eye movements, and with phase, the asynchrony in degrees between eye and stimulus movements. As expected, gain decreased and phase lags increased with age at about the same rate for both stimulus types. Visual–vestibular interactions were studied by comparing gain and phase when the observers were rotated in the same direction as the stimuli, thereby enhan-

cing the vestibular response, or in the opposite direction, thereby suppressing the response. Enhancement improved gain and phase for all groups; suppression resulted in increased gain for higher frequency and a fall off in phase for frequencies above and below 1 Hz. Thus the age differences observed reflect declines in both the visual and vestibular systems.

Using similar procedures, Demer (1994) studied age differences in pitching movements under conditions of predictable and unpredictable velocity impulses. The visual enhancement and suppression effects were similar to those of Paige. In general, the pattern of results indicates that the visual control of the vestibular-ocular response is truncated with older age.

E. Sensitivity to Light

1. Dark Adaptation and Scotopic Vision

Controversy continues about age differences in the rate of change (not the final level) of the photopic segment of the dark adapation function. Herse (1995) found that the rate of change per minute to the asymptotic level of photopic adaptation declined with age from 77, 74, 56, and 54% for subjects in age groups with midpoints of 15, 30, 50, and 70 years, respectively. In contrast, the rates of adaptation of the rods to asymptote were similar in the same persons.

2. Photopic Sensitivity

Rubin and colleagues (1997) provided population-based data on contrast sensitivity for photopic vision for adults ranging in age from 65 to 84 years, reporting a 28% decline in sensitivity per decade. Research by Pardhan, Gilchrist, Elliott, and Beh (1996) and Bennett, Sekuler, and Ozin (1999) indicated that age differences in photopic contrast sensitivity could not be attributed to optical factors, as suggested by earlier research.

3. Color Discrimination

Largely because of age differences in sensitivity to luminance, research on color perception in relation to age has been particularly sensitive to variations in research techniques (See Fozard, 1990; Kline & Scialfa, 1996, for details). Results of several studies using a variety of techniques indicate an age-related loss of color sensitivity (Fioretini, Porciatti, Morrone, & Burr, 1996; Johnson & Marshall, 1995; Swanson & Fish, 1996). A study by Kraft and Werner (1999a) illustrates one of the psychophysical approaches used. In one interval a broadband light was presented; in the other the broadband light plus a monochromatic light ranging from 420–680 nm was presented, and the observer chose the one with the chromatic component. Discrimination was poorer for the older observers at all levels and markedly so when the target luminance was low. Analyses indicated a loss in sensitivity to short- and medium-plus long-wavelength stimuli with age across the spectrum. The difference between this and earlier findings is attributed to better control of luminance levels for young and old observers and the use of an improved psychophysical method. In related studies, Kraft and Werner (1999b) demonstrated significant color constancy across age indicating compensation for age-related losses in cone sensitivity and elevated thresholds for chromatic discrimination (Kraft & Werner, 1994). Together, the recent studies provide evidence for age differences in color vision that can be attributed to loss of photoreceptors with age across a wide range of retinal eccentricities. The detailed explanation of color constancy across age in view of these changes offered by Kraft and Werner (1999b) is particularly interesting and will generate further study.

4. Glare

Population-based data on glare sensitivity was provided by Rubin and colleagues (1997), who required observers to identify letters surrounded by a glare source. The number of letters lost with glare in comparison to the nonglare condition increased from an average of 1 to over 2 between ages 65–84.

Steen, Whittaker, Elliott, and Wilds (1994) examined the effects of disability glare on contrast color sensitivity for gratings with red-green, blue-yellow, or luminance differences. Without glare, the age effect on sensitivity was significant only for the blue-yellow lights. Contrast sensitivity decreased with the addition of glare for the red-green and luminance conditions because the glare effectively desaturated the component colors, thereby reducing sensitivity.

5. Suprathreshold Contrast Sensitivity

Sehefrin, Bieber, McLean, and Werner (1998) evaluated age differences in spatial summation in scotopic vision in order to determine whether postretinal neurological factors contribute to the observed effects of age. Because a constant amount of energy is needed for the threshold response to a light of given size and intensity (Ricco's Law), the largest area that will yield a threshold response, for it defines the area over which complete summation—Ricco's area—is possible. The hypothesis was that losses of rods and ganglion cells with age would result in age-related increases in Ricco's area. The results supported the hypothesis; Ricco's area increased with age, about 15% per decade.

F. Spatial Vision

There is much new research dealing with this topic; the following is not exhaustive (see Haegerstrom-Portnoy, Schneck, & Brabyn, 1999).

1. Static Acuity

The Beaver Dam Eye Study provides epidemiological estimates of incidence and 5-year changes in best-corrected—as opposed to usual corrected—visual acuity (R. Klein, Klein, & Lee, 1996). Near visual acuity was not assessed. Over 5 years, impaired vision developed in 3% of the population, aged 43–84 years. The changes were almost entirely confined to the 75+ population whose odds of developing impaired vision, severe impairment, doubling of visual angle, or improvement were about 12, 78, 10, and 2, respectively. The relatively low level of acuity observed in this study most likely reflects the high level of participation. The finding that the 5-year decline was most pronounced in persons over 75 years parallels the longitudinal findings in men (Gittings & Fozard, 1986) and women (Gittings, personal communication, July, 2000) from the Baltimore Longitudinal Study of Aging.

As with other measures of visual spatial function, the estimates of the usual age differences in acuity vary significantly with illumination, size and style of stimuli, contrast, and color (Elliott, Yang, & Whitaker, 1995; Research Institute of Human Engineering for Quality Life, 1999). Haegerstrom-Portnoy, Schneck, and Brabyn (1999) evaluated visual acuity and contrast sensitivity for letters under high and low contrast and luminance. The effects of viewing conditions on acuity were profound. Median visual acuity for successive 2-year age groups beginning at age 58 declined from about 20/20 to 20/50 and from 20/50 to 20/260 for high and low luminance conditions, respectively. The corresponding figures for high and low contrast were 20/20 to 20/50 and 20/30 to 20/125. The effect of glare on low contrast near vision resulted in lowering of acuities from about 20/50 to 20/1000.

2. Contrast Sensitivity

Are age differences in contrast sensitivity (Fozard, 1990) an artifact of testing procedures? Yager and Beard (1994) reanalyzed studies that used two alternative forced choice procedures to determine the degree to which results were affected by individual differences in criteria and internal noise. They concluded that the observed age-related differences in contrast sensitivity were not artifacts of the psychophysical methods, which is similar to the conclusion reached by Haegerstrom-Portnoy, Schneck, and Brabyn (1999) cited above.

3. Visual Processing in the Periphery

Results from several studies indicate that the density of photoreceptors in the periphery decline with age (Thibos, 1998; Wild, Cubbidge, Pacey, & Robinson, 1998).

Scialfa, Thomas, and Joffe (1994) studied age differences in the frequency and latency of eye movements involved in identifying a target presented from 4 to 14 d from central fixation. The number of eye movements increased with eccentricity and distractors much more in older observers who "rechecked" a location previously searched much more than younger ones.

4. Presbyopia and Accommodation

The loss of accommodative power of the lens is the major factor that affects near acuity. How big is the loss? Atchison, Capper, and McCabe (1994) reported that accommodation fell from 5 to 2 D from the 20s to the 40s as opposed to the 8 to 4 D usually reported in earlier large-scale studies.

Koretz, Cook, and Kaufman (1997) related experimentally induced changes in accommodation to the sagittal dimensions of the lens and anterior segment in screened observers ranging in age from 18 to 70. With increasing age, the mean anterior depth decreased while lens thickness increased. The most important finding was that the relationships between the changes in lens dimensions and level of accommodation did not change over age even though the range of values for accommodation and the lens dimensions were different.

Bruce, Atchison, and Bhoola (1995) measured age differences in the relationship between accommodation and convergence in screened observers ranging in age from 17 to 42. The ratio of the induced change in convergence to the change in accommodation increased with age because the difference between accommodation and convergence increased with age more than accommodation. The ratio of the induced change in accommodation to the change in convergence decreased strongly with age because the difference between convergence minus accommodation diminished to nearly zero—reflecting the loss of accommodation—while accommodation did not change. The results support the hypothesis that with increasing age, greater effort is required to produce a unit change in accommodation. The importance of the ciliary muscle in the accommodation—convergence dynamic also comes from animal studies showing that lens thickness makes ciliary muscle contractions less effective (Neider, Crawford, Daurman, & Bito, 1990).

G. Temporal Summation, Resolution, and Motion Perception

1. Temporal Summation

Zhang and Sturr (1995) measured contrast thresholds for a 0.5 c/d grating for presentation times ranging from 10–1000 ms presented at 4 luminance levels ranging from .44 to about 259 cd/m². The shape of the function relating threshold to stimulus duration was the same in young and old age groups, declining from 10 to 100 ms

and changing little between 100 and 1000 ms. The effect of luminance on the thresholds was greater at the two lower levels than at the higher ones. The results indicate that aging shifted the position of the threshold duration function up without changing the shape of the function and that increased luminance affected both position and shape of the function. The authors conclude that optical factors did not completely account for the age differences observed because the interaction between luminance and threshold were different in the two age groups.

2. Temporal Resolution

Using 89 screened observers aged 18–77 years of age, Kim and Mayer (1994) measured foveal contrast sensitivity for a flickering red stimulus. Sensitivity was greatest between 5–10 Hz and declined systematically at frequencies up to 50 Hz. The response functions were shallower in observers in the 55–64 and 65–77-year-old groups after adjusting for optical and decision criteria. The authors hypothesize that contrast sensitivity for flickering stimuli involve two or three mechanisms, a band pass filter centered at 20 Hz and two at low frequencies, 5 and 10 Hz.

3. Perception of Motion

Optic flow refers to information about motion available to stationary or moving persons. It is studied in the laboratory by creating moving displays of dot patterns that radiate from a central point, radial movement, or move in a plane, lamellar motion.

Andersen and Atchley (1995) and later, Atchley and Andersen (1998) measured age differences in detection of lamellar and radial movement in a variety of conditions and varying retinal eccentricities. Detection thresholds were higher with increasing eccentricity and lower for slower movement velocity for young and elderly observers, but more so for the older observers. The authors propose a three-stage model involving two processing systems. The first stage of analysis is the extraction of two-dimensional information, which is processed first by motion analyzers for velocities and second by anlyzers for types of motion (e.g., curl, divergence, shear), which provide the basis for perceiving heading and object motion, including impressions of three-dimensional surfaces.

Using different research procedures, Wojciechowski, Trick, and Steinman (1995) also concluded that there are age-sensitive independent pathways serving motion detection.

Tran, Silverman, Zimmerman, and Feldon (1998) studied lamellar motion detection for dot patterns in which the percentage of dots moving in the same direction varied. They also measured the presence of optokinetic nystagmus to the patterns. The linear correlations between both measures and age of screened observers ranging in age from 20–92 was about 0.36. The detection of motion defined psychophysically and by the initiation of optokinetic nystagmus was not the same. The authors hypothesize that the optokinetic pathways involve a number of cortical and subcortical loops, while the perception of motion depends on other pathways as described above.

Kramer, Martin-Emerson, Larish, and Andersen (1996) studied visual search for a moving target to evaluate the hypothesis that attention to movement is mediated by specialized cells in the medio-temporal region of the cortex. The alternative hypothesis is that the context of stationary and moving distractors determine the ability to identify the moving target, the common fate hypothesis. In a motion search task, a single target letter (e.g., o), is moved in a display of stationary o's of varying size. In the nontarget condition, the o was stationary. As expected, the younger adults were faster than the older; the times were longer in nontarget conditions for both. In the form-feature search task, the nontargets were also moving, and in the conjunctive feature task, nontargets were either stationary or moving. In the latter two situations the slope relating display size to response speed increased for both target and nontarget conditions, but more so for the older adults in the non-target conditions. The older subjects benefited as much from the additional information provided by the stationary items in the display as younger ones.

H. Visual Attention and Search

1. Attention

The beneficial effects of prompting observers about the probable location of a target has been the topic of many studies. McCalley, Bouwhuis, and Juola (1995) cued target location in three concentric rings from 2–6 d from central fixation on 80% of the trials. The target letter was presented from 250–1000 ms after the cue. Both young and elderly observers did better with the cue than in the control condition in which the entire area was cued. Times and errors were longer for older observers, especially at greater distances from fixation; they were also more sensitive to the longer intervals between the cue and the target. In a second experiment the size of the letters were increased with greater target eccentricity, resulting in an improvement in performance by the older observers, whose performances were then similar to those of younger adults. Evaluation of three models of attention allocation indicated that the same model of attention accounted for the data of young and old observers. When visibility was controlled, a resource allocation model positing that attention may be allocated to different regions around the fovea in response to a cue accounted for data for both groups. In a somewhat similar study, Gottlob and Madden (1998) found that

when stimulus display time and luminance were adjusted for younger and
older participants, attentional allocation
of resources was similar in both groups.
Together, the results of these studies
indicate that when age differences in
sensory factors are controlled in central
vision, age differences in response to
cuing of attention are similar.

2. Search

Explanations of age differences in visual
search emphasize the number of nontargets and the similarity between target and
nontarget as the main determinants of the
age effect. Arguing that research on visual
search has not taken into account age
differences in latency and speed of saccadic eye movements, useful field of view,
and working memory capacity, Scialfa
and Thomas (1994) adapted a task by
Nickerson (1965). The positions of the
target and comparison stimuli in perifo-
veal view were constant and differed only
in two levels each of three dimensions of
color, shape, or size. For young and elderly adults, response times were shortest
on same judgments, longest when the stimuli were most similar, and progressively
shorter as the number of similar dimensions decreased. Response times and errors were greater in the older group, most
obviously when the target and nontarget
differed on only one dimension. The findings are consistent with the hypothesis
that search requires a self-terminating
search process of the features of the stimuli. The fact that this theory would incorrectly predict the longest times for
identical stimuli is explained by a response bias toward identical stimuli that
occur more frequently than different stimuli, an explanation that was substantiated
in part by data from an auxiliary study.

Much of the recent research on visual
search in both static and moving displays
(as discussed above) compares age differences in two search processes, feature and

conjunction. Feature means that a target
is uniquely differentiated from nontargets
(e.g., the only letter x). Conjunction means
that the target shares one or more dimensions with nontargets, (e.g., a red x target
among blue x's and red and blue o's as
nontargets). The slopes relating response
time to display size is smaller in feature
than conjunctive search tasks, and age differences between the two are larger in the
latter (see Kotary & Hoyer, 1995, and
Oken, Kishiyama, and Kaye, 1994).

Madden and Allen (1995) evaluated age
differences in visual feature search in
terms of the relation between response
time and errors. Results supported an ac-
cumulator model predicting a positive
correlation between reaction time and
error rate and longer response times to
errors. Older persons were slower in accumulating "evidence" for the presence
of a target (see also Allen, Patterson, &
Propper, 1994, for similar conclusions
based on a different research approach).
By design, Madden and Allen did not con-
strain presentation times. Harpur, Scialfa,
and Thomas (1995) found that when older
observers are forced to respond to briefly
presented stimuli, they required more
time for feature extraction, particularly
if the nontargets were incompatible with
the targets. Latencies of correct responses
increased with longer presentation times,
more so with older observers. The results
provide strong evidence for the importance of context effects in feature search
tasks involving very short display times
(see also Brown, Kosslyn, and Dror, 1998).

Another approach to understanding age
differences in visual search was provided
by Fisk, Rogers, Cooper, and Gilbert
(1997), who studied training and transfer
in a hybrid memory scanning and perceptual search task. In a consistent mapping
memory scanning task, participants decide whether a single test item is a member of the memorized set, e.g., varying
numbers of animal names (Rogers, Fisk,
& Hertzog, 1994). In the visual search

version of the task, participants identify the exemplar of the memorized set (e.g., animal names in a display with one or more distractors). The task differs from the other studies described above in that the physical target presented in successive trials in the search task is one of several in the memorized set. The major age difference in the perceptual search task was that the training benefit for the older observers was limited to the specific words in the category, whereas the young adults' learning generalized to other words within the category. Older participants showed no positive transfer of training when exemplars of the category on which they had received training were introduced. Accordingly, the benefits of training for older adults resulted from reduced demands on working memory.

3. Expectancy

The role of expectations and life experiences on illusions, ambiguous figures, and so on received little attention in the period covered by this review. The exception is the large number of studies of age differences in the interference condition of the Stroop test in which observers are required to read the name of a color (e.g., red) that is printed in a different color (e.g., green). In a meta-analysis, Verhaeghen and De Meersman (1998) concluded that the apparent age sensitivity of the interference effect appears to be an artifact of general slowing.

I. Vision in Complex Behavior

1. Proprioception and Balance

Measuring sway on a static or moving force plate surface with firm and soft surfaces with eyes open or closed is a basic tool for identifying the contribution to balance by vision and proprioception. Colledge and colleagues (1994) found that sway increased with age equally in men and women, always worse with eyes closed. Relatively poorer performance on the soft surface shows the increased dependence on proprioception when that information becomes uncertain. The authors attribute the age increase in sway to slowing of central nervous system integration of information. In a large study of women, Lord and Ward (1994) found that when information to visual and peripheral sensation systems were removed or diminished, there was an increased reliance on vision to maintain balance through age 65, beyond which the relative contribution of vision declined (see also Turano, Rubin, Herdman, Chee, and Fried, 1994). In a study of static and dynamic balance by Perrin, Jeandel, Perrin, and Beene (1997) that included electromyographic measurement of muscle action, all measured components of sway became worse with older age, especially the integration of nerve conduction from muscles and central integration of proprioception. In their study of dynamic balance of a group of community-dwelling elders, Judge and colleagues (1995) demonstrated that knee strength made a significant contribution. Finally, using different methods to manipulate various sensory inputs, Tang, Moore, and Wollacott (1998) also demonstrated that restriction to focal or central vision made a significant impact on balance, and that sway was increased equally by diminished or complete blocking of visual information. The rapidly growing literature on vision in relation to age difference in speed of walking, gait, stumbles, and falls is further reviewed by Fozard (2000), Fozard and Heikkinen (1998), and B. Klein, Klein, Lee, and Cruikshank (1998).

2. Vision, Hearing, and Cognitive Abilities

Lindenberger and Baltes (1994) with data from the Berlin Aging Study and then with other data from younger adults (Baltes & Lindenberger, 1997) demonstrated a strong correlation between visual acuity, auditory pure tone thresholds and several measures of intellectual functioning. The correlations were larger in the oldest adults, but positive and significant in younger groups as well. The increasing correlations with older cohorts were interpreted to reflect a common pattern of brain aging that affected both kinds of measures. The alternative hypothesis of sensory deprivation in older age resulting in poorer scores was less attractive. A similar conclusion was reached by Salthouse, Hancock, Holly, Meinz, and Hambrick (1996) and Stevens, Cruz, Marko, and Lakatos (1998) using other measures.

3. Vision and Driving

Growing evidence from laboratory studies of driving and self-reported visual problems related to driving (Kline et al., 1992) are defining the contribution of visual problems to poor driving and accidents. Owsley and colleagues (Owsley, Ball, et al, 1998; Owsley, McGwin, & Ball, 1998) reported that of many visual functions evaluated, restrictions in the useful field of view and glaucoma were significant risk factors for accidents. In road tests, Perryman and Fitten (1996) found that in comparison to younger drivers, healthy older drivers drove slower, made fewer braking actions, made fewer steering and eye movement excursions, and drifted across center line more frequently. Steering errors increase with age relatively more with poor illumination (Owens & Tyrrell, 1999).

J. Environmental Interventions

1. Contrast and Illumination

As part of a handbook on design for older adults, Steenbekkers (1998) published a table of lower-case Times Roman letter sizes (about 3–12 points) required for reading text with near vision by Dutch adults of different ages under three levels of illumination (10,100, and 1,000 lx) and four levels of contrast ranging from 10 to 100%. The age differences in performance were profound; the differences between the 30- and 80-year-old adults were about two fold throughout except at the highest level of illumination under the best contrast. At 10 lx, better contrast improved reading for young but not old adults, most of whom could not read the text under that level. At the 1000 lx level, the effects of improving contrast on performance of the oldest adults was most measurable. The importance of high levels of illumination for reading as well as other visual tasks is evident from all of the basic and applied research reviewed in this chapter. As pointed out by Halloin (1995) and Charness (1998, Fig. 7), the lighting levels of many homes and some offices do not meet existing standards for lighting.

2. Linking Application and Laboratory Results

As indicated by Charness and Bosman (1994), field studies are needed to "bridge the gap between survey self-reports and laboratory studies and to determine the cost and benefits of redesign" (p. 45). One approach is to involve active participation of observers in determining the optimal combinations of illumination, contrast, and glare in laboratory simulations of everyday visual tasks (Fozard, Rietsema, Bouma, & Graafmans, 2000), an idea partially implemented in current Japanese research (Research Institute for Human Quality of Life, 1999). The design of road signs is often evaluated in terms of the time needed to react (Lerner, 1994). Kline (1994) describes advances in using optical simulation of visual loss and contrast sensitivity in conjunction with imaging processing to create better displays for older persons.

III. Hearing

Behavioral and electrophysiologic studies are elucidating the source of the auditory problems of older people. The largest communication complaint of this population is difficulty understanding speech, particularly in degraded listening environments. Although much of this problem can be attributed to age-related loss of sensitivity, recent findings clearly suggest that deficits in central auditory processing capacity and cognitive decline further act to diminish speech understanding in everyday situations. However, wide individual variability and gender differences exist on age-related changes in hearing sensitivity, reactions to hearing loss, and speech understanding problems. This section will review recent findings from the hearing and aging literature that focus particularly on the interplay and relative contributions of peripheral, central, and cognitive factors in hearing abilities.

A. What Older People Say about Their Hearing

Hearing problems are the most frequent type of impairment reported by individuals aged 65 years and over (National Center for Health Statistics, 1995). Older individuals with mild-to-moderate hearing impairment report a significant impact on communication in social situations and a significant emotional reaction as a result of communication difficulties (Mulrow et al., 1990). Interestingly, older people with hearing loss report *less* hearing handicap than do younger people with matched hearing sensitivity (Gordon-Salant, Lantz, & Fitzgibbons, 1994). Garstecki and Erler (1996) found that older adults reported fewer communication problems, less importance to perceiving communication in work-related situations, and fewer challenges in their usual communication environment than younger adults. Older adults also appeared to be more accepting of their hearing loss than younger adults. This surprising age effect may be associated with the subtle nature of the progressive hearing loss or fewer demands on hearing among older individuals.

Sex differences do exist on attitudes about hearing loss (Garstecki & Erler, 1999). Older women are more likely to admit communication problems, assign more importance to effective communication, and use nonverbal strategies to circumvent communication problems, such as moving their seat to a well-lit area at a party. Personal adjustment to hearing loss differs for older men and women also, with women more often expressing feelings of frustration, anger, and stress associated with their hearing loss. Socioeconomic factors, such as marital status and personal income, are likely associated with these differences.

B. Auditory System

Presbycusis, a hearing loss attributed to age effects, is impossible to distinguish from hearing loss caused by hereditary factors, noise exposure, disease processes, ototoxicity, and other exogenous events that occur throughout the life span (Willott, 1991). Consequently, the reported findings may reflect the additive and cumulative effects of aging and other factors. Animal models of aging are included because the environment, diet, and medical history of the animals can be completely controlled.

1. Cochlea and Auditory Nerve

The best-documented age changes in the auditory system occur in the inner ear and nerve of hearing. In the cochlea, there is loss of inner and outer hair cells and supporting cells in the basal turn of the cochlea (Schuknecht, 1993). The loss of inner hair cells in this region reduces afferent neural transmission of high-frequency signals. The loss of outer hair cells decreases the active feedback loop, possibly causing hearing loss, limited frequency selectivity, and a reduced dynamic range. Objective measures of outer hair cell function using otoacoustic emissions have shown that although the emissions increase linearly with increasing age, this effect is confounded by the presence of hearing loss among older subjects (Stover & Norton, 1993). When hearing loss is controlled between younger and older groups, there are no differences in otoacoustic emissions (He & Schmiedt, 1996; Strouse, Ochs, & Hall, 1996), suggesting that age per se does not alter measurable outer hair cell function.

Another alteration in the cochlea of older people is a decrease in the volume of strial tissue on the lateral cochlear wall (Schukencht, 1993; Schulte & Schmiedt, 1992). The stria vascularis maintains the ionic concentration of the endolymphatic fluid that fills the cochlea, and is the source of the +80 mV endocochlear potential of the scala media. Animal models indicate that age-related deterioration of the strial tissue on the lateral cochlear wall is correlated with a reduction of the endocochlear potential (Gratton, Schmiedt, & Schulte, 1996; Schulte & Schmiedt, 1992). One theory is that a shift in the endocochlear potential is the cause of age-related hearing loss; hence, chemical alteration of the source of the endocochlear potential may eventually prove to reduce or delay hearing loss in older people (Schulte, 1997).

The neuronal population comprising the auditory nerve is markedly reduced in aged human subjects (Schuknecht, 1993; Spoendlin & Schrott, 1989, 1990). The loss of neurons reduces afferent transmission of acoustic signals and affects the frequency selectivity, temporal resolution, and amplitude growth functions of the auditory system. Aged gerbils show reduced compound action potentials (CAP), auditory brainstem response (ABR) amplitudes, and slopes of ABR input–output functions compared to younger gerbils, independent of hearing loss (Boettcher, Mills, & Norton, 1993a,b; Hellstrom & Schmiedt, 1990). Single-unit data in these animals indicate that CAP amplitudes are reduced due to a decrease in the number of synchronized auditory nerve fibers. The reduction in CAP amplitude could cause a reduction in ABR amplitudes.

2. Central Auditory Nervous System

The central auditory nervous system (CANS) is involved in afferent transmission, recoding, binaural correlation, frequency coding, and final processing of acoustic signals. Efferent pathways in the CANS suggest that it plays a role also in regulating function at lower levels. Aging human auditory systems are characterized by a reduction in the number of neurons in each nucleus of the auditory brainstem, and a dramatic decline in the neuronal population in the auditory cortex (Willott, 1991). These alterations are thought to affect processing of complex acoustic stimuli, including degraded speech and sequential nonspeech signals.

Age-related changes in cochlear structures affect the input to the CANS causing alterations in the response of the CANS. For example, modifications of high-frequency input to the inferior colliculus (IC) and auditory cortex of C57 mice result in increasing responses to lower frequency stimuli in the high-frequency regions of these structures (Willott, 1996; Willott & Bross, 1990; Willott, Aitken, & McFadden, 1993; Willott, Bross, & McFadden). These findings suggest the possibility of neural plasticity in the CANS in older animals.

A reduction in neurotransmitters with increasing age has been observed among certain animal strains. Findings from

Fischer 344 rats indicate a reduction in the inhibitory neurotransmitter gamma aminobutyric acid (GABA) in the IC (Caspary, Razza, Lawhorn Armour, Pippen, & Americ, 1990). Additionally, an increase in spontaneous neural activity has been observed in the IC of C57 and CBA mice strains (Willott, 1991). These age-related changes could produce an increase in neural noise or a reduction in suppression of external noise, both of which could degrade perception of acoustic signals in noise.

C. Hearing Thresholds

In the Framingham Cohort, the prevalence of some degree of hearing loss is 83% among 2351 participants aged 57–89 years (Moscicki, Elkins, Baum, & McNamara, 1985). With hearing loss defined as the pure-tone average at 500–4000 Hz exceeding 25 dB HL, 47% have a loss in the better ear. The corresponding figure in the Beaver Dam Cohort is 45.9% among 3753 participants (Cruickshanks et al., 1998). The hearing losses among the participants in both studies are largely attributed to disease, noise-exposure, and heredity.

Hearing thresholds of 1097 participants carefully screened for known risk factors were measured over time in a study conducted at the Baltimore Longitudinal Study on Aging (Pearson et al., 1995). Declines in hearing sensitivity vary with age, frequency, gender, and individuals. The decline in hearing sensitivity is apparent at all frequencies by age 30 in men and by age 50 in women, with the rate of change in hearing level more than twice as fast in men than in women at certain ages. The hearing sensitivity of men is better than that of women at frequencies below 1000 Hz, whereas that of women is better at frequencies above 1000. Nevertheless, even at age 70 years, the average person in this sample exhibited normal hearing sensitivity, based on pure-tone

averages of either 500, 1000, and 2000 Hz or 1000, 2000, and 4000 Hz, and a criterion of < 20 dB HL. These findings suggest that much of the hearing loss observed in older people is associated with factors other than the aging process *per se*.

Hearing sensitivity in the extended high frequencies (EHF) may be useful as an early predictor of age-related hearing loss. Declines in hearing sensitivity at extended high frequencies (> 8000 Hz) appear to be greater than declines in the lower audiometric frequencies (250–8000 Hz) among older adults (Matthews, Lee, Mills, & Dubno, 1997; Wiley, et al., 1998b). Moreover, EHF thresholds are even poorer among older individuals with hearing loss in the audiometric range compared to individuals with normal hearing (Matthews et al., 1997). In a large population-based study of 3396 participants, Wiley et al. (1998) found that men had poorer thresholds than women at lower EHFs (9–14 kHz), but comparable thresholds at the higher frequencies (16–20 kHz). They also found that EHF hearing sensitivity worsens at all frequencies from 9 kHz through 20 kHz at all ages between 48 and 92 years. Additionally, EHF thresholds were highly correlated with thresholds at the higher frequencies in the audiometric range (4 kHz and 8 kHz). Thus, early monitoring of EHF thresholds among young and middle-aged adults may be useful for predicting the onset of hearing loss and for aggressively recommending strategies to prevent or reduce hearing loss among individuals at early risk.

D. Psychoacoustic Measures

Performances of young and elderly listeners with either normal hearing or matched hearing losses have been compared on a range of psychoacoustic (non-speech) measures. Although age-related deficits are observed on many of these measures, the extent of aging effects is largely influenced by the complexity of the stimuli and task.

1. Temporal Processing

Gap detection is the ability to detect a brief silent interval, or temporal gap, in the stimulus waveform. Snell (1997) found that older listeners with normal hearing exhibit gap detection thresholds that are about 1/3 larger than those of younger listeners with matched audiograms, for noise-burst stimuli. Age-related differences increase with added stimulus complexity (e.g., the addition of a noise floor) (Snell, 1997). Schneider and Hamstra (1999) found that age-related differences in gap-detection thresholds were largely dependent on the duration of the stimulus markers that precede and follow the gap. Compared to younger subjects' brief (<3 ms) gap-detection thresholds across marker duration, older subjects' thresholds are significantly higher (<200 ms), but not for longer, 500-ms duration markers. Age effects were not observed among younger and older normal-hearing listeners when psychometric functions for detection of gaps were measured in a yes–no paradigm, rather than the usual adaptive paradigm (He, Horwitz, Dubno, & Mills, 1999). Age-related differences in detection of temporal gaps were observed, however, in conditions where the location of the gap was unpredictable and the gap was located near the onset or offset of the signal. In summary, elderly listeners have some limitations in temporal resolution independent of peripheral hearing loss, but the extent is influenced considerably by the listening task.

Clear age-related performance deficits in discriminating differences in the duration of sounds have been observed by Fitzgibbons and Gordon-Salant (1994, 1995, 1998). For simple tonal stimuli or silent intervals between tonal stimuli, the just noticeable difference for stimulus duration is about 50% larger for elderly listeners compared to younger listeners with matched hearing sensitivity (Fitzgibbons & Gordon-Salant, 1994). Unlike gap-detection thresholds, the duration-discrimination thresholds are unaffected by hearing loss, making them an ideal measure of temporal processing for elderly listeners who may have acquired hearing loss. Age effects on measures of duration discrimination become exaggerated considerably in conditions of increased stimulus complexity, such as with target stimuli embedded in a sequence of tones, and stimulus uncertainty in which the location of the target varies from trial to trial (Fitzgibbons & Gordon-Salant, 1995, 1998). The age-related deficits in auditory duration discrimination, particularly for complex stimuli and tasks, are ascribed to age-related changes in central auditory function.

Temporal processing can also be measured with a backward masking paradigm, detection of a brief signal measured in quiet and in the presence of a subsequent masker, presented at various delays. Older subjects with normal hearing experience more masking and a longer time course of temporal masking than do younger listeners (Gehr & Sommers, 1999). Because both central and peripheral factors appear to contribute to backward masking, these findings suggest that there are alterations in both loci in older listeners, even in the presence of normal hearing.

Perception of the presentation order of acoustic elements in a sequence is a basic auditory ability underlying speech perception. Trainor and Trehub (1989) reported that older listeners were significantly poorer than younger listeners on judgments of temporal order discrimination and identification for four-tone stimulus sequences. The magnitude of age-related performance differences was independent of the task, amount of practice, or presentation rate of stimuli in the sequence. Fitzgibbons and Gordon-Salant (1998) found that elderly listeners showed similar performance patterns to younger listeners on a temporal order discrimination task in which frequency shifts were in a uniform direction (rising or falling) and on temporal order identification tasks with relatively long component durations (750 ms to 250 ms). Age-related differences emerged on a discrimination task for more complex pitch patterns and on an identification task for faster stimulus presentation rates. These performance patterns suggest that both stimulus complexity and processing speed may interact to cause an age-related deficit in information processing.

2. Frequency and Intensity Discrimination

Humes (1996) reported that older subjects exhibited deficits in both intensity and frequency discrimination compared to younger listeners who were noise-masked to simulate the hearing loss of the older listeners. Although the frequency discrimination deficits were attributed to the effects of hearing loss, the intensity-discrimination deficits were associated exclusively with aging. He, Dubno, and Mills (1998) found that elderly subjects with normal hearing showed elevated differential thresholds in both frequency and intensity, compared to younger subjects with normal hearing. Age-related differences on both measures were largest at 500 Hz and decreased with increasing frequency. This frequency-dependent aging effect on measures of both intensity and frequency discrimination suggests a common mechanism underlying the age-related deficit.

E. Speech Perception

Investigations during the last 5 years have sought to elucidate whether the older person's speech-recognition deficit is en-

tirely attributed to the loss of hearing sensitivity, or whether there is an additional age-related component that acts to further diminish performance. Age-related deficits emerge on suprathreshold speech recognition tasks, but the effects are highly dependent on the type and extent of speech degradation, and on the demands of the listening task. Gender differences among older adults have also been observed on some speech-recognition tasks.

1. Speech in Noise

Effects of aging in noise conditions were observed in two recent studies. Hargus and Gordon-Salant (1995) controlled for the effects of hearing loss by comparing nonsense syllable and sentence recognition of older listeners with hearing loss to that of young noise-masked listeners with normal hearing. An audibility-based predictive algorithm (the Speech Intelligibility Index, SII) was used to predict the speech-recognition scores of both subject groups for a variety of stimuli and noise conditions. SII-predictive accuracy was poorer for the elderly subjects than for the younger subjects in all conditions, indicating that the deficits of elderly listeners could be attributed to factors other than sensitivity differences. Wiley and colleagues (1998a) reported data from 3189 adults ranging in age from 48–92 years, from the Beaver Dam Epidemiology of Hearing Loss Study. Among this population, monosyllabic word-recognition scores in competing messages were worse for older groups than younger age groups, and poorer for men than women in each age decade, even after statistically adjusting for the degree of sensorineural hearing loss.

Other findings contradict these reports. Souza and Turner (1994) assessed monosyllabic word recognition in several types of background noises for young listeners with normal hearing and for young and elderly listeners who were matched for sensorineural hearing loss. Groups with hearing loss performed more poorly than the normal-hearing group in all conditions; age effects were not observed in any condition. Elderly listeners' word-recognition deficits in noise were thus attributed exclusively to the presence of sensorineural hearing loss and not to an age-specific deficit *per se*. Dubno, Lee, Matthews, and Mills (1997) compared performance on a battery of speech-recognition tests of three groups of older men and women, ranging in age from 55 to 84 years, who were matched for degree of hearing loss. Age-related differences were not observed within this narrow age span. However, age differences were found for the males on several speech measures when partial correlations were used to adjust for the association between score and age with average thresholds. Studebaker, Sherbecoe, McDaniel, and Gray (1997) assessed monosyllabic word recognition in 140 subjects ranging in age from 20 to 90 years. Audibility was held constant by selecting subjects with normal hearing sensitivity between 250 and 2000 Hz, band-pass filtering the speech in this frequency range, and mixing the speech with a wide-band noise. Consistent and significant age effects were not observed except for those over 80 years of age. The performance deficit of the oldest group could not be explained by audibility differences. The conclusion from this wide array of findings is that age differences can be observed on speech-recognition-in-noise tasks, but they are most likely to emerge with an older cohort of elderly subjects (>80 years) and with careful methodology to account for audibility differences between younger and older subjects.

2. Temporally Distorted Speech

Unlike speech recognition in noise, elderly listeners' ability to recognize tem-porally distorted speech shows clear and consistent age-related deficits. Reverberation, a continuation of sound in an enclosed space, effectively causes a smearing of the individual speech elements and speech-on-speech masking. The longer the reverberation time, the greater the detrimental effects on speech recognition. Elderly listeners with normal hearing and with hearing loss show poorer recognition scores than younger listeners with matched hearing sensitivity for reverberant speech in a range of reverberation times (Gordon-Salant & Fitzgibbons, 1993). Divenyi and Haupt (1997a) also reported an age-related deficit when audibility differences between younger and older subjects were partialled out. Recognition of reverberant speech is inversely related to duration-discrimination thresholds, indicating that temporal-processing deficits are associated with problems in recognizing reverberant speech (Gordon-Salant & Fitzgibbons, 1993). However, measures of gap detection do not appear to be related to recognition of reverberant speech (Divenyi & Haupt, 1997b; Gordon-Salant & Fitzgibbons, 1993), suggesting that a fine-grained analysis of temporal processing abilities is necessary to reveal relationships between psychoacoustic and speech-processing abilities.

Older listeners consistently perform more poorly than younger listeners in recognizing speeded speech, created either by a speaker talking unusually fast or with a computerized algorithm (called time compression). Older listeners exhibit poorer scores than younger listeners for time-compressed speech with varying time-compression ratios and discard intervals (Letowski & Poch, 1996). Age effects are observed among younger and older listeners who are matched for normal hearing sensitivity and for sensorineural hearing loss (Gordon-Salant & Fitzgibbons, 1993). Age-related deficits are exacerbated when time compression is combined with other forms of degradation such as noise or reverberation (Gordon-Salant & Fitzgibbons, 1995). A recent study of age-related performance differences on a range of temporally based measures concluded that the most important speech measures for distinguishing the performances of younger and older listeners involved time compression of speech (Gordon-Salant & Fitzgibbons, 1999). This robust finding strongly indicates that aging imposes a limitation on the ability to process rapid speech elements. Deficits in recognition of time-compressed speech exceed those associated with peripheral hearing loss in elderly subjects, so one source of this deficit is likely localized at higher levels of processing than the auditory periphery.

3. Cognitive Factors and Speech Recognition Performance

The findings from time-compressed speech studies are generally attributed to an age-related decline in processing speed (Wingfield, 1996). When the linguistic and semantic cues in the speech signal are reduced or enhanced, the age effects of the speeded speech are correspondingly exacerbated or diminished (Wingfield, Poon, Lombardi, & Lowe, 1985). Contextual cues also enhance recognition of speech degraded by other temporal interruptions and noise, particularly for elderly listeners with hearing loss (Gordon-Salant & Fitzgibbons, 1997).

Evidence for memory deficits in word-recognition performance derives from several recent studies. Pichora-Fuller, Schneider, and Daneman (1995) showed that older listeners performed more poorly than younger listeners on a word-recall task presented in noise, in which subjects recalled the final words of sentences immediately after each sentence and following presentation of two, four, or six sentences. Older subjects consistently identified fewer target words than

younger subjects in adverse noise conditions, providing further support for reduced availability of working memory functions under adverse conditions of noise or age-related deterioration of the auditory system. In another study examining effects of memory demands, older listeners showed poorer sentence recall than younger listeners when silent intervals of increasing duration were inserted between each pair of words in the sentences (Gordon-Salant & Fitzgibbons, 1997). These findings confirm that added memory demands have a detrimental effect on elderly listeners' speech-understanding performance. Both of these investigations found that the older listeners' performance difficulties with added memory demands were reduced considerably when semantic contextual cues were provided. The convergent findings from the foregoing studies strongly indicate that age-related cognitive decline can play a role in speech understanding, particularly in difficult listening situations. However, older listeners' knowledge of the language enables them to compensate for many of the apparent deficits when contextual cues are available. This consistent finding serves as a guiding principle in aural rehabilitation programs that seek to improve the older listener's ability to take advantage of all available auditory, visual, and situational cues.

F. Rehabilitation

At present, there is no medical intervention for sensorineural hearing loss attributed to deterioration of hair cells, the stria vascularis, or neural fibers. The principal form of remediation is amplification, using either personal hearing aids or assistive listening devices (ALDs). Contemporary hearing aids amplify and process the acoustic signal using either analog or digital components, which permit varying amounts of gain for different frequencies and input signal levels.

Efforts to reduce amplification of background noise that occurs simultaneously with amplification of the speech signal include high-pass filtering the amplified signal, noise cancellation with multiple microphone arrays, and directional microphones. Many additional features are available with digitally programmable hearing aids. Despite the major technological advances in hearing aids over the past decade, only 20% of older hearing-impaired individuals purchase hearing aids and use them consistently. Some of the most important factors affecting hearing aid satisfaction and use are amplification of speech in noise, the availability of a good hearing aid dispenser, naturalness of the sound quality, cost, quality of the user's own voice, and feedback (Cox & Alexander, 1999; Dillon, Birtles, & Lovegrove, 1999).

Older people with hearing loss derive benefit from amplification. As a group, elderly listeners demonstrate significant improvements in speech understanding performance in quiet and noise, and a decrease in self-perceived hearing handicap with the use of amplification (Humes, Halling, & Coughlin, 1996). However, this benefit is not observed in all subjects. In a comparison of different hearing aid circuits, Newman and Sandridge (1998) found that elderly listeners show significant improvements in signal audibility, speech-recognition scores, and perceived hearing handicap while using linear, compression, and programmable hearing aids. Although most participants expressed a preference for the high-end programmable hearing aid, this preference changed for one-third of the participants when they were informed of the cost of this device. A cost–benefit analysis is clearly an important issue in hearing aid recommendations.

Personality factors and gender play a role in hearing aid satisfaction and benefit. Elderly individuals who are more extroverted report more speech communication benefit from their hearing aids (Cox, Alexander, & Gray, 1999). Additionally, older people who perceive a lower locus of control find environmental sounds to be more unpleasant with their hearing aids than people who feel that they have control over the rewards and penalties they receive. Women report fewer communication difficulties in noise than men. Men report a greater aversion to amplified sounds compared to women. Both observations could be associated with differing amounts of high-frequency amplification recommended for men and women on the basis of different high-frequency pure tone thresholds.

Many elderly people continue to reject the use of amplification. The multiple demands of understanding speech in everyday listening situations, which include limited audibility, background noise, reverberation, rapid speech, different talkers, minimal contextual cues, and varying memory load, may exceed the processing resources available to older people. Aural rehabilitation programs, which train hearing-impaired individuals to capitalize on available contextual cues, use communication intervention strategies, and understand information preserved in reduced auditory cues, are essential for improving communication in everyday settings.

IV. Conclusions and Future Directions

During the period covered by this review, the research on age changes in hearing and vision has expanded dramatically while becoming more specialized. Five broad trends are evident in this literature. The first concerns the breadth and sophistication of the scientific description of age-related differences in vision and hearing resulting from new reports of population-based epidemiological and longitudinal studies. These studies validate published laboratory-based studies and provide a link to demographic differences and modifiable health-related risk factors, thereby laying the groundwork for aggressive programs of prevention to be developed. Also, significant improvements in laboratory-based research have occurred relative to the characterization and screening of research volunteers and the development and use of a variety of experimental procedures that effectively match young and old observers on important age differences, particularly in peripheral aspects of sensory function. Such advances directly address the variability of the aging process, thereby increasing the value of research findings.

Second, the increased use of forced-choice and other sophisticated psychophysical procedures has reduced the impact of possible age differences in decision-making criteria on the results of psychophysical studies. These developments were apparent in new studies of age differences in responses to patterns of stimulus frequency and intensity, but most strongly in studies of detection and discrimination of temporal changes. Several research reports revealed significant age deficits in auditory temporal processing for complex sequences of sounds and temporally distorted speech signals that contribute to higher order limitations in rapid information processing. Comparable trends were identified in studies of age differences in motion detection, temporal resolution, and visual attention.

Third, significant contributions of higher level neural processing to age differences in auditory and visual perception—both within and among different sensory systems—have been discovered. Recent data show that higher level behavioral slowing and cognitive decline affect both vision and hearing. Studies of auditory and visual sensory evoked responses, PET, and studies of binocular depth perception in vision have revealed a complex pattern of age differences in neural function that are experimentally distinguishable from age differences in end organ function. With the rapid development of imaging technology, this research direction will increase rapidly. In vision, important studies of the interactions of vestibular and visual systems in motion detection and between vision in relation to proprioception and muscle action on balance, falls, stumbles, and walking gait have been described.

Fourth, the reported research identifies an increasingly wide range of possibilities for improving sensory and perceptual functioning of older persons through environmental interventions. In hearing, the sophistication of signal enhancement through digital processing and transmission technology have markedly improved the quality of assistive hearing devices. In both vision and hearing, research has been published relative to improving signal intensity, as well as improving contrast between signal and noise through control of glare or background noise. Practical research on vision research using person–environment interaction paradigms has been reported. At the same time, research focusing on training older persons to use context information to improve perceptual performance has increased. Although the principles underlying these developments are not new, we can anticipate significant increases in their application over the next few years.

Fifth, the present review only mentioned current advances in molecular biology and in biochemical engineering with animal models that demonstrate the feasibility of chemical alteration, neural plasticity, and regeneration possibilities that may significantly reduce or eliminate losses in visual and auditory functioning. Advanced signal processing in the middle ear and implants in the cochlea, retina, and brain stem are receiving much research attention at present. It can be expected that future reviews of age differences in sensory function will devote increasing space to these topics.

Acknowledgments

During his research internship with the Florida Geriatric Research Program (FGRP), Mr. John Lersch of the Biology Faculty of Clearwater High School, Clearwater, Florida, carefully screened approximately 800 titles and abstracts used by the authors in preparing this chapter. We are grateful to him as well as to Ms. Karen Roth, Manager of the Morton Plant Mease Health Care Medical Libraries and her staff for obtaining copies of several hundred references reviewed. Ms. Margaret Mawinney and Ms. Barbara Sleicher, both volunteers with the FGRP and Ms. Diane Kirk, FGRP secretary prepared the references. Mr. Neil Gittings performed the anlayses of sex differences in longitudinal age changes in visual acuity described in the text; the unpublished data were from the Baltimore Longitudinal Study of Aging. Dr. James Birren provided many excellent suggestions, especially during the difficult task of condensing and organizing the description of the unexpectedly large amount of research reviewed.

References

Allen, P. A., Patterson, M. B., & Propper, R. E. (1994). Influence of letter size on age differences in letter matching. *Journal of Gerontology, 49*, 24–28.

Andersen, G. J., & Atchely, P. (1995). Age-related differences in the detection of three-dimensional surfaces from optic flow. *Psychology and Aging, 10*, 650–658.

Atchison, D. A., Capper, E. J., & McCabe, K. L. (1994). Critical subjective measurement of amplitude of accommodation. *Optometry and Vision Science, 71*, 699–706.

Atchley, P. & Andersen, G. J. (1998). The effect of age, retinal eccentricity, and speed on the detection of optic flow components. *Psychology and Aging, 13*, 297–308.

Baltes, P. B., & Lindenberger, U. (1997). Emergence of a powerful connection between sensory and cognitive functions across the adult life span: A new window to the study of cognitive aging. *Psychology and Aging, 12*, 12–21.

Bennett, P. J., Sekuler, A. B., & Ozin, L. (1999). Effects of aging on calculation efficiency and equivalent noise. *Journal Optical Society of America, 16*, 654–668.

Boettcher, F. A., Mills, J. H., & Norton, B. L. (1993a). Age-related changes in auditory evoked potentials of gerbils. I. Response amplitudes. *Hearing Research, 71*, 137–145.

Boettcher, F. A., Mills, J. H., & Norton, B. S. (1993b). Age-related changes in auditory evoked potentials of gerbils. II. Response latencies. *Hearing Research, 71*, 146–156.

Brant, L. J., Gordon-Salant, S., Pearson, J. D., Klein, L. L., Morrell, C. H., Metter, E. J., & Fozard, J. L. (1996). Risk factors related to age-associated hearing loss in the speech frequencies. *Journal of the American Academy of Audiology, 7*, 152–160.

Brown, H. D., Kosslyn, S. M., & Dror, I. E. (1998). Aging and scanning of imagined and perceived visual images. *Experimental Aging Research, 24*, 181–194.

Bruce, A. S., Atchison, D. A., & Bhoola, H. (1995). Accommodation-convergence relationships and age. *Investigatiave Ophthalmology and Visual Science, 36*, 406–413.

Caspary, D. M., Raza, A., Lawhorn Armour, B. A., Pippin, J., & Arneric, S. P. (1990). Immunocytochemical and neurochemical evidence for age-related loss of GABA in the inferior colliculus: Implications for neural presbycusis. *Journal of Neuroscience, 10*, 2363–2372.

Charness, N. (1998). Interactions and gerontechnology. In J. Graafmans, V. Taiipele, & N. Charness (Eds.), *Gerontechnology: A sustainable investment in the future* [pp. 62–74]. Amsterdam: IOS Press.

Charness, N., & Bosman, E. A. (1994). Age-related changes in perceptual and psychomotor performance: Implications for engineering design. *Experimental Aging Research, 20*, 45–59.

Colledge, N. R., Cantley, P., Peaston, I., Brash, H., Lewis, S., & Wilson, J. A. (1994). Aging and balance: The measurement of spontaneous sway by posturography. *Gerontology, 40*, 273–278.

Cox, R. M., & Alexander, G. C. (1999). Measuring satisfaction with amplification in daily life: The SADL Scale. *Ear and Hearing, 20*, 306–320.

Cox, R. M., Alexander, G. C., & Gray, G. (1999). Personality and the subjective assessment of hearing aids. *Journal of the American Academy of Audiology, 10*, 1–13.

Cruickshanks, K. J., Wiley, T. L., Tweed, T. S., Klein, B. E. I., Klein, R., Mares-Perlman, J. A., & Nondahl, D. M. (1998). Prevalence of hearing loss in older adults in Beaver Dam, WI: The epidemiology of hearing loss study. *American Journal of Epidemiology, 148*, 879–886.

Demer, J. L. (1994). Effect of aging on vertical visual tracking and visual-vestibular interaction. *Journal of Vestibular Research, 4*, 355–370.

Dillon, H., Birtles, G., & Lovegrove, R. (1999). Measuring the outcomes of a National Rehabilitation Program: Normative data for the Client Oriented Scale of Improvement (COSI) and the Hearing Aid User's Questionnaire (HAUQ). *Journal of the American Academy of Audiology, 10*, 67–79.

Divenyi, P. J., & Haupt, K. M. (1997a). Audiological correlates of speech understanding deficits in elderly listeners with mild-to-moderate hearing loss. II. Correlation analysis. *Ear and Hearing, 18*, 100–113.

Divenyi, P. J., & Haupt, K. M. (1997b). Audiological correlates of speech understanding deficits in elderly listeners with mild-to-moderate hearing loss. III. Factor representation. *Ear and Hearing, 18*, 189–201.

Dubno, J. R., Lee, F-S., Matthews, L. J., & Mills, J. H. (1997). Age-related and gender-related changes in monaural speech recognition. *Journal of Speech, Language, and Hearing Research, 40*, 444–452.

Elliott, D. B., Yang, K. C. H., & Whitaker, D. (1995). Visual acuity changes throughout adulthood in normal healthy eyes: Seeing beyond 6/6. *Optometry and Vision Science, 72*, 186–191.

Fiorentini, A., Porciatti, V., Morrone, M. C., & Burr, D. C. (1996). Visual aging: unspecific decline of the responses to luminance and color. *Vision Research, 36*, 3557–3566.

Fisk, A. D., Rogers, W. A., Cooper, B. P., & Gilbert, D. K. (1997). Automatic category search and its transfer: Aging, type of search, and level of learning. *Journal of Gerento-*

logy: Psychological Sciences, 52B(2), P91–P92.

Fitzgibbons, P. J., & Gordon-Salant, S. (1994). Age effects on measures of auditory duration discrimination. *Journal of Speech and Hearing Research, 37*, 662–670.

Fitzgibbons, P. J., & Gordon-Salant, S. (1995). Duration discrimination with simple and complex stimuli: Effects of age and hearing sensitivity. *Journal of the Acoustical Society of America, 98*, 3140–3145.

Fitzgibbons, P. J., & Gordon-Salant, S. (1998). Auditory temporal order perception in younger and older adults. *Journal of Speech, Language, and Hearing Research, 41*, 1052–1060.

Fozard, J. L. (1990). Vision and hearing in aging. In J. E. Birren & K. W. Schaie (Eds), *Handbook of the psychology of aging* (3rd ed.) (pp. 150–170). San Diego, CA: Academic Press.

Fozard, J. L. (2000). Sensory and cognitive changes with age. In K. W. Schaie & M. Pietrucha (Eds), *Mobility and transportation in the elderly* (pp. 1–44) New York: Springer.

Fozard, J. L., & Heikkinen, E. (1998). Maintaining movement ability in old age. In J. Graafmans, V. Taipele, & N. Charness (Eds.), *Gerontechnology: A sustainable investment in the future*, (pp. 48–61) Amsterdam: IOS Press.

Fozard, J. L., Rietsema, J., Bouma, H., & Graafmans, J. A. M. (2000). Gerontechnology: Creating enabling environments for the challenges and opportunities of aging. *Educational Gerontology, 26*, 331–344.

Garstecki, D., & Erler, S. F. (1996). Older adult performance on the Communication Profile for the Hearing Impaired. *Journal of Speech, Language, and Hearing Research, 39*, 28–42.

Garstecki, D., & Erler, S. F. (1999). Older adult performance on the Communication Profile for the Hearing Impaired: Gender difference. *Journal of Speech, Language, and Hearing Research, 42*, 735–796.

Gehr, S. E., & Sommers, M. S. (1999). Age differences in backward masking. *Journal of the Acoustical Society of America, 106*, 2793–2799.

Gittings, N. S., & Fozard, J. L. (1986). Age changes in visual acuity. *Experimental Gerontology, 21*, 423–434.

Gordon-Salant, S., & Fitgibbons, P. J. (1993). Temporal factors and speech recognition performance in young and elderly listeners. *Journal of Speech and Hearing Research, 36*, 1276–1285.

Gordon-Salant, S., & Fitzgibbons, P. J. (1995). Comparing recognition of distorted speech using an equivalent signal-to-noise ratio index. *Journal of Speech and Hearing Research, 38*, 706–713.

Gordon-Salant, S., & Fitzgibbons, P. J. (1997). Selected cognitive factors and speech recognition performance among young and elderly listeners. *Journal of Speech, Language, and Hearing Research, 40*, 423–431.

Gordon-Salant, S., & Fitzgibbons, P. J. (1999). Profile of auditory temporal processing in older listeners. *Journal of Speech, Language, and Hearing Research, 42*, 300–311.

Gordon-Salant, S., Lantz, J., & Fitzgibbons, P. J. (1994). Age effects on measures of hearing disability. *Ear and Hearing, 15*, 262–265.

Gottlob, L. R., & Madden, D. J. (1998). The course of allocation of visual attention after equating for sensory differences: An age-related perspective. *Psychology and Aging, 13*, 138–149.

Grady, C. L., Maisog, J. M., Horwitz, B., Ungerleider, L. G., Mentis, M. J., Salerno, J. A., Pietrini, P., Wagner, E., & Haxby, J. V. (1994). Age-related changes in cortical bloodflow activation during visual processing of faces and location. *The Journal of Neuroscience, 14*(3), 1450–1462.

Gratton, M. A., Schmiedt, R. A., & Schulte, B. A. (1996). Age-related decreases in endococchlear potential are associated with vascular abnormalities in the stria vascularis. *Hearing Research, 94*, 116–124.

Guiaro, A., Gonzale, G., Redondo, M., Geraghty, E., Norrby, S., & Artal, P. (1999). Average optical performance of the human eye as a function of age in a normal population. *Investigative Ophthalmology & Visual Science, 40*, 203–213.

Haegerstrom-Portnoy, G., Schneck, M. E., & Brabyn, J. A. (1999). Seeing into old age: Vision function beyond acuity. *Optometry and Vision Science, 76*, 141–158.

Halloin, J. (1995). Application of current knowledge in lighting to the needs of the homebound aged. *Journal of Long-Term Home Health Care, 14*, 32–39.

Hargus, S. E., & Gordon-Salant, S. (1995). Accuracy of speech intelligibility index predictions for noise-masked young listeners with normal hearing and for elderly listeners with hearing impairment. *Journal of Speech and Hearing Research, 38*, 234–243.

Harpur, L. L., Scialfa, C. T., & Thomas, D. M. (1995). Age differences in feature search as a function of exposure duration. *Experimental Aging Research, 21*, 1–15.

He, N., & Schmiedt, R. A. (1996). Effect of aging on the fine structure of the 2f1–f2 acoustic distortion product. *Journal of the Acoustical Society of America, 99*, 1002–1015.

He, N., Dubno, J. R., & Mills, J. H. (1998). Frequency and intensity discrimination measured in a maximum-likelihood procedure from young and aged normal-hearing subjects. *Journal of the Acoustical Society of America, 103*, 553–565.

He, N., Horwitz, A. R., Dubno, J. R., & Mills, J. H. (1999). Psychometric functions for gap detection in noise measured from young and aged subjects. *Journal of the Acoustical Society of America, 106*, 966–978.

Hellstrom, L. I., & Schmiedt, R. A. (1990). Comparisons of compound action potential input/output functions in aged and young gerbils. *Association for Research in Otolaryngology Abstracts, 12*, 43.

Herse, P. (1995). A new method for quatification of the dynamics of dark adaptation. *Optometry and Vision Science, 72*, 907–910.

Humes, L. E. (1996). Speech understanding in the elderly. *Journal of the American Academy of Audiology, 7*, 161–167.

Humes, L. E., Halling, D., & Coughlin, M. (1996). Reliability and stability of various hearing-aid outcome measures in a group of elderly hearing-aid wearers. *Journal of Speech, Language, and Hearing Research, 39*, 923–935.

Johnson, C. A., & Marshall Jr. D. (1995). Aging effects for opponent mechanisms in the central visual field. *Optometry and Vision Science, 72*, 75–82.

Judge, J. O., King, M. B., Whipple, R., Clive, J., & Wolfson, L. I. (1995). Dynamic balance in older persons: Effects of reduced visual and proprioceptive-input. *Journal of*

Gerontology: Medical Sciences, 50A(5), M263–M270.

Kim, C. B. Y., & Mayer, M. J. (1994). Floceal flicker sensitivity in healthy aging eyes. II. Cross-sectional aging trends from 18 through 77 years of age. *Journal of the Optical Society of America, 11*, 1958–1969

Klein, B. E. Klein, R., Lee, K. E., & Cruickshanks, K. J. (1998). Performance-based and self-assessed measures of visual function as related to history of falls, hip fractures, and measured gait time. *Ophthalmology, 105*, 160–164.

Klein, R., Klein, B. E., & Lee, K. E. (1996). Changes in visual acuity in a population *Ophthalmology, 103*, 1169–1178.

Kline, D. W. (1994). Optimising the visibility of displays for older observers. *Experimental Aging Research, 20*, 11–23.

Kline, D. W., Kline, T. J. B., Fozard, J. L., Kosnik, W., Schieber, F., & Sekuler, R. (1992). Vision, aging and driving: The problems of older drivers. *Journal of Gerontology: Psychological Sciences, 47*, P27–P34.

Kline, D. W., & Scialfa, C. T. (1996). Visual and auditory aging. In J. E. Birren & K. W. Schaie (Eds.), *Handbook of the psychology of aging* (4th ed.), (pp. 181–203). San Diego, CA: Academic Press.

Koretz, J. F., Cook, C. A., & Kaufman, P. L. (1997). Accommodation and presbyopia in human eye. *Investigative Ophthalmology and Visual Science, 38*, 569–578.

Kotary, L., & Hoyer, W. J. (1995). Age and the ability to inhibit distractor information in visual selective attention. *Experimental Aging Research, 21*, 159–171.

Kraft, J. M., & Werner, J. S. (1994). Spectral efficiency across the life span: Flicker photometry and brightness matching. *Journal of the Optical Society of America, 11*, 1213–1221.

Kraft, J. M., & Werner, J. S. (1999a). Aging and the saturation of colors. 1. Colorimetric pruity discrimination. *Journal of the Optical Society of America, 16*, 223–230.

Kraft, J. M., & Werner, J. S. (1999b). Aging and the saturation of colors. 2. Scaling of color appearance. *Journal of the Optical Society of America, 16*, 231–234.

Kramer, A. F., Martin-Emerson, R., Larish, J. F., & Andersen, G. J. (1996). Aging and filtering by movement in visual search. *Journal of*

Gerontology: Psychological Sciences, 51B, P201–P216.

Lerner, N. (1994). Giving the older driver enough perception-reaction time. *Experimental Aging Research, 20*, 25–33.

Letowski, T., & Poch, N. (1996). Comprehension of time-compressed speech: Effects of age and speech complexity. *Journal of the American Academy of Audiology, 7*, 447–457.

Lindenberger, U., & Baltes, P. B. (1994). Sensory functioning and intelligence in old age: A strong connection. *Psychology and Aging, 9*, 339–355.

Lord, S. R., & Ward, J. A. (1994). Age-associated differences in sensori-motor function and balance in community dwelling women. *Age and Aging, 23*, 452–460.

Madden, D. J., & Allen, P. A. (1995). Aging and the speed/accuracy relation in visual search: Evidence for an acculator model. *Optometry and Vision Science, 72* (3), 210–216.

Mangione, C. M., Lee, P. P., Pitts, J., Guterrez, P., Berry, S., & Hays, R. D., for the NEI-VFQ Field Test Investigators. (1998). Psychometric properties of the National Eye Institute Visual Function Questionnaire (NEI-VFQ). *Archives of Ophthalmology, 116*, 1496–1504.

Matthews, L. J., Lee, F-S., Mills, J. H., & Dubno, J. R. (1997). Extended high-frequency thresholds in older adults. *Journal of Speech, Language, and Hearing Research, 40*, 208–214.

McCalley, L. T., Bouwhuis, & Juola, J. F. (1995). Age changes in the distribution of visual attention. *Journal of Gerontology: Psychological Sciences, 50B*, P316–P331.

McLeod, S. D., West, S. K., Quigley, H. A., & Fozard, J. L. (1990). A longitudinal study of the relationship between intraocular pressure and blood pressures. *Investigative Opthalmology and Visual Science, 31*, 2351–2366.

Morrison, J. D., & Reilly, J. (1989). The pattern evoked cortical response in human ageing. *Quarterly Journal of Experimental Physiology, 74*, 311–328.

Moscicki, E. K., Elkins, E. F., Baum, H. F., & McNamara, P. M. (1985). Hearing loss in the elderly: an epidemiologic study of the Framingham Heart Study Cohort. *Ear and Hearing, 6*, 184–190.

Muir, J. A., Barlow, H. L., & Morrison, J. D. (1996). Invariance of the pattern electroretinogram evoked by psychophysically equivalent stimuli in human aging. *Journal of Physiology, 49,* 825–835.

Mulrow, C. D., Aguilar, C., Endicott, J. E., Velex, R., Tuley, M. R., Charlip, W. S., & Hill, J. A. (1990). Association between hearing impairment and the quality of life of elderly individuals. *Journal of the American Geriatrics Society, 38,* 45–50.

National Center for Health Statistics (1995). *Vital and Health Statistics. Trends in the Health of Older Americans: United States, 1994.* Series 3: Analytic and Epidemiological Studies, No. 30. U.S. Department of Health and Human Services Publication No. 95–1414.

Neider, M. W., Crawford, K., Daurman, P. L. & Bito, L. Z. (1990). In vivo videography of the rhesus monkey accommodative apparatus. *Archives of Ophthalmology, 108,* 69–74.

Newman, C. W., & Sandridge, S. A. (1998). Benefit from, satisfaction with, and cost-effectiveness of three different hearing aid technologies. *American Journal of Audiology, 7,* 115–128.

Nickerson, R. S. (1965). Response times for "same"–"different" judgments. *Perceptual and Motor Skills, 24,* 543–554.

Oken, B. S., Kishiyama, S. S., & Kaye, J. A. (1994). Age-related differences in visual search task performance: Relative stability of parallel but not serial search. *Journal of Geriatric Psychiatry and Neurology, 7,* 163–168.

Owens, D. A., & Tyrrell, R. A. (1999). Effects of luminance, blur, and age on nighttime visual guidance: A test of the selective degradation hypothesis. *Journal of Experimental Psychology: Applied, 5* (2), 1–14.

Owsley, C., Ball, K., McGwin, G., Sloane, M. E., Roenker, D. L., White, M. F., & Overley, T. (1998). Visual processing impairment and risk of motor vehicle crash among older adults. *Journal of the American Medical Association, 279,* (14) 1083–1088.

Owsley, C., McGwin Jr., G., & Ball, K., (1998). Vision impairment, eye disease, and injurious motor vehicle crashes in the elderly. *Ophthalmic Epidemiology, 5,* 101–113.

Paige, G. D. (1994). Senescence of human visual-vestibular interactions: Smooth pursuit, optokinetic, and vestibular control of eye movements with aging. *Experimental Brain Research, 98,* 355–372.

Pardhan, S. (1996). A comparison of binocular summation in young and older patients. *Current Eye Research, 15,* 315–319.

Pardhan, S., Gilchrist, J., Elliott, D. B., & Beh, G. K. (1996). A comparison of sampling efficiency and internal noise level in young and old subjects. *Vision Research, 36* (1), 1641–1648.

Pearson, J. D., Morrell, C. H., Gordon-Salant, S., Brant, L. J., Metter, E. J., Klein, L. L., & Fozard, J. L. (1995). Gender differences in a longitudinal study of age-associated hearing loss. *Journal of the Acoustical Society of America, 97,* 1196–1205.

Perrin, P. P., Jeandel, C., Perrin, C. A., & Beene, M. C. (1997). Influence of visual control, conduction, and central integration on static and dynamic balance in healthy older adults. *Gerontology, 43,* 223–231.

Perryman, K. M., & Fitten, J. (1996). Effects of normal aging on the performance of motor vehicle operational skills. *Journal of Geriatric Psychiatry and Neurology, 9,* 136–141.

Pichora-Fuller, M. K., Schneider, B. A., & Daneman, M. (1995). How young and old adults listen to and remember speech in noise. *Journal of the Acoustical Society of America, 97,* 593–608.

Research Institute of Human Engineering for Quality Life. (1999). *Human sensory measurement application technology project, 1990–1998.* Osaka, JA: 2–5 1-chome, Dojima, Kita-ku, Osaka, 530.

Rogers, W. A., Fisk, A. D., & Hertzog, C., (1994). Do ability-performance relationships differentiate age and practice effects in visual search? *Journal of Experimental Psychology, 20,* 710–738.

Rubin, G. S., Roche, K. B., Prasada-Rao, P., & Fried, L. P. (1994). Visual impairment and disability in older adults. *Optometry and Vision Science, 71* (12), 750–760.

Rubin, G. S., West, S. K., Munoz, B., Bandeen-Roche, K., Zeger, S., Schein, O., Fried, L. P., & the SEE Project Team (1997). A comprehensive assessment of visual impairment in a population of older Americans. *Investigative Ophthalmology & Visual Science, 38,* 557–568.

Salthouse, T. A., Hancock, Holly, E., Meinz, E. J., & Hambrick, D. Z. (1996) Interrelations of age, visual acuity, and cognitive functioning. *Journal of Gerontology: Psychological Sciences, 51B*, 317–330.

Schefrin, B. E., Bieber, M. L., McLean, R., & Werner, J. S. (1998). The area of complete scotopic spatial summation enlarges with age. *Journal of Optical Society of America, 15*, 340–348.

Schneider, B. A., & Hamstra, S. J. (1999). Gap detection thresholds as a function of tonal duration for younger and older listeners. *Journal of the Acoustical Society of America, 106*, 371–380.

Schuknecht, H. F. (1993). *Pathology of the ear.* (2nd ed.). Philadelphia: Lea & Febiger.

Schulte, B. (1997, April). *Auditory aging.* Presentation at the 9th Annual Convention of the American Academy of Audiology, Fort Lauderdale.

Schulte, B. A., & Schmiedt, R. A. (1992). Lateral wall Na, K-ATPase and endocochlear potentials decline with age in quiet-reared animals. *Hearing Research, 46*, 35–46.

Scialfa, C. T., Esau, S. P., & Joffe, K. M. (1998). Age, target-distractor similarity, and visual search. *Experimental Aging Research, 24*, 337–358.

Scialfa, C. T., & Thomas, D. M. (1994). Age differences in same-different judgments as a function of multidimensional similarity. *Journal of Gerontology: Psychological Sciences, 49*(4), 173–178.

Scialfa, C. T., Thomas, D. M., & Joffe, K. M. (1994). Age differences in the useful field of view: An eye movement analysis. *Optometry And Vision Science, 71*, 736–742.

Snell, K. B. (1997). Age-related changes in temporal gap detection. *Journal of the Acoustical Society of America, 101*, 2214–2220.

Souza, P. E., & Turner, C. W. (1994). Masking of speech in young and elderly listeners with hearing loss. *Journal of Speech and Hearing Research, 37*, 665–661.

Spoendlin, H., & Schrott, A. (1990). Quantitative evaluation of the human cochlear nerve. *Acta Oto-Laryngologica Supplement, 470*, 61–70.

Spoendlin, H., & Schrott, A. (1989). Analysis of the human auditory nerve. *Hearing Research, 43*, 25–38.

Steen, R., Whitaker, D., Elliott, D. B., & Wilds, J. M. (1994). Age-related effects of glare on luminance and color contrast sensitivity. *Optometry and Vision Science, 71*, 792–796.

Steenbekkers, L. P. A. (1998). Visual contrast sensitivity. In L. P. A. Steenbekkers & C. E. M. van Beijsterveldt (Eds.), *Design-relevant characteristics of ageing users.* (pp. 131–136). Delft, The Netherlands: Delft University of Technology Press.

Stevens, J. C., Cruz, L. A., Marks, L. E., & Lakatos, S. (1998). A multimodal assessment of sensory thresholds in aging. *Journal of Gerontology: Psychological sciences, 54*, P263–P272.

Stover, L., & Norton, S. J. (1993). The effects of aging on otoacoustic emissions. *Journal of the Acoustical Society of America, 94*, 2670–2681.

Strouse, A. L., Ochs, M. T., & Hall, J. W. III (1996). Evidence against the influence of aging on distortion-product otoacoustic emissions. *Journal of the American Academy of Audiology, 7*, 339–345.

Studebaker, G. A., Sherbecoe, R. L., McDaniel, D. M., & Gray, G. A. (1997). Age-related changes in monosyllabic word recognition performance when audibility is held constant. *Journal of the American Academy of Audiology, 8*, 150–162.

Swanson, W. H., & Fish, G. E. (1996). Age-related changes in the color-match-area effect. *Vision Research, 36*, 2079–2085.

Tang, P-F, Moore, S., & Woollacott, M. H. (1998). Correlation between two clinical balance measures in older adults: Functional mobility and sensory organization test. *Journal of Gerontology: Medical Sciences, 53A*, M140–M146.

Thibos, L. N. (1998). Acuity perimetry and the sampling theory of visual resolution. *Optometry and Vision Science, 75*, 399–406.

Tobimatsu, S. (1995). Aging and pattern visual evoked potentials. *Optometry and Vision Science, 72*, 192–197.

Trainor, L. J., & Trehub, S. E. (1989). Aging and auditory temporal sequencing: Ordering the elements of repeating tone patterns. *Perception and Psychophysics, 45*, 417–426.

Tran, D. B., Silverman, S. E., Zimmerman, K., & Feldon, S. E. (1998). Age-related deterioration of motion perception and detection.

Graefe's Archives of Clinical and Experimental Ophthalmology, 236, 269–273.

Turano, K., Rubin, G. S., Herdman, S. J., Chee, E., & Fried, L. P. (1994). Visual stabilization of posture in the elderly: Fallers vs. nonfallers. *Optometry and Vision Science, 71*(12), 761–769.

Verhaeghen, P., & DeMeersman, L. (1998). Aging and the stoop effect: A meta-analysis. *Psychology and Aging, 13,* 120–126.

Wahl, H. W., Oswald, F., & Zimprich, D. (1999). Everyday competence in visually impaired older adults: A case for person-environment perspectives. *The Gerontologist, 39,* 140–149.

West, S. K., Munoz, B., Rubin, G. S., Schein, O. D., Bandeen-Roche, K., Zeger, S., German, P. S., Fried, L. P., & SEE Project Team. (1997). Function and visual impairment in a population-based study of older adults. *Investigative Ophthalmology & Visual Science, 38,* 72–82.

Wild, J. M., Cubbidge, R. P., Pacey, I. E., & Robinson, R. (1998). Statistical aspects of the normal visual field in short-wavelength automated perimetry. *Investigative Ophthalmology & Visual Science, 39,* 54–63.

Wiley, T. L., Cruickshanks, K. J., Nondahl, D. M., Tweed, T. S., Klein, R., & Klein, B. E. K. (1998a). Aging and word recognition in competing message. *Journal of the American Academy of Audiology, 9,* 191–198.

Wiley, T. L., Cruickshanks, K. J., Nondahl., D. M., Tweed, T. S., Klein, R., & Klein, B. E. K. (1998b). Aging and high-frequency hearing sensitivity. *Journal of Speech, Language, and Hearing Research, 41,* 1061–1072.

Willott, J. F. (1991). *Aging and the Auditory System.* San Diego: Singular Publishing Group.

Willott, J. F. (1996). Anatomic and physiologic aging: A behavioral neuroscience perspective. *Journal of the American Academy of Audiology, 7,* 141–151.

Willott, J. F., & Bross, L. (1990). Morphology of the octopus cell area of the ventral cochlear nucleus in young and aging C57BL/6J and CBA/J mice. *Journal of Comparative Neurology, 300,* 61–81.

Willott, J. F., Aitkin, L. M., & McFadden, S. M. (1993). Plasticity of auditory cortex associated with sensorineural hearing loss in adult C57BL/6J mice. *Journal of Comparative Neurology, 329,* 402–411.

Willott, J. F., Bross, L., & McFadden, S. L. (1992). Morphology of the dorsal cochlear nucleus in young and aging C57BL/6J and CBA/J mice. *Journal of Comparative Neurology, 321,* 666–678.

Wingfield, A. (1996). Cognitive factors in auditory performance: context, speed of processing, and constraints of memory. *Journal of the American Academy of Audiology, 7,* 175–182.

Wingfield, A., Poon, L. W., Lombardi, L., & Lowe, D. (1985). Speed of processing in normal aging: effects of speech rate, linguistic structure, and processing time. *Journal of Gerontology, 40,* 579–585.

Wojciechowski, R., Trick, G. L., & Steinman, S. B. (1995). Topography of the age-related decline in motion sensitivity. *Optometry and Vision Science, 72,* 67–74.

Wood, J., & Bullimore, M. A. (1996). Interocular differences in visual function in normal subjects. *Ophthalmological and Physiological Optics, 16,* 507–512.

Yager, D., & Beard, B. L. (1994). Age differences in contrast sensitivity are not the result of changes in subjects' criteria or psychophysical performance. *Optometry and Visual Science, 71,* 778–82.

Zhang, L., & Sturr, J. F. (1995). Aging, background luminance, and threshold-duration functions for detection of low spatial frequency sinusoidal gratings. *Optometry and Vision Science, 72,* 198–204.

Eleven

Understanding the Role of Attention in Cognitive Aging Research

Wendy A. Rogers and Arthur D. Fisk

I. Historical Perspective

The concept of attention is an important one in the field of psychology. Early theorists such as James (1950/1890), Ribot (1903), and Titchener (1908), along with empiricists such as Bryan and Harter (1899) and Solomons and Stein (1896) considered issues of attention to be of primary relevance to everyday skills and activities; that is, to psychology. Even given this long history of importance, defining "attention" is no simple matter. In our view, and as has been suggested by many before us, attention is a multidimensional construct that involves processes that focus, select, divide, sustain, and inhibit (Parasuraman & Davies, 1984).

As a starting point to the development of our chapter, we reviewed how the concept of attention had been addressed in the previous editions of the *Handbook of the Psychology of Aging* (Birren & Schaie, 1977, 1985, 1990, and 1996). In the first edition, no chapters were devoted to the topic of attention. Instead, discussion of age-related changes in attention was incorporated into the memory chapter (Craik, 1977). Age-related differences

in the dichotic listening paradigm were reported to indicate that memory for attended items was intact for older adults, but there was an age difference in recall of items presumably stored preperceptually. Thus the focus was not on attention, per se, but on the use of an attentional paradigm to study aspects of memory. Similarly, divided attention studies, which typically reveal age-related differences in performance, were discussed as the results related to aspects of memory. Thus, that chapter emphasized the use of attention as a manipulation to enable investigations of other constructs such as memory. We shall return to this point later.

In the 1985 edition, the construct of attention was again incorporated in the chapter on memory (Poon, 1985). After reviewing the basic patterns of age-related changes in memory, Poon's review focused on potential explanations of such changes. As one possibility, Poon considered theories of biological changes in attention such as Kinsbourne's view of neuronal depletion as it might affect attentional processes (e.g., Kinsbourne, 1980). Thus in that edition of the handbook, the primary emphasis on attention

Handbook of the Psychology of Aging

revolved around the viability of age-related changes in attention as a root cause of age-related changes in other behaviors, primarily memory.

The third edition of the handbook included an entire chapter devoted to attention (McDowd & Birren, 1990). That chapter reviewed the prevailing understanding at the time of age-related differences in four main categories of attention: divided, switching, sustained, and selective. The focus was on the attentional processes themselves, and whether they changed with age. McDowd and Birren's review of research conducted prior to 1990 led to the following conclusions about these attentional processes: (a) there was a robust age-related difference in divided attention; (b) results were mixed for attention switching; (c) generally, age-related differences were observed in sustained attention; and (d) selective attention was also age-sensitive. One of their recommendations for future research was to continue the efforts to understand age-related considerations in the varieties of attention.

Attention was not the focus of a chapter in the 1996 edition, perhaps because as Birren and Schaie stated in the preface to that volume, certain topics were "not represented...because we decided that there had not been sufficient progress since the previous handbook edition to warrant a new presentation" (p. xvi). As such, references to attention in that edition are found only in terms of how arousal might influence achievement motivation (Filippe, 1996), and selective attention in the context of visual search (Kline & Scialfa, 1996).

We were invited to contribute a chapter on attention for the present volume perhaps because, as we believe, there has indeed been much recent progress within the field broadly defined as attention and aging. The progress has occurred on numerous fronts that can be categorized as understanding attention as a manipulation for investigating age-related behavioral differences (i.e., as a tool), better understanding the hypothetical construct per se, and for understanding and developing practical solutions to important real-world problems.

The history of how attention has been conceptualized and discussed in the previous handbook volumes is revealing and likely representative of how attentional issues have been investigated in cognitive aging research. We see three primary themes in these reviews. First is the idea that attentional manipulations provide a tool to investigate age-related changes in other aspects of human behavior such as memory. For example, presuming that attention is required for encoding, and attentional resources are reduced through a divided attention manipulation, the effects of divided attention on memory can be investigated (and compared across age groups). The second theme represents the focus on attentional processes themselves as the focus of interest. That is, where the goal is to understand age-related changes in attentional process such as selection. The third general theme is the appeal to attentional changes as the underpinnings of age-related changes in other behaviors. The focus is on explanation of age effects in other aspects of behavior, rather than manipulation of attention or on the attentional process, per se. These three themes provide the context for the present chapter. An additional thread that runs through all of the themes is the idea that studies of aging contribute to and test basic theories of attention.

II. Overview of Chapter

Given the existing recent reviews of attention and aging (e.g., Hartley, 1992; McDowd & Shaw, 2000; Rogers, 2000), we have focused primarily on recent research, post-1990, and on the role of the construct of attention in understanding behavioral aspects of aging more generally. Our approach to understanding the role of attention in the field of psychology of aging was to classify research into three broad categories. First is research wherein attentional resources are manipulated in some way to assess other variables of interest. For example, requiring an individual to share attention between two tasks can provide an index of the attentional requirements of one of the tasks. In this category of research, attention is manipulated as a means to understanding other aspects of cognition.

The second category of research consists of studies wherein attention itself is the process of interest. It has long been assumed that there are varieties of attention (e.g., James, 1950/1890; Parasuraman & Davies, 1984). As such, it is important to document and understand the aspects of attention that show age-related changes. Research in this category includes studies of selective attention, sustained attention, focused attention, divided attention, and the transition from attention-demanding processing to automatic processing of task components. These aspects of attention, and age-related differences therein, are the focus of most reviews of attention research. As such, our review provides illustrative examples, rather than an exhaustive review of relevant research. Instead we point the reader to the recent, and very complete, review by McDowd and Shaw (2000).

The third category of research in our framework comprises studies wherein the focus is on attention as an explanatory construct for age-related differences in other aspects of cognition or in everyday activities. Age-related differences in an aspect of attention are thus used as an explanation for age-related differences in more complex cognition.

Our conceptualization of attention research into these three general categories enabled us to provide a perspective on how understanding of attention and aging contributes to our broader understanding of the psychology of aging. The material discussed in each section is not meant to be exhaustive but illustrative of the nature and extent of the progress in each category. We will end the chapter by discussing current and future directions for research that may advance the broad field of attention and aging even further. Such fruitful areas, in our view, include neuropsychology and practical applications.

III. Manipulation of Attention

Experimental psychologists sometimes use an attention manipulation in their study as a method of investigating some other aspect of cognitive performance. For example, the logic of manipulating attention in the context of studies of memory is based on the contention that memory (e.g., the strength of the memory trace) is influenced by the attention allocated to the processing of the stimulus (e.g., Craik, 1977).

A popular attentional manipulation is to require young adults to divide their attention as a method of "mimicking" the aging process. In fact, some researchers argue that aging and a reduction in attentional capacities are functionally the same. For example, Jennings and Jacoby (1993) tested the prediction that aging and dividing attention would both influence the controlled recollective aspect of a memory test (and not influence the automatic component). These two components of memory can be differentiated using the process-dissociation procedure, wherein participants are either actively trying to recollect items or are influenced by automatic aspects of memory. Jennings and Jacoby compared older adults and young adults who either were or were not required to divide their attention with a secondary task during the acquisition of a list of names. They concluded that aging and dividing attention both result in a reduction in the amount of consciously controlled processing that is available to be allocated to a task.

However, contrary to the Jennings and Jacoby (1993) conclusion, there are data that show that with some task experience, age-related deficits in controlled processing are eliminated (e.g., Fisk & Rogers, 1991). That is, in many cases initial performance differences may be due to extraneous factors such as unfamiliarity with the testing environment or the instructions. In addition, dual-task studies show that age-related deficits presumed to be due to attention may be due to other factors, such as different learning for each age group (Kramer & Larish, 1996; Rogers, Bertus, & Gilbert, 1994) or conservative response biases that change with practice (e.g., Batsakes & Fisk, 2000). Hence age-related differences in attention-demanding tasks are not necessarily the result of enduring characteristics and they are not necessarily immutable. Therefore, a strong message from the literature is that when division of attention is used as a manipulation, care must be taken about the conclusions drawn.

Additional evidence against equating the general effects of aging with a reduction in attentional resources comes from findings wherein young and older adults show similar patterns of an attentional manipulation. Presumably, older adults should be more affected by such manipulations, if they are already faced with an attentional deficit. In one study, Mutter and Goedert (1997) investigated age-related differences in frequency judgment. Frequency information is presumably based on memory traces associated with repeated occurrences of an event or item. Although early research in this area indicated that such frequency judgments were immune to the deleterious effects of aging (e.g., Hasher & Zacks, 1979),

this claim is not without controversy (e.g., Fisk & Schneider, 1984). Mutter and Goedert compared the ability of young and older adults to make absolute and relative frequency judgments after either a focused- or a divided-attention encoding context. Their results showed that having to devote some attentional resources to a secondary task influenced the ability to make frequency judgments, but not differentially across age groups.

A similar pattern of age-related effects was observed in a study of speech processing by Tun, Wingfield, Stine, and Mecsas (1992). They also found that adding a secondary task did not differentially impact the performance of older adults relative to younger adults. Having to divide attention by processing pictorial information reduced speech memory performance in a similar fashion for both age groups.

The requirement to divide attention yielded similar deficits in performance for young and older adults in another test of the process-dissociation procedure conducted by Schmitter-Edgecombe (1999). For both age groups the attentional manipulation influenced the conscious recollection component of memory, but not the automatic component. On the contrary, Anderson (1999) observed greater divided attention costs for older, relative to young adults during the encoding and retrieval phases of a free-recall task.

The manipulation of attention is a useful tool for understanding age-related differences in performance on cognitive tasks, but researchers cannot simply assume that young adults under divided-attention conditions will mimic mechanisms of aging. Although this approach has historical precedence in the field, the pattern of results is mixed in terms of showing age-related effects as a function of an attention manipulation (for a review, see Kramer & Larish, 1996). Thus the manipulation of attention may be an avenue for insight into age-related differences in cognitive processing, but convergent evidence should be sought to establish that the pattern of results are truly due to attentional factors and not other variables (see Perfect & Rabbitt, 1993, for a similar argument). What appear to be deficits due to attention may actually be due to other psychological mechanisms, such as response bias or differential rates of learning.

IV. Attention as a Process

In his introduction to *The Attentive Brain*, Parasuraman (1998) suggested that there are three primary components of attention: selection, vigilance, and control (see Posner & Peterson, 1990, for a similar view). Together, these aspects of attention comprise the processes that are critical for enabling individuals to perform a wide variety of functions. We will use this framework to guide our review of research on age-related differences in specific attentional processes.

A. Selective Attention

At any moment in time, we are bombarded by stimulation to all of our senses. However, we are quite adept at the selection of the information that is most relevant to our task goals. Reading a novel requires the processing of the words on the page (much of which is performed automatically for skilled readers) as well as the inhibition of distracting stimulation, such as a television in the next room. Another example is making a decision about which stimuli to attend to when making a left turn at an intersection.

Selective attention involves at least two processes: selection of relevant information and inhibition of irrelevant information. It may be difficult to pinpoint the specific role of each process in a selective attention task. However, studies of age-related differences have focused primarily on either selection or inhibition.

Selective attention requires detecting a particular stimulus or class of stimuli while ignoring other irrelevant stimuli. Visual search tasks have frequently been used to assess age-related differences in the visual selection process. In a visual search task, the individual must determine either where a target item is located or whether a target item is present in a display.

Generally, older adults are less adept on selective attention tasks (for a review see Plude, Enns, & Brodeur, 1994). However, age differences are minimal for simple feature searches (Foster, Behrmann, & Stuss, 1995; Humphrey & Kramer, 1997; Plude & Doussard-Roosevelt, 1989) or if participants are given sufficient practice, such that the task measures selection processes, per se, rather than general familiarity with computers and task instructions (e.g., Fisk & Rogers, 1991).

Also contributing to successful selection of information is inhibition of irrelevant information. Hasher and Zacks (1988) suggested that an age-related difference in inhibition could account for a wide variety of age-related differences in other aspects of cognition (working memory in particular). Thus inhibition was proposed as an explanation of other cognitive performance differences (we return to this point in section V). The Hasher and Zacks concept of inhibition failure as an aspect of aging served as a catalyst for studies that focused on inhibition as an attentional process to be studied directly. Scores of experiments have been carried out in the intervening years. The results of the research suggest that there is not a simple relationship between age, inhibition, and other cognitive functions (see the special section on "Inhibitory Function and Aging" published in the *Journal of Gerontology: Psychological Sciences* in 1997 featuring articles by Burke, McDowd, and Zacks & Hasher).

To illustrate the complexity of the results of inhibition studies, consider the following set of studies. Using a negative priming study, Hasher, Stoltzfus, Zacks, and Rypma (1991) found that older adults did not reliably inhibit to-be-ignored distractors (this effect was replicated by others, e.g., McDowd & Oseas-Kreger, 1991). Age deficits were observed primarily for identity (or meaning) priming. Connelly and Hasher (1993) found that older adults did show negative priming for location information, thereby suggesting that there may be two inhibitory mechanisms, one of which is intact across age.

However, negative priming of identity information has been found to be intact for older adults by Sullivan and Faust (1993). They speculated that inhibition may be intact for older adults if (a) older adults adopt the same response criterion as younger adults, (b) the task is sensitive enough to show a substantial negative priming effect, and (c) task factors are considered such as display and target duration, distractor location, prime response required, and target response characteristics. They also found correlations between negative priming and interference and suggested that those two constructs may be governed by a single mechanism (see also Little & Hartley, 2000). Similarly, Kramer, Humphrey, Larish, Logan, and Strayer (1994) found intact negative priming for young and older adults. They suggested that the finding of age similarity was dependent on the difficulty of the selection task; that is, more difficult selection on one trial leads to more inhibition on the next (i.e., more processing initially leads to more inhibition when done). However, they reported a pattern of correlations among measures to support the idea of independent varieties of inhibitory function.

In an effort to directly contrast selection versus inhibition differences, Allen, Weber, and Madden (1994) designed two visual search experiments to disambiguate activation from inhibition. They argued that their results pointed to an age difference in the selection (i.e., activation) component of the search task, rather than an age deficit in inhibitory capability. It is possible that for the class of search task they investigated, activation ability was more directly relevant to performance. However, it is also possible that their results provide another case where age differences in inhibition are not evident. The particular strength of this research is the comparison of the two processes within the same task. This approach applied to other task domains might prove to be very enlightening for a better understanding of age-related differences in selective attention.

In sum, although age differences are apparent in selective attention tasks that require more than simple feature search, the mechanism responsible for the age-related difference remains indeterminate. There is evidence to support an inhibition deficit, but this conclusion is certainly not definitive. Consequently, studies of aging and selective attention will, and must, continue.

B. Vigilance (Sustained Attention)

Vigilance, also referred to as sustained attention, involves the maintenance of attention across time. Watching a cream sauce for the moment it begins to boil, listening for one's number at the deli counter, and monitoring a computer display for a critical signal all require vigilance for adequate performance. Successful vigilance is dependent on a number of variables ranging from the intensity of the stimulus itself to the cost of missing the appearance of the signal information.

The relationship between age and vigilance is not clear. For vigilance tasks that require making a perceptual discrimination, age-related differences are found (e.g., Deaton & Parasuraman, 1993), but not if the discrimination is made very salient and demands on memory are minimized (Giambra & Quilter, 1988), or if older adults are screened for visual deficits (Giambra, 1995). Practice on the vigilance tasks also reduces age-related differences (Parasuraman & Giambra, 1991).

For vigilance tasks with a cognitive component, such as those that require identification of an item or a decision about an item, older adults have been found to be worse than young adults in some cases (Deaton & Parasuraman, 1993). However, such age differences are not observed if the memory demands of the task are tailored to the individual's memory ability (Tomporowski & Tinsley, 1996).

Clearly there is not a simple answer to the question of whether sustained attention declines with age. The answer is, it depends. It depends on the characteristics of the task, the goals of the individual, and the nature of the stimuli. However, we should not really expect a simple answer to how aging affects this aspect of attention because the nuances of vigilance tasks, which have been studied for decades (see Warm & Dember, 1998, for a review), point to the complexity of this construct.

C. Attentional Control

Attentional control can be conceptualized as an individual's ability to focus, switch, and divide attention. The idea is that the person can control the allocation of attention. We will discuss each aspect of attentional control as it has been studied in the context of aging.

One aspect of attentional control involves focusing attention on a particular stimulus or location in space, especially in the presence of distraction. (The primary distinction between focused attention and selective attention tasks is that the location in space or time of the target

of attention is known in a focused attention task, whereas the target must be searched for in a selective attention task.) Shifting one's focus of attention also requires control. There are three categories of findings relevant to older adults' ability to focus attention.

First, if the participants know where to focus their attention, age-related differences are minimal (e.g., Madden & Gottlob, 1997). Similarities across young and older adults in focused attention are observed even if participants are required to focus attention on two noncontiguous locations and ignore intervening distractors (Hahn & Kramer, 1995).

Second, if a valid cue is provided to aid the shifting of attention, older adults are generally able to benefit from the cue (for a review, see Hartley, 1992). With a 100% valid cue, older adults' pattern of attention allocation is identical to younger adults' (Madden, 1990). Similarities have also been observed across age groups in costs associated with 100% invalid cues (Folk & Hoyer, 1992). Greenwood and Parasuraman (1999) found that older adults actually showed greater effects of both valid and invalid cues, relative to younger adults. Similar cue benefits for young and older adults have even been found for attentional shifts in three-dimensional space (Atchley & Kramer, 1998).

The third general finding in the focused attention research is that the rate at which older individuals are able to shift their attention may be slowed. For example, Madden, Connelly, and Pierce (1994) found that when older adults were required to shift attention to a target presented with distractors, their attention shift time was more than twice that of the younger adults (83 ms vs. 39 ms). Similar conclusions were drawn from earlier studies (Madden, 1990, 1992). However, more recent research indicates that these studies may be misleading in attributing the source of the age differences to an attentional phenomenon. In an effort to disambiguate attentional factors from perceptual factors, Gottlob and Madden (1998) conducted a study wherein target duration was individually determined to equate sensory factors across individuals and age groups. Their results suggested that attention allocation, per se, is not slowed for older adults. Instead, they argued that more peripheral sensory-processing differences account for previously reported differences in rate of attention allocation.

An appeal to a perceptual source of age differences in attention allocation was also made by McCalley, Bouwhuis, and Juola (1995). They modeled data from younger and older adults and discovered that a different model for each age group best defined the attention allocation process. A resource allocation model indicating flexible allocation of attention best described the young adults' performance. A zoom lens model indicating a more general spreading of attention better described the performance of older adults. In a second experiment designed to control for age difference in visual acity, results indicated that the performance of both age groups was well defined by the more flexible resource allocation model. McCalley et al. argued that making allowances for age differences in peripheral acuity would yield comparable patterns of attention allocation across young and older adults (but see Gottlob & Madden, 1999, for evidence that attention allocation may be slowed for more cognitively demanding tasks).

Various circumstances require us to divide our attention between two (or more) sources of information. Consider just a few examples: driving while carrying on a conversation, preparing a multiple-course meal, or talking on the phone while tending to children. The oft-quoted claim that the requirement to divide attention nearly always yields age-related differences in performance (e.g., Craik, 1977) is in need of revision. Instead, in

answer to the question of whether older adults have more difficulty dividing their attention, the appropriate answer again is that it depends. Task variables to consider include the complexity of the tasks, the amount and type of practice provided on each task, and the degree to which each task requires attention.

If the tasks are not memory demanding, older adults may be successfully able to divide their attention (e.g., Somberg & Salthouse, 1982). However, for more complex tasks, age-related differences emerge (e.g., McDowd & Craik, 1988). Age differences may be minimized for well-practiced tasks (for a review see Rogers, 2000) or when participants are trained with flexible priority strategies (Kramer, Larish, & Strayer, 1995; Kramer, Larish, Weber, & Bardell, 1999). However, if the young adults are able to automatize one of the task components after practice, and older adults are not, age differences will reemerge (e.g., Rogers et al., 1994).

One additional caveat in interpreting the literature on age-related differences in divided attention abilities relates to the variability in the methodologies used to assess such differences in performances. Methodological issues include selecting tasks that would be expected to compete for attentional resources, measuring (and maintaining) single-task performance levels appropriately, and selecting metrics to assess dual-task performance decrements (for more discussion of these issues see Fisk, Derrick, & Schneider, 1986–1987; Salthouse, Fristoe, Lineweaver, & Coon, 1995).

Consequently, it may not be a simple matter to predict where age-related differences might be observed. Moreover, when such differences do occur, their source remains in dispute: Some of the ideas that have been considered include the following:

- Divided attention tasks are merely more "complex" than single tasks, and the added complexity is the source of the age differences (e.g., McDowd & Craik, 1988).

- Age differences in divided attention tasks are due primarily to age-related differences in the component tasks themselves (e.g., Salthouse et al., 1995).
- The coordinative requirements to divide attention, that is, the executive processing involved, is the source of age-related differences (e.g., Baddeley, 1986).
- Strategic aspects of control of attention may be contributing factors (Batsakes & Fisk, 2000; Sit & Fisk, 1999).

D. Automaticity

To fully understand attention one needs to also understand why and when attention is not required (see Shiffrin, 1988; Underwood, 1993). Processing that is not attention demanding is often described as "automatic." More completely, an automatic process is a process that occurs obligatorily when a specific eliciting stimulus is present; it can occur without intention, and once initiated, will run to completion; it does not reveal itself to conscious awareness, nor does it consume attentional resources. The pattern of age-related changes in automatic processing is complex, thus we will discuss it only in general terms (for a recent review of automaticity and aging, see Rogers, 2000). In short, there are varieties of automaticity only some of which seem to be influenced by aging.

Visual processing that requires only simple feature discrimination is similar for younger and older adults (e.g., Plude & Doussard-Roosevelt, 1989). Similarly, the automatic aspects of memory do not differ (e.g., Jennings & Jacoby, 1993; Salthouse, Toth, Hancock, & Woodard, 1997). Also maintained are automatic processes acquired at a young age such as word reading (Dulaney & Rogers, 1994; Light, 1992)

or arithmetic fact retrieval (Rogers & Fisk, 1991).

Evidence for age-related differences in automatic processing comes primarily from studies of the acquisition of new automatic process. Even here the picture is relatively complex. Older adults are able to automatize memory-based components of tasks if sufficient practice is provided (e.g., Fisk & Rogers, 1991). For tasks such as visual search that require attention training related to perceptual processes (see Shiffrin & Schneider, 1977), older adults do not show evidence of automatic process development even after extensive practice (e.g., Fisk & Rogers, 1991; Rogers, 1992; but see Anandam & Scialfa, 1999).

To summarize our knowledge about age-related differences in automatic processes, there are two basic questions. First, are automatic processes that were acquired at a younger age maintained into old age? The answer here appears to be yes. This finding is very encouraging because it means that we may rely on automatic processes throughout our lives, provided we first acquire them prior to senescence. However, there is some evidence that fine motor skills and gross motor movements that were habitual may begin to require attention as individuals age. This is not a new idea, as illustrated by a now classic anecdote recounted by Miles (1933, cited in Welford, 1958): when Charles Eliot, the president of Harvard University, was 84 he recounted that "the chief change he noticed in his powers as he grew older was that he had to give direct visual attention to the performance of manual habit. 'If I lift a glass of water I must now keep watch on it or the glass may slip from my hand. A few years ago, the hand itself would entirely take care of such a matter'" (Welford, 1958, p. 186–187). The degree to which attention must be devoted to formerly automatic motor movements such as walking has experienced a resurgence of interest in more recent studies (e.g., Li, Lindenberger, Freund, & Baltes, 2000; Marsiske, Delius, Maas, Lindenberger, Scherer, & Tesch-Römer, 1999).

The second question is how well can older adults acquire new automatic processes? Here the answer is, it depends on the type of task. For tasks dominated by improvement based on associative learning, older adults may take longer, but they can successfully automatize the task. However, for tasks that involve more perceptual learning such as visual search tasks, older adults' performance may improve but the task may require attention, even after thousands of trials of consistent practice.

V. Attention as an Explanation

Age-related differences in attention have been proposed to explain age-related differences in other cognitive processing. The most well-known recent example of this type of research is invoking the idea of an age-related deficit in inhibition as an explanation of age-related differences on working memory tasks in general, in reading comprehension, or for other everyday activities (see Hasher & Zacks, 1988; Zacks & Hasher, 1997). Another example is the idea that age-related changes in the ability to allocate attention to multiple goals results in intrusion errors on a Stroop task (i.e., naming the ink color of a color word such as GREEN printed in red ink, West, 1999).

Age-related changes in attention may also explain changes in the instantiation or carrying out of well-learned skills. There is evidence to suggest that well-learned skills acquired at a young age may be maintained as individuals grow older (e.g., Charness, 1985; Salthouse, 1984). However, the precision with which some fine motor skills are performed may change with age. Molander and Bäckman (1994) found a correlation

between self-perceived distractibility and performance for highly skilled miniature golf players in the context of a competition. They used the Test of Attentional and Interpersonal Style to assess individual differences in the ability to handle attentional distractions. Molander and Bäckman found that this measure of distractibility was higher for middle-aged and older individuals (compared to adolescents and young adults) and was correlated with golf score. A regression analysis revealed that this distractibility factor (referred to as overload) significantly predicted performance in competitive play above and beyond age and baseline performance. Molander and Bäckman argued that attentional focusing (i.e., ignoring distractions) was a potential causative factor in age-related differences in the precise motor skill of miniature golf. The relationship between attention and performance in other sports and other precise motor movements should be experimentally investigated in future studies to investigate whether there is a causal relationship.

Of course there are limitations to the explanatory capacity of age-related changes in attention. For example, it has been suggested that attentional decline is a primary reason for age-related differences in memory tasks (e.g., Craik, 1977; Craik & McDowd, 1987). Yet a large-scale study suggests that attentional declines may not underlie age differences in at least episodic memory. Nyberg, Nilsson, Olofsson, and Bäckman (1997) tested one thousand individuals ranging in age from 35 to 80. Their results showed that reducing attentional capacity (via a divided attention task) yielded similar performance declines for all age groups. From these data, they argued that age-related declines in attentional capacity were not sufficient to explain age-related differences in episodic memory (see also Light, 1991; Light & Prull, 1995).

VI. Future Directions for Attention and Aging Research

A. Neurological Bases of Attention

Perhaps the most promising arena in which to advance attentional theory with respect to aging involves neuroscience. A currently prominent area of research in this field involves understanding the neurocognitive aspects of attention (see Parasuraman, 1998). Substantial progress has been made using techniques such as positron emission tomography (PET), functional magnetic resonance imaging (fMRI), and event-related brain potentials (ERPs) to identify the areas of the brain that relate to the different functions of attention (i.e., selection, vigilance, and control). In addition, efforts are underway to develop animal models of attention as a method to better understand the neurological bases of attention (see Bushnell, 1998, for a review).

As we have reviewed in earlier sections of this chapter, changes in attentional performance accompany aging. It is also known that aging tends to have differential impact on areas of the brain. Age may thus serve as a crucible for testing general theories in neuroscience, as the term was used by Underwood (1975). For example, Johnson (1998) reviewed research in the field of neurodevelopment and attention; that is, tracking the development of aspects of attention in infants and children as such developmental changes may relate to brain areas critical for that aspect of attention (see also Posner & DiGirolamo, 1998). At the other end of the life span, evidence for age-related declines in aspects of attention may correspond to those areas of the brain that show physiological changes with either normal aging or dementia. For example, neocortical areas that are affected early in the progression of Alzheimer's disease are also involved in aspects of attention (Parasuraman & Greenwood, 1998).

Research in the area of selective spatial attention and neurological underpinnings is illustrative. Attentional processes govern the selection of information from locations in space. Such processes have been studied extensively in healthy younger adults (for reviews see Driver & Baylis, 1998; Kanwisher & Driver, 1992) and older adults (reviewed in Hartley, 1992; Plude, Enns, & Brodeur, 1994). Others have investigated these selection processes for older individuals with Alzheimer's disease (e.g., Parasuraman, Greenwood, Haxby, & Grady, 1992).

Recent efforts in neuroscience are attempting to integrate the findings from these populations through an investigation into the specific brain areas involved in the attentional processes as they relate to brain areas and functions influenced by age and disease. The benefits of having a cue to direct spatial attention appear to be comparable for younger and older adults (Hartley, 1992, 1993) and for Alzheimer's patients and age-matched controls (Parasuraman et al., 1992). However, there are greater costs of invalid cues for Alzheimer's patients, presumably due to the need to disengage and shift attention (Faust & Balota, 1997; Parasuraman et al., 1992). This deficit pattern is consistent with the effects of Alzheimer's disease on the parietal lobe (Parasuraman & Greenwood, 1998). Importantly, according to Parasuraman and Greenwood, the patterns of attentional deficits differ for Alzheimer's disease and other dementia such as Parkinson's disease, which have a different etiology.

Research on the neuropsychology of aging, disease, and spatial attention is in its nascent stages. However, such research has the potential to (a) allow tests of behaviorally based theories of spatial attention, and (b) enable predictions of expected declines in performance for normal aging and for Alzheimer's patients.

Little is currently known about the brain–behavior relationships of other aspects of attention (e.g., vigilance and control) and the influence of age and disease on these processes. These are thus fertile research areas to increase our understanding of the complex cognitive processes involved in attention. For example, Zeef, Sonke, Kok, Buiten, and Kenemans (1996) have conducted psychophysiological studies as a method to inform our understanding of age-related changes in focused attention. The results are somewhat mixed, but Zeef et al. proposed a potential explanation of an increased size of the attentional spotlight for older adults. Their explanation is consistent with behavioral data and apparently also with putative cortical structures (see also Greenwood & Parasuraman, 1999).

Another example comes from work by Madden and his colleagues (1999) in a PET study suggesting that the need for allocation of attentional resources (measured by regional cerebral blood flow) to a memory task decreases with practice for young adults, but does not show a comparable reduction for older adults. The brain activity data are thus used to suggest attention allocation differences across age groups.

Cognitive neuroscience can also provide direction for testing theories about aging and attention in the area of inhibitory control. Kramer et al. (1994) endeavored to contrast the dorsal-ventral theory of inhibitory changes with age (Connelly & Hasher, 1993) and the frontal lobe theory (e.g., Hartley, 1993). As such, Kramer et al. selected a battery of tasks that would differentially tap various brain areas, and hence provide support (or lack thereof) for either of the theories. Their study was behavioral in nature but it relied on an understanding of neuropsychological data to select the appropriate tasks for theory testing. Although they did not rule out the dorsal-ventral theory, their pattern of data was more consistent with a frontal lobe model wherein the tasks for which age-related deficits in in-

hibitory function were observed were associated with frontal lobe function (i.e., the Wisconsin Card Sorting Task and a stopping task). Tasks for which inhibition was apparently intact across age were those tasks carried out via visual pathways and less dependent on the frontal lobe.

Pharmacologic studies of attention and aging are also being conducted to advance our knowledge of the neurological bases of attentional functions. One theory supposes that aging results in a reduction in the functioning of the cholinergic system, and the cholinergic system is important for cognitive functions such as memory and attention. This idea has been supported by a study wherein the drug scopolamine (which is an anticholinergic agent) was found to impair older adults to a greater degree than younger adults (Molchan et al., 1992).

In addition to informing the field about attention, aging, and neurological functions, drug studies may ultimately lead to pharmacological interventions that will reduce age-related attentional declines. To provide just one example of a study, Missonnier, Ragot, Derouesné, Guez, and Renault (1999) reported benefits of a noradrenergic drug (which facilitated neurotransmission) on the automatic orienting of attention in Alzheimer's patients. This type of work will undoubtedly be vigorously pursued in the future.

B. Practical Applications

Much of the early research on attention (e.g., Broadbent, 1958) was motivated by practical problems. As has been alluded to throughout the chapter, attentional processes are involved in a myriad of activities. Consequently, it is critically important to extend the study of attention from well-controlled laboratory environments to the complexity of the outside world. Such extensions provide important tests of the external validity of attentional theories, as well as strong tests of the explanatory power of the theories. Moreover, theories of attention can provide guidance for the design and development of systems with which individuals must interact. Attention research provides an excellent example of success in increasing our understanding of cognitive functions and solving problems on the everyday lives of individuals (Rogers, Rousseau, & Fisk, 1999).

Knowledge of changes in attention that accompany aging can provide specific guidance for system designs for older individuals. In addition, tests of attentional theories for complex tasks may illuminate the limits of such theories and provide feedback for their refinement and elaboration.

1. Driving

The opportunity to continue to drive, as one ages, is necessary for maintaining functional independence for many older individuals. A brief analysis of the task of driving illustrates the relevance of the attentional components of selection, vigilance, and control. Navigating through traffic requires the selection and processing of critical cues such as entering vehicles, changes in traffic signals, speed changes in the flow of traffic. The role of vigilance may be most important for long stretches of driving where fatigue may be problematic. Control of attention is involved in the shifting of attention among the various sources of information.

The attention-demanding aspects of the task of driving were summarized by Underwood (1993) as follows:

An analysis of the task requirements could well conclude that it is impossible to drive. The competing inputs include the traffic circumstances, road and route signs, dashboard instruments (to say nothing of car 'phones), and engine behaviour, and the sources are varying dynamically. It is not just the present behaviour of the approaching car that must be evaluated, but we must also, anticipate what the car is likely to do as it moves nearer. As current and anticipated stimuli are understood and a mental model of the world constructed, then we have the problems of deciding what to do about it, and how to make those changes. Changes to the immediate world include steering the car and changing gear, which itself might require coordinated actions of feet and hand as well as manipulation of instrument controls. These are attention-demanding activities." (pp. xiii)

One aspect of driving that may be particularly attention demanding involves maneuvering through intersections—there are multiple sources of stimulus information, many of which are of direct relevance to the decisions being made by the driver. Consequently, the needs for dividing and shifting attention are quite high in this context. Not surprisingly then, left-turn intersections are a frequent site of traffic accidents for all drivers, but particularly older adults. Older drivers have been found to be nine times more likely than younger drivers to be turning left when involved in an accident (U.S. Department of Transportation, 1994).

Understanding age-related differences in divided attention tasks leads to the prediction that older adults would have more difficulty at intersections where the attention demands are high (see Brouwer, Waterink, Wolffelaar, & Rothengatter, 1991). At the same time, understanding that older adults can benefit from attentional cues (Hartley, 1992) provides direction for improving the traffic system to minimize accidents in these situations. Staplin and Fisk (1991) tested young and older drivers in a simulated driving context wherein they were required to make a decision to either make a left turn or wait. Older adults made the wrong decision (elected to make the turn when they did not have the right-of-way) significantly more frequently than young adults. However, age differences in incorrect responses were minimized when a red light was presented along with a sign to wait for the left turn signal. In addition, both young and older drivers benefited from the provision of signs in advance that provided right-of-way information. Priming the drivers about the proper behavior for the intersection improved accuracy as well as latency of decision making.

Age-related declines in the ability to divide attention may result in other hazards related to driving, namely in the use of cellular phones while driving. McKnight and McKnight (1993) assessed the ability to engage in a conversation while simultaneously driving a simulator through highway traffic for young (17–25), middle-aged (age 26–49), and older drivers (50–80). Overall, carrying on an intense conversation on a cellular phone caused 44% of the participants to miss critical events that occurred in the driving task (e.g., failure to brake in the presence of a pedestrian in the roadway), relative to the 34% of participants who did not respond even in the nondistraction control condition. Age differences were not observed in the control condition, but older individuals were the most likely to fail to respond for both casual telephone conversations (about general topics) and intense telephone conversations (which involved solving memory problems).

The potential for dangerous distractions due to cellular phone conversations is being recognized in some areas of the country where talking on a cellular phone is prohibited by the driver of a vehicle when that vehicle is in motion. The findings of McKnight and McKnight (1993) suggest that older drivers should especially be encouraged to minimize optional distractions (such as cellular phones) while driving.

Driving difficulties due to attentional declines are exacerbated for individuals with dementia of the Alzheimer's type. In fact, Parasuraman and Nestor (1991) reported that those aspects of attention that tend to be critically important for driving, such as selective and switching attention, are also the aspects of cognitive function that show early evidence of decline in individuals with Alzheimer's disease.

Given the importance of attentional processes to the task of driving, attentional capabilities may mediate the ability of older drivers. As such, it is critically important to develop methods of predicting at-risk drivers, as well as developing training for such drivers to minimize their risk. The concept of a *useful field of view* (UFOV) is quite promising for both of these goals. The UFOV may be defined generally as the visual field that can be processed during a brief glance (Sanders, 1970). Importantly, UFOV has an attentional component in addition to a visual component; that is, the UFOV involves the detection of objects in the periphery, to which attention may then be focused. Larger visual fields will allow for earlier detection of peripheral objects than smaller visual fields, thus allowing for more time to respond. Older adults tend to have a reduced UFOV (Owsley, Ball, Sloane, Roenker, & Bruni, 1991). Moreover, individual differences in UFOV are correlated with accident rates. Ball and Owsley (1991) found that a measure of UFOV alone accounted for 13% of the variance of all accidents in a sample of older drivers and 21% of the variance of intersection accidents. In fact, UFOV was a better predictor of accidents than traditional measures of driver functioning, such as general visual function (e.g., foveal and peripheral visual acuity). The argument is that UFOV measures attentional processing as well as visual processing and is thus more highly correlated with driving behavior.

The promising aspect of UFOV research is the evidence that training might reduce age-related declines. In an earlier study, Ball, Beard, Roenker, Miller, and Griggs, (1988) found that restricted UFOVs can be improved through training by as much as 133% after only five days of training and that these training gains were maintained even after 6 months. Thus, the construct of UFOV provides a potentially valuable technique for identifying at-risk drivers and for providing training to potentially minimize such risks.

2. Technology Use

Computer technology has permeated our lives such that it is nearly impossible to avoid interacting with computers in some way, shape, or form. In a series of focus groups conducted with older individuals, Rogers, Meyer, Walker, and Fisk (1998) found that older adults reported interacting with computers frequently in their daily activities. There were two important trends in the Rogers et al. data. First, older individuals reported some frustrations in dealing with technologies that were not easy to use (e.g., videocassette recorders). Second, the participants were very interested in learning to use new technologies such as fax machines, photocopiers, and computers in general. The main caveat was that they wanted to be provided with training to learn to use such new systems and not be expected to teach themselves.

Computers can enhance the lives of older individuals by enabling them to maintain functional independence, access services, and interact with friends and relatives (see Czaja, 1996). However, it is critically important that computer systems be designed with consideration for the motor, perceptual, and cognitive capabilities of the older user.

Consider the World Wide Web. Older adults are the fastest growing segment of the population, and a recent survey suggests that they are already using the web or are interested in learning to use it (Morrell, Mayhorn, & Bennett, 2000). There is a proliferation of web sites that are designed for an older population, particularly in the domain of health-related issues (e.g., sites that provide information or sell products). Awareness of age-related abilities and limitations in the area of

attention are directly relevant to the design of web sites intended to be accessible to older users.

Consider some of the attentional capabilities that decline with age, as reviewed herein. The ability to selectively attend to information is impaired as is, at least to some degree, the ability to inhibit irrelevant information. Mead, Lamson, and Rogers (in press) reviewed existing health-oriented web sites and discovered that they are typically not designed with consideration for older individuals (see also Stronge, Walker, & Rogers, in press). Mead et al. provided guidance for web designers, based on the cognitive aging literature. For example, the following recommendations were made to compensate for age-related declines in selective attention:

- Do not place patterned backgrounds behind text.
- Avoid unnecessary graphics and animation.
- Limit the amount of information presented per page.
- Avoid using pop-up menus and drop lists that overlay other interface elements.
- Use identical link names, fonts, and graphics for all links to a given page.
- Mark all links with an underline or other convention (e.g., a button graphic).

These recommendations represent only those that pertain to attentional issues; Mead et al. also presented suggestions based on age-related changes in movement control, perception, language comprehension, and decision making. The important point is that an understanding of basic cognitive changes that typically accompany aging has direct applicability to the design of computer interfaces. In addition, empirical testing of the benefits of such interface changes might inform and extend basic theories of cognitive aging. For example, it may be true that the ability to select relevant information is impaired for older adults on laboratory-based tasks. However, the recommendations for computer interface design are based primarily on logical inferences from these documented age-related changes in attention. These recommendations remain to be empirically verified. Moreover, little is known about older adults' attentional capabilities in contextually rich task domains such as computer applications. Attempts to scale-up basic theories to more complex real-world tasks can serve as a test bed and source of additions and modifications to such theories.

VII. Conclusion

This chapter was not meant to be an exhaustive review of all work in the area of attention and aging since the last handbook chapter on this topic (i.e., McDowd & Birren, 1990). Instead, our goal was to illustrate the relevance of the construct of attention as an experimental tool, as a topic of study, as an explanation, and as a means of testing theories and solving practical problems.

Our review points to the fact that progress has been made in areas that provide us with a better theoretical understanding of the interplay between attention and aging. Maturity of a scientific field is often shown by the application of that field's theoretical work to important and challenging problems associated with daily living. We believe that the broad field of attention and aging has emerged on its path to maturity.

Acknowledgments

The authors were supported in part by grants from the National Institutes of Health (National Institute on Aging): Grant P50 AG11715 under the auspices of the Center for Aging and Cognition: Health, Education, and Technology, Grant P01 AG17211 under the auspices of the Center for Research and Education on Aging and Technology Enhancement (Edward R. Roybal Centers for Research on Applied Gerontology), Grant R01 AG07654, and Grant R01 AG18177. The authors are grateful to Jim Birren, Art Kramer, and an anonymous reviewer for their constructive comments, and to Aideen Stronge for her assistance in gathering the reference material.

References

Allen, P. A., Weber, T. A., & Madden, D. J. (1994). Adult age differences in attention: Filtering or selection? *Journal of Gerontology: Psychological Sciences, 49,* P213–P222.

Anandam, B. T., & Scialfa, C. T. (1999). Aging and the development of automaticity in feature search. *Aging, Neuropsychology, and Cognition, 6,* 117–140.

Anderson, N. D. (1999). The attentional demands of encoding and retrieval in younger and older adults: 2. Evidence from secondary task reaction time distributions. *Psychology and Aging, 14,* 645–655.

Atchley, P., & Kramer, A. F. (1998). Spatial cuing in a stereoscopic display: Attention remains "depth-aware" with age. *Journal of Gerontology: Psychological Sciences, 53B,* P318–P323.

Baddeley, A. (1986). *Working memory.* New York: Oxford University Press.

Ball, K., Beard, B., Roenker, D., Miller, R., & Griggs, D. (1988). Age and visual search: Expanding the useful field of view. *Journal of the Optical Society of America, 5,* 2210–2219.

Ball, K., & Owsley, C. (1991). Identifying correlates of accident involvement for the older driver. Special Issue: Safety and mobility of elderly drivers: Part I. *Human Factors, 33,* 583–595.

Batsakes, P. J., & Fisk, A. D. (2000). Age and dual-task performance: Are performance gains retained? *Journal of Gerontology: Psychological Sciences, 55B,* P332–342..

Birren, J. E., & Schaie, K. W. (1977). *Handbook of the psychology of aging.* New York: Van Nostrand Reinhold.

Birren, J. E., & Schaie, K. W. (1985). *Handbook of the psychology of aging* (2nd ed.). New York: Van Nostrand Reinhold.

Birren, J. E., & Schaie, K. W. (1990). *Handbook of the psychology of aging* (3rd ed.). San Diego: Academic Press.

Birren, J. E., & Schaie, K. W. (1996). *Handbook of the psychology of aging* (4th ed.). San Diego: Academic Press.

Broadbent, D. E. (1958). *Perception and communication.* Oxford: Pergamon Press.

Brouwer, W. H., Waterink, W., Wolffelaar, P. C. V., & Rothengatter, T. (1991). Divided attention in experienced young and older drivers: Lane tracking and visual analysis in a dynamic driving simulator. *Human Factors, 33,* 573–582.

Bryan, W. L., & Harter, N. (1899). Studies on the telegraphic language: The acquisition of a hierarchy of habits. *Psychological Review, 6,* 345–375.

Burke, D. M. (1997). Language, aging, and inhibitory deficits: Evaluation of a theory. *Journal of Gerontology: Psychological Sciences, 52B,* P254–P264.

Bushnell, P. J. (1998). Behavioral approaches to the assessment of attention in animals. *Psychopharmacology, 138,* 231–259.

Charness, N. (1985). Aging and problems solving performance. In N. Charness (Ed.), *Aging and human performance* (pp. 225–259). Chichester: Wiley.

Connelly, S. L., & Hasher, L. (1993). Aging and inhibition of spatial location. *Journal of Experimental Psychology: Human Perception and Performance, 19,* 1238–1250.

Craik, F. I. M. (1977). Age differences in human memory. In J. E. Birren & K. W. Schaie (Eds.), *Handbook of the psychology of aging* (pp. 384–420). New York: Van Nostrand Reinhold.

Craik, F. I. M., & McDowd, J. M. (1987). Age differences in recall and recognition. *Journal of Experimental Psychology: Learning, Memory, and Cognition, 13,* 474–479.

Czaja, S. J. (1996). Aging and the acquisition of computer skills. In W. A. Rogers, A. D. Fisk, & N. Walker (Eds.), *Aging and skilled performance* (pp. 201–220). Mahwah, NJ: Lawrence Erlbaum Associates.

Deaton, J. E., & Parasuraman, R. (1993). Sensory and cognitive vigilance: Effects of age on performance and subjective workload. *Human Performance, 6,* 71–97.

Driver, J., & Baylis, G. C. (1998). Attention and visual object segmentation. In R. Parasuraman (Ed.), *The attentive brain* (pp. 299–325). Cambridge, MA: MIT Press.

Dulaney, C. L., & Rogers, W. A. (1994). Mechanisms underlying reduction in Stroop interference with practice for young and old adults. *Journal of Experimental Psychology: Learning, Memory, and Cognition, 20,* 470–484.

Faust, M. E., & Balota, D. A. (1997). Inhibition of return and visuospatial attention in healthy old adults and individuals with dementia of the Alzheimer type. *Neuropsychology, 11,* 13–29.

Filippe, S. (1996). Motivation and emotion. In J. E. Birren & K. W. Schaie (Eds.), *Handbook of the psychology of aging* (4th ed.) (pp. 218–235). San Diego: Academic Press.

Fisk, A. D., Derrick, W. L., & Schneider, W. (1986–1987). A methodological assessment and evaluation of dual-task paradigms. *Current Psychological Research and Reviews, 5,* 315–327.

Fisk, A. D., & Rogers, W. A. (1991). Toward an understanding of age-related memory and visual search effects. *Journal of Experimental Psychology: General, 120,* 131–149.

Fisk, A. D., & Schneider, W. (1984). Memory as a function of attention, level of processing, and automatization. *Journal of Experimental Psychology: Learning, Memory, and Cognition, 10,* 181–197.

Folk, C. L., & Hoyer, W. J. (1992). Aging and shifts of visual spatial attention. *Psychology and Aging, 7,* 453–465.

Foster, J. K., Behrmann, M., & Stuss, D. T. (1995). Aging and visual search: Generalized cognitive slowing or selective deficit in attention? *Aging and Cognition, 2,* 279–299.

Giambra, L. M. (1995). Sustained attention and aging: Overcoming the decrement? *Experimental Aging Research, 23,* 145–161.

Giambra, L. M., & Quilter, R. (1988). Sustained attention in adulthood: A unique large-sample, longitudinal and multi-cohort analysis using the Mackworth Clock Test. *Psychology and Aging, 3,* 75–83.

Gottlob, L. R., & Madden, D. J. (1998). Time course of allocation of visual attention after equating for sensory differences: An age-related perspective. *Psychology and Aging, 13,* 138–149.

Gottlob, L. R., & Madden, D. J. (1999). Age differences in the strategic allocation of visual attention. *Journal of Gerontology: Psychological Sciences, 54B*, P165–P172.

Greenwood, P. M., & Parasuraman, R. (1999). Scale of attention focus in visual search. *Perception and Psychophysics, 1*, 837–859.

Hahn, S., & Kramer, A. F. (1995). Attentional flexibility and aging: You don't need to be 20 years of age to split the beam. *Psychology and Aging, 10*, 597–609.

Hartley, A. A. (1992). Attention. In T. A. Salthouse & F. I. M. Craik (Eds.), *Handbook of aging and cognition* (pp. 3–49). Hillsdale, NJ: Erlbaum.

Hartley, A. A. (1993). Evidence for the selective preservation of spatial selective attention in old age. *Psychology and Aging, 8*, 371–379.

Hartley, A. A., & Kieley, J. M. (1995). Adult age differences in the inhibition of return of visual attention. *Psychology and Aging, 10*, 670–683.

Hasher, L., Stoltzfus, E. R., Zacks, R., & Rypma, B. (1991). Age and inhibition. *Journal of Experimental Psychology: Learning, Memory, and Cognition, 17*, 163–169.

Hasher, L., & Zacks, R. T. (1979). Automatic and effortful processes in memory. *Journal of Experimental Psychology: General, 108*, 356–388.

Hasher, L., & Zacks, R. T. (1988). Working memory, comprehension, and aging: A review and a new view. In G. K. Bower (Ed.), *The psychology of learning and motivation* (Vol. 22, pp. 193–225). San Diego: Academic Press.

Humphrey, D. G., & Kramer, A. F. (1997). Age differences in visual search for feature, conjunction, and triple-conjunction targets. *Psychology and Aging, 12*, 704–717.

James, W. (1950). *The principles of psychology* (Vol. 1). New York: Holt, Rhinehart & Winston. Original work published 1890.

Jennings, J. M., & Jacoby, L. L. (1993). Automatic versus intentional uses of memory: Aging, attention, and control. *Psychology and Aging, 8*, 283–293.

Johnson, M. H. (1998). Developing an attentive brain. In R. Parasuraman (Ed.), *The attentive brain* (pp. 427–443). Cambridge, MA: MIT Press.

Kanwisher, N. G., & Driver, J. (1992). Objects, attributes, and visual attention: Which, what, and where. *Current Directions in Psychological Science, 1*, 26–31.

Kinsbourne, M. (1980). Attentional dysfunction in the elderly: Theoretical models and research perspectives. In L. W. Poon, J. L. Fozard, L. S. Cermak, D. Arenberg, and L. W. Thompson (Eds.), *New directions in memory and aging* (pp. 113–129). Hillsdale, NJ: Erlbaum.

Kline, D. W., & Scialfa, C. T. (1996). Visual and auditory aging. In J. E. Birren & K. W. Schaie (Eds.), *Handbook of the psychology of aging* (4th ed.) (pp. 181–203). San Diego: Academic Press.

Kramer, A. F., Humphrey, D. G., Larish, J. F., Logan, G. D., & Strayer, D. L. (1994). Aging and inhibition: Beyond a unitary view of inhibitory processing in attention. *Psychology and Aging, 9*, 491–512.

Kramer, A. F., & Larish, J. F. (1996). Aging and dual-task performance. In W. A. Rogers, A. D. Fisk, and N. Walker (Eds.), *Aging and skilled performance: Advances in theory and application* (pp. 83–112). Hillsdale, NJ: Erlbaum.

Kramer, A. F., Larish, J. F., & Strayer, D. L. (1995). Training for attentional control in dual task settings: A comparison of young and old adults. *Journal of Experimental Psychology: Applied, 1*, 50–76.

Kramer, A. F., Larish, J. F., Weber, T. A., & Bardell, L. (1999). Training for executive control: Task coordination strategies and aging. In D. Gopher & A. Koriat (Eds.), *Attention and performance XVII: Cognitive regulation of performance: Interaction of theory and application* (pp. (pp. 617–652), Cambridge, MA: MIT Press.

Light, L. L. (1991). Memory and aging: Four hypotheses in search of data. *Annual Review of Psychology, 42*, 333–376.

Light, L. L. (1992). The organization of memory in old age. In F. I. M. Craik and T. A. Salthouse (Eds.), *The Handbook of Aging and Cognition* (pp. 111–165). Hillsdale, NJ: Erlbaum.

Light, L. L., & Prull, M. W. (1995). Aging, divided attention, and repetition priming. *Swiss Journal of Psychology, 54*, 87–101.

Little, D. M., & Hartley, A. A. (2000). Further evidence that negative priming in the Stroop color-word task is equivalent in older and younger adults. *Psychology and Aging, 15,* 9–17.

Li, K. Z. H., Lindenberger, U., Freund, A. M., & Baltes, P. B. (2000, April). *Walking while memorizing: Age differences in external aid use and task priority as compensation during concurrent task performance.* Paper presented at the Cognitive Aging Conference, Atlanta, GA.

Madden, D. J. (1990). Adult age differences in the time course of visual attention. *Journal of Gerontology: Psychological Sciences, 45,* P9–P16.

Madden, D. J. (1992). Selective and visual search: Revision of an allocation model and application to age differences. *Journal of Experimental Psychology: Human Perception and Performance, 18,* 821–836.

Madden, D. J., Connelly, S. L., & Pierce, T. W. (1990). Adult age differences in shifting focused attention. *Psychology and Aging, 9,* 528–538.

Madden, D. J., & Gottlob, L. R. (1997). Adult age differences in strategic and dynamic components of focused visual attention. *Aging, Neuropsychology, and Cognition, 4,* 185–210.

Madden, D. J., Turkington, T. G., Provenzale, J. M., Denny, L. L., Hawk, T. C., Gottlob, L. R., & Coleman, R. E. (1999). Adult age differences in the functional neuroanatomy of verbal recognition memory. *Human Brain Mapping, 7,* 115–135.

Marsiske, M., Delius, J., Maas, I., Lindenberger, U., Scherer, H., & Tesch-Römer, C. (1999). Sensory systems in old age. In P. B. Baltes and K. U. Mayer (Eds.), *The Berlin aging study: Aging from 70 to 100* (pp. 360–383). Cambridge, UK: Cambridge University Press.

McCalley, L. T., Bouwhuis, D. G., & Joula, J. F. (1995). Age changes in the distribution of visual attention. *Journal of Gerontology: Psychological Sciences, 50B,* P316–P331.

McDowd, J. M. (1997). Inhibition in attention and aging. *Journal of Gerontology: Psychological Sciences, 52B,* P265–P273.

McDowd, J. M., & Birren, J. E. (1990). Aging and attentional processes. In J. E. Birren, & K. W. Schaie (1990). *Handbook of the psychology of aging* (third edition, pp. 222–233). San Diego: Academic Press.

McDowd, J. M., & Craik, F. I. M. (1988). Effects of aging and task difficulty on divided attention performance. *Journal of Experimental Psychology: Human Perception and Performance, 14,* 267–280.

McDowd, J. M., & Oseas-Kreger, D. M. (1991). Aging, inhibitory processes, and negative priming. *Journals of Gerontology, 46,* P340–P345.

McDowd, J. M., & Shaw, R. J. (2000). Attention and aging: A functional perspective. In F. I. M. Craik & T. A. Salthouse (Eds.), *Handbook of aging and cognition* (2nd ed.) (pp. 221–292). Mahwah, NJ: Erlbaum.

McKnight, A. J., & McKnight A. S. (1993). The effect of cellular phone use upon driver attention. *Accident Analysis and Prevention, 25,* 259–265.

Mead, S. E., Lamson, N., & Rogers, W. A. (in press). Human factors guidelines for web site usability: Health-oriented web sites for older adults. In R. W. Morrell (Ed.), *Older adults, health information, and the World Wide Web.* Mahwah, NJ: Erlbaum.

Missonnier, P., Ragot, R., Derouesné, C., Guez, D., & Renault, B. (1999). Automatic attentional shifts induced by a noradrenergic drug in Alzheimer's disease: Evidence from evoked potentials. *International Journal of Psychophysiology, 33,* 243–251.

Molander, B., & Bäckman, L. (1994). Attention and performance in miniature golf across the lifespan. *Journal of Gerontology: Psychological Sciences, 49,* P35–P41.

Molchan, S. E., Martinez, R. A., Hill, J. L., Weingartner, H. J., Thompson, K., Vitiello, B., & Sunderland, T. (1992). Increased cognitive sensitivity to scopolamine with age and a perspective on the scopolamine model. *Brain Research Reviews, 17,* 215–226.

Morrell, R. W., Mayhorn, C. B., & Bennett, J. (2000). A survey of World Wide Web use in middle-aged and older adults. *Human Factors, 42,* 175–182.

Mutter, S. A., & Goedert, K. M. (1997). Frequency discrimination vs. frequency estimation: Adult age differences and the effect of divided attention. *Journal of Gerontology: Psychological Sciences, 52B,* P1–P328.

Nyberg, L., Nilsson, L. G., Olofsson, U., & Bäckman, L. (1997). Effects of division of attention during encoding and retrieval on age differences in episodic memory. *Experimental Aging Research*, 23, 137–143.

Owsley, C., Ball, K., Sloane, M. E., Roenker, D. L., & Bruni, J. R. (1991). Visual/cognitive correlates of vehicle accidents in older adults. *Psychology and Aging*, 6, 403–415.

Parasuraman, R. (1998). The attentive brain: Issues and prospects. In R. Parasuraman (Ed.), *The attentive brain* (pp. 3–15). Cambridge, MA: MIT Press.

Parasuraman, R., & Davies, D. R. (1984). *Varieties of attention*. San Diego: Academic Press.

Parasuraman, R., & Giambra, L. (1991). Skill development in vigilance: Effects of event rate and age. *Psychology and Aging*, 6, 155–169.

Parasuraman, R., & Greenwood, P. M. (1998). Selective attention in aging and dementia. In R. Parasuraman (Ed.), *The attentive brain* (pp. 461–487). Cambridge, MA: MIT Press.

Parasuraman, R., Greenwood, P. M., Haxby, J. V., & Grady, C. L. (1992). Visuospatial attention in dementia of the Alzheimer type. *Brain*, 115, 711–733.

Parasuraman, R., & Nestor, P. G. (1991). Attention and driving skills in aging and Alzheimer's disease. *Human Factors*, 33, 539–557.

Perfect, T. J., & Rabbitt, P. M. A. (1993). Age and the divided attention costs of category exemplar generation. *British Journal of Developmental Psychology*, 11, 131–142.

Plude, D. J., & Doussard-Roosevelt, J. A. (1989). Aging, selective attention and feature integration. *Psychology and Aging*, 1, 4–10.

Plude, D. J., Enns, J. T., & Brodeur, D. (1994). The development of selective attention: A life-span overview. *Acta Psychologica*, 86, 227–272.

Poon, L. W. (1985). Differences in human memory with aging: Nature, causes, and clinical implications. In J. E. Birren & K. W. Schaie (Eds.), *Handbook of the psychology of aging* (2nd ed.) (pp. 427–462). New York: Van Nostrand Reinhold.

Posner, M. I., & DiGirolamo, G. J. (1998). Executive attention: Conflict, target detection, and cognitive control. In R. Parasuraman (Ed.), *The attentive brain* (pp. 401–423). Cambridge, MA: MIT Press.

Posner, M. I., & Petersen, P. T. (1990). The attention system of the human brain. *Annual Review of Neuroscience*, 13, 25–42.

Ribot, T. (1903). *The psychology of attention*. Chicago: Open Court Publishing.

Rogers, W. A. (2000). Attention and aging. In D. C. Park & N. Schwarz (Ed.), *Cognitive aging: A primer* (pp. 57–73). Philadelphia: Psychology Press.

Rogers, W. A. (1992). Age differences in visual search: Target and distractor learning. *Psychology and Aging*, 7, 526–535.

Rogers, W. A., Bertus, E. L., & Gilbert, D. K. (1994). A dual-task assessment of age differences in automatic process development. *Psychology and Aging*, 9, 398–413.

Rogers, W. A., & Fisk, A. D. (1991). Age-related differences in the maintenance and modification of automatic processes: Arithmetic Stroop interference. *Human Factors*, 33, 45–56.

Rogers, W. A., Meyer, B., Walker, N., & Fisk, A. D. (1998). Functional limitations to daily living tasks in the aged: A focus group analysis. *Human Factors*, 40, 111–125.

Rogers, W. A., Rousseau, G. K., & Fisk, A. D. (1999). Applications of attention research. In F. T. Durso, R. S. Nickerson, R. W. Schvaneveldt, S. T. Dumais, D. S. Lindsay, & M. T. H. Chi (Eds.), *Handbook of applied cognition* (pp. 33–55). Chichester: Wiley.

Salthouse, T. A. (1984). Effects of age and skill in typing. *Journal of Experimental Psychology: General*, 113, 345–371.

Salthouse, T. A., Fristoe, N. M., Lineweaver, T. T., & Coon, V. E. (1995). Aging and attention: Does the ability to divide decline? *Memory and Cognition*, 23, 59–71.

Salthouse, T. A., Toth, J. P., Hancock, H. E., & Woodard, J. L. (1997). Controlled and automatic forms of memory and attention: Process purity and the uniqueness of age-related influences. *Journal of Gerontology: Psychological Sciences*, 52B, P216–P228.

Sanders, A. F. (1970). Some aspects of the selective process in the functional field of view. *Ergonomics*, 13, 101–117.

Schmitter-Edgecombe, M. (1999). Effects of divided attention and time course on automatic and controlled components of memory in older adults. *Psychology and Aging*, 14, 331–345.

Shiffrin, R. M. (1988). Attention. In R. C. Atkinson, R. J. Herrnstein, & R. D. Luce (Eds.), *Stevens' handbook of experimental psychology* (pp. 739–811). New York: Wiley.

Shiffrin, R. M., & Schneider, W. (1977). Controlled and automatic human information processing: II. Perceptual learning, automatic attending, and a general theory. *Psychological Review, 84*, 127–190.

Sit, R. A., & Fisk, A. D. (1999). Age-related performance in a multiple-task environment. *Human Factors, 41*, 26–34.

Solomons, L., & Stein, G. (1896). Normal motor automatism. *Psychological Review, 3*, 492–512.

Somberg, B., & Salthouse, T. A. (1982). Divided attention abilities in young and old adults. *Journal of Experimental Psychology: Human Perception and Performance, 8*, 651–665.

Staplin, L., & Fisk, A. D. (1991). A cognitive engineering approach to improve signalized left-turn intersections. *Human Factors, 33*, 559–571.

Stronge, A. J., Walker, N., & Rogers, W. A. (in press). Searching the World Wide Web: Can older adults get what they need? In W. A., Rogers & A. D. Fisk (Eds.), *Human factors interventions for the health care of older adults*. Mahwah, NJ: Erlbaum.

Sullivan, M. P., & Faust, M. E. (1993). Evidence for identity inhibition during selective attention in old adults. *Psychology and Aging, 8*, 589–598.

Titchener, E. B. (1908). *Lectures on the elementary psychology of feeling and attention*. New York: Arno Press.

Tomporowski, P. D., & Tinsley, V. F. (1996). Effects of memory demand and motivation on sustained attention in young and older adults. *American Journal of Psychology, 2*, 187–204.

Tun, P. A., Wingfield, A., Stine, E. A. L., & Mecsas, C. (1992). Rapid speech processing and divided attention: Processing rate versus processing resources as an explanation of age effects. *Psychology and Aging, 7*, 546–550.

Underwood, B. J. (1975). Individual differences as a crucible in theory construction. *American Psychologist, 30*, 128–134.

Underwood, G. (1993). *The psychology of attention: Volume I*. New York: New York University Press.

U.S. Department of Transportation (1994). *Traffic safety facts*. Washington, DC: National Center for Statistics and Analysis.

Warm, J. S., & Dember, W. N. (1998). Tests of a vigilance taxonomy. In R. R. Hoffman, M. F. Sherrick, & J. S. Warm (Eds.), *Viewing psychology as a whole: The integrative science of William N. Dember* (pp. 87–112). Washington, DC: American Psychological Association.

Welford, A. T. (1958). *Ageing and human skill*. Westport, CT: Greenwood Press.

West, R. (1999). Age differences in lapses of intention in the Stroop task. *Journal of Gerontology: Psychological Sciences, 54B*, P34–P43.

Zacks, R., & Hasher, L. (1997). Cognitive gerontology and attentional inhibition: A reply to Burke and McDowd. *Journal of Gerontology: Psychological Sciences, 52B*, P274–P283.

Zeef, E. J., Sonke, C. J., Kok, A., Buiten, M. M., & Kenemans, J. L. (1996). Perceptual factors affecting age-related differences in focused attention: Performance and psychophysiological analyses. *Psychophysiology, 33*, 555–565.

Twelve

Speed and Timing of Behavioral Processes

David J. Madden

I. Introduction

Virtually all measures of task performance are related in some way to either
speed or accuracy. These measures, together with underlying theories of the
information-processing requirements of
tasks, allow researchers to draw conclusions regarding changes in performance as
a function of both the demands of tasks
and the abilities of individuals. Speed has
a special status in this scientific endeavor
because speed is often viewed not only as
a behavioral measure but also as a fundamental property of the central nervous
system. This unique status of speed in
psychological research extends historically at least to the measurement of the
speed of the nervous impulse by Helmholtz in 1850 (Boring, 1957). The subtraction method used by Helmholtz was
applied by Donders (1969/1869) to the
measurement of reaction time (RT) in
tasks involving judgment and is the
basis of modern research on mental
chronometry (Sternberg, 1969). Measures
involving speed are thus of considerable
importance for understanding the changes
in performance associated with human
aging.

The majority of the research included
in this review is based on cross-sectional
comparisons between younger adults (usually in their 20s) and older adults (usually
over 60 years of age), and thus the results
reflect cohort differences as well as the
effects of age per se (Hertzog, 1996). In
this research, the dependent variable is
typically either manual or vocal RT, but
the goal is often to estimate the duration
of the component processes of task performance rather than the combined duration of all the components (i.e., total RT).
The research issues thus include the timing of these component processes as well
as the overall speed of performance. Technically, speed is a rate measure (e.g.,
events per unit time). Results are usually
expressed in terms of an absolute measure, RT, with the assumption that if cohort differences can be minimized, then
age differences in RT reflect underlying
age-related changes in the speed of information processing.

To provide focus for the present review,
the emphasis is on the implications of
speed for cognitive functioning. Age-
related changes in the speed of motor processes have been addressed in previous
editions of this handbook (Spirduso &

Handbook of the Psychology of Aging
Copyright © 2001 by Academic Press.
All rights of reproduction in any form reserved.

MacRae, 1990; Welford, 1977). The present focus will also be weighted towards investigations from experimental psychology in which RT is used as a dependent variable for testing various theories of information processing. These types of studies address theoretical issues associated with the identification of component processes rather than the definition of normative values for performance. Standardization of testing procedures and definition of normative values are more important in the psychometric literature, and excellent reviews of psychometric studies of cognitive aging have been provided by Salthouse (1991b, 1992b).

Psychometric studies are useful as a starting point, however, because it is in this context that a fundamental aspect of age-related change in cognitive function was observed. From the earliest investigations of age-related changes in performance on psychometric tests, it was apparent that although there were roughly linear age-related declines in a variety of ability measures, these changes were not uniform across the different measures. In general, tests relying primarily on accumulated knowledge (e.g., vocabulary measures) exhibited relatively little or no age-related decline, whereas scores on tests involving the efficiency of current processing (e.g., measures of spatial and reasoning abilities) exhibited declines of approximately 5–10% per decade beginning at 30–40 years of age (Salthouse, 1982). This differential decline in psychometric performance has been categorized in a variety of ways, perhaps the best known being the distinction between crystallized and fluid abilities (Cattell, 1943; Horn, 1982).

The speed of elementary perceptual-motor processes plays a significant role in this decline. Analyses of both longitudinal (Schaie, 1989) and cross-sectional (Hertzog, 1989; Salthouse, 1987; Salthouse & Mitchell, 1990) data indicate that the age differences in psychometric tests of verbal and spatial and reasoning abilities are reduced substantially by controlling statistically for paper-and-pencil measures of perceptual-motor speed. Longitudinal analyses in addition suggest that although a decline in various measures of cognitive functioning is predictive of mortality, speed-based measures are particularly important in this regard. For example, Smits, Deeg, Kriegsman, and Schmand (1999) found that after self-reported health was controlled statistically, general cognitive functioning and learning ability did not predict mortality, whereas information-processing speed, fluid intelligence, and memory were significant predictors. Bosworth, Schaie, and Willis (1999) reported that after controlling for demographic variables and psychomotor speed, only a psychometric measure of perceptual speed remained a significant risk factor for mortality. Thus, the results from psychometric studies suggest that age-related changes in perceptual speed may be a primary marker of central nervous system aging, reflecting an adaptive capacity to resist the cumulative effects of disease (Birren, 1965).

II. Assessing Age-Related Changes in Speed

If slowing is a fundamental dimension of age-related change in cognitive function, what is the best method for characterizing this dimension? There are two approaches to this issue, which Salthouse (2000b) has described as the *micro*- and *macro* approaches. These correspond roughly to the difference between the experimental and psychometric research mentioned in the previous section. In the microapproach, the focus is on the potential interactions between age and other task-specific variables, with the goal of identifying age-related changes within the context of a particular task. The microapproach relies heavily on the methodology of experimental psychology, especially the subtraction and additive factors methods for identifying stages of information processing (Sternberg, 1969). The macroapproach is concerned less with the componential analysis of individual tasks and is concerned more with distinguishing general and task-specific components of age-related change. A fundamental type of macroanalysis is the characterization of the systematic relation between younger and older adults' performance across various tasks (Brinley, 1965; Salthouse, 1992c). The macroapproach also emphasizes statistical techniques, such as hierarchical regression and path analysis, which identify the role of age as a mediating variable, among other variables, as a predictor of cognitive performance (Salthouse, 1992a, 1993b).

A. Microapproach

Investigations using the microapproach often involve the measurement of RT when the task can be performed at a high level of accuracy. These are "resource-limited" conditions (Norman & Bobrow, 1975), in which performance is limited more by participants' cognitive abilities than by the quality of the sensory information. Experiments in this tradition have yielded an extensive body of findings regarding age-related changes in several aspects of cognitive function, especially memory and attention.

1. Memory

Several experiments have reported age-related slowing in components of episodic (context-dependent) memory. The features of short-term memory have been investigated in Sternberg-type recognition tasks in which a brief (e.g., 1–7 items) set of letters or digits is presented on each trial. A consistent finding is that both search time per item (as reflected in

the slope of function relating RT to memory set size), and the duration of encoding and response processes (as reflected in the zero intercept of the RT-set size function) are longer for older adults than for younger adults (Anders, Fozard, & Lillyquist, 1972; Eriksen, Hamlin, & Daye, 1973). Anders and Fozard (1973) found that the speed of retrieval from long-term episodic memory, as assessed with pre-memorized lists of letters and digits, also decreased as a function of adult age. Anders and Fozard proposed that the older adults' retrieval rate (in terms of items/sec) was approximately half that of younger adults, for both short-term and long-term memory.

Age-related slowing in the retrieval of semantic (context-independent) information has also been observed in some tasks. Petros, Zehr, and Chabot (1983) found that when participants made different types of judgments regarding word pairs (i.e., whether the two words were physically identical, similar in name, or belonged to the same semantic category), there was a disproportionate increase in older adults' RT for the category judgments. When the judgment type was held constant across task conditions, however, the proportional age difference was constant (Madden, 1985), indicating that decision and response processes may have contributed to the Petros et al. finding. similarly, experiments on the efficiency of access to lexical (word-level) information have yielded mixed results. Balota and Duchek (1988) used a delayed pronunciation task and found that older adults benefited more than younger adults from a preexposure of the target word, suggesting an age-related slowing of lexical access. Several experiments have investigated the effect of word frequency (i.e., rare versus familiar words) on naming and word–nonword discrimination (lexical decision). The assumption is that the effect of word frequency on RT (i.e., decreasing familiarity leading to slower responses) is at least to some extent related to lexical access (Monsell, Doyle, & Haggard, 1989). The effect of word frequency on naming RT has been found both to remain constant (Allen, Madden, & Slane, 1995; Bowles & Poon, 1981) and to increase (Balota & Ferraro, 1993) as a function of age. The age-related increase may represent a slowing of lexical access, but could also be due to other factors such as an increased reliance on lexical rather than orthographic features of words (Spieler & Balota, 2000).

Investigations measuring the activation of semantic information associated with a priming context have consistently indicated that this aspect of semantic processing does not undergo substantial age-related slowing. RT for naming or decisions regarding a target word, for example, is influenced by the presentation of a priming word prior to the target: Decisions are faster when the prime and target are related semantically (relative to a neutral prime) and are slower when the prime and target are unrelated (i.e., priming benefits and costs; Neely, 1991). Both the benefit and cost component of priming effects are typically at least as great in magnitude for older adults as for younger adults, suggesting that the activation of semantic information in this type of task is resistant to age-related slowing (Laver & Burke, 1993; Madden, 1992a). Although the majority of semantic priming research has focused on verbal information, comparable results are obtained when the target is a picture rather than a word (Mitchell, 1989; Thomas, Fozard, & Waugh, 1977). The time course of semantic activation, as inferred from the manipulation of the interval between the prime and the target items (Balota & Duchek, 1988; Burke, White, & Diaz, 1987; Madden, Pierce, & Allen, 1993) is also generally similar for younger and older adults. This age constancy may reflect the architecture of the semantic system, in which summation of activation

over multiple connections among words, extending from the priming context, can compensate for any deficits in individual connections (Burke & Laver, 1990).

MacKay and Abrams (1996) emphasized that studies of memory cannot be completely independent of studies of language. Memory abilities involving verbal material and language abilities are not separate but unitary, even though different verbal memory tasks tap into these unitary language-memory abilities in different ways. Research to date, however, has focused on the recognition of isolated words rather than on the use of higher order linguistic structure (Kellas, Paul, & Vu, 1995). Stine (1990) analyzed the word-by-word reading times for single sentences presented in a recall task. The reading times for younger and older adults were affected by word-level and constituent-level variables in a similar manner. The older adults, however, were less likely than younger adults to allocate additional reading time at the end of a sentence, and more likely to allocate time at a minor clause boundary, which may reflect age-related limitations in working memory. Allen, Stadtlander, Groth, Pickle, and Madden (2000) found that syntactic regularity (e.g., intact vs. scrambled sentences) affected the speed of letter search in a similar manner for younger and older adults, implying an age constancy in the formation of sentence-level codes.

Mental arithmetic abilities are one domain in which there is semantic information with relatively limited linguistic structure. Research on age-related changes in mental arithmetic is consistent with studies of lexical processing in that, once slowing in relatively peripheral components of task performance is accounted for, there is a substantial preservation of mental addition and multiplication ability as a function of adult age. For example, there is age-related slowing in encoding digits and verbally producing an answer, but not in the rate of retrieving the arithmetic facts from long-term memory (Allen, Smith, Jerge, & Vires-Collins, 1997; Geary & Wiley, 1991; Sliwinski, 1997).

2. Attention

The topic of age-related changes in attention has been an active area of inquiry for investigations of processing speed, because attention is invoked frequently as a fundamental processing component of perceptual and memory tasks (A. A. Hartley, 1992; McDowd & Shaw, 2000). Research in this area addresses questions regarding how cognitive processing is selectively allocated, both externally, as in attending to a particular spatial location, and internally, as in attending to a set of items held in short-term memory. Attention experiments often involve analyses of RT to briefly presented visual displays. As a result, age-related decline in the extraction of feature-level information may contribute to the results, depending on task demands (Hoyer & Plude, 1982; Madden, 1992b; Scialfa, 1990). Rabbitt (1965a, b) conducted seminal work in this area, demonstrating that age differences in visual search RT were affected more by increases in the number of irrelevant items (distractors) in the display than by the number of response categories. Rabbitt proposed that older adults' performance is based on a more redundant set of perceptual cues than that of younger adults.

Attention has been investigated frequently in terms of spatial cuing, under the assumption that a visually presented cue regarding target location leads to the allocation of attention to that location (LaBerge, 1995). In general, older adults are as efficient as younger adults in using spatial cues to improve RT performance (Hahn & Kramer, 1995; A. A. Hartley, Kieley, & Slabach, 1990; Plude & Hoyer, 1986). When attentional alloca-

tion requires the use of higher order combinations of display features, however, age-related declines have been observed under some conditions (Folk & Lincourt, 1996; Madden, Pierce, & Allen, 1996; but cf. Humphrey & Kramer, 1997). After extensive practice (several thousand trials) in visual search, the allocation of attention to target and distractor items is different for younger and older adults (Fisk & Rogers, 1991).

As was evident in the work of Rabbitt (1965 a,b), an important component of attention, and perhaps one particularly vulnerable to age-related decline, is the inhibition of task-irrelevant information. Hasher, Zacks, and colleagues have conducted extensive research in this domain using RT measures, focusing on the relation between attentional inhibition and memory (Hasher & Zacks, 1988; May, Kane, & Hasher, 1995). Several findings suggest an age-related decline in inhibitory functioning. The increase in RT associated with targets that had been distractors on previous trials (i.e., negative priming), for example, is in some contexts greater for younger adults than for older adults, which has been interpreted as less efficient inhibition of the distractors by older adults than by younger adults. Interference in some Stroop tasks has been found to be disproportionately greater for older adults, suggesting an age-related decline in the effectiveness of inhibition (Spieler, Balota, & Faust, 1996). Tasks that would be expected to yield age differences in inhibition do not invariably do so, however (Kramer, Humphrey, Larish, Logan, & Strayer, 1994), and the role of inhibition as a critical source of age differences in attention tasks is actively debated (Burke, 1997; McDowd, 1997; Zacks & Hasher, 1997).

3. Evaluation of the Microapproach

The microapproach has used RT as a dependent variable to identify age-related changes (and constancy) in task-specific components of information processing. Measures of RT on an absolute scale (e.g., milliseconds) have the advantage of yielding estimates of the actual duration of information-processing components. This approach provides interpretations of age-related performance differences in terms of the theoretical models that are available currently in experimental psychology. There are important limitations, however, to this analytic approach. Some of these limitations are related to the use of between-groups designs in which the interaction between group and task condition is of primary interest. For example, the absolute magnitude of RT differences among task conditions is often magnified for the group with the higher baseline RT (e.g., older adults). This creates a scaling problem: Interactions between age and task conditions may be observed for these absolute measures even when the proportional changes are constant. It is consequently difficult to separate age differences associated with the specific demands of task conditions from those that represent a generalized age-related slowing in response to task complexity (Cerella, Poon, & Williams, 1980; Salthouse, 1985b). Another problem is that because the microapproach is focused primarily on the interaction between age and task conditions, the relative contribution of age and the other independent variables in accounting for variance in RT is not assessed. Interpretation of results using the microapproach is also complicated by the difficulty in meeting certain assumptions associated with RT analyses, such as the normality of RT distributions and the similarity between groups of participants in the relative emphasis on speed versus accuracy (Salthouse & Hedden, in press). These limitations have led researchers to adopt methods of investigation focusing on the macrolevel.

B. Macroapproach

1. Method of Systematic Relations

One widely used macroapproach focuses on the systematic relation, across task conditions, between younger and older adults' performance (Salthouse, 1992c). The development of this method was motivated by an observation reported by Brinley (1965). When the mean RTs of older adults, for a group of task conditions, are plotted in relation to the corresponding means of younger adults, the result is frequently a monotonic function with a slope greater than 1.0. The data points (task condition means) usually lie quite close to the line of best fit, and changes in task demands tend to change the positions of the data points along this line rather than the degree of fit. This function, often referred to as a task complexity function or Brinley plot, can be highly monotonic even when interactions between age group and task condition are significant statistically. The task complexity function illustrates the scaling problem associated with the microapproach, in which task condition effects are greater in absolute magnitude for the group of participants with the higher RT values. The important and extensively investigated implication of Brinley's finding is that the age differences in RT associated with performance of a particular task may represent a generalized (systematic) age-related slowing of cognitive performance, which holds across a variety of task conditions, rather than changes in specific information-processing components (Cerella, 1985; Salthouse, 1985b).

A central concern of the method of systematic relations has been the investigation of changes in the parameters of the task complexity function. Under the assumption that the task complexity function is linear, the slope can be viewed as the magnitude of age-related slowing, and multiple regression procedures can be applied to estimate changes in the function in relation to age and task condition (Myerson, Ferraro, Hale, & Lima, 1992). The slope has been observed to change in relation to several variables, but it is not clear that there is an underlying dimension associated with this change. Cerella (1985), in a meta-analysis of previously published studies, proposed that tasks involving computational processing exhibited a higher slope than those primarily involving sensorimotor processing. Madden (1988) reported that increasing perceptual difficulty (obtained by lowering the visual quality of the display items) led to an increase in task complexity slope. Lima, Hale, and Myerson (1991) proposed that the lexical versus nonlexical task domain is an important determinant of the slope.

Hale, Myerson, and their colleagues have suggested that data from task complexity metaanalyses are often best fit by a positively accelerated power function rather than a linear function, especially when the data are derived from nonverbal tasks (Hale, Myerson, & Wagstaff, 1987). Myerson, Hale, Wagstaff, Poon, and Smith (1990) developed a generalized-slowing model based on a power function characterization of task complexity effects. In this model, the duration of a processing step is inversely proportional to the information available, and age leads to the loss of information between steps. The information-loss model can also characterize task complexity effects representing individual differences in RT rather than age (Myerson, Hale, Chen, & Lawrence, 1997).

2. Mediational Models

A second type of macroapproach focuses on the evaluation of the relative magnitude of shared and unique age-related influences on variables found to exhibit age-related change (Salthouse, 1985a, 1992a, 1996a,b). A central goal of this approach is to identify variables that mediate the relation between age and criterion variables (e.g., cognitive performance). The primary methods that are used in this approach are hierarchical linear regression and what Salthouse (2000a) referred to as shared influence analysis. In hierarchical linear regression, different regression models for predicting a criterion variable are compared. A critical comparison is made between one model that includes only age as a predictor and another model in which the variance associated with a mediating variable is estimated (i.e., controlled) before the age-related variance is estimated. The degree to which the age-related variance is attenuated in the second model, as compared to the first model, is an indication of the degree to which the effect of age in the criterion measure is related to the mediator variable.

The shared influence analyses include different methods for identifying the variance that a set of variables has in common (e.g., identifying the first principal component in a principal components factor analysis). The age-related effects on that shared component are then controlled before the age-related effects on individual variables are examined. The relations among the variables and the common component are often expressed quantitatively in a structural equation model (path analysis), which uses the covariation in the data to depict hypothesized causal relationships (paths) among variables.

The application of these types of methods to cross-sectional data has led to two conclusions. First, relatively few cognitive measures have much unique age-related variance. Second, the speed of elementary perceptual motor processing (as measured from tests similar to the Digit Symbol Substitution subtest of the Wechsler Adult Intelligence Scale; Wechsler, 1981) is ubiquitous as a mediator of age-related changes in cognitive performance.

Several investigators have used this approach to identify mediators of age-related change in cognitive function. Salthouse (1991a) examined the contribution of speed and working memory to age differences in a composite measure of spatial and integrative reasoning. The hierarchical regression analyses indicated that after controlling for either speed or working memory, age accounted for no more than 18% of the variance in the composite measure of cognition. The effects of working memory, in addition, were attenuated by controlling the variance associated with perceptual speed. These results were confirmed by path analyses, in which coefficients for the direct (i.e., unmediated) path between age and cognition were generally rather small. Similarly, Salthouse and Coon (1994) found that the age-related variance in mental arithmetic performance was eliminated after controlling for perceptual speed. Lindenberger, Mayr, and Kliegl (1993) found that speed continued to mediate most of the age-related variance changes in psychometric measures of knowledge, reasoning, memory, and fluency even when all of the participants were more than 70 years of age. Lindenberger et al. also found, however, that the difference in age trends in fluid and crystallized abilities that is frequently observed in comparisons of younger and older adults (Salthouse, 1991b) was not present in this older sample. Lindenberger et al. concluded that age-related decline in processing speed leads to a convergence, or dedifferentiation, of abilities in later adulthood.

Age-related changes in episodic memory performance appear to be influenced by perceptual speed. Bryan and Luszcz (1996) and Salthouse (1996a) investigated the degree to which processing speed mediated age differences in the free recall of word lists. In the Bryan and Luscz study, hierarchical regression analyses indicated that an independent measure of processing speed (digit symbol substitution) was an important mediator of age differences in free recall. Salthouse also included, as potential mediators, derived measures, which were designed to reflect the speed of specific memory-relevant processes such as search, rehearsal, association, reorganization, and retrieval. Structural equation modeling indicated that most of the age-related influences on the individual speed variables, as well on memory performance, was mediated through a general or common speed factor, rather than through the derived measures. Park et al. (1996) used structural equation modeling to estimate the contribution of speed to long-term memory tasks that varied in their degree of difficulty. Their results confirmed that speed is a fundamental mechanism that mediates age-related changes in long-term memory performance across a range of levels of difficulty.

Age-related changes in different forms of attentional functioning are also related closely to an underlying speed factor. Salthouse and Meinz (1995) examined the influence of measures of attentional inhibition (from Stroop tasks) on working memory performance. Using the inhibition measures as mediating variables led to substantial attenuation of age-related effects in working memory. The attenuation was just as great, however, when the mediating variable was either a speed measure from the neutral condition of the Stroop task or from other elementary perceptual comparison tasks. Salthouse, Fristoe, McGuthry, and Hambrick (1998) demonstrated that although an age-related decline was evident in the ability to switch between tasks (often viewed as reflecting the efficiency of attention), the relation of age to cognitive performance was mediated by processing speed (baseline RT) rather than by task switching.

Salthouse (1996b) integrated the findings from research on mediational models, as well as the results of research using the microapproach, into a general theory of age-related changes in fluid cognition. Two central components of the theory are a limited time mechanism and a simultaneity mechanism. Salthouse proposed that changes in these mechanisms, at an elementary level, lead to changes that are observed in a variety of cognitive tasks. For example, the time available to perform higher order cognitive operations would be limited by an increase in the proportion of the available time occupied by initial processing stages. Similarly, if initial processing is slowed, then the products of this processing may not be available simultaneously as required by later operations.

3. Evaluation of the Macro Approach

Research using this approach has made a valuable contribution by demonstrating that there is a general component to age-related slowing that is shared across a variety of cognitive tasks. An important implication of this research is that before age differences in performance can be attributed to specific cognitive processes, the potential contribution of generalized slowing should be addressed. As was the case with the microapproach, however, several interpretive difficulties exist. A fundamental limitation of the method of systematic relations is that it is a primarily descriptive approach that does not easily lend itself to the development of explanatory constructs. In the context of the information-loss model, for example, there is no inherent reason for the rate of information loss to be greater for nonlexical information than for lexical information. Critics of this method have noted several other problems. Salthouse (1988) pointed out that it is important to recognize findings that are not well accounted for by task complexity. Semantic priming effects, for example, tend to be greater in magnitude for older adults than for younger adults, but not to the degree that would be expected on the basis of task complexity alone (Laver & Burke, 1993; but cf. Hale & Myerson, 1995). It is in addition difficult to rely entirely on the Brinley plot as means of discriminating generalized and task-specific age effects (Fisk & Fisher, 1994; Sliwinski & Hall, 1998).

The interpretation of changes in task complexity slope (e.g., Cerella, 1985; Madden, 1988) is problematic. Although such changes are sometimes presented as evidence disconfirming a generalized-slowing interpretation of a particular task, the variation in slope simply means that a specific model, one based on a single linear function, does not provide the best fit to the data. It is unrealistic to assume a strict dichotomy between general and task-specific models. Changes in task complexity slope are perhaps better viewed as reflecting different sources of slowing, some of which is general and some of which may be related to task-specific demands.

Ratcliff, Spieler, and McKoon (2000) proposed that the slope of the Brinley plot is not a measure of generalized slowing but rather a measure of the relative standard deviations of older versus younger adults' RTs. These authors emphasized that explanations of age-related slowing should not focus exclusively on Brinley plot slopes, but also account for accuracy, the shape of the RT distribution, and the relative speeds of correct and error responses. Ratcliff et al. developed a more theory-based approach by demonstrating how a specific model of performance of choice RT performance, the diffusion model (Ratcliff, 1978), can account for age-related slowing in terms of specific model parameters.

One limitation of the mediational modeling discussed in this section is that the distinction among different cognitive operations may only be possible at a relatively coarse level, as when, for example, perceptual speed variables are analyzed in the same model as variables representing higher-order cognitive functions (Salthouse, 2000a). Thus, whether perceptual speed is a unitary construct or can be decomposed further is an open question. The significance of the attenuation of age-related variance, by perceptual speed, is also a matter of perspective. Age often remains a significant predictor of the criterion measure even when it follows speed in the regression equation, and this age-related variance (though attenuated) may be relevant for a particular theory of cognitive aging (J. T. Hartley, 1986; Light, 1996; Madden et al., 1996). Exceptions to the fundamental nature of the age–speed relation have also been reported. Raz and colleagues found that working memory was more influential than speed as a mediator of age differences in mental imagery performance (Briggs, Raz, & Marks, 1999; Raz, Briggs, Marks, & Acker, 1999). It is also important to note that in virtually all of the modeling conducted to date, age has been measured cross-sectionally, and conclusions from the analysis of longitudinal data may be different. For example, Hultsch, Hertzog, Dixon, and Small (1998) reported that working memory was more important than semantic processing speed as a mediator of longitudinal change in episodic memory performance over a 6-year interval.

III. Alternative Approaches

A. Data Transformations

The limitations of RT as a measure of age differences in cognitive functioning have motivated the development of several alternative approaches. One alternative approach is to transform RT data in a way that (in theory) addresses the scaling problem associated with measuring RT in groups who exhibit different levels of baseline RT. Two related methods are the use of proportion scores (e.g., Burke

et al., 1987; Madden, 1985; Maylor & Lavie, 1998; Petros et al., 1983) and the use of a logarithmic transformation (e.g., Lindholm & Parkinson, 1983; Madden, 1990). The proportion transform can be used to express either the change in RT across task conditions within age groups (i.e., the RT difference between control and an experimental conditions, divided by RT in the control condition), or the proportional age-related increase in RT within each task condition. Similarly, transforming RT to log RT treats equal ratios as equal intervals. These transformations consequently represent an attempt to take into account the increase in task condition effects often exhibited by participants with higher baseline RTs (i.e., older adults). Although this approach is appealing in its simplicity, a problem is that once the data are transformed, interpretation should be based on the transformed scale, and thus the goal of interpreting changes in performance in terms of real time is lost. In addition, the proportional and logarithmic transformations involve the assumption that the task complexity intercept for the untransformed data is zero, whereas such intercepts often have negative values.

Madden, Pierce, and Allen (1992, 1993) introduced a transformation method that corrects for the age difference in baseline RTs but retains the metric of real time. In this method, a Brinley plot is calculated for the task condition means, and then the young adults' RTs are transformed by the best-fitting Brinley plot function. The assumption is that the young adults' transformed RTs are now comparable to those of the older adults, in terms of whatever pattern of generalized slowing was evident in the Brinley plot. The new data set, with transformed RTs for younger adults and untransformed RTs for older adults, can be analyzed by standard parametric methods. In an analysis of variance context, interactions between age group and task condition that remain significant following the transformation can be viewed as representing effects beyond those associated with generalized age-related slowing. As noted by Faust, Balota, Spieler, and Ferraro (1999), this transformation is limited in that it uses a single function to transform data at the individual level, and thus individual differences in the degree of slowing are not taken into account.

Faust et al. (1999) developed a technique for transforming RT that is sensitive to individual differences. These authors developed a rate-amount model in which the expected RT for a particular task is modeled as the ratio of the amount of information processing (task difficulty) over the rate of processing (the relative cognitive speed of the individual). The model proposes further that RTs for different individuals are general linear transformations of each other. In this approach, information-processing rate and amount parameters are estimated from Brinley plots obtained at the level of the individual (i.e., an individual's task condition means plotted against the overall means). The rate and amount model parameters can then be used to transform each individual's RTs to a common scale. Faust et al. reanalyzed a data set representing younger and older adults' choice-RT performance on seven nonlexical tasks (Hale, Myerson, Faust, & Fristoe, 1995) and demonstrated that interactions between age group and task condition could be detected in data transformed by the rate-amount model, even though there was a highly linear relation between the task condition means of the two groups. That is, the model could be used to identify task-specific age differences that were independent of the age-related increase in baseline RT.

B. Distributional Analyses

In the vast majority of RT investigations of age differences, performance in each task condition is estimated from the central tendency (e.g., mean or median) of a series of trials. Age differences in performance are assessed by means of parametric analyses (e.g., analysis of variance) of the mean or median RT for each combination of participant and task condition. In this approach, however, potentially valuable information is lost. Reaction time distributions (i.e., probability density functions of RT values) are typically not normal (Gaussian) in form, but are positively skewed, reflecting the fact that unusually slow responses are more common than unusually fast responses. As a result, an increase in the central tendency of the distribution may result either from a shift in the whole distribution or from an increase in the proportion of higher RT values. Several investigators have sought to recover this additional information through analyses of RT distributions.

The analysis of RT distributions is particularly useful for estimating the relative contribution of shared and unique age-related variance. Salthouse (1993a) reasoned that when the complete distribution of RTs for each participant was examined, a task-specific process such as attentional blocking (e.g., a lapse of concentration or failure of inhibition) would be evident as an increase in the magnitude of age differences for the higher RT values of the distribution (i.e., slower responses) relative to the lower RT values. Although this pattern was present, hierarchical regression analyses indicated that the age-related variance in the higher RTs was attenuated almost entirely by entering the lower RTs before age in the regression equation. Salthouse (1998) observed a similar pattern in five other RT tasks, which suggests that age-related performance changes are not attributable entirely to specific processes such as attentional lapses or inhibition failure, but instead are evident throughout the complete distribution of RTs for each individual. Anderson (1999), however, obtained evidence for unique as well as shared age-related effects. In hierarchical regression analyses of secondary-task RTs for memory tasks, she found that in some task conditions involving recall, age continued to be a significant predictor of the slower (90th percentile) secondary-task responses, even after the RTs for the faster (10th percentile) responses had been entered in the regression model. Age-related variance in the secondary-task RTs for recognition, in contrast, was attenuated entirely by controlling for the variance associated with the faster responses. Anderson concluded that two mechanisms, one reflecting generalized slowing (evident throughout the RT distribution) and one reflecting task-specific attentional demands (evident in the higher RT values), contributed to age differences in the measures of memory encoding and retrieval.

Other investigators have attempted to distinguish shared and unique age-related influences by fitting empirical RT distributions to mathematical functions with known properties. Fozard, Thomas, and Waugh (1976) used the gamma function in this manner, in an analysis of stimulus repetition effects in choice RT. Fozard et al. estimated a psychomotor component representing peripheral sensory and response processes (which would be relatively constant across trials) and a decision component (which would vary with task demands). The results indicated that increased age was associated with a shift in the whole RT distribution, and that the psychomotor component was a more important determinant of age differences in RT than the decision component.

Several experiments have used an ex-Gaussian model to characterize age-related changes in RT distributions. The positively skewed RT distribution is well described, at an empirical level, as a convolution of two component functions: exponential and Gaussian (Hohle, 1965;

Ratcliff, 1979). In the three-parameter ex-Gaussian model, the mean (mu) and variance (sigma) of the Gaussian component characterize the leading edge of the distribution (i.e., the shortest RTs), and the mean of the exponential component (tau) characterizes the tail of the distribution. Whether these parameter estimates can be mapped onto distinct components of information processing is less clear. As in the Fozard et al. (1976) work with the gamma function, it has been suggested that the parameters do reflect different aspects of processing, with the exponential component representing a task-dependent decision process and the Gaussian component representing residual processes, such as feature-level coding and response selection (Hockley, 1984; Ratcliff & Murdock, 1976). Spieler et al. (1996) found that Stroop interference was comparable for younger and older adults in the mu parameter, but that an age-related change was evident in the tau parameter. These authors concluded that the greater amount of interference observed in the older adults' tau values resulted from an increase in the number of attentional inhibitory lapses. These lapses, though a transient effect occurring on a few trials, prevented older adults from successfully inhibiting the interfering effect of the response-incongruent words.

West and Baylis (1998) obtained related results, reporting that Stroop interference had an influence throughout the RT distribution for older adults, leading to an increase in both mu and tau, but led to an increase only in the tau parameter for younger adults. Similarly, West (1999) examined age differences in the RT distributions associated with a working memory task, and found that the RT cost associated with working memory demands (responses to one-back stimuli) were observed in both mu and tau parameters for older adults, but only in the tau parameter for younger adults. West interpreted the RT distribution changes, however, in terms of whether the task condition effects were evident in a relatively few long responses or throughout the complete distribution of RTs, rather than in terms of an association between the ex-Gaussian parameters and specific aspects of information processing.

C. Speed–Accuracy Functions

Microanalytic investigations of age-related changes in speed usually focus on RT as the dependent variable of primary interest. The assumption is that in resource-limited tasks with relatively high levels of accuracy (e.g., greater than 90%), the changes in accuracy across the task conditions are relatively unimportant. Even when overall accuracy is high, however, the relative emphasis on speed versus accuracy may vary across individuals, which has consequences for the interpretation of RT. When participants are instructed to adopt a range of speed–accuracy emphases, accuracy is lowest when responses are the most rapid and highest when responses are slowest. Between these two extremes there is a monotonic increase in accuracy as a function of increasing RT (Pachella, 1974). Thus, a difference in RT between two groups of participants may not be due entirely to a difference in processing speed but rather to their preferred location on the speed–accuracy function (i.e., a response criterion effect).

The middle portion of the speed–accuracy function is often linear, and the slope (i.e., increase in accuracy per unit RT) has been viewed as representing the rate of information extraction (Pachella & Fisher, 1969). Several investigators have used response deadline and accuracy instructions to obtain a range of values on the speed–accuracy function for younger and older adults. Salthouse and Somberg (1982), using a two-choice RT task with highly discriminable stimuli (left and right arrows corresponding to left and right response keys), found equivalent speed–accuracy slopes for younger and older adults. In more complex tasks (e.g., mental rotation), however, the rate of information extraction (as reflected in the speed–accuracy slope) has been found to be relatively slower for older adults (Band & Kok, 2000; Hertzog, Vernon, & Rypma, 1993). In these latter experiments older adults also used a relatively more cautious response criterion, in the sense of being less willing to increase response speed to a level that would lower accuracy.

D. Accuracy Measures

A more extreme approach to solving the problems associated with RT measures involves forsaking RT altogether and measuring accuracy instead. This approach, by definition, has the advantage of avoiding some of the limitations associated with RT measures, although other issues remain. The effects of generalized slowing, in terms of the limited time mechanism and simultaneity mechanism (Salthouse, 1996b), for example, would be evident in accuracy measures as well as in RT. Brinley (1965) noted that the monotonic relation between younger and older adults' performance in various task conditions held for both accuracy and RT. In addition, as noted previously (section II), RT measures are typically obtained under resource-limited conditions (Norman & Bobrow, 1975), in which accuracy is high. Using accuracy rather than RT often requires data-limited conditions, in which performance is limited by the sensory quality of the displays rather than the cognitive resources available. Performance measured under resource limitations and data limitations may not be directly comparable (Santee & Egeth, 1982).

Investigations measuring accuracy have addressed issues relevant to age-related changes in speed by manipulating the temporal properties of stimulus presentation. In this approach, speed and timing are properties of the task under the control of the experimenter (independent variables) rather than features of participants' responses (dependent variables). The emphasis in this research, until recently, has been on the early stages of visual perception. Eriksen, Hamlin, and Breitmeyer (1970) examined the reciprocity between time and intensity for the identification of threshold-adjusted Landolt Cs. The critical duration or time unit over which light energy is integrated increased with age, for participants between 30–55 years of age. This result indicates that older adults can compensate for a heightened sensory threshold for light by integrating energy over a longer time period, thus effectively increasing the intensity of the stimulus. Several studies have used a backward masking paradigm, in which two stimuli (usually letters) are presented in rapid succession, and the degree to which the second (masking) stimulus disrupts the identification of the first stimulus is measured. The results indicate that the interstimulus interval necessary to avoid backward masking is relatively greater for older adults, indicating an age-related slowing of perceptual processing (Walsh, Till, & Williams, 1978).

Tasks that involve the temporal integration of two stimuli (e.g., dot matrices) into a single percept, rather than backward masking, yield a somewhat different pattern of age effects: In an analysis of four adult age groups, Di Lollo, Arnett, and Kruk (1982) found that although a form of age-related perceptual slowing was evident in both types of tasks, the age-related changes occurred earlier (before 60 years of age) for backward masking tasks than for temporal integration tasks (after 60 years of age). These authors concluded that the two types of tasks reflect different forms of age-related slowing: an increase in the duration of visible persist-

ence in the case of temporal integration and a slowing in the rate of perceptual categorization in the case of backward masking, mechanisms that may have different developmental trajectories.

J. Zacks and Zacks (1993) used accuracy to estimate age differences in the processes involved in a somewhat more complex task, visual search through a multi-item display. Zacks and Zacks used a forced-choice task combined with a staircase psychophysical technique to estimate, for displays with varying numbers of items, the duration at which a target could be detected with a fixed level of accuracy. Search rate was estimated from the duration-display size functions. The search was estimated to be more rapid when it was measured with this accuracy-based method than when it was measured from RT to longer duration displays. This result suggests that strategic processes, such as participants' rechecking their decisions before responding, may contribute to RT-based estimates of search rate. An age-related slowing of search was evident, however, in both the accuracy and the RT methods.

Ellis, Goldberg, and Detweiler (1996) developed a mathematical model to characterize age differences in the perceptual encoding and central decision-making aspects of a multiple-frame search task. The best-fitting model indicated that younger participants processed task information with a two-channel parallel system, whereas older participants relied to a greater extent on serial processing. In addition, age differences were most pronounced in the model component representing encoding speed. The duration of the average encoding time was nearly twice as long for older adults (68 ms) as for younger adults (35 ms). A related model is that of Madden, Gottlob, and Allen (1999), who found that age differences in visual search accuracy were influenced more by target detectability than by changes in response criteria.

Kliegl, Mayr, and Krampe (1994) introduced an accuracy-based method, the determination of time–accuracy functions, with potential application for a variety of cognitive tasks. In this method, presentation time is varied so that performance reaches a particular accuracy level. Kliegl et al. found that the time–accuracy function was well characterized by a negatively accelerated exponential. Analyses of the parameters of this function indicated that older adults required additional presentation time to match the performance of younger adults in each task condition. More importantly, these age differences were greater for high complexity tasks (cued recognition and figural reasoning) than for low complexity tasks (figural and word scanning) and held for proportional measures as well as for absolute ones. Kliegl et al. concluded that the interpretation of their results required task-specific assumptions regarding the type of cognitive processing involved, and that a generalized slowing model could not account for all of the age differences in performance. An important dimension, for example, appeared to be whether the task involved sequential complexity (variation in the number of independent processing steps) or coordinative complexity (organization and transfer of information between processing steps). The working memory demands of coordinative complexity led to an increased likelihood that an age-related decline in performance will be evident (Mayr & Kliegl, 1993).

IV. Functional Neuroanatomy of Age-Related Changes in Speed

A. Effects of Health Status

As noted in the Introduction, speed has a special status because it is not only a dependent variable but also a property of central nervous system functioning.

Although substantial progress in understanding age-related changes in speed can be made by measuring behavior under various task conditions, it is also important to recognize that age-related slowing is ultimately the result of changes in the central nervous system (Birren, 1965). One way of approaching this issue is to examine the influence that the general efficiency of central nervous system functioning, as reflected in health status, has on age-related slowing. The incidence of a variety of diseases (e.g., hypertension) is relatively greater in older adults, and these health problems often have measurable, though not necessarily clinically significant, negative effects on cognitive functioning (Elias, Elias, & Elias, 1990; Siegler & Costa, 1985). It is consequently important to determine the interaction between health status and speed as mediators of age-related cognitive change.

For relatively healthy individuals, investigations of the relation between health status (as measured by self-report) and age-related change in cognitive performance have yielded mixed results (Perlmutter & Nyquist, 1990; Salthouse, Kausler, & Saults, 1990). Structural equation modeling of the effects of self-rated health status indicate that this variable is a significant mediator of age-related changes in speed, although the direct effect of age on speed is greater than the indirect effect of age as mediated by health (Earles, Connor, Smith, & Park, 1997; Earles & Salthouse, 1995). When physiological measures of cardiovascular fitness are used as indicators of health status, a greater age-related slowing in some RT measures has been observed for less fit individuals (Bunce, Warr, & Cochrane, 1993), though not consistently (Stones & Kozma, 1988). The type of RT task may be critical. Kramer et al. (1999) reported that older adults, following 6 months of aerobic exercise, exhibited selective improvement on the types of

RT tasks whose performance has been postulated to be mediated by prefrontal cortical regions (i.e., executive control processes).

B. Alzheimer's Disease

Dementia, especially Alzheimer's disease (AD), leads to structural and functional changes that are distributed widely throughout the brain but are most prominent in the parietal and temporal lobes (Boller & Duyckaerts, 1997; Hoffman, 1997). Progressive impairment in memory is the hallmark of this debilitating illness and is a significant determinant of AD patients' ability to live independently. As noted previously, a decline in memory performance would be expected to result from a generalized slowing of information processing (Myerson et al., 1990; Salthouse, 1996b). Is it consequently possible to characterize AD as an exaggerated form of normal aging, in which additional damage to neural tissue accelerates the process of age-related slowing? Several experiments have used the macroanalytic techniques reviewed in section II to address this issue. The results suggest that there is a generalized component to AD patients' performance of RT tasks, as represented by a linear task complexity function (Myerson, Lawrence, Hale, Jenkins, & Chen, 1998). When younger adults are included as a comparison group, the task complexity slope is higher for AD patients than for age-matched, healthy older adults (Madden, Welsh-Bohmer, & Tupler, 1999; Nebes & Madden, 1988).

The cognitive performance of AD patients also differs qualitatively from that of healthy older adults, however, in ways that are not consistent with a one-dimensional slowing model. The increased task complexity slope, for example, indicates that the task condition RTs of the AD patients are not on the same continuum as those of the healthy older adults; a different task complexity function is required. In addition, in analyses of a semantic (lexical decision) task, Madden, Welsh-Bohmer, and Tupler (1999) found that the relation between RT and accuracy was different for AD patients and healthy older adults. Sliwinski and Buschke (1997) conducted hierarchical regression analyses of AD patients' and healthy older adults' performance on cued recall and text memory, using perceptual processing speed as a mediating variable. The results indicated that controlling processing speed statistically provided a much greater degree of attenuation for age-related variance than for dementia-related variance. That is, although the effects of age on memory performance could be viewed as being secondary to generalized slowing, because the age effects were mediated almost entirely by processing speed, memory impairment in dementia was primary in the sense that it was not mediated by generalized slowing.

C. Neuroimaging

Another approach to clarifying the contribution of changes in the central nervous system to age-related slowing involves the application of neuroimaging techniques such as magnetic resonance imaging (MRI), positron emission tomography (PET), and event-related potentials (ERPs). The application of these techniques to age-related issues is relatively recent and is accompanied by interpretive challenges (Cabeza, 2001; Grady, 1998; Madden & Hoffman, 1997; Raz, 2000). The results have demonstrated age-related changes in both brain structure (e.g., a reduction in volume of both gray and white matter) and function (e.g., a reduction in resting metabolic rate). The pattern of task-dependent activation across brain regions, as measured by PET and functional MRI (fMRI), differs with age. In some task conditions there is an age-related decline in activation, especially in occipitotemporal regions (Grady et al., 1994; Madden et al., 1997). In other task conditions older adults exhibit higher levels of activation, often in prefrontal regions, which may represent the recruitment of additional neural regions in response to cognitive task demands (i.e., functional compensation; Grady, 1998).

To determine whether changes in specific neural systems mediate age-related slowing, it will be necessary to characterize the relation between neuroimaging measures of cortical activation and behavioral measures of performance. Little is currently known, however, regarding this issue. Madden and colleagues (Madden, Gottlob, et al., 1999, Madden, Turkington, et al., 1999c), in a PET study of verbal recognition memory, reported that the covariation between activation and retrieval-related RT measures involved more cortical regions for older adults than for younger adults. Thus, older adults' recruitment of additional neural systems to support task performance may lead to increased RT. A related finding is that of Rypma and D'Esposito (2000), obtained in an fMRI study of working memory. These authors noted that within a particular brain region (dorsolateral prefrontal cortex) the correlation between activation and RT for working memory retrieval was positive for younger adults but negative for older adults. Rypma and D'Esposito suggested that older adults may require a higher level of neural activation to achieve optimal response discriminability.

As in investigations based entirely on behavioral measures, it is likely that there are both general and specific neural influences on age-related slowing. The reduction in the volume of both gray matter and white matter that occurs throughout the brain, as well as an age-related increase in cerebrovascular lesions (e.g., white matter hyperintensities), potentially contribute to age-related slowing independently of specific task demands. These general changes may lead to the

compensatory recruitment of specific neural regions. As measured by PET or fMRI, this interaction is expressed as an age-related change in the pattern of cortical activation, with older adults exhibiting a decreased activation in some neural regions and increased activation in other regions. It is also likely that there are significant contributions to age-related slowing from structural and functional changes in subcortical nuclei such as the basal ganglia (Hicks & Birren, 1970; Rubin, 1999). These nuclei receive projections from throughout the cortex and project to frontal regions. The age-related loss of dopaminergic receptors in the pathways between the basal ganglia and frontal cortex may have a central role in slowing, especially with regard to motor response processes (Bashore, 1993; Raz, 2000).

Event-related potentials recorded from scalp electrodes provide less information regarding the spatial location of cortical activation than PET or fMRI, but provide greater resolution regarding the temporal course of cortical activity, and are thus particularly relevant to issues of speed and timing. Bashore, Osman, and Heffley (1989) performed a meta-analysis of data from experiments measuring both RT and the P300 component of the ERP for younger and older adults. The P300 component has been postulated to represent the latency of cognitive events occurring prior to the response. Bashore et al. found that both the RT and ERP data yielded linear task complexity functions. As in previous RT meta-analyses of age differences in performance, the RT function exhibited a slope higher than 1.0. The P300 function, in contrast, exhibited a slope near 1.0, indicating that RT measures of age-related slowing may be influenced significantly by response processes. The intercept for the P300 task complexity function was also higher than that for the RT data, indicating an age-related slowing in some processes, perhaps encoding-related, to which the P300 component is sensitive. This latter finding is consistent with the results of the accuracy studies (e.g., Madden, Gottlob, & Allen, 1999; Zacks & Zacks, 1993) suggesting age-related performance changes are not attributable entirely to response processes. It will consequently be useful to incorporate both physiological and behavioral measures in analyses of age-related slowing (Bashore, 1994; Bashore, Ridderinkhof, & van der Molen, 1998).

V. Conclusions

As has been true historically, RT measures continue to be used extensively in investigations of age-related changes in cognitive functioning. These investigations approach the issue of age-related slowing from either a micro-or macroperspective, in the former instance focusing on the interactions between age and specific task conditions, and in the latter instance defining the unique contribution of age relative to other variables. The microapproach has several limitations, including the difficulty of both meeting underlying assumptions and distinguishing task-specific age-related slowing from a generalized effect related to task complexity. Analyses associated with the macroapproach, such as the method of systematic relations and mediational modeling, avoid some of these limitations but typically do not provide a fine-grained analysis of the components of task performance.

What has emerged from research using these different perspectives is that a substantial proportion of age-related variance in the speed and timing of performance is shared across a wide range of cognitive tasks, and that some age-related slowing is specific to particular task demands. Although generalized slowing and task-specific interpretations are often presented as irreconcilable alternatives, this type of characterization is overly simplistic. It is likely that both generalized and task-specific effects can be discerned in the results of any investigation of age-related slowing.

As analyses of age-related slowing develop further, it will be important to determine how both types of effects contribute to domains of cognitive functioning. Thus, when interpreting an age-related decline in a particular ability, such as the efficiency of memory retrieval or selective attention, a critical issue is the relative contribution of generalized and task-specific effects to the age differences in that ability. Confronting that difficult issue can be assisted by different analytic methods: The scaling problem associated with age differences in baseline RT can be addressed by the use of proportional scores or by the use of a transformation based on the task complexity function. The age-related variance unique to the task of interest can be estimated from mediational modeling techniques (e.g., hierarchical regression and path analysis) and the analysis of RT distributions. Other analytic methods, such as the application of psychophysiological and neuroimaging measures, will be useful for determining the contribution of changes in specific neural systems to age-related changes in the speed and timing of performance.

Acknowledgments

Preparation of this chapter was supported by research grants R37 AG02163 and R01 AG11622 from the National Institute on Aging.

References

Allen, P. A., Madden, D. J., & Slane, S. D. (1995). Visual word encoding and the effect of adult age and word frequency. In P. A. Allen & T. R. Bashore (Eds.), *Age differences in word and language processing* (pp. 30–71). Amsterdam: North Holland.

Allen, P. A., Smith, A. F., Jerge, K. A., & Vires-Collins, H. (1996). Age differences in mental multiplication: Evidence for peripheral but not central decrements. *Journal of Gerontology: Psychological Sciences, 52B*, P81–P90.

Allen, P. A., Stadtlander, L. M., Groth, K. E., Pickle, J. L., & Madden, D. J. (2000). Adult age invariance in sentence unitization. *Aging, Neuropsychology, and Cognition, 7*, 54–67.

Anders, T. R., & Fozard, J. L. (1973). Effects of age upon retrieval from primary and secondary memory. *Developmental Psychology, 9*, 411–415.

Anders, T. R., Fozard, J. L., & Lillyquist, T. D. (1972). Effects of age upon retrieval from short-term memory. *Developmental Psychology, 6*, 214–217.

Anderson, N. D. (1999). The attentional demands of encoding and retrieval in younger and older adults: 2. Evidence from secondary task reaction time distributions. *Psychology and Aging, 14*, 645–655.

Balota, D. A., & Duchek, J. M. (1988). Age-related differences in lexical access, spreading activation, and simple pronunciation. *Psychology and Aging, 3*, 84–93.

Balota, D. A., & Ferraro, F. R. (1993). A dissociation of frequency and regularity effects in pronunciation performance across young adults, older adults, and individuals with senile dementia of the Alzheimer's type. *Journal of Memory and Language, 32*, 573–592.

Band, G., & Kok, A. (2000). Age effects on response monitoring in a mental-rotation task. *Biological Psychology, 51*, 201–221.

Bashore, T. R. (1993). Differential effects of aging on the neurocognitive functions subserving speeded mental processing. In J. Cerella, J. Rybash, W. (J.) Hoyer, & M. L. Commons (Eds.), *Adult information processing: Limits on loss* (pp. 37–76). San Diego: Academic Press.

Bashore, T. R. (1994). Some thoughts on neurocognitive slowing. *Acta Psychologica, 86*, 295–325.

Bashore, T. R., Osman, A., & Heffley, E. F. (1989). Mental slowing in elderly persons: A cognitive psychophysiological analysis. *Psychology and Aging, 4*, 235–244.

Bashore, T. R., Ridderinkhof, K. R., & van der Molen, M. W. (1998). The decline of cognitive processing speed in old age. *Current Directions in Psychological Sciences, 6*, 163–169.

Birren, J. E. (1965). Age changes in speed of behavior: Its central nature and physiological correlates. In A. T. Welford & J. E. Birren (Eds.), *Behavior, aging, and the nervous system* (pp. 191–216). Springfield, IL: Charles C. Thomas.

Boller, F., & Duyckaerts, C. (1997). Alzheimer disease: Clinical and anatomic aspects. In T. E. Feinberg & M. J. Farah (Eds.), *Behavioral neurology and neuropsychology* (pp. 521–544). New York: McGraw-Hill.

Boring, E. G. (1957). *A history of experimental psychology*. New York: Appleton-Century-Crofts.

Bosworth, H. B., Schaie, K. W., & Willis, S. L. (1999). Cognitive and sociodemographic risk factors for mortality in the Seattle Longitudinal Study. *Journal of Gerontology: Psychological Sciences, 54B*, P273–P282.

Bowles, N. L., & Poon, L. W. (1981). The effect of age on speed of lexical access. *Experimental Aging Research, 7*, 417–426.

Briggs, S. D., Raz, N., & Marks, W. (1999). Age-related deficits in generation and manipulation of mental images: I. The role of sensorimotor speed and working memory. *Psychology and Aging, 14*, 427–435.

Brinley, J. F. (1965). Cognitive sets, speed and accuracy of performance in the elderly. In A. T. Welford, & J. E. Birren (Eds.), *Behavior, aging, and the nervous system* (pp. 114–149). Springfield, IL: Thomas.

Bryan, J., & Luszcz, M. A. (1996). Speed of information processing as a mediator between age and free-recall performance. *Psychology and Aging, 11*, 3–9.

Bunce, D. J., Warr, P. B., & Cochrane, T. (1993). Blocks in choice responding as a function of age and physical fitness. *Psychology and Aging, 8*, 26–33.

Burke, D. M. (1997). Language, aging, and inhibitory deficits: Evaluation of a theory. *Journal of Gerontology: Psychological Sciences, 52B*, P254–P264.

Burke, D. M., & Laver, G. D. (1990). Aging and word retrieval: Selective age deficits in language. In E. A. Lovelace (Ed.), *Aging and cognition: Mental processes, self awareness and interventions* (pp. 281–300). Amsterdam: North-Holland.

Burke, D. M., White, H., & Diaz, D. L. (1987). Semantic priming in young and older adults: Evidence for age constancy in automatic and attentional processes. *Journal of Experimental Psychology: Human Perception and Performance, 13,* 79–88.

Cabeza, R. (2001). Functional neuroimaging of cognitive aging. In R. Cabeza & A. Kingstone (Eds.), *Handbook of functional neuroimaging of cognition* (pp. 331–377). Cambridge, MA: MIT Press.

Cattell, R. B. (1943). The measurement of adult intelligence. *Psychological Bulletin, 40,* 153–193.

Cerella, J. (1985). Information processing rates in the elderly. *Psychological Bulletin, 98,* 67–83.

Cerella, J., Poon, L. W., & Williams, D. M. (1980). Age and the complexity hypothesis. In L. W. Poon (Ed.), *Aging in the 1980s: Psychological issues* (pp. 332–340). Washington, DC: American Psychological Association.

Di Lollo, V., Arnett, J. L., & Kruk, R. V. (1982). Age-related changes in rate of visual information processing. *Journal of Experimental Psychology: Human Perception and Performance, 8,* 225–237.

Donders, F. C. (1969). On the speed of mental processes. Translation by W. G. Koster in W. G. Koster (Ed.), *Attention and performance II* (pp. 412–431). Amsterdam: North Holland. Original work published 1869.

Earles, J. L. K., Connor, L. T., Smith, A. D., & Park, D. C. (1997). Interrelations of age, self-reported health, speed, and memory. *Psychology and Aging, 12,* 675–683.

Earles, J. L. (K.), & Salthouse, T. A. (1995). Interrelations of age, health, and speed. *Journal of Gerontology: Psychological Sciences, 50B,* P33–P41.

Elias, M. F., Elias, J. W., & Elias, P. K. (1990). Biological and health influences on behavior. In J. E. Birren & K. W. Schaie (Eds.), *Handbook of the psychology of aging* (3rd ed.), (pp. 79–102). San Diego: Academic Press.

Ellias, R. D., Goldberg, J. H., & Detweiler, M. C. (1996). Predicting age-related differences in visual information processing using a two-stage queuing model. *Journal of Gerontology: Psychological Sciences, 51B,* P155–P165.

Eriksen, C. W., Hamlin, R. M., & Breitmeyer, R. G. (1970). Temporal factors in visual perception as related to aging. *Perception & Psychophysics, 7,* 354–356.

Eriksen, C. W., Hamlin, R. M., & Daye, C. (1973). Aging adults and rate of memory scan. *Bulletin of Psychonomic Society, 1,* 259–260.

Faust, M. E., Balota, D. A., Spieler, D. H., & Ferraro, F. R. (1999). Individual differences in information-processing rate and amount: Implications for group differences in response latency. *Psychological Bulletin, 125,* 777–799.

Fisk, A. D., & Fisher, D. L. (1994). Brinley plots and theories of aging: The explicit, muddled, and implicit debates. *Journal of Gerontology: Psychological Sciences, 49,* P81–P89.

Fisk, A. D., & Rogers, W. A. (1991). Toward an understanding of age-related memory and visual search effects. *Journal of Experimental Psychology: General, 120,* 131–149.

Folk, C. L., & Lincourt, A. E. (1996). The effects of age on guided conjunction search. *Experimental Aging Research, 22,* 99–118.

Fozard, J. L., Thomas, C. J., & Waugh, N. C. (1976). Effects of age and frequency of stimulus repetitions on two-choice reaction time. *Journal of Gerontology, 31,* 556–563.

Geary, D. C., & Wiley, J. G. (1991). Cognitive addition: Strategy choice and speed-of-processing differences in young and elderly adults. *Psychology and Aging, 6,* 474–483.

Grady, C. L. (1998). Brain imaging and age-related changes in cognition. *Experimental Gerontology, 33,* 661–673.

Grady, C. L., Maisog, J. M., Horwitz, B., Ungerleider, L. G., Mentis, M. J., Salerno, J. A., Pietrini, P., Wagner, E., & Haxby, J. V. (1994). Age-related changes in cortical blood flow activation during visual processing of faces and location. *The Journal of Neuroscience, 14,* 1450–1462.

Hahn, S., & Kramer, A. F. (1995). Attentional flexibility and aging: You don't need to be 20 years of age to split the beam. *Psychology and Aging, 10,* 597–609.

Hale, S., & Myerson, J. (1995). Fifty years older, fifty percent slower? Meta-analytic regression models and semantic context effects. *Aging and Cognition, 2,* 132–145.

Hale, S., Myerson, J., Faust, M., & Fristoe, N. (1995). Converging evidence for domain-specific slowing from multiple nonlexical tasks and multiple analytic methods. *Journal of Gerontology: Psychological Sciences, 50B*, P202–P211.

Hale, S., Myerson, J., & Wagstaff, D. (1987). General slowing of nonverbal information processing: Evidence for a power law. *Journal of Gerontology, 42*, 132–136.

Hartley, A. A. (1992). Attention. In F. I. M. Craik & T. A. Salthouse (Eds.), *The handbook of aging and cognition* (pp. 3–50). Hillsdale, NJ: Erlbaum.

Hartley, A. A., Kieley, J. M., & Slabach, E. H. (1990). Age differences and similarities in the effects of cues and prompts. *Journal of Experimental Psychology: Human Perception and Performance, 16*, 523–537.

Hartley, J. T. (1986). Reader and text variables as determinants of discourse memory in adulthood. *Psychology and Aging, 1*, 150–158.

Hasher, L., & Zacks, R. T. (1988). Working memory, comprehension, and aging: A review and a new view. In G. H. Bower (Ed.), *The psychology of learning and motivation* (Vol. 22, pp. 193–225). Orlando: Academic Press.

Hertzog, C. (1989). Influences of cognitive slowing on age differences in intelligence. *Developmental Psychology, 25*, 636–651.

Hertzog, C. (1996). Research design in studies of aging and cognition. In J. E. Birren & K. W. Schaie (Eds.), *Handbook of the psychology of aging* (4th ed.) (pp. 24–37). San Diego, CA: Academic Press.

Hertzog, C., Vernon, M. C., & Rypma, B. (1993). Age differences in mental rotation task performance: The influence of speed/accuracy tradeoffs. *Journal of Gerontology: Psychological Sciences, 48*, 150–156.

Hicks, L. H., & Birren, J. E. (1970). Aging, brain damage, and psychomotor slowing. *Psychological Bulletin, 74*, 377–396.

Hockley, W. E. (1984). Analysis of response time distributions in the study of cognitive processes. *Journal of Experimental Psychology: Learning, Memory, and Cognition, 10*, 598–615.

Hoffman, J. M. (1997). Positron emission tomography studies in dementia. In K. R. R. Krishnan & P. M. Doraiswamy (Eds.), *Brain imaging in clinical psychiatry* (pp. 533–574). New York: Marcel Dekker.

Hohle, R. H. (1965). Inferred components of reaction times as functions of foreperiod duration. *Journal of Experimental Psychology, 69*, 382–386.

Horn, J. L. (1982). The theory of fluid and crystallized intelligence in relation to concepts of cognitive psychology and aging in adulthood. In F. I. M. Craik & S. Trehub (Eds.), *Aging and cognitive processes* (pp. 237–278). New York: Plenum.

Hoyer, W. J., & Plude, D. J. (1982). Aging and the allocation of attentional resources in visual information processing. In R. Sekuler, D. Kline, & K. Dismukes (Eds.), *Aging and human visual function* (pp. 245–263). New York: Alan R. Liss, Inc.

Hultsch, D. F., Hertzog, C., Dixon, R. A., & Small, B. J. (1998). *Memory change in the aged*. Cambridge, England: Cambridge University Press.

Humphrey, D. G., & Kramer, A. F. (1997). Age differences in visual search for feature, conjunction, and triple-conjunction targets. *Psychology and Aging, 12*, 704–717.

Kellas, G., Paul, S. T., & Vu, H. (1995). Aging and language performance: From isolated words to multiple sentence contexts. In P. A. Allen & T. R. Bashore (Eds.), *Age differences in word and language processing* (pp. 87–109). Amsterdam: North Holland.

Kliegl, R., Mayr, U., & Krampe, R. T. (1994). Time-accuracy functions for determining process and person differences: An application to cognitive aging. *Cognitive Psychology, 26*, 134–164.

Kramer, A. F., Hahn, S., Cohen, N. J., Banich, M. T., McAuley, E., Harrison, C. R., Chason, J., Vakil, E., Bardell, L., Boileau, R. A., & Colocombe, A. (1999). Ageing, fitness, and neurocognitive function. *Nature, 400*, 418–419.

Kramer, A. F., Humphrey, D. G., Larish, J. F., Logan, G. D., & Strayer, D. L. (1994). Aging and inhibition: Beyond a unitary view of inhibitory processing in attention. *Psychology and Aging, 9*, 491–512.

LaBerge, D. (1995). *Attentional processing: The brain's art of mindfulness*. Cambridge, MA: Harvard University Press.

Laver, G. D., & Burke, D. M. (1993). Why do semantic priming effects increase in old age? A meta-analysis. *Psychology and Aging, 8*, 34–43.

Light, L. L. (1996). Memory and aging. In E. L. Bjork & R. A. Bjork (Eds.), *Memory* (pp. 443–490). San Diego, CA: Academic Press.

Lima, S. D., Hale, S., & Myerson, J. (1991). How general is general slowing? Evidence from the lexical domain. *Psychology and Aging, 6,* 416–425.

Lindenberger, U., Mayr, U., & Kliegl, R. (1993). Speed and intelligence in old age. *Psychology and Aging, 8,* 207–220.

Lindholm, J. M., & Parkinson, S. R. (1983). An interpretation of age-related differences in letter-matching performance. *Perception & Psychophysics, 33,* 283–294.

MacKay, D. G., & Abrams, L. (1996). Language, memory and aging: Distributed deficits and the structure of new-versus-old connections. In J. E. Birren & K. W. Schaie (Eds.), *Handbook of the psychology of aging* (4th ed.) (pp. 251–265). San Diego, CA: Academic Press.

Madden, D. J. (1985). Age-related slowing in the retrieval of information from long-term memory. *Journal of Gerontology, 40,* 208–210.

Madden, D. J. (1988). Adult age differences in the effects of sentence context and stimulus degradation during visual word recognition. *Psychology and Aging, 3,* 167–172.

Madden, D. J. (1990). Adult age differences in the time course of visual attention. *Journal of Gerontology: Psychological Sciences, 45,* P9–P16.

Madden, D. J. (1992a). Four to ten milliseconds per year: Age-related slowing of visual word identification. *Journal of Gerontology: Psychological Sciences, 47,* P59–P68.

Madden, D. J. (1992b). Selective attention and visual search: Revision of an allocation model and application to age differences. *Journal of Experimental Psychology: Human Perception and Performance, 18,* 821–836.

Madden, D. J., Gottlob, L. R., & Allen, P. A. (1999). Adult age differences in visual search accuracy: Attentional guidance and target detectability. *Psychology and Aging, 14,* 683–694.

Madden, D. J., Gottlob, L. R., Denny, L. L., Turkington, T. G., Provenzale, J. M., Hawk, T. C., & Coleman, R. E. (1999). Aging and recognition memory: Changes in regional cerebral blood flow associated with

components of reaction time distributions. *Journal of Cognitive Neuroscience, 11,* 511–520.

Madden, D. J., & Hoffman, J. M. (1997). Application of positron emission tomography to age-related cognitive changes. In K. R. R. Krishnan & P. M. Doraiswamy (Eds.), *Brain imaging in clinical psychiatry* (pp. 575–613). New York: Marcel Dekker.

Madden, D. J., Pierce, T. W., & Allen, P. A. (1992). Adult age differences in attentional allocation during memory search. *Psychology and Aging, 7,* 594–601.

Madden, D. J., Pierce, T. W., & Allen, P. A. (1993). Age-related slowing and the time course of semantic priming in visual word identification. *Psychology and Aging, 8,* 490–507.

Madden, D. J., Pierce, T. W., & Allen, P. A. (1996). Adult age differences in the use of distractor homogeneity during visual search. *Psychology and Aging, 11,* 454–474.

Madden, D. J., Turkington, T. G., Provenzale, J. M., Denny, L. L., Hawk, T. C., Gottlob, L. R., & Coleman, R. E. (1999). Adult age differences in the functional neuroanatomy of verbal recognition memory. *Human Brain Mapping, 7,* 115–135.

Madden, D. J., Turkington, T. G., Provenzale, J. M., Hawk, T. C., Hoffman, J. M., & Coleman, R. E. (1997). Selective and divided visual attention: Age-related changes in regional cerebral blood flow measured by $H_2^{15}O$ PET. *Human Brain Mapping, 5,* 389–409.

Madden, D. J., Welsh-Bohmer, K. A., & Tupler, L. A. (1999). Task complexity and signal detection analyses of lexical decision performance in Alzheimer's disease. *Developmental Neuropsychology, 16,* 1–18.

May, C. P., Kane, M. J., & Hasher, L. (1995). Determinants of negative priming. *Psychological Bulletin, 118,* 35–54.

Maylor, E. A., & Lavie, N. (1998). The influence of perceptual load on age differences in selective attention. *Psychology and Aging, 13,* 563–573.

Mayr, U., & Kliegl, R. (1993). Sequential and coordinative complexity: Age-based processing limitations in figural transformations. *Journal of Experimental Psychology: Learning, Memory, and Cognition, 19,* 1297–1320.

McDowd, J. M. (1997). Inhibition in attention and aging. *Journal of Gerontology: Psychological Sciences, 52B*, P265–P273.

McDowd, J. M., & Shaw, R. J. (2000). Attention and aging: A functional perspective. In F. I. M. Craik & T. A. Salthouse (Eds.), *The handbook of aging and cognition* (2nd ed.,) (pp. 221–292). Mahwah, NJ: Erlbaum.

Mitchell, D. B. (1989). How many memory systems? Evidence from aging. *Journal of Experimental Psychology: Learning, Memory, and Cognition, 15*, 31–49.

Monsell, S., Doyle, M. C., & Haggard, P. N. (1989). Effects of frequency on word recognition tasks: Where are they? *Journal of Experimental Psychology: General, 118*, 43–71.

Myerson, J., Ferraro, F. R., Hale, S., & Lima, S. D. (1992). General slowing in semantic priming and word recognition. *Psychology and Aging, 7*, 257–270.

Myerson, J., Hale, S., Chen, J., & Lawrence, B. (1997). General lexical slowing and the semantic priming effect: The roles of age and ability. *Acta Psychologica, 96*, 83–101.

Myerson, J., Hale, S., Wagstaff, D., Poon, L. W., & Smith, G. A. (1990). The information loss model: A mathematical theory of age-related cognitive slowing. *Psychological Review, 97*, 475–487.

Myerson, J., Lawrence, B., Hale, S., Jenkins, L., & Chen, J. (1998). General slowing of lexical and nonlexical information processing in dementia of the Alzheimer type. *Aging, Neuropsychology, and Cognition, 5*, 182–193.

Nebes, R. D., & Madden, D. J. (1988). Different patterns of cognitive slowing produced by Alzheimer's disease and normal aging. *Psychology and Aging, 3*, 102–104.

Neely, J. H. (1991). Semantic priming effects in visual word recognition: A selective review of current findings and theories. In D. Besner, & G. W. Humphreys (Eds.), *Basic processes in reading: Visual word recognition* (pp. 264–336). Hillsdale, NJ: Erlbaum.

Norman, D. A., & Bobrow, D. G. (1975). On data-limited and resource-limited processes. *Cognitive Psychology, 7*, 44–64.

Pachella, R. G. (1974). The interpretation of reaction time in information-processing research. In B. Kantowitz (Ed.), *Human information processing: Tutorials in performance and cognition* (pp. 41–82). Hillsdale, NJ: Erlbaum.

Pachella, R. G., & Fisher, D. F. (1969). Effect of stimulus degradation and similarity on the trade-off between speed and accuracy in absolute judgments. *Journal of Experimental Psychology, 81*, 7–9.

Park, D. C., Smith, A. D., Lautenschlager, G., Earles, J. L., Frieske, D., Zwahr, M., & Gaines, C. L. (1996). Mediators of long-term memory performance across the life span. *Psychology and Aging, 11*, 621–637.

Perlmutter, M., & Nyquist, L. (1990). Relationships between self-reported physical and mental health and intelligence performance across adulthood. *Journal of Gerontology: Psychological Sciences, 45*, P145–P155.

Petros, T. V., Zehr, H. D., & Chabot, R. J. (1983). Adult age differences in accessing and retrieving information from long-term memory. *Journal of Gerontology, 38*, 589–592.

Plude, D. J., & Hoyer, W. J. (1986). Age and the selectivity of visual information processing. *Psychology and Aging, 1*, 4–10.

Rabbitt, P. (1965a). Age and discrimination between complex stimuli. In A. T. Welford, & J. E. Birren (Eds.), *Behavior, aging, and the nervous system* (pp. 35–53). Springfield, IL: Charles C. Thomas.

Rabbitt, P. (1965b). An age-decrement in the ability to ignore irrelevant information. *Journal of Gerontology, 20*, 233–238.

Ratcliff, R. (1978). A theory of memory retrieval. *Psychological Review, 85*, 59–108.

Ratcliff, R. (1979). Group reaction time distributions and an analysis of distribution statistics. *Psychological Bulletin, 86*, 446–461.

Ratcliff, R., & Murdock, B. B. Jr. (1976). Retrieval processes in recognition memory. *Psychological Review, 83*, 190–214.

Ratcliff, R., Spieler, D., & McKoon, G. (2000). Explicitly modeling the effects of aging on response time. *Psychonomic Bulletin & Review, 7*, 1–25.

Raz, N. (2000). Aging of the brain and its impact on cognitive performance: Integration of structural and functional findings. In F. I. M. Craik & T. A. Salthouse (Eds.), *The handbook of aging and cognition* (2nd ed.) (pp. 1–90). Mahwah, NJ: Erlbaum.

Raz, N., Briggs, S. D., Marks, W., & Acker, J. D. (1999). Age-related deficits in generation and manipulation of mental images: II. The role of dorsolateral prefrontal cortex. *Psychology and Aging, 14*, 436–444.

Rubin, D. C. (1999). Frontal-striatal circuits in cognitive aging: Evidence for caudate involvement. *Aging, Neuropsychology, and Cognition, 6*, 241–259.

Rypma, B., & D'Esposito, M. (2000). Isolating the neural mechanisms of age-related changes in human working memory. *Nature Neuroscience, 3*, 509–515.

Salthouse, T. A. (1982). *Adult cognition: An experimental psychology of human aging.* New York: Springer-Verlag.

Salthouse, T. A. (1985a). *A theory of cognitive aging.* Amsterdam: North-Holland.

Salthouse, T. A. (1985b). Speed of behavior and its implications for cognition. In J. E. Birren & K. W. Schaie (Eds.), *Handbook of the psychology of aging* (2nd ed.), (pp. 400–426). New York: Van Nostrand Reinhold.

Salthouse, T. A. (1987). The role of representations in analogical reasoning. *Psychology and Aging, 2*, 357–362.

Salthouse, T. A. (1988). The complexity of Age x Complexity functions: Comment on Charness and Campbell. *Journal of Experimental Psychology: General, 117*, 425–428.

Salthouse, T. A. (1991a). Mediation of adult age differences in cognition by reductions in working memory and speed of processing. *Psychological Science, 2*, 179–183.

Salthouse, T. A. (1991b). *Theoretical perspectives on cognitive aging.* Hillsdale, NJ: Erlbaum.

Salthouse, T. A. (1992a). *Mechanisms of age-cognition relations in adulthood.* Hillsdale, NJ: Erlbaum.

Salthouse, T. A. (1992b). Reasoning and spatial abilities. In F. I. M. Craik & T. A. Salthouse (Eds.), *The handbook of aging and cognition* (pp. 167–211). Hillsdale, NJ: Erlbaum.

Salthouse, T. A. (1992c). Shifting levels of analysis in the investigation of cognitive aging. *Human Development, 35*, 321–342.

Salthouse, T. A. (1993a). Attentional blocks are not responsible for age-related slowing. *Journal of Gerontology: Psychological Sciences, 48*, P263–P270.

Salthouse, T. A. (1993b). Speed mediation of adult age differences in cognition. *Developmental Psychology, 29*, 722–738.

Salthouse, T. A. (1996a). General and specific speed mediation of adult age differences in memory. *Journal of Gerontology: Psychological Sciences, 51B*, P30–P42.

Salthouse, T. A. (1996b). The processing-speed theory of adult age differences in cognition. *Psychological Review, 103*, 403–428.

Salthouse, T. A. (1998). Relation of successive percentiles of reaction time distributions to cognitive variables and to age. *Intelligence, 26*, 153–166.

Salthouse, T. A. (2000a). Aging and measures of processing speed. *Biological Psychology.*

Salthouse, T. A. (2000b). Steps toward the explanation of adult age differences in cognition. In: T. Perfect & E. Maylor (Eds.), *Theoretical debate in cognitive aging* (pp. 19–49). Oxford: Oxford University Press.

Salthouse, T. A., & Coon, V. E. (1994). Interpretation of differential deficits: The case of mental arithmetic. *Journal of Experimental Psychology: Learning, Memory, and Cognition, 20*, 1172–1182.

Salthouse, T. A., Fristoe, N., McGuthry, K. E., & Hambrick, D. Z. (1998). Relation of task switching to speed, age, and fluid intelligence. *Psychology and Aging, 13*, 445–461.

Salthouse, T. A., & Hedden, T. (in press). Interpreting reaction time measures in between-group comparisons. *Journal of Clinical and Experimental Neuropsychology.*

Salthouse, T. A., Kausler, D. H., & Saults, J. S. (1990). Age, self-assessed health status, and cognition. *Journal of Gerontology: Psychological Sciences, 45*, P156–P160.

Salthouse, T. A., & Meinz, E. J. (1995). Aging, inhibition, working memory, and speed. *Journal of Gerontology: Psychological Sciences, 50B*, P297–P306.

Salthouse, T. A., & Mitchell, D. R. D. (1990). Effects of age and naturally occurring experience on spatial visualization performance. *Developmental Psychology, 26*, 845–854.

Salthouse, T. A., & Somberg, B. L. (1982). Time-accuracy relationships in young and old adults. *Journal of Gerontology, 37*, 349–353.

Santee, J. L., & Egeth, H. E. (1982). Do reaction time and accuracy measure the same aspects of letter recognition? *Journal of Experimental Psychology: Human Perception and Performance, 8*, 489–501.

Schaie, K. W. (1989). Perceptual speed in adulthood: Cross-sectional and longitudinal studies. *Psychology and Aging, 4*, 443–453.

Scialfa, C. T. (1990). Adult age differences in visual search: The role of non-attentional processes. In J. T. Enns (Ed.), *The development of attention: Research and theory* (pp. 509–526). Amsterdam: Elsevier.

Siegler, I. C., & Costa, P. T. (1985). Health behavior relationships. In J. E. Birren & K. W. Schaie (Eds.), *Handbook of the psychology of aging* (2nd ed.), (pp. 144–166). New York: Van Nostrand Reinhold.

Sliwinski, M. (J.) (1997). Aging and counting speed: Evidence for process-specific slowing. *Psychology and Aging, 12*, 38–49.

Sliwinski, M. (J.), & Buschke, H. (1997). Processing speed and memory in aging and dementia. *Journal of Gerontology: Psychological Sciences, 52B*, 308–318.

Sliwinski, M. J., & Hall, C. B. (1998). Constraints on general slowing: A meta-analysis using hierarchical linear models with random coefficients. *Psychology and Aging, 13*, 164–175.

Smits, C. H. M., Deeg, D. J. H., Kriegsman, D. M. W., & Schmand, B. (1999). Cognitive functioning and health as determinants of mortality in an older population. *American Journal of Epidemiology, 150*, 978–986.

Spieler, D. H., & Balota, D. A. (2000). Factors influencing word naming in younger and older adults. *Psychology and Aging, 15*, 225–231.

Spieler, D. H., Balota, D. A., & Faust, M. E. (1996). Stroop performance in healthy younger and older adults and in individuals with dementia of the Alzheimer's type. *Journal of Experimental Psychology: Human Perception and Performance, 22*, 461–479.

Spirduso, W. W., & MacRae, P. G. (1990). Motor performance and aging. In J. E. Birren & K. W. Schaie (Eds.), *Handbook of the psychology of aging* (3rd ed.) (pp. 183–200). San Diego: Academic Press.

Sternberg, S. (1969). The discovery of processing stages: Extensions of Donders' method. In W. G. Koster (Ed.), *Attention and performance II*. Amsterdam: North Holland.

(Reprinted from *Acta Psychologica*, 1969, *30*, 276–315.)

Stine, E. A. L. (1990). On-line processing of written text by younger and older adults. *Psychology and Aging, 5*, 68–78.

Stones, M. J., & Kozma, A. (1988). Physical activity, age, and performance. In M. L. Howe & C. J. Brainerd (Eds.), *Cognitive development in adulthood* (pp. 273–322). New York: Springer.

Thomas, J. C., Fozard, J. L., & Waugh, N. C. (1977). Age-related differences in naming latency. *American Journal of Psychology, 90*, 499–509.

Walsh, D. A., Till, R. E., & Williams, M. V. (1978). Age differences in peripheral perceptual processing: A monoptic backward masking investigation. *Journal of Experimental Psychology: Human Perception and Performance, 4*, 232–243.

Wechsler, D. (1981). *Wechsler Adult Intelligence Scale-Revised*. New York: Psychological Corporation.

Welford, A. T. (1977). Motor performance. In J. E. Birren & K. W. Schaie (Eds.), *Handbook of the psychology of aging* (pp. 450–496). New York: Van Nostrand Reinhold.

West, R. (1999). Visual distraction, working memory, and aging. *Memory & Cognition, 27*, 1064–1072.

West, R., & Baylis, G. C. (1998). Effects of increased response dominance and contextual disintegration on the Stroop interference effect in older adults. *Psychology and Aging, 13*, 206–217.

Zacks, J. L., & Zacks, R. T. (1993). Visual search times assessed without reaction times: A new method and an application to aging. *Journal of Experimental Psychology: Human Perception and Performance, 4*, 798–813.

Zacks, R. (T.), & Hasher, L. (1997). Cognitive gerontology and attentional inhibition: A reply to Burke and McDowd. *Journal of Gerontology: Psychological Sciences, 52B*, P274–P283.

Thirteen

Age-Related Declines in Motor Control

Caroline J. Ketcham and George E. Stelmach

I. Introduction

With increased age come well-known declines in motor control, including sensorimotor changes, generalized slowing, and decrements in balance and gait. This chapter briefly reviews and synthesizes many of these declines in motor performance on individuals of advanced age. For the most part, research on older adults has been concerned with documenting the declines in motor functions. Motor control declines have been tied to an array of changes in the central and peripheral nervous systems (Salthouse, 1985; Stelmach & Worringham, 1985; Welford, 1977). In most of the studies reviewed, movements performed by older adults are compared to young adults, and even after extensive practice older adults still perform at lower levels than controls (Chaput & Proteau, 1996a; Seidler-Dobrin & Stelmach, 1998). Understanding why motor functions decline is critically important to elucidating how aging processes effect the motor system and to the development of intervention programs aimed at reducing or even reversing the typical declines in motor control and coordination.

This chapter is intended to summarize the decrements and abnormalities that occur with aging, specifically those related to motor control. The sensorimotor changes that occur are addressed including reductions in brain structure, muscle composition and activation, and proprioception as well as declines in sensorimotor integration. Elucidating the multiple changes with advanced age provides a framework for understanding many of the age-related deficits. We discuss age-related deficits by examining studies that have used outcome measurements, including movement times and reaction times, as well as those that have decomposed movements through kinematics. Force control, coordination, movement variability, and increased reliance on visual feedback are also discussed in the context of movement slowing and increased variability. Subsequently, a discussion of how these changes are related to postural control is presented. Training programs established to benefit older adults by restoring or minimizing age-related motor decrements is also reviewed.

Handbook of the Psychology of Aging

II. Sensorimotor Systems

It is well known that individuals of advanced age have structural and functional changes that accrue over time and contribute significantly to decrements and abnormalities in movement control (Birren 1974; Brown, 1996; Welford, 1984). There are several sensorimotor changes that occur with increased age, including neuroanatomical reductions (Adams, 1987; Alexander, 1994; Hirai et al., 1996; Mano et al., 1992; Mink & Thach, 1991; Pujol, Jungue, Vandell, Grag & Capdevila, 1992; Sjobeck, Dahlen, & Emyloyd, 1999; Thach, 1998; Wang et al., 1998), muscular changes (Brown, 1972; Erim, Beg, Burke, & De Lucas, 1999; Galganski, Fuglevand, & Enoka, 1993; Metter et al., 1999; Welford, 1984; Roos, Rice, Connelly, & Vandervourt, 1999; Roos, Rice, & Vander roost, 1997), reduced proprioception (Ferrell, Crighton, & Sturrock, 1992; Hurley, Rees, & Newham, 1998; Pai, Rymer, Chang, & Sharma, 1997; Petrella, Lattanzio, & Nelson, 1997), and decrements in sensorimotor integration (Chaput & Proteau, 1996a, b; Hay, 1996; Teasdale, Stelmach, & Breunig, 1991; Teasdale, Stelmach, Breunig, & Meeuwsen, 1991; Warabi, Nodag & Kato, 1986). Although it is apparent that these changes contribute to the decline in motor control, their role in the cause of specific deficits is not well understood.

A. Brain Structure

Fundamental changes that occur with aging are modifications in the central nervous system (CNS), specifically neural reductions in brain regions. Although most regions undergo dramatic changes with advanced age, only those primarily related to movement are briefly reviewed here. Age-related degeneration of neurons occurs in the basal ganglia (Alexander, 1994; Mano et al., 1992; Mink & Thach, 1991; Mortimer, 1988; Pujol et al., 1992;

Rinne, Lonnberg, & Marjamski, 1990; Wang et al., 1998), the cerebellum (Sjobeck et al., 1999; Thach, 1998) and the motor cortex (Adams, 1987; Allen et al., 1983; Brody, 1976; Hirai et al., 1996). Degeneration of these regions has been linked to functional changes in the motor system in individuals of advanced age.

The basal ganglia are thought to be involved in the initiation, timing, planning, and learning of complex movements (Contreras-Vidal & Stelmach, 1995; Marsden, 1984; Mink & Thach, 1991). Lesions to the basal ganglia result in a lack of inhibition of motor function and deficits in initiation and timing of complex movements, as seen in Parkinson's disease (Alexander, 1994; Munro-Davies, Winter, Aziz, & Stein, 1999; Pirozzolo, Mahurin, & Swihart, 1991). Basal ganglia degeneration are also associated with normal aging (Naoi & Maruyama, 1999; Pirozzolo et al., 1991). Dopamine neurons in the basal ganglia decline as a result of aging by 5–10% per decade (Naoi & Maruyama, 1999). Pujol and colleagues (1992) found shrinkage of basal ganglia specifically of the substantia nigra in healthy older adults and suggested that this neuronal loss may contribute to the declines in movement spontaneity and coordination. Furthermore, dopamine concentrations have also been found to be significantly lower in older adults, with up to 50% reductions of dopamine receptors (McGreer, McGreer, & Suzuki, 1977; Rinne et al., 1990;. Wang et al., 1998). Cell losses in the basal ganglia and dopaminergic system are presumed to lead to progressive changes in the motor system such as slowing of movement as seen in older adults (Mortimer, 1988; Pirrozzolo et al., 1991; Rinne et al., 1990).

The cerebellum is thought to be involved in the coordination and timing of complex movements and contributes to the maintenance of muscle tone, stretch reflexes, gait, postural control, sensory integration, and motor learning (Bickford, Shukitt-Hale, & Joseph, 1999; Ivry, Keele, & Diener, 1988; Thach, 1998). Considerable neuronal cell losses in the cerebellum and brain stem and related declines are pronounced in the late stages of life (Luft et al., 1999; Pirozzolo et al., 1991; Sjobeck et al., 1999; Torvik, Torp, & Lindhoe, 1986). Cerebellar atrophy has been found to be nonlinear across age (Luft et al., 1999), and highly variable among individuals (Torvik et al., 1986). Although the exact cause of the neuronal degeneration is unknown, it is suggested that it may be related to a reduced supply of oxygen due to decreased cerebral blood flow, changes in metabolic supply, reduced energy production, or due to deafferentation (Bickford et al., 1999; Luft et al., 1999; Sjobeck et al., 1999). Bellgrove, Phillips, Bradshaw, and Galluci (1998) have reported similarities between aging and individuals with cerebellar dysfunction. It has been proposed that this accelerated cerebellar cell loss is associated with the increase in the number of falls as the cerebellum is important in the regulation of equilibrium and control of muscles involved in posture, mobility, balance, and smooth movements (Bellgrove et al., 1998; Ivry et al., 1988; Sjobeck et al., 1999).

Hirai and colleagues (1996) found that after age 60, activity of the motor cortex measured by a magnetic resonance imaging system decreased as seen by signal intensity. Further, Schiebel, Lindsay, Tomiyasu, and Scheibel (1975) found dendritic degeneration in the motor cortex. These changes in the motor cortex may lead to weakness and deficits in motor function (Ghez, 1981). Along with anatomical changes in the basal ganglia, cerebellum, and motor cortex, Leonard, Matsumato, Diedrich, and McMillan (1997) found that older adults showed similar relative levels of activation and inhibition of alpha motoneurons during the execution of voluntary movement compared to the young. Furthermore, the

modulation of these alpha motoneurons was delayed, resulting in temporal sequencing changes in distal muscle activity (Mankowsky, Mints, & Lisenyak, 1982). These deficits may be a result of a change in the control of synaptic transmission in the older adults' CNS. Buchart, Farguhar, Part, and Roberts (1993) found that these changes lead to the inability of older adults to reach and sustain torque levels equivalent to those of the young adults.

Changes in brain regions lead to progressive deficits in motor function in older adults. The understanding of declines in brain structure provide researchers with insight into behavioral decrements observed in adults of advanced age. However, it should be noted that even with the extended research on brain structure and function it is difficult to associate changes that occur with motor control impairments observed. Movement control impairments could be a result of a specific change in a brain structure or in how that structure relates to another. Research on the elderly has not been very successful in distinguishing between primary and secondary associations.

B. Muscle Composition and Activation

One important change that occurs with advanced age is the loss of muscle mass. Muscle fiber or muscle mass losses in older adults lead to decreases in voluntary contractile strength (Doherty, Vandervart, & Brown, 1993; Lexell, 1996; Metter et al., 1999; Rogers & Evans, 1991; Roos et al., 1997; Roos et al. 1999). There is some evidence that muscle fibers decrease as a consequence of alpha motor neuron losses in the spinal cord, which denervates many of the muscle fibers (Campbell, McConas, & Petito, 1973; Doherty et al., 1993; McComas, Quartly, & Griggs, 1997). Muscle biopsies have shown that a large portion of muscle fiber loss occurs in the type II fibers (fast twitch), which are significantly reduced with advanced age (40% reduction), whereas type I fibers (slow twitch) are less diminished compared to young adults' cross-sectional biopsies (Aniansson, Hedbera, Henning, & Grimby, 1986; Lexell, 1996; Singh et al., 1999; Welford, 1984). However, muscle loss alone cannot explain the motor coordination deficits in older adults, although it may be associated with some neurological changes that influence voluntary force production (Roos et al., 1997). It has also been found that the velocity of contracting muscle fibers decreases with advanced age (Davies & White, 1983; Larsson, Li, & Frontera, 1997; Ng & Kent-Braun, 1999; Roos et al., 1997), but this slowing does not necessarily appear to result in decreased force production (Ng & Kent-Braun, 1999).

The loss in muscle fibers has been assumed to be involved in the degeneration and reorganization of existing motor units (Doherty et al., 1993). For example, Campbell and colleagues (1973) found that subjects over 60 years in age exhibited substantial loss in motor units and significant increases in the average size of the remaining motor units. Fewer motor units to relative muscle mass has been documented by others (Brown, 1972; McComas, Fawcett, Campbell, & Sica, 1971; Roos et al., 1999, 1997). These motor units have been shown to produce stepwise forces instead of smooth ramped forces (Clamann, 1993; Cooke, Browne, & Cunningfhan, 1989; Darling et al., 1989; Davies & White, 1983; Galganski, Fuglerand, & Emica, 1993; Milner-Brown, Stein, & Yemm, 1973), as well as lower force production levels (Doherty et al., 1993; Izquierdo, Aquado, Ganzalez, Lopez, Hakkinen, 1999; Singh, 1999; Roos et al., 1999, 1997; Milner, Cloutier, Leger, & Franklin, 1995). All of these factors contribute to the loss of voluntary strength in older adults and to the reduced capability

to fully activate their muscles (Roos et al., 1999; Yue, Ranganathan, Siemionov, Liu, & Sahgal, 1999).

Muscle activation patterns have been examined in an attempt to better understand their contributions to changes in motor control and coordination. For most movements, activation patterns are organized in a triphasic pattern that consists of two bursts of activity in the agonist muscle separated by a single burst of activity in the antagonist muscle (Berardelli et al., 1996). Functionally, this agonist–antagonist–agonist pattern of muscle activation produces a smooth single-action trajectory of the limb, first to initiate movement and overcome inertial forces of the limb, and then decelerate the movement to the desired location (Berardelli et al., 1996; Brown, 1996; Buneo, Soechting, & Flanders, 1994; Darling, Cooke, & Brown, 1989; see Figure 13.1). Asymmetrical movement trajectories may be a result of modified muscle activation patterns and contribute to longer deceleration phases during discrete movements (Berardelli et al., 1996; Brown, 1996; Seidler-Dobrin, He, & Stelmach, 1998). Darling and colleagues (1989) demonstrated that older adults had a normal initial agonist burst, but the antagonist burst was abnormal. This antagonist burst was temporally disrupted compared to young, which resulted in an agonist–antagonist coactivation instead of reciprocal phasic patterns of activation (Darling et al., 1989; Seidler-Dobrin et al., 1998). Coactivation of agonist–antagonist muscles reduces movement variability and increases accuracy, however it also reduces the ability to accelerate rapidly (Seidler-Dobrin et al., 1998). Hakkinen and colleagues (1998) found that strength training increased agonist activation and decreased coactivation of antagonist muscles in elderly adults. The magnitude of increase was smaller than in young and may be explained by neural control changes as well as muscle changes. Figure

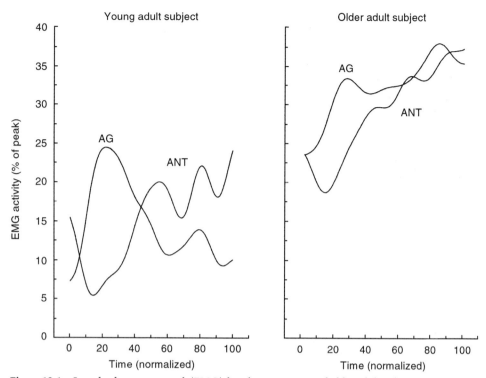

Figure 13.1 Sample electromyograph (EMG) data from a young and older adult subject. AG, agonist; ANT, antagonist. The older adult subject does not phase activation patterns in the same manner as the young adult subject, and coactivation is present in the older adult subject. (Reprinted by permission, from R. D. Seidler-Dobrin, J. He, and G. E. Stelmach, 1998, "Coactivation to reduce variability in the elderly," *Motor Control, 2* (4), 323).

13.1 shows the phase activation pattern differences between young and elderly, as well as coactivation of agonist (AG) and antagonist (ANT) muscles in the elderly.

C. Proprioception

Proprioception involves the ability to perceive where one's body is in space and how body segments relate to each other arising from receptors in the joints and muscles. Proprioception provides information of limb postures as well as an ongoing reference as to when the segment position changes. In addition, proprioception provides feedback that aids in maintaining stable balance. Classical measures of proprioception were done in the late 1950s using a tuning fork or mechanical vibration to assess subjects' sensitivity of detection. Diminished sensitivity was examined in people between 65–70 years of age using these methods (Levin & Benton, 1973). Modern methods of proprioceptive capabilities are commonly assessed by passively moving a subject's limb to a defined location using a manipulandum with vision obstructed. The limb is momentarily held in that position before returning to the starting position. Once at the starting position, subjects are asked to reproduce the defined location. Errors in absolute and signed form are used to assess proprioception. Researchers have assessed proprioceptive capabilities using this method and found that older adults have reduced joint position sense (Ferrell et al., 1992;

Hurley et al., 1998; Kaplan, Nixon, Reitz, Rindfleish, & Jucker, 1985; Levin & Benton, 1973; Pai et al., 1997; Petrella et al., 1997; Skinner, Barrack, & Cook, 1984; Lord, Rogers, Hawland, & Fitzpatrick, 1999). Commonly knee position and joint angle is assessed to measure joint position sense. Petrella and colleagues (1997) found older adults had errors of ± 1.2 degrees compared to young subjects, who only had errors of ±0.4 degrees. Similar differences were found by Kaplan and colleagues (1985) with varying time delays. Skinner and colleagues (1984) found larger errors in older adults compared to young adults in the reproduction task as well. They formulated a prediction equation, which estimates that for each additional year of age, one is expected to increase their absolute error in detection by 0.06 degrees. Similar results were also found when testing positioning sense in finger joints, with older adults producing errors of ± 3.2 degrees in the reproduction of joint position (Ferrell et al., 1992). Along these same lines, but from a psychophysical standpoint, threshold of proprioceptive detection has also been assessed. Skinner and colleagues (1984) examined proprioceptive declines in older adults and formulated an equation, which predicts the threshold of knee joint position sense as a function of age. For every year older a person is, they increase their error detection threshold by .05 degrees. Pai and colleagues (1997) also found that older adults had higher thresholds of proprioception detection. Positioning sense is impaired in various body segments in older adults and may contribute to motor function declines. It has been noted that these reproduction paradigms have a potential methodological confound in that they may be testing memory of defined target location if the reproduction movement is delayed.

Another method is therefore also commonly used to assess position sense by asking subjects to match limb position or joint angles between limbs. Kaplan and colleagues (1985) used this method in detecting joint sense in the knee. They found error of ± 4 degrees in young adults and ± 7 degrees in older adults, with the largest error at the largest matching angle. They further analyzed the errors and found that older adults had a tendency to underestimate their joint angle. Stelmach and Sirica (1986) also assessed proprioception using the matching method and observed that older adults were unable to match limb position as accurately as young subjects. These results suggested that older adults were not able to use afferent information that arises from joint and muscle receptors as well as young adults. Interestingly, when older adults participated in defining the final forearm location, they were able to overcome much of the difference in position sense. These results suggest that older adults were able to compensate for a deficit in proprioception acuity if they were allowed to select and then organize their movement to the target location (Kaplan et al., 1985; Stelmach & Sirica, 1986; Stelmach & Worringham, 1985).

D. Sensorimotor Integration

Coordinated movement is a result of integration of information from a variety of sensory receptors across several modalities. Individual sources of information including visual, proprioceptive, and vestibular feedback deteriorate with advanced age (Stelmach & Worringham, 1985). Stelmach and Sirica (1986) suggest that inaccurate sensorimotor integration, specifically proprioception, result in longer latencies to incorporate sensory information, which leads to slower and more variable movements. However, Chaput and Proteau (1996a,b) found that older subjects can use proprioceptive information effectively, but are impaired in integrating several modes of afferent feedback and appear to process them independently. Sensorimotor integration combines sensory and motor information about the environment and the initial position of the body in that environment. Several sensory modalities send afferent information to the CNS to be processed and implemented into the planned movement. These multiple inputs often provide redundant sources of sensory information about limb postures and movements. Therefore, if one source of information is disrupted, the control and coordination of the movement can continue. Warabi and colleagues (1986) performed a study in which subjects were asked to move their eyes to a target on a screen, and move a laser attached to their wrist to a target on the screen in a subsequent condition. During these conditions at random times, the target was extinguished for 1 sec following the first saccade of the eye. These researchers found that corrective movements of older adults took significantly longer than young adults on all conditions, and were additionally increased when target information was removed and saccadic movements accompanied hand movements (Warabi et al., 1986). The slower corrective adjustments were thought to be a result of reduced or distorted sensory feedback being processed and integrated, seemingly taking more time (Pohl, Winstein, & Fisher, 1996; Warabi et al., 1986).

Another line of research has assessed sensory integration in posture. Posture allows researchers to disrupt one sensory source and examine the effects on the system. Longer latencies in response to sensory feedback lead to less time to correct postural instability and may contribute to a fall (Stelmach & Worringham, 1985). Several authors have reported that conflicting or occluded visual and proprioceptive information result in substantial declines in the maintenance of postural stability (Chaput & Proteau, 1996a; Hay, 1996; Hay, Bard, Fleury,

Teasdale, 1996; Lord et al., 1999; Quoniam, Hay, Roll, & Harley, 1995; Teasdale et al., 1991a, 1992; Woollacott, 1993). Information processed and integrated can be used to confirm a postural disturbance. If integration of these multiple sources is compromised, a person of advanced age performs at less than optimal levels. Furthermore, the switching between sensory systems is a common occurrence when one modality is abruptly occluded. Teasdale and colleagues (1991a) performed an experiment in which both vision and surface were altered to assess older adults' performance on different combinations of these two variables. These conditions manipulated visual, proprioceptive, and vestibular information, which allowed researchers to assess sensory integration. Older adults had a greater range, variability, velocity, and dispersion of postural sway compared to the young. They found that older adults were substantially more impaired when the task required transitions between visual and proprioceptive information. These authors suggest this is a result of poor central integrative mechanisms (Teasdale et al., 1991a, 1992). Changes in information input from one or more modalities reduce the capability to integrate sensory information. Similarly, Hay and colleagues (1996) manipulated vision as well as proprioception by using vibration to distort incoming information. They found that the latencies in postural response from proprioceptive input were delayed as age increased. The reinterpretation of incoming proprioceptive information after deprivation resulted in increases in velocity and variability of center of pressure in older adults, and again was further amplified when vision was occluded. Hay and colleagues (1996) suggest that this is a consequence of an impaired ability to utilize multiple modes of sensory information and a higher reliance on vision. They further suggest that the multiple sources of sensory information in young adults results in redundancy, but in older adults becomes transient noise due to slow signal detection (Hay, 1996; Hay et al., 1996; Welford, 1981).

III. Movement Control

Motor actions generally become slower and more variable with age. For the most part, investigators have sought to determine which aspects of performance are most impaired. The results from these studies have helped characterize how the motor system of the older adults is compromised with advanced age. Further, the understanding of how segments of the body are controlled and coordinated in the older adults provides insight into how degradations of the sensorimotor system affect the control and coordination of complex movement, such as lifting, reaching, handwriting, and other everyday tasks. Assessment of movement from the behavioral level is typically done through kinematic, kinetic, and duration measures. Kinematics involves calculating the velocity and acceleration profiles from the position data, dividing them into different components, and examining the characteristics of the movement features recorded. Kinematics is a tool used to assess dynamical properties of a movement when temporal and spatial factors are considered. Relatedly, kinetics focus on the forces that act on the individual joints, as well as how they interact with other joints. Unfortunately, little research has been done on the kinetic differences in upperlimb movements of older adults.

A. Reaction Time

Reaction time (RT) is the time required to initiate a movement response following a stimulus presentation. This is a measure that is commonly used to assess the amount of time spent detecting a stimu-

lus and preparing the appropriate response. The intent of RT experiments is to assess the speed of information transmission in the CNS (Stelmach & Goggin, 1988). Experiments in which the response is predetermined assess the processing time from stimulus detection to initiation of a motor response (simple reaction time, SRT). Although results vary across experiments, all indicate RT is prolonged across age. Welford (1984) estimates that RT latencies increase 1.5 ms per year, or 26% from the age of 20 to the age of 60. Several researchers have found SRTs to be greater than 25% longer in older adults compared to young adults (Amrhein et al., 1991; Walker, Philbin, & Fisk, 1997; Stelmach, Goggin, & Amrhein, 1988; Cerella, 1985; Cerella, Poon, & Williams, 1980). Cerella and colleagues (1980) performed a meta-analysis of RTs and found that the slope of the line created by plotting RT of older subjects versus RT of younger subjects was greater than 1.0 (1.36) or on the order 26% slower compared to young. The authors suggest that this indicates that speed of processing is slowed in older individuals as estimated by the regression line (Cerella et al., 1980). These findings are supported by event-related potential (ERP) studies in which latencies between phases of brain activity were longer with advanced age, which results in longer processing time and slower RTs (Bashore, Oshmans & Heffley, 1997). The Baltimore Longitudinal Study followed and tested 1265 subjects in 2-yr intervals and observed changes in RT as they advanced in age. The authors found that SRT was lengthened 0.5 ms/yr, indicating that as adults advance in age, time to process information lengthens (Fozard, Vercruyssen, Reynolds, Hancock, & Quilter, 1994). Gottsdanker (1982) measured SRT in 220 subjects from 18–93 yr of age. In this study subjects were asked to press a button when they heard an auditory stimulus. To account for anticipation, the tone came at random times while a cursor moved across a projection screen. The results revealed that SRT increased approximately 2 ms/decade. Furthermore, researchers manipulated the time subjects had to prepare for a response by lengthening the time before the auditory stimulus was presented. This additional time potentially requires the older adults to maintain preparation for a specified period of time. They found that as preparation time was increased, the difference between older adults and young adults magnified, suggesting that older adults had a difficult time remaining fully prepared (Amrhein et al., 1991; Gottsdanker, 1982). Several researchers have indicated that older adult subjects have a reduced capability to maintain a prepared response and therefore do not benefit from extended preparation times (Amrhein et al., 1991; Gottsdanker, 1980, Salthouse, 1985; Smith & Brewer, 1995; Stelmach et al., 1988; Stelmach, Goggin, & Garcia-Colera, 1987; Wickens, Braune, & Stokes, 1987). However, Bellgrove and colleagues (1998) found that older adults produced slower less efficient movements when they could not completely program their movement. In order to further understand how processing time is compromised in older individuals, it is important to compare SRT results to choice reaction time (CRT) tasks where subjects must select among several response choices.

A CRT task includes additional processing time to identify a stimulus, select the appropriate response, and initiate an action. A CRT task requires the subject to choose among multiple responses. For example, a red light may mean respond with the left hand, and a green light may mean respond with the right hand. In this paradigm, the subjects may only prepare and execute the movement when the imperative stimulus is presented, because prior to that there are two possible response choices. Therefore, the differences between SRT and CRT are thought to reflect the added time it takes to complete response selection process. A consistent finding in young adults is that as the number of choices increases, RT lengthens in a linear fashion (Hick's Law, Hick, 1952). In CRT tasks researchers have found older adults to be 30–60% slower than young adults (Seidler & Stelmach, 1996; Simon, 1967; Jordan & Rabbitt, 1977; Welford, 1984). Fozard and colleagues (1994) found that CRT increased 1.6 ms/yr in the Baltimore Longitudinal Study, and this amplified as the number of CRT choices rose. Amrhein and colleagues (1991) found 29% slowing on CRTs in older adults. Furthermore, older adults were impaired when stimulus discriminability was more difficult, by reducing the view of the stimulus by a translucent plexiglas barrier (Simon & Pouraghabagher, 1978). As the number of possible choices increase, differences in RTs are amplified between young and older adults. Walker and colleagues (1997) used a 2-, 4-, and 7-item CRT paradigm to assess differences between young and older adults on RT for a baseline measure to further experiments. They found that older adults were 39%, 40%, and 45% slower respectively on these tasks. Combining the findings of CRT studies, it is apparent that older adults follow the same patterns as young adults (Hick's Law); however, older adults start with slower RTs and prolong them at a greater rate as response choice increases. This is evidence that decision-making processes are slowed in older adults in addition to the overall slowing, and that additional response choices also influence RT (Cerella, 1985; Cerella et al., 1980, Fozard et al., 1994).

The increased RTs between young and older adults on CRT tasks compared to SRT tasks may be due to the opportunity available to prepare a response in advance of an imperative signal. With the presentation of a precue, and if it contains necessary information about the upcoming stimulus, CRT can be reduced to the level of SRT. Most researchers have interpreted this finding as evidence that the precue allows subjects to prepare the appropriate response prior to stimulus preparation. These precues typically are varied in accuracy between 20 and 100%. The precue is thought to decrease RT if the subjects are capable of using the precue information. It follows then that if the precues are used to prepare the upcoming movement, subjects should produce faster RTs. However, since the accuracy of the precue varies between 100 and 20%, 20% of the time the precue is invalid. If the subject used the precue information to prepare a response when the stimulus appears, the incorrect preparation must be discarded and a new one prepared "on-line." For the most part, the older adults are able to use the precue information. Older adults were 31% slower than young adults on RT when a precue was given (Amrhein et al., 1991). Stelmach and colleagues (1988) found proportional benefits of a precue in both young and older adults. When the precue was valid, older adults had 33% slower RTs than young adults. Similarly with an invalid precue, older adults were 32% slower. Comparing the young and older adults on the beneficial effects of a valid precue, young were 35% faster in the valid precue condition, and older adults were 34% faster (Stelmach et al., 1988). Overall, older adults benefit the same proportion as young adults from a precue, but differences are apparent when varying durations of preparation time are available. It takes the elderly longer to discard the prepared action and to organize a new one (Amrhein et al., 1991; Goggin & Stelmach, 1990; Larish & Stelmach, 1982; Stelmach, Goggin, & Garcia-Colera, 1987).

Another RT procedure commonly used to assess age-related deficits in processing speed is a stimulus–response (S-R) mapping task where the compatibility between the stimulus and the response is varied. When the S-R mapping is high, RT are fast because the spatial compatibility is very congruent. However, when the mapping is low, it requires that the subject make one or more translations prior to making the correct response. A typical example of an incompatible S-R pair is press the left button with the left finger when a light in the right visual field is illuminated, or hit the right button with the right button when a left light is illuminated. Diggles-Buckles and Vercruyssen (1990) performed a S-R compatibility study in which there were three levels of S-R compatibility. First, direct S-R mapping, in which the stimulus is compatible with the response. Second, reversed S-R mapping, in which the stimulus and response are incompatible. Third, arbitrary S-R mapping, in which there was no obvious association between the stimulus and response (Diggles-Buckles & Vercruyssen, 1990). These authors found older adults to be differentially impaired in the arbitrary mapping condition compared to the young. In the reversed mapping condition, older adults, although slower, processed the information in the same fashion as young. However, in the arbitrary condition, where the S-R associates are not so apparent, the older adults were differentially impaired. This study is consistent with that of Simon (1967) in which older adults were 63% slower with incompatible S-R mapping compared to the compatible pairing, whereas young had only a 36% slowing. Combined, these findings suggest that with advanced age, spatial-motor translations become more difficult as observed by longer response latencies (Diggles-Buckles & Vercruyssen, 1990; Simon, 1967; Welford, 1977, 1984). Overall, data from SRT, CRT, precue, and S-R mapping paradigms have demonstrated that older adults have slower RTs than young adults, and further are more prolonged as complexity of the task increases, whether it is having more choices to respond to, or having to make multiple spatial transitions (Amrhein et al., 1991; Bashore et al., 1997; Cerella, 1985; Cerella et al., 1980; Diggles-Buckles & Vercruyssen, 1990; Stelmach et al., 1987).

B. Movement Time

The generalized slowing hypothesis postulated by Birren (1974) and restated by Salthouse (1985), suggests that all fundamental neural events become slower with advanced age for all cognitive and motor functions. General slowing of movements have been shown in everyday tasks such as reaching and grasping (Bennett & Castiello, 1994; Carnahan, Vanderroort, & Swanson, 1998), point-to-point movement tasks (Amrhein et al., 1991; Cerella, 1985; Cooke et al., 1989; Diggles-Buckles & Vercruyssen, 1990; Goggin & Meeuwsen, 1992; Gottsdanker, 1980, 1982; Stelmach et al., 1988), and continuous movements (Greene & Williams, 1996; Pohl et al., 1996; Wishart, Lee, Murdoch, & Hodges, 2000). Movement time (MT) is formally classified as the time from the initiation of the movement to the termination of the move-

ment. It has generally been found that as task difficulty increases, older adults are slower, with increases in movement duration compared to the young (Amrhein et al., 1991; Bellgrove et al., 1998; Cooke et al., 1989; Diggles-Buckles & Vercruyssen, 1990; Goggin & Meeuwsen, 1992; Gottsdanker, 1980, 1982; Ketcham, Seidler Van Gemmert, & Stelmach, Simon & Pouraghabagher, 1978; Stelmach et al., 1988; Strayer, Wickens, & Braune, 1987; Welford, 1977, 1984 (Figure 13.2)). MTs are approximately 30% longer in the older adults compared to the young adults in tasks ranging from simple to complex movements (Welford, 1977). Stelmach and colleagues (1988), in a simple point-to-point movement task, found older adults to have as large as 69% slower MTs compared to young adults, 421 ms compared to 132 ms respectively. Amrhein and colleagues (1991) found MTs of older adults to be 47% slower than young adults. These results vary greatly from study to study, as Walker and colleagues (1997) found slowing on the order of 26% in older adults compared to young adults in a point-to-point movement task. On a continuous bimanual and unimanual task, Greene and Williams (1996) found older adults were unable to execute the

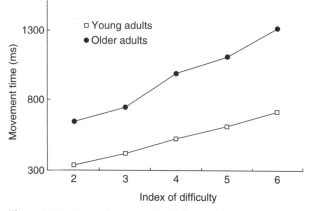

Figure 13.2 Movement times (ms) for young and older adult subjects as index of difficulty increases (adapted from Ketcham et al., 2000).

task at the same frequencies as young adults, 2.07 Hz compared to 3.76 Hz respectively on the bimanual task. Conversely, Carnahan and colleagues (1998) found older adults to be 3% faster than young adults when reaching and grasping a stationary object, and 13% faster when grasping a moving target. Similarly, Brown (1996) and Cooke and colleagues (1989) found virtually little to no movement slowing in older adults compared to young, with correlations on the order of 0.98–1.0 on a point-to-point movement task. Although they are important to assessing movement slowing, MTs do not provide information on the source of the slowing or the control of movement. Many researchers have attempted to identify components of movement slowing by decomposing movement data. Overall, researchers have found longer times to peak velocity, lower peak velocities, and longer deceleration phases of the movement. The kinematics of the movement are discussed in further detail in the subsequent section.

Another way researchers assess age-related movement slowing is to manipulate task difficulty and/or the information processed in a stepwise fashion. A common way to achieve this is using a Fitts' Law task. Fitts' Law (Fitts, 1954) states that as index of difficulty (ID) increases, movement time will lengthen in a linear fashion:

$$ID = -\log_2 2A/W \text{ bits/response,}$$

where W is target width and A is movement amplitude. Index of difficulty is an objective way to raise task difficulty in a stepwise fashion by manipulating target-size or movement amplitude or both in a point-to-point aiming task. In such tasks, movements are performed by subjects to targets of varying widths and distances apart or from the home position. Movement durations are analyzed to assess the processing rates of subjects. Older adults tend to move slower, but do not necessar-

ily make more errors (Bashore et al., 1989; Goggin & Meeuwsen, 1992; Hines, 1979; Ketcham et al., 2000; Salthouse, 1988). Ketcham and colleagues (2000) found the average MT in the older adults at an ID of 2 was 642 ms compared to 333 ms in the young controls. At an ID of 6, the average elderly MT was 1304 ms compared to 717 ms for the young controls. These results are evidence that older adults are considerably slower than the young across varying levels of difficulty. Similar results were examined by Pohl and colleagues (1996) on a continuous task in which MTs for older adults again were slower than young adults. The difference in MTs in young and older adults were amplified as task difficulty increased, with an 80-ms time difference at the high ID (5.21) compared to a 29-ms difference at the low ID (0). Others have adapted Fitts' Law and essentially found the same results (Brogmus, 1991; Fozard et al., 1994; Welford, 1977). Further understanding of age-related slowing is assessed by manipulating target width or movement amplitude separately. Researchers have found that older adults were differentially affected by increases in movement amplitude compared to the young (Goggin & Meeuwsen, 1992; Ketcham et al., 2000). However, they were not substantially different from young when target-size was manipulated. This research further suggests that the decrements in performance with larger movement amplitudes could be a result of producing and maintaining forces to execute the desired movement and result in slower MTs. Furthermore, older adults performed the task with higher accuracy than young subjects (Goggin & Meeuwsen, 1992). This research suggests that older adults tend to emphasize accuracy of their response, which also offers an explanation of why older adults are consistently slower than young adults (Goggin & Meeuwsen, 1992; Goggin & Stelmach, 1990; Larish & Stelmach, 1982).

C. Movement Components

Kinematic analysis can identify features of a movement that are altered through the aging process and contribute to slower MTs (Slavin, Phillips, & Bradshaw, 1996). Kinematic profiles provide researchers with an objective way of analyzing movement performance by dividing movements into components, including an acceleration and deceleration phase. Early attempts examined the acceleration and deceleration aspects of movement between targets. Researchers have shown that young subjects maintain a bell-shaped velocity profile when the accuracy constraint is high, whereas older adults produce a velocity curve that shows substantially longer deceleration phase times, or a lengthened tail to the curve (Bennett & Castiello, 1994; Brown, 1996; Cooke et al., 1989; Darling et al., 1989; Goggin & Stelmach, 1990; Marteniuk et al., 1987; Figure 13.3). Figure 13.3

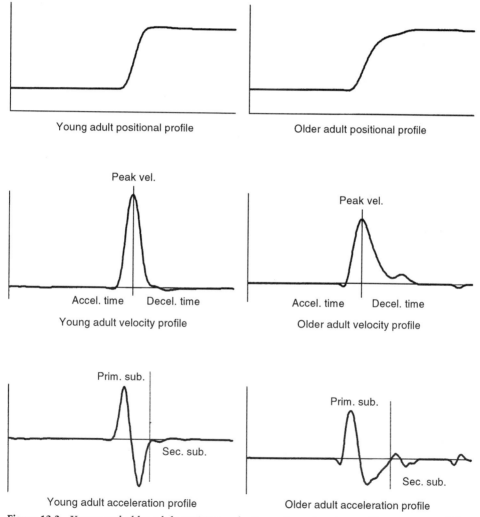

Figure 13.3 Young and older adult position, velocity, and acceleration profiles to portray differences in kinematics including acceleration and deceleration phases, as well as primary and secondary submovements. (adapted from Ketcham et al., 2000).

illustrates the differences between young controls and older adults in movement control. The acceleration phase consists of the portion of the movement before peak velocity, whereas the deceleration phase is the portion of the movement after peak velocity. The deceleration phase is considered as the "homing in phase" and constitutes a slowing down of the movement as it reaches a desired position. The acceleration phase has been found by many researchers to be shortened and the deceleration phase lengthened in older adults compared to young controls, suggesting more of their aiming movements are under feedback or corrective control (Bellgrove et al., 1998; Brown, 1996; Cooke et al., 1989; Darling et al., 1989; Goggin & Meeuwsen, 1992; Pratt et al., 1994; Warabi et al., 1986; Seidler & Stelmach, 1996). Goggin and Meeuwsen (1992) reported that older adults spent 403 ms in the deceleration phase, whereas young spent 274 ms. Similar results were reported by Brown (1996), in which the ratio of acceleration phase to deceleration phase had a range in older adults of 0.61–0.78 ms compared to young who had ratios ranging from 0.78–0.96 ms. In this analysis, a score of 1 constitutes symmetric bell-shaped velocity profiles. Cooke and colleagues (1989) found acceleration-to-deceleration ratio to be lower in older adults as well and suggest that older adults do not have deficits in the initiation of movements but more in the appropriate control of the deceleration phase. These same results have been documented by others in tasks such as wrist rotations (Pratt et al., 1994), reaching and grasping (Bennett & Castiello, 1994), and continuous point-to-point movements (Morgan et al., 1994). Morgan and colleagues (1994) controlled movement speed and analyzed associated movement kinematics. They reported that older adults performed similarly to young adults on acceleration and deceleration profiles when speed was con-

strained. They found older adults had similar times to peak acceleration compared to young, and therefore movement slowing occurred in the latter portion. They suggest that movement slowing in older adults was related to hesitation and corrections within their movements to maintain coordinated outcomes. Goggin and Meeuwsen (1992) underwent further analysis of the effects of ID on the deceleration phase of the movement. They reported that older adults were differentially affected by ID in the deceleration phase of their movement, which explained the increased MTs. Furthermore, they showed more inflections in their deceleration phase compared to young, as well as lower peak velocities.

Lower peak velocity and acceleration amplitudes have also been documented as a kinematic characteristic of older adults' movements (Bellgrove et al., 1998; Brown, 1996; Cooke et al., 1989; Goggin & Meeuwsen, 1992; Ketcham et al., 2000; Pratt et al., 1994). Young produced higher peak velocities and accelerations compared to older adults on the order of 70% greater acceleration amplitudes (Goggin & Meeuswen, 1992; Morgan et al., 1994). Pohl and colleagues (1996) found in a continuous task, peak acceleration and deceleration where 27% lower in older adults compared to young adults. Ketcham et al. (2000) found similar differences in amplitude of peak velocity, on the order of 45% lower amplitudes in older adults. Furthermore, velocity did not increase to the same degree in older adults when movement distance was increased. Gutman, Latash, Almeida, and Gottleib (1993) suggest that some of the differences in kinematics may be a result of physical differences in speed and joint dynamics and not necessarily an aspect of the control system.

To further analyze and assess movements and possible sources of slower movements in older adults, velocity and acceleration profiles can also be divided into primary and secondary submovements as proposed in the movement optimization model (Meyer, Abrams, Kornblum, Wright, & Smith, 1988; Figure 13.3). The primary submovement is thought to represent the planned or ballistic movement, whereas the secondary submovements represent corrective feedback-oriented movements. Adjustments to the microstructure of movements, as noted by the parsing of movements, indicate how movements are adjusted to certain accuracy constraints (Meyer et al., 1988). The basic tenet of the optimized submovement model is that individuals respond to movement difficulty by adjusting the submovement structure both in terms of the length and speed of the underlying primary submovement, and in the number of secondary submovements they make. The model suggests that under heightened task difficulty, performance is optimized by shortening the primary submovement and increasing the number of secondary, corrective submovements. Older adults cover proportionally less distance with their primary submovement, and consequently they have to make more secondary, corrective submovements (Bellgrove et al., 1998; Darling et al., 1989; Hsu, Huang, Isuang, & Sun, 1997; Ketcham et al., 2000; Pratt et al., 1994; Walker et al., 1997). Pratt and colleagues (1994) found that older adults spent 50% of the distance traveled in the primary submovement, which was significantly less than young adults, who spent 70% in the primary submovement. Walker and colleagues (1997) found that older adults traveled approximately 10% less distance in primary submovement compared to young adults. Ketcham and colleagues (2000) found older adults traveled 25% less distance than young controls in the primary submovement. The shortening of the primary submovement may be a result of the inability of older adults to prepare and organize the movement, reduced proprioception, or

abnormal muscle activation patterns. The consequence on making a short primary submovement is a longer distance to travel in the secondary submovements. Analyses have shown that compared to the young adults, older adults made many more secondary, corrective submovements as they approach a target, making on average one or more corrective movements (Goggin & Meeuwsen, 1992; Hsu et al., 1997; Ketcham et al., 2000; Pohl et al., 1996; Pratt et al., 1994; Seidler & Stelmach, 1996; Seidler-Dobrin et al., 1998; Walker et al., 1997). Two suggestions have been brought forth by these researchers as explanations to these shortened primary submovements: (a) that older adults rely more on feedback, primarily visual, to control their movements to the desired position (see section III. F, Visual Monitoring); (b) that older adults are unable to produce enough force to propel their limb to the desired target (see section III. D, Force Control). This movement subparsing analysis has given researchers an additional tool to identify components of movement slowing and variability in older adults.

D. Force Control

Another area of research, which has received a great deal of attention, is force control and regulation in older adults. Force control is an elementary component of movement production and can provide insight into how movements are initiated and controlled. Researchers have found that with advanced age force production and regulation decreases, which can limit the ability to make fast and accurate movements (Brown, 1996; Campbell et al., 1973; Clamann, 1993; Cooke et al., 1989; Darling et al., 1989; Davies & White, 1983; Doherty et al., 1993; Galganski et al., 1993; Izquierdo et al., 1999; Karlsson, & Larsson, 1978; Milner-Brown et al., 1973; Milner et al., 1995; Roos et al., 1999; Singh et al., 1999;

Stelmach, Teasdale, & Worringham, 1989). Similarly, fine motor skills such as precision grip are also limited (Cole & Beck, 1994; Cole, Rotella, & Harper, 1999; Lazarus & Haynes, 1997; Kinoshita & Francis, 1996). The knowledge that older adults produce lower isometric and dynamic forces has been established in early studies of force (Campbell et al., 1973; Larsson & Karlsson, 1978; McDonagh, White, & Davies, 1984). Recent research has assessed force production and rate of force production from a functional and physiological standpoint. Researchers attempt to assess and understand deficits in force production and variability. Kinoshita and Francis (1996) suggest that older adults show a decline in force production capacity exhibited by an inability to reach target forces with a single burst. In contrast to young adults, the older adults produced multiple force bursts to reach a desired force level, not a smooth ramping of force (Brown, 1996; Galganski et al., 1993). These findings were substantially pronounced at low levels of force production and less apparent at high levels. This suggests that forces can be produced by older adults, but the smoothness of production is reduced in older adults (Galganski et al., 1993). However, it has been shown when force production is normalized that older subjects show an inability to reach and maintain force levels comparable to young controls, and therefore may be related to more than muscle atrophy (Bruce, Newton, & Woledge, 1989). Stelmach and colleagues (1989) documented amplitude and variability on isometric force contractions and found that older adults generated lower peak forces and more variability than young adults. These researchers showed that older adults had substantially lower peak velocities at 45% of subjects maximum, approximately 15 N, and had slightly longer rate of peak force production, approximately 20 ms. Ng and Kent-Braun (1999) have similarly found

that older adults have 20 ms longer times to peak force production as well as 60 N lower peak force production. They relate these changes to motor unit reorganization and muscle composition changes. Similar speculations have been made by several researchers in the recent past (Erim et al., 1999; Galganski et al., 1993; Hakkinen et al., 1996; Yue et al., 1999). Izquierdo and colleagues (1999) have related these declines to lower muscle mass, with 13% less mass in older adults compared to young controls. It is important to examine the physiological changes associated with advanced age (motor unit reconfiguration, loss of muscle mass, changes in fiber-typed ratios, and conduction velocity of neuromuscular connections) and relate them to deficits in the control of force output (Brown, 1996; Bruce et al., 1989).

The suggestion from movement subparsing analyses is that the differences between young and older adults may be attributed to the inability to produce the necessary forces to propel the limb all the way to a target in a single step (Walker et al., 1997). In this study, they compared peak amplitudes of the force produced when there were no target accuracy constraints. Under those conditions, the older adults produced forces that were identical to those of the young. These data suggest that it is not an inability to produce rapid force that causes the shortened primary submovements (Cooke et al., 1989; Darling et al., 1989; Pratt et al., 1994; Seidler-Dobrin et al., 1998).

Furthermore, the variability of force production and control gives researchers another element to assess and understand movement slowing in older adults. Variability of movement in older adults has been contributed to an inaccurate production of sequential force outputs to move the limb to the desired target location (Brown, 1996; Erim et al., 1999; Galganski et al., 1993; Seidler & Stelmach, 1996). Erim and colleagues (1999) showed that older adults had multiple inflections in their force-time curve when asked to maintain a given force. Older adults produced lower and more variable force outputs compared to young adults. This pattern has been shown by others as well (Galganski et al., 1993; Yue et al., 1999). Stelmach and colleagues (1989) showed relative peak force variability to be higher in older adults compared to young, with 9.4% variability compared to 8.4% variability respectively. Yan (1999) found older adults had large variability in the production of force on a digitizing tablet. On average older adults had $25 \, g/cm^2$ force variability when performing linear and curvilinear arm movements.

Older adults do not always produce less than desired forces. Cole and colleagues (1999) showed that compared to young subjects, the older adults produced too much force during a precision grip task. Older adults produced excessive grip forces that created excessive safety margins averaging twice that of young controls (Cole et al., 1999; Kinoshita & Francis, 1996). The safety margin reflects the excessive force produced beyond those required to grasp and lift the object. Long delays have also been reported in older adults between the time they grasp the object and begin to lift it (Cole et al., 1999; Kinoshita & Francis, 1996). Furthermore, older adults although able to maintain grip force, were unable to modulate the forces in conjunction with lifting forces and therefore produced less smooth forces as well (Cole & Beck, 1994; Kinoshita & Francis, 1996). Cole and colleagues (1999) assessed grip force in older adults and the differences with various surfaces (silk or sandpaper) and with various weights (4 N and 2 N). Subjects were instructed to lift and hold the object for 4 sec and then return it to the table, or were asked to slowly release their grip and allow the object to drop. Grip forces for older subjects were 35–73% higher in the sandpaper condition and 18–32% higher

in the silk condition. Safety margins were on the order of two times greater for the sandpaper condition in older adults. Safety margins with increased loads were 41–104% greater that young adults. Older subjects' force production was often delayed by approximately 250 ms, which may account for the excessive force or high safety margins in compensation to a central delay (Cole et al., 1999). Lazarus and Haynes (1997) further examined grip force in a dual-task paradigm in which subjects performed the learning of dynamic isometric force production in a pinching task in conjunction with a pursuit-tracking paradigm. Older subjects produced excessive force in the first few trials, but were able to complete task demands during the following trials (Lazarus & Haynes, 1997), which has been shown by Cole and colleagues (1999) as well. The greater number of errors older adults produced on the isometric pinching task were attributed to peripheral decrements, including tactile insensibility, muscle reorganization, and slow afferent information processing (Cole et al., 1999; Cole & Beck, 1994; Kinoshita & Francis, 1996; Lazarus & Haynes, 1997).

E. Movement Variability and Coordination

Heightened movement variability is another characteristic of movements produced by older adults (Brown, 1996; Cooke et al., 1989; Greene & Williams, 1996; Seidler-Dobrin et al., 1998). Cooke and colleagues (1989) found older adults to have significantly greater coefficients of variation compared to young adults on measures including peak velocity, movement duration, ratio of maximum velocity to average velocity, and ratio of acceleration to deceleration phases. Furthermore, the variability was amplified in movements of small amplitudes compared to larger amplitude movements.

This variability has been documented with kinematics and end-point measures (Brown, 1996). Trajectory variability is also a main feature in older adults (Brown, 1996; Goggin & Meeuwsen, 1992; Ketcham et al., 2000). Brown (1996) found the largest variability in the acceleratory phase of the movement. Similar findings were reported by Greene and Williams (1996), who found movement variability to be approximately 5 degrees higher in older adults compared to young adults on a dynamic bimanual coordination task. Seidler-Dobrin and colleagues (1998) examined variability of movements in older adults and simulated their results with a model. They found that elderly subjects spent a larger portion of their movements coactivating antagonist and agonist muscles during movement, which resulted in abnormal muscle activation patterns, which contributed to increased movement variability (Figure 13.1). The abnormal agonist–antagonist pattern led to the inability to accelerate rapidly, but it does reduce movement variability. Furthermore, older adults exhibited asymmetrical velocity profiles with longer deceleration phases of the movement, again in an effort to maintain accuracy and reduce variability. To examine the underlying mechanisms, these researchers simulated muscle coactivation patterns in the older adults and found that the simulated forces increased normalized jerk, and increased coactivation lowered the normalized jerk score.

The coordination of movements in older adults is another area of research that is conducted to understand age-related changes in movement control. Coordination has been assessed in such tasks as reach-to-grasp (Bennett & Castiello, 1994; Carnahan et al., 1998), handwriting (Teulings & Stelmach, 1993), and bimanual tasks (Greene & Williams, 1996; Swinnen et al., 1998; Wishart et al., 2000). In reach-to-grasp and prehension tasks, older adults show less stable coupling between the transport and manipulation phases of the movement (Bennett & Castiello, 1994). Furthermore, grip aperture occurs significantly earlier in the movement of older adults compared to young adults (Bennett & Castiello, 1994; Carnahan et al., 1998). Carnahan and colleagues (1998) found that the time to peak wrist velocity was approximately 50 ms longer than young adults. However, they found older adults were faster than young adults on intercepting a moving target. They attribute these findings to the experience of older adults to correctly anticipate control of a moving object. Handwriting studies have shown that although older adults are able to maintain stroke size, they show significant reductions in peak accelerations and stroke durations compared to young adults, which is related to reductions in fine motor coordination (Teulings & Stelmach, 1993). In bimanual coordination, Swinnen and colleagues (1998) found that older adults are not able to overcome preferred modes of coordination compared to young adults which result in less smooth movements. Greene and Williams (1996) assessed bimanual coordination in older adults during a dynamic movement task. They found that older adults were able to maintain in-phase coordination at high speeds, but antiphase coordination tasks moved to in-phase movements at significantly lower speeds than younger adults, approximately 1 Hz slower. These findings were replicated and extended by Wishart and colleagues (2000). They found older adults performed as well as young adults on in-phase movements up to 2.5 Hz speeds, but showed breakdowns in coordination of antiphase movements at 1.5 and 2.0 Hz where young adults were able to maintain coordination. Similar findings have been found in circle drawing with older adults, where their movement tends toward a stable state at lower speeds than young adults (Dounskaia et al., 2000).

F. Visual Monitoring

It has been thought that reductions in central planning, proprioception, force production and regulation, and irregular muscle patterns in the elderly reduce the capability to control volitional actions, thereby creating a need to use vision to guide and regulate movements, particularly during the terminal phase (Chaput & Proteau, 1996b; Larish & Stelmach, 1982; Gottlob & Madden, 1999; Seidler-Dobrin & Stelmach, 1998; Slavin et al., 1996; Yan, Thomas, & Stelmach, 1998). Thus, visual monitoring of an ongoing movement is thought to compensate for sensorimotor information loss during execution. The consequences of the increased reliance on vision is that movements are typically performed slower with more variability, and exhibit prolonged deceleration phases. Haaland, Harrington, and Grice (1993) found that when visual information was removed regarding arm position during movements, the performance of older adult subjects' on an aiming task was impaired compared to the young subjects. These results showed that older adults increased movement duration and end point errors. Chaput and Proteau (1996b) reported similar findings in a point-to-point movement task. Older adults performed significantly different when visual feedback was not available compared to when it was; movement times were 100 ms longer and movement errors were on average 9.3 mm larger. These results have also been documented in other point-to-point movement tasks (Larish & Stelmach, 1982; Seidler-Dobrin & Stelmach, 1998; Slavin et al., 1996; Yan et al., 1998), a continuous tapping task (Pohl et al., 1996), and in postural stability tasks (Peterka & Black, 1990; Whipple, Wolfson, Derby, Singh, & Tobin, 1993; Woollacott, 1993). Because visual processing requires continuous adjustment in online central control of a movement, it is often assumed that this is the reason the older adults produce slower more variable movements (Goggin & Stelmach, 1990; Seidler-Dobrin & Stelmach, 1998; Walker et al., 1997).

Support for increased reliance on vision to guide a movement comes from studies that have deprived subjects of complete or partial vision of the limb during movement to a visible target. The kinematics of the movement are then examined to determine if they are altered in the absence of vision (Seidler-Dobrin & Stelmach, 1998; Darling et al., 1989; Warabi et al., 1986). Seidler-Dobrin and Stelmach (1998) investigated reliance of visual feedback in older adults after substantial amounts of practice and found that practice did not reduce a subject's dependence on vision. Subjects were instructed to move as fast and accurate as possible for 180 trials on a point-to-point movement task. Blocks of trials consisted of a pretest block with disrupted vision, an extensive practice block with vision, and finally a posttest block to see how practice influenced the kinematic structure of the movement when vision was again disrupted. The results documented that both young and older adults relied on visual feedback in the early practice trials. After considerable practice, the young subjects were able to lengthen the proportion of the movement that initially propelled the limb to the target, thus showing their reduced reliance on vision. In contrast, older adults did not demonstrate such a benefit from practice, as they were not able to extend the length of the initial ballistic phase of the movement; consequently they remained highly dependent on vision to guide a greater proportion of the movement. The reviewed studies provide evidence that older adults are much more dependent on vision to guide and control a movement. The reasons for increased dependence of visual monitoring is not well understood; however, several investigators have suggested that it is likely due to limitations in central planning, force production and reg-ulation, proprioception, and/or sensori-motor integration capabilities (Amrhein, 1996; Pohl et al., 1996; Seidler & Stel-mach, 1995a, Stelmach & Sirica, 1986).

IV. Posture and Gait

Mobility is an extremely important con-cern in the elderly population. If the abil-ity to ambulate is reduced, there is a tremendous amount of independence lost. Disturbances in gait produce disabil-ities in roughly 13% of older adults (Lar-ish et al., 1988). Teresi, Golden, and Gurland (1984) have shown that mobility and functional independence are highly correlated. It is projected that by the year 2020, over 400,000 hip fractures will occur from falls in individuals over 65 years of age. Twenty percent of individ-uals who experience hip fractures will not survive the next year, and a substantial number who survive the first year will not regain the ability to ambulate with-out assistance (Schneider & Guralnik, 1990; Schultz, 1992).

A. Posture and Balance

The ability to stabilize posture is not only important for upright stance, but also when performing a variety of upper extremity movements. Balance and pos-ture control is assessed to understand motor decrements that contribute to in-stability. Visual, proprioceptive, and ves-tibular information are sent to the CNS for integration, and appropriate adjust-ments are made to the motor control sys-tem in order to maintain upright posture. Deficits in any or many of these systems can lead to unstable posture and an in-creased risk for falls. Postural stability is commonly measured in two situations. First, analyzing postural sway during quiet standing, and second, analyzing how the postural system responds follow-ing a platform perturbation or a destabil-izing thrust to the torso. Older adults have been shown to have deficits during both quiet stance and induced sway bal-ance tests (Maki, Holliday, & Fernie, 1990). A classic study done by Sheldon (1963) found that postural sway velocity and range increased with advanced age in a quiet stance and was more pronounced when vision was occluded (Hay, 1996; Schieppati, Grasso, Siliotto, & Nardore, 1993 woolacott, 1993;). This inherit in-crease in the velocity and range of the center of pressure has been studied in la-boratory situations for many years to elu-cidate why postural instability increases with advanced age.

In the laboratory setting, analysis of posture control is measured by perturbing the surface on which subjects are stand-ing. In these induced postural distur-bances, older adults show greater deficits in velocity and range of the induced sway (Hu & Woollacott, 1994; Maki et al., 1990; Woollacott, Moore, & Hu, 1993). Magnified postural sway dispersion in older adults implies a deficit in, or slow-ing of, the central integrative mechan-isms responsible for compensation and reconfiguration of the control system (Hu & Woollacott, 1994; Maki et al., 1990; Teasdale, Stelmach, & Breunig, 1991; Teasdale, Stelmach, Breunig, & Meeuwsen, 1991). These studies found that the combination of visual occlusion and altered surface conditions resulted in increased variability, velocity, range, and dispersion of postural sway. Collins, De-Luca, Burrowr, and Lipsitz (1995) studied postural control mechanisms when sen-sory feedback was available to update control of the task, and when it was not available. Older adults were substantially more unstable when feedback was not available, and were actually more stable in the feedback situation compared to young controls (Collins et al., 1995).

Larger variability in postural sway in the absence of vision in older adults has been well documented (Peterka & Black, 1990; Whipple et al., 1993; Woollacott, 1993). These researchers summarized the changes in postural sway under various vision occlusion or distortion conditions in conjunction with surface perturbations. Although older adults showed slight increases in postural sway compared to young adults when vision was occluded or distorted on an undisturbed surface, deficits were amplified when the surface was perturbed (Whipple et al., 1993; Woollacott, 1993). This reliance on vision in this postural control situation appears to be the primary source of feedback, however, with several trials older adults were able to maintain postural control without vision, suggesting they change reliance to another mode of control (Woollacott, 1993). Older adults had significant trouble maintaining balance when the eyes were closed and when inaccurate visual information was given, with a large portion of subjects falling with inaccurate visual feedback (Whipple et al., 1993). However, even with this decline, vision is still relied upon. Stelmach and Worringham (1985) reported that with vision, proprioceptive deterioration was not present, but when vision was absent, substantial declines were apparent. These data suggest that there was a decline in proprioceptive efficiency. Older adults were particularly disadvantaged if they had only proprioceptive information and had to rely on it to correct or perform movements (Stelmach & Worringham, 1985). Furthermore, attention is important to postural stability. Older adults have to allocate more attention to the maintenance of postural stability following a destabilizing activity (Brown, Shumway-Cook, & Woollacott, 1999; Shumway-Cook Woollacott, Kerns, & Baldwin, 1997; Stelmach, Meeuwsen, & Zelaznt, 1990). Older adults need more time to completely recover from a destabilizing perturbation compared to young adults, which may be a result of

the attentional demands associated with the task (Hay et al., 1996). Older adults need the additional time to process sensory feedback and therefore redundant sources of sensory information increase task demands. Overall, the results of these studies establish that compared to the young, older adults rely more on visual feedback to execute movements and maintain stability. The reliance on visual feedback may be a consequence of the impaired ability to prepare and organize a movement or due to reductions in other somatosensory feedback mechanisms.

Along with these changes in vision and proprioceptive feedback, the ability to produce a rapid and accurate force is also an important aspect to maintaining stability. Force production is slower in older adults, muscle coordination is decreased, and attentional demands are increased to maintain stability (Cole & Beck, 1994; Cole et al., 1999; Kinoshita & Francis, 1996; Lazarus & Haynes, 1997; Stelmach & Nahom, 1992, 1993). Higher levels of torque suggest increased force production of the muscles, which in turn suggests greater strength. In older adults, strength is decreased which leads to decreased torque and power of body segments (Whipple et al., 1993; Hall, Woollacott, & Jenaen, 1999). Thelen, Schultz, and Alexander (1996) previously found that the inability of older adults to quickly produce muscular forces led to a greater incidence of falls.

There are a variety of types of falls ranging from slips and trips to falls that invoke serious injury. Howell (1949) estimated that by the age of 80, one in three people would experience a damaging fall. Tinetti, Speechley, and Ginter (1988) assessed risk factors for falls in the elderly. They assessed both balance and gait rated on a functional scale and associated them with the likelihood of falls in the 336 older adults observed. They statistically reduced the assessment of balance and gait abnormalities to give a total mobility score, which was correlated with the incidence of falls. Lower scores were associated with a higher likelihood of falls. Measures of balance and gait included assessment of larger postural sway, slower walking speed, large deviation of walking path, and inability to withstand perturbations to upright stance. Subjects were rated as to whether they could or could not perform the array of tasks. The question is what age-related declines lead to the increased risk for falls, and what interventions can reduce these risks. Changes in the sensorimotor system that lead to slips, trips, and falls include declines in proprioception, muscle mass, force control, and sensorimotor integration (Stelmach & Worringham, 1985). It has also been established that MT, RTs, and preparation times are all slower in older adults and may contribute to the frequency of falls (Bashore et al., 1989; Fozard et al., 1994; Goggin & Meeuwsen, 1992; Larish & Stelmach, 1982; Salthouse, 1988; Seidler & Stelmach, 1996). All of these decrements result in slowed response and delayed initiation of movement. Stelmach and Worringham (1985) report that a response time of less than 300 ms is necessary to correct an unstable movement, and that older adults tend to frequently have response time that are beyond these limits. Perhaps a delayed response to a perturbation or unstable step is enough to result in a fall before the reactive mechanisms respond (Doherty et al., 1993; Roos et al., 1999; Stelmach & Worringham, 1985; Woollacott & Manchester, 1993). These delayed responses result in reduced time for protective or corrective movements in older adults. As a result, older adults may compensate by coactivating postural muscles intending to decrease sway, which in turn reduces the adaptability to respond to unforeseen postural disturbances (Stelmach & Worringham, 1985).

Fernie, Gryfe, Holliday, and Llewellyn (1982) performed a double-blind study to examine if postural sway and incidence of falls were related. Forty-two percent of the subjects tested had reported a previous fall history. The researchers found that postural sway was higher in subjects who had a previous histories of falls, but not necessarily linear by age (Fernie et al., 1982). The combination of prolonged latencies in reaction onset and decreased magnitudes of postural responses result in ineffective corrective balance strategies and lead to a greater number of falls (Tang & Woollacott, 1998; Woollacott, Inglin, & Manchester, 1988). Older adults also have an increased risk for falls or loss of balance when attention is focused on a simultaneous task regardless of its nature, suggesting that postural control is an attentionally demanding task (Brown et al., 1999; Shumway-Cook et al., 1997).

B. Gait

Gait changes in older adults include a decreased preferred speed of walking, shorter stride lengths, increased stride frequency, a wider stance, and longer support times, which lead to more time in the stance phase than the swing phase (Baumann, 1994; Larish et al., 1988; Ringsberg, Gerdhem, 1999; Fernandez, 1993; Samson, Crave, Duvrsma, Desseno, 1998; Ho, Verbaea, Woo, Yuen, Shan, & Chan, 1997). Baumann (1994) suggests that step length decreased because of deficits in balance, muscle strength, muscle mass, and range of motion. There is also an age-related decline in preferred walking speed in the older adults, with a higher metabolic cost than young adults (Larish et al., 1988). Decreased leg strength was associated with reductions in gait speed and increases in the number of steps taken (Ringsberg et al., 1999; Lipsitz et al., 1994; Schultz, 1992). Similarly, a study comparing older men and women found that muscular power on a leg extension test highly correlated with walking speed and stability (Rantanen &

Avela, 1997). Force control is also important in mobility, as the coordination of forces is extremely vital to the timing of gait. Inaccurate coordination of forces and increased coactivation may contribute to these findings (Larish et al., 1988; Woollacott et al., 1988; Seidler-Dobrin et al., 1998). Peak ground reaction forces in older adults were 15% lower than young on heel contact and was thus an interaction between ground reaction forces and speed (Larish et al., 1988). Gait characteristics have not been correlated with the incidence of falls, although many falls occur during walking (Gehlsen, Mitchell, & Whaley, 1990). However, falls are usually reported to be associated with changes in the walking surface or some external perturbation and may indeed be related to slower sensory feedback (Tinetti et al., 1988).

Although muscular strength, power, and force control are important components to walking stability, other contributors such as flexibility and range of motion are also significant factors in gait deficits. Advanced age leads to limited range of motion and flexibility and greater joint stiffness (Golding, 1998). Flexibility decreases with age and is due in part to the lack of physical activity in older adults; however, training and stretching increases flexibility and extends range of motion. Range of motion was reported to decline by approximately 20% in hip rotation from 45 to 70 years of age (Allander, Biornsson, Olafsson, Sigfusson, & Thorstensson, 1974). Advanced age led to 50% less range of motion in lower extremities compared to young (Hortobagyi & DeVita, 1999). In a downward stepping motion, older adults had 92% less dorsiflexion, 28% less knee flexion, 42% less ankle range of motion, and 57% less knee range of motion in a downward stepping motion. Suggested contributions to these deficits are increased coactivation in the hamstring muscles around the knee joint and more type I (slow twitch) muscle fibers (Hortobagyi & DeVita, 1999). The effects of decreased range of motion on daily activities are not well studied, but Badley, Wagstaff, and Wood (1984) found that adults of all ages with arthritis had significantly decreased abilities to move around one's surroundings when knee flexion was limited. The same association was made with hips, arms, and wrists, and limited range of motion again correlated with the ability to interact efficiently with the environment in lower and upper extremity movements (Badley et al., 1984).

C. Training Programs

The sensorimotor and physiological changes that accompany aging have adverse effects on activity in everyday tasks in older adults. Exercise training has provided some evidence that the adverse affects of aging can be slowed (Cress et al., 1999). It is observed that people who begin exercising even at the age of 80 will benefit from the training. Exercise training increases muscle mass and flexibility, and has been shown to reduce the risk for falls and is important for such tasks as driving an automobile (Allander et al., 1974; Hortobagyi & DeVita, 1999; Stelmach & Nahom, 1993, 1992). Related to motor control impairments, exercise includes physical activity that can increase muscle mass, strength, and flexibility. Moderate aerobic exercise and stretching have been found to substantially increase physical functioning including flexibility, strength, range of motion, and coordination (Drowatzky & Drowatzky, 1999; Morey et al., 1999). However, it may be important to include programs that specifically target muscle function to reduce the risk of falls and injuries (Pendergast, Fisher, & Calkins, 1993). Strength training is gaining recognition in the older adult population, as it has been found that resistance training increases muscle mass and the production and maintenance of force output (Drowatzky & Drowatzky, 1999; Keen, Yue, & Enoka, 1994; Singh et al., 1999). Strength training has been shown to increase the percentage of type II fibers by 20% (Drowatzky & Drowatzky, 1999). Strength training has also been shown to increase maximum torque in plantarflexors of older adults (Blanpied & Smidt, 1993).

Training specific to balance and postural stabilization, including multisensory training that requires the processing of several types of sensory information simultaneously, has been shown to improve postural responses in older adults (Daubney & Culham, 1999; Hu & Woollacott, 1994; Tang & Woollacott, 1996). A study in which enhanced sensory implants were put in the soles of subjects' shoes found that this intervention improved the efficiency of stabilizing reactions elicited by unpredictable postural perturbations (Maki, Perry, Norne, & McIlroy, 1999). Furthermore, in a review done by Tang and Woollacott (1996) on balance training in older adults, it is suggested that multifactorial balance-training regimes were the most productive. Training programs should target specific subsystems, work on specific individual needs, and most importantly be progressive. Shumway-Cooke and colleagues (1997) suggest that balance-training programs should include tasks that involve multiple processes, thereby increasing the attentional demands associated with balance control. This could include such tasks as interlimb coordination to increase the postural response resources and improve compensatory strategies (Tang & Woollacott, 1998). Rose and Clark (2000) have reported that a biofeedback-based balance intervention results in improvement in balance control in older adults. Subjects on the intervention were able to make quicker corrections to perturbations and able to recover from larger sway dispersions, suggesting more

control of their center of gravity. Proprioceptive and gait training has also been observed to be beneficial to older adults to maintain balance and control of their bodies and prevent falls (Galindo-Ciocon, Ciocon, & Galindo, 1995; Gauchard, Jeandel, Tessier, & Perrin, 1999). Training programs can have a positive impact on physical functioning in older adults, whether it is through enhancing sensory information, increasing muscle strength and mass, increasing flexibility and range of motion, or improving balance.

V. Motor Learning

The ability to learn a motor skill in older adults is important for implications in the development and application of retraining programs. Unfortunately, there is not substantial research on motor learning in older adults, but what is available suggests they do not learn as well as young. Seidler-Dobrin and Stelmach (1998) conducted a study to determine if reliance on visual feedback changes with practice. Subjects were instructed to move as fast and accurately as possible for a total of 180 trials (expanded description in Reliance on Vision). They found that young subjects increased their distance in the initial ballistic portion of the movement, suggesting a greater portion of the movement was preplanned or programmed with practice. Older adults, however, did not lengthen their distance in the initial ballistic movement, suggesting that even with practice their movement microstructure does not change (Seidler-Dobrin & Stelmach, 1998). Pratt and colleagues (1994) found similar results and relate these findings to the inability to rapidly generate forces. With practice, older subjects have shown changes in kinematics, such as shorter deceleration phases and less movement variability; however, coactivation was still present and time in the primary submovement remains constant (Brown, 1996; Darling et al., 1989; Pratt et al., 1994; Seidler-Dobrin et al., 1998).

Research examining skill acquisition has found that older adults, although able to learn new skills, learn at a slower rate, but perform with the same error rates as younger adults when normalized for quantity (Czaja & Sharit, 1998; Harrington & Haaland, 1992; Lazarus & Haynes, 1997; Strayer & Kramer, 1994). Older adults need more time practicing a skill to show performance improvements. Judge, King, Whipple, Clive, and Wolfson (1995) performed a study, which administered a challenging balance test to older individuals. Overall, the older subjects showed deficits when vision and proprioceptive feedback were occluded. However, with substantial practice, learning occurred, although in the oldest adults not to a significant degree. Older adults have also been shown to have trouble learning new associative relations compared to young adults when accuracy levels are similar, suggesting performance differences and adoption of a more conservation response bias (Strayer & Kramer, 1994). These results support the idea that older adults are primarily concerned with accuracy. In a study by Dixon and colleagues (1993), which assessed handwriting performance in young and elderly adults as a function of familiarity and practice, older adults were slower than younger adults on all task conditions. Age differences were magnified if the subjects were unfamiliar with the task but lessened with familiarity (Dixon, Kurzman, & Iriesen, 1993; Seidler & Stelmach, 1995a,b). It was found in the study of handwriting that with practice older adults do improve, but performance level remained below those of young controls (Dixon et al., 1993). Learning in older adults also occurs at a slower rate compared to young on a postural perturbation task; however, again it does occur (Woollacott, 1993). Perhaps this slower

rate of motor learning is not only a result of a reduced plasticity of the elderly motor system, but also the result of the need to process different sources of sensory information independently (Chaput & Proteau, 1996b). In an interlimb coordination study performed by Swinnen and colleagues (1998), older adult subjects did not improve their performance level with practice. These researchers suggest from a kinetic perspective, that older adults have a decreased capability to overcome preferred coordination modes, which is often required to maintain competence in complex actions.

In a study by Kramer, Hahn, and Gopher (1999), the ability to switch between two different cognitive tasks was assessed. They found that early in the practice sessions, older adults had large time delays when switching was measured by RTs. However, with practice these differences diminished between young and older adults so that delay times were equivalent. Interestingly, older adults were able to maintain the acquired capability after a 2-month period. It has been suggested that to enhance learning, older adults should use cognitive learning strategies to perform motor skills (Greenwood, Meeuwsen, & Irench, 1993; Proteau, Charest, & Chaput, 1994). Cognitive strategy has been shown to help older adults achieve success at a quicker rate, which in turn enhances the experience and will lead to less attrition rates in intervention programs. Learning occurs in older adults; however, it is many times slower than young. It should be noted, however, that the variability between older adult subjects is much greater than young, suggesting individuals age at different rates and to different degrees.

VI. Summary and Conclusions

Literature related to declines in motor control in older adults were reviewed in this chapter. Sensorimotor changes including alterations in brain structures related to motor function, changes in muscle composition, and reorganization of motor units contribute to motor changes with advanced age. Other changes in sensorimotor systems that relate to movement deficits include declines in proprioception and slower sensorimotor integration. Although all of these decrements result in slow discoordinated movements, they do not accumulate in a linear manner (Walker et al., 1997). The aging motor system compensates for a variety of the changes observed. There is evidence that the elderly are capable of learning new motor tasks just as the young, but at a slower rate of improvement, thus practice and training programs may minimize declines in motor function. Foregoing modifications in the motor system produce many changes in the motor output, particularly slower, more variable movements. Although many behavioral and physiological explanations have been summarized in this chapter, many researchers commonly allude to two other possible explanations for movement slowing in older adults, *neural noise* (Brown, 1996; Chaput & Proteau, 1996a; Seidler & Stelmach, 1995b; Seidler & Stelmach, 1996; Teuling's & Stelmach, 1993; Welford, 1984), and strategy (Hines, 1979; Goggin & Meeuwsen, 1992; Larish & Stelmach, 1982; Morgan et al., 1994; Salthouse, 1988; Walker et al., 1997). Little empirical data have been collected on either of these topics, primarily due to the nature of the question.

Any increase in irregular neural activity in the brain and throughout the CNS with increased age is termed *neural noise* and could affect a wide range of sensorimotor and cognitive performance abilities (Welford, 1977, 1984). Welford introduced the term neural noise to the research on elderly in the late 1970s, and it has remained a viable explanation of why older adults become slower and produce move-

ments that exhibit considerable variability. Older adults are thought to have higher neural noise compared to young subjects when asked to generate forces of the same amplitude (Seidler & Stelmach, 1996; Walker et al., 1997; Teulings & Stelmach, 1993; Welford, 1984). This neural noise disturbs the processing of central and peripheral signals, delaying their interpretation and implementation. The implications for movement output are disturbances and longer latencies in the ability to organize and execute goal-oriented actions. Neural noise may explain movement slowing in older adults by reductions in signal-to-noise ratios (SNRs). The SNR expresses the ratio between the amount of modulation due to the invariant or programmed component (signal) and the modulation in the invariant component due to random activity due to increased age (noise) (Teulings & Stelmach, 1993). Therefore, a high SNR indicates low variability, and a low SNR indicates high variability. Older adults were found to be more variable in force production, duration, and size in a handwriting task demonstrated by low SNRs compared to young subjects (Seidler & Stelmach, 1995b; Teuling & Stelmach, 1993). Walker and colleagues (1997) assess neural noise in older adults on a point-to-point movement task. They assessed neural noise in a noise-to-force ratio by minimizing accuracy constraints and assessing target end point in a single-step movement with no corrective movements. They regressed standard deviation of the end point on peak acceleration in young and older adults. Older adults differed from young adults by a factor of 3, which was indication of a higher noise-to-force ratio and neural noise. This further suggests that higher neural noise results in increased variability in the task. The on-line variability is noticed in all forms of performance including sensory, cognitive, and motor systems (Brown, 1996; Chaput & Proteau, 1996a;

Seidler & Stelmach, 1996; Welford, 1984). The obvious consequence of the reduced SNRs is slower and more variable movement performance by older individuals (Teulings & Stelmach, 1993; Welford, 1984).

The other possibility that remains an explanation in movement slowing, is a strategy used by older adults to reduce movement variability. Many researchers have found that older adults are concerned with performing the task as accurately as possible (Goggin & Meeuwsen, 1992; Hines, 1979; Morgan et al., 1994; Larish & Stelmach, 1982; Salthouse, 1988; Walker et al., 1997). With higher speeds, error rates rose; therefore, the older adults' movements are slowed to execute accurate movements. The strategy to maintain accuracy at the cost of speed becomes an issue that is difficult to control for in MT studies. Morgan and colleagues (1994) performed a study in which the experimental design controlled for strategy by training all subjects to move the same speed and then assess differences between older adults and young controls. Even with this training, older adult subjects showed greater hesitancies and submovements, which suggests that their performance was a result of declines in motor coordination not necessarily strategy with advanced age (Morgan et al., 1994). Therefore, although strategy remains a possibility of movement slowing, many decrements contribute to age-related changes. One major problem of research on older adults is physiological and chronological ages do not always coincide. Compiling anatomical, physiological, and behavioral research can provide guidelines for how the motor, sensory, and cognitive systems are altered in older adults. Age-related changes in the motor system are well documented and always on the path of understanding how the brain controls movement at all ages.

References

Adams, I. (1987). Comparison of synaptic changes in the precentral and postcentral cerebral cortex of aging humans: A quantitative ultrastructural study. *Neurobiology of Aging, 8(3)*, 203–212.

Alexander, G. E. (1994). Basal ganglia-thalmocortical circuits: Their role in control of movements. *Journal of Clinical Neurophysiology, 11(4)*, 420–431.

Allander, E., Bjornsson, O. J., Olafsson, O., Sigfusson, N., & Thorstensson, J. (1974). Normal range of joint movements in shoulder, hip, wrist, and thumb with special reference to side: A comparison between two populations. *International Journal of Epidemiology, 3*, 253–261.

Allen, S. J., Benton, J. S., Goodhardt, M. J., Haan, E. A., Sims, N. R., Smith, C. C. T., Spillane, J. A., Bowen, D. M., & Davison, A. M. (1983). Biochemical evidence of selective nerve cell changes in the normal aging human and rat brain. *Journal of Neurochemistry, 41*, 256–265.

Amrhein, P. C. (1996). Age-related slowing in movement parameterization studies: Not what you might think. In A. M. Fernandez & N. Teasdale (Eds.), *Changes in sensory motor behavior in aging* (vol 114). Elsevier Science BV: North Holland.

Amrhein, P. C., Goggin, N. L., & Stelmach, G. E. (1991). Age differences in the maintenance and restructuring of movement preparation. *Psychology and Aging, 6(3)*, 451–466.

Aniansson, A., Hedberg, M., Henning, G. B., & Grimby, G. (1986). Muscle morphology, enzymatic activity, and muscle strength in elderly men: a follow-up study. *Muscle and Nerve, 9(7)*, 585–591.

Badley, E., Wagstaff, S., & Wood, P. H. N. (1984). Measures of functional ability (disability) in arthritis in relation to impairment of range of joint movement. *Annuals of Rheumatoid Disorders, 43*, 563–569.

Bashore, T. R., Ridderinkhof, R., & van der Molen, M. W. (1997). The decline of cognitive processing speed in old age. *A Journal of the American Psychological Society, 6(6)*, 163–169.

Bashore, T. R., Oshman, A., & Heffley, E. F. (1989). Mental slowing in elderly persons: A cognitive psychophysiological analysis. *Psychology and Aging, 4(2),* 235–244.

Baumann, J. U. (1994). Gait changes in elderly people. *Orthopade, 23(1),* 6–9.

Bellgrove, M. A., Phillips, J. G., Bradshaw, J. L., & Galluci, R. M. (1998). Response (re-)programming in aging: A kinematic analysis. *Journal of Gerontology, 53A(3),* M222–M227.

Bennett, K. M. B., & Castiello, U. (1994). Reach to grasp: Changes with age. *Journal of Gerontology, 49B(1),* P1–P7.

Berardelli, A., Hallett, M., Rothwell, J. C., Agostino, R., Manfredi, M., Thompson, P. D., & Marsden, C. D. (1996). Single-joint rapid arm movements in normal subjects and in patients with motor disorders. *Brain, 119,* 661–674.

Bickford, P. C., Shukitt-Hale, B., & Joseph, J. (1999). Effects of aging on cerebellar nonandrenergic function and motor learning: Nutritional interventions. *Mechanisms of Ageing and Development, 111,* 141–154.

Birren, J. E. (1974). Translations in gerontology—from lab to life. Psychophysiology and speed of response. *American Psychology, 29(11),* 808–815.

Blanpied, P., & Smidt, G. L. (1993). The difference in stiffness of the active plantarflexors between young and elderly human females. *Journal of Gerontology, 48A(2),* M58–M63.

Brody, H. (1976). An examination of cerebral cortex and brainstem aging. In R. D. Terry & S. Gershon (Eds)., *Aging, 3.* New York: Raven.

Brogmus, G. E. (1991). Effects of age and sex on speed and accuracy of hand movements and the refinements they suggest for Fitts' law. *Proceeding of the Human Factors Society 35th Annual Meeting,* 208–212.

Brown, L. A., Shumway-Cook, A., & Woollacott, M. H. (1999). Attentional demands and postural recovery: The effects of aging. *Journal of Gerontology, 54A(4),* M165–M171.

Brown, S. H. (1996). Control of simple arm movements in the elderly. In A. M. Fernandez & N. Teasdale (Eds.), *Changes in sensory motor behavior in aging* (Vol. 114). Elsevier Science BV: North Holland.

Brown, W. F. (1972). A method for estimating the number of motor units in thenar muscles and the changes in motor unit count with ageing. *Journal of Neurology, Neurosurgery, and Psychiatry, 35,* 845–852.

Bruce, S. A., Newton, D., & Woledge, R. C. (1989). Effect of age on voluntary force and cross-sectional area of human adductor pollicis muscle. *Quarterly Journal of Experimental Psychology, 74,* 359–362.

Buchart, P., Farquhar, R., Part, N. J., & Roberts, R. C. (1993). The effect of age and voluntary contraction on presynaptic inhibition of soleus muscle la afferent terminals in man. *Experimental Physiology, 78(2),* 235–242.

Buneo, C. A., Soechting, J. F., & Flanders, M. (1994). Muscle activation patterns for reaching: The representation of distance and time. *Journal of Neurophsyiology, 71(4),* 1546–1558.

Campbell, M. J., McComas, A. J., & Petito, F. (1973). Physiological changes in ageing muscles. *Journal of Neurology, Neurosurgery, and Psychiatry, 36(2),* 174–82.

Carnahan, H., Vandervoort, A. A., & Swanson, L. R. (1998). The influence of aging and target motion on the control of prehension. *Experimental Aging Research, 24,* 289–306.

Cerella, J. (1985). Information processing rates in the elderly. *Psychological Bulletin, 98(1),* 67–83.

Cerella, J., Poon, L. W., & Williams, D. M. (1980). Age and the complexity hypothesis. In L. Poon (Ed.), *Aging in the 1980's: Psychological issues.* Washington, DC: American Psychological Association.

Chaput, S., & Proteau, L. (1996a). Aging and motor control. *Journal of Gerontology, 51B(6),* P346–P355.

Chaput, S., & Proteau, L. (1996b). Modification with aging in the role played by vision and proprioception for movement control. *Experimental Aging Research, 22,* 1–21.

Clamann, H. P. (1993). Motor unit recruitment and the gradation of muscle force. *Physical Therapy, 73(12),* 830–843.

Cole, K. J., & Beck, C. L. (1994). The stability of precision grip force in older adults. *Journal of Motor Behavior, 26(2),* 171–177.

Cole, K. J., Rotella, D. L., & Harper, J. G. (1999). Mechanisms for age-related changes of fingertip forces during precision gripping and lifting in adults. *The Journal of Neuroscience, 19(8),* 3238–3247.

Collins, J. J., DeLuca, C. J., Burrows, A., & Lipsitz, L. A. (1995). Age-related changes in open-loop and closed-loop postural control mechanisms. *Experimental Brain Research, 104*, 480–492.

Contreras-Vidal, J. L., & Stelmach, G. E. (1995). A neural model of basal ganglia-thalamocortical relations in normal and Parkinsonian movement. *Biological Cybernetics, 73(5)*, 467–476.

Cooke, J. D., Brown, S. H., & Cunningham, D. A. (1989). Kinematics of arm movements in elderly humans. *Neurobiology of Aging, 10*, 159–165.

Cress, M. E., Buchner, D. M., Questad, K. A., Essclman, P. C., deLateur, B. J., & Schwartz, R. S. (1999). Exercise: Effects on physical functional performance in independent older adults. *Journal of Gerontology, 54A(5)*, M242–M248.

Czaja, S. J., & Sharit, J. (1998). Ability-performance relationships as a function of age and task experience for a data entry task. *Journal of Experimental Psychology: Applied, 4(4)*, 332–351.

Darling, W. G., Cooke, J. D., & Brown, S. H. (1989). Control of simple arm movements in elderly humans. *Neurobiology of Aging, 10*, 149–157.

Daubney, M. E., & Culham, E. G. (1999). Lower-extremity muscle force and balance performance in adults aged 65 years and older. *Physical Therapy, 79(12)*, 1177–1185.

Davies, R. J., & White, M. J. (1983). The contractile properties of elderly human triceps surae. *Gerontology, 29*, 19–23.

Diggles-Buckles, V., & Vercruyssen, M. (1990). Age-related slowing, S-R compatibility, and stages of information processing. *Proceedings of the Human Factors Society 34th Annual Meeting*, 154–157.

Dixon, R. A., Kurzman, D., & Friesen, I. C. (1993). Handwriting performance in younger and older adults: Age, familiarity, and practice effects. *Psychology and Aging, 8(3)*, 360–370.

Doherty, T. J., Vandervoort, A. A., & Brown, W. F. (1993). Effects of ageing on the motor unit: A brief review. *Canadian Journal of Applied Physiology, 18(4)*, 331–358.

Dounskaia, N., Ketcham, C. J., & Stelmach, G. E. (2000). Commonalities and differences in control of a large set of drawing movements. Unpublished manuscript, *Arizona State University*.

Drowatzky, K. L., & Drowatzky, J. N. (1999). Physical training programs for the elderly. *Clinical Kinesiology, 53(3)*, 52–62.

Erim, Z., Beg, M. F., Burke, D. T., & De Luca, C. J. (1999). Effects of aging on motor-unit control properties. *Journal of Neurophysiology, 82*, 2081–2091.

Ferrell, W. R. Crighton, A., & Sturrock, R. D. (1992). Age-dependent changes in position sense in human proximal interphalangeal joints. *Neuroreport, 3(3)*, 259–261.

Fernandez, A. M. (1993). Modulations of gait in normal aging and Parkinson's disease. In G. E. Stelmach & V. Homberg (Eds.), *Sensorimotor Impairment in the elderly*, (pp. 209–230). Elsevier Science BV: North Holland.

Fernie, G. R., Gryfe, C. I., Holliday, P. J., & Llewellyn, A. (1982). The relationship of postural sway in standing to the incidence of falls in geriatric subjects. *Age and Ageing, 11*, 11–16.

Fitts, P. M. (1954). The information capacity of the human motor system in controlling the amplitude of movement. *Journal of Experimental Psychology, 47*, 381–391.

Fozard, J. L., Vercruyssen, M., Reynolds, S. L., Hancock, P. A., & Quilter, R. E. (1994). Age differences and changes in reaction time: The Baltimore Longitudinal Study of Aging. *Journal of Gerontology, B 49(4)*, P179–P189.

Galganski, M. E., Fuglevand, A. J., & Enoka, R. M. (1993). Reduced control of motor output in a human hand muscle of elderly subjects during submaximal contractions. *Journal of Neurophysiology, 69(6)*, 2108–2115.

Galindo-Ciocon, D. J., Ciocon, J. O., & Galindo, D. J. (1995). Gait training and falls in the elderly. *Journal of Gerontological Nursing, June*, 11–17.

Gauchard, G. C., Jeandel, C., Tessier, A., & Perrin, P. P. (1999). Beneficial effect of proprioceptive physical activities on balance control in elderly human subjects. *Neuroscience Letters, 273*, 81–84.

Gehlsen, G. M., Mitchell, H., & Whaley, M. S. (1990). Falls in the elderly: Part I, gait. *Archives of Physical and Medical Rehabilitation, 71*, 735–738.

Ghez, C. (1981). Cortical control of voluntary movement. In E. R. Krandel & J. H.

Schwartz (Eds.), *Principles of neural science.* New York: Elsevier Science Publishers.

Goggin, N. L., & Meeuwsen, H. J. (1992). Age-related differences in the control of spatial aiming movements. *Research Quarterly for Exercise and Sport, 63(4)*, 356–372.

Goggin, N. L., & Stelmach, G. E. (1990). Age-related differences in a kinematic analysis of precued movements. *Canadian Journal on Aging, 9*, 371–385.

Golding, L. A. (1998). Older adults. *ACSM's Health and Fitness Journal, 2(2)*, S24–S27.

Gottsdanker R. (1980). Aging and the maintaining of preparation. *Experimental Aging Research, 6(1)*, 13–27.

Gottsdanker R. (1982). Age and simple reaction time. *Journal of Gerontology, 37(3)*, 342–348.

Gottlob, L. R., & Madden, D. J. (1999). Age differences in the strategic allocation of visual attention. *Journal of Gerontology, 54B(3)*, P165–P172.

Greene, L. S., & Williams, H. G. (1996). Aging and coordination from the dynamic pattern perspective. In A. M. Fernandez & N. Teasdale (Eds.), *Changes in sensory motor behavior in aging.* Elsevier Science, B V: North Holland.

Greenwood, M., Meeuwsen, H., & French, R. (1993). Effects of cognitive learning strategies, verbal reinforcement, and gender on the performance of closed motor skills in older adults. *Activities, Adaptation and Aging, 17(3)*, 39–53.

Gutman, S. R., Latash, M. L., Almeida, G. L., & Gottlieb, G. L. (1993). Kinematic description of variability of fast movements: analytical and experimental approaches. *Biological Cybernetics, 69*, 485–492.

Haaland, K. Y., Harrington, D. L., & Grice, J. W. (1993). Effects of aging on planning and implementing arm movements. *Psychology and Aging, 8(4)*, 617–32.

Hakkinen, K., Kallinen, M., Izquierdo, M., Jokelaninen, K., Lassila, H., Malkia, E., Kraemer, W. J., Newton, R. U., & Alen, M. (1998). Changes in agonist-antagonist EMG, muscle CSA, and force during strength training in middle-aged and older people. *Journal of Applied Physiology, 84(4)*, 1341–1349.

Hakkinen, K., Kraemer, W. J., Kallinen, M., Linnamo, V., Pastinen, U. M., & Newton, R. U. (1996). Bilateral and unilateral neuromuscular function and muscle cross-sectional area in middle-aged and elderly men and women. *Journal of Gerontology, 51A(1)*, B21–B29.

Hall, C. D., Woollacott, M. H., & Jensen, J. L. (1999). Age-related changes in the rate and magnitude of ankle torque development: implication for balance control. *Journal of Gerontology, 54A(10)*, M507–M513.

Harrington, D. L., & Haaland, K. Y. (1992). Skill learning in the elderly: diminished implicit and explicit memory for a motor sequence. *Psychology and Aging, 7(3)*, 425–434.

Hay, L. (1996). Posture control and muscle proprioception in the elderly. In A. M. Fernandez & N. Teasdale (Eds.), *Changes in sensory motor behavior in aging.* Elsevier Science BV: North Holland.

Hay, L., Bard, C., Fleury, M., & Teasdale, N. (1996). Availability of visual and proprioceptive afferent messages and postural control in elderly adults. *Experimental Brain Research, 108*, 129–139.

Hick, W. E. (1952). On the rare of gain of information. *Quarterly Journal of Experimental Psychology, 4*, 11–26.

Hines, T. (1979). Information feedback, reaction time and error rates in young and old subjects. *Experimental Aging Research, 5(3)*, 207–215.

Hirai, T., Korogoi, Y., Sakamoto, Y., Hamatake, S., Ikushima, I., & Takahashi, M. (1996). T2 shortening in the motor cortex: Effect of aging and cerebrovascular diseases. *Radiology, 199(3)*, 799–803.

Ho, S. C., Woo, J., Yuen, Y. K., Sham, A., & Chan, S. G. (1997). Predictors of mobility decline: the Hong Kong old-old study. *Journal of Gerontology, 52A(6)*, M356–M362.

Hortobagyi, T., & DeVita, P. (1999). Altered movement strategy increases lower extremity stiffness during stepping down in the aged. *Journal of Gerontology: Biological Sciences, 54(2)*, B63–B70.

Howell, T. H. (1949). Serial deterioration of the central nervous system: Clinical study. *British Medical Journal, 1*, 56–58.

Hsu, S. H., Huang, C. C., Tsuang, Y. H., & Sun, J. S. (1997). Age differences in remote pointing performance. *Perceptual Motor Skills, 85*, 2515–2527.

Hu, M. H., & Woollacott, M. H. (1994). Multisensory training of standing balance in older adults: II. Kinematic and electromyographic postural responses. *Journal of Gerontology, 49A(2)*, M62–M71.

Hurley, M. V., Rees, J., & Newham, D. J. (1998). Quadriceps function, proprioceptive acuity and functional performance in healthy young, middle-aged, and elderly subjects, *Age Ageing, 27(1)*, 55–62.

Ivry, R. B., Keele, S. W., & Diener, H. C. (1988). Dissociation of the lateral and medial cerebellum in movement timing and movement execution. *Experimental Brain Research, 73(1)*, 167–180.

Izquierdo, M., Aguado, X., Gonzalez, R., Lopez, J. L., & Hakkinen, K. (1999). Maximal and explosive force production capacity and balance performance in men of different ages. *European Journal of Applied Physiology, 79*, 260–267.

Jordan, T. C., & Rabbitt, P. M. A. (1977). Response times to stimuli of increasing complexity as a function of ageing. *British Journal of Psychology, 68*, 189–201.

Judge, J. O., King, M. B., Whipple, R., Clive, J., & Wolfson, L. I. (1995). Dynamic balance in older persons: Effects of reduced visual and proprioceptive input. *Journal of Gerontology, 50A(5)*, M263–M270.

Kaplan, F. S., Nixon, J. E., Reitz, M., Rindfleish, L., & Tucker, J. (1985). Age-related changes in proprioception and sensation of joint position. *Acta Orthopaedica Scandinavica, 56*, 72–74.

Keen, D. A., Yue, G. H., & Enoka, R. M. (1994). Training-related enhancement in the control of motor output in elderly humans. *Journal of Applied Physiology, 77(6)*, 2648–2658.

Ketcham, C. J., Seidler, R. D., VanGemmert, A. W. A., & Stelmach, G. E. (2000). Movement kinematics and speed-accuracy constraints in aging. Unpublished manuscript, *Arizona State University*.

Kinoshita, H., & Francis, P. R. (1996). A comparison of prehension force control in young and elderly individuals. *European Journal of Applied Physiology, 74*, 450–460.

Kramer, A. F., Hahn, S., & Gopher, D. (1999). Task coordination and aging: Explorations of executive control processes in the task switching paradigm. *Acta Psychologica, 101(2–3)*, 339–378.

Larish, D. D., Martin, P. E., & Mungiole, M. (1988). Characteristic patterns of gait in the healthy old. *Annals of the New York Academy of Science, 515*, 18–32.

Larish, D. D., & Stelmach, G. E. (1982). Preprogramming, programming, and reprogramming of aimed hand movements as function of age. *Journal of Motor Behavior, 14(4)*, 322–240.

Larsson, L., Li, X., & Frontera, W. R. (1997). Effects of aging on shortening velocity and myosin isoform composition in single human skeletal muscle cells. *American Journal of Physiology, 272, (Cell Physiology 41)*, C638–C649.

Larsson, L., & Karlsson, J. (1978). Isometric and dynamic endurance as a function of age and skeletal muscle characteristics. *Acta Physiologica Scandanavica, 104*, 129–136.

Lazarus, J. C., & Haynes, J. M. (1997). Isometric pinch force control and learning in older adults. *Experimental Aging Research, 23*, 179–200.

Leonard, C., Matsumoto, T., Diedrich, P., & McMillan, J. (1997). Changes in neural modulation and motor control during voluntary movement of older individuals. *Journal of Gerontology, 52A(5)*, M320–M325.

Levin, H. S. & Benton, A. L. (1973). Age effects in proprioceptive feedback performance. *Gerontologica Clinica, 15*, 161–169.

Lexell, J. (1996). What is the cause of the ageing atrophy? Assessment of the fiber type composition in whole human muscles. In G. E. Stelmach and V. Homberg (Eds.), *Sensorimotor Impairment in the Elderly*, 143–153, Elsevier Science BV: North Holland.

Lipsitz, L. A., Nakajima, I., Gagnon, M., Hirayama, T., Connelly, C. M., Izumo, H., & Hirayama, T. (1994). Muscle strength and fall rates among residents of Japenese and American nursing homes: An international cross-cultural study. *Journal of American Geriatric Society, 42(9)*, 953–959.

Lord, S. R., Rogers, M. W., Howland, A., & Fitzpatrick, R. (1999). Lateral stability, sensorimotor function and falls in older people. *JAGS, 47*, 1077–1081.

Luft, A. R., Skalej, M., Schulz, J. B., Welte, D., Kolb, R., Burk, K., Klockgether, T., & Voigt, K. (1999). Patterns of age-related shrinkage in cerebellum and brainstem observed in vivo using three-dimensional MRI volumetry. *Cerebral Cortex, 9,* 712–721.

Maki, B. E., Perry, S. D., Norrie, R. G., & McIlroy, W. E. (1999). Effect of facilitation of sensation from plantar foot-surface boundaries on postural stabilization in young and older adults. *Journal of Gerontology: Medical Sciences, 54A(6),* M281–M287.

Maki, B. E., Holliday, P. J., & Fernie, G. R. (1990). Aging and postural control: A comparison of spontaneous—and induced—sway balance tests. *American Geriatrics Society, 38,* 1–9.

Mankowsky, N. B., Mints A. Y., & Lisenyuk, V. P. (1982). Age peculiarities of human motor control in aging. *Gerontology, 28,* 314–322.

Mano, Y., Nakamuro, T., Ikoma, K., Sugata, T., Morimoto, S., Takayanagi, T., & Mayer, R. F. (1992). Central motor conductivity in aged people. *Internal Medicine, 31(9),* 1084–1087.

Marsden, C. D. (1984). The pathophysiology of movement disorders. *Neurology Clinical, 2,* 435–459.

Marteniuk, R. G., MacKenzie, C. L., Jeannerod, M., Athenes, S., & Dugas, C. (1987). Constraints of human am movement trajectories. *Canadian Journal of Psychology, 41(3),* 365–378.

McComas, A. J., Quartly, C., & Griggs, R. C. (1997). Early and late losses of motor units after poliomyelitis. *Brain, 120(8),* 1415–21.

McComas, A. J., Fawcett, P. R., Campbell, M. J., & Sica, R. E. (1971). Electrophysiological estimation of the number of motor units within a human muscle. *Journal of Neurology Neurosurgery and Psychiatry, 34(2),* 121–31.

McDonagh, M. J. N., White, M. J., & Davies, C. T. M. (1984). Different effects of ageing on the mechanical properties of human arm and leg muscles. *Gerontology, 30,* 49–54.

McGreer, P. L., McGreer, E. G., & Suzuki, J. S. (1977). Aging and extrapyramidal function. *Archives of Neurology, 34,* 33–35.

Metter, E. J., Lynch, N., Conwit, R., Lindle, R., Tobin, R., & Hurley, B. (1999). Muscle quality and age: Cross-sectional and longitudinal comparisons. *Journal of Gerontology, 54A(5),* B207–B218.

Meyer, D. E., Abrams, R. A., Komblum, S., Wright, C. E., & Smith J. E. K. (1988). Optimality in human motor performance: Ideal control of rapid aimed movements. *Psychological Review, 95,* 340–370.

Milner-Brown, H. S., Stein, R. B., & Yemm, R. (1973). The contractile properties of human motor units during voluntary isometric contractions. *Journal of Physiology, 228(2),* 285–306.

Milner, T. E., Cloutier, C., Leger, A. B., & Franklin, D. W. (1995). Inability to activate muscles maximally during cocontraction and the effect on joint stiffness. *Experimental Brain Research, 107,* 293–305.

Mink, J. W., & Thach, W. T. (1991). Basal ganglia motor control. III. Pallidal ablation: Normal reaction time, muscle cocontraction, and slow movement. *Journal of Neurophysiology, 65(2),* 330–351.

Morey, M. C., Schenkman, M., Studenski, S. A., Chanler, J. M., Crowley, G. M., Sullivan Jr., R. J., Pieper, C. F., Doyle, M. E., Higginbotham, M. B., Horner, R. D., MacAller, H., Puglisi, C. M., Morris, K. G., & Weinberger, M. (1999). Spinal-flexibility-plus-aerobic versus aerobic only training: Effects of a randomized clinical trial on function in at-risk older adults. *Journal of Gerontology, 54A(7),* M335–M342.

Morgan M., Phillips, J. G., Bradshaw, J. L., Mattingly, J. B., lasek, R., & Bradshaw, J. A. (1994). Age-related motor slowness: simply strategic? *Journal of Gerontology, 49A(2),* M133–M139.

Mortimer, J. A. (1988). Human motor behavior and aging. *Annals New York Academy of Sciences, 515,* 54–69.

Munro-Davies, L. E., Winter, J., Aziz, T. Z., & Stein, J. F. (1999). The role of the pedunculopontine region in basal-ganglia mechanisms of akinesia. *Experimental Brain Research, 129,* 511–517.

Naoi, M., & Maruyama, W. (1999). Cell death of dopamine neurons in aging and Parkinson's disease. *Mechanisms of Ageing and Development, 111,* 175–188.

Ng, A. V., & Kent-Braun, J. A. (1999). Slowed muscle contractile properties are not associated with a decreased EMG/force relationship in older humans. *Journal of Gerontology, 54A(10),* B452–B458.

Pai, Y. C., Rymer, W. Z., Chang, R. W., & Sharma, L. (1997). Effect of age and osteoarthritis on knee proprioception. *Arthritis Rheum, 40(12)*, 2260–2265.

Pendergast, D. R., Fisher, N. M., & Calkins, E. (1993). Cardiovascular, neuromuscular, and metabolic alteration with age leading to frailty. *The Journals of Gerontology, 48(SI)*, 61–67.

Peterka, R. J., & Black, F. O. (1990). Age-related changes in human posture control sensory organization tests. *Journal of Vestibular Research, 1*, 73–85.

Petrella, R. J., Lattanzio, P. J., & Nelson, M. G. (1997). Effect of age and activity on knee joint proprioception. *American Journal of Physical Medicine and Rehabilitation, 76(3)*, 235–241.

Pirozzolo, F. J., Mahurin, R. K., & Swihart, A. A. (1991). Motor function in aging and neurodegenerative disease. In F. Boller & J. Grafman (Eds.), *Handbook of Neuropsychology, 3*. Elsevier Science Publishers, BV.

Pohl, P. S., Winstein, C. J., & Fisher, B. E. (1996). The locus of age-related movement slowing: sensory processing in continuous goal-directed aiming. *Journal of Gerontology, 51B(2)*, P94–P102.

Pratt, J., Chasteen, A. L., & Abrams, R. A. (1994). Rapid aimed limb movements: age differences and practice effects in component submovements. *Psychology and Aging, 9(2)*, 325–334.

Proteau, L., Charest, I., & Chaput, S. (1994). Differential roles with aging of viual and proprioceptive afferent information for fine motor control. *Journal of Gerontology, 49B(3)*, P100–P107.

Pujol, J., Junque, C., & Vendrell, P., Grau, J. M., & Capdevila, A. (1992). Reduction of the substantia nigra width and motor decline in aging and Parkinson's disease. *Archives of Neurology, 49*, 1119–1122.

Quoniam, C., Hay, L., Roll, J. P., & Harlay, F. (1995). Age effects on reflex and postural response to propriomuscular inputs generated by tendon vibration. *Journal of Gerontology, 50A(3)*, B155–B165.

Rantanen, T., & Avela, J. (1997). Leg extension power and walking speed in very old people living independently. *Journal of Gerontology, 52A(4)*, M225–M231.

Ringsberg, K., Gerdhem, P., Johansson, J., & Obrant, K. J. (1999). Is there a relationship between balance, gait performance and muscular strength in 75-year-old women? *Age Aging, 28(3)*, 289–293.

Rinne, J. O., Lonnberg, P., & Marjamski, P. (1990). Age-dependent decline in human brain dopamine D1 and D2 receptors. *Brain Research, 508(2)*, 349–352.

Rogers, M. A., & Evans, W. J. (1993). Changes in skeletal muscle with aging: effects of exercise training. *Exercise Sport Sciences Review, 21*, 65–102.

Roos, M. R., Rice, C. L., Connelly, D. M. & Vandervoort, A. A. (1997). Age-related changes in motor unit function. *Muscle and Nerve, 20(6)*, 679–690.

Roos, M. R., Rice, C. L., Connelly, D. M. & Vandervoort, A. A. (1999). Quadriceps muscle strength contractile properties, and motor unit firing rates in young and old men. *Muscle and Nerve, 22(8)*, 1094–1103.

Rose, D. J. & Clark, S. (2000). Can the control of bodily orientation be significantly improved in a group of older adults with a history of falls? *Journal of the American Geriatrics Society, 48*, 275–282.

Salthouse, T. A. (1988). Cognitive aspects of motor functioning. *Annals of the New York Academy of Science, 515*, 33–41.

Salthouse, T. A. (1985). A theory of cognitive aging. In G. E. Stelmach & P. A. Vroon (Eds.), *Advances in Psychology, 28*, Elsevier Science BV: North Holland.

Samson, M. M., Crowe, A., Duursma, S. A., Dessens, J. A., & Verhaar, H. J. (1998). Spatial-temporal analysis of mobility over the adult age range using the Postural-Locomotor-Manual Test. *Journal of Gerontology, 53A(3)*, M242–M247.

Schiebel, M. E., Lindsay, R. D., Tomiyasu, U., & Schiebel, A. B. (1975). Progressive dendritic changes in aging human cortex. *Experimental Neurology, 47(3)*, 392–403.

Schieppati, M., Grasso, M., Siliotto, R., & Nardone, A. (1993). Effect of age, chronic diseases and Parkinsonism on postural control. In G. E. Stelmach & V. Homberg (Eds.), *Sensorimotor impairments in the elderly*, (pp. 355–373) Elsevier Science BV: North Holland.

Schneider, E. L., & Guralnik, J. M. (1990). The aging of America-impact on health care costs. *Journal of the American Medical Association, 263,* 2335–2340.

Schultz, A. B. (1992). Mobility impairment in the elderly: Challenges for biomechanics research. *Journal of Biomechanics, 25(5),* 519–528.

Seidler, R. D. & Stelmach, G. E. (1995a). Reduction in sensorimotor control with age. *Quest, 47,* 386–394.

Seidler, R. D. & Stelmach, G. E. (1995b). Reduction in control with aging: Temporal and spatial declines. In S. N. Blair (Ed.), *Physical activity, fitness, and health,* Champaign, ILL: Human Kinetics.

Seidler, R. D., & Stelmach, G. E. (1996). Motor control. *Encyclopedia of Gerontology, 2,* 177–185.

Seidler-Dobrin, R. D., & Stelmach, G. E. (1998). Persistence in visual feedback control by the elderly. *Experimental Brain Research, 119,* 467–474.

Seidler-Dobrin, R. D., He, J., & Stelmach, G. E. (1998). Coactivation to reduce variability in the elderly. *Motor Control, 2,* 314–330.

Sheldon, J. H. (1963). The effect of age on the control of sway. *Gerontology Clinical, 5,* 129–138.

Shumway-Cook, A., Woolacott, M., Kerns, K. A., Baldwin, M. (1997). The effects of two types of cognitive tasks on postural stability in older adults with and without a history of falls. *Journal of Gerontology, 52A(4),* M232–M240.

Simon, J. R. (1967). Choice reaction time as a function of auditory S-R correspondence, age and sex. *Ergonomics, 10(6),* 659–664.

Simon, J. R. & Pouraghabagher, A. R. (1978). The effect of aging on the stages of processing in a choice reaction time task. *Journal of Gerontology, 33(4),* 553–561.

Singh, M. A. F., Ding, W., Manfredi, T. J., Solares, G. S., O'Neill, E. F., Clements, K. M., Ryan, N. D., Kehayias, J. J., Fielding, R. A., & Evans, W. J. (1999). Insulin-like growth factor I in skeletal muscle after weight-lifting exercise in frail elders. *American Journal of Physiology, 277 (Endocrinology and Metabolism 40),* E135–E143.

Sjobeck, M., Dahlen, S., & Englund, E. (1999). Neuronal loss in the brainstem and cerebellum–part of the normal aging process? A morphometric study of the vermis cerebelli

and inferior olivary nucleus. *Journal of Gerontology, 54A(9),* B363–B368.

Skinner, H. B., Barrack, R. L., & Cook, S. D. (1984). Age-related decline in proprioception. *Clinical Orthopaedics and Related Research, 184,* 208–211.

Slavin, M. J., Phillips, J. G., & Bradshaw, J. L. (1996). Visual cues in the handwriting of older adults: a kinematic analysis. *Psychology and Aging, 11(3),* 521–526.

Smith, G. A. & Brewer, N. (1995). Slowness and age: Speed-accuracy mechanisms. *Psychology and Aging, 10(2),* 238–247.

Stelmach, G. E. & Goggin, N. L. (1988). Psychomotor decline with age. *Physical Activity and Aging, 22,* 6–17.

Stelmach, G. E., Goggin, N. L., & Amrhein, P. C. (1988). Aging and the restructuring of precued movements. *Psychology and Aging, 3(2),* 151–157.

Stelmach, G. E., Goggin, N. L., & Garcia-Colera, A. (1987). Movement specification time with age. *Experimental Aging Research, 13(1),* 39–46.

Stelmach, G. E., Meeuwsen, H., & Zelaznik, H. (1990). Control deficits in the elderly. In T. Brandt, W. Paulus, W. Bles, M. Dieterich, S. Krafczyk, & A. Straube (Eds.), *Disorders of posture and gait: Xth International Symposium of the Society for Postural and Gait Research.* New York: Georg thieme Verlag Stuttgart.

Stelmach, G. E., & Nahom, A. (1992). Cognitive-motor abilities of the elderly driver. *Human Factors, 34(1),* 53–65.

Stelmach, G. E., & Nahom, A. (1993). The effects of age on driving skill cognitive-motor capabilities. In B. Peacock & W. Karwowski (Eds.), *Automotive ergonomics.* London: Taylor Francis.

Stelmach, G. E., & Sirica, A. (1986). Aging and proprioception. *Age, 9,* 99–103.

Stelmach, G. E., Teasdale, J., & Worringham, C. J. (1989). Force production characteristics in Parkinson's disease. *Experimental Brain Research, 76,* 165–172.

Stelmach, G. E., & Worringham, C. J. (1985). Sensorimotor deficits related to postural stability: implications for falling in the elderly. *Clinical Geriatric Medicine, 1(3),* 679–694.

Strayer, D. L., & Kramer, A. F. (1994). Aging and skill acquisition: Learning-performance distinctions. *Psychology and Aging, 9(4),* 589–605.

Strayer, D. L., Wickens, C. D., & Braune, R. (1987). Adult age differences in the speed and capacity of information processing: 2, an eletrophysiological approach. *Psychology and Aging, 2(2),* 99–110.

Swinnen, S. P., Verschueren, S. M. P., Bogaerts, H., Dounskaia, N., Lee, T. D., Stelmach, G. E., & Serrien, D. J. (1998). Age-related deficits in motor learning and differences in feedback processing during the production of a bimanual coordination pattern. *Cognitive Neuropsychology, 15(5),* 439–466.

Tang, P. F. & Woollacott, M. H. (1998). Inefficient postural response to unexpected slips during walking in older adults. *Journal of Gerontology, 53A(6),* M471–M480.

Tang, P. F. & Woollacott, M. H. (1996). Balance control in older adults: Training effects on balance control and the integration of balance control into walking. In A. M. Fernandez & N. Teasdale (Eds.), *Changes in sensory motor behavior in aging* (pp. 339–367). North Holland: Elsevier Science BV.

Teasdale, N., Bard, C., Dadouchi, F., Fleury, M., Larue, J., & Stelmach, G. E. (1992). Posture and elderly persons: Evidence for deficits in the central integrative mechanisms. In G. E. Stelmach & J. Requin (Eds.), *Tutorials in motor behavior II.* North Holland: Elsevier Science Publishers, B. V.

Teasdale, N., Stelmach, G. E., & Breunig, A. (1991). Postural sway characteristics of the elderly under normal and altered visual and support surface conditions. *Journal of Gerontology, 46A(6),* B238–B244.

Teasdale, N., Stelmach, G. E., Breunig, A., & Meeuwsen, H. J. (1991). Age differences in visual sensory integration. *Experimental Brain Research, 85,* 691–696.

Teresi, J., Golden, R., & Gurland, B. (1984). Concurrent and predictive validity of indicator scales developed for the comprehensive assessment and referral evaluation interview scale. *Journal of Gerontology, 39,* 158–165.

Teulings, H. L. & Stelmach, G. E. (1993). Signal-to-noise ratio of handwriting size, force, and time: cues to early markers of Parkinson's disease. In G. E. Stelmach & V. Homberg (Eds.), *Sensorimotor impairment in the elderly,* (pp. 311–327). North Holland: Elsevier Science BV.

Thach, W. T. (1998). A role for the cerebellum in learning movement coordination. *Neurobiology of Learning and Memory, 70,* 177–188.

Thelen, D. G., Schultz, A. B., & Alexander, N. B. (1996). Effects of age on rapid ankle torque development. *Journal of Gerontology, 51A,* M226–M232.

Tinetti, M. E., Speechlcy, M., & Ginter, S. F. (1988). Risk factors for falls among elderly persons living in the community. *New England Journal of Medicine, 319,* 1701–1707.

Torvik, A., Torp, A., & Lindboe, C. F. (1986). Atrophy of the cerebellar vermis in ageing. A morphometric and histological study. *Journal of Neurological Science, 76(2–3),* 283–294.

Walker, N., Philbin, D. A., & Fisk, A. D. (1997). Age-related differences in movement control: adjusting submovement structure to optimize performance. *Journal of Gerontology, 52B(1),* P40–P52.

Wang, Y., Chan, G. L., Holden, J. E., Dobko, T., Mak, E., Schulzer, M., Huser, J. M., Snow, B. J., Ruth, T. J., Calne, D. B., & Stoessl, A. J. (1998). Age-dependent decline of dopamine D1 receptors in human brain: A PET study. *Synapse, 30(1),* 56–61.

Warabi, T., Noda, H., & Kato, T. (1986). Effect of aging on sensorimotor functions of eye and hand movements. *Experimental Neurobiology, 93,* 686–697.

Welford, A. T. (1977). Motor Performance. In J. E. Birren & K. W. Schaie (Eds.), *Handbook for the psychology of aging.* New York: Van Nostrand Reinhold.

Welford, A. T. (1981). Signal, noise, performance, and age. *Human Factors, 23(1),* 97–109.

Welford, A. T. (1984). Between bodily changes and performance: some possible reasons for slowing with age. *Experimental Aging Research, 10(2),* 73–88.

Whipple, R., Wolfson, L., Derby, C., Singh, D., & Tobin, J. (1993). Altered sensory function and balance in older persons. *The Journal of Gerontology, 48(SI),* 71–76.

Wickens, C. D., Braune, R., & Stokes, A. (1987). Age differences in the speed and capacity of information processing: 1. A dual-task approach. *Psychology and Aging, 2(1),* 70–78.

Wishart, L. R., Lee, T. D., Murdoch, J. E., & Hodges, N. J. (2000). Effects of aging on automatica and effortful processes in bimanual coordination. *Journal of Gerontology, 53B(2),* P85–P94.

Woollacott, M. H. (1993). Age-related changes in posture and movement. *The Journals of Gerontology, 48(SI),* 56–60.

Woollacott, M. H., & Manchester, D. L. (1993). Anticipatory postural adjustments in older adults: are changes in response characteristics due to changes in strategy? *Journal of Gerontology, 48A(2),* M64–M70.

Woollacott, M. H., Moore, S., & Hu, M. H. (1993). Improvements in balance in the elderly through training in sensory organization abilities. In G. E. Stelmach & V. Homberg (Eds.), *Sensorimotor Impair-*

ment in the Elderly (pp. 377–392). North Holland: Elsevier Science BV.

Woollacott, M. H., Inglin, B., & Manchester, D. (1988). Response preparation and posture control: neuromuscular changes in the older adult. *Annals New York Academy of Sciences, 515,* 42–53.

Yan, J. H. (1999). Tai Chi practice reduces movement force variability for seniors. *Journal of Gerontology, 54A(12),* M629–M634.

Yan, J. H., Thomas, J. R., & Stelmach, G. E. (1998). Aging and rapid aiming arm movement control. *Experimental Aging Research, 24,* 155–168.

Yue, G. H., Ranganathan, V. K., Siemionow, V., Liu, J. Z., & Sahgal, V. (1999). Older adults exhibit a reduced ability to fully activate their biceps brachii muscle. *Journal of Gerontology, 54A(4),* M249–M253.

Fourteen

Aging and Memory
Cognitive and Biological Perspectives

Lars Bäckman, Brent J. Small, and Åke Wahlin

I. Introduction

No single variety of human memory is completely immune to the negative influence of aging on performance. Thus, age-related deficits have been documented in tasks assessing episodic memory, semantic memory, short-term memory, procedural memory, as well as different forms of priming (Bäckman, Small, Wahlin, & Larsson, 1999; Craik & Jennings, 1992). Despite this seemingly general effect, the most consistent age-related impairment is observed in the domain of episodic memory. There is also ample evidence that older adults vary greatly with regard to the magnitude of age-related memory impairments. These facts are reflected in the present overview.

The chapter is organized as follows. We first provide brief reviews of the effects of aging on all nonepisodic forms of memory. This is followed by a more extensive discussion of the ways in which aging influences episodic memory functioning, including the generality, sources, and variability of the effect. As to the latter, we adopt a broad perspective on individual differences encompassing demo-graphic (e.g., sex, education), lifestyle (e.g., social and physical activity levels), health-related (e.g., vitamin B_{12} and folic acid deficiency, circulatory disease, depression, dementia), and genetic (e.g., apolipoprotein E) factors. A progressive area of activity in current research on cognitive aging is the use of brain-imaging techniques (e.g., positron emission tomography [PET], functional magnetic resonance imaging [fMRI]) to investigate neural correlates of age-related performance changes. We will make reference to this emerging literature.

Finally, we discuss recent observations indicating that a large portion of the age-related variance in memory, other cognitive (e.g., speed, reasoning, and fluid intelligence), and sensory and motor functioning is shared (Anstey, Lord, & Williams, 1997; Baltes & Lindenberger, 1997; Lindenberger & Baltes, 1994; Salthouse, Hambrick, & McGuthry, 1998; Verhaeghen & Salthouse, 1997). Assuming that such patterns of data reflect common origins of age-related changes, an important task is to delineate ways in which these origins may be identified. For many of the domains and issues raised in this chapter,

Handbook of the Psychology of Aging
Copyright © 2001 by Academic Press.
All rights of reproduction in any form reserved.

there are excellent reviews available to which the reader is referred.

II. Nonepisodic Forms of Memory

Tulving (1999) suggested that all forms of learning and memory, except episodic memory, share the feature that they are oriented toward the present or the future at the time of retrieval. Thus, for nonepisodic forms of memory, it does not matter how the information was acquired. Although there is no necessity for any conscious access to the past, these forms of memory are important because they shape and effectively enhance the individual's interaction with present or future environments. In the following subsections, we briefly review relevant research on the effects of aging on procedural memory, priming, semantic memory, and short-term memory.

A. Procedural Memory

Procedural memory underlies the acquisition of skills and other aspects of knowledge that are not directly accessible to consciousness and the presence of which can only be demonstrated indirectly by action (e.g., walking, skating). It involves the acquisition of motor, perceptual, or cognitive operations that occurs gradually as a function of practice (Nyberg & Tulving, 1996). Unlike semantic and episodic information that can be acquired quickly, acquisition of most procedural skills occurs slowly. At an early point, the acquisition of any skill poses demands on other types of memory, but practice will transfer the performance of the skill to procedural memory (e.g., learning to drive, learning to type). In contrast to other types of knowledge, procedural knowledge is little influenced by the passage of time, which is reflected by the fact that we can adequately perform skills that we may not have practiced for years.

Unfortunately, relatively little research has addressed the relationship between different categories of procedural learning and aging, although it is commonly held that procedural memory is largely unaffected by age, particularly when contrasted against the pattern of findings in episodic memory tasks (e.g., Light & La Voie, 1993). Evidence in favor of the robustness of skill acquisition in old age was reported by Schugens, Daum, Spindler, and Birbaumer (1997). In this study, skill learning within the context of a mirror reading task was unaffected by age, whereas explicit recall of verbal and visual materials declined steadily with increasing age.

However, there is evidence that aging may affect procedural memory negatively, and there are indications that age differences may vary as a function of the complexity of the task. Specifically, age-related deficits have been reported in both nonmotor and motor procedural tasks, including the pursuit rotor task (Wright & Payne, 1985), learning to read inverted sentences (Moscovitch, Winocur, & McLachlan, 1986), and partial word identification (Hashtroudi, Chrosniak, & Schwartz, 1991). Interestingly, in the Hashtroudi et al. study, age differences were present only when stimuli were presented at a short presentation rate or at a high degree of degradation.

One reason for the somewhat mixed evidence in research on aging and procedural memory may be differences among studies with regard to the requirement of strategies, which may draw on cognitive abilities other than procedural memory (e.g., working memory, visuospatial skill, reasoning). Thus, age-related deficits in these other abilities may underlie age differences in procedural memory. Related to this is the issue of whether baseline performance or rate of acquisition constitutes the primary outcome measure. Whereas baseline performance in procedural tasks likely reflects a variety of factors (e.g., strategies, working memory), learning rate across trials should reflect the ability to acquire procedural knowledge. Indeed, several reports demonstrate age invariance in learning rate in procedural tasks, although the young outperform the old at baseline (Howard & Howard, 1989; Moscovitch et al., 1986; Vakil & Agmon-Ashkenazi, 1997).

A final point to note is that preservation of procedural memory in old age may not be expected considering that both lesion (Brown & Marsden, 1988) and brain imaging (Grafton, Hazeltine, & Ivry, 1995) data indicate that this form of memory draws on a frontostriatal circuitry that is affected in aging (Rubin, 1999). However, the primary motor cortex, which is relatively well preserved in old age (Raz, 1999), is also typically recruited during procedural memory tasks (Cabeza & Nyberg, 2000). Thus, various procedural memory tasks may differ in the extent to which specific brain regions are recruited, and the extent to which these regions are affected by aging. Also, older adults may be able to compensate for changes in some regions or networks by more effective utilization of others (cf. Cabeza, 2001).

B. Priming

Repetition priming refers to the unconscious facilitation of performance following prior exposure to a target item or a related stimulus (Schacter, 1987). Similar to procedural memory tasks, priming tasks have been referred to as "implicit," because the test instructions do not inform the participants to actively think back at a previous study episode. Implicit retrieval is often contrasted with "explicit" retrieval, as measured by standard episodic memory tasks in which subjects are told to recollect information from the study session (Graf & Mandler, 1984).

A basic distinction in the priming literature is that between perceptual and conceptual priming tasks. Whereas analysis of perceptual features at study and test largely determine the size of the priming effect in perceptual priming tasks (e.g., word identification, word-stem completion, word-fragment completion), conceptual priming tasks (e.g., word association, category exemplar generation, fact completion) involve processes related to the meaning of the target information (Roediger & McDermott, 1993).

The initial work on the effects of aging in priming tasks revealed nonexistent differences between young and older adults (e.g., Light & Albertson, 1989; Light, Singh, & Capps, 1986; Mitchell, 1989). Although this pattern of results has been largely confirmed in more recent studies, a meta-analysis indicated a small overall priming advantage for young over older adults (La-Voie & Light, 1994). One controversial issue has been whether age-related priming deficits are more likely to occur for conceptual compared with perceptual tests (Jelicic, Craik, & Moscovitch, 1996; Rybash, 1996; Small, Hultsch, & Masson, 1995). In a recent overview, Fleischman and Gabrieli (1998) found no support for this hypothesis: The dominant pattern for both perceptual and conceptual priming tests is age equivalence, and there is little evidence for differential impairment in aging for either class of priming test.

Based on some findings that age-related priming deficits may be larger in tasks that put higher demands on production at retrieval than in those that largely involve identifying an item (Chiarello & Hoyer, 1988; Davis et al., 1990; Rybash, 1994; Winocur, Moscovitch, & Stuss, 1996), Fleischman and Gabrieli (1998) suggested that the production–identification distinction may be useful in accounting for patterns of age differences and similarities in priming (see also Gabrieli et al., 1999). Although this proposal makes intuitive sense and is consistent with portions of the relevant data, it fails to account for other findings, including age equivalence in conceptual priming tasks with considerable demands on production (e.g., Maki & Knopman, 1996). Conceivably, the presence or absence of age-related differences in priming depends on multiple interactions between subject-related and experimental factors as well as factors related to statistical power and test reliability.

The general pattern of small or nonexistent age differences in priming is substantiated in brain-imaging research on word-stem completion. The standard finding in imaging research on perceptual priming with young adults is a deactivation in posterior cortical areas during priming relative to baseline conditions (Buckner et al., 1995; Schacter, Alpert, Savage, Rauch, & Albert, 1996). The deactivation observed during priming is thought to reflect a shaping of the relevant neuronal population so that less neural activity is required to process a stimulus at a subsequent compared with a previous encounter (Ungerleider, 1995). A similar pattern of deactivation in posterior neocortex during priming has been demonstrated in older adults (Bäckman, Almkvist, et al., 1997; Bäckman, Almkvist, Nyberg, & Andersson, 2000), suggesting that the neural basis for perceptual priming is unaffected in old age.

Research using other methodologies has corroborated the view that age-related deficits in implicit memory are relatively small. In Jacoby's (1991) Process Dissociation Procedure, the relative contributions of automatic (implicit) and controlled (explicit) processes to memory can be separated. Using this procedure, investigators have reported age-related deficits in the controlled component along with no age differences in the automatic component (Jennings & Jacoby, 1993; Salthouse, Toth, Hancock, & Woodard, 1997; Titov & Knight, 1997). In the know–remember paradigm (Gardiner & Java, 1993), memory is partitioned into items that subjects consciously recollect having encountered (remember) versus those for which they

merely have a feeling of familiarity (know). Research indicates that the overall advantage of young adults in both cued recall and recognition is attributable to a greater proportion of remember responses; age-related differences are minimal for know responses (Mäntylä, 1993; Parkin & Walter, 1992).

C. Semantic Memory

Semantic memory deals with our general knowledge of the world, including meanings about words, concepts, and symbols, their associations as well as rules for manipulating these concepts and symbols (Tulving, 1983). The information in semantic memory is stored without reference to the temporal and spatial context present at the time of acquisition.

An important aspect of semantic memory is what has been referred to as the internal lexicon. The internal lexicon is thought of as consisting of a network of nodes that represents words, concepts, and associations between different representations (e.g., Collins & Loftus, 1975). It is assumed that the information is organized hierarchically, following a top-to-bottom structure. The superordinate category (e.g., fruit) is represented at the top of the hierarchy, its more specific attributes (e.g., yellow, sour) further down the hierarchy, followed by lower order categories (e.g., banana, lemon).

Several lines of evidence suggest that the organization and associative structure of the internal lexicon remain stable across the adult life span (Laver & Burke, 1993). For example, young and older adults typically do not differ in the types of word associations emitted (Burke & Peters, 1986), they access categorical information alike (Balota & Duchek, 1988), and vocabulary scores remain stable or even increase from early to late adulthood (Bäckman & Nilsson, 1996; Salthouse, 1988). Furthermore, the pattern of semantic priming effects are similar in young and older adults (Howard, Heisey, & Shaw, 1986; Nebes, Boller, & Holland, 1986). However, although Howard et al. (1986) reported similar semantic priming effects across age in a lexical decision task, the young subjects showed priming at shorter latencies compared with the older subjects. This outcome suggests that the semantic network is intact, but that lexical access may be slower in old age. Small or nonexistent age differences have also been reported in tasks assessing the ability to describe objects (Stine, 1986), release from proactive inhibition (Puglisi, 1980), and monitoring of general knowledge (Lachman, Lachman, & Thronesberry, 1979).

However, not all aspects of semantic memory are resistant to aging. Older adults have been found to exhibit more blockages of lexical information than do younger adults, as exemplified by age-related increases in tip-of-the-tongue experiences that may reflect problems in accessing phonological representations of words from semantic cues (Burke, MacKay, Worthley, & Wade, 1991). Word-finding problems in old age are also illustrated by difficulties among older adults in remembering proper names (Crook & West, 1990), generating items in tests of verbal fluency (Bäckman & Nilsson, 1996), naming common objects (Au et al., 1995; Mitrushina & Satz, 1995), and producing words from definitions (Maylor, 1990).

Additional evidence for the view that semantic memory difficulties among older adults are due to retrieval failures rather than to structural changes was provided by Hultsch, Hertzog, Small, McDonald-Miszczak, and Dixon (1992). These authors reported an age-related decline across a 3-year period in tasks with high retrieval demands (fact recall and verbal fluency), but not for a task with a high level of retrieval support (vocabulary). The pattern of semantic memory deficits in normal aging differs from that seen in Alzheimer's disease (AD). Not only are semantic memory deficits markedly exacerbated in AD; they are also characterized by both access problems (Bonilla & Johnson, 1995) and alterations in the structure of the semantic network (Chan, Butters, Paulsen, Salmon, & Swenson, 1993). However, note that some research suggests that age-related reductions in vocabulary size may occur in very old age (Gilinsky & Judd, 1994; Lindenberger & Baltes, 1994).

Thus, at least until late senescence, it is unlikely that age-related deficits in semantic memory reflect a degradation of the semantic network; conceptual knowledge seems to be organized in a similar fashion in early and late adulthood. A more probable account is that such deficits stem largely from problems in accessing lexical information rapidly (for a review, see Light, 1992).

D. Short-Term Memory

Short-term memory operations can be roughly divided into those that deal with merely holding information in consciousness (primary memory) and those that involve processing information while maintaining other information as well as task-relevant goals and strategies at a conscious level (working memory; Baddeley, 1986).

There is converging evidence that measures of primary memory functioning such as digit span forward or primary memory scores derived from the Tulving and Colotla (1970) lag method yield small or nonexistent age-related differences (Corey-Bloom et al. 1996; Gregoire & Van der Linden, 1997; Howieson, Holm, Kaye, Oken, & Howieson, 1993; Wahlin et al., 1993; Wahlin, Bäckman, & Winblad, 1995). Such results suggest that maintaining information in mind in a relatively untransformed fashion for a brief period of time is little affected by the normal aging process.

To be sure, primary memory has emerged as a domain that is little affected by numerous conditions with serious repercussions for cognitive functioning, including AD (Morris, 1996; Simon, Leach, Winocur, & Moscovitch, 1995). Thus, we should not be surprised by the fact that normal old persons perform relatively well in primary memory tasks.

The pattern of results observed for primary memory tasks may be contrasted against that seen in working memory tasks: When the task requires simultaneous storage and processing of information, age-related deficits are robust. Such findings have been documented in various tasks assessing working memory span, including reading span, computational span, and listening span (Brébion, Ehrlich, & Tardieu, 1995; Gilinsky & Judd, 1994; Hultsch, Hertzog, & Dixon, 1990; Hultsch et al., 1992; Norman, Kemper, & Kynette, 1992; Salthouse & Babcock, 1991). Moreover, the size of the age-related working memory deficit increases with increasing cognitive demands (Craik & Rabinowitz, 1984; Salthouse, 1994). Obviously, working memory is not a unitary concept. In an attempt to determine whether age-related working memory deficits reflect problems in storage, processing, or executive function, Salthouse and Babcock (1991) found evidence that deficits in the processing component of working memory constitute the major source of the difficulty. Furthermore, evidence suggests that the magnitude of age-related working memory deficits depends on the type of strategies older persons can use to cope with the conflicting demands characteristic of a working memory test (Brébion, Smith, & Ehrlich, 1997).

The general pattern of small age-related differences in primary memory along with pronounced age-related differences in working memory was substantiated in a meta-analysis (Verhaeghen, Marcoen, & Goossens, 1993), demonstrating a considerably larger effect size for age in working memory tasks compared with primary memory tasks.

Recent brain-imaging work indicates that prefrontal regions are typically activated during working memory performance (for a review, see Cabeza & Nyberg, 2000). Of interest in this context are findings suggesting age-related decreases in specificity of neural processing during working memory performance. Specifically, the relative dominance of the right or left prefrontal cortex (depending on the task conditions) appears to be altered in old age, where the pattern of prefrontal activation in working memory tasks is more bilateral (Grady et al., 1998; Reuter-Lorenz et al., 2000). A recent study by Rypma and D'Esposito (2000) demonstrated no age-related differences in the ventrolateral prefrontal cortex during working memory performance, although there were age-related decreases of activity during working memory retrieval in the dorsolateral prefrontal cortex. These patterns of age similarities and differences in activation are consistent with the behavioral data reviewed above, as the ventrolateral prefrontal cortex has been linked to more passive short-term memory operations, whereas the dorsolateral prefrontal cortex has been associated with higher level working memory operations (Petrides, 1995)

III. Episodic Memory

Episodic memory deals with the acquisition and retrieval of information that is acquired in a particular place at a particular time. It involves traveling back in time to remember personally experienced events through conscious recollective processes. This orientation toward the past makes episodic memory phenomenologically different from other varieties of memory. In the laboratory, episodic memory is typically assessed by asking persons to recall or recognize some information encountered in the experimental setting.

A. General Patterns

As summarized in several excellent reviews on learning and memory in earlier editions of this handbook (Craik, 1977; Hultsch & Dixon, 1990; Poon, 1985; Smith, 1996), there is strong evidence for age-related deficits in episodic memory functioning. Three general aspects concerning the pattern of episodic memory performance across adulthood are noteworthy. First, the onset of decline appears to occur earlier in life than perhaps commonly thought. Second, episodic memory deteriorates from early to late adulthood in a continuous rather than in a discrete fashion. Third, the rate of decline is relatively slow. These observations were evident in two recent large-scale studies involving subjects from the mid-30s through 80 years of age (Nilsson et al., 1997) and from the late teens through the mid-90s (Salthouse, 1998).

These characteristics of adult episodic memory functioning are interesting to consider in light of other observations, and may have implications for understanding the source(s) of the age-related impairment. First, the fact that episodic memory peaks in early adulthood is consistent with the observation that autobiographical memories from around 20 years of age tend to be most vivid, although other factors likely contribute to this phenomenon (Rubin, Rahhal, & Poon, 1998). Second, the early onset and gradual nature of the age-related episodic memory decline should be taken into account in attempts to determine biological or other origins of the decline. Specifically, whatever the proposed origin may be, it would strengthen the case if the causative factor would show a similar onset and trajectory as the behavioral data. Third, the slow rate of decline may be an important reason for the relatively small age-related

changes observed in many longitudinal studies on episodic memory using short retest intervals (Albert et al., 1995; Hultsch et al., 1992). Indeed, Zelinski and Burnight (1997) argued that reliable age-related changes may not be expected for follow-up periods shorter than 6 years.

An important issue in research on aging and episodic memory has been whether the size of the age-related impairment varies systematically across different encoding and retrieval conditions. Because of age-related deficits in self-initiated processing (Craik, 1983) and recoding operations (Bäckman, 1985), it was argued that differences in memory performance between young and older adults should be magnified when the task offers little cognitive support and attenuated when task conditions are more supportive (e.g., free vs. cued recall of words; word vs. object recognition). Although the observation that age differences in general increase from recognition through cued recall to free recall (Bäckman & Larsson, 1992; Craik & McDowd, 1987) provides partial support for this view, numerous other studies do not (for reviews, see Bäckman, Mäntylä, & Herlitz, 1990; Craik & Jennings, 1992).

In particular, although single studies have demonstrated selective gains from the provision of cognitive support in both older (Park, Smith, Morrell, Puglisi, & Dudley, 1990; Sharps & Gollin, 1988) and younger (Puglisi & Park, 1987; Rabinowitz, 1989) adults, the typical finding is one of parallel gains from cognitive support across the adult life span (e.g., Bäckman, 1991; Cohen, Sandler, & Schroeder, 1987; Dixon & Gould, 1998; Johnson, Schmitt, & Pitrukowicz, 1989; Rabinowitz & Craik, 1986). The conflicting results likely reflect complex interactions among multiple subject-related and experimental variables (Bäckman et al., 1990; Craik & Jennings, 1992).

The notion that the age-related episodic memory deficit is rather global receives further support from two other sources. First, research indicates that the deficit generalizes across different materials, including words, sentences, prose passages, faces, and actions; and sensory modalities, including vision, hearing, touch, and smell (Bäckman, Small, & Larsson, 2000). Second, the fact that the magnitude of the deficit is not appreciably different in laboratory-based tasks and tasks that may be more representative of everyday remembering is yet another indication of its generality (Allaire & Marsiske, 1999).

In the research reviewed above, episodic memory was assessed using retrospective recall or recognition of item information. Next, we discuss the patterns of age differences observed in research focusing on other aspects of episodic remembering, namely source memory, false memory, and prospective memory.

B. Source Memory

Most of our memories are likely to be externally derived in the sense that they include information we have heard other people say, events we have witnessed, or acts we have performed. However, memories may also originate from internal sources and be generated from our imaginations, dreams, plans, and so on (Johnson, Hashtroudi, & Lindsay, 1993). In current conceptualizations of source memory, the term *source* refers to the specific conditions that were present when a certain memory was acquired (e.g., the temporal, spatial, and social context of the event; the modality through which it was perceived).

Johnson et al. (1993) distinguished among three types of source monitoring discriminations. First, the process of discriminating between internally generated and externally derived information (e.g., to discriminate between fantasy and perceived experiences) is referred to as reality

monitoring. Second, internal source monitoring involves discriminating between different internally generated memories (e.g., discriminating one's thoughts from what one says). Third, external source monitoring requires distinguishing between different external sources (discriminating statements made by one person from statements made by another person).

Most aging research on source memory has focused on external source monitoring. In general, this research indicates age-related deficits in remembering the contexts in which target items were presented, including color (Park & Puglisi, 1985), input modality (Larsson & Bäckman, 1998), and font (Naveh-Benjamin & Craik, 1995). However, some research suggests that the magnitude of the age effect depends on the nature of the source memory task. For example, Ferguson, Hashtroudi, and Johnson (1992) found that older adults were impaired when the source was one of two women, that is, when perceptual cues were similar. However, this age deficit was overcome when perceptual cues were made more distinctive, in this case when the information was presented by a man and a woman. This outcome suggests that the requirement of perceptual and cognitive differentiation may determine the size of age-related source memory deficits (see also Bayen, Murnane, & Erdfelder, 1996; Johnson, De Leonardis, Hashtroudi, & Ferguson, 1995).

Another finding in this literature is that age-related deficits in both external and internal source monitoring may be observed, although young and older adults perform equally well in reality monitoring tasks (Degl'Innocenti & Bäckman, 1996; Hashtroudi, Johnson, & Chrosniak, 1989). To the extent that reality monitoring requires a less distinctive encoding of perceptual and cognitive features than external or internal source monitoring (Raye & Johnson, 1980), these findings too are in agreement with the view that the degree of elaboration required to discriminate between sources is a critical factor for the presence or absence of age differences. The fact that age-related deficits may occur also in reality-monitoring tasks when the sources are less salient (Brown, Jones, & Davis, 1995; Hashtroudi, Johnson, Vnek, & Ferguson, 1994) provides additional evidence for this view.

In this research, source memory scores are typically conditionalized on item memory scores. Thus, the presence of age-related deficits in source memory indicates that such deficits are larger than those observed for item memory (see Spencer & Raz, 1994, for a meta-analysis). However, this should not be taken to mean that item and source memory draw on qualitatively different processes. As noted by Johnson et al. (1993), different memory tasks require different degrees of differentiation such that, for example, a recognition task requires less perceptual and cognitive differentiation than a source monitoring task. Empirical evidence in favor of this view comes from research indicating that source decisions require more processing time than do recognition decisions (Johnson, Kounios, & Reeder, 1992). Thus, the finding of a selective age deficit in source memory may reflect that older adults have problems in binding perceptual features with target information at encoding, and to reconstruct this information at retrieval (Chalfonte & Johnson, 1996; Schacter, Osowiecki, Kaszniak, Kihlstrom, & Valdiserri, 1994).

C. False Memory

An area of research that has received considerable attention in recent years is that of false memories. In part, this research has been motivated by a need to understand the nature of false memories in legal contexts. In experimental research on this topic, Deese's false memory paradigm has often been employed (Deese, 1959; Roediger & McDermott, 1995). In this paradigm, participants are exposed to a list of semantically related items (e.g., candy, sour, sugar, bitter) and the subsequent recall or recognition of a related nonpresented word (e.g., sweet) is examined. The influence of the semantic associates is quite powerful and can result in high recall levels as well as a high degree of confidence for nonpresented words (Schacter, Norman, & Koutstaal, 1998). A number of studies have examined this and related paradigms among older adults (e.g., Schacter, Koutstaal, & Norman, 1997). In general, results indicate that although older adults recall or recognize fewer of the presented items, their recall of nonpresented items is comparable to that of younger adults (Balota et al., 1999; Kensinger & Schacter, 1999). As a result, when false recall is calculated as a proportion of total recall, older adults produce more false memories than their younger counterparts. Koutstaal, Schacter, Galluccio and Stofer (1999) instructed younger and older participants to employ more careful scrutiny of items at encoding and retrieval. Although these manipulations reduced the number of false memories for both age groups, they did not completely eliminate the age-related increase in false recognition rate.

This pattern of results has been attributed to a greater reliance upon gist or general features of the information in older compared with young adults (Tun, Wingfield, Rosen, & Blanchard, 1998). Toward this end, it is interesting to note that an increased tendency of older adults to focus on more general aspects of the information to be remembered has been reported before in both the text recall (Dixon, Hultsch, Simon, & von Eye, 1984) and word recall (Mäntylä & Bäckman, 1990) literature. As a final comment, it is likely that impairments in source memory functioning as described above make it more difficult for older adults to discriminate between what was actually present versus just inferred (Rybash & Hrubi-Bopp, 2000).

D. Prospective Memory

Prospective memory involves remembering to do something in the future (Brandimonte, Einstein, & McDaniel, 1996). Despite some initial research indicating small or nonexistent age differences in prospective memory using both laboratory-based (Einstein & McDaniel, 1990) and naturalistic (Dobbs & Rule, 1987) tasks, the bulk of research demonstrates that the pattern of age-related differences in prospective memory resembles closely that observed in retrospective memory (e.g., Einstein, McDaniel, Cunfer, & Guynn, 1995; Mäntylä, 1994; Maylor, 1993).

Although age-related deficits in prospective memory are legion, the size of the impairment may be greater for some tasks than for others. For example, older adults may do as well as young adults in remembering future actions when they can rely on external reminders, but not when internal reminding has to be utilized (Maylor, 1990). Relatedly, age-related deficits are more easily observed in time-based (e.g., remembering to call a colleague on Friday) compared to event-based (e.g., remembering to tell your friend to read a particular book the next time you meet her) prospective memory tasks (e.g., Einstein & McDaniel, 1990; Einstein et al., 1995).

Typically, an event-based task involves some form of external event that cues retrieval, whereas time-based tasks require more self-initiated processing for successful performance. Indeed, several studies indicate that it is not the time-based versus event-based nature of the prospective memory task that determines the magnitude of age-related differences. Rather, the salience of the prospective cue that triggers remembering appears to be the critical factor, with age differences increasing as a function of decreasing cue salience (Mäntylä, 1994; Maylor, 1993, 1996; Park, Hertzog, Kidder, Morrell, & Mayhorn, 1997). Recent research indicates that an age-related decline in accessing relevant cues may cause momentary lapses of intention, which in turn result in prospective memory failures among older adults (West & Craik, 1999).

Thus, there is an interesting similarity between prospective and retrospective memory for both items and sources: Across all these classes of tasks, age-related performance deficits seem to be magnified when the demands on self-initiated processing are high (Craik & Kerr, 1996). Additional evidence for this view comes from research demonstrating that age-related deficits in prospective memory are most pronounced when subjects are engaged in a highly demanding task in the context of remembering something prospectively (Einstein, Smith, McDaniel, & Shaw, 1997).

IV. Theoretical Notions

In the following subsections, we review current attempts to account for age-related memory deficits focusing on cognitive and biological factors.

A. Cognitive Accounts

Until some years ago, attempts to explain age-related deficits in remembering largely involved specific memory processes operationalized within an experimental context (e.g., elaboration, organization). Although experimentally based accounts of age-related episodic memory deficits such as integration and reconstruction of contextual information (Schacter et al., 1994), encoding and use of temporal information (Wingfield, Lindfield, & Kahana, 1998), and efficiency of strategy use (Dunlosky & Hertzog, 1998) still populate the literature, in recent years they have been successively replaced by more general explanatory constructs (e.g., processing speed, working memory capacity). The power of such constructs in accounting for age-related deficits is typically assessed using correlational rather than experimental approaches.

There is compelling evidence that statistical control of indices of speed or working memory attenuates greatly or even eliminates age-related differences in episodic memory (Luszcz, Bryan, & Kent, 1997; Park et al., 1996; Hultsch, Hertzog, Dixon, & Small, 1998; Salthouse & Babcock, 1991). Based on such findings, it has been suggested that age-related changes in a complex cognitive activity such as episodic remembering may be mediated by changes in more fundamental processing resources (Salthouse, 1996, 1998). The mediational approach has radically altered the field of aging and memory, by moving the level of explanation from the domain- or even task-specific level to a more general level, thereby highlighting the multivariate cognitive space in which remembering takes place. However, several authors have noted that the exact way(s) in which the lower order construct affects the criterion measure is poorly understood (Salthouse & Craik, 1999; Zacks, Hasher, & Li, 1999). A more detailed specification of these links may help understanding of why speed has emerged as the strongest mediator of age-related differences in episodic memory in some studies (Park et al., 1996), whereas working memory has done the best job in others (Hultsch et al., 1998). Relatedly, more knowledge is needed concerning the relationship between the lower order mediators and more specific memory-related processes, such as contextual integration and strategy use. The finding that improvement on a popular measure of a basic resource (i.e., substitution coding as a measure of speed) may be more strongly related to memory (i.e., an often

used criterion variable) than to other measures of speed (Piccinin & Rabbitt, 1999) also urges caution in interpreting some findings within this analytical framework.

In addition, Lindenberger and Pötter (1998) expressed concerns with regard to some basic features of the mediational approach to age-related cognitive deficits. Essentially, they demonstrated that the estimate of age-related variance that is reduced by the inclusion of a mediator can vary greatly depending on the correlation between the mediator and outcome variables. Thus, the legitimacy of this method hinges on both the potential for the mediator to account for age-related variance, and the relationship between the mediator and the outcome variable themselves. This is not to say that the mediational approach, instantiated through the use of multiple regression or structural equation modeling, is inherently flawed. Rather, more consideration should be placed on this potentially biasing relationship by authors who embrace this method of data analysis. Finally, Lindenberger and Pötter advocate the examination of longitudinal patterns of performance, rather than relying solely upon cross-sectional designs.

B. Biological Accounts

The effects of aging on episodic memory are interesting in view of the fact that numerous other more or less devastating conditions (e.g., AD, Korsakoff's syndrome, depression, alcohol intoxication, sleep deprivation) exert strong effects on episodic memory, while typically leaving other forms of memory less affected (Bäckman et al., 2000). Tulving (1999) speculated that the apparent vulnerability of episodic memory to multiple conditions with diverse affects on brain functioning may reflect the fact that it evolved late phylogenetically (Suddendorf & Corballis, 1997) and lags behind other forms of memory ontogenetically (Perner & Ruffman, 1995). Perhaps as a consequence of its advanced nature, episodic memory is a biologically complex cognitive ability. Lesion (for a review, see Prull, Gabrieli, & Bunge, 1999) and imaging (for a review, see Cabeza & Nyberg, 2000) studies indicate that episodic memory draws on a widespread network of brain structures, including the hippocampus and related regions, diencephalon, anterior cingulate gyrus, precuneus and other parietal structures, cerebellum, and frontal cortex. The susceptibility of episodic memory to human aging and multiple other conditions may thus reflect that performance could be disrupted because of changes at multiple sites in a large distributed network.

In addition, brain structures that may be particularly relevant to episodic memory are known to be affected by aging. Specifically, moderate age-related shrinkage of the hippocampus (Golomb et al., 1994; Jernigan et al., 1991) and a more sizable loss of frontal volume in old age (Raz et al., 1997; Raz, Gunning-Dixon, Head, Dupuis, & Acker, 1998) has been reported. In general, attempts to link volumetric measurements of these structure to age-related episodic memory deficits have been successful, with most studies reporting moderate to strong relationships (for a review, see Raz, 1999).

The pattern of outcome from studies in which the brain activity of young and older adults is compared during encoding and retrieval is less consistent, likely reflecting differences across studies in tasks, methods, and subject selection procedures, as well as small sample sizes. Nevertheless, there are several findings in this literature that may contribute to our understanding of age-related episodic memory deficits. Grady et al. (1995) found an age-related decrease in hippocampal activity during encoding of faces. Such a decrease was not observed during recognition (see also Bäckman et al., 1997; Schacter et al., 1996). This suggests that age-

related functional changes in the hippocampus are more likely to occur at encoding than at retrieval. There is also evidence of age-related decreases of activity in left inferior frontal cortex during episodic encoding (Cabeza et al., 1997). This region has been implicated in semantic elaboration during encoding in imaging research with young adults (Kapur et al., 1994). Of interest is also the finding that young adults show decreased activity in left frontal cortex under conditions of divided attention (Idaka, Anderson, Kapur, Cabeza, & Craik, 2000). In addition, in young adults prefrontal activation is lateralized for episodic memory, such that left prefrontal activity dominates during encoding and right prefrontal activity dominates at retrieval (for a review, see Nyberg, Cabeza, & Tulving, 1996). Several studies demonstrate that this encoding–retrieval asymmetry is markedly reduced in old age (Bäckman et al., 1997; Cabeza et al., 1997; Madden et al., 1999), possibly reflecting age-related decreases in specificity of neural processing during episodic remembering (see Cabeza, 2001).

C. Individual Differences among Older Adults

Although older adults, in general, perform more poorly than young adults in episodic memory tasks, there is great variability within the older population with regard to the size of the impairment. In the following section, we review relevant individual-difference research focusing on demographic, lifestyle, health-related, and genetic factors. Note that most of the specific factors discussed appear to affect memory performance in a similar fashion across adulthood. Thus, knowledge of these relationships is not very useful in determining the sources of age-related performance deficits, although it is informative in understanding late-life variability in memory performance.

1. Demographic Factors

Age, education, and sex are all related to episodic memory performance in late life. The age-related deterioration from early to late adulthood continues in a fairly linear fashion in very old age, and qualitative differences in patterns of performance are rarely observed when people in the 70s and the 90s are compared (Wahlin et al., 1993; Zelinski & Burnight, 1997). There is a positive relationship between education and memory performance in old age, although the relative importance of factors occurring before (e.g., genetic and social selection), during (e.g., learning of memory-relevant skills, dendritic growth), and after (e.g., cognitive stimulation during the active work period, health behaviors) the educational experience for this relationship remains unknown (Bäckman et al., 1999). There is also emerging evidence for an advantage of women over men in episodic memory that is not seen for other forms of memory (Herlitz, Nilsson, & Bäckman, 1997). Both biological (e.g., Collaer & Hines, 1995) and social (e.g., Eagly & Wood, 1999) factors have been proposed to account for this sex difference that appears to generalize across adulthood (Meinz & Salthouse, 1998).

2. Lifestyle Factors

Two classes of lifestyle factors have been especially targeted as potential correlates of episodic memory functioning in old age, namely activity patterns and substance use. There is strong cross-sectional evidence for a positive relationship between engagement in social, cognitive, and physical activities and memory performance in aging (e.g., Christensen et al., 1996; Hill, Wahlin, Winblad, & Bäckman, 1995; Hultsch, Hammer, & Small, 1993). Obviously, such findings are not very informative concerning the causal relationship between activity levels and memory.

A longitudinal study examined the relationship between self-reported health, activity life-style, and cognitive performance (Hultsch, Hertzog, Small, & Dixon, 1999). Although the authors failed to observe a link between changes in health status and cognitive performance across a 6-year follow-up period, a relationship was observed between changes in intellectually stimulating activities and changes in cognitive functioning. However, this pattern of results could also be interpreted as cognitively able individuals leading active lives up until the point where decline in cognitive abilities limits this activity. Overall, Hultsch et al. failed to observe strong evidence for a causal relationship between changes in health and lifestyle patterns and cognitive performance in late life. To be sure, evidence for or against such relationships is dependent upon methodological factors, such as the length of the follow-up interval and the ways in which health and activity lifestyle are conceptualized (Hertzog, Hultsch & Dixon, 1999; Pushkar et al., 1999).

Attempts to link use of alcohol and tobacco to memory performance have yielded mixed results. Although some research indicates that substance use may be negatively associated with memory functioning in old age (Hill, 1989), other research demonstrates positive effects (Elias, Elias, D'Agostino, Silberhatz, & Wolf, 1999; Hultsch et al., 1993), and still other research reveals no effects (Hill et al., 1995). Note also that when effects from substance use have been found, these have been relatively small. Thus, the safest conclusion from the available data is that use of tobacco and alcohol has limited effects on memory performance in old age.

3. Health-Related Factors

Many specific conditions that are detrimental to memory functioning increase dramatically in old age, including AD and vascular disorders (Brody & Schneider, 1986; Fozard, Metter, & Brant, 1990). In cognitive aging research, investigators have predominantly relied on self-reported measures in examining the relationship between health and memory. In general, such measures are related to objectively verified indicators of health (e.g., Busch, Miller, Golden, & Hale, 1989), although the size of the relationship varies across conditions (Haapanen, Miilunpalo, Pasanen, Oja, & Vuori, 1997). In addition, self-reported measures of health are typically related to memory performance (e.g., Earles, Connor, Smith, & Park, 1997; Perlmutter & Nyquist, 1990).

Examining the relationship between specific conditions and memory performance should provide more exact information concerning the health–memory link. In the following, we describe the effects of a select number of conditions on memory performance in old age. Much research has addressed the influence on memory of different types of diseases related to the circulatory system, ranging from hypertension (e.g., Launer, Masaki, Petrovitch, Foley, & Havlik, 1995) through neurologically "silent" cerebral infarctions (e.g., Price et al., 1997) to stroke (e.g., Bowler, Hadar, & Wade, 1994) and vascular dementia (e.g., Ricker, Keenan, & Jacobson, 1994). In general, this research suggests that circulatory disturbance has negative effects on memory performance, the size of the effect varying with the severity of the condition and the site affected.

Impaired memory performance in elderly adults with diabetes is routinely observed (e.g., Croxon & Jagger, 1995; Zelinski, Crimmins, Reynolds, & Seeman, 1998). Interestingly, nondiabetic older persons with impaired glucose tolerance also show memory impairment, although the size of the deficit is smaller than in diabetics (Kalmijn, Feskens, Launer, Stijnen, & Kromhout, 1995). This suggests a continuum of memory problems in diabetes that progresses from the subclinical to the clinical stage. A similar continuum has been observed in depression. Specifically, it is well established that old age depression is related to deficits in episodic memory functioning (for reviews, see Burt, Zembar, & Niederehe, 1995; Kindermann & Brown, 1997). It has also been found that subclinical variations in depressive symptomatology are related to memory performance, with those persons who suffer from some depressive symptoms occupying an intermediate position between the nonsymptomatic and the clinically depressed on a dimension reflecting degree of memory impairment (Bäckman & Forsell, 1994; Bäckman, Hill, & Forsell, 1996).

Evidence also indicates that subclinical vitamin B_{12} and folic acid deficiency (Hassing, Wahlin, Winblad, & Bäckman, 1999; Wahlin, Hill, Winblad, & Bäckman, 1996) as well as thyroid disturbance (Wahlin, Robins-Wahlin, Small, & Bäckman, 1998) may exert relatively strong effects on episodic memory in old age. Although the biological mechanism(s) for these effects remain unclear, both vitamin deficiency and thyroid disturbance have been linked to alterations of protein synthesis in the brain (Wahlin et al., 1996; Wahlin et al., 1998), a process which is known to be critical to the consolidation of information in episodic memory (Davis & Squire, 1984).

The most powerful individual-difference variable in cognitive aging is dementia. Dementia diseases, such as AD and vascular dementia, have profound effects on memory functioning even early on in the pathogenesis (for a review, see Morris, 1996). In current research on normal aging and memory, clinically demented individuals are not likely to be included because of the screening procedures adopted. However, several studies have demonstrated that there is a long preclinical period in AD during which cognitive deficits, especially episodic memory deficits, are detectable (e.g., Small, Fratiglioni, Viitanen, Winblad, & Bäckman, 2000; Tierney et al., 1996). Considering that the incidence of dementia increases drastically in old age (e.g., Fratiglioni et al., 1997), the number of preclinical AD cases will increase with advancing age. Sliwinski, Lipton, Buschke, and Stewart (1996) demonstrated how these facts have a bearing on our conclusions regarding normative age-related changes in memory and cognition. Specifically, these investigators showed that eliminating persons who developed dementia across a 4-year interval reduced the size of the age-related differences in memory and other cognitive domains at baseline.

The phenomenon of terminal decline constitutes an analogous case in point. Terminal decline refers to the fact that there is a relationship between proximity to death and cognitive performance (Kleemeier, 1962). Numerous studies have found evidence for terminal decline in memory and other cognitive functioning (for reviews, see Berg, 1996; Small & Bäckman, 1999). As with preclinical AD, the fact that the probability of dying increases in late life implies that the magnitude of normal age-related differences in performance may be overestimated because of the influence of impending death.

As alluded to, some of the conditions discussed in this section are typically screened for in normal cognitive aging research (e.g., dementia, depression). However, others are most often not assessed (e.g., vitamin deficiency, thyroid disturbance) and still others are, for obvious reasons, impossible to take into account in cross-sectional research (e.g., impending dementia and death). The important point is that although most conditions may affect memory and cognition equally across adulthood, the mere fact that their prevalence increases in old age inevitably implies that failure to account

for these conditions will overestimate the size of normal age-related deficits (Bäckman et al., 1999).

4. Genetic Factors

Studies that have examined the relationship between genetics and memory in late life have approached this issue in one of two ways. One class of studies has examined the broad influence of genetics by comparing the performance of monozygotic and dizygotic twins. For example, Johansson et al. (1999) reported that among their measures of primary memory, 47% of the variability in backward digit span and 27% of the variability in forward digit span could be ascribed to heritability. Among the measures of episodic memory, the heritability estimates ranged from 4% for prose recall to 47% for picture recognition. Swan et al. (1999) examined the influence of genes and environment on memory variables derived from the California Verbal Learning Test. In this study, over half (56%) of the variance in a factor defined by measures of verbal learning and memory was linked to heritability. By contrast, no genetic influence was detected for a recognition memory factor. Taken together, although evidence indicates that memory performance is influenced by genetic factors, the magnitude of the influence appears to vary greatly both within and across the domains examined.

The other class of studies have focused on the impact of specific genes on functioning. The gene coding for apolipoprotein E (APOE) has received the most attention due to its relevance as a risk factor for AD (Strittmatter et al., 1993). In these studies, memory performance is compared across individuals with or without the ε4 allele, the allelic variant that conveys the greatest susceptibility to AD. Some studies have found ε4-related deficits in memory performance also among nondemented older persons (Haan, Shemanski, Jagust, Manolio, &

Kuller, 1999; O'Hara et al., 1998), whereas others have failed to observe such a relationship (Small et al., 2000; Smith et al., 1998). Several authors have argued that ε4-related effects on memory performance in nondemented samples may not necessarily reflect an influence of the genotype in normal aging (Bondi et al., 1995; Small, Basun, & Bäckman, 1998). For example, Bondi, Salmon, Galasko, Thomas, and Thal (1999) found that the ε4–non-ε4 group difference disappeared after individuals with preclinical dementia were excluded. As noted, there is an increased risk of developing AD among ε4 carriers, and the preclinical period in AD can last for many years (Petersen et al., 1999; Small et al., 2000). Thus, the cognitive deficits that are observed among nondemented ε4 carriers may be related to an overrepresentation of preclinical dementia cases, rather than to a direct influence of the genotype itself on cognitive performance.

It is anticipated that genetic influences on memory performance will remain an important and active area of research in the future. Wahlsten (1999) argued that as we learn more about the human genome, our focus may shift from the single gene–behavior approach to examining the interaction between multiple genetic and environmental factors and their impact on performance.

D. Shared Variance between Cognitive and Noncognitive Variables

Much of the age-related variance in memory tasks is shared with that in other cognitive tasks, including those assessing not only speed and working memory but also verbal and visuospatial skill and reasoning (e.g., Salthouse, 1998; Salthouse et al., 1998). Moreover, the age-related variance in memory and cognition overlaps to a great extent with that observed in measures of sensory (Baltes & Lindenberger, 1997; Lindenberger & Baltes, 1994) and motor (Anstey et al., 1997) function-

ing. These strong interrelationships among multiple cognitive and noncognitive variables have led many investigators to propose that a common cause may underlie the age-related changes in all these variables (e.g., Anstey, 1999; Baltes & Lindenberger, 1997; Salthouse, Hancock, Meinz, & Hambrick, 1996).

Although the common cause hypothesis is theoretically sensible, it may prove difficult to achieve consensus concerning what the common cause actually represents. At a general (and superficial) level, it is obvious that the common cause is brain aging. However, at a more specific level, finding the biological parameter that would adequately account for the age-related variance in cognitive and other functioning may be doomed to fail, because of the inherent complexity at both the biological and behavioral level.

Rather, determining the biological underpinnings of age-related changes may require consideration of a multitude of factors at different levels of analysis. In this chapter, we have briefly reviewed research using both structural and functional imaging techniques that has provided valuable insights concerning the neural basis of age-related memory deficits. However, it is clear that the activation patterns in functional imaging (Cabeza & Nyberg, 2000) and the volume-performance correlations in structural imaging (Raz, 1999) vary quite substantially across different forms of memory and cognition and even within a certain variety of memory (e.g., episodic) as a function of different task characteristics.

Thus, as a complement to domain or task-specific correlates of age-related memory changes, it would be useful to identify biological variables that may be expected to have a more general influence on age-related changes in cognitive functioning. We would like to close this chapter by noting two lines of research of potential interest in this regard. First, age-related changes in subcortical and cortical white matter are well documented (Kemper, 1994; Strassburger, et al., 1997). White-matter lesions result from loss of myelin, which has been linked to cognitive and motor slowing (Kail, 1998; Tang, Nyengaard, Pakkenberg, & Gundersen, 1997), both of which are characteristic of normal aging. Although white-matter lesions may exert a general influence on cognitive functioning, the empirical evidence for a relationship between white-matter abnormalities and age-related cognitive changes is mixed (e.g., O'Brien, Desmond, Ames, Schweitzer, & Tress, 1997; Raz, Millman, & Sarpel, 1990). This may reflect the fact that the degree of white-matter changes must reach a certain threshold before significant cognitive effects are observed (DeCarli et al., 1995). However, if this is the case, it is unclear how white-matter changes can account for age-related deficits in those cognitive functions (i.e., episodic memory and speed) that are characterized by an early onset and a gradual progression across the adult life span (Nilsson et al., 1997; Salthouse, 1998).

Second, there are gradual losses in the striatal dopamine system across the adult life span. From early to late adulthood, linear decreases in dopaminergic function average 6–10% per decade (Rinne et al., 1993; Wong et al., 1984). Note that this developmental trajectory resembles closely that seen for episodic memory and speed. The cognitive relevance of dopamine is demonstrated in studies of basal ganglia disorders such as Huntington's disease, in which PET-derived measures of dopamine D_1 and D_2 receptor densities show sizable relationships to speed, executive functions, and working and episodic memory (Bäckman, Robins Wahlin, Lundin, Ginovart, & Farde, 1997; Lawrence et al., 1998). Importantly, there is a functional influence of dopaminergic neurotransmission through the parallel cortico-striatal-pallidal-thalamo circuits that form a fundamental basis for information processing in the brain (Gerfen, 1989; Parent & Hazrati, 1995). Indeed, the popular view that age-related cognitive changes largely reflect changes in the frontal cortex (e.g., Shimamura, 1994; West, 1996) was recently challenged by Rubin (1999). In brief, Rubin argued that proponents of this view may have overlooked the potential role of age-related striatal changes in producing deficits in speed, executive functions, and memory.

Two studies are directly relevant to this argument. Volkow et al. (1998) demonstrated parallel age-related reductions for dopamine D_2 receptor binding in caudate and putamen and tasks assessing cognitive speed and executive functions. An interesting finding was that the relationship between D_2 binding and cognitive performance remained after age was partialed out. This suggests that dopaminergic activity may influence cognitive performance irrespective of age. Bäckman et al. (2000) showed that the rather large age-related variance in speed and episodic memory was completely eliminated when controlling for striatal D_2 binding. By contrast, D_2 binding accounted for a substantial proportion of the performance variation independent of age. Thus, these studies suggest that age-related changes in striatal dopamine function are important to consider in determining biological origins of age-related cognitive changes.

V. Concluding Comments

Extant evidence suggests that age-related deficits in primary memory and various forms of priming are small or nonexistent. For procedural and semantic memory, age-related deficits may or may not be observed depending on various demand characteristics. By contrast, tasks assessing working memory and episodic memory typically exhibit a marked performance deterioration from early to late adulthood. In this chapter, we focused on the nature, causes, and variability of age-related episodic memory deficits.

The age-related episodic memory impairment generalizes across (a) different materials and input modalities, (b) multiple domains of assessment (e.g., item memory, source memory, prospective memory), and (c) laboratory and everyday tasks. Although there is partial evidence for the view that the size of age-related memory deficits increases as a function of decreasing retrieval support, most research indicates similar gains from the provision of cognitive support across adulthood. The vulnerability of episodic memory to human aging and multiple other conditions that affect brain functioning may be due to the neural complexity of this form of memory, reflecting its evolved nature, both phylogenetically and ontogenetically.

Despite the generally downward trajectory of episodic memory functioning across the adult life span, there are large performance differences among older adults as a function of various demographic, lifestyle, health-related, and genetic factors. Most of these individual-difference variables exert similar effects on memory performance across adulthood. However, the fact that the majority of cognitively relevant conditions increase in prevalence in old age implies that failure to account for such conditions may overestimate the magnitude of normative age-related differences in memory performance.

Process- or task-specific explanations of age-related memory deficits no longer dominate the scene. In the last decade, such accounts have been challenged by numerous studies demonstrating that the age-related variance in memory performance may be mediated by changes in more fundamental cognitive resources (e.g., speed of processing). Although the mediational approach has produced some of the most consistent data in the cognitive aging literature, some potential statistical and conceptual weaknesses associated with this approach have been identified recently.

An important observation is that the age-related variance in memory performance may be shared both with that in other cognitive domains and in noncognitive domains (e.g., sensory and motor functioning). This fact has led several investigators to propose that a common cause may underlie the overlapping patterns of age-related changes: brain aging. There are several promising lines of research using both structural and functional imaging techniques to determine neural correlates of age-related memory changes. Some of these approaches (e.g., activation studies) will continue to provide important knowledge concerning age-related changes in specific memory processes, whereas others (e.g., receptor studies) may have a greater potential in furthering our understanding of age-related cognitive changes across a wider range of domains.

We believe that future attempts to increase our knowledge of adult life span changes in memory functioning may profit from combining biological indicators at different analytical levels (e.g., blood flow during task performance and receptor densities), as well as from combining various biological parameters with other factors known to produce systematic performance variation (e.g., lifestyle, health-related, and genetic factors).

Acknowledgments

Writing of this chapter was supported by a grant from the Swedish Council for Research in the Humanities and the Social Sciences to Lars Bäckman.

References

Albert, M. S., Jones, K., Savage, C. R., Berkman, L., Seeman, T., Blazer, D., & Rowe, J. C. (1995). Predictors of cognitive change in older persons: MacArthur studies of successful aging. *Psychology and Aging, 10,* 578–589.

Allaire, J. C., & Marsiske, M. (1999). Everyday cognition: Age and intellectual ability correlates. *Psychology and Aging, 14,* 627–644.

Anstey, K. J. (1999). Sensorimotor variables and forced expiratory volume as correlates of speed, accuracy, and variability in reaction time performance in late adulthood. *Aging, Neuropsychology, and Cognition, 6,* 84–95.

Anstey, K. J., Lord, S. R., & Williams, P. (1997). Strength in the lower limbs, visual contrast sensitivity, and simple reaction time predict cognition in older women. *Psychology & Aging, 12,* 137–144.

Au, R., Joung, P., Nicholas, M., Obler, L. K., Kass, R., & Albert, M. L. (1995). Naming ability across the adult life span. *Aging and Cognition, 2,* 300–311.

Bäckman, L. (1985). Compensation and recoding: A framework for aging and memory research. *Scandinavian Journal of Psychology, 26,* 193–207.

Bäckman, L. (1991). Recognition memory across the adult life span: The role of prior knowledge. *Memory and Cognition, 19,* 63–71.

Bäckman, L., Almkvist, O., Andersson, J. L. R., Nordberg, A., Winblad, B., Reineck, R., & Långström, B. (1997). Brain activation in young and older adults during implicit and explicit retrieval. *Journal of Cognitive Neuroscience, 9,* 378–391.

Bäckman, L., Almkvist, O., Nyberg, L., & Andersson, J. L. R. (2000). Functional changes in brain activity during priming in Alzheimer's disease. *Journal of Cognitive Neuroscience, 12,* 134–141.

Bäckman, L., & Forsell, Y. (1994). Episodic memory functioning in a community-based sample of old adults with major depression: Utilization of cognitive support. *Journal of Abnormal Psychology, 103,* 361–370.

Bäckman, L., Ginovart, N., Dixon, R. A., Robins Wahlin, T.-B., Wahlin, Å., Halldin, C., & Farde, L. (2000). Age-related cognitive deficits mediated by changes in the striatal dopamine system. *American Journal of Psychiatry, 157,* 635–637.

Bäckman, L., Hill, R. D., & Forsell, Y. (1996). The influence of depressive symptomatology on episodic memory among clinically nondepressed older adults. *Journal of Abnormal Psychology, 105,* 97–105.

Bäckman, L., & Larsson, M. (1992). Recall of organizable words and objects in adulthood: Influences of instructions, retention interval, and retrieval cues. *Journal of Gerontology: Psychological Sciences, 47,* 273–278.

Bäckman, L., Mäntylä, T., & Herlitz, A. (1990). The optimization of episodic remembering in old age. In P. B. Baltes & M. M. Baltes (Eds.), *Successful aging: Perspectives from the behavioral sciences* (pp. 118–163). New York: Cambridge University Press.

Bäckman, L., & Nilsson, L.-G. (1996). Semantic memory functioning across the adult life span. *European Psychologist, 1,* 27–33.

Bäckman, L., Robins Wahlin, T.-B, Lundin, A., Ginovart, N., Farde, L. (1997). Cognitive deficits in Huntington's disease are predicted by dopaminergic PET markers and brain volumes. *Brain, 120,* 2207–2217.

Bäckman, L., Small, B. J., & Larsson, M. (2000). Memory. In J. G. Evans, T. F. Williams, B. L. Beattie, J.-P. Michel, & G. K. Wilcock (Eds.), *Oxford textbook of geriatric medicine* (2nd ed.) (pp. 906–916). Oxford: Oxford University Press.

Bäckman, L., Small, B. J., Wahlin, Å., & Larsson, M. (1999). Cognitive functioning in very old age. In F. I. M. Craik & T. A. Salthouse (Eds.), *Handbook of cognitive aging* (Vol. 2, pp. 499–558). Mahwah, NJ: Erlbaum.

Baddeley, A. D. (1986). *Working memory.* Oxford, UK: Clarendon Press.

Balota, D. A., Cortese, M. J., Duchek, J. M., Adams, D., Roediger, III, H. L., McDermott, K. B., & Yerys, B. E. (1999). Veridical and false memories in healthy older adults and in dementia of the Alzheimer's type. *Cognitive Neuropsychology, 16,* 361–384.

Balota, D. A., & Duchek, J. M. (1988). Age-related differences in lexical access, spreading activation, and simple pronounciation. *Psychology and Aging, 3,* 84–93.

Baltes, P. B., & Lindenberger, U. (1997). Emergence of a powerful connection between sensory and cognitive functions across the adult life span: A new window to the study of cognitive aging? *Psychology and Aging, 12,* 12–21.

Bayen, U. J., Murnane, K., & Erdfelder, E. (1996). Source discrimination, item detection, and multinomial models of source monitoring. *Journal of Experimental Psychology: Learning, Memory, & Cognition, 22*, 197–215.

Berg, S. (1996). Aging, behavior, and terminal decline. In J. E. Birren & K. W. Schaie (Eds.), *Handbook of the psychology of aging* (4th ed.) (pp. 323–337). San Diego: Academic Press.

Bondi, M. W., Salmon, D. P., Galasko, D., Thomas, R. G., & Thal, L. J. (1999). Neuropsychological function and Apolipoprotein E genotype in the preclinical detection of Alzheimer's disease. *Psychology and Aging, 14*, 295–303.

Bondi, M. W., Salmon, D. P., Monsch, A. U., Galasko, D., Butters, N., Klauber, M. R., Thal, L. J., & Saitoh, T. (1995). Episodic memory changes are associated with the APOE-ε4 allele in nondemented older adults. *Neurology, 45*, 2203–2206.

Bonilla, J. L., & Johnson, M. K. (1995). Semantic space in Alzheimer's disease patients. *Neuropsychology, 9*, 345–353.

Bowler, J. L., Hadar, U., & Wade, J. P. H. (1994). Cognition in stroke. *Acta Neurologica Scandinavica, 90*, 424–429.

Brandimonte, M., Einstein, G. O., & McDaniel, M. A. (Eds.). (1996). *Prospective memory: Theory and applications.* Hillsdale, NJ: Erlbaum.

Brébion, G., Ehrlich, M.-F., & Tardieu, H. (1995). Working memory in older subjects: Dealing with ongoing and stored information in language comprehension. *Psychological Research, 58*, 225–232.

Brébion, G., Smith, M. J., & Ehrlich, M. -F. (1997). Working memory and aging: Deficit or strategy differences. *Aging, Neuropsychology, and Cognition, 4*, 58–73.

Brody, J. A., & Schneider, E. L. (1986). Disease and disorders of aging: A hypothesis. *Journal of Chronic Disorders, 39*, 871–876.

Brown, A. S., Jones, E. M., & Davis, T. L. (1995). Age differences in conversational source monitoring. *Psychology & Aging, 10*, 111–122.

Brown, R. G., & Marsden, C. D. (1988). Subcortical dementia: The neuropsychological evidence. *Neuroscience, 25*, 363–387.

Buckner, R. L., Petersen, S. E., Ojemann, J. G., Miezin, F. M., Squire, L. R., & Raichle, M. E. (1995). Functional anatomical studies of explicit and implict memory retrieval tasks. *Journal of Neuroscience, 15*, 12–29.

Burke, D. M., MacKay, D. G., Worthley, J. S., & Wade, E. (1991). On the tip of the tongue: What causes word-finding failures in young and older adults? *Journal of Memory and Language, 30*, 542–579.

Burke, D. M., & Peters, L. (1986). Word associations in old age: Evidence for consistency in semantic encoding during adulthood. *Psychology and Aging, 1*, 283–292.

Burt, D. B., Zembar, M. J., & Niederehe, G. (1995). Depression and memory impairment: A meta-analysis of the association, its pattern and specificity. *Psychological Bulletin, 117*, 285–305.

Busch, T. L., Miller, S. R., Golden, A. L., & Hale, W. E. (1989). Self-report and medical record report agreement of selected medical conditions in the elderly. *American Journal of Public Health, 79*, 1554–1556.

Cabeza, R. (2001). Functional neuroimaging of cognitive aging. In R. Cabeza & A. Kingstone (Eds.), *Handbook of functional neuroimaging of cognition* (pp. 331–377). Cambridge, MA: MIT Press.

Cabeza, R., & Nyberg, L. (2000). Imaging cognition II: An empirical review of 275 PET and fMRI studies. *Journal of Cognitive Neuroscience, 12*, 1–47.

Cabeza, R., Grady, C. L., Nyberg, L., McIntosh, A. R., Tulving, E., Kapur, S., Jennings, J., Houle, S., & Craik, F. I. M. (1997). Age-related differences in neural activity during memory encoding and retrieval: A positron emission tomography study. *Journal of Neuroscience, 17*, 391–400.

Chalfonte, B. L., & Johnson, M. K. (1996). Feature memory and binding in young and older adults. *Memory & Cognition, 24*, 403–416.

Chan, A. S., Butters, N., Paulsen, J. S., Salmon, D. P., & Swenson, M. R. (1993). An assessment of the semantic network in patients with Alzheimer's disease. *Journal of Cognitive Neuroscience, 5*, 254–261.

Chiarello, C., & Hoyer, W. J. (1988). Adult age differences in implicit and explicit memory: Time course and encoding effects. *Psychology and Aging, 3*, 358–366.

Christensen, H., Korten, A., Jorm, A. F., Henderson, A. S., Scott, R., & Mackinnon, A. J. (1996). Activity levels and cognitive functioning in an elderly community sample. *Age and Ageing, 25*, 72–80.

Cohen, R. L., Sandler, S. P., & Schroeder, K. (1987). Aging and memory for action events: Effects of item repetition and list length. *Psychology and Aging, 2,* 280–85.

Collaer, M. L., & Hines, M. (1995). Human behavioral sex differences: A role for gonadal hormones during early development. *Psychological Bulletin, 118,* 55–107.

Collins, A. M., & Loftus, E. F. (1975). A spreading activation theory of semantic processing. *Psychological Review, 82,* 407–428.

Corey-Bloom, J., Wiederholt, W. C., Edelstein, S., Salmon, D. P., Cahn, D., & Barett-Connor, E. (1996). Cognitive and functional status of the oldest old. *Journal of the American Geriatrics Society, 44,* 671–674.

Craik, F. I. M. (1977). Age differences in human memory. In J. E. Birren & K. W. Schaie (Eds.), *Handbook of the psychology of aging* (pp. 384–420). New York: Van Nostrand Reinhold.

Craik, F. I. M. (1983). On the transfer of information from temporary to permanent memory. *Philosophical Transactions of the Royal Society of London, B302,* 341–359.

Craik, F. I. M., & Jennings, J. M. (1992). Human memory. In F. I. M. Craik & T. A. Salthouse (Eds.), *Handbook of aging and cognition* (pp. 51–110). Hillsdale, NJ Erlbaum.

Craik, F. I. M., & Kerr, S. A. (1996). Prospective memory, aging, and lapses of intention. In M. Brandimonte, G. O. Einstein, & M. A. McDaniel (Eds.), *Prospective memory: Theory and applications* (pp. 227–237). Hillsdale, NJ: Erlbaum.

Craik, F. I. M., & McDowd, J. M. (1987). Age differences in recall and recognition. *Journal of Experimental Psychology: Learning, Memory and Cognition, 13,* 474–479.

Craik, F. I. M., & Rabinowitz, J. C. (1984). Age differences in the acquisition and use of verbal information. In H. Bouma & D. G. Bouwhuis (Eds.), *Attention and performance* (Vol. 10, pp. 471–500). Hillsdale, NJ: Erlbaum.

Crook, T. H., & West, R. L. (1990). Name recall performance across the adult life span. *British Journal of Psychology, 81,* 335–349.

Croxon, S. C. M., & Jagger, C. (1995). Diabetes and cognitive impairment: A community-based study of elderly subjects. *Age and Ageing, 24,* 421–424.

Davis, H. P., Cohen, A., Gandy, M., Colombo, P., Van Dusseldorp, G., Smolke, N., & Roman, J. (1990). Lexical priming deficits as a function of age. *Behavioral Neuroscience, 104,* 288–297.

Davis, H. P., & Squire, L. R. (1984). Protein synthesis and memory: A review. *Psychological Bulletin, 96,* 518–559.

DeCarli, C., Murphy, D. G. M., Tranh, M., Grady, C. L., Haxby, J. V., Gillette, J. A., Salerno, J. A., Gonzales-Aviles, A., Horwitz, B., Rapoport, S. I., & Schapiro, M. B. (1995). The effect of white-matter hyperintensity volume on brain structure, cognitive performance, and cerebral metabolism of glucose in 51 healthy adults. *Neurology, 45,* 2077–2084.

Deese, J. (1959). On the prediction of occurrence of particular verbal intrusions in immediate recall. *Journal of Experimental Psychology, 58,* 17–22.

Degl'Innocenti, A., & Bäckman, L. (1996). Aging and source memory: Influences of intention to remember and associations with frontal lobe tests. *Aging, Neuropsychology, and Cognition, 4,* 307–319.

Dixon, R. A., & Gould, O. N. (1998). Younger and older adults collaborating on retelling everyday stories. *Applied Developmental Science, 2,* 160–171.

Dixon, R. A., Hultsch, D. F., Simon, E. W., & von Eye, A. (1984). Verbal ability and text structure effects on adult age differences in text recall. *Journal of Verbal Learning and Verbal Behavior, 23,* 569–578.

Dobbs, A. R., & Rule, B. G. (1987). Prospective memory and self-reports of memory abilities in older adults. *Canadian Journal of Psychology, 41,* 209–222.

Dunlosky, J., & Hertzog, C. (1998). Aging and deficits in associative memory: What is the role of strategy production? *Psychology and Aging, 13,* 597–607.

Eagly, A. H., & Wood, W. (1999). The origins of sex differences in human behavior: Evolved dispositions versus social roles. *American Psychologist, 54,* 408–423.

Earles, J. L. K., Connor, L. T., Smith, A. D., & Park, D. C. (1997). Interrelations of age, self-reported health, speed, and memory. *Psychology and Aging, 12,* 675–683.

Einstein, G. O., & McDaniel, M. A. (1990). Normal aging and prospective memory. *Journal of Experimental Psychology: Learning, Memory, and Cognition, 16,* 717–26.

Einstein, G. O., McDaniel, M. A., Cunfer, A. R., & Guynn, M. J. (1995). Aging and prospective memory: Examining the influence of self-initiated retrieval processes and mind wandering. *Journal of Experimental Psychology: Learning, Memory, and Cognition*, 21, 996–1007.

Einstein, G. O., Smith, R. E., McDaniel, M. A., & Shaw, P. (1997). Aging and prospective memory: The influence of increased task demands at encoding and retrieval. *Psychology and Aging*, 12, 479–488.

Elias, P. K., Elias, M. F., D'Agostino, R. B., Silberhatz, H., & Wolf, P. A. (1999). Alcohol consumption and cognitive performance in the Framingham Heart Study. *American Journal of Epidemiology*, 150, 580–589.

Ferguson, S. A., Hashtroudi, S., & Johnson, M. K. (1992). Age differences in using source-relevant cues. *Psychology and Aging*, 7, 443–452.

Fleischman, D. A., & Gabrieli, J. D. E. (1998). Repetition priming in normal aging and Alzheimer's disease: A review of findings and theories. *Psychology and Aging*, 13, 88–119.

Fozard, J. L., Metter, E. F., & Brant, L. J. (1990). Next steps in describing aging and disease in longitudinal studies. *Journal of Gerontology: Psychological Sciences*, 45, 116–127.

Fratiglioni, L., Vitanen, M., von Strauss, E., Tontodonati, V., Herlitz, A., & Winblad, B. (1997). Very old women at highest risk of dementia and Alzheimer's disease: Incidence data from the Kungsholmen Project, Stockholm. *Neurology*, 48, 132–138.

Gabrieli, J. D. E., Vaidya, C. J., Stone, M., Francis, W. S., Thompson-Schill, S. L., Fleischman, D. A., Tinklenberg, J. R., Yesavage, J. A., & Wilson, R. S. (1999). Convergent behavioral and neuropsychological evidence for a distinction between identification and production forms of repetition priming. *Journal of Experimental Psychology: General*, 128, 479–498.

Gardiner, J. M. & Java, R. I. (1993). Recognizing and remembering. In A. F. Collins, S. E. Gathercole, M. A. Conway, & P. E. Morris (Eds.), *Theories of memory* (pp. 163–188). Hillsdale, NJ: Erlbaum.

Gerfen, C. R. (1989). The neostriatal mosaic: Striatal patch-matrix organization is related to cortical lamination. *Science*, 246, 385–388.

Gilinsky, A. S., & Judd, B. B. (1994). Working memory and bias in reasoning across the adult life span. *Psychology and Aging*, 9, 356–371.

Golomb, J., Kluger, A., de Leon, M. J., Ferris, S. H., Convit, A., Mittelman, M. S., Cohen, J., Rusnick, H., De Santi, S., & George, A. E. (1994). Hippocampal formation size in normal human aging: A correlate of delayed secondary memory performance. *Learning & Memory*, 1, 45–54.

Grady, C. L., McIntosh, A. R., Horwitz, B., Maisog, J. M., Ungerleider, L. G., Mentis, M. J., Pietrini, P., Schapiro, M. B., & Haxby, J. V. (1995). Age-related reductions in human recognition memory due to impaired encoding. *Science*, 269, 218–221.

Grady, C. L., McIntosh, A. R., Bookstein, F., Horwitz, B., Rapoport, S. I., & Haxby, J. V. (1998). Age-related changes in regional cerebral blood flow during working memory for faces. *Neuroimage*, 8, 409–425.

Graf, P., & Mandler, G. (1984). Activation makes words more accessible, but not necessarily more retrievable. *Journal of Verbal Learning and Verbal Behavior*, 23, 553–568.

Grafton, S. T., Hazeltine, E., & Ivry, R. (1995). Functional mapping of sequence learning in normal humans. *Journal of Cognitive Neuroscience*, 7, 497–510.

Gregoire, J., & Van der Linden, M. (1997). Effects of age on forward and backward digit span. *Aging, Neuropsychology, and Cognition*, 4, 140–149.

Haan, M. N., Shemanski, L., Jagust, W. J., Manolio, T. A., & Kuller, L. (1999). The role of APOE-ε4 in modulating effects of other risk factors for cognitive decline in elderly persons. *Journal of the American Medical Association*, 282, 40–46.

Haapanen, N., Miilunpalo, S., Pasanen, M., Oja, P., & Vuori, I. (1997). Agreement between questionnaire data and medical records of chronic diseases in middle-aged and elderly Finnish men and women. *American Journal of Epidemiology*, 145, 762–769.

Hashtroudi, S., Chrosniak, L. D., & Schwartz, B. L. (1991). Effects of aging on priming and skill acquisition. *Psychology and Aging*, 6, 605–615.

Hashtroudi, S., Johnson, M., & Chrosniak, L. D. (1989). Aging and source monitoring. *Psychology and Aging*, 4, 106–112.

Hashtroudi, S., Johnson, M. K., Vnek, N., & Ferguson, S. A. (1994). Aging and the effects of affective and factual focus on source monitoring and recall. *Psychology & Aging, 9,* 160–170.

Hassing, L., Wahlin, Å., Winblad, B., & Bäckman, L. (1999). Further evidence on the effects of vitamin B_{12} and folate levels on episodic memory functioning: A population-based study of very old adults. *Biological Psychiatry, 45,* 1472–1480.

Herlitz, A., Nilsson, L.-G., & Bäckman (1997). Gender differences in episodic memory. *Memory and Cognition, 25,* 801–811.

Hertzog, C., Hultsch, D. F., & Dixon, R. A. (1999). On the problem of detecting effects of lifestyle on cognitive changes in adulthood: Reply to Pushkar et al. (1999). *Psychology and Aging, 14,* 528–534.

Hill, R.D. (1989). The residual effects of cigarette smoking on cognitive performance in normal aging. *Psychology and Aging, 4,* 251–254.

Hill, R. D., Wahlin, Å., Winblad, B., & Bäckman, L. (1995). The role of demographic and life style variables in utilizing cognitive support for episodic remembering among very old adults. *Journal of Gerontology: Psychological Sciences, 50,* 219–227.

Howard, D. V., Heisey, J. G., & Shaw, R. J. (1986). Aging and the priming of newly learned associations. *Developmental Psychology, 22,* 78–85.

Howard, D. V., & Howard, J. H. (1989). Age differences in learning serial patterns: Direct versus indirect measures. *Psychology and Aging, 4,* 357–364.

Howieson, D. B., Holm, L. A., Kaye, J. A., Oken, B. S., & Howieson, J. (1993). Neurologic function in the optimally healthy oldest old: Neuropsychological evaluation. *Neurology, 43,* 1882–1886.

Hultsch, D. F., & Dixon, R. A. (1990). Learning and memory in aging. In J. E. Birren & K. W. Schaie (Eds.), *Handbook of the psychology of aging* (3rd ed.) (pp. 258–274). San Diego, CA: Academic Press.

Hultsch, D. F., Hammer, M., & Small, B. J. (1993). Age differences in cognitive performance in later life: Relationships to self-reported health and activity life style. *Journal of Gerontology: Psychological Sciences, 48,* 1–11.

Hultsch, D. F., Hertzog, C., & Dixon, R. A. (1990). Ability correlates of memory performance in adulthood and aging. *Psychology and Aging, 5,* 356–338.

Hultsch, D. F., Hertzog, C., Dixon, R. A., & Small, B. J. (1998). *Memory change in the aged.* Cambridge: Cambridge University Press.

Hultsch, D. F., Hertzog, C., Small, B. J., & Dixon, R. A. (1999). Use it or lose it: Engaged lifestyle as a buffer of cognitive decline in aging? *Psychology and Aging, 14,* 245–263.

Hultsch, D. F., Hertzog, C., Small, B. J., McDonald-Miszczak, L., & Dixon, R. A. (1992). Short-term longitudinal change in cognitive performance in later life. *Psychology and Aging, 7,* 571–584.

Idaka, T., Anderson, N. D., Kapur, S., Cabeza, R., & Craik, F. I. M. (2000). The effect of divided attention on encoding and retrieval in episodic memory revealed by positron emission tomography. *Journal of Cognitive Neuroscience, 12,* 267–280.

Jacoby, L. L. (1991). A process dissociation framework: Separating automatic from intentional uses of memory. *Journal of Memory and Language, 30,* 513–541.

Jelicic, M., Craik, F. I. M., & Moscovitch, M. (1996). Effects of aging on different explicit and implicit memory tasks. *European Journal of Cognitive Psychology, 8,* 225–234.

Jennings, J. M., & Jacoby, L. L. (1993). Automatic versus intentional uses of memory: Aging, attention and control. *Psychology and Aging, 8,* 283–293.

Jernigan, T. L., Archibald, S. L., Berhow, M. T., Sowell, E. R., Foster, D. S., & Hesselink, J. R. (1991). Cerebral structure on MRI: Part I. Localization of age-related changes. *Biological Psychiatry, 29,* 55–67.

Johansson, B., Whitfield, K., Pedersen, N. L., Hofer, S. M., Ahern, F., & McClearn, G. E. (1999). Origins of individual differences in episodic memory in the oldest-old: A population-based study of identical and same-sex fraternal twins aged 80 and older. *Journal of Gerontology: Psychological Sciences, 54,* 173–179.

Johnson, M. K., Hashtroudi, S., & Lindsay, D. S. (1993). Source monitoring. *Psychological Bulletin, 114,* 3–28.

Johnson, M. K., DeLeonardis, D. M., Hashtroudi, S., & Ferguson, S. A. (1995). Aging and single versus multiple cues in source monitoring. *Psychology and Aging, 10,* 507–517.

Johnson, M. K., Kounios, J., & Reeder, J. A. (1992, November). *Time course studies of reality monitoring and recognition.* Paper presented at the 33rd Annual Meeting of the Psychonomic Society, St. Louis, MO.

Johnson, M. M. S., Schmitt, F. A., & Pitrukowicz, M. (1989). The memory advantages of the generation effect: Age and process differences. *Journal of Gerontology, 44*, 91–94.

Kail, R. (1998). Speed of information processing in patients with multiple sclerosis. *Journal of Clinical and Experimental Neuropsychology, 20*, 98–106.

Kalmijn, S., Feskens, E. J. M., Launer, L. J., Stijnen, T., & Kromhout, D. (1995). Glucose intolerance, hyperinsulinaemia and cognitive function in a general population of elderly men. *Diabetologia, 38*, 1096–1102.

Kapur, S., Craik, F. I. M., Tulving, E., Wilson, A. A., Houle, S., & Brown, G. M. (1994). Neuroanatomical correlates of encoding in episodic memory: Levels of processing effect. *Proceedings of the National Academy of Sciences, USA, 91*, 2008–2011.

Kemper, T. L. (1994). Neuroanatomical and neuropathological changes during aging and in dementia. In M. L. Albert & E. J. E. Knoepfel (Eds.), *Clinical neurology of aging* (2nd ed.) (pp. 3–67). New York: Oxford University Press.

Kensinger, E. A., & Schacter, D. L. (1999). When true memories suppress false memories: Effects of aging. *Cognitive Neuropsychology, 16*, 399–415.

Kindermann, S. S., & Brown, G. G. (1997). Depression and memory in the elderly: A meta-analysis. *Journal of Clinical and Experimental Neuropsychology, 19*, 625–642.

Kleemeier, R. W. (1962). Intellectual changes in the senium. *Proceedings of the American Statistical Association, 1*, 290–295.

Koutstaal, W., Schacter, D. L., Galluccio, L., & Stofer, K. A. (1999). Reducing gist-based false recognition in older adults: Encoding and retrieval manipulations. *Psychology and Aging, 14*, 220–237.

Lachman, J. L., Lachman, R., & Thronesberry, C. (1979). Metamemory through the adult life span. *Developmental Psychology, 15*, 543–551.

Larsson, M., & Bäckman, L. (1998). Modality memory across the adult life span. Evidence for selective olfactory deficits. *Experimental Aging Research, 24*, 63–82.

Laver, G. D., & Burke, D. M. (1993). Why do semantic priming effects increase in old age: A meta-analysis. *Psychology and Aging, 8*, 34–43.

LaVoie, D., & Light, L. L. (1994). Adult age differences in repetition priming: A meta-analysis. *Psychology and Aging, 9*, 539–553.

Lawrence, A. D., Weeks, R. A., Brooks, D. J., Andrews, T. C., Watkins, L. H. A., Harding, A. E., Robbins, T. W., & Sahakian, B. J (1998). The relationship between striatal dopamine receptor binding and cognitive performance in Huntington's disease. *Brain, 121*, 1343–1355.

Launer, L. J., Masaki, K., Petrovitch, H., Foley, D., & Havlik, R. J. (1995). The association between midlife blood pressure levels and late-life cognitive function: The Honolulu-Asia Aging Study. *Journal of the American Medical Association, 274*, 1846–1851.

Light, L. L. (1992). The organization of memory in old age. In F. I. M. Craik & T. A. Salthouse (Eds.), *Handbook of aging and cognition* (pp. 111–165). Hillsdale, NJ: Erlbaum.

Light, L. L., & Albertson, S. A. (1989). Direct and indirect tests of memory for category exemplars in young and older adults. *Psychology and Aging, 4*, 487–492.

Light, L. L., & La Voie, D. (1993). Direct and indirect measures of memory in old age. In P. Graf & M. E. J. Masson (Eds.), *Implicit memory: New directions in cognition, development, and neuropsychology* (pp. 207–230). Hillsdale, NJ: Erlbaum.

Light, L. L., Singh, & Capps, J. L. (1986). Dissociation of memory and awareness in young and older adults. *Journal of Clinical and Experimental Neuropsychology, 8*, 62–74.

Lindenberger, U., & Baltes, P. B. (1994). Sensory functioning and intelligence in old age: A strong relation. *Psychology and Aging, 9*, 339–355.

Lindenberger, U., & Pötter, U. (1998). The complex nature of unique and shared effects in hierarchical linear regression: Implications for developmental psychology. *Psychological Methods, 3*, 218–230.

Luszcz, M. A., Bryan, J., & Kent, P. (1997). Predicting episodic memory performance of very old men and women: Contributions from age, depression, activity, cognitive ability, and speed. *Psychology and Aging, 12*, 340–351.

Madden, D. J., Turkington, T. G., Provenzale, J. M., Denny, L. L., Hawk, T. C., Gottlob, L.

R., & Coleman, E. (1999). Adult age differences in functional neuroanatomy of verbal recognition memory. *Human Brain Mapping, 7*, 115–135.

Maki, P. M., & Knopman, D. S. (1996). Limitations of the distinction between conceptual and perceptual implicit memory: A study of Alzheimer's disease. *Neuropsychology, 10*, 464–474.

Mäntylä, T. (1993). Knowing but not remembering: Adult age differences in recollective experience. *Memory & Cognition, 21*, 379–388.

Mäntylä T. (1994). Remembering to remember: Adult age differences in prospective memory. *Journal of Gerontology: Psychological Sciences, 49*, 276–282.

Mäntylä, T., & Bäckman, L. (1990). Encoding variability and age-related retrieval failures. *Psychology and Aging, 5*, 545–550.

Maylor, E. A. (1990). Age, blocking, and the tip of the tongue state. *British Journal of Psychology, 81*, 123–134.

Maylor, E. A. (1993). Aging and forgetting in prospective and retrospective memory tasks. *Psychology and Aging, 3*, 420–428.

Maylor, E. A. (1996). Age-related impairment in an event-based prospective-memory task. *Psychology and Aging, 11*, 74–78.

Meinz, E. J., & Salthouse, T. A. (1998). Is age kinder to females than to males? *Psychonomic Bulletin and Reviews, 5*, 56–70.

Mitchell, D. B. (1989). How many memory systems? Evidence from aging. *Journal of Experimental Psychology: Learning, Memory, and Cognition, 15*, 31–49.

Mitrushina, M., & Satz, P. (1995). Repeated testing of normal elderly with the Boston Naming Test. *Aging: Clinical and Experimental Research, 7*, 123–127.

Morris, R. G. (Ed.). (1996). *The cognitive neuropsychology of Alzheimer's disease.* Oxford: Oxford University Press.

Moscovitch, M., Winocur, G., & McLachlan, D. (1986). Memory as assessed by recognition and reading time in normal and memory-impaired people with Alzheimer's disease and other neurological disorders. *Journal of Experimental Psychology: General, 115*, 331–347.

Naveh-Benjamin, M., & Craik, F. I. M. (1995). Memory for context and its use in item memory: Comparisons of younger and older persons. *Psychology and Aging, 10*, 284–293.

Nebes, R. D., Boller, F., & Holland, A. (1986). Use of semantic context by patients with Alzheimer's disease. *Psychology and Aging, 1*, 261–269.

Nilsson, L. -G., Bäckman, L., Erngrund, K., Nyberg, L., Adolfsson, R., Bucht, G., Karlsson, S., Widing, M., & Winblad, B. (1997). The Betula prospective cohort study: Memory, health, and aging. *Aging, Neuropsychology, and Cognition, 4*, 1–32.

Norman, S., Kemper, S., & Kynette, D. (1992). Adults' reading comprehension: Effects of syntactic complexity and working memory. *Journal of Gerontology: Psychological Sciences, 47*, 258–265.

Nyberg, L., Cabeza, R., & Tulving, E. (1996). PET studies of encoding and retrieval: The HERA model. *Psychonomic Bulletin & Review, 3*, 135–148.

Nyberg, L., & Tulving, E. (1996). Classifying human long-term memory: Evidence from converging dissociations. *European Journal of Cognitive Psychology, 8*, 163–183.

O'Brien, J. T., Desmond, P., Ames, D., Schweitzer, I., & Tress, B. (1997). Magnetic resonance imaging correlates of memory impairment in the healthy elderly: Association with medial temporal lobe atrophy but not white-matter lesions. *International Journal of Geriatric Psychiatry, 12*, 369–374.

O'Hara, R., Yesavage, J. A., Kraemer, H. C., Mauricio, M., Friedman, L. F., & Murphy, G. M. (1998). The APOE epsilon 4 allele is associated with decline on delayed recall performance in community-dwelling older adults. *Journal of the American Geriatrics Society, 46*, 1493–1498.

Parent, A., & Hazrati, L. N. (1995). Functional anatomy of the basal ganglia. I. The cortico-basal-ganglia-thalamo-cortical loop. *Brain Research and Reviews, 20*, 91–127.

Park, D. C., Hertzog, C., Kidder, D. P., Morrell, R. W., & Mayhorn, C. B. (1997). Effect of age on event-based and time-based prospective memory. *Psychology and Aging, 12*, 314–327.

Park, D. C., & Puglisi, J. T. (1985). Older adults memory for the color of pictures. *Journal of Gerontology, 40*, 198–204.

Park, D. C., Smith, A. D., Morrell, R. W., Puglisi, J. T., & Dudley, W. N. (1990). Effects of contextual integration on recall of pictures by older adults. *Journal of Gerontology: Psychological Sciences, 45*, 52–57.

Park, D. C., Smith, A. D., Lautenschlager, G., Earles, J. L., Frieske, D., Zwahr, M., & Gaines, C. L. (1996). Mediators of long-term memory performance across the life span. *Psychology and Aging, 11*, 621–637.

Parkin, A. J., & Walter, B. M. (1992). Recollective experience, normal aging, and frontal dysfunction. *Psychology and Aging, 7*, 290–298.

Perlmutter, M., & Nyquist, L. (1990). Relationships between self-reported physical and mental health and intelligence performance across adulthood. *Journal of Gerontology: Psychological Sciences, 45*, 145–155.

Perner, J., & Ruffman, T. (1995). Episodic memory an autonoetic consciousness: Developmental evidence and a theory of childhood amnesia. *Journal of Experimental Child Psychology, 59*, 516–548.

Petersen, R. C., Smith, G. E., Waring, S. C., Ivnik, R. J., Tangalos, E. G., & Kokmen, E. (1999). Mild cognitive impairment: Clinical characterization and outcome. *Archives of Neurology, 56*, 303–308.

Petrides, M. (1995). Functional organization of the human frontal cortex for mnemonic processing: Evidence from neuroimaging studies. *Annals of the New York Academy of Sciences, 769*, 85–96.

Piccinin, A. M., & Rabbitt, P. A. (1999). Contribution of cognitive abilities to performance and improvement on a substitution coding task. *Psychology and Aging, 14*, 539–551.

Poon, L. W. (1985). Differences in human memory with aging: Nature, causes, and clinical implications. In J. E. Birren & K. W. Schaie (Eds.), *Handbook of the psychology of aging* (2nd ed.) (pp. 427–462). New York: Van Nostrand Reinhold.

Price, T. R., Manolio, T. A., Kronmal, R. A., Kittner, S. J., Yue, N. C., Robbins, J., Anton-Culver, H., & O'Leary, D. H. (1997). Silent brain infarction on magnetic resonance imaging and neurological abnormalities in community-dwelling older adults: The Cardiovascular Health Study. *Stroke, 28*, 1158–1164.

Prull, M. W., Gabrieli, J. D. E., & Bunge, S. A. (1999). Age-related changes in memory: A cognitive neuroscience perspective. In F. I. M. Craik & T. A. Salthouse (Eds.), *Handbook of cognitive aging*, (Vol. 2, pp. 91–153). Mahwah, NJ: Erlbaum.

Puglisi, J. T. (1980). Semantic encoding in older adults as evidenced from release from proactive inhibition. *Journal of Gerontology, 35*, 743–745.

Puglisi, J. T., & Park, D. C. (1987). Perceptual elaboration and memory in older adults. *Journal of Gerontology, 42*, 160–162.

Pushkar, D., Etezadi, J., Andres, D., Andres, D., Arbuckle, T., Schwartzman, A. E., & Chaikelson, J. (1999). Models of intelligence in late life: Comment on Hultsch et al. (1999). *Psychology and Aging, 14*, 520–527.

Rabinowitz, J. (1989). Age deficits in recall under optimal study conditions. *Psychology and Aging, 4*, 378–380.

Rabinowitz, J., & Craik, F. I. M. (1986). Prior retrieval effects in young and old adults. *Journal of Gerontology, 41*, 368–375.

Raye, C. L., & Johnson, M. K. (1980). Reality monitoring vs. discriminating between external sources of memories. *Bulletin of the Psychonomic Society, 15*, 405–408.

Raz, N. (1999). Aging of the brain and its impact on cognitive performance: Integration of structural and functional findings. In F. I. M. Craik & T. A. Salthouse (Eds.), *Handbook of cognitive aging* (Vol. 2, pp. 1–90). Mahwah, NJ: Erlbaum.

Raz, N., Gunning, F. M., Head, D. P., Dupuis, J. H., McQuain, J. M., Briggs, S. D., Thornton, A. E., Loken, W. J., & Acker, J. D. (1997). Selective aging of human cerebral cortex observed in vivo: Differential vulnerability of the prefrontal grey matter. *Cerebral Cortex, 77*, 268–282.

Raz, N., Gunning-Dixon, F. M., Head, D. P., Dupuis, J. H., & Acker, J. D. (1998). Neuroanatomical correlates of cognitive aging: Evidence from structural MRI. *Neuropsychology, 12*, 95–114.

Raz, N., Millman, D., & Sarpel, G. (1990). Cerebral correlates of cognitive aging: Grey-white matter differentiation in the medial-temporal lobes and fluid vs. crystallized abilities. *Psycholobiology, 18*, 475–481.

Reuter-Lorenz, P., Jonides, J., Smith, E. S., Hartely, A., Miller, A., Marshuetz, C., & Koeppe, R. A. (2000). Age differences in the frontal lateralization of verbal and spatial working memory revealed by PET. *Journal of Cognitive Neuroscience, 12*, 1–14.

Ricker, J. H., Keenan, P. A., & Jacobson, M. W. (1994). Visuoperceptual-spatial ability and visual memory in vascular dementia of the Alzheimer type. *Neuropsychologia, 32,* 1287–1296.

Rinne, J. O., Hietala, J., Ruotsalainen, U., Sako, E., Laihinen, A., Nagren, K., Lehikonen, P., Oikonen, V., & Syvalahti, E. (1993). Decrease in human striatal dopamine D_2 receptor density with age: A PET study with [^{11}C] raclopride. *Journal of Cerebral Blood Flow and Metabolism, 13,* 310–314.

Roediger, H. L., & McDermott, K. B. (1993). Implicit memory in normal human subjects. In H. Spinnler & F. Boller (Eds.), *Handbook of neuropsychology* (pp. 63–131). Amsterdam: Elsevier.

Roediger, H. L., III., & McDermott, K. B. (1995). Creating false memories: Remembering words not presented in lists. *Journal of Experimental Psychology: Learning, Memory, and Cognition, 21,* 803–814.

Rubin, D. C. (1999). Frontal-striatal circuits in cognitive aging: Evidence for caudate involvement. *Aging, Neuropsychology, and Cognition, 6,* 241–259.

Rubin, D. C., Rahhal, T. A., & Poon, L. W. (1998). Things learned in early adulthood are remembered best. *Memory & Cognition, 26,* 3–19.

Rybash, J. M. (1994). Aging, associative priming, and test awareness. *Aging and Cognition, 1,* 158–173.

Rybash, J. M. (1996). Implicit memory and aging: A cognitive neuropsychological perspective. *Developmental Neuropsychology, 12,* 127–179.

Rybash, J. M., & Hrubi-Bopp, K. L. (2000). Source monitoring and false recollection: A life span developmental perspective. *Experimental Aging Research, 26,* 75–87.

Rypma, B., & D'Esposito, M. (2000). Isolating the neural mechanisms of age-related changes in human working memory. *Nature Neuroscience, 3,* 509–515.

Salthouse, T. A. (1988). Effects of aging on verbal abilities: Examination of the psychometric literature. In L. Light & D. M. Burke (Eds.), *Language, memory, and aging* (pp. 17–35). New York: Cambridge University Press.

Salthouse, T. A. (1994). The aging of working memory. *Neuropsychology, 8,* 535–543.

Salthouse, T. A. (1996). The processing-speed theory of adult age differences in cognition. *Psychological Review, 103,* 403–428.

Salthouse, T. A. (1998). Independence of age-related influences on cognitive abilities across the life span. *Developmental Psychology, 34,* 851–864.

Salthouse, T. A., & Babcock, R. L. (1991). Decomposing adult age differences in working memory. *Developmental Psychology, 27,* 763–776.

Salthouse, T. A., & Craik, F. I. M. (1999). Closing comments. In F. I. M. Craik & T. A. Salthouse (Eds.), *Handbook of cognitive aging* (Vol. 2, pp. 689–703). Mahwah, NJ: Erlbaum.

Salthouse, T. A., Hambrick, D. Z., & McGuthry, K. E. (1998). Shared age-related influences on cognitive and noncognitive variables. *Psychology and Aging, 13,* 486–500.

Salthouse, T. A., Hancock, H. E., Meinz, E. J., & Hambrick, D. Z. (1996). Interrelations of age, visual acuity, and cognitive functioning. *Journal of Gerontology: Psychological Sciences, 51,* 317–330.

Salthouse, T. A., Toth, J. P., Hancock, H. E., & Woodard, J. L. (1997). Controlled and automatic forms of memory and attention: Process purity and the uniqueness of age-related differences. *Journal of Gerontology: Psychological Sciences,* 216–228.

Schacter, D. L. (1987). Implicit memory: History and current status. *Journal of Experimental Psychology: Learning, Memory, and Cognition, 13,* 477–494.

Schacter, D. L., Alpert, N. M., Savage, C. R., Rauch, S. L., & Albert, M. S. (1996). Conscious recollection and the human hippocampal formation: Evidence from positron emission tomography. *Proceedings of the National Academy of Sciences, USA, 93,* 321–325.

Schacter, D. L., Koutstaal, W., & Norman, K. A. (1997). False memories and aging. *Trends in Cognitive Sciences, 1,* 229–236.

Schacter, D. L., Norman, K. A., & Koutstaal, W. (1998). The cognitive neuroscience of constructive memory. *Annual Review of Psychology, 49,* 289–319.

Schacter, D. L., Osowiecki, D., Kaszniak, A. W., Kihlstrom, J. F., & Valdiserri, M. (1994). Source memory: Extending the boundaries of age-related deficits. *Psychology and Aging, 9,* 81–89.

Schugens, M. M., Daum, I., Spindler, M., & Birbaumer, N. (1997). Differential effects of aging on explicit and implicit memory. *Aging, Neuropsychology, and Cognition, 4,* 33–44.

Sharps, M. J., & Gollin, E. S. (1988). Aging and free recall for objects located in space. *Journal of Gerontology: Psychological Sciences, 43,* 8–11.

Shimamura, A. P. (1994). Neuropsychological perspectives on memory and cognitive decline in normal human aging. *Seminars in the Neurosciences, 6,* 387–394.

Simon, E., Leach, L., Winocur, G., & Moscovitch, M. (1995). Intact primary memory in mild to moderate Alzheimer's disease: Indices from the California Verbal Learning Test. *Journal of Clinical and Experimental Neuropsychology, 16,* 414–422.

Sliwinski, M., Lipton, R. B., Buschke, H., & Stewart, W. (1996). The effects of preclinical dementia on estimates of normal cognitive functioning in aging. *Journal of Gerontology: Psychological Sciences, 51,* 217–225.

Small, B. J., & Bäckman, L. (1999). Time to death and cognitive performance. *Current Directions in Psychological Science, 8,* 168–172.

Small, B. J., Basun, H., & Bäckman, L. (1998). Three-year changes in cognitive performance as a function of Apolipoprotein E genotype: Evidence from very old adults without dementia. *Psychology and Aging, 13,* 80–87.

Small, B. J., Fratiglioni, L., Viitanen, M., Winblad, B., & Bäckman, L. (2000). The course of cognitive impairment in preclinical Alzheimer's disease: 3-and 6-year follow-up of a population-based sample. *Archives of Neurology, 57,* 839–844.

Small, B. J., Graves, A. B., McEvoy, C. L., Crawford, F. C., Mullan, M., & Mortimer, J. A. (2000). Is APOE-ε4 a risk factor for cognitive impairment in normal aging? *Neurology, 54,* 2082–2088.

Small, B. J., Hultsch, D. F., & Masson, M. E. J. (1995). Adult age differences in perceptually based, but not conceptually based implicit tests of memory. *Journal of Gerontology: Psychological Sciences, 50,* 162–70.

Smith, A. D. (1996). Memory. In J. E. Birren & K. W. Schaie (Eds.), *Handbook of the psychology of aging* (4th ed.) (pp. 236–250). San Diego: Academic Press.

Smith, G. E., Bohac, D. L., Waring, S. C., Kokmen, E., Tangalos, E. G., Ivnik, R. J., & Petersen, R. C. (1998). Apolipoprotein E genotype influences cognitive "phenotype" in patients with Alzheimer's disease but not in healthy control subjects. *Neurology, 50,* 355–362.

Spencer, W. D., & Raz, N. (1994). Memory for facts, source, and context: Can frontal lobe dysfunction explain age-related differences? *Psychology and Aging, 9,* 149–159.

Stine, E. L. (1986). Attribute-based similarity perception in young and older adults. *Experimental Aging Research, 12,* 89–94.

Strassburger, T. L., Lee, H. C., Daly, E. M., Szcepanik, J., Krasuski, J. S., Mentis, M. J., Salerno, J. A., DeCarli, C., Schapiro, M. B., & Alexander, G. E. (1997). Interactive effects of age and hypertension on volumes of brain structures. *Stroke, 28,* 1410–1417.

Strittmatter, W. J., Saunders, A. M., Schmechel, D., Pericak-Vance, M., Enghild, J., Salvesen, G. S., Roses, A. D. (1993). Apolipoprotein E: High avidity binding to beta-amyloid and increased frequency of type 4 allele in late-onset familial Alzheimer's disease. *Proceedings of the National Academy of Sciences, 90,* 1977–1981.

Suddendorf, T., & Corballis, M. C. (1997). Mental time travel and the evolution of the human mind. *Genetic, Social, & General Psychology Monographs, 123,* 133–167.

Swan, G. E., Reed, T., Jack, L. M., Miller, B. L., Markee, T., Wolf, P. A., DeCarli, C., & Carmelli, D. (1999). Differential genetic influence for components of memory in aging adult twins. *Archives of Neurology, 56,* 1127–1132.

Tang, Y., Nyengaard, J. R., Pakkenberg, B., & Gundersen, J. G. (1997). Age-induced white-matter changes in the human brain: A stereological investigation. *Neurobiology of Aging, 18,* 609–618.

Tierney, M. C., Szalai, J. P., Snow, W. G., Fisher, R. H., Nores, A., Nadon, G., Dunn, E., & St. George-Hyslop, P. H. (1996). Prediction of probable Alzheimer's disease in memory-impaired patients: A prospective longitudinal study. *Neurology, 46,* 661–665.

Titov, N., & Knight, R. G. (1997). Adult age differences in controlled and automatic memory processing. *Psychology and Aging, 12,* 565–573.

Tulving, E. (1983). *Elements of episodic memory*. Oxford: Oxford University Press.

Tulving, E. (1999). On the uniqueness of episodic memory. In L.-G. Nilsson & H. Markowitsch (Eds.), *Cognitive neuroscience of memory* (pp. 11–42). Göttingen, Germany: Hogrefe & Huber.

Tulving, E., & Colotla, V. (1970). Free recall of trilingual lists. *Cognitive Psychology, 1*, 86–98.

Tun, P. A., Wingfield, A., Rosen, M. J., & Blanchard, L. (1998). Response latencies for false memories: Gist-based processes in normal aging. *Psychology and Aging, 13*, 230–241.

Ungerleider, L. G. (1995). Functional brain imaging studies of cortical mechanisms for memory. *Science, 270*, 769–775.

Vakil, E., & Agmon-Ashkenazi, D. (1997). Baseline performance and learning rate of procedural and declarative memory tasks: Younger versus older adults. *Journal of Gerontology: Psychological Sciences, 52*, 229–234.

Verhaeghen, P., Marcoen, A., & Goossens, L. (1993). Facts and fiction about memory aging: A quantative integration of research findings. *Journal of Gerontology: Psychological Sciences, 48*, 157–171.

Verhaeghen, P., & Salthouse, T. A. (1997). Meta-analyses of age-cognition relations in adulthood: Estimates of linear and nonlinear age effects and structural models. *Psychological Bulletin, 122*, 231–249.

Volkow, N. D., Gur, R. C., Wang, G.-J., Fowler, J. S., Moberg, P. J., Ding, Y.-S., Hitzemann, R. R., Smith, G., & Logan, J. (1998). Association between decline in brain dopamine activity with age and cognitive and motor impairment in healthy individuals. *American Journal of Psychiatry, 155*, 344–349.

Wahlin, Å., Bäckman, L., Mäntylä, T., Herlitz, A., Viitanen, M., & Winblad, B. (1993). Prior knowledge and face recognition in a community-based sample of healthy, very old adults. *Journal of Gerontology: Psychological Sciences, 48*, 54–61.

Wahlin, Å., Bäckman, L., & Winblad, B. (1995). Free recall and recognition of slowly and rapidly presented words in very old age: A community-based study. *Experimental Aging Research, 21*, 251–271.

Wahlin, Å., Hill, R. D., Winblad, B., & Bäckman, L. (1996). Effects of serum vitamin B_{12} and folate status on episodic memory performance in very old age: A population-based study. *Psychology and Aging, 11*, 487–496.

Wahlin, Å, Robins Wahlin, T.-B., Small, B. J., & Bäckman, L. (1998). Influences of Thyroid Stimulating Hormone on cognitive functioning in very old age. *Journal of Gerontology: Psychological Sciences, 53*, 234–239.

Wahlsten, D. (1999). Single-gene influences on brain and behavior. *Annual Review of Psychology, 50*, 599–624.

West, R. L. (1996). An application of prefrontal cortex function theory to cognitive aging. *Psychological Bulletin, 120*, 272–292.

West, R. L., & Craik, F. I. M. (1999). Age-related decline in prospective memory: The roles of cue accessibility and cue sensitivity. *Psychology and Aging, 14*, 264–272.

Wingfield, A., Lindfield, K. C., & Kahana, M. J. (1998). Adult age differences in the temporal characteristics of category free recall. *Psychology & Aging, 13*, 256–266.

Winocur, G., Moscovitch, M., & Stuss, D. T. (1996). Explicit and implicit memory in the elderly: Ervidence for a double dissociation involving medial temporal- and frontal-lobe functions. *Neuropsychology, 10*, 57–65.

Wong, D. F., Wagner, H. N., Dannals, R. F., Links, J. M., Frost, J. J., Ravert, H. T., Wilson, A. A., Rosenbaum, A. E., Gjedde, A., Douglass, K. H., Petronis, J. D., Folstein, M. F., Thomas Toungm J. K., Burns, D., & Kuhar. M. J. (1984). Effects of age on dopamine and serotonin receptors measured by positron tomography in the living human brain. *Science, 226*, 1393–1396.

Wright, B. M., & Payne, R. B. (1985). Effects of aging on sex differences in psychomotor reminiscence and tracking proficiency. *Journal of Gerontology, 40*, 179–184.

Zacks, R. T., Hasher, L., & Li, K. Z. H. (1999). Human memory. In F. I. M. Craik & T. A. Salthouse (Eds.), *Handbook of cognitive aging* (Vol. 2, pp. 689–703). Mahwah, NJ: Erlbaum.

Zelinski, E. M., & Burnight, K. P. (1997). Sixteen-year longitudinal and time lag changes in memory and cognition in older adults. *Psychology & Aging, 12*, 503–513.

Zelinski, E. M., Crimmins, E., Reynolds, S., & Seeman, T. (1998). Do medical conditions affect cognition in older adults? *Health Psychology, 17*, 504–512.

Fifteen

Language Production and Comprehension

Susan Kemper and Tracy L. Mitzner

I. Introduction

Language production and comprehension by older adults have come under increased scrutiny as a domain for testing alternative models of cognitive aging. Two questions have dominated: How do capacity limitations affect older adults' ability to produce and comprehend language, and how do inhibitory deficits affect older adults' production and comprehension? Recent reviews (Burke, 1997; Caplan & Waters, 1999; Kemper & Kliegl, 1999; Wingfield & Stine-Morrow, 2000; Zacks & Hasher, 1997) have addressed these questions. This chapter summarizes the current status of these debates and turns to two emergent areas of research: research examining the effects of Alzheimer's disease on language production and comprehension and research evaluating alternative strategies for enhancing communication with older adults, especially those with Alzheimer's disease. The effects of Alzheimer's disease on language may be distinct from those resulting from normal aging, although capacity limitations and inhibitory deficits may also contribute to the linguistic problems of adults with Alzheimer's disease. Older adults with Alzheimer's disease as well as those spared this disease may benefit from speech accommodations, particularly those designed to minimize processing demands.

II. Effects of Working Memory

Studies of older adults' reading comprehension and memory have been concerned with determining how processing limitations affect older adults. Comprehension imposes many simultaneous demands on the reader to process information on a number of levels (e.g., syntactic, semantic, and pragmatic) and to generate a hierarchical representation of this information. Readers must recognize individual words, parse the words into phrases and clauses, establish logical and temporal connections among the clauses, determine the referents of pronouns, and infer unstated causes and consequences of events. It has been generally assumed that these simultaneous processing demands are handled by working memory, a limited-capacity storage and processing component of the human information-processing system (Baddeley, 1986, 1996;

Handbook of the Psychology of Aging
Copyright © 2001 by Academic Press.
All rights of reproduction in any form reserved.

Daneman & Merikle, 1996; Just & Carpenter, 1992; Kemper, 1992). Other characterizations of working memory also assume general capacity limitations on the temporary maintenance of information (Engle, Tuholski, Laughlin, & Conway, 1999); some, however, would partition working memory into multiple temporary buffers with distinct capacities, time courses, and representational formats (Caplan & Waters, 1999; Martin, Shelton, & Yaffee, 1994).

Support for the hypothesis that capacity limitations account for age-related language-processing problems is largely correlational. Older adults have typically been found to have smaller working memory spans than young adults, and such span measures have been found to correlate with language-processing measures (Norman, Kemper, Kynette, Cheung, & Anagnopoulos, 1991; Stine & Wingfield, 1990; Tun, Wingfield, & Stine, 1991). Van der Linden et al. (1999) sought to distinguish the effects of working memory limitations from those due to reductions of processing speed or a breakdown of inhibitory processes by examining performance on a wide range of language tasks using structural equation modeling. Young and older adults were tested on their ability to understand texts and recall sentences and words. They were also given a large battery of tests designed to measure processing speed, working memory capacity, and the ability to inhibit distracting thoughts. The analysis indicated that these three general factors (speed, working memory, inhibition) did account for age differences in performance on the language-processing tasks. Further, the analysis indicated that "age-related differences in language, memory and comprehension were explained by a reduction of the capacity of working memory, which was itself influenced by reduction of speed, [and] increasing sensitivity to interference" (p. 48).

The hypothesis that working memory limitations affect language processing has

been carefully examined by Caplan and Waters (1996, 1999), who have considered a number of lines of evidence from studies of young and older adults as well as individuals with aphasia and dementia. They distinguish between immediate, interpretative syntactic processing and postinterpretative semantic and pragmatic processing. Caplan and Waters argue that there is little evidence to support the hypothesis that working memory limitations affect immediate syntactic processes; rather, they conclude that working memory limitations affect postinterpretative processes involved in retaining information in memory in order to recall it or use it (e.g., to answer questions or match sentences against pictures). In a variety of studies comparing adults stratified into groups based on measures of working memory, Caplan and Waters (1996) note that effects of syntactic complexity do not differentially affect high versus low span readers or listeners. And they report that secondary tasks that impose additional processing demands on working memory do not differentially affect the processing of complex sentences. Caplan and Waters consider aphasic patients, such as B. O., who had a digit span of only two or three digits but who was able to perform as well as normal healthy older adults on a wide range of tasks with complex sentences. They also note that patients with Alzheimer's dementia, who also show severely limited working memory capacity, are able to make speeded acceptability judgments of complex sentences as accurately as nondemented controls.

Two sentence-processing studies support Caplan and Waters's (1999) conclusion that postinterpretative processes, but not immediate syntactic processes, are affected by aging. Kemtes and Kemper (1997) used a word-by-word reading paradigm to assess younger and older adults' on-line comprehension of temporarily ambiguous sentences (e.g., *Several angry workers warned about low wages...*) that were resolved with either a main verb (MV) interpretation (e.g., *Several angry workers warned about low wages during the holiday season*), or a reduced relative clause (RRC) interpretation (e.g., *Several angry workers warned about low wages decided to file complaints*). Mac-Donald, Just, and Carpenter (1992) had previously reported differential patterns of word-by-word reading times for young adults as a function of working memory span. The primary finding from Kemtes and Kemper's (1997) replication was that although older adults' on-line reading times were slower than those of younger adults, syntactic ambiguity did not differentially impair older adults' on-line comprehension of the sentences. High-span and low-span young adults exhibited the same pattern of reading time latencies as did high- and low-span older adults. In contrast, older adults' off-line question comprehension was influenced by the syntactic ambiguity manipulation, in that question comprehension was reliably worse, relative to young, for the syntactically ambiguous sentences. These findings pose a challenge to the hypothesis that working memory limitations affect syntactic processing; not only did Kemtes and Kemper fail to replicate MacDonald et al.'s (1992) finding that high-and low-span young adults allocate reading times differentially; they also failed to link age differences on the comprehension test to on-line processing differences.

A similar outcome has been reported by Kemtes and Kemper (1999), who conducted two experiments to compare young and older adults' processing of complex sentences involving quantifier scope ambiguities. Young adults were hypothesized to use a mix of syntactic processing strategies to interpret sentences, such as *Every actor used a prop* or *An actor used every prop*. Older adults, particularly those with limited working memories, were hypothesized to rely on

a simple pragmatic principle. Participants read the quantifier sentences and judged whether a continuation sentence "made sense." Reading times for the quantifier sentences and continuation sentence acceptability judgments were analyzed. Whereas young and older adults exhibited similar patterns of reading times for the quantifier sentences, they preferred different continuations for the *Every...a* quantifier sentences. As predicted, both young adults and older adults interpreted a quantifier sentence, such as *An actor used every prop*, as referring to a single entity; this resulted in a preference for continuations, such as *The actor was on the stage*. In contrast, young and older adults made different interpretations of a quantifier sentence, such as *Every actor used a prop*. Young adults preferred continuations postulating multiple entities such as *The props were on the stage*; in contrast, older adults, particularly those with working memory limitations, preferred continuations with a single entity, such as *The prop was on the stage*. These results support the Caplan and Waters (1999) model of the effects of aging on language processing in which immediate syntactic analysis is not affected by aging or working memory limitations, whereas postcomprehension processes are affected by aging and/or working memory limitations.

Other factors than working memory limitations must, therefore, affect older adults' reading and listening comprehension. Kemtes and Kemper (1999) suggest that young and older adults adopt different strategies in order to interpret quanifier sentences. Strategy differences may also underline other age differences in language comprehension. In a clever series of experiments, Stine and her colleagues (Soederberg Miller & Stine-Morrow, 1998; Stine, 1990; Stine, Cheung, & Henderson, 1995; Stine-Morrow, Loveless, & Soderberg, 1996) have looked for evidence of such strategy differences by examining how young and older adults allocate reading time to individual words in a text. These studies examine word-by-word reading times, regressing young and older adults' reading times on a variety of word-level, sentence-level, and text-level features. In general, young and older adults have been found to allocate time very similarly; however, age differences in reading time allocation have been reported for specific aspects of syntactic and semantic processing.

Stine (1990) found that both young and older adults allocate reading time to word-level and constituent-level processing. However, they found qualitative differences in how time was allocated at clause and sentence boundaries. Young adults spent extra time reading words that occurred at sentence boundaries, minor clause boundaries, and major clause boundaries. Although older adults also allocated extra time to major and minor clause boundaries, they did not spend extra time at sentence boundaries.

Stine et al. (1995) examined word-by-word reading times in relation to various text features. Their results were similar to Stine's (1990) findings. In general, young and older adults allocated reading time similarly to most text features. However, recall ability and age did interact to affect reading time allocations. Although young adults who were good recallers paused longer at minor, major, and sentence boundaries, older adults who were good recallers only paused longer at minor sentence boundaries. Both studies suggest that older adults spend less time on sentence-level integration than young adults.

Stine-Morrow et al. (1996) let young and older adults read syntactically coherent text at their own pace. Both young and older adults who achieved good recall allocated extra reading time to syntactically complex sentences. However, some age differences were found with regard to other time-allocation strategies used to achieve good recall. For young adults, good recall was related to the allocation of additional reading time to infrequent words and to new concepts first mentioned in the text. However, for older adults, good recall was related to the allocation of additional reading time as they progressed serially through the text. These findings indicate that older adults use a different strategy than young adults to achieve good recall. Whereas young adults rely on recalling key words and concepts, older adults may rely on recalling a global text structure that is built up serially.

If so, contextual constraints may be particularly beneficial to older adults. Soederberg Miller and Stine-Morrow (1998) explored the effects of background knowledge on reading strategies. In one condition, a passage title established a meaningful context. The titles did facilitate conceptual integration at sentence boundaries, particularly for older adults. When no titles were provided, the readers spent more time accessing low-frequency words and read more slowly as the text progressed serially, suggesting they were spending additional time building up a context in which to interpret individual words and sentences. The latter effect was exacerbated for older readers, again suggesting that older readers rely on a global or situational model in order to interpret what they read. Successful older readers may be those who are best able to differentially allocate reading time and other cognitive resources (see also Morrow, Leirer, Altieri, & Fitzsimmons, 1994; Morrow, Stine-Morrow, Leirer, Andrassy, & Kahn, 1997).

III. Effects of Inhibitory Deficits

A different account of older adults' language problems has been put forth by Hasher and Zacks (1988). They proposed that inhibitory mechanisms weaken with age and permit the intrusion of irrelevant thoughts, personal preoccupations, and idiosyncratic associations during text encoding and retrieval. These irrelevant thoughts compete for processing resources, such as working memory capacity, and impair older adults' comprehension and recall. Hence, older adults' comprehension may be affected by distractions or intrusive thoughts. For example, when a text contains distracting words printed in a different typeface, young adults are able to ignore the distracting material, even when it is related to the text, whereas older adults are not able to ignore the distracting material, which slows their reading, impairs their comprehension, and renders them subject to memory distortions (Carlson, Hasher, Connelly, & Zacks, 1995; Connelly, Hasher, & Zacks, 1991; Zacks & Hasher, 1997).

Hasher, Zacks, and May (1999) postulate three functions of inhibition: preventing irrelevant information from entering working memory, deleting irrelevant information from working memory, and restraining probable responses until their appropriateness can be assessed. They argue that older adults suffer from a variety of processing impairments that can be attributed to decreased inhibitory mechanisms. Hence, older adults' language processing may mirror that of young adults whenever the task requires the active application of processing strategies because excitatory mechanisms are spared, whereas older adults' language processing may be impaired, relative to young adults', whenever inhibitory mechanisms are required to block out distractions, clear away irrelevancies, or switch between activities. Individuals with poor inhibitory mechanisms may not only be more susceptible to distraction, but they may also be less able to switch rapidly from one task to another and they may rely on well-learned "stereotypes, heuristics, and schemas" (Yoon, May, & Hasher, 1998, p. 123).

This hypothesis received support from a study by Kwong See and Ryan (1995). Kwong See and Ryan examined individual differences in text processing attributable to working memory capacity, processing speed, and efficiency of inhibitory processes, estimated by backward digit span, color naming speed, and Stroop interference, respectively. Their analysis suggested that older adults' text-processing difficulties can be attributed to slower processing and less efficient inhibition, rather than to working memory limitations. In light of these data suggesting age-related inhibitory deficits, it is important to note that a limitation of the Carlson et al. (1995) and Connelly et al. (1991) studies, like that of Kwong See and Ryan (1995), is that inhibitory breakdown was inferred from performance on probe questions or a global measure of reading speed. Despite the availability of techniques for assessing reading on-line, these methods have not been used to examine, for example, the distribution of reading times to text segments, word-by-word reading times, or other measures that may directly reflect the distribution of attention to key elements in a text.

Two studies by Connelly et al. (1991) compared young and older adults' reading to provide key support for inhibitory deficit theory. Connelly et al. compared passage reading times and answers to probe comprehension questions for young and older adults for texts that did not have distracting material interspersed amid target texts. The texts were approximately 125 words in length. In the distracting version, distracting words and phrases were inserted every three to four words. The distractors were presented in a different typeface. The distractors consisted of words or phrases conceptually related to the content of the target text (in Experiment 1) and recurred over and over again throughout the target text. Connelly et al. reported that young adults not only read the texts containing the distracting material more rapidly than older adults but that they also showed greater comprehension of the target material. This simple phenomena has provided the clearest and strongest support for inhibitory-deficit theory. Older adults are more distractible than young adults because they are less able to suppress or inhibit reading task-irrelevant words and phrases.

In their second experiment, Connelly et al. (1991) compared three types of distractors: words related in meaning to the passage, words unrelated in meaning, and meaningless strings of x's. They found that related distractors slowed older adults' reading times more than unrelated ones and that the x's slowed older adults' reading times relative to a baseline condition. They also found that young adults' reading times were slowed by the x's as well as by distractor words but that related versus unrelated distractors did not differentially affect the young adults. They suggest that the related distractor words "produce what might be a greater breadth of spontaneous activation" for older adults who may also expend "greater effort to understand" (p. 539) the related distractors and text passage. Despite their efforts to understand the text, older adults are ultimately less successful than young adults in terms of performance on the comprehension probes.

Connelly et al.'s (1991) conclusion has been challenged by Dywan and Murphy (1996), who modified the procedure to include a surprise word recognition test for the interposed material. They found that the young adults had superior recognition memory for the distractor words, a result which is difficult to explain if the young adults are assumed to have been successful at inhibiting processing of the distractors. Burke (1997) also argues that research on semantic priming, the activation of word meanings, and the detection of ambiguity provides "no support" for claims that "older adults are deficient

in suppressing contextually irrelevant meaning or that they activate more irrelevant semantic information than young adults or that they retrieve more high frequency, dominant, or typical information than young adults" (p. P257).

Additional support for the inhibitory deficit theory comes from more recent studies using a variety of paradigms and experimental procedures. Although most research exploring inhibitory processes in language and aging has been based on visual language processing (see Burke, 1997; and McDowd, 1997, for reviews), Sommers and Danielson (1999) examined older adults' ability to use context to identify spoken words. Some of the words were hard to identify because they are phonetically similar to many other words (e.g., *cat* is similar to *kit*, *cot*, *scat*); other words were easy to identify because they have few, phonologically similar competitors. The authors also varied predictability by using different contexts. Consistent with the predictions of inhibitory deficit theory, older adults did not perform as well as young adults identifying hard words in single-word and low-probability contexts. However, older adults were able to supress phonologically similar competitors of the hard-to-identify words when they were presented in a highly predictable context. In addition, Sommers and Danielson found that individuals who performed less well on tests of inhibition, such as an auditory version of the classic Stroop test, had more difficulty recognizing hard-to-identify words than individuals who performed better on the inhibition tests. Based on these results, Sommers and Danielson concluded that older adults have difficulty recognizing words with many phonologically similar competitors because of age-related inhibitory deficits.

This conclusion has been challenged by Murphy, McDowd, and Wilcox (1999) who measured young and older adults' ability to process unattended auditory information. In three experiments using different paradigms to assess processing of the unattended information, younger and older adults did not differ in terms of their processing of the unattended information, although the older adults performed more poorly with regards to processing the attended information. Young and older adults' perceptions of homophones were equally influenced by semantic cues presented as distractors, biasing words, or sentences presented in the unattended channel. Inhibitory deficit theory would predict that the older adults should process more of the unattended information because they should be less able to disregard it or inhibit processing this information.

Inhibition has also been examined in relation to processing "garden-path" sentences (Hartman & Dusek, 1994; Hartman & Hasher, 1991; Hasher, Quig, & May, 1997). These sentences lead the participant to think of a highly predictable final word and then they are surprised with an alternative unexpected word which must be remembered, as in *Before you go to bed, turn off the...stove*. An indirect memory test then is used to probe for recall of the predicted but disconfirmed word (e.g., *light*), or the unexpected word (e.g., *stove*). Participants are asked to complete sentence fragments; a breakdown of inhibition is inferred whenever the predicted but disconfirmed word is as likely to be used to complete the fragments as the unexpected word. The original report of this procedure indicated that young adults tend to produce only the unexpected word, whereas older adults tend to produce both. According to inhibition deficit theory, older adults are unable to inhibit processing the predicted but disconfirmed word, whereas young adults can suppress processing of the predicted word once the actual unexpected final word is presented.

Hartman (1995) challenged this intepretation. She noted that the participants

were required to generate the predictable word before the actual final word was presented. Consequently, she suggested, older adults might have been confused as to which word they were to remember. In addition, the unexpected final words may have been less memorable just because they were not predictable from the context and so they were less well integrated with the context to form a durable memory representation. More recently, May, Zacks, Hasher, and Multhaup (1999) have challenged Hartman's interpretation, using an additional series of task manipulations. What seems to be common to the variants of the garden-path paradigm that produced age differences in performance on the implicit memory task is that the participants are required to generate the competing word during the initial phase of the experiment. This observation suggests that a source memory problem (Spencer & Raz, 1995) contributes to the age differences in performance on the implicit memory task.

The most controversial and intriguing debate over the role of inhibitory deficits in language processing involves studies of off-target verbosity. Gold, Andres, Arbuckle, and Schwartzman (1988) observed that a minority of older adults not only talk a lot but drift from topic to topic, weaving into their conversations many unrelated and irrelevant topics. Off-target verbosity appears to be related to poor performance on tests of frontal lobe functioning as well as to psychosocial stress, extraversion, limited social support, and smaller social networks (Arbuckle & Gold, 1993; Pushkar Gold, Arbuckle, & Andres, 1994; Pushkar Gold & Arbuckle, 1995).

Whereas off-target verbosity has been cited as providing strong support for inhibitiory deficit theory, Burke (1997) argues that this speech style is limited to social settings in which older adults' construe their task differently than do young adults—as monologue, responsive to an internal chain of associations. James, Burke, Austin, and Hulme (1998) examined speech samples collected from young and older adults. Those from the older adults were, indeed, more verbose but only when they were describing personal, autobiographical topics. However, these autobiographical narratives were rated as more informative and interesting than the more focused, less verbose narratives produced by young adults.

Pushkar, et al. (2000) and Arbuckle, Nohara-LeClair, and Pushkar (2000) have carefully examined the speech, social skills, convestational style, and referential communication skill of older adults identified as demonstrating high levels of off-target verbosity. From a panel of 455 older adults, they scored off-target verbosity defined as copious speech and a high degree of content unrelated to the questions during a structured interview. The 35 highest scoring participants were designated as the high off-target verbose participants. This group did more poorly on inhibition tasks including the Stroop test; however, they were not distinguishable from the other participants in terms of their scores on a variety of measures of social support and social skills. During "get acquainted" conversations with other participants, they also talked more, revealed more personal information, and tended to ask fewer questions of their partners and to recall less about their partners (Pushkar et al., 2000). On a referential communication task, they were less efficient in giving directions in that they produced more hedged or qualified directions and gave more redundant directions (Arbuckle et al., 2000). Pushkar et al. conclude that these older adults are self-absorbed and self-preoccupied. They also emphasize that off-target verbosity characterizes a minority of older adults, and is not a general characteristic of older adults. They conclude, "It is possible that older people who are experiencing losses generated by declining cognitive skills are more motivated by self-affirmation as a communicative goal, leading them to more egocentric behavior in conversational settings" (p. 373). This view of off-target verbosity, therefore, suggests that off-target verbosity, while linked to a breakdown of inhibition, represents a qualitatively different phenomena than that described by Hasher and Zacks (1988). For Hasher and Zacks, off-target verbosity is a general characteristic of older adults resulting from the breakdown of a general mechanism that controls the access of information to working memory, the deletion of information from working memory, and responses based on the contents of working memory. For Pushkar et al. and Arbuckle et al., off-target verbosity is an infrequently concommitant of old age, arising from neuropsychology and psychosocial pathologies.

IV. Emerging Research Areas

The debates over working memory capacity limitations and inhibitory deficits are centermost to the general study of gerontology. These core research issues have been supplemented by two emerging topics: research examining the effects of AD on language production and comprehension and research examining how to improve older adults' comprehension of language.

A. Effects of Alzheimer's Disease

Clinical markers of the onset of Alzheimer's disease are difficult to distinguish from nonclinical age-related lapses of attention or memory sometimes termed "benign senescent forgetfulness" or "nonpathological age-associated memory impairments" (Kral, 1962, p. 257). A new diagnostic category, *mild cognitive impairment* (Smith, Petersen, Ivnik, Malec,

& Tangelos, 1996) has also emerged in recent years to refer to individuals who experience memory problems without other symptoms of dementia. Distinguishing *normative* age-related changes to language from *nonnormative* or pathological changes may be important for the early diagnosis, hence possible treatment, of Alzheimer's disease and related disorders. The early detection and diagnosis of Alzheimer's disease may be improved by measuring the extent of linguistic impairments (Bayles, Tomoeda, & Trosset, 1992); however, age of onset of the disease may also contribute to the nature and extent of observed linguistic impairment (Grossee, Gilley, & Wilson, 1991), as some aspects of language may decline more rapidly than others.

One focus of the Nun Study has been the investigation of the relationship between linguistic ability and the risk for Alzheimer's disease and longevity. The Nun Study is an ongoing longitudinal, epidemiological study of aging, directed at investigating risk factors for the development of Alzheimer's disease (Snowdon, 1997). Snowdon et al. (1996) analyzed language samples from participants in the Nun Study, all members of the School Sisters of Notre Dame. The participants wrote autobiographies at the time they took their vows and became members of the religious congregation, at 18–32 years of age. When the participants were 75 to 93 years of age, they were given a battery of tests of cognition and memory designed to assess probable Alzheimer's dementia. Low linguistic ability in young adulthood was associated with increased risk for poor performance on the cognitive and memory tests in late adulthood and with increased neuropathology characteristic of Alzheimer's disease for a small number of nuns who had died. In a follow-up study, Snowdon, Greiner, Kemper, Nanayakkara, and Mortimer (1999) linked low linguistic ability in young adulthood to increased all-cause mortality among the participants. Linguistic ability may be a general measure of cognitive and neurological development; low linguistic ability in young adulthood may reflect suboptimal neurocognitive development which, in turn, may increase susceptibility to age-related decline due to Alzheimer's or other diseases.

Alzheimer's disease appears to spare syntactic production (Bates, Harris, Marchman, Wulfeck, & Kritchevsky, 1995; Lyons et al., 1993). Some simplifications of syntax result but the speech of individuals with Alzheimer's dementia does not appear to become agrammatic. For example, Kemper et al. (1993) examined single sentences produced by older adults undergoing a neurological examination as part of the Mini-Mental State Examination (Folstein, Folstein, & McHugh, 1975). The adults were classified as nondemented or diagnosed with probable Alzheimer's disease and rated as very mildly, mildly, or moderately demented. The sentences were evaluated for propositional content, length, and grammatical form. The sentences produced by the moderately demented adults were shorter and simpler, both in content and form, than those produced by the nondemented and very mildly demented adults. Despite these differences, the sentences from the moderately demented adults were as grammatical as the sentences from the nondemented and mildly demented adults. Hence, basic syntax is preserved, although working memory limitations associated with Alzheimer's disease reduce sentence length and complexity.

Studies of syntactic processing in individuals with Alzheimer's dementia have found conflicting results. For example, della Sala, Lorenzi, Spinnler, Zuffi (1993) found that individuals with Alzheimer's dementia performed more poorly on a syntactic comprehension task relative to age-, education-, and sex-matched controls. Tomoeda, Bayles, Boone, and Kaszniak

(1990) examined speech rate and syntactic comprehension of normal adults and adults with Alzheimer's dementia and found that both groups performed more poorly when the syntactic complexity increased, although rate of presentation was not an influential factor. However, adults with Alzheimer's dementia performed more poorly than normal adults regardless of rate or syntactic complexity condition.

Syntactic complexity does not always impair comprehension by adults with Alzheimer's dementia. Rochon, Waters, and Caplan (1994), Waters, Caplan, and Rochon (1995), and Waters, Rochon, and Caplan (1998) tested normal older adults and adults with dementia on a sentence-picture matching task in which to-be-matched sentences differed in terms of syntactic and propositional complexity; concurrent digit loads were presented on some of the trials. In all three studies, the performance of adults with dementia was minimally impaired on the syntactically complex sentences, whereas increasing propositional content and imposing a concurrent digit load severely impaired sentence comprehension for adults with dementia. Thus, it may be that task demands, attentional lapses, response biases, or other cognitive deficits contribute to the syntactic comprehension problems of adults with dementia.

A similar conclusion was reached by Kempler, Almor, MacDonald, and Anderson (1999) from a series of studies using on- and off-line tests of sentence comprehension. They contrasted simple and complex sentences using a sentence-picture verification task and a cross-modal naming procedure. In this procedure, a person listens to an introductory sentence followed by a sentence fragment and then names, as rapidly as possible, a word presented visually. The word is either a "good" or a "bad" continuation of the sentence. For example, *The students were doing well. The young girl*...might be followed by WAS or WERE. The "good" continuation "was" should be named more rapidly than the bad continuation "were" if the individual is sensitive to the grammatical rules governing subject–verb agreement.

Kempler et al. (1999) found that syntactic complexity affected the ability of adults with Alzheimer's disease to correctly match a sentence to a picture. In addition, the number of protagonists mentioned in the sentence (or perhaps the number of entities depicted in the picture) also affected the patient's performance. The cross-modal naming task suggested that other factors than just syntax affect sentence processing by individuals with Alzheimer's dementia. They could name "good" continuations to the auditory sentence fragments more rapidly than "bad" continuations when subject–verb agreement was probed, indicating this aspect of syntactic competence was spared. However, when the stimuli tested the ability to select a pronoun in a discourse context (e.g., *The children loved the silly clown at the party. During the performance, the clown threw candy to... THEM or HIM*), the patients with Alzheimer's disease exhibited no naming advantage for "good" continuations. This suggested that they were not sensitive to discourse factors that determine the appropriateness of pronouns.

In a related study, Almor, Kempler, MacDonald, Andersen, and Tyler (1999) compared pronoun production and comprehension in Alzheimer's patients using spontaneous speech, a cross-modal naming procedure probing sensitivity to appropriate and inappropriate uses of pronouns, and a paragraph comprehension test comparing usage of pronouns to full noun phrase referents. Whereas the patients used many pronouns spontaneously, they were not sensitive to appropriate versus inappropriate uses. However, the patients were better able to remember information if full noun phrases were used than if pronouns were used in the paragraphs.

Kempler et al. (1999) and Almor et al. (1999) conclude that the "computational" demands imposed by particular combinations of task and sentence stimuli will determine whether patients with Alzheimer's dementia will experience language-processing problems or not. Pronouns are "computationally" easy to produce but "computationally" hard to understand, whereas the reverse is true of full noun phrases.

Semantic and lexical processes are particularly disrupted by Alzheimer's dementia. A number of researchers have found that resource-demanding explicit tests of lexical processing such as word recall and recognition reveal that the word knowledge of adults with Alzheimer's dementia is severely impaired relative to normal older adults (e.g., Grossman & White-Devine, 1998). Grossman, Mickanin, Onishi, and Hughes (1995) tested normal older adults and adults with Alzheimer's disease on their understanding of mass versus count terms: mass terms refer to aggregates, such as *milk*, which can be quantified by *much* or *little*, whereas count terms refer to individual items that are quantified by *many* or *few*. On the sentence-picture verification task, the participants were given, for example, a choice of a picture of large number of pencils, a picture of a small number of pencils, a picture of large mass of a substance, or a picture of small mass of a substance, and they had to select the picture corresponding to the target sentence (e.g., *Point to the picture with many*). On a sentence-acceptability task, the participants had to rate the acceptability of, for example, *The jar contains much pencils*. On both tasks, the adults with Alzheimer' disease were less accurate than normal older adults; they were less likely to select the correct picture corresponding to *Point to the picture with many* and to detect sentences violating the mass–count distinction, such as *The jar contains much pencils*.

Grossman, Mickanin, Onishi, and Hughes (1996) collected sentence-acceptability ratings from normal adults and adults with Alzheimer's disease. The adults with Alzheimer's disease tended to accept such sentences as *Steve heard the room* or *Cathy thought at her house* as well as *Sally gazed that the light was bright* or *Bob listened that the story was long*. The first type of sentence violates linguistic constraints on the pairing of verbs and predicates: the predicate object of a verb like *heard* must be an auditory event or a noise, whereas the predicate object of *thought* must be an idea; the second type of sentence violates linguistic constraints on pairing verbs and sentence complements: *gaze* and *listen* are typically used with prepositional phrases such as *at the bright light* or *to the long story*. Robinson, Grossman, White-Devine, and D'Esposito (1996) report that individuals with Alzheimer's dementia have more difficulty with semantic judgment tasks involving verbs than those involving nouns.

Grossman, Mickanin, Onishi, Robinson, and D'Esposito (1996) suggest that individuals with Alzheimer's dementia have difficulty learning verb argument structures, although they could learn the meaning of novel verbs. Nondemented individuals were able to learn, from a few uses, the meaning and use of a novel verb such as "wamble" (meaning "to return home"), as well as its argument structure: that it cannot be used with a direct object as in *The eagle wambles the nest* or with an inanimate agent as in *Books wamble into the store*. The individuals with AD were able to correctly select pictures to match the meaning of "wamble" but found the novel sentences to be grammatical. These studies suggest that the disruption of semantic memory by Alzheimer's disease is not limited to nominals but extends to verbs and other parts of speech.

In contrast, many researchers have found that tests of implicit word knowledge reveal few differences between dementing adults and normal older adults (Ober, Shenaut, Jagust, & Stillman, 1991). Preserved lexical knowledge is commonly found in studies of lexical priming in sentence contexts. For example, Nebes (1994) found that sentence-level priming, in which the message conveyed by the sentence facilitates a decision about a target presented after the sentence, remains intact in adults with Alzheimer's dementia. Nebes and Halligan (1995) presented normal adults and adults with dementia with sentences in which the last word of the sentence was replaced by a picture. The authors also varied the degree to which sentence context constrained the interpretation of the sentence-final picture. Participants were to decide whether or not the picture was a sensible ending to the sentence. The effect of contextual constraint was similar for adults with Alzheimer's disease and normal young and older adults. Hence, adults with Alzheimer's disease must still have access to an intact semantic system of lexical features and word associations. A similar conclusion was reached by Nebes and Halligan (1996), who asked normal adults and adults with Alzheimer's disease to verify sentences about attributes of a target primed by sentence context, as in *Jill's cat was tangled up in the telephone. Does a telephone have a cord?* or which were not primed by the sentence context, such as *In the distance he heard his neighbor's telephone. Does a telephone have a cord?* Again, adults with Alzheimer's disease and normal adults benefited equally from the sentence context.

Some researchers have concluded that the structure of semantic knowledge is destroyed by Alzheimer's dementia (Abeysinghe, Bayles, & Trosset, 1990; Chan, Butters, Paulsen, et al., 1993; Chan, Butters, Salmon, & McGuire, 1993; Gonnerman, Andersen, Devlin, Kempler, & Seidenberg, 1997; Haut et al., 1998; Hodges, Patterson, Graham, & Dawson, 1996; Hodges, Salmon, & Butters, 1992). As a result, performance on verbal-fluency tasks, such as generating exemplars of categories or words beginning with a specific letter, is impaired; picture and object naming is hindered, and word associations are destroyed. Henderson, Mack, Freed, Kempler, and Anderson (1990) compared errors made on a confrontation naming task administered on two occasions 6 months apart; 80% of the errors were consistent on both occasions, suggesting that lexical information is indeed lost.

Others have concluded that the semantic network of adults with Alzheimer's dementia is intact but becomes inaccessible (Atell & Harley, 1996; Grossman et al. 1996; Margolin, Pate, & Friedrich, 1996; Nebes & Brady, 1990; Nebes & Halligan, 1996; Ober, Shenaut, & Reed, 1995). From this perspective, semantic priming in reaction-time tasks involving word naming and lexical decisions is preserved. Consistent with this view is the finding by Bayles, Tomoeda, and Rein (1996) that older adults with Alzheimer's dementia are bothered by both length and meaninglessness on a phrase repetition task; repeating a phrase such as *tornadoes judged long eggplant booklets* was more challenging than repeating a meaningful phrase such as *active volcanoes spew hot lava*, which would not be expected if semantic memory is lost or severely degraded by the disease.

Nebes (Madden, Nebes, & Allen, 1992; Nebes & Brady, 1992) has suggested that Alzheimer's disease results in the general, task-independent slowing of cognitive processes including lexical access. Myerson, Lawrence, Hale, Jenkins, and Chen (1998) also supported the general slowing hypothesis by comparing the performance of adults with Alzheimer's disease to age-matched, healthy adults on a series of speeded tasks. They report that the adults with Alzheimer's disease responded 1.8 times more slowly than the age-matched controls and that slowing on lexical tasks was equivalent to slowing on nonlexical tasks. They also suggest that general slowing increased progressively with disease severity.

Faust, Balota, Duchek, Gernsbacher, and Smith (1997) have suggested that a breakdown of inhibitory processes may contribute to the semantic processing problems of individuals with Alzheimer's dementia (see also Duchek, Balota, & Thessing, 1998). Faust et al. used a sentence comprehension task in which individuals were asked to judge whether a word was related to a target sentence. On the critical trials, the target sentence ended with an ambiguous word, such as *He dug with a spade*; the word was related to either a contextually appropriate meaning, GARDEN, or to the alternative meaning, ACE. Whereas nonimpaired individuals were able to quickly and reliably reject the contextually inappropriate words, individuals with Alzheimer's dementia tended to accept these words as consistent with the sentence. This pattern of results indicates that the alternative meaning of the ambiguous word was not suppressed, consistent with the view that Alzheimer's dementia is associated with a breakdown of inhibitory processes. This breakdown of inhibitory processes may contribute to many of the word retrieval problems experienced by adults with Alzheimer's disease.

In sum, recent research on the effects of Alzheimer's disease on language suggests that adults with Alzheimer's disease present a unique profile of spared and impaired language: basic syntax is preserved, whereas working memory limitations restrict the use of long and complex constructions; on the other hand, explicit and implicit access to lexical items and semantic knowledge is progressively disrupted by general slowing and the break-

down of inhibition. This profile was confirmed by Kemper (1997) using a metalinguistic judgment task with normal adults and adults with Alzheimer's disease. One type of sentences tested linguistic constraints on phrase structure, such as the contrast in acceptability for *Jane gave the library a book* versus *Jane donated the library a book* or *The bed was slept on by Washington* versus *Tuesday was slept on by Washington*. Young adults and healthy older adults tended to reject the sentences that violated linguistic constraints on phrase structure, whereas adults with Alzheimer's disease tended to find *Jane donated the library a book* and *Tuesday was slept on by Washington* to be acceptable. This finding suggests that adults with Alzheimer's disease are not sensitive to subtle aspects of verb meaning that regulate their use in various phrase structures, consistent with the hypothesis that implicit and explicit access to the semantic system is disrupted by Alzheimer's disease. The second type of sentence involved linguistic constraints on syntactic transformations of linguistic structure. Some alternative forms of sentences can be legitimately derived, whereas others are blocked by linguistic constraints. Both *The fact is irrelevant that John gave Bill all his old books* and *The fact that John gave Bill all his old books is irrelevant* are permitted, whereas *The fact that John gave Bill is irrelevant all his old books* is blocked by a linguistic constraint. Kemper found that young adults' metalinguistic judgments match the predictions of linguistic theory, whereas older adults and adults with Alzheimer's disease tend to find all three variants to be acceptable. This pattern was correlated with working memory capacity, suggesting that the older adults and adults with Alzheimer's disease were unable to fully process the long, multiclause sentences due to working memory limitations; hence, they were unable to detect the violation of the linguistic constraint.

B. Effects of Elderspeak

A special speech register, sometimes termed *elderspeak*, has been described as an accommodation to communicating with older adults, especially those with dementia; elderspeak may be evoked by the actual communicative needs as well as by negative stereotypes of older adults. Hence, elderspeak is addressed to older adults with dementia as well as to other older adults who are often presumed to have dementia (Kemper, 1994; Ryan, Bourhis, & Knops, 1991; Ryan, Giles, Bartolucci, & Henwood, 1986). Elderspeak has been characterized as involving a simplified speech register with exaggerated pitch and intonation, simplified grammar, limited vocabulary, and slow rate of delivery. It appears to be a robust phenomenon that occurs in a wide range of settings involving older adults such as craft classes, legal seminars, and congregate meals as well as nursing homes for demented and nondemented older adults (Kemper, 1994) although it is most often associated with nursing homes and other health care facilities (Ryan, Hummert, & Boich, 1995). Many of the characteristics of elderspeak, such as its slow rate, exaggerated prosody, and simplified syntax and vocabulary, resemble the characteristics of other speech registers, such as those directed at young children, foreigners, and household pets (Warren & McCloskey, 1997). Elderspeak is assumed to have these special characteristics because it enhances or facilitates communication with older adults.

Harwood, Giles, and Ryan (1995) argue that the use of elderspeak, as well as other age-based behavioral modifications, contributes to development of an "old" identity, reinforcing negative stereotypes of older adults, and lowering older adults' self-esteem. Following Ryan et al. (1986), they further argue that a downward spiral can result such that elderspeak contributes to the social isolation and cognitive decline of older adults, triggering further speech simplifications. Ryan et al. (1986) term this the *communicative predicament of aging*. The predicament is that elderspeak can lead to a negative spiral of perceived and actual communicative impairments but the failure to use appropriate speech accommodations for older adults may also lead to social isolation and cognitive decline. Other observational studies as well as simulation studies using scripted interactions have noted that elderspeak conveys a sense of disrespect towards its recipients, limits their conversational interactions, and implies that they are cognitively impaired (Edwards & Noller, 1993; Ryan et al., 1991; Ryan, Hamilton, & Kwong See, 1994; Ryan, MacLean, & Orange, 1994). O'Connor and Rigby (1996), following Ryan et al. (1991), suggest that older adults, especially those in nursing homes, adapt to situational demands by becoming more accepting of elderspeak.

Using a controlled referential communication task, Kemper and her colleagues (Kemper, Ferrell, Harden, Finter-Urczyk, & Billington, 1998; Kemper, Finter-Urczyk, Ferrell, Harden, & Billington, 1998; Kemper, Othick, Gerhing, Gubarchuk, & Billington, 1998; Kemper, Othick, Warren, Gubarchuk, & Gerhing, 1996; Kemper, Vandeputte, Rice, Cheung, & Gubarchuk, 1995) have investigated elderspeak addressed by young adults to older adults in a laboratory setting. This series of studies suggests that the speech register is composed of two sets of parameters. One set of correlated parameters is linked to the perception that the older listener is cognitively impaired; these parameters affect how much information is conveyed and include semantic elaborations, such as expansions and repetitions of previous map directions. The other set of correlated parameters includes modifications to fluency, prosody, and grammar; these parameters are influenced by practice and task familarity.

Whereas the first set of elderspeak parameters may benefit older adults, the modifications to fluency, prosody, and grammar do not appear to benefit older listeners.

Overall, young adults' use of elderspeak improved the performance of the older listeners. However, the older adults also reported experiencing more receptive and expressive communication problems when they were paired with a young adult who used elderspeak than when they were paired with another older adult. The use of elderspeak by the young partners appeared to trigger older adults' perceptions of themselves as cognitively impaired, consistent with the communicative predicament of aging model of Ryan et al. (1986).

In a final series of experimental studies, Kemper and Harden (1999) systematically tested the efficacy of such manipulations of prosody as well as other components of elderspeak including speech rate. These experiments demonstrated that it is possible to develop a form of elderspeak that benefits older adults and that does not give rise to negative self-assessments of communicative competence and which is not perceived as insulting or patronizing. This form of elderspeak would provide semantic elaborations by repeating or expanding instructions or requests. It would also reduce syntactic complexity by eliminating subordinate and embedded clauses and thus lowering processing demands. Reducing sentence length per se, without reducing syntactic complexity, has no effect on older adults' performance and it increases communication problems. Chopping up directions into short two- to five-word sentences does not benefit older adults and may actually impair their comprehension by dribbling out information over multiple sentences, thus taxing working memory. The exaggerated prosody of elderspeak appears to convey no positive benefit to older adults in terms of performance on the referential communication task and may actually hurt performance. High pitch and/or slow speaking rate contribute to older adults' negative assessment of their own communicative competence as well as to negative evaluations of the speaker. To be addressed in a "baby talk" version of elderspeak made up of short, simple sentences delivered slowly with contrastive pitch seems to convey the impression to older adults that they are cognitively impaired and have communication problems.

Some form of elderspeak may enhance communication with older adults, especially those with Alzheimer's dementia (Orange, Ryan, Meredith, & MacLean, 1955; Ryan, Meredith, MacLean, & Orange, 1995), but there has been little systematic research assessing intervention and training program. Ripich (1994) developed the FOCUSED program for training caregivers to use functional communication strategies. This program emphasizes *f*ace-to-face communication, *o*rientation through repetition of key words, *c*ontinuity of topic, "*u*nsticking" patients who are unable to retrieve a word by suggesting candidate words, *s*tructuring questions by providing one or two options, *e*xchanging normal conversation on normal topics, and using *d*irect, short, and simple sentences and nouns. Ripich reports that this training program promotes more positive attitudes toward patients and more satisfying communication with patients. To date, she has not assessed whether the FOCUSED program actually enhances patients' comprehension or or the frequency or quality of their interactions with nursing staff and other caregivers.

Not all of the componets of this training program may be necessary or appropriate. In a study of sentence–picture comprehension, Small, Kemper, and Lyons (1997) found that older adults with Alzheimer's disease did not benefit from reductions in speech rate, although repetition, either verbatim repetition or paraphrasing, did improve the performance of the impaired older adults. The older adults with Alzheimer's disease, also benefited from grammatical simplifications, yet they were able to understand complex sentences that were repeated either verbatim or in paraphrase form. A slow speech rate may actually impair comprehension by individuals with severe working memory limitations (Small, Andersen, & Kempler, 1997). Alternative strategies for enhancing communication with adults with Alzheimer's dementia must be developed by combining clinical observation with empirical research.

V. Conclusions

The past decade has seen heated debates over the effects of working memory capacity limitations and inhibitiory deficits on older adults' comprehension and production of language. In the heat of these debates, it is important not to lose sight of several general points. First, many aspects of language processing are age invariant, particularly lexical access and semantic memory, yet vulnerable to the ravages of Alzheimer's disease. Other aspects of language, particularly syntax, may be resistant to Azheimer's disease yet susceptible to age-related decline due to working memory limitations or inhibitory deficits. Resolving these observations within a general frame constitues the major challenge for the next decade. Second, there has been a gradual shift away from the standard "workhorses" of cognitive psychology, recall, recognition, imitation, to more sophisticated methodologies such as the decomposition of self-paced reading times. This shift will surely gain momentum as cognitive aging researchers begin to investigate eye movement patterns, evoked potential recordings, and brain activation patterns using PET

and fMRI. Third, the shift toward developing and evaluating practical applications, exemplified by the growing body of research on elderspeak, will continue. The linkage of basic research on language processing with everyday practicalities has led to the development of consumer standards and guidelines for presenting medical information (Park, Morrell, & Shifren, 1999) and for electronic and telecommunications (Charness, Park, & Sabel, 2001).

Acknowledgments

Preparation of this chapter was supported by NIA grants AG009952 and AG00226 to the University of Kansas.

References

Abeysinghe, S. C., Bayles, K. A., & Trosset, M. W. (1990). Semantic memory deterioration in Alzheimer's subjects: Evidence from word association, definition, and associate ranking tasks. *Journal of Speech and Hearing Research, 33*, 574–582.

Almor, A., Kempler, D., MacDonald, M. C., Andersen, E. S., & Tyler, L. K. (1999). Why do Alzheimer patients have difficulty with pronouns? Working memory, semantics, and reference in comprehension and production in Alzheimer's disease. *Brain and Language, 67*(3), 202–227.

Arbuckle, T., & Gold, D. P. (1993). Aging, inhibition, and verbosity. *Journal of Gerontology: Psychological Sciences, 48*, P225–P232.

Arbuckle, T., Nohara-LeClair, M., & Pushkar, D. (2000). Effects of off-target verbosity on communication efficiency in a referential communication task. *Psychology and Aging, 15*, 65–77.

Astell, A. J., & Harley, T. A. (1996). Tip-of-the-tongue states and lexical access in dementia. *Brain and Language, 54*, 196–215.

Baddeley, A. (1986). *Working memory.* Oxford: Clarendon Press.

Baddeley, A. D. (1996). The concept of working memory. In S. Gathercole (Ed.), *Models of short-term memory* (pp. 1–28). Hove, UK.: Psychology Press.

Bates, E., Harris, C., Marchman, V., Wulfeck, B., & Kritchevsky, M. (1995). Production of complex syntax in normal aging and Alzheimer's disease. *Language and Cognitive Processes, 10*, 487–539.

Bayles, K. A., Tomoeda, C. K., & Rein, J. A. (1996). Phrase repetition in Alzheimer's disease: Effect of meaning and length. *Brain and Language, 54*, 246–261.

Bayles, K. A., Tomoeda, C. K., & Trosset, M. W. (1992). Relation of linguistic communication abilities of Alzheimer's patients to stage of disease. *Brain and Language, 42*, 454–472.

Burke, D. (1997). Language, aging, and inhibitory deficits: Evaluation of a theory. *Journal of Gerontology: Psychological Sciences, 52B*, 254–264.

Caplan, D., & Waters, G. S. (1996). Syntactic processing in sentence comprehension under dual-task conditions in aphasic patients. *Language and Cognitive Processes, 11*, 525–551.

Caplan, D., & Waters, G. (1999). Verbal working memory and sentence comprehension. *Behavioral and Brain Sciences, 22*, 114–126.

Carlson, M. C., Hasher, L., Connelly, S. L., & Zacks, R. T. (1995). Aging, distraction, and the benefits of predictable location. *Psychology and Aging, 10*, 427–436.

Chan, A. S., Butters, N., Paulsen, J. S., Salmon, D. P., Swenson, M., & Maloney, L. (1993). An assessment of the semantic network in patients with Alzheimer's disease. *Journal of Cognitive Neuroscience, 5*, 254–261.

Chan, A. S., Butters, N., Salmon, D. P., & McGuire, K. A. (1993). Dimensionality and clustering in the semantic network of patients with Alzheimer's disease. *Psychology and Aging, 8*, 411–419.

Charness, N., Park, D. C., & Sabel, B. A. (2001). *Communication, technology, and aging: Opportunities and challenges for the future*. New York: Springer.

Connelly, S. L., Hasher, L., & Zacks, R. T. (1991). Age and reading: The impact of distraction. *Psychology and Aging, 6*, 533–541.

Daneman, M., & Merikle, P. M. (1996). Working memory and language comprehension: A meta-analysis. *Psychonomic Bulletin and Review, 3*, 422–433.

della Sala, S., Lorenzi, L., Spinnler, H., & Zuffi, M. (1993). Components in the breakdown of verbal communication in Alzheimer's disease. *Aphasiology, 7*, 285–299.

Duchek, J. M., Balota, D. A., & Thessing, V. C. (1998). Inhibition of visual and conceptual information during reading in healthy aging and Alzheimer's disease. *Aging, Neuropsychology, and Cognition, 5(3)*, 169–181.

Dywan, J., & Murphy, W. E. (1996). Aging and inhibitory control in text comprehension. *Psychology and Aging, 11*, 199–206.

Engle, R. W., Tuholski, S. W., Laughlin, J. E., & Conway, A. R. A. (1999). Working memory, short-term memory, and general fluid intelligence: A latent-variable approach. *Journal of Experimental Psychology: General, 128*, 309–331.

Edwards, H., & Noller, P. (1993). Perceptions of overaccommodations used by nurses in communication with the elderly. *Journal of Language and Social Psychology, 1*, 207–223.

Faust, M. E., Balota, D. A., Duchek, J. M., Gernsbacher, M. A., & Smith, S. (1997). Inhibitory control during sentence comprehension in individuals with dementia of the Alzheimer type. *Brain and Language, 57*, 225–253.

Folstein, M. F., Folstein, S. E., & McHugh, P. R. (1975). Mini-Mental State: A practical method for grading the cognitive state of patients for the clinician. *Journal of Psychiatric Research, 12*, 189–198.

Gold, D., Andres, D., Arbuckle, T., & Schwartzman, A. (1988). Measurement and correlates of verbosity in elderly people. *Journal of Gerontology: Psychological Sciences, 43*, 27–33.

Gonnerman, L. M., Anderson, E. S., Devlin, J. T., Kempler, D., & Seidenberg, M. S. (1997). Double dissociation of semantic categories in Alzheimer's disease. *Brain and Language, 57*, 254–279.

Grosse, D. A., Gilley, D. W., & Wilson, R. S. (1991). Episodic and semantic memory in early versus late onset Alzheimer's Disease. *Brain and Language, 41*, 531–537.

Grossman, M., Mickanin, J., Onishi, K., & Hughes, E. (1995). An aspect of sentence processing in Alzheimer's disease: Quantifier-noun agreement. *Neurology, 45*, 85–91.

Grossman, M., Mickanin, J., Onishi, K., & Hughes, E. (1996). Verb comprehension deficits in probable Alzheimer's disease. *Brain and Language, 53*, 369–389.

Grossman, M., Mickanin, J., Onishi, K., Robinson, K. M., & D'Esposito, M. (1996). Anomaly judgements of subject-predicate relations in Alzheimer's disease. *Brain and Language, 54,* 216–232.

Grossman, M., & White-Devine, T. (1998). Sentence comprehension in Alzheimer's disease. *Brain and Language, 62,* 186–201.

Hartman, M. (1995). Aging and interference: Evidence from indirect memory tests. *Psychology and Aging, 10,* 659–669.

Hartman, M., & Dusek, J. (1994). Direct and indirect memory tests: What they reveal about age differences in interference. *Aging and Cognition, 1*(4), 292–309.

Hartman, M., & Hasher, L. (1991). Aging and suppression: Memory for previously irrelevant information. *Psychology and Aging, 6,* 587–594.

Harwood, J., Giles, H., & Ryan, E. B. (1995). Aging, communication, and intergroup theory: Social identity and intergenerational communication. In J. Nussbaum & J. Coupland (Eds.), *Handbook of communication and aging.* Hillsdale, NJ: Erlbaum Associates.

Hasher, L., & Zacks, R. T. (1988). Working memory, comprehension, and aging: A review and a new view. In G. H. Bower (Ed.), *The psychology of learning and motivation* (Vol. 22, pp. 193–226). New York: Academic.

Hasher, L., Zacks, R. T., & May, C. P. (1999). Inhibitory control, circadian arousal, and age. In D. Gopher & A. Koriat (Eds.), *Attention and performance XVII: Cognitive regulation of performance: Interaction of theory and application.* Cambridge, MA: MIT Press.

Hasher, L., Quig, M. B., & May, C. P. (1997). Inhibitory control over no-longer-relevant information: Adult age differences. *Memory and Cognition, 25*(3), 286–295.

Haut, M. W., Roberts, V. J., Goldstein, F. C., Martin, R. C., Keefover, R. W., & Rankin, E. D. (1998). Working memory demands and semantic sensitivity for prose in mild Alzheimer's disease. *Aging, Neuropsychology, and Cognition, 5*(1), 63–72.

Henderson, V. W., Mack, W., Freed, D. M., Kempler, D., & Andersen, E. S. (1990). Naming consistency in Alzheimer's disease. *Brain and Language, 39,* 530–538.

Hodges, J. R., Salmon, D. P., & Butters, N. (1992). Semantic memory impairment in Alzheimer's disease: Failure of access or degraded knowledge? *Neuropsychologia, 30,* 301–314.

Hodges, J. R., Patterson, K., Graham, N., & Dawson, K. (1996). Naming and knowing in dementia of Alzheimer's type. *Brain and Language, 54,* 302–325.

James, L. E., Burke, D. M., Austin, A., & Hulme, E. (1998). Production and perception of "verbosity" in younger and older adults. *Psychology and Aging, 13,* 355–368.

Just, M. A., & Carpenter, P. A. (1992). A capacity theory of comprehension: Individual differences in working memory. *Psychological Review, 99,* 122–149.

Kemper, S. (1992). Language and aging. In F. I. M. Craik & T. A. Salthouse (Eds.), *Handbook of aging and cognition* (pp. 213–270). Hillsdale, NJ: Lawrence Erlbaum.

Kemper, S. (1994). Elderspeak: Speech Accommodations to Older Adults. *Aging and Cognition, 1,* 17–28.

Kemper, S. (1997). Metalinguistic judgments in normal aging and Alzheimer's disease. *Journal of Gerontology: Psychological Sciences, 52,* 147–155.

Kemper, S., Ferrell, P., Harden, T., Finter-Urczyk, A., & Billington, C. (1998). The use of elderspeak by young and older adults to impaired and normal older adults. *Discourse Processes, 5,* 43–55.

Kemper, S., Finter-Urczyk, A., Ferrell, P., Harden, T., & Billington, C. (1998). Using elderspeak with older adults. *Discourse Processes, 25,* 55–74.

Kemper, S., & Harden, T. (1999). Disentangling what is beneficial about elderspeak from what is not. *Psychology and Aging, 14,* 656–670.

Kemper, S., LaBarge, E., Ferraro, R., Cheung, H. T., Cheung, H., & Storandt, M. (1993). On the preservation of syntax in Alzheimer's disease: Evidence from written sentences. *Archives of Neurology, 50,* 81–86.

Kemper, S., & Kliegl, R. (1999). Concluding observations. In S. Kemper & R. Kliegl (Eds.), *Constraints on language: Aging, memory, and grammar* (pp. 299–307). New York: Kluwer Academic.

Kemper, S., Othick, M., Gerhing, H., Gubarchuk, J., & Billington, C. (1998). Practicing speech accommodations to older adults. *Applied Psycholinguistics, 19,* 175–192.

Kemper, S., Othick, M., Warren, J., Gubarchuk, J., & Gerhing, H. (1996). Facilitating older adults' performance on a referential communication task through speech accommodations. *Aging, Neuropsychology, and Cognition, 3*, 37–55.

Kemper, S., Vandeputte, D., Rice, K., Cheung, H., & Gubarchuk, J. (1995). Speech adjustments to aging during a referential communication task. *Journal of Language and Social Psychology, 14*, 40–59.

Kempler, D., Almor, A., MacDonald, M. C., & Andersen, E. S. (1999). Working with limited memory: Sentence comprehension in Alzheimer's disease. In S. Kemper & R. Kliegl (Eds.), *Constraints on language: aging, grammar, and memory* (pp. 227–248). Boston: Kluwer Academic.

Kemtes, K. A., & Kemper, K. (1997). Younger and older adults' on-line processing of syntactically ambiguous sentences. *Psychology and Aging, 12*(2), 362.

Kemtes, K. A., & Kemper, S. (1999). Aging and the resolution of quantifier scope ambiguities. *Journal of Gerontology: Psychological Sciences, 54B*, P350–P360.

Kral, V. A. (1962). Senescent forgetfulness: Benign and malignant. *The Canadian Medical Association Journal, 86*, 257–260.

Kwong See, S. T., & Ryan, E. B. (1995). Cognitive mediation of adult age differences in language performance. *Psychology and Aging, 10*, 458–468.

Lyons, K., Kemper, S., LaBarge, E., Ferraro, F. R., Balota, D., & Storandt, M. (1993). Language and Alzheimer's disease: A reduction in syntactic complexity. *Aging and Cognition, 50*, 81–86.

MacDonald, M., Just, M. A., & Carpenter, P. A. (1992). Working memory constraints on the processing of syntactic ambiguity. *Cognitive Psychology, 24*, 56–98.

Madden, D. J., Nebes, R. D., & Allen, P. A. (1992). Cognitive slowing in Alzheimer's disease as a function of task type and response type. *Developmental Neuropsychology, 8*(4), 459–471.

Margolin, D. I., Pate, D. S., & Friedrich, F. J. (1996). Lexical priming by pictures and words in normal aging and in dementia of the Alzheimer's type. *Brain and Language, 54*, 275–301.

Martin, R., Shelton, J. R., & Yafee, L. S. (1994). Language processing and working memory: Neuropsychological evidence for separate phonological and semantic capacities. *Journal of Memory and Language, 38*, 83–111.

May, C. P., Zacks, R. T., Hasher, L., & Multhaup, K. S. (1999). Inhibition in the processing of garden-path sentences. *Psychology and Aging, 14*, 304–313.

McDowd, J. M. (1997). Inhibition in attention and aging. *Journals of Gerontology: Series B: Psychological Sciences and Social Sciences, 52B*(6), 265–273.

Morrow, D., Leirer, V., Altieri, P., & Fitzsimmons, C. (1994). Age differences in creating spatial models from narratives. *Language and Cognitive Processes, 9*(2), 203–220.

Morrow, D. G., Stine-Morrow, E. A. L., Leirer, V. O., Andrassy, J. M., & Kahn, J. (1997). The role of reader age and focus of attention in creating situation models from narratives. *Journals of Gerontology: Series B: Psychological Sciences and Social Sciences, 52B*(2), 73–80.

Murphy, D. R., McDowd, J. M., & Wilcox, K. A. (1999). Inhibition and Aging: Similarities between younger and older adults as revealed by the processing of unattended auditory information. *Psychology and Aging, 14*, 44–59.

Myerson, J., Lawrence, B., Hale, S., Jenkins, L., & Chen, J. (1998). General slowing of lexical and nonlexical information processing in dementia of the Alzheimer type. *Aging, Neuropsychology, and Cognition, 5*(3), 182–193.

Nebes, R. D. (1994). Contextual facilitation of lexical processing in Alzheimer's disease, Intralexical priming or sentence level priming? *Journal of Clinical and Experimental Neuropsychology, 16*, 489–497.

Nebes, R. D., & Brady, C. B. (1990). Preserved organization of semantic attributes in Alzheimer's disease. *Psychology and Aging, 5*, 574–579.

Nebes, R. D., & Brady, C. B. (1992). Generalized cognitive slowing and severity of dementia in Alzheimer's disease: Implications for the interpretation of response-time data. *Journal of Clinical and Experimental Neuropsychology, 14*(2), 317

Nebes, R. D., & Halligan, E. M. (1995). Contextual constraint facilitates semantic decisions about object pictures by Alzheimer patients. *Psychology and Aging, 10,* 590–596.

Nebes, R. D., & Halligan, E. M. (1996). Sentence context influences the interpretation of word meaning by Alzheimer patients. *Brain and Language, 54,* 233–245.

Norman, S., Kemper, S., Kynette, D., Cheung, H., & Anagnopoulos, C. (1991). Syntactic complexity and adults' running memory span. *Journal of Gerontology, 46,* 346–351.

Ober, B. A., Shenaut, G. K., Jagust, W. J., & Stillman, R. C. (1991). Automatic semantic priming with various category relations in Alzheimer's disease and normal aging. *Psychology and Aging, 6,* 647–660.

Ober, B. A., Shenaut, G. K., & Reed, B. R. (1995). Assessment of associative relations in Alzheimer's disease: Evidence for preservation of semantic memory. *Aging and Cognition, 2,* 254–267.

O'Connor, B. P., & Rigby, H. (1996). Perceptions of baby talk, frequency of receiving baby talk, and self-esteem among community and nursing home residents. *Psychology and Aging, 11,* 147–154.

Orange, J. B., Ryan, E. B., Meredith, S. D., & MacLean, M. J. (1995). Application of the communication enhancement model for long-term care residents with Alzheimer's disease. *Topics in Language Disorders, 15,* 20–35.

Park, D. C., Morrell, R. W., & Shifren, K. (Eds.). (1999). *Processing of medical information in aging patients: Cognitive and human factors perspectives.* Mahwah, NJ: Lawrence Erlbaum Associates.

Pushkar, D., Basevitz, P., Arbuckle, T., Nohara-LeClair, M., Lapidus, S., & Peled, M. (2000). Social behavior and off-target verbosity in elderly people *Psychology and Aging, 15,* 361–374.

Pushkar Gold, D., & Arbuckle, T. Y. (1995). A longitudinal study of off-target verbosity. *Journals of Gerontology: Series B: Psychological Sciences and Social Sciences, 50B*(6), 307–315.

Pushkar Gold, D., Arbuckle, T. Y., & Andres, D. (1994). Verbosity in older adults. In M. L. Hummert, J. M. Wiemann, & J. F. Nussbaum (Eds.), *Interpersonal communication in older adulthood: Interdisciplinary theory and research* (pp. 107–129). Thousand Oaks, CA: Sage Publications.

Ripich, D. N. (1994). Functional communication with AD patients: A caregiver training program. *Alzheimer's Disease and Associated Disorders, 8,* 95–109.

Robinson, K. M., Grossman, M., White-Devine, T., & D'Esposito, M. (1996). Category-specific difficulty naming with verbs in Alzheimer's disease. *Neurology, 47,* 178–182.

Rochon, E., Waters, G. S., & Caplan, D. (1994). Sentence comprehension in patients with Alzheimer's disease. *Brain and Language, 46,* 329–349.

Ryan, E. B., Bourhis, R. Y., & Knops, U. (1991). Evaluative perceptions of patronizing speech addressed to elders. *Psychology and Aging, 6,* 442–450.

Ryan, E. B., Giles, H., Bartolucci, G., & Henwood, K. (1986). Psycholinguistic and social psychological components of communication by and with the elderly. *Language and Communication, 6,* 1–24.

Ryan, E. B., Hamilton, J. M., & Kwong See, S. (1994). Younger and older adult listeners' evaluations of baby talk addressed to institutionalized elders. *International Journal of Aging and Human Development, 39,* 21–32.

Ryan, E. B., Hummert, M. L., & Boich, L. H. (1995). Communication predicaments of aging: Patronizing behavior toward older adults. *Journal of Language and Social Psychology, 14,* 144–166.

Ryan, E. B., MacLean, M., & Orange, J. B. (1994). Inappropriate accommodation in communication to elders: Inferences about nonverbal correlates. *International Journal of Aging and Human Development, 39,* 273–291.

Ryan, E. B., Meredith, S. D., MacLean, M. J., & Orange, J. B. (1995). Changing the way we talk with elders: Promotion health using the communication enhancement model. *International Journal of Aging and Human Development, 41,* 89–107.

Small, J. A., Andersen, E. S., & Kempler, D. (1997). Effects of working memory capacity on understanding rate-altered speech. *Aging, Neuropsychology, and Cognition, 4,* 126–139.

Small, J. A., Kemper, S., & Lyons, K. (1997). Sentence comprehension in Alzheimer's disease: Effects of speech rate, syntactic complexity, and repetition. *Psychology and Aging, 12*(1), 3–11.

Smith, G. E., Petersen, R. C., Ivnik, R. J., Malec, J. F., & Tangelos, E. G. (1996). Subjective memory complaints, psychological distress, and longitudinal change in objective memory performance. *Psychology and Aging, 11*, 272–279.

Snowdon, D. A. (1997). Aging and Alzheimer's disease: Lessons from the Nun Study. *Gerontologist, 37*, 150–156.

Snowdon, D. A., Greiner, L. A., Kemper, S., Nanayakkara, N., & Mortimer, J. A. (1999). Linguistic ability in early life and longevity: Findings from the Nun Study. In J. M. Robine, B. Forette, C. Franchesci, & M. Allard (Eds.), *The paradoxes of longevity* (pp. 103–113). Amsterdam: Springer.

Snowdon, D. A., Kemper, S. J., Mortimer, J. A., Greiner, L. H., Wekstein, D. R., & Markesbery, W. R. (1996). Cognitive ability in early life and cognitive function and Alzheimer's disease in late life: Findings from the Nun study. *Journal of the American Medical Association, 275*, 528–532.

Soederberg Miller, L. M., & Stine-Morrow, E. A. L. (1998). Aging and the effects of knowledge on on-line reading strategies. *Journal of Gerontology: Psychological Sciences, 53B*, 223–33.

Sommers, M. S., & Danielson, S. M. (1999). Inhibitory processes and spoken word recognition in young and older adults: The interaction of lexical competition and semantic context. *Psychology and Aging, 14*, 458–472.

Spencer, W. D., & Raz, N. (1995). Differential effects of aging on memory for content and context: A meta-analysis. *Psychology and Aging, 10*, 527–539.

Stine, E. A. L. (1990). On-line processing of written text by younger and older adults. *Psychology and Aging, 5*, 68–78.

Stine, E. A. L., Cheung, H., & Henderson, D. (1995). Adult age differences in the on-line processing of new concepts in discourse. *Aging and Cogntion, 2*, 1–18.

Stine, E. A. L., & Wingfield, A. (1990). How much do working memory deficits contribute to age differences in discourse memory? *European Journal of Cognitive Psychology, 2*, 289–304.

Stine-Morrow, E. A. L., Loveless, M. K., & Soederberg, L. M. (1996). Resource allocation in on-line reading by younger and older adults. *Psychology and Aging, 11*, 475–486.

Tomoeda, C. K., Bayles, K. A., Boone, D. R., & Kaszniak, A. W. (1990). Speech rate and syntactic complexity effects on the auditory comprehension of Alzheimer patients. *Journal of Communication Disorders, 23*, 151–161.

Tun, P. A., Wingfield, A., & Stine, E. (1991). Speech-processing capacity in young and older adults: A dual task study. *Psychology and Aging, 6*, 3–9.

Van der Linden, M., Hupet, M., Feyereisen, P., Schelstraete, M. -A., Bestgen, Y., Bruyer, R., Lories, G., El Ahmadi, A., & Seron, X. (1999). Cognitive mediators of age-related differences in language comprehension and verbal memory performance. *Aging, Neuropsychology, and Cognition, 6*, 32–55.

Warren, A., & McCloskey, L. A. (1997). Language in social contexts. In J. Berko Gleason (Ed.), *The development of language* (4th ed., pp. 210–258). Boston: Allyn and Bacon.

Waters, G. S., Caplan, D., & Rochon, E. (1995). Processing capacity and sentence comprehension in patients with Alzheimer's disease. *Cognitive Neuropsychology, 12*, 1–30.

Waters, G. S., Rochon, E., & Caplan, D. (1998). Task demands and sentence comprehension in patients with dementia of the Alzheimer's type. *Brain and Language, 62*, 361–397.

Wingfield, A., & Stine-Morrow, E. A. L. (2000). Language and Speech. In F. I. M. Craik & T. A. Salthouse (Eds.), *Handbook of aging and cognition* (2nd ed., pp. 359–416). Mahwah, NJ: Erlbaum Associates.

Yoon, C., May, C. P., & Hasher, L. (1998). *Aging, circadian arousal patterns, and cognition*. Philadelphia, PA: Psychology Press.

Zacks, R., & Hasher, L. (1997). Cognitive gerontology and attentional inhibition: A reply to Burke and McDowd. *Journal of Gerontology: Psychological Sciences, 52B*, P274–P283.

Sixteen

Emotions over the Life Span

Carol Magai

Emotions intersect and interpenetrate every aspect of human life from the moment of birth till the end of life. Not only are they integral to our sense of well-being or lack of well-being, but emotions are also the motivational sine qua non of behavior. They are what make individuals care about outcomes, and care in particular ways, with fear, revulsion, joy, shame, excitement, guilt, indignation, and so forth. Emotions are at the very heart of social relations, with the expressive qualities of emotions constituting one of the major communicative links that allows us to function as social creatures within the context of family, kinship systems, and culture.

Until recently, research and theory with respect to emotional development was limited to infancy and the childhood years (Magai, in press). However, with the burst of research activity in adult development and aging that occurred during the second half of the 20th century, there have evolved theoretical models of emotional development that embrace a life span view. In this chapter, I begin by reviewing the major theories of emotional development that take a life-course perspective, considering their assertions regarding the topics of change and continuity in emotions within the domains of subjective experience, regulatory behavior, expressive behavior, social process, and personality. The evidence in support of these theories is then presented, and the theories are critiqued.

I. Theoretical Contributions

A. Differential Emotions Theory

Although a number of theories regarding human emotions evolved during the 1960s and 1970s, Carroll Izard's differential emotions theory (1971, 1977, 1991) was unique in drawing attention to developmental processes. The term, *differential emotions*, derives its name from the theory's emphasis on the qualitatively different nature of the primary or basic emotions. Primary emotions, like anger, joy, or sadness, are said to have different neurophysiological, phenomenological, physiognomic, and motivational properties. They are prewired and functional within the opening months of life, and the emotion system is viewed as the primary organizer of human thought and

Handbook of the Psychology of Aging
Copyright © 2001 by Academic Press.
All rights of reproduction in any form reserved.

behavior. Although the greater mass of research and theory emanating from Izard's laboratory has dealt with infancy and early childhood, differential emotions theory has always had an inherent application to life span development as well, and more recent formulations have explicitly addressed the issue (Dougherty, Abe, & Izard, 1996; Izard & Ackerman, 1998).

The theory assumes that there are certain aspects of the emotion system that contribute to constancy as well as change across development. In terms of stable aspects, one of the tenets of differential emotions theory is that the feeling states that accompany the various discrete emotions are not altered with time or development (Izard & Malatesta, 1987). This means that the qualitative experiential core of elation, fear, anger, or shame, for example, do not change with age, although the feelings may become more cognitively complex and elaborated. This constancy in emotional experience is attributed, in part, to the fact that each discrete emotion produces a distinct feeling that drives thought and action in a particular direction and toward a particular goal. The pairings of emotion with motivation and emotion with mental state are thought to be hardwired in the nervous system and to remain stable from infancy to old age. Thus, whether one is a toddler, teenager, or middle-aged adult, shame will always be experienced as heightened awareness of the self and the desire to retreat from the view of others, anger will always be experienced as a forceful tendency to approach and challenge obstacles, and so forth.

The stability of this fundamental aspect of the emotion system across the life span serves several adaptive functions (Dougherty et al., 1996; Izard & Ackerman, 1998). With an underlying constancy of experience, individuals can move through broad developmental changes in cognition and behavior with a stable sense of self and without experiencing confusion or identity diffusion. In addition, because interpersonal functioning is dependent on the cross-temporal correspondence between emotion states and their associated motivational propensities and interpersonal sensitivities, damage to the neural substrate of the emotion system results in impaired social skills and social functioning (Dougherty et al., 1996). Finally, the stability of the subjective experience of an emotion ensures that individuals will be motivated to engage in appropriate adaptive behaviors. Otherwise, developmental changes in what it feels like to be afraid or to be angry, for example, might result in failing to perform behaviors that are required in situations of danger or blocked goals.

Despite the elements of stability thus far described, differential emotions theory also proposes that certain elements of emotional behavior and experience are modifiable over the course of development. According to the theory, the capacity for significant developmental change is not located within the emotion system itself, but rather in the connections that exist among the emotion, cognition, and action systems. One example of an emotion–cognition connection that changes over time is the acquisition of the ability to anticipate the emotional responses of other people. Although the connection is initially dependent on the growth of cognitive capabilities in the young child, a lifetime of accumulated interpersonal experience fosters an increasingly sophisticated and multifaceted ability to anticipate emotions in others. Another example of an emotion–cognition connection that undergoes change over time is improved facility at modulating expressive behavior to meet the more subtle understanding of interpersonal processes. In turn, these developmental changes create feedback and feedforward loops that influence an individual's social interactions, ideally facilitating the development and maintenance of social support systems. Other elements of change include the association of discrete emotions with images and thoughts that greatly increase the associative neural network and the capacity for creative and artistic work. A further aspect of the emotion system that changes with maturation is expressive behavior. Although the emotion expressions of young infants are nstinct-like in nature, and there is little ability to postpone or alter the quality or amplitude of the response, older children show increasing modulatory control in growing response to social expectations and conventions. These changes in the formal aspects of emotion expression are thought to occur throughout the life span.

In summary, differential emotions theory proposes that certain aspects of emotional life are stable, and others, such as the connections between the emotion's and other subsystems of personality, and aspects of physiognomy, are inherently capable of change and increasing complexity. Compared to the other theories discussed below, differential emotions theory provides the most well-developed theory of emotions, and is particularly systematic in considering how the different components of emotions develop. In terms of stability, it suggests that the fundamental feeling states, patterns of expression, and neurophysiological patterns associated with discrete emotions are stable over the life course, but that increasing sophistication within the cognitive and behavioral subsystems of personality permits greater modulation in expressive behavior, greater complexity of emotional experience, and a keener understanding of interpersonal processes. Because of its roots in the functional consideration of emotions, differential emotions theory is less a theory of personality or social interaction than some other life span theories, although its conceptualization of emotions as representing the fundamental motivating and organizing forces in human existence holds an inherent application to many other research domains.

B. Cognitive–Affective Developmental Theory

Gisela Labouvie-Vief offers a life span theory of emotion that situates emotional development within the context of developing cognitive and ego processes (Labouvie-Vief, 1996; Labouvie-Vief, DeVoe, & Bulka, 1989; Labouvie-Vief, Hakim-Larson, DeVoe, & Schoeberlein, 1989). The theory suggests that emotional experiences are qualitatively restructured as the maturing individual (a) acquires more complex forms of cognition with which to reflect upon the world and (b) develops a more differentiated and integrated self. Based on neo-Piagetian and postformal cognitive models, her theory asserts that the increasing cognitive sophistication that comes with maturation provides an ever more complex scaffolding on which differentiated experiences of emotion and emotion regulation can occur.

Although Labouvie-Vief does not delineate fixed stages of emotional development, her theory does propose a trajectory of adult emotional development linked to levels of cognitive and personality development. In infancy and early childhood, emotion regulation is seen as operating at a presystemic level, being governed through the actions of external social agents. During adolescence and early adulthood, with the advent of formal operations, an "intrasystemic" period emerges, allowing the individual to regulate emotions according to abstract ideals and societal standards. At this point, emotional process is characterized by internal regulation that remains highly dependent on the conventions and rules of the culture, which define standards of competent emotional behavior. As such, the cognitive–affective system remains grounded in conventional language, symbols, and norms that emphasize conformity rather than change and transformation. The theory assumes that in order to achieve true emotional maturity, the individual must advance to the point where he or she reintegrates internal subjectivity and self-reference into the cognitive–emotional system.

From early adulthood through middle age there is an emerging intersystemic level integration. That is, there is a gradual shift away from the conventional orientation towards one that becomes increasingly contextualistic. Rules and norms for behavior are no longer viewed as absolute, but rather as relativistic and context-moderated. Cognitions and behavior become more individualized and customized to particular conditions and circumstances, and subjectivity, autonomy, and self-exploration increase. These advances in cognitive and ego complexity produce an important reorganization of self that has a direct impact on emotional development. Labouvie-Vief refers to the process that leads to this "vertical integration" as a de-repression of emotions that comes to be more prominent during the middle years. Greater conceptual and emotional complexity during the middle years permits increased flexibility of self-regulation and more modulated emotion expression. However, at the emotional level, the greater awareness of differentiated inner states, in which opposing feelings may conflict with one another, makes for a certain degree of tension. Some individuals may not be capable of sustaining or resolving the tension, which may prompt a retreat into more defensive modes of operating. Alternatively, an individual may intensify his or her efforts at reconciliation and integration, and advance in ego level as well as further emotional maturity. Additional

growth may accrue in later life, as well, though there may be limits imposed by cognitive and physical decline.

In a manner similar to differential emotions theory, Labouvie-Vief describes affective organization and change in terms of *cognitive–affective complexity*, differentiating between two aspects of affect regulation related to the self that also have different aims. One seeks to maximize positive affect and minimize or dampen negative affect; the goal is to maintain a positively valenced view of the self and entails regulating the self's behavior and values so as to align with social norms and to avoid conflict. The other aspect of emotional development, affective complexity, involves intrapsychic differentiation, greater blending of positive and negative affect, greater cognitive complexity, tolerance of ambiguity, and flexible affect regulation. Its aim is to maintain an open and undistorted view of reality. The theory thus entertains the thesis that there may be both general, developmental trends reflecting improvement with age (although experience, ego level, and other cognitive phenomena, rather than age per se are implicated), as well as individual differences in the extent to which an individual has a preference for positivity or complexity.

In summary, Labouvie-Vief's theory maintains that the course of emotional development over the adult years involves qualitative changes in the subjective aspects of emotional life that involve increasing cognitive–affective complexity. Her theory emphasizes the consideration of emotional regulation and experience as stemming from more general developmental changes in cognitive capacities and the self. In terms of emotion, her theory suggests that with development, culturally defined proscriptions for affective behavior lessen and a more self-authored system of management emerges. In later life these trends may be partially reversed, though perhaps not for all individuals.

C. Control Theory of Emotion

In recent work, Richard Schulz has expanded a life span theory of control, which previously excluded emotion, to treat the functional significance of emotion in the development of the individual over the life span (Schulz & Heckhausen, 1996, 1998). According to the theory, *control* is a central theme for characterizing human development and relates to the human desire to influence the environment and to experience events as contingent upon the self's behavior. Two types of control are differentiated. Primary control involves attempts to achieve effects in the immediate environment through direct influence on the external world, whereas secondary control targets the self and attempts to achieve changes from within the individual. Emotions enter the picture insofar as they provide the feedback that enables individuals to regulate their control strivings, signaling the status of primary control efforts, and, in conjunction with secondary control processes, help moderate primary control. Emotions are construed as a kind of energy or fuel that enhances control efforts thus maximizing the chances for success and survival. This regulatory aspect of emotion is the primary focus of the aspect of the theory relevant to emotion, although other functions of emotion are acknowledged. Mastery of behavior–event contingencies is associated with positive affect, and the resultant contingency experiences serve to reinforce the maintenance of, and continuing pursuit of, primary control strivings. Losses and failures result in negative affect, which serves to increase or redirect control efforts.

In combination, the two kinds of control processes help to optimize development over the life course, but they have differential trajectories. According to the model's formulations, primary control follows an inverted U-shaped function over the life span, accelerating during infancy and throughout adolescence, peaking around age 45–50, and then declining in later life. Secondary control efforts that target the self and the self's internal processes have a later onset and steadily increase over the life span, even into old age. The theory thus implies that there is a significant shift from an external focus to an internal focus during later middle age, and a corresponding increase in the attention paid to emotional processes. According to Schulz, this shift allows for greater regulatory control over affect as individuals move toward old age. Although his theory offers little in the way of explanation for *why* this change occurs, he does suggest that primary control effort failures engendered by the behavioral and cognitive declines associated with aging provoke negative affect, a consequence that can be assuaged by a shift to internal control processes.

In summary, control theory stresses the instrumental nature of emotions, their feedback functions, and the place of emotion regulation. A developmental trajectory is outlined in which outer-directed control shifts to inner-directed control during midlife, with increasingly effective self-regulatory management of emotion. The theory stresses the broad role of positive and negative affect with only limited attention to the role of particular emotions, and has little to say about how the different components of emotions develop.

D. Optimization and Selectivity Theories of Emotion

Like Schulz, Powell Lawton and Laura Carstensen have also focused on changes in affect regulation over the life course, but for them, emotions are central psychological processes rather than the means towards another end. Both authors propose that adults become more sophisticated at emotion regulation over the adult years.

Lawton (e.g., Lawton, 1989; Lawton, Kleban, Rajagopal, & Dean, 1992; Lawton, Van Haitsma, & Klapper, 1996) suggests that gains in the management of affect over time results from both personality factors as well as adaptations to changes in social contexts and life events. Although he suggests that there are three dimensions of affective experience that undergo change in later life (responsiveness or reactivity to emotional stimuli, affect dynamics—frequency, rise time, duration, intensity—and self-regulatory processes), his emphasis is on self-regulation. He suggests that older adults deliberately attempt to control the mix of emotionally stimulating versus insulating features towards the general goal of *affective optimization*. That is, older adults are increasingly proactive in seeking the kinds of social environments that allow them to avoid negative affect and conflict and which permit sufficient intellectual and emotional stimulation.

In a similar vein, Carstensen's (1992, 1995) socioemotional selectivity theory indicates that older individuals exercise deliberate choice with respect to interpersonal relationships, which is linked to emotion regulation goals and the conservation of energy. According to Carstensen, there are three primary social motives: emotion regulation, development and maintenance of self-concept, and information seeking. The priority of these motives changes in middle and later life, as information seeking becomes less important and emotional goals become more central. The latter goals include achieving emotional satisfaction in the context of fulfilling interpersonal relationships, maintaining a positively valenced emotional life, and optimal emotion regulation. Although a part of this shift has to do with the maturing

individual's acquisition of experience and knowledge, such that fewer people can provide information that is novel, the change is also caused by the construal of time remaining as more limited. Although this motive force can be activated in adults of any age, it is particularly notable in older adults and leads to emotional goals becoming more important than information goals. This theory then is an attempt to explain the commonly observed narrowing of social networks in later life, and offers an alternative to disengagement theory (Cummings & Henry, 1961). Indeed, older adults are said not to withdraw and reduce their emotional involvement with the world, but rather to selectively narrow their relationships to accentuate those that are emotionally gratifying; close friends and relatives become more important, relationships that are new or only of superficial depth are shed (Carstensen, 1992; Carstensen, Graff, Levenson, & Gottman, 1996; Carstensen, Gottman, & Levenson, 1995).

These age-related changes in the interpersonal realm form the basis of changes that occur in emotion experience and emotion regulation over the course of the adult life span. According to selectivity theory, controlling the frequency and quality of social engagement is an adaptive strategy people use to regulate emotion. The strategy is particularly important for the maintenance of well-being in later life because age is associated with increased energy depletion, heightened physiological arousability, and increased physical debilitation. Social contacts become limited to relationships that offer the maximization of positive outcomes (social support, companionship, and assistance) and the minimization of depleting negative affect, such as interpersonal conflict. The observed changes in social relationships in old age, when viewed within this context, can be seen as highly adaptive and as contributing to successful aging, rather than withdrawal and decline.

The move away from the pursuit of novelty and new information toward the satisfaction of emotional goals does not occur suddenly in old age, but is a gradual process. Although the goal of pursuing knowledge about the self and the social world—highly salient during adolescence and young adulthood—may still be paramount and even occur at the expense of emotional satisfaction in midlife, given the continued demands of establishing a career and family, this gradually subsides to give way to a more paramount goal in later life—the goal of maintaining positive affect (Carstensen, 1992). From middle adulthood until later adulthood, frequency of contact with acquaintances is expected to decrease, contact with intimate social partners to increase, and emotion regulation to improve.

In summary, the theoretical formulations of Lawton and Carstensen have primarily focused on emotion regulatory characteristics, processes, and functions over the adult years. Both view aging as involving a general change in goal priorities and the concurrent acquisition of more accomplished and efficient regulatory skills. Together, these changes both motivate and assist aging individuals to reduce peripheral social interactions and the experience of negative affect. Carstensen's theory in particular offers clear predictions regarding emotional experience and social behaviors in older adults.

E. Attachment Theory as a Life Span Theory of Emotion

John Bowlby (1979) described attachments as integral to human well-being "from the cradle to the grave" (p. 129). Unlike the discrete emotions theories that argue that emotions are the primary organizing force in development over the life span, attachment theory views attachment-related strivings as the central force in human development. Neverthe-less, feelings and emotions are viewed as the basic substrate out of which attachments develop, and the differential emotional substrates that accrue during development are at the heart of differential attachment styles and patterns of relating. Although the bulk of early formulations and research with respect to attachment focused on infancy and childhood, the literature has grown steadily to encompass the study of attachments in adulthood—stimulated largely by the work of Mary Main and colleagues in developmental psychology (e.g., Main, Kaplan & Cassidy, 1985), and Cindy Hazan and Phil Shaver within the social personality field (e.g., Hazan & Shaver, 1987).

According to Bowlby, attachment styles forged in infancy are carried forward, from infancy to childhood and beyond, through the development of "internal working models" of the primary attachment relationship, which then generalize to other social partners. In general, researchers distinguish among three distinct attachment patterns—secure, avoidant, and ambivalent. The three attachment styles are associated with different styles of proximity seeking, attentional strategies, affective communication, and strategies for emotion regulation, as well as with different behavioral, representational, and emotional profiles. Secure attachment is associated with an ease of approach to social partners when distressed, and with a balanced affective repertoire and ability to contend with negative events without ignoring them or becoming dysregulated. The avoidant or dismissive style is associated with interpersonal avoidance under conditions of distress, with dampened expressivity, a tendency to shunt negative affect from consciousness, and a tendency to engage in avoidance coping. The ambivalent or preoccupied pattern is associated with interpersonal approach–avoidance conflict, heightened affect expression, hypervigilance for distress, and emotionally demanding behavior (Magai, 1999; Magai & McFadden, 1995).

Attachment theory suggests that attachment styles, whether they be secure, avoidant, or ambivalent, should remain relatively stable once formed, although changes in these patterns are possible through adjustments in internal working models based on subsequent life experiences. Attachment styles in adulthood, just as in childhood, should be integrally associated with different patterns of affective expression and emotion regulation. Moreover, because attachment relationships are imbued with emotion, another prediction from the theory might be that changes in attachment patterns would be preceded by significant emotional perturbations within interpersonal relationships, either of a positive or negative nature. Finally, because attachment patterns are known to respond to adverse family conditions in the form of increased insecurity (Cassidy & Shaver, 1999), cohort differences in the distribution of attachment styles might be anticipated in cohorts born earlier in the century.

In summary, although attachment theory has been more thoroughly investigated in light of its applications as a personality theory, the theory has always retained an inherent application to emotional development. Different attachment styles are known to be associated with different emotional profiles, emotion communication styles, and patterns of affect regulation in childhood, as well as over the adult life span. Although individual attachment styles and their emotional correlates have typically been conceptualized as being relatively stable once established, changes are provided for within the attachment framework. Indeed, although relatively little is known of changes in adult attachment styles, the study of such changes might provide another means of organizing, predicting, and explaining changes in emotional experience across the life span. The attachment framework also leads to the expectation that changes in interpersonal relationships may precipitate some of the more disturbing emotional experiences of life and act as a catalyst for changes in the structure of emotional organizations.

F. Discrete Emotions Functionalist Theory

In this theory, Carol Malatesta-Magai has attempted to integrate personality theory with discrete emotions theory. In the early 1980s, the author first proposed a life span perspective on emotional development as a challenge to the prevailing models limited to children (Malatesta, 1981, 1982). This was later followed by two papers that began to outline some of the theory's basic tenets (Malatesta & Wilson, 1988; Izard & Malatesta, 1987). As a theory within the discrete emotion tradition, it traces its roots to the work of Darwin (1872), Tomkins (1962), and Izard (1971), although a number of aspects are unique, for example, its integral lifespan orientation. It also offers more focused treatments of certain areas of emotional development, such as a greater emphasis on the role of emotional traits or biases in personality development, attention to expressive changes in adult development, and the addition of dynamic systems principles to describe patterns of emotion and personality change over the life course (e.g., Malatesta, 1982, 1990; Malatesta & Izard, 1984; Magai & Nusbaum, 1996, Magai & Haviland, in press). Its description as a functionalist theory calls attention to the functional properties of the different emotions and the adaptational goals that they serve in personality.

Personality patterns are seen as being closely linked to patterns of experienced emotion. In early development, certain emotional states, experienced repeatedly, become highly centered in experience; by the same token, some feeling states may be selectively disowned, disavowed, or dissociated from the self, and thus by their very absence in the affective repertoire, also reflect a characteristic aspect of the self. Over time, these emotional organizations become ever more consolidated and take on a trait-like quality. These traits then contribute to emotionally biased ways of processing the world that affect attention, perception, judgment, memory, and other cognitive processes. It is assumed that particular birth cohorts may show distinctive emotional profiles, given that different cohorts encounter systematically different historical, economic, and sociocultural experiences that may impinge on families and hence on individual development and for which different emotional responses are required for adaptation (Magai & McFadden, 1995). Likewise, different cultures may emphasize emotion regulatory processes such as denial or confrontation, or differential expression of or control of certain emotions, and thus shape a culture's profile with respect to emotions (Dilworth-Anderson, 1998). The operative process in each of these formative familial, cohort-specific, and cultural-specific circumstances is the repetitive exposure to events and conditions that draw upon the distinctive adaptational properties of particular emotions.

Earlier accounts of the theory were primarily focused on describing the role that structuralized emotion played in personality functioning, whereas more recent formulations have attempted to address the role of emotions in precipitating change in personality structure. In fact, Magai (in press) has suggested that one of the more challenging questions today is that of determining the processes underlying personality change. It is her thesis that emotional events and experiences are not only formative features of personality and lend them a triat-like aspect, but that emotions also are largely responsible for changes in the personality structure.

Just as interpersonal process is assumed to play a key role in the development of emotional biases in children, interpersonal process is assumed to constitute a crucial factor in the destabilization of emotion traits in adult development. This aspect of Magai's theory uses dynamic systems modeling to account for changes in personality structure with respect to emotional organizations. According to the dynamic systems approach to development, complex adaptive systems, including human biological and psychological systems, are composed of component parts capable of interacting in a nearly infinite number of ways. However, due to inherent self-organizing tendencies, the interacting parts of systems tend to coalesce around certain recurrent patterns referred to as "attractors."

With respect to personality, interacting elements, such as emotions and cognitions, tend to gravitate toward certain preferred emotion states or moods. Although the feedback and feedforward processes in development tend to produce progressively more stable personality configurations across the life span, dynamic systems are inherently flexible. Small perturbations in any of the personality subsystems can create systemwide destabilization, ultimately producing what is termed a *phase shift* or comprehensive reorganization of its structure. Similarly, the attractors that comprise the mood states or emotion biases of personality can be destabilized by precipitous events. As such, it is hypothesized that changes in emotion organization and personality may be more common than most personality theorists have assumed. Given that there are often significant changes in work and family roles and alterations in interpersonal relationships during middle adulthood, this may be a period of particular opportunity for structural changes in the personality. The latter part of life, however, may be different. Over the life span, individuals acquire increasingly sophisticated emotion regulatory capacities. As such, in spite of the fact that there is a great density of life changes involving social networks (loss of parents, spouse, friends) the greater regulatory capacities that seem to characterize old age may act as a stabilizing factor, mitigating further structural change in the personality.

In terms of expressive behavior, Magai's theory assumes that emotional expressions undergo transformation with neurological, intellectual, and social maturation, as individuals acquire and internalize the display rules of both the family and the larger culture and learn to modulate expressive behavior in accordance with these conventions. Aspects of expressive behavior that are hypothesized to undergo change include the frequency, range, discreteness, and complexity of expressive behavior (Izard & Malatesta, 1987; Malatesta & Izard, 1984).

Having elements in common with differential emotions theory, but drawing in principles from dynamic systems theory, the discrete emotions functionalist perspective suggests a combination of consistency and change in emotional development across the life span. Like Izard, Magai's view of emotions offers a differentiated view of emotional development, describing and predicting changes in a number of the component aspects of the emotion system. Additionally, this approach to emotional development makes emotions central to personality development. Individuals are said to develop emotional dispositions or biases that affect a wide array of social, intellectual, and behavioral processes. Nevertheless, according to Magai's view, there is an inherent dynamism in personality structure and functioning. Personalities are ultimately affective structures, and the emotional responses associated with critical interpersonal life events can precipitate personality change.

G. Concluding Remarks on Life Span Theories of Emotions

Although the increasing elaboration of life span theories of emotion represents an important and much needed development in the aging literature, the theories reviewed above are, for the most part, still young. Primarily, this relative immaturity is made manifest in the comparatively specific aspects of development each addresses and in a lack of theoretical elaboration. The theories of Schulz, Lawton, and Carstensen, for example, are predominantly focused on the regulatory aspects of emotions, and only attend to other aspects of emotional development when they are relevant to this overarching concern. These theories have tended to emphasize a consistent normative change in regulatory styles across the life span, with comparatively little attention paid to the more stable aspects of emotional development. In contrast, the theories of Labouvie-Vief, and Magai, as well as attachment theory, evidence a greater emphasis on the life span development of emotions as relevant to personality and the self, although each also attends to how emotional experience relates to patterns of stability and change in these domains. Finally, of the theories reviewed here, Izard's is the most well developed and systematic in considering how the different components of emotions both develop and remain the same across the life span. These strengths no doubt derive from the theory's roots as a full theory of emotion, as well as reflecting the three decades worth of thought and research that have gone into the development of differential emotions theory.

As will become clear, the comparative specificity of each theory's conceptual domain makes the theories difficult to tease apart empirically. In some senses, the particular emphases of the different theories mean that they become "related" theories about very different phenomena, with a consequence that the predictions made within each are in some ways less relevant to the other theories. Moreover, the specificity of the theories means that data typically have the appearance of having been gathered under a particular umbrella and thus cannot realistically be thought of as providing a test between theories. These distinctions noted, data can nonetheless be treated as more or less consistent with the tenets of each theoretical body, the focus of the following section.

II. Empirical Work on Emotional Development over the Life Course

As indicated in the foregoing review, theory with respect to emotional development over the life span has grown substantially since the 1980s. These developments have had a salutary effect, stimulating a groundswell of new research on emotional processes. In this section I examine the supporting evidence for the theoretical models reviewed above. The treatment is organized in much the same way as the theories themselves, considering issues of stability and/ or change in the subjective, regulatory, expressive, and social aspects of the emotion system, and in the structure of personality. As will become clear, the data generally suggest that as adults age, emotional functioning improves, certainly through middle age and perhaps well beyond, although some authors urge caution with respect to this interpretation (Labouvie-Vief, 1996; Magai & Passman, 1997).

A. Stability and Change in the Subjective Experience of Emotion

Studies conducted 20 to 40 years ago using largely institutionalized samples of older adults suggested that aging is accompanied by a blunting of emotion and an increase in negative affect (Malatesta, 1981). Results of more recent studies based on community-dwelling adults have begun to challenge those assumptions. The review below groups studies in terms of stability and change in the intensity and quality of subjective emotional experience, including changes in hedonic tone, discrete emotions, and emotional complexity.

1. Affective Intensity

Cross-sectional studies reveal inconsistent findings with respect to age-related difference in the intensity of emotion over the adult years. Studies that have gathered information on adults' reflections on how they experience their emotions in general have found that older adults had lower scores on affective intensity for negative affect (Barrick, Hutchinson, & Deckers, 1989) or both positive and negative affect (Diener, Sandvik, & Larsen, 1985; Lawton et al., 1992). However, in another type of study, where younger and older adults were asked to report on whether they thought their emotions had become less intense with age, older adults maintained that the intensity of their experiences had not diminished over the years (Malatesta & Kalnok, 1984). More recently, Gross, Carstensen, Tsai, Skorpen, and Hsu (1997) asked respondents about the intensity of their "impulse strength," that is, the strength of those emotional impulses that are difficult to control. Older European Americans and African Americans, but not Chinese Americans, reported lower impulse strength than their younger counterparts.

Studies that have avoided the use of retrospective accounts of experience do not support the existence of age changes in emotional intensity. In an experience sampling study of a wide age range of adults, Carstensen and colleagues gathered data on emotional experiences as they occurred in everyday life, repeatedly sampling the same subjects many times a day over the period of 1 week (Carstensen, Pasupthi, & Mayr, in press). No age differences in subjective intensity of positive or negative emotion were found. Laboratory studies in which adults of different ages are asked to re-experience and recount emotionally salient events drawn from their own lives have shown no age differences (Levenson, Carstensen, Friesen, & Ekman, 1991; Malatesta, Izard, Culver, & Nicolich, 1987).

2. Qualitative Aspects of Subjective Emotional Experience

A number of studies have investigated changes in either hedonic tone or in the balance of positive and negative affect. Others have looked at the level of specific moods or emotion, and still others have investigated developmental changes in the complexity of affective experience.

a. Changes in Hedonic Tone Several studies indicate that the frequency or level of positive affect either remains the same or increases over the adult years until very late life, when there is a decline. A cross-national study of nearly 170,000 people across 16 countries found that reported level of happiness was comparable from ages 15 to 65+ (Inglehart, 1990). There are three large-scale studies that examined both positive and negative affect in a broad age spectrum of adults. The National Health and Nutrition Examination Survey (NHANES) surveyed 4942 men and women ranging in age from 24 to 74 years twice over a 9 year period. There were no differences across age in general well-being, although both positive and negative affect were lower in the older groups. Because the cross-sectional differences in positive and negative affect were not replicated by longitudinal change, these authors speculate that co-

hort effects may have accounted for previous findings of difference, with individuals born earlier in the century being less willing to express their feelings. Because the NHANES study was a national survey, with a carefully drawn sample representing nearly 5000 Caucasian and African American men and women and used a well-validated measure of well-being, it makes a strong case for the lack of maturational changes in psychological well-being, as defined by positive and negative affect, in adulthood at least up through the early 70s.

Mroczek and Kolarz (1998) also assessed patterns of positive and negative affect in a large sample of adults ranging in age from the mid-20s to mid-70s. Although significant age effects were found for both positive and negative affect, the age effects were small, accounting for less than 1% of the variance, and these differences are possibly due to cohort effects as in the NHANES survey. Negative affect was highest among the two youngest groups and lowest in the oldest age group, and vice versa for positive affect, again suggesting that cohort differences in the predisposition to report affective experiences may be at play. Finally, the Berlin Aging Study (Baltes & Mayer, 1999), which sampled individuals well up into their 90s, found that there was a modest decline in positive affect in very late life (>85 years), although there was no corresponding increase in negative affect.

In summary, there do not appear to be major age-related changes in either positive or negative affect, except perhaps in the very oldest groups. Although positive affect ratings tend to increase, and negative affect to decease as individuals age, the effects of age are typically small. These findings are perhaps most consistent with the predictions of optimization and selectivity theories, although they might also be seen as consistent with control theory. Neither differential emotions theory nor discrete emotions functionalist theory has made predictions regarding global affective states, consistent with their emphases on discrete emotions.

b. Changes in Specific Emotions Lawton, Kleban, and Dean (1993) had young, middle-aged, and older adults indicate how often they experienced various affects over the past year. There was no overall age difference in positive affect, but older adults were less depressed, anxious, hostile, and shy than one or both younger groups, and more content. In a similar vein, Gibson (1997) administered the state version of the POMS mood scale to 247 community-dwelling Australian adults ranging in age from 60–98. In addition to replicating the factor structure of the instrument as originally normed in college samples, he, like Lawton et al. (1993), found that the older subjects exhibited lower mean scores on most dimensions of mood including depression, anxiety, anger, fatigue, and vigor. What is of particular interest about this study is that it included a control measure of social desirability. This finding is important for there is some suggestion in the literature that older individuals may exhibit a greater tendency to portray themselves in a good light (Raskin, 1979). In Gibson's study, age was significantly and positively correlated with increasing scores on the Lie Scale of the Eysenck Personality Questionnaire, a measure of the tendency to portray the self in a good light by endorsing only socially desirable items. Significant inverse relations were found between the desire to portray the self in a good light and self-reported levels of anxiety, depression, and anger. Higher Lie Scale scores were associated with greater positive mood, such as feelings of vigor and friendliness. Most importantly, when the Lie Scale scores were used as covariates in partial correlations, age was no longer associated with mood, the one exception being self-reported levels of anger, which showed a significant decrease with advancing age.

Gross and colleagues (1997) asked respondents about the frequency of happiness, anger, sadness, fear, and disgust in two studies—one involving community-dwelling Norwegian respondents 20 to 70+ years of age—and the other a sample of nuns from a large, midwestern community of religious sisters, ranging in age from 24 to 101 years. In the Norwegian sample, aging was associated with a decreased frequency of the experience of anger in older women versus younger women, but no such difference was found across men. In the sample of nuns, aging was associated with decreased emotional experiences of anger, sadness, and fear, but not disgust, and with increased experiences of happiness.

Overall, the literature on the intensity and quality of affect suggests that when emotions are activated, affective intensity may remain the same across the adult years. However, there may be an age-related decrease in the frequency of some discrete emotions, most notably anger, but possibly also in anxiety and sadness. These findings are consistent with the hedonic and social tenets of both selectivity and optimization theory, although they are also in line with the functionalist view of emotion as portrayed by Izard's and Magai's theories. As noted above, control theory has little to say about changes in specific affects, and, if anything, attachment theory would be more likely to predict stability than change in this domain.

c. Changes in Affective Complexity Some of the most recent empirical studies indicate that affective experience becomes more complex with age. Carstensen and colleagues' (2000) experience-sampling study of emotion found that greater age was accompanied by the report of more complex emotional experiences. That is, older respondents related more mixed and bittersweet emotions and more poignant experiences within the same sampled moment. Emotions apparently become more complex and experienced more keenly, even as affect regulation is in general improved. As noted earlier, selectivity theory suggests that as people age mortality becomes more salient, and there emerges a sharper appreciation of the mixedness and value of life. Thus the emotional complexity that comes with aging, although bittersweet, is seen as an ultimately rewarding and deepening experience.

Labouvie-Vief and colleagues have been engaged in research on affective complexity, defined as the interaction between emotion and cognition and their integration, on an ongoing basis for a number of years. In an early study, researchers from this laboratory content analyzed emotion narratives collected from younger and middle-aged adults and found a developmental trend with respect to changes in subjective experience (Labouvie-Vief et al., 1989). Younger individuals rarely referred to inner subjective feelings and were likely to describe their experiences in terms of normative proscriptions. They also indicated that they controlled their emotions through such metacognitive strategies as forgetting, ignoring, or distracting the self. The middle-aged adults, in contrast, were able to acknowledge complex feelings, were less influenced by conventional norms and standards, and could sustain feelings of ambivalence and tension without resolving them prematurely. Later research with adults ranging across the adult life span found that affective–conceptual complexity peaks in midlife, with young and old individuals scoring lower than middle-aged adults (Labouvie-Vief, Chiodo, Goguen, Diehl, & Orwoll, 1995; Labouvie-Vief, Diehl, Chiodo, & Coyle, 1995).

From the above studies it would appear that emotional complexity—the interaction between emotion and cognition and their integration—is enhanced with age, though it seems to peak during the middle years. Such findings provide partial support for the theories of Labouvie-Vief and Izard. It should be noted, however, that the general trend towards increasing affective complexity up to and throughout the middle years does not hold for all individuals (Diehl, Coyle, & Labouvie-Vief, 1996; Labouvie-Vief, 1996). Moreover, the research of Labouvie-Vief and colleagues suggests that adults who do not have a well-developed capacity for cognitive–affective complexity may be limited in their use of the more mature coping strategies that are necessary for adaptive emotion regulation. Thus, for some adults, increasing age may be associated with greater limitation in emotion functioning rather than a deepening of experience.

B. Changes in Emotion Regulation

Emerging data seem to indicate a change in emotion regulation strategies with age. Given the greater physical frailty and reduced energy reserves associated with old age, it might be expected that later life would see a shift towards a preference for maintaining a positive equilibrium for the self. Indeed, emerging data seem to indicate a change in emotion regulation strategies with age. In a sample of individuals ranging from age 10 to older than 70, Diehl et al. (1996) found that older persons showed a preference for avoiding conflict and delaying expression. They used a combination of coping and defense strategies indexing greater impulse control and the tendency to positively appraise conflict situations.

Lawton and colleagues (1992, 1993) asked young, middle-aged, and older participants to complete a questionnaire that tapped the ways people view their own internal and external reactivity, emotional dynamics (intensity, frequency, duration), and volitional ability to influence the occurrence and content of emotion. They found that age was associated with increased emotional control, decreased surgency, greater stability of mood, greater moderation of affect, decreased psychophysiological responsiveness, and reduced sensation seeking. The data also indicated that affective responsiveness and dynamics become moderated with older age. However, the differences were not great, by the authors' own acknowledgment, and there was considerable individual variation.

In the context of the same studies mentioned earlier, Gross and colleagues (1997) also examined self-reports of the tendency to control the inner experience of five target emotions: happiness, sadness, fear, anger, and disgust in samples of Norwegian adults and American nuns. In the Norwegian sample there were age-related increases in emotional control for each of the five emotions and an interaction effect indicating that older women reported a greater ability to control the internal experience of anger than younger women. In terms of external control of emotions, there were no age-related changes. In the sample of nuns, aging was associated with increased inner control of happiness, sadness, fear, and anger. As far as the control of the external expression of emotion, aging was positively associated with increased outer control of happiness and sadness and negatively associated with the control of disgust. Finally, a study by McConatha and Huba (1999) examined the relation between perceptions of primary control and four kinds of secondary control—defined as emotion control strategies—in a sample of young, middle-aged, and older adults. They found an inverse relation between age and primary control, with primary control decreasing and secondary control increasing with age. As age increased, aggression control, impulsiveness control, and inhibition control increased, at the same time, the tendency

to ruminate about emotionally upsetting events decreased with age.

The foregoing studies, though cross-sectional in nature, collectively suggest that the emotion regulation capacities of individuals improve with age, in the sense that people get better at avoiding negative affect. There appears to be a general trend in which regulatory efforts move from more instrumental or environment-focused efforts towards internal strategies. This finding is consistent with the theories of Izard, Labouvie-Vief, Carstensen, and Schulz, although the explanatory emphasis in accounting for this change differs across the theorists. Izard's theory, and to a lesser extent the theory of Labouvie-Vief, explains this change in terms of cognitive and social development, whereas the theories of Carstensen and Lawton emphasize changes in motivation and an increased importance of maximizing the positive nature of experience with age.

C. Expressing Emotion and Reading the Expressive Behavior of Others

A number of studies have looked at changes in the expression of emotion as well as at changes in sensitivity to the perception of emotion in others.

1. Changes in the Expression of Emotion

There are three channels of nonverbal communication that index emotional states: face, voice, and body, with the vast bulk of research having focused on facial expressions. Research has shown that there is increasing conventionalization of facial expressions across the childhood years, which in large measure involves adopting familial and cultural display rules and includes a general dampening of expressive behavior. However, changes accrue during adulthood as well. Malatesta-Magai, Jonas, Shepard, and Culver (1992) studied the facial expressions of younger and older individuals using an emotion-induction procedure in which participants relieved and recounted emotionally charged experiences involving anger, fear, sadness, and interest. Older individuals were found to be more emotionally expressive than younger subjects in terms of the frequency of expressive behavior under all four emotion-induction conditions.

The facial expressive behavior of older adults also appears to be more expressive in another sense. Malatesta and Izard (1984) videotaped and subsequently coded the facial expressions of a group of young, middle-aged, and older women as they recounted emotional experiences. The facial expressions of the middle-aged and older women showed fewer component muscle movements than younger women in their expressions; however, at the same time they were more complex and consisted of more instances in which different emotions combined in the same expression.

Part of the difficulty in reading older faces may stem from the fact that dispositional tendencies with respect to the emotions become crystallized on the face with age. Malatesta and colleagues (1987) had older adults fill out an emotion trait measure that reported on the frequency with which they expressed various emotions. They also were asked to encode five facial expressions. Other individuals—naïve judges serving as decoders—were asked to ascertain the emotions that the encoders had been asked to communicate. These naïve decoders found the older faces more difficult to judge. The decoders had difficulty owing to the fact that encoders' emotional dispositions leaked through and overrode the task demands. Despite their attempt to encode different emotion states, anger-prone adults were perceived to be expressing anger, sadness-prone adults sadness, contempt-prone adults contempt, and guilt-prone adults guilt.

Moreno, Borod, Welkowitz and Alpert (1990) examined age differences in the laterality of expressive behavior. Laterality was examined using measures of facial symmetry during an emotion-induction task involving a neutral condition and four emotions: surprise, joy, sadness, and disgust. The sample consisted of young, middle-aged, and older adults. In addition to assessing laterality, raters also judged the degree of intensity of the facial expressions. The authors found that there was no main effect for age on laterality. However, there was an emotion by age effect such that the older participants were rated as showing more intense disgust. They also were seen as having more intense "neutral expressions." The finding with respect to more intense neutral expressions may also relate to the structural changes that occur in the face with age.

Two studies have also looked at expressive behavior in late life and under conditions of dementia. Using a behavioral coding system and direct observation, Lawton and colleagues (1996) found that the emotions of anger, sadness, pleasure, and anxiety were relatively infrequent, whereas contentment and interest were more common. All of the emotions were seen as present to some degree or another in the dementia patients, all but anger in the nondemented residents. Pleasure, interest, and contentment ratings were greater in cumulative duration among the nondemented versus demented residents, whereas anxiety was less. Magai, Cohen, Comberg, Malatesta, and Culver (1996) also evaluated the emotional expressions of mid-to late-stage dementia patients using a behavioral coding scheme and direct observation. The observations took place during a family visit, with facial expressions of interest, anger, contempt, sadness, joy, disgust, and fear recorded on a second-to-second basis by trained coders. The incidence of fear and disgust were too infrequent for parametric analysis, and all of them occurred in the oldest and most deteriorated patients. Recognizable facial expressions of emotion were observed across the spectrum of cognitive deterioration, including the most severely impaired patients, although there were changes with advancing intellectual impairment. Only one emotion was found to be lower at the end stage of the disease than at earlier stages, namely joy. Thus, this study indicated that the ability to express affect, as observed in interpersonal contexts, remains intact during the course of dementia, even in the most deteriorated individuals. Moreover, other data from the study, such as the finding that sadness expressions of residents were typically restricted to family leave taking, indicated that the emotion system is not only behaviorally intact in these patients, but functionally intact as well, and that emotion expressions were not just random discharges of facial activity but that they are related to the patients' feelings and goals.

2. Changes in Sensitivity to the Expressive Behavior of Others

Only a handful of studies have looked at potential age-related changes in the ability to decode the expressive behavior of social partners. McDowell, Harrison, and Demaree (1994) found that older adults were significantly less accurate than younger adults in their identification of negative and neutral facial expressions. Similarly, in the Malatesta et al. (1987) study mentioned previously, there were age differences in the accuracy with which decoders judged the emotion states of encoders. Older subjects in general did more poorly, although results varied depending on the age congruence between judges and emotion expressors, suggesting a decoding advantage accruing through social contact with like-aged peers. Older individuals may thus have a greater facility in discounting the "noise" of facial wrinkling so as to discern the essential emotional messages of older social partners.

Two other studies examined sensitivity to other nonverbal emotion cues. Allen and Brosgole (1993) found an overall decline in the ability of older adults to identify specific emotions from vocal cues. Montepare, Koff, Zaitchik, and Albert (1999) examined age-related differences in the ability of adults to decode emotion through body movements and gestures. Although both younger and older adults made accurate emotion identification well above chance levels, older adults made more errors overall, especially for negative emotions. Moreover, they were especially likely to misidentify emotional displays as neutral in content. However, the actors who depicted the emotional gestures were young adults, and the Malatesta et al. (1987) study of facial expressions showed that age congruence between encoders and decoders may facilitate recognition of emotion encoded in the face, a pattern that may well extend to expressive gestures as well.

In summary, though the data from the above studies are cross-sectional in nature and need to be replicated in longitudinal research, there appear to be developmental trends indicating increased complexity of facial expressions in terms of greater interindividual variability and the presence of more blended affects, supporting the theories of Izard and Magai. Changes in facial musculature appear to obscure the meaning of affective signals in older people, but not appreciably so. The ability to understand the emotional signals of others, whether they are facial, vocal, or gestural appears to undergo a slight decline with age, with some compensation if the social partners are peers of the same age.

D. Social Relations and Attachment Patterns

Available data on changes in patterns of social relations over the adult years are found within the context of research on marital relations and other close relationships and in studies of attachment relationships.

1. Affect in Marital and Other Close Relationships

The literature on subjective experiences of emotion and expressive patterns, reviewed earlier, comprises one source of information on how emotional experience and expression may vary as a function of age. However, because most emotion experience is socially grounded (Magai & Passman, 1997; Malatesta & Kalnok, 1982), an examination of emotion occurring in social contexts, especially close relationships, comprises another especially important venue in which to examine age-related differences in emotion experience and expression.

a. Within Marriage Levensen and colleagues (e.g., Carstensen, Gottman, & Levensen, 1995; Levenson, Carstensen, & Gottman, 1994) studied patterns of emotion communication in long-term marriages. Two groups of married couples, one middle-aged, the other older, were asked to interact with one another in three exchanges: conversations about events of the day, a problem area of continuing disagreement in their marriage, and a mutually agreed upon pleasant topic. Each conversation lasted 15 minutes, during which time each partner's emotional expressions and physiological activity were recorded. Spouses later returned to view their recorded interactions and provided a continuous report of their subjective affective experience during each of the interactions using a rating dial. Results indicated that older couples, compared to middle-aged couples, expressed lower levels of anger, disgust, belligerence and whining, as well as higher levels of affection during discussion of a marital problem, a finding that holds even

when controlling for the severity of the problem discussed. In general, marital interaction in the older couples was more affectively positive and involved lower physiological arousal than was the case with the younger couples. These investigators found that older unhappy couples were less likely than older happy, or middle-aged happy and unhappy couples to engage in sequences in which one spouse's neutral affect was followed by the expression of negative affect by the other spouse; that is, the couples tended to avoid "negative start-up". The authors speculate that these couples had learned to achieve some control over the activation of negative affect. However, in the part of the session in which couples were to discuss an area of continuing conflict in the marriage, the exchanges of older unhappy couples, like those of younger unhappy couples, were characterized by the expression of high levels of negative emotion, negative affect reciprocity, female engagement, and male withdrawal.

b. The Broader Social Network Carstensen and colleagues have found in both longitudinal and cross-sectional studies that the narrowing of social networks in later life is selective in nature and involves shedding peripheral relationships while retaining those that are most intimate and emotionally gratifying (Carstensen, 1992; Lang & Carstensen, 1994). Moreover, reductions in social contact did not occur only due to deaths or other barriers to contact, because the data indicated that older people had fewer acquaintances, but not fewer confidants. Two studies have also indicated that social selectivity in older adults has to do with the affective potential of prospective social partners rather than the potential for future contact and the potential to gain information. Older adults placed greatest emphasis on the potential for emotionally meaningful contact, whereas younger people placed comparable emphasis on all three aspects (Carstensen, 1995; Fredrickson & Carstensen, 1990).

In accord with the thesis that age-related reduction in social contact has more to do with an appreciation of limited time rather than being an intrinsic aspect of aging, Carstensen and colleagues have shown that the preference for familiar and intimate social partners over novel social partners can be demonstrated in other age groups, depending on perceptions of the nearness of death or by manipulating subjects' times frame. For example, in a sample of gay men who were either HIV-negative, HIV-positive, or had active AIDS, it has found that the different life expectancies of the groups affected the way they responded to a card-sort measure of desirable qualities of prospective social partners. The healthy subsample oriented equally to the prospects for future contact, information seeking, and affective potential, whereas for the infirm subsample affective potential assumed central prominence (Carstensen, 1995).

In summary, the literature on social networks and close relationships supports the formulations of selectivity and optimization theories of emotion to the extent that as individuals mature, they enact emotional behaviors in close relationships that help avoid or de-escalate negative affect, and choose social partners that help them to satisfy the need for emotionally rewarding interpersonal relations.

2. Emotion and Attachment Relationships

Because there are no long-term longitudinal studies of attachment patterns in adults, the literature on emotion in attachment relationships during adulthood and aging is concentrated on two areas of concern that are indirectly relevant to the question of the stability or change in attachment patterns. Do the different attachment patterns in adults versus children cohere in the same way with respect to affective profiles? Are there cohort or age differences in the distribution of attachment patterns across the adult years that might reflect on changes in attachment style with the passage of time?

a. Patterns of Emotion in Different Attachment Styles The literature on adult attachment, which has grown to over 800 articles and chapters since 1987 (Crowell, Fraley, & Shaver, 1999), is concentrated mainly on young adulthood. This literature has shown convincingly that the different attachment styles identified in the original attachment literature on infants and children are linked to different emotion traits and dispositions, emotion regulation patterns, coping patterns, and with a variety of interpersonal processes (Cassidy & Shaver, 1999). In brief, secure individuals are characterized by a predisposition to express positive affect, and they possess good modulatory skills when it comes to negative affect. Avoidant individuals, at least those that can be described as dismissively avoidant, tend to be hostile, to defend against negative affect, and to inhibit affect expression. Ambivalent individuals tend to be anxious, to have frustrated attachment aims, to be overalert to distress, and to be expressively disinhibited to an extreme degree (Magai, 1999).

There is far less literature on emotion patterns in the attachment relationships of middle-aged or older adults. In a study by Magai, Hunziker, Mesias, and Culver (2000) adults ranging in age from the mid-20 to the mid-80s, with a mean age of 63 years, were assessed for attachment style, emotion traits, and internal working models of relationships; the latter involved assessing facial affect decoding biases and thematic biases in narrative material. The participants were also videotaped during an emotion-induction session, in which they were asked to relate affectively charged events involving anger, sadness, fear, and interest. The expressive behavior was subsequently coded.

Regression analyses indicated that attachment security was predicted by facial expressions of joy, a facial affect-decoding bias favoring shame, a disinclination to route negative emotion from consciousness, and a disinclination for depressive affect. Fearful avoidance was predicted by facial expressions of shame, attributions of sadness to ambiguous facial expressions, wish-fulfillment fantasies of approval from others, and trait anxiety. Preoccupation was predicted by facial expressions of disgust, wish-fulfillment fantasies of closeness and affiliation, trait anger, and female gender. Finally, dismissive attachment was predicted by mixed or ambivalent facial activity, the disinclination to see anger in faces, the routing of negative emotion from consciousness, inner conflict expressed in stories, and the denial of anxiety.

Magai and Cohen (1998) also looked at the relation between attachment style and emotion-regulation patterns in a sample of patients undergoing diagnosis for dementia; caregivers described the patients' premorbid attachment style as well as premorbid pattern of emotion regulation. The researchers found that an avoidant premorbid attachment pattern was associated with premorbid elevations on the emotions of contempt, anger, inhibition, and reserve and with lower sociability; the ambivalent premorbid attachment style was associated with the premorbid emotions of anxiety and sadness.

The findings discussed here regarding the emotional profile of the different attachment styles in older adults are congruent with the general patterns disclosed in samples of younger adults, underscoring the significance and coherence of emotional–attachment patterns as a life-long phenomenon.

b. Distribution of Attachment Patterns In the majority of studies involving predominantly young adults, the distribution of attachment styles resembles that found in the original studies with infants and children. That is, about 55 to 65% of samples using self-report measures have been found to be secure, 22–30% avoidant (dismissing), and 15–20% ambivalent (e.g., Hazan & Shaver, 1987; Feeney & Noller, 1990; Kirkpatrick & Davis, 1994; Davila, Burge, & Hammen, 1997). In three studies using an interview-based assessment, 52–62% have been found to be secure, 22–28% avoidant, and 16–20% ambivalent (Cassidy & Shaver, 1999).

These patterns are not sustained in the few studies that have evaluated older respondents. In brief, the avoidant attachment style tends to be more prominent in older adults and secure attachment less prominant, as indicated in five studies that included a significant number of older adults. For example, in a sample of adults with a mean age of 63 years, Magai et al., (2000) found that security of attachment, as assessed by an adult attachment interview, was negatively correlated with age and that dismissing attachment (a form of avoidant attachment that devalues relatedness and attachment) was positively correlated with age. Diehl, Elnick, Bourbeau, and Labouvie-Vief (1998), who assessed attachment styles in a sample of adults from a relatively affluent Midwestern suburb, found that whereas 16% the young adult sample were dismissing, the figure for the oldest sample was 37%. A similar figure was obtained by Magai and Cohen (1998) in a sample of dementia caregivers asked to rate their family member's attachment style before the patient became ill; the mean age of the patients was 76 years. In a study of older Caucasian and Asian adults by Webster

(1997), 52% of adults were classified as dismissing and 33% were classified as secure. Finally, in a large, randomly drawn sample of urban elders living in an economically disadvantaged community, 78% were found to be avoidant (Magai et. al., 2001).

Thus although the proportion of avoidant–dismissing and secure individuals varies across samples and appears to have something to do with economic background of the participants, the data clearly show that the distributions of attachment styles in older adults are quite at variance with those of younger samples. Diehl and colleagues (1996) have suggested that the higher proportion of avoidant older adults might be due to a greater number of losses experienced by older persons. To test this, Magai and colleagues (1999) subdivided their own sample into a younger cohort born between 1922 and 1932, and an older cohort born between 1911 and 1921. The younger cohort had significantly lower numbers of persons with secure attachment than did the older cohort. However, there was no difference between the two age cohorts in terms of the number of close relatives or friends who had died within the past 5 years. The authors surmised that the difference in the proportion of secure and dismissing attachment in the two cohorts represents the influence of Watsonian behaviorism—which advocated the withholding of affection from children—and which would have reached its apex of influence between the 1920s and 1930s, thus affecting the younger versus older cohort.

In summary, the literature on attachment patterns in adults indicates that avoidant attachment is far more common in older adults and secure attachment more uncommon, much in contrast to the findings with young adults and children. However, qualitative differences in emotion regulatory patterns, attentional strategies, emotion traits, and coping patterns that distinguish attachment patterns in younger and older adults are quite similar to those found in children. Because there are no long-term longitudinal data on attachment styles in adults, it is not clear whether the differences between younger and older adults are due to cohort effects or are linked to age-related losses or other circumstances of late life, but cohort effects seem likely.

E. Change in Emotion Traits

Summarizing the literature on emotion and personality, Rusting (1998) differentiates three streams of research that relate to trait-like aspects of emotion. The first concerns broad traits of positive–negative affectivity, defined as stable individual differences in the tendency to experience positive and negative moods. A second line of research has involved the examination of specific emotion traits such as anxiety, depression, and hostility, and the third category of traits related to emotion concerns individual differences in emotion regulation.

There is now fairly consistent evidence that broad dimensions of positive and negative affect are stable over both short and longer periods of time. For example, Epstein (1979) sampled reports of positive and negative emotion in a group of young adults repeatedly over a period of weeks; the odd-even stability coefficients over 12 days reached above .80 for positive affect and above .70 for negative affect. Similarly, Diener and Larsen (1984) found that the three-week stability for positive affect among college students across a variety of situations, as measured during an experience sampling method, was .79; the stability for negative affect was .81 (see also Segerstrom, Taylor, Kemeny, & Fahey, 1998). There is also considerable stability for specific moods and traits. Berenbaum, Fujita, and Pfennig (1995) had students record ratings on three negative emotions in a daily diary for 6 weeks and found that the mean of the first 3 weeks was significantly correlated with the mean of the second 3 weeks: .74, .80, and .78 for sadness, anger, and fear, respectively. Moreover, these correlations remained significant for the individual emotions even after controlling for the variance shared by the other two negative emotions. These findings suggest that emotional moods may represent enduring dispositions, although there are but a few studies that provide estimates of stability over a longer period of time. In terms of positive and negative moods, Watson and Slack (1993) reported stability coefficients over an average time span of 27 months of .74 and .63, respectively, while Ormel and Schaufeli (1991) reported retest coefficients for negative affect of .57 and .52 over 7 and 8 years.

In terms of discrete emotions, Izard, Libero, Putnam, and Haynes (1993) assessed the stability of 12 emotions in a group of postpartum women. The 3-year test–retest stabilities ranged from a low of .33 for fear to a high .71 for contempt, with an average of .56. Magai (1999b) obtained 8-year stability coefficients for anxiety, depression, interest, anger-in, anger-out, and total anger, ranging from .47 to .75. Only anger-out showed significant change, in this case, decline, over the 8 years. In a national sample of nearly 5000 men and women ranging in age from 24 to 87 (Costa et al., 1987), the 9-year stability coefficient for scores on a general well-being scale was .48; stability coefficients for the three-item positive affect subscale, the five-item negative affect subscale, and the two-item health concern subscale ranged from .37 to .44. The above figures indicated that broad dimensions of positive and negative affect as well as specific mood states are fairly stable and typify adult personality functioning.

Individual differences in the way that persons habitually attend to or avoid disturbing or threatening stimuli is captured by the constructs of repression and sensitization. Repressors tend to disattend to threatening stimuli or truncate awareness, whereas sensitizers monitor the environment for the presence of such stimuli. Sensitization is strongly related to trait anxiety, and thus stability for this characteristic may be seen as reflecting on the stability of trait fear (Rusting, 1998). Measures of repressive defensiveness, as indexed by verbal-autonomic dissociation—that is, autonomic reactivity accompanied by reduced awareness of distress—has been found to be stable over a period of 8 months in a sample of middle-aged individuals who had suffered bereavement (Bonanno, Keltner, Holen, & Horowitz, 1995).

There are only a handful of studies that have examined factors associated with *changes* in personality characteristics and emotional organizations, but they suggest that affectively charged interpersonal events are important precipitants. For example, Miller and C'deBaca (1994) studies individuals who underwent radical change and found that interpersonal processes were prominent—one-fifth of the respondents had been in therapy, and a number of narratives were striking for their depiction of the respondent's involvement in a group, workshop, or retreat, where intense affiliative relationships were experienced (see also Ullman, 1989).

With respect to the more clearly affective qualities of personality, Magai (1999b) examined the factors that may mediate changes in personality in a sample of 63 adults (mean age 63 years) who provided self-report data on the degree to which they felt their perspectives, goals, personality, feelings, and ways of relating had changed over 8 years. Respondents reported moderate changes in all five areas, and their reports of change were significantly correlated with reports by independent informants who were acquainted with the participants for all areas but goals. Overall personality change (an aggregate measure of all indices) was associated with positive and negative interpersonal life events of an intimate nature such as marriage, divorce, and death of loved ones, and was unassociated with other emotional high and low points in people's lives involving careers, changes in residence, and more distant social relationships.

In summary, there is considerable evidence of stability in aspects of personality that have to do with emotional organization. On the other hand, structural change in the personality is also possible under certain circumstances. The studies reviewed lend support to Magai's thesis that traits associated with emotion are relatively stable as well as the thesis that emotion-related changes in personality in the face of emotional events are more likely to obtain in cases that involve interpersonal process—events that involve the initiation or termination of intimate relationships or other intense affiliative experiences, although additional longitudinal work is necessary.

III. Summary of Empirical Studies

The studies reviewed above, based on a wide range of methodologies, generally support the theories of emotional development described in the introduction. Collectively, the last two decades of data on subjective experience of emotion and emotion regulation suggest that age does not affect emotional intensity nor bring with it an increase in negative mood and decrease in positive mood as suggested by the earlier literature based largely on samples of institutionalized persons (Malatesta, 1981). In terms of specific emotions, one recurrent finding in both cross-sectional and longitudinal research is that there is a decrease in anger with age (Gibson, 1997; Gross et al., 1997; Lawton et al., 1993; Magai, 1999b;

McContha & Huba, 1999). The decrease in anger with age can be interpreted from the discrete emotions functionalist perspective, a control theory perspective, and from the perspective of socioemotional selectivity and optimization theories. The motivational function of anger is to overcome obstacles and barriers to goals. To the extent that age brings with it changes in the incidence of blocked goals, its prevalence should decline. In a similar vein, because anger is an emotion that is designed to effect changes in the external environment, a decrease in anger could well be explained by a reduction in primary control and a shift to secondary control after middle age. Finally, anger is also an interpersonal "repellor" (Magai & Haviland-Jones, in press) that can put strains on intimate interpersonal relationships. To the extent that social networks become narrowed in later life and limited to a few important relationships, anger would pose a threat to these relationships.

Another discrete emotion effect observed in the literature pertains to that of disgust. Moreno et al. (1990) found that disgust was more common in older faces. Gross and colleagues (1997) found that the experience of disgust was level across age groups, whereas for all other negative emotions, older subjects reported lower rates than younger subjects; as well, respondents reported decreasing control over the external signs of disgust. Finally, Magai and colleagues (1996) found that disgust and fear were only evident in dementia patients in the last stages of the disease. A functionalist account of the meaning of disgust offers intriguing speculation. Within the theoretical literature, the emotion of disgust— a rejecting affect—has been described variously as a reaction to unwanted intimacy, as a defense against infection, and as a primary means of internalizing cultural prohibitions (Rozin, Haidt, & McCauley, 1993). To the extent that older cohorts appear to be characterized by more dismissing attachment styles than younger cohorts and thus more avoidant of intimacy, they may be expected to display more disgust. Alternatively, the aging process itself seems to result in a narrowing of social networks, which also may provoke activation of disgust as a means of gaining distance from persons in the more peripheral social network. Older persons are also more vulnerable to disease and infection and thus may be more vigilant for contaminants. Finally, there is accumulating longitudinal evidence that as people age, they show greater endorsement of norm orientation (Helson & Kwan, in press); events and objects that violate societal conventions are rejected. It is difficult to decide on the appropriate interpretation; perhaps they are not mutually exclusive.

The literature also indicates that there may be a deepening of affective experience with age, at least up to and through middle-age, and an improvement in the ability to regulate emotional states, at least until very old age. With aging, whether through social selectivity, increasing integration of affect and cognition, or a shift in focus to regulating the self rather than the environment, cross-sectional data suggest that adults may learn to modulate their negative emotions more effectively over the years, especially by the active selection of environments. However, some caution should be exercised in interpreting the results in this way. A number of authors have noted that some of the apparent effects of aging may be related to cohort effects indexing historical changes in child-rearing practices and changing cultural values with respect to the desirability of controlling or expressing emotion. Mroczek and Kolarz (1998) and Malatesta-Magai et al. (1992) have also pointed out that the seeming improvement in emotional well-being and emotion functioning with age found in the various cross-sectional studies may be linked to a selective survivorship effect. It may be that happier and more expressive people live longer or that chronic unhappiness and emotion inhibition is associated with dying younger. The finding that older adults are characterized by more dismissing attachment styles may mean that reports of positive affect and contentment are linked to repressive coping rather than nondefended positivity. Longitudinal research by Carstensen and Labouvie-Vief, presently underway, should eventually help to clarify whether emotion regulation does actually improve with age and whether distributional differences in attachment styles observed in cross-sectional studies are related to cohort or aging effects.

References

Allen, R., & Brosgole, L. (1993). Facial and auditory affect recognition in senile geriatrics, the normal elderly, and young adults. *International Journal of Neuroscience, 68,* 33–42.

Baltes, P. B., & Mayer, K. U. (Eds.), (1999). *The Berlin aging study: Aging from 70 to 100.* Cambridge, UK: Cambridge University Press.

Barrick, A. L., Hutchinson, R. L., & Deckers, L. H. (1989). Age effects on positive and negative emotions. *Journal of Social Behavior and Personality, 4,* 421–429.

Berenbaum, H., Fujita, F., & Pfennig, J. (1995), Consistency, specificity, and correlates of negative emotions. *Journal of Personality and Social Psychology, 68,* 342–352.

Bonanno, G. A., Keltner, D., Holen, A., & Horowitz, M. J. (1995). When avoiding unpleasant emotion might not be such a bad thing: Verbal-autonomic response dissociation and midlife conjugal bereavement. *Journal of Personality and Social Psychology, 46,* 975–989.

Bowlby, J. (1979). *The making and breaking of affectional bonds.* London: Tavistock.

Carstensen, L. L. (1992). Social and emotional patterns in adulthood: Support for socioemotional selectivity theory. *Psychology and Aging, 7,* 331–338.

Carstensen, L. L. (1995). Evidence for a life-span theory of socioemotional selectivity. *Current Directions in Psychological Science, 4,* 151–156.

Carstensen, L. L., Gottman, J. M., & Levenson, R. W. (1995). Emotional behavior in long-term marriage. *Psychology and Aging, 10,* 140–149.

Carstensen, L. L., Graff, J., Levenson, R. W., & Gottman, J. M. (1996). Affect in intimate relationships. In C. Magai & S. H. McFadden (Eds.), *Handbook of emotion, adult development, and aging* (pp. 227–242). San Diego, CA: Academic Press.

Carstensen, L. L., Pasupathi, M., & Mayr, U. (2000). Emotional experience in everyday life across the adult life span. *Journal of Personality and Social Psychology, 79,* 644–655.

Cassidy, J., & Shaver, P. R. (1999). (Eds.), *Handbook of attachment.* New York: Guilford Press.

Costa, P. T., Jr., McCrae, R. R., & Zonderman, A. B. (1987). Environmental and dispositional influences on well-being: Longitudinal follow-up of an American national sample. *British Journal of Psychology, 78,* 299–306.

Crowell, J. A., Fraley, R. C., & Shaver, P. R. (1999). Measurement of individual differences in adolescent and adult attachment. In J. Cassidy & P. R. Shaver (Eds.), *Handbook of attachment: Theory, research, and clinical applications* (pp. 434–465). New York: Guilford.

Cummings, E., & Henry, W. E. (1961). *Growing old: The process of disengagement.* New York: Basic Books.

Darwin, C. R. (1872). *The expression of emotions in man and animals.* London: John Murray.

Davila, J., Burge, D., & Hammen, C. (1997). Why does attachment style change? *Journal of Personality and Social Psychology, 73,* 826–838.

Diehl, M., Elnick, A. B., Bourbeau, L. S., & Labouvie-Vief, G. (1998). Adult attachment styles: Their relations to family context and personality. *Journal of Personality and Social Psychology, 74,* 1656–1669.

Diehl, M., Coyle, N., & Labouvie-Vief, G. (1996). Age and sex differences in strategies of coping and defense across the life span. *Psychology and Aging, 11,* 127–139.

Diener, E., & Larsen, R. J. (1984). Temporal stability and cross-situational consistency of affective, behavioral, and cognitive responses. *Journal of Personality and Social Psychology, 47,* 871–883.

Diener, E., Sandvik, E., & Larsen, R. J. (1985). Age and sex effects for emotional intensity. *Developmental Psychology, 21,* 542–546.

Dilworth-Anderson, P. (1998). Emotional well-being in adult and later life among African Americans: A cultural and sociocultural perspective. In K. W. Schaie & M. P. Lawton (Eds.), *Annual review of gerontology and geriatrics, Vol. 17,* (pp. 282–303). New York: Singer Publishing Co.

Dougherty, L. M., Abe, A., & Izard, C. (1996). Differential emotions theory and emotional development in adulthood and later life. In C. Magai & S. H. McFadden (Eds.), *Handbook of emotion, adult development, and aging* (pp. 27–38). San Diego, CA: Academic Press.

Epstein, S. (1979). The stability of behavior: I. On predicting most of the people much of the time. *Journal of Personality and Social Psychology, 37,* 1097–1126.

Feeney, J. A., & Noller, P. (1990). Attachment style as a predictor of adult romantic relationships. *Journal of Personality and Social Psychology, 38,* 281–291.

Fredrickson, B. L., & Carstensen, L. L. (1990). Choosing social partners: How old age and anticipated endings make people more selective. *Psychology and Aging, 5,* 335–347.

Gibson, S. J. (1997). The measurement of mood states in older adults. *Journal of Gerontology: Psychological Sciences, 52B,* P167–P174.

Gross, J. J. & Carstensen, L. L., Tsai, J., Skorpen, C. G., & Hsu, A. Y. C. (1997). Emotion and aging: Experience, expression, and control. *Psychology and Aging, 12,* 590–599.

Hazan, C., & Shaver, P. (1987). Romantic love conceptualized as an attachment process. *Journal of Personality and Social Psychology, 52,* 511–524.

Helson, R., & Kwan, V. S. Y (in press). Personality change in adulthood: The broad picture and processes in one longitudinal sample. In S. Hampson (Ed.), *Advances in personality psychology,* (Vol. 1). London: Routledge.

Inglehart, R. (1990). *Culture shift in advanced industrial society.* Princeton, NJ: Princeton University Press.

Izard, C. E. (1971). *The face of emotion*. New York: Appleton-Century-Crofts.

Izard, C. E. (1977). *Human emotions*. New York: Plenum Press.

Izard, C. E. (1991). *The psychology of emotions*. New York: Plenum Press.

Izard, C. E., & Ackerman, B. P. (1998). Emotions and self-concepts across the life span. In K. W. Schaie & M. P. Lawton (Eds.). *Annual review of gerontology and geriatrics* (Vol. 17, pp. 1–26). New York: Singer Publishing Co.

Izard, C. E., Libero, D. Z., Putnam, P., & Haynes, O. M. (1993). Stability of emotion experiences and their relations to traits of personality. *Journal of Personality and Social Psychology, 64*, 847–860.

Izard, C. E., & Malatesta, C. Z. (1987). Emotional development in infancy. In J. Osofsky (Ed.), *Handbook of infant development* (2nd ed.) (pp. 494–554). New York: Wiley.

Kirkpatrick, L. A., & Davis, K. E. (1994). Attachment style and relationship stability: A longitudinal analysis. *Journal of Personality and Social Psychology, 66*, 3, 502–512.

Labouvie-Vief, G. (1996). Emotion, thought and gender. In C. Magai & S. H. McFadden (Eds.), *Handbook of emotion, adult development, and aging* (pp. 101–115). San Diego, CA: Academic Press.

Labouvie-Vief, G., Chiodo, L. M., Goguen, L. A., Diehl, M., & Orwoll, L. (1995). Representations of self across the life span. *Psychology and Aging, 10*, 404–415.

Labouvie-Vief, G., DeVoe, M., & Bulka, D. (1989). Speaking about feelings: Conceptions of emotion across the life span. *Psychology and Aging, 4*, 425–437.

Labouvie-Vief, G., Diehl, M., Chiodo, L. M., & Coyle, N. (1995). Representations of self and parents across the life span. *Journal of Adult Development, 2*, 207–222.

Labouvie-Vief, G., Hakin-Larson, J., DeVoe, M., & Schoeberlein, S. (1989). Emotions and self-regulation: A lifespan view. *Human Development, 32*, 279–299.

Lang, F. R., & Carstensen, L. L. (1994). Close emotional relationships in late life: Further support for proactive aging in the social domain. *Psychology and Aging, 9*, 315–324.

Lawton, M. P. (1989). Environmental proactivity and affect in older people. In S. Spacapan & S. Oskamp (Eds.), *The social psychology of aging* (pp. 135–163). Newbury Park: Sage.

Lawton, M. P., Kleban, M. H., & Dean, J. (1993). Affect and age: Cross-sectional comparisons of structure and prevalence. *Psychology and Aging, 8*, 165–175.

Lawton, M. P., Kleban, M. H., Rajagopal, D., & Dean, J. (1992). The dimensions of affective experience in three age groups. *Psychology and Aging, 7*, 171–184.

Lawton, M. P., Van Haitsma, K., & Klapper, J. (1996). Observed affect in nursing home residents with Alzheimer's Disease. *Journals of Gerontology, Psychological Sciences, 51B*, 3–14.

Levenson, R. W., Carstensen, L. L., Friesen, W. V., & Ekman, P. (1991). Emotion, physiology, and expression in old age. *Psychology and Aging, 6*, 28–35.

Levenson, R. W., Carstensen, L. L., & Gottman, J. M. (1994). The influence of age and gender on affect, physiology, and their interrelations: A study of long-term marriages. *Journal of Personality and Social Psychology, 67*, 56–68.

Magai, C. (in press). Emotional development in adulthood. In N. J. Smelser & P. B. Baltes (Eds.), *International encyclopedia of the social and behavioral sciences*. London: Pergamon Press.

Magai, C. (1999a). Affect, imagery, attachment: Working models of interpersonal affect and the socialization of emotion. In J. Cassidy & P. Shaver (Eds.), *Handbook of attachment theory and research* (pp. 787–802). New York: Guilford.

Magai, C. (1999b). Personality change in adulthood: Loci of change and the role of interpersonal process. *International Journal of Aging and Human Development, 49*, 339–352.

Magai, C., & Cohen, C. (1998). Attachment style and emotion regulation in dementia patients and their relation to caregiver burden. The *Journal of Gerontology: Psychological Science, 53B*, P147.

Magai, C., Cohen, C., Milburn, N., Thorpe, B., McPherson, R., Peralta, D. & Evans-Ross, A. (Nov., 1999). A paper presented at the Gerontological Society of America, San Francisco.

Magai, C., Cohen, C., Milburn, N., Thorpe, B., McPherson, R., & Peralta, D. (2001). Attachment styles in European American and African American adults. *Journals of Gerontology, Psychological Sciences, 46B*, S1–S8.

Magai, C., Cohen, C., Gomberg, D., Malatesta, C., & Culver, C. (1996). Emotion expression in late stage dementia. *International Psychogeriatrics, 8*, 383–396.

Magai, C., & Haviland-Jones, J. (in press). *The genius of emotion: Dynamic trajectories of lives.* New York: Cambridge University Press.

Magai, C., Hunziker, J., Mesias, W., & Culver, C. (2000). Adult attachment styles and emotional biases. *International Journal of Behavioral Development.*

Magai, C., & McFadden, S. H. (1995). *The role of emotions in social and personality development: History, theory, and research.* New York: Plenum Press.

Magai, C., & Nusbaum, B. (1996). Personality change in adulthood: Dynamic systems, emotions, and the transformed self. In C. Magai & S. McFadden (Eds.), *Handbook of emotion, adult development and aging* (pp. 403–420). San Diego, CA: Academic.

Magai, C., & Passman, V. (1997). The interpersonal basis of emotional behavior and emotion regulation. In M. P. Lawton & K. W. Schaie (Eds.), *Annual review of gerontology and geriatrics* (Vol. 17, pp. 104–137). New York: Springer.

Main, M., Kaplan, N., & Cassidy, J. (1985). Security in infancy, childhood, and adulthood: A move to the level of representation. In I. Bretherton & E. Waters (Eds.), *Growing points of attachment theory and research. Monographs of the Society for Research in Child Development* (Vol. 50, pp. 66–106) (1–2).

Malatesta, C. (1981). Affective development over the lifespan: Involution or growth? *Merrill-Palmer Quarterly, 27*, 145–73.

Malatesta, C. (1982). The expression and regulation of emotion: A lifespan perspective. In T. M. Field & A. Fogel (Eds.), *Emotion and early interaction.* Hillsdale, NJ: Erlbaum Associates.

Malatesta, C., Fiore, M. J. & Messina, J. (1987). Affect, personality, and facial expressive characteristics of older individuals. *Psychology and Aging, 1*, 64–69.

Malatesta, C., & Izard, C. E. (1984). Facial expression of emotion in young, middle-aged, and older adults. In C. Malatesta & C. E. Izard (Eds.), *Emotion in adult development.* Beverly Hills: Sage Publications.

Malatesta, C., & Izard, C. E. (1984). The ontogenesis of human social signals: From biological imperative to symbol utilization. In N. Fox & R. Davidson (Eds.), *The psychobiology of affective development* (pp. 161–206). Hillsdale, NJ: Erlbaum.

Malatesta, C., Izard, C. E., Culver, C., & Nicolich, M. (1987). Emotion communication skills in young, middle-aged and older women. *Psychology and Aging, 2*, 193–203.

Malatesta, C., & Kalnok, M. (1984). Emotional experience in younger and older adults. *Journal of Gerontology, 39*, 301–308.

Malatesta, C., & Wilson, A. (1988). Emotion/cognition interaction in personality development: A discrete emotions, functionalist analysis. *British Journal of Social Psychology, 27*, 91–112.

Malatesta-Magai, C., Jonas, R., Shepard, B., & Culver, C. (1992). Type A personality and emotional expressivity in younger and older adults. *Psychology and Aging, 7*, 551–561.

McConatha, J. T., & Huba, H. M. (1999). Primary, secondary, and emotional control across adulthood. *Current Psychology: Developmental, Learning, Personality, Social. 18*, 164–170.

McDowell, C. L., Harrison, D. W., & Demaree, H. A. (1994). Is right hemisphere decline in the perception of emotion a function of aging? *International Journal of Neuroscience, 70*, 1–11.

Miller, W. R., & C'deBaca, R. (1994). Quantum change: Toward a psychology of transformation. In T. F. Heatherton and J. L. Weinberger (Eds.), *Can personality change?* (pp. 253–280). Washington, DC: American Psychological Association.

Montepare, J., Koff, E., Zaitchik, D., & Albert, M. (1999). The use of body movements and gestures as cues to emotions in younger and older adults. *Journal of Nonverbal Behavior, 23*, 133–152.

Moreno, C. R., Borod, J. C., Welkowitz, J., & Alpert, M. (1990). Lateralization for the expression and perception of facial emotion as a function of age. *Neuropsychologia, 28*, 199–209.

Mroczek, D. K., & Kolarz, C. M. (1998). The effect of age on positive and negative affect: a developmental perspective on happiness. *Journal of Personality and Social Psychology, 75*, 1333–1349.

Ormel, J., & Schaufeli, W. B. (1991). Stability and change in psychological distress and their relationship with self-esteem and locus of control: A dynamic equilibrium model. *Journal of Personality and Social Psychology, 60,* 288–299.

Raskin, A. (1979). Signs and symptoms of psychopathology in the elderly. In A. Raskin & L. F. Jarvick (Eds.), *Psychiatric symptoms and cognitive loss in the elderly* (pp. 3–18). Washington, DC: Hemisphere.

Rozin, P., Haidt, J., & McCauley, C. R. (1993). Disgust. In M. Lewis & J. M. Haviland (Eds.), *Handbook of emotions* (pp. 575–594). New York: Guilford.

Rusting, C. L. (1998). Personality, mood, and cognitive processing of emotional information: Three conceptual frameworks. *Psychological Bulletin, 124,* 165–196.

Schultz, R., & Heckhausen, J. (1996). A life span model of successful aging. *American Psychologist, 51,* 702–714.

Schulz, R., & Heckhausen, J. (1998). Emotion and control: A life-span perspective. In & K. W. Schaie & M. P. Lawton (Eds.), *Annual Review of Gerontology and Geriatrics* (Vol. 17, pp. 185–205). New York: Springer.

Segerstrom, S. C., Taylor, S. E., Kemeny, M. E., & Fahey, J. L. (1998). Optimism is associated with mood, coping, and immune change in response to stress. *Journal of Personality and Social Psychology, 74,* 1646–1655.

Tomkins, S. (1962). *Affect, imagery, consciousness. Vol. I: The positive affects.* New York: Springer.

Ullman, C. (1989). *The transformed self: The psychology of religious conversion.* New York: Plenum.

Watson, D., & Slack, A. K. (1993). General factors of affective temperament and their relation to job satisfaction over time. *Organizational Behavior and Human Decision Processes, 54,* 181–202.

Webster, J. D. (1997). Attachment style and well-being in elderly adults: A preliminary investigation. *Canadian Journal on Aging, 16,* 101–111.

Seventeen

Social Relations
An Examination of Social Networks, Social Support, and Sense of Control

Toni C. Antonucci

I. Introduction

One result of the mounting evidence demonstrating the influence of psychological factors on physical and mental health has been the emergence of social relations as an important focus of study. The contribution of social relations to the health and well-being of the elderly is particularly important in shaping successful aging. Aging is associated with increasing physical and mental changes. Although the medical, biological, physical, and other life sciences have contributed to our understanding of these changes, there is increasing evidence that social relations help individuals prepare for, cope with, and recover from many of the exigencies of life that are associated with aging. Thus, an examination of social relations is an especially appropriate topic for the *Handbook of the Psychology of Aging*.

The study of social relations has most often included the related concepts of social networks and social support. In this chapter we extend these related concepts to include social cognition, more specific-

ally a sense of control. Recent theoretical and empirical research exploring the processes and mechanisms through which social relations affect well-being have implicated the central role of social cognition. Although it is not possible to review all of the relevant work in this chapter, it is my intention to provide the reader with a brief overview of the field and to include a sampling of some of the most interesting, related work currently being reported in the literature. This chapter is organized as follows. It begins with a short history of important developments in the field. Next, issues and problems of definition, measurement, design, and analyses are considered, and exciting new advancements in these areas are recognized. The major focus of the chapter, however, is on important theoretical developments and recent empirical evidence. The implications of what we know and how we can best utilize what we know are also considered. Finally, some thoughts are offered on what we still need to know, that is, how future research might most profitably be directed.

Handbook of the Psychology of Aging
Copyright © 2001 by Academic Press.
All rights of reproduction in any form reserved.

II. History

Psychologists have long recognized the importance of interpersonal factors on individual mental health, but it was only when the importance of these factors on physical health and mortality was documented that the research became interesting to a broader array of scientists, researchers, and clinicians. Although both Cassel (1976) and Cobb (1976) provided the theoretical grounding for this perspective, the empirical turning point can perhaps best be identified with the early work of Berkman and Syme (1979). Using the Alameda county longitudinal epidemiological data, which followed a large representative sample of residents from the California county, Berkman and Syme were able to document that people who reported more social ties with friends and organizations were significantly more likely than people with no or fewer ties to be alive 9 years later. Subsequent studies essentially replicated these findings with respect to mortality in Tecumseh, Michigan (House, Robbins, & Metzner, 1982) and Evans County, Georgia (Blazer, 1982). Thus began a series of studies, both in the United States and abroad, documenting the association between social relations and numerous aspects of physical and mental health, including depression, cancer, heart disease, experience of pain, recovery from major health events, and the occurrence of dementia (e.g. Antonucci, Fuhrer, & Dartigues, 1997; Berkman, 1985; Fratiglioni, Wang, Ericsson, Maytan, & Winblad, 2000; George, Blazer, Hughes & Fowler, 1989; Holahan, Moos, Holahan, & Brennan, 1995; Kaplan, Salonen, Cohen, Syme, & Puska, 1988; Orth-Gomer, & Johnson, 1987; Oxman, Berkman, Kasl, Freeman, & Barrett, 1992; Oxman & Hull, 1997; Vaillant, Meyer, Mukamal, & Soldz, 1998; see Bowling & Grundy, 1998, for a more recent review).

A. Definitional Issues

Early research in the field of social relations was characterized by vague definitions, poor and inadequate samples, and inappropriate generalizations. Things have improved considerably. We have developed much clearer definitions, and we have come to recognize the ways in which definitional differences affect data collection (e.g., Knipscheer & Antonucci, 1990). We have made great strides in terms of samples, now having a number of regionally and nationally representative samples and several longitudinal studies that include important social relations measures.

In an effort to promote greater specificity, the generalized term *social relations* is proposed to describe the broad array of factors and interpersonal interactions that characterize social exchanges among people. Under this rubric, we consider three terms in this chapter: social networks, social support, and sense of control.

Social networks can best be understood in terms of the objective characteristics that describe the people with whom an individual maintains interpersonal relations. Thus, one can describe one's social network members in terms of their age, gender, role relationship, years known, residential proximity, frequency of contact, and the like. Describing a social network reveals critical information about the people with whom an individual has a relationship, but nothing about the nature, content, or quality of those relationships (Faber & Wasserman, in press; Glass, Mendes De Leon, Seeman, & Berkman, 1997).

To describe the content and quality of social relations we use the term social support. Social support refers to the actual exchange of support. Although it has been defined in various ways, for the purposes of this chapter we describe social support as an interpersonal transaction involving one of three key elements: aid, affect, or affirmation (Kahn & Antonucci, 1980). Aid refers to instrumental or tangible support, such as lending money, helping with chores, or providing sick care. Affect refers to emotional support, such as love, affection, and caring. Affirmation refers to agreement or acknowledgment of similarities or appropriateness of one's values or point of view. Several characteristics of social support exchanges have also been shown to be important. These include such factors as the source of support (e.g., family, friend, neighbor); satisfaction with the support received (i.e., its quality, content, or quantity); and even the perception that the support was provided, whether or not it actually was (e.g., Barrera, 1986; Chappell, 1992).

Sense of control refers to the degree to which individuals feel that they have control over a situation. It can be thought of as a type of social cognition, which is the study of how people think about social situations. Of particular interest to the study of social relationships is the emphasis in social cognition on examining how individuals cognitively represent information about people and social situations and then use that information to guide their behavior. Many factors are thought to influence how a person processes and represents information. Among these factors are fundamental cognitive processes, as well as memories of the past, perceptions of self, and attributions about others (Hess, 1994; Hess & Blanchard-Fields, 1999). The study of social cognition, generally, can be very helpful to understanding fundamental aspects of social relations. Reis and Downey (1999) recognize this when they consider the role of social cognition in relationships. These authors remind us that "thinking is for relating," (p. 97). In this chapter, however, it is the degree to which social relations lead to, influence, or are influenced by social cognition, especially a sense of control, that is especially relevant

(Bisconti & Bergeman, 1999). It is this association that will be explored in later sections of this chapter.

B. Methodological Issues

Recognition of these different social relations concepts and the distinctly different definitions associated with them leads directly to the myriad of problems that have been associated with their measurement. Fortunately, measurement of these concepts has evolved significantly over the last several years. Multiple assessment strategies and measurement techniques have been employed in recent studies. Measurement strategies include in-depth ethnographic and laboratory studies, as well as large representative, epidemiological surveys (e.g., Johnson 1999a,b; Sarason, Sarason, & Pierce, 1990; Seeman, Bruce, & McAvay, 1996). Open-ended questions, focus groups, daily diary studies, and structured interviews are examples of the measurement techniques that have been used successfully (e.g., Barrera, 1986; Cohen, Kessler, & Gordon, 1995; Fingerman, 1997; Morgan, 1997). Because of the breadth of definitions, methods, and measures employed in social relations research, it is important to be cognizant of how these differences fundamentally influence the kind of information obtained. The use of so many different methodologies, addressing related but different questions, has increased our basic knowledge about social relations in important ways. Furthermore, advances in statistical techniques mean that we are now a far cry from the simple frequencies offered by early researchers. In addition to more traditional analytic techniques used by many psychologists, such as analysis of variance and multiple regression analyses, techniques such as structural equation, hierarchical linear, and latent growth curve modeling offer new and unique possibilities in the exploration of social relations.

Reviews and sourcebooks are now available that summarize the latest measures and analytic techniques that have been successfully applied to the study of social relations (e.g., Pierce, Lakey, Sarason, & Sarason, 1997; Wasserman & Faust, 1994).

C. Theoretical Perspectives

We are fortunate to have a sizable collection of theorists focusing on theories of aging (e.g., Birren & Bengtson, 1988; Bengtson & Schaie, 1999; Marshall, 1996; Sarason, Sarason, & Pierce, 1994). Recently, several theoretical perspectives for conceptualizing social relations have been offered (see Levitt, 2000, for an overview). It is now generally recognized that a life span perspective provides a critical underlying base to developmental theory (Elder, 1998). It is also central to the study of social relations. The most important social relations usually involve long-lasting, significant, close relationships, such as those between parent and child, siblings, or husband and wife (Pierce, Sarason, & Sarason, 1996). Interpersonal relationships are life span in nature either because they are relationships that have existed over the life course or because current relationships are built upon the numerous interpersonal relationships that individuals have experienced over their lifetimes. To understand how an individual experiences a relationship at any one point in time, it is most useful to understand the history of that specific relationship as well as other relationships in the person's life. Thus, the study of a 50-year-old woman and her 70-year-old mother is best conceptualized as a relationship that has continued from when the 50-year-old was an infant through her early childhood, adolescence, young adulthood, and into the current state of middle age. Similarly, her mother was at one time a young 20-year-old mother who has loved and cared for her child through-

out the subsequent 50 years. The resultant mother–child relationship is likely to be understood very differently depending on these lifetime-accumulated experiences. One might even argue that a specific negative experience could and would be forgiven because of a lifetime of positive experiences. Or, on the contrary, a contemporaneous positively supportive interaction may be unable to make up for a lifetime of disappointment or neglect (e.g., Parrott & Bengston, 1999).

III. The Convoy Model

I have suggested the convoy model (e.g., Antonucci, 1990; Kahn & Antonucci, 1980) as a framework within which to study social relationships because it utilizes a life span perspective as the fundamental basis upon which to conceptualize the longitudinal nature of social relations. The convoy can be thought of as a structural concept shaped by personal (age, gender, personality) and situational (role expectations, resources, demands) factors that influence the support relations experienced by the individual. People form the convoy and the convoy, under ideal conditions, provides a protective, secure base or cushion that allows the individual to learn about and experience the world. These personal and situational factors and social relations, in turn, affect that individual's health and well-being both contemporaneously and longitudinally. The protective base provided by convoy members leads to better mental health and less psychological distress because it allows the individual to optimally grow and develop and successfully meet the challenges of life. Evidence has been accumulating supporting the convoy model (e.g. Antonucci & Akiyama, 1987, 1991; Levitt, Guacci-Franco, & Levitt, 1993; Peek & Lin, 1999). This protective base is both objective and subjective, providing the individual with practical help, but also, and perhaps most importantly, a psychological basis upon which to view the world. This is critical, as subjective and perceived support can be far more influential than objective and actual support in affecting the health and well-being of the individual (Antonucci et al., 1997; George et al., 1989; Oxman et al., 1992). It should be noted that the greater influence of subjective over objective support leads to the conclusion that it is the cognitive construction and interpretation of the situation that is crucial in explaining how and why social relations have an effect on the individual's health and well-being.

Most unique about the convoy model is the conceptualization of the individual as part of a dynamic network that moves through time, space, and the life course surrounding, embracing, and supporting the individual through the multiple experiences of life. The individual changes, grows, and develops. The situation within which that individual exists changes; it may become more or less complex, and it may involve more or less people. The interaction between the individual and the situation changes in response to both the individual's changes and the situational changes. The convoy reflects this dynamic aspect of social relations. As the individual ages, people are added to the convoy, subtracted from the convoy, move in and out the convoy in response to both internal and external events. Under optimal conditions, this dynamic aspect of the convoy allows it to meet and be responsive to the changing needs of the individual.

IV. Empirical Evidence: Social Networks

Details about network membership and composition is important because it provides information about who is potentially available as a support provider. The increase in the number and quality of empirical studies that have examined social networks provides some basic cornerstones upon which to build knowledge in the field. Although there is still much to learn about the way in which social networks and social support operate, there is quite a bit that we do already know. There are both sociodemographic and cultural similarities and differences in the nature of social relations (Chatters, Taylor, & Jayakody, 1994; Jackson & Antonucci, 1992; Levitt, Guacci-Franco, & Weber, 1992; Tucker, Taylor, & Mitchell-Kernan, 1993). We know, for example, that most people report immediate family—mother, father, spouse, child, and siblings—as their closest relationships (Antonucci & Akiyama, 1995; Chen & Silverstein, 2000; Connidis, 2001; Fingerman & Birditt, in press; Wenger, 1997). We also know that people differentiate their relationships hierarchically, from very close to much less close. All these relationships can be important, but it is clear that the closest relationships are most importantly linked to well-being. However, it is worth remembering that there is strength in weak ties (Granovetter, 1973). Although close relationships are pervasively important, there can be special circumstances under which a person generally not considered very close can have significant influence on the individual. A supervisor whom one would not consider a friend, but who goes out of his or her way to extend praise or deliver criticism can be such a person. As is the friend of a friend who knows someone who has the unique skills that are needed to solve a problem. Generally, however, as with people of all ages, the social networks of the elderly consist mainly, though not exclusively, of close family and friends.

Research examining majority and minority cultures in this country, as well as research in Europe and Asia, is now providing information about fundamental similarities in the structure and function of social networks, as well as documenting differences. There has been much interesting and important comparative work on social relations in recent years. Because of space limitations, I have selected four illustrative areas to consider: age, gender, race, and culture.

A. Age

The question of network size over time is important, because it has now been documented that people with larger networks get more help in times of illness. It has also been shown that more informal support at an earlier period leads to less decline in health at a later period in time (Choi & Wodarski, 1996). It was long assumed that the size of social networks and the exchange of social support decreases with age. Data are now available that make it clear that this is an overly simplistic view. Studies using large representative samples indicate that there are relatively few changes in social relations over time. Although it may be true that the total number of social relations decreases with age, the number of close social relationships and the amount of emotional support is relatively stable across the life span until very old age (Due, Holstein, Lund, Modvig, & Avlund, 1999). Furthermore, people clearly become more positive and less negative about their social relations with age (Carstensen, Gross, & Fung, 1997; Fingerman & Birditt, in press). Carstensen has suggested that with less time left to live, individuals reduce the number of people with whom they wish to maintain relationships. According to socioemotional selectivity theory, people actively select those relationships in which they wish to invest and from which they get the most pleasure. Carstensen argues that as people age they are likely to drop relationships that are less important to them or that create bad feelings. Research evidence has been accumulating in support of this perspective (Carstensen, Isaacowitz, & Charles,

1999; Lang, 2000; Lansford, Sherman, & Antonucci, 1998).

Examination of the stability of social relations across age have yielded relatively consistent findings across cultures. Data from the Berlin Aging Study indicate considerable social network stability in old age until very late in life (Baltes & Mayer, 1999). This is a finding that is replicated in our own work (Antonucci et al., 2000) and appears to be true for most of the countries about which we currently have data. There is no doubt, however, that as one reaches 80, 90, and 100 years old, significantly fewer people who have been close supporters are still alive. At the same time, these relationships are typically so close and long lasting that they are not easily replaced.

An interesting question arises over the issue of frequency of interactions by age. Although there seems to be a general decrease in the quantity of interactions with age, some data suggest that there is an increase (e.g., Wenger, 1997). It may very well be that there is a general decline in contact frequency with age under normal conditions. With the onset of a crisis, however, there is a concomitant increase in network contact, especially among close relations, to meet the needs brought on by the crisis (Hogan & Spencer, 1993). Thus, the simple question of whether network size increases, decreases, or remains the same with age appears to have a complex answer. Available evidence suggests that network size remains the same until advanced old age. However, networks may appear to increase in size as the existing, though perhaps dormant, network is activated under certain specialized "crisis" conditions.

B. Gender

Perhaps the most complex and controversial issue in the study of social relations is the study of gender differences. It has been widely recognized that men and women have social relations with the same people (e.g., spouse, children, other family and friends), but the nature of these relationships is quite different (Antonucci, 1994; Troll, 1994). It has been assumed that women are benefited by their relationships because they are more intimate, of higher quality, and are generally more intense. These facts are still assumed to be true, but more recent research has begun to question the benefits of these differences. Although women's relationships do seem to be more intimate, this also translates to a much greater, more in-depth sharing of problems and concerns. Relationships have been thought to be of higher quality among women, mainly because of the expression of greater closeness with larger numbers of people. However, evidence suggests that, in fact, women have both more positive and more negative relationships with others, often the same people (Antonucci, Akiyama, & Lansford, 1998; Canary, Cupach, & Messman; 1995; Fincham & Linfield, 1997; Levitt, Silver, & Franco, 1996; Rook, 1992). Thus, women are more likely to feel strong, positive feelings of affection towards their spouse, children, family, and friends, but they are also more likely to report higher levels of conflict, disagreement, and frustration with these same relationships. With respect to the intensity of their relationships, men and women may both express concern about the problems and crises faced by their close relationships, but women are more likely to feel responsible for and try to solve the problems of their network members, whereas men, although wishing them well, do not feel personally responsible.

Women's networks were once described as linked to spouse, family, and friends, whereas men's networks were linked to spouse who in turn linked them to family and friends. Some thought this disadvantaged men because it distanced them from close relationships.

However, it now appears that, under normal circumstances, this style of network relationship may be advantageous, because men are not fundamentally affected by the problems and concerns of others. As women have been shown to reflect this concern through lower levels of happiness and higher levels of depressive symptomatology (Antonucci et al., 1998; Connidis, 2001; Rook, 1992), one might conclude that being linked more distally to one's social network can be an advantage (Wellman & Worley, 1990). Although this may be true, other work indicates that men can be disadvantaged by their lack of a support network, especially if their link to that network, namely their wife, is unavailable (Connidis, in press; Rubenstein, 1986). A study of older married couples also provides some insight into the gender differences evident in social relations. One study found that while the wife's view of exchanges and reciprocity within the martial relationship directly predicted her marital and overall well-being, the husband's view of these same relationship characteristics was not significantly related to either his marital or overall well-being (Acitelli & Antonucci, 1991). Walen and Lachman (2000) also found that among middle-aged women, family strain was more often predictive of well-being for women than men, but that friends and family were also more likely to serve a buffering role for women than men. A recent study of gender differences in social relationships analyzed differences among the elderly by age. This study replicated many of the gender differences just reported with the younger portions of their sample, but found that these differences disappeared among people over 70 years of age (Tucker, Schwartz, Clark, & Friedman, 1999). It may be that at the later stages of the life course, as the number of people in one's network declines, the kinds of gender differences that were evident at younger ages no longer apply.

The increasing labor participation among women might be thought to have important implications for their social relations. Thus far, our data suggest that women at midlife do not have fewer people in their networks. It appears that they maintain the same, if not more (adding on co-workers), relationships, but have less time to spend with them (Antonucci, Akiyama, & Merline, 2001). One might speculate on both the positive and negative implications of these changes. On the one hand, women have less time to invest in other people's problems but, on the other, they may also have less time to garner support from their network members. Current research on the effects of multiple roles on women suggests that these multiple roles may lead to more stress, but they also lead to more potential sources of satisfaction (Crosby, 1993).

One additional body of literature is relevant to the exploration of gender differences in social relations, that is, the literature on social relations and mortality. Interestingly, in light of the gender differences just examined, several studies show a protective effect from social relations for men, but not women (House et al., 1982; Schoenbach, Kaplan, Fredman, & Kleinbaum, 1986). For this reason, Shye, Mullooly, Freeborn, and Pope (1995) have argued that the association between social relationships and mortality is male gender-specific, but little is known about the nature of this specificity. One might speculate that the benefits of social relations can be offset for women by their overinvestment in the problems and concerns of their network members. In sum, although men and women have close social relations with the same people, the nature, content and effect of these relationships appear to differ by gender.

C. Race, Ethnicity, and Culture

Renewed attention has been given to recognizing the importance of understanding and defining race, ethnicity, and culture (Brown, Sellers, Brown, & Jackson, 1999). With this recognition comes the crucial next step of understanding when there are racial, ethnic, and cultural universals in social relations and when there are unique differences. Improved quality and type of available data now provide a basic framework within which to understand racial and ethnic similarities and differences in support relationships (Dilworth-Anderson & Burton, 1999; Dilworth-Anderson, Williams, & Cooper, 1999; Dressel, Minkler, & Yen, 1997; Jackson, 1991; Jackson, Chatters, & Tayor, 1993; Pugliesi & Shook, 1998; Roschelle, 1997; Taylor, Jackson, & Chatters, 1997). For example, Wenger (1997), in her review of social relations in several European countries, has demonstrated that there appear to be fundamental characteristics of social relationships that transcend national boundaries. Thus, she notes that most support networks consist of close family members. However, different groups seem to have different customs and sometimes different characteristics, which influence support relationships. The following examples illustrate this point.

Social relations, in particular social networks and social support, have served important adaptive strategies among ethnic minorities (Harrison, Wilson, Pine, & Chan 1990; Jackson, 1991, 1993). For example, the roles of family, friends, and the church as support providers are especially important among the African-American community (Levin, Taylor, & Chatters, 1994; Taylor & Chatters, 1986; Taylor, Chatters, Tucker, & Lewis, 1990; Wilkinson, 1993). Barker, Morrow, and Mittness (1998) studied elderly urban African Americans and found that women had larger networks consisting primarily of friends and children, while male networks consisted primarily of spouses, kin, and friends. Married men had relatively close contact with their children, but men who were not married or who remarried had much less contact with them.

Taylor, Hardison, and Chatters (1999) reviewed the literature on kin and nonkin as sources of help among African Americans, concluding that both are crucial and major sources of informal assistance for African Americans. However, they also note that, with the quality of data now available, it is possible to further specify the circumstances leading to support seeking from family versus nonfamily. According to Taylor et al. (1996), being married is the most influential circumstance likely to increase the probability that help will be sought from family in times of trouble. This is true for whites as well, but the fact that African Americans are more likely than whites to be never married, separated, divorced, or widowed suggests that fewer African Americans will have this source of support available to them.

Ajrouch, Antonucci, and Janevic (2000) examined a representative sample of the Detroit metropolitan area and found that African Americans, when compared to whites, have smaller networks that consist of more family, with whom they have more contact. African Americans and whites were similar with regard to proximity of network members. These findings are consistent with those of Cantor, Brennan, and Sainz (1994), George (1988) and Kim and McHenry (1998). Ajrouch et al., (in press) also addressed the question raised by Ferraro and Farmer (1996) concerning the relative effects of age and race on social relations. Age was more predictive than race of differences in social networks, with older people having smaller, less frequently seen, and less proximal networks with a higher proportion of family. Furthermore, race differences were moderated by age, in that differences between whites and African Americans in frequency of contact and proportion of kin disappeared in the older age categories. Silverstein and Waite (1993) found it impossible to establish whether support given and received differed by age or race. Their analyses indicate that support exchange is predicted not only by age and race but also by specific life circumstances.

Other racial and ethnic groups within the United States also show distinctive patterns of social relations. Dense and supportive networks of nuclear and extended family often found among Hispanics have been noted as critical in the lives of elder Hispanics (Vega, 1990). Tsai and Lopez (1998), studying Chinese immigrants in the United States, found that children were the primary support providers of the elderly, followed by friends and family. In the United States, in general, the daughter is often the most significant support provider and caregiver for older parents. However, in Japan, daughters-in-law are more likely to provide support than daughters, because the traditional living arrangements in Japan require the daughter-in-law to live with her husband in his parents' house.

Wenger (1997) reviewed the available empirical evidence for Western Europe concerning social networks and support relationships of the elderly. She concludes that there are a great many similarities in both size and composition of social networks. Most people have networks that average about three to seven members, with the closest members being spouse, children, other family members, and friends. These figures agree with House and Kahn's (1985) conclusion that the essential composition of a support network could be captured with the documentation of five network members. Data from Asian countries, such as Japan and China, agree with these findings. Very few data are yet available from Africa and South America.

In one unique study, Kim and McKenry (1998) examined four different ethnic groups in the United States and suggested that, in some circumstances, it may be socioeconomic status (SES) rather than ethnicity that shapes social relations. Comparing the social networks of African Americans, Asian Americans, Caucasian Americans, and Hispanic Americans, these authors found far more similarities than differences once education was controlled. They note that increased education is likely associated with greater financial resources and greater independence, which may explain the decreased reliance on family seen in higher SES groups. With limited resources, elders in all ethnic groups turn to family, especially children, for support. Once more resources are available, other family members and nonkin may also be called upon in times of crisis. This was most evident among Caucasians in Kim and McKenry's study, but it was equally true for those in the other ethnic groups who were at the same education levels.

D. Socioeconomic Status

It has been known for quite some time (e.g., Gurin, Veroff, & Feld, 1960) that social networks and social support differ by SES. To put it succinctly, people at lower SES levels have smaller networks, which tend to be sex segregated and to consist mainly of family members (Antonucci, Ajrouch, & Janevic, 1999). They exchange support with fewer people and are often, though not always, less satisfied with the support they do receive. Generally speaking, social relations are more strained among people at the lower end of the SES continuum (i.e. among people with lower levels of education, income, or occupational status). Specific SES factors affecting social relations, such as financial strain, have been identified in current research (e.g., Krause, 1999).

Recently there has been renewed interest on the part of government agencies and social science researchers in the ef-

fects of examining social inequalities on both physical and mental health. This renewed interest can benefit from our increased knowledge of the complexity of social relations and socioeconomic indicators. Greater sophistication with respect to SES measurement is especially helpful. Assessment of SES has generally included multiple factors that focus on personal characteristics, most notably education, occupation, and income (Kaplan & Keil, 1993; Liberatos, Link, & Kelsey, 1988). These indicators are often assumed to offer consistent information. However, recent literature indicates that problems exist both in the definition and assessment of these contributing factors and in the assumption of consistency (Anderson & Armstead, 1995; Williams, 1990). Berkman (1988) notes that assessing SES among the elderly can be particularly problematic for a number of reasons. First, current income may not indicate their overall standard of living. Second, educational achievement early in the century was not related as linearly to occupational achievement as it is today. Finally, job title among people now retired may not give an accurate picture of the actual occupational status of that position, given the rapidly evolving industrial world through which the current elderly have lived.

In light of these issues, researchers have recently examined the question of SES and social relations in much greater detail, resulting in more careful analyses of these associations. Ross and Mirowsky (1989), for example, found that education, a common measure of SES, was positively related to support, but another common indicator of SES, family income, was completely unrelated. Ensel (1986) demonstrated that although relationships among people of lower SES may be of lesser quality than those of higher SES overall, no such SES differences are evident in the appraisal of close relationships. Antonucci et al. (2000) found that low-SES men who have an adult child on whom they can rely are as healthy as high-SES men, but low SES men who cannot rely on an adult child are significantly less healthy. One interpretation of this finding is that the key to the SES–health link for low-SES men may be close family ties. These ties are associated with less loneliness, better self-care, better immunological functioning, and consequently better health. Finally, a recent meta-analysis (Pinquart & Sorensen, 2000) documents differences in specific SES measures with respect to their association with social relations variables and feelings of competence, strongly supporting the need for a detailed examination of the associations among these variables. Thus, it appears that sweeping generalizations concerning the association of social relations and SES are inappropriate. Greater specificity is required to accurately document and understand this association across all ages, but especially among the elderly.

As the link between SES and mortality has been demonstrated repeatedly (e.g., Kaplan, Pamuk, Lynch, Cohen, & Balfour, 1996; Pappas, Queen, & Hadden, 1993), links between an individual's social relationships and mortality have also been documented (Berkman & Syme, 1979; Blazer, 1982; Shye et al., 1995; Yasuda et al., 1997; House et al., 1982; Orth-Gomer & Johnson, 1987; Sugisawa, Liang, & Liu, 1994). Despite evidence that the meaning and impact of social relations are likely to vary across socioeconomic strata, there has been little previous work linking SES, social relations, and mortality. There is reason to think that these links might be significant; for example, indirect mechanisms linking social relations and health—such as facilitating access to medical care—may operate differently among people of lower SES (Berkman, 1985). It is, therefore, important to explore how social relations and SES interact in their effects on mortality.

There have been some inconsistencies in the findings regarding social relations and mortality. These inconsistencies may be due to heterogeneity of measures across studies and differences in study populations (Seeman et al., 1993) or to lack of measurement specificity. Most studies have used measures of network structure and only a few have measured social support variables (Hanson, Isacsson, Janzon, & Lindell, 1990; Ho, 1991; Kaplan et al., 1994). The links between network structure and mortality may be heavily influenced by support quality. Although only a small fraction of studies have included quality of social relations measures (Antonucci et al., 1997; Blazer, 1982; George et al., 1989; Hanson et al., 1990; Kaplan et al., 1994; Oxman et al., 1992), the results consistently indicate that support quality is a critical factor influencing morbidity and mortality outcomes. Thus, when exploring how the association between social relationships and mortality may vary by SES, greater specificity may be necessary. A potentially profitable line of recent research is the examination of the mediating and moderating effects of support, specifically support quality, on the SES–health relationship (e.g., Krause, 1997b; Lachman & Weaver, 1998a,b).

In sum, there are both similarities and differences in social relations as a function of sociodemographic characteristics, such as age, gender, race, ethnicity, and culture, and SES. Such group level variables are generally of lesser interest to psychologists than to sociologists or epidemiologists who aim to identify aggregate, societal level distributions across the variables of interest. These particular sociodemographic variables of age, gender, and race, ethnicity, and culture, however, are of special interest to psychologists in the study of social relations for descriptive purposes and because they provide important insights into how membership in these groups influences an individual's social relations experiences. The specific characteristics of the social relations experienced by people who are members of different sociodemographic groups may provide meaningful information about that person's psychological development. Thus, in addition to knowing that low SES compromises one's health, we now know that it also strains both the formation and existence of social relations. What is most exciting about linking these two bodies of research is that it enables us to demonstrate that some aspects of the negative link between low SES and health can be offset by social relations (Antonucci et al., 2000).

Examination of age, gender, SES, and race, ethnicity, and culture differences in social relations helps us to understand the complexities of social relations and their association with other characteristics. Variations in social relations associated with age represent the accumulating events and interpersonal experiences of social relations over time and by proxy give us some idea of how these have effected the individual. Age similarities in network size provide normative information, while age changes highlight potential vulnerabilities. So too with gender. Of interest to the psychologist is not simply that men and women differ in their social relations, but that men and women differ in how these social relations have been experienced and are interpreted. We learn that men and women have close relationships with the same people, but the intimacy of those relationships varies considerably with gender, as does the effects of those relationships on the individual. Whereas women have multiple close relationships of great intimacy and high quality, they are not necessarily advantaged by these relationships. The psychological impact of these relations can be beneficial in helping to cope with a problem, but can also be disadvantageous when women feel responsible for resolving the problems their close network

members face. On the other hand, husbands, while having the same general network composition as their wives, are neither as burdened by these relationships nor as benefited by them especially when the closest relationship, that of spouse, is unavailable. These findings have important implications for how to interpret social interactions and how to understand their impact on the well-being of the elderly.

As we examine race, ethnicity, and culture, we gain a fuller understanding of how the context and expectations of membership in these groups increase similarities across groups or distinguish members of one group from another, and how these factors enhance or diminish personal well-being. It is not so much skin color or country of origin that is of interest, but the fact that group membership is associated with specific advantages, disadvantages, expectations, and dependencies that may fundamentally influence the individual's experience and interpretation of social relations. And finally, SES is of interest because it helps us to understand how social relations are experienced differently by people of lower (or higher) education or income levels.

I turn now to a consideration of social support variables. Again, because of space limitations, I have chosen four illustrative examples: source of support, support quality, reciprocity, and perceived versus received support.

E. Source of Support

One area of inquiry that has provided some interesting information about social support is empirical evidence about who provides support to whom. Potential providers typically include spouse, children, siblings, extended family, and friends. Perhaps the most information available is about spousal support and, indeed, spouses do seem to be the preferred support provider. Both men and women feel more comfortable with support from their spouse and are most likely to report that their spouse provides both instrumental and emotional support (Cantor, 1979; Cantor et al., 1994). However, with age, the probability of being married decreases considerably, especially among women and some minority groups. Under these circumstances, older people often turn to their children, especially for instrumental, but also for emotional support (Fingerman, & Birditt, in press).

Research indicates that both the parent and adult child generally assume that the child will provide support to the parent as needed, but the actual exchange of needed support is sometimes accompanied by hostility and resentment (e.g., Murphy et al., 1997) or, at the very least, ambivalence (Luescher & Pillemer, 1998). Parent–child relationships can be both a source of support and a source of conflict (Suitor, Pillemer, Keeton, & Robinson, 1996). The parent–child relationship is lifetime in nature. Although most children readily provide support to their parents, relationships with parents are influenced by the child's lifetime of interactions with them. Parent–child pairs that have always been conflictual are not likely to become suddenly harmonious when the parent becomes old (e.g., Parrot & Bengtson, 1999; Suitor & Pillemer, 1991). In fact, the elder abuse literature suggests that elder abuse is often a continuation of a lifetime of conflict, sometimes beginning with child abuse.

Not to be ignored when considering the child as a source of support is the fact that parents and their children are simply not peers. No matter how good the relationship has been, there is still a generational divide. Thus, the status differential is likely to contribute some awkwardness to the relationship. Siblings and friends represent peer relationships and often occupy a special role for this reason. An increasing amount of research has focused on siblings in late life (Bedford,

1995; Campbell, Connidis, & Davies, 1999; Cicirelli, 1991; Connidis, 2001; Gold, 1987). Siblings provide important emotional support in late life, and they often step in as providers of instrumental support, especially among the never married. Several researchers have focused on the single and never married in late life, and have noted that these people have also developed networks of friends and other more extended relations who are critical support providers (Barrett, 1999). Friends in general have been shown to have a unique and important role in the lives of older people (e.g., Adams & Blieszner, 1994). These are peer, nonobligatory relationships, and they provide individuals at all ages, but particularly, the elderly, with a special type of positive feedback and mutual appreciation (O'Connor; 1995; Lansford, 2000).

F. Quality of Support

The perceived quality of support relationship has been shown to contribute to the health and well-being of the individual, over and above what might be expected based on the objective data. People clearly interpret relationships and perceive them as supportive, satisfactory, and adequate, or as nonsupportive, unsatisfactory, and inadequate. Positive aspects of support relationships appear to provide a sense of security that makes individuals feel positive about themselves and their world. People who feel more supported cope better with illness, stress, and other difficult life experiences. On the other hand, data are accumulating that suggest that some supportive relationships can have a negative effect either because they provide negative feedback or because they support negative behaviors (Rook, 1992). Relationship quality has both psychological effects, affecting, for example, levels of depression, happiness, and perceived quality of life (Antonucci et al., 1997; Hall & Nelson, 1996; Oxman, et al.,

1992; Russell & Cutrona, 1991) and physical effects, in that relationship quality is associated with frequency of illness, mortality, and immunological functioning (Fratiglioni et al., 2000; House, Landis, & Umberson, 1988; Uchino, Cacioppo, & Kiecolt-Glaser, 1996).

G. Support Reciprocity

Support exchanges are perceived as either reciprocal or nonreciprocal. Because reciprocity has classically been considered the norm of social relationships (Gouldner, 1960), it is useful to consider how people assess the reciprocity of their relationships. Interestingly, this norm has recently been reconsidered. Uehara (1995) essentially verifies the norm and notes that the bulk of the empirical evidence suggests that people prefer to underbenefit rather than overbenefit when relations are nonreciprocal. Smith and Goodnow (1999) found that people of all ages disliked receiving unsolicited support. They suggest that people interpret unsolicited support as implying incompetence.

As one gets older, it is often the case that one requires more support, both emotionally and instrumentally, to cope with the challenges of life. Older people may then come to perceive their relationships as nonreciprocal and feel that they are overbenefited (i.e., receive more support than they provide) in these exchanges. Levitt, Guacci-Franco, and Weber (1992), for example, found that older women perceive themselves to be overbenefited with respect to support exchanges with their middle-age daughters. There is then the danger that this perception of greater benefit would lead to a sense of indebtedness. However, many people are quite resourceful about maintaining relationship equity by using what has been termed a *support bank* (Antonucci, 1985) accounting system. Older people have been known to consider support provided by them to others earlier in life as contributions to a support bank from which they can make withdrawals, as needed, later in life. They may view their earlier provision of support as support loans that are in a sense being repaid at this later date. This interpretation of support exchanges can be especially useful for understanding how some older people cope with crises by accepting considerable support from others, without the disadvantage of feeling overly indebted by the receipt of more aid than they are currently able to reciprocate. Also interesting is the phenomenon whereby the older person recalibrates support received of one type to equal support provided of another type. Thus, a drive to the doctor's office can be completely reciprocated by a freshly baked pan of rolls. Some might argue that the ability to cognitively construct an equitable exchange is not necessarily a reality assessment, but rather an exercise in adaptive illusions (Taylor, Kemeny, Reed, Bower, & Gruenewald, 2000). It is important to address not only the relationship between reciprocity and well-being, but also what makes some people evaluate their relationships as reciprocal while others evaluate the exact same relationships as nonreciprocal.

H. Perceived and Received Support

The final question to be considered here is related to perceived versus received support. The psychological nature of social relations is highlighted, as perceived support and received support are rarely synonymous. Fortunately, an impressive body of literature has been accumulating. Wallsten, Tweed, Blazer, and George (1999) found that older people who positively appraised their network were less depressed than people who appraised their network less positively. Especially interesting was the finding that although social support mitigates the depressive effect of disability when the network's efforts are appraised positively, this was not true for instrumental support. Wallsten et al. conclude that, "One's perception of the network's helpfulness appears to be more potent than the actual help provided by friends and family" (p. 145). Recent studies by Ikkink and colleagues (Ikkink & van Tilburg, 1998; Ikkink, van Tilburg, & Knipscheer, 1999) explored the perspective of the parent and child in the receipt of support by the elderly parents. Reports were only moderately correlated, with parents reporting that they receive less than the children report providing. Lynch et al. (1999) examined the actual network structure and perceived support of depressed patients. Among older adult patients, pessimistic thinking was associated with lower perceived social support. In fact, pessimistic thinking was a better predictor of lower perceived support than actual received instrumental support.

Krause (1997a) makes the distinction between received and anticipated support. In a prospective study of older people, he found that anticipated support was associated with reduced mortality, but received support was associated with increased mortality. These findings vary by SES, with upper SES elderly showing greater benefits from anticipated support. A study of midlife men and women by Dras, Williams, Kaplan, and Siegler (1996), consistent with earlier reported gender differences, found that women perceived greater availability of support than men, but they also provided more support than men. They report that self-esteem was the best predictor of perceived support, again suggesting that there is a critical psychological element to the perception of support. In an interesting laboratory study with a related finding, Ross, Lutz, and Lakey (1999) found that those with higher levels of perceived support hypothesized that ineffective support was caused by temporary or unstable factors, whereas those with lower levels of perceived support attributed ineffective support to more stable,

internal, and global factors. Unfortunately, this study included only younger participants, but the findings suggest that differential attributions are associated with variations in support perceptions. There are clearly current and past or predisposing psychological factors that influence whether or not an individual perceives their support network as supportive. Cross-cultural research further illustrates this point. A recent study (van Tilburg, Gierveld, Lecchini, & Marsiglia, 1998) comparing older people in the Netherlands, who often live alone, with older people in Italy who most often live with their children, found the Italians reporting less social integration and more loneliness than the Dutch. These findings serve to underscore that social relations are fundamentally influenced by the cognitive interpretation applied to those relationships. Objective support networks affect well-being only in so far as they are subjectively interpreted. Actual support is predictive of outcomes only to the degree that support is perceived to be present. The fact that perceived support, in turn, is significantly predictive of health and well-being both implicates the role of social cognition and has important implications for prevention or intervention work with the elderly.

I. Sense of Control

Researchers have begun to search for theoretical frameworks to explain how social support positively effects health and well-being (Rook, 1995). They have suggested that a critical next step in the field is to begin to understand the processes and mechanisms through which social support affects health (Cohen, 1988; Krause, Liang, & Keith, 1990; Pearlin, 1985). It is here that the rapidly developing field of social cognition (Hess & Blanchard-Fields, 1999), in particular, research on the individual's sense of control, shows particular promise. The descriptive phase of social relations research has now given way to the next stage, where more sophisticated investigations have revealed associations among variables previously thought to be unimportant or unrelated, and documented a lack of or limited associations among variables formerly assumed to be highly related. Findings that women are more affected by relationships than men in the same relationships, or that subjective support is more highly related to health and well-being than objective support, are examples that serve as a reminder that we must reinsert psychology into the study of social relations. Fundamentally, relationships reflect not only objective interactions among equal entities, but also interactions among individuals who have prior, current and future views of their social relationships. These views influence how their relationships are experienced and what their effects will be.

Several models, building upon the established literatures of social control, self-efficacy and mastery, have been proposed in the literature. These are often presented as separate constructs, but there is considerable overlap among them (Gecas, 1989; Ross & Sastry, 1999). In the seventies (Rodin & Langer, 1977; Rodin, 1976; Schulz, 1976) and eighties (Baltes & Baltes, 1986; Lachman, 1985), researchers documented the positive role of control on the health and survival of older people. Though Rook, Thuras, and Lewis (1990) did not find a positive effect of social control on health behaviors among older people, Lachman (1985; Lackman & Weaver, 1998b) has documented differential and significant patterns of social versus other types of control in relation to health. Oxman, Freeman, and Manheimer (1995) suggested that social support can stimulate feelings of control and self-efficacy. McAvay, Seeman, and Rodin (1996) found that greater interpersonal efficacy is related to more frequent emotional and instrumen-

tal support, but that over time low instrumental support was related to a reduction in activities of daily living.

Self-efficacy, especially as influenced by a supportive spouse, is positively associated with recovery from myocardial infarction (Bandura, 1997; Taylor, Bandura, Ewart, Miller, & DeBusk, 1985). Mutran et al. (1995) also report that support from husband was associated with better recovery by the wife from surgery. Bisconti and Bergeman (1999) examined perceived control as a mediator of the relationships among social support, well-being, and health. Interestingly, their data indicate that control mediates the support–health association, but support does not mediate the control–health association. But there can be a negative side. If there is more support than really needed, especially instrumental support, the individual is likely to experience a reduction in efficacy and well-being. Newsom and Schulz (1998) found that too much help provided by a caregiver in a long-term caregiving situation was perceived negatively and effectively reduced the self-esteem and perceived control of the care recipient. Overall, current findings suggest that self-efficacy may be a mechanism through which social support affects health.

Antonucci and Jackson (1987) have proposed a support–efficacy model that directly incorporates self-efficacy as the cognitive mechanism through which social relations affect health and well-being. The model suggests how social support can have such wide reaching and seemingly unrelated effects on an individual. Specifically, it is the cumulative expression of support by one or several individuals to another that communicate to the target person that he or she is an able, worthy, and capable person—or perhaps in the case of an elderly person, continues to be an able, worthy, and capable person. Assuming that the support recipient perceives the support provided as accurate and altruistically motivated, the support recipient will come to internalize this belief in self-worth and competence that is being communicated by the supportive other. Thus, with multiple and accumulating exchanges of this type, the supported person develops a belief in his or her own ability that, under optimal conditions, will enable that person to face and succeed in the multiple goals and challenges one confronts throughout life. Consistent with this model of support and efficiency, Lang, Featherman, and Nesselroade (1997) found that people who felt supported, as measured by perceived support availability, had higher levels of self-efficacy than those who did not. Krause (1997b) also finds considerable support in the literature concerning a reciprocal association between social support and personal control, consistent with the support–efficacy model.

Unfortunately, as noted earlier, not all people receive support from those who surround them, and not all support is positive (Rook, 1992). Thus, some people, instead of being told that they are competent, capable and worthy, may instead be led to believe that they are incompetent, incapable and unworthy. Just as the cumulative effect of positive exchanges can have an ameliorative effect on an individual's health and well-being, so, too, can the opposite have a devastating and cumulative negative effect on health and well-being (Antonucci, 1994). Research is now available that demonstrates, at the psychoimmunological level, that people who are lonely or have more hostile interactions with others are much more likely to become ill, to develop heart disease, and to take longer to recover once they develop a health problem (Uchino et al., 1996). Recognition should also be given to the fact that some support networks can have a negative effect by supporting or encouraging behaviors that are detrimental to one's health and well-being. Drug buddies, drinking buddies, eating buddies, and buddies who discourage exercise are all examples. These are people who help or "support" behaviors that simply are not health-promoting.

In sum, individuals believe they can solve a problem and successfully meet life's challenges only because they have come to interpret and internalize supportive others' communications to them that they are able and competent to control their destiny and solve their problems. Perhaps most impressive is the degree to which the experience and interpretation of social relations have now been shown to effect psychoimmunological functioning. How you feel about others and how you think others feel about you affects not only how you feel about yourself and your abilities, morbidity, and mortality, but also how well your immunological systems operates. The effect of social relations is pervasive. It is critical that we reach a better understanding of the processes and mechanisms through which these influences occur.

V. Future Directions

In addition to achieving a better understanding of the fundamental processes and mechanisms that underlie social relations, the next important challenge in this area of research is to find ways to incorporate what we know about social relations into prevention and intervention programs targeted at improving the physical and mental health of the elderly. The research reviewed here strongly suggests that these programs can profitably focus on social networks, social support, and sense of control. Several exciting research endeavors have now impressively demonstrated that social relations interventions can be practically introduced in a manner that will improve the health and well-being of the elderly. A few examples of such pioneering research have been reported in the literature and are briefly summarized below.

Stevens and van Tilburg (2000) recently conducted a successful pilot intervention, which was designed to increase the number of friendships among lonely older women. This intervention effectively increased the size of the social networks of the women in the intervention program. Stevens and van Tilburg developed a friendship course that involved several sessions, including educational and homework activities, role playing, and tips on developing and maintaining friendships. The women who participated in the friendship course, compared to those in the control group, expressed less loneliness and developed new friendships thus increasing the number of people in their social networks. An interesting intervention by Harris, Brown, and Robinson (1999) involved the provision of support through friendship. A community sample of chronically depressed women were matched with briefly trained community volunteers who met with them weekly for 1 year. Seventy-six percent of the chronically depressed women in the befriended group remained in remission, compared to 38% who saw a volunteer only once, and 63% who participated in only 2 to 6 months of the year-long program. This is an impressive, community-based intervention providing chronically depressed women with social support from nonprofessional volunteers.

Szendre and Jose (1996) developed a program that targeted the provision of telephone support by older community residents to inner city adolescents. Adolescents were invited to call "grandparents" to discuss any matter of interest to them, either positive or negative. Although the program only targeted adolescents, the effect of the intervention was, in fact, reciprocal. Both the older grandparent and younger adolescent participants in this intervention reported increased well-being and life satisfaction.

The adolescents enjoyed and benefited from having an adult take special interest in them, while the older people enjoyed being able to provide support and having a positive impact on the teenager.

As the literature reviewed in this chapter indicates, support programs need to be developed that are sensitive to individual differences, help an individual maintain their sense of control, and do not encourage or induce dependence. In their study of intergenerational support, Silverstein, Chen, and Heller (1996) found that support from children was psychologically beneficial up to a point, after which it had the opposite affect of increasing dependence and reducing well-being. Among their most intriguing findings is the fact that overbenefiting was psychologically more harmful than underbenefiting. Recall van Tilburg et al.'s (1998) finding, which indicated that despite the apparent objective occurrence of support as indicated by the Italians living with their children, it was the Dutch elders living independently who felt more love and concern from their families. The perception of support, at least in the van Tilburg study, was not related to what might be considered the objective receipt of support suggested by co-residence. These last two studies, though not intervention studies, clearly suggest how intervention programs must be designed.

An important target of intervention is the caregiving relationship. Newsom and Schultz's study (1998) document another situation where too much support has a negative effect. They report that if the caregiver provided too much support, the result was a reduction in self-esteem and loss of control in the care recipient. Another type of intervention, which directly targeted the caregivers of patients with Alzheimer's disease, was more successful. Mittelman et al. (1995) provided a comprehensive support intervention program for caregivers of Alzheimer's disease patients. Over the course of a year the level of depressive symptomatology remained stable for the supported caregivers, whereas the control caregivers became increasingly more depressed. In this case the support intervention positively effected the well-being of the caregiver. Since caregiving well-being is known to directly affect the status and well-being of the care recipient, the positive effects of this intervention are twofold. These almost opposite findings clearly demonstrate that caution is needed in the design and execution of intervention programs.

Social relations are most beneficial when they instill in the individual a feeling of being valued and competent, of being worthy and capable. As noted above, we are just beginning to understand how this happens. Controlled intervention research would expand our knowledge regarding the extent to which support enhances a sense of control and whether enhanced control in turn promotes psychological and physical health. In general, the potential of carefully designed intervention and prevention programs can serve a very important function in optimizing the ability of older people to successfully meet the challenges of age.

References

Acitelli, L. K., Antonucci, T. C. (1994). Gender differences in the link between marital support and satisfaction in older couples. *Journal of Personality and Social Psychology, 67*, 688–698.

Adams, R. G., & Blieszner, R. (1994). An integrative conceptual framework for friendship research. *Journal of Social and Personal Relationships, 11*, 163–184.

Ajrouch, K. J., Antonucci, T. C., & Janevic, M. R. (2001). Social networks among blacks and whites: The interaction between race and age. *Journal of Gerontology: Social Sciences, 56B*, 5112–118.

Anderson, N. B., & Armstead, C. A. (1995). Toward understanding the association of socioeconomic status and health: A new challenge for the biophysical approach. *Psychosomatic Medicine, 57*, 213–225.

Antonucci, T. C. (1985). Personal characteristics, social support, and social behavior. In R. H. Binstock & E. Shanas (Eds.), *Handbook of aging and the social sciences* (pp. 94–128). New York: Van Nostrand Reinhold.

Antonucci, T. C. (1990). Social supports and social relationships. In R. H. Binstock & L. K. George (Eds.), *The handbook of aging and the social sciences* (3rd ed.) (pp. 205–226). San Diego, CA: Academic Press.

Antonucci, T. C. (1994). A life-span view of women's social relations. In B. F. Turner & L. E. Troll (Eds.), *Women growing older: Psychological perspectives* (pp. 239–269). Thousand Oaks, CA: Sage Publications.

Antonucci, T. C., Ajrouch, K. J., & Janevic, M. R. (1999). Socioeconomic status, social support, age and health. In N. E. Adlar, M. Marmat, B. S. McEwen & J. Stewart (Eds.) *Socioeconomic status and Health in Industrial Nations* New York: New York academy of Sciences.

Antonucci, T. C., & Akiyama, H. (1987) Social networks in adult life and a preliminary examination of the convoy model. *Journal of Gerontology, 42*, 519–527.

Antonucci, T. C., & Akiyama, H. (1991). Convoys of social support: Generational issues. *Marriage and Family Review, 16*, 103–124.

Antonucci, T. C., & Akiyama, H. (1995). Convoys of social relations: Family and friendships within a life span context. In R. Blieszner & V. H. Bedford (Eds.), *Handbook of aging and the family* (pp. 355–372). Westport, CT: Greenwood Press.

Antonucci, T. C., Akiyama, H., & Lansford, J. E. (1998). The negative effects of close social relations among older adults. *Family Relations, 47*, 379–384.

Antonucci, T. C., Akiyama, H., & Merline, A. (2001). Dynamics of social relationships in midlife. In M. Lachman (Ed.), *Handbook of midlife development* New York: John Wiley & Sons.

Antonucci, T. C., Fuhrer, R., & Dartigues, J. F. (1997). Social relations and depressive symptomatology in a sample of community-dwelling French older adults. *Psychology and Aging, 12*, 189–195.

Antonucci, T. C., & Jackson, J. S. (1987). Social support, interpersonal efficacy and health. In L. L. Carstensen, & B. A. Edelstein (Eds.), *Handbook of clinical gerontology*, 291–311.

Antonucci, T. C., Lansford, J. E., Schaberg, L., Smith, J., Akiyama, H., Takahashi, K., Fuhrer, R., & Dartigues, J. F. (in press). *Widowhood, financial strain, and illness: A comparison of social network characteristics in France, Germany, Japan, and the United States. Psychology and Aging*.

Baltes, P. B., & Baltes, M. M. (Eds.). (1986). *The psychology of control and aging*. Hillsdale: Erlbaum.

Baltes, P., & Mayer K. (Eds.). (1999). *The Berlin Aging Study: Aging from 70 to 100*. New York: Cambridge University Press.

Bandura, A. (Ed.). (1997). *Self-efficacy: The exercise of control*. New York: W. H. Freeman.

Barker, J. C., Morrow, J., & Mittness, L. S. (1998). Gender, informal social support networks, and elderly urban African Americans. *Journal of Aging Studies, 12*, 199–222.

Barrera, M. (1986). Distinctions between social support concepts, measures, and models. *American Journal of Community Psychology, 14*, 413–455.

Barrett, A. E. (1999). Social support and life satisfaction among the never married. *Research on Aging, 21*, 46–72.

Bedford, V. H. (1995). Sibling relationships in middle and old age. In R. Blieszner & V. H. Bedford (Eds.), *Handbook of aging and the family* (pp. 201–222). Westport, CT: Greenwood Press.

Bengtson, V. L., & Schaie, K. W. (Eds.). (1999). *Handbook of theories of aging*. New York: Springer Publishing Co.

Berkman, L. F. (1985). The relationship of social network and social support to morbidity and mortality. In S. Cohen & L. S. Syme (Eds.), *Social support and health* (pp. 241–262). New York: Academic Press.

Berkman, L. F. (1988). The changing and heterogeneous nature of aging and longevity: A social and biomedical perspective. *Annual Review of Gerontology and Geriatrics, 8*, 37–88.

Berkman, L. F., & Syme, S. L. (1979). Social networks, host resistance, and mortality: A nine-year follow-up study of Alameda County residents. *American Journal of Epidemiology, 109*, 186–204.

Birren, J. E., & Bengtson, V. L. (Eds.). (1988). *Emergent theories of aging*. New York: Springer.

Bisconti, T. L., & Bergeman, C. S. (1999). Perceived social control as a mediator of the relationships among social support, psychological well-being and perceived health. *The Gerontologist, 39*, 94–101.

Blazer, D. G. (1982). Social support and mortality in an elderly community population. *American Journal of Epidemiology, 115*, 684–694.

Bowling, A., & Grundy, E. (1998). The association between social networks and mortality in later life. *Reviews in Clinical Gerontology, 8*, 353–361.

Brown, T. N., Sellers, S. L., Brown, K. T., & Jackson, J. S. (1999). Race, ethnicity and culture in the sociology of mental health. In C. S. Aneshensel & J. C. Phelan (Eds.), *Handbook of the sociology of mental health* (pp. 167–182). New York: Kluwer Academic/Plenum Publishers.

Campbell, L. D., Connidis, I. A., & Davies, L. (1999). Sibling ties in later life: A social network analysis. *Journal of Family Issues, 20*, 114–148.

Canary D. J., Cupach, W. R., & Messman, S. J. (Eds.). (1995). *Relationship conflict: Conflict in parent–child, friendship, and romantic relationships*. Thousand Oaks: Sage Publications.

Cantor, M. H. (1979). Neighbors and friends: An overlooked resource in the informal support system. *Research on Aging, 1*, 434–463.

Cantor, M. H., Brennan, M., & Sainz, A. (1994). The importance of ethnicity in the social support systems of older New Yorkers: A longitudinal perspective (1970–1990). *Journal of Gerontological Social Work, 22*, 95–128.

Carstensen, L. L., Gross, J. J., & Fung, H. H. (1997). The social context of emotional experience. In K. W. Schaie & M. P. Lawton (Eds.), *Annual review of gerontology and geriatrics: Vol. 17. Focus on emotion and adult development* (pp. 325–352). New York: Springer.

Carstensen, L. L., Isaacowitz, D. M., & Charles, S. T. (1999). Taking time seriously: A theory of socioemotional selectivity. *American Psychologist, 54*, 165–181.

Cassel, J. (1976). The contribution of the social environment to host resistance. *American Journal of Epidemiology, 104*, 107–123.

Chappell, N. (Ed.). (1992). *Social support and aging.* Toronto: Butterworths Canada.

Chatters, L. M., Taylor, R. J., & Jayakody, R. (1994). Fictive kinship relations in black extended families. *Journal of Comparative Studies, 25*, 297–312.

Chen, X., & Silverstein, M. (2000). Intergenerational social support and the psychological well-being of older parents in China. *Research on Aging, 22*, 43–65.

Choi. N. G., & Wodarski, J. S. (1996). The relationship between social support and health status of elderly people: Does social support slow down physical and functional deterioration? *Social Work Research, 20*, 52–63.

Cicirelli, V. G. (1991). Sibling relationships in adulthood. *Marriage and Family Review, 16*, 291–310.

Cobb, S. (1976). Social support as a moderator of life stress. *Psychosomatic Medicine, 38*, 300–314.

Cohen, S. (1988). Psychosocial models of the role of social support in the etiology of physical disease. *Health Psychology, 7*, 269–297.

Cohen, S., Kessler, R. C., & Gordon, L. U. (Eds.). (1995). *Measuring stress: A guide for health and social scientists.* New York: Oxford University Press.

Connidis, I. A. (2001). *Family ties and aging.* Thousand Oaks, CA: Sage Publications.

Crosby, F. J. (1993). *Juggling: The unexpected advantages of balancing families.* New York: Free Press.

Dilworth-Anderson, P., & Burton, L. M. (1999). Critical issues in understanding family support and older minorities. In T. P. Miles (Ed.), *Full color aging* (pp. 93–106). Washington, DC: The Gerontological Society of America.

Dilworth-Anderson, P., Williams, S. W., & Cooper, T. (1999). Family caregiving to elderly African Americans: Caregiver types and structures. *Journal of Gerontology: Social Sciences, 54B*, S237–S241.

Dras, D., Williams, R. B., Kaplan, B. H., & Siegler, I. C. (1996). Correlates of perceived social support and equality of interpersonal relationships at mid-life. *International Journal of Aging and Human Development, 43*, 199–217

Dressel, P., Minkler, M., & Yen, G. (1997). Gender, race, class and aging: Advances and opportunities. *International Journal of Health Services, 27*, 579–600.

Due, P., Holstein, B., Lund, R., Modvig, J., & Avlund, K. (1999). Social relations: Network, support and relational strain. *Social Science and Medicine, 48*, 661–673.

Elder, G. H. (1998). The life course as developmental theory. *Child Development, 69*, 1–12.

Ensel, W. M. (1986). Social support and depressive symptomatology. In N. Lin, A. Dean, & W. Ensel (Eds.), *Social support, life events, and depression* (pp. 249–266). Orlando: Academic Press.

Faber, A. D., & Wasserman, S. (in press). Social support and social networks: Synthesis and review. In B. Levy & J. A. Pescosolido, (Eds.), *Social networks and health.*

Ferraro, K. F., & Farmer, M. M. (1996). Double jeopardy, aging as leveler, or persistent health inequality? A longitudinal analysis of white and black Americans. *Journal of Gerontology: Social Sciences, 51B*, S319–S328.

Fincham, F. D., & Linfield, K. J. (1997). A new look at marital quality: Can spouses feel positive and negative about their marriage? *Journal of Family Psychology, 11*, 489–502.

Fingerman, K. L. (1997). Aging mothers' and adult daughters retrospective ratings of conflict in their past relationships. *Current Psychology, 16*, 131–154.

Fingerman, K. L., & Birditt, K. S. (in press). Do age differences in close and problematic family networks reflect variation in living relatives? *Journal of Gerontology: Psychological Sciences.*

Fratiglioni, L., Wang, H., Ericsson, K., Maytan, M., & Winblad, B. (2000). Influence of social network on occurence of dementia: A community-based longitudinal study. *The Lancet, 355*, 1315–1319.

Gecas, V. (1989). The social psychology of self-efficacy. *Annual Review of Sociology, 15*, 291–316.

George, L. K. (1988). Social participation in later life: Black-white differences. In J. S. Jackson (Ed.), *The Black American elderly: Research on physical and psychosocial health* (pp. 99–126). New York: Springer.

George, L. K., Blazer, D. G., Hughes, D. C., & Fowler, N. (1989). Social support and the outcome of major depression. *British Journal of Psychiatry, 154,* 487–485.

Glass, T. A., Mendes De Leon, C. F., Seeman, T. A., & Berkman, L. F. (1997). Beyond single indicators. *Social Science and Medicine, 44,* 1503–1517.

Gold, D. T. (1987). Siblings in old age: Something special. *Canadian Journal on Aging, 6,* 199–215.

Gouldner, A. W. (1960). The norm of reciprocity: A preliminary statement. *American Sociological Review, 25,* 161–178.

Granovetter, M. S. (1973). The strength of weak ties. *American Journal of Sociology, 78,* 1360–1380.

Gurin, G., Veroff, J., & Feld, S. (Eds.). (1960). *Americans view their mental health: A nationwide interview survey.* New York: Basic Books.

Hall, G. B., & Nelson, G. (1996). Social networks, social support, personal empowerment, and the adaptation of psychiatric consumers/survivors: Path analytic models. *Social Science and Medicine, 43,* 1743–1754.

Hanson, B. S., Isacsson, S. O., Janzon, L., & Lindell, S. E. (1990). Social network and social support influence mortality in elderly men. *American Journal of Epidemiology, 7,* 16–18.

Harris, T., Brown, G. W., & Robinson, R. (1999). Befriending as an intervention for chronic depression among women in an inner city. *British Journal of Psychiatry, 174,* 219–224.

Harrison, A. O., Wilson, M. N., Pine, C. J., & Chan, S. Q. (1990). Family ecologies of ethnic minority children. *Child Development, 61,* 347–362.

Hess, T. M. (1994). Social cognition in adulthood: Aging-related changes in knowledge and processing mechanisms. *Developmental Review, 14,* 373–412.

Hess, T. M., & Blanchard-Fields, F. (Eds.). (1999). *Social cognition and aging.* San Diego: Academic Press.

Ho, S. C. (1991). Health and social predictors of mortality in an elderly Chinese cohort. *American Journal of Epidemiology, 133,* 907–21.

Hogan, D., & Spencer, L. J. (1993). Kin structure and assistance in aging societies. In G.

L. Maddox (Ed.), *Annual review of gerontology and geriatrics, Vol. 13. Focus on kinship, aging, and social change* (pp. 169–186). New York: Springer.

Holahan, C. J., Moos, R. H., Holahan, C. K., & Brennan, P. L. (1995). Social support, coping and depressive symptoms in a late-middle-aged sample of patients reporting cardiac illness. *Health Psychology, 14,* 152–163.

House, J. S., & Kahn, R. L., (1985). Measures and concepts of social support. In S. Cohen & S. L. Syme (Eds.), *Social support and health* (pp. 83–108). Orlando: Academic Press.

House, J. S., Landis, K., & Umberson, D. (1988). Social relationships and health. *Science, 241,* 540–545.

House, J. S., Robbins, C., & Metzner, H. L. (1982). The association of social relationships and activities with mortality: Prospective evidence from the Tecumseh community health study. *American Journal of Epidemiology, 116,* 123–140.

Ikkink, K. K., & van Tilburg, T. V. (1998). Do older adults' network members continue to provide instrumental support in unbalanced relationships? *Journal of Social and Personal Relationships, 15,* 59–75.

Ikkink, K. K., van Tilburg, T. V., & Knipscheer, K. (1999). Perceived instrumental support exchanges in relationships between elderly parents and their adult children: Normative and structural explanations. *Journal of Marriage and the Family, 61,* 831–844.

Jackson, J. S. (Ed.). (1991). *Life in Black America.* Newbury Park, CA: Sage.

Jackson, J. S. (1993). African American experiences through the adult years. In R. Kastenbaum (Ed.), *Encyclopedia of adult development* (pp. 18–26). Phoenix, AZ: Orvx Press.

Jackson, J. S., & Antonucci, T. C. (1992). Social support processes in the health and effective functioning of the elderly. In M. L. Wykle, E. Kahana, & J. Kowal (Eds.), *Stress and health among the elderly* (pp. 72–95). New York: Springer.

Jackson, J. S., Chatters, L. M., & Taylor, R. J. (Eds.). (1993). *Aging in Black America.* Newbury Park, CA: Sage.

Johnson, C. L. (1999a). Family life of older black men. *Journal of Aging Studies, 13,* 145–160.

Johnson, C. L. (1999b). Fictive kin among oldest old African Americans in the San Francisco Bay area. *Journal of Gerontology: Social Sciences, 54B*, S368–S375.

Kahn, R. L., & Antonucci, T. C. (1980). Convoys over the life course: Attachment, roles, and social support. *Life Span Development, 3*, 253–286.

Kaplan, G. A., & Keil, J. E. (1993). Socioeconomic factors and cardiovascular disease: A review of the literature. *Circulation, 88*, 1973–1988.

Kaplan, G. A., Pamuk, E. R., Lynch, J. W., Cohen, R. D., & Balfour, J. L. (1996). Inequality in income and mortality in the United States: Analysis of mortality and potential pathways. *British Medical Journal, 312*, 999–1003.

Kaplan, G. A., Salonen, J. T., Cohen, R. D., Syme, S. L., & Puska, P. (1988). Social connections and mortality from all causes and from cardiovascular-disease: Prospective evidence from Eastern Finland. *American Journal of Epidemiology, 128*, 370–380.

Kaplan, G. A., Wilson, T. W., Cohen, R. D., Kauhanen, J., Wu, M., & Salonen, J. T. (1994). Social functioning and overall mortality: Prospective evidence for the Kuopio ischemic heart disease risk factor study. *Epidemiology, 5*, 494–500.

Kim, H. K., & McKenry, P. C. (1998). Social networks and support: A comparison of African Americans, Asian Americans, Caucasians, and Hispanics. *Journal of Comparative Family Studies, 29*, 313–334.

Knipscheer, K., & Antonucci, T. C. (Eds.). (1990). *Social network research: Methodological questions and substantive issues*. Amsterdam: Swets & Zeitlinger.

Krause, N. (1997a). Received support, anticipated support, social class, and mortality. *Research on Aging, 19*, 387–422.

Krause, N. (1997b). Social support and feelings of personal control in later life. In G. R. Pierce, B. Lakey, I. G. Sarason, & B. R. Sarason (Eds.), *Sourcebook of social support and personality* (pp. 335–355). New York: Plenum Press.

Krause, N. (1999). Mental disorder in late life: Exploring the influence of stress and socioeconomic status. *Handbook of sociology of mental health* (pp. 183–208). New York: Kluwer Academic/Plenum Publishers.

Krause, N., Liang, J., & Keith, V. (1990). Personality, social support, and psychological distress in later life. *Psychology and Aging, 5*, 315–326.

Krause, N., Liang, J., & Keith, V. (1990). Personality, social support, and psychological distress in later life. *Psychology and Aging, 5*, 315–326.

Lachman, M. E. (1985). Personal efficacy in middle and old age: Differential and normative patterns of change. In G. H. Elder (Ed.), *Life-course dynamics: Trajectories and transitions* (pp. 182–213). Ithaca: Cornell University Press.

Lachman, M. E., & Weaver, S. J. (1998a). Sociodemographic variations in the sense of control by domain: Findings from the MacArthur studies of midlife. *Psychology of Aging, 13*, 553–562.

Lachman, M. E., & Weaver, S. L. (1998b). The sense of control as a moderator of social class differences in health and well-being. *Journal of Personality and Social Psychology, 74*, 763–773.

Lang, F. R. (2000). Endings and continuity of social relationships: Maximizing intrinsic benefits within personal networks when feeling near to death. *Journal of Social and Personal Relationships, 17*, 155–182.

Lang, F. R., Featherman, D. L., & Nesselroade, J. R. (1997). Social self-efficacy and short-term variability in social relationships: The MacArthur Successful Aging Studies. *Psychology and Aging, 12*, 657–666.

Lansford, J. E. (2000). *Family relationships, friendships, and well-being in the United States and Japan*. Unpublished Doctoral dissertation, University of Michigan, Ann Arbor.

Lansford, J. E., Sherman, A. M., & Antonucci, T. C. (1998). Satisfaction with social networks: An examination of socioemotional selectivity theory across cohorts. *Psychology and Aging, 13*, 544–552.

Levin, J. S., Taylor, R. J., & Chatters, L. M. (1994). Race and gender differences in religiosity among older adults: Findings from four national surveys. *Journal of Gerontology: Social Sciences, 49*(3), S137–S145.

Levitt, M. J. (2000). Social relations across the life span: In search of unified models. *International Journal of Aging and Human Development, 51*, 71–84.

Levitt, M. J., Guacci-Franco, N., & Levitt, J. L. (1993). Convoys of social support in childhood and early adolescence: Structure and function. *Developmental Psychology, 29*, 811–818.

Levitt, M. J., Guacci-Franco, N., & Weber, R. A. (1992). Intergenerational support, relationship quality, and well-being: A bicultural analysis. *Journal of Family Issues, 13*, 465–481.

Levitt, M. J., Silver, E., & Franco, N. (1996). Troublesome relationships: A part of human experience. *Journal of Social and Personal Relationships, 13*, 523–536.

Libertos, P., Link, B. G., & Kelsey, J. L. (1988). The measurement of social class in epidemiology. *Epidemiologic Reviews, 10*, 87–121.

Luescher, K., & Pillemer, K. (1998). Intergenerational ambivalence: A new approach to the study of parent–child relations in later life. *Journal of Marriage and the Family, 60*, 413–425.

Lynch, T. R., Medelson, T., Robins, C. J., Krishnan, R., George, L. K., Johnson, C. S., & Blazer, D. G. (1999). Perceived social support among depressed elderly, middle-aged, and young-adult samples: Cross-sectional and longitudinal analyses. *Journal of Affective Disorders, 55*, 159–170.

Marshall, V. W. (1996). The state of theory in aging and the social sciences. In R. H. Binstock & L. K. George (Eds.), *Handbook of aging and the social sciences* (pp. 12–30). San Diego: Academic Press.

McAvay, G., Seeman, T. E., & Rodin, J. (1996). A longitudinal study of change in domain-specific self-efficacy among older adults. *Journal of Gerontology: Psychological Science, 51B*, 243–253.

Mittelman, M. S., Ferris, S. H. Shulman, E., Steinberg, G., Ambinder, A., Mackell, J. A., & Cohen, J. (1995). A comprehensive support program: Effect on depression in spouse-caregivers of AD patients. *The Gerontologist, 35*, 792–802.

Morgan, D. (1997). *Focus groups as qualitative research*. Thousand Oaks: Sage.

Murphy, B., Schofield, H., Nankervis, J., Bloch, S., Herrman, H., & Singh, B. H. (1997). Women with multiple roles: The emotional impact of caring for ageing parents. *Ageing and Society, 18*, 277–291.

Mutran, E. J., Reitzes, D. C., Mossey, J., & Fernandes, M. E. (1995). Social support, depression, and recovery of walking ability following hip Fracture Surgery. *Journal of Gerontology*: Social Sciences, 50, 354–361.

Newsom, J. T., & Schulz, R. (1998). Caregiving from the recipient's perspective: Negative reactions to being helped. *Health Psychology, 17*, 172–181.

O'Connor, B. P. (1995). Family and friend relationships among older and younger adults: Interaction motivation, mood, and quality. *International Journal of Aging and Human Development, 40*, 9–29.

Orth-Gomer, K., & Johnson, J. V. (1987). Social network interaction and mortality: A 6–yr follow-up study of a random sample of the Swedish population. *Journal of Chronic Diseases, 40*, 949–957.

Oxman, T. C., Berkman, L. F., Kasl, S., Freeman, D. H., & Barrett, J. (1992). Social support and depressive symptoms in the elderly. *American Journal of Epidemiology, 135*, 356–368.

Oxman, T. E., Freeman, D. H., & Manheimer, E. D. (1995). Lack of social participation or religious strength and comfort as risk factors for death after cardiac surgery in the elderly. *Psychosomatic Medicine, 57*, 5–15.

Oxman, T. E., & Hull, J. G. (1997). Social support, depression, and activities of daily living in older heart surgery patients. *Journal of Gerontology: Psychological Sciences, 52*, 1–14.

Pappas, G., Queen, S., & Hadden, W. (1993). The increasing disparity in mortality between socioeconomic groups in the United States. *The New England Journal of Medicine, 329*, 103–109.

Parrot, T. M., & Bengtson, V. L. (1999). The effects of earlier intergenerational affection, normative expectations, and family conflict on contemporary exchanges of help and support. *Research on Aging, 21*, 173–105.

Pearlin, L. I. (1985). Social structure and the processes of social support. In S. Cohen & S. L. Syme. (Eds.), *Social support and health* (pp. 43–60). Orlando: Academic Press.

Peek, M. K., & Lin, N. (1999). Age differences in the effects of network composition on psychological distress. *Social Science and Medicine, 49*, 621–636.

Pierce, G. R., Lakey, B., Sarason, I. G., & Sarason, B. R. (1997). *Sourcebook of social support and personality*. New York: Plenum Press.

Pierce, G. R., Sarason, B. R., & Sarason I. G. (Eds.) (1996). *Handbook of social support and the family*. New York, Plenum.

Pinquart, M., & Sorensen, S. (2000). Influences of socioeconomic status, social network, and competence on subjective well-being in later life: A meta-analysis. *Psychology and Aging, 15*, 187–224.

Pugliesi, K., & Shook, S. L. (1998). Gender, ethnicity, and network characteristics: Variation in social support resources. *Sex Roles, 38*, 215–238.

Reis, H. T., & Downey, G. (1999). Social cognition in relationships: Building essential bridges between two literatures. *Social Cognition, 17*, 97–117.

Rodin, J. (1976). Density, perceived choice, and response to controllable and uncontrollable outcomes. *Journal of Experimental Social Psychology, 12*, 564–578.

Rodin, J., & Langer, E. H. (1977). Long-term effects of a control relevant interaction with the institutional aged. *Journal of Personality and Social Psychology, 35*, 897–902.

Rook, K. S. (1992). Detrimental aspects of social relationships: Taking stock of an emerging literature. In H. O. F. Veiel & U. Baumann (Eds.), *The meaning and measurement of social support* (pp. 157–169). New York: Hemisphere.

Rook, K. S. (1995). Support, companionship, and control in older adults' social networks: Implications for well-being. In J. F. Nussbaum & J. Coupland (Eds.), *Handbook of communication and aging research* (pp. 437–463). Mahwah, NJ: Erlbaum.

Rook, K. S., Thuras, P. D., & Lewis, M. A. (1990). Social control, health risk taking, and psychological distress among the elderly. *Psychology and Aging, 5*, 327–334.

Roschelle, A. R. (Ed.). (1997). *No more kin: Exploring race, class, and gender in family networks*. Thousand Oaks: Sage.

Ross, L. T., Lutz, C. J., & Lakey, B. (1999). Perceived social support and attributions for failed support. *Personality and Social Psychology Bulletin, 25*, 896–909.

Ross, C. E., & Mirowsky, J. (1989). Explaining the social patterns of depression: Control and problem solving or support and talking? *Journal of Health and Social Behavior, 30*, 206–219.

Ross, C. E., & Sastry, J. (1999). The sense of personal control: Social-structural causes and emotional consequences. In C. S. Aneshensel & J. C. Phelan (Eds.), *Handbook of sociology of mental health* (pp. 369–394). New York: Kluwer Academic/Plenum Publishers.

Rubenstcin, R. L. (Ed.). (1986). *Singular paths: Old men living alone*. New York: Columbia University Press.

Russell, D. W., & Cutrona, C. E. (1991). Social support, stress, and depressive symptoms among the elderly: Test of a process model. *Psychology and Aging, 6*, 190–201.

Sarason, B. R., Sarason, I. G., & Pierce, G. R. (1990). Traditional views of social support and their impact on assessment. In B. R. Sarason, I. G. Sarason, & G. R. Pierce (Eds.), *Social support: An interactional view* (pp. 9–25). New York: Wiley.

Sarason, I. G., Sarason, B. G., & Pierce, G. R. (1994). Relationship-specific social support: Towards a model for the analysis of supportive interactions. In B. E. Burleson, T. L. Albrecth, & I. G. Sarason (Eds.), *Communication of social support: Messages, interactions, relationships and community* (pp. 91–112). Thousand Oaks: Sage.

Schoenbach, V. J., Kaplan, B. H., Fredman, L., & Kleinbaum, D. G. (1986). Social ties and mortality in Evans County, Georgia. *American Journal of Epidemiology, 123*, 577–591.

Schulz, R. (1976). Effects of control and predictability on the physical and psychological well-being of the institutionalized aged. *Journal of Personality and Social Psychology, 33*, 563–573.

Seeman, T. E., & Berkman, L. F. (1988). Structural characteristics of social networks and their relationship with social support in the elderly: Who provides support? *Social Science and Medicine, 26*, 737–749.

Seeman, T. F., Berkman, L. F., Kohout, F., Lacroix, A., Glenn, R., & Blazer, D. (1993). Intercommunity variations in the association between social ties and mortality in the elderly. *Annals of Epidemiology, 3*, 325–335.

Seeman, T. E., Bruce, M. L., & McAvay, G. J. (1996). Social network characteristics and onset of ADL disability: MacArthur studies of successful aging. *Journal of Gerontology: Social Sciences, 51B*, 191–200.

Shye, D., Mullooly, J. P., Freeborn, D. K., & Pope, C. R. (1995). Gender differences in the relationship between social network support and mortality: A longitudinal study of an elderly cohort. *Social Science and Medicine, 41*, 935–947.

Silverstein, M., Chen, X., & Heller, K. (1996). Too much of a good thing? Intergenerational social support and the psychological well-being of older parents. *Journal of Marriage and the Family, 58*, 970–982.

Silverstein, M., & Waite, L. J. (1993). Are blacks more likely than whites to receive and provide social support in middle and old age? Yes, no, and maybe so. *Journal of Gerontology: Social Sciences, 48*, 212–222.

Smith, J., & Goodnow, J. (1999). Unasked-for support and unsolicited advice: Age and the quality of social experience. *Psychology and Aging, 14*, 108–121.

Stevens, N., & van Tilburg, T. (2000). Stimulating friendship in later life: A strategy for reducing loneliness among older women. *Educational Gerontology: Special Issue: International research and practice, 26*, 15–35.

Sugisawa, H., Liang, J., & Liu, X. (1994). Social networks, social support and mortality among older people in Japan. *Journal of Gerontology: Social Sciences, 49*, 3–13.

Suitor, J. J., & Pillemer, K. A. (1991). Family conflict when adult children and elderly parents share a home. In K. Pillemer & McCartney (Eds.), *Parent–child relations throughout life* (pp. 179–201). Hillsdale, NJ: Lawrence Erlbaum.

Suitor, J. J., Pillemer, K. A., Keeton, S., & Robinson, J. (1996). Aged parents and aging children: Determinants of relationship quality. In R. Blieszner & V. H. Bedford (Eds.), *Handbook of aging and the family* (pp. 223–242). Westport, CT: Greenwood Press.

Szendre, E. N., & Jose, P. E. (1996). Telephone support by elderly volunteers to inner-city children. *Journal of Community Psychology, 24*, 87–96.

Taylor, C. B., Bandura, A., Ewart, C. K., Miller, N. H., & Debusk, R. F. (1985). Raising spouse's and patient's perception of his cardiac capabilities after clinically uncomplicated acute myocardial function. *American Journal of Cardiology, 55*, 635–638.

Taylor, R. J., & Chatters, L. M. (1986). Patterns of informal support to elderly black adults: Family, friends, and church members. *Social Work, 31*, 432–438.

Taylor, R. J., Chatters, L. M., Tucker, M. B., & Lewis, E. (1990). Developments in research on black families: A decade review. *Journal of Marriage and the Family, 52*, 993–1014.

Taylor, R. J., Hardison, C. B., & Chatters, L. M. (1996). Kin and nonkin as sources of informal assistance. In H. W. Neighbors & J. S. Jackson (Eds.), *Mental health in black America* (pp. 130–145). Thousand Oaks: Sage.

Taylor, R. J., Jackson, J. S., & Chatters, L. J. (Eds.) (1997). *Family life in black America* (pp. 293–316). Thousand Oaks: Sage.

Taylor, S. E., Kemeny, M. E., Reed, G. M., Bower, J. E., & Gruenewald, T. L. (2000) *American Psychologist; 55*, 99–109

Troll, L. E. (1994). Family connectedness of old women. In B. F. Turner & L. E. Troll (Eds.), *Women growing older* (pp. 169–201). Thousand Oaks, Sage.

Tsai, D. T., & Lopez, R. A. (1998). The use of social supports by elderly Chinese immigrants. *Journal of Gerontological Social Work, 29*, 77–94.

Tucker, J. S., Schwartz, E., Clark, K. M., & Friedman, H. S. (1999). Age-related changes in the associations of social network ties with mortality risk. *Psychology and Aging, 14*, 564–571.

Tucker, M. B., Taylor, R. J., & Mitchell-Kernan, C. (1993). Marriage and romantic involvement among aged African Americans. *Journal of Gerontology: Social Sciences, 48*, S123–S132.

Uchino, B. N., Cacioppo, J. T., & Kiecolt-Glaser, J. K. (1996). The relationship between social support and physiological processes: A review with emphasis on underlying mechanisms and implications for health. *Psychological Bulletin, 119*, 488–531.

Uehara, E. S. (1995). Reciprocity reconsidered: Gouldner's 'moral norm of reciprocity' and social support. *Journal of Social and Personal Relationships, 12*, 483–502.

Vaillant, G. E., Meyer, S. E., Mukamal, K., & Soldz, S. (1998). Are social supports in late midlife a cause or a result of successful physical ageing? *Psychological Medicine*, *28*, 1159–1168.

van Tilburg, T. (1998). Losing and gaining in old age: Changes in personal network size and social support in a four-year longitudinal study. *Journal of Gerontology*, *53B*, S313–323.

van Tilburg, T., & Gierveld, J., Lecchini, L., & Marsiglia, D. (1998). Social integration and loneliness: A comparative study among older adults in the Netherlands and Tuscany, Italy. *Journal of Social and Personal Relationship*, *15*, 740–754.

Vega, W. A. (1990). Hispanic families in the 1980s: A decade of research. *Journal of Marriage and the Family*, *52*, 1015–1024

Walen, H. R., & Lachman, M. E. (2000). Social support and strain from, partner, family, and friends: Costs and benefits for men and women in adulthood. *Journal of Social and Personal Relationships*, *17*, 5–30.

Wallsten, S. M., Tweed, D. L., Blazer, D. G., & George, L. K. (1999). Disability and depressive symptoms in the elderly: The effects of instrumental support and its subjective appraisal. *International Journal of Aging and Human Development*, *48*, 145–159.

Wasserman, S., & Faust, K. (Eds.). (1994). *Social network analysis: Methods and applications*. Cambridge: Cambridge University Press.

Wellman, B., & Worley, S. (1990). Different strokes from different folks: Community ties and social support. *American Journal of Sociology*, *96*, 558–588.

Wenger, G. C. (1997). Review of findings on support networks of older Europeans. *Journal of Cross-Cultural Gerontology*, *12*, 1–21.

Wilkinson, D. (1993). Family ethnicity in America. In H. P. McAdoo (Ed.), *Family and ethnicity: Strength in diversity* (pp. 15–59). Newbury Park, CA: Sage.

Williams, D. R. (1990). Socioeconomic differentials in health: A review and redirection. *Social Psychology Quarterly*, *53*, 81–99.

Yasuda, N., Zimmerman, S. I., Hawkes, W., Fredman, L., Hebel, J. R., & Magaziner, J. (1997). Relation of social network characteristics to a 5-year mortality among young-old versus old-old white women in an urban community. *American Journal of Epidemiology*, *145*, 516–523.

Eighteen

Gender and Aging
Gender Differences and Gender Roles

Jan D. Sinnott and Kim Shifren

I. Introduction

Gender and aging is a difficult topic to summarize because definitions and subject areas have been inconsistent and because the research and scholarship in this area have been fragmented. Many gender-related studies have emerged from the discipline of sociology or from biology or medicine. Although an interdisciplinary perspective is preferable in research and practice, and the subject at hand clearly lends itself to an interdisciplinary treatment, consideration of the space limits of this volume of the handbook demands confining this discussion to traditional topics in psychology.

Gender and aging has been an important topic for the psychology of aging. We are experiencing a period of significant global cultural transformation, a period during which the utility of life-long traditional gender roles for both the person and the society is being reevaluated. Individual differences and the overall quality of the individual's experience are of more interest now than at other points in history. The concepts of femaleness and maleness are undergoing very rapid transformation in industrialized nations such as the United States. In addition, the discipline of psychology is becoming one based on data from both women and men. The growth of the aging population is forcing us to consider gender-related aspects of identity for aging humans of both genders.

In this chapter aging will be defined as the passage of chronological time in an organism's life span, concentrating on the period starting with middle age. In the first section of this chapter, we will review the role of gender in past research and scholarship, define it, and set limits on its use in this chapter. In the second section distinctions will be made among the members of the family of terms related to gender: sex, sexuality, sexual identity, sex role, and sex role stereotypes. Cultural expectations, cohort issues, and cross-cultural issues will be examined. Next, in the third section, we will consider what the important developmental aspects of gender may be in the later stages of life, those that stretch beyond the parental imperative for most individuals. New models for studying gender and aging will be described. Methodological issues will be discussed. In section IV we will examine gender role

Handbook of the Psychology of Aging

development and aging, including the theories of gender role reversal, androgyny, and gender role transcendence. We will consider the question of the meaning (considering issues raised above) of differential performance of women and men in aging research that is *not* related to gender roles and gender studies per se. Every section will include suggestions for future directions in research and theory related to gender and aging.

II. Gender in the Literature

A. Main Types of Gender Studies

Literature on the psychology of aging is replete with studies that take into account some aspect of gender, or, using the older terminology, sex, in the behavior of older adults. Gender has seldom been the main focus of the study. Both female and male respondents have appeared in aging psychology studies, much more often than has happened in psychological studies as a whole, possibly because women are the most numerous older respondents. If both genders are included it is possible to contrast their performance.

We have also seen an increase in studies of women (only) (e.g., Coyle, 1997; Wheeler, 1997) and aging since the rise of the women's movement. Much of the material in these new volumes would be labeled sociology, biology, or medicine, but some is within the traditional domain of psychology, our present concern.

Growing interest in varieties of aging experience has led to studies of aging and gender in diverse populations (e.g., Stanford & Dubois, 1992). Some of the diverse populations, namely lesbians, gay men, and transgendered persons, are defined by gender-related terms, and therefore may be of interest to psychologists examining gender and aging (e.g., Berger, 1984).

Historically, the primary purpose of specifically gender-related psychology aging studies has been to compare and contrast male and female performance data (obtained for other purposes), usually without specifying precisely what aspect of gender is meant and by what mechanism gender might be causing some effect. Examples of research with gender performance data are provided later in this chapter in the section on gender differences. In the main three bodies of work that have been related to psychology, gender has been specified to mean biological sex, and the mechanism of causation has been considered to be biological. Those three areas are studies on the different life spans and health of women and men of equal ages, studies of sexuality, and studies of the social impact of the typically longer life spans of female respondents. This set of studies for the most part has avoided deeper psychological considerations related to gender.

Overall, most gender-by-performance comparisons are done in passing, not as planned comparisons based on theory, and so it is not surprising that gender as a variable usually sheds no particular light on the behavior of interest to the investigator, even when gender differences are found. (For example, one partial review of the experimental literature on sex differences in aging appears in Obler, 1982). We would be forced to conclude, based on these results alone, that in matters related to psychological aging, few important gender differences have been documented. Alternatively, we might hypothesize that investigators have made so few planned gender comparisons that we have no clear and comprehensive idea which gender differences have an impact on behavior or why.

One more well-known fact compounds this problem: females and males vary widely within their own gender categories and do not all respond the same way, even when we speak of purely biological responses. So, for many reasons, our performance comparisons to date are not very useful.

The second main purpose of studies of gender in our field has been to examine the nature of changes in some aspect of gender identity and changes in gender roles. Does identity change? Do gender roles and stereotypes stay the same from childhood through parenthood and into advanced old age? This second set of studies has been more developmental in quality, looking at changes over time, either those changes that (theoretically) occur because of specific developmental life changes, or those that simply happen to coincide with the passage of time. However, most of these studies also suffer from the same limitations noted above.

A third set of gender-related studies relates gender role differences to social roles and social power of a more general type, drawing psychological implications from the actions of society on older women and men. Obviously, this research could be important because it may demonstrate that any gender effects are developed due to societal beliefs and pressures! These studies are of special interest in political and social policy arenas. For example, some studies examine gender in relation to differential caregiving roles, attitudes toward retirement, differential treatment of older women and men, and the social power of male and female elders in our own and in other cultures.

B. Historical Use of the Term *Gender* in Research and Theory

Sex and gender may mean several different concepts (see below), any one (or several) of which a writer has chosen to explore and, possibly, to describe to readers. Given that there are several concepts, we need to know how the writer is conceptually and operationally defining gender. On what, exactly, are we dividing our respondents when we make gender comparisons? Unfortunately this clarification seldom happens in the literature. Although most writers simply assume that readers share their particular understanding of the term, others do consciously select one of the meanings from this family of terms and describe their concept to readers. But few writers seem to take into account the fact that there are additional gender-related concepts among the terms, concepts that might be important to whatever they are investigating. Since results often have implications for research, theory, public policy, and client care, overt clarity about the aspect of gender under consideration is important, and greater breadth in concepts considered may be useful.

In our field, most gender-related studies consider gender as a term enfolding all related meanings described below. The main underlying concept of gender, for most writers, seems to be a biological one, though writers may suggest nonbiological aspects of the term in discussion sections of papers. For example, a study of interpersonal relations of aging nursing home residents may label respondents female and male, and appear to interpret results as if simple biological sex differences are being examined. However, whatever gender differences do occur could logically be related to female sex-stereotypic role and male sex-stereotypic role, a different member of the gender family of terms. This possibility might be suggested at the end of the paper, but not before. Even if a writer is thinking in terms of role, the reader seeing "Effects of gender on..." often mentally summarizes the findings in terms of biology, the conceptual lens through which most readers view gender. Unless these sorts of distinctions are made clear in the research from the start, the reader may close the journal muttering that men and women were just born different and unchangeable. In contrast, the writer, who really considered gender to be a role-related variable, is already making plans for an intervention to change the nursing home community's view of appropriate roles so that men and women can enjoy social interactions equally. That researcher will face opposition in implementing the intervention, though, if he or she is surrounded by professionals who only see gender in simple biological terms. The use of the term gender in psychology aging research has been problematic and therefore has led to unfortunate limitations on the utility of research findings and the direction of intervention research.

C. Plan of This Chapter

Our discussion here must be limited to traditional topics in psychology. One focus of this chapter will be on the limits and the meaning of work in this area, and on changes in an individual's gender roles, stereotypes, or identity over time during mature adulthood and old age. Our discussion, review, and analysis of specific studies that mention gender will be concentrated on recent work on the topics of cognitive functioning, personality, health, and caregiving.

III. Concepts Related to the Term Gender

A. Definitions

1. Sex versus Gender

Several distinctions need to be made to avoid confusion. First we must distinguish between sex and gender. Unger (1979) argued that sex should be limited to the biological bases for producing the two genders: the presence of XX or XY chromosomes, hormonal output from the gonads, internal and external reproductive anatomy, and secondary physical sex characteristics. Gender is what culture does with the evidence of biological sex. Sex is mainly considered to be a bio-

logical variable; gender is mainly considered to be a psychosocial variable.

2. Gender (or Sex) Roles Versus Gender (or Sex) Role Stereotypes

Gender roles include the actual behaviors of females and males, which have considerable within-group variability. Gender role stereotypes are oversimplified socially shared perceptions of idealized male or female actions, perceptions which usually allow for little variability. Societies usually promote the stereotypical behavior and punish behavior that runs counter to these stereotypes. Both of these variables are mainly considered to be psychosocial variables.

3. Sexuality versus Sex Roles

Sexuality is the behavior directly associated with having sexual relations or being sexually aroused. Sex roles (see gender roles, above) are behaviors of *many* kinds, behaviors that may have little or nothing to do with actual sexual relations. Sexuality is mainly considered to be a biological and psychological variable.

4. Gender Identity versus Gender Roles and Sexuality

Gender identity is one's sense of being essentially male or female, whatever the biological or social circumstances that have led to that feeling. One's identity may or may not be reflected in one's roles or sexuality, and may or may not be congruent with one's apparent biological gender. Gender identity is sometimes considered to be a psychological variable and sometimes a biological variable.

5. Gender Schemes

Gender schemes are the cognitive constructs used to conceptualize roles or identity. Although these concepts may be central to a person's worldview, they may or may not be congruent with the person's behavior. Gender scheme is mainly considered to be a psychological variable.

6. Gender Differences

This is a judgment, usually based on an average of some behavior across all individuals in a gender category. Variability is usually of minor interest in the current literature. A problem occurs in deciding how much difference constitutes a true or meaningful difference. For almost all measures, the curves describing females' and males' responses overlap to a great degree, even when investigators find statistically significant differences between genders. Whether a gender difference matters (like whether racial or culture of origin differences matter) is sometimes decided in terms of statistical significance, effect size, clinical considerations, or political stance.

B. Cohort Issues and Cross-Cultural Issues

When we consider gender and aging psychology together, we need to consider the impact of birth cohort and nature of the culture. This is necessary because the complex definitions of gender include cohort and culture elements (e.g., see Coyle (1997.))

The cohort into which an older person was born partly shapes his or her definitions of gender, due to the psychosocial nature of most of the meanings of gender described above. That person then will behave in accord with the cultural expectations related to gender and will hold concepts related to gender that fit the cultural milieu of that time. If that person is a researcher, she or he will create scales that test the cohort-specific concepts about gender of his or her cohort. If she or he is a clinician, that clinician most

likely will expect clients to adapt to the gender demands articulated by the theory of gender held by the clinician and the clinician's cohort or to those suitable at the time of treatment. We might question whether a gender-measuring device ever really captures what gender is about, free of the artifact of history.

For example, some tests of sex roles include an item related to dependency and expect women to state that they themselves are dependent as part of their femininity. Dependency may have been a middle-class feminine trait earlier in history, but it is less so today. Including dependency on the femininity scale is invalid for one cohort of elders but valid for another. What, then, is the nature of gender role if it changes from cohort to cohort? How can we perform complex time-lag studies when our measures may not be valid for successive cohorts?

A similar problem occurs when the measure was created for a younger age group, but used with an older age group (the opposite seldom occurs). Is femininity really the same for a teen, a mother of teens, and an 80-year-old woman? Although gender identity may remain constant over the life span, the way in which it or sexuality is expressed is likely to vary based on cohort and stage of life.

Cross-cultural factors and differences due to socioeconomic status (SES) also influence the validity of these psychosocial and sometimes biological measures. Different cultures and socioeconomic groups have differing norms for and concepts of gender-related behaviors at different points in the life span. Culture and SES imply differences in health status, too, which has an impact on the more biological of gender variables.

For example, going back to that dependency question, Sinnott once interviewed an older women whose culture of origin and SES group taught her that once she passed menopause she, as a woman, should become a strong support for her extended family and be "above" physical sexual relations. She therefore rejected dependency and sexual relations as part of her older femininity, in contrast to some traits that had been part of her younger femininity. However her health status (the side effects of diabetes and high blood pressure often found in her group) had rendered her a near-invalid in need of frequent help, rather than a stalwart matriarch. Her husband was willing to help, but only if she was willing to resume sexual intercourse with him. She needed the help. As she became more dependent and resumed having sexual relations to obtain it, she considered herself less and less of a woman. This gender-related change would not have been anticipated or understood using typical questionnaires and measures that were not culture, SES, and age sensitive.

IV. What Is the Meaning of Gender to Persons in Later Life?

In this section we will consider what the developmental aspects of gender may be in the later stages of life, those which stretch beyond the parental imperative. The parental imperative model is based on the idea that the core qualities that are stereotypically linked to men and women have developed in response to the demands of the parenting role. New models for studying gender and aging will be described. Methodological issues will be discussed.

A. Beyond the Parental Imperative

The family of terms related to gender evolved from consideration of stage-related needs of younger persons. Studies of gender-related personality traits, of gender identity, of sex roles, and of sexuality relied on reports by younger individuals in childhood, the teens, and young

adulthood. Scales were suitable and valid for these groups. Would gender-related terms mean the same thing to individuals in middle and old age?

Let us consider gender meanings in light of a developmental theory such as Erikson's (1950, 1985). In later life individuals are said to be using their psychological energy to begin to address the conflicts between generativity and stagnation, and between integrity and despair. They are attempting to create meaning in their lives, conscious of their ever-shortening lifetime. They are dealing with physical changes and reporting less interest in sexual relationships. They want to know more deeply the people they care about, and spend less time in superficial, role-driven relationships. Perhaps they are developing complex thought, developing wisdom, becoming less focused on achievement and more focused on spirituality. With focus shifting to issues of the wholeness and meaning of life, and issues of death, and shifting away from socially stereotypic roles of Mom and Dad, gender role categories may no long matter to the individual. In old age gender may be psychologically transcended. Will these changes in psychological emphasis mean that older adults see gender concepts differently? If so our psychological study of gender and aging should take this into account.

It appears from several theories and related data discussed below that some gender concepts change in meaning as a lifetime passes. Looking at the gender-related terms defined above, let's discuss the possible changes in the meaning of these terms and concepts after the parental imperative. The modified concepts could be investigated and may influence how we interpret earlier findings related to gender in later years. Sex would still be the biological basis of producing males and females, as before. Gender would still be what culture does with this biological statement. Gender and sex roles would change, as a concept. We would have to find out what the organized patterns of interpersonal behavior, congruent with a culture, related to maleness and femaleness, might be for persons in mature and old groups. Role stereotypes are also open to major redefinition because we have little organized information on cultural expectations for older stereotypic femininity and masculinity. What is a real man like if he's an old man? What is a real woman like if she is an old woman? Our own responses to these two questions may be slightly stereotyped and may have shown how far we still are from seeing older persons as ordinary males and females, rather than some other gender group! What other (if any) measurable gender role are they expected to have if they can't fit the stereotypic roles? Sexuality may be a term for which we have an old age variant in mind, but not a very good one: asexual. Sexuality as a concept still seems dominated by ideas of youth and fertility in spite of a graying population and overpopulation! What might older adults consider sexy, and what is sexuality about, from their vantage point of a longer lifetime? We are probably safe in saying that the term gender identity is equally meaningful for the later part of life, although a surprising number of older individuals are redefining their gender identities and talking about it in recent years. Gender schemes would be a likely candidate for redefinition for older adults whose concepts of what it means to be a certain gender seem to expand with the changes mentioned above. With the change and individual variability in gender-related concepts, gender differences therefore might be harder to find in this age period.

B. Models: Metaphors for Transcendence and Belonging

Unfortunately, despite continual efforts by a few researchers (e.g., Gutmann,

1994; Huyck, 1996, 1998; Sinnott, 1997; Smith & Baltes, 1998) to integrate theory into work on gender and aging, much research shows little to no theoretical reasoning behind the examination of gender similarities and differences as we age. Though no model is perfect, without theoretical models we would have no structure to our discussions of gender and aging (Sinnott, 1997).

In this section we will define a model broadly, in an Aristotelian way, as a brief description of the form and nature of a behavioral event or process. Models are our lenses through which we see the concept of gender (Bem, 1993). Where the older Western philosophies emphasized a small number of polarized concrete roles that might be exchanged, the newer approaches emphasized the continuum of roles and the process of ongoing change and transformation. They may provide models of human behavior and development that can accommodate individuality, community, and transcendence as they relate to gender.

All models may differ along several dimensions: whether they attempt to give descriptive versus inferential information; how detailed they are; their genesis and historical period of origin; whether they are based on a single factor or multifactorial antecedent conditions; whether they are mechanistic, organismic or constructionist; whether they are analog or digital; the degree to which they are nested in explicit theory; the type of issue to which they are applied; the degree to which they are developmental and life span; the degree to which they are assumed to be generalizable to most humans; the degree to which the model is nomothetic (seeking information on average behavior) versus idiographic (seeking information on changes within a single self who is also a reference point at any one time for other states of the self); the complexity of their view of women and men; the degree to which the assumptions inherent in the model are made conscious; whether they permit respondents a sense of meaning; whether data within them can be abstract or narrative quality data; whether they permit qualitative or quantitative analyses; and whether the model is based on Newtonian science versus new physics science (see Sinnott, 1981b), chaos and complexity theory, and systems theory. Of course there could be many more characteristics.

Because of global change, the most useful models for future work appear to be those that give both descriptive and inferential information; contain meaningful detail; give analog information; are constructionist; are at least potentially multifactorial (e.g., biopsychosocial); are nested in theory; can be applied to a wide range of issues; are developmental and life span; are both nomothetic and idiographic, thereby allowing for summaries and for individual differences; make assumptions conscious; permit meaning and narrative; permit both qualitative and quantitative analyses; and are based on new physics sciences and systems theory.

Here is a brief listing of some newer multidisciplinary research models which, by virtue of both their content and their underlying assumptions, are more complex (see Sinnott, 1997, for references.) These areas might be used as a stimulus for some important future research on gender and aging:

1. Chaos theory and complexity theory
2. General Systems Theory
3. Eastern philosophy
4. New physics, relativity theory, quantum theory
5. Environmental psychology
6. Theories of psychological archetypes
7. Humanistic psychology
8. Transpersonal psychology
9. Existential psychology
10. Mind–body studies
11. Postformal reasoning
12. Creation of community
13. New biology, cooperative evolution
14. Lifetime learning, plasticity
15. Learning through intense or long-term relationships
16. Search for personal meaning and spirituality
17. Nonpolarized roles or descriptors
18. Theories of individuals as creators of their own experiences

Recall for a moment the dimensions of models presented earlier in this section, for example, that a model might provide descriptive versus inferential information. The 18 areas just mentioned can generally produce research possessing both dimensions discussed, both descriptive and inferential data produced in this case, because they are more complex models. Most of the 18 areas naturally generate studies that are both single factor and multifactorial; they naturally generate mechanistic and organismic and constuctionist studies. Each of the 18 areas represents a complex idea of a person in society evolving over time. Each is abstract enough to transcend the trap of considering just one historical period or just one detailed operational definition as the whole truth. Each provides information that can be analyzed as nomothetic or idiographic information, mathematical models, and narrative analyses. On the whole they are more representative of the complexity of the transcendent person-in-community-over-time model than most simpler models. They can be applied to studies of gender and aging.

V. Gender Differences

Since Huyck's seminal work on gender and aging in the third edition of the *Handbook of Psychology and Aging* (Huyck, 1990), there has been a plethora of research on gender issues and aging. Many studies have been conducted covering a wide range of topics including self-efficacy, body attitudes, self-reported health, intelligence, verbal ability, caregiving, sense of control, social ties, personality, and medical decision-making processes. The large number of studies on gender and aging has resulted in recent literature reviews and meta-analyses for certain topic areas (e.g., Feingold, 1994; Seeman, 1996; Yee & Schulz, 2000). In this section of the chapter we shall briefly discuss research from several topic areas that focus on gender and aging issues, including (a) cognitive functioning, (b) personality, (c) health, and (d) caregiving.

A. Cognitive Functioning

There is a vast literature on age differences in cognitive functioning. Much of this research is theory driven (Kausler, 1991) and has provided researchers and practitioners with important information on cognitive functioning as we age. For example, theoretical models of the relation between age, speed of processing information, and individuals' working memory capacity have been eloquently described (Park et al., 1996). From this theoretically driven research, we know that older adults have slower processing speed than younger adults (Salthouse, 1996), and less working memory capacity than younger adults (Park et al., 1996).

As discussed earlier in this chapter, much research has focused on gender differences in performance on various tasks. This is true for research on cognitive functioning. Gender differences are examined, but no theoretical models are provided to direct hypothesis testing and assessment and discussion of findings. What we currently know is that there are gender differences in performance on a variety of cognitive tasks including, verbal tasks, mathematical tasks, and spatial relations. There are male–female differences in performance on math tests (Steele, 1997), and females continue to get higher scores than males in writing

performance (U. S. Dept. of Education, 1997). There is also evidence of interactions between gender and age on performance on cognitive tasks, but again, no theoretical models appear to drive the research.

Norman, Evans, Miller, and Heaton (2000) studied individuals, 17 to 101 years old, and they found that age, education, ethnicity, and gender were all significant predictors of performance on the California Verbal Learning Test. Wilson et al. (1999) studied women and men, 65 and over (sample over 6000), for the frequency and kinds of cognitive activities they performed. Wilson et al. (1999) found that Caucasian males with higher income and education participated in activities that were more cognitively demanding than African American males and Caucasian and African American females. They also found that younger Caucasian females (young–old group) with high income and more education frequently participated in cognitive activities, but these activities were not as demanding as those cognitive activities of Caucasian men. Brown, Lahar, and Mosley (1998) used a direction-giving paradigm to examine gender and age differences in both frequency and accuracy rate on direction-giving tasks. They found that middle-aged females spent more time studying urban maps, and had higher frequency of strategies compared to younger groups of women and men and middle-aged men. However, accuracy was the same for older and younger groups of men and women. Capitani, Laiacona, and Basso (1999) examined men and women, 18–81 years old, for sensitivity to a phonetically cued word fluency task. Females appeared to have an advantage over males on this task, and there was no significant decline in performance with age. There appears to be a greater sensitivity to aging in males than females on this task.

There are some studies, however, that do not show gender differences in cognitive performance as we age. Lowe and Reynolds (1999) studied adults, 54–89 years old, and they found no significant relation between error scores and age and gender on verbal ability, fluency, set-shifting, and rule inductions. Interesting cross-cultural research on verbal perform-ance and gender shows that of Chinese native speakers, 7–95 years old, the num-ber of items generated on a category flu-ency test increased with age, peaking in 19–30-year-old age range, and then de-clined in later life (Chan & Poon, 2000). Chan and Poon (2000) did *not* find gender differences in performance on this cat-egory fluency test. Unterrainer et al. (2000) found that asymmetric type of pro-cessing was necessary for better visuo-spatial brain performance, regardless of gender. Minor and Park (1999) found no gender differences in spatial working memory in a schizophrenic sample.

Gender differences in cognitive func-tioning are likely shaped, in part, by our environment. However, there is also evi-dence of a biological connection between gender, age, and cognitive functioning. Again, there is no consistent presence of theoretical models in this research. Interestingly, normal aging men given testosterone showed improved per-formance on visual-spatial tests (Ja-nowsky, Oviatt, & Orwall, 1994). Cherrier (2000) also found preliminary evidence of improvements in spatial and verbal memory in men, 59–76 years old, who were administered testosterone. Older women with estrogen supplements show reduced incidence of Alzheimer's disease (AD) (Paganini-Hill, Buckwalter, Logan, & Henderson, 1993). However, not all studies involving hormones pro-vide support for a biological explanation of gender differences in cognition as we age. For example, Barrett-Connor and Kritz-Silverstein (1999) studied women and men, 65–95 years old, and found no support for estrogen deficiency being associated with a decline in cog-nitive functioning in postmenopausal women.

Is gender an important aspect of indi-viduals to examine when assessing cogni-tive functioning as we age? Well, there appears to be a difference of opinion on this topic. Halpern (1997) has noted that there is much interest in the possibility that gender difference in cognition is decreasing, because of less sex role stereo-types and other lessening of sex-differen-tiated environment. However, an earlier meta-analysis by Lytton and Romney (1991) on parents' sex-role socialization practices showed that parents had no less sex differentiation over the past two decades of parenting. Hedges and Nowell (1995) conducted a meta-analysis of read-ing, writing, math, and science, and they found that gender differences in cognition appear stable over a 30-year period. Des-pite suggestions that gender differences in cognition may be decreasing, the evi-dence is not sufficient to support this idea. The evidence we do have warrants the development of theoretical models on gender and age in relation to certain cog-nitive tasks.

B. Personality

There is both theory and some evidence that personality is stable over time (Costa & McCrae, 1993), and this has resulted in less focus on research that includes gen-der-by-age interactions on personality fac-tors. However, as stated earlier, life span developmental psychologists have theory behind their beliefs that there is both sta-bility and change in individuals' person-ality as they age (Ruth & Coleman, 1996; Ryff, 1991; Shifren, 1996). There is also recent evidence for both stability and change in personality as we age. For ex-ample, a recent meta-analysis (Roberts & DelVecchio, 2000) shows that tempera-ment characteristics (e.g., adaptability, negative emotionality, activity level, rhythmicity), the Big Five (e.g., extraversion, agreeableness, neuroticism conscienciousness, openness to experience), coding of items for masculinity and femininity, and Type A personality revealed a linear and somewhat steplike pattern to trait consistency as we age, with a peak sometime after age 50. Roberts and Del-Vecchio (2000) did *not* find gender differences in these personality traits as we age.

There is a growing body of literature on age differences in generativity (McAdams, 1993). In particular, there is a greater exploration of generativity in women as they age. A recent group of studies by Stewart and colleagues has addressed generativity from womens' perspectives as they age. Their studies focus on middle adulthood and not older adulthood. Interestingly, Stewart and Ostrove (1998) report that by middle age, college-educated women show an increased sense of their personal identity and confidence in personal efficacy. This is accompanied by women's increasing preoccupation with the aging process itself. Stewart and Vandewater (1998) discuss the idea that womens' "felt capacity for generativity" rises from early to mid-adulthood, but then the felt capacity declines somewhat in women after this age period. Also, young and middle-aged adults perceive greater control, especially over their health, than do older adults (Leventhal et al., in press).

Most recently, Stewart, Ostrove, and Helson (in press) examined three samples of women in their 40s and 50s looking at identity, generativity, confident power, and awareness of aging. They found that all of these aspects of women were more evident in middle age than in early adulthood. Women in their 50s reported a greater sense of personal identity, greater vision of self in the social world, and women believed they had the capacity to impact the world. Melia (1999) found that womens' identity and ego integrity were reestablished and revised over time in a study of elderly Catholic nuns. Specific-

ally, the important themes that occurred in the nuns' lives were repeated over the life span allowing for revision of identity and ego.

There is both theory and evidence of gender differences in personality as we age. Early work has shown that by midlife men and women describe themselves less in terms of the gender stereotypes of society than younger individuals (Sinnott, 1986). Gutmann (1994) suggests that older males become peacemakers in midlife, and they rework the more aggressive personality style from their youth. Women shift from a personality style that was passive and yielding to a style that is more assertive and in more control. These personality styles fall under the rubric of stereotypic personality characteristics more recently discussed as instrumental and expressive traits (Shifren, Furnham, & Bauserman, 1998). Huyck (1998) cautions against the notion that men and women can be easily categorized as "masculine," "feminine," or "androgynous" in any kind of simplistic way as has been done in prior research. From research on her Parkville sample, Huyck (1996) showed that there is no simple model of androgyny that is useful. Huyck found that men and women's scores on a measure of global masculine and feminine characteristicis separated into three masculine and three feminine factors. She found that androgyny could be based on high scores on a variety of these factors; consequently, different combinations might relate very differently to outcomes. Labouvie-Vief, Hakim-Larsen, Devoe, and Schoeberlein (1989) also point out that masculine–feminine is a duality. In midlife adults are capable of more complex thinking; consequently, the duality of thinking can be diminished as we age (see Labouvie-Vief, Orwoll & Manion, 1995).

For some personality characteristics such as locus of control, the evidence for gender-by-age effects has been mixed and theory is not as evident. A meta-analysis by Feingold (1994) showed that men and women did not differ in control beliefs. However, gender differences do occur for certain domains such as marriage and health issues. A recent study on control in marital relations contradicts the conclusions of the earlier meta-analysis (Lachman & Weaver, 1998). Lachman and Weaver (1998) found that men perceived higher personal mastery than women, whereas women reported greater perceived restraints and less perceived control over their marriages. In another study, researchers examined elderly men and women (65–94 years old), and they found that women have significantly lower perceived internal control and significantly lower scores on a powerful others scale than men (Perrig-Chiello, Perrig, & Staehelin, 1999).

C. Health

There is a long history of evidence for gender differences in health as we age (Verbrugge, 1989; Wheeler, 1997). Certainly, some theoretical models on health include gender and age as predictors of health outcomes. However, much research on health outcomes does not include theoretical models of the interaction of gender and age on health outcomes. What do we know about gender, health, and age? There might be more quantity to womens' lives, but it also appears that there is less quality to the lives of older women. For example, Smith and Baltes's (1998) Berlin Aging Study on 70 to 103 year olds found that women were overrepresented in clusters of less desirable profiles including more depression, loneliness, frailty, and cognitive impairment compared to men. What follows here is a mixed bag of evidence for and against gender-by-age interactions on a variety of health measures.

Plaud, Schweigman, and Welfy (1998) found that of American Indian men and women, 48–82 years old, they had equivalent scores on depression, cigarette use, and seat belt use. However, men and women differed on alcohol consumption and cholesterol. Women had higher cholesterol and glucose, and men had higher frequency and quantity of alcohol-consumption rates. Latimer and Sheahan (1998) examined individuals, 65 and over, and found subtle but important differences in older adults' health. They found that income impacted older womens' health, but living alone impacted men's health. Furthermore, Unger, McAvay, Bruce, Berkman, and Seeman (1999), in a study on men and women 70–80 years old, found that social ties had a stronger protective effect for men than women as seen by performance on a physical functioning scale that measures pushing, pulling, stooping, lifting, and writing. This provides further support for Seeman's (1996) review concluding that support impacts heart health and mortality in men. Tomiak, Berthelot, Guimond, and Mustard (2000) examined a representative sample of all people, 65 and over, in Manitoba in 1986. Besides age, they found that marital status is an important factor for nursing home entry in men, and education was important as a factor for nursing home entry in women. When it comes to providing self-care rather than care to others, women over 70 perform more instrumental activities for longer durations than men when they are widowed women, even after controlling analyses for age, long-term-care residence, income, and education (Horgas, Wilms, & Baltes, 1998).

There are also studies where no relation between gender, age, and health has been found. For example, Wilcox (1998) examined men and women, 20–80 years old, and she found that men and women report similar scores on body attitude items. Wilcox (1998) found no age, gender, or interactive effects for body attitudes in her sample. In a cross-cultural study including Tampere and Florence, no gender differences were found in 60–74 and 75–89 year olds on self-reported health, even after adjusting analyses for age, education, disease, and disability factors (Jylhä, Guralnik, Ferrucci, Jokela, & Schoeberlein, 1998).

D. Caregiving

There is no doubt that the caregiving role can be stressful for individuals. The stressors of caregiving are greatly enhanced when one is caregiving for a relative with a dementing illness (Schulz & Williamson, 1991). Despite the abundance of research on caregiving, little attention has been paid to developing and testing theoretical models including gender and age for caregiving samples. This is surprising because the caregiving literature has shown some evidence of gender differences in the caregiving experience as we age (see meta-analysis by Miller & Cafasso, 1992). In the most recent literature review to date, Yee and Schulz (2000) researched the caregiving literature for gender differences in psychiatric morbidity. They found that women caregivers report psychiatric symptoms more than men caregivers, including more depression, anxiety, and lower life satisfaction. They suggest that there may be several reasons for gender differences in caregiving experiences, including (a) women respond differently at all stages of the stress process than men, (b) they have more caregiving demands than male caregivers, and (c) they provide more intensive care day to day than men. Not surprisingly, women caregivers have higher amounts of objective stressors, and this relates to womens' higher perceived stress. Yee and Schulz (2000) point out that little has been done to directly test the importance of these factors in explaining differences in men and women caregivers for psychiatric morbidity. Obviously, this is an area that deserves further study.

In another recent study comparing AD caregivers to Parkinson's disease (PD) caregivers, researchers looked at gender differences in mental health and coping techniques (Hooker, Manoogian-O'Dell, Monahan, Frazier, & Shifren, 2000). Hooker et al. (2000) found no gender differences in the PD caregivers; however, for AD caregivers, women were more depressed, stressed, and anxious than men. Furthermore, men AD caregivers were more likely to use problem-focused coping techniques than women AD caregivers. Hooker et al. (2000) suggest that marital relation losses in the AD caregiving group might influence women AD caregivers' overall well-being. However, it is also possible to derive positive meaning, positive mood, and even positive expectations about the future from the caregiving experience (Motenko, 1989; Shifren & Hooker, 1995). Unfortunately, there has been little study including gender differences in positive aspects of caregiving as we age. This is an area that deserves further exploration.

In the final section of this chapter, the history of gender role development research is discussed along with where we need to go in terms of theory in adult development and aging. Also, the important role that postformal operations may have in adult gender role development is discussed along with major conflicts in the field.

VI. Gender Role Development and Aging

Theories of life span sex roles attempt to describe how behavior is connected to the stereotypic gender-related role behavior of men and women, which changes developmentally over time (e.g., Bem, 1993; Carter, 1987; Rogers, Sinnott, & van Dusen, 1991, summarized in Sinnott, 1998; Sinnott, 1977, 1980a,b,c, 1981a, 1982a,b, 1984a, 1984–85, 1986, 1987,

1989a,c, 1994b, 1997; Sinnott, Block, Gaddy, Grambs, & Davidson, 1980; Sinnott, Rogers, & Spencer, 1996). The theories in their current manifestations suggest that roles are first polarized into male and female roles. Then roles are reversed or are combined into a complex role. Ultimately roles are transcended to the point that sex roles matter relatively little to the individual or to the construction of the individual's identity.

Looking at the qualities underlying these sex role theories we see that some information related to them is descriptive, but much less is inferential, despite the existence of several standard measurement tools. Although gender roles themselves have existed for millennia, this area of study originated with Freudian psychology, social learning theory, cross-cultural studies, the feminist movement, and awareness of the rapidly changing American experience. Although sex role theory was originally a rather simple enterprise, we currently find more and more associated variables and context effects and ways of scaling dimensions (Bem, 1974, 1993; Spence & helmreich, 1979; Spence, Helmreich, & Stapp, 1975). Organismic models (e.g., Freud's) have been challenged by mechanistic ones (e.g., Bandura's) and later by constructivist ones (e.g., Kohlberg's). Most approaches have been digital, labeling respondents in a polarized way, rather than analog (asking, for example, "To what degree am I masculine or feminine?"). Sex role studies are nested in explicit theory; they are usually applied to clinical, personality, and developmental issues, such as adaptivity. Sex role theory has been assumed to be generalizable to all humans. Investigators seek information about average behavior and generally are not very complex in their view of women and men. This work does not present qualitative analyses of respondents' narratives and does not analyze information

about the meaning of sex roles in their lives. Quantitative analyses are the norm. The model uses Newtonian logic. This set of theories, then, rests on models that are good for both specific detailed investigations and painting the broader picture, but still are essentially intra-personal and uncritically accepting of arguments about women's and men's traditional places and behavior as defined by society. They do not address the transcendent meanings mature and older persons try to bring to their role-related experiences because there is no room in the model for this.

A. Role Permanence

Early views of gender role development considered roles as biologically based and, once established in childhood, consistent throughout the life span. Masculinity and femininity were conceptualized as two end points of a continuum and were tested accordingly, or they were conceptualized as separate variables and tested accordingly. An individual was assumed to be optimally adjusted if biological sex and role were the same.

In early biologically based psychological theories, an individual who deviated from a prescribed role was thought to be one whose psychosexual development was inadequate. This reflected the Freudian view that successful resolution of Oedipal and Electra conflicts led to permanent identification of boys with fathers and girls with mothers. Individuals then copied the same-sex role behaviors, showing objective evidence of identification. Later neuropsychologically based theories focused on the aspects of roles that might be biologically built into the female and male brains and neuroendocrine systems.

Whereas Freud and other functionalist implied that roles unfolded from innate potential, social learning theorists posited that roles were learned by simple observation and imitation of the same-sex adult. Reinforcement then led to establishment of enduring patterns. Although changes in reinforcement contingencies allowed the possibility for role variability, it was assumed that roles were lifelong. However, research that has focused on modeling of adult behavior or global personality traits shared by parent and child has not found that children closely follow the behavior or personality of the same-sex adult.

Cognitive developmental approaches held that the child's perception of gender role identification precedes role-appropriate behavior. The child discovered that there were girls and boys, adopted one of those labels, then copied the reinforced behavior congruent with the labeled concept. The roles then were kept consistent over the life span.

Learning perspectives on role development have received support from researchers such as Bandura. Results suggested the very strong impact of socialization on role behavior. Learning approaches were also supported by anthropological work comparing roles in primitive societies and exploring the survival value of roles. Because roles were not universally consistent, proponents of the learning approach could argue for the greater impact of environment. However, opponents to learning theory could argue for evolutionary change within special environmental conditions. Recent theories suggest that gender is less a personality attribute than an emergent property of social groups (Maccoby, 1998).

B. Adult Theories

The consideration of life span gender role development has been a relatively recent phenomenon, with the majority of work done in the 1970s and 1980s. A review of publications during that period, and of some classic references, are presented in Sinnott (1987). At the beginning of this historical wave of interest, Neugarten, Crotty, and Tobin (1964), Gutmann (Gutmann, 1975, 1987; Neugarten & Gutmann, 1968) and Block (1973) explored changes in role expectations during adulthood that were based upon social expectations and major developmental tasks. Block (1973) and Riegel (1973) viewed the manifestation of cultural gender roles as a function not only of biological demands and past learning experiences but of the nature of economic systems, of the historical moment, and of the philosophical system within which they are defined. Thus, roles in this perspective imply dynamic change based upon individual change and social and cultural climate. Loevinger's (1977) milestones of ego development and their extrapolations to gender role development formed the basis of Block's (1973) approach. In the earliest period, the main developmental concerns of the child are genderless, and identity constitutes a mere naming of gender. Later, conformity to learned patterns becomes the main task, reflected in the development of role stereotypes. Here differentiation of roles results. The highest most integrated level of functioning finds the individual evolving a complex identity that combines aspiration, experience, and previously polarized traits. This is the period of androgyny. Investigators have attempted to measure later-life development of androgyny (e.g., Hyde & Phyllis, 1979; Sinnott, 1982a; Sinnott, Block, Gaddy, Grambs, & Davidson, 1980; Windle & Sinnott, 1985, Windle 1986), and examine its relation to social expectations in later life (Sinnott, 1984a), to mental health (Livson, 1976; Sinnott, 1984–85), and to other factors in life context (Sinnott, 1982a).

Following the lead of Jung (1982) who wrote that opposite-sex behavior would begin to surface for a person in the later half of life, Gutmann (Gutmann, 1987; Neugarten & Gutmann, 1968) describes the role reversal that comes after child rearing is completed. Based on data from a wide variety of cultures, gathered using Thematic Apperception Tests (TAT), older women and men reverse roles. Men take a more feminine (by younger definitions) stance toward life; women act in more masculine (by younger definitions) ways. These reversals are thought to represent more adaptive behaviors for the aging individuals.

Hefner, Rebecca, and Oleshansky (1975) proposed a life span hierarchical stage progression through roles, leading to role transcendence. The stages include global undifferentiated, polarized traditional, and combined or transcendent roles. Although the young child most likely has not defined a role, and the adolescent most likely has overdefined it, the adult synthesizes the masculine and feminine roles. But rather than stopping at this androgyny-like stage, adults may go beyond traditional roles. At that final point adjustment is no longer tied to roles at all; roles just do not matter much as organizers of identity.

Garnets and Pleck (1979) presented a concept called sex role strain analysis. Combining learning and development, they see psychological harm resulting from conflict at any time in the life span between the individual's self-perception of roles and his or her perception of social expectations about appropriate roles. When considering the importance of this strain, they also measure the salience of roles for the individual.

Sinnott (1984b, 1986, 1987, 1989b, 1994a, 1995, 1998) described a postformal theory of adult role development. A number of investigators have addressed the topic of postformal operations (i.e., those structures of thought that are a stage more complex in organization than Piaget's formal operations). The question of interest here is, how might this complex thought, which develops in adulthood, relate to more complex sex role development in adulthood? To address this question it is necessary to examine more closely some aspects of postformal operations and the argument itself. The argument is a postmodern one. Social relations, including sex roles, may be seen as based on cognitive skills. As cognitive skills develop, the social role also can be thought of in more complex ways, and therefore can be lived in more complex ways. Postformal operations have the following characteristics: they subsume and organize several formal operational logical systems, and they have a quality of necessary subjectivity (that is, the knower realizes that truth is partly created by the way he or she conceptualizes things). So complex adult sex roles, viewed postformally, are roles that are not absolute but that are consciously created to some degree by the actor selecting a view of truth. This approach has the quality of the new physics realities. The role taken becomes what is agreed upon as true by those in the interaction. Role behaviors become attempts to solve ill-structured everyday problems about identity and how to behave. Postformal thought-based roles in adulthood and old age might permit greater creativity in using strategies to solve problems about social interactions where the goal is unclear, a characteristic of most everyday problems, especially social ones.

A general systems theory of sex roles is based on the idea that interacting processes influence each other over time to permit the continuity of some larger whole (see, for example, Ford, 1987; Miller, 1978; von Bertalanfy, 1968). In Miller's discussion of living systems, individuals, societies, and cells all appear to use similar processes to create boundaries, to take in stimulation, to process information, to act and to change. As living systems develop and age, they appear to proceed through a regular set of stages. They begin in disorder, with few parts concretely defined; they gradually become more orderly; they end when they

are too rigid to face challenges successfully. How does this relate to sex role
development over the life span? Consider
the person and society as living systems,
each seeking continuity and meeting survival needs, including control of information and energy flow. Sex roles are ways
that person and social systems can regulate that flow of energy and information.
The early stages are disorderly (i.e., no
roles); later, roles become more concretely feminine and masculine. Deadly
final stages would find the roles too rigid
to respond to new needs of later adulthood. In middle age and old age, the post-
parental imperative results in the need to
change structured roles or risk foundering
on dysfunctionally rigid roles.

C. Major Conflicts in the Field

Five major conflicts have emerged in the
field, conflicts that could form the basis
for some important future research. First,
are roles fixed or flexible? Life span sex
role developmentalists would tend to
pick the latter. Second, how central are
sex roles to personality and identity? Life
span sex role developmentalists would
answer, not central. Third, should sex
roles be measured taking into account
age-appropriate norms, context, and self-
perception? Life span theorists such as
Barrows and Zuckerman (1976) and
Windle and Sinnott (1985) would want to
go beyond actual behavior to examine
what the behavior means in each context
and developmental stage. Fourth, are
stereotypes, sexism, power, and politics
inherent in sex roles, and therefore something to be factored out in studies? Life
span investigators have shown little
tendency to take stereotypes, sexism,
and power and politics into account;
most grant that they do matter, however.
Fifth, should we study change and adaptive qualities of roles over time?
Although the obvious answer would
seem to be yes for life span investigators,

aging studies addressing or assuming
change and adaptation are relatively infrequent. Sixth, should sex roles be linked to
cognitive processes and to other living
system processes, using those literatures
to guide the generation of research questions? Life span investigators are moving
in the direction of such multifactorial
approaches. Seventh, must sex roles be
polarized concepts, mandating clearly
masculine and feminine behaviors in
well-adapted persons? Life span developmental theorists are moving in the direction of conceptualizing roles as more
individualistic, defined and given differential value by each developing individual in concert with society, creating a
wide spectrum of role behavior possibilities (e.g., McGee & Wells, 1982). Along
with this transformation, roles are more
often seen as distinct from other related
concepts such as gender identity.

VII. Summary and Conclusions

Studies of gender and aging in the adult
life span literature have often been hap-
hazard and opportunistic. They have contributed the most sophisticated and
useful information on the topics of development of sex and gender roles over the
life span. In spite of difficulties with operational and conceptual definitions of
the term gender, and in spite of known
challenges of measurement, subject selection, and design, a body of theory and
data has emerged to form a basis for
future work. Sophisticated multifactorial
models are needed to address the form
and processes of gender role development
in adulthood so that the influences of, for
example, culture and birth cohort are not
confounded with the influence of biology
and time. Gender role development in old
age appears to involve transforming and
even transcending such roles, at least as
they are conceptualized in earlier life, to
continue the construction of identity,

meaning, and community for the aging person. Gender may be an emergent property of social groups, as Maccoby (1998) suggests, even in later years.

With regard to research on gender differences in cognitive functioning, personality, health, and caregiving, several issues are important to note. First, there is enough evidence of gender differences in these different domains to warrant further investigation of these gender differences. Rather than asking the question, Is there a gender difference as we age?, we sould be asking, Why is there a gender difference as we age? Second, gender-by-age interactions on various tasks may indicate a complex interaction between biology and the environment. We need more theoretically driven models for the relation between gender and age on different outcomes. Models that address the "why" of gender-by-age interactions on outcomes will be useful in shaping future interventions for health care.

The discussion of gender differences in research on cognition, personality, health, and caregiving was meant to provide a brief update on the research in these domains. However, it was not meant to be an extensive literature review of each area of research. We hope that researchers will continue to study gender-by-age interactions on these important topic areas. However, we encourage more theory-driven models behind the research. There is enough evidence of gender differences to warrant more theoretically derived studies and less studies based solely on performance data.

References

Barrett-Connor, E., & Kritz-Silverstein, D. (1999). Gender differences in cognitive function with age: The Rancho Bernardo Study. *Journal of the American Geriatics Society, 47,* 159–164.

Barrows, G. W., & Zuckerman, M. (1976). Content validity of three masculinity-femininity tests. *Journal of Counseling and Clinical Psychology, 34,* 1–7.

Bem, S. (1974). The measurement of psychological androgyny. *Journal of Consulting and Clinical Psychology, 42,* 155–162.

Bem, S. L. (1985). Androgyny and gender schema theory: A conceptual and empirical integration. In T. B. Sonderegger (Ed.), *Nebraska symposium on motivation 1984; Psychology and gender* (vol. 32). Lincoln: University of Nebraska Press.

Bem, S. (1993). *The lenses of gender: Transforming the debate on sexual equality.* New Haven, CT: Yale University Press.

Berger, R. M. (1984, January-February). Realities of gay and lesbian aging. *Social Work,* 57–62.

Block, J. H. (1973). Conceptions of sex role. *American Psychologist, 28,* 512–526.

Brown, L. A., Lahar, C. J., & Mosley, J. L. (1998). Age and gender-related differences in strategy use for route information. A "map-present" direction-giving paradigm. *Environment and behavior, 30,* 123–143.

Capitani, E., Laiacona, M., & Basso, A. (1999). Phonetically cued word-fluency, gender differences and aging: A reappraisal. *Cortex, 34,* 779–783.

Carter, D. B. (Ed.) (1987). *Current conceptions of sex roles and sex typing.* New York: Praeger.

Chan, A. S., & Poon, M. W. (2000). Performance of 7 to 95 year old individuals in a Chinese version of the category fluency test. *Journal of the International Neuropsychological Society, 5,* 525–533.

Cherrier, M. M. (2000). Androgens, ageing, behavior and cognition: Complex interactions and novel areas of inquiry. *New Zealand Journal of Psychology, 28,* 4–9.

Costa, P. T., & McCrae, R. R. (1993). Psychological stress and coping in old age. In L. Goldberger & S. Breznitz (Eds.), *Handbook of stress: Theoretical and clinical aspects* (2nd ed.) (pp. 403–412). New York: Free Press.

Coyle, J. M. (Ed.) (1997). *Handbook on women and aging.* Westport, CT: Greenwood Press.

Erikson, E. (1950). *Childhood and society.* New York: Norton.

Erikson, E. (1985). *The life cycle completed.* New York: Bantam.

Feingold, A. (1994). Gender differences in personality: A meta-analysis. *Psychological Bulletin, 116,* 429–456.

Ford, D. (1987). *Humans as self-constructing systems: A developmental perspective.* Hillsdale, NJ: Erlbaum.

Garnets, L., & Pleck, J. H. (1979). Sex role identity, androgyny, and sex role transcendence: A sex role strain analysis. *Psychological of Women Quarterly, 3,* 270–283.

Gutmann, D. (1975). Parenthood: A key to the comparative study of the life cycle. In N. Datan & L. Ginsberg (Eds.), *Life-span developmental psychology: normative crises* (pp. 167–184). New York: Academic Press.

Gutmann, D. L. (1977). The cross-cultural perspective: Notes toward a comparative psychology of aging. In J. E. Birren & K. W. Schaie (Eds.), *Handbook of the psychology of aging* (pp. 302–306). New York: Van Nostrand Reinhold.

Gutmann, D. (1987). *Reclaimed powers: Toward a new psychology of men and women in later life.* New York: Basic Books.

Gutmann, D. L. (1994). *Reclaimed powers: Toward a new psychology of men and women in later life.* Evanston, IL: Northwestern University Press.

Halpern, D. F. (1997). Sex differences in intelligence: Implications for education. *American Psychologist, 52,* 1091–1102.

Hedges, L. V., & Nowell, A. (1995, July 7). Sex differences in mental test scores, variability, and numbers of high-scoring individuals. *Science, 269,* 41–45.

Hefner, R., Rebecca, M., & Oleshansky, B. (1975). Development of sex role transcendence. *Human Development, 18,* 143–158.

Hooker, K., Manoogian-O'Dell, M., Monahan, D. J., Frazier, L. D., & Shifren, K. (2000). Does type of disease matter? Gender differences among Alzheimer's and Parkinson's disease spouse caregivers. *The Gerontologist, 40,* 568–573.

Horgas, A. L., Wilms, H.-U., & Baltes, M. M. (1998). Daily life in very old age: Everyday activities as expression of successful living. *The Gerontologist, 38,* 556–568.

Huyck, M. H. (1990). Gender differences in aging. In J. Birren & K. W. Schaie (Ed.), *Handbook of the psychology of aging* (pp. 125–132). San Diego: Academic Press.

Huyck, M. H. (1996). Continuities and discontinuities in gender identity. In V. Bengtson, (Ed.), *Adulthood and aging: Research on continuities and discontinues* (pp. 98–121). New York: Springer.

Huyck, M. H. (1998). Gender roles and gender identity in midlife. In S. L. Willis & J. D. Reid (Eds.), *Life in the middle: Psychological and social development in middle age* (pp. 209–232). San Diego, CA: Academic Press.

Hyde, J. S., & Phyllis, E. E. (1979). Androgyny across the lifespan. *Developmental Psychology, 15,* 334–336.

Janowsky, J. S., Oviatt, S. K., & Orwoll, E. S. (1994). Testosterone influences spatial cognition in older men. *Behavioral Neuroscience, 108,* 325–332.

Jung, C. (1982). *The complete works.* London: Routledge & Kegan Paul.

Jylhä, M., Guralnik, J. M., Ferrucci, L., Jokela, J., & Heikkinen, E. (1998). Is self-rated health comparable across cultures and genders? *Journal of Gerontology: Social Sciences, 53B,* S144–S152.

Kausler, D. H. (1991). *Experimental psychology, cognition, and human aging* (2nd ed.). New York: Springer-Verlag.

Labouvie-Vief, G., Hakim-Larson, J., Devoe, M., & Schoeberlein, S. (1989). Emotions and self-regulation: A life span view. *Human Development, 32,* 279–299.

Labouvie-Vief, G., Orwoll, L., & Manion, M. (1995). Narratives of mind, gender, and the life course. *Human Development, 38,* 239–257.

Lachman, M. E., & Weaver, S. L. (1998). Sociodemographic variations in the sense of control by domain: Findings from the MacArthur studies of midlife. *Psychology and Aging, 13,* 553–562.

Latimer, M., & Sheahan, S. L. (1998). Gender differences in the causal factors affecting the health status of older adults. *American Journal of Health Behavior, 22,* 298–307.

Leventhal, H., Leventhal, E.A., & Cameron, L. (in press). Representations, procedures, and affect in illness self-regulation: A perceptual-cognitive model. In A. Baum, T. Revenson, & J. Singer (Eds.), *Handbook of health physiology,* New York, New York: Lawrence Erlbaum.

Livson, F.B. (1976). Patterns of personality development in midle-aged women: A longitudinal study. *International Journal of Aging and Human Development, 7*, 107–115.

Loevinger, J. (1977). *Ego development.* San Francisco: Jossey-Bass.

Lowe, P. A., & Reynolds, C. R. (1999). Age, gender, and education may have little influence on error patterns in the assessment of set-shifting and rule induction among normal elderly. *Archives of Clinical Neuropsychology, 14*, 303–315.

Lytton, H., & Romney, D. M. (1991). Parents' differential socialization of boys and girls: A meta-analysis. *Psychological Bulletin, 109*, 267–296.

Maccoby, E. E. (1998). *The two sexes: Growing apart, coming together.* Cambridge, MA: Harvard University Press.

McAdams, D. P. (1993). *The stories we live by: Personal myths and the making of the self.* New York: William Morrow.

McGee, J., & Wells, K. (1982). Gender typing and androgyny in later life: New directions for theory and research. *Human Development, 25*, 116–139.

Melia, S. P. (1999). Continuity in the lives of elder Catholic women nuns. *International Journal of Aging and Human Development, 48*, 175–189.

Miller, B., & Cafasso, L. (1992). Gender differences in caregiving: Fact or artifact? *The Gerontologist, 32*, 498–507.

Miller, J. (1978). *Living systems.* New York: McGraw-Hill.

Minor, K., & Park, S. (1999). Spatial working memory: Absence of gender differences in schizophrenia patients and healthy control subjects. *Biological Psychiatry, 46*, 1003–1005.

Motenko, A. K. (1989). The frustrations, gratifications, and well-being of dementia caregivers. *The Gerontologist, 29*, 166–172.

Neugarten, B. (1964). *Personality in middle and late life.* New York: Prentice-Hall.

Neugarten, B., Crotty, G., & Tobin, S. (1964). Personality types in an aging population. In B. Neugarten (Ed.), *Personality in middle and late life.* New York: Prentice Hall.

Neugarten, B., & Gutmann, D. (1968). Age-sex roles and personality in middle age. In B. Neugarten (Ed.), *Middle age and aging* (pp.

58–71). Chicago: University of Chicago Press.

Norman, M. A., Evans, J. D., Miller, S. W., & Heaton, R. K. (2000). Demographically corrected norms for the California Verbal Learning Test. *Journal of Clinical and Experimental Neuropsychology, 22*, 80–94.

Obler, L. K. (1982). Sex differences in aging: The experimental literature. *Resources for Feminist Research, 11*, 209–210.

Paganini-Hill, A., Buckwalter, J. G., Logan, C. G., & Henderson, V. W. (1993). Estrogen replacement and Alzheimer's disease in women. *Society for Neuroscience Abstracts, 19*, 1046.

Park, D.C., Smith, A.D., Lautenschlager, G., Earles, J., Frieske, D., Zwahr, M., & Gaines, C. (1996). Mediators of long-term memory performance across the life span. *Psycholoical and Aging, 11*, 621–637.

Perrig-Chiello, P., Perrig, W. G., & Staehelin, H. B. (1999). Health control beliefs in old age: Relationship with subjective and objective health, and health behaviour. *Psychology, Health and Medicine, 4*, 83–94.

Plaud, J. J., Schweigman, K., & Welty, T. K. (1998). Health-related and cultural gender differences in an aging American Indian population. *Journal of Clinical Geropsychology, 4*, 111–118.

Riegel, K. F. (1973). Dialectical operations: The final period of human development. *Human Development, 16*, 346–370.

Roberts B. W., & DelVecchio, W. F. (2000). The rank-order consistency of personality traits from childhood to old age. A quantitative review of longitudinal studies. *Psychological Bulletin, 126*, 3-25.

Rogers, D. R. B., Sinnott, J. D., & Van Dusen, L. (1991). *Marital adjustment and social cognitive performance in everyday logical problem solving.* Paper presented at the Sixth Adult Development Symposium, Suffolk University, Boston.

Ruth, J.-E., & Coleman, P. (1996). Personality and aging: Coping and management of the self in later life. In J. E. Birren & K. W. Schaie's (Eds.), *Handbook of the psychology of aging* (4th ed.) (pp. 308–322). San Diego, CA: Academic Press.

Ryff, C. D. (1991). Possible selves in adulthood and old age: A tale of shifting horizons. *Psychology and Aging, 6*, 286–295.

Salthouse, T. A. (1996). General and specific speed mediation of adult age differences in memory. *Journal of Gernotology: Psychological Sciences, 51B*, P30–P42

Schulz, R., & Williamson, G. M. (1991). A two-year longitudinal study of depression among Alzheimer's caregivers. *Psychology and Aging, 6*, 569–578.

Seeman, T. E. (1996). Social ties and health. *Annals of Epidemiology, 6*, 442–451.

Shifren, K. (1996). Individual differences in the perception of optimism and disease severity: A study among individuals with Parkinson's disease. *Journal of Behavioral Medicine, 19*, 241–271.

Shifren, K., Furnham, A., & Bauserman, R. L. (1998). Instrumental and expressive traits and eating attitudes: A replication across American and British students. *Personality and Individual Differences, 25*, 1–17.

Shifren, K., & Hooker, K. (1995). Stability and change in optimism: A study among spouse caregivers. *Experimental Aging Research, 21*, 59–76.

Silver, R. (1999). Differences among senior and young, men and women in attitudes and cognition. U. S. Department of Education. *Office of Educational Research and Improvement*. 1–25. Document report.

Sinnott, J. D. (1977). Sex-role inconstancy, biology, and successful aging: A dialectical model. *Gerontologist, 17*, 459–463.

Sinnott, J. D. (1980a). *Contributions of dialectical theory to a study of elders' sex-role development.* Paper presented at American Psychological Association Convention, Montreal, Canada.

Sinnott, J. D. (1980b). *Correlates of sex-role complexity in older adults.* Paper presented at the Eastern Psychological Association, Hartford, Connecticut.

Sinnott, J. D. (1980c). *Role flexibility: Is it a coping mechanism?* Paper presented at Gerontological Society, San Diego, CA.

Sinnott, J. D. (1981a). *Sex roles in old age.* Paper presented at Meeting of the International Gerontological Society, Hamburg, Germany.

Sinnott, J. D. (1981b). The theory of relativity: A metatheory for development? *Human Development, 24*, 295–311.

Sinnott, J. D. (1982a). Correlates of older adults' performance on the BSRI (Bem Sex Role Inventory). *Journal of Gerontology, 37*, 587–594.

Sinnott, J. D. (1982b). *Older women, older men: Are their perceived sex roles similar?* Paper presented at Eastern Psychological Association, Baltimore, MD.

Sinnott, J. D. (1984a). Older woman, older men: Are their perceived sex roles similar? *Sex Roles, 10*, 847–856.

Sinnott, J. D. (1984b). Postformal reasoning: The relativistic stage. In M. Commons, F. Richards & C. Armon (Eds.), *Beyond formal operations* (pp. 298–325). New York: Praeger.

Sinnott, J. D. (1984–85). Stress, health, and mental older women and men. *International Journal of Aging and Human Development, 20*, 123–132.

Sinnott, J. D. (1986). *Sex roles and aging: Theory and research from a systems perspective.* New York: Karger.

Sinnott, J. D. (1987). Sex roles in adulthood and aging years. In D. B. Carter (Ed.), *Current conceptions of sex roles and sex typing* (pp. 155–177). New York: Praeger.

Sinnott, J. D. (1989a). *A general systems theory perspective on sex roles and social change.* Paper presented at National Women' Studies Association Conference, Baltimore, MD.

Sinnott, J. D. (1989b). Adult differences in the use of postformal operations. In M. Commons, J. D. Sinnott, F. Richards, & C. Armon (Eds.), *Adult development: Comparison and application of developmental models* (pp. 239–278). New York: Praeger.

Sinnott, J. D. (1989c). The general systems metatheory: A conceptual system to study changes and explain resistance to change in sex roles and gender identity. *Women's Studies International Forum, 12* (5), p. XVI.

Sinnott, J. D. (Ed.) (1994a). *Interdisciplinary handbook of adult lifespan learning.* Westport, CT: Greenwood Press.

Sinnott, J. D. (1994b). Sex roles. In V. S. Ramachandran (Ed.), *Encyclopedia of human behavior* (pp. 151–158). NY: Academic Press.

Sinnott, J. D. (1995). The development of complex reasoning: Postformal thought. In F. Blanchard-Fields & T. Hess (Eds.), *Perspectives on cognitive change in adulthood and aging.* New York: McGraw-Hill.

Sinnott, J. D. (1997). Developmental models of midlife and aging in women: Metaphors for transcendence and for individuality in community. In J. M. Coyle (Ed.), *Handbook on women and aging* (pp. 149–163). Westport, CT: Greenwood.

Sinnott, J. D. (1998). *The development of logic in adulthood: Postformal thought and its applications*. New York: Plenum Press.

Sinnott, J. D., Block, M., Gaddy, C., Grambs, L., & Davidson, J. (1980). *Sex roles in mature adults: Antecedents and correlates*. College Park, Maryland: University of Maryland, Center on Aging. (Also available through *Journal Supplement Abstract Service*, 1981, *11*, 82.

Sinnott, J. D., Rogers, D., & Spencer, F. (1996). Reconsidering sex roles and aging: Preliminary data on some influences of context, cohort, time. *ERIC*, Document # ED 391 139/ CG 026 796.

Smith, J., & Baltes, M. M. (1998). The role of gender in very old age: Profiles of functioning and every day life patterns. *Psychology and Aging, 13*, 676–695.

Spence, J. T., Helmreich, R. L. (1979). On assessing "androgyny". *Sex Roles, 5*, 721–738.

Spence, J. T., Helmreich, R. L., & Stapp, M. (1975). Ratings of self and peers on sex-role attributes and their relation to concepts of self-esteem in males and females. *Journal of Personality and Social Psychology, 32*, 29–39.

Stanford, E. P., & DuBois, B. C. (1992). Gender and ethnicity patterns. In J. E. Birren, R. B. Sloane, & G. D. Cohen (Eds.), *Handbook of mental health and aging* (pp. 99–119). San Diego: Academic Press.

Steele, C. M. (1997). A threat in the air: How stereotypes shape intellectual identity and performance. *American Psychologist, 52*, 613–629.

Stewart, A. J., & Ostrove, J. M. (1998). Women's personality in middle age: Gender, history, and midcourse corrections. *American Psychologist, 53*, 1185–1194.

Stewart, A. J., Ostrove, J. M., & Helson, R. (in press). Middle aging in women: Patterns of personality change from the 30s to the 50s. *Journal of Adult Development*.

Stewart, A. J., & Vandewater, E. A. (1998). The course of generativity. In D. P. McAdams &
E. de St. Aubin (Eds.), *Women's lives through time* (pp. 235–258). San Francisco: Jossey-Bass.

Tomiak, M., Berthelot, J.-M., Guimond, E., & Mustard, C. A. (2000). Factors associated with nursing-home entry for elders in Manitoba, Canada. *Journal of Gerontology: Medical Sciences, 55A*, M279–M287.

Unger, J. B., McAvay, G., Bruce, M. L., Berkman, L., & Seeman, T. (1999). Variation in the impact of social network characteristics on physical functioning in elderly persons: MacArthur studes of successful aging. *Journal of Gerontology: Social Sciences, 54B*, S245–S251.

Unger, R. K. (1979). Toward a redefinition of sex and gender. *American Psychologist, 34*, 1084–1094.

Unterrainer, J., Wranek, U., Staffen, W., Gruber, T., & Ladurner, G. (2000). Lateralized cognitive visuospatial processing: Is it primarily gender-related or due to quality of performance? A HMPAO-SPECT study. *Neuropsychobiology, 41*, 95–101.

U. S. Department of Education. (1997). *National assessment of educational progress* (Indicator 32: Writing Proficiency; prepared by the Educational Testing Service). Washington, DC: Author. Available: http:// www.ed.gov/nces

Verbrugge, L. M. (1989). Gender, aging, and health. In K. S. Markides (Ed.), *Aging and health: Perspectives on gender, race, ethnicity, and class* (chapter 2). Newbury Park: Sage.

von Bertalanfy, L. (1968). *General systems theory*, New York: Braziller.

Wheeler, H. R. (1997). *Women and aging: A guide to the literature*. Boulder, CO: Lynne Rienner.

Wilcox, S. (1998). Age and gender in relation to body attitudes: Is there a double standard of aging? *Psychology of Women Quarterly, 21*, 549–565.

Wilson, R. S., Bennett, D. A., Beckett, L. A., Morris, M. C., Gilley, D. W., Bienias, J. L., Scherr, P. A., & Evans, D. A. (1999). Cognitive activity in older persons from a geographically defined population. *Journals of Gerontology: Psychological and Social Sciences, 54B*, P155–P160.

Windle, M. (1986). Sex role orientation, cognitive flexibility, and life satisfaction among older adults. *Psychology of Women Quarterly, 10,* 263–273.

Windle, M., & Sinnott, J. D. (1985). A psychometric study of the Bem Sex Role Inventory with an older adult sample. *Journal of Gerontology, 40,* 336–343.

Yee, J. L., & Schulz, R. (2000). Gender differences in psychiatric morbidity among family caregivers: A review and analysis. *The Gerontologist, 40,* 147–164.

Nineteen

Personality and Aging
Flourishing Agendas and Future Challenges

Carol D. Ryff, Christine M. L. Kwan, and Burton H. Singer

I. Introduction

Personality, broadly defined, refers to the study of individual differences in diverse human characteristics, such as traits, goals and motives, emotion and moods, self-evaluative processes, coping strategies, and well-being. Thanks to the vision of early leaders in the fields of gerontology and life-course development, personality and aging has been a vibrant forum of theoretical and empirical inquiry for more than 40 years. Drawing on prior chapters in this series, we first glimpse at earlier targets of personality research. Looking to the past serves as a departure point for examining current studies where the range of contemporary topics is abundant, underscoring the vitality of research on individual differences. We also give attention to how aspects of personality have been *put together*—for example, how traits, goals, or coping strategies have been used to predict well-being. Adopting an evaluative stance, we discuss problematic issues, such as construct overlap among personality variables and reliance on single sources of data.

Following this critique, we call for multidisciplinary expansion of personality research in adulthood and aging, reaching *outward* to macrolevel, social structural influences that may contour individual-difference variables as well as *inward* toward biological factors that underlie personality profiles. How individual-difference variables contribute to successful aging, particularly later life resilience, is offered as a useful query that integrates broad scientific terrain (personality, neurophysiological mechanisms, health outcomes). We provide illustrations of such integrative research and conclude with observations about methodological advances needed to carry out multidisciplinary science.

II. Looking Back: Prior Incarnations of Personality and Aging

Fittingly, the first chapter on personality in the first edition of the *Handbook of the Psychology of Aging* was written by Bernice Neugarten (1977), the matriarch of

Handbook of the Psychology of Aging

"personality and aging." Along with her classic in social gerontology, *Middle Age and Aging* (Neugarten, 1968) and other seminal works (Neugarten, 1973), Neugarten defined many of the core issues that shaped subsequent decades of personality research: How does aging affect personality? Does personality affect aging? Does personality *develop* in the second half of life? Neugarten's vision was wide, encompassing such novel ideas as the "executive processes" of personality in the middle years (e.g., managing complexity, leadership, decision making); the timing of events in the life course and "social clocks" surrounding them that serve as "prods and brakes" on behavior; and the internal subtleties of growing old, such as shifting from thinking of one's age as years remaining, rather than years since birth.

Vibrant input to personality and aging also insued from psychodynamic and ego development circles, such as Jung's (1933) formulation of turning inward in later life and his ideas of gender crossovers in adulthood; Erikson's psychosocial stages, especially midlife generativity and old-aged integrity (1959); and Bühler's (Bühler & Massarik, 1968) "basic life tendencies" that worked toward the fulfillment of life. These works catalyzed new eras of research that continue into the present. For example, research on generativity (see next section) is teeming with current activity.

In the second edition of the handbook, the field of personality was disaggregated into realms of the self and traits (Bengston, Reedy, & Gordon, 1985), emotion and affect (Schulz, 1985), and coping and adaptation (Whitbourne, 1985). This division contributed useful diversification of theoretical and empirical inquiry, but illustrates the rather arbitrary boundary conditions that surrounded personality variables (e.g., are traits distinct from affect and emotion? where does coping and adaptation end and the self begin?). Bengtson et al. (1985) brought forward

cognitive, affective, and motivational perspectives on the self, reviewing studies on such topics as self-esteem, locus of control, sex-role identity, temperament, traits, and body image. These were organized around the overarching question of whether diverse aspects of self-concept show age changes (longitudinal studies) or age differences (cross-sectional studies). The evidence was mixed and diverse, pointing toward needed future studies with better research designs (longitudinal, sequential), psychometrically sound measures, and more representative samples.

Schulz (1985) brought emotion and affect squarely into the field of aging, noting emotion researchers rarely addressed questions of adult development, whereas those studying adulthood and aging showed little interest in emotion. The time was ripe to pursue a host of new questions: Does the intensity or duration of emotional experience vary with aging? Are there aging differences in arousal, affect, and mood? Do events that elicit emotion change with aging? These questions generated many subsequent studies, some of which are described in the summary of current work that follows.

Whitbourne's (1985) chapter in the second edition elaborated the realms of stress, coping, and adaptation. Studies of stressful life events were reviewed, giving considerable emphasis to the appraisals (threatening, positive, benign) of such events. This chapter also summarized the literature on subjective well-being and global satisfaction. Across these, Whitbourne called for more explicit developmental, life-course formulations and put forth the life span construct as an integrative model.

In the third edition of the handbook, Kogan (1990) emphasized trait, contextual, and developmental models of personality. Regarding the former, empirical findings were summarized on structural invariance of personality over time, rank-order stability, and mean-level change.

Contextual models involved examining evidence of personality change associated with social clocks (timing and sequencing of events) as well as interactions between temperament and life roles. Developmental stage models continued evaluation of work built on Erikson's psychosocial model of adult development as well as oevinger's formulation of ego development and Levinson's conception of adult development.

In the fourth edition of the handbook, the chapter on personality and aging brought coping into high relief (Ruth & Coleman, 1996), focusing on how aged individuals cope with later life events, and what resources (internal and external) contribute to their later life adaptation. Basic patterns and ways of coping were defined and juxtaposed with major life events of old age. The formulation of internal resources included personality traits, sense of control, ego level, and adaptive competence. External resources included socioeconomic status, education, and coping strategies. This chapter also elaborated aging and self-concept, emphasizing proactive and motivational features of the self. Stability and change were prominent questions throughout, and the need for methodological innovation (e.g., work on narratives and individual-level analyses) was underscored.

Also in the fourth edition, Filipp (1996) summarized work on motivation and emotion, drawing distinctions between cognitive approaches and arousal or activation approaches. The experience and expression of later life emotion was reviewed, both in self-reported states (e.g., positive and negative affect) as well as arousal of the autonomic nervous system. Filipp (1996) highlighted the paradox of well-being in old age (i.e., that many older persons appear positive and contented, despite the losses and threats of aging. How this comes about was examined in terms of various social relational and social comparative processes as well

as coping strategies. Aging and achievement motivation, both cognitive and social, was also addressed, drawing attention to the wide variability among the aged.

This brief look at personality in prior editions of the *Handbook of the Psychology of Aging* reveals notable continuity in guiding topics: traits, the self, coping, and emotion have been repeatedly examined, and across them, questions of life-course change and stability have been persistently centerstage. The contexts and events of aging lives, frequently formulated in terms of later life stresses, have also been recurrent themes. Methodological issues have often involved how to assess change or stability (e.g., structural invariance, correlational, and mean-level analyses) as well as how to disentangle age and cohort effects. Theoretical guidance has faded in and out, with considerable work being descriptive (i.e., does *variable X* change with age?), although increasingly studies have adopted more explanatory, predictive, or process-oriented approaches. The section below provides recent installments across these diverse realms of inquiry.

III. Varieties of Individual Differences: Current Agendas

Personality research in adulthood and later life is flourishing. There are many vibrant avenues of research, some growing out of the above agendas, but others revealing important new directions. Greater interplay is also evident with mainstream personality psychology, an exchange that has contributed promising new topics, but also underscored the neglect of life-course issues in the larger field of personality. Five key areas of inquiry are selectively reviewed below: (a) traits and development; (b) well-being, affect, and quality of life; (c) stress and coping; (d) goals, projects, and striving, and (e) studies of the self. What is covered in each area is illustrative, with selections made on the basis of studies that are well conceptualized and carefully implemented, and/or that point to promising new directions.

A. Constructive Tensions: Traits and Development

More than any query, studies of personality in adulthood and aging have been dominated by the seemingly straightforward question—does personality change as people grow older, or is it stable? Neugarten likely never imagined that this simple query could prompt such extensive and sustained empirical investigation. After decades of research, based on studies of increasing sophistication in design, assessment procedures, sample selection, and data analyses, the answer is resoundingly *yes to both*: personality in adulthood and later life is characterized by stability AND change. What is increasingly clear, however, is that there is considerable variation in how much change (or stability) occurs, and for whom. An important contributor to teasing apart these profiles of change and stability has been developmental theory.

Early formulations of development, from Jung, Erikson, Buhler, and later, Neugarten, and still later, Levinson, Gould, Vaillant, and Loevinger (for reviews see Ryff, 1984; Wrightsman, 1994) fueled the idea that personality was dynamic and evolving through time. As Costa and McCrae rightfully argued, these perspectives needed rigorous empirical testing and validation, not just enthusiastic endorsement. Hence, they called for a "look at the facts" in a realm of "personal impressions" (McCrae & Costa, 1990, p. 17). Drawing on factor analytically derived trait models, they amassed extensive evidence in support of personality stability in five major dimensions of personality: neuroticism, extraversion, openness, agreeableness, and conscientiousness (Costa & McCrae, 1980, 1988;

Costa, McCrae, & Zonderman, 1986; McCrae, 1993). Their findings were based on longitudinal and cross-sectional analyses, self and other reports (e.g., spouse), and included detailed evaluations of whether the obtained effects were best interpreted as due to age, period, or cohort effects.

Additional evidence of life-course stability came from other investigators as well (e.g., Caspi, 1993; Caspi & Herbener, 1990; Von Dras & Siegler, 1997). Caspi, for example, probed the question of why maladaptive behaviors persist, and further looked to influences that promote personality continuity, such as whom one marries. This work has been valuable for taking personality research into more penetrating realms of understanding *how* stability is maintained. For example, individuals can select themselves into particular environments that reinforce established characteristics, and they can evoke from others responses that contribute to their persistent, sometimes maladaptive, profiles. Marriage is one forum in which such effects can be played out.

Nonetheless, at the same time evidence mounted on behalf of personality stability, there were persistent findings, guided by developmental thinking (frequently Erikson) that personality change occurred with aging. Focusing on early adulthood, Whitbourne used both longitudinal and sequential designs to document shifts in identity and intimacy statuses over a 22-year period (Whitbourne & Waterman, 1979; Whitbourne, Zuschlag, Elliott, & Waterman, 1992). The longitudinal work of Helson and colleagues also drew richly on developmental theories, including those postulating gender crossovers (e.g., Gutmann, 1975; Jung, 1933) and add further evidence of change in personality in women from early adulthood into their mid-fifties (Helson & Moane, 1987; Helson & Roberts, 1994; Helson & Wink, 1992). These studies were based on well-standardized personality inventories (e.g., the California Personality Inventory) that were creatively linked to developmental theory. Further evidence of personality change, in self-confidence, cognitive commitment, outgoingness, and dependability, emerged in long-term analyses of the Berkeley Guidance and Oakland Growth Studies (Jones & Meredith, 1996).

Other researchers explored perceived changes in personality. Flccson and Heckhausen (1997) examined anticipated and recalled change in personality and wellbeing, finding that more losses than gains are expected in late adulthood compared to young adulthood, although all target ages showed evidence of some gains. Krueger and Heckhausen (1993) also documented subjective conceptions of personality that showed more growth than decline and more desirable than undesirable traits. Others documented subjective change across the decades of adult life in accord with developmental theory (Ryff, 1984).

An important contribution of developmental theory has been identification of particular personality challenges linked to specific life periods. This is no better represented than with Erikson's formulation of generativity, a developmental task centered in midlife that requires individuals to move beyond the self-concerns of identity, or the interpersonal focus of intimacy (Erikson's two prior states), into broader concern for others (children, younger colleagues, co-workers) and assuming roles of leadership and guidance in one's community.

The construct of generativity has undergone a dramatic rebirth in recent years, capturing the interest of many investigators (e.g., Keyes & Ryff, 1998; McAdams & St. Aubin, 1998; McAdams, St. Aubin, & Logan, 1993; Peterson & Klohnen, 1995). These studies provide evidence of life-course shifts into and out of midlife generativity and also detail the diverse forms through which generativity can be assessed and enacted. How

generativity is linked to other aspects of personality, and how it is contoured by social structural influences (e.g., level of education) have also been topics of study. This construct is not present in extant trait models, and as such, clarifies that unique topics follow from adopting a developmental perspective on personality.

The intersection of changing lives and changing historical contexts has also received important attention in recent years. Roberts and Helson (1997), for example, tracked the influence of individualism in their longitudinal sample of women. From the 1950s to the 1980s, a period in which American culture was perceived as becoming increasingly individualistic, they found evidence of increased self-focus and decreased norm adherence over this period. Importantly, they were able to predict *for whom* these changes were most likely to occur by using their young adult measures of ego strength and adjustment. Agronick and Duncan (1998) also explored the intersections of personality and social change, via a focus on the women's movement. Working with longitudinal data from early adulthood to midlife, they found that how women reacted to the women's movement was predicted by their early personality profiles and experiential life paths (e.g., timing and focus of commitments to family or career).

Taken as a whole, this trajectory of studies, revolving around core questions of personality change and stability as well as change in surrounding historical contexts, reveals productive tensions, thoughtfully described by Helson (1993). Whether one finds evidence of personality change or stability is driven powerfully by how one conceptualizes personality and how one measures change. Cumulative evidence, based on psychometrically sound assessment procedures and longitudinal or sequential designs, clearly documents stability and continuity in personality, at the same time that it provides unequivocal support for change and discontinuity. Thus, rather than seek categorical either–or answers to whether personality is stable or changing, Helson offered a variety of ingenious tools, both in collecting and analyzing data and in working creatively across samples and designs to advance understanding of *all these realities*. Jack Block, a luminary in longitudinal personality research (author of *Lives Through Time*, 1971), offered wisdom many years ago, when he asked "Do people change?" His reply was, "Some do and some don't." Current inquiries add another reality to this terse response those who both do and don't—individuals who show stability in traits *and* change in developmental characteristics. Thus, the scientific challenge has matured to one of using well-crafted longitudinal studies to discern the full range of change and stability processes and, more importantly, to understand why they occur.

B. Well-Being, Affect, and Quality of Life

Another tradition in research on personality and aging, also emanating from the early strides of investigators such as Neugarten, Havighurst, and Tobin (1961), and other contributors such as Lawton (1984), has been the interest in assessing positive psychological qualities such as life satisfaction, well-being, and morale. This work affords a counterpoint to studies of psychological distress (e.g., depression, anxiety), and as such, represents a tradition that has recently been bolstered by interest in positive psychology (Ryff & Singer, in press; Seligman & Csikszentmihalyi, 2000).

Early approaches to quality of life and successful aging were organized primarily around life satisfaction (see Cutler, 1979; Larson, 1978). Theory was not strongly evident in development of this construct or its assessment; rather, the emphasis was on applied research and program de-

velopment (Sauer & Warland, 1982). The early literature on subjective well-being (Diener, 1984; Veroff, Douvan, & Kulka, 1981) was also not strongly guided by theory, although there were considerable efforts to specify structure of the well-being domain based on extant measures of life satisfaction and happiness, or positive and negative affect (Bryant & Veroff, 1982; Liang, 1985; Stock, Okun, & Benin, 1986).

Drawing on numerous realms of theory, including conceptions of adult development (e.g., Buhler & Massarik, 1968; Erikson, 1959; Jung, 1933; Neugarten, 1968, 1973), but also social psychological, humanistic, and existential theories (e.g., Allport, 1961; Maslow, 1968; Rogers, 1961), and formulations of mental health (Jahoda, 1958), Ryff (1989a) generated a multidimensional conception of psychological well-being. The points of convergence in these prior formulations comprised *six key dimensions* of positive psychological functioning, for which assessment tools were subsequently developed. Although theoretically attractive, such conceptions had received little empirical study due to a lack of psychometrically sound measures.

First, to be psychologically well, one needs to have positive feelings about oneself and one's past life, including a capacity to accept personal limitations (*self-acceptance*). The most universally endorsed aspect of well-being is that one have quality, caring, trusting, connections to others (*positive relations with others*). Being able to manage the demands of daily life and create living contexts suitable to one's needs and capacities (*environmental mastery*) is another key dimension. A feature of well-being emerging from conceptions of individuation and self-actualization is the capacity to follow one's own convictions, even if they go against conventional wisdom (*autonomy*). Existential features of well-being include the need to find meaning in one's life, which includes having goals that give direction (*purpose in life*) as well as the sense of continued development and realization of personal talents and potential through time (*personal growth*).

Structural analyses on a national sample of young, midlife, and older aged adults support a six-factor model of well-being (with a single, higher-order factor) (Ryff & Keyes, 1995). Two aspects of well-being (i.e., environmental mastery, self-acceptance) correlate highly with prior measures of life satisfaction, morale, and affect balance, but the remaining dimensions (autonomy, personal growth, positive relations with others, purpose in life) do not, thereby underscoring the empirical distinctiveness of these theory-guided dimensions of well-being.

With regard to life-course trajectories, findings from community samples and national surveys document replicable age differences (Ryff, 1989a, Ryff & Keyes, 1995). Some aspects of well-being—self-acceptance and positive relations with others—show notably little age variation across the periods of young adulthood, midlife, and old age. Other aspects, notably environmental mastery and autonomy—show upward age trends. And still others, purpose in life and personal growth, consistently show downward (sometimes dramatically) age trajectories. Given differing depths of measurement, with local samples employing lengthy instruments (14 or 20 items per scale), and national samples employing short instruments (3 items per scale), the consistency of these effects is noteworthy. Adding to the cross-sectional effects, longitudinal inquiries have underscored the dynamics of well-being, documenting change in numerous aspects of positive functioning surrounding later life transitions, such as community relocation (Kling, Ryff, & Essex, 1997; Kling, Seltzer, & Ryff, 1997).

The downward trajectories on life purpose and personal growth evident across all samples raise concerns about later life well-being, regardless of whether effects are due to maturational processes, cohort influences, or both. Similar outcomes have emerged in a nationally representative sample of Canadian seniors (Clarke, Marshall, Ryff, & Rosenthal, 2000). If older persons no longer care about purposeful pursuits and continued growth, the findings might underscore that later life involves marching to a different drummer. However, when ideals of well-being have been examined (Ryff, 1991), the aged, like those younger in age, show continued endorsement of these existential aspects of well-being. Qualitative, open-ended assessments convey similar messages about how middle-aged adults and the aged conceive of well-being (Ryff, 1989b).

From a sociological perspective, the findings may implicate the "structural lag" phenomenon (Riley, Kahn, & Foner, 1994), which posits that contemporary social institutions have not kept up with the added years of life many older persons now experience. Seen in this light, lower profiles of life purpose and continued growth among the aged may be individual-level manifestations of a society that has yet to address the needs for purposeful engagement and talent utilization among its growing older population. It is important to remember that these late-life vulnerabilities co-occur with numerous aspects of positive functioning on which the aged show robust profiles compared with those younger in age.

Psychological well-being is similar to life satisfaction in that both involve generally cognitive evaluations of self and life. However, also important are realms of affect and emotion, as emphasized by structural analyses (Bryant & Veroff, 1982; Liang, 1985) that underscore distinctions between cognitive and affective features of being well. Quality of life, in fact, has come to refer to the combination of both features of well-being (Lawton,

1996). Because emotion is addressed in another chapter in this edition, comments here are restricted to studies of affect pertaining to well-being. Illustrative of work in this area is a study by Mroczek and Kolarz (1998) that investigated associations between age and positive and negative affect in a national sample of adults aged 25 to 74. Controlling for numerous sociodemographic, personality, and contextual influences, they found that positive affect shows an *upward* age trajectory, whereas negative affect shows a *downward* trajectory. Together, these findings convey a generally upbeat message about affect in later life, although the findings also underscored the influence of sociodemographic (gender, marital status) and personality variables (extraversion) in understanding age and affect.

How quality of life and well-being are maintained in the later years is increasingly linked to affect management. Lawton (1996) draws on adaptation-level theory to discuss later life affect regulation. Carstensen (1993, 1995), in turn, targets the social realm as a forum in which emotion regulation is played out, via increased later life selectivity in partners for social interaction. Alternatively, Panksepp and Miller (1996) summarize abundant evidence of decline in various neurochemical systems with age, thus underscoring biological angles on affective reactivity. Critically needed are future studies of the interplay between affect regulation, characterized as a realm of proactive, self-management, and affective change framed as an age-related process of neurophysiological decline.

Finally, although affective research has traditionally been heavily weighted on the side of negative emotion and distress, there is increasing interest in the role of positive emotions (Fredrickson, 1998). From the perspective of how well-being is maintained, positive emotions may be important in undoing the aftereffects of negative emotion (i.e., speeding recovery from fear, anxiety, or sadness) (see Fredrickson, & Levenson, 1998). These observations come from the field of emotion and have yet to be examined in life-course studies. A further important avenue for future work is how positive and negative affect interact and influence each other as individuals confront life challenges.

C. Stress and Coping

Those who study later life stress and coping generally give greater emphasis to the actual experiences of old age, whether they be acute events or chronic challenges. Many have focused on specific contexts of coping, such as caring for frail older adults (DeVries, Hamilton, Lovett, & Gallagher-Thompson, 1997), or for an adult child with mental illness or mental retardation (Seltzer, Greenberg, & Kraus, 1995), or by contrasting coping in the face of different later life challenges (e.g., caregiving vs. relocation) (Kling et al., 1997). These investigations identify differences in the frequency or type of coping (e.g., emotion-focused, problem-focused) as a function of age, gender, caregiving status, and type of life challenge, and these differences have been shown to contribute to variations in well-being.

Other investigators study age differences in coping more generally (not in response to specific life stresses). Aldwin, Sutton, Chiara, and Spiro (1996) used the Normative Aging Study to investigate age differences in stress, appraisal, and coping, and found that many older-aged men reported having no problems, whereas middle-aged men more likely appraised their challenges as both problems and annoyances. No age differences were evident in perceived stressfulness of problems, number of emotions reported, or coping efficacy, leading the authors to suggest that later life shifts from episodic to chronic stresses may affect coping and appraisal processes.

Drawing on psychodynamic theory, Diehl, Coyle, and Labouvie-Vief (1996) contrasted coping and defense strategies across age and gender groups. They found that older adults used a combination of coping and defense strategies indicating greater impulse control and the tendency to positively appraise conflict situations. Adolescents and younger adults used more outwardly aggressive and psychologically undifferentiated strategies, indicating lower levels of impulse control and self-awareness. Women also used more internalizing defenses than men. The authors suggested that men and women may face different developmental tasks in the process to maturity in adulthood.

Continuing themes of positive meaning and emotion, Folkman (1997) critiqued coping theory for being overly focused on the management of distress, thereby ignoring consequential roles of positive psychological states in dealing with life challenge. She argued that the capacity to find meaning and experience periods of positive affect are particularly consequential in coping with the severe stresses of cargiving and bereavement. A related realm of growing interest is research on optimism and pessimism, both of which have been actively studied as influences on mental and physical health (Scheier & Carver, 1985, 1992; Segerstrom, Taylor, Kemeny, & Fahey, 1998; Taylor et al., 2000), although how optimism is involved with meeting the challenges of aging is not well understood. Schulz, Bookwala, Knapp, Scheier, and Williamson (1996) found that a pessimistic life orientation is a risk factor for mortality, but only among younger cancer patients. In a midlife longitudinal sample of women, Bromberger and Matthews (1996) found that those who were more pessimistic, anxious, and reported more stressful events were more likely to show increments in depressive symptoms. Based on a midlife and older-aged sample, Robinson-Whelen, Kim, MacCallum, and Kiecolt-Glaser (1997) showed that optimism and pessimism are separate and weakly correlated factors among caregivers, although both appear to be affected by the caregiving experience.

In sum, research on later life stresses, chronic or acute, is a rich arena of innovative studies investigating how adults successfully negotiate—via effective coping strategies, defense mechanisms, optimism, and positive illusions—the life challenges and health threats that accompany growing old.

D. Goals, Projects, and Adult Life Tasks

A further realm of vibrant activity pertains to the study of motivated, proactive, striving aspects of individual differences. These directions were clearly evident among early leaders of the field of aging, as in Buhler's (Buhler & Massarik, 1968) life tasks that worked toward the fulfillment of life, and Havighurst's (1952) model of developmental tasks. Cantor (Cantor & Langston, 1989) revived interest in life tasks, defined as concrete goals that individuals work on in particular life periods and in specific life contexts. Much of this work has been done with college students, although Harlow and Cantor (1996) used Terman's longitudinal study of gifted individuals to examine later life tasks of social participation and community service activities. They found that engagement in such tasks predicted life satisfaction (after controlling for health, social support, baseline satisfaction, and several psychosocial variables). Also working with the Terman study, Holahan (1988) found that the maintenance of life goals (i.e., striving for autonomy, involvement, and achievement) contributed to health and well-being among those aged 65 to 75.

Emmons (1992) describes "personal strivings" as individually organized patterns of goals. Studies of students and community volunteers of diverse age show that strivings predict life satisfaction as well as positive and negative affect. Conflict among strivings has also been linked with well-being and physical illness, and high-level striving has been linked with psychological distress. Little (1996) construes "personal projects" as the middle ground between personal strivings (which represent more internal, self-defining aspects of human action) and life tasks (which reflect external, culturally mandated forms of action). Linking personal projects to well-being, McGregor and Little (1998) found that goal efficacy (how likely one's projects are to be successful) was associated with happiness, whereas goal integrity (how consistent one's projects are with core aspects of self) was associated with meaning. Little (1999) has also elaborated how individuals appraise meaning from their life projects as well as how projects contribute to community involvement.

Clarifying that not all goal pursuits lead to well-being, Ryan, Sheldon, Kasser, and Deci (1995) showed that external goals (e.g., money, fame, good looks) are associated with poorer mental health than pursuits of goals related to needs for autonomy, competence, and relatedness (needs deemed essential by self-determination theory). Brunstein, Schultheiss, and Grässmann (1998) found that progress toward goals predicted emotional well-being, but only for goals congruent with higher order motives. Brandtstädter's formulation of tenacious goal pursuit and flexible goal adjustment offers the most explicitly adulthood and aging perspective on the realm of proactive, intentional striving (Brandtstädter, Wentura, Rothermund, 1999). He construes human development as a series of assimilative and accommodative processes, the balance of which shifts as individuals grow older. Specifically, accommodative flexible goal adjustment increasingly predominates over assimilative persistent, tenacious goal pursuit as individuals confront the irreversible losses and fading action resources of aging. This perspective suggests that goals and projects of intentional self-development must be continually adjusted to changes in constraints and developmental reserves. Brandtstädter argues that accommodative processes have received insufficient attention in goal theories and action frameworks, despite their significance for understanding later life.

The theme of choice, and more specifically *selectivity*, recurs in studies of personality and aging. Heckhausen and Schulz (1999) underscore the fundamental significance of goal choice, claiming that regulation of choice becomes ever more salient when considered ontogenetically. Different life choices define distinctive life paths. Baltes and Baltes (1990) propose selective optimization with compensation as a framework for understanding successful aging. Freund and Baltes (1998) show in a subsample of the Berlin Aging Study that reports of these processes predict several global indicators of successful aging (e.g., satisfaction, lack of agitation, positive emotions, absence of loneliness). Carstensen also addresses ideas of selection and compensation, particularly in the social relational realm and its influence on emotion regulation (Carstensen, 1993, 1995). A further theme across many of these formulations is psychological control: age changes and constraints on psychological control (Heckhausen & Schulz, 1995; Lachman, 1986); primary and secondary control strategies involved in the compensation of later life losses (Heckhausen, 1997); stabilizing sense of control through accommodating goals (Brandtstädter et al., 1999).

E. Aging Studies of the Self and Self-Evaluative Processes

Much of the above work is framed as research on intentional self-development. There are, however, additional realms of inquiry about the aging self that are not primarily motivational in nature. The content and structure of the aging self-concept has also been examined (Markus & Herzog, 1992), with emphasis on how self-schemas organize experience, regulate affect, and influence behavior. Bringing life experience into the self arena, Diehl (1999) considers the role of critical events in life-course self-development, drawing extensively on Riegel's (1976) dialectical view of adult development. Crisis, in this framework, can be a catalyst toward continued development.

Other investigators have focused on self-evaluation via social comparison processes and perceived feedback from others (reflected appraisals). Heidrich and Ryff (1993a) found that older women in poorer health made more frequent comparisons with others than those in better health. Moreover, those who saw themselves comparing favorably with others showed higher levels of psychological well-being. Benefits of positive comparisons were particularly evident among those with health problems. A further study (Heidrich & Ryff, 1993b) elaborated different aspects of the "self-system" (e.g., social comparisons, self-discrepancies) and demonstrated their role in mediating relationships between physical and mental health in later life. Applying self-evaluative processes to negotiation of a life transition, Kling, Ryff, and Essex (1997) found that older women with flexible self-concepts (i.e., those who showed change in central aspects of their self-definition) showed greater longitudinal gains in well-being following community relocation than those with more inflexible self-definitions. These studies draw extensively on social psychological formulations of the unique human capacity to protect and enhance the self.

F. Intersections among Individual-Difference Variables

The above progression across diverse topical areas reveals an emergent shift toward more *process-oriented studies*. That is, descriptive studies of whether traits, well-being, coping strategies, goals, or the self-concept change with aging are increasingly replaced with studies that attempt to formulate and test how particular individual-difference variables work together to account for mental or physical health outcomes. For example, as illustrated above, many investigators use coping strategies or goal orientations to predict variations in well-being. In fact, personality researchers frequently document that individual-difference variables matter through demonstrating their capacity to predict (cross-sectionally) or account for changes (longitudinally) in various aspects of psychological well-being, life satisfaction, or positive affect. Other personality variables, particularly those coming from theories of self and intentional action (e.g., social comparison processes, reflected appraisals, goal orientations) are increasingly investigated as factors that mediate, or moderate, the impact of various life challenges or losses on well-being and health.

The progression toward theory-driven investigations of *how* personality influences aging outcomes is a significant stride forward. And yet, it is an advance that generates growing concern regarding issues of construct redundancy. That is, specifying (and testing) intersections among the individual-difference variables is neither simple nor straightforward due to the fact that boundary conditions between various constructs are far from clear. Where does personality end and the self begin? Are goal orientations distinctive from, or part of development and well-being? How much are affect and emotion included in assessments of traits, coping, and well-being?

The difficulties that ensue from blurred, overlapping constructs are usefully illustrated, with the growing interest in links between personality and well-being (see Schmutte & Ryff, 1997). Traits such as neuroticism have been used to predict negative affect and depressive symptoms (e.g., Costa & McCrae, 1980; Emmons & Diener, 1985; McCrae & Costa, 1990; 1984). These queries are fraught with problems of both construct and source overlap (i.e., negative affect is part of what defines neuroticism, and both are typically measured via self-report from the same respondent). High levels of variance explained are likely fueled by internal tautologies.

Such problems demand greater attention by personality researchers. The difficulties can be partially addressed by careful evaluation of theoretical starting points and measurement instruments as well as use of diverse methods (e.g., self-reports, spousal reports, behavioral observations). At a more general level, however, there is need for caution regarding the reification of constructs (traits, well-being, coping, goals, the self), all of which likely share overlapping space in the parsing of differences between individuals. Extending personality research beyond its own confines (i.e., connecting individual-difference variables to other disciplines and domains) is another response to the problem of construct redundancy. Two such examples of bridging inquiries are described in the next section.

IV. Promising New Venues

A. Personality and Social Structure

A long tradition of research exists on the boundaries between psychology, sociology, and anthropology, in which person-ality variables are related to surrounding social structural factors (see House, 1981; Ryff, 1987), be they broad influences of cultural and social class, or proximal influences of social roles, norms, and socialization processes. The field of aging has shown long-standing interest in how society and individuals co-constitute each other (Marshall, 1996). Recently, Ryff and Marshall (1999) rekindled interest in macro–micro linkages by proffering connections between current exemplars of individual-difference variables and social structural factors, such as socioeconomic hierarchies or cultural influences.

For example, Franks, Herzog, Holmberg, and Markus (1999) investigated how aging selves are defined and represented as a function of educational attainment. They document that those with more education have more complex and detailed selves, and suggest that this bolstering of self-definition and process (e.g., self-esteem, sense of control) may be implicated in understanding variability in later life health and well-being. Diehl (1999), examining the role of critical life events in self-development, argued for greater attention to self-determined versus uncontrollable life events. The latter, he clarifies, disproportionately accrue to those of lower socioeconomic status, whereas the former (which may enhance mastery and autonomy) more likely occur for those with socioeconomic advantage. Invoking Riegel's (1976) dialectical theory, Diehl examines how critical events of low controllability can nonetheless provide impetus for growth and continued development.

Ryff, Magee, Kling, and Wing (1999) summarize findings from numerous studies showing that those with higher levels of income and education tend to have higher levels of well-being (e.g., self-acceptance, purpose in life, personal growth) (see Marmot, Ryff, Bumpass, Shipley, & Marks, 1997). Drawing on social psychological theory, they further show that social comparison processes and "perceived inequalities" constitute mechanisms through which socioeconomic hierarchies penetrate individual levels of well-being. Themes of inequality are also evident in midlife studies of generativity (Keyes & Ryff, 1998), which show that those with higher educational levels exhibit more diverse aspects of as well as higher levels of generativity. Similarly, Lachman and Weaver (1998) show that adults with lower incomes have lower mastery and higher constraint profiles. However, control beliefs play a moderating role, such that those with low incomes, but high sense of control, report levels of health and well-being comparable to high-income groups.

Socioeconomic structures are but one avenue for examining macrolevel influences on personality. The burgeoning literatures on culture and the self (Markus & Kitayama, 1991) and culture and emotion (Kitayama & Markus, 1994) illustrate other directions for connecting individual-difference variables to broad external forces that shape, and are shaped by, personality. Life-course and aging angles on the intersections of personality and culture are much needed. Numerous other individual-difference variables described above (e.g., coping strategies, goal orientations) would be enriched by probing connections with social structural factors.

B. Personality and Health: Integrative Studies of Later Life Resilience

In addition to reaching outward to connect personality to social structural influences, the field is usefully extended inward toward biology and health. This, of course, is not novel territory. In the second edition of the *Handbook of the Psychology of Aging*, Siegler and Costa (1985) identified a variety of connections between personality traits, assessed longitudinally, and hypertension, cardiovascular disease, or death and illness-related

sample attrition. They explicitly emphasized behavior and health relationships as a two-way, reciprocal street, providing illustrations of both, and encouraged psychologists to become interested in areas traditionally the purview of public health and medical sociology. Since that time, health psychology has blossomed (Taylor, 1999), such that extensive new areas of inquiry connect behavior, personality, and emotion to health processes and outcomes.

At the same time, the preponderance of these connections has revolved around negative spirals between risk behaviors or personal maladjustment and adverse health outcomes. Remarkably little work has probed connections between psychological well-being, positive emotion, coping effectiveness, life-course development, and health. In an effort to activate interest in positive health, Ryff and Singer (1998) called for a new era of research on the "physiological substrates of flourishing" (i.e., the connections between positive psychological and social factors and underlying neural circuitry and downstream endocrinological and immunological function). Illustrative of such research are studies that demonstrate the life-extending benefits of optimism, social support, and emotional expression (Berkman, Leo-Summers, & Horwitz, 1992; Spiegel & Kimerling, in press; Taylor et al., 2000). How these positive psychosocial factors contribute to disease resistance, faster recovery from illness, and longer survival times is an essential venue for future research in which individual-difference variables, as described above, will contribute richly to the science and practice of prevention and positive health promotion (Ryff & Singer, 2000a).

A promising arena for such integrative biopsychosocial research pertains to the interpersonal realm—that is, relational flourishing (Ryff & Singer, 2000b). Numerous studies in social epidemiology document that those who are more socially integrated show lower profiles of morbidity and delayed mortality (Berkman, 1995; Seeman et al., 1993). Understanding how these effects occur and variations within them requires greater exchange between those who map the defining features of close personal relationships (e.g., Berscheid & Reis, 1998), including their emotional configurations. Moreover, it is in the social relational realm that strides are currently occurring in building bridges to neuroendocrine systems and immunology (e.g., Kiecolt-Glaser et al., 1997; Seeman & McEwen, 1996).

A further realm of enormous promise for aging researchers pertains to the construct of resilience. Although studies of resilience initially focused on early life (e.g., Garmezy, 1991; Rutter, 1990; Werner, 1995), increasing interest has been given to resilience in adulthood and later life (Klohnen, 1996; Ryff, Singer, Love, & Essex, 1998; Staudinger, Marsiske, & Baltes, 1995). Formulations of successful aging, in fact, are frequently framed in terms of resilience (Brandtstädter & Lerner, 1999). It is important to underscore, however, that high well-being and positive adjustment in later life are, in themselves, insufficient to demonstrate resilience, which fundamentally entails thriving *in the face of challenge or adversity*. There is wide variation in the aged population regarding the accumulation of adversity. Thus, research on later life resilience ideally must include longitudinal assessment of (a) the actual life challenges and losses confronting older individuals; (b) their psychosocial strengths in responding to them, drawing on individual-difference variables detailed above; (c) their health outcomes (profiles of morbidity, disability, mortality); and (d) neurobiological mechanisms that offer inroads for understanding how personal and interpersonal factors afford resistance against illness and disease. Examples of

such mechanisms include left prefrontal activation (Davidson, 1998), allostasis (McEwen & Stellar, 1993), and immune competence (Cohen & Herbert, 1996).

Singer and Ryff (1999) have probed pieces of this larger agenda by investigating, in a 40-year longitudinal study, links between persistent economic adversity (i.e., the life challenge), persistent social relational well-being, such as having caring ties with parents in childhood and multiple forms of intimacy with spouse in adulthood (i.e., interpersonal strengths), and allostatic load (i.e., an index of cumulative wear and tear on multiple physiological systems). Measured with numerous risk factors (cardiovascular, metabolic, neuroendocrine, sympathetic nervous system), high allostatic load has been shown in longitudinal aging research to predict not only incident cardiovascular disease, but also declines in cognitive and physical functioning and mortality (Seeman, Singer, Rowe, Horwitz, & McEwen, 1997). The latter constitute relevant health outcomes, but Singer and Ryff probed life-course antecedents, showing that cumulative adversity in the form of economic deprivation as well as poor relational ties predict high allostatic load. However, underscoring the theme of resilience, they further documented that those exposed to long-term economic disadvantage escaped the risk of high allostatic load if they were on positive relational pathways. These preliminary results warrant further investigation, linking as they do psychosocial strengths to physiological mechanisms implicated in later life health.

C. Methodological Innovation: Integrative Analyses and Person-Centered Approaches

Prior chapters on personality and aging in this series have frequently emphasized methodological priorities. For example, the question of whether personality changes or is stable across adult life was accompanied by extensive attention to issues of research design (cross-sectional, longitudinal, sequential), assessment tools (clinical interviews, projective tests, structured self-report procedures), and strategies of data analysis (structural invariance, correlational and mean-level change).

The methodological issue we underscore in the present volume pertains to the task of understanding *pathways to particular health outcomes* (mental and physical) in later life. Pursuing the integrative agendas suggested above, that on the one hand, link individual differences to macrolevel structural factors, and on the other, to internal biological processes, and do so with emphasis on cross-time dynamics, will require innovative analytic approaches. The basic challenge is how to use longitudinal data across different domains to represent whole lives, aggregating them into meaningful taxonomies that facilitate understanding of how given outcomes come about. Despite considerable interest in this task across multiple disciplines (see e.g. Elder & Clipp, 1988; Glueck & Glueck, 1968; Vaillant, 1983), there has been a dearth of analytical strategies providing for flexible integration of life history evidence (quantitative and qualitative) on the same groups of people.

In recent years, two broad classes of methodological techniques, referred to as *person-centered methods*, have been introduced in response to this challenge: bottom-up and top-down strategies. The bottom-up strategies begin with idiosyncratic individual histories, and the analytical steps identify important commonalities and differences across lives, leading to *aggregation* of histories into relatively homogeneous groups. The top-down strategies begin with coarse-grained descriptions of heterogeneous—in terms of details of life histories—populations

and *partition* them into progressively more homogeneous subgroups, each of which is described using information over time from multiple life domains. Developmental researchers are increasingly interested in the use of such person-centered methods (Cairns, Bergman, & Kagan, 1998).

Illustrating such efforts, Singer, Ryff, Carr, and Magee (1998) used bottom-up person-centered techniques to understand pathways to midlife psychological resilience, operationalized as recovery of high well-being following major depression. This work integrated extensive life history information over more than three decades to delineate four primary pathways to midlife resilience. These differed in the timing and nature of life adversities confronted as well as the degree of compensating life advantages. Manton, Stallard, Woodbury, Tolley, and Yashin (1987), in turn, used a top-down technique—Grade-of-Membership modeling—to characterize the health and functional status histories of elderly persons who eventually entered nursing homes as permanent residents versus those who lived independently, or in residential communities providing limited assistance to mildly disabled persons.

Both studies utilized longitudinal survey data as the raw information from which life history representations were constructed. The methodology of Singer et al. (1998) used narratives (i.e., writing text summaries of whole lives based on quantitative survey data) as a beginning step in an analytical strategy that culminated in complex Boolean statements to characterize life histories. An important alternative for representing and aggregating complex individual histories is the use of multivariate, replicated, single-subject, repeated measures (MRSRM) designs and the combination of P-technique and dynamic factor analysis (Shifren, Hooker, Wood, & Nesselroade, 1997; Jones & Nesselroade, 1990). This methodology is relevant once the raw survey responses have been combined and coded into numerical scales. The development of text summaries of whole lives, and the subsequent judgmental steps leading to scale specification and definition of composite variables described in Singer, Ryff, Carr, and Magee (1998) are essential steps that precede the subtle use of P-technique and dynamic factor analysis to produce a final taxonomy of individual histories.

Numerous investigations are based on qualitative life history data, and separate techniques are increasingly available to carry out *aggregation* of them into homogeneous groups representing distinct pathways to health outcomes. In addition, the studies of criminal careers by Laub and Sampson (1998) exemplify the evolving techniques for integrating narrative and numerical data on the same individuals. Focused specifically on aging, Singer and Ryff (in press) review a range of person-centered methodologies, including grade-of-membership models, recursive partitioning, and the integration of narratives and numbers, as routes to understanding how later life health outcomes come about. There is, nevertheless, need for further methodological innovation to facilitate the integrative agendas reaching outward to social structure and inward to biology.

V. Summary

The overriding message in this chapter is that personality research in adulthood and later life is thriving. There are diverse avenues of inquiry actively in progress on a rich array of individual-difference variables. Questions of stability and change continue to be prominent, with evidence increasingly supporting the co-occurrence of persistent traits and unfolding development linked to changing life tasks. In addition, process studies, using constructs such as coping, goal orientations, and

self-evaluative processes to predict well-being, affect, and life satisfaction, are demonstrating how individual-difference variables can be usefully combined. Such investigations raise concerns pertaining to the boundary conditions between core personality constructs. A useful direction for future research, which provides a partial response to this problem, is to extend personality research in multidisciplinary directions, both outward toward broad, macrolevel factors that contour individual differences, and inward toward biological processes that link the personality realm to health. Methodological innovation, particularly in the form of person-centered techniques, will be needed to carry out such multidisciplinary integration.

References

Agronick, G. S., & Duncan, L. E. (1998). Personality and social change: Individual differences, life path, and importance attributed to the women's movement. *Journal of Personality and Social Psychology, 74*, 1545–1555.

Aldwin, C. M., Sutton, K. J., Chiara, G., & Spiro, A. III. (1996). Age differences in stress, coping, and appraisal, findings from the Normative Aging Study. *Journals of Gerontology: Series B: Psychological Sciences and Social Sciences, 51B*, P179–P188.

Allport, G. W. (1961). *Pattern and growth in personality.* New York: Holt, Rinehart, & Winston.

Baltes, P. B., & Baltes, M. M. (1990). *Successful aging: Perspectives from the behavioral sciences.* New York: Cambridge University Press.

Bengston, V. L., Reedy, M. N., & Gordon, C. (1985). Aging and self-conceptions: Personality processes and social contexts. In J. E. Birren & K. W. Schaie (Eds.), *Handbook of the psychology of aging* (2nd ed), (pp. 544–593). New York: Van Nostrand Reinhold.

Berkman, L. F. (1995). The role of social relations in health promotion. *Psychosomatic Medicine, 57*, 245–254.

Berkman, L. F., Leo-Summers, L., & Horwitz, R. I. (1992). Emotional support and survival after myocardial infarction. *Annals of Internal Medicine, 117,* 1003–1009.

Berscheid, E., & Reis, H. T. (1998). Attraction and close relationships. In D. T. Gilbert, S. T. Fiske, & G. Lindzey (Eds.), *Handbook of social psychology* (4th ed.) (Vol. 2, pp. 193–281). Boston, MA: McGraw-Hill.

Block, J. (1971). *Lives through time.* Berkeley, CA: Bancroft Books.

Brandtstädter, J., Lerner, R. M. (Eds.), *Action and self-development through the life span.* Thousand Oaks, CA: Sage Publications.

Brandtstädter, J., Wentura, D., & Rothermund, K. (1999). Intentional self-development through adulthood and later life: Tenacious pursuit and flexible adjustment of goals. In J. Brandtstädter & R. M. Lerner (Eds.), *Action and self-development: Theory and research through the life span* (pp. 373–400). Thousand Oaks, CA: Sage Publications.

Bromberger, J. T., & Matthews, K. A. (1996). A longitudinal study of the effects of pessimism, trait anxiety, and life stress on depressive symptoms in middle-aged women. *Psychology and Aging, 11,* 207–213.

Brunstein, J. C., Schultheiss, O. C., & Grässmann, R. (1998). Personal goals and emotional well-being: The moderating role of motive dispositions. *Journal of Personality and Social Psychology, 75,* 494–508.

Bryant, F. B., & Veroff, J. (1982). The structure of psychological well-being: A sociohistorical analysis. *Journal of Personality and Social Psychology, 43,* 653–673.

Bühler, C., & Massarik, F. (Eds.) (1968). *The course of human life.* New York: Springer.

Cairns, R., Bergman, L., & Kagan, J. (Eds.) (1998). *Methods and models for studying the individual.* Thousand Oaks, CA: Sage.

Cantor, N., & Langston, C. A. (1989). Ups and downs of life tasks in a life transition. In L. A. Pervin (Ed.), *Goal concepts in personality and social psychology* (pp. 127–168). Hillsdale, NJ: Erlbaum.

Carstensen, L. L. (1993). Motivation for social contact across the life-span: A theory of socioemotional selectivity. In J. E. Jacobs (Ed.), *Nebraska Symposium on Motivation: Vol. 40. Developmental perspectives on motivation* (pp. 209–254). Lincoln, NE: University of Nebraska Press.

Carstensen, L. L. (1995). Evidence for a life-span theory of socioemotional selectivity. *Current Directions in Psychological Science, 4,* 151–156.

Caspi, A. (1993). Why maladaptive behaviors persist: Sources of continuity and change across the life span. In D. C. Funder, R. D. Parke, C. Tomlinson-Keasey, & K. Widaman (Eds.), *Studying lives through time: Personality and development* (pp. 343–376). Washington, DC: American Psychological Association.

Caspi, A., & Herbener, E. S. (1990). Continuity and change: Assortative marriage and the consistency of personality in adulthood. *Journal of Personality and Social Psychology, 58,* 250–258.

Clarke, P. J., Marshal, V. W., Ryff, C.D., Rosenthal, C. J. (2000). Well-being in Canadian seniors: Findings from the Canadian study of Health and Aging. *Canadian Journal on Aging, 19,* 139–159.

Cohen, S., & Herbert, T. B. (1996). Health psychology: Psychological factors and physical disease from the perspective of human psychoneuroimmunology. *Annual Review of Psychology, 47,* 113–142.

Costa, P. T., & McCrae, R. R. (1980). Still stable after all these years: Personality as a key to some issues in aging. In P. B. Baltes & O. G. Brim, Jr. (Eds.), *Life-span development and behavior* (Vol. 3, pp. 66–102). New York: Academic Press.

Costa, P. T., Jr., & McCrae, R. R. (1988). Personality in adulthood: A six-year longitudinal study of self-reports and spouse ratings on the NEO Personality Inventory. *Journal of Personality and Social Psychology, 54,* 853–863.

Costa, P. T., Jr., McCrae, R. R., & Zonderman, A. B. (1986). Cross-sectional studies of personality in a national sample: 2. Stability in neuroticism, extraversion, and openness. *Psychology and Aging, 1,* 144–149.

Cutler, N. E. (1979). Age variations in the dimensionality of life satisfaction. *Journal of Gerontology, 34,* 573–578.

Davidson, R. J. (1998). Affective style and affective disorders: Perspectives from affective neuroscience. *Cognition and Emotion, 12,* 307–330.

DeVries, H. M., Hamilton, D. W., Lovett, S., & Gallagher-Thompson, D. (1997). Patterns of coping preferences for male and female caregivers of frail older adults. *Psychology and Aging, 12,* 263–267.

Diehl, M. (1999). Self-development in adulthood and aging: The role of critical life events. In C. D. Ryff & V. W. Marshall (Eds.), *The self and society in aging processes* (pp. 150–183). New York: Springer.

Diehl, M., Coyle, N., & Labouvie-Vief, G. (1996). Age and sex differences in strategies of coping and defense across the life span. *Psychology and Aging, 11,* 127–139.

Diener, E. (1984). Subjective well-being. *Psychological Bulletin, 92,* 542–575.

Elder, G., & Clipp, E. (1988). Wartime losses and social bonding: Influences across 40 years in men's lives. *Psychiatry, 51,* 177–198.

Emmons, R. A. (1992). Abstract versus concrete goals: Personal striving level, physical illness, and psychological well-being. *Journal of Personality and Social Psychology, 62,* 292–300.

Emmons, R. A., Diener, E. (1985). Personality correlates of subjective well-being. *Personality and Social Psychology Bulletin, 11,* 89–97.

Erikson, E. (1959). Identity and the life cycle. *Psychological Issues, 1,* 18–164.

Filipp, S. (1996). Motivation and emotion. In J. E. Birren & K. W. Schaie (Eds.), *Handbook of the psychology of aging* (4th ed.) (pp. 218–235). San Diego, CA: Academic Press.

Fleeson, W., & Heckhausen, J. (1997). More or less "me" in past, present, and future: Perceived lifetime personality during adulthood. *Psychology and Aging, 12,* 125–136.

Folkman, S. (1997). Positive psychological states and coping with severe stress. *Social Science and Medicine, 45,* 1207–1221.

Franks, M. M., Herzog, A. R., Holmberg, D., & Markus, H. R. (1999). Educational attainment and self-making in later life. In C. D. Ryff & V. W. Marshall (Eds.), *The self and society in aging processes* (pp. 223–246). New York: Springer.

Fredrickson, B. L. (1998). What good are positive emotions? *Review of General Psychology, 2,* 300–319.

Fredrickson, B. L., & Levenson, R. W. (1998). Positive emotions speed recovery from the cardiovascular sequalae of negative emotions. *Cognition and Emotion, 12,* 191–220.

Freund, A. M., & Baltes, P. B. (1998). Selection, optimization, and compensation as strategies of life management: Correlations with subjective indicators of successful aging. *Psychology and Aging, 13,* 531–543.

Garmezy, N. (1991). Resiliency and vulnerability of adverse developmental outcomes associated with poverty. *American Behavioral Scientist, 34,* 416–430.

Glueck, S., & Glueck, E. (1968). *Delinquents and nondelinquents in perspective.* Cambridge, MA: Harvard University Press.

Gutmann, D. L. (1975). Parenthood: Key to the comparative psychology of the life cycle. In N. Datan & L. Ginsberg (Eds.), *Life-span developmental psychology: Normative life crises* (pp. 167–184). San Diego, CA: Academic Press.

Harlow, R. E., & Cantor, N. (1996). Still participating after all these years: A study of life task participation in later life. *Journal of Personality and Social Psychology, 71,* 1235–1249.

Havighurst, R. J. (1952). *Developmental tasks and education.* New York: David McKay.

Heckhausen, J. (1997). Developmental regulation across adulthood: Primary and secondary control of age-related challenges. *Developmental Psychology, 33,* 176–187.

Heckhausen, J., & Schulz, R. (1995). A life-span theory of control. *Psychological Review, 102,* 284–304.

Heckhausen, J., & Schulz, R. (1999). Selectivity in life-span development: Biological and societal canalizations and individuals' developmental goals. In J. Brandtstädter & R. M. Lerner (Eds.), *Action and self-development: Theory and research through the life span* (pp. 67–103). Thousand Oaks, CA: Sage Publications.

Heidrich, S. M., & Ryff C. D. (1993a). The role of social comparison processes in the psychological adaptation of elderly adults. *Journal of Gerontology: Psychological Sciences, 48,* P127–P136.

Heidrich, S. M., & Ryff C. D. (1993b). Physical and mental health in later life: The self-system as mediator. *Psychology and Aging, 8,* 327–338.

Helson, R. (1993). Comparing longitudinal studies of adult development: Toward a paradigm of tension between stability and change. In D. C. Funder, R. D. Parke, C. Tomlinson-Keasey, & K. Widaman (Eds.), *Studying lives through time: Personality and development* (pp. 93–119). Washington, DC: American Psychological Association.

Helson, R., & Moane, G. (1987). Personality change in women from college to midlife. *Journal of Personality and Social Psychology, 53,* 176–186.

Helson, R., & Roberts, B. W. (1994). Ego development and personality change in adulthood. *Journal of Personality and Social Psychology, 66,* 911–920.

Helson, R., & Wink, P. (1992). Personality change in women from the early 40s to the early 50s. *Psychology and Aging, 7,* 46–55.

Holahan, C. K. (1988). Relation of life goals at age 70 to activity participation and health and psychological well-being among Terman's gifted men and women. *Psychology and Aging, 3,* 286–291.

House, J. S. (1981). Social structure and personality. In M. Rosenberg & R. H. Turner (Eds.), *Social psychology: Sociological perspectives* (pp. 525–561). New York: Basic Books.

Jahoda, M. (1958). *Current concepts of positive mental health.* New York: Basic Books.

Jones, C., & Meredith, W. (1996). Patterns of personality change across the life span. *Psychology and Aging, 11,* 57–65.

Jones, C., & Nesselroade, J. R. (1990). Multivariate, replicated, single-subject, repeated measures designs and P-technique factor analysis: A review of intraindividual change studies. *Experimental Aging Research, 16,* 171–183.

Jung, C. G. (1933). *Modern man in search of a soul* (W. S. Dell & C. F. Baynes, Trans.). New York: Harcourt, Brace, & World.

Keyes, C. L. M., & Ryff, C. D. (1998). Generativity in adult lives: Social structural contours and quality of life consequences. In D. P. McAdams & E. de St. Aubin (Eds.), *Generativity and adult development: Psychosocial perspectives on caring for and contributing to the next generation* (pp. 227–263). Washington, DC: American Psychological Association.

Kiecolt-Glaser, J. K., Glaser, R., Cacioppo, J. R., MacCallum, R. C., Snydersmith, M.,

Cheongtag, K., & Malarkey, W. B. (1997). Marital conflict in older adults: Endocrinological and immunological correlates. *Psychosomatic Medicine, 59,* 339–349.

Kitayama, S., & Markus, H. R. (Eds.) (1994). *Emotion and culture: Empirical studies of mutual influence.* Washington, DC: American Psychological Association.

Kling, K. C., Ryff, C. D., & Essex, M. J. (1997). Adaptive changes in the self-concept during a life transition. *Personality and Social Psychology Bulletin, 23,* 989–998.

Kling, K. C., Seltzer, M. M., & Ryff, C. D. (1997). Distinctive late life challenges: Implications for coping and well-being. *Psychology and Aging, 12,* 288–295.

Kogan, N. (1990). Personality and aging. In J. E. Birren & K. W. Schaie (Eds.), *Handbook of the psychology of aging* (3rd ed.) (pp. 330–346). San Diego, CA: Academic Press.

Krueger, J., & Heckhausen, J. (1993). Personality development across the adult life span, Subjective conceptions vs. cross-sectional contrasts. *Journal of Gerontology: Psychological Sciences, 48,* P100–P108.

Lachman, M. E. (1986). Personal control in later life: Stability, change, and cognitive correlates. In M. M. Baltes & P. B. Baltes (Eds.), *The psychology of control and aging* (pp. 207–236). Hillsdale, NJ: Lawrence Erlbaum.

Lachman, M. E., & Weaver, S. L. (1998). The sense of control as a moderator of social class differences in health and well-being. *Journal of Personality and Social Psychology, 74,* 763–773.

Larson, R. (1978). Thirty years of research on the subjective well-being of older Americans. *Journal of Gerontology, 33,* 109–125.

Laub, J., Sampson, R. (1998). Integrating quantitative and qualitative data. In J. Z. Giele & G. H. Elder (Eds.), *Methods of life course research: Qualitative and Quantitative approaches* (pp. 213–230). Thousand Oaks, CA: Sage.

Lawton, M. P. (1984). The varieties of well-being. In C. Z. Malatesta & C. E. Izard (Eds.), *Emotion in adult development* (pp. 67–84). Beverly Hills, CA: Sage.

Lawton, M. P. (1996). Quality of life and affect in later life. In C. Magai & S. H. McFadden (Eds.), *Handbook of emotion, adult development, and aging* (pp. 327–348). San Diego, CA: Academic Press.

Liang, J. (1985). A structural integration of the Affect Balance Scale and the Life Satisfaction Index. *Journal of Gerontology, 40,* 552–561.

Little, B. R. (1996). Free traits, personal projects and idio-tapes: Three tiers for personality psychology. *Psychological Inquiry, 7,* 340–344.

Little, B. R. (1999). Personal projects and social ecology: Themes and variation across the life span. In J. Brandtstädter & R. M. Lerner (Eds.), *Action and self-development: Theory and research through the life span* (pp. 197–221). Thousand Oaks, CA: Sage Publications.

Manton, K. G., Stallard, E., Woodbury, M. A., Tolley, H. D., & Yashin, A. I. (1987). Grade-of-membership techniques for studying complex event history processes with unobserved covariates. In C. Clogg (Ed.), *Sociological methodology* (pp. 309–346). Washington, DC: American Sociological Association.

Markus, H. R., & Herzog, A. R. (1992). The role of self-concept in aging. *Annual Review of Gerontology and Geriatrics, 11,* 111–143.

Markus, H. R., & Kitayama, S. (1991). Culture and the self: Implications for cognition, emotion, and motivation. *Psychological Review, 98,* 224–253.

Marmot, M., Ryff, C. D., Bumpass, L. L., Shipley, M., & Marks, N. F. (1997). Social inequalities in health: Converging evidence and next questions. *Social Science and Medicine, 44,* 901–910.

Marshall, V. W. (1996). The state of theory in aging and the social sciences. In R. H. Binstock & L. George (Eds.), *Handbook of aging and the social sciences* (4th ed.) (pp. 12–30). San Diego, CA: Academic Press.

Maslow, A. H. (1968). *Toward a psychology of being* (2nd ed.). New York: Van Nostrand.

McAdams, D. P., & St. Aubin, E. (Eds.) (1998). *Generativity and adult development: How and why we care for the next generation.* Washington, DC: American Psychological Association.

McAdams, D. P., St. Aubin, E., & Logan, R. L. (1993). Generativity among young, midlife, and older adults. *Psychology and Aging, 8,* 221–230.

McCrae, R.R. (1993). Moderated analyses of longitudinal personality stability. *Journal*

of Personality and Social Psychology, 65, 577–585.

McCrae, R. R., & Costa, P. T., Jr. (1990). *Personality in adulthood.* New York: Guilford Press.

McEwen, B. S., & Stellar, E. (1993). Stress and the individual: Mechanisms leading to disease. *Archives of Internal Medicine, 153,* 2093–2101.

McGregor, I., & Little, B. R. (1998). Personal projects, happiness, and meaning: On doing well and being yourself. *Journal of Personality and Social Psychology, 74,* 494–512.

Mroczek, D. K., & Kolarz, C. M. (1998). The effect of age on positive and negative affect: A developmental perspective. *Journal of Personality and Social Psychology, 75,* 1333–1349.

Neugarten, B. L. (1968). *Middle age and aging.* Chicago: University of Chicago Press.

Neugarten, B. L. (1973). Personality change in later life: A developmental perspective. In C. Eisdorfer & M. P. Lawton (Eds.), *The psychology of adult development and aging* (pp. 311–335). Washington, DC: American Psychological Association.

Neugarten, B. L. (1977). Personality and aging. In J. E. Birren & K. W. Schaie (Eds.), *Handbook of the psychology of aging* (pp. 626–649). New York: Van Nostrand Reinhold.

Neugarten, B. L., Havighurst, R. J., & Tobin, S. (1961). The measurement of life satisfaction. *Journal of gerontology, 16,* 134–143.

Panksepp, J., & Miller, A. (1996). Emotions and the aging brain: Regrets and remedies. In C. Magai & S. H. McFadden (Eds.), *Handbook of emotion, adult development, and aging* (pp. 3–26). San Diego, CA: Academic Press.

Peterson, B. E., & Klohnen, E. C. (1995). Realization of generativity in two samples of women in midlife. *Psychology and Aging, 10,* 20–29.

Riegel, K. F. (1976). The dialectics of human development. *American Psychologist, 31,* 689–699.

Riley, M. W., Kahn, R. L., & Foner, A. (1994). *Age and structural lag.* New York: Wiley.

Roberts, B. W., & Helson, R. (1997). Changes in culture, changes in personality: the influence of individualism in a longitudinal study of women. *Journal of Personality and Social Psychology, 72,* 641–651.

Robinson-Whelen, S., Kim, C., MacCallum, R. C., & Kiecolt-Glaser, J. K. (1997). Distinguishing optimism from pessimism in older adults: Is it more important to be optimistic or not to be pessimistic? *Journal of Personality and Social Psychology, 73,* 1345–1353.

Rogers, C. R. (1961). *On becoming a person.* Boston: Houghton Mifflin.

Ruth, J., & Coleman, P. (1996). Personality and aging: Coping and management of the self in later life. In J. E. Birren & K. W. Schaie (Eds.), *Handbook of the psychology of aging* (4th ed., pp. 308–322). San Diego, CA: Academic Press.

Rutter, M. (1990). Psychosocial resilience and protective mechanisms. In J. Rolf, A. S. Masten, D. Cicchetti, K. H. Neuchterlein, & S. Weintraub (Eds.), *Risk and protective factors in the development of psychopathology* (pp. 181–214). New York: Cambridge University Press.

Ryan, R. M., Sheldon, K. M., Kasser, T., & Deci, E. L. (1995). All goals are not created equal: An organismic perspective on the nature of goals and their regulation. In P. M. Gollwitzer & J. A. Bargh (Eds.), *The psychology of action: Linking cognition and motivation to behavior* (pp. 7–26). New York: Guilford Press.

Ryff, C. D. (1984). Personality development from the inside: The subjective experience of change in adulthood and aging. In P. B. Baltes & O. G. Brim, Jr. (Eds.), *Life-span development and behavior* (Vol. 6, pp. 244–279). San Diego, CA: Academic Press.

Ryff, C. D. (1987). The place of personality and social structure research in social psychology. *Journal of Personality and Social Psychology, 53,* 1192–1202.

Ryff, C. D. (1989a). Happiness is everything, or is it? Explorations on the meaning of psychological well-being. *Journal of Personality and Social Psychology, 57,* 1069–1081.

Ryff, C. D. (1989b). In the eye of the beholder: Views of psychological well-being among middle-aged and older adults. *Psychology and Aging, 4,* 195–210.

Ryff, C. D. (1991). Possible selves in adulthood and old age: A tale of shifting horizons. *Psychology and Aging, 6,* 286–295.

Ryff, C. D., & Keyes, C. L. M. (1995). The structure of psychological well-being revisited. *Journal of Personality and Social Psychology, 69,* 719–727.

Ryff, C. D., Magee, W. J., Kling, K. C., & Wing, E. H. (1999). Forging macro-micro linkages in the study of psychological well-being. In C. D. Ryff & V. W. Marshall (Eds.), *The self and society in aging processes* (pp. 247–278). New York: Springer.

Ryff, C. D., & Marshall, V. W. (Eds.) (1999). *The self and society in aging processes.* New York: Springer Publishing.

Ryff, C. D., & Singer, B. (1998). The contours of positive human health. *Psychological Inquiry, 9,* 1–28.

Ryff, C. D., & Singer, B. (2000a). Biopsychosocial challenges of the new millennium. *Psychotherapy and Psychosomatics, 69,* 170–177.

Ryff, C. D., & Singer, B. (2000b). Interpersonal flourishing: A positive health agenda for the new millennium. *Personality and Social Psychology Review, 4,* 30–44.

Ryff, C. D., & Singer, B. (in press). Ironies of the human condition: Health and well-being on the way to mortality. In L. G. Aspinwall & U. M. Staudinger (Eds.), *A psychology of human strengths: Perspectives on an emerging field.* Washington, DC: American Psychological Association.

Ryff, C. D., Singer, B., Love, G. D., & Essex, M. J. (1998). Resilience in adulthood and later life. In J. Lomranz (Ed.), *Handbook of aging and mental health* (pp. 69–94). New York: Plenum.

Sauer, W. J., & Warland, R. (1982). Morale and life satisfaction. In D. A. Mangen & W. A. Peterson (Eds.), *Research instruments in social gerontology: Vol. 1. Clinical and social psychology* (pp. 195–240). Minneapolis, MN: University of Minnesota Press.

Scheier, M. F., & Carver, C. S. (1985). Optimism, coping, and health: Assessment and implications of generalized outcome expectancy on health. *Health Psychology, 4,* 219–247.

Scheier, M. F., & Carver, C. S. (1992). Effects of optimism on psychological and physical well-being: Theoretical overview and empirical update. *Cognitive Therapy and Research, 16,* 201–228.

Schmutte, P. S., & Ryff, C. D. (1997). Personality and well-being: Reexamining methods and meanings. *Journal of Personality and Social Psychology, 73,* 549–559.

Schulz, R. (1985). Emotion and affect. In J. E. Birren & K. W. Schaie (Eds.), *Handbook of the psychology of aging* (2nd ed.) (pp. 531–543). New York: Van Nostrand Reinhold.

Schulz, R., Bookwala, J., Knapp, J. E., Scheier, M., & Williamson, G. M. (1996). Pessimism, age, and cancer mortality. *Psychology and Aging, 11,* 304–309.

Seeman, T. E., Berkman, L.F., Kohout, F., Lacroix, A., Glynn, R., Blazer, D. (1993). Intercommunity variation in the association between social ties and mortality in the elderly: A comparative analysis of three communities. *Annals of Epidemiology, 3,* 325–335.

Seeman, T. E., & McEwen, B. S. (1996). Impact of social environment characteristics on neuroendocrine regulation. *Psychosomatic Medicine, 58,* 459–471.

Seeman, T. E., Singer, B. H., Rowe, J. W., Horwitz, R. I., & McEwen, B. S. (1997). The price of adaptation: Allostatic load and its health consequences: MacArthur Studies of Successful Aging. *Archives of Internal Medicine, 157,* 2259–2268.

Segerstrom, S., Taylor, S. E., Kemeny, M. E., & Fahey, J. L. (1998). Optimism is associated with mood, coping, and immune change in response to stress. *Journal of Personality and Social Psychology, 74,* 1646–1655.

Seligman, M. E. P., & Csikszentmihalyi, M. (2000). Positive psychology: An introduction. *American Psychologist, 55,* 5–14.

Seltzer, M. M., Greenberg, J. S., & Krauss, M. W. (1995). A comparison of coping strategies of aging mothers of adults with mental illness or mental retardation. *Psychology and Aging, 10,* 64–75.

Shifren, K., Hooker, K., Wood, P., & Nesselroade, J. R. (1997). Structure and variation of mood in individuals with Parkinson's Disease: A dynamic factor analysis. *Psychology and Aging, 12,* 328–339.

Siegler, I. C., & Costa, P. T. Jr. (1985). Health behavior relationships. In J. E. Birren & K. W. Schaie (Eds.), *Handbook of the psychology of aging,* (2nd ed.) (pp. 144–166). New York: Van Nostrand Reinhold.

Singer, B. H., & Ryff, C. D. (in press). Understanding aging via person-centered methods and the integration of numbers and narratives. In R. H. Binstock & L. K. George (Eds.), *Handbook of aging and the social sciences* (5th ed.). San Diego, CA: Academic Press.

Singer, B. H., & Ryff, C. D. (1999). Hierarchies of life histories and associated health risks. In N. D. Adler, B. S. McEwen & M. Marmot (Eds.), *Socioeconomic status in industrialized countries. Annals of the New York Academy of Sciences, 896,* 96–115.

Singer, B. H., Ryff, C. D., Carr, D., & Magee, W. J. (1998). Life histories and mental health: A person-centered strategy. In A. Raftery (Ed.), *Sociological methodology* (pp. 1–51). Washington, DC: American Sociological Association.

Spiegel, D., & Kimmerling, R. (2001). Group psychotherapy for women with breast cancer: Relationships among social support, emotional expression, and survival. In C. D. Ryff, & B. Singer (Eds.), *Emotion, social relationships, and health.* pp. 97–123 New York: Oxford University Press.

Staudinger, U. M., Marsiske, M., & Baltes, P. B. (1995). Resilience and reserve capacity inlater adulthood: Potentials and limits of development across the life span. In D. Cicchitti & D. J. Cohen (Eds.), *Developmental psychopathology, Vol. 2: Risk, disorder, and adaptation* (pp. 801–847). New York: John Wiley & Sons.

Stock, W. A., Okun, M. A., & Benin, M. (1986). Structure of subjective well-being among the elderly. *Psychology and Aging, 2,* 91–102.

Taylor, S. E. (1999). *Health psychology* (4th ed.). Boston, MA: McGraw-Hill.

Taylor, S. E., Kemeny, M. E., Reed, G. M., Bower, J. E., & Gruenewald. (2000). Psychological resources, positive illusions, and health. *American Psychologist, 55,* 99–109.

Vaillant, G. (1983). *The natural history of alcoholism.* Cambridge, MA: Harvard University Press.

Veroff, J., Douvan, E., & Kulka, R. A. (1981). *The inner American: A self-portrait from 1957 to 1976.* New York: Basic Books.

Von Dras, D. D., & Siegler, I. C. (1997). Stability in extraversion and aspects of social support in midlife. *Journal of Personality and Social Psychology, 72,* 233–241.

Werner, E. E. (1995). Resilience in development. *Current Directions in Psychological Science, 4*, 81–85.

Whitbourne, S. K. (1995). The psychological construction of the life span. In J. E. Birren & K. W. Schaie (Eds.), *Handbook of the psychology of aging* (2nd ed., pp. 594–618). New York: Van Nostrand Reinhold.

Whitbourne, S. K., & Waterman, A. S. (1979). Psychosocial development during the adult years: Age and cohort comparisons. *Developmental Psychology, 15*, 373–378.

Whitbourne, S. K., Zuschlag, M. K., Eliott, L. B., & Waterman, A. S. (1992). Psychosocial development in adulthood: A 22-year sequential study. *Journal of Personality and Social Psychology, 63*, 260–271.

Wrightsman, L. S. (1994). *Adult personality development: Theories and concepts* (Vol. I). Thousand Oaks, CA: Sage.

Twenty

Wisdom and Creativity

Robert J. Sternberg and Todd I. Lubart

I. Introduction

When we seek out people who are wise, we often turn to elders, often people older than ourselves, perhaps believing that, in the imagined placidity of old age, "still water runs deep." But when we seek out people who are creative, we often turn to the young, perhaps believing "you can't teach an old dog new tricks." What, exactly, are wisdom and creativity, and does their respective development really run in opposite directions? Is wisdom the residual glow as the flame of creativity burns ever more dimly?

The body of psychological work on creativity and its development is much more substantial and wide-ranging than the body of work on wisdom and its development. Many more researchers have studied creativity than have studied wisdom, and there are many more theories as well as empirical studies on creativity. Some of the reasons may be that wisdom is harder to define, quantify, and study than is creativity, and it is easier to point to examples of creative people and products than to examples of wise ones.

In discussing the development of creativity, therefore, we can draw on a more substantial base of information than in the discussion of wisdom. We are also less limited, in discussing the development of creativity, to work within particular theoretical frameworks. In discussing wisdom, therefore, we shall review specific approaches to studying wisdom and the wisdom within these approaches. Our need to do so stems specifically from the fact that what we know about wisdom and aging derives mostly from research within specific theoretical frameworks. In discussing creativity, however, we shall concentrate on creative works and discuss implications of what is known within a generalized theoretical framework that represents an amalgam of theories. The theoretical framework we use is a generalized confluence model (Amabile, 1996; Collins & Amabile, 1999; Sternberg & Lubart, 1995, 1996), which includes such attributes of creativity as abilities, knowledge, styles of thinking, personality, motivation, and environmental influences.

In this chapter, we will discuss, first wisdom and its development, then creativity and its development. Finally, we will discuss whether they truly run in opposite directions as time moves on.

Handbook of the Psychology of Aging
Copyright © 2001 by Academic Press.

II. Wisdom and Its Development

Wisdom can be defined as the "power of judging rightly and following the soundest course of action, based on knowledge, experience, understanding, etc." (*Webster's New World College Dictionary*, 1997, p. 1533). Such a power would seem to be of vast importance in a world that at times seems bent on destroying itself.

III. Major Approaches to Understanding Wisdom

A number of psychologists have attempted to understand wisdom in different ways. The approaches underlying some of these attempts are summarized in Sternberg (1990a). The approaches might be classified as philosophical, implicit-theories approaches, and developmental approaches.

A. Philosophical Approaches

Philosophical approaches have been reviewed by Robinson (1990; see also Robinson, 1989, with regard to the Aristotelian approach in particular, and Labouvie-Vief, 1990, for a further review). Robinson notes that the study of wisdom has a history that long antedates psychological study, with the Platonic dialogues offering the first intensive analysis of the concept of wisdom. Robinson points out that, in these dialogues, there are three different senses of wisdom: wisdom as (a) *sophia*, which is found in those who seek a contemplative life in search of truth; (b) *phronesis*, which is the kind of practical wisdom shown by statesmen and legislators; and (c) *episteme*, which is found in those who understand things from a scientific point of view.

Implicit in the Platonic notion is the idea that wisdom results from a search, a search that presumably takes time. One develops wisdom as one conducts this search, and hence ages. The philosopher-kings who Plato hoped might someday form a government were visualized as mature adults who had been trained over long periods of time.

Aristotle distinguished between *phronesis*, the kind of practical wisdom mentioned above, and *theoretikes*, or theoretical knowledge devoted to truth. Robinson (1989) notes that, according to Aristotle, a wise individual knows more than the material, efficient, or formal causes behind events. This individual also knows the final cause, or that for the sake of which the other kinds of causes apply. In Aristotle's thinking, as in Plato's, wisdom develops with time.

B. Implicit-Theoretical Approaches

Implicit-theoretical approaches to wisdom have in common the search for an understanding of people's folk conceptions of what wisdom is. Thus, the goal is not to provide a "psychologically true" account of wisdom, but rather an account that is true with respect to people's beliefs, whether these beliefs are right or wrong.

Some of the earliest work of this kind was done by Clayton (1975, 1976, 1982; Clayton & Birren, 1980), who multidimensionally scaled ratings of pairs of words potentially related to wisdom for three samples of adults differing in age (younger, middle-aged, older). In her earliest study (Clayton, 1975), the terms that were scaled were ones such as *experienced, pragmatic, understanding*, and *knowledgeable*. In each study, participants were asked to rate similarities between all possible pairs of words. The main similarity in the results for the age cohorts for whom the scalings were done was the elicitation of two consistent dimensions of wisdom, which Clayton referred to as an affective dimension and a reflective dimension. There was also a suggestion of a dimension relating to age. The greatest difference among the age cohorts was that mental representations of wisdom seemed to become more differentiated with increases in the ages of the participants, in line with differentiation theories of development in general. Thus, this work suggested, consistent with the Greek view, that wisdom develops with age.

Holliday and Chandler (1986) also used an implicit-theories approach to understanding wisdom. Approximately 500 participants were studied across a series of experiments. The investigators were interested in determining whether the concept of wisdom could be understood as a prototype (Rosch, 1975) or central concept. Principal-components analysis of one of their studies revealed five underlying factors: exceptional understanding, judgment and communication skills, general competence, interpersonal skills, and social unobtrusiveness. To the extent that these skills depend on age, they might be expected to show some sort of increase with age, at least up to a point.

Sternberg (1985b, 1990b) has reported a series of studies investigating implicit theories of wisdom. In one study, 200 professors each of art, business, philosophy, and physics were asked to rate the characteristicness of each of the behaviors obtained in a prestudy from the corresponding population with respect to the professors' ideal conception of each of an ideally wise, intelligent, or creative individual in their occupation. Laypersons were also asked to provide these ratings but for a hypothetical ideal individual without regard to occupation. Correlations were computed across the three ratings. In each group except philosophy, the highest correlation was between wisdom and intelligence; in philosophy, the highest correlation was between intelligence and creativity. The correlations between wisdom and intelligence ratings ranged from .42 to .78 with a median of

.68. For all groups, the lowest correlation was between wisdom and creativity. Correlations between wisdom and creativity ratings ranged from −.24 to .48 with a median of .27. The only negative correlation (−.24) was for ratings of professors of business.

The fact that the lowest correlations were obtained between wisdom and creativity is consistent with the notion that there is something fundamentally different between wisdom and creativity, whereas there is not something fundamentally different between wisdom and creativity, whereas there is not something fundamentally different between wisdom and intelligence. In the case of the business professors, the suggestion is that as people become wiser, they become *less* creative. Indeed, Sternberg (1997b) has argued that creativity is associated with a liberal style of thinking, whereby a person welcomes change and innovation. It is not clear, however, that wisdom is more associated with a conservative style, and results to be presented later challenge any such positive association (Staudinger, Lopez, & Baltes, 1997).

In a second study, 40 college students were asked to sort three sets of 40 behaviors each into as many or as few piles as they wished. The 40 behaviors in each set were the top-rated wisdom, intelligence, and creativity behaviors from the previous study. The sortings then each were subjected to nonmetric multidimensional scaling. For wisdom, six components emerged: reasoning ability, sagacity, learning from ideas and environment, judgment, expeditious use of information, and perspicacity.

In a third study, 50 adults were asked to rate descriptions of hypothetical individuals for intelligence, creativity, and wisdom. Correlations between ratings were .94 for wisdom and intelligence, .62 for wisdom and creativity, and .69 for intelligence and creativity, again suggesting that wisdom and intelligence are highly correlated in people's implicit theories, but not wisdom and creativity.

Most studies of implicit theories have looked at populations that were neither selected for nor particularly trained for wisdom. An interesting approach was taken by Levitt (1999), who interviewed monks in a monastery in the Himalayan region of India. These monks were being taught to be wise, at least in terms of the Buddhist tradition of wisdom. Key attributes of wisdom that emerged from the interviews were the ability to distinguish good from evil, being efficient in projects, being beyond suffering, being compassionate toward others, and showing honesty, humility, respect for others, and treating all creatures as worthy and equal. Self-knowledge was also seen as an important ingredient of wisdom.

C. Explicit-Theoretical Approaches

Explicit theories are constructions of (supposedly) expert theorists and researchers rather than of laypeople. In the study of wisdom, most explicit-theoretical approaches are based on constructs from the psychology of human development.

1. Wisdom as the Orchestration of Mind and Virtue

The most extensive program of research has been that conducted by Baltes and his colleagues. For example, Baltes and Smith (1987, 1990) gave adult participants life-management problems, such as, "A fourteen-year-old girl is pregnant. What should she, what should one, consider and do?" and "A fifteen-year-old girl wants to marry soon. What should she, what should one, consider and do?" Baltes and Smith tested a five-component model on participants' protocols in answering these and other questions. The five components in the model are (a) rich factual knowledge (general and specific know-

ledge about the conditions of life and its variations), (b) rich procedural knowledge (general and specific knowledge about strategies of judgment and advice concerning matters of life), (c) life span contextualism (knowledge about the contexts of life and their temporal [developmental] relationships), (d) relativism (knowledge about differences in values, goals, and priorities), and (e) uncertainty (knowledge about the relative indeterminacy and unpredictability of life and ways to manage). An expert answer should reflect more of these components, whereas a novice answer should reflect fewer of them. The data were generally supportive of their model.

Over time, Baltes and his colleagues (e.g., Baltes, Smith, & Staudinger, 1992; Baltes & Staudinger, 1993, 2000) have collected a wide range of data showing the empirical utility of the proposed theoretical and measurement approaches to wisdom. For example, Staudinger, Smith and Baltes (1992) showed that human-services professionals outperformed a control group on wisdom-related tasks.

Staudinger et al. (1997) sought to understand psychometric correlates of wisdom. They were able to account for 40% of the variation in wisdom-related performance by measures of intelligence and personality. In particular, a measure of fluid ability correlated .28 with wisdom and a measure of crystallized ability, .34. With regard to personality, openness to experience correlated .42 and psychological mindedness, .28. They also found that certain thinking styles from the theory of mental self-government (Sternberg, 1997b) showed correlations with wisdom. The judicial style showed a correlation of .25, but the conservative style correlated −.36, the oligarchic style, −.38, the monarchic style, −.12, and the external style, .10. Creativity correlated .37.

The Baltes group also has showed that older adults performed as well on such tasks as did younger adults, and that older adults did better on such tasks if there was a match between their age and the age of the fictitious characters about whom they made judgments. Baltes, Staudinger, Maercker, and Smith (1995) found that older individuals nominated for their wisdom performed as well as did clinical psychologists on wisdom-related tasks. They also showed that up to the age of 80, older adults performed as well on such tasks as did younger adults. In a further set of studies, Staudinger and Baltes (1996) found that performance settings that were ecologically relevant to the lives of their participants and that provided for actual or "virtual" interaction of minds increased wisdom-related performance substantially.

Staudinger (1999) has sought in particular to understand the relationship between age and wisdom. Her findings dispute the fairy-tale and proverbial notions that old age and wisdom are closely intertwined. She found (see above), in a meta-analysis of four studies ($N = 533$) that between 20 and 75 or even 80 years of age, there is no relationship at all between age and wisdom (see also Staudinger & Baltes, 1996). Had she left things there, the finding might have been merely puzzling. But fortunately, her analysis is deeper than that.

Her argument is that the life experience and knowledge one needs to develop wisdom comes with age, but often so does deterioration in the basic intellectual functioning as well as personality changes that tend to be associated with decreases in wisdom. In particular, fluid abilities may decline later in life (Horn, 1994), as may openness to experience (Costa & McCrae, 1994; McCrae, 1996). At the same time, cognitive rigidity may increase. Staudinger has found, however, that when older people are given time to discuss a life-related problem with a peer, and then given time to reflect on the discussion, they profit more from such opportunities than do younger people. Thus,

giving older people a chance to develop "interactive minds" may be particularly facilitative for their showing their potential for wisdom.

A particularly interesting finding in this line of work is what Baltes, Staudinger, and their colleagues (Smith & Baltes, 1990, Smith, Staudinger, & Baltes, 1994; Staudinger, 1989, 1999; Staudinger et al., 1992) refer to as an *age-match effect*. The basic idea is that younger and older adults show greater wisdom in the solution of problems that are age-relevant to them. In a sense, then, the question of whether people get older and wiser may be an oversimplification. People become wiser at a given age with respect to the problems that confront them at that point in their lives.

Sternberg (1990b) also proposed an explicit theory, suggesting that the development of wisdom can be traced to six components: (a) knowledge, including an understanding of its presuppositions and meaning as well as its limitations; (b) processes, including an understanding of what problems should be solved automatically and what problems should not be so solved; (c) a judicial intellectual style, characterized by the desire to judge and evaluate things in an in-depth way; (d) personality, including tolerance of ambiguity and of the role of obstacles in life; (e) motivation, especially the motivation to understand what is known and what it means; and (f) environmental context, involving an appreciation of the contextual factors in the environment that lead to various kinds of thoughts and actions.

2. Wisdom as Postformal-Operational Thinking

Some theorists have viewed wisdom in terms of postformal-operational thinking, thereby viewing wisdom as extending beyond the Piagetian stages of intelligence (Piaget, 1972). Wisdom thus might be a stage of thought beyond Piagetian formal operations. Although this stage might begin in late adolescence, it would continue to unfold throughout the life span. For example, some authors have argued that wise individuals are those who can think reflectively or dialectically. In the case of dialectical thinking, the argument is that individuals come to realize that truth is not always absolute. Rather, it evolves in an historical context of theses, antitheses, and syntheses (e.g., Basseches, 1984; Kitchener, 1983, 1986; Kitchener & Brenner, 1990; Kitchener & Kitchener, 1981; Labouvie-Vief, 1980, 1982, 1990; Pascual-Leone, 1990; Riegel, 1973; Sternberg, 1999a). Consider a very brief review of some specific dialectical approaches.

Kitchener and Brenner (1990) suggested that wisdom requires a synthesis of knowledge from opposing points of view. Similarly, Labouvie-Vief (1990) has emphasized the importance of a smooth and balanced dialogue between logical forms of processing and more subjective forms of processing. Pascual-Leone (1990) has argued for the importance of the dialectical integration of all aspects of a person's affect, cognition, conation (motivation), and life experience. Similarly, Orwoll and Perlmutter (1990) have emphasized the importance to wisdom of an integration of cognition with affect. Kramer (1990) has suggested the importance of the integration of relativistic and dialectical modes of thinking, affect, and reflection. And Birren and Fisher (1990), putting together a number of views of wisdom, have suggested as well the importance of the integration of cognitive, conative (motivational/personality), and affective aspects of human abilities.

Other theorists have suggested the importance of knowing the limits of one's own extant knowledge and of then trying to go beyond them. For example, Kitchener and Brenner (1990) have emphasized the importance of knowing the limita-tions of one's own knowledge. Arlin (1990) has linked wisdom to problem finding, the first step of which is the recognition that how one currently defines a problem may be inadequate. Arlin views problem finding as a possible stage of postformal operational thinking. Such a view is not necessarily inconsistent with the view of dialectical thinking as a postformal-operational stage. Dialectical thinking and problem finding could represent distinct postformal-operational stages, or two manifestations of the same postformal-operational stage.

3. *Wisdom as a Resource That Diminishes over the Life Span*

One of the proponents of the view that wisdom inheres in knowing the limitations of one's own knowledge is Meacham (1990). Meacham has suggested that an important aspect of wisdom is an awareness of one's own fallibility and the possession of knowledge of what one does and does not know. Meacham has gone one step further, however, and argued that, although most theorists believe that wisdom increases with age (e.g., Clayton & Birren, 1980; Erikson, 1963, 1982), the opposite may well be true, namely, that wisdom decreases with age. Meacham believes that the greatest wisdom is shown in childhood, and that it is downhill after that!

The evidence that Meacham (1990) offers is largely anecdotal, but at least worth considering. First, he notes that the prototypical example of wisdom, that of Solomon in devising a procedure to figure out which of two women was truly the mother of a baby (I Kings 4:16–28), was the wisdom of Solomon in his youth. Meacham notes that according to the Bible (I Kings 11), Solomon in his old age became rich, powerful, and turned away from God. A second source of evidence adduced by Meacham is proverbs, such as "A wise son makes a glad father"

(Proverbs 10:1), "A wise son heareth his father's instruction" (Proverbs 13:1), and "Great men are not always wise; neither do the aged understand judgment" (Job 32:9). A third source cited by Meacham is the diary of Anne Frank (1952), written while Anne was between 13 and 15 years of age, but full of wisdom about the Second World War and its human consequences.

Meacham may be correct, but the evidence cited seems, as Meacham himself notes, to be in need of serious supplementation. Probably no one would question the existence of at least some exceptionally wise children, and some exceptionally foolish adults or older adults. But the fact that such people exist speaks little about how generalizable findings from them are likely to be. Solomon and Anne Frank would be scarcely typical cases from which one would want to generalize. On the contrary, they were about as exceptional as individuals in history come. Similarly, it is dangerous to generalize from proverbs, as anyone knows who has pondered at the same time, "absence makes the heart grow fonder" and "out of sight, out of mind." Probably, one can dig up a proverb to make almost any point one might wish ultimately to make.

4. An Evolutionary Approach

Although most developmental approaches to wisdom are ontogenetic, Csikszentmihalyi and Rathunde (1990) have taken a philogenetic or evolutionary approach, arguing that constructs such as wisdom must have been selected for over time, at least in a cultural sense. They define wisdom as having three basic dimensions of meaning: (a) that of a cognitive process, or a particular way of obtaining and processing information; (b) that of a virtue, or socially valued pattern of behavior; and (c) that of a good, or a personally desirable state or condition.

5. The Balance Theory

A further view of wisdom is the balance theory of wisdom (Sternberg, 1998, 1999b). This view has at its core the notion of tacit knowledge (Polanyi, 1976), which is defined as action-oriented knowledge, acquired without direct help from others, that allows individuals to achieve goals they personally value (Sternberg et al., 2000; Sternberg & Wagner, 1993; Sternberg, Wagner, & Okagaki, 1993; Sternberg, Wagner, Williams, & Horvath, 1995). Tacit knowledge has three main features: (a) it is procedural; (b) it is relevant to the attainment of goals people value; and (c) it is acquired with little help from others over the course of one's life.

Tacit knowledge is thus a form of "knowing how" rather than of "knowing that" (Ryle, 1949). It may be viewed as condition-action sequences (production systems) as a useful formalism for understanding the mental representation of tacit knowledge (Horvath et al., 1996; Sternberg, et al., 1995). For example, if one needs to deliver bad news to one's staff but it is the day before the beginning of Christmas vacation, then it is better to wait until after Christmas vacation to deliver the bad news. Note that tacit knowledge is always wedded to particular uses in particular situations or classes of situations. It increases as a result of learning from experience, rather than from experience per se.

Tacit knowledge also is practically useful. It is instrumental to the attainment of goals people value. Thus, people use this knowledge in order to achieve success in life, however they may define success. Abstract academic knowledge about procedures for solving problems with no relevance to life would not be viewed, in this perspective, as constituting tacit knowledge.

Finally, tacit knowledge is acquired without direct help from others. At best, others can guide one to acquire this knowledge. Often, environmental support for the acquisition of this knowledge is minimal, and sometimes organizations actually suppress the acquisition of tacit knowledge. For example, an organization might not want its employees to know how personnel decisions are really made, as opposed to how they are supposed to be made. From a developmental standpoint, this view suggests that wisdom is not taught so much as indirectly acquired. One can provide the circumstances for the development of wisdom and case studies to help students develop wisdom, but one cannot teach particular courses of action that would be considered wise, regardless of circumstances. Indeed, tacit knowledge is wedded to contexts, so that the tacit knowledge that would apply in one context would not necessarily apply in another context. To help someone develop tacit knowledge, one would provide mediated learning experiences rather than direct instruction as to what to do, when.

Why should tacit knowledge be relatively independent of academic abilities, and thus wisdom be seen as relatively independent of IQ-like abilities? The reason is that real-world problems—the types that require wisdom—are different in kind from many academic problems (Neisser, 1979). In particular, academic problems tend to be (a) formulated by others; (b) often of little or no intrinsic interest; (c) having all needed information available from the beginning; (d) disembedded from an individual's ordinary experience; (e) well defined; (f) characterized by a "correct" answer; and (g) characterized by a single method of obtaining the correct answer. In contrast, practical problems tend to be (a) unformulated or in need of reformulation; (b) of personal interest; (c) lacking in information necessary for solution; (d) related to everyday experience; (e) poorly defined; (f) characterized by multiple "correct" or at least "acceptable" solutions, each with liabilities as well as assets; and (g) character-

ized by multiple methods for picking a problem solution (Sternberg, et al., 1995).

Several of the theories described above emphasize the importance of various kinds of integrations or balances in wisdom. At least three major kinds of balances have been proposed: among various kinds of thinking (e.g., Labouvie-Vief, 1980), among various self-systems, such as the cognitive, conative, and affective (e.g., Kramer), and among various points of view (e.g., Kitchener & Brenner, 1990). Hartshorne (1987) has further emphasized the role of moderation in wisdom.

The definition of wisdom in the balance theory draws both upon the notion of tacit knowledge, as described above, and on the notion of balance. In particular, wisdom is defined as the application of tacit knowledge toward the achievement of a common good through a balance among (a) intrapersonal, (b) interpersonal, and (c) extrapersonal interests in order to achieve a balance among (a) adaptation to existing environments, (b) shaping of existing environments, and (c) selection of new environments, over the long term as well as the short term.

Thus, wisdom is similar to practical intelligence in that it draws upon tacit knowledge, but it differs in one fundamental way. Practical intelligence has been defined in terms of maximizing one's own outcomes. For example, when one manages oneself, others, or tasks (Wagner, 1987; Wagner & Sternberg, 1985), one's ultimate goal typically is to maximize one's self-interest. Wisdom is not just about maximizing one's own self-interest, however, but about balancing off various self-interest (intrapersonal) with the interests of others (interpersonal) and of other aspects of the context in which one lives (extrapersonal), such as one's city or country or environment or even God. Wisdom is quite different from creativity, however, which often involves taking a position that sticks oneself out on a limb and that is far from balanced.

When one applies practical intelligence, one may seek deliberately outcomes that are good for oneself and bad for others. In wisdom, one certainly may seek good ends for oneself, but one also seeks good outcomes for others. If one's motivations are to maximize certain people's interests and minimize other people's, wisdom is not involved. In wisdom, one seeks a common good, realizing that this common good may be better for some than for others. An evil genius may be academically intelligent; he may be practically intelligent; he cannot be wise.

We refer here to "interests," which are related to the multiple points of view that are a common feature of many theories of wisdom (as reviewed in Sternberg, 1990a). Diverse interests encompass multiple points of view, and thus the use of the term "interests" is intended to include "points of view." Interests go beyond points of view, however, in that they include not only cognitive aspects of divergences, but affective and motivational divergences as well.

Problems requiring wisdom always involve at least some element of intrapersonal, interpersonal, and extrapersonal interests. For example, one might decide that it is wise to go to college, a problem that seemingly involves only one person. But many people are typically affected by an individual's decision to go to college—parents, friends, present or future significant others and children, and the like. And the decision always has to be made in the context of what the whole range of available options is. Similarly, a decision about whether to have an abortion requires wisdom because it involves not only oneself, but the baby who would be born, others to whom one is close, such as the father, and the rules and customs of the society.

As is true with practical intelligence (Sternberg, 1985b, 1997a; Sternberg et al., 2000), wisdom involves a balancing not only of the three kinds of interests, but also of three possible courses of action in response to this balancing. These courses of action are adaptation of oneself or others to existing environments; shaping of environments in order to render them more compatible with oneself or others; and selection of new environments over the long and short terms. In adaptation, the individual tries to find ways to conform to the existing environment that forms his or her context. Sometimes adaptation is the best course of action under a given set of circumstances. But typically one seeks a balance between adaptation and shaping, realizing that fit to an environment requires not only changing oneself, but changing the environment as well. When an individual finds it impossible or at least implausible to attain such a fit, he or she may decide to select a new environment altogether, leaving, for example, a job, a community, a marriage, or whatever.

Wisdom manifests itself as a series of processes, which are typically cyclical and can occur in a variety of orders. These processes are related to what have been referred to as "metacomponents" of thought (Sternberg, 1985a). They include (a) recognizing the existence of a problem, (b) defining the nature of the problem, (c) representing information about the problem, (d) formulating a strategy for solving the problem, (e) allocating resources to the solution of a problem, (f) monitoring one's solution of the problem, and (f) evaluating feedback regarding that solution. In deciding about whether to place a parent in an institutional setting, for example, one first has to recognize that the parent can no longer care for him- or herself and has no family member willing or able to provide care. A problem cannot be solved before it is recognized and defined.

The balance theory suggests that wisdom is at least partially domain specific, in that tacit knowledge is acquired within a given context or set of contexts. It is typically acquired by selectively encoding new information that is relevant for one's purposes in learning about that context; selectively comparing this information to old information in order to see how the new fits with the old; and selectively combining pieces of information in order to make them fit together into an orderly whole (Sternberg et al., 1993).

Although tacit knowledge is acquired within a domain, it more typically applies to a field, following a distinction made by Csikszentmihalyi (1988, 1996). Csikszentmihalyi refers to the domain as the formal knowledge of a socially defined field. So, for example, knowing how to construct, conduct, or analyze the results of experiments would be knowledge important to the domain of experimental psychology. But knowing how to speak about the results persuasively, how to get the results published, or knowing how to turn the results into the next grant proposal would constitute knowledge of the field. Thus, academic intelligence would seem to apply primarily in the domain, practical intelligence and wisdom in the field. Because the field represents the social organization of the domain, it is primarily in the field that intrapersonal, interpersonal, and extrapersonal interactions take place. Interestingly, domain knowledge is obtained largely through schooling and field knowledge through life experience, which accumulates over a long period of time.

Perhaps the ideal problems for measuring wisdom, in light of the balance theory proposed here, are complex conflict-resolution problems involving multiple competing interests and no clear resolution of how these interests can be reconciled (see, e.g., Sternberg & Dobson, 1987; Sternberg & Soriano, 1984). For example, one might be asked to resolve a conflict between a couple over whether the husband's mother should be allowed to come to live with the couple. Given the relevance of such problems, it makes sense that Baltes and his colleagues (Smith et al., 1994) would have found that clinical psychologists would do particularly well on wisdom-related tasks. Another group who might be expected to do well would be experienced foreign-service officers and other negotiators who have helped nations in conflict reach resolutions of their disagreements.

There is one source of evidence that suggests that wisdom and intelligence might be rather different "kettles of fish." We know that IQs have been rising substantially over the past several generations (Flynn, 1987). The gains have been experienced both for fluid and for crystallized abilities, although the gains are substantially greater for fluid than for crystallized abilities. Yet it is difficult to discern any increase in the wisdom of the peoples of the world. Of course, tests administered over time might have revealed otherwise. But the levels of conflict in the world show no sign of de-escalating, and conflicts recently have intensified in many parts of the world where formerly they lay dormant (as in former Yugoslavia). So maybe it is time that psychologists, as a profession, take much more seriously the measurement of wisdom, and the formulation of theories and theory-based measures of wisdom. Although there has certainly been work in the area, the amount of work is dwarfed by work on intelligence. And perhaps we even need to think about how we might create experiences that would guide people to develop wisdom, much as we have been concerned in some quarters about developing intelligence (see, e.g., Perkins & Grotzer, 1997). Perhaps if schools put into wisdom development even a small fraction of the effort they put into the development of an often inert knowledge base, some of the conflicts that have arisen so quickly would also quickly disappear. We cannot know for sure, but is it not worth the effort to find out?

IV. Creativity and Its Development

Creativity can be defined as the ability to produce work that is (a) novel, (b) high in quality, and (c) task-appropriate (Barron, 1988; Jackson & Messick, 1967; Lubart, 1994, 1999; MacKinnon, 1962; Ochse, 1990; Stein, 1953; Sternberg & Lubart, 1995). How does the ability to produce such work change over age?

A. Creativity across the Life Span

1. Variations in Quantity of Creative Work

Lehman (1953) and Simonton (1988, 1990a, 1990b, 1999) have thoroughly documented age-related variations in the quantity of creative work. Productivity (i.e., the quantity of creative work) can be measured by counting the number of works that an individual produces during a certain span of time, such as a decade. In general, productivity increases rapidly with age to a peak, often around the age of forty. Productivity then tends to decrease slowly through the rest of the life span, often declining until productivity is one-half of its peak rate. This general relationship between productivity and age has been found in both artistic and scientific fields, and across different cultures (Simonton, 1988).

In conjunction with this general trend, it is important to note three things. First, the exact location of the peak and the rate of change in productivity depend on the field of endeavor. In some fields, such as pure mathematics, the productivity peak is early (e.g., age 30), and productivity declines rapidly with age to one-quarter of the peak performance level. In contrast, domains such as history and philosophy show a later age peak for productivity (e.g., age 50), with small decreases beyond the peak. Second, although the productivity of creative work typically declines

asymptotically, there are numerous cases of creative work by people in their eighties and older. Third, there are large individual differences in the change in productivity with age. McLeish (1976) identified several "Ulysseans" who showed high productivity during old age (e.g., Thomas Mann published three major novels after he was 70 years of age).

2. Variation in the Quality of Creative Work

In contrast to productivity, which varies over the life span, the quality of creative work tends to follow a constant-probability-of-success model (Simonton, 1990b). The number of masterworks during a specified period is a probabilistic function of the number of works produced in the period. In other words, during very productive periods of a person's life, there is a higher chance that a creative masterwork will be produced. The ratio of high-quality works to total number of works in any given period, however, does not show any developmental pattern. For example, Simonton (1985) used citation counts to establish major and minor works in the careers of ten eminent psychologists. The ratio of major (high-quality) works to total publications per unit of time showed no systematic changes with age. The same result was demonstrated with 10 classical composers (Simonton, 1977).

Changes in productivity, therefore, seem to drive the basic age function for creativity. When people produce less, they have a reduced probability of making a creative "hit."

3. Variation in the Form of Creative Work

Analysis of creative works suggests that the form and substance of creativity differs with age. Arieti (1976), for example, proposed that "young creators," those in their twenties or thirties, produce spontaneous, intense, and "hot from the fire" works. Older creators, age forty and above, "sculpt" their products with more intermediate processing. Simonton (1975) supported this idea in this study of 420 literary creators. Creators were drawn from 25 centuries using histories, anthologies, and biographical dictionaries of Western, Near Eastern, and Far Easter literature. Poets produced their most frequently cited works at a significantly younger average age than did imaginative prose writers and informative prose writers. Poetry is often seen as a literary form involving emotional content and play with language. In other words, then, poetry involves creativity "hot from the fire" (Cohen-Shalev, 1986). Gardner (1993) has made a similar kind of proposal, namely, that creative works of younger people tend more to defy previous traditions, whereas creative works of older people tend to integrate traditions.

Several researchers have suggested that as creativity evolves over the life span, certain features emerge in the creative products of elderly adults. Although the details depend on the domain of work, an "old-age style" with four main characteristics can be identified. First, creative work by older adults tends to emphasize subjective rather than objective experience. For example, in the domain of writing, this feature may involve the use of an introspective approach and a focus on inner harmony (see Simonton, 1989). In art, this concept can be expressed through even tonality, muted colors, and decreased tension and dynamics. Third, creative achievements during old age often involve a summing up or integration of ideas (Lehman, 1953). Creative work in basic science, social science, and philosophy often consists of writing memoirs, histories of a field, and textbooks, or recording observations accrued over a life span. Fourth, there is a recur-

rent emphasis on aging in the content of older creators' work. Issues of living with old age and coping with death emerge in novels, scholarly works, and musical compositions (Beckerman, 1990; Lehman, 1953; Wyatt-Brown, 1988).

B. Accounting for Life Span Variations in Creativity

How can the observed patterns of age-related changes in creative productivity, quality of creative work, and the form and content of creative work over the life span be explained? Following a generalized confluence model (Sternberg & Lubart, 1991, 1995), we will consider the phenomena described above in theoretical terms.

1. Changes in Cognition

Cognition includes intellectual processes and knowledge. Changes in intellectual processes and knowledge may be related to changes in creative productivity as well as to changes in the nature of creative work with age. The intellectual processes involved in creativity include defining and redefining problems, choosing appropriate problem-solving strategies, divergent thinking, and using insight processes to solve problems (Sternberg, 1985a; Sternberg & Lubart, 1991, 1995). These insight processes include selective encoding (sifting out information that is relevant for one's purposes and seeing as relevant information that others may pass over), selective comparison (seeing connections between present and past ideas), and selective combination (the meaningful synthesis of disparate information fragments).

The intellectual processes involved in creative performance are subject to both positive and negative age influences. On the positive side, problem definition, strategy selection, and selective encoding, comparison, and combination can become more efficient with experience (Berg & Sternberg, 1985). Also, dialectical thinking is believed to develop with age (see discussion above in the section of the article on wisdom). Dialectical thinking could also contribute to the harmony and decreased tension that forms part of the putative old-age style of creativity.

On the negative side, fluid abilities—the abilities used in thinking rapidly and flexibly, and that are used to handle new kinds of situations, to produce divergent thinking, and to generate selective attention (which is relevant to selective encoding)—show declines with age (Belsky, 1990; Horn, 1994; McCrae, Arenberg, & Costa, 1987; McDowd & Birren, 1990; Salthouse, 1996; Salthouse & Somberg, 1982; Simonton, 1990b). These declines may be reversible (Schaie & Willis, 1986), however. The declines in these abilities, however, may be partly due to the use of domain-general tests, whereas the abilities needed for creative success may become increasingly domain specific with age (Salthouse, 1990; Schaie, 1990; Simonton, 1988). Some declines also may be spurious and appear due to use of cross-sectional methodology (Schaie, 1989, 1996). The most insidious effect of age is probably a generalized slow-down of information processing, which could cause changes in productivity of creative work (Cerella, 1990; Salthouse, 1996). Some researchers believe that the slowdown is most pronounced in the final 10 years or so of life, but not before.

In addition to the intellectual processes, an informed creative contribution in any domain requires knowledge. Hayes (1989), for example, examined over 500 notable musical compositions produced by 76 "great" composers. Only three pieces were composed before year 10 of the composers' careers, and the literature on expertise strongly supports the importance of knowledge in a given field (e.g., Chase & Simon, 1973; Chi, Glaser, & Rees, 1982; Ericsson, 1990, 1996).

As noted earlier, domains vary in the age at which peak creativity occurs. Fields also vary on the average age at which the earliest contributions occur. This variation is found across disparate fields (e.g., mathematics and history) and even within subdisciplines of a large domain such as science (e.g., chemistry and physics) (Simonton, 1991). These age-related variations may be caused, in part, by differences in the amount of start-up knowledge that a field requires before creative work is possible (Amabile, 1983). Differences in peak ages may be due to the mix of fluid and crystallized abilities required at different ages, with fields more demanding of fluid abilities tending to show earlier peaks (see Horn, 1994).

With regard to knowledge, aging usually involves increases in general knowledge, life experience, and career experience. In Gruber's (1989; Gruber & Wallace, 1999) evolving-systems approach to creativity, creative work can only develop over time as many disparate systems of thinking are learned and integrated. For older adults a large knowledge base can help buffer decrements that may occur in the intellectual processes (Salthouse, 1990). Also, changes in the content of knowledge, such as a greater awareness of the aging processes and disease, can move a creator's work in new directions (Gardner & Monge, 1977). This change in the content of creative work is one feature of the putative old-age style, described earlier.

While noting the benefits of knowledge, research indicates that as people become more expert, they may lose flexibility and become entrenched in a standard or "correct" way of approaching a problem (Frensch & Sternberg, 1989; Langer, 1989, 1997). As a result of entrenchment, the rate of knowledge acquisition may decrease with age. As the author of one (nevertheless highly creative) book wrote, "many of these examples are somewhat old—but then again, so am I"

(Abelson, 1995, p. xiv). With less novelty in the knowledge base, there may be less idea generation and less creative productivity. Also, if an individual fails to keep up with changes in the domain of work, his or her work may become dated. The tendency for knowledge to become outdated more quickly in some domains as compared with others can account for variation across fields in the average age of final creative contributions (Simonton, 1991).

2. Changes in Personality and Motivation

Changes in personality and motivation may also play a key role in life span changes in creative productivity, and subsequently, the quality of creative work. Several personality attributes have been linked to creativity. First, consider tolerance of ambiguity, necessary during those periods of creative endeavor in which things are not quite fitting together, but in which premature closure would negate the likelihood of creative contribution (Barron & Harrington, 1981; Golann, 1963). In one study with 111 teachers (ages 20–83), scores on the Barron-Welsh Art Scale (a measure of tolerance of ambiguity) declined with age, especially beyond age 50 (Alpaugh & Birren, 1977). A second attribute important for creativity is perseverance, because creative ideas often threaten those who have a stake in the existing order (Golann, 1963; Roe, 1952). It has often been suggested that old age is accompanied by decreased stamina and decreased willingness to battle frustration (Abra, 1989; Lehman, 1953). There are, of course, counterexamples such as Renoir, who continued to work although rheumatism forced him to have a paint brush tied to his hand (Simonton, 1990b).

A third attribute, willingness to grow and openness to new experiences, becomes especially important as one attempts to go beyond one's past contributions to make new ones that are genuinely different and perhaps different in kind (McCrae, 1987). Older workers may be content with their earlier accomplishments. They must also compete with their own records when they produce new work (Abra, 1989; Lehman, 1953). Due, in part, to the possibility of devaluing their own work, Planck (1949) and others have proposed that older achievers in a discipline are less receptive than are younger achievers to new ideas. Hull, Tessner, and Diamond (1978) tested this hypothesis with historical records of British scientists who reacted to Darwin's theory of evolution in the decade after it was published. Scientists who accepted the theory were significantly younger (by approximately 11 years of age, on average) than were those who rejected the theory. Moreover, it may be that the same scientists who once rejected the establishment willingly become a part of that establishment as they grow older.

A fourth attribute, willingness to take risks (Glover, 1977; Lubart & Sternberg, 1998; McClelland, 1956; Sternberg & Lubart, 1995), is important during creative work, because there is a potential for gain (internal and external rewards) or loss and the outcome is uncertain. Botwinick (1984) documented the tendency for increased cautiousness with age. Several studies have measured risk taking through a set of hypothetical situations that involve choice dilemmas. Elderly participants showed a tendency to avoid risk in these scenarios by refusing to endorse the risky course of action "no matter what the probability" of success. On cognitive tests, elderly participants prefer to omit answers rather than guess incorrectly and, when possible, choose problems that offer a high probability of success (Okun & DiVesta, 1976).

A fifth attribute is individuality and a supporting courage of one's convictions (Barron & Harrington, 1981; Dellas &

Gaier, 1970; Golann, 1963; MacKinnon, 1962, 1965). One needs to value oneself and one's difference from others, and to believe in one's ideas even as they go against the entrenched ones. Individuality appears to decline in older adults. Adults aged 60 and older display more conformity than do younger adults on projective tests such as the Thematic Apperception Test (TAT) and in experimental settings (Botwinick, 1984). Klein (1972), for example, tested young adults (16–21 years of age) and older adults (60–86 years) in a perceptual judgment task. When given false feedback about other participants' judgments, the older participants conformed significantly more often, and this tendency was even stronger for more difficult versions of the task.

Motivation may be especially linked to life span-related trends in career advancement and retirement policies (Mumford & Gustafson, 1988). A few studies have shown changes in the level of specific motivations, which may affect creative productivity, such as shifts in achievement motivation with age (Kausler, 1990; Veroff, Reuman, & Feld, 1984).

3. Changes in the Environment

The final element influencing creative productivity, described here, is environmental context. Environments may provide physical or social stimulation, which helps new ideas to form, and can foster or hinder the development of these fledgling ideas (Amabile, 1983). Aging is associated with a host of environmental changes. First, older people often experience decreased income and decreased social networks for support (Belsky, 1990). These elements create a context in which creative work is difficult. Second, as a person advances in a field, and becomes more well known, there are requests for lectures, committees on which to serve, and other chores. Essentially, with age, people have increased responsibilities for

the maintenance of their field. These "taxes" limit the time available for creative productivity (Bjorksten, 1946). Third, there may be cohort differences in the overall economic climate and the availability of benefactors to support creative work (Simonton, 1988). Additionally, publication practices and the amount of competition in a field can also change over time (Botwinick, 1984; Simonton, 1977).

Beyond these effects, the social environment also serves to evaluate products and performances. The very same contribution viewed as creative by one group of judges may be viewed as mundane by another (Csikszentmihalyi, 1988, 1999). Changes in life span creativity can be traced, in part, to changes in implicit standards for creativity over time, and to rater bias against the elderly. For example, each age cohort may have a different standard for creativity (Romaniuk & Romaniuk, 1981). Cohorts may have their own preferred genres of work, as well as distinct preferences of artists or musicians that were novel during the cohort's youth. Products that an older cohort may consider novel could very well be deemed ordinary or boring by a younger cohort because that novelty has been incorporated into the culture. Indeed, there is some evidence for cohort-matching effects, whereby judges tend to rate as more creative products emanating from peers of their own cohort (Sternberg & Lubart, 1995). Bias against work produced by elderly person also seems to occur. Elderly creators, in some critics' eyes, may be constrained by their early products to follow a developmental course in their work. Unusual works may be dismissed as evidence for senility (Cohen-Shalev, 1989). Also, critics may set unrealistic standards for elderly creators, believing that the products of old age must offer a profound message and surpass the creator's earlier works in order to be considered creative.

V. Final Comments

In this essay, we have concentrated on what wisdom and creativity are, and how they develop in later adulthood. In this brief final section, we wish to discuss why we believe that wisdom and creativity are undervalued and worthy of far more theory, research, and practice, both in life-span developmental psychology and in the world at large.

In psychology, the field of intelligence is far larger than the field of wisdom or the field of creativity. This difference in size can be seen in number of publications, number of citations of publications, number of people contributing to the field, number of books devoted to the topic, or really, whatever reasonable measure one choose to use. There are perhaps several reasons why psychology, in particular, and society, in general, has placed more emphasis on intelligence than on wisdom and creativity.

First, it is easier to conceptualize intelligence than it is to conceptualize either wisdom or creativity. Intelligence traditionally has been defined in terms of the ability to adapt to environments, and people know what that means—it is the ability to get ahead in some set of environments. Creativity involves shaping environments, and it often is not clear just how that can or should be done. Wisdom involves some balance of intelligence and creativity, and the nature of how to balance two constructs can be no more clear, and probably will be less clear, than the nature of the two constructs themselves.

Second, intelligence—or at least intelligence as it is usually defined in a relatively narrow way—is easier to measure than is either wisdom or creativity. Science and society always have and probably always will tend to turn their attention to the things that can be quantified and thus be understood more easily operationally. Indeed, the tendency often is to equate the operationalization of a concept with the concept itself.

Third, intelligence counts for more in school than do either wisdom or creativity. Students with higher levels of conventionally defined intelligence are likely to do better in school. Students with higher levels of wisdom or creativity—especially those who question teachers, schools, and institutions—are likely to do worse in school. They will not be appreciated by those whose steadfast beliefs are called into question, especially because those individuals are older than the students who question them.

Finally, fields tend to build upon themselves. Those that have success tend to grow "richer" in the resources allocated to them, whereas those that have less success tend to grow "poorer." The field of intelligence has had success, at least as measured by the extraordinary growth of intelligence testing and of research on such testing. The fields of wisdom and creativity have been smaller and at many times have seemed to be close to shrinking into oblivion.

In a rapidly changing world, however, such as the one we live in, creativity and wisdom may become progressively more important for survival. The need *flexibly* to adapt and to shape environments is greater than ever before. At times in the past, most people stayed in the same job throughout their lifetime, and the nature of their job stayed pretty much the same. Today the world is changing much more rapidly: Many people shift jobs frequently, and even those who do not find that the nature of a given job changes. Those of us who are middle-aged professors, for example, started our careers in a day when there were no small computers, no electronic mail, no Internet. Much of what we need to do today is completely different from what we once needed to do. We need the creativity to adapt to and shape this changing world, and we need the wisdom to make sense of it—to come to grips with the things that change, but also to understand the things that do not—to realize that the principles and values underlying the search for scientific understanding remain the same, regardless of the technology available to conduct this search.

Acknowledgments

Preparation of this chapter was supported by a government grant from the National Science Foundation, a contract from the Army Research Institute, and under a grant from the Javits Act Program (Grant No. R206R000001) as administered by the Office of Educational Research and Improvement, U. S. Department of Education. Grantees undertaking such projects are encouraged to express freely their professional judgment. This chapter, therefore, does not necessarily represent the positions or the policies of the U.S. government, and no official endorsement should be inferred.

References

Abelson, R. P. (1995). *Statistics as principled argument*. Hillsdale, NJ: Lawrence Erlbaum Associates.

Abra, J. (1989). Changes in creativity with age: Data, explanations, and further predictions. *International Journal of Aging and Human Development, 28*, 105–126.

Alpaugh, P. K., & Birren, J. E. (1977). Variables affecting creative contributions across the adult life span. *Human Development, 20*, 240–248.

Amabile, T. M. (1983). *The social psychology of creativity*. New York: Springer-Verlag.

Amabile, T. M. (1996). *Creativity in context*. Boulder, CO: Westview-Harper Collins.

Arieti, S. (1976). *Creativity: The magic synthesis*. New York: Basic Books.

Arlin, P. K. (1990). Wisdom: the art of problem finding. In R. J. Sternberg (Ed.), *Wisdom: Its nature, origins, and development* (pp. 230–243). New York: Cambridge University Press.

Assman, A. (1994). Wholesome knowledge: Concepts of wisdom in a historical and cross-cultural perspective. In D. L. Featherman, R. M. Lerner, & M. Perlmutter (Eds.), *Life-span development and behavior* (Vol. 12, pp. 188–224). Hillsdale, NJ: Erlbaum.

Baltes, P. B., & Smith, J. (1987, August). *Toward a psychology of wisdom and its ontogenesis*. Paper presented at the Ninety-Fifth Annual Convention of the American Psychological Association, New York City.

Baltes, P. B., & Smith, J. (1990). Toward a psychology of wisdom and its ontogenesis. In R. J. Sternberg (Ed.), *Wisdom: Its nature, origins, and development* (pp. 87–120). New York: Cambridge University Press.

Baltes, P. B., Smith, J., & Staudinger, U. M. (1992). Wisdom and successful aging. In T. Sonderegger (Ed.), *Nebraska Symposium on Motivation* (Vol. 39, pp. 123–167). Lincoln, NE: University of Nebraska Press.

Baltes, P. B., & Staudinger, U. M. (1993). The search for a psychology of wisdom. *Current Directions in Psychological Science, 2*, 75–80.

Baltes, P. B., & Staudinger, U. M. (2000). Wisdom: A metaheuristic to orchestrate mind and virtue towards excellence. *American Psychologist, 55*, 122–135.

Baltes, P. B., Staudinger, U. M., Maercker, A., & Smith, J. (1995). People nominated as wise: A comparative study of wisdom-related knowledge. *Psychology and Aging, 10*, 155–166.

Barron, F. (1988). Putting creativity to work. In R. J. Sternberg (Ed.), *The nature of creativity* (pp. 76–98). New York: Cambridge University Press.

Barron, F., & Harrington, D. M. (1981). Creativity, intelligence, and personality. *Annual Review of Psychology, 32*, 439–476.

Basseches, J. (1984). *Dialectical thinking and adult development*. Norwood, NJ: Ablex.

Beckerman, M. B. (1990). Leos Janácek and "the late style" in music. *The Gerontologist, 30*, 632–635.

Belsky, J. K. (1990). *The psychology of aging: Theory, research, & interventions* (2nd ed.). Pacific Grove, CA: BrooksCole.

Berg, C. A., & Sternberg, R. J. (1985). A triarchic theory of intellectual development during adulthood. *Developmental Review, 5*, 334–370.

Birren, J. E., & Fisher, L. M. (1990). The elements of wisdom: Overview and integration. In R. J. Sternberg (Ed.), *Wisdom: Its nature, origins, and development* (pp. 317–332). New York: Cambridge University Press.

Bjorksten, J. (1946). The limitation of creative years. *Scientific Monthly, 62,* 94.

Botwinick, J. (1984). *Aging and behavior* (3rd ed.). New York: Springer.

Britt, C. R. & Ball-Kilbourne, G. (Eds.). (1997). *1 & 2 Kings, 1 & 2 Chronicles (Genesis to Revelation).* Nashville, TN: Abingdon Press.

Cantor, N., & Kihlstrom, J. F. (1987a). *Personality and social intelligence.* Englewood Cliffs, NJ: Prentice-Hall.

Cattell, R. B. (1971). *Abilities: Their structure, growth, and action.* Boston: Houghton-Mifflin.

Cerella, J. (1990). Aging and information-processing rate. In J. E. Birren & K. W. Schaie (Eds.), *Handbook of the psychology of aging* (3rd ed.) (pp. 201–221). San Diego, CA: Academic Press.

Chandler, M. J., & Holiday, S. (1990). Wisdom in a postapocalyptic age. In R. J. Sternberg (Ed.), *Wisdom: Its nature, origins, and development* (pp. 121–141). New York: Cambridge University Press.

Chase, W. G., & Simon, H. A. (1973). The mind's eye in chess. In W. G. Chase (Ed.), *Visual information processing.* New York; Academic Press.

Chi, M., Glaser, R., & Rees, E. (1982). Expertise in problem solving. In R. J. Sternberg (Ed.), *Advances in the psychology of human intelligence* (Vol. 1, pp. 7–76). Hillsdale, NJ: Erlbaum.

Clayton, V. (1975). Erickson's theory of human development as it applies to the aged: wisdom as contradictory cognition. *Human Development, 18,* 119–128.

Clayton, V. (1976). *A multidimensional scaling analysis of the concept of wisdom.* Unpublished doctoral dissertation, University of Southern California.

Clayton, V. (1982). Wisdom and intelligence: The nature and function of knowledge in the later years. *International Journal of Aging and Development, 15,* 315–321.

Clayton, V., & Birren, J. E. (1980). The development of wisdom across the life-span: a reexamination of an ancient topic. In P. B. Baltes & O. G. Brim (Eds.), *Life-span devel-

opment and behavior* (Vol. 3, pp. 103–135). New York: Academic Press.

Cohen-Shalev, A. (1986). Artistic creativity across the adult life span: An alternative approach. *Interchange, 17*(4), 1–16.

Cohen-Shalev, A. (1989). Old age style: Developmental changes in creative production from a life-span perspective. *Journal of Aging Studies, 3*(1), 21–37.

Collins, M. A., & Amabile, T. M. (1999). Motivation and creativity. In R. J. Sternberg (Ed.), *Handbook of creativity* (pp. 297–312). New York: Cambridge University Press.

Costa, P. T., Jr., & McCrae, R. R. (1994). Set like plaster? Evidence of the stability of adult personality. In T. F. Hetherington & J. L. Weinberger (Eds.), *Adult development: Comparisons and applications of developmental models* (Vol. 1). New York: Praeger.

Csikszentmihalyi, M. (1988). Society, culture, and person: A systems view of creativity. In R. J. Sternberg (Ed.), *The nature of creativity* (pp. 325–339). New York: Cambridge University Press.

Csikszentmihalyi, M. (1996). *Creativity.* New York: HarperCollins.

Csikszentimihalyi, M. (1999). Implications of a systems perspective for the study of creativity. In R. J. Sternberg (Ed.), *Handbook of creativity* (pp. 313–335). New York: Cambridge University Press.

Csikszentmihalyi, M., & Rathunde, K. (1990). The psychology of wisdom: an evolutionary interpretation. In R. J. Sternberg (Ed.), *Wisdom: Its nature, origins, and development* (pp. 25–51). New York: Cambridge University Press.

Dellas, M., & Gaier, E. L. (1970). Identification of creativity: The individual. *Psychological Bulletin, 73,* 55–73.

Ericsson, K. A. (1990). The nature of exceptional performance. In P. B. Baltes, D. L. Featherman, & R. M. Lerner (Eds.), *Life-span development and behavior* (pp. 187–217). Hillsdale, NJ: Erlbaum.

Ericsson, K. A. (Ed.) (1996). *The road to excellence.* Mahwah, NJ: Lawrence Erlbaum Associates.

Erikson, E. H. (1963). *Childhood and society* (2nd ed.). New York: Norton.

Erikson, E. H. (1982). *The life cycle completed.* New York: Norton.

Flynn, J. R. (1987). Massive IQ gains in 14 nations. *Psychological Bulletin, 101,* 171–191.

Frank, A. (1952). *Anne Frank: The diary of a young girl.* New York: Doubleday & Company.

Frensch, P. A., & Sternberg, R. J. (1989). Expertise and intelligent thinking: when is it worse to know better? In R. J. Sternberg (Ed.), *Advances in the psychology of human intelligence* (Vol. 5, pp. 157–188). Hillsdale, NJ: Erlbaum.

Gardner, E. G., & Monge, R. H. (1977). Adult age differences in cognitive abilities and educational background. *Experimental Aging Research, 3,* 337–383.

Gardner, H. (1993). *Creating minds.* New York: Basic Books.

Glover, J. A. (1977). Risky shift and creativity. *Social Behavior and Personality, 5,* 317–320.

Golann, S. E. (1963). Psychological study of creativity. *Psychological Bulletin, 60,* 548–565.

Goleman, D. (1995). *Emotional intelligence.* New York: Bantam Books.

Gruber, H. E. (1989). The evolving systems approach to creative work. In D. B. Wallace & H. E. Gruber (Eds.), *Creative people at work: Twelve cognitive case studies* (pp. 3–24). New York: Oxford University Press.

Gruber, H. E., & Wallace, D. B. (1999). The case study method and evolving systems approach for understanding unique creative people at work. In R. J. Sternberg (Ed.), *Handbook of creativity* (pp. 93–115). New York: Cambridge University Press.

Hartshorne, C. (1987). *Wisdom as moderation: a philosophy of the middle way.* Albany: State University of New York Press.

Hayes, J. R. (1989). Cognitive processes in creativity. In J. A., Glover, R. R. Ronning, & C. R. Reynolds (Eds.), *Handbook of creativity* (pp. 135–146). New York: Plenum.

Hedlund, J., Horvath, J. A., Forsythe, G. B., Snook, S., Williams, W. M., Dennis, M., & Sternberg, R. J. (1998). *The acquisition of tacit knowledge for military leadership: Implications for training.* Manuscript in preparation.

Holliday, S. G., & Chandler, M. J. (1986). *Wisdom: explorations in adult competence.* Basel, Switzerland: Karger.

Horn, J. L. (1994). Fluid and crystallized intelligence, theory of. In R. J. Sternberg (Ed.), *Encyclopedia of human intelligence* (Vol. 1, pp. 443–456). New York: Macmillan.

Horvath, J. A., Sternberg, R. J., Forsythe, G. B., Sweeney, P. J., Bullis, R. C., Williams, W. M., & Dennis, M. (1996). *Tacit knowledge in military leadership: Supporting instrument development* (Technical Report 1042). Alexandria, VA: U. S. Army Research Institute for the Behavioral and Social Sciences.

Hull, D. L., Tessner, P. D., & Diamond, A. M. (1978). Planck's principle: Do younger scientists accept new scientific ideas with greater alacrity than older scientists? *Science, 202,* 717–723.

Jackson, P. W., & Messick, S. (1967). The person, the product, and the response: Conceptual problems in the assessment of creativity. In J. Kagan (Ed.), *Creativity and learning* (pp. 1–19). Boston: Houghton Mifflin.

Kausler, D. H. (1990). Motivation, human aging, and cognitive performance. In J. E. Birren & K. W. Schaie (Eds.), *Handbook of the psychology of aging* (3rd ed.) (pp. 171–182). San Diego, CA: Academic Press.

Kitchener, K. S. (1983). Cognition, metacognition, and epistemic cognition: A three-level model of cognitive processing. *Human Development, 4,* 222–232.

Kitchener, K. S. (1986). Formal reasoning in adults: A review and critique. In R. A. Mines & K. S. Kitchener (Eds.), *Adult cognitive development.* New York: Praeger.

Kitchener, K. S., & Brenner, H. G. (1990). Wisdom and reflective judgment: Knowing in the face of uncertainty. In R. J. Sternberg (Ed.), *Wisdom: Its nature, origins, and development* (pp. 212–229). New York: Cambridge University Press.

Kitchener, K. S., & King, P. M. (1981). Reflective judgment: concepts of justification and their relationship to age and education. *Journal of Applied Developmental Psychology, 2,* 89–116.

Kitchener, K. S., & Kitchener, R. F. (1981). The development of natural rationality: Can formal operations account for it? In J. Meacham & N. R. Santilli (Eds.), *Social development in youth: Structure and content.* Basel, Switzerland: Karger.

Klein, R. L. (1972). Age, sex, and task difficulty as predictors of social conformity. *Journal of Gerontology, 27,* 229–236.

Kramer, D. A. (1990). Conceptualizing wisdom: the primacy of affect-cognition relations. In R. J. Sternberg (Ed.), *Wisdom: Its nature, origins, and development* (pp. 279–313). New York: Cambridge University Press.

Labouvie-Vief, G. (1980). Beyond formal operations: uses and limits of pure logic in life span development. *Human Development, 23,* 141–161.

Labouvie-Vief, G. (1982). Dynamic development and mature autonomy. *Human Development, 25,* 161–191.

Labouvie-Vief, G. (1990). Wisdom as integrated thought: historical and developmental perspectives. In R. J. Sternberg (Ed.), *Wisdom: Its nature, origins, and development* (pp. 52–83). New York: Cambridge University Press.

Langer, E. J. (1989). *Mindfulness.* New York: Addison-Wesley.

Langer, E. J. (1997). *The power of mindful learning.* Needham Heights, MA: Addison-Wesley.

Lehman, H. C. (1953). *Age and achievement.* Princeton, NJ: Princeton University Press.

Levitt, H. M. (1999). The development of wisdom: An analysis of Tibetan Buddhist experience. *Journal of Humanistic Psychology, 39,* 86–105.

Lubart, T. I. (1994). Creativity. In R. J. Sternberg (Ed.), *Thinking and problem solving* (pp. 289–332). New York: Academic Press.

Lubart, T. I. (1999). Creativity across cultures. In R. J. Sternberg (ed.). *Handbook of creativity* (pp. 339–350). New York: Cambridge University Press.

Lubart, T. I., & Sternberg, R. J. (1998). Life span creativity: an investment theory approach. In C. Adams-Price (Ed.), *Creativity and successful aging: Theoretical and empirical approaches* (pp. 21–41). New York: Springer.

MacKinnon, D. W. (1962). The nature and nurture of creative talent. *American Psychologist, 17,* 484–495.

MacKinnon, D. W. (1965). Personality and the realization of creative potential. *American Psychologist, 20,* 273–281.

Mayer, J. D., & Salovey, P. (1993). The intelligence of emotional intelligence. *Intelligence, 17,* 433–442.

McClelland, D. C. (1956). The calculated risk: An aspect of scientific performance. In C. W. Taylor (Ed.), *The 1955 University of Utah research conference on the identification of creative scientific talent* (pp. 96–110). Salt Lake City, UT: University of Utah Press.

McCrae, R. R. (1987). Creativity, divergent thinking, and openness to experience. *Journal of Personality and Social Psychology, 52,* 1258–1265.

McCrae, R. R. (1996). Social consequences of experiential openness. *Psychological Bulletin, 120,* 323–337.

McCrae, R. R., Arenberg, D., & Costa, P. T., Jr. (1987). Declines in divergent thinking with age: Cross-sectional, longitudinal, and cross-sequential analyses. *Psychology and Aging, 2,* 130–137.

McDowd, J. M., & Birren, J. E. (1990). Aging and attentional processes. In J. E. Birren & K. W. Schaie (Eds.), *Handbook of the psychology of aging* (3rd ed.) (pp. 222–233). San Diego, CA: Academic Press.

McLeish, J. A. B. (1976). *The ulyssean adult: Creativity in the middle and later years.* New York: McGraw-Hill Reyerson.

Meacham, J. (1983). Wisdom and the context of knowledge: Knowing that one doesn't know. In D. Kuhn & J. A. Meacham (Eds.), *On the development of developmental psychology* (pp. 111–134). Basel, Switzerland: Karger.

Meacham, J. (1990). The loss of wisdom. In R. J. Sternberg (Ed.), *Wisdom: Its nature, origins, and development* (pp. 181–211). New York: Cambridge University Press.

Mumford, M. D., & Gustafson, S. B. (1988). Creativity syndrome: integration, application, and innovation. *Psychological Bulletin, 103,* 27–43.

Neisser, U. (1979). The concept of intelligence. In R. J. Sternberg & D. K. Detterman (Eds.), *Human intelligence: Perspectives on its theory and measurement* (pp. 179–189). Norwood, NJ: Ablex.

Ocshe, R. (1990). *Before the gates of excellence.* New York: Cambridge University Press.

Okun, M. A., & DiVesta, F. J. (1976). Cautiousness in adulthood as a function of age and instructions. *Journal of Gerontology, 31,* 571–576.

Orwoll, L., & Perlmutter, M. (1990). The study of wise persons: Integrating a personality perspective. In R. J. Sternberg (Ed.), *Wisdom: Its nature, origins, and development* (pp. 160–177). New York: Cambridge University Press.

Pascual-Leone, J. (1990). An essay on wisdom: Toward organismic processes that make it possible. In R. J. Sternberg (Ed.), *Wisdom: Its nature, origins, and development* (pp. 244–278). New York: Cambridge University Press.

Perkins, D. N., & Grotzer, T. A. (1997). Teaching intelligence. *American Psychologist, 52,* 1125–1133.

Piaget, J. (1972). *The psychology of intelligence.* Totowa, NJ: Littlefield-Adams.

Planck, M. (1949). *Scientific autobiography and other papers,* (F. Gaynor, Trans). New York: Philosophical Library.

Polanyi, M. (1976). Tacit knowledge. In M. Marx & F. Goodson (Eds.), *Theories in contemporary psychology* (pp. 330–344). New York: Macmillan.

Riegel, K. F. (1973). Dialectical operations: The final period of cognitive development. *Human Development, 16,* 346–370.

Robinson, D. N. (1989). *Aristotle's psychology.* New York: Columbia University Press.

Robinson, D. N. (1990). Wisdom through the ages. In R. J. Sternberg (Ed.), *Wisdom: Its nature, origins, and development* (pp. 13–24). New York: Cambridge University Press.

Roe, A. (1952). *The making of a scientist.* New York: Dodd, Mead.

Romaniuk, J. G., & Romaniuk, M. (1981). Creativity across the life span: a measurement perspective. *Human Development, 24,* 366–381.

Rosch, E. (1975). Cognitive representations of semantic categories. *Journal of Experimental Psychology: General, 104,* 192–233.

Ryle, G. (1949). *The concept of mind.* London: Hutchinson.

Salovey, P., & Mayer, J. D. (1990). Emotional intelligence. *Imagination, Cognition, and Personality, 9,* 185–211.

Salthouse, T. A. (1990). Cognitive competence and expertise in aging. In J. E. Birren & K. W. Schaie (Eds.), *Handbook of the psychology*

of aging (3rd ed.), (pp. 310–319). San Diego, CA: Acdemic Press.

Salthouse, T. A. (1996). The processing-speed theory of adult age differences in cognition. *Psychological Review, 103,* 403–428.

Salthouse, T. A., & Somberg, B. L. (1982). Skilled performance: Effects of adult age and experience on elementary processes. *Journal of Experimental Psychology: General, 111,* 176–207.

Schaie, K. W. (1989). Perceptual speed in adulthood: Cross-sectional and longitudinal studies. *Psychology and Aging, 4,* 443–453.

Schaie, K. W. (1990). Intellectual development in adulthood. In J. E. Birren & K. W. Schaie (Eds.), *Handbook of the psychology of aging* (3rd ed), (pp. 291–309). San Diego, CA: Academic Press.

Schaie, K. W. (1996). *Intellectual development in adulthood: The Seattle Longitudinal Study.* New York: Cambridge University Press.

Schaie, K. W., & Willis, S. L. (1986). Can decline in intellectual functioning in the elderly be reversed? *Developmental Psychology, 22,* 223–232.

Simonton, D. K. (1975). Interdisciplinary creativity over historical time: A correlational analysis of generational fluctuations. *Social Behavior & Personality, 3*(2), 181–188.

Simonton, D. K. (1977). Creative productivity, age, and stress: A biographical time-series analysis of 10 classical composers. *Journal of Personality and Social Psychology, 35,* 791–804.

Simonton, D. K. (1985). Quality, quantity, and age: The careers of 10 distinguished psychologists. *International Journal of Aging and Human Development, 21,* 241–254.

Simonton, D. K. (1988). Age and outstanding achievement: What do we know after a century of research? *Psychological Bulletin, 104,* 251–267.

Simonton, D. K. (1989). The swan-song phenomenon: Last-works effects for 172 classical composers. *Psychology and Aging, 4,* 42–47.

Simonton, D. K. (1990a). Creativity in the later years: Optimistic prospects for achievement. *The Gerontologist, 30,* 626–631.

Simonton, D. K. (1990b). Creativity and wisdom in aging. In J. E. Birren & K. W. Schaie (Eds.), *Handbook of the psychology of aging*

(3rd ed) (pp. 320–329). San Diego, CA: Academic Press.

Simonton, D. K. (1991). Career landmarks in science: individual differences and interdisciplinary contrasts. *Developmental Psychology, 27,* 119–130.

Simonton, D. K. (1999). Creativity from a historiometric perspective. In R. J. Sternberg (Ed.), *Handbook of creativity* (pp. 116–133). New York: Cambridge University Press.

Smith, J., & Baltes, P. B. (1990). Wisdom-related knowledge: Age/cohort differences in responses to life planning problems. *Developmental Psychology, 26,* 494–505.

Smith, J., Staudinger, U. M., & Baltes, P. B. (1994). Occupational settings facilitating wisdom-related knowledge: The sample case of clinical psychologists. *Journal of Consulting and Clinical Psychology, 66,* 989–999.

Staudinger, U. M. (1989). *The study of life review: An approach to the investigation of intellectual development across the life span.* Berlin: Sigma.

Staudinger, U. M. (1999). Older and wiser? Integrating results on the relationship between age and wisdom-related performance. *International Journal of Behavioral Development, 23,* 641–664.

Staudinger, U. M., & Baltes, P. M. (1996). Interactive minds: a facilitative setting for wisdom-related performance? *Journal of Personality and Social Psychology, 71,* 746–762.

Staudinger, U. M., Lopez, D. F., & Baltes, P. B. (1997). The psychometric location of wisdom-related performance. *Personality and Social Psychology Bulletin, 23,* 1200–1214.

Staudinger, U. M., Smith, J., & Baltes, P. B. (1992). Wisdom-related knowledge in life review task: age differences and the role of professional specialization. *Psychology and Aging, 7,* 271–281.

Stein, M. I. (1953). Creativity and culture. *Journal of Psychology, 36,* 311–322.

Sternberg, R. J. (1985a). *Beyond IQ: A triarchic theory of human intelligence.* New York: Cambridge University Press.

Sternberg, R. J. (1985b). Implicit theories of intelligence, creativity, and wisdom. *Journal of Personality and Social Psychology, 49,* 607–627.

Sternberg, R. J. (Ed.) (1990a). *Wisdom: Its nature, origins, and development.* New York: Cambridge University Press.

Sternberg, R. J. (1990b). Wisdom and its relations to intelligence and creativity. In R. J. Sternberg (Ed.), *Wisdom: Its nature, origins, and development* (pp. 142–159). New York: Cambridge University Press.

Sternberg, R. J. (1997a). *Successful intelligence.* New York: Plume.

Sternberg, R. J. (1997b). *Thinking styles.* New York: Cambridge University Press.

Sternberg, R. J. (1998). A balance theory of wisdom. *Review of General Psychology, 2,* 347–365.

Sternberg, R. J. (1999a). A dialectical basis for understanding the study of cognition. In R. J. Sternberg (Ed.), *The nature of cognition* (pp. 51–78). Cambridge, MA: MIT Press.

Sternberg, R. J. (1999b). Schools should nurture wisdom. In B. Z. Presseisen (Ed.), *Teaching for intelligence* (pp. 55–82). Arlington Heights, IL: Skylight.

Sternberg, R. J., & Dobson, D. M. (1987). Resolving interpersonal conflicts: An analysis of stylistic consistency. *Journal of Personality and Social Psychology, 52,* 794–812.

Sternberg, R. J., Forsythe, G. B., Hedlund, J., Horvath, J., Snook, S., Williams, W. M., Wagner, R. K., & Grigorenko, E. L. (2000). *Practical intelligence in everyday life.* New York: Cambridge University Press.

Sternberg, R. J., & Lubart, T. I. (1991). An investment theory of creativity and its development. *Human Development, 34,* 1–31.

Sternberg, R. J., & Lubart, T. I. (1995). *Defying the crowd: Cultivating creativity in a culture of conformity.* New York: Free Press.

Sternberg, R. J., & Lubart, T. I. (1996). Investing in creativity. *American Psychologist, 51,* 677–688.

Sternberg, R. J., & Grigorenko, E. L. (1997). The cognitive costs of physical and mental ill-health: Applying the psychology of the developed world to the problems of the developing world. *Eye on Psi Chi, 2*(1), 20–27.

Sternberg, R. J., & Smith, C. (1985). Social intelligence and decoding skills in nonverbal communication. *Social Cognition, 2,* 168–192.

Sternberg, R. J., & Soriano, L. J. (1984). Styles of conflict resolution. *Journal of Personality and Social Psychology, 47,* 115–126.

Sternberg, R. J., & Wagner, R. K. (1993). The g-ocentric view of intelligence and job performance is wrong. *Current Directions in Psychological Science, 2,* 1–5.

Sternberg, R. J., Wagner, R. K., & Okagaki, L. (1993). Practical intelligence: The nature and role of tacit knowledge in work and at school. In H. Reese & J. Puckett (Eds.), *Advances in lifespan development* (pp. 205–227). Hillsdale, NJ: Erlbaum.

Sternberg, R. J., Wagner, R. K., Williams, W. M., & Horvath, J. A. (1995). Testing common sense. *American Psychologist, 50,* 912–927.

Veroff, J., Reuman, D., & Feld, S. (1984). Motives in American men and women across the adult life span. *Developmental Psychology, 20,* 1142–1158.

Wagner, R. K. (1987). Tacit knowledge in everyday intelligent behavior. *Journal of Personality and Social Psychology, 52,* 1236–1247.

Wagner, R. K., & Sternberg, R. J. (1985). Practical intelligence in real-world pursuits: The role of tacit knowledge. *Journal of Personality and Social Psychology, 49,* 436–458.

Webster's New World Dictionary (3rd ed.) (1997). New York: Simon & Schuster.

Wyatt-Brown, A. M. (1988). Late style in the novels of Barbara Pym and Penelope Mortimer. *The Gerontologist, 28,* 835–839.

Twenty-One

Mental Health and Aging at the Outset of the Twenty-First Century

Margaret Gatz and Michael A. Smyer

I. Introduction

If success has a thousand parents and failure has none, mental health issues for older adults is an orphan. For decades, two professional sectors have neglected these issues—those concerned with programs and policies to improve the lives of older Americans, and those focused on mental health. In this chapter, we look at how the situation has changed during the 1990s and at what we can anticipate in the decade ahead. This endeavor builds on two previous exercises: Gatz, Smyer, and Lawton (1980) and Gatz and Smyer (1992).

We begin in section II by reviewing the demographic context and the epidemiology of mental disorders. This chapter is not the place for a comprehensive consideration of demographic trends. Instead, we focus on how changes at the population level inform mental health and aging concerns. We turn next to the epidemiology of mental disorders, in particular, the numbers of older adults with mental disorders. Here we focus on rates of disorder, not on etiology. In section III, we consider where older people with mental disorders are being treated and what treat-

ments are available. Then we turn to the policy context. In section III.B, we discuss trends in mental health policy—managed care, prescription privileges, and practice guidelines—and the greater engagement with mental health issues that has recently been evidenced by advocacy organizations in aging. In our discussion of practice guidelines, we consider outcome studies with respect to treatment of mental disorders in older adults. In section IV, we nominate four emerging influences, from the just completed Decade of the Brain to increased attention given by social science to spirituality, and suggest how they might affect the mental health of older adults in next decade. In section V, we touch on the role of the psychologist in the decade ahead.

At the outset, it may be useful to comment on the concepts of mental health and mental illness in later life. Mental health is a complex concept that encompasses a range from symptom-free psychosocial functioning to optimal functioning (Birren & Renner, 1980; Qualls & Smyer, 2001). Two elements contribute to definitions of mental illness—subjective distress and objective limitations in psychological functioning. Throughout this chapter, we will focus on both mental health and mental illness as we consider the complex determinants of well-being in later life.

II. The Larger Context

A. Demographics

In the United States and in most western European countries, the proportion of the population who are aged 60 and older is already high. For example, in the United States in 1996, 16.5% were aged 60 and older; in Norway, 19.8%; and in Belgium, 21.5% (U.S. Bureau of the Census, 2000a). Instead of a population pyramid, in which there are more members of younger age groups and progressively fewer members of each older age group, the distribution is becoming rectangularized, with equal proportions of individuals at each decade from birth through 70 (U.S. Bureau of the Census, 2000b). In addition, the elderly population in the United States is becoming more culturally and ethnically diverse (Miles, 1999).

The size of the older population is a global concern. In developing countries, the pace of increase in the older population is far greater than in North America and Europe. For example, in China, which in 1996 had only 9.5% of individuals aged 60 and older, the proportion of the population who are aged will be skyrocketing, in part as an unintended consequence of the one child per family policy inaugurated in 1979 to control total population growth (Zhu & Xu, 1992). By 2025, the number of persons aged 60 and older in China is projected to reach a staggering 290,640,000, or 20.3% of the population (U.S. Bureau of the Census, 2000a).

The implications for mental health and aging are that, with more older adults, the crude numbers of those with mental disorders will rise, even if prevalence rates were to stay unchanged. In addition, associated with rectangularization of the age distribution, there are changes in the availability of family and others to provide various forms of assistance to older generations. There are also differences in family norms about providing care in different nationalities and cultural groups.

Internationally, inequality is expanding. In the United States, disparities between the richest and the poorest segments of the population are widening. The wealthiest one fifth account for greater than half of all income earned by individuals ("Cutting the Cookie," 1999). Nations that have tended toward social democracy, for example, in Northern Europe, are seeing greater differences in pay between top executives and ordinary workers, possibly as a consequence of globalization of the economy, and the ascendance of liberty over equality as a value ("Liberty, Equality, Humility," 1999). Developing countries have learned that open economies favor a few while leaving vast majorities in poverty.

Because inequalities in resources available to older adults parallel other inequalities, societal inequalities have consequences for the mental and physical well-being of older persons. For example, social class differences are evident on a number of chronic conditions and limitations in activities of daily living (ADLs) in a U.S. sample (House et al., 1992). Similarly, social class differences are evident in peak expiratory flow, performance measures of ADLs, joint pain, and mobility in a study of the oldest old in Sweden (Parker, Thorslund, & Lundberg, 1994). These findings are particularly interesting because Sweden has a social welfare system aimed at reducing social inequalities. In three different studies of incident cases of Alzheimer's disease (AD), lower occupational prestige or having held a less skilled occupation predicted incidence (Evans et al., 1997; Nielsen, Lolk, Anderson, Anderson, & Kraugh-Sorensen, 1999; Stern et al., 1994). Across a variety of older adult samples, lower education and lower income have both been found to be related to higher levels of depressive symptoms (George, 1995). Possible mechanisms include the role of poor health as a risk factor for depressive symptoms, or the lesser availability of personal resources to older adults of lower socioeconomic status (Krause, 1999).

B. Epidemiology

Currently available information about rates of mental disorders in older adults is not much different from a decade ago. We are still relying on Epidemiologic Catchment Area survey data, now collected over 15 years ago (George, Blazer, Winfield-Laird, Leaf, & Fischbach, 1988; Robins, et al., 1984). Recent population-based information about rates of dementia is available, although there is some variability in the figures. At the extreme, Evans et al. (1989) suggested that the prevalence of AD rose to 47.2% for those aged 85 and older. More usual estimates find rates of AD to be around 13.1% for those aged 85 and older, and rates of all dementias to be around 23.8% (Bachman et al., 1992). Prevalence of dementia is fairly comparable in different countries (Fratiglioni, DeRonchi, & Agüero-Torres, 1999). Variability lies mainly in types of dementia (e.g., there may be higher rates of vascular dementia and differences in risk factors for Asian Americans and African Americans compared to European Americans, Shadlen & Larson, 1999).

In 1992 we estimated that 22% of older adults met criteria for a mental disorder (Gatz & Smyer, 1992). This figure includes dementia as well as other mental disorders, such as depression. The estimate relied on developing our own composite opinion based on reading the epidemiological literature. To encompass both community-dwelling and institutionalized, adults, we included rates of disorder in nursing homes weighted by the proportion of older adults in nursing homes. Jeste and colleagues (1999) engaged in a more recent exercise of combining sources and emerged with a comparable estimate of 19.6%.

We need good data, especially, data that will distinguish rates of new disorders arising in old age from rates of disorders that had their onset earlier in life but have continued into old age or reoccurred. Jeste et al. (1999) believe that there may be increased rates of mental disorder among older adults in the near future. This projection is based on analyses (Klerman & Weissman, 1989; Lewinsohn, Rohde, Seeley, & Fischer, 1993) suggesting increased depression in cohorts born after World War II. Thus, more people may be bringing disorders with them to old age. There is no equal reason to project an increase in late-onset disorder, except for predictions of increased AD if gains in longevity outstrip advances in neuroscience.

III. The Older Adult in the Mental Health Treatment System

A. Where Are Older Adults Being Treated?

The last three decades have brought changes in rates of treatment of mentally ill elderly, the site of treatment, and views about the most appropriate setting for treatment. Among the settings where older adults with mental disorders may be seen are formal mental health settings (such as outpatient offices or clinics), general hospitals (including both psychiatric units and patients seen in medical units), nursing homes, unregulated settings (board and care, assisted living apartments, senior housing complexes), and primary care physicians' offices.

There is emerging appreciation of the pivotal role of primary care providers, including primary care providers in managed care settings, with respect to access by older adults to mental health services. Regier et al. (1993) used data from the Epidemiological Catchment Area survey to look at visits to professionals in the past 6 months by persons with mental disorders. These data show that at any age most people with mental disorders do not see a professional. At all ages, people with mental disorders are more likely to see a general medical provider than a specialty mental health provider. In addition, compared to other age groups, older adults are less likely to see a professional at all; and, when they do see a professional, it is less likely that the professional will be a mental health specialist. In the past, these data have been viewed as a call for increased referrals to mental health professionals. Recently, a more nuanced interpretation has emerged that focuses on identifying and treating mental disorders within the primary care setting itself.

With adults of all ages, Wells, Schoenbaum, Unützer, Lagomasino, and Rubenstein (1999) found that out of 1204 outpatients in managed care settings who were depressed when they visited their physician, 43% of those with both depression and dysthymia and 29% of those with depression received some form of treatment (most often antidepressants). These sorts of data lead to the suggestion that primary care physicians need to be encouraged to be more alert for depression in their patients. Gallo, Ryan, and Ford (1999) surveyed primary care physicians and found that most saw it as their responsibility to diagnose depression and treat it with antidepressants. However, there was a strong tendency for physicians to view depression in older adults as understandable in light of their physical illnesses and disabilities and the deaths of friends and family. Physicians also tended to question whether psychotherapy was effective in older adults. These data point to a need for physician education.

Economic arguments for improved detection of depression are now being offered as well. For example, Unützer et al. (1997) demonstrated that older adults with significant depressive symptoms use more medical services in managed care settings, after controlling for the severity of their chronic illnesses. A meta-analysis by Chiles, Lambert, and Hatch (1999) demonstrated savings in medical costs resulting from the implementation of various psychological interventions, with older adults showing a larger offset than adults under age 65. Thus, it makes economic sense to recognize and treat depression, anxiety, and other forms of psychological distress.

Cohort issues may interact with service delivery issues. In the past, mental health and aging experts often attributed underutilization of mental health services by older adults to their cohort, and to the images of mental health they learned as young adults. The implication was that it would be different for that cohort who were psychologically sophisticated and who grew up on TV and movie psychotherapists. The leading edge of this more psychologically minded cohort is beginning to arrive in old age.

In one study assessing the new cohort of older adults, Belcher, Haley, Becker, and Polivka (1999) compared older adults' bias against mental health services with other age groups. In their results, older adults were equal to younger adults in thinking that it was appropriate to seek professional help for mental problems. There were differences in referral sources, with older adults predominantly turning first to their primary care physician. Older adults were equal to younger adults in likelihood of seeking treatment for severe problems, such as suicidal feelings, but were more likely to find other ways to manage lesser problems, such as bereavement. The biggest barrier was cost, not stigma.

We need to remind ourselves that it is the baby boomers who will be swelling the ranks of the aged in the near future. Although we do not know for certain how this cohort will behave as elders, it is conceivable that there will be changes with respect to rates of disorder, willingness to seek treatment, knowledgeability of consumers, and demand to be involved in decision making. However, due to comorbidity and perhaps due to the structuring of the health care system, it will still be the case that most older adults with mental disorders will show up at a primary care physician's office. The elder will already be at the physician's office for physical illnesses. Thus, we will still need mechanisms to connect patients to mental health care.

Pointing specifically to one potentially influential role for physicians are data showing that older adults who commit suicide are very apt to have seen a physician quite recently, some 70 to 75% within the past month, a subset of whom saw a physician within the past 24 hours (Carney, Rich, Burke, & Fowler, 1994). Based on this logic, PROSPECT (*PRevention Of Suicide in Primary care Elderly Collaborative Trial*) is being conducted by National Institute of Mental Health (NIMH) Intervention Research Centers at Cornell, University of Pennsylvania, and University of Pittsburgh. The intervention, which is being compared to usual care, educates primary care settings to screen for and treat depression, following the Agency for Health Care Policy and Research (AHCPR) guidelines, with pharmocologic treatment as the first line, and interpersonal therapy as the second line intervention (Katz, 1999b). Another study—Primary Care Research in substance Abuse and Mental Health for the Elderly (PRISMe)—is comparing an integrated approach within the primary care setting to an approach based on mental health referrals. Eleven sites are participating, including Veterans Administration Medical Centers, university health science centers, and community health centers (Wohlford & McDonel, 2000).

There are examples of similar efforts in other countries. In London, depressed older adults identified through comprehensive community screening were either referred to a primary care nurse to implement an individual care plan, generated by a multidisciplinary team, or received treatment as usual from the primary care physician. Examples of the interventions included prescribing antidepressants, recommending attendance at a social program such as a day care center, and formal counselling. Those who received the intervention improved in their depression scores compared to controls (Blanchard, Waterreus, & Mann, 1995).

In the decade ahead, we can expect continued emphasis on collaborative models of care involving primary practice settings, and we will have evaluation results from PROSPECT and from PRISMe. An open question is how active a role psychologists will play as these models are implemented.

B. Health and Mental Health Policy

1. Overview of Developments

For over three decades, mental health policy has been affected by and has mimicked policy developments in health-care provision and professional practice. At the same time, health-care planners have rarely regarded mental disorders as the equal of physical disorders, as evidenced by health insurers' more restricted reimbursement for mental health than for physical health care. In turn, various organized groups, including professional organizations such as the American Psychological Association (APA) and consumer groups, have been active in seeking parity for mental health.

Parity means that mental health policies—including reimbursement—should be on a par with policies concerning physical health care. Older adults have argely been overlooked by spokespersons for mental health policy, although Medicare figured into campaigns for parity.

In 1999, there was a White House Conference on Mental Health, an event historically unprecedented in providing visibility for mental health. The White House Conference was motivated by reducing stigma toward mental disorders and by seeking parity for mental health. Following the White House Conference on Mental Health, there was a separate undertaking by the Surgeon General's Office, resulting in a report on the nation's mental health (Surgeon General, 1999). The Surgeon General's report also calls for parity and emphasizes reducing stigma. In particular, the report recommends educating the public that mental illnesses are like physical illnesses, meaning that there are real (i.e., biochemical) bases for these disorders and that there are effective treatments. Most notably, the Surgeon General's report is an exception to the usual practice of overlooking older adults, in that the report includes an entire chapter on older adults.

Financing of mental health care services for older adults is a barrier to both older consumers and to those contemplating a career in mental health and aging (Koenig, George, & Schneider, 1994). Hartman-Stein (1999) has documented some of the ways in which audits of Medicare claims are serving to discourage conscientious, competent psychological practitioners from providing care to frail older adults. One of the most dominant developments in health care financing, and one which has led to dissatisfaction by psychologists, has been the explosion in managed care.

2. Managed Care

During the last decade, managed care has become a major source of funding for mental health care for older adults. Unfortunately, much of the current approach to organizing and reimbursing mental health services under managed care has developed with little research on the impact of different delivery mechanisms on client outcomes (Durham, 1998; Seligman & Levant, 1998). Durham (1998) has suggested that the research agenda should focus on key issues: cost, quality, access, satisfaction, and functional outcomes associated with managed mental health care. Bullen (1999) emphasized the need to define quality of managed behavioral care, but also warned that "defining quality in behavioral health is in its infancy" (p. 7).

Although occasional attention has been paid to the impact of managed care on issues of parity (e.g., Burnam & Escarce, 1999) and on access to mental health services (e.g., Salkever, Shinogle, & Goldman, 1999). most writing about managed care has focused on the impact of managed mental health or behavioral health care on the core mental health disciplines of psychiatry (e.g., Meyer & McLaughlin, 1998) and psychology (e.g., Berman, 1998; Cummings, Pallak, & Cummings, 1996). At times, the discussion of access or quality in managed care has intersected with a call for an enhanced role for a profession (e.g., psychology) (Bobbitt, Marques, & Trout, 1998). Kiesler (2000) argues that some of these concerns are misplaced and that integrating mental health services into a larger general health-care plan could bring substantial benefits both for patients and psychologists. He makes the case that for patients with both mental health and physical health problems, it would be more cost effective to treat all of the patient's conditions within one managed care plan, and that integrated services might also lead to improved treatment.

What is striking, however, is how little geropsychology has factored into the discussions of managed care. This disjunction was embodied, for example, in a February 1998 issue of *Professional Psychology*, which happened to be composed of two special sections: one on geropsychology (Knight & McCallum, 1998; LaRue & Watson, 1998; Qualls, 1998); the other, a series of articles on managed care surveys (e.g., Benedict & Phelps, 1998; Phelps, Eisman, & Kohout, 1998). There was virtually no overlap in the two segments.

Since the time that the special issue of *Professional* Psychology appeared, there has been increased attention in the research and scholarly literature to the intersection of managed care and geriatric mental health issues. For example, Bartels and his colleagues (Bartels, Levine, & Shea, 1999) highlighted the gap between the promise of integrated service and effective service delivery for a targeted group: older persons with severe and persistent mental illness. Similarly, a special issue of the *Journal of Geriatric Psychiatry* focused on mental health care for older adults in the age of managed care (Silver, 1999).

Over the next decade, we can predict continued efforts more fully to include mental health treatment of older adults in the larger developments in managed care (Maxwell & Levkoff, 1999). Geriatric concerns will need to be incorporated into emerging managed care protocols and guidelines, in multiple arenas, and on many levels: discussions of integrating medical and psychological treatment (e.g., Chiles et al., 1999); targeting specific disorders—such as depression (e.g., Merrick, 1998); developing and implementing public-sector approaches to managed care (e.g., Sabin & Daniels, 1999); or developing policy-relevant research paradigms (e.g., Frank, McGuire, Normand, & Goldman, 1999). In each case, the special concerns of mentally ill elderly will need to be represented.

Maxwell and Levkoff (1999) summarized the challenge well: "Policy makers and advocacy groups for the elderly need to work with managed care plans to improve geriatric care in general, and to focus greater attention on addressing the specific mental health needs of the elderly" (p. 39). We would only add our concern that psychologists should be a part of that collaboration, bringing clinical and research expertise into the discussion.

3. Prescription Privileges

Along with advocacy for parity for mental health, during the last decade, the APA has sought to expand the practice of psychology to include prescription privileges (Cullen & Newman, 1997). In 1995, the governing body of the APA passed a resolution that outlined the changing professional definition and its implications for education and training. This resolution followed earlier study of the issue and the recommendation of an APA Task Force that educational models and training curricula be in place before seeking such privileges (Lorion, 1996; Smyer et al., 1993).

Since the 1995 action, there has been considerable debate within the profession regarding the potential impact of prescription privileges on the profession's self-definition, its efficacy as a distinctive service provider, and the effects on consumers (Gutierrez & Silk, 1998). Proponents (e.g., DeLeon & Wiggins, 1996) and opponents (e.g., DeNelsky, 1996; Hayes & Heiby, 1996) continue to disagree on the appropriate course for the profession. However, as in the managed care debate, the absence of aging issues in the discussion is striking.

Older adults commonly rely upon prescription medicines to maintain health and well-being in later life (Smyer & Downs, 1995). Moreover, for those with mental disorders, a complicated regimen to manage physical and mental health problems requires astute prescribing and monitoring expertise (Cooper, 1994). Age-related changes in biological functions (e.g., drug clearance rates, etc.) assure that prescribing for older adults requires more skill and sensitivity to individual differences (Beizer, 1994). Thus, if anything, older adults' medication concerns should get more attention—not less—as the profession of psychology develops its training curricula to support prescribing privileges.

In the decade ahead, geropsychologists will face three challenges in the prescribing arena: first, staying attuned to changes at the state level in legal and regulatory definitions of the practice of psychology; second, assuring that information regarding the special concerns of older clients is included in psychopharmacology training and educational materials; third, assessing the efficacy of prescribing psychologists for mentally ill elderly. This last emphasis—focusing on outcomes—represents the intersection of the managed care and prescribing issues in shaping the context for geropsychology in the coming decade.

4. Practice Guidelines and Evidence-Based Practice

The past decade has seen a proliferation of guidelines, consensus statements, and authoritative summaries of clinical outcome studies. With respect to depression, the AHCPR has issued clinical practice guidelines in *Depression in Primary Care: Detection and Diagnosis* (vol. 1) and *Treatment of Major Depression* (vol. 2) (U.S. Dept. of Health and Human Services, 1993, a, b). These were developed to assist primary care providers (e.g., general practitioners, family practitioners, internists, nurse practitioners, registered nurses, mental health nurse specialists, physician assistants, and others). Additionally, the American Psychiatric Association (1994) issued a practice guideline for major depressive disorder in adults,

and there is a consensus statement update from the National Institutes of Health on diagnosis and treatment of depression in later life (Lebowitz et al., 1997).

Specific to aging, there are guidelines for AD diagnosis from the American Association for Geriatric Psychiatry (Small et al., 1997) and guidelines for AD management developed by the California Workgroup (*Guidelines for Alzheimer's Disease Management*) in conjunction with the Los Angeles Chapter of the Alzheimer's Association (Alzheimer's Association, 1998). The Los Angeles Chapter of the Alzheimer's Association is, at the same time, working actively with managed care and other physician providers to determine how to convey the guidelines in ways that will affect practice. Similarly, when psychologists became concerned about the level of mental health care being made available to nursing home residents, a workgroup drafted *Standards for Psychological Services in Long Term Care Facilities* (Lichtenberg et al., 1998).

Guidelines are based on reviewing clinical trials and abstracting those practices supported by the evidence. Clinical psychology took a somewhat different approach and established criteria for empirically supported treatments (Chambless et al., 1998). Based on these criteria, there is a list of treatments that qualify and a directory of manuals for those treatments (Woody & Sanderson, 1998). The list of treatments that qualify has been extended to older adults (Gatz et al., 1998).

A variety of volumes summarize treatment outcomes studies in psychotherapy research (e.g., Roth & Fonagy, 1996; Nathan, Gorman, & Salkind, 1999). Both include chapters on older adults (Niederehe & Schneider, 1998; Woods & Roth, 1996). With respect to research evaluating the effect of psychological interventions with older adults (and at all ages), depression is the most studied disorder. We expect the next decade to bring progress in evaluating interventions for anxiety and for cognitive training.

For depression, there is a great deal of evidence that psychotherapy works (Cole, 1996). There are a growing number of good outcome studies, and a mounting number of meta-analyses or other summaries of treatment outcome studies with older adults. The first of these, by Scogin and McElreath (1994), covered 17 studies using various psychosocial treatments. Their meta-analysis combined outcome studies in which the older adults qualified for major depressive disorder with studies that used depressive symptoms as an outcome but did not limit the intervention to those who were clinically depressed. The conclusion was that intervention made a difference.

The Scogin and McElreath (1994) publication has been followed by other summaries and other meta-analyses. The Cuijpers (1998) meta-analysis again encompasses both those with clinical depression and those with a lesser level of symptoms. The effect size was large and comparable to effect sizes for mixed age adult psychotherapy. Cognitive behavioral treatment had a significantly larger effect than other approaches. An average dropout rate of 23% was found across 14 studies. Gerson, Belin, Kaufman, Mintz, and Jarvik (1999) conducted a massive meta-analysis of both psychological and pharmacological treatments in older adults. There were no differences in response rates to psychotherapy, tricyclic antidepressants, or selective serotonin reuptake inhibitors. Dropout averaged just over 30% for various medications. Results from Thompson, Coon, Gallagher-Thompson, Sommer, and Koin (in press) extend this conclusion. Older adult patients with major depression disorder were randomly assigned to a 16–20-session cognitive behavioral therapy (CBT) protocol, pharmacotherapy with a tricyclic antidepressant, or combined CBT and drug treatment. Both CBT alone and the combined treatment were superior to drug alone, and there was no difference between CBT alone and the combined treatment.

For anxiety, although most older adults who are troubled by symptoms of anxiety do receive pharmacologic treatment from physicians, psychological treatments for anxiety in older adults are a demonstrably effective alternative (Wetherell, 1998). In particular, relaxation training, alone or combined with other components, seems to make a difference in treated patients compared to randomized controls. In a review of treatment of anxiety in older adults, Krasucki, Howard, and Mann (1999) concluded that prescribing practices and clinical recommendations have outstripped available data. Benzodiazepines are the most frequently described medications, often continued over a long term despite the fact that clinical trials tend to focus on 1 month or less. Benzodiazepines have also been associated with such side effects as memory loss, dependence and withdrawal, and hip fractures (Krasucki et al., 1999).

Treatments that are offered map unevenly on the evidence. For example, Katz (1999a) comments that the expanding use of psychopharmacological treatment has overshadowed other effective modalities. Most of the current initiatives targeted at identifying and treating geriatric depression rely on pharmacotherapy. As Katz notes, the empirical evidence would equally point to offering cognitive-behavioral, problem-solving, interpersonal, or brief psychodynamic psychotherapy as first-line treatments (except for profound depression).

C. Aging Network Policy

In the past, there has been little attention to mental health by the aging network, which is the term used to describe the collection of national, state, and local agencies whose mission is to oversee delivery of services to older adults, primarily, but not exclusively, in the community. However, the past 5 years have witnessed increased attention to mental health issues within the aging network.

In 1995 there was a White House Conference on Aging (WHCoA). Such conferences have been held nearly every decade, and their outcome has shaped aging policies over the several years following each one. For example, the 1961 WHCoA produced momentum for Medicare, and the 1971 WHCoA helped to establish the National Institute on Aging. Mental health has been strikingly absent from WHCoA agendas. However, preceding the 1995 WHCoA, a group called the Coalition on Mental Health and Aging sponsored a conference on Emerging Issues in Mental Health and Aging (see Gatz, 1995). Among the cosponsors was the AARP (formerly called the American Association of Retired Persons), an organization that has traditionally avoided seemingly negative topics such as mental illness. Due to lobbying efforts by the Coalition, a resolution sent forward by the conference on emerging issues was passed at the WHCoA. Thus, the 1995 WHCoA report contains perhaps the strongest language with respect to mental health that has ever been part of a WHCoA proceedings (see Table 21.1).

Currently, the Administration on Aging is proposing a mental health initiative, aimed at training practitioners to identify mental health problems in older adults and make appropriate referrals and at developing innovative approaches to delivering mental health services to older adults (Takamura, 2000). It will be of interest to track these steps into the new decade.

IV. Emerging Influences

Four remarkably diverse influences will affect conceptualizations and treatment of the mental health needs of older adults in the coming decade: the exponential growth of knowledge about the genetic bases of disorders; a renaissance in the behavioral and social sciences; recognition by professionals and scientists of the power of spirituality; and, finally, the Internet.

A. The Genetic Revolution

The decade just completed was designated the Decade of the Brain, during which—among other research initiatives—there has been a massive effort to map the human genome. The upshot has been an emphasis on genetic influences on disease, and a hope that increased knowledge about the genome will translate into prevention and treatment. The translation process will be intricate. From a genetic perspective, there are two sorts of diseases. Some are relatively uncommon and can be attributed to a single genetic defect, typically inherited following Mendelian rules. Others are complex diseases, which are relatively common, and with multiple genes and/or a combination of genetic and environmental influences involved in causing the disorder. Examples of complex diseases include diabetes, cancers, Parkinson's disease, AD, and depression. For many complex diseases, such as AD, there are subtypes associated with a single gene mutation, accounting for a tiny proportion of the disease, while the vast majority of cases are truly complex (Plassman & Breitner, 1997; Sprott & Pereira-Smith, 2000).

Mental health research and practice are influenced in multiple ways by the genetic revolution. Patients may be more likely to blame their genes rather than their upbringing or their personal choices, which could make it easier to seek treatment, because there is less sense of blame or shame. There may simultaneously be increased preference for somatic treatments, aiming biological cures at

Table 21.1
Resolution at the 1995 White House Conference on Aging

Meeting Mental Health Needs

WHEREAS quality of life and optimal functioning depend upon physical and mental health;

WHEREAS mental disorders of late life (e.g., Alzheimer's Disease, depression) represent major burdens to older Americans and their families;

WHEREAS substantial numbers of older persons residing in the community have mental health needs and approximately half of all nursing home residents have serious, often undiagnosed, untreated mental disorders;

WHEREAS research indicates the efficacy of mental health interventions, illness prevention, and health promotion in producing positive health outcomes;

WHEREAS there is an insufficient supply of practitioners, including primary care providers, who are adequately prepared for the promotion of optimal mental health and the recognition and treatment of mental disorders among diverse populations; and

WHEREAS older adults are experienced, knowledgeable, and effective in meeting their own and other's mental health needs;

THEREFORE, BE IT RESOLVED by the 1995 White House Conference on Aging to support policies that:

1. Amend Medicaid to include provisions that ensure the availability of home and community-based mental health services;

2. Assure access to an affordable, comprehensive range of quality mental and physical health care, including outreach, in-home, preventive, acute, and long-term care services;

3. Amend all statutes that regulate public and private health and long-term care insurance plans to achieve parity in coverage and reimbursement for mental and physical health disorders, eliminate exclusions based on pre-existing conditions, set standards for health plans, and ensure consumer rights;

4. Expand professional and continuing education programs for: a) all providers of services to older people, including primary care physicians, nurses, social workers, and so forth; b) all specialists in the provision of mental health services and treatment for older people; and c) faculty in schools which prepare a variety of professionals for geriatric practice, such as schools of medicine, nursing, allied health professions, social work;

5. Expand educational and training programs in mental health and aging for older persons, their families, and friends, and others in the community, such as letter carriers, police and fire personnel, bank tellers, and shop keepers, who are likely to come in contact with older persons at risk;

6. Support an expedited mental health and aging research agenda that includes funding for basic, clinical, services research, and ensures that findings are widely disseminated;

7. Distribute culturally sensitive information about accessing community-based mental health services;

8. Ensure that Federal, State, and local public policies shall recognize older adults as a primary resource for maintenance and achievement of mental health, and that consumers shall be significantly involved in the planning and development of mental health research, systems, services, and programs.

---

biological ailments. Likewise, for researchers, it becomes easy to forget the environmental contribution to the disease equation (McCullough, Wilson, Rymes, & Teasdale, 2000; Rowe & Gatz, 2000).

Psychological research can contribute to showing that pathways between biology and behavior go both directions (e.g., caregivers' neuroimmune functioning has been shown to be affected by stress) (Kiecolt-Glaser et al., 1987). This insight means that discovering that mental disorders have biological bases does not lead inexorably to purely biological interventions.

B. The Decade of Behavior

Following the Decade of the Brain, there has also been a growing appreciation that for the diseases of the 21st century (heart disease, stroke, chronic lung disease), a very large proportion of prevalence is attributable to behavior (e.g., whether we smoke, whether we eat a high-fat diet, whether we wear helmets when we bicycle, whether we bicycle or do any exercise at all, whether we follow th instructions on the pill bottle). The years 2000–2010 have been declared the Decade of

Behavior by 44 scientific societies, in recognition of the importance of behavioral science to tackling problems such as obesity, diabetes, depression, unintentional injuries, and scientific and technological illiteracy (Decade of Behavior National Advisory Committee, 2000). Of course, the role of behavioral factors in health has been recognized for many decades (Ory, Abeles, & Lipman, 1992). The Decade of Behavior represents a renewed effort to draw public and policy attention to these factors.

Behavior encompasses preventive actions such as modifying one's lifestyle, compensatory steps in the face of functional impairments, and compliance with regimens designed to maintain control over chronic disease and prevent relapse or worsening. Lifestyle risk factors (e.g., smoking, inadequate physical activity, and poor nutrition) reflect both genetic and environmental influences (Pedersen et al., 1989); thus, modifying these behaviors must take individual differences into account. Social inequalities in health have also been singled out by the Decade of Behavior, including the challenge of disentangling the source of disparities in health for those who are more and less advantaged, whether it be lifestyle risk factors, unhealthy environments, or lack of access to care (Decade of Behavior National Advisory Committee, 2000). Thus, there is a whole new set of roles for behavioral scientists outside of mental health, in which the emphasis is modifying health-related behaviors using some of the same behavioral tools that are relevant to addressing mental health problems. These issues are particularly cogent for aging, as older adults have more disabling conditions than other age groups, and the diseases that will be most prominent in the 21st century are chronic conditions such as heart disease and arthritis (National Academy on an Aging Society, 1999). Kiesler (2000) also argues that greater integration of mental health care and medical care will facilitate behavioral interventions.

Perhaps reflecting renewed interest in behavior, prevention may be enjoying a modest return to popularity. In a call to action, Schneider (1999) warns that without an investment in research on disease prevention, the demand for long-term care for older adults with chronic conditions will explode during the third millennium. The Institute of Medicine (IOM) model (Mrazek & Haggerty, 1994) distinguishes universal, selective, and indicated strategies. Indicated refers to treating subthreshold symptoms to prevent or forestall disease (Mossey, Knott, Higgins, & Talerico, 1996); selective targets those at risk (e.g., caregivers) (Schulz, O'Brien, Bookwala, & Fleissner, 1995); universal includes wellness programs and efforts to build networks of mutual assistance (e.g., Dellman-Jenkins, 1997). The continuum of interventions in the IOM model also includes maintenance and rehabilitation, where the goal is preventing excess disability and premature institutionalization (e.g., techniques to improve adherence to pharmacologic regimens, behavioral strategies to compensate for impairment, and use of assistive devices) (Deatrick, 1997; Gitlin, 1995). The range of interventions in the IOM model fits with the behavioral emphasis and is readily applicable to aging.

C. Spirituality

During the last decade there has been increasing attention to the impact of spiritual and religious concerns on health and well-being in later life (e.g., George, 1998; Koenig, 1994; Moody & Carroll, 1998). Some gerontologists have focused on the process of coping with the basic meaning of life and death—from an existential and philosophical framework (e.g., Manheimer, 1999; Tornstam, 1999).

Although some of the research literature has focused on the link between religiosity and mental health (e.g., Koenig, George, & Peterson, 1998), much has reflected the positive impact of religious involvement on health status (e.g., Koenig, George, Cohen, Hays, Larson, & Blazer, 1998; Koenig et al., 1999). McFadden and Levin (1996) summarized the possible explanations for this positive association: (a) religious commitment may affect health behaviors (e.g., smoking, alcohol consumption); (b) religious participation may affect social support; (c) religious worship and prayer may produce positive emotional experiences; (d) religious beliefs may be consistent with positive health beliefs; (e) religious belief may lead to optimism and a positive mental attitude; and (f) a combination of these elements may produce the positive association.

A recent national conference focused attention on the links between religious commitment and mental health, as well as physical health (Larson, Sawyers, & McCullough, 1998). Although Larson and his colleagues did not focus on aging concerns, their summary of areas for priority investigation provide clear directions for those interested in the intersection of geropsychology and the psychology of religion: improving the theoretical models of mental-health-related effects of religiousness and spirituality in later life; improving measurement approaches in this domain; specifying under what conditions which aspects of mental health functioning will be affected by religiousness and spirituality; developing, implementing, and evaluating intervention programs (prevention and treatment) that integrate a spiritual or religious dimension; and effectively disseminating the results of these "clinical trials" to the practice community. In the decade ahead, we can anticipate that geropsychologists will be involved in each of these elements.

D. Technology and the Internet

Technological advances have spillover into issues of mental illness, for example, in-home electronic monitoring and emergency alert systems can bring greater peace of mind to older adults and/or their families, advances in neuroimaging techniques have enabled identifying brain changes associated with different disorders, and professionals can communicate more rapidly by means of fax, electronic mail, teleconferencing, and mobile phone. Of particular interest is the spread of the Internet, including use not only by professionals but also by consumers and potential consumers of mental health services. Information about numbers of older users and senior citizen web sites is in flux, although it is suggested that possibilities currently outstrip actual use (Rogers, 1999). What seems likely is that as adults now in midlife become aged, they will continue to use the Internet. Yet, there are currently inequalities in access to communication technologies among younger generations (Ball-Rokeach, 2000), inequalities that have the potential of continuing into old age.

There are barriers to bringing older adults together with computers, ranging from the physical (bifocals may be wrong for the height of the screen; keys may be too small for arthritic fingers), to the psychological, to the inaccessibility of technical support for in-home computer users. Psychologists trained in human factors can help. Cody, Dunn, Hoppin, and Wendt (1999) presented one example of a training program to connect more older adults to the Internet, and White et al. (1999) introduced Internet and e-mail access into a retirement community. Both found that using computers was associated with increased sense of social support and decreased loneliness, as well as lessened numbers of computer problems and lower computer anxiety.

Informal evidence suggests that the main use of the Internet by older adults is e-mail contact with family, similar to the pattern observed by Ball-Rokeach (2000) across all age groups, in which contact with family and friends was more common than building of new relationships. There is a wealth of senior-specific web sites, encompassing genealogy, travel planning, financial management, buying or selling a house, and health information. Directories of sites are available through the Administration on Aging (http://www.aoa.dhhs.gov) or AARP (http://www.aarp.org).

Two aspects invite our speculation. First is the use of computers to get information about health, and—presumably—about mental health. Older adults have been shown to be more reluctant than younger adults to ask questions of their physicians (if anything, they ask about the symptoms that are not physically threatening, while not mentioning symptoms that might have serious implications). However, they are equally likely to turn to informal resources, such as friends and newspaper articles (Turk-Charles, Gatz, & Meyerowitz, 1997). It seems plausible that the Internet will be a medium that older adults will feel comfortable using to obtain information, which could in turn make older adults more informed about their own health. Helwig, Lovelle, Guse, and Gottlieb (1999), for example, tested the use of on-line patient information. Increasingly, as well, older adults may secure information about their health conditions from the Internet and bring this information with them to their appointment with their physician. By extension, the Internet might serve a powerful role in raising awareness of mental health symptoms and further reducing stigma about mental health.

A second new direction is the use of computer technologies for counseling. For example, on-line support groups have been reported by users to be helpful, particularly for those who have mobility limitations (e.g., LeClaire, 1997). Major issues about confidentiality are raised (American Psychological Association, 1997). Nonetheless, it seems inevitable

that there will be greater use of computer counseling. Psychologists might think of the computer as a psychoeducational tool, just as bibliotherapy is used today (Scogin, 1998). Some of the types of self-monitoring taught through cognitive behavioral and behavioral interventions could readily be adapted for computer-assisted self-monitoring.

V. The Role of the Psychologist

Aging processes and the mental health issues of older adults are inherently interdisciplinary, both with respect to research issues and clinical intervention. Psychologists have struggled to clarify what they have to bring to the interdisciplinary table. Numbers of board-certified geriatric psychiatrists (Jeste et al., 1999) have grown far faster than the number of clinical psychologists working in aging. Qualls (1998) summarized the gap between the need for trained clinical geropsychologists and programs available to provide training.

A. Interprofessional and Transdisciplinary Activities

Interdisciplinary teams are especially suited for gerontological practice because the problems of older adults are complex (Zeiss & Steffen, 1996). Interdisciplinary teams include members from several disciplines, organized nonhierarchically, working together to develop, implement, and evaluate a plan of treatment. Psychologists have not tended to be advocates of interdisciplinary care, perhaps due to concern about their own power and prestige. Zeiss and Steffen (1996) suggest that roles be diagrammed, with each discipline represented by a circle that has areas of overlap with other circles. This exercise can clarify unique and shared roles. For interdisciplinary teams to work, training and team building are required. The Veterans Administration has been a leader in this area (Zeiss & Steffen, 1996).

For geropsychologists, learning to work with other disciplines is among the necessary areas of competence (Niederehe, 2000). Qualls and Czirr (1988) note that each profession has distinct assumptions regarding the logic of assessment (e.g., ruling out vs. ruling in factors), the appropriate focus of professional effort (e.g., acute care/symptom relief vs. chronic care/functional ability), and the pace of action (crisis vs. maintenance). For psychologists to become more integral to interdisciplinary teams may require simultaneously clarifying what psychologists have to offer (see next sections) and deemphasizing guild issues.

B. Behavioral Change

Psychologists are experts in human behavior. As we have reviewed, there are effective behavioral treatments for depression, anxiety, and the behavioral problems associated with Alzheimer's disease. In addition, there are behaviorally based interventions that may help with pain management, urinary incontinence, and sleep hygiene. Older adults do not partition their ailments, nor do they draw bright lines between traditional and alternative medicine. Although the current reimbursement system conspires against it, we would hope to see behavioral interventions for a wide variety of diseases included in the portfolio of psychologists who practice with older adults.

Increasing knowledge about genetics is putting practitioners in an entirely different position with respect to treating disease (Caplan, 1997). It will be increasingly possible to obtain a profile of what diseases one is genetically at risk for, to choose the best drugs based on genetic information from the patient, and to begin to replace other biological treatments with gene therapies. Drugs will also be used preventively to reduce risk for diseases in accordance with genetic characteristics. Psychologists can help with educating people about the meaning of genetic risk and pursuant choices.

It seems possible that learning that one is at genetic risk for a certain disease could lead to enhanced motivation to undertake behavioral change to reduce risk (Capron, 2000). For instance, will learning that one is at greater risk for heart disease lead to better adherence to an exercise program? Thus, the decade of behavior should bring attention to the intersection of genetic and behavioral influences.

C. Assessing Competency and Decision-Making Capacity

In the coming decade, older adults and their families seem likely to call for greater involvement in health-care decision making and in deciding the disposition of personal property. These issues are at the intersection of legal definitions, clinical practice, and the emerging knowledge base of geropsychology (Smyer, Schaie, & Kapp, 1996). Psychologists can be expected to contribute to the increasingly sophisticated assessments of older adults' capacity to consent to treatment, competence to stand trial, and to execute wills (Frank & Smyer, 1998). Underlying these capacities are assessments of several areas of psychological functioning (e.g., mental status, memory, language, reasoning, etc.). In each area, psychologists will be helpful in developing, implementing, and evaluating psychometrically reliable and valid measures of functioning. For example, Marson and his colleagues (Marson, Chatterjee, Ingram, & Harrell, 1996) identified cognitive predictors of competency performance among Alzheimer's patients, using three different legal standards of competency. In doing so, they also developed a prototype instrument for making such assessments (Marson, Ingram, Cody, & Harrell, 1995).

Other psychologists (e.g., Diehl, 1998) have focused attention on the link between cognitive functioning and "everyday competence" (i.e., the underlying abilities necessary to function in daily life). Both of these areas—assessment of capacity within legal frameworks and assessment of everyday competence—will increase in importance in the coming decade and provide opportunities for input from psychological research.

VI. Conclusions

During this first decade of the 21st century, the pace of change is likely to be great, affecting both individuals' adaptation to later life and psychologists' ability to assist in that adaptation. On the population level, we know that the baby boomer generation will be approaching old age and that, by the end of this decade, the characteristics of this cohort will define the "young old". What remains unclear, however, is the impact of cohort succession on mental health demands and service delivery mechanisms.

In addition to changing cohorts, we can expect significant changes in our understanding of basic disease processes and treatment mechanisms. The explosive growth in our knowledge of genetics will alter our approach to mental disorders. We can expect significant advances, from neurosciences to psychoneuorimmunology and psychopharmacology. For geropsychologists, the challenge will be to extend those developments to the field of aging

In the policy arena, health-care reform remains on the national agenda. We can anticipate incremental changes in the conduct of managed care and some steps in the direction of parity. One challenge for psychologists in the next decade is to continue to participate in health services research, assessing the effectiveness of psychotherapeutic and combined intervention approaches, and actively disseminating these results in ways that will enhance practice.

The emphasis on behavior and on prevention provides fresh opportunities for psychologists to shape practice and policy. Although it appears that mental health of older adults is finally receiving attention, it is too soon to know whether that attention will translate into a coherent system that effectively addresses the needs of today's and tomorrow's older adults. What is clear, however, is that psychologists have much to contribute to the changing landscape of geriatric mental health research and care.

Acknowledgements

The authors thank Tricia Huei-Yi Sung and Brianna Garcia for their diligence in tracking down information for this chapter.

References

AARP (2001). Web site list. [on-line]. Available: http: //www.aarp.org

Administration on Aging (2001). Aging related web site. [on-line]. Available: http://www.aoa.dhhs.gov

Alzheimer's Association (1998). *Guidelines for Alzheimer's disease management*. [On-line]. Available: http://www.alzla.org

American Psychological Association (1997, November 15). *Services by telephone, teleconferencing, and Internet: A statement by the Ethics Committee of the American Psychological Association*. [On-line]. Available: http://www.apa.org/ethics/stmnt01.html

American Psychiatric Association. (1994). Practice guideline for major depressive disorder in adults. *American Journal of Psychiatry, 151*, 625–626.

Bachman, D. L., Wolf, P. A., Linn, R., Knoefel, J. E., Cobb, J., Belanger, A., D'Agostino, R. B., & White, L. R. (1992). Prevalence of dementia and probable senile dementia of the Alzheimer type in the Framingham Study. *Neurology, 42*, 115–119.

Ball-Rokeach, S. (2000). *Globalization of everyday life: Visions and reality.* [Online]. Available: http://metamorph.org/vault/summaryglobal.html

Bartels, S. J., Levine, K. J., & Shea, D. (1999). Community-based long-term care for older persons with severe and persistent mental illness in an era of managed care. *Psychiatric Services, 50,* 1189–1197.

Beizer, J. L. (1994). Medications and the aging body: Alterations as a function of age. *Generations, 18,* 13–17.

Belcher, C. R., Haley, W. E., Becker, M. A., & Polivvka, L. A. (1999). Attitudes about mental health services among older adults [Abstract]. *Gerontologist, 39,* 534.

Benedict, J. G., & Phelps, R. (1998). Introduction: Psychology's view of managed care. *Professional Psychology, 29,* 29–30.

Berman, W. H. (1998). Psychology in managed care: Introduction. *Clinical Psychology, 5,* 51–52.

Birren, J. E., & Renner, J. (1980). Concepts and issues of mental health and aging. In J. E. Birren & R. B. Sloane (Eds.) *Handbook of mental health and aging* (pp. 3–33). Englewood Cliffs, NJ: Prentice-Hall.

Blanchard, M. R., Waterreus, A., & Mann, A. H. (1995). The effect of primary care nurse intervention upon older people screened as depressed. *International Journal of Geriatric Psychiatry, 10,* 289–298.

Bobbitt, B. L., Marques, C. C., & Trout, D. I. (1998). Managed behavioral health care: Current status, recent trends, and the role of psychology. *Clinical Psychology, 5,* 53–66.

Bullen, B. M. (1999). Managed behavioral health in the public sector. *Psychiatric Services, 50,* 7.

Burnam, A., & Escarce, J. J. (1999). Equity in managed care for mental disorders. *Health Affairs, 18,* 22–31.

Caplan, A. L. (1997). *Am I my brother's keeper? The ethical frontiers of biomedicine.* Indianapolis, IN: Indiana University Press.

Capron, A. M. (2000). Genetics and insurance: Accessing and using private information. *Social Philosophy & Policy, 18,* 235–275.

Carney, S. S., Rich, C. L., Burke, P. A., & Fowler, R. C. (1994). Suicide over 60: The San Diego Study. *Journal of the American Geriatrics Society, 42,* 174–180.

Chambless, D. L., Baker, M. J., Baucom, D. H., Beutler, L. E., Calhoun, K. S., Crits-Christoph, P., Daiuto, A., DeRubeis, R., Detweiler, J., Haaga, D. A. F., Johnson, S. B., McCurry, S., Mueser, K. T., Pope, K. S., Sanderson, W. C., Shoham, V., Stickle, T., Willias, D. A., & Woody, S. R. (1998, Winter). Update on empirically validated therapies, II. *Clinical Psychologist, 51,* 3–16.

Chiles, J. A., Lambert, M. J., & Hatch, A. L. (1999). The impact of psychological interventions on medical cost offset: A meta-analytic review. *Clinical Psychology: Science and Practice, 6,* 204–220.

Cody, M. J., Dunn, D., Hoppin, S., & Wendt, P. (1999). Silver surfers: Training and evaluating Internet use among older adult learners. *Communication Education, 48,* 269–286.

Cole, M. (1996). Major depression in old age: Outcome studies. In K. I. Shulman, M. Tohen, & S. P. Kutcher (Eds.), *Mood disorders across the life span* (pp. 361–397). New York: Wiiley-Liss.

Cooper, J. W. (1994). Drug-related problems in the elderly patient. *Generations, 18,* 19–26.

Cuijpers, P. (1998). Psychological outreach programs for the depressed elderly: A meta-analysis of effects and dropout. *International Journal of Geriatric Psychiatry, 13,* 41–48.

Cullen, E. A., & Newman, R. (1997). In pursuit of prescription privileges. *Professional Psychology, 28,* 101–106.

Cummings, N. A., Pallak, M. S., & Cummings, J. L. (1996). *Surviving the demise of solo practice: Mental health practitioners prospering in the era of managed care.* Madison, CT: Psychosocial Press.

Cutting the cookie. (1999, September 11). *The Economist, 352,* 52.

Deatrick, D. (1997). Senior-Med: Creating a network to help manage medications. *Generations, 11,* 59–60.

Decade of Behavior National Advisory Committee (2000). *Health and behavior.* Unpublished manuscript [Available from: Richard McCarty, Executive Director for Science, American Psychological Association, 750 First St., NE, Washington, D. C. 20002–4242.]

DeLeon, P. H., & Wiggins, J. G. (1996). Prescription privileges for psychologists. *American Psychologist, 51,* 225–229.

Dellman-Jenkins, M. (1997). A senior-centered model of intergenerational programming with young children. *Journal of Applied Gerontology, 16,* 495–506.

DeNelsky, G. Y. (1996). The case against prescription privileges for psychologists. *American Psychologist, 51,* 207–212.

Diehl, M. (1998). Everyday competence in later life: Current status and future directions. *Gerontologist, 38,* 422–433.

Durham, M. L. (1998). Mental health and managed care. *Annual Review of Public Health, 19,* 493–505.

Evans, D. A., Funkenstein, H. H., Albert, M. S., Scherr, P. A., Cook, N. R., Chown, M. J., Hebert, L. E., Hennekens, C. H., & Taylor, J. O. (1989). Prevalence of Alzheimer's disease in a community population of older persons: Higher than previously reported. *Journal of the American Medical Association, 262,* 2551–2556.

Evans, D. A., Hebert, L. E., Beckett, L. A., Scherr, P. A., Chown, M. J., Pilgrim, D. M., & Taylor, J. O. (1997). Education and other measures of socioeconomic status and risk of incident Alzheimer disease in a defined population of older persons. *Archives of Neurology, 54,* 1399–1405.

Frank, L., & Smyer, M. (1998). Understanding decisional capacity in older adults. In B. Edelstein (Ed.), *Comprehensive clinical psychology (vol. 7): Clinical geropsychology* (pp. 114–131). New York: Elsevier Science.

Frank, R. G., McGuire, T. G., Normand, S.-L. T., & Goldman, H. H. (1999). The value of mental health care at the system level: The case of treating depression. *Health Affairs, 18,* 71–88.

Fratiglioni, L., DeRonchi, D., & Agüero-Torres, H. (1999). Worldwide prevalence and incidence of dementia. *Drugs and Aging, 15,* 365–375.

Gallo, J. J., Ryan, S. D., Ford, D. E. (1999). Attitudes, knowledge, and behavior of family physicians regarding depression in late life. *Archives of Family Medicine, 8,* 249–256.

Gatz, M. (Ed.) (1995). *Emerging issues in mental health and aging.* Washington DC: American Psychological Association.

Gatz, M., Fiske, A., Fox, L. S., Kaskie, B., Kasl-Godley, J. E., McCallum, T. J., & Wetherell, J. L. (1998). Empirically-validated psychological treatments for older adults. *Journal of Mental Health and Aging, 4,* 9–46.

Gatz, M., & Smyer, M. (1992). The mental health system and older adults in the 1990s. *American Psychologist, 47,* 741–751.

Gatz, M., Smyer, M. A., & Lawton, M. P. (1980). The mental health system and the older adult. In L. W. Poon (Ed.), *Aging in the 1980s: Psychological issues* (pp. 5–19). Washington, DC: American Psychological Association.

George, L. K. (1998). Religion and aging comes of age. *Gerontologist, 38,* 508–510.

George, L. K. (1995). Social factors and illness. In R. H. Binstock & L. K. George (Eds.), *Handbook of aging and the social sciences* (pp. 229–252). San Diego: Academic Press.

George, L. K., Blazer, D. F., Winfield-Laird, I., Leaf, P. J., & Fischbach, R. L. (1988). Psychiatric disorders and mental health service use in later life: Evidence from the Epidemiologic Catchment Area program. In J. Brody & G. Maddox (Eds.), *Epidemiology and aging* (pp. 189–219). New York: Springer.

Gerson, S., Belin, T. R., Kaufman, A., Mintz, J., & Jarvik, L. (1999). Pharmacological and psychological treatments for depressed older patients: A meta-analysis and overview of recent findings. *Harvard Review of Psychiatry, 7,* 1–28.

Gitlin, L. N. (1995). Why older people accept or reject assistive technology. *Generations, 14,* 41–46.

Gutierrez, P. M. & Silk, K. R. (1998). Prescription privileges for psychologists: A review of the psychological literature. *Professional Psychology, 29,* 213–222.

Hartman-Stein, P. E. (1999). Expect harsh, intensive scrutiny if your Medicare claims are audited. *The National Psychologist, 8*(6), 6–8.

Hayes, S. C., & Heiby, E. (1996). Psychology's drug problem. *American Psychologist, 51,* 198–206.

Helwig, A. L., Lovelle, A., Guse, C. E., & Gottlieb, M. S. (1999). An office-based Internet patient education system: A pilot study. *Journal of Family Practice, 48*(2), 123–127.

House, J. S., Kessler, R. C., Herzog, A. R., Mero, R. P., Kinney, A. M., & Breslow, M. J. (1992). Social stratification, age, and health. In K. W. Schaie, D. Blazer, & J. House (Eds.). *Aging, health behaviors, and health outcomes* (pp. 1–37). Hillsdale, NJ: Lawrence Erlbaum Associates.

Jeste, D. V., Alexopoulos, G. S., Bartels, S. J., Cummings, J. L., Gallo, J. J., Gottlieb, G. L., Halpain, M. C., Palmer, B. W., Patterson, T. L., Reynolds, C. F., & Lebowitz, B. D. (1999). Consensus statement on the upcoming crisis in geriatric mental health: Research agenda for the next 2 decades. *Archives of General Psychiatry, 56*, 848–853.

Katz, I. R. (1999a). Expanding the place of geriatric mental health within health systems: Integrated care, prevention, and rehabilitation. *Gerontologist, 39*, 626–630.

Katz, I. R. (1999b). Opportunities to leverage findings from SAMHSA, NIMH, and The Hartford Foundation Initiative on Mental Health [Abstract]. *Gerontologist, 39*, 594.

Kiecolt-Glaser, J., Glaser, R., Shuttleworth, E. C., Dyer, C. S., Ogrocki, P., & Speicher, C. E. (1987). Chronic stress and immunity in family caregivers of Alzheimer's disease victims. *Psychosomatic Medicine, 49*, 523–535.

Kiesler, C. A. (2000). The next wave of change for psychology and mental health services in the health care revolution. *American Psychologist, 55*, 481–487.

Klerman, G. L., & Weissman, M. M. (1989). Increasing rates of depression. *Journal of the American Medical Association, 261*, 2229–2235.

Knight, B. G., & McCallum, T. J. (1998). Adapting psychotherapeutic practice for older clients: Implications of the contextual, cohort-based, maturity, specific challenge model. *Professional Psychology, 29*, 15–22.

Koenig, H. G. (1994). *Aging and God: Spiritual pathways to mental health in midlife and later years.* New York: Haworth Pastoral Press, Inc.

Koenig, H. G., George, L. K., & Peterson, B. L. (1998). Religiosity and remission of depression in medically ill older patients. *American Journal of Psychiatry, 155*, 536–542.

Koenig, H. G., George, L. K., & Schneider, R. (1994). Mental health care for older adults in the year 2020: A dangerous and avoided topic. *Gerontologist, 34*, 674–679.

Koenig, H. G. Hays, J. C., Larson, D. B., George, L. K., Cohen, H. J., McCullogh, M. E., Meador, K. G., & Blazer, D. G. (1999).

Does religious attendance prolong survival? *Journal of Gerontology: Medical Sciences, 54A*, M370–M376.

Koenig, H. G., George, L. K., Cohen, H. J., Hays, J. C., Larson, D. B., & Blazer, D. G. (1998). The relationship between religious activities and cigarette smoking in older adults. *Journal of Gerontology: Medical Sciences, 53A*, M426–M434.

Krasucki, C., Howard, R., & Mann, A. (1999). Anxiety and its treatment in the elderly. *International Psychogeriatrics, 11*, 25–45.

Krause, N. (1999). Mental disorder in late life: Exploring the influences of stress and socioeconomic status. In C. S. Aneshensel & J. C. Phelan (Eds.), *Handbook of the sociology of mental health* (pp. 183–208). New York: Kluwer Academic/Plenum.

Larson, D. B., Sawyers, J. P., & McCullough, M. E. (Eds.). (1998). *Scientific research on spirituality and health.* Rockville, MD: National Institute for Healthcare Research.

LaRue, A., & Watson, J. (1998). Psychological assessment of older adults. *Professional Psychology, 29*, 5–14.

Lebowitz, B. D., Pearson, J. L., Schneider, L. S., Reynolds, C. F., Alexopoulos, G. S., Bruce, M. L., Conwell, Y., Katz, I. R., Meyers, B. S., Morrison, M. F., Mossey, J., Niederehe, G., & Parmelee, P. (1997). Diagnosis and treatment of depression in late life: Consensus statement update. *Journal of the American Medical Association, 278*, 1186–1190.

LeClaire, R. B. (1997). How a computer and SeniorNet changed my life. *Generations, 21* (3), 36–37.

Lewinsohn, P. M., Rohde, P., Seeley, J. R., & Fischer, S. A. (1993). Age-cohort changes in the lifetime occurrence of depression and other mental disorders. *Journal of Abnormal Psychology, 102*, 110–120.

Liberty, equality, humility. (1999, September 11). *The Economist, 352*, 15–16.

Lichtenberg, P. A., Smith, M., Frazer, D., Molinari, V., Rosowsky, E., Crose, R., Stillwell, N., Kramer, N., Hartman-Stein, P., Qualls, S., Salamon, M., Duffy, M., Parr, J., & Gallagher-Thompson, D. (1998). Standards for psychological services in long-term care facilities. *Gerontologist, 38*, 122–127.

Lorion, R. P. (1996). Applying our medicine to the psychopharmacology debate. *American Psychologist, 51*, 219–224.

Manheimer, R. (1999). A philosophical time of life. *Generations, 23,* 15–20.

Marson, D. C., Chatterjee, A., Ingram, K. K., & Harrell, L. E. (1996). Toward a neurologic model of competency: Cognitive predictors of capacity to consent in Alzheimer's disease using three different legal standards. *Neurology, 46,* 666–672.

Marson, D. C., Ingram, K. K., Cody, H. A., & Harrell, L. E. (1995). Assessing the competency of patients with Alzheimer's disease under different legal standards. *Archives of Neurology, 52,* 949–954.

Maxwell, J. H., & Levkoff, S. (1999). Behavioral health care for the elderly: The promise and practice of managed care. *Journal of Geriatric Psychiatry, 32,* 15–42.

McCullough, L. B., Wilson, N. L., Rhymes, J. A., & Teasdale, T. A. (2000). Ethical issues in genetics and aging: Diagnosis, treatment, and prevention in the era of molecular medicine. *Generations, 24*(1), 72–78.

McFadden, S. H., & Levin, J. S. (1996). Religion, emotions, and health. In C. Magi & S. H. McFadden (Eds.), *Handbook of emotion, adult development, and aging* (pp. 349–365). San Diego, CA: Academic Press.

Merrick, E. L. (1998). Treatment of major depression before and after implementation of a behavioral health carve-out plan. *Psychiatric Services, 49,* 1563–1567.

Meyer, R. E., & McLaughlin, C. J. (1998). *Between mind, brain, and managed care: The now and future world of academic psychiatry.* Washington, DC: American Psychiatric Press.

Miles, T. P. (Ed.). (1999). *Full color aging.* Washington DC: Gerontological Society of America.

Moody, H. R., & Carroll, D. (1998). *The five stages of the soul: Charting the spiritual passages that shape our lives.* New York: Anchor Doubleday.

Mossey, J. M., Knott, K. A., Higgins, M., & Talerico, K. (1996). Effectiveness of a psychosocial intervention, interpersonal counselling, for subdysthymic depression in medically ill elderly. *Journal of Gerontology: Medical Sciences, 51A,* M172–M178.

Mrazek, P. J., & Haggerty, R. J. (Eds.). (1994). *Reducing risks of mental disorders: Frontiers for preventive intervention research.*

Washington, D. C.: National Academy Press.

Nathan, P. E., Gorman, J. M., & Salkind, N. J. (1999). *Treating mental disorders: A guide to what works.* New York: Oxford University Press.

National Academy on an Aging Society. (1999). *Chronic conditions: A challenge for the 21st century.* Washington, DC: Gerontological Society of America.

Niederehe, G. (2000). *Training guidelines for practice in clinical geropsychology* [On-line]. Available: http://bama.ua.edu/~appgero/apa12_2/qualifications/qualificationsmain.html

Niederehe, G., & Schneider, L. S. (1998). Treatments for depression and anxiety in the aged. In P. E. Nathan & J. M. Gorman (Eds.), *A guide to treatments that work* (pp. 270–287). New York: Oxford University Press.

Nielsen, H., Lolk, A., Andersen, K., Andersen, J., & Kragh-Sorensen, P. (1999). Characteristics of elderly who develop Alzheimer's disease during the next two years–A neuropsychological study using CAMCOG: The Odense Study. *International Journal of Geriatric Psychiatry, 14,* 957–963.

Ory, M. G., Abeles, R. P., & Lipman, P. D. (Eds.) (1992). *Aging, health, and behavior.* Newbury Park, CA: Sage Publications.

Parker, M. G., Thorslund, M., & Lundberg, O. (1994). Physical function and social class among Swedish oldest old. *Journal of Gerontology: Social Sciences, 49,* 196–201.

Pedersen, N. L., Lichtenstein, P., Plomin, R., deFaire, U., McClearn, G. E., & Matthews, K. A. (1989). Genetic and environmental influences for Type A-like measures of related traits: A study of twins reared apart and twins reared together. *Psychosomatic Medicine, 51,* 428–440.

Phelps, R., Eisman, E. J., & Kohout, J. (1998). Psychological practice and managed care: Results of the CAPP Practitioner survey. *Professional Psychology, 29,* 31–36.

Plassman, B. L., & Breitner, J. C. S. (1997). The genetics of dementia in late life. *Psychiatric Clinics of North America, 20,* 59–76.

Qualls, S. H. (1998). Training in geropsychology: Preparing to meet the demand. *Professional Psychology, 29,* 23–28.

Qualls, S. H., & Czirr, R. (1988). Geriatric health teams: classifying models of professional and team functioning. *Gerontologist, 28*, 372–376.

Qualls, S. H., & Smyer, M. A. (2001). Mental health. In G. Maddox (Ed.), *Encyclopedia of aging.* 3rd edition, (pp. 679–681). New York: Springer Publishing Co.

Regier, D. A., Narrow, W. E., Rae, D. S., Manderscheid, R. W., Locke, B. Z., & Goodwin, F. K. (1993). The de facto U.S. mental and addictive disorder service system: Epidemiologic Catchment Area prospective one-year prevalence rates of disorders and services. *Archives of General Psychiatry, 50*, 85–94.

Robins, L. N., Helzer, J. E., Weissman, M. M., Orvaschel, H., Gruenberg, E., Burke, J. D., & Regier, D. A. (1984). Lifetime prevalence of specific psychiatric disorders in three sites. *Archives of General Psychiatry, 41*, 949–958.

Rogers, W. (1999, November). Senior citizens and the internet. [On-line]. Available: http://www.iota.org/Fall99/seniors.html

Roth, A., & Fonagy, P. (1996). *What works for whom?* New York: Guilford Press.

Rowe, J. W., & Gatz, M. (2000). Implications of genetic knowledge for public policy. *Generations, 24*(1), 79–83.

Sabin, J. E., & Daniels, N. (1999). Public-sector managed behavioral health care: II. Contracting for Medicaid Services—the Massachusetts Experience. *Psychiatric Services, 50*, 39–41.

Salkever, D. S., Shinogle, J., & Goldman, H. (1999). Mental health benefit limits and cost-sharing under managed care: A national survey of employers. *Psychiatric Services, 50*, 1631–1633.

Schneider, E. L. (1999). Aging in the third millennium. *Science, 283*, 796–797.

Schulz, R., O'Brien, A. T., Bookwala, J., & Fleissner, K. (1995). Psychiatric and physical morbidity effects of dementia caregiving. Prevalence, correlates, and causes. *Gerontologist, 35*, 771–791.

Scogin, F. (1998). Bibliotherapy: A nontraditional intervention for depression. In P. E. Hartman-Stein (Ed.), *Innovative behavioral healthcare for older adults: A guidebook for changing times* (pp. 129–144). San Francisco, CA: Jossey-Bass.

Scogin, F., & McElreath, L. (1994). Efficacy of psychosocial treatments for geriatric depression: A quantitative review. *Journal of Consulting and Clinical Psychology, 62*, 69–74.

Seligman, M. P., & Levant, R. F. (1998). Managed care policies rely on inadequate science. *Professional Psychology, 29*, 211–212.

Shadlen, M. F., & Larson, E. B. (1999). Unique features of Alzheimer's disease in ethnic minority populations. In T. P. Miles (Ed.), *Full color aging* (pp. 33–51). Washington DC: Gerontological Society of America.

Silver, M. (1999). Introduction. *Journal of Geriatric Psychiatry, 32*, 3–4.

Small, G. W., Rabins, P. V., Barry, P. P., Buckholtz, N. S., DeKosky, S. T., Ferris, S. H., Finkel, S. I., Gwyther, L. P., Khachaturian, Z. S., Lebowitz, B. D., McRae, T. D., Morris, J. C., Oakley, F., Schneider, L. S., Streim, J. E., Sunderland, T., Teri, L. A., & Tune, L. E. (1997). Diagnosis and treatment of Alzheimer disease and related disorders: Consensus statement of the American Association for Geriatric Psychiatry, the Alzheimer's Association, and the American Geriatrics Society. *Journal of the American Medical Association, 278*, 1363–1371.

Smyer, M., Schaie, K. W., & Kapp, M. B. (Eds.). (1996). *Older adults' decision-making and the law.* New York: Springer Publishing Co.

Smyer, M. A., & Downs, M. (1995). Psychopharmacology: An essential element in educating clinical psychologists for working with older adults. In B. Knight, L. Teri, P. Wohlford, & J. Santos (Eds.), *Mental health services for older adults: Implications for training and practice in geropsychology* (pp. 73–84). Washington, DC: American Psychological Association.

Smyer, M. A., Balster, R. L., Egli, D., Johnson, D. L., Kilbey, M. M., Leith, N. J., & Puente, S. E. (1993). Summary of the Report of the Ad Hoc Task Force on Psychopharmacology of the American Psychological Association. *Professional Psychology, 24*, 394–403.

Sprott, R. L., & Pereira-Smith, O. M. (2000). The genetics of aging: Introduction. *Generations, 24*(1), 6–7.

Stern, Y., Gurland, B., Tatemichi, T. K., Tang, M. X., Wilder, D., & Mayeux, R. (1994). Influence of education and occupation on the incidence of Alzheimer's disease. *Journal of the American Medical Association, 271,* 1004–1010.

Surgeon General. (1999). *Mental Health: A report of the Surgeon General.* [On-line]. Available: http://www.surgeongeneral.gov/library/mentalhealth/index.html

Takamura, J. C. (2000, February 9). *Statement at Hearing of the House Subcommittee on Labor, Health and Human Services and Education* [On-line]. Available: http://www.aoa.gov/Oaa/2000/jct02-09-2000.html

Thompson, L. W., Coon, D. W., Gallagher-Thompson, D., Sommer, B., & Koin, D. (in press). Comparison of desipramine and cognitive/behavioral therapy in the treatment of late-life depression. *American Journal of Geriatric Psychiatry.*

Thorslund, M., & Lundberg, O. (1994). Health and inequalities among the oldest old. *Journal of Aging and Health, 6,* 51–69.

Tornstam, L. (1999). Transcendence in later life. *Generations, 23,* 10–14.

Turk-Charles, S., Gatz, M., & Meyerowitz, B. E. (1997). Age differences in information-seeking among cancer patients. *International Journal of Aging and Human Development, 45,* 85–98.

Unützer, J., Patrick, D. L., Simon, G., Grembowski, D., Walker, E., Rutter, C., & Katon, W. (1997). Depressive symptoms and the cost of health services in HMO patients aged 65 years and older: A 4-year prospective study. *Journal of the American Medical Association, 277,* 1618–1623.

U.S. Bureau of the Census. (2000a). *International Data Base.* [On-line]. Available: http://www.census.gov/ipc/www/idbnew html

U.S. Bureau of the Census. (2000b). *National population projections.* [On-line]. Available: http://www.census.gov/population/www/projections/natproj.html

U.S. Dept. of Health and Human Services. (1993a). *Depression in primary care: Volume 1. Detection and diagnosis* (AHCPR Publication No. 93–0550). Rockville, MD: Author.

U.S. Dept. of Health and Human Services. (1993b). *Depression in primary care: Volume 2. Treatment of major depression* (AHCPR Publication No. 93–0551). Rockville, MD: Author.

Wells, K. B., Schoenbaum, M., Unützer, J., Lagomasino, I. T., & Rubenstein, L. V. (1999). Quality of care for primary care patients with depression in managed care. *Archives of Family Medicine, 8,* 529–536.

Wetherell, J. L. (1998). Treatment of anxiety in older adults. *Psychotherapy, 35,* 444–458.

White, H., McConnell, E., Clipp, E., Bynum, L., Teague, C., Navas, L., Craven, S., & Halbrecht, H. (1999). Surfing the Net in later life: A review of the literature and pilot study of computer use and quality of life. *Journal of Applied Gerontology, 18,* 358–378.

Wohlford, P., & McDonel, B. (2000). *Mental health/substance abuse services for older adults through primary care.* [On-line]. Available: http://www.hms.harvard.edu/aging/mhsa

Woods, R., & Roth, A. (1996). Effectiveness of psychological interventions with older people. In A. Roth & P. Fonagy (Eds.), *What works for whom?* (pp. 321–340). New York: Guilford Press.

Woody, S. R., & Sanderson, W. C. (Eds.). (1998). Manuals for empirically supported treatments: 1998 update. *Clinical Psychologist, 51,* 17–21.

Zeiss, A. M., & Steffen, A. M. (1996). Interdisciplinary health care teams: The basic unit of geriatric care. In L. L. Carstensen, B. A. Edelstein, & L. Dornbrand (Eds.), *The practical handbook of clinical gerontology* (pp. 423–450). Thousand Oaks, CA: Sage Publications.

Zhu, C. Y., & Xu, Q. (1992). Family care of the elderly in China: Changes and problems. In J. I. Kosberg (Ed.), *Family care of the elderly: Social and cultural changes* (pp. 67–81). Newbury Park, CA: Sage Publications.

Part Four

Behavior in Social Contexts

Twenty-Two

Technological Change and the Older Worker

Sara J. Czaja

I. Introduction

A number of existing and emerging demographic trends have generated renewed interest in the older worker. It is well established that the percent of older people in the population is increasing, and that this trend will continue into the next decade. By the year 2030 the number of persons aged 65+ years will represent 18% of the population. At the same time that the population is aging, the overall workforce is aging. In 1996, the median age of the labor force was 38 years and by 2006 it is expected to increase to approximately 41 years. Also, although the number of older people in the labor force has been declining, current projections indicate that by the year 2030 the number of older workers, including both males and females will slightly increase. It is estimated that the annual growth rate of workers 55+ yr will be 3.7% between the years 1996 to 2006 (Fullerton, 1997).

Despite these projections a number of analysts (e.g., Herzog, House, & Morgan, 1991) maintain that there will be an increase in the old-age dependency ratio with potentially serious social and economic consequences. In fact, policy makers have turned their attention towards increasing employment opportunities for older workers because of the serious demand that may be placed on alternative sources of income such as Social Security benefits. The average length of retirement, measured as the increase in the period of nonworking after age 65, has increased since the adoption of the Social Security system. Between 1940 and 1980 the average length of retirement increased by 18% for males and 37% for females; by 2040 this increase is projected to be 31% for males and 54% for females (Rappaport & Plumley, 1989). In response to these projections, the Social Security Act was amended in 1983 to raise the minimum age of retirement for the receipt of full benefits from 65 to 67. In addition, the Age Discrimination in Employment Act ws amended in 1986 to eliminate a mandatory age for most occupational groups (Kovar &LaCroix, 1987).

Employers have also turned their attention towards older workers because of the changing demographics of the workforce. By 2000 the number of workers aged 18–24 years declined about 5%, and workers aged 25–34 years declined about 6%. This implies a likely labor shortage in the future, especially for entry-level positions. Some companies are turning to older workers to fill these positions. For example, Days Inn, Hartford Insurance, and the Travelers Insurance Companies have established successful programs for older workers as have other corporations such as Burger King. Similar trends are being observed in other countries such as Japan (Miyazaki, 1988).

Trends in the labor market also influence the employment of older people. In periods of prosperity and high employment, such as the 1980s, the labor market conditions for older people were generally favorable. Labor shortages created a need for employers to recruit and hire older workers. However, the recession in the 1990s resulted in high displacement rates for workers, and older people were particularly vulnerable. Many older workers were also offered early retirement packages during this time. The current economic boom is again creating a need for employers to turn to older workers. Many industries such as the service sector are experiencing labor shortages. Thus there are opportunities for older people to remain employed or to return to work following retirement.

Finally, given that many older people are healthy and active, they may desire or need to continue working for financial or social reasons. For example, the declines in the real value of pension benefits and declines in retiree health-care coverage creates a need for many older people to return to work after retirement from their primary occupation. A recent study, examining the relation of work and retirement to health and well-being (Herzog et al., 1991), suggests that those older people who have voluntarily retired might be induced to continue working if the nature of the work and the working conditions were significantly more attractive and flexible. Ucello (1998), in a recent study examining factors influencing retirement, found that workers in physically

demanding jobs retire earlier than those in less physically demanding jobs. In addition, the majority of retirees reported that they were in good health and did not have any functional limitations that limit work. Hayward, Grady, Hardy, and Sommers (1989) found that two aspects of work activity, substantive complexity and physical demands, are significant determinants of the decision to retire. Workers in jobs which are cognitively demanding and less physically demanding are less likely to retire than those in jobs with low substantive demands and high physical demands. They also found that health limitations have a strong impact on the decision to retire. Other investigators (e.g., Belbin, 1955) have also found that older workers are more likely to transfer to jobs that are less physically demanding. Powell (1973), in a study examining factors affecting the age at which men leave coal mining, found that the heavy physical demands associated with mining was one of the primary reasons older men (40+ years) transferred to other occupations. These finding suggests that most people over aged 65 are able to continue working and that the trend towards less physically demanding jobs will help extend their working lives. In fact, data from the current population survey (Herz, 1995) indicates that a return to full and part-time work is increasing among retired men.

All of these reasons point to a need to develop strategies that allow for successful integration of older people into today's work environment. In order to develop these strategies, it is important to understand the impact that age-related changes in abilities have on work performance. This is far from a trivial task, considering that aging is associated with substantial variability in performance and that older adults as a group are very heterogeneous. For many indices of performance there are greater differences within the older population than between older and younger age groups. Thus although we can discuss trends in performance in the context of chronological age, predictions about an individual's ability to perform a particular job should be based on his or her functional capacity relative to the demands of that job. In the discussion that follows, the available knowledge on aging and work performance is summarized in order to unravel some of the myths and realities associated with older workers, and to identify areas of needed research. An emphasis is given to the implications of computer and automation technologies for older workers, as most of today's jobs involve the use of some form of technology.

II. Employment Patterns of Older Workers

Workers over age 45 are most likely to be employed in three particular industries—manufacturing, service, and trade, with differences according to gender. Men between the ages of 45 and 64 are most likely to be involved in manufacturing, and those over 65 are most likely to be in the service sector. Women age 45 ± are also most likely to have jobs in the service industry. With respect to occupation, the major occupations for males 45 to 64 are crafts (21%), management (19%), and professional/technical occupations (17%). For males 65+ the major occupations are management (18%), professional/technical (15%), and service occupations (13%). The pattern for females is different. The majority of women aged 45 to 64 (40%) are found in clerical jobs, and about 21% and 19% are found in service and professional/technical jobs, respectively. Women aged 65± are most likely to be found in clerical (25%) and service jobs (21%) (Office of Technology Assessment, 1985). Knowledge of the types of jobs where older people are likely to be employed is useful for targeting research efforts.

With respect to the future it is difficult to project industry and occupation by age. However, general projections regarding the labor force can be used to gain some understanding of employment opportunities for older people. In the next few years most of the growth in the labor force is expected in the service industry. The trade industry is also expected to show large growth, whereas manufacturing will only show moderate growth. If the labor force distribution of older workers remains the same, these projections indicate that older people are in industries that are likely to experience growth (Office of Technology Assessment, 1985). However, this does not necessarily mean that employment opportunities will expand for older workers, as there are a number of other factors that influence this equation, such as the job and skill requirements of these industries and receptivity to older workers by employers and organizations.

The data also suggest that technology will have a major impact on the future structure of the labor force, changing the types of jobs that are available and the way in which jobs are performed. Most workers need to interact with some type of computer technology to perform their job. For example, during the 1990s computer technology affected approximately 7 million factory jobs and 38 million office jobs (Sauter, Murphy, & Hurrell, 1990). These numbers will continue to increase as developments in technology continue. Furthermore, the number of people who are telecommuting is rapidly increasing. In 1995 at least three million Americans were telecommuting for purposes of work, and this number is expected to increase by 20% per year (Nickerson & Landauer, 1997).

Technology changes the nature of work. A major issue associated with rapid technological change is the question of how workers will upgrade their knowledge, skills, and abilities, to avoid problems with obsolescence. Continuous changes in technology imply that people will need to learn new systems and new activities at multiple points during their working life. Workers not only have to learn to use technical systems, but they must also learn new ways of performing jobs. Issues of skill obsolescence and worker retraining are highly significant for older workers, as they are less likely than younger workers to have had exposure to technology such as computers. Most studies that have assessed age differences in experience with computers (e.g., Czaja & Sharit, 1998) indicate that current cohorts of older adults have significantly less experience with technology than do younger people. This is important, as research (Czaja & Sharit, 1998) has indicated that prior experience with computers is an important predictor of performance on computer- based tasks. Although older people are capable of learning new skills, they often encounter some difficulty especially within unfamiliar domains. Furthermore, because of myths associated with older workers, they are often bypassed for training or retraining opportunities (Griffiths, 1997).

As discussed by Sterns and Barrett (1992) technological innovation may affect older workers in several ways, including (a) rendering existing skills and knowledge obsolete, (b) requiring the development of new knowledge and skills, (c) changing attitudes and job satisfaction, (d) creating new opportunities for employment, and (e) creating conditions of unemployment. The impact of technology on the older worker will vary according to the organizational climate, type of technology, and the willingness and ability of older people to upgrade their skills to keep pace with changing job demands.

The following section will provide a general summary of what is known about aging and work. This will be followed be a discussion of the implications of workplace technologies for older people.

III. Aging and Work Performance

A.   Productivity: An Overview

Older workers are often perceived negatively by employers and co-workers because of myths regarding their skills and productivity. Common beliefs about older workers are that they are physically unable to do their job, have a high rate of absenteeism, have a high rate of accidents, are less productive, less motivated, and less receptive to innovations than younger people, and that they are unable to learn (Peterson & Coberly, 1989). Although these are rather commonly held beliefs, there is actually little data to support these assumptions; in fact, most research studies that are available indicate that these stereotypes are inaccurate. This is not to suggest that we have an entirely clear picture of the impact of aging on work performance.

In general, information regarding aging and work performance is limited, especially for technology-based jobs, and the information that is available is somewhat contradictory (Table 22.1). Rhodes (1983) conducted a comprehensive review of the studies of age and work performance and concluded that there is equal evidence in support of the observation that job performance increases with age, decreases with age, or remains the same. She maintains that the relationship is dependent on the type of performance measure, the nature of the job, and other factors such as experience. Stagner (1985) also conducted a comprehensive review of the aging and work performance literature and found similarly contradictory results.

Waldman and Avolio (1986) conducted a meta-analysis on 40 samples containing data pertaining to age and job performance, and their results have provided

Table 22.1
Summary of Findings Regarding Aging and Work Performance

Investigator	Job type method	Findings
Rhodes (1983)	Comprehensive literature review	Equal evidence that job performance increased with age, decrease with age, not related to age
Waldman & Avolio (1986)	Meta-analysis of 40 samples	Results varied according to type of performance measure and job type; age accounted for only small degree of variance
McEvoy & Casio (1989)	Meta-analysis of 65 samples	Age and job performance are unrelated
Drury & Sheehan (1971)	Industrial inspection	Age-related declines
Evans (1951)	Industrial inspection	No age-related declines
Davies & Parasuraman (1982)	Vigilance task	No age-related declines
Parasuraman & Giambra (1991)	Vigilance task	Age decrements in performance
Clay (1956)	Production task	Peak in performance to age 40 followed by a gradual decline
Greenberg (1960)	Industrial tasks	Peak in performance to age 35 followed by a gradual decline
Salvendy (1972)	Manufacturing	No age-related declines
Giniger, Despenzieri & Eisenberg (1983)	Manufacturing	No age-related declines
Kutscher & Walker (1960)	Clerical workers	Age-related decline in productivity
U.S. Department of Labor (1960)	Office workers	No age-related declines
Streufest, Pogash, Piasecki & Post (1990)	Management performance	Age differences in number of decisions, decision strategies and less optimal use of information
Salthouse (1996)	Synthetic, complex-time sharing task	Age-related declines in performance
Czaja & Sharit (1993, 1998, 1999)	Computer-based work tasks (data entry, database inquiry, accounts balancing)	Age-related declines in performance
Morrow and Colleagues (1990, 1991, 1993)	Simulated flight performance	Minimal age difference in primary flight tasks; age decrements in Air traffic control communication

some clarity on this issue. They found that the relationship between age and productivity depended to some degree on the type of performance measure used and on occupation. For production records, age, and performance were positively correlated, whereas supervisory ratings were negatively correlated with age. They also found that age-related performance declines were less likely for professionals than nonprofessionals. They concluded that age only accounted for a small portion of the variance in individual differences in work behavior. McEvoy and Cascio (1989) also performed a meta-analysis of over 65 studies and concluded that age and job performance were unrelated. However, they cautioned that most of the studies were cross-sectional and involved small sample sizes. Avolio

(1992) points out that much of the research pertaining to aging and work performance has not included a detailed analysis of contextual factors, such as opportunities for retraining, which have an impact on work ability. He suggests that a "levels of analysis" framework would be useful when studying aging and work behavior, as it can be used to clarify links between individual changes and the context within which such changes take place within work settings. For example, grouping jobs according to job demands (e.g., complexity, pacing, or type of work experience) may help explain variance in age performance relationships.

B. Blue Collar Jobs

With respect to specific jobs or occupations, the findings in the literature are also mixed. For example, Drury and Sheehan (1971) and Czaja and Drury (1981) found age-related declines in the performance of a visual inspection, whereas Evans (1951) reported no age differences in inspection performance. More recently, Parasuraman and Giambra (1991) found age decrements in the performance of a vigilance tasks even when the task was well practiced. Considering production tasks, Clay (1956) examined production records of machine compositors, hand compositors, and proofreaders from two printing plants. The general pattern of performance was an increase in performance to a peak in the 40s, followed by a gradual decline. However, there were differneces according to job, such that the performance of the oldest age group was always higher than that of the youngest age group (20–29) when the machine compositors were removed from the analyses. Caution must be exercised with respect to these findings, as there were only small samples of older employees in some jobs. The United States Department of Labor (Greenberg, 1960) examined output records in a range of industries. Data from several industries indicated that performance improved up to age 35 and thereafter exhibited a gradual decline, although the performance of older people was only moderately below peak performance.

In contrast, Salvendy (1972) and Giniger, Despenzieri, and Eisenberg (1983) found no age differences in performance for manufacturing jobs. The jobs studied by Giniger et al. (1983) were in the light manufacturing industry and not very physically demanding. They suggested that the older people in their study may have compensated for any declines in physical stamina with strategies developed through experience. They found, in fact, that experience was the primary determinant of job performance.

Sparrow and Davies (1988) examined the effects on performance of age, tenure, job complexity, and training among a sample of service engineers. They found an inverted-U relation between age, quality, and speed of performance. However, three other important findings emerged from their study. One is that job complexity did not moderate the effect of age and performance; in fact, for all age groups performance was higher for the more complex tasks. Second, age only accounted for a small portion of the variance in performance. Finally, training was an important mediating variable between age and performance. Finally, training was an important mediating variable between age and performance. Older engineers who had received recent task training performed better than those who had not received recent training. This suggests that training can mediate age declines in performance.

C. White Collar Jobs

The findings are similar for white collar jobs. Kutscher and Walker (1960) reported a decline in productivity with age for clerical workers, whereas a Department of Labor study (1960) reported no age differences in output per work hour for office workers.

Considering age and performance in professional and managerial jobs, the data are again limited and inconclusive. Different results are obtained among fields and within fields, depending on the output measure used in the analysis. For example, Stumpf and Ravinowitz (1981) found a negative relationship between age and peer assessment of performance.

Streufert, Pogash, Piasecki, and Post (1990) studied age and team management performance among a sample of male managers who performed simulated decision-making tasks. They found that performance by young and middle-aged teams was generally similar. The older managers made fewer decisions and were less strategic and less responsive to incoming information. However, older teams used opportunities and handled a simulated emergency as effectively as their younger peers. They caution, however, that their results may be due to cohort differences, such as recent job assignments or training. Dalton and Thompson (1970, 1971) investigated the relationship between age and performance among a sample of professional engineers in the aerospace industry. They found that performance peaked in the mid-30s and gradually declined with advances in age. Some of these effects were related to skill obsolescence due to rapid development of new technologies.

Avolio, Waldman, and McDaniel (1990) found that experience was a better predictor of job performance than age. They examined data from individuals employed in the private sector across 111 jobs. The database used was from the United States Employment Service. Across occupations they found experience to be more highly correlated with performance than age. However, there were differences according to occupation in that both age and experience predicted performance for jobs requiring higher levels of complexity. The investigators indicated that the occupational differences suggest that there are other aspects of work context that affect the age and performance relationship.

A recent review of cognitive proficiency and flight performance in older pilots (Hardy & Parasuraman, 1997) found that for simulated flight performance there were no differences between younger and older pilots for primary flight tasks despite differences in basic perceptual and cognitive abilities. However, there were age-related differences in voice communications with Air Traffic Control (ATC). Generally, older pilots were found to be less accurate in reading back commands and also had more difficulty executing ATC commands. With respect to actual flight performance, the most recent data indicate that older pilots do not have more accident rates than younger pilots.

Smith, Staudinger, and Baltes (1994) found that elderly clinical psychologists performed as well as their younger colleagues in tasks involving the application of wisdom-related knowledge. Similarly, a study of university professors suggests that age-related declines in some aspects of cognition such as prose recall may be mitigated in cognitively active people. This finding is consistence with the notion that as long as older people are in jobs where the demands of a job remain stable, few age deficits will be observed.

D. Accidents and Absenteeism

With respect to other measures of job behavior, the findings, although limited, are a bit more conclusive. Regarding accidents, older workers tend to have lower accident rates than younger workers; however, older workers tend to remain off the job longer if they are injured. In 1981, workers age 55 and older made up 13.6% of the labor force, but accounted for only 9.7% of all workplace accidents

(U.S. Administration on Aging, 1984). Absenteeism and turnover rates also appear to be lower for older adults. Martoccio (1989) completed a meta-analysis across 34 samples that included data regarding age and absenteeism. The results indicated that both voluntary absence, based on a frequency index and based on a lost-time index, were inversely related to age.

E. Summary

In general, the relationship between age and job performance is complex and far from understood. One problem is that the data that are available are sometimes unreliable. For example, studies that rely on supervisory rating of performance may be unreliable if the rater has negative attitudes about older workers. Finkelstein, Burke, and Raju (1995) found that in simulated employment settings, younger workers tended to rate older workers less favorably when they were not provided with job-relevant information about the workers and when they concurrently rated older and younger workers. Also, many studies involve small samples, restricted age ranges, or they are cross- sectional—which may confound age effects with factors such as experience, education, or exposure to technology. The results also vary according to type of task and type of performance. Finally, the number of recent studies conducted in actual employment settings has been limited.

Overall, the empirical literature offers little support for the widely held belief that job performance declines significantly with age. The information that is available suggests that certain types of tasks, such as those that are associated with heavy physical demands or are externally placed, may be unsuitable for older workers. This might include, for example, tasks such as construction work, firefighting, law enforcement, or aspects of manufacturing. However, these conclusions are speculative, and there are little data regarding specific jobs or occupations.

In this regard, one important area of needed research is developing a knowledge base that links age-related changes in skills and abilities to specific skill requirements of jobs. For example, currently, the relationships among aging, cognition, and work productivity are unclear. Generally, the literature indicates (Schmidt, Hunter, Outerbridge, & Goff, 1988) that cognitive ability is related to both job knowledge and job performance. Thus one would expect to find a negative relationship between age and performance on work tasks that are characterized by cognitive demands. Yet, many older adults successfully perform jobs that are cognitively demanding. In this regard, Salthouse (1990) suggests that experience results in higher levels of job knowledge or competence and may compensate for declines in abilities. In fact, several studies have shown (e.g., Charness, Salthouse, 1984) that for tasks where older people have expertise, age differences in performance are diminished. Other investigators have found that practice considerably improves the performance of older people. For example, Czaja and Sharit (1998, 1999) found task experience improved the ability of people of all ages to perform computer- based work. However, they also found that experience did not mitigate age–performance differences

Park (1994) suggests four possible explanations for understanding the relationships between aging, cognition, and work. One is that older workers remain in jobs in which they are highly experienced. Thus they are not in "resource-demanding" situations. A second possible explanation is that experience prevents declines in cognitive abilities underlying work behavior. A third possibility is that job knowledge structures increase with age and compensate for ability declines. Finally, it may be that older adults increasingly rely on environmental supports to compensate for declines in cognition. Clearly, examining issues related to aging, cognition, and work performance is a fruitful area for research. A more complete understanding of these relationships would help direct the development of intervention strategies for older workers.

IV. The Implications of Technology for Older Workers

Knowledge regarding aging and work is particularly important in the domain of computer-based work. During the past decade, computer and communication technologies and other forms of automation such as robotics and flexible manufacturing systems have been introduced into most occupational settings. For example, secretaries and office personnel now need to use word processing, electronic mail, and data-base management packages to perform standard office tasks. Manager, bank tellers, sales clerks, and cashiers are also using computers on a regular basis to carry out routine tasks and activities, such as sales transactions, inventory management, and decision making. This means that workers have to learn new skills to operate computers and use software to meet job demands. Computer-interactive tasks are also becoming prevalent within the general manufacturing, chemical, and nuclear power industries. For example, computer-aided manufacturing (CAM) now involves both directed and in-directed applications of computers in the manufacturing process. This includes computer-aided control of machines, process control, inventory management, and scheduling. The fastest growing occupations are also centered around technology and include computer engineers, computer support specialists, systems analysts, and database administrators (Fullerton, 1997). Furthermore, projections for the period of 1996–2006 indicated that high-tech-related employment is growing more than twice as fast at employment in the economy as a whole. Specifically, in 2006, high-tech employment is expected to account for about 16% of total employment (Hecker, 1999).

One unanswered question is how the influx of this technology into work settings will alter the work life of the elderly. Technology obviously changes the nature of work. In some cases, both the context and demands are altered. In general, for example, computer tasks place greater emphasis on cognitive skills than do traditional work methods. These demands may have a negative impact on the employment of older adults because of diminished cognitive abilities (e.g., declines in processing speed), skill obsolescence, and limited opportunities to offset declines in skill with experience. Salthouse (1985) suggests that in a society rapidly becoming more automated, the slowness of many older adults may place them at a great disadvantage relative to younger adults.

Czaja and Sharit (1993) found that age-related slowing had an impact on the performance of some computer-based tasks. In that study, women, ranging in age from 25 to 70 years, performed three computer-based tasks: a data entry task, a file maintenance task, and an inventory management task. The results indicated that the response times of the older participants were significantly longer than those of the younger subjects for all three tasks. This difference was found even when controlling for differences in prior computer experience and typing speed. However, actual task experience was limited, and as shown by several investigators (e.g., Salthouse, 1984, and Bosman, 1993), older people often develop strategies as they gain experience on a task to compensate for declines in speed. In a more recent study, Czaja and Sharit (1998) examined the relationship between component cognitive abilities, such as processing speed, and performance on simulated real-world data entry task. They found that psychomotor speed and working memory and prior computer experience were significant predictors of performance, and after controlling for differences on these abilities, age no longer predicted performance.

Other age-related declines in cognition may also make it difficult for older people to interact with workplace technologies. For example, declines in working memory may make it difficult for older adults to learn new concepts, such as those associated with computer technologies, or recall complex and/or uncommon operational procedures. Declines in attentional capacity may make it difficult for an older person to perform concurrent activities or to switch their attention between competing displays of information. They also may have problems attending to or selecting target information on complex displays. Salthouse (1996) studied age-related differences on a synthetic complex work task that required multiple concurrent demands. These differences persisted even with 2 hours of task practice. The older adults were less able to deal successfully with several concurrent tasks than the younger adults.

On the positive side, because in many cases technology reduced the physical demands of work, employment opportunities for older people may be increased with the influx of workplace technologies. Computer technology also makes work at home a more likely option. This is beneficial for older people who find it difficult to leave home because of health or transportation problems. Clearly the questions of how well older workers will cope with the changing context and demands of computer-based work is important.

Unfortunately, although the empirical literature on human computer interaction is vast, few studies have concerned themselves with evaluating computer-based work for older adults. Most of the studies that have been done have concerned the ability of older people to acquire text-editing skills. Overall research in this area suggests that older people are receptive to using technology and that they are able to acquire the skills needed to perform computer tasks. However, they may need more training and practice than younger people. Furthermore, the literature that is available suggests that older people may not perform at the same level as younger people. The following sections will provide a summary about what is known about aging and the acquisition of computer skills and the performance of computer-based tasks.

A. Older Adults and the Acquisition of Computer Skills

As shown in Table 22.2, a number of studies have examined the ability of older adults to learn to use computer technology. These studies span a variety of computer applications and also vary with respect to training strategies, such as conceptual versus procedural training (Morrell, Park, Mayhorn, & Echt, 1995) or computer-based or instructor-based versus manual-based training (Czaja, Hammond, Blascovich, & Swede, 1989). In addition, the influence on learning of such variables as attitude towards computers and computer anxiety have been examined. Overall, the results of these studies indicate that older adults are, in fact, able to use computers for a variety of tasks. However, older adults often have more difficulty acquiring computer skills than younger people and require more training and more help during training. Also, when compared to younger adults on performance measures such as speed,

Table 22.2
Summary of Computer Training and Older Adults

Study	Age Range	Application	Findings
Caplan & Schooler (1990)	18–60	Drawing Software	Conceptual model detrimental for older adults; older adults had lower performance.
Charness, Schuman, & Boritz (1989)	25–81	Word processing	Older adults took longer to complete training and required more help.
Czaja, Hammond, Blascovich, & Swede (1989)	25–70	Word processing	Older adults took longer to complete task problems and made more errors.
Czaja, Hammond, & Joyce (1989)	25–70	Word processing	Older adults took longer to complete task problems and made more errors; goal-oriented training improved performance.
Egan & Gomez (1985)	28–62	Word processing	Age and spatial memory were significant predictors of performance.
Elias, Elias, Robbins, & Gage (1987)	18–67	Word processing	Older adults had longer learning times and required more help.
Garfein, Schaie, & Willis (1988)	49–67	Spreadsheet	No age differences
Gist, Rosen, & Schwoerer (1988)	Mean = 40	Spreadsheet	Older adults performed more poorly on a posttraining test; modeling improved performance.
Hartley, Hartley, & Johnson (1984)	18–75	Line-editor	No age differences in performance efficiency; older adults took longer to complete training and required more help.
Morell, Park, Mayhorn, & Echt (1995)	Young-old $(X = 68.6)$ Old-old $(X = 79.9)$	Electronic bulletin board	Procedural training superior to conceptual; age effects
Zandri & Charness (1989)	20–84	Calendar and notepad	Advanced organizer not beneficial; age effects for training time and needed more help

adult adults often achieve lower levels of performance.

For example, Egan and Gomez (1985) conducted a series of experiments in an attempt to identify individual-difference variables that predict ability to learn text editing. They found that age and spatial memory were significant predictors of learning difficulty. Both of these variables contributed to the prediction of first-try errors and execution time per successful edit change. In particular, age was associated with difficulty producing the correct sequence of symbols and patterns to accomplish the desired editing change.

Elias, Elias, Robbins, and Gage (1987) conducted a study to examine age differences in the acquisition of text-editing skills and to identify sources of difficulty encountered by older adults. The training program included an audiotape and a training manual. The results indicated that all participants were able to learn the fundamentals of word processing; however, the older adults required more time to complete the training program and required more help. The older people also performed more poorly on a review examination. Garfein, Schaie, and Willis (1988) examined the ability of older adults to learn a spreadsheet package. They also attempted to identify component abilities that are predictive for computer novice to acquire computer skills. The results of their study indicated that all participants were able to operate a computer and use the spreadsheet package after only two brief 90-minute sessions of training. There were no significant age effects for the performance measures. However, this may be because the age range of the participant was restricted and only included people ranging in age from 49 to 67 years. In terms of other factors affecting computer proficiency, they found that fluid intelligence was an important predictor of performance. Gist, Rosen, and Schwoerer (1988) also examined the influence of age and training method on the acquisition of a spreadsheet program. The training program consisted of two approaches: tutorial or bahavioral modeling. The tutorial approach involved a computer-based step-by-step interactive instructional package. The behavioral modeling involved watching a videotape of a middle-aged male demonstrating the use of the software and then practicing the procedure. The results indicated that the modeling approach was superior to the tutorial approach for both younger and older participants. They also found that older adults performed more poorly on a posttraining test.

Zandri and Charness (1989) investigated the influence of training method on the ability of older people to use a calendar and notepad system. Specifically, they examined if providing an advanced organizer would impact on the acquisition of computer skills for younger and older adults. They also examined if learning with a partner would have an influence on learning. The results indicated an age-by-training method (learning alone or with a peer) by organizer (with or without an organizer) interaction for performance on a final test. For the older adults who received training without a partner, the advanced organizer resulted in better performance. For the other group of older people, there was no performance effect. For the younger subjects, having the advanced organizer resulted in worse performance if they learned alone, but it made no difference if they learned in partners. These results suggest that the provision of an advanced organizer may be differentially effective for older people under some learning conditions. Furthermore, the older people were about 2.5 times slower than the younger people in the training sessions, and they required about 3 times as much as help.

In a follow-up study, Charness, Schuman, and Boritz (1992) examined the impact of training techniques and computer anxiety on the acquisition of word-processing skills in a sample of younger and older adults. In the first study, 16 computer novices ranging in age from 25–81 yr. learned word processing skills under a self-paced training program. Half of the participants received the organizer prior to training. Overall, the provision of organizer did not improve performance. The results also indicated that older adults took about 1.2 times more than younger adults did to complete training and they required more help. In a second study, the investigator attempted to control the nature of the training session. Thirty computer novices were assigned to an either self-paced learning condition where they were actively involved in the tutorial or a fixed-paced condition where they passively observed a predetermined sequence of activities. The results indicated that both the younger and older adults performed better in the self-paced training condition relative to fixed-paced condition. Again the older adults took about 1.2 times more than the younger adults to complete training and required more help.

Czaja, Hammond, Blascovich, and Swede (1989) evaluated three training strategies for novice adults in learning to use a word-processing program. The training strategies were instructor-based, manual-based, and on-line training. The results indicated that younger adults were more successful learning the word-processing program. The older adults were slower and made more errors. The results also indicated that the manual and instructor-based training were superior to on-line training for all participants. The investigators also found that there were age differences in performance on the post-training tasks. The older adults took more time to complete the tasks and made more errors.

In a more recent study, Czaja, Hammond, and Joyce (1989) attempted to identify a training strategy that would minimize age differences in learning text editing. Two training programs were evaluated, a goal-oriented program and a traditional approach that included a manual and lecture. The goal-oriented approach introduced the elements of text editing in an incremental fashion, moving from more simple to the more complex task. The training sessions included problem-solving tasks with objectives of discovering and achieving methods for completing the tasks. The manual was written as a series of goal-oriented units. It used simple language, similarities were drawn between computer and familiar concepts, and the amount of necessary reading was minimized. The results indicated that posttraining performance was better for participants who were trained using the goal-oriented approach. These participants took less time to complete the tasks and made fewer mistakes. In spite of training manipulation, the performance still was lower for older adults than for younger adults. Older adults required more time to complete tasks, completed fewer editing changes, and made more mistakes.

Caplan and Schooler (1990) evaluated whether providing the participants with a conceptual model of the software would improve their ability to learn a painting software program. They provided half of the participants with an analogical model of a painting software program before training. The results indicated that the model was beneficial for younger adults but detrimental for older adults. Similar results were found by Morrell, Park, Mayhorn, and Echt (1995) study. They examined the ability of young-old (ages 60–74 years) and old-old (ages 75–89) adults to perform tasks on ELDER-COMM, a bulletin board system. The participants were presented with procedural instructional materials or a combination of conceptual information and procedural instructions. The results indicated that all participants performed better with the procedural instruction material. They also found that the young-old adults had better performance than the old-old adults; the old-old adults made more performance errors. The investigator concluded that conceptual training may not be beneficial for older adults because they need to translate the model into actions which may increase working memory demands.

Rogers, Fisk, Mead, Walker, and Cabrera (1996) assessed the efficacy of several instructional methods in teaching older adults to use automatic teller machines. The results indicated that training method did have an influence on performance such that an on-line tutorial was superior, which provided specific practice on the task components, and it was superior to written instructions and written instructions accompanied by graphics. The authors discuss the importance of providing older adults with actual training on technologies such as ATM machines: sole reliance on instructional materials or self-discovery may not be optimal for this population especially for more complex technological applications such as the Internet. Identification of training strategies that are efficacious for older adults is especially important given that continual developments in technology will require life-long learning for people of all ages. In this regard, Mead and Fisk (1998) examined the impact of the type of information presented during training on the initial and retention performance of younger and older adults learning to use ATM technology. Specifically, they compared two types of training: concept and action. The concept training presented factual information, whereas the action training was procedural in nature. The action training was found to be superior for older adults. They showed superior speed and accuracy immediately after training and superior speed following the retention interval. They concluded that presenting procedural information to older adults during training was more important than presenting conceptual information.

Mead, Spauding, Sit, Meyer, and Walker (1997) examined the effects of type of training on efficiency in a World Wide Web search activity. The participants were trained with a "hands-on" Web navigation tutorial or a verbal description of available navigation tools. The hands-on training was found to be superior, especially for older adults. Older adults who received hands-on training increased the use of efficient navigation tools. These findings suggest that type of training strategy does impact on the ability of older people to use complex computer technologies. Generally, the data suggest that procedural "hands-on" training with an action component is superior for older adults. However, more research is needed to identify training strategies that facilitate the ability of older people to acquire computer-based skills. Generally, the literature indicates that older adults are able to use computers for routine tasks and that they are able to learn a wide variety of computer

applications. However, they are typically slower to acquire computer skills than younger adults and generally require more help and "hands-on" practice. Furthermore, they typically need training on basic computer concepts, such as mouse and windows management, in addition to training on the application area of interest. They may also require information of the types of technologies that are available, the potential benefits associated with using these technologies, and where and how to access these technologies. Finally, greater attention needs to be given to the design of training and instructional materials to accommodate age-related changes in perceptual and cognitive abilities.

In summary, when considering skill acquisition, training, and older adults, there are three important conclusions. First, older people are quite capable of learning new skills, tasks, and procedures. Second, training strategies may need to be modified for older people, and these modifications may significantly improve the learning efficiency of older adults. Finally, it is important to recognize that costs associated with additional training or extended practice may be offset by lower turnover and absenteeism among older people. Table 22.3 outlines some general guidelines that are important when developing training programs for older people.

B. Aging and Computer Task Performance

There have only been a handful of studies that have examined the ability of older people to perform computer-based tasks, especially tasks that are common in work settings. In an early study Czaja and Sharit (1993) examined age differences in the performance of three simulated real-world computer tasks—a data entry task, a file modification task, and an inventory management task. They also evaluated

Table 22.3
Summary of Training Recommendations for
Older Adults

1. Allow extra time for training; self-paced learning schedules appear to be optimal.
2. Ensure that help is available and easy to access; create a supportive learning environment.
3. Ensure that the training environment is free from distractions.
4. Training material should be well organized and important information should be highlighted.
5. Address any concerns the learner has about use of the equipment (e.g., Will I break the computer if I do this?).
6. Minimize demands on spatial abilities and working memory.
7. Provide sufficient practice on task components.
8. Provide an active learning situation; allow the learner to discover ways of accomplishing tasks.

Source: Rogers, 2000.

differences in subjective assessments of task difficulty and stress. For all three tasks, the older people exhibited longer times and a greater number of errors than the younger people. They also found the tasks to be more stress inducing and perceptions of workload such that the older people found the tasks, especially the inventory management task (the most demanding of the three tasks), to be more difficult and mentally challenging than the younger people. Furthermore, the older participants reported more fatigue following performance of all three tasks. Analysis of the physiological data indicated that the older people experienced increased arousal on a number of measures of respiration during task performance and exhibited longer recovery to baseline than the younger participants (Czaja & Sharit, 1993). These findings have implications for issues such as job design and work rest scheduling. It may be that older people need longer or more frequent rest breaks than younger people or that particular types of

computer tasks such as data entry that are often fast-paced are unsuitable for older workers.

In a follow-up study Czaja and Sharit (1998, 1999) examined age differences in a simulated data entry task, customer service representative (information search and retrieval), and an accounts balancing task (commonly performed in the banking industry). They also examined the influence of task experience on performance and the relationship between component cognitive abilities and performance. For all three tasks the older workers performed at lower levels than the younger workers with respect to work output (Figure 22.1) and these differences remained with 9 hours of task experience. However, there were no age differences in accuracy for the data entry task after controlling for differences in work output (Figure 22.2). Furthermore, interventions such as redesigning the screen and reconfiguring the timing of the computer mouse improved the performance of all participants. The results also indicated that prior computer experience and component cognitive abilities such as working memory and psychomotor speed were important predictors of performance for all three tasks. These findings have important implications for training and interface design. More work in this area is needed. Studies are needed to identify the locus of the age–performance differences and to determine how modifications in training strategies and interface design can help mitigate age performance differences. In addition to changes in interface design, alternative input devices such as voice might prove to be beneficial to older people. Furthermore, the relationship between age and performance needs to be examined over longer periods of task experience. The findings from the Czaja and Sharit (1998, 1999) study indicate that performance of the older people improved with experience and that they had not reached asymptotic levels of

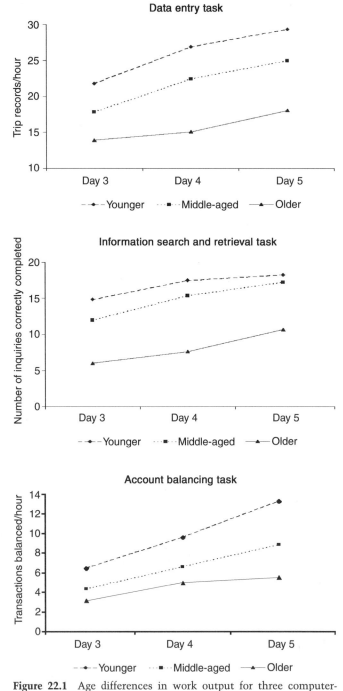

Figure 22.1 Age differences in work output for three computer-based tasks.

performance. It is likely that performance would continue to improve with more experience. Furthermore, the finding regarding the importance of prior computer experience to task performance points to the need to provide people with training

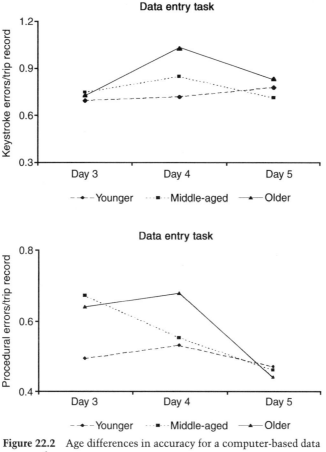

Figure 22.2 Age differences in accuracy for a computer-based data entry task.

on the actual technology as well as on the task.

Other investigators have examined age as a potential factor impacting on ability to use the computer for information search and retrieval. This is an important area of investigation given the prevalence of this type of activity within work environments. In many work settings, such as department stores, airlines, hotels, utility and health insurance companies, and educational institutions, workers are required to search through computer databases and access information to respond to customer requests. This type of activity is also central to use of the World Wide Web.

Generally, the findings from these studies indicate that although older adults are capable of performing these types of tasks, there are age-related differences in performance that appear to be in some way related to age differences in cognitive abilities. For example, Westerman, Davies, Glendon, Stammers, and Matthews (1995) examined the relationship between spatial ability, spatial memory, vocabulary skills, and age and the ability to retrieve information from a computer database, which varied according to how the database was structured (e.g., hierarchical vs. linear). In general, they found that the older subjects were slower in retrieving the information than the younger adults, however, there were no age-related differences in accuracy. The learning rates also differed for the two groups such that the older people were slower than the younger people. They found that the slower response on the part of the older adults was more dependent on general processing speed than other cognitive abilities.

Freudenthal (1997) examined the degree to which latencies on an information-retrieval task were predicted by movement speed and other cognitive variables in a group of younger and of older adults. The participants were required to search for answers to questions in a hierarchical menu structure. Results indicated that the older subjects were slower than the younger subjects on overall latencies for information retrieval and that this slowing increased with each consecutive step in the menu. Similar to Westerman et al. (1995), Freudenthal also found that movement speed was a significant predictor of overall latency. He also found that other cognitive abilities such as reasoning speed, spatial ability, and memory were also predictive of response latencies. However, memory and spatial abilities are only predictors for latency on steps further into the menu structure. Freudenthal (1997) suggests that deep menu structures may not be appropriate for older adults, as navigation through these types of structures is dependent on spatial skills that tend to decline with age. Vicente, Hayes, and Williges (1987) also found that age, spatial ability, and vocabulary were highly predictive of variance in search latency for a computer-based information retrieval task. They postulated that people with low spatial ability tend to "get lost" in the database. Czaja and Sharit (1999), in their investigation of this type of task, which simulated a customer service representative for a health insurance company, also found that spatial skills were important predictors of performance, as were response speed and

prior computer experience. As discussed they also found age-related performance differences.

V. Conclusions

The topic of aging and work is becoming increasingly important given the current demographic trends. However, the empirical data regarding the impact of aging on work performance is limited, especially for present-day jobs and those likely to exist in the public sector in the future. There is a critical need for further research in this area. For example, we need more information on the relationship between age-related changes in functioning and the specific skill requirements of jobs. Studies investigating the impact of age-related changes in abilities on the performance of work activities has been limited. Although there are age-related declines in most aspects of functioning, the decline is nearly always gradual, and most jobs do not demand constant performance at the level of maximum capacity. The majority of the population of older adults remains healthy and functionally able until very late in life. It is also important to recognize that conclusions regarding age–performance differences are often based on the comparison of averages. As shown in Figure 22.3, in many cases there are a number of older adults who function at the same level or above that of younger adults.

In order to understand these age effects on work performance, we need to examine abilities relative to the demands of specific jobs. Using a Human Factors Engineering framework, the issue becomes one of determining the degree of fit between these demands and the capabilities of older persons. This type of framework would identify specific components of jobs that are limiting for older adults and target areas where interventions such as job, equipment, or workplace redesign

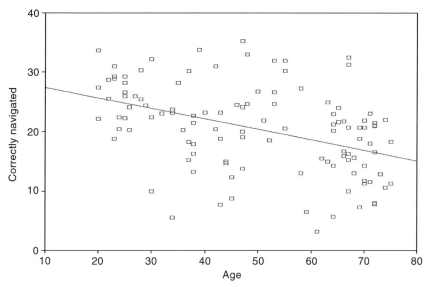

Figure 22.3 Scatter plot of age and performance for number of inquiries correctly navigated for a computer-based information search-and-retrieval task.

could be used to enhance the ability of older people to meet their job requirements.

Another important area of research is identifying interventions that enhance the ability of older people to function effectively in work environments. These workplace interventions might include job redesign, workplace and equipment redesign, and/or the development of innovative training strategies. It is generally accurate to assert that in cases where age-related declines exist, many of the performance decrements can be greatly reduced by practice or changes in design.

We also need sound, research-based information about the impact of technology on an aging workforce. In addition, we need information on how other factors such as family caregiving impact on work performance. Currently, an estimated 14.4 million workers are balancing work and caregiving responsibilites. This number is likely to increase given the aging of the population.

In general, research attention directed toward those aspects of work that could become more difficult, less productive, or less satisfying with age could make a worthwhile contribution to improving the work life of older adults. Such research would also help to assure the availability of appropriate employment opportunities for older people and broaden the pool of potential employees for public agencies competing for increasingly scarce labor.

References

Avolio, B. J. (1992) A levels of analysis perspective of aging and work research. In K. W. Schaie & M. P. Lawton (Eds.), *Annual review of gerontology and geriatrics* (pp. 239–260). New York: Springer Publishing Company.

Avolio, B. J., Waldman, D. A., & McDaniel, M. A. (1990). Age and work performance in non-managerial jobs: The effects of experience and occupational type. *Academy of Management Journal, 33,* 407–422.

Belbin, R. M. (1955). Older workers and heavy work. *British Journal of Industrial Medicine, 12,* 309–319.

Bosman, E. (1993). Age-related differences in motoric aspects of transcription typing skill. *Psychology and Aging, 8,* 87–102.

Caplan, L. J., & Schooler, C. (1990). The effects of analogical training models and age on problem-solving in a new domain. *Experimental Aging Research, 16,* 151–154.

Charness, N., Schumann, C. E., & Boritz, G. A. (1992). Training older adults in word processing: Effects of age, training technique and computer anxiety. *International Journal of Aging and Technology, 5,* 79–106.

Clay, H. M. (1956). A study of performance in relation to age at two printing works. *Journal of Gerontology, 4,* 417–442.

Czaja, S. J., & Drury, C. G. (1981). Age and pretraining in industrial inspection. *Human Factors, 23,* 485–494.

Czaja, S. J., Hammond, K., & Joyce, J. B. (1989). *Word processing training for older adults.* Final report submitted to the National Institute on Aging (Grant # 5 R4 AGO4647-03).

Czaja, S. J., Hammond, K., Blascovich, J., & Swede, H. (1989). Age-related differences in learning to use a text- editing system. *Behavior and Information Technology, 8,* 309–319.

Czaja, S. J., & Sharit, J. (1993). Age differences in the performance of computer based work as a function of pacing and task complexity. *Psychology and Aging, 8,* 59–67.

Czaja, S. J., & Sharit, J. (1998). Ability-performance relationships as a function of age and task experience for a data entry task. *Journal of Experimental Psychology: Applied, 4,* 332–351.

Czaja, S. J., & Sharit, J. (1999). Age differences in a complex information search and retrieval task. *Annual Meeting of American Psychological Association,* Boston.

Dalton, G. W., & Thompson, D. H. (1970). *Age obsolescence and performance.* Unpublished Report.

Dalton, G. W., & Thompson, D. H. (1971). Accelerating obsolescence of older engineers. *Harvard Business Review, 49,* 57–67.

Davies, D. R., & Parasuraman, R. (1982). *The psychology of vigilance.* New York: Academic Press.

Drury, C. G., & Sheehan, J. J. (1971). Ergonomics and economic factors in an industrial inspection task. *International Journal of Production Research, 7,* 333–341.

Egan, D. E., & Gomez, L. M. (1985). Assaying, isolating, and accommodating individual differences in learning a complex skill. *Individual Differences in Cognition, 2,* 174–217.

Elias, P. K., Elias, M. F., Robbins, M. A., & Gage, P. (1987). Acquisition of word-processing skills by younger, middle-aged, and older adults. *Psychology and Aging, 2,* 340–348.

Evans, R. N. (1951). Training improves micrometer accuracy. *Personal Psychology, 4,* 231–242.

Finkelstein, L. M., Burke, M., & Raju, N. S. (1995). Age discrimination in employment contexts: An integrative analysis. *Journal of Applied Psychology, 80,* 652–653.

Freudenthal, D. (1997). *Learning to use interactive devices: Age differences in the reasoning process.* Master's thesis, Eindhoven University of Technology.

Fullerton, H. N. (1997). Employment outlook: 1996–2006. Labor force 2006: Slowing down and changing composition. *Monthly Labor Report, November.*

Garfein, A. J., Schaie, K. W., & Willis, S. L. (1988). Microcomputer proficiency in later-middle-aged adults and older adults: Teaching old dogs new tricks. *Social Behavior, 3,* 131–148.

Giniger, S., Despenzieri, A., & Eisenberg, J. (1983). Age, experience, and performance on speed and skill jobs in an applied setting. *Journal of Applied Psychology, 68,* 469–475.

Gist, M., Rosen, B., & Schwoerer, C. (1988). The influence of training method and trainee age on the acquisition of computer skills. *Personal Psychology, 41,* 255–265.

Greenberg, L. (1960). Productivity of older workers. *Gerontologist, 1,* 38–41.

Griffiths, A. (1997). Ageing, health and productivity: A challenge for the new millennium. *Work & Stress, 11,* 197–214.

Hardy, D. J., & Parasuraman, R. (1997). Cognition and flight performance in older pilots. *Journal of Experimental Psychology: Applied, 3,* 313–348.

Hartley, A. A., Harley, J. T., & Johnson, S. A. (1984). The older adult as a computer user. In P. K. Robinson, J. Livingston, & J. E. Birren (Eds.), *Aging and technological advances,* New York: Plenum Press, pp. 347–348.

Hayward, M. D., Grady, W. R., Hardy, M. A., & Sommers, D. (1989). Occupational influences on retirement, disability and death. *Demography, 26,* 393–409.

Hecker, D. (1999). High-technology employment: A broader view. *Monthly Labor Review, June,* 18–28.

Herz, D. E. (1995). Work after early retirement: An increasing trend among men. *Montly Labor Review, April,* 13–20.

Herzog, A. R., House, J. S., & Morgan, J. N. (1991). Relations of work and retirement to health and well-being in older age. *Psychology and Aging, 6,* 202–211.

Kovar, M. G., & LaCroix, A. Z. (1987). Aging in the eighties: Ability to perform work-related activities, data from supplement on aging to the national health interview survey, U.S. 1984, *Advance Data From Vital and Health Statistics, No. 136. DHHS Pub No. (PHS) 87–1250.* Public Health Service. Hyattsville, Md.

Kutscher, R. E., & Walker, J. F. (1960). Comparative job performance of office workers by age. *Monthly Labor Review, 83,* 39–43.

Martocchio, J. J. (1989). Age related differences in employee absenteeism: A meta-analysis, *Psychology and Aging, 4,* 409–414.

McEvoy, G. M., & Cascio, W. F. (1989). Cumulative evidence of relationship between employee age and job performance. *Journal of Applied Psychology, 74,* 11–17.

Mead, S. E., & Fisk, A. D. (1998). Measuring skill acquisition and retention with an ATM simulator: The need for age-specific training. *Human Factors, 40,* 516–523.

Mead, S. E., Spaulding, V. A., Sit, R. A., Meyer, B., & Walker, N. (1997). Effects of age and training on World Wide Web navigation strategies. *Proceedings of the Human Factors and Ergonomics Society 41st Annual Meeting,* 152–156.

Mijazaki, T. (1988). Microelectronic technology and aging of the labor force. *Advanced Robotics, 2,* 299–310.

Morrell, R. W., Park, D. C., Mayhorn, C. B., & Echt, K. V. (1995). Older adults and electronic communication networks: Learning to use ELDERCOMM. *Paper presented at the 103 Annual Convention of the American Psychological Association.* New York, New York.

Morrow, D., Leirer, V., & Yesavage, J. (1990). The influence of alcohol and aging on radio communication during flight. *Aviation, Space, and Environmental Medicine, 61,* 12–20.

Morrow, D., Leirer, V., Yesavage, J., & Tinklenberg, J. (1991). Alcohol, age, and piloting: Judgement, mood, and actual performance. *The International Journal of the Addictions, 26,* 669–683.

Morrow, D., Yesavage, J., Leirer, V., & Tinklenberg, J. (1993). Influence of aging and practice on piloting tasks. *Experimental Aging Research, 19,* 53–70.

Nickerson, R. S., & Landauer, T. K. (1997). Human-computer interaction: Background and issues. In M. G. Helander, T. K., Landauer, and P. V. Prabhu. *Handbook of human-computer interaction* (2nd ed., pp. 3–32). Amsterdam, The Netherlands: Elsevier.

Office of Technology Assessment (1985). *Technology and aging in America.* Washington, DC: U.S. Government Printing Office.

Parasuraman, R., & Giambra, L. (1991). Skill development in vigilance: Effects of event rate and age. *Psychology and Aging, 6,* 155–170.

Park, D. C. (1994). Aging, cognition, and work. *Human Performance, 7,* 181–205.

Peterson, D., & Coberly, S. (1989). The older worker: Myths and realities. In R. Morris & S. A. Bass (Eds.), *Retirement reconsidered: Economic and social roles for older people* (pp. 116–128). New York: Springer Publishing Co.

Powell, M. (1973). Age and occupational change among coal miners. *Occupational Psychology, 47,* 37–49.

Rabbitt, P. (1997). The Alan Welford Memorial Lecture – Ageing and human skill: A 40th anniversary. *Ergonomics, 40,* 962–981.

Rappaport, A. M., & Plumley, P. (1989). Changing demographic profiles in maturing societies. In R. Morris and S. A. Bass (Eds.), *Retirement reconsidered: economic and social roles for older people* (pp. 35–58). New York: Springer Publishing Co.

Rhodes, S. R. (1983). Age-related differences in work attitudes and behavior: A review and conceptual analysis. *Psychological Bulletin, 93,* 328–367.

Rogers, W. A., Fisk, A. D., Mead, S. E., Walker, N., & Cabrera, E. F. (1996). Training older adults to use automatic teller machines. *Human Factors*, *38*, 425–433.

Salthouse, T. A. (1984). Effects of age and skill in typing, *Journal of Experimental Psychology: General*, *113*, 345–371.

Salthouse, T. A. (1985). Speed of behavior and its implication for cognition. In J. E. Birren and K. W. Schaie (Eds.), *Handbook of the Psychology of Aging* (2nd ed.) (pp. 400–426) New York: Van Nostrand Reinhold.

Salthouse, T. A. (1996). Constraints on theories of cognitive aging. *Psychonomic Bulletin & Review*, *3*, 287–299.

Salvendy, G. (1972). Effects of age on some test scores on production criteria. *Studia Psychologica*, *14*, 186–189.

Sauter, S. L., Murphy, L. R., & Hurrell, J. T. (1990). Prevention of work-related psychological disorders: A national strategy proposed by the National Institute for Occupational Safety and Health, *American Psychologist*, *45*, 1146–1158.

Schmidt, F. L., Hunter, J. E., Outerbridge, A. N., & Goff, S. (1988). Joint relation of experience and ability with job performance: Tests of three hypotheses. *Journal of Applied Psychology*, *73*, 46–57.

Smith, J., Staudinger, M., & Baltes, P. (1994). Occupational settings facilitating wisdom-related knowledge: The sample case of clinical psychologist. *Journal of Consulting and Clinical Psychology*, *62*, 989–999.

Sparrow, P. R., & Davies, D. R. (1988). Effects of age, tenure, training, and job complexity on technical performance. *Psychology of Aging*, *3*, 307–314.

Stagner, R. (1985). Aging in industry. In J. E. Birren and K. W. Schaie (Eds.), *Handbook of the psychology of aging* (2nd ed.) (pp. 299–332). New York: Van Nostrand Reinhold.

Sterns, H. L., & Barrett, G. V. (1992, August). *Work (paid employment) and aging*. Paper presented at National Institute of Aging Workshop, Bethesda, MD.

Streufert, S., Pogash, R., Piasecki, M., & Post, G. M. (1990). Age and management team performance. *Psychology and Aging*, *5*, 4, 551–559.

Stumpf, P. A., & Rabinowitz, S. (1981). Career stages as a moderator of performance relationships with facets of job satisfaction and role perceptions. *Journal of Vocational Behaviors*, *16*, 282–298.

Ucello, C. E. (1998). *Factors influencing retirement: Their implications for raising retirement age*. American Association of Retired Persons: Washington Public Policy Institute.

U.S. Administration on Aging (1984). *Promoting employment of older workers: A handbook for area agencies on aging*. Washington, D.C.: U.S. Government Printing Office.

Vicente, K. J., Hayes, B. C., & Williges, R. C. (1987). Assaying and isolating individual differences in searching a hierarchical file system. *Human Factors*, *29*, 349–359.

Waldman, D. A., & Avolio, B. J. (1986). Meta-analysis of age differences in job performance, *Journal of Applied Psychology*, *71*, 33–38.

Westerman, S. J., Davies, D. R., Glendon, A. I., Stammer, R. B., & Matthews, G. (1995). Age and cognitive ability as predictors of computerized information retrieval. *Behaviour and Information Technology*, *14*, 313–326.

Zandri, E., & Charness, N. (1989). Training older and younger adults to use software. *Educational Gerontology*, *15*, 615–631.

Twenty-Three

Elder Abuse and Victimization

Kathleen H. Wilber and Dennis P. McNeilly

I. Introduction

Elder abuse is a new topic in this hand-book, reflecting the increasing awareness and study of a variety of situations that fall under the terms *abuse* and *victimiza-tion*. This chapter examines this rapidly evolving area from several different per-spectives. It begins with a definition and delineation of what constitutes elder abuse and victimization. It also clarifies what criteria are used to determine the incidence and prevalence of elder abuse. We then offer a brief history of elder abuse that illustrates the rapid change that has occurred in the field over the last two decades. Notably, although some early assumptions have proven to be mislead-ing, they continue to persist in the litera-ture, in public policy, and in clinical practice. Insights from several perspec-tives lead us to a discussion of competing paradigms and frameworks that offer ex-planations for the etiology and treatment of abuse. We discuss various treatment approaches and note that little is known about their viability. We conclude the chapter with a discussion of future re-search needs.

II. Definitions of Elder Abuse and Victimization

There is no national policy on elder abuse. Rather, each state legislates its own policies on what constitutes abuse and how and by whom it is to be ad-dressed. All states have procedures in place to report elder abuse (Wolf & Li, 1997), although the reporting require-ments, including the range of behaviors and situations that constitute elder abuse, vary from state to state. The ma-jority of states mandate professionals to report known or suspected instances of abuse; a few states make reporting volun-tary based on the judgment of the profes-sional. As we discuss below, concepts of elder abuse have developed from multiple paradigms that include spousal abuse, child abuse and neglect, and financial victimization. Variations in both state policies and conceptual approaches have resulted in a variety of definitions of abuse that make comparisons of policies and across studies problematic. As Wolf (1996) noted, behavior that is labeled abuse in one state may not be considered abuse in another state. To further

Handbook of the Psychology of Aging
Copyright © 2001 by Academic Press.
All rights of reproduction in any form reserved.

complicate matters, there are few existing instruments designed to measure abuse.

Since elder abuse was first recognized as a social problem over two decades ago, inconsistent and shifting definitions have plagued the field. In an effort to address this problem, an advisory committee of experts in elder abuse, including members from the National Committee on Elder Abuse and the National Elder Abuse Incidence Study (NEAIS), analyzed and revised definitions of physical, sexual, emotional, and financial abuse, abandonment, neglect, and self-neglect (Tatara, Thomas, & Cyphers, 1998). Their definitions are provided in Table 23.1.

III. Studies of Incidence and Prevalence

With a few recent exceptions, which we discuss below, most elder abuse studies have relied on small convenience samples of suspected or substantiated abuse that has come to the attention of service providers or protective services (Pillemer & Finkelhor, 1988). Because such studies have not been generalizable, it has been difficult to determine the extent of elder abuse, although it has been suggested that reported cases of elder abuse represent the "tip of the iceberg" (National Center for Elder Abuse [NCEA], 1998). As with other forms of abuse, elder abuse is often difficult to study because reliable information from both victims and perpetrators is not easily obtained (Reis & Nahmiash, 1998). Other factors believed to contribute to keeping elder abuse hidden include victims' fear of social stigma or reprisal, societal ageism, lack of knowledge on the part of victims of where to turn for assistance, and lack of information and intervention protocols for treatment professionals (Quinn & Tomita, 1997). As mentioned above, lack of common definitions across studies also have made it

Table 23.1

1. *Physical abuse*: the use of physical force that may result in bodily injury, physical pain, or impairment. Physical punishments of any kind are examples of physical abuse.

2. *Sexual abuse*: nonconsensual sexual contact of any kind with an elderly person.

3. *Emotional or psychological abuse*: infliction of anguish, pain, or distress.

4. *Financial or material exploitation*: the illegal or improper use of an elder's funds, property, or assets.

5. *Abandonment*: the desertion of an elderly person by an individual who had physical custody or otherwise had assumed responsibility for providing care for an elder or by a person with physical custody of an elder.

6. *Neglect*: refusal or failure to fulfill any part of a person's obligations or duties to an elder.

7. *Self-neglect*: the behaviors of an elderly person that threaten his or her own health or safety. The definition of self-neglect excludes a situation in which a mentally competent older person (who understands the consequences of his or her decisions) makes a conscious and voluntary decision to engage in acts that threaten his or her health or safety.

difficult to determine the extent of elder abuse.

The first studies to develop preliminary estimates of the frequency of elder abuse specific to certain geographic regions were conducted during the late 1970s and early 1980s (see Hudson, 1986, for a review). Typically, these studies queried professionals or older persons themselves about their knowledge of abuse. Sometimes surveys were coupled with retrospective analyses of elder abuse case records. One early study of prevalence (Block & Sinnott, 1979) found that approximately 4% of the older adult population had been victims of elder abuse. Despite the authors' acknowledgment that methodological weaknesses made the statistic unreliable, a 4% prevalence rate was widely used in subsequent articles and policy discussions.

Almost a decade later, the problem of generalizing prevalence from nonprobability samples was addressed with the publication of the first large-scale random sample study of elder abuse (Pillemer & Finkelhor, 1988). This study focused on the physical abuse, psychological abuse (defined as chronic verbal aggression), and neglect of community-residing adults, aged 65 and older, who resided in the Boston metropolitan area. To identify victims, subjects—or in some cases their proxies—were screened for abuse by telephone or in person, with follow-up interviews conducted with identified victims. The study yielded an abuse rate of 32 elders per 1,000 interviews. Two-thirds of identified elder abuse situations involved physical abuse, with spouses identified as the perpetrator in about one-half (51%) of the cases.

The prevalence of elder abuse was informed by a second representative study, a national survey conducted on elder abuse in Canada (Podnieks, 1992; Podnieks, Pillemer, Nicholson, Shillington, & Frizzel, 1990). This study incorporated telephone interviews of a modified random sample of 2008 individuals aged 65 and over. Self-reports by victims were used to identify the prevalence rates of four different types of abuse by others: physical, psychological, neglect, and financial abuse (which had not been a category in the Boston study). Overall prevalence rates, which were surprisingly similar to Block and Sinnott's (1979) study, were found to be 40 cases per 1,000. Financial abuse of older adults, at 25 cases per 1,000, was the most common type of abuse identified. The Canadian study supported Pillemer and Finkelhor's (1988) findings that physical abuse and psychological abuse were most often perpetrated by spouses.

Two additional studies, one in Finland and one in Britain, both found prevalence rates to be about 5% (Wolf, 1996). A study, conducted in Amsterdam, the Netherlands, on a population-based sample (N = 1,797) found that the 1-year prevalence of elder abuse was 5.6%, with verbal aggression the most common type of abuse identified at 3.2%. Financial abuse was found in 1.4% of the older sample; the prevalence of physical aggression was 1.2%, and neglect was .2% of the older adult sample (Hannie, Pot, Smit, Bouter, & Cees, 1998).

Because no large, nationally representative study of the incidence of elder abuse and neglect had ever been conducted in the United States, Congress authorized such a study in 1992 to focus on elder abuse and self-neglect in domestic (e.g., noninstitutional) settings. The National Elder Abuse Incidence Study, completed in 1998, was funded by the U.S. Department of Health and Human Services. The immediate purpose of the study was to estimate the incidence, defined as the number of new cases of elder abuse and neglect, in the United States during 1996. More long-range goals included developing strategies for preventing violence in the home and reducing self-neglect. The study used a nationally representative sample of 20 countries in 15 states. Data were collected from substantiated reports of abuse to adult protective service (APS) agencies responsible for receiving and investigating elder abuse in each county. In addition, key informants or "sentinels" who worked in a variety of community agencies that had frequent contact with older adults were trained to identify abuse (NCEA, 1998). This study estimated that in 1996, among the population of community-residing persons aged 60 and over in the United States, approximately 550,000 experienced abuse, neglect, and/or self-neglect. Of this total, only about one in five cases of abuse or neglect were reported to and substantiated by APS agencies.

Two problems should be noted with the practice of relying on APS as a means to identify the prevalence or incidence of abuse. The first, noted in the NEAIS, is the "tip of the iceberg" problem. This problem suggests that a large proportion of cases go unreported and untreated. A second problem—the possibility that some percentage of reported cases are false positives—tends to be overlooked. For example, a study in North Carolina documented that only 23 (19%) out of 123 reported cases were confirmed (Shiferaw et al., 1994). A study of elder abuse in Illinois and one in Wisconsin found markedly higher rates of verification of abuse reports: 2,577 out of 3,727 reports (69%) in the Illinois study (Neale, Hwalek, Goodrich, & Quinn, 1996) and 1,420 out of 2,489 cases or 57% in the Wisconsin study (Sharon, 1991). In practice, it also is important to bear in mind that persons seen in treatment settings are more likely to be victims of abuse than would be found in a random sample of older adults. For example, in the United States, the prevalence of elder abuse among persons seen in health or social service settings was found to be about 13% (Reis & Nahmiash, 1998).

Finally, following most of the literature, we have discussed abuse by discrete types. However, it is important to point out that more than one type of abuse may occur at the same time. For example, a study by Wolf, Godkin, and Pillemer (1984) found that close to three-quarters (73%) of elder abuse cases involved more than one type of victimization. Similarly, Segal and Iris (1989) noted that a majority of cases in their study (59%) involved multiple types of abuse.

IV. Who Are the Perpetrators?

The present section reviews what is known about categories of abusers. In addition to significant others, organizations, and strangers, we discuss several categories of abuse in which "the self" is the perpetrator.

A. Family Members

Abuse of older adults most often occurs in the context of family relations. For example, results from the NEAIS indicated that family members were the perpetrator in almost 90% of the elder abuse and neglect incidents where the abuser was identified. Two- thirds of perpetrators were spouses or adult children (NCEA, 1998). Other studies support these findings. Pillemer and Finkelhor (1988) in the Boston probability study discussed earlier, noted that older adults were most likely to be abused by persons with whom they lived. Their research indicated that 58% of abusers were spouses compared to 24% who were adult children. To some extent, this finding was attributed to the reality that older adults are more likely to live with spouses than with their adult children. Pittaway and Westhues's (1993) study of elder abuse and neglect of Canadians age 55 and older who had accessed health and social services, found most cases of physical and psychological abuse and all the cases of sexual abuse were committed by spouses.

B. Nonfamily Caregivers

Abuse and neglect in nursing homes was identified as a concern as long ago as the early 1960s, well before elder abuse gained recognition as a societal problem. Yet, there are relatively few studies of abuse in institutional settings. A random sample survey of nurses and nurses aides employed in nursing homes by Pillemer and Moore (1989) indicated that in the preceding year, over one-third (36%) had witnessed an incident of physical abuse, and 10% admitted that they themselves had physically abused a resident. High levels of stress and staff burnout were associated with abuse (Pillemer & Moore, 1989; Pillemer & Moore, 1990). Several studies found that nurses aides, the category of staff who have the most direct patient contact and the least formal training, are the most likely category of abuser among nonfamily caregivers (Office of Inspector General, 1990; Payne & Cikovic, 1995). There also has been research on less overt forms of abuse in nursing homes, including subtle indignities, insensitivities (Nebocat, 1990), and unintended consequences of objectifying elders, under the guise of therapeutic mandates or treatment protocols (e.g., forcing a resident to take a bath, overuse of psychotropic medication).

C. Others

Elder abuse viewed from a domestic violence perspective has tended to overlook the less overt forms of relational exploitation, such as financial abuse (Sprey & Matthews, 1989). Some state statutes refer to the need to protect older adults from "designing persons, swindlers, or their own improvidence" (Wilber, 1990). Other terms used to describe this type of abuse include abuse by a person in a position of trust, undue influence, or fraud. Although such abuse may be committed by family members, we focus here on other acquaintances who either act alone or work with others to separate an older person from his or her money and/or other resources. As Quinn (1998) noted, someone in a position of trust is also in a position to take advantage. Those in a position of trust include persons with a formal financial relationship with the older adult (i.e., bankers, accountants, bookkeepers), as well as other professionals such as psychologists, caregivers, and clergy, all of whom, by virtue of the power they wield, are obliged to serve the best interests of the older adult and to avoid conflict of interest and self-dealing (Kapp, 1999; Quinn, 1998).

Although the magnitude of financial abuse by strangers is not known, one type of abuse, telemarketing fraud against older adults, appears to be a significant and growing problem. Perpetrators of telemarketing fraud have been characterized as clever street psychologists who understand and prey on the fears and needs of their targets by tapping into their victims' emotional Achilles heel (i.e., loneliness, greed, ego, desire to please, need to help, etc.) (Gross, 1999). Current estimates are that fraudulent sales over the telephone cost victims in the United States over 40 billion annually (Federal Bureau of Investigation, 1998). A more extensive discussion of financial abuse is presented later in the chapter.

D. The Self as Perpetrator

At least two areas of elder abuse involve self-destructive behaviors: self-neglect and various forms of addictive behaviors, such as substance abuse and problem gambling. These types of situations raise the question of whether problem behaviors are long-standing or appear related to such areas as cognitive changes from a dementing illnesses, late-life depression, or bereavement.

Self-neglect is the inability of an adult to perform essential self-care activities, including providing for food and shelter, medical care, and general safety (Quinn & Tomita, 1997). Although the NEAIS suggests that self-neglect is the most common types of abuse, it is also the least understood (NCEA, 1998). An extreme form of self-neglect is the Diogenes syndrome, whereby an individual engages in marked social withdrawal, domestic squalor, and severe self-neglect. Diogenes syndrome is often (but not always) characterized by a tendency to hoard excessively and a denial manifested in a resistance to treatment or the accession of the medical care system. Among older adults, compulsive hoarders are most likely to be female, never married, and living alone (Frost, 1999). These individuals most frequently collect newspapers and containers, as well as animals—with an estimated 700–2,000 cases of animal hoarding reported nationally in the United States each year (Patronek, 1999). The majority of animal hoarders are older females in single-person households, who have kept a median number of 39 animals, such as cats, dogs, farm animals, and birds (Patronek, 1999).

Gambling is another area of recent concern for potential abuse among older adults. The growth in popularity and availability of gambling through bingo, lotteries, keno, "pull tabs," instant scratch tickets, and casinos has provided increasing numbers of older adults new forms of entertainment and recreation. Promotional programs offered by casinos and often marketed to older adults include inexpensive meals, free transportation, coupons, slot clubs, bingo days, dance clubs, and discount prescription offers.

The potential public health question of problem gambling among older adults has only recently begun to be examined. Of particular concern to treatment professionals has been a progressive number of older adults who have accessed problem gambling hotlines (Fowler, 1999; Karpin, 1998), and been presented for treatment of affective disorders with underlying problem gambling behaviors (McNeilly & Burke, 2000). Treatment professionals have observed that these individuals appear to gamble as a means to "relieve or escape" their negative dysphoric feelings of isolation, boredom, depression, or to avoid difficult situations.

Few studies have directly investigated older adults and gambling, and those few that have examined this subgroup of the population, have often been drawn from methodologically weak observational data (Campbell, 1976), or were conducted prior to the recent expanded availability of gambling in this country (Kallick, Suits, Deilman, & Hybels, 1979; Li & Smith, 1976, Mok & Hraba, 1991). A more recent study found gambling, specifically bingo followed by casino gambling,

to be the most highly attended social activity for the 6,957 active senior citizens represented, and as reported by the activities directors of senior and retirement centers (McNeilly & Burke, in press).

Although the determination of prevalence rates for problem and pathological gambling in demographic groups considered potentially vulnerable, such as older adults, has yet to be determined, a recent National Gambling Impact Study Commission found an increase in those aged 65 and older who ever gambled between 1975 and 1997 (National Opinion Research Council, 1999). Small studies of older adults have begun to examine the behaviors, attitudes, and levels of depression among older adult gamblers (McNeilly & Burke, 2001), and have found older adults who were sampled at gambling venues were more likely to have higher levels of disordered gambling than older adults from the community, as measured by the South Oaks Gambling Screen-Revised (SOGS-R). The older adult gamblers also cited relaxation, boredom, passing time, and getting away for the day as the most likely reported motivations for their gambling. However, a specific determination has yet to be made as to whether those older adults involved in disordered and/or pathological gambling are new to gambling or lifetime gamblers who have begun to gamble since it has become increasingly available outside of Nevada and Atlantic City.

V. Historical Perspective

In this section, we examine the history of how elder abuse came to be identified as a social problem, compare elder abuse to other types of abuse, and explore the early efforts to identify risk factors for abuse. Our focus includes the period from the 1960s until the end of the twentieth century. Prior to any discussion of this very recently identified problem, it is important to point out that elder abuse and neglect are not new phenomena. Evidence suggests that elder mistreatment has existed across cultures and throughout history. However, it is only recently that this problem has been named and studied, and efforts have been undertaken to provide treatment (Wolf & Pillemer, 1989).

A. Similarities to Child Abuse

Several authors have compared child abuse, spousal abuse, and elder abuse (see, for example, Hudson, 1986, and Wolf & Pillemer, 1989). Chronologically, child abuse was "discovered" first, in the 1960s. By 1968, all 50 states had enacted laws that mandated the reporting of child abuse and provisions for a protective service system for abused children. Wolf and Pillemer (1989) noted that extensive efforts by professionals (i.e., physicians, social workers, attorneys) to define and address the problem of child abuse resulted in legalizing and medicalizing responses and treatment. In contrast, spousal abuse, which was identified as a problem in the 1970s, failed to generate attention from policymakers, legal advocates, or academics. Rather, it gained recognition through the grass roots efforts of victims and feminists, who directly shaped responses and interventions such as the shelter movement. Interest in elder abuse developed in the context of these two dissimilar efforts to address different aspects of abuse and violence.

Although the "discovery" of elder abuse as a social problem did not occur until the mid- to late 1970s, the groundwork was laid a decade earlier, when federal funding established state-based APS programs to provide an array of services to "dependent adults" who needed protection (Wolf, 1999). Wolf and Pillemer (1989) have suggested that because elder abuse was professionally discovered and championed, responses to elder abuse

more closely resemble child abuse than spousal abuse. Given the widespread notion of older adult dependency, it is perhaps not surprising that beliefs about elder abuse and approaches to interventions developed largely from a child abuse paradigm rather than a domestic violence perspective (Baumann, 1989). As with child abuse, initial efforts to intervene focused primarily on mandatory reporting by professionals. Such reports trigger investigations by APS in cases of domestic elder abuse—or the Ombudsman program when the abuse occurs in a long-term care facility. This focus on reporting has served as a mechanism to identify persons at risk and in need of treatment, and created more visibility and awareness of the problem. Such a strategy has not been without controversy, however, particularly related to the concern that resources have been focused too extensively on reporting at the expense of treatment and services (Crystal, 1987).

Despite the similarities, Wolf and Pillemer (1989) have suggested that a key difference in the development of child abuse and elder abuse legislation was timing. Child abuse was discovered during a period of expansion in federal and state spending on social programs. Elder abuse came to the fore during a period of constriction in federal spending on social welfare and an increased emphasis on state responsibility for social programs. During the late 1970s and early 1980s, as programs for older persons expanded, elder abuse was reframed from a public welfare problem to an aging issue (Wolf, 1999) and some support was provided through the Older Americans Act.

B. Efforts to Identify Risk Factors

Elder abuse was first publically mentioned in the United States at a Congressional hearing in 1978 (Wolf &

Pillemer, 1989). This attention resulted in increasing public and policy recognition, including recommendations for research on elder abuse. Hudson (1986) identified and reviewed 29 studies of elder abuse published between 1979 and 1985, noting that, in general, these early studies were exploratory and descriptive. Although as Hudson pointed out, differences in definitions of abuse, sampling, and data collection prevented systematic comparison between the studies, some consistent patterns of risk emerged. In general, these studies suggested that elder abuse resulted from intrafamily violence and emphasized the vulnerability of the victim as a result of advanced age, dependency, and disability. Early pilot studies (e.g., Block & Sinnott, 1979; Lau & Kosberg, 1979; McLaughlin, Nickell, & Gill, 1980; O'Malley, Segars, Perez, Mitchell, & Kneupfel, 1979) consistently found that victims were frail (physically and/or cognitively impaired), primarily women, over the age of 75, who typically lived with their abusers. Because of the greater number of women in the population age 65 and over, it might be expected that more women than men were found in samples of elder abuse victims. Even so, the percentage of women victims in most studies was high (approximately 75–80%). Subsequent studies, however, suggested that the picture was more complicated. For example, findings from the Boston probability study (Pillemer & Finkelhor, 1988) indicated that men had slightly higher absolute rates of victimization than women (52% compared to 48%). The authors attributed this to the fact that, even with fewer men in the population 65 years or older, men have a greater likelihood of living with another, usually a spouse, thus increasing their risk of abuse. Yet, a more recent study by the NCEA (1998) supported findings from the earlier studies that women were more likely to be abused than men. The NCEA results also indicated that the oldest old (80 years and over) were abused and neglected at two to three times their proportion of the older adult population. An explanation for these discrepancies is provided by Pillemer and Finkelhor (1988) who suggested that women tend to suffer more serious forms of abuse, which is more likely to be reported to the authorities. Thus, the conflicting findings on gender may be a result of the increasing proportion of women in older cohorts coupled with greater severity and higher visibility of abuse among women and among oldest old victims.

In addition to examining characteristics of victims, the consensus of the early studies was that abuse typically involved family members who cared for frail elders. As a result, researchers began to consider the role played by caregiver stress and burden. The case was made that family perpetrators of elder abuse most often were overstressed caregivers, typically adult children, unable to cope with the difficulties of caring for a dependent, highly impaired parent. Interestingly, two studies that compared matched samples of abused and nonabused older adults did not find elder dependence to be a risk factor for abuse (Phillips, 1983, and Pillemer, 1985). After separating subjects drawn from caseload reports of public health nurses into abused and nonabused groups, Phillips (1983) found that abused elders had lower expectations and had higher levels of social isolation and depression. Pillemer (1985), as part of a three-state Model Projects Study, using case controls matched by sex and living arrangements, also found that abused elders tended to be more socially isolated. Although Pillemer's sample was similar to that of earlier studies in that it was comprised largely of older women, his research added an interesting twist to the question of dependency. He found a strong association between physical abuse and financial dependency, but the dependency was reversed; the perpetrator was financially dependent on the older adult victim.

Wolf, Strugnell, and Godkin (1982), also using data from the three-state Model Projects Study, identified correlates of abuse with characteristics of the perpetrator such as mental illness, substance abuse, and financial dependence on the victim. Several years later, as part of their work on the prevalence of elder abuse, Pillemer and Finkelhor (1988, 1989) examined two different concepts of abuse: (a) the extent to which caregiver stress generated by caring for dependent older adults explained elder abuse, and (b) the role played by the individual pathology of the abuser. As with the Model Projects research, they found the strongest predictors of abuse were the abuser's deviant behavior such as substance abuse, personality disorders, and perpetrator dependency on the victim.

Using Pillemer and Finkelhor's (1988) prevalence rates, a study of risk factors for violent abuse among community-dwelling Alzheimer patients and their primary caregivers found that cognitively impaired older persons with Alzheimer's disease had 2.5 times greater risk for abuse than the community-based probability sample (Paveza et al., 1992). When both caregiver and care receiver were considered, 17.4% reported violent behavior by one or both parties in the year since diagnosis. Risk factors were not related to characteristics of the care receiver, all of whom had AD, but rather to caregiver characteristics (depression) and living arrangements (living with another). In addition to caregivers as perpetrators, this study suggested that persons caring for family members with dementing illnesses may themselves be at high risk of violent behavior from the care receiver (Paveza et al., 1992).

A study of elder abuse in Illinois that focused specifically on the role of substance abuse by the perpetrator (Hwalek, Neale, Goodrich, & Quinn, 1996) noted important differences between cases where substance abuse was and was not an issue. Substance abuse, which was found in 13% of cases, was more prevalent among male adult children who were not in a caregiving role. Abuse cases where perpetrator substance abuse was identified was more likely to involve physical or emotional abuse and less likely to involve neglect.

Over the last two decades, studies of risk factors for abuse have yielded conflicting results. Inconsistent findings have been attributed to methodological shortcomings, including the cross-sectional and retrospective nature of elder abuse research. To determine longitudinal risk factors for abuse prospectively, Lachs, Williams, O'Brien, Hurst, and Horwitz (1997) linked 9-year longitudinal data from the Established Populations for Epidemiologic Studies in the Elderly (EPESE) with protective service records of abuse. Identified risk factors included age, poverty, race, functional and cognitive impairment, particularly the onset of new cognitive impairment, and living with someone. Gender was not a risk factor. The authors noted that the protective service system focus of the study may have resulted in overestimation of race and poverty as risk factors. They advise clinicians to be alert to high-risk situations in which functional and/or cognitive impairment are evident.

VI. Theories and Concepts

Elder abuse, rather than falling under a single framework, is multidimensional and multidisciplinary, reflecting an array of divergent ideas (Harbison, 1999). To some extent these varied perspectives reflect different views about the extent to which elder abuse is similar to other types of family violence or is related to characteristics of aging, specifically age-related dependency. In this section we discuss several models of elder abuse, including the situational stress model, transgenerational violence, double direction violence, psychopathology of the perpetrator, and social exchange. We then compare the models to empirical evidence from recent studies. Finally, we discuss the need to expand the theoretical perspectives to include unique dynamics found in financial abuse as well as factors related to self-neglect.

A. The Situational Stress Model

One of the most popular and intuitively appealing theories of elder abuse (Quinn & Tomita, 1997), the Situational Stress Model, has its roots in social-psychological concepts derived from child abuse and intrafamily violence. According to this perspective, elder abuse results when overburdened caregivers who suffer from the overwhelming stress related to caregiving take out their frustrations on the person requiring care (Phillips, 1986). The notion that high levels of stress coupled with inappropriate coping skills result in abuse fits with similar ideas of child abuse. Over the years, additional support for this perspective came from elder abuse reports to state protective service agencies, which indicated that adult children caregivers, most often daughters, were abusing or neglecting frail older adults (Wolf, 1998) or both. Yet, as we discussed in the section on risk factors, empirical evidence has not supported the premise that increased levels of caregiver stress and burden, per se, is associated with abuse (Wolf & Pillemer, 1989).

B. Transgenerational Violence

The transgenerational violence model of elder abuse suggests that violent behavior learned within the family is transmitted from one generation to the next. According to this view, abusers grow up in violent families only to reenact the parent–child cycle of violence once the dependency roles shift from child to parent. Caregivers may also seek to settle scores by punishing past injustices (Phillips, 1986). Transgenerational violence builds upon findings that perpetrators of domestic violence are more likely to have grown up in violent homes where they witnessed spousal abuse and/or were victims of child abuse themselves. Moreover, battered women, as well as their abusers, are more likely to batter their children. The rate of transmission of abusive violence from one generation to the next is estimated to be about 30% compared to a 3% rate of abusive violence in the general population (Quinn & Tomita, 1997). Despite its strong support in the family violence literature, there is little evidence to support transgenerational violence in studies of elder abuse. One of the few studies to investigate the link found no association between physical punishment as a child and becoming a perpetrator of elder abuse as an adult (Wolf & Pillemer, 1989). Wolf and Pillemer (1989) noted that conceptually there is a different dynamic at work in that previously abused adult children who abuse elderly parents have experienced child abuse not elder abuse. Thus, rather than a "cycle of violence," they are responding with direct, albeit delayed, retaliation.

C. Double-Directional Violence

Double-directional violence describes interactions between the caregiver and older care receiver in which both parties are abusive. Steinmetz (1988), who coined the term, noted that some families attempt to control each other by screaming or hitting. Caregivers also may use force to administer treatment, threaten to use force, or use intimidation by threatening to send the older person to a nursing home. Steinmetz's research suggested that much of the overt violence was single direction, perpetrated by the care receiver. Older adult care receivers were more likely to hit, slap, or throw objects (22%) than caregivers who used this approach 3% of the time. Some corroboration for Steinmetz's findings was provided by several more recent studies. In research on care receivers with dementia (Paveza et al., 1992) discussed earlier, the prevalence of violent behavior between caregivers and care receivers was 15.8% by care receivers and 5.4% by caregivers; 3.8% of caregiver–care receiver pairs experiencing two-way violence. Similarly, Pillemer and Suitor (1992) found that caregiver violence was associated with violence on the part of the care receiver.

D. Psychopathology of the Perpetrator

As indicated in the section on risk factors, although early studies supported the notion that elder dependency and caregiver stress were major factors in elder abuse, more recent studies, particularly those that used comparison group study designs, have found that risk is associated with characteristics of the abuser. Problem behaviors such as substance abuse, mental disorders, and *abuser* dependency on the victim have been shown to be related to abuse. For example, Anetzberger, Korbin, and Austin (1994) found that caregiver abusers were more likely to be identified as problem drinkers. K. Quinn, Hwalek, and Goodrich (1993) found that substance abuse of the perpetrator was associated with the victim remaining at high risk of further abuse over time.

In one study, Wolf and Pillemer (1989) found that approximately two-thirds of perpetrators of physical abuse were financially dependent on their victims. They further noted that abusers of older adults are more likely to suffer from psychological problems, such as mental disorders or substance abuse or to be developmentally disabled, than the general population and even than perpetrators of

domestic violence. A related idea, offered by Quinn and Tomita (1997) is that some abusers may represent a population that was formerly institutionalized. In the absence of adequate resources in the community, they are dependant on their parents for support. When adult children with severe mental disorders turn to aging parents, it raises the question of who is really the caregiver.

E. Social Exchange Theory

Social exchange is built on the idea of reciprocity or a fair distribution of rewards within relationships. According to this perspective, expectations within relationships are that patterns of exchange are mutually beneficial and that each person in a relationship has both rights to receive benefits and responsibilities to contribute. Imbalances in social exchange indicate power imbalances in the relationship. Individuals within relationships try to maximize rewards and minimize punishments. Some individuals, by virtue of dependency or lack of resources, may violate the norms of reciprocity in that they are powerless, vulnerable, and have little to contribute. In some situations, lack of reciprocity may be justification for abuse. Yet, because of psychological, social, or economic dependancy, the older adult may believe that he or she has little choice but to maintain the relationship. In such situations, the party with the most power has little to lose by being unjust (Phillips, 1986). Aging affects this equation in two ways. First, older individuals may have less access to obtaining exchange resources. Second, as a result of ageism, older adults may feel devalued and have lower social status (Finkelhor & Pillemer, 1988). Lower social status implies that the older individual is a less attractive partner in the relationship or even a burden who must provide higher levels of compensation as part of the exchange bargain. Although older adults typically control their financial resources, some may have fewer options to choose alternative relationships. Moreover, abusers may attempt to exert greater control by socially isolating the older adult, thus reducing further other options and limiting interventions.

F. Empirical Evidence

Although intuitively appealing, recent research suggests that the assumptions of caregiver stress and abuse should be re-examined. One area that merits further attention is that the quality of the relationship prior to caregiving is an important factor (Homer & Gilleard, 1990). Although caregiving may result in high levels of emotional distress and burden, studies have not supported the notion that elder dependency per se leads to abuse (Hamel et al., 1990). Several studies reviewed by Wolf (1998), as well as those discussed in this chapter in the section on double-direction violence, suggest that one trigger for abuse may be abusiveness of the care receiver toward the caregiver. Studies have supported the notion that characteristics of the abuser, particularly psychopathology and financial dependency of the abuser on the victim, are risk factors for abuse (Quinn et al., 1993; Wolf & Pillemer, 1989). It is interesting that the social exchange model is actually reversed in research that shows abuser dependency on the caregiver. One explanation is that when the abuser feels powerless, he or she compensates by abusive behavior.

Building on two decades of elder abuse literature, a study by Reis and Nahmiash (1998) examined two types of abuse indicators, characteristics of the caregiver and characteristics of the care receiver or victim. Caregiver characteristics included substance abuse, cognitive impairment, mental disorders, lack of experience in caregiving, economic difficulties, abused as a child, stress, social isolation, blaming others or lacking empathy, hypercritical attitude, lacking understanding, unrealistic expectations, financial dependency, involved in other family or marital conflict, reluctant to give care. Characteristics of the victim included being older, female, dependent, alcohol abuser, socially isolated, a history of past abuse, other family or marital conflicts, difficult behavior (e.g., demanding, unappreciative), and unrealistic expectations. From these indicators, 48 items were listed for a preliminary screen that discriminated abuse from nonabuse. Of these, 27 problems and 2 demographic characteristics formed a scale that was successful in discriminating abuse from nonabuse cases 78–84% of the time. Problems comprising the screen include (a) intrapersonal problems of the caregiver (substance abuse, mental disorder, behavior problems), (b) interpersonal problems of the caregiver (e.g., family or marital conflict, poor relationship with care receiver), and (c) social characteristics of the care receiver (e.g., lack of social support, past abuse). The authors note that the pathology of the caregiver is the most salient red flag of abuse. Other key indicators include social isolation, past abuse of the victim, and financial dependency of the abuser.

G. Financial Elder Abuse

Paradigms of elder abuse derived from child abuse and domestic violence do not explain financial elder abuse, particularly abuse that occurs outside the family. Financial abuse generally occurs when the perpetrator uses a position of trust to further his or her own ends. Typically the strategy used is subtle persuasion, misrepresentation, or psychological manipulation to substitute the will of the abuser with the authentic desires of the victim (Wilber & Reynolds, 1996). Through the use of a personal relationship with the older adult, the perpetrator may persuade the victim to change his or her will, grant expensive gifts, deed over the home or other property, or make the perpetrator the beneficiary of a trust.

In addition to individual abusers who build a trusting relationship over time, organizations may engage in financial abuse. These include fraudulent home repair businesses, bogus sweepstakes companies, and telemarketing fraud. Telemarketing fraud includes fraudulent investment opportunities, pyramid schemes, credit repair scams, phony charities, land swindles, and insurance fraud. Many of these forms of abuse involve prizes that can only be "awarded" if the recipient sends a check to "release" their prize (Schuett & Burke, 2000). For example, the second author was introduced to the problem of elder abuse by an 82-year-old client in the early stages of Alzheimer's disease whose family referred her for mental health treatment. This woman spent between $65,000–$100,000 on various sweepstakes entries and magazine subscriptions in order to increase her chances of winning several sweepstakes and lotteries. She increasingly refused to leave her home, because she did not want to miss the "prize patrol" who she believed might stop by to award her prize "at any time." Older adults may be the target of such schemes because perpetrators view them as affluent, easily accessible (more likely to be at home), more likely to be socially isolated or lacking someone with whom to discuss the proposed purchase, more likely to suffer from cognitive impairment, more trusting, and less likely to recognize and to report fraud (Gross, 1999; Shadel & T., 1994).

VII. The Treatment of Elder Abuse

To effectively address elder abuse, it is necessary to understand the underlying causes of mistreatment and the consequences of abuse. Given the lack of common definitions, conflicting models of abuse, and the relative newness of the field, it is not surprising that interventions to both avoid and address abuse have not been well studied (Gross, 1999; Quinn & Tomita, 1997). For this reason, much of what we discuss in this section is descriptive rather than evaluative.

Most studies have focused on the prevalence or incidence of abuse rather than the damage caused by the abuse, the severity and intensity of the mistreatment, and what type of help is required (Comijs, Pot, Smit, & Jonkers, 1998). Because research by Comijs et al. (1998) found that a majority of victims were able to take steps on their own to stop abuse, they suggested that treatment should be focused on those (43% in their study) who are not able to stop the abuse or to seek out effective remedies. Griffin (1999) takes this idea of abuse one step further by cautioning that researchers and professionals run the risks of mislabeling the problem and developing ineffective treatments if they fail to understand how older adults perceive, define, experience, and address elder abuse. She stressed the importance of understanding the role of cultural diversity and the cultural context in which beliefs and attitudes about abuse are formed. Focusing on cultural diversity, Rittman, Kuzmeskys, and Flum (1999) suggested that failure to understand culturally based beliefs about the importance of the community or family versus the individual may result in inaccurate identification of abuse and ineffective approaches for addressing abuse. For example, in a cross-cultural study in which older women were asked questions about behaviors presented in a series of vignettes, Korean-American women were much less likely than African-American or Caucasian women to view a situation as abusive and more likely to focus on family harmony (Moon & Williams, 1993). This study also found that a higher percentage of African Americans than Caucasians or Korean Americans identified situations as abusive. As these results suggest, different strategies may be necessary to prevent and address abuse in different communities (Benton, 1999).

Earlier in this chapter, we presented several models for conceptualizing elder abuse. In considering interventions, it is important to point out that each model suggests different approaches. For example, the caregiver stress model evokes sympathy for the abuser and suggests intervention aimed at stress reduction and caregiver support. Similarly, assumptions in the transgenerational and double-directional violence model suggest focusing on family counseling and support. In contrast, a focus on the pathology of the perpetrator is more likely to lead to criminalization of elder abuse and criminal justice solutions. Finally, social exchange theory implies a need for social support as well as efforts to combat ageism and the devaluation of older adults.

Another issue in designing and implementing treatment strategies to address the broad area of elder abuse is that different types of abuse (i.e., physical abuse, financial abuse, neglect) are likely to require different types of interventions (Podnieks, 1992; Podnieks, Pillemer, Nicholson, Shillington & Frizzel, 1990). For example, treatments aimed at addressing family violence are quite different from those developed to deal with telemarketing fraud. Given the lack of conceptual clarity and conflicting definitions, it is not surprising that there are a number of different approaches to prevention, detection, and treatment. In this section we focus on several of the most prominent efforts, including abuse reporting and investigation, training and interdisciplinary collaboration, protective placement, the legal system, and mental health services.

A. Reporting and Investigation

Building on state policies to address child abuse, all states have enacted laws concerning the identification and reporting of elder abuse. Most states mandate that professionals report abuse of dependent adults to designated protective services agencies or law enforcement. In a handful of states, reporting is left to the discretion of the professional. Some states use age as a proxy for need by specifically identifying persons over a certain age (e.g., 60 or 65) as a protected class. Other states use the category "dependent adult" as the protected category with the understanding that older adults with cognitive or physical impairments that make them vulnerable to abuse are included.

Once abuse is reported, an investigation is undertaken to substantiate the abuse. Neale, Hwalek, Goodrich, and Quinn (1996), in their study of the Illinois APS system, found that the average amount of time spent on an investigation before verifying that abuse had occurred was 388 minutes (over 6 hours). In cases where abuse was verified (approximately two-thirds of reported cases), workers spent an average of 668 additional minutes (about 11 hours) per case.

In addition to reporting laws and designated investigating agencies, the majority of states have enacted legislation that criminalizes abuse and neglect by paid caregivers in institutional settings (MacLean, 1999). Because laws vary by state, it is important for mental health professionals to become familiar with the relevant state laws (Kapp, 1999). To ensure that reporting is effective, health and mental health professionals and others who are in positions to identify victims of abuse need training on risk factors, what to look for, and how to report identified problems.

B. Education, Training, and Collaborative Efforts

Efforts have been undertaken to increase awareness and reduce barriers to reporting and treatment among a variety of professionals. Examples include emergency room physicians (Clarke & Pierson, 1999), primary care physicians (Krueger & Patterson, 1997), social work students (Wolf & Pillemer, 1994), judges (American Bar Association, 1996; American Bar Association 1997), and bank officers (Price & Fox, 1997). Education efforts also have been undertaken to help older adults and the public in general avoid and address abuse. For example, the American Psychological Association (APA) has developed a brochure for the general public available through its web site (APA, 1999). AARP has developed films and consumer education materials to help older consumers recognize and prevent abuse situations in the home (AARP, 1992) and to avoid telemarketing fraud (AARP, 1997). Other consumer education efforts aimed at preventing telemarketing fraud have expanded rapidly in recent years, including general education efforts directed toward potential victims, education of service providers including bank personnel, reverse "boiler-rooms" in which law enforcement and volunteers contact identified victims of "hit lists" and warn them about scams (Gross, 1999), and the development of money management programs targeting at-risk older adults (Wilber & Buturain, 1993).

In addition to educating consumers and professionals, multidisciplinary teams comprised of individuals with different areas of expertise are increasingly used to address complex elder abuse cases. For example, Dyer et al. (1999) described a hospital-based geriatric assessment team developed to address the problem of elder neglect that includes caseworkers from APS. Wolf and Pillemer (1994) discussed a multidisciplinary team composed of a variety of professionals who met monthly to review and assess multiproblem multiagency elder abuse cases. The team focused on cases that require clarification of agency roles and case disagreements between agencies, recommendations for

nontypical cases and those that defied resolution, and consultation on legal and medical questions not otherwise available. To address financial abuse, Los Angeles has developed the Fiduciary Abuse Specialist Team that brings together police, case managers, attorneys, APS workers, and other service providers in a monthly case conference (Hankin, Flanagan, Zuzga, Babcock, & Reyes, 1994). Benefits of multidisciplinary teams include avoiding situations in which there is too little or too much agency involvement, the promotion of a family systems approach to case conceptualization and treatment, the introduction of service providers to one another, and the production of a comprehensive care plan (Wolf & Pillemer, 1994).

C. Protective Placement

With the exception of restraining orders against the perpetrator, protective interventions generally focus on removing the older person from the home and/or placing him or her under guardianship. Such restrictions, which are similar to remedies used to combat child abuse, raise ethical questions about autonomy and self-determination when the victim is an adult. Involuntary placement and guardianship rely on the power of *parens patriae*, which authorizes the state to protect persons who lack capacity to protect themselves from harm. Yet, approaches that let the abuser remain at large while institutionalizing and/or placing the older adult under guardianship appear to punish the victim and run counter to basic rights of client self-determination. In addition, anecdotal evidence suggests that fear of such interventions may contribute to victims' resistance to ask for or to accept help. Interestingly, in one study, older adults whose abuse was substantiated were more likely to refuse service than those whose abuse was unsubstantiated (Sharon, 1991). There also is some evidence that older adults are unlikely to use less restrictive approaches such as shelters for battered women (Vinton, 1992) and that shelters specifically designed for older persons are rare.

In pursuing protective interventions, a general guideline is that freedom trumps safety unless the individual lacks the capacity to make a reasoned decision (Quinn & Tomita, 1997). This is because, in contrast to minor children, mentally competent adults have the right to refuse investigation and treatment. In practice, given the complexity of the problem of assessing risk and capacity, reporting elder abuse to APS and the use of multi-disciplinary teams to assess high-risk situations offer potential safeguards.

When safety is the primary goal, protective interventions have been found to reduce risk for some. For example, research that analyzed statewide elder abuse data from Illinois indicated that the most frequent reason for case closure (29% of the 552 substaintiated cases that were closed) was that the victim entered a nursing home (Neale et al., 1996). An additional 24% of those offered placement ($n = 96$) refused, and 53% of those offered housing services ($n = 64$) refused. Findings sugested that neglect cases were more likely than other forms of abuse to result in improvement (defined as reduced risk or no longer at risk), because victims of neglect were most likely to be placed in skilled nursing facilities (Quinn et al. 1993).

D. The Legal System

In addition to protective interventions, the legal system offers remedy through both criminal and civil law suits. In describing the role of a legal service program for older adults, Eisenberg (1991) suggested that the initial interview should focus on information (i.e., rights and recourse) and protection (i.e., placing assets beyond the reach of a third party; actions to remedy past abuses) to ensure that the

abuser does not take control and thwart the attorney's efforts. Recently the legal system has also been used in several states to bring class-action suits against fraudulent telemarketing organizations.

Traditionally, the role of protective services has been to focus on the needs of victims, rather then ensuring that perpetrators avoid victimizing others through criminal prosecution (Wolf, 1999). Increasingly, however, local and state prosecutors have moved to protect abuse victims by criminally prosecuting abusers. Unfortunately, in many areas, criminalization becomes a default approach because effective treatments for perpetrators have been rare and alternatives such as psychotherapy, education or problem-solving interventions, and enhanced social supports have received little attention. Although behavioral problems of abusers (e.g., substance abuse, financial dependency, poor coping skills) create difficult challenges for APS workers, providing services to both parties has the potential to reduce risk. For example, Quinn et al. (1993) noted that one unanticipated finding of their research was the importance of providing medical and psychiatric services treatment to the abuser to reduce risk to the victim. Also, such approaches may be more acceptable to victims, who may be less willing to cooperate if criminal prosecutions is the outcome. Nevertheless, studies of the efficacy of abuser treatment are lacking.

E. Mental Health Treatment Issues

Several cross-sectional studies have suggested that elder abuse is associated with depression (Comijs et al., 1999; Dyer, Pavlik, Murphy, & Hyman, 2000) and cognitive impairment of the victim (Dyer, Pavlik, Murphy & Hyman, 2000). Moreover, studies have found that victims of elder abuse had higher levels of psychological distress than a comparison group of nonvictims (Comijs al., 1999). Although mental health services would seem to be an important means to address problems of elder abuse, few empirical studies have been conducted on mental health interventions. A study by Neale et al. (1996) on elder abuse services in Illinois found relatively few referrals to mental health services. Of 552 substantiated cases with treatment data, there were 52 referrals for mental health services; more than half (54%) of those referred refused the service. As we discussed earlier in our introduction to this section, victims may not perceive mental health services as a treatment for elder abuse.

A number of studies have identified lack of social support as a risk factor for abuse. Although a study by Comijs et al. (1998) indicated that victims typically do not seek help from family or friends, subsequent research (Comijs et al., 1999) found that elder abuse victims with higher levels of social support had less psychological distress. Wolf and Pillemer (1994) described two "best practice" models of social support, a peer group and self-help group. In the first, volunteers aged 60 and over were recruited from AARP membership lists and assigned to those who had experienced or were at risk for abuse, neglect, or self-neglect. Benefits included the supplemental emotional and concrete support the peer volunteers provided to the elder abuse clients, and the improved self-awareness volunteers obtained through their participation with elder-abuse victims. The elder- abuse victim support group model of intervention (Wolf & Pillemer, 1994) recruited individuals 60 and older identified through community agencies or hospital outpatient and inpatient departments as victims of abuse and neglect inflicted by a family member. Members of the victim support group were extensively screened and provided transportation to the 10-member 10-session cycle meetings facilitated by two co-leaders. In addition, a buddy system was used where each group member kept in contact and provided support to another member. Benefits to group members included an eased sense of isolation, buffered feelings of victimization and a stronger sense of control, increased socialization, and prevention or decreased frequency and severity of abuse.

VIII. Current Issues and Suggestions for Further Research

The field of elder abuse is a relatively new area for research. Like many new areas, studies have been largely descriptive, cross-sectional, and based on convenience samples. Recent efforts to expand knowledge of elder abuse suggest a number of areas in which additional research is needed. Although considerable progress has been made over the last two decades, research should continue to focus on the etiology of elder abuse. As our discussion about the conceptual underpinnings of elder abuse suggest, more studies are needed that test underlying dynamics of abuse. Particularly useful are multimodel studies as illustrated in the work of Reis and Nahmiash (1998). Moreover, building on their work by refining instruments to screen for elder abuse from identified risk factors should help to better target resources and test strategies to prevent and treat abuse. In addition, more longitudinal studies are needed to explore how relationships change over time and to identify the precursors and consequences of abuse. One of the issues that requires further clarification is the extent to which elder abuse reflects domestic violence and exploitive patterns over the life course versus the extent to which various types of abuse are associated with late-life change, particularly disease associated with late life that increase dependency. Another related area is the consequences of abuse. For example, a recent study indicated that community-residing victims of abuse had higher rates of mortality even after controlling for other factors associated with increased mortality (Lachs et al., 1998). The underlying reasons for this finding are unclear but certainly merit further attention.

As we discussed earlier, evidence suggests that problem gambling may be increasing among older adults. Thus, there is a need for a national study of this potential source of financial abuse among older adults. Important in such research would be a distinction between recent versus lifetime older problem and pathological gamblers, and a finer distinction of the behaviors associated with problem vs. pathological gambling in older adults that is described in the *DSM-IV* (APA, 1994) distinction of abuse versus dependence and found in the substance abuse literature.

Research also is needed to evaluate the effectiveness of interventions. Strategies to reduce elder abuse include both prevention and treatment. Treatment may focus on the victim, the perpetrator, or more broadly on the relationship between victim and abuser. Little is known about the effectiveness of either preventive strategies or treatment approaches. Nor have studies been conducted on the effectiveness of various public policies, such as mandatory reporting, designating elders as a protected class, or increasing the penalties for abuse. Such research requires efforts to identify and ultimately measure the outcomes of various interventions. In the area of prevention, education has been a prominent strategy to reduce victimization. Although intuitively appealing, there have been no studies of the effectiveness of educational approaches in reducing abuse. Related to the effectiveness of interventions, attention is beginning to be directed toward culture and the implications of cultural preferences. This is a promising area in that cultural preferences affect how abuse is defined and what treatment approaches may be most

accepted. A related area is the question of values. For example, within the broad definitions of abuse, what specific behaviors are considered abuse or not abuse and does this vary among researchers, practitioners, older adults, and the populations at large? Another dimension of preferences and values is the role that religious institutions play in the identification and treatment of abuse. Anecdotal evidence suggests that some churches are offering financial management services to older adults at risk of abuse. Future research might be directed at the extensiveness and effectiveness of such services as well as the role that church and community support play in addressing victimization. Ultimately, effective approaches to prevent and to treat abuse require a better understanding of the problem and preferred remedies from the experiences, perceptions, and preferences of older adult victims and those at risk of abuse.

IX. The Challenge to Psychologists

Social, cognitive, and clinical psychologists, particularly those trained in gerontology, have much to offer to efforts to address the problems of elder abuse and neglect. The role of cognitive impairment as a risk factor for abuse, particularly decreased executive functioning and decision-making abilities, memory, and judgment has not been well understood or evaluated. Interviews with perpetrators suggest that older persons who are cognitively compromised are more likely to be targeted for financial scams, though little is known about the level at which an individual's cognitive impairment increases their risk for telemarketing, sweepstakes, and lottery scams. Other research (Lachs et al., 1997) suggests that new cognitive impairment is a risk factor for abuse. Nevertheless, the relationship between cognitive impairment and risk is unclear and requires further study. For example, as a first step to address this issue, Wilber and her colleagues have recently launched a study to test the hypothesis that impaired executive functioning is associated with both financial abuse and self-neglect. Impaired executive functioning may also play a role in problem gambling, telemarketing, lottery and sweepstakes scams, which should be tested by research on risk factors for problems in these areas. For example, a study recently undertaken by McNeilly and Burke has begun to initially clarify and identify the risk factors for disordered gambling behaviors among older adults new to gambling versus lifetime gamblers.

In addition to a focus on the individual, elder abuse is also symptomatic of relationships and family dynamics gone awry. As such, there is a need for elder abuse research grounded in social and family systems contexts. More work is needed to understand elder abuse in terms of family systems dynamics, the role of underlying family stressors, and how family and social norms and values affect attitudes and practices related to abuse. Social support has been found to buffer the negative affects of abuse; continued work in this area offers the promise of developing better treatment approaches. Both social isolation and living with others are risk factors for abuse. Research by social psychologists is needed to sort out these somewhat paradoxical issues and improve our understanding of how both supportive and dysfunctional relationships relate to abuse.

Clinical psychologists play a central role in furthering assessment knowledge and building theory to improve the treatment of elder abuse. As we have noted, the development and systematic evaluation of effective treatment has received little attention. Currently, practitioners lack the tools to adequately treat elder abuse because there has been a void in the development of systematically evaluated educational and therapeutic interventions, for both victims and perpetrators. Unfortunately, criminal justice solutions for abusers and protective interventions (i.e., guardianship, institutionalization) are too often the default treatments available to victims. Given these approaches, it is not surprising that many victims refuse to participate in investigation or interventions.

After more than two decades of research, the basic descriptive groundwork has been laid and a number of lessons have been learned about risk factors associated with abuse and the extent of the problem. We believe that it is now necessary to move to more effective approaches to address the problems discussed in this chapter. The complexities of elder abuse require a multidisciplinary research focus. Participation and leadership by psychologists in this effort, particularly those attuned to the needs of older adults, are essential to meet the challenge of addressing the complex problem of elder abuse.

References

AARP (1992). *Abused elders or older battered women?* Report on AARP Forum, October 29–30. Washington, DC: Author

AARP (1997). *Don't fall for a telephone line* (Video). Washington, DC: Author.

American Bar Association. (1996). *Recommended guidelines for state courts handling cases involving elder abuse.* Washington, DC: American Bar Association

American Bar Association. (1997). *Elder abuse in the state courts: Three curricula for judges and court staff.* Washington, DC: American Bar Association.

American Psychiatric Association. (1994). *Diagnostic and statistical manual of mental disorders* (4th ed.) Washington, DC: American Psychiatric Press.

American Psychological Association (1999). *Elder abuse and neglect: In search of solutions.* [on-line] Available: http://www.apa. org/pi/aging/onlinebr.html

Anetzberger, G. T., Korbin, J. E., & Austin, C. (1994). Alcoholism and elder abuse. *Journal of Interpersonal Violence, 9*, 184–193.

Baumann, E. A. (1989). Research rhetoric and the social construction of elder abuse. In J. Best (Ed.), *Images of issues: Typifying contemporary social problems*, (pp. 55–74). New York: Aldine de Gruyter.

Benton, D. M. (1999). African Americans and elder mistreatment: Targeting information for a high-risk population In T. Tatara (Ed.), *Understanding elder abuse in minority populations* (pp. 49–64). Philadelphia, PA: Taylor & Francis.

Block, M. R., & Sinnott, J. D. (1979). *The battered elder syndrome: An exploratory study.* College Park, MD: University of Maryland, Center on Aging.

Campbell, F. F. (1976). The future of gambling. *The Futurist* (10), Bethesda: MD World Future Society.

Clarke, M. E., & Pierson, W. (1999). Management of elder abuse in the emergency department. *Emergency Medicine Clinics of North America, 17*, 631–644.

Comijs, H. C., Penninx, R. W. J. H., Knipscheer, K. P. M., & van Tilburg, W. (1999). Psychological distress in victims of elder mistreament: The effects of social support and coping. *Journal of Gerontolog: Psychological Sciences, 54B*, 240–245.

Comijs, H. C., Pot, A. M., Smit, J. H., & Jonker, C. (1998). Elder abuse in the community: Prevalence and consequences. *Journal of the American Geriatrics Society, 46*, 885–888.

Crystal, S. (1987). Elder abuse: The latest "crisis." *The Public Interest, 88*, 56–66.

Dyer, C. B., Pavlik, V. N., Murphy, K. P., & Hyman, D. J. (2000). The high prevalence of depression and dementia in elder abuse and neglect. *Journal of the American Geriatrics Society. 48*, 205–208.

Dyer, C. B., Gleason, M. S., Murphy, K. P., Pavlik, V. N., Portal, B., Regev, T., & Hyman, D. J. (1999). Treating elder neglect: Collaboration between a geriatrics assessment team and adult protective services. *Southern Medical Journal, 92*, 242–244.

Eisenberg, H. B. (1991). Combating elder abuse through the legal process. *Journal of Elder Abuse and Neglect, 3*, 65–94.

Federal Bureau of Investigation. (1998). *FBI's major investigations—Operation double barrel—telemarketing crime problem.* [Online] Available: http://www.fbi.gov

Finkelhor, D., & Pillemer, K. (1988). Elder abuse: Its relationship to other forms of domestic violence. In G. T. Hotaling, D. Finkelhor, J. T. Kirkpatrick, & M. A. Strauss (Eds.), *Family abuse and its consequences: New directions in research* (pp. 224–254). Newbury Park: Sage.

Fowler, P. (1999). *Hot-line accession rates by seniors.* Executive Director, Florida Council on Compulsive Gambling, Unpublished raw data.

Frost, R. (1999). Unmarried status linked to more severe hoarding symptoms. *Clinical Psychiatry News, 27*, 25.

Griffin, L. W. (1999). Elder maltreatment in the African American community: You just don't hit our momma!!! In T. Tatara (Ed.), *Understanding elder abuse in minority populations* (pp. 27–48). Philadelphia, PA: Taylor & Francis.

Gross, E. A. (1999). *Telemarketing fraud.* Unpublished doctoral dissertation, Department of Educational Counseling. University of Southern California, Los Angeles.

Hamel, M., Gold, D. P., Andres, D., Reis, M., Dastoor, D., Grauer, H., & Bergman, H. (1990). Predictors and consequences of aggressive behavior by community-based dementia patients. *The Gerontologist, 30*, 206–211.

Hankin, M. B., Flanagan, W., Zuzga, C., Babcock, K., & Reyes, C. (1994). Coordinating law enforcement, public interest and private legal services to prevent fiduciary abuse. Symposium presented at the Conference on *Silent Suffering: Elder abuse in America* by FHP Foundation and University of California, Irvine, Long Beach, California.

Hannie, C. C., Pot, A. M., Smit, J. H., Bouter, L. M., & Cees, J. (1998). Elder abuse in the community: Prevalence and consequences. *Journal of the American Geriatrics Society, 46*, 885–888.

Harbison, J. (1999). Models of intervention for 'elder abuse and neglect': A Canadian perspective on ageism, participation, and empowerment. *Journal of Elder Abuse and Neglect, 10*, 1–17.

Homer, A. C., & Gilleard, C. (1990). Abuse of elderly people by the carers. *British Medical Journal, 301*, 1359–1362.

Hudson, M. (1986). Elder mistreatment: Current research. In K. Pillemer & R. S. Wolf (Eds.), *Elder abuse: Conflict in the family.* Dover, MA: Auburn House.

Hwalek, M. A., Neale, A. V., Goodrich, C. S., & Quinn, K. (1996). The association of elder abuse and substance abuse in the Illinois elder abuse system. *The Gerontologists, 36,* 694–700.

Kallick, M., Suits, D., Dielman, T., & Hybels, J., (1979). Gambling participation. In Kallick, M., Suits, D., Dielman, T., & Hybels, J. (Eds.), *A survey of American gambling attitudes and behavior.* Ann Arbor, MI: Survey Research Center, Institute for Social Research, University of Michigan.

Kapp, M. B. (1999). *Geriatrics and the law: Patient rights and professional responsibilities* (3rd ed.). New York: Springer Publishing Company.

Karpin, R. (1998). *Senior callers to helpline.* Senior Outreach Coordinator, Council on Compulsive Gambling of New Jersey. [Online] Available: http://www.800gambler. org/. Unpublished raw data.

Krueger, P., & Patterson, C. (1997). Detecting and managing elder abuse: Challenges in primary care. *Canadian Medical Association Journal, 157,* 1095–1100.

Lachs, M. S., Williams, C., O'Brien, S., Hurst, L., & Horwitz, R. (1997). Risk factors for reported elder abuse and neglect: A nine-year observational cohort study. *The Gerontologist, 37,* 469–474.

Lachs, M. S., Williams, C. S., O'Brien, S., Pillemer, K. A., & Charlson, M. E. (1998). The mortality of elder mistreatment. *JAMA, 280,* 428–432.

Lau, E. A., & Kosberg, J. I. (1979). Abuse of the elderly by informal care providers. *Aging,* 10–15.

Li, W. L., & Smith, M. H. (1976). The propensity to gamble: Some structural determinants. In W. R. Eadington (Ed.), *Gambling and society,* Springfield, IL: Charles D. Thomas Publishers.

MacLean, D. S. (1999). Preventing abuse and neglect in long-term care. Part 1: Legal and political aspects. *Annals of Long-Term Care, 7,* 452–458.

McLauglin, J. S., Nickell, J. P., & Gill, L. (1980). An epidemiological investigation of elderly abuse in southern Maine and New Hampshire. In *Elder abuse* (Pub. No. 68–463), U. S. House of Representatives, Select Committee on Aging.

McNeilly, D. P. & Burke, W. J. (2000). Late life gambling: The attitudes and behaviors of older adults. *Journal of Gambling Studies, 16*(4), 393–415.

McNeilly, D. P., & Burke, W. J. (2001). Casino gambling as a social activity of older adults. *International Journal of Aging & Human Development, 52*(1), 19–28.

McNeilly, D. P., & Burke W. J. (in press). Disposable time and disposable income: Problem gambling behaviors in older adults. *Journal of Clinical Geropsychology.*

Mok, W. P., & Hraba, J. (1991). Age and gambling behavior: A declining and shifting pattern of participation. *Journal of Gambling Studies, 7*(4), 313–336.

Moon, A., & Williams, O. (1993). Predictors of morale among Korean immigrant elder in the United States. *Journal of Cross Cultural Gerontology, 11,* 386–395.

National Center for Elder Abuse (1998). *National Elder Abuse Incidence Study.* Washington, DC. [On-line] Available: http://www.aoa.gov/abuse/report/default.htm

National Opinion Research Council (1999). *Gambling impact and behavior study.* Chicago: University of Chicago.

Neale, A. V., Hwalek, M. A., Goodrich, C. S., & Quinn, K. M. (1996). The Illinois elder abuse system: Program description and administrative findings. *The Gerontologist, 36,* 502–511.

Nebocat, S. A. (1990). Elder abuse and neglect. Borderline situations. In Ronald Roesch, D. G. Dutton & V. F. Sacco (Eds.), *Family violence: Perspectives on treatment, research, and policy* (pp. 151–160). Burnaby, BC: British Columbia Institute on Family Violence.

Office of the Inspector General. (1990). *Resident abuse in nursing homes: Understanding and preventing abuse.* Washington, DC: Office of Evaluations and Inspections.

O'Malley, H., Segars, H., Perez, R. Mitchell, V., & Kneupfel, G. M. (1979). *Elder abuse in Massachusetts: A survey of professionals and paraprofessionals.* Boston: Legal Research and Services for the Elderly.

Patronek, G. J. (1999). Hoarding of animals: An under-recognized public health problem in a difficult-to-study population. *Public Health Report, 114*, 81–87.

Paveza, G. J., Cohen, D., Eisdorfer, C., Freels, S. Semla, T., Ashford, J. W., Gorelick, P., Hirschman, R., Luchman, R., Luchins, D., & Levy, P. (1992). Severe family violence and Alzheimer's disease: Prevalence and risk factors. *The Gerontologist, 32*, 493–497.

Payne, B. K., & Cikovic, R. (1995). An empirical examination of the characteristics, consequences, and causes of elder abuse in nursing home. *Journal of Elder Abuse and Neglect, 7*, 61–74.

Phillips, L. R. (1983). Abuse and neglect of the frail elderly at home: An exploration of theoretical relationships. *Journal of Advanced Nursing, 8*, 379–392.

Phillips, L. R. (1986). Theoretical explanations of elder abuse: Competing hypotheses and unresolved issues. In K. A. Pillermer & R. S. Wolf (Eds.), *Elder abuse: Conflict in the family* (pp. 197–217). Dover, MA: Auburn House Publishing Company.

Pillemer, K. (1985). *Domestic violence against the elderly: A case-controlled study*. Unpublished doctoral dissertation, Department of Sociology, Brandeis University.

Pillemer, K., & Finkelhor, D. (1988). The prevalence of elder abuse: A random sample survey. *The Gerontologist, 28*, 51–57.

Pillemer, K., & Finkelhor, D. (1989). Causes of elder abuse'' Caregiver stress versus problem relatives. *American Journal of Orthopsychiatry, 59*, 179–187.

Pillemer, K., & Moore, D. W. (1989). Abuse of patients in nursing homes: Findings from a survey of staff. *The Gerontologist, 29*, 321–327.

Pillemer, K., & Moore, D. W. (1990). Highlights from a study of abuse of patients in nursing home. *Journal of Elder Abuse and Neglect, 2*, 5–29.

Pillemer, K., & Suitor, J. (1992). Violence and violent feelings: What causes them among family caregivers? *Journal of Gerontology: Social Sciences, 47*, 165–172.

Pittaway, E. D., & Westhues, A. (1993). The prevalence of elder abuse and neglect of older adults who access health and social services in London, Ontario, Canada. *Journal of Elder Abuse and Neglect, 5*, 77–93.

Podnieks, E. (1992). Emerging themes from a follow-up study of Canadian victims of elder abuse. *Journal of Elder Abuse and Neglect, 4*, 59–111.

Podnieks, E., Pillmer, K., Nicholson, J. P., Shillington, T. & Frizzel A. (1990). *National survey on abuse of the elderly in Canada*. Ryerson Polytechnical Institute. Ottawa: Health and Welfare Department, Canada.

Price, G., & Fox, C. (1997). The Massachusetts bank reporting project: An edge against elder financial exploitation. *Journal of Elder Abuse and Neglect, 8*, 59–72.

Quinn, K. M., Hwalek, M., & Goodrich, C. S. (1993). *Determining effective interventions in a community-based elder abuse system*. Final Report to the Administration on Aging.

Quinn, M. J. (1998). Undue influence: an emotional con game. *Aging Today XIX, 9*, 11

Quinn, M. J., & Tomita, S. K. (1997). *Elder abuse and neglect: Causes, diagnosis, and intervention strategies* (2nd ed.). New York: Springer Publishing Company.

Reis, M., & Nahmiash, D. (1998). Validation of the indicators of abuse (IOA) screen. *The Gerontologist, 38*, 471–480.

Rittman, M., Kuzmeskys, L. B., & Flum, M. A. (1999). A synthesis of current knowledge on minority elder abuse. In T. Tatara (Ed.) *Understanding elder abuse in minority populations* (pp. 221–242). Philadelphia, PA: Taylor & Francis.

Schuett, A., & Burke, W. J. (2000). *The hazards of participating in sweepstakes by the elderly*. Unpublished raw data.

Segal, S. R., & Iris, M. A. (1989). The use of interventions in a systems approach to casework. In R. Filinson & S. R. Ingman (Eds.), *Elder abuse: Practice and policy* (pp. 51–61). New York: Juman Sciences Press, Inc.

Shadel, D. P., & T., J. (1994) *Schemes and scams : A practical guide for outwitting today's con artist for the 50+ generation*. North Hollywood, CA: Newcastle Publishing.

Sharon, N. (1991). Elder abuse and neglect substantiations: What they tell us about the problem. *Journal of Elder Abuse and Neglect, 3*, 19–43.

Shiferaw, B., Mittelmark, M. B., Wofford, J. L., Anderson, R. T., Walls, P., & Rohrer, B. (1994). The investigation and outcome of reported cases of elder abuse: The Forsyth County aging Study. *The Gerontologist, 34*, 123–125.

Sprey, J., & Matthews, S. H. (1989). The perils of drawing policy implications from research: The case of elder mistreatment. In R. Filinson & S. R. Ingman (Eds.), *Elder abuse: Practice and policy* (pp. 51–61). New York: Human Sciences.

Steinmetz, S. K. (1988). *Duty bound: Elder abuse and family care.* Beverly Hills, CA: Sage.

Tatara, T., Thomas, C., & Cyphers, G. (1998). *The National Elder Abuse Incidence Study.* Final Report. Prepared for the Administration for Children and Families and the Administration on Aging. Washington DC: The National Center on Elder Abuse.

Vinton, L. (1992). Battered women's shelters and older women: The Florida experience. *Journal of Family Violence, 7*, 63–72.

Wilber, K. H. (1990). Material abuse of the elder: When is guardianship a solution? *Journal of Elder Abuse and Neglect, 2*, 89–104.

Wilber, K. H., & Buturain, L. (1993). Developing a daily money management service model: Navigating the uncharted waters of liability and viability. *The Gerontologist, 33*, 687–691.

Wilber, K. H., & Reynolds, S. L. (1996). Introducing a framework for identifying elder abuse. *Journal of Elder Abuse and Neglect, 8*, 61–80.

Wolf, R. S. (1996). Elder abuse and family violence: Testimony presented before the U. S. Senate Special Committee on Aging. *Journal of Elder Abuse and Neglect, 8*, 81–96.

Wolf, R. S. (1998). Studies believe caregiver stress as key to elder mistreatment. *Aging Today, XIX,* 9, 12.

Wolf, R. S. (1999). *The criminalization of elder abuse.* Paper presented at the Pan American Congress, San Antonio, Texas.

Wolf, R. S., Godkin, M. A., & Pillemer, K. (1984). *Elder abuse and neglect: Report from three model projects.* Worcester, MA: University of Massachusetts Medical Center.

Wolf, R. S., & Li, (1997, November). *Factors affecting the rate of elder abuse reporting to a state protective services program.* Paper presented at the Annual Scientific Meeting of the Gerontological Society of America, Cincinnati, Ohio.

Wolf, R. S., & Pillemer, K. (1989). *Helping elderly victims: The reality of elder abuse.* New York: Columbia University Press.

Wolf, R. S., & Pillemer, K. (1994). What's New in Elder Abuse Programming? Four bright ideas. *The Gerontologist, 34*, 126–129.

Wolf, R. S., Strugnell, C., & Godkin, M. A. (1982). *Preliminary findings from three model projects on elder abuse.* Worcester, MA: University of Massachusetts Medical Center, Center on Aging.

Twenty-Four

Quality of Life and the End of Life

M. Powell Lawton

Over the past decade the study of death and the dying process has taken a different turn from the approach taken in the mid-20th-century, when pioneers like Feifel (1959), Glaser and Strauss (1965), Kastenbaum (1966), and Weisman (1974) introduced the topic to the psychological and social sciences. The emphasis at that time was on subjective representations and fear of death, on the one hand, and on the structures society had provided to accommodate an unwelcome and therefore only grudgingly acknowledged event. Although these basic psychosocial themes have not disappeared, the individual perspective has become more behavioral in relation to treatment at the end of life and the social perspective more focused on the health-care delivery system. Quality of life (QOL) is a construct that links the individual and society in a variety of ways, but it has taken a special place in the realm of health. Specifically, chronic illness, intrusive treatment, and the dying process erode QOL for the individual. Because these illness-related factors also are the occasion for large expenditures on health care, QOL has become the medium of exchange by which the worth of

health both to the individual and society is gauged. The emphasis on QOL brings concern over dying and death back to the psychological realm, which is where the present chapter is focused; the influences of cultural, social, and environmental structures are acknowledged but treated in less detail here (see deVries, 1999).

In keeping with a developmental view of life, time is either an explicit or implicit dimension in every process involved in the move from life to death. Beyond this central element, how to organize discussion of the important features of the end of life is unclear because of gaps in knowledge about many of the features and their interrelationships. Therefore, this chapter is organized around a small number of themes, with the hope that later research will help explicate their relationships with each other. These topics are health and time; quality-of-life trajectories; the decline of health and end-of-life decisions; behavioral outcomes and end-of-life wishes; and a model to represent the multivariate influences of personal, social, and environmental factors on the quality of dying.

I. Health and Time: Good Health and Health Preferences

Although many health problems become increasingly likely as age increases, this relationship is rough at best. Therefore, chronological age is a less reliable focus for examining the track from full health to death than one whose basic dimension is health-related. One way of dividing this time track is to conceive, in order, of full physical health, good health plus intimations of mortality, physical illness, and death. "Dying" is absent from this stage-related nomenclature because its beginning has thus far defied empirical definition. Physicians have been notably inaccurate in forecasting death (Lynn et al., 1996). An alternative possible marker of the beginning of the dying phase might be the patient's recognition of that state. Although this phase is worthy of study in its own right, there are so many other influences on self-recognition of impending death as to make it an equally fallible indicator that the dying process has begun. Therefore the end-of-life phase is defined as the beginning of an illness that is characterized by any of the three dimensions of severity (Lawton, Ward, & Yaffe, 1967): diagnosis of a potentially fatal illness, the beginning of a functional limitation in one's ability to perform any of the basic physical activities of daily living (ADLs), or the advent of pain or physical symptoms that are either or both (a) a major distress to the person and (b) prodromal to death.

This roughly defined end-of-life phase is clearly the focus of this chapter. If this is so, why then include the period of good health in this discussion? The answer, of course, is that attitudes, expectations, anxieties, and planning revolving around death are common human experiences regardless of age or state of health and therefore provide the context within which actual health decisions will eventually be made. The complex of such experiences is referred to as a "mortality schema." During the period of relatively good health, these processes are often far from awareness. Therefore, the term "latent mortality schema" is a more accurate designation. Although age alone may motivate concern over one's mortality, good health counteracts recognition. The period during which the latent mortality schema becomes manifest thus is still difficult to identify. An additional reason for including the period of good health is that much of the research on end-of-life planning has been performed on adults in good health. As will be seen, relatively little research on planning for and wishes regarding end-of-life care has been performed on people who have entered the end-of-life phase.

The term *planning* is used to subsume the thoughts, feelings, and intentions that people experience in relation to the end of their lives, processes clearly conditioned by personality, family environment, social, and cultural factors. The research on healthy people will be considered from two related perspectives. The first is organized around several conceptions of health: health state, health-related quality of life, and health utility. The second perspective is the study of how people in good health anticipate various end-of-life treatments and how they plan for this period.

A. Constructs Representing Health

There are ambiguities in some of the terms used to describe the major constructs in this type of research. Health state, health-related QOL, and health utility need to be differentiated from one another.

Health state seems best reserved to describe health as measured traditionally in objective fashion (i.e., by an observer or some external standard), whether as a diagnosis, a scaled or counted number of comorbidities (e.g., the Health

Conditions subscale of the Multilevel Assessment Instrument; Lawton, Moss, Fulcomer, & Kleban, 1982), other-rated global health, or functional health (as in ADLs, Katz, Ford, Moskowitz, Jackson, & Jaffe, 1963). An essential aspect of what is referred to as "health state" in this chapter is the origin of the judgment of health in an external source. If a measure typically included in the health-related QOL category (see below) is used by an external rater, this measure belongs in the health state category. Another type of external standard derives not from the rating of a single subject but from the consensus of many raters who have judged a set of conditions rather than specific people. Specific individuals may be characterized in these terms, but the reference point for that individual's health rating is a set of consensually established weights for an array of conditions. The most-used measure of this type is the Quality of Well-Being Scale (Fanshel & Bush, 1970). The basis for the Quality of Well-Being Scale is a rating scale whose total ranges from 1.00 (perfect health) to 0.00 (death), each item of which is composed of a description (with an attached fractional weight) of a single level of functioning in each of the three domains of mobility, physical activity, role activity, plus a list of 27 health symptoms. Severity judgments of syndromes composed of combinations of these poor health states were made by about 900 community residents of all ages. These ratings resulted in weights assigned to every point on the three function scales and symptoms, weights which are then subtracted from 1.00 to yield a well-being score. Because the Quality of Well-Being Scale components each have a weight established on the metric of 0.0 to 1.0 (or 0 to 100), health states have often been judged on that rating scale or a variant of it; for example, "If 0 represents death and 100 represents perfect health, what number would you use to describe patient A's health?"

B. How Universal Are the Weights Assigned to Health States?

The Quality of Well-Being Scale weights established by consensus are thought to reflect normative social judgments of the extent to which symptoms, problems, and dysfunctions detract from perfect health. These weights are used as if invariant across population groups and sometimes are used as indicators of health utility. Hays et al. (1996), recognizing that this scale lacked a number of conditions prevalent in very old people with chronic illnesses (e.g., incontinence, sleep problems), studied 50 cognitively intact residents of an assisted-living facility. Their data not only allowed the addition of 11 additional weighted symptoms to the Quality of Well-Being Scale, but also tested how well the standardization population and the old-old agreed in the way the basic consensual health-utility indicators were weighted. Although the health-utility judgments of old-old subjects were highly correlated with those of the population sample, they were slightly but systematically lower, that is, the same complexes of poor health conditions were rated as slightly more severe by the old subjects. Among a very large sample of patients from community medical practices given both time trade-off and standard gamble choices, Sherbourne, Keeler, Unützer, Lenert, and Wells (1999) found that age alone occasioned almost no additional willingness to give up years of life in return for better health. The use of the Quality of Well-Being Scale as a consensual health state measure thus seems to be defensible.

C. Health-Related Quality of Life

One of the dominant themes of medical research of the past decade has been study of the extent to which the symptoms of various illnesses and some of their therapies intrude upon normal quality of everyday life (see Spilker, 1996, for an exhaustive treatment of this topic). Health-related QOL refers to the extent to which physical dysfunction, pain, and distress result in limitations of people's everyday behaviors, social activities, psychological well-being, and other aspects of overall quality of life, as judged by the person. Similar decrements may also result from treatments such as radiation, chemotherapy, amputation, pharmacological treatment, and so on. There are three critical defining features of health-related QOL. First is that the impact on QOL is due to an illness or treatment. Second is that the effects are decrements from "normal." Third is that health-related QOL judgments are made by the person for him- or herself only.

Health-related QOL research has not been concerned with how factors outside the health arena associated with QOL increments above the average range affect overall QOL and preferences for treatment. Judgments of the health aspect of QOL should be limited to those attributable to a health state, as one of the most-used measures, the Sickness Impact Profile (Bergner, Bobbitt, Carter, & Gilson, 1981) does. It should be noted that health-related QOL research has been very much attuned to the fact that effects on QOL differ considerably by disease state. Thus there has been a flood of disease-specific measures of QOL (see Patrick & Deyo, 1989; Spilker, 1996) in addition to generalized measures. Self-rated health, although it can serve as a useful proxy indicator for "objective" health (Mossey & Shapiro, 1982), is also strongly related to subjective well-being and mental health and may be less useful because it straddles the physical and emotional health domains. Because it reflects this subjective standard, self-rated health, whether in its frequent single-item form ("is your health excellent, good, fair, or poor?") or anchored on a rating scale from 0 (death) to 100 (perfect health), is

included among the health-related QOL indicators, as is self-rated ADL.

D. Health Utility

Health utility was a term originally applied to health in the economic sense, that is, to denote preference for years of life or for treatment when confronted with a set of potential gains and losses in the health arena. Health utility has been operationalized in two distinct ways. The first is the time–trade-off, a method by which people are asked to make personal choices in a hypothetical judgment task between length of chronological life in one health condition (often portrayed in a scenario depicting a compromised health condition) versus a shorter number of years in perfect health.

The time–trade-off inquiry begins by asking whether the person would prefer living 12 months in his or her present health, 11 months in perfect health, or whether the two are equal. If 11 months in perfect health is preferred, the person is then asked whether 10 months (or 9—equal intervals are not necessary) in perfect health would be preferred to 12 months in present health. Months in good health are diminished until the fewer months is rejected or considered equally preferable. The score is the proportion of 12 represented by the number of acceptable months (e.g., 9 months = .75 of 12), the time–trade-off score that has also been called "quality-adjusted life years" (or "well years" in Kaplan & Anderson's, 1996, terms). In this example, .75 quality years are the equivalent of one year of chronological life in the current condition; if computed over an expected life span of four more years, that would represent 3 quality-adjusted life years. The response thus reflects a personal reference point ("your current state of health") and a personal wish ("would you prefer for yourself..."). Another technique, the standard gamble, is based explicitly on decision theory, where the choice is forced between a risk of death (e.g., a treatment that might kill you) or the uncertain benefit of x years in perfect health (Kahneman & Tversky, 1984). Respondents are asked what minimum probability of success they would require of the treatment in order for them to be willing to try it. This is a more difficult task than other methods. Both the standard gamble and the consensual Quality of Well-Being Scale for an individual may be converted into a quality-adjusted life years metric, although the time–trade-off, standard gamble, and Quality of Well-Being Scale have been shown to differ somewhat in their estimates of health utility (Revicki & Kaplan, 1993).

For the present purpose, it is suggested that the term "personal health utility" be reserved for measures where the person makes the rating for him-or herself, as is done in the time–trade-off and standard gamble. Consensual utilities measure socially agreed-upon average judgments of the severity of standard health conditions and thus represent a measure of the person's health state more than health utility. Personal health utilities express more individualistic values, where not only health but other nonhealth-related values enter into the choices made.

Personal health utility methods other than the time–trade-off and the standard-gamble have been used. Schneiderman, Pearlman, Kaplan, Anderson, and Rosenberg (1992) devised the Quality of Life Scale, which presents the respondent with a series of health scenarios and asks how long the person would wish to live under each set of conditions (i.e., varying levels of functional health, cognitive function, pain, and home versus institutional residence), which Lawton, Moss, et al. (1999) termed *years of desired life*. Although the response to years of desired life is easy to frame, there is a high rate of nonresponse because many people have difficulty assuming such a hypothetical perspective. For example, Lawton, Moss, et al. (1999) found that only about 60% of such judgments of 10 vignettes depicting poor health states were possible for a sample ages 70 and over to make using numerical estimates of such questions. The remaining responses were nonnumerical, such as "don't know," "only God can tell," or "as long as possible."

Defining and operationalizing health have given researchers problems for years. Even though there are many ambiguities, it seems essential to display the aspects of health and their defining characteristics, as just discussed (Table 24.1). In summary, age alone seems to account for little variation in people's willingness to sacrifice chronological years for better quality years. The research on health utilities deals with relatively abstract health states. The next topic deals with a different perspective on health preferences. Much research on the end of life concerns the concrete choices that might be made about treatment decisions regarding life prolongation and responsibility for those decisions.

E. Anticipating End-of-Life Decisions

The Patient Self-Determination Act of 1990 mandated that patients admitted to hospitals be told about their right to determine the nature of their treatment. An advance directive may either designate who might speak for the patient should he or she not be able to make a treatment decision (durable power of attorney for health-care decisions) or to express the person's own wishes for treatment that might extend life under conditions of low QOL such as extreme distress or unconsciousness. A great deal of research on these questions has been performed on people in good health, presuming that planning for end-of-life care while in sound mind would be beneficial for the

Table 24.1
Three Health Constructs[a]

Construct	Definition	Source of data	Typical measures
Health state	Current health judged as objectively as possible	Observer, normative scaling (normative health utility).	Physician's diagnoses Number of diagnoses Quality of Well-Being Scale (Fanshel & Bush (1970). Rating scale (0 death, 100 perfect) Observer-rated ADL (Katz et al., 1963)
Health-related QOL	Personal health state or other domains of QOL negatively affected by health.	Self-rated health state.	Self-rated health item Rating scale (0 death, 100 perfect). Sickness Impact Profile (Bergner et al., 1981) SF 36 (Ware & Sherbourne, 1992) Self-rated ADL
Personal health utility	Choice between longer health-compromised chronological life or shorter but healthier life	Self-rated preferences	Time–trade-off Standard gamble Quality of Life Scale (Schneiderman et al., 1992) Years of desired life

[a]ADLs, activities of daily living; QOL, quality of life.

person and helpful for potential later decision makers, such as family and medical professionals (see Circirelli, 2001, for a detailed review of such research). A number of good reasons have been found for the type of planning in which people articulate their preferences for treatment and decision-making power. Advance directives may be pondered and thought out over time rather than being made in times of crisis. An advance directive assures that such preferences are expressed when cognitive functioning is normal, rather than sought when dementing illness or limited consciousness might intrude. The advance directive gives people the opportunity to express the conditions under which life extension would be consistent with their unique goals. Finally, the opportunity to control one's own destiny is seen as of intrinsic value.

Considerable research has been performed to determine what influences treatment preferences. Although age and gender have not been shown to have consistent effects, cultural background is important. African Americans are less likely to reject life-prolonging treatment, whereas Asian-American elderly are more likely to reject such measures than Anglo Americans (Eleazer et al., 1996). Better educated elders are also more likely to refuse such measures (Cicirelli, 1998), while those espousing greater religious orientation and greater fear of death are more accepting (Cicirelli, 1997). Factors related to the illness and to the treatment are also determinants of such attitudes. Schonwetter, Walker, Solomon, Indurkhya, and Robinson (1996) found that 66% of a community-resident sample would accept cardiopulmonary resuscitation (CPR) in their present state of health, but only 8% would if they knew they were terminally ill. Hypothetical conditions portraying pain and dementia also elicit lower treatment preferences (Coppola et al., 1999; Lawton et al., 2001). Many investigators have compared various treatments. Among the five most commonly studied (see Lawton, 2000, Table 1), hospitalization and surgery are the most acceptable, whereas preferences for CPR, tube feeding, and ventilation decrease radically as the gravity of the illness portrayed in the hypothetical questions increases. Some treatments are difficult for research participants to comprehend as described in research questions. Major changes in judgments have been elicited after subjects first responded to a briefly phrased item and then were given a more complete explanation of the procedures or recounting of the prognoses for particular treatments (Murphy et al., 1994; O'Brien et al., 1995).

Given the advantages to advance planning in general and the predictors of treatment preferences just reviewed, a larger look at the topic suggests several reasons why people might wish to limit the extent of their treatment. First, most people do recognize that some illnesses and some treatments either cause or prolong poor quality of life, especially pain and dysfunction. Second, many reject the thought of being a burden on family and on the specific personal indignities of dependence. Third, the cost of treatment that may be medically futile is seen as undesirable for both self and society. On the opposite side of the argument, some people feel the motivation to cling to life for its own sake. Some find that every stage of life offers new or redefined personal goals that might be attained with a little more time to live. Some do not want to reject any possible deferral of death in the hope that a cure might be found. A strong reliance on the will of God leads some to wish to use any available method to stay alive until a predesignated time for death has occurred, although some use the same reliance on God's will as a basis for refusing "artificial" means of delaying death.

Looking back at the topics presented thus far, the discussion has focused on the utility of advance decisions for healthy people attempting to plan for better ends of their lives. How well are people able to foresee their future selves, and specifically how will they feel about the value of their various life qualities in balance with a health state they have not yet experienced? Difficulty predicting future behavior from earlier attitudes is a generic problem in psychology. In health-care decision making it may be especially problematic because a one-time but outdated statement of treatment preference may be all there is on which to base a decision regarding a life-or-death matter. This issue will be discussed later in this chapter. Actual health-care decisions have deliberately not been referred to yet because the discussion dealt largely with people in relatively good health whose mortality schemas were frequently latent. In this type of research, thoughts about health and death are frequently brought to the surface only by researchers' questions. Responses may reflect social stereotypic ways of thinking rather than well thought-out personal values. Decisions were not really being made by most participants in these studies. What was studied were attitudes, expectations, and affective schemas that might form the background for future decisions.

II. Quality-of-Life Trajectories

A trajectory represents the course over time of any attribute in this discussion, to the point of death. In the present case, it is convenient to distinguish health trajectories from QOL trajectories (see Bradley, Kasl, Fried, & Idler, 2001). Disease state trajectories may be classified as sudden death, steady decline, and episodic decline (Institute of Medicine, 1997). As noted earlier, however, poor health is more than the existence of a disease diagnosis. At the very least, it also has components of pain or distress and impaired function (ADL and other daily tasks). As suggested by Bradley et al. (2001), QOL trajectories other than health are important to study both for their own sake and for their special relevance to the end of life. Although a trajectory can be established with only two points of measurement, mapping multiple trajectories over multiple points in the time preceding death affords a detailed picture of the quality of the dying process and of the great variety of individual experiences.

A. What Are the Major QOL Dimensions That Characterize the End of Life?

Several issues arise in addressing this question. First, does the end of life demand the use of dimensions of QOL different from those relevant to life in general? Second, what level of globality or specificity is appropriate? Third, what is the consensus on the most important domains of QOL? Finally, what empirical data exist to help map the trajectories of QOL domains through the period of dying?

End-of-life-specific domains of QOL are strongly advocated by Bradley et al. (2001), Miller, Mor, Gage, and Coppola (2001), Stewart, Teno, Patrick, and Lynn (1999), and Teno, McNiff, and Lynn (2001). There is no consensus on the ideal list of QOL domains. Some who have offered such lists when writing about the end of life include Bradley et al. (2001), Teno et al. (2001), and Lawton, Moss, and Glicksman (1990). A great deal of the literature also makes such nominations. Rather than reviewing the lists and commenting on them separately, my suggestions will be offered together with a rationale for the choices. In keeping with my general view of QOL (Lawton, 1991), a number of domains of QOL, like health, may be assessed from the outside (objective QOL) or the inside (subjective QOL).

Four categories are suggested within which a number of more specific domains fall: physical QOL, social QOL, perceived QOL, and psychological QOL. *Physical QOL* has already been discussed in terms of health states and health-related QOL. This domain is the one most closely tied to biology. Pain, symptoms, functional limitations, and cognitive function appear on almost every QOL list. Although no symptom is limited to the end of life, there has been relatively good consensus that the quality of death may be vastly improved if sufficient attention is given to treating symptoms such as constipation, diarrhea, nausea, dyspnea, dry mouth, swallowing problems, coughing, anorexia, insomnia, or fever. Dementia may also be considered an instance of poor life quality. In addition, an optimal level of consciousness has to be established by balancing the patient's desired level of consciousness with amount and type of pain medication.

The realm of *social QOL* includes relatively objective indicators of engagement with the outside world. That optimal level clearly varies with the individual so that more is not necessarily better for all. Measures include size of social network, frequency of contact, participation in discretionary activities, and social space. A specialized form of social interchange mentioned by many writers on the end of life is interpersonal communication explicitly about the focal topics of health, death, details of the illness, wishes and feelings of the aging person regarding other people, personal goals, and anxieties. As in the general social domains, how much and what a dying person wishes to communicate is highly individual and can be judged by an outsider only through sensitive listening. "Social space" represents the radius and frequency of traversals in and out of the home. This space may be grossly reduced near the end of life, but may be psychologically enlarged within the smaller radius ("miniaturization," Rubinstein, 1989; Lawton, 1985) by redefinition of what is important to control and how contact with the world is maintained (visual, auditory, or technological, rather than behavioral, traversal).

The *perceived QOL* category generally represents the subjective analogues of social QOL such as family quality, friends quality, time quality, and economic security. Although the types of engagement that produce high perceived quality near the end of life may differ from those in less-ill or healthy people, dying people with a reasonable level of consciousness will probably continue to experience differing levels of satisfaction in these domains. Bradley et al. (2001) have called special attention to the possibility that some people's end of life may be decremented by worries about the burden on the family, the cost of their illness, and the economic state of their survivors.

Psychological QOL is composed of the possible affects and dysphoric symptoms and personal needs and outlooks that have the most generalized effect on overall QOL. Although fear of death does not seem to be particularly prevalent at the end of life (Mishara, 2000), it can be quite intense for some individuals. Depression and anxiety are relatively prevalent (see next section). In the one study over the last year of life to address the issue, higher self-rated spirituality and religious attendance were associated with a variety of other favorable outcomes (Idler & Kasl, 1998). Schulz and Heckhausen (1996) have offered a model of psychological well-being in which a sense of personal control (primary or secondary) is the central element. Writers on the end of life (Bradley et al., 2001; Miller et al., 2001) have hypothesized that the loss of control during end-of-life health care reduces the quality of dying. However, no empirical data have been located to determine whether making end-of-life decisions for oneself has a psychological advantage. Basic psychological perspectives such as meaning, sense of coherence, and self-esteem are clearly highly valued states for everyone. In contrast, the locations of care (e.g., hospital, nursing home, at home), the equipment used, and dependence on others for one's bodily needs near the end of life have often been viewed as evidence of indignity and loss of esteem.

Quality of care is clearly relevant to the end of life. A statement signed by 41 health-related organizations named 10 types of quality of care appropriate to the end of life (Lynn, 1997). Teno et al. (2001) argue strongly that people rearrange their hierarchy of needs near the end of life, so that "dignity, spirituality, and transcendence" may become more important than physical health. Hurley, Volicer, and Mahoney (2001) emphasize comfort at that time but also mention transcendence and freedom to control one's own destiny. Teno et al. (2001) also review the efforts of several stakeholder groups to specify quality-of-care outcomes (e.g., Emanuel & Emanuel, 1998). In addition to those already mentioned, other favorable outcomes include death occurring in the patient's preferred location, being surrounded by those one loves, staff sensitivity to the wishes of patient and family for recognizing and assimilating knowledge of impending death, and successful attention to the sense of bereavement within the family.

B. Studies of QOL Trajectories

Although these aspects of QOL have face validity as important features of the end of life, many have not been studied quantitatively and related explicitly to the trajectory of decline at the end of life. In this section such quantitative information will be collated. Table 24.2 displays the major facets of these studies. The first four studies attempted to map the trajectories by determining QOL indicators at more than one time prior to death. The last two gathered information on only one occasion that attempted to characterize the entire last year of life. Results (for the last occasion prior to death, if more than one was studied) are summarized in the rightmost column. Where appropriate, percentages were converted so

Table 24.2

Studies of Quality of Life Near the End of Life[a]

Study	Participants	Occasions	Source of data	Results: Time reference and indicators of good QOL
Brock, Foley, & Lozonczy (1987)	N = 1500 from 4000 65+ sampled from Fairfield City, CT, death records, 82% completion rate.	State at 1 year, 1 month, and 1 day before death	Single interview with informant named on death certificate, 10 months postdeath	Day before death: pain low 65%; consciousness clear 51% *; mobility unlimited 13%.* Symptoms: no dyspnea 52% *; no nausea, 87%; no diarrhea 90%; continent 30%.* *QOL diminished over 1 year.
Deeg et al. (1988)	88 residents of Dutch home for aged.	Quarterly assessments, last 4 before death	Staff ratings on four investigator-constructed measures, contemporaneous	ADL, cognition, morale, behavioral symptoms all diminished in QOL over 1 year (last measure not available)
Lawton et al. (1990)	200 decedents 65+ from Philadelphia death records, 150 matched nonmoribund, 49% completion of death group.	QOL at each of the 12 months before death.	Single interview with informant named on death certificate, 4–6 months postdeath.	1 month before death: pain low 42%; consciousness clear 73%; ADL independent 42%. Positive QOL (various metrics): social 67%; time quality 64%; depression low 62%; interest high 57%; hope high 74%. All but social diminished in quality over 1 year.
Morris et al. (1988)	1023 hospice patients	State at 5, 3, and 1 week prior to death.	Self or informant interview rating, contemporaneous	Percent better than two worst categories: pain (73%); emotional QOL (75%); awareness (67%); social QOL (91%); ADL (45%); overall QOL (70%). One week before death* *Quality diminished on all measures except social quantity from week 5 to week 1.
Lynn et al. (1997)	3357 (all ages) SUPPORT (Tsevat et al., 1995) sample and HELP (Tsevat et al., 1998) sample	State during last 3 days of life.	Single interview with informant, 4–10 weeks postdeath.	Conscious 55% (other data only for the fully conscious): 88% no nausea; 20% no fatigue: Mean POMS Anxiety (range 0–4) = .7 to 1.7. 83% not alone and isolated, during last 3 days of life.
Seale & Cartwright (1994)	All-ages samples of all deaths in England, 1969 and 1987. 785 in 1969 (75% 65+) 639 in 1987 (77% 65)	State during last 12 months of life.	With informant, single interview, 6–8 months postdeath.	No pain * (31%); no dyspnea (53%); no nausea (68%); sleep OK (55%); cognitively intact (64%); not depressed (64%); not anorexic (52%); not constipated (68%); continent (bladder 65%); continent (bowel 75%). No ADL assistance (35%). All judged over 12 months preceding death. * % for each symptom approximate average of 2 survey years.

[a]QOL, quality of life; ADL, activities of daily living; POMS, Profile of Mood States.

that all represent the percentages displaying a positive quality.

A number of methodological problems are evident in these studies. The worst of them is the difficulty of obtaining ratings directly from people as they near death. Morris, Suissa, Sherwood, Wright, and Greer (1986) sought data from hospice patients but substituted the judgments of caregivers and research assistants when patients were too sick. For the last rating prior to death (Table 24.2), for example, 64% of the ratings were by caregivers. Nonetheless these ratings, as well as those by staff in the study by Deeg, van Loveren-Huyben, and von der Bom (1988), were at least based on contemporary observations rather than retrospectively rated signs. All the remaining studies depended on the retrospective memories of informants, who were asked to think back to the death 3 to 12 months previously and then reconstruct a period of up to 12 months before that time. Whether there is more retrospection error in the studies that asked informants to integrate a full year's worth of QOL or in those who reported multiple time points in constructing a trajectory is uncertain; neither is ideal. Another problem is that the trajectories of cancer victims and those with other illnesses are often quite different. Thus there are limitations to estimates based either on a mix that includes all diseases or on cancer only. Addington-Hall, Altmann, and McCarthy (1998) studied and reported separately on large samples of both; only in the estimate of pain (greater in cancer) was there a notable difference in level of QOL. These investigators also were the only team that removed "sudden" and "unexpected" deaths from their sample. Although establishing absolute estimates of QOL and their trajectories does not require a comparison group, an anchoring point is needed for determining how good or bad the QOL measure is. Only Lawton et al. (1990) reported comparisons with a year in

the life of elders who had not died or been selected for poor health. Not surprisingly, in all domains except family contact, QOL was poorer for the last-year people.

Lawton et al. (1990, pp. 21–22) attempted a ledger composed of nine dimensions of QOL over the last 12 months of life, where each domain was dichotomized in terms of relatively high versus low QOL. "High" quality was defined each month if the majority (i.e., five or more) of the domains were reported as being in the good end of a good versus bad dichotomy defined for each domain. Pain and ADL dependence displayed the worst quality in the last month of life, but by the five out of nine criterion, almost two-thirds of the decedents were reported to have been in the good QOL range across five or more domains in the month before death.

With these cautions in mind, a few generalizations from the findings shown in Table 24.2 are possible. First, most indicators of QOL diminished over time when multiple time points were studied, with the exception of the social arena, where support from family did not diminish. Half or more decedents were reported to have experienced some bothersome pain shortly before death, but at least half retained some level of consciousness. Dyspnea and nausea were the most prevalent distressing symptoms. Psychological symptoms were not measured by most studies, but their prevalence when reported was 30–70%. Few deaths could really be characterized as "good" deaths. A substantial number of the intrusions on good quality are targets for improvement in care and medical practices.

III. The Decline of Health

The relationship between health or change in health and QOL constitutes the core of the psychology of the ending of life. Death in old age comes after a lifetime of personal cognitive and affective representations of one's own inevitable death that move from the latent toward the manifest, influenced at every step by personal values and social and cultural schemas of how death ought to be viewed. This chapter began with a section on the way relatively healthy people look ahead toward future ill health and its treatment. This section reviews knowledge regarding decline in health and outcomes of QOL, health utility, and actual end-of-life behaviors and medical care. The section begins with a brief review of data regarding the relationship between health state and health utility.

A. Health State and Health Utility

The studies of advance planning by people in relatively good health showed a clear preference for quality over quantity as evidenced in the "discounting" expressed by relatively healthy people of years of life if degraded by pain or dysfunction. These cognitive attitudes projected into the future need to be distinguished from judgments made by people who are actually experiencing contemporaneously reduced health-related QOL of this type. If people's present health states are substantially correlated with their individualized health utilities, we should conclude that the earlier life hypothetical discounting of poor-quality life years is a process that simply endures as poor health intrudes. Such a situation would also support the suggestion that the will to live diminishes as health declines. If health utility is weakly related to health state when health is declining, we should infer an adaptation process with the result that people devalue their own poor health to a lesser extent than they thought they might.

A large all-ages sample studied by Sherbourne et al. (1999) used both a time–trade-off and standard-gamble approach to measuring health utility. Eighty percent were unwilling to give up any

months of life and the mean 1-year time–trade-off metric (expressed in quality-adjusted life years) was .94 (i.e., willingness to give up a mean of 23 days in 1 year). Age was unrelated to either measure of health utility, but the quality-adjusted life years decreased as number of poor health conditions increased: 0 conditions, quality-adjusted life years = .95; 1–2 conditions, quality-adjusted life years = .94; 3–6 conditions, quality-adjusted life years = .91; 6+ conditions, quality-adjusted life years = .85 (Sherbourne, Sturm, & Wells, 1999). Nonetheless, several health-state measures together accounted for only 3% of the variance in time–trade-off. By contrast, quality-adjusted life year estimates from a severely ill hospital patient population of all ages was .73 (Tsevat et al., 1995) and from a hospitalized, aged 80+ sample (median age 84), .81 (Tsevat et al., 1998). In these relatively ill samples, and another large older sample (Lawton, Moss, et al., 1999) health-state versus health-utility correlations (using several different health measures) ranged from .09 to .26.

Another test of the effect of health state on health utilities is provided by comparing groups who are experiencing a health condition with a group that does not. Notable among such studies was Sackett and Torrance's (1978) study of community residents and renal-disease patients. The latter were willing to relinquish significantly fewer months under the dialysis condition than were non kidney-disordered participants. The most stringent test of the dependence of health utility on health state is given when health changes are studied longitidinally. Llewellyn-Thomas, Sutherland, and Thiel (1993) studied laryngeal cancer patients before and after treatment. Their time–trade-off scenarios were based on disease-specific symptoms. There was no overall change in health utility after treatment. The utilities of the most severe scenario judged by the patients whose outcomes were worst, however, increased after treatment, whereas the less-severe outcome groups' utilities did not change. Although the statistical interaction was not analyzed, inspection of the data suggests that the worst scenario had come to seem less malignant to those whose outcomes were poorest (Llewellyn-Thomas et al., 1993, Table 8). The most convincing documentation of change in health utilities over time was from two multisite studies. The Study to Understand Prognosis and Preferences for Outcomes and Risks of Treatments (SUPPORT, Tsevat et al., 1995) recruited and analyzed data from 1438 hospitalized patients (median age 63) who displayed a physiological profile suggesting an average 6-month life expectancy. Among the 593 who survived and completed 2-month and 6-month follow-up assessments, their time–trade-off utility assessment, expressed in quality-adjusted life years, increased significantly from .78 year at baseline to .85 and .86 at follow-up assessments. These increases in utility were correlated only slightly with improvement in functional health (ADL, $r = .10$).

Another multisite study recruited 622 hospitalized people 80 and over—the Hospitalized Elderly Longitudinal Project (HELP, Tsevat et al., 1998), with assessments being performed at baseline (4 days after admission to hospital) and 12 months later. Among the 176 who survived and were survived at the 12-month follow-up, there were significant though small increases in health utility (2 less weeks willing to be traded in the time–trade-off personal utility measure). As in the SUPPORT study, health state was only marginally associated with personal health utility, although the sizes of these relationships were higher at follow-up than at 4 days after admission (ADL $r = .15$, pain $r = -.17$).

As noted earlier in this chapter, healthy people discount survival time substan-

tially when comparing hypothetical poor health states with perfect health. When people whose health is poor respond, however, although personal health utilities change as health state changes, the size of this relationship is relatively small. Empirical evidence that afflicted people judge their own health state more favorably than do people without the state is scant, but very convincing in the renal-dialysis study (Sackett & Torrance, 1978). The overall import of these differences between judgments by healthy and less healthy people is that poor health seems to be less eroding of QOL than people anticipate it might be.

B. Health Utility and Indicators of QOL

It has long been established that health state is positively correlated with mental health and other aspects of QOL (Okun, Stock, Haring & Witter, 1984). The number of empirical studies of health utility's relationship to QOL is still relatively small, however. Both the SUPPORT and HELP studies reported an association between health utility and diverse measures of QOL and mental health. More importantly, increases in utility over the longitudinal study periods were correlated with improvement in some of these measures of well-being. The SUPPORT study (Tsevat et al., 1995) indicated that increase in health utility between the 2-month and 6-month intervals was associated with decreased anxiety and depression. A similar pattern was observed in the HELP study (Tsevat et al., 1998), which also showed a significant correlation between increase in personal health utility and increase in overall QOL. When people are asked to judge personal health utility, as in the time–trade-off, standard-gamble, or Years of Desired Life situation, it seems reasonable to suppose that depression would limit one's attachment to life and therefore that personal utility might be lower.

Although depression does increase at the end of life (see earlier QOL section and review by Lawton, 2000), the relationship between depression and health utility is less certain. If we view the intention to use life-extending treatment as another indicator of health utility, a number of relevant findings have been reported (reviewed by Lawton, 2000). Some found no association between depression and acceptance or rejection of treatment (Cohen-Mansfield, Droge, & Billig, 1992; Michelson, Mulvihill, Hsu, & Olsen, 1991; Uhlmann & Pearlman, 1991). However, in both cross-sectional and longitudinal study of a large sample (Garrett, Harris, Norburn, Patrick, & Danis, 1993; Danis, Garrett, Harris, & Patrick, 1994), depressed community-resident elders were more likely to desire life-supportive treatment than nondepressed. In contrast, O'Brien et al. (1995) found that depressed nursing home residents were less likely to express a wish for CPR, as were depressed veterans in Lee and Ganzini's research (1992). In this latter study, however, depressed and nondepressed did not differ in the wish for life-extending treatment under the three poorest-prognosis scenarios. Lee and Ganzini (1994) and Ganzini, Lee, Heintz, Bloom, and Fenn (1994) studied these veteran inpatients before and after treatment for depression. Despite group improvement in depression, the mean number of life-extending treatments desired did not change following therapy. However, one subgroup displayed a marked increase in treatment wishes; at baseline this group had been significantly more depressed and treatment-pessimistic (i.e., they wished for fewer life-supporting treatments) than the group who had not changed in their wishes for life-extending treatments as their depression lifted. It thus may be that it is only the most depressed who are selectively at risk for refusing life-extending treatment.

Another indicator of health utility is simply the answer to questions regarding the wish to die. Chochinov et al. (1995) studied a hospital-based palliative care sample. By their measure of strong desire to die, 8.5% of 200 cancer patients would wish to die early. The more depressed expressed a stronger wish to die. Although only 8% of those who did not wish to die were depressed, 59% of those wishing to die were depressed. These investigators also found that among the small group of six patients who expressed the wish to die and were evaluated again 2 weeks later, four had changed their minds and only two showed stability of this wish.

Taking into account the divergent findings and the usually small size of relationships between depression and personal health utility, it nonetheless does seem that depression is a risk factor for devaluation of one's life and measures that might extend life. The opposite conclusions reached by Danis et al. (1994) and Lee and Ganzini (1994) illustrate the uncertainty of knowledge. It may be that depression has a curvilinear relationship to the wish for treatment. Mild depression increases the wish for life-supporting treatment but beyond some threshold of intensity, there is no wish for such treatment. There is also the likelihood of a reverse direction of effect, that is, the most life-threatening and least treatable conditions cause depression.

C. Intervening Variables in the Relationship between Health State and Personal Health Utility

Although the foregoing pages have centered on personal health utility as the expression of people's willingness to live, this review has illustrated that although people in poor health do express lower personal utility, this effect is surprisingly small. Sherbourne, Keeler et al. (1999), for example, estimated that 97% of the variation in time–trade-off utility was attributable to factors other than health. This finding raises the question as to what other factors might explain variations in health utility. It is very likely that a substantial portion of the unexplained variance is due to error. All measures of utility force the respondent to make judgments that are based on hypothetical conditions. The concepts themselves are unfamiliar to most people, to say nothing of the awkward response forms of the time–trade-off and the standard-gamble studies. A class of possible intervening explanatory variables is the QOL indicators reviewed earlier, some of which clearly were related to health utility. Surprisingly few attempts to include both health and nonhealth-related QOL in the analysis of health utility have been located.

The author and colleagues (Lawton et al., 1999: Lawton et al., 2001; Crawford, Hoffman, Lawton, & Moss, 1999) made such an attempt in their longitudinal study of 600 community residents 70 and over, recruited to represent both very health elders as well as those with major chronic diseases. They found that indicators of QOL, including depression, were related to health utility (measured in terms of years of desired life, Lawton et al., 2001) independently of a variety of background and health factors. They also predicted that a cognitive–affective schema termed "valuation of life" would also contribute to health utility. Valuation of life comprises cognitions like hope, purpose, futurity, and perseverance while carefully excluding content related to health, psychopathology, or end of life. It was thus seen as a subjective perspective that would lead to a stronger wish to live (years of desired life). Valuation of life was shown to be associated cross-sectionally with years of desired life under 8 of 10 hypothetical health-compromising conditions, independently of background factors, health, several measures of QOL,

three measures of positive mental health, and three traditional measures of mental health (mastery, positive affect, and depression, Lawton, Moss et al., 1999). Among a partial sample who had a 24-month follow-up interview, valuation of life was shown to moderate the effect of health over those 2 years (highly significant interaction of Time-1 valuation of life and decline in ADL in predicting change in years of desired life, Crawford et al., 1999).

This demonstration that a mental attitude like valuation of life bore both a mediating and moderating relationship to a health-utility measure strengthens the need to search for other antecedents (and better measures) for the resolute will to live even under very adverse conditions. This search would proceed with the very firm evidence from most health-utility research that people in good health do express diminished health utility when thinking about a future state of poor health. This relationship is much weaker when people in poor contemporaneous health are included. The issue to be addressed is whether other aspects of a person's life, such as modes of coping, reduce the expected decrement in health utility in the way that valuation of life did.

IV. Behavioral Outcomes and End-of-Life Wishes

The first section of this chapter reviewed knowledge regarding end-of-life wishes as expressed in attitudes toward advance directives and treatment preferences by people who were either relatively healthy or who at least had not been selected for research because their lives were at risk. Does proximity to death or severe illness affect people's wishes or the actual outcomes of the quality of care and quality of death? This section will consider several factors that might affect QOL outcomes at the end of life: the stability of end-of-life wishes over time and as health changes; the ability of other people to represent dying people's wishes when they cannot express them personally; and the type and quality of the treatment actually given near the time of death and how it relates to earlier wishes.

A. Stability of Wishes for End-of-Life Treatment

The question was raised earlier about whether a wish stated at one time in a person's life continues to represent what the person would choose at later stages of life. A first question concerns the stability of treatment preferences, given a relatively stable state of health. Although there have been several studies of stability, the time lapse over which stability was estimated has often been relatively short. Longer periods were studied by Danis et al. (1994). They found that about 70% of community-resident elders who would have refused treatment at the outset would still choose that course 2 years later, whereas original acceptors were as likely to reject as to accept on the later occasion. Carmel and Mutran (1999) conducted three interviews over a 2-year period and reported the same overall stability rate as Danis et al. The relationship of health state to stability and direction of change is an important aspect of the course of the end of life. In both studies, the weight of change from acceptance to nonacceptance was about double the percentage change in the opposite direction, (i.e., toward wanting more treatment). Several more short-term studies were performed on people with health problems (Emanuel, Emanuel, Stoeckle, Hummel, & Barry, 1994; Everhart & Pearlman, 1990; Schneiderman et al., 1992), with very similar 1-month to 1-year stability rates ($\pm$ 70%). Both the SUPPORT and the HELP studies also examined changes in the wish for CPR

and a choice of treatment goals expressed as a preference for life extension versus relief of pain (Tsevat et al., 1995, 1998). Tsevat et al. (SUPPORT, 1995) reported among their broader age-ranged sample that those with higher utility were more likely to wish for CPR and to prefer life extension over pain relief. Over 6 months most did not change in CPR preferences. Those who originally wished for CPR but at 6 months no longer felt that way did not change in health-utility judgments. But among those who would have rejected CPR at first but later would have accepted it, a significant increase of .21 in time–trade-off utility occurred. Among the 176 longitudinal participants in the study of the very old (HELP, Tsevat et al., 1998), time–trade-off health utility and treatment wishes were congruent, as reported in the SUPPORT study, at both the 4-day and 12-month occasions. If we accept these estimates, that around 30% of people's wishes for the several most intrusive treatments changes over time (10% want more, while 20% want less treatment), there does seem to be clear reason for making assertive effort to provide opportunities for people to revise their preferences over time and as their health changes. This conclusion is reinforced by the knowledge that some proportion of these "changers" are those whose wishes for treatment are congruent with generalized increase in personal health utility.

A unique study that mapped daily and hourly changes in a visual-analogue will-to-live scale (a concept related to health utility) was done by Chochinov, Tataryn, Clinch, and Dudgeon (1999) with 138 palliative-care patients followed as much as possible until their death. Although median levels of the will to live were reasonably stable (<10% change) over 12-hr, 24-hr, 7-day, and 30-day intervals, there were wide variations within individuals across time as measured by maximum-change scores for each patient. Will to live was less among those with a lower sense of well-being, greater anxiety, and more dyspnea. The dual facts that will to live changes and that anxiety and depression are associated with short-term declines in will-to-live ratings constitutes further evidence in favor of intensive monitoring of people's end-of-life wishes and changes in wishes.

B. How Well Do Others Perceive the Wishes of People at Risk?

This question is extremely relevant to quality at the end of life because actual treatment decisions are so frequently made by physicians or family members. Most of the knowledge about this issue has been gained from parallel inquiries of research participants, on the one hand, and their families (surrogates) or professional medical personnel, on the other. Not surprisingly most elder groups compared in this way were relatively healthy at the time. Comparison of elders' and physicians' preferences for several types of life-sustaining treatment vary to some extent with the treatment. One large probability sample of Israeli community-resident adults expressed a lesser willingness to undergo such treatments as compared to an unrelated sample of physicians who made judgments of what would be appropriate treatment (Carmel, 1999), whereas in other studies of less healthy (Gramelspacher, Zhou, Hanna, & Tierney, 1997; Uhlmann et al., 1988) or life-threateningly ill (Schneiderman, Kaplan, Pearlman, & Tretzel, 1993) older people rated by their own physicians, there was a plurality of conditions under which the patients would be more accepting of these measures than their physicians when judging the same patient. In the SUPPORT study (Teno et al., 1995), despite an effort to increase communication between physician and very ill patients, the patients' physicians were wrong one-third of the time in predicting the patients' preference for CPR. Uhl-

mann et al. (1988) found that physicians agreed with patient choices only at a chance level, and that even spouses agreed significantly in only half of the scenarios presented.

Cicirelli (2001) in reviewing data on comparative acceptance by elder and surrogate (usually family) indicates that choices by surrogates usually are more favorable to life-sustaining treatment than are elders' own (see for example, Uhlmann et al., 1988). Not all findings support this point of view. Jacobson et al. (1995) interviewed survivors, who reported that 17% of their deceased family members "would have wanted" assisted suicide and 15% euthanasia. These same informants' own wishes on behalf of their deceased relatives were, however, 24% and 21% respectively. A similar study by Koenig, Wildman-Hanlon, and Schmader (1996) revealed that 40% of patients but 60% of relatives would favor physician-assisted suicide in the hypothetical instance of terminal illness. We thus conclude that opposing forces may operate. At the actual time of decision, a family member may feel driven to wish that maximum help be extended. But in hypothetical judgments or retrospective wishes, the family member as the outsider may devalue the judged health utility of the ill person.

What are the mechanisms responsible for the difficulty that both trained professionals and close family members have in predicting the wishes of their ill patients? Many reasons have been advanced that will not be reviewed here (see Circirelli, 2001; Teno et al., 1995). One possibility worth further attention is the difference in perspectives between the subject and an outsider who is relatively healthy in their judgments of the subject's health. In the SUPPORT study, a rating scale anchored at 0 = death and 100 representing perfect health (Tsevat, Dawson, & Matchar, 1990) was used, rated by self, physician, and surrogate. Patients' mean rating was 57.9, physicians 42.5, and surrogates' 49.5, patient ratings being very significantly higher than those of either observer group (Tsevat et al., 1995). Patients' personal health-utility judgments (quality-adjusted life years = .73) were also significantly higher than those of proxy ratings by surrogates (quality-adjusted life years = .65). Berlowitz, Du, Kazis, and Lewis (1995) found that VA nursing home residents rated their own health and quality of life more highly than either their physicians or nurses on most domains assessed by the SF-36 (Ware & Sherbourne, 1992). This limitation in the outsider's perspective is one of the factors leading to error in the ability of others to empathize with the judgment of the individual. Observers' excess discounting of health state in turn is one of the factors that limits effective proxy health-care decision making.

This section depicted the relatively primitive state of knowledge regarding what vulnerable people, their significant others, and the health-care system can do to improve the quality of the end of life. We need to understand better possible means of helping dying people to attain their wishes and helping professionals and surrogates to comprehend and act on these wishes.

V. A Rudimentary Model of the Quality of the End of Life

As noted at the beginning of this chapter, concepts in this area consist more of a list of themes than a coherent depiction of the dynamics of quality at the end of life. At this point, however, it seems worthwhile to propose such a model, emphasizing the psychological perspective (Figure 24.1). Central to the model is the hypothesis that the mortality schema is a thread that continues through the life span that people construct to prepare and account for their eventual dying process.

A. The Mortality Schema

The mortality schema is influenced directly by cultural and social-normative traditions shaped by family influence and personal disposition and indirectly through personal value systems (elements on left side of model). Although constantly changing and sometimes surfacing into high conscious salience, the mortality schema is largely a latent force, reflecting the assumption of immortality characteristic of most people through much of their life span. This latent mortality schema has been the object of most of the study of death and dying as experienced by people in general. At varying times of chronological life and usually so slowly as to be unrecognized by the person at first, the latent mortality schema becomes manifest. Many classic gerontologists have noted this increasing awareness of one's own mortality (Butler, 1963; Cumming & Henry, 1961; Kastenbaum, 1966) as a developmental stage. In the present model, it is a hypothetical construct not yet operationalized nor yet viewed as occupying an antecedent or consequent position in the model (hence the dashed-line boxes). The usual QOL model (Lawton, Winter, Kleban, & Ruckdeschel, 1999) with mental health as the outcome thus does not include latent mortality. As the mortality schema becomes manifest, the personalization of death is the occasion for a reconstructed model of well-being. Interposing the manifest mortality schema and its path to health utility begins the process of defining goals of life beyond mental health that acknowledge the relevance of the mysterious state of death and its precursors. Health-related QOL (a consequence of health state) is not, of course, unique to the trajectory of dying, but it becomes statistically more relevant during chronic illness and dying. In the latent mortality schema period, QOL contributes strongly to the end states of mental health

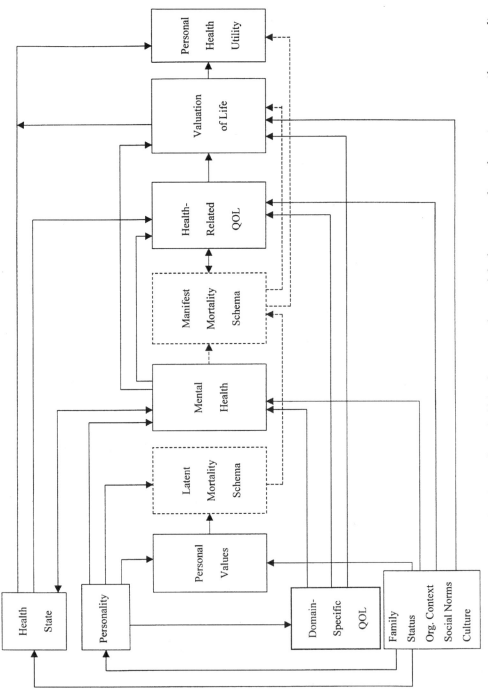

Figure 24.1 Conceptual model of quality at the end of life, showing evolution of the latent mortality schema into a manifest mortality schema as the end of life becomes more salient. QOL, quality of life.

(Lawton et al., 2001). As the death-specific elements are added to the model, domains of QOL that are central to the person are also hypothesized to exert direct effects on health-related QOL. For example, using the time–trade-off, Ditto, Druley, Moore, Danks, and Smucker (1996) found that health-related QOL was lower to the extent that hypothetical poor health states were viewed as interfering with participants' most valued activities.

B. Other Model Elements

Many of the antecedent paths shown in Figure 24.1 are familiar in the literature and will not be detailed here. The social-cultural influences shown at the lower left have been neglected in this chapter because of its emphasis on psychological phenomena. The lack of support given by the health-care context to the fulfillment of patient wishes, however, is an example of the influence of organizational context to health-related QOL.

Valuation of life is one attempt to represent intervening processes, schematized in Figure 24.1 to show both a mediating effect between health-related QOL and health utility and a moderating effect on the relationship between health and health utility. Valuation of life contributes to the subjective reconstruction of one's present and future life, whose purpose is to make sense of one's present position. Of course the search for meaning does not begin at this stage of life, but its usefulness in coping with matters of life and death is new. In fact, valuation of life is not in any way death-specific, nor are other similar modes of reconstructing meaning, such as spirituality or existential reordering of personal goals.

These active and adaptational moves help explain the resilience displayed by many people in the face of major health stresses. As noted earlier, the psychological mechanism of adaptation undoubtedly allows people, if given time, to alter their behaviors and expectations in such a way as to limit the negative consequences of a lowered health state. A great deal of decline in health is either very slow or episodic, with plateaus of stability interspersed. These are conditions that favor slow learning and adoption of new behaviors and attitudes that counteract the negative effects of poor health. Adaptation has its limits, of course. It is clear that further research is needed to determine how the tipping point beyond which low QOL overwhelms everything is reached. Better understanding of how people in this state reshape their balance of primary and secondary control (Schulz & Heckhausen, 1996) should be useful in counseling dying people.

As the ultimate outcome in the model, personal health utility is represented by various primitive efforts to measure, such as years of desired life or the will to live, all error-laden constructs and measures. The most serious lack of knowledge is in specifying the mechanism by which people calculate the balance among the inputs from health, non health-related QOL, mental health, and health-related QOL to arrive at a point of clinging to life or feeling that the costs of living exceed the gains.

VI. Conclusion

The ultimate goal of applying psychological concepts to the study of the end of life is a hope that new knowledge thus generated will lead to improvement in the quality of this unwelcome end of the human developmental cycle. Although life is usually preferable to death, research in this area has demonstrated that the quality of dying varies across a very broad range and that in some instances, there may be varieties of living that are worse fates than death. The psychological perspective assumed in this chapter was organized in such a way as to identify the end-of-life outcomes preferred by older people and the antecedents of such outcomes.

In brief, more favorable outcomes seem probable when people have had an extended period during which they could ponder the possible alternatives and particularly to develop a mode to process what is important in their lives. The mortality schema probably begins very early in a person's life and slowly becomes more and more tied to means and ends relating to death, ideas that take on increasing reality as health diminishes, or as statistical life expectancy decreases. Are there ways by which this preparatory period can become more effective in strengthening people's ability to make good decisions? Little is known about such a question. The answer probably will be found more in the subject matter of earlier-life developmental psychology and in the social and cultural study of death than in gerontology.

Once the reality becomes more salient (the manifest mortality schema), the means and the end come within better range of people's motivational and behavioral systems. People may benefit from conscious thought about their preferences for quality versus quantity of life or about the specifics of the kind of treatment and the context one prefers for one's death. The mechanisms used by such people to shield themselves from the worst of physical and emotional pain deserve intensive study. Knowing that some ill people evaluate their conditions as less serious than do those in good health, and that health utility does not necessarily diminish as health state declines, makes the intervening mechanisms a significant target for future research.

References

Addington-Hall, J., Altmann, D., & McCarthy, M. (1998). Variations by age in symptoms and dependency levels experienced by people in the last year of life, as reported by surviving family, friends, and officials. *Age and Aging, 27*, 129–136.

Bergner, M. B., Bobbit, R. A., Carter, W. B., & Gilson, B. S. (1981). The Sickness Impact Profile: Development and final revision of a health status measure. *Medical Care, 19*, 787–798.

Berlowitz, D. R., Du, W., Kazis, L., & Lewis, S. (1995). Health-related quality of life of nursing home residents: Differences in patient and provider perceptions. *Journal of the American Geriatrics Society, 43*, 799–802.

Bradley, E. H., Kasl, S. V., Fried, T. R., & Idler, E. (2001). Quality of life trajectories of elders in the end of life. In M. P. Lawton (Ed.), *Annual review of gerontology and geriatrics* (Vol. 20): *Emphasis on end-of-life issues.* (pp. 64–96). New York: Springer.

Brock, D. B., Foley, D. J., & Lozonczy, K. G. (1987). A survey of the last days of life: Overview and initial results. *Proceedings of the American Statistical Association, Social Statistics Section*, 306–311.

Butler, R. N. (1963). The life review: An interpretation of reminiscence in the aged. *Psychiatry, 119*, 721–728.

Carmel, S. (1999). Life-sustaining treatments: What doctors do, what they want for themselves and what elderly persons want. *Social Science and Medicine, 49*, 1401–1408.

Carmel, S., & Mutran, E. J. (1999). Stability of elder persons' exposed preferences regarding the use of life-sustaining treatments. *Social Science and Medicine, 49*, 305–311.

Chochinov, H. M., Tataryn, D., Clinch, J. J., & Dudgeon, D. (1999). Will to live in the terminally ill. *Lancet, 354*, 816–819.

Chochinov, H. M., Wilson, K. G., Enns, M., Mowchum, N., Lander, S., Levitt, M., & Clinch, J. J. (1995). Desire for death in the terminally ill. *American Journal of Psychiatry, 152*, 1185–1191.

Cicirelli, V. G. (1998). Relationship of psychosocial and background variables to older adults' end-of-life decisions. *Psychology and Aging, 12*, 72–83.

Cicirelli, V. G. (1998). Views of elderly people concerning end-of-life decisions. *Journal of Applied Gerontology, 17*, 186–203.

Cicirelli, V. G. (2001). Healthy elders' early decisions for end-of-life living and dying. In

M. P. Lawton (Ed.), *Annual review of gerontology and geriatrics (Vol. 20): Emphasis on end-of-life issues* (pp. 163–192). New York: Springer.

Cohen-Mansfield, J., Droge, J. A., & Billig, N. (1992). Factors influencing hospital patients' preferences in the utilization of life-sustaining treatments. *The Gerontologist, 32,* 89–95.

Coppola, K. M., Bookwala, J., Ditime-tradeoff, P. H., Lockhart, L. K., Danks, J. H., & Smucker, W. D. (1999). Elderly adults' preferences for life-sustaining treatments. *Death Studies, 23,* 617–634.

Crawford, W. Y., Hoffman, C. J., Lawton, M. P., & Moss, M. S. (1999, November). *Changes in valuation of life over time.* Paper presented at the annual meeting of the Gerontological Society of America, San Francisco.

Cumming, E., & Henry, W. E. (1961). *Growing old: The process of disengagement.* New York: Basic Books, Inc.

Danis, M., Garrett, J., Harris, R., & Patrick, D. L. (1994). Stability of choices about life-sustaining treatments. *Annals of Internal Medicine, 120,* 567–573.

Deeg, D. J. H., Van Loveren-Huyben, C. M. S., & van der Bom, J. A., (1988). Changes in health-related factors during the last year of life. In M. G. H. Jansen & W. H. van Schnur (Eds.), *The many faces of multivariate analysis* (pp. 133–148). Groningen Netherlands: Institut voor Ondersvijsonderzock, Rijksuniversiteit Groningen.

de Vries, B. (Ed.) (1999). *End of life issues.* New York: Springer.

Ditto, P. H., Druley, J. A., Moore, K. A., Danks, J. H., & Smucker, W. D. (1996). Fates worse than death: The role of valued activities in health-state evaluations. *Health Psychology, 15,* 332–343.

Eleazer, G. P., Hornung, C. A., Egbert, C. B., Egbert, J. R., Eng, C., Hedgepeth, J., McCann, R., Strothers, H., Sapir, M., Wei, M., & Wilson, M. (1996). The relationship between ethnicity and advance directives in a frail older population. *Journal of the American Geriatrics Society, 44,* 938–943.

Emanuel, E. J., & Emanuel, L. L. (1998). The promise of a good death. *Lancet, 351* (suppl. II), 21–29.

Emanuel, L. L., Emanuel, E., Stoeckle, J. D., Hummel, L. R., & Barry M. J. (1994). Advance directives: Stability of patients' treatment choices. *Archives of Internal Medicine, 154,* 209–217.

Everhart, B. S., & Pearlman, R. A. (1990). Stability of patient preferences regarding life-sustaining treatments. *Chest, 97,* 159–164.

Fanshel, S., & Bush, J. W. (1970). A health-status index and its application to health-service outcomes. *Operations Research, 10,* 1021–1066.

Feifel, H. (Ed.) (1959). *The meaning of death.* New York. McGraw-Hill.

Ganzini, L., Lee, M. A., Heintz, R. J., Bloom, J. D., & Fenn, D. S. (1994). The effect of depression treatment on elderly patients preferences for life-sustaining medical therapy. *American Journal of Psychiatry, 151,* 1631–1636.

Garrett, J. M., Harris, R. P., Norburn, J. K., Patrick, D. L., & Danis, M. (1993). Life sustaining treatments during terminal illness: Who wants what? *Journal of General Internal Medicine, 8,* 361–368.

Glaser, B. G., & Strauss, A. L. (1965). *Awareness of dying.* Chicago IL: Aldine.

Gramelspacher, G. P., Zhou, X. H., Hanna, M. P., & Tierney, W. M. (1997). Preferences of physicians and their patients for end-of-life care. *Journal of General Internal Medicine, 12,* 346–351.

Hays, R. D., Siu, A. L., Keeler, E., Marshall, G. N., Kaplan, R. M., Simmons, S., El Monchi, D., & Schnelle, J. F. (1996). Long-term care residents' preferences for health states on the Quality of Well-Being Scale. *Medical Decision Making, 16,* 254–261.

Hurley, A. C., Volicer, L., & Mahoney, T. K. (2001). Comfort in older adults at the end of life. In M. P. Lawton (Ed.) *Annual review of gerontology and geriatrics. (Vol. 20): Emphasis on end-of-life issues* (pp. 120–143). New York: Springer.

Idler, E. L., & Kasl, S. (1998). Patterns of religiousness and spirituality in the last year of life: Normative trends and the impact on quality of life. *The Gerontologist, 39,* 30.

Institute of Medicine (1997). *Approaching death.* Washington, DC: National Academy Press.

Jacobson, J. A., Dasworm, E. M., Battin, M. P., Botkin, J. R., Francis, L. P., & Green, D. (1995). Decedents' reported preferences for physician-assisted death. *Journal of Clinical Ethics, 6,* 149–157.

Kahneman, D., & Tversky, A. (1984). Choices, values, and frames. *American Psychologist, 39,* 340–350.

Kaplan, R. M., & Anderson, J. P. (1996). The general health policy model: An integrated approach. In B. Spilker (Ed.), *Quality of life and pharmoeconomics in clinical trials* (pp. 309–322). Philadelphia PA: Lippincott-Raven.

Kastenbaum, R. (1966). Death as a research problem in social gerontology. *The Gerontologist, 7,* 67–69.

Katz, S., Ford, A. B., Moskowitz, R. W., Jackson, B. A., & Jaffee, N. W. (1963). Studies of Illness in the Aged. The index of ADL: A standardized measure of biological and psychosocial function. *Journal of the American Medical Association, 185,* 914–919.

Koenig, H. G., Wildman-Hanlon, D., & Schmader, K. (1996). Attitudes of elderly patients and their families toward physician-assisted suicide. *Archives of Internal Medicine, 156,* 2240–2248.

Lawton, M. P. (1985). The elderly in context: Perspectives from environmental psychology and gerontology. *Environment and Behavior, 17,* 501–519.

Lawton, M. P. (1991). A multidimensional view of quality of life in frail elders. In J. E. Birren, J. Lubben, J. C. Rowe, & D. E. Deutchman (Eds.), *The concept and measurement of quality of life* (pp. 3–27). New York: Academic Press.

Lawton, M. P. (2000). Quality of life depression, and end-of-life attitudes and behaviors. In G. M. Williamson, P. A. Parmelee, & D. R. Shaffer (Eds.), *Physical illness and depression in older adults* (pp.147–171). New York: Plenum.

Lawton, M. P., Moss, M., Fulcomer, M., & Kleban, M. H. (1982). A research and service-oriented Multilevel Assessment Instrument. *Journal of Gerontology, 37,* 91–99.

Lawton, M. P., Moss, M., & Glicksman, A. (1990). The quality of the last year of life in older persons. *Milbank Quarterly, 68,* 1–28.

Lawton, M. P., Moss, M. S., Hoffman, C., Grant, R., Ten Have, T., & Kleban, M. H. (1999). Health, valuation of life, and the wish to live. *The Gerontologist, 39,* 406–416.

Lawton, M. P., Moss, M., Hoffman, C., Kleban, M. H., Ruchdeschel, K., & Winter, L. (2001).

Valuation of life: A concept and a scale. *Journal of Aging and Health.*

Lawton, M. P., Ward, M., & Yaffe, S. (1967). Indices of health in an aging population. *Journal of Gerontology, 22,* 334–342.

Lawton, M. P., Winter, L., Kleban, M. H., & Ruckdeschel, K. (1999). Affect and quality of life: Objective and subjective. *Journal of Aging and Health, 11,* 169–198.

Lee, M. A., & Ganzini, L. (1992). Depression in the elderly: Effect on patient attitudes toward life-sustaining therapy. *Journal of the American Geriatrics Society, 40,* 983–988.

Lee, M. A., & Ganzini, L. (1994). The effect of recovery from depression on preferences for life-sustaining therapy in older patients. *Journal of Gerontology: Medical Sciences, 49,* M15–M21.

Llewellyn-Thomas, H. A., Sutherland, H. J., & Thiel, E. C. (1993). Do patients' evaluations of a future health state change when they actually enter that state? *Medical Care, 31,* 1002–1012.

Lynn, J. (1997). Measuring quality of care at the end of life: A statement of principles. *Journal of the American Geriatrics Society, 45,* 526–527.

Lynn, J., Harrell, F. E., Cohn, F., Hamel, M. B., Dawson, N., & Wu, A. W. (1996). Defining the "terminally ill": Insights from SUPPORT. *Duquesne Law Review, 35,* 311–336.

Lynn, J., Teno, J. M., Phillips, R. S., Wu, A. W., Desbiens, N., Harrold, J., Claessens, M. T., Wenger, N., Kreling, B., & Connors, A. F. (1997). Perceptions by family members of the dying experience of older and seriously ill patients. *Annals of Internal Medicine, 126,* 97–106.

Michelson, C., Mulvihill, M., Hsu, M. A., & Olsen, E. (1991). Eliciting medical care preferences from nursing home residents. *The Gerontologist, 31,* 358–363.

Miller, S. C., Mor, V., Gage, B., & Coppola, K. (2001). Hospice and its role in improving end-of-life care. In M. P. Lawton (Ed.), *Annual review of gerontology and geriatrics (Vol. 20): Emphasis on end-of-life issues* (pp. 193–223). New York: Springer.

Mishara, B. (2000). Suicide research. Special state-of-the-art article. *Omega, 40,* 1–76.

Morris, J. N., Suissa, S., Sherwood, S., Wright, S. M., & Greco, D. (1986). Last days: A study of the quality of life of terminally ill cancer patients. *Journal of Chronic Diseases, 39,* 47–62.

Mossey, J., & Shapiro, E. (1982). Self-rated health: A predictor of mortality among the elderly. *American Journal of Public Health, 72,* 800–808.

Murphy, D. J., Burows, D., Santilli, S., Kemp, A. W., Tenner, S., Kreling, B., & Teno, J. (1994). The influence of the probability of survival on patients' preferences regarding cardiopulmonary resuscitation. *New England Journal of Medicine, 330,* 545–549.

O'Brien, L. A., Grisso, J. A., Maislin, G., La-Pann, K., Krotki, K. P., Greco, P. J., Siegert, E. A., & Evans, L. K. (1995). Nursing home residents' preferences for life-sustaining treatments. *Journal of the American Medical Association, 274,* 1775–1779.

Okun, M. A., Stock, W. A., Haring, M. J., & Witter, R. (1984). Health and subjective well-being: A meta-analysis. *International Journal of Aging and Human Development, 19,* 111–132.

Patrick, D. L., & Deyo, R. A. (1989). Generic and disease-specific measures in assessing health status and quality of life. *Medical Care, 27,* (3, Supplement), S217–S232.

Revicki, D. A., & Kaplan, R. M. (1993). Relationship between psychometric and utility-based approaches to the measurement of health-related quality of life. *Quality of Life Research, 2,* 477–487.

Rubinstein, R. L. (1989). The home environments of older people: Psychosocial processes relating person to place. *Journal of Gerontology: Social Sciences, 44,* S45–S53.

Sackett, D. L., & Torrance, G. W. (1978). The utility of different health states as perceived by the general public. *Journal of Chronic Diseases, 31,* 697–704.

Schneiderman, L. J., Kaplan, R. M., Pearlman, R. A., & Taetzel, H. (1993). Do physicians' own preferences for life-sustaining treatment influence their perception of patients' preferences? *Journal of Clinical Ethics, 4,* 28–33.

Schneiderman, L. J., Pearlman, R. A., Kaplan, R. M., Anderson, J. P., & Rosenberg, E. M. (1992). Relationship of general advance directive instructions to specific life-sustaining treatment preferences in patients with serious illness. *Archives of Internal Medicine, 152,* 2114–2122.

Schonwetter, R. S., Walker, R. M., Solomon, M., Irdhurkhya, A., & Robinson, B. E. (1996). Life values, resuscitation preferences, and the applicability of living wills in an older population. *Journal of the American Geriatrics Society, 44,* 954–958.

Schulz, R., & Heckhausen, J. (1996). A life-span model of successful aging. *American Psychologist, 51,* 702–714.

Seale, C., & Cartwright, A. (1994). *The year before death.* Aldershot, UK: Avebury.

Sherbourne, C. D., Keeler, E., Unützer, J., Lenert, L., & Wells, K. B. (1999). Relationship between age and patients' current health state preferences. *The Gerontologist, 39,* 271–278.

Sherbourne, C. D., Sturm, R., & Wells, K. B. (1999). What outcomes matter to patients? *Journal of General Internal Medicine, 14,* 357–363.

Spilker, B. (Ed.) (1996). *Quality of life and pharmacodynamics trials.* Philadelphia PA: Lippincott-Raven.

Stewart, A. L., Teno, J. M., Patrick, D. L., & Lynn, J. (1999). The concept of quality of life of dying persons in the context of health care. *Journal of Pain and Symptom Management, 17,* 93–102.

Teno, J. M., Hakim, R. B., Knaus, W. A., Wenger, N., Phillips, R. s., Wu, A. W., Layde, P., Connors, A. F., Dawson, N. V., & Lynn, J. (1995). Preferences for cardiopulmonary resuscitation. *Journal of General Internal Medicine, 10,* 179–186.

Teno, J. M., McNiff, K., & Lynn, J. (2001). Measuring quality of medical care for dying persons and their families. In M. P. Lawton (Ed.), *Annual Review of Gerontology and Geriatrics (Vol. 20): Emphasis on end-of-life issues* (pp. 97–119). New York: Springer.

Tsevat, J., Cook, E. F., Green, M. L., Matchar, D. B., Dawson, N. V., Broste, S. K., Wu, A. W., Phillipa, R. S., Oye, R. K., & Goldman, L. (1995). Health values of the seriously ill. *Annals of Internal Medicine, 122,* 514–520.

Tsevat, J., Dawson, N. V., & Matchar, D. B. (1990). Assessing quality of life and preferences in the seriously ill using utility theory. *Journal of Clinical Epidemiology, 43,* (Suppl.), 73S–77S.

Tsevat, J., Dawson, N. V., Wu, A. W., Lynn, J., Soukop, J. R., Cook, E. F., Viduilett, H., &

Phillips, R. S. (1998). Health values of hospitalized patients 80 years or older. *Journal of the American Medical Association, 279,* 371–375.

Uhlmann, R. F., & Pearlman, R. A. (1991). Perceived quality of life and preferences for life-sustaining treatment in older adults. *Archives of Internal Medicine, 151,* 495–497.

Uhlmann, R. F., Pearlman, R. A., & Cain, K. (1988). Physicians' and spouses' predictions of elderly patients' resuscitation preferences. *Journal of Gerontology, 43,* 115–121.

Ware, J. E., & Sherbourne, C. D. (1992). The MOS 36-item Short-Form Health Survey (SF-36). *Medical Care, 30,* 473–483.

Weisman, A. D. (1974). *The realization of death.* New York: Jason Aronson.

Author Index

Subject Index